Kenya

THE ROUGH GUIDE

There are more than one hundred and fifty Rough Guide titles
covering destinations from Amsterdam to Zimbabwe

Forthcoming titles include

Cuba • Dominican Republic • Las Vegas • Sardinia • Switzerland

Rough Guide Reference Series

Classical Music • Drum 'n' Bass • European Football • House
The Internet • Jazz • Music USA • Opera • Reggae
Rock Music • World Music

Rough Guide Phrasebooks

Czech • European • Dutch • French • German • Greek • Hindi & Urdu
Hungarian • Indonesian • Italian • Japanese • Mandarin Chinese
Mexican Spanish • Polish • Portuguese • Russian • Spanish • Swahili
Thai • Turkish • Vietnamese

Rough Guides on the Internet
www.roughguides.com

ROUGH GUIDE CREDITS

Text editor: Helena Smith
Series editor: Mark Ellingham
Editorial: Martin Dunford, Jonathan Buckley, Jo Mead, Kate Berens, Amanda Tomlin, Ann-Marie Shaw, Paul Gray, Judith Bamber, Kieran Falconer, Orla Duane, Olivia Eccleshall, Ruth Blackmore, Sophie Martin, Geoff Howard, Claire Saunders, Gavin Thomas, Alexander Mark Rogers, Polly Thomas, Joe Staines, Lisa Nellis, Andrew Tomičić (UK); Andrew Rosenberg, Mary Beth Maioli (US)
Production: Susanne Hillen, Andy Hilliard, Link Hall, Helen Ostick, Julia Bovis, Michelle Draycott, Anna Wray, Katie Pringle, Robert Eyers

Cartography: Melissa Baker, Maxine Burke, Nichola Goodliffe, Ed Wright
Picture research: Louise Boulton
Online editors: Alan Spicer, Kate Hands (UK); Kelly Cross (US)
Finance: John Fisher, Katy Miesiaczek, Gary Singh, Ed Downey, Catherine Robertson
Marketing & Publicity: Richard Trillo, Niki Smith, David Wearn, Jemima Broadbridge (UK); Jean-Marie Kelly, Simon Carloss, Myra Campolo (US)
Administration: Tania Hummel, Charlotte Marriott, Demelza Dallow

ACKNOWLEDGEMENTS

The author would like to thank everyone who worked on this book – particularly Helena Smith for calm and efficient editing, Katie Pringle for excellent typesetting, Maxine Burke, Ed Wright and Sam Kirby for a fine new set of maps and Louise Boulton for gorgeous jacket work. Grateful thanks also to Cameron Wilson for Australia Basics, Sean Harvey for US Basics, Gillian Armstrong for proofreading, Judith Bamber for indexing and cross-references, Doug Paterson for musical input and Isabelle Prondzynski for field-testing chapters. Lastly, awed gratitude to the tireless Jens who, in six months, took more notes, made more discoveries, slept in more B&Ls and ate in more *hotelis* than seems humanly possible – and would have done even more given half a chance. Thank you for everything, Jens, and thank you especially for all the first-rate background research and endless emails.

On previous editions, for aid, ideas and encouragement in diverse forms, continuing indebtedness to Jeremy

Torr for the fantastic bike that got me round Kenya on the first trip, Michelle Cox and Bruce Buckland, Mark Dubin, David Else, Emma Gregg, Rosie Mercer, Tony Stones, Jackie Switzer, Tony Zurbrugg, Robert Gordon and family, and the Khan family in Kisii. Lastly, as ever, to Teresa, Alex, David and Phoebe, all my love and gratitude for putting up with so much for so long.

Jens would like to thank Oby Obyerodhyambi and all at Mzizi Cultural Centre; Jabob Lelenguiya in Maralal for proving beautifully that the Samburu do in fact play instruments; the Hedges family (Safari Camp Services) and the Njau family (Paa Ya Paa) for their hospitality; Dr Mwenda Ntarangwi for lending me his thesis on Taarab music; Dr Paul Lane at the British Institute; Professor Osaga Odak at the Institute of African Studies; and to all those throughout Kenya who helped feed my hunger for traditional music. Many (pointless) thanks also to the frogs at various locations who set me dreaming about rhythm and life without the aid of drugs. Asante sana. Croak.

PUBLISHING INFORMATION

This sixth edition published September 1999 by Rough Guides Ltd, 62–70 Shorts Gardens, London, WC2H 9AB.
Previous editions published in 1987, 1988, 1991, 1993, 1996
Distributed by the Penguin Group:
Penguin Books Ltd, 27 Wrights Lane, London W8 5TZ
Penguin Books USA Inc., 375 Hudson Street, New York 10014, USA
Penguin Books Australia Ltd, 487 Maroondah Highway, PO Box 257, Ringwood, Victoria 3134, Australia
Penguin Books Canada Ltd, 10 Alcorn Avenue, Toronto, Ontario, Canada M4V 1E4
Penguin Books (NZ) Ltd, 182–190 Wairau Road, Auckland 10, New Zealand
Typeset in Linotron Univers and Century Old Style to an original design by Andrew Oliver.
Printed in England by Clays Ltd, St Ives plc.
Illustrations in Part One and Part Three by Edward Briant.

Illustration on p.1 by Jane Smith and on p.601 by Henry Iles
© Richard Trillo 1999
No part of this book may be reproduced in any form without permission from the publisher except for the quotation of brief passages in reviews.
Photographs in the "Wildlife of East and Southern Africa" section © Bruce Coleman Picture Library
736pp – Includes index
A catalogue record for this book is available from the British Library
ISBN 1-85828-448-1

Kenya

THE ROUGH GUIDE

written and researched by

Richard Trillo

this edition researched and updated by

Jens Finke

with additional contributions by

Doug Paterson

THE ROUGH GUIDES

TRAVEL GUIDES • PHRASEBOOKS • MUSIC AND REFERENCE GUIDES

 We set out to do something different when the first Rough Guide was published in 1982. Mark Ellingham, just out of university, was travelling in Greece. He brought along the popular guides of the day, but found they were all lacking in some way. They were either strong on ruins and museums but went on for pages without mentioning a beach or taverna. Or they were so conscious of the need to save money that they lost sight of Greece's cultural and historical significance. Also, none of the books told him anything about Greece's contemporary life – its politics, its culture, its people, and how they lived.

So with no job in prospect, Mark decided to write his own guidebook, one which aimed to provide practical information that was second to none, detailing the best beaches and the hottest clubs and restaurants, while also giving hard-hitting accounts of every sight, both famous and obscure, and providing up-to-the-minute information on contemporary culture. It was a guide that encouraged independent travellers to find the best of Greece, and was a great success, getting shortlisted for the Thomas Cook travel guide award,

and encouraging Mark, along with three friends, to expand the series.

The Rough Guide list grew rapidly and the letters flooded in, indicating a much broader readership than had been anticipated, but one which uniformly appreciated the Rough Guide mix of practical detail and humour, irreverence and enthusiasm. Things haven't changed. The same four friends who began the series are still the caretakers of the Rough Guide mission today: to provide the most reliable up-to-date and entertaining information to independent-minded travellers of all ages on all budgets.

We now publish more than 150 titles and have offices in London and New York. The travel guides are written and researched by a dedicated team of more than 100 authors, based in Britain, Europe, the USA and Australia. We have also created a unique series of phrasebooks to accompany the travel series, along with an acclaimed series of music guides, and a best-selling pocket guide to the Internet and World Wide Web. We also publish comprehensive travel information on our Web site:

www.roughguides.com

HELP US UPDATE

We've gone to a lot of effort to ensure that the sixth edition of *The Rough Guide to* Kenya is accurate and up-to-date. However, things change – places get "discovered", opening hours are notoriously fickle, restaurants and rooms raise prices or lower standards. If you feel we've got it wrong or left something out, we'd like to know, and if you can remember the address, the price, the time, the phone number, so much the better.

We'll credit all contributions, and send a copy of the next edition (or any other Rough Guide if you prefer) for the best letters. Please mark letters: "Rough Guide Kenya Update" and send to:
Rough Guides, 62–70 Shorts Gardens, London WC2H 9AB, or
Rough Guides, 375 Hudson St, 9th floor, New York NY 10014.
Or send email to: mail@roughguides.co.uk
Online updates about this book can be found on Rough Guides' Web site at www.roughguides.com

THE AUTHOR

Richard Trillo was conceived in Canada in 1956 and born in England. He spent most of his youth dreaming about travelling and plotting his big escape. There were several attempts, and then a hitchhiking trip to Timbuktu with a friend and $100 cash between them: they had to be helped home. Since then he has travelled extensively in Africa, writing and co-writing the Rough Guides to Kenya and West Africa along the way. He is Rough Guides' Director of Marketing, Publicity and Rights, and is married, with three children.

READERS' LETTERS

This sixth edition owes a huge debt to readers and users of the fifth edition of the *Rough Guide to Kenya* who wrote in with comments, updates and corrections:

Michael Adams, Christine Albrecht, Terese Allen, Lyn Arnold, Gareth Banks and Penny Lacey-Smith, Jim Bardoe, Jonathan Booth and Liz Baker, Jillian and Lisa Berry, Monika Bleckmann, Paul Booth, Nick Burton, John Breitweiser and Stuart Wilber, Julia Brown, Birgit Bunke, Beryl and Mike Butcher, Eleanor Chowns and Bryn Higgs, Robert Clark, Alison Clarke, Sam Corcoran, Graham Coster, David Cowe, Deborah Cox, Celia Crowley, Ronald Davey, Annabel Deuchar, R.A. Duncan, Iain Dryden, Geoffrey Edwards, Roland Evans, Barbara Feichtinger, Rosemary and Paul Gardner, Paul Gehringer, Steven Gibson, Caroline and Mike Gidney, Isabelle Graillet, Maria Grimm, Fiona Hawkins, Petra Henkel, Nancy Holmstrom and Richard Smith, Herbert E. Huppert, Nancy J. Johnson, Roger Kaibunga, Alexandra Kainz, Dave Kennedy, Denise Kiehn, Reinhard Koeppe, Hartmut Kroll, Ulrike Küfer, Henry Kwah, Rebecca Lake and Alice Shiner, Jason Lam, Ian Lancaster, Ivor and Simone Lawton, Kiki and Marion Lenz, Philipp Leonhartsberger, Silvia Mayer, Kirsty McDowell, Sean McQuaid and Deborah Szymanski, Frank Moerschel, James Mumford, Georg G. Neudecker, Joanne Nicel and Mitra Feldman, Carrie Oelberger, Mark Ogilvie, Joe Oram, Edward Orrell, A. Padmore, Sanjeev Parmar, Julia Payne, Marcus Pearce, Juliet Pearson, Karin Pfund, Caroline Piper, Daniel Pollard, Jörg Reinecke, Tania Sadek, Cynthia Salvadori, Steffi Schaub, Bob Schneider, Graham Simons, Anthony Skipper, Bill and Sue Smith, Steve Smith, Nicky State, Morag Stonehouse, Sandy Swann, Mr and Mrs D.C. Sweeting, Joanna Tarratt, Maggi Tomkins, Sally Tomkins, Rico Torriani, Keith Turner, Leon D. Urbain, Anke Vetter, Jos Vogler, Laura Wade, Harriet Watford, Helen Wendholt, Samantha Witman, Rona Williams.

Many thanks to the following people who helped so generously on this edition, either on the ground or by replying to queries. Keep us posted!

In particular, we would like to extend a warm thank you to: Raymond Matiba and Chris Modigell at Alliance Hotels; Jane Clark of Children's Holiday Resort, Erika Kanja and Tony Gathiri at Block Hotels; David Chianda at Gametrackers; Ashwin Bhatt at Kenia Tours & Safaris; Festus Gatheca Kibugu at Kentrout; Jim Flannery and John Maliti at KTB; Judy Kepher-Gona and Wafula Nabutola at KWS; Moses Mungai at Kilimanjaro Safari Club; Tony Farrell at Kimbla; S.M. Marriott of Lewa Wildlife Conservancy, Liz Nicholas and Rica Robinson at Lonhro; Tinu Mhajan at Mada Holdings; Lars and Carol Korschen at Peponi; Selina and Harm at Pili Pipa; Sammy and Paul at Sangare; Francis Mwariga at Savannah Camps and Lodges; Nishit Lakhani at Suntrek Tours & Travel; Jake Grieves-Cook at Tropical Places; and Malcolm Gascoigne at Yare. Also to Alan, Brenda and Eric, and Let's Go Travel in Nairobi for putting up with many Monday morning questions and emails.

CONTENTS

Introduction xi

• CHAPTER 2: THE CENTRAL HIGHLANDS 183–231

• CHAPTER 3: THE RIFT VALLEY 232–269

• CHAPTER 4: WESTERN KENYA 270–335

• CHAPTER 5: THE MOMBASA ROAD AND MAJOR GAME PARKS 336–407

• CHAPTER 6: THE COAST 408—544

• CHAPTER 7: THE NORTH 545—599

PART THREE CONTEXTS 601

LIST OF MAPS

MAP SYMBOLS

Regional Maps

———	Unpaved motor track
═══	Paved road
= = =	4WD only
- - - - -	Footpath
▬▬■▬■	Railway
— —	Ferry route
··············	River
■—■—■	International border
———-	Chapter division boundary
⌒⌒	Mountain range
▲	Mountain peak
⚞	Escarpment
🗻	Cliff
⛰	Hill
⌖	Viewpoint
☀	Crater
⌓	Cave
⚱	Waterfall
〰	Marshland
✿	Spring
◆	Ruin or other monument
⚲	Lighthouse
⊓	Picnic area
⤳	Gate
⌂	Lodge

⚠	Campsite
✈	Airport
✦	Airstrip
▦	National Park
▨	Beach
🌲	Forest
⬡	Glacier

Town Maps

═══	Roads (mainly unpaved)
★	Bus stop
⛽	Petrol station
ⓘ	Information office
☏	Telephone
✉	Post office
⛪	Monastery
✡	Synagogue
☪	Mosque
⛩	Temple
✚	Church
■	Building
⬭	Stadium
⊞	Cemetery
▦	Park

INTRODUCTION

With its long, **tropical beaches** and dramatic **wildlife parks**, **Kenya** has an exotic tourist image. Justifiably, for this is one of the most beautiful lands in Africa and a satisfyingly exciting and relatively easy place to travel, whether on a short holiday or an extended stay. The glossy hype of the brochures ignores the country's less salubrious images – its share of post-colonial poverty and political tension – but is true in its way and a valid enough reason for visiting. Treating Kenya as a succession of tourist sights, however, is neither the best nor the most enjoyable way of experiencing the country. **Travelling independently**, or at least with eyes open (something this book is designed to facilitate), you can enter the more genuine and very different world inhabited by most Kenyans: a ceaselessly active, contrasting landscape of farm and field, of streams and bush paths, of wooden and corrugated-iron shacks, tea shops and lodging houses, of crammed buses and pick-up vans, of overloaded bicycles, and of streets wandered by goats and chickens and toddlers.

You'll find a rewarding degree of openness and curiosity in Kenya's towns and villages, especially off the more heavily trodden tourist routes. Out in the wilds, there is an abundance of authentic scenic glamour – vistas of rolling savannah dotted with **Maasai** and their herds, high **Kikuyu** moorlands, dense **forests** bursting with bird song and insect noise, and stony, shimmering **desert** – all of which comes crisply into focus when experienced in the intense African context of an economically beleaguered country nearly four decades after Independence.

On the **Indian Ocean coast**, the palm-shaded strands of beach and an almost continuous, reef-protected lagoon are even better than the holiday brochures would have you imagine – no photo can really do it justice. And, of course, everywhere you go, Kenya's **wildlife** (see the colour section in the centre of this book and the complementary piece in Contexts) adds a startling and rapidly addictive dimension.

Shape and divisions

Physically, Kenya consists mostly of broad plateaux. The majority of the population live in the rugged highland areas in the **southwest** quarter of the country, where the ridges are a sea of *shamba* smallholdings and plantations. Ripping through the heart of these highlands sprawls the **Great Rift Valley**, an archetypal east African scene of dry, thorn-tree savannah, splashed with lakes and hot springs and studded by volcanoes. The walls of the Rift, and **Mount Kenya** itself, dominate the horizon for much of the time. **Nairobi**, the capital, feels like the centre of Kenya, but it lies at the highlands' southeastern edge, only a three-hour drive from the Tanzanian border. The famous **game parks**, watered by seasonal streams, are mostly located in savannah country on the highland fringes.

Further west, towards **Lake Victoria**, lies gentler countryside, less often visited. And in the **north** the land is **desert** or semi-desert – a surprise for many visitors – broken only by the natural highlight of **Lake Turkana**, almost unnaturally blue and gigantic in the wilderness.

Southeast of the highlands, separating the interior from the Indian Ocean, there are further arid lands. There, the barrier of the **Taru Desert** accounts in large part for the very different history and culture of **the coast**: a surprising and quite distinct Islamic **Swahili** civilization with a long historical record in its mosques, tombs, and ruins of ancient towns cut from the jungle.

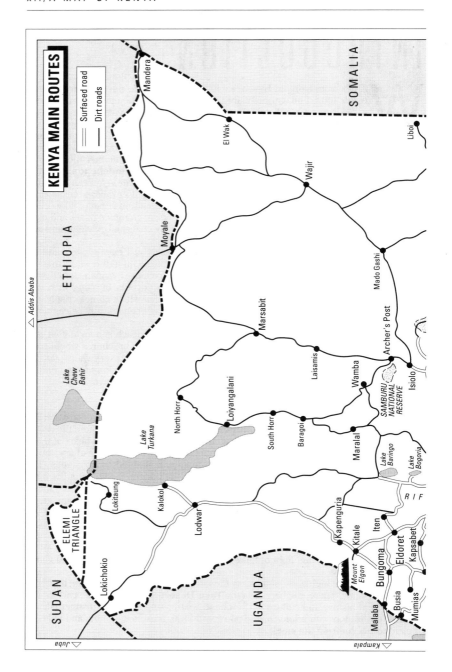

KENYA MAIN ROUTES

Surfaced road
Dirt roads

ETHIOPIA

SOMALIA

Mandera

El Wak

Wajir

Liboi

△ Addis Ababa

Moyale

Mado Gashi

Lake Chew Bahir

Marsabit

Laisamis

Archer's Post

Lake Turkana

North Horr

Loiyangalani

South Horr

Baragoi

Wamba

Isiolo

SAMBURU NATIONAL RESERVE

Lokitaung

Kalokol

Lodwar

Maralal

Lake Baringo

Lake Bogoria

SUDAN

ELEMI TRIANGLE

Kapenguria

Kitale

Iten

R I F

Lokichokio

Mount Elgon

Bungoma

Eldoret

Kapsabet

Malaba

Busia

Mumias

UGANDA

△ Juba

△ Kampala

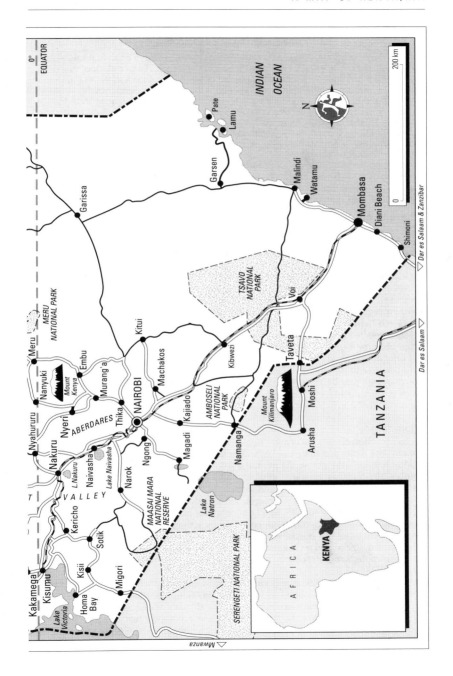

FACTS AND FIGURES

Kenya's **area** of 582,000 square kilometres makes it about two and a half times the size of Britain and nearly one and a half times the size of California. The **population**, which, for many years had a growth rate faster than that of any other country in the world, is now around 30 million, but the rate of increase has at last begun to slow down. Most people are engaged in subsistence agriculture to scrape a living. The main sources of the foreign currency needed for vital imports are **coffee and tea exports** and **tourism**. **Politically**, although Kenya now has opposition MPs in parliament, they are hamstrung by internal divisions and by the ruthless power hunger of the ruling Kenya African National Union (KANU) party, which restricts genuine debate. Daniel Arap Moi has been the president since 1978 and his term of office has now exceeded in length that of Kenya's first president, Jomo Kenyatta. The country's **independence** was returned to it in 1963 after nearly eighty years of British occupation and colonial rule.

Where to go

Where to travel clearly depends on your personal interests, and the time you have available. **Nairobi** (p.79) is usually only used as a gateway. **The coast** (p.408) and major **game parks** (p.356) are the most obvious targets, and if you come to Kenya on an inclusive tour you're likely to have your time divided between these two attractions. If you like the idea of walking or climbing, there's the hot, dry **Rift Valley** (p.232) and the high forests and moors of the **Central Highlands** – Mount Kenya itself is a major target and feasible for most people (p.190). For the best immersion in Kenyan life and culture, the **western** region (p.270) stands out as accessible and untouristy. For serious adventure, **the north** (p.545) is one of the most spectacular and memorable of all African regions.

More detailed rundowns on the specific character and appeal of each area are given in the **chapter introductions**. There too, and at times within the main text, you will find brief backgrounds on the various **Kenyan peoples**. The ten main language groups can no longer be wholly identified with the regions (and moves towards the cities and intermarriage are blurring distinctions), but some understanding of cultural differences is worth achieving. See also "People and Languages" (p.71) and "Religion and Etiquette" (p.73) in Basics.

When to go

As far as **climate** is concerned, Kenya has complicated and unpredictable shifts. Broadly, the pattern is that January and February are hot and dry, while from March to May it is hot and wet – this period is known as the "long rains". From June until October the weather is warm and dry, and then come the "short rains", making November and December warm and wet.

Temperatures, though, are determined largely by altitude. Nairobi's are surprisingly moderate compared with, say, London's (see box opposite). You can reckon on a drop of 6°C (or 11°F) in temperature for every 1000m you climb from sea level. The low-lying coast and the north remain hot all year round, while the highlands (which range to over 4000m and peak above 5000m) are generally warm or mild during the day but much cooler at night. Nairobi, higher than the Cairngorms or the Appalachians, can drop to 5°C (41°F).

At the highest altitudes, it may **rain** at almost any time. Western Kenya has a scattered rainfall pattern influenced by Lake Victoria. Temperatures tend to climb towards the end of the dry seasons, particularly in late February and early March, when it can become very humid before the rains break. It's worth noting that Kenya's climate has been drying out in recent years – the chart opposite paints a slightly rainier picture than you'll find in the country now.

The main **tourist seasons** tie in with the rainfall patterns: the biggest influxes are in December and January and, to a lesser extent, July and August. **Dry season** travel does have a number of advantages, not least a greater visibility of wildlife as animals are concentrated along the diminishing watercourses. July and August are probably the **best months**, overall, for game-viewing. October to January are the months with the clearest seas for **snorkelling** and **diving** – especially November. In the "long rains", the mountain parks are sometimes closed, as tracks are no longer drivable. But the **rainy seasons** shouldn't deter travel unduly: the rains usually come only in short afternoon or evening cloudbursts, and the landscape is strikingly green and fresh even if the skies may be cloudy. There are bonuses, too, in the lack of tourists: hotel and often car rental prices are reduced and people generally have more time for you.

If you're concerned about being part of a horde of tourist arrivals, don't let it bother you too much. Kenya's million-odd annual visitors are few compared with the tens of millions that descend on many Mediterranean countries. There is nothing to prevent you escaping the predictable bottlenecks and tourist "oases" for a completely separate experience and, even on an organized tour, you should not feel constrained to follow the prescribed plan.

KENYA'S CLIMATE

	JAN	FEB	MAR	APR	MAY	JUN	JUL	AUG	SEPT	OCT	NOV	DEC
NAIROBI (Alt 1661m)												
Av day temp (°C)	25	26	25	24	22	21	21	21	24	24	23	23
Av night temp (°C)	12	13	14	14	13	12	11	11	11	13	13	13
Days with rainfall	5	6	11	16	17	9	6	7	6	8	15	11
Rainfall (mm)	38	64	125	211	158	46	15	23	31	53	109	86
MOMBASA (sea level)												
Av day temp (°C)	31	31	31	30	28	28	27	27	28	29	29	30
Av night temp (°C)	24	24	25	24	24	23	22	22	22	23	24	24
Days with rainfall	6	3	7	15	20	15	14	16	14	10	10	9
Rainfall (mm)	25	18	64	196	320	119	89	66	63	86	97	61
KISUMU (Alt 1135m)												
Av day temp (°C)	29	29	28	28	27	27	27	27	28	29	29	29
Av night temp (°C)	18	19	19	18	18	17	17	17	17	18	18	18
Days with rainfall	6	8	12	14	14	9	8	10	8	7	9	8
Rainfall (mm)	48	81	140	191	155	84	58	76	64	56	86	102

LONDON'S CLIMATE

	JAN	FEB	MAR	APR	MAY	JUN	JUL	AUG	SEPT	OCT	NOV	DEC
LONDON (Sea level)												
Av day temp (°C)	6	7	10	13	17	20	22	21	19	14	10	7
Av night temp (°C)	2	2	3	6	8	12	14	13	11	8	5	4
Days with rainfall	15	13	11	12	12	11	12	11	13	13	15	15
Rainfall (mm)	54	40	37	37	46	45	57	59	49	57	64	48

PART ONE

THE
BASICS

GETTING THERE FROM BRITAIN AND IRELAND

Flying to Kenya is invariably the cheapest way of getting there from Great Britain, and London the best departure point. Alternatively, buying an inclusive package holiday can make a lot of sense as some, based around charter flights to Mombasa and mid-range coast hotels, are very cheap. If you choose carefully, you shouldn't feel too packaged. Some of the tour brochures contain quite interesting safari itineraries and a number of independent companies specialize in adventure packages. Another option would be to make your way to Kenya overland, currently only practicable from southern Africa, Ethiopia or Uganda, but not from the Mediterranean or West Africa – wars in Congo and Sudan and the ethnic conflict in Rwanda and Burundi have closed those routes for the time being.

FLIGHTS

Many British travel agents offer tickets for sched-uled flights at substantially **discounted rates** – well below the official fares agreed by IATA, the association to which most airlines belong (see "Airlines' Own Fares" on p.7). In the past, airlines prepared to sell off their tickets through these agents were generally the less reputable carriers left with the most unsold seats. But more and more major carriers are cashing in – though some admittedly are doing so as part of a "restricted eligibility" arrangement where the passenger has to be a student, for example, or under a certain

age. There are also a number of short-stay, "flight only" package deals on **charter flights** to Mombasa from London or Manchester. For full details of scheduled flights from London to Nairobi, see the "Airlines" box on p.6.

There are no direct flights to Kenya from Ireland. From **Belfast**, the only good connections are on British Airways (daily, via London Gatwick, overnight). Other airlines will get you there, but you'll have to change planes twice: possibilities include Air France via London Heathrow and Paris. From **Dublin**, the picture is slightly better, with convenient through-connections on British Airways (daily via London Gatwick, overnight); Sabena via Brussels (Mon, Wed & Fri, overnight); KLM via Amsterdam (Mon, Wed & Fri); and Air France via Paris Charles de Gaulle (Mon, Thurs, Fri, Sat and Sun, overnight).

Flight times are: London–Nairobi non-stop from 8hr 30min to 9hr; London–Mombasa, includ-ing a one-hour refuelling stop, 10hr 30min. Remember Kenya is two hours ahead of Britain in summer and three hours ahead in winter. Because of the small time difference, you won't experience any jet lag.

BOOKING SEATS AND BUYING TICKETS

Your local travel agent should be able to fix you up with a cheap flight on either a charter or scheduled flight. However, travel agents are allo-cated a limited number of tickets, so if you have no luck, try the "Discount agents" listed in the box on p.4. If you phone around, you'll quickly get an idea of the set-up by throwing a few destinations at them.

When **booking**, don't expect to see your ticket until you've paid in full; while many agents have ticketing agreements with certain airlines and can write tickets on the premises, they may have to order some tickets from the nominated **consol-idator** of the airline concerned, which usually means another agent.

Always ask what **refund** you'll get if anything goes wrong and find out how easy it will be to change your reservation dates once you've got your ticket. You can sometimes leave a return tick-et "open-dated" on its return portion, but in that case you'll have to make a seat reservation your-self with the airline in Kenya. It's just as easy, and more prudent, to have a confirmed seat and change the date if necessary (and if seats are available). Note that if you book through a discount agency, you cannot deal direct with the airline on your booking until you have your ticket, though you can always quote them the details and ask them to check the reservation is held under your name. If it's not, don't panic: it will probably be held under the agent's block seat allocation.

Airline **seasons** for Kenya vary a little but generally departures in July, August and December will be the most expensive. Most airlines have low-season rates from February to June, and often again from October to early December. This also ties in with student and youth fares which are always more in summer and Christmas holiday periods.

Book as far **in advance** as you can. Six months isn't too long, and that's when you can pick up the cheapest scheduled tickets. Before the 1997–98 slump in tourism, some airlines were full to capacity at peak periods, especially Christmas, and discounted seat availability was often snapped up quickly. On the other hand, if you find early on that flights seem to be "full", check the same outlets again nearer your departure date – assuming you haven't got something by then – for reservations not taken up and released allocations.

TYPES OF TICKET

Return tickets are generally of three types – short excursions (usually one month), three-month excursions and one year (never more). A **one-way** fare (valid one year) is normally half the relevant "yearly" fare. You may be able to fly out to Nairobi and back from somewhere else (an "open jaw" flight), depending on the airline and the agent's contract.

In rare cases, you may also be able to purchase tickets *back* from East Africa before you leave –

DISCOUNT AGENTS IN BRITAIN AND IRELAND

Africa Travel Centre, 4 Medway Court, 21 Leigh St, London WC1H 9QX (☎0171/387 1211, fax 383 7512, *africatravel@easynet.co.uk*). Helpful and resourceful.

Apex Travel, 59 Dame St, Dublin 2 (☎01/671 5933). Long-haul flights, including Africa.

Bridge the World, 47 Chalk Farm Road, Camden Town, London NW1 8AN (☎0171/911 0900, fax 813 3350). Competitive independent travel firm, for one-off flights or tailor-made round-the-world itineraries.

Brightways Travel, 94 The Green, Southall, Middlesex UB2 4BG (☎0181/574 2622, fax 621 8880). Good fares to Nairobi via Paris.

Council Travel, 28a Poland St, London W1V 3DB (☎0171/437 7767, fax 287 9414). Student discount agent.

Joe Walsh Tours, 8–11 Baggot St, Dublin (☎01/676 3053). General budget fares agent.

North South Travel, Moulsham Mill Centre, Parkway, Chelmsford, Essex CM2 7PX (☎ & fax 01245/608291). Friendly, competitive travel agency, offering discounted fares worldwide – profits are used to support projects in the developing world, especially the promotion of sustainable tourism.

Quest Worldwide Travel, Quebec House, 10 Richmond Rd, Kingston-upon-Thames, Surrey KT2

5HL (☎0181/547 3322, fax 547 3320). Small, personal agent. Recommended.

Sam Travel, 14 Broadwick St, London W1V 1FH (☎0171/434 1523, fax 494 3560); and 803–805 Romford Rd, London E12 5AN (☎0181/478 8911, fax 553 4374). General discount agent.

Soliman Travel, 113 Earl's Court Rd, London SW5 9RL (☎0171/244 6855, fax 835 1394). Particularly good on Egyptair flights via Cairo.

Somak Travel, 545 High Rd, Wembley, Middlesex, HA0 2DJ (☎0181/903 8526, fax 902 8434). Good deals on BA, Kenya Airways and Caledonian.

STA Travel Main office: 86 Old Brompton Rd, London SW7 (☎0171/361 6262); Africa Desk: 117 Euston Rd, London NW1 (☎0171/465 0486, fax 388-0944); 25 Queens Rd, Bristol BS8 1QE (☎0117/929 4399); 38 Sidney St, Cambridge CB2 3HX (☎01223/366966); 88 Vicar Lane, Leeds LS1 7JH (☎0113/244 9212); 75 Deansgate, Manchester M3 21BW (☎0161/834 0668); 36 George St, Oxford, OX1 4AH (☎01865/792800). Large range of fares and airlines for Kenya, from 24 offices in the UK and over 100 worldwide. Special fares for students and young people as well as a specialist Africa Desk.

Superstar Holidays, UK House, 180 Oxford St, London W1N 0EL (☎0171/957 4300, fax 957 useful if you're travelling out overland. Egyptair tickets can be bought like this, though the ticket is collected from their office in the city in question. Such arrangements, known as PTAs, are surprisingly reliable.

If you want to travel onwards from Kenya and only need a one-way flight, check the cancellation charge for cashing in the unused half of a return ticket. While it doesn't apply much to the land borders, passing through immigration at the airport is always smoother if you have a flight out again.

STUDENT AND YOUTH FARES

If you're a **student**, academic or under 32, ask if the agent has special fares — some of the better airlines (including British Airways, the only airline flying London–Nairobi non-stop) grant various **restricted eligibility fares** to certain selected agents which are not available in theory to the general public. Note that the advantage of some of these discretionary fares may lie more in the length of stay they offer and an easing of booking regulations than purely in their price. They are not automatically cheaper than anything else, but they may, all considered, be much better value.

DISCOUNTED AGENTS' FARES

As regards **discount prices**, you can pay anything from under £250 to over £700 for a discounted London–Nairobi return (round-trip) ticket. One-ways will always be over £200, often only fractionally less than the return fare. The airlines to watch for the **cheapest fares** are Aeroflot, Egyptair, Gulf Air and Emirates.

Aeroflot tickets are always valid for a full year and, on a one-way, these are generally the cheapest. Weekly or fortnightly flights connect through Moscow, with a current stop-over of about eight hours (or a basic hotel at their expense). Some

---

4399). Official consolidator for El Al tickets, with special six-month fares.

Tradewings, 1st Floor, Room 31-36, 320 Regent St, London W1R 5AG (☎0171/631 1840, fax 636 1705). Happy to shop around for good deals to Nairobi.

Trailfinders, 42–48 Earl's Court Rd, London W8 6EJ (☎0171/938 3366); and 58 Deansgate, Manchester M3 2FF (☎0161/839 6969). Respected discount flights agency with a convenient range of other services. Some reasonable fares, but not especially geared up for Africa.

Travel Cuts, 295 Regent St, London W1 (☎0171/255 2082). Student and youth (under 26) travel specialists.

Twohigs, 8 Burgh Quay, Dublin 2 (☎01/677 2666); 13 Duke St, Dublin 2 (☎01/670 9750). Long-haul flights including Africa.

Unique Tours & Travel, 2nd Floor, 169 Piccadilly, London W1V 9DD (☎0171/495 4848, fax 491 9693). Specializes in Aeroflot flights via Moscow (currently every Wednesday).

Usit, Fountain Centre, College St, Belfast BT1 6ET (☎01232/324 073); 10–11 Market Parade, Patrick St, Cork (☎021/270 900); 33 Ferryquay St, Derry (☎01504/371 888); 19 Aston Quay, Dublin 2 (☎01/602 1700); Victoria Place, Eyre Square, Galway (☎091/565 177); Central Buildings, O'Connell St, Limerick (☎061/415 064); 36–37

Georges St, Waterford (☎051/872 601). Student and youth specialists.

Usit CAMPUS (*www.campustravel.co.uk*), 52 Grosvenor Gardens, London SW1W 0AG (☎0171/730 8111); 541 Bristol Rd, Selly Oak, Birmingham B29 6AU (☎0121/414 1848); 61 Ditchling Rd, Brighton BN1 4SD (☎01273/570226); 37–39 Queen's Rd, Clifton, Bristol BS8 1QE (☎0117/929 2494); 5 Emmanuel St, Cambridge CB1 1NE (☎01223/324283); 53 Forest Rd, Edinburgh EH1 2QP (☎0131/225 6111, telesales 668 3303); 122 George St, Glasgow G1 1RS (☎0141/5531818); 166 Deansgate, Manchester M3 3FE (☎0161/833 2046, telesales 273 1721); 105–106 St Aldates, Oxford OX1 1BU (☎01865/242067). Student/youth travel specialists, with branches also in YHA shops and on university campuses all over Britain.

Wexas, 45 Brompton Rd, London SW3 1DE (☎0171/589 3315, fax 589 8418). If you're unable to visit others, this membership-only organization handles everything competently by post. Detailed brochures and fare and airline information.

World Express Travel Ltd, Suite 252–254, The Linen Hall, 162–168 Regent St, London W1R 5TB (☎0171 434 1654, fax 734 2550). Official UK consolidators for Kenya Airways, Alliance Air and Ethiopian Airlines.

World Travel Centre, 35 Pearse St, Dublin 2 (☎01/671 7155). Long-haul flights including Africa.

AIRLINES FROM LONDON TO NAIROBI

The following **airlines** currently fly London Heathrow to Nairobi (except British Airways, which flies from Gatwick). Mombasa is served only by Kenya Airways connections via Nairobi and by direct charter flights. Departures are given as overnight (meaning arrival the next morning) or by day (meaning arrival same evening). Try to avoid a flight which arrives at night – definitely not the best time for a first encounter with Nairobi. If that isn't possible, don't be alarmed, it's worth seeing how much a pre-booked hotel room would cost (STA and Trailfinders can be helpful here). Alternatively, reserve directly with one of the better hotels listed on p.48–50 (the cheaper places tend to be shut at night).

Aeroflot (SU) 70 Piccadilly, London W1 (☎0171/355-2233, fax 493-1892); reservations in Dublin ☎01/679 1453, Shannon ☎061/472299. Variable schedule, either weekly or fortnightly; out overnight Wed; back overnight Thurs; change in Moscow (8hr stop-over).

Air France (AF) Colet Court, Hammersmith Rd, London W6 7JP (☎0181/742 6600, fax 750 4488); Mezzanine floor, Dublin Airport, Dublin (☎01/677 8899). Out daily except Tues, Wed; back overnight daily except Tues, Wed; change in Paris.

Alitalia (AZ) 205 Holland Park Ave, London W11 (☎0171/602-7111); 63 Dawson St, Dublin 2 (☎01/677 5171). Out by day Wed or overnight Fri; back overnight Thurs & Sun; change in Rome.

British Airways (BA) 156 Regent St, London W1 (☎0181/897-4000 or linkline ☎0345/222111); 9 Fountain Centre, College St, Belfast BT1 6ET (☎0345/222111); Dublin reservations (☎1800/626747). Out from Gatwick daily overnight; back daily overnight; all non-stop.

Egyptair (MS) 29–31 Piccadilly, London W1V OPT (☎0171/437 6426, fax 287 1728). Out overnight Thurs, Sun; back by day Mon, Fri; change in Cairo.

El Al (LY), UK House, 180 Oxford St, London W1N (☎0171/957 4100, fax 957 4299). Out overnight Mon but no same-day connection from London; back Tues (arrives in Tel Aviv at 11.05pm); change in Tel Aviv.

Emirates (EK) Gloucester Park, 95 Cromwell Road, London SW7 4DL (☎0171/808 0808, fax 808 0080). Out overnight daily, with better connections Sun, Mon, Wed & Sat; back overnight daily; change in Dubai.

Ethiopian Airlines (ET) 166 Piccadilly, London W1V 9DE (☎0171/491 2125, fax 491 1892). Out Mon, Wed, Fri (Mon & Fri have overnights at Addis Ababa, Wed has a good connection); back by day Mon, Fri, Wed; change in Addis Ababa.

Gulf Air (GF) 10 Albemarle St, London W1X 4LS (☎0171/408 1717, fax 629 3989). Out Tues (changes in Bahrain and Muscat), Fri (change in Muscat), Sat (change Abu Dhabi; back overnight).

Kenya Airways (KQ) Cirrus House, CSC Building, Bedfont Rd, London Heathrow Airport, Staines, Middlesex, TW19 7NL (☎01784/888222, reconfirmations ☎01784/888333, fax 888299). Out daily overnight from Heathrow, mostly direct but some flights (Thur, Fri & Sun) routed via Amsterdam; back daily overnight.

KLM Royal Dutch Airlines (KL) 8 Hanover St, off Regent St, London W1 (☎0990/750900, fax 778095). Out by day daily; back overnight daily; change in Amsterdam.

Sabena (SN) 1 Swiss Court, Swiss Centre, Leicester Square, London W1V 4BJ (reservations: ☎0181/780-1444, fax 780-1502). Out by day Mon, Wed, Fri and Sat; back overnight same days; change in Brussels.

Saudia (SV) 171 Regent St, London W1R 7FB (☎0181/995-7777, fax 995-3803). Out overnight Fri; back by day Sat (very early start); change in Jeddah.

Swissair (SR) Swiss Centre, 10 Wardour St, London W1V 4BJ (☎0171/434-7300, fax 434-7219); 54 Dawson St, Dublin 2 (☎01/677 8173). Out overnight Mon, Wed, Sat; back by day Tues, Thurs, Sun; change in Zurich.

agents won't deal with Aeroflot because they're slow to make refunds.

Other good deals can be obtained on **British Airways**, **Air France** and **Kenya Airways**. Low-season, limited-availability discounts offered by these airlines have been known to bring the price of a return flight down to under £250. With **Alitalia** (via Rome), **Emirates** (via Dubai) or **Sabena** (via Brussels), it's usually possible to fly for under £405 return (low season) or £525 (high season).

Lastly, you might ask about **Saudia** and **Ethiopian Airlines**, both of which are reputable carriers with good fares, but often forgotten by agents; Ethiopian offers the option of stop-overs in Addis Ababa.

AIRLINES' OWN FARES

In principle, the **airlines' own fares** should all be about the same (see the "Airlines" box on p.6 for addresses). Current **British Airways** return fares from London Gatwick to Nairobi (valid for a 14–45 day stay) start at £400 (all year round) – the trick is to buy your ticket early to guarantee a cheap seat: once the plane fills up, remaining seats can cost over £700. Tickets can be bought up to twelve months in advance. A book-anytime, non-seasonal one-way fare is £444 plus £24.90 tax. If you want to do some detective work, ask the airline to give you details of their consolidators. Some are only too happy; others refuse.

"FLIGHT-ONLY" CHARTER PACKAGES

If you're happy to fly into Mombasa, there are several **charter operators** with whom you can get seats from as little as £350: finding these is simply a question of getting your travel agent to trawl the computer network for availability. Somak is one of the few agents to offer flight-only charter deals on a regular basis, but you may also find a seat through the Africa Travel Shop. Hayes and Jarvis, Tropical Places, Inspirations and Cosmos occasionally have flight-plus-accommodation offers that work out at less than the cost of a scheduled flight.

It's important to realize that these are strictly **holiday flights**, not scheduled services. There's usually a maximum stay of four or six weeks, with the price depending on the number of days you stay, and you won't be able to change your dates. These are not comfortable flights. Mombasa, their destination, is further than Nairobi and most flights refuel en route (and you can't get off the plane), which adds a couple of hours to the journey time. You'll fly by Airbus A300, DC-10 or 767, and the seating is tight: people of above-average dimensions are likely to find it a trial. The experience is particularly tedious with small children (under-twos don't get their own seats and on some charter flights baby bassinets are not available). Families might seriously consider spending the extra for greater comfort, and a better start to the holiday, on a scheduled flight to Nairobi.

PACKAGE HOLIDAYS

Using charter flights, **packages** of flight and two weeks' dinner and bed and breakfast (half-board) in a beach hotel can cost to as little as £499. If you take on board the drawbacks of the flight described above, it does make sense to consider this option for a short holiday. You don't have to stick with the crowd all the time – or even stay at the hotel – and you could do several short independent trips around the country.

Coast hotels vary greatly in price, atmosphere and amenities. Find out as much as possible about the establishment, and beware of spending hundreds of pounds more on a place that isn't actually a lot nicer than the one next door. The tropical beach environment is so impressive in itself that much of what you're paying extra for (staff in smarter uniforms, pricier furniture, carpets) is likely to be almost irrelevant to your enjoyment. While there are a few quite dismal hotels, some of the nicest places are also the most reasonable.

It's important to realize, too, that a **safari** component in a package tour always knocks the bill up a lot: a week on the beach may look cheap, but add a week's safari and £750 will be the absolute minimum cost, inclusive of flight – and that's in May or June during the long rains (Tropical Places).

TYPES OF SAFARI

Before arranging the details, think about whether you want comfort or a more authentic experience. Internal flights (an "**air safari**") will add enormously to the cost and comfort of your trip and give you spectacular views but a much less intimate feel of Africa. On the other hand, long bumpy drives to meet the demands of an itinerary can be completely exhausting (and impossible for the physically infirm) while hours of your time may be eaten away in a cloud of dust. Note that the "**balloon safaris**" you see advertised are short balloon flights, not complete tours. They take place at dawn and last a couple of hours at most. They can be done in several parks, most popularly in the Maasai Mara, and the bill is a big one – $360–400 (sometimes slightly cheaper if pre-booked with a package from the UK). There are more details on p.397.

Many safaris take you from one game park hotel (known as **lodges**) to another, using **minibuses** with lift-up roofs for picture-taking. Make sure you have a window seat and ask about the number of passengers and whether the vehicle is shared by several operators or is for your group only. More details about the food and accommodation you can expect from a package are covered in relevant sections further on.

UK PACKAGE TOUR OPERATORS

Below are listed both mainstream operators whose brochures are likely to be found in every high street travel agent, and several more unusual companies. All of them offer **safaris**, at prices considerably higher than those offered in Kenya itself. You may, however, find it's a small price to pay to avoid the potential hassle and pitfalls of arranging something yourself – read the section on organizing safaris from Nairobi (p.134) or Mombasa (p.435) if you're considering this. If you're looking for a package, look also at the companies in the "Overland and Adventure Tour Operators" box on p.10.

Abercrombie and Kent, Sloane Square House, Holbein Place, London SW1W 8NS (☎0171/730-9600, fax 730-9376, *www.abercrombiekent.com*). Very upmarket long-haul specialists, with unusual offerings, a dedicated and very flexible manner and a wide knowledge of Kenya, where the company originated. Busy Nairobi operation.

About Africa, 10 Barley Mow Passage, Chiswick, London W4 4PH (☎0181/747-0177, fax 995-2055). Sales agents for Southern Cross Safaris in Nairobi (p.136), a reputable mid-range safari and tailor-made holiday package company.

Art of Travel, 21 The Bakehouse, Bakery Place, 119 Altenburg Gardens, London SW11 1JQ (☎0171/738-2038, fax 738-1893). Innovative travel stylists with a personal approach, specializing in tailor-made trips. Tempting combinations of game driving, walking, horse riding and beach lounging, with accommodation in luxury lodges or off-the-beaten track farmhouses (from around £3000 for two weeks).

British Airways Holidays, Astral Towers, Betts Way, London Rd, Crawley, West Sussex RH10 2XA (☎01293/723181, fax 722650). Impressive range of safari and beach combinations; some keen prices but you'll find certain hotel packages offered for less elsewhere.

Elite Vacations, Elite House, 98 Bessborough Rd, Harrow, Middlesex HA1 3DT (☎0181/864 4431, fax 426 9178, *elite@alphauk.co.uk*). Numerous holiday options including the combination of a classic Kenyan safari with four to seven nights spent on Mauritius or the Seychelles (from £1425 and up).

Grenadier Safaris 11 West Stockwell St, Colchester Essex CO1 1HN (☎01206/549585, fax 561337). General operator which takes bookings for some upmarket lodges.

Hayes and Jarvis, Hayes House, 152 King St, London W6 0QU (☎0181/748 5050, fax 741 0299). Long-established, experienced operator, originally from Kenya, whose wide-ranging options stretch from budget self-catering and no-frills safaris to luxury escorted tours.

The Imaginative Traveller, 14 Barley Mow Passage, Chiswick, London W4 4PH (☎0181/742

The alternative to a standard lodge safari is a **camping safari**, also in a minibus, where the crew – or you, if it's a budget trip – put up your tents at the end of the day. With this kind of trip you have to be prepared for a degree of discomfort along with the self-sufficiency: insects can occasionally be a menace, you may not get a shower every night, the food won't be so lavish and the beer not so cold.

The minibus safaris fitted into most of the inexpensive charter packages venture no further afield than the three national parks easily accessible from the coast – Tsavo East, Tsavo West and Amboseli (trips up to Samburu or west to Maasai Mara are more expensive, and therefore cheaper if arranged from Nairobi). There are more details on what to expect and how to improve it on p.64.

On the best camping safaris, you travel in a fairly **rugged vehicle** – a four-wheel-drive land

cruiser or even an open-sided lorry – giving more flexibility about where you go and how long you stay. The more expensive camping safaris come very expensive indeed and tend to model their style on images culled from *Out of Africa*; they can easily cost over £200 a day. At the other end of the scale, you can pre-book a week-long camping safari from the UK for hardly any more than this – without flights. Decide where and how you want to go, and find a tour to fit. You can do this in advance or when you get there (see the list of operators on p.135).

Most high-street travel agents can fix you up with brochures for the more **mainstream tour operators** whose packages generally (though not always) fall into the lodge and minibus category. For more **off-beat adventure trips**, or a better selection of camping safaris, you should contact the operator directly. Note that the **single-person supplement** tends to be high on convention-

8612, fax 742 3045, *info@imaginative-traveller.com*). Inspired range of hotel/lodge-based and camping safaris, with the option of adding on a mountain trek, a spell on the coast, or an escape to the Seychelles.

Inspirations, Saxley Court, Horley, Surrey RH6 7AS (☎01293/822244, fax 821732). A plentiful choice of reasonably priced beach holidays with safari options.

Kuoni, Kuoni House, Dorking, Surrey RH5 4AZ (☎01306/740888 or 743000, fax 744222). Reputable long-haul holiday operator, with a flexible approach and lots of experience. Good choice of safaris and coastal destinations.

Safari Consultants, Orchard House, Upper Road, Little Cornard, Sudbury, Suffolk CO10 0NZ (☎01787/228494, 228096). Deals in less usual destinations and arrangements.

Somak Holidays, Somak House, Harrovian Village, Bessborough Road, Harrow on the Hill, Middlesex HA1 3EX (☎0181/423 3000, fax 423 7700). Long-established Kenyan company with busy offices in Nairobi (PO Box 48495, ☎02/557832, fax 535175) and Mombasa (PO Box 90738, ☎011/313871, fax 315514). Wide selection of safaris including tailor-mades. Good-value charter flights, BA and Kenya Airways flights. Recommended.

Thomson, Greater London House, Hampstead Rd, London NW1 7SD (☎0990/502399 or 0171/707 9000; late availability offers on p.289

of Teletext). The big one as far as British visitors are concerned. Lots of choice, spread over two comprehensive brochures (Faraway Shores and Worldwide). Fourteen-day safari and beach from £795; fourteen-day beach only from £625. Some strikingly good-value holidays.

Tropical Places, Freshfield House, Lewes Rd, Forest Row, East Sussex RH18 5ES (☎01342/825123, fax 822364; information and special offers on p.259 & 269 of ITV Teletext). Good-value coast packages using a choice of scheduled or charter flights from London Gatwick or Manchester to Mombasa (from £299 for a seven-day B&B package, or £850-900 for a fourteen-day full-board coastal holiday including a one-night safari).

Wildlife Discovery, 29a Bell St, Reigate, Surrey RH2 7AD (☎01737/223903, fax 241104, *mail@wildlifediscovery.com*). Individual operator with a firm emphasis on high-quality safaris using good accommodation. Tailor-made arrangements, or fixed-itinerary safari including BA flight and professional guides. Excellent value. Office in Nairobi.

Worldwide Journeys and Expeditions, 8 Comeragh Rd, London W14 9HP (☎0171/381 8638, fax 381 0836, *wwj@wjournex.demon.co.uk*). Well-designed trips with unusual emphases, including "homestead" safaris, staying on private estates as the guests of experienced guides and wildlife experts. From around £1850 for two weeks all inclusive.

---

al beach and safari packages and somewhat less (or you can share) on the more adventure-spirited trips, where prices are per person, but depend also on the size of the group, which can make things extremely expensive if there's only two or three people.

WORK CAMPS

The **Kenya Voluntary Development Association** is a locally inspired organization, founded in 1962, with international friendship and grass roots development its twin goals. It exists to bring Kenyans and foreigners together for a few weeks or a few months on work camps – digging irrigation trenches, making roads, building schools, or just making as many mud bricks as possible. An international work camp is no holiday, and conditions are usually primitive, with volunteers sharing the local water supply problems,

eating very basic food and organizing their own sanitary, washing and cooking facilities. But they can be a lot of fun, too, and are undoubtedly worthwhile. There is no upper age limit but volunteers older than 25 are unusual; the minimum age is 18, and the groups are very mixed in terms of nationality.

The registration fee is $200 or, if you're very energetic, $300 for two consecutive work camps (they last about three or four weeks). Write to KVDA, PO Box 48902 Nairobi, Kenya (☎02/225379).

CYCLING HOLIDAYS

The energetic might like to try an organized **bicycle tour** of Kenya (though of a far cheaper option is simply to bring your own bike and do it yourself). Leisure Activity Safaris, 19 Bishops Court, Bishopsteignton, Devon, TQ14 9RS, England

(☎01626/775070, fax 777903), offer various long and short bike safaris. Or contact Bicycle Africa, 4887 Columbia Drive South, Seattle, WA 98108-1919, who offer mountain-bike trips with a pioneering spirit and a wide variety of accommodation. 23 Tours, Route d'Arnier 14, 1092 Belmont, Switzerland (fax 41 21 7291795, *captain23@ compuserve.com*) offer mountain bike rides (up to five days) in Maralal District and Samburu, based at Yare campsite in Maralal. The owner is also the organizer of Kenya's national mountain-biking series.

You can fix up similar arrangements in Kenya through a number of agents and operators (addresses on p.131) and book short jaunts to Hell's Gate and lakes Naivasha, Nakuru, Baringo and Bogoria.

Cycling Kenya by Kathleen Bennett is a worthwhile supplementary guide that won't weigh down your bar bag. Also see the section on cycling independently in Kenya, on pp.43–44.

UK OVERLAND AND ADVENTURE TOUR OPERATORS

The **"overland"** catch-all means a loosely packaged trip from A to B in a converted truck, taking a set number of weeks (or months), traditionally from the UK to Cape Town via Nairobi. Unfortunately, wars in Congo and Sudan and the continuing convulsions in Burundi and Rwanda means that no operator currently goes further south or east than Cameroon, from where you have to fly to Nairobi. As a result, Nairobi has become the main base for the southern continuations of these trips, invariably heading down via Harare to South Africa, with an optional few weeks in Uganda to see the gorillas (briefly suspended after the killing of eight tourists in Bwindi National Park in 1999). The option of flying out direct to Nairobi, touring around by truck, and flying back from South Africa, is an increasingly popular one. You don't have to take the entire trip, and can join or leave the truck at a number of places en route.

Note that operators sometimes run trips "in association" with each other. Most run occasional evening slide and video sessions, when you can decide if a packaged adventure is for you. A number of other, smaller operators also advertise regularly in *BBC Wildlife* magazine. If you're interested in one of the more **inexpensive expedition companies** – sometimes regrettably one-off outfits – that advertise in the classified columns of national dailies, it's worth paying them a visit. It seems unfair to throw blanket disapproval over them, but even more unfair on you if things go disastrously wrong. Scrutinizing their blurb gives a good indication of their probable preparedness and real know-how. And if the blurb looks cheap or hasty you should forget it. As well as the operators listed here, check "Package Tour Operators" on p.8 and "Discount Agents" on p.4. Many of the latter are agents for companies below. When getting quotes, find out whether flights are included, and how much your contribution to the communal "kitty" is, as this can add up to thirty percent to the total cost.

The following operators all do the five- to eight-week Nairobi–Harare–Cape Town run, and most also offer three- or four-week diversions in Uganda. Unless stated, prices quoted include the "kitty" (communal fund), but exclude flights from Europe or within Africa.

Absolute Africa, 41 Swanscombe Rd, Chiswick, London W4 2HL (☎0181/742 0226, fax 995 6155, *absaf@actual.co.uk*). Eight weeks from Nairobi to Cape Town (around £900), or twelve weeks via Uganda (around £1400).

African Trails, 3 Flanders Rd, Chiswick, London W4 1NQ (☎0181/742 7724, fax 742 8621, *aftrails@globalnet.co.uk*). Seven-week Nairobi-Cape Town including Uganda for under £900, plus trans-Africa trips when conditions permit.

Africa Travel Shop, 4 Medway Court, 21 Leigh St, London WC1H 9QX (☎0171/387 1211, fax 383 7512). Helpful agents for several overland companies.

Bukima Africa, 55 Huddlestone Rd, Willesden Green, London NW2 5DL (☎0181/451 2446, fax 830 1889). Long-established overlanders, pricier than most, running the usual trips from Nairobi: Uganda (four weeks; £830), and a bumper twelve-week ride to Cape Town (£2035).

Dragoman, 96 Camp Green, Kenton Rd, Debenham, Suffolk IP14 6LA (☎01728/861133, fax 861127, *www.dragoman.co.uk*). Personal and creative with notably good trucks and competitive prices. Regular East, southern and trans-African departures (fly-over from Cameroon to Nairobi). Five weeks Nairobi to Cape Town via Harare costs around £1350.

Encounter Overland, 267 Old Brompton Rd, London SW5 9JA (☎0171/370 6951, fax 244 9737, *www.encounter-overland.com*). Well-respected operator offering one- to eight-week trips through

OVERLAND TO KENYA

Opportunities to **travel overland** to Kenya from Europe are liable to change as Africa's borders open and close in the wake of political and military conflicts.

OVERLAND VIA EGYPT AND SUDAN

This is not currently advisable, although a handful of hardy travellers do manage to find their way through every year. Heading south from the Mediterranean, the main route is from Egypt into Sudan, and thence overland via Eritrea and Ethiopia into Kenya, with the option of diverting south via the Red Sea. However, you should carefully watch developments in Egypt regarding the threat to tourists from fundamentalists. Sudan has been mostly out of bounds since 1984 and the **Nile route** through Sudan is impassable, with most of the countryside in the south controlled by

East and southern Africa, including an unusual fifteen-day spin in Ethiopia (£650, plus flight from Nairobi). Straightforward no-extras pricing.

Exodus Expeditions, 9 Weir Rd, Balham, London SW12 0LT (☎0181/675 5550, fax 673 0779, *www.exodustravels.co.uk*). Long-established outfit, offering a wider variety than most. Three-week trips from Nairobi to southern Africa (from £790, excluding kitty); 22-day round trip exploring the Kenyan, Tanzanian and Ugandan Rift Valley from Nairobi (from £1000 excluding kitty); combined walking tours of Mount Kenya and Kilimanjaro (seventeen days, from £1730 including flight); and a camping tour of western Kenya and Tanzania (fifteen days, from £670 excluding kitty).

Explore Worldwide, 1 Frederick St, Aldershot, Hampshire, GU11 1LQ (☎01252/319448, fax 343170 or 760001, *www.explore.co.uk*). Highly respected small groups operator which runs an interesting Rift Valley tour, and a Samburu–Baringo–Nakuru–Mara safari with the fine bonus of walking in the Loita Hills (sixteen days from about £1100, excluding flights). Ten-day Rift Valley lakes camping (from £1125 including flight), Kenyan parks and Zanzibar.

Footloose Adventure Travel, 105 Leeds Rd, Ilkley, West Yorkshire LS29 8EG (☎01943/604030, fax 604070). Small, enthusiastic independent outfit offering a classic Mount Kenya–Kilimanjaro trek for mountain enthusiasts; they'll tailor-make a safari to fit your budget and interests, offer advice on overland travel options, and track down good-value flights.

Guerba Expeditions, Wessex House, 40 Station Rd, Westbury, Wiltshire BA13 3JN (☎01373/826611, fax 858351, *www.guerba.co.uk*). The acknowledged African experts, running a string of Kenya trips, including a nine-day camping safari for under £500 (you can find cheaper in Nairobi) and a seven-day lodge safari for under £800, plus longer East African trips. Office in Nairobi.

Kumuka Expeditions, 40 Earls Court Rd, London W8 6EJ (☎0171/937 8855, fax 937 6664). Three different overland trips from Nairobi to Harare or vice versa, all of them taking in the Rift Valley and the Maasai Mara (five–ten weeks, £845–1495 excluding kitty), and short adventure tours in Kenya and Tanzania, including climbing tours of Mount Kenya and Kilimanjaro (from £425 for five days; again, you'll find cheaper in Kenya).

Phoenix Expeditions, College Farm, Far St, Wymeswold, Leicestershire LE12 6TZ (☎01509/881818, fax 881822, *www.phoenixexpeditions.co.uk*). Well-equipped outfit offering a fourteen-week overland trip from Istanbul to Nairobi via Cairo (from £1650, including Cairo–Addis Ababa flight, excluding kitty), plus trips through East and southern Africa (eight weeks Nairobi–Cape Town £1325).

Sherpa Expeditions, 131a Heston Rd, Hounslow, Middlesex TW5 0RD (☎0181/577 2717, fax 572 9788, *www.sherpa-walking-holidays.co.uk*). Trekking specialists, with a combined seventeen-day Mount Kenya–Kili trip to satisfy the most masochistic (from £1750–2050, flight included, excludes kitty).

Tracks Africa, The Flots, Brookland, Romney Marsh, Kent TN29 9TG (☎0171/937 3028, fax 01797/344135, *trek.europe@virgin.net*). Short, well-priced safaris in Kenya, or Kenya plus Tanzania or Uganda (eg eight-day highlights from £460, four-week safari from £820, both excluding flight).

Truck Africa, 6 Hurlingham Studio, Ranelagh Gardens, Fulham, London SW6 3PA (☎0171/731 6142, fax 371 7445, *www.truckafrica.com*). Personal but professional and enthused over by past clients, with a big trans-Africa expedition from London to Kenya/Zimbabwe (currently overflying from Douala to Nairobi). Also East Africa trips based out of Nairobi. From around £550 for five weeks (excluding flights and kitty).

the various factions of the anti-government Sudanese People's Liberation Army: Sudan south of Khartoum should be avoided at all costs. The same applies to **Somalia**, which has been without central government since 1991. Travel in Ethiopia itself is usually fine, but be aware of its on-off border conflict with Eritrea, which has made a habit of picking fights with all its neighbours, and should be avoided at present.

Unless you find something discounted, the necessary flight from Khartoum to Nairobi will cost over £260 ($390). If the route is reopened, Nile steamers ply upriver as far as Juba in the rainy season (April–Oct) from where a rough road connects with Lodwar in Kenya. Juba is currently a battleground between Ugandan and Sudanese troops. The Ethiopian border with Kenya at Moyale is passable with a minimum of fuss.

OVERLAND VIA NORTH AND WEST AFRICA

The journey across **the Sahara** and via West Africa is a long one, and currently the Sahara traverse is all but closed while Algerian fundamentalists wage a guerrilla war against secular society. As a viable alternative, it's possible for convoys and overland groups to travel down the coast **from Morocco to Mauritania**, an option which may soon be open to individual traffic if the eternally-delayed UN-sponsored referendum in the Moroccan-occupied Western Sahara finally takes place.

Once in West Africa, the main route is through Nigeria, thence south through Cameroon, east across the Central African Republic, southeast through Congo (a flight will be necessary, as the Congo, formerly Zaire, has plunged into yet another bloody civil war). The West African portion of this trip is covered in the *Rough Guide to West Africa*.

DRIVING OVERLAND TO KENYA

Driving yourself, or entering into partnership with others (sometimes located through classified ads) to fix up a vehicle and head off to Africa – is obviously peppered with potential pitfalls. If the war in central Africa is resolved and Centrafrique and Congo become once again safe to drive traverse, then driving the whole way is perfectly feasible. Equally possible is simply setting off alone, or with a companion, using **public transport**, hitching lifts and walking. This is without any doubt the richest, most satisfying way of travelling in Africa, offering daily contact with ordinary people. You'll get to share their lives and you'll finish with memories and experiences that would otherwise take a lifetime to acquire. This latter, evidently more economical, option in fact also has a higher chance of success, bearing in mind the possible breakdowns that can befall a vehicle. One practical warning: don't go into an independent overland trip via North and West Africa if you have less than six months, as the adventure, otherwise, becomes a race.

BY SHIP TO KENYA

It is still possible to get to East Africa **by ship**, a romantic idea, but you can expect to pay considerably more for a berth for the four-week passage than you would for an air ticket (in fact you pay roughly the same as the first-class air fare). Strand Voyages, Charing Cross Shopping Concourse, The Strand, London WC2N 4HZ (☎0171/836-6363, fax 497-0078, *www.strand-travel.co.uk*), is the main agent in Britain for passenger-carrying cargo ship voyages. There are currently no scheduled passenger services, so it's

---

FLIGHTS FROM AFRICAN CITIES

Within Africa, direct (and sometimes non-stop) flights to Nairobi are available from Abidjan, Accra, Addis Ababa, Brazzaville, Bujumbura, Cairo, Dar es Salaam, Douala, Entebbe/Kampala, Gaborone, Harare, Johannesburg (see "Getting There from South Africa", p.19), Khartoum, Kigali, Kinshasa, Lagos, Lomé, Lusaka, the Seychelles and Zanzibar.

Flights from other capitals connect through these cities, often with long delays.

Fares, which are rarely discounted, can seem a little high – around £420 ($630) one-way Accra–Nairobi for example, and around £600 ($900) for a one-month excursion. If you're planning on taking Nairobi in as part of broader air travel in Africa, you may well find some saving in making separate trips out of London. The main transcontinental carriers operating to and from Kenya are Ethiopian Airlines (for central and west Africa) and Kenya Airways and South African Airlines, operating as Alliance Air (for southern and East Africa).

a matter of contacting them to find out when the next irregular sailing is. It takes approximately 28 days from Felixstowe to Mombasa, through the Med via Livorno and Naples and the Suez Canal to Port Sudan, Djibouti: longer if the ship docks first at Dar es Salaam and Tanga before heading back north to Mombasa. The price is around £2080 one-way.

GETTING THERE FROM THE USA AND CANADA

There are no direct flights from the USA or Canada to East Africa: you have to change planes and, quite possibly, airlines. The fastest routes to Nairobi are from New York via Paris on Air France or via London on British Airways. These are daytime flights, arriving the following morning. For such convenience, you're not likely to get much discount, if any, below the airlines' own fares. Unless time is a big consideration you will probably make an overall saving by flying to London – usually the cheapest departure point in Europe – stopping over for a day or two and picking up a discounted flight there.

Regardless, you'll find the cheapest fares during low season (April 1–June 24 & Aug 20–Dec 9), with the rates slightly higher during shoulder season (Jan 11–March 31) and at their most expensive during high season (June 25–Aug 19, Dec 10–Jan 10). For more details on buying discount flights – and complete information on the airlines that fly into Nairobi – see "Getting to Kenya from Britain and Ireland" on p.3.

Other locations for cheap flights to Nairobi – useful if you plan to tie in your trip to Africa with further travels – include **Athens**, **Cairo** and **Tel Aviv**. These cities are accessible by direct flights from New York, and the national carriers, Olympic, Egyptair and El Al, fly to Nairobi.

Buying an **all-inclusive vacation** can, however, make a lot of sense if time rather than money is a limiting factor: spending half a week travelling in each direction takes a lot out of a three-week trip. And even if time is not a problem, a "package holiday" out of the UK can be an economical way of visiting Kenya. Prices have plummeted in recent years with charter flights operating direct from London to Mombasa. Note, however, that this tends to be travel at the level of bargain vacations to Hawaii or Mexico – distinctly unglamorous in all aspects, from the packed planes to the minibus safaris. Choose carefully.

The last option, if you have all the time in the world, is to get to Europe, then **travel overland** to Kenya (more details on p.11).

FLIGHTS FROM THE USA

Any flight from Europe to Nairobi can be tacked on to a transatlantic routing. But the flights usually advertised, with reasonable connections, all hub through New York and then connect with a flight to Nairobi in one or other of the following European capitals – Amsterdam, Brussels, Geneva, London, Paris, Rome or Zurich.

Purchasing direct from the airline, the low-season, mid-week price out of New York extends upwards from $1300 and out of Los Angeles from $2590; travelling on weekends will increase this fare by $100–200. Keep in mind also that these rates can be cut somewhat by going through one of the discount brokers listed below.

For those intending to build a trip to Kenya into an extensive travel plan, **round-the-world fares** from discount agents start at roughly $2600 for economy and around $5000 for first-class. As a general rule you must decide your itinerary and stop-over cities in advance, travelling in a single direction, either eastbound or westbound with no backtracking. You set a date for the first outbound flight in advance, and then reserve the others as you go, completing the entire journey within either six months or a year.

GENERAL DISCOUNT AGENTS IN THE USA

Flytime, 45 W 34th St, Suite 305, New York, NY 10001 (☎212/760-3737).

Hariworld, 25 W 45th St, New York, NY 10036 (☎212/997-3300).

Interworld, 800 Douglas Rd, Coral Gables, FL 33134 (☎305/443-4929).

Magical Holidays, 501 Madison Ave, New York, NY 10022 (☎212/486-9600 or 1-800/228-2208).

Pan Express Travel, 55 W 39th St, New York, NY 10018 (☎212/719-9292 or 1-800/518-7726);

209 Post St, Suite 921, San Francisco, CA 94108 (☎415/989-8282).

Sendant Travel International, 801 Royal Parkway, Suite 200, Nashville, TN 37214 (☎1-800/221-8139).

Swan Travel, 400 Madison Ave, New York, NY 10017 (☎212/421-1010).

UniTravel, Box 12485, 11737 Administration Dr, Suite 120, St Louis, MO 63146 (☎1-800/325-2222 or 314/569-2501).

COUNCIL TRAVEL OFFICES IN THE USA

Head office: 205 E 42nd St, New York, NY 10017 (☎212/822-2700 or 1-800/226-8624, *www.counciltravel.com*).

Other main offices at:

530 Bush St, Ground Floor, San Francisco, CA 94108 (☎415/421-3473);

10904 Lindbrook Drive, Los Angeles, CA 90024 (☎310/208-3551);

1138 13th St, Boulder, CO 80302 (☎303/447-8101);

3300 M St NW, 2nd Floor, Washington, DC 20007 (☎202/337-6464);

1160 N State St, Chicago, IL 60610 (☎312/951-0585);

273 Newbury St, Boston, MA 02116 (☎617/266-1926);

1501 University Ave SE, Room 300, Minneapolis, MN 55414 (☎612/379-2323);

2000 Guadalupe St, Suite 6, Austin, TX 78705 (☎512/472-4931);

1314 NE 43rd St, Suite 210, Seattle, WA 98105 (☎206/632-2448).

STA TRAVEL OFFICES IN THE USA

☎1-800/777-0112 (nationwide information number), *www.statravel.com*.

Main offices at:

10 Downing St, New York, NY 10014 (☎212/627-3111);

6560 N Scottsdale Rd, Suite F-100, Scottsdale, AZ 85253 (☎1-800/777-0112);

ASUC Travel Center, MLK Jr Bldg, 2nd Floor, UC, Telegraph at Bancroft Way, Berkeley, CA 94720 (☎510/642-3000);

920 Westwood Blvd, Los Angeles, CA 90036 (☎310/824-1574);

51 Grant Ave, San Francisco, CA 94108 (☎415/391-8407);

J Wayne Reitz Union, Suite G6, Museum Rd, University of Florida, Gainsville, FL 32611 (☎352/338-0068);

2401 Pennsylvania Ave, Washington DC 20037 (☎202/887-0912);

297 Newbury St, Boston, MA 02115 (☎617/266-6014);

Rittenhouse Plaza, 1905 Walnut St, Philadelphia, PA 19103 (☎215/568-7999).

TRAVEL CUTS OFFICES IN CANADA

Head Office: 187 College St, Toronto, ON M5T 1P7 (☎416/979-2406, *www.travelcuts.com*).

Other main offices at:

MacEwan Hall Student Centre, University of Calgary, Calgary, AB T2N 1N4 (☎403/282-7687);

10127A 124th St, Edmonton, AB T5N 1P5 (☎403/488-8487);

Student Union Building, Dalhousie University, Halifax, NS B3H 4J2 (☎902/494-2054);

1613 rue St Denis, Montréal, QC H2X 3K3 (☎514/843-8511);

222 Laurier Ave East, 2nd floor, Ottawa, ON K1N 6P2 (☎613/238-8222);

Universite Laval Pavillion, Maurice – Pollack, L – 1258, Ste Foy, Quebec, PQ G1V 1T1 (☎418/654-0224);

1 Campus Drive, Place Riel, University of Saskatchewan, Saskatoon, SA S7N 5A3 (☎306/975-3722);

567 Seymour St, Vancouver, BC V6B 3H6 (☎604/659-2830);

University Centre, University of Manitoba, Winnipeg, MA R3T 2N2 (☎204/269-9530).

USEFUL AIRLINES FOR KENYA FROM THE USA AND CANADA

Air Canada (in BC ☎1-800/663-3721; in Alberta, Saskatchewan and Manitoba ☎1-800/542-8940; in eastern Canada ☎1-800/268-7240; in US ☎1-800/776-3000, *www.aircanada.ca*).

Air France (☎1-800/237-2747; in Canada ☎1-800/667-2747, *www.airfr.fr*).

Alitalia (☎1-800/223-5730; in New York ☎1-800/442-5860; in Canada ☎1-800/361-8336, *www.alitalia.com*).

British Airways (in US ☎1-800/247-9297; in Canada ☎1-800/668-1059, *www.british-airways.com*).

Egyptair (☎1-800/334-6787 or ☎212/315-0900).

El Al (☎1-800/223-6700).

Gulf Air (☎1-800/553-2824).

KLM (in US ☎1-800/447-4747; in Canada ☎1-800/361-5073, *www.klm.com*).

Sabena (☎1-800/955-2000, *www.sabena.com*).

Swissair (in US ☎1-800/221-4750; in Canada ☎1-800/267-9477, *www.swissair.com*).

TWA (domestic ☎1-800/221-2000; international ☎1-800/892-4141, *www.twa.com*).

FLIGHT DEALS FROM THE EASTERN USA

Especially if you're a student, youth (under 26) or teacher, check out Council Travel, with cheap New York–London round-trips, and New York–Nairobi from $1170 (students/under-26s, on Air France) or $1375 (non-students, on Gulf Air). STA Travel, who have a large international network of offices, offer round-trip fares to Nairobi from $1000 (on Air France), on the basis of restricted eligibility and depending on season.

Classified advertisers in the Sunday travel section of *The New York Times* offer various **discounted seat fares** open to all on good airlines (Virgin or BA, and Kenya Airways, for example), though the cheapest "bucket shops" will find you something at a lower price using one of the less convenient European airlines. Good one-way deals are very rare.

FLIGHT DEALS FROM THE WESTERN USA

Give Council and STA Travel a call first – STA's LA–Nairobi fares start at around $1400 for students (on Air France) and sometimes they have deals open to all. Then check out the agents listed opposite or make a search of the Sunday travel pages of the *Los Angeles Times* or the *San Francisco Examiner/Chronicle* for discounted round-trip fares.

FLIGHTS FROM CANADA

The airlines' Toronto–Nairobi Apex fares start at around CDN$3800, but if you book through a Canadian travel agent you can take advantage of the frequent "Net" fares offered to agencies by the airlines in Canada, which can cut the rate to as low as CDN$1450. Travel Cuts also offers a few deals to Nairobi, some of which, using transatlantic charters, are open to all: from Toronto, fares are CDN$1385–1920 round-trip depending on season. Currently, the lowest fares are offered by El Al and Alitalia.

INCLUSIVE TOURS

A large number of tour operators offer **inclusive vacation and safari packages** to Kenya. When checking with them, remember that most of the quotes you'll be given are for the land arrangements only, with flight extra (which may be purchased from the travel operator or from another source). Prices, not including flights, start at around $1000 per week, with most of the tour spent on safari. Hotel-based beach extensions work out somewhat cheaper and are more subject to seasonal variation.

WARNING: BAGGAGE LIMITS

North American passengers who expect to use **transatlantic baggage quotas** – two unweighed pieces of hold luggage – may have problems flying on to Kenya from Europe where a **20kg weight limit** (44lb) applies. The 20kg rule is most likely to be enforced if you have broken your journey in Europe: you won't have any difficulty if you are connecting through. Coming back from Kenya, however, you are, to some extent, subject to the whim of the handler you deal with.

AFRICA AND ADVENTURE TRAVEL SPECIALISTS

Most agents are representatives not only for North American companies but also for many of the **adventure travel operators** whose head offices are in Britain (see pp.10–11), and can offer flight deals.

US AGENTS AND TOUR OPERATORS

Abercrombie & Kent,1520 Kensington Rd, Suite 212, Oak Brook, IL 60523 (☎1-800/323-7308 or 708/954-2944). Leading upscale operator with over thirty years of experience organizing African safaris. Comprehensive and professional programme in Kenya; offices in Nairobi. Tour options include The Adventurer Safari (classic Kenya safari, fourteen days from $2670 land only), The Kenya Family Safari (fifteen days from $3860 adults, $2500 under-12s, land only), Pearls of Africa (eighteen-day safari escorted by Lynne Leakey or Wendy Corroyer, $7400), plus deluxe air safaris and Kenya–Tanzania or Kenya–Egypt combinations.

Adventure Center, 1311 63rd St, Suite 200, Emoryville, CA 94608 (☎1-800/227-8747 or 510/654-1879). Wide range of affordable adventure tours and safaris.

Africa Tours, 217 Merrick Rd, Suite 212, Amityville, NY (☎516/264-2800 or 1-800/235-3692, *www.africasafaris.com*). A variety of Kenya safaris from $1800 land only, or $3800 air included.

African Adventure Company, 5353 N Federal Highway, Suite 300, Ft Lauderdale, FL 33308 (☎1-800/882-WILD or 954/491-8877). One of the best agencies in the business, offering over a hundred programmes to Africa and thousands of safari options, from $1850 land only.

Geo Expeditions, PO Box 3656, Sonora, CA 95370 (☎1-800/351-5041, *www.geoexpeditions.com*). Fifteen-day Kenya safaris and combination Kenya/Tanzania safaris ($4000).

Holbrook Travel, 3540 NW 13th St, Gainesville, FL 32609 (☎352/377-7111). Top-quality natural history tours and safaris led by experts, from $3500 including flight.

Journeys, 1536 NW 23rd Ave, Portland, OR 97210 (☎503/226-7200, *travel@journeys.com*). Tailor-made trips for individuals and groups, plus flights through consolidators.

Ker & Downey, Westchase Square, 2825 Wilcrest Drive, Suite 600 Houston TX 77042 (☎800-423-4236 or 713-917-0048, fax 713-917-0123, *info@kerdowney.com*). Renowned upmarket safaris under canvas in style, with an "Edwardian feel". Also runs to South Africa, Botswana and Tanzania.

Luxury Adventure Safaris, 4635 Via Vistosa, Santa Barbara, CA 93110 (☎805/967-1712, *www.davidanderson.com*). No expense spared here: escorted wildlife safaris and first-class accommodation; $3000–6000, land only.

Mountain Travel Sobek, 6420 Fairmount Ave, El Cerrito, CA 94530 (☎1-800/227-2384 or 510/527-8100). Mountaineering, hiking, white-water rafting and other activity tours, from $1900.

Nature Expeditions International, 7860 Peters Rd, Suite F103, Plantation, FL 33324 (☎954/693-8852 or 1-800/869-0639, *www.naturexp.com*). Education and adventure in travel, offering wildlife, natural history and cultural expeditions. East Africa Wildlife Safari (18–23 days) led by expert naturalist, from $4300 land only.

Safari Center, 3201 N Sepulveda Blvd, Manhattan Beach, CA 90266 (☎1-800/223-6046 or 310/546-4411, *www.safaricenter.com*). Deluxe, economy or adventure safari options, as well as off-the-beaten track safaris; $800–4000.

Somak Safaris, 5250 West Century Blvd, # 311, Los Angeles, CA 90045 (☎310/642-3700 or 1-800/757-6625, *www.somaksafaris.com*). A wide range of safaris to Kenya and all of Africa, starting at $1995, with some special promotions that are even less expensive.

Spector Travel, 2 Park Plaza, Boston, MA 02116 (☎617/338-0111 or 1-800/TRY AFRICA, *www.spectortravel.com*). African specialist with a good record.

Tamsin & Cooke, PO Box 8, Franklin Lakes, NJ 07417 (☎201/337-6151, fax 201/337-0212, *tamsincook@aol.com*). Customized itineraries based on thirty years' residence in Africa, with emphasis on luxury, away-from-it-all accommodation and safaris on foot, horseback and by camel.

Wilderness Travel, 1102 Ninth St, Berkeley, CA 94710 (☎510/558-2488 or 1-800/368-2794). Small-group expeditions to the great game parks of Kenya, led by an experienced Maasai guide (thirteen days, lodge and camping, $3795), a nineteen-day East African Wildlife Safari ($4895), and Perspectives on East Africa, a symposium and safari programme with Jane Goodall and other experts ($5595 plus flight).

CANADIAN AGENTS AND OPERATORS

Blyth & Co, 13 Hazelton Ave, Toronto, ON M5R 2E1 (☎416/964-2569 or 1-800/387-1387). Custom tours to Kenya.

Western Treks/Adventure Center, 8412 109th St, Edmonton T6G 1E2 (☎403/439-9118 or 1-800/227-8747, fax 403/439-5494).

Worldwide Quest, 1170 Sheppard Ave W, Unit 45, Toronto, ON M3K 2A3 (☎416/221-3000 or 1-800/387-1483, *www.worldwidequest.com*). Natural history safaris, from $3395 (seventeen days, land only).

GETTING THERE FROM AUSTRALIA AND NEW ZEALAND

There are no direct flights from Australia or New Zealand – all require a stopover either in Asia, South Africa, or in the carrier's home city. The most direct flights are via either Harare or Mauritius. Another option is to take a round-the-world flight via Harare, including Nairobi as a side trip.

From Australia, the best deals are on Gulf Air via Singapore and Bahrain (from A$1850), and Egyptair via Singapore and Cairo (from A$1850 out of Sydney or Melbourne; A$2015 out of Brisbane; A$2080 out of Adelaide or Hobart). Another inexpensive option is Ansett/Air Mauritius via Mauritius (from A$1850 out of Sydney, Brisbane or Melbourne; A$1720 out of Perth). Qantas and Air Zimbabwe "code-share" flights to Harare twice weekly from eastern cities (from A$2349) and Perth (from A$2190).

In the high season (mid-Nov to mid-Jan), expect to pay an extra $300 or so. As an alternative to taking the Harare–Nairobi flight connection, you could take the train through Zambia and Tanzania, go overland by local transport, or hook up with any number of foreign-operated overland trips from Harare to Nairobi, most of which are very good value for money and take a month or so for the trip.

AIRLINES IN AUSTRALIA AND NEW ZEALAND

Air New Zealand, 5 Elizabeth St, Sydney (☎13 2476); 139 Queen St, Auckland (☎09/357 3000).

Air Mauritius, Level 3, 84 Pitt St, Sydney (☎02/9233 6588); no NZ office.

Air Zimbabwe, Level 17, 456 Kent St, Sydney (☎02/9285 6822); c/o 101 Great South Rd, Remuera, Auckland (☎09/524 2526).

Ansett Australia, 32 Martin Place, Sydney (☎13 1414); branches throughout Australia.

Ansett New Zealand, 2/50 Grafton Rd, Auckland (☎09/379 6409); branches throughout New Zealand.

British Airways, Level 19, 259 George St, Sydney (☎02/8904 8800); 154 Queen St, Auckland (☎09/356 8690).

Egyptair, Level 16/130 Pitt St, Sydney (☎02/9232 6677); no NZ office.

Gulf Air, 64 York St, Sydney (☎02/9244 2199); no NZ office.

Qantas, 70 Hunter St, Sydney (☎13 1211); Qantas House, 154 Queen St, Auckland (☎09/357 8900).

AFRICA AND INDEPENDENT TRAVEL SPECIALISTS

Many of these agents are representatives not only for Australian companies but also for adventure travel operators whose head offices are in Britain (see p.10).

AUSTRALIA

Abercrombie & Kent, 90 Bridport St, Albert Park, Melbourne, VIC 3206 (☎03/9699-9766). Long-established, upmarket operator selling its own exclusive holidays.

Adventure World, 73 Walker St, North Sydney (☎02/956-7766, toll-free 1800/221-931); 8 Victoria Ave, Perth (☎09/221-2300). Accommodation, car rental, discounted air fares and a varied selection of tours from city mini-stays in Nairobi and Mombasa to camping and overland safaris.

Africa Travel Centre, Level 12, 456 Kent St, Sydney, NSW 2000 (☎02/9267-3048). Sister company of the London-based Africa Travel Shop: accommodation, self-drive, Nairobi and Mombasa stop-overs and a comprehensive range of safaris.

Africa Wildlife Safaris, 1st Floor, 259 Coventry St, South Melbourne, VIC 3205 (☎03/9696-2899).

Specialists in upmarket camping and lodge-based safaris.

Exodus Expeditions, Suite 5, Level 5, 1 York St, Sydney (☎02/9521-5430, toll-free 1800/800-724). Wholesaler, offering a seventeen-day Aberdares/Mount Kenya game-viewing trek (A$3000).

Flight Centres, Circular Quay, Sydney (☎02/9241-2422); Bourke St, Melbourne (☎03/650-2899); plus other branches nationwide.

Peregrine, 258 Lonsdale St, Melbourne (☎03/9663-8611). Beach stays, overland trips and all-inclusive game safaris; offices in Brisbane, Sydney, Adelaide, Perth and Hobart.

STA Travel, 732 Harris St, Ultimo, Sydney (☎02/9212-1255, toll-free 1800/637-444); 256 Flinders St, Melbourne (☎03/9347 4711); other offices in Townsville, state capitals and major universities.

NEW ZEALAND

Abercrombie & Kent, Floor 14, Brandon Brookfield House, 17 Victoria St, Auckland (☎09/358-4200).

Adventure Travel Shop, 50 High St, Auckland (☎09/303-1805).

Adventure World, 101 Great South Rd, Remuera, PO Box 74008, Auckland (☎09/524-5118). Agents for Exodus Expeditions and Peregrine, Australia.

Africa Travel Centre, 21 Remuera Rd, PO Box 9365, Newmarket, Auckland (☎09/520-2000). From the same stable as the Australian company.

Flight Centres, National Bank Towers, 205–225 Queen St, Auckland (☎09/309 6171); Shop 1M, National Mutual Arcade, 152 Hereford St, Christchurch (☎09/379 7145); 50–52 Willis St, Wellington (☎04/472 8101); other branches countrywide.

STA Travel, Travellers' Centre, 10 High St, Auckland (☎09/366 6673); 233 Cuba St, Wellington (☎04/385 0561); 223 High St, Christchurch (☎03/379 9098); other offices in Dunedin, Palmerston North, Hamilton and major universities.

From New Zealand, Ansett-Air Mauritius fly twice weekly to Nairobi via Melbourne and Mauritius (from NZ$2500). Alternatively, it's possible to pick up a cheap combination ticket via Singapore or Bangkok, or to fly to Harare and then on to Nairobi. There are twice-weekly flights via Sydney and Harare on Air New Zealand–Air Zimbabwe (from NZ$2505) and Qantas (from NZ$2600).

A **round-the-world** fare that could include Nairobi as a side trip is Qantas/BA/Cathay's "Global Explorer", which allows six free stop-overs worldwide, from A$2399/NZ$2899 (additional stop-overs can be purchased for around A$100/NZ$200, depending on the extra mileage involved).

GETTING THERE FROM SOUTH AFRICA

Direct **flights from Johannesburg** (the only departure point) to Nairobi are operated by South African Airways (Mon, Tues, Fri & Sun; ☎011/978 1111, fax 773 8988, *www.saa.co.za*) and Kenya Airways (Mon, Weds, Thurs & Sat; ☎011/881 9747, fax 881 9749). Booking direct with the airlines, fares start at R2900 for a one-month trip on an Apex ticket; open yearly returns start at R3500.

Useful **tour operators and travel agents** include:

Adventures, 9 Sunbird Place, Swallow Drive, Fourways, Johannesburg (☎011/465 1288, fax 465 9320, *fsal@global.co.za*). Exclusive package tours.

African Outposts, PO Box 4593, Rivonia 2128 (☎011/884 6848, fax 883 8690, *www.tourism.co.za/af-out*). Specialists in "environmental education through tourism".

African Routes, PO Box 1835, Tourist Junction corner of Pine St and Gardener, Durban 4000 (☎031/569 3911 or 569 3912, fax 569 3908, *aroutes@iafrica.com*). Overland operator and agent.

African Safari Shop, PO Box 3714, Cresta 2118 (☎011/888 6364, Fax 782 7557, *www.safarishop.co.za*). Wide range of options at many budgets.

Africa Travel Centre, corner of Military Rd and New Church St, Cape Town 8001 (☎021/4235 555, fax 4230 065, *www.backpackers.co.za*). Local branch of the London-based Africa overland specialist.

Drifters, PO Box 48434, Roosevelt Park 2129 (☎011/888 1160, fax 888 1020, *drifters@drifters.co.uk*). Fortnightly overland departures to Nairobi.

Student Travel Centre, off Craddock Ave, opposite Rosebank, Rosebank 2196, Johannesburg (☎011/447 5551, fax 447 5775, *info@statravel.co.za*). Good youth and student fares.

Wild Frontiers, PO Box 844, Halfway House, Johannesburg 1685 (☎011/315 4838, fax 315 4850, *www.wildfrontiers.com*). A range of mid-priced tours.

TAKING CHILDREN

Kenya is a terrific country for families. If you're considering taking young children, however, you should ask yourself if you can really be bothered with all the hassle. It's a good start if your children are already enchanted with the idea of Africa and its wildlife. But pre-school children have few notions about such things and derive little thrill from experiencing them for themselves.

The following is aimed principally at families with babies and under-fives. For the under-fives, Kenya is a mixture of fun – in the pool, on the beach, with other kids – and tedium – in the car or plane, on a game drive, in a restaurant.

CHILDREN'S HEALTH

Health issues figure most prominently in most people's minds: with the exception of malaria, however, you can discount fears about your children getting tropical diseases in Kenya. Remember how many healthy second-generation expatriate children have been brought up there. (The biggest health problem for Kenyan children is poverty.)

It can, however, be very difficult to persuade small children to take **malaria** pills, under any guise: chloroquine is available as a syrup, but is really not much use in Kenya, while Paludrine is only in tablet form. Breast-feeding babies will be as protected as their mother. With toddlers you may have to choose between ramming pills down their throats – inducing hysterical tears – or giving in and risking it. In the latter case, up-country Kenya is much safer territory than the coast, but you should be extremely careful to cover them with Deet repellent early each evening and be sure they sleep under secure nets. Take a small net for babies, or try to get something like Fisher-Price's "Pop-Up Baby Cabana", a fully enclosed miniature mosquito net tent, discontinued, but previously available in the USA for about $80. For more on malaria, see p.28.

As for sanitation, if you use disposable nappies, bring your own supply for a short stay. Any longer and you'd want to buy them in Kenya (from modern supermarkets), but they are expensive at around Ksh1000 for 36. Baby foods are also available in large supermarkets, but here you'll have few problems if you're staying in hotels as there's usually a good variety of fresh food and staff who, given some warning, are happy to prepare it for infants' tastes.

Unless your time is to be spent exclusively on the coast, bring some **warm clothing** for up-country mornings and evenings. Temperatures in some parts drop low and hotels are not heated.

Probably the most important health concern is the **sun**. On the equator, even when the altitude keeps temperatures down, the effect of thirty minutes' ultra-violet on delicate skin can be severe. Keep them thoroughly smothered in factor 40 (seriously) and insist they wear hats. Children should also wear T-shirts when swimming, and especially if snorkelling. Sunglasses, too, are a good idea, even for babies, to reduce the intense glare: you can always find little novelty ones that will fit. And of course, make sure they drink plenty of water.

TRAVELLING WITH CHILDREN

Air travel with under-twos (who get no seat for their ten percent fares) can be a nightmare. Make every possible effort to get – and retain – bulk-head seats and a bassinet (hanging cradle) for the baby. These requests should be a priority in your plans. When you reconfirm 48 hours before flying, double-check you still have them. If you have lively children who won't easily settle, consider the simple drugging method: trimeprazine (one brand is called Vallergan) can be obtained on prescription and they'll sleep right through the flight and wake up refreshed.

For a young family, going on a group **safari** (whether organized from home as part of a package or booked in Kenya) is probably not on. **Hiring a car** is quite feasible, however, and gives you the flexibility and privacy you need for changing nappies, toilet stops and shouting at each other. For babies and children too small for seat belts, you'll need a **car seat** which, if you have the right model, also works as an all-purpose carrier, pool-side recliner and picnic throne.

If you have a light, easily collapsible **buggy**, bring it. Many hotels and lodges have long paths from the central public areas to the rooms or cottages. A **child-carrier** backpack is another very useful accessory.

For flying with all this baggage, remember you have a full luggage allowance for each passenger with a seat.

SAFARIS AND HOTELS

On safari with young children in tow, your driving time is more likely to be spent in getting from one lodge to the next than in purposeful game drives, but if the children are old enough to enjoy spotting the animals, make sure they have their own **binoculars**.

Small children find it frustrating trying to pick out animals at great distances. And **long drives** are always a big turn-off. For these reasons, some parks are more child-friendly than others. **Nairobi National Park** is great (if you can divert their attention from the planes landing at the airport) and **Lake Nakuru** is a hit as well, as distances are small and the animals close. Equally, **Amboseli**'s small size and the presence of large numbers of elephants make it popular with younger children.

Most **hotels**, **lodges** and **tented camps** do not specifically exclude children of any age, but a number of organized tours have a **minimum age** of seven, while several of the more exclusive tented camps and all four of the "tree hotels" have minimum ages (seven, eight or even ten; restrictions, where they exist, are noted in our reviews).

The **coast hotels** are on sandy beaches facing a warm sea, safely protected by the reef. Particularly suitable family hotels are mentioned in the text.

PROBLEMS AND REWARDS

In hotels, the biggest recurring problem is **meal times**. Some have children's menus and early sittings but it's not something you can count on and it doesn't solve the problem of when the parents eat: it's always a good idea to stick to your established routines if possible. If you're eating as a family, young children will often need something to amuse them (take a good stock of puzzle and colouring books, and as many of their favourite toys as possible).

In the evenings, you'll need a **babysitter**. Very few hotels make permanent provision for this. The management will usually find a local woman to come in, given a few hours' notice, but they tend to leave the question of payment up to you. To avoid inflating the economy, Ksh200 would normally be fine if the arrangement is informal, but Ksh500 for a full evening is the most you should ever pay. Alternatively, if the children are asleep, speak to the restaurant manager and arrange for an *askari* (night watch) to sit outside.

Swimming pools, focus of attention for most children, are only sure to be warm on the coast. In the higher, up-country regions, including Nairobi, unheated pools are always chilly, which can be a big disappointment for keen splashers.

If your child only thrives with **friends** the same age, being stuck with you in a beautiful hotel for a day or two can be numbingly boring. It's obvi-ously not difficult to track down other, child-infested guests and suggest the kiddies amuse themselves together, but if this doesn't work you may want to look for children in the neighbour-hood – not as far-fetched as it sounds in, for example, Naivasha or the suburbs of Nairobi.

Wherever you go, the reaction of **local people** to families and their children is warm and exceptionally welcoming. Waiters and other hotel staff invariably have kids of their own (usually liv-ing far away) and greet and talk to children unselfconsciously. Mothers will find their status breaks the ice with local women (if any needed breaking) and visits with your children to Maasai *enkangs* and similar "ethnic tourism" will always be more rewarding than going on your own.

TRAVELLERS WITH DISABILITIES

Although by no means easy, Kenya does not pose insurmountable problems for people with disabilities. While there is little gov-ernment involvement in improving access, tourist industry staff – not to mention passers-by – are usually prepared to help whenever necessary. Considering, princi-pally, wheelchair-users, many hotels have ground-floor rooms; a number on the coast have ramped access walks to public areas; and larger hotels in Nairobi have elevators. Safari vehicles can usually manage wheel-chair-users.

GETTING THERE

British Airways and Kenya Airways offer the only **non-stop flights** from London to Kenya (note that Kenya Airways "direct" flights to Mombasa do require a plane change to a domestic Kenya Airways flight in Nairobi). These airlines, togeth-er with Air France, KLM and Swissair are the best airlines for disabled passengers. They're some-times more costly, but less physically demanding than the cheapies. If you're flying by **charter**, you'll arrive at Mombasa, which has very basic facilities, but no steps or long distances to nego-tiate – just the steps down from the plane, where you will have to be carried.

From **North America to Europe**, Virgin and Air Canada come out top in terms of disability awareness (and seating arrangements) and may be worth contacting first for any information they can provide.

If you're looking for an all-in tour, contact the upmarket Kenya specialists Abercrombie & Kent (addresses in the "Getting There" sections above) who have some experience in carrying disabled passengers on their regular itineraries.

IN KENYA

Attitudes to disabled people are generally good – there are always willing hands to help you over any obstacle. All the international-class **hotels** in Nairobi have elevators, as do several of the cheaper places (details in the text). **Getting around** the city, however, to do some of its limit-ed sightseeing or to book safaris, is difficult in a wheelchair. While distances are short, there is lit-tle ramping of pedestrian areas and drivers are not used to wheelchairs crossing the road. The capacious London taxi cabs, however, are a boon.

Safari vehicles have superb springing, but taking a pressure cushion is a wise precaution. Even then, off-road trips can be very arduous, especially on the awful roads in and around Maasai Mara, where flying in is recommended. It's perhaps better to use Nairobi as a base, and go on one of the many one-day excursions, to Nakuru, Naivasha or the Outspan near Mount Kenya for example. If you are determined, howev-er, any of the luxury lodges and tented camps should be accessible, with help, making a proper

CONTACTS FOR TRAVELLERS WITH DISABILITIES

BRITAIN AND IRELAND

Access Travel, 16 Haweswater Ave, Astley, Lancashire M29 7BL (☎01942/888844, fax 891811). Tour operator that can arrange flights, transfer and accommodation. This is a small business, personally checking out places before recommendation. ATOL bonded, established six years.

Holiday Care Service, 2nd floor, Imperial Building, Victoria Rd, Horley, Surrey RH6 7PZ (☎01293/774535, fax 784647; minicom ☎01293/776943). Provides free lists of accessible accommodation abroad; information on financial help for holidays available.

RADAR (Royal Association for Disability and Rehabilitation), 12 City Forum, 250 City Rd, London EC1V 8AF (☎0171/250 3222; minicom ☎0171/250 4119). A good source of advice on holidays and travel abroad.

Tripscope, The Courtyard, Evelyn Rd, London W4 5JL (☎0181/994 9294, fax 994 3618). This registered charity provides a national telephone information service offering free advice on international transport for those with a mobility problem.

USA AND CANADA

Directions Unlimited, 123 Green Lane, Bedford Hills, NY 10507 (☎1-800/533-5343). Tour operator specializing in custom tours for people with disabilities.

Jewish Rehabilitation Hospital, 3205 Place Alton Goldbloom, Chomedy Laval, Quebec, H7V 1R2 (☎514/688-9550 ext 227). Guidebooks and travel information.

Mobility International USA, PO Box 10767, Eugene, OR 97440 (Voice and TDD: ☎503/343-1284). Information and referral services, access guides, tours and exchange programmes. Annual membership $20 (includes quarterly newsletter).

Society for the Advancement of Travel for the Handicapped (SATH), 347 Fifth Ave, Suite 610, New York, NY 10016 (☎212/447-7284,

www.sittravel.com). Non-profit travel-industry referral service that passes queries on to its members as appropriate; allow plenty of time for a response.

Travel Information Service, Moss Rehabilitation Hospital, 1200 W Tabor Rd, Philadelphia, PA 19141 (☎215/456-9603). Telephone information and referral service.

Twin Peaks Press, Box 129, Vancouver, WA 98666 (☎360/694-2462 or 1-800/637-2256). Publisher of the *Directory of Travel Agencies for the Disabled* ($19.95), listing more than 370 agencies worldwide; *Travel for the Disabled* ($19.95); the *Directory of Accessible Van Rentals* ($9.95) and *Wheelchair Vagabond* ($14.95), loaded with personal tips.

AUSTRALIA AND NEW ZEALAND

ACROD (Australian Council for Rehabilitation of the Disabled), PO Box 60, Curtin, ACT 2605 (☎06/682-4333); 55 Charles St, Ryde (☎02/9809-4488).

Disabled Persons Assembly, PO Box 10, 138 The Terrace, Wellington (☎04/472-2626).

safari quite feasible, especially if you fly. One or two places even have baths (as well as showers), and are mentioned in the guide. Only on the most adventurous trips, with temporary camps set up in the bush, and long-drop toilets, would wheelchair-users really have problems.

The all-night **Nairobi–Mombasa sleeper train** sounds improbable but, again, is possible. On this, though, you would have to be carried – with some difficulty – from your cabin to the toilets and dining car, as the corridors are very narrow. Your wheelchair would go in the luggage van, too, so expect a delay in retrieving it on arrival. With the exception of the "luxury" coaches plying between Nairobi and Mombasa, other public transport in Kenya is not at all wheelchair-friendly.

RED TAPE AND VISAS

Obvious, but still worth stating, check that your passport is current. And check that it will remain valid for at least six months beyond the end of your projected stay in Kenya. If you're travelling further afield in Africa, you'll need to allow for this, and ensure your passport has plenty of spare pages for stamps. Indian, Pakistani, Canadian, Australian, New Zealand, Sri Lankan and Nigerian citizens need a visa to enter Kenya. Other Commonwealth nationals, and passport holders from Britain, Ireland, Germany, Denmark, Finland, Ethiopia, Sweden, Spain, and Turkey can enter Kenya freely, with just a visitor's pass, issued routinely on arrival. South Africans do not require a visa unless they intend to stay for more than a month. However, the situation has become fluid of late, and all visitors are advised to check in advance with a Kenyan embassy, consulate or high commission as to whether a visa will be required.

VISAS AND VISITORS' PASSES

Visas can be obtained in advance from any Kenyan embassy, consulate or high commission, or from a British embassy in countries where Kenya has no diplomatic representation. Visas normally take 24–48 hours to process, require two passport-size photos and usually an **air ticket** out of the region (not just to Uganda or Tanzania). This requirement is usually waived if

the embassy is satisfied of your alternative arrangements or financial responsibility. Standard fees are £35 (US$50)/A$80 for Britons and New Zealanders; £25 or US$40 (or equivalent) for French and Canadians; and £18, US$30 or A$40 for Americans, Australians and other nationalities. Multiple entry visas cost roughly double. Remember that Kenyan diplomatic missions are closed on Kenyan public holidays (see p.60 for a list of holidays). Transit visas (valid for seven days) can be bought on arrival for around $15. Visas are normally valid for entry within three months of the date of issue.

It's possible to get a **visa on arrival** at the airport (sterling or dollars cash only), though it's best avoided if you're arriving at night. Although this is generally a hassle-free formality, it does leave you open to potential problems caused by corrupt officials preying on your fear of being refused a visa. It also generally requires you to stand in line and take up to an hour. So get in quick!

On arrival in Kenya you will be issued with a visitor's pass limiting the **length of stay** actually granted to you (whether or not you require a visa to enter). Various factors may determine the length of time granted, including your appearance, how much money you have and (fortunately) how long you actually want to stay. They normally give visitors' passes of up to three months.

If you're planning on visiting Uganda or Tanzania out of Kenya, you can cross the border freely within the validity of your Kenya visa (assuming of course you have a visa for Uganda or Tanzania if you need one), but for other trips outside Kenya, you will need to reapply for a visa to re-enter.

EXTENDING YOUR STAY

It's important to know just how long a stay you've been granted in Kenya, particularly, perhaps, if you don't require a visa. There have recently been a number of cases of travellers **overstaying** the limits of their visitors' passes by a few days and finding themselves invited to spend the night behind bars while a suitable fine was discussed – anything up to the equivalent of £100 (US$150). The problem can arise if, for example, you can't decipher KVP5W/H ("Kenya Visitors' Pass 5-Week Holiday"). Ask what's been stamped when you arrive and renew well in advance. You will certainly have to renew after three months.

Extensions to **visitors' passes** and **visa renewals** can be done at the immigration offices in Nairobi, Mombasa, Lamu or Kisumu. Addresses for these are given in the relevant "Listings" sections in the guide. You can only renew your pass for a further three months (six months in all), after which you'll have to leave East Africa.

If your passport requires a visa and you have stayed a total of **six months** in the country and don't have resident's status, you will have to leave not only Kenya, but East Africa, in order to obtain a new visa to allow you to return.

For **neighbouring countries' embassies** in Nairobi see "Nairobi Listings".

CUSTOMS

If you're stopped at the **customs** benches, you will normally be asked if you have any photographic equipment, video camcorders, cassette players and so on. Unless you're some kind of professional, with mountains of specialist gear, there shouldn't be any question of paying duty on personal equipment, though some customs officers like to make notes of it all in your passport to ensure it is re-exported. If you have friends in Kenya, however, and are taking presents for them, you are likely to have to pay duty if you declare the items. If you are asked for a bribe, refuse (the corrupt officer will usually give up on you after half an hour), or kick up a loud fuss.

KENYAN EMBASSIES, CONSULATES AND HIGH COMMISSIONS

AUSTRALIA: 33 Ainslie Ave, PO Box 1990, GPO Canberra (☎02/6247-4748); also serves New Zealand.

AUSTRIA: Rotenturmstrasse 22, 1010 Vienna (☎01/63 32 42).

BELGIUM: Av Joyeuse Entrée 1–5, Brussels (☎02/230 30 65).

CANADA: 415 Laurier Ave East, Ottawa, Ontario K1N 6R4 (☎613/563-1773).

CONGO: Plot 5002, ave de l'Ouganda, BP 9667, Zone Gombe, Kinshasa (☎12/30117).

EGYPT: 20 Boulos Hanna St, PO Box 362, Dokki, Cairo (☎02/704455).

ETHIOPIA: Hiher 16, Kebelle 01, Fikre Mariam Rd, PO Box 3301, Addis Ababa (☎1/18 00 33).

FRANCE: 3 rue Cimarosa, 75116 Paris (☎1/45.53.35.00).

GERMANY: Villichgasse 17, 5300 Bonn 2 (☎0228/35 60 41).

INDIA: 66 Vasant Marg, Vasant Vihar, New Delhi (☎11/672280).

ITALY: CP 10755, 00144 Rome (☎6/808 2718).

JAPAN: 24-20 Nishi-Azabu 3-Chome, Minato-Ku, Tokyo (☎03/479 4006).

NETHERLANDS: Konninginnegracht 102, The Hague (☎70/350 42 15).

NIGERIA: PO Box 6464, 53 Queen's Drive, Ikoyi, Lagos (☎01/682768).

RUSSIA: Bolshaya Ordinka, Dom 70, Moscow (☎095/237 4702).

RWANDA: Blvd de Nyabugogo, PO Box 1215, Kigali (☎772774).

SAUDI ARABIA: PO Box 95458, Riyadh 11693 (☎01/488-2484).

SUDAN: Street 3, Amarat, PO Box 8242 Khartoum (☎11/40386 or 43758).

SWEDEN: Birger Jarlsgatan 37, 2st 11145 Stockholm (☎08/21 83 00).

TANZANIA: 4th Floor, NIC Investment House, Samora Ave, PO Box 5231, Dar es Salaam (☎51/31502).

UGANDA: 60 Kira Rd, PO Box 5220 Kampala (☎41/231861).

UNITED ARAB EMIRATES: PO Box 3854 Abu Dhabi (☎02/366300).

UNITED KINGDOM: 45 Portland Place, London W1N 4AS (☎0171/636-2371).

USA: Embassy, 2249 R St NW, Washington, DC 20008 (☎202/387-6101); Consulate, 424 Madison Ave, New York, NY 10017 (☎212/486-1300); 9150 Wilshire Blvd, Suite 160, Beverly Hills, CA 90212 (☎310/274-6635).

ZAMBIA: 5207 United Nations Ave, PO Box 50298, Lusaka (☎01/212531).

ZIMBABWE: 95 Park Lane, PO Box 4069, Harare (☎04/792901).

MONEY AND COSTS

Kenya's currency, the Kenyan shilling (Ksh), is a colonial legacy based on the old British currency. It's now worth less than a fifth of its original 5 pence sterling (one shilling) equivalent. People occasionally talk in "pounds", meaning Ksh20, and often in "bob", meaning shillings. You'll also hear "quids" for pounds. There are Ksh1000, 500, 200, 100 and 50 notes (the Ksh20 note is being phased out) and coins of Ksh20, 10, 5, 1, 50 cents (half a shilling), 20 cents, 10 cents and 5 cents, though in practice you will rarely come across coins of less than Ksh1. It is possible to export up to Ksh100,000 and some foreign banks stock shillings should you wish to buy some before you arrive in Kenya, but at rates about ten percent under what you might find in Kenya.

At the beginning of 1993, Kenya successively devalued its currency, dropped IMF and World Bank free market policies, floated the currency and then returned to the donors' fold once more, sending the Kenyan shilling all over the place. More fun and games came in 1997, when the IMF suspended a $220 million loan over corruption, which led to a thirty percent fall in the value of the shilling at one point, though it subsequently refound its previous equilibrium rate of around Ksh55–65: $1 and Ksh95–100: £1. At the time of writing, the **rates of exchange** were Ksh100: £1 and Ksh60: $1. There's no longer a black market for foreign currency – don't change money on the street.

MONEY

You can **exchange** hard currencies in cash or travellers' cheques (passport and sometimes receipt required) at banks and foreign exchange bureaux ("forex") all over the country, and at most large hotels for a substantially poorer rate. US dollars and British pounds sterling are always the most acceptable and will cause the least delay where the rates aren't immediately to hand; always ask first what commission and charges will be deducted, as they vary mysteriously even within branches of the same bank (it shouldn't be more than one percent, plus Ksh15 per cheque). Cash invariably attracts better rates than travellers' cheques. Comparative tables of bank and forex bureau rates are published daily (except Sun) in the *Nation* newspaper.

Banks in cities are usually open Monday to Friday (9am–3pm) and on the first and last Saturday of the month from 9–11am. Rural banks and those in small towns are generally open Monday to Friday (8.30am–2.30pm), and every Saturday (8.30–10.30am).

Branches of Barclays and the Commercial Bank of Africa, as well as forex bureaux, are normally fastest, and Standard Chartered are also reasonable. The Kenya Commercial Bank (KCB) is ubiquitous but usually slow and in places charges outrageous commission (fifteen percent). In out-of-the-way places, you may have to wait till 10am to change money, as the rates take ages being sent up from Nairobi. Lastly, if a clerk is being unhelpful or otherwise difficult, a polite but firm demand to see the manager can work miracles.

CARRYING IT AND KEEPING IT

Travellers' cheques are the obvious way to carry your funds. Despite the marginally better rates, there's really little advantage to **cash** and it can't be replaced if lost or stolen. It's definitely worth shopping around for the cheapest travellers' cheques, as some banks levy large charges.

It's wise to carry valuable hard currency (as opposed to Kenyan shillings), as well as passport and air ticket, in a very **safe place**, ideally in a leather pouch or money belt under your belt or waistband, but wrap your things in a plastic bag to avoid damage by sweat. Pouches hanging around your neck are pretty stupid, and ordinary wallets are a disaster. Similarly, the voluminous "bum bags" worn back to front by many tourists over their clothing invite a mugging. As for Kenyan shillings, you'll be carrying around large quantities of coins and paper money. Be aware that, except in the towns, Ksh1000 bills can be hard to change (few people have that sort of money) — so make sure you have a safe purse or secure zip pocket to stuff all the small denominations in.

CREDIT CARDS AND CASH MACHINES

As for **plastic**, VISA and American Express are widely accepted for tourist services such as upmarket hotels and restaurants, flights, safaris, and car rental; Mastercard/Access and Diners' Card are more limited. There's usually a two- to five-percent mark-up on top of the price but, as establishments are charged a fixed percentage of their transactions, this is obviously negotiable. A credit card can be very useful for leaving a deposit for car rental (frequently tens of thousands of shillings).

Most branches of Barclays Bank and Standard Chartered give **cash advances** in shillings (no charge), US dollars or sterling (one percent charge) on Visa and Mastercard, whilst some post offices do cash advances in shillings, slapping on a hefty seven percent commission. The maximum amount you can withdraw is usually your card limit, although large withdrawals may entail an interrogation to screen for potential fraud.

Also useful are the 24-hour **ATM cash machines** recently introduced by many branches of Barclays and Standard Chartered, even in some tiny villages, where you can use your PIN to with-draw cash up to a maximum of Ksh80,000 (£800) per day. The machines accept cards with VISA, VISA Electron, Mastercard, Plus or Cirrus symbols. Obviously, **security** is a concern if you're using ATMs (you're a tempting target with your back turned to the street), so if you're wary get a friend to come along and look out for you. Some Nairobi branches of Barclays have machines inside the building. The actual rate you'll be charged for ATM withdrawals depends on the day that the advance is processed by the credit card company, so it's something of a lottery: some cards offer a floating rate that holds for thirty days or so and actually gets one of the lower rates, but in general the rates are worse than if you were changing cash or travellers' cheques.

Abuse of **credit cards** is not uncommon in Kenya. If you're paying a sum in shillings by cred-it card, make sure that the voucher specifies the currency before you sign. If it doesn't, it's all too easy for the vendor to fill in a dollar sign in front of the total after you've left. Also fill in the lead-ing digits with zeroes. Be especially careful not to let the card get out of your sight (for example in hotels and restaurants), to ensure that only one slip is filled in.

COSTS

Most **prices** in this guide are given in Kenyan shillings, a relatively stable currency. However, we've given prices in US$ for those establish-ments, especially tourist services such as safaris and car rental, which still quote their rates in the "hard" dollar. Almost all the more expensive hotels and lodges also charge non-Kenyans in dol-lars, though you are legally entitled to pay in Ksh, usually at inferior rates of exchange.

HAVING MONEY SENT TO KENYA

Try to avoid **sending home for money**, not so much for the expense (the sender pays the bulk), but to avoid the hassle of transfers getting lost or delayed, and bureaucracy: avoid drafts and money orders, as they cannot be cashed but have to be credited to a Kenyan bank account, and telexed draft orders can take weeks to reach you at the counter even though the normal delay should be four or five working days. More work-able is to send funds via interbank telegraphic transfer (eg SWIFT), for which arrangements can be made if you don't have a Kenyan account (best sent to Barclays' Queensway House or Moi Avenue branches in Nairobi). The service costs you Ksh200, much more for the sender. Western Union also sends money to Kenya, which can be picked up at the Nairobi, Kisumu or Mombasa branches of Kenya Post Bank (details in the rele-vant chapters under "Listings"). This service costs around £20 ($30), and can be effected in under an hour from an overseas bureau de change.

If you're planning a trip to Kenya using moderate or expensive accommodation, it's useful to know that a lot of money can be saved by not going in the high season. With slight variations on date, **resort hotels** and **safari lodges** have separate low-, mid- and high-season rates (it applies much less to town hotels). The seasons of many of the coastal, cottage-type establishments are tied closely to the school year, with the Easter and Christmas holidays, plus July and August, being considered "high". Low-season rates can be anything from a third to a half of the high-season tariff.

Low season: After Easter to June 30 or July 15 (coinciding with the "Long Rains").

Mid season: July 1–16 to November 30 or December 15 (coinciding with the "Short Rains").

High season: December 1–16 to Easter (hot and sunny weather until March).

Kenya can be expensive if you want to hire a car or go on organized safaris. But by staying in the more economical hotels, eating in local places and using public transport, you can get by easily enough on **£10/$16** a day, less if you choose carefully or stay in the cheapest dives or else camp and buy your own food (many Kenyans who survive on the fringes of the money economy manage on less than Ksh300/£3 a week). On a daily average budget of **£20/$32**, you would be living very well most of the time, even staying in the occasional more luxurious tourist hotel.

Staying put you'll find it much easier to live cheaply: a week or so in Lamu on the coast or Lake Naivasha in the Rift Valley need not cost you much more than **£8/$13** a day.

Getting around by **bus** and **pick-up van** (*matatu*) is very cheap (rarely more than £4/$6.65 for the longest journey), but the crucial disadvantage is that they can't drive you around the game parks. In order to do that, **renting a vehicle** – and paying for fuel – will add at least £50 ($75) a day to your costs, though shared between two or more this isn't cripplingly expensive for a week or so; see "Car rental and driving" on p.41. You can also find all-inclusive **camping safaris** from around £40 ($64) a day, sometimes less – see the "Camping Safaris" section on p.64.

BARGAINING

You'll need to get into **bargaining** quickly (see p.59), but be cautious, at first, over your purchases, until you've established the value of things. Once you start, it's surprising how little is sold at a strictly fixed price: it's nearly always worth making an offer. In places that see tourists and travellers, prices sometimes vary considerably through the year. This "seasonal factor" seems to be increasing in importance, too, especially given the near-collapse of the tourist industry in 1997–98.

HEALTH

For arrivals by air from Europe, Australia, or North America, Kenya has no required inoculations. Entering overland, though, you may well be required to show International Vaccination Certificates for both yellow fever and cholera. If you fly on an airline that stops en route in Africa, you should have the yellow fever shot before you leave and get a form that looks like a cholera vaccination certificate but doesn't mean you've had the jab (in Britain, most GPs will give you this – the cholera shot is widely considered completely ineffective). You may otherwise be subjected to them at the airport. Plan ahead and start organizing your jabs at least six weeks before departure. Remember that a yellow fever certificate only becomes valid ten days after you've had the jab. You should also start taking malaria tablets before departure and don't forget to continue taking them for the prescribed time after you return.

OTHER JABS

You should have **tetanus** and **polio** boosters and doctors usually recommend **typhoid** jabs (beware that these take you out of action for a couple of days). For **hepatitis A**, Havrix is now commonly prescribed, and needs a booster after six months to knock up your immunity to ten years. The much cheaper gamma-globulin (or immunoglobulin) shots are only effective for a few months, sometimes it seems not at all, and so are good only for a short once-in-a-lifetime trip to the tropics. The disease itself is debilitating, taking up to a year to clear up.

To reduce the risk of contracting hepatitis, be extra careful about cleanliness and in particular about contamination of water – a problem wherever a single cistern holds the whole water supply in a cockroach-infested toilet/bathroom, as often happens in Lamu.

MALARIA

Protection against **malaria** is absolutely essential. The disease – caused by a parasite carried in the saliva of some mosquitoes – is endemic in tropical Africa; many people carry it in their bloodstream and get occasional bouts of fever. It has a variable **incubation period** of a few days to several weeks so you can get it long after being bitten (but you can't get it soon after arrival). If you get malaria, you'll probably know: the fever, shivering and headaches are something like severe flu and come in waves. If a child gets malaria, however, you might not know: take any fever very seriously indeed. Malaria is not infectious but it can be very dangerous and sometimes even fatal if not treated quickly. The destruction of red blood cells by the *falciparum* type of malaria parasite can lead to **cerebral malaria** (blocking of the brain capillaries) and is the cause of a nasty complication called **blackwater fever** in which the urine is stained by excreted blood cells.

PREVENTION

It is essential to do everything possible to avoid being bitten, and it's normally considered vital to take anti-malaria tablets (the oft-promised vaccine has yet to materialize).

In the UK, **anti-malarials** are only available on private prescription. Your doctor or clinic will advise as to which to take: the drug most often prescribed is **mefloquine** (trade name **Lariam**), which was run through the wringer by the media after its release in the early 1990s. It is expensive, and can cause nasty psychological side effects, the most insidious being mild depression, at worst full-blown hallucinations and paranoia. Although the manufacturers claim that the risks are minimal compared to the dangers of contracting malaria, official figures suggest that 22 percent of patients taking Lariam are likely to suffer mild bouts of nausea or dizziness, and reports from travellers suggest that the official figure of around one in ten thousand experiencing neuropsychiatric problems such as depression and sleep disturbance is a vast underestimate. The manufacturers advise against taking the prophylactic for periods of over two months (which means one month travel). It is not suitable for pregnant women, people with liver or kidney problems, epileptics, or infants under three years. The dose is one tablet per week, for a minimum of six weeks, starting two weeks before entry into a malarial zone and continuing for at least two weeks after leaving.

For those for whom Lariam is counter-indicated – or if you're simply not convinced by the manu-

IMMUNIZATIONS AND ADVICE

In **Britain**, your first source of advice and probable supplier of jabs and prescriptions is your general practitioner. Family doctors are often well informed and are likely to charge you a (relatively low) flat fee for routine injections. For yellow fever and other exotic shots you'll normally have to visit a specialist clinic, often in a county town health authority headquarters.

In London, advice and low-cost **inoculations** are available from the Travel Clinic, Mortimer Market Centre, off Tottenham Court Rd, WC1E 6AU (Mon–Fri 9am–5pm; ☎0171/387 4411, fax 388 7645). They produce a series of useful fact sheets, and you can make an appointment for a consultation and/or a course of jabs. With a referral from your GP, they can also give you a complete **check-up** on your return if you think it may be worth it.

Also in London, the British Airways Travel Clinic, 156 Regent St, London W1 (☎0171/439 9584), is open Monday to Friday 9.30am–5.15pm, and Saturday 10am–4pm (no appointment required). They can provide you with a wide variety of unusual shots like plague, anthrax and rabies as well as the usual ones, anti-malarial tablets and various hardware. There are more than thirty similar BA Travel Clinics around England, plus one in Cardiff (☎01222/811425) and one each in Edinburgh (☎0131/336 3038) and Aberdeen (☎01224/624669). Call ☎01276/685040 for the address of your nearest one.

The travel agency Trailfinders has its own travel clinic (see "Discount Agents" box, p.4). You might also visit the Nomad Traveller's Medical Centre, 3–4 Wellington Terrace, Turnpike Lane, London N8 0PX (☎0181/889 7014), for jabs, prescriptions, and medical kits (pharmacist on site Wed & Thurs 2–5.30pm, Sat 9am–5.30pm). It's attached to the excellent Nomad equipment shop, which has a free travel reference centre, with a selection of books, brochures, and accommodation details.

If you don't live near a clinic, or you're passing through the UK, you may want to check out the services of MASTA (Medical Advisory Services for Travellers Abroad, Bureau of Hygiene and Tropical Diseases, Keppel St, London WC1E 7HT; ☎0171/631-4408) who provide very detailed, personalized "Health Briefs" for whichever country you're visiting. They advise on which inoculations you need and when to get them, give rundowns on all the diseases you may fall victim to and include up-to-date health news from the countries concerned. The "Concise Brief" seems pretty complete but the "Comprehensive" one is amazingly so and a delight for hypochondriacs (students half-price). MASTA also sell Neat Deet insect repellent, various mosquito nets and Sterile Emergency Kits – basically sterile needles and drip.

Other major tropical disease centres in the UK are:
Communicable Diseases Unit, Ruchill Hospital, Glasgow G20 9NB (☎0141/946 7120). Telephone helplines (24hr recorded information):
Hospital for Tropical Diseases Healthline (☎0839/337733). User-friendly service offering comprehensive advice over the phone or fax.
Liverpool School of Tropical Medicine, Pembroke Place, Liverpool L3 5QA (☎0151/708 9393).
London School of Hygiene and Tropical Medicine Malaria Helpline (☎0891/600350). Advice on malaria prevention.
MASTA Healthline (☎0891/224100). Health Brief ordering system (written information sent by post if you leave details of your itinerary) followed by general advice.

In **Ireland**, Travel Medicine Services, PO Box 254, 16 College St, Belfast 1 (☎01232/315220), and the Tropical Medical Bureau, Grafton St Medical Centre, Dublin 2 (☎01/671 9200), offer medical advice before a trip and medical help afterwards in the event of a tropical disease.

In the **USA** and **Canada**, all travellers heading for Kenya should call at one of the Centers for Disease Control and Prevention (international travellers hotline: ☎888/232-3228, CDC autofax 888/232-3299, *www.cdc.gov*) and ask for "Health Information for International Travel" – a very informative booklet giving details on jabs and bugs and general advice. Their 24-hour Voice Information System (☎404/332-4555) gives recorded information on general health concerns for travellers, and their Web site, *www.cdc.gov/travel/index.htm*, has up-to-the-minute health advice for every country in the world. The Travelers Medical Center, 31 Washington Square, New York, NY 10011 (☎212/982-1600), offers a consultation service on immunizations and treatment of diseases. Travel Medicine, 351 Pleasant St, Suite 312, Northampton, MA 01060 (☎1-800/872-8633), sells first-aid kits, mosquito netting, water filters and other health-related travel products.

In **Australia**, vaccination clinics include the Travellers' Medical and Vaccination Centre, 7/428 George St, Sydney (☎02/9221 7133); 2/393 Little Bourke St, Melbourne (☎03/9602 5788); 6/29 Gilbert Place, Adelaide (☎08/8212 7522); 6/247 Adelaide St, Brisbane (☎07/3221 9066); and 5 Mill St, Perth (☎08/9321 1977). The general info/health line number is ☎1902/261 560. In **New Zealand**, contact 1/170 Queen St, Auckland (☎09/373 3531); 147 Armagh St, Christchurch (☎03/379 4000, *www.tmvc.com.au*).

GOING DOWN WITH MALARIA

If you go down with **malaria**, you'll need to take a cure. Don't compare yourself with local people who may have considerable immunity. The priority, if you think you might be getting a fever, is treatment. Delay is very risky.

First, confirm your diagnosis by getting to a doctor and having a **blood test** to identify the strain. Use your own sterile needle pack, even if it might offend. Be aware that Lariam can lead to an inconclusive result. If a test isn't possible, and you're not on the coast, **quinine tablets** are recommended as the best treatment – 600mg twice a day for five days, and then three Fansidar tablets. If you notice no improvement after the first dose of quinine, it's a safe bet that your

malaria is chloroquine-resistant – take three Fansidar tablets straight away. If you're on the coast and can't get to a doctor, any malarial symptoms should be treated as chloroquine-resistant *falciparum*, so take three Fansidar tablets immediately. Fansidar is effective but is not sold in the West due to its very rare but dangerous side-effects. Lariam (mefloquine) can also be taken as a cure: take three tablets, then two more after six hours, then one more 24 hours after the first dose.

While giving the cure time to work you should dose up on painkillers to help ease the worst of the discomfort, take plenty of fluids, and keep eating (but avoid milk-based products).

facturers' claims about its minimal risks – it's worth taking an alternative regime of anti-malarials. A combination of **proguanil** (trade name **Paludrine**; taken daily) and **chloroquine** (trade name **Avloclor**; taken weekly) still provides a high enough level of protection to make them worth persevering with, although chloroquine on its own provides less than 75 percent protection. Again, keep a careful routine and cover the period before and after your trip with doses. These too may leave you feeling nauseous; the dose is best taken at the end of the day, and never on an empty stomach.

Once in Kenya, chloroquine-based tablets (eg Nivaquin, Aralen and Resochin), as well as Paludrine and Daraprim, can be bought everywhere, but the newer drugs to which *falciparum* malaria is less resistant – Lariam, Halfan and Fansidar – are only available in big towns. Fansidar is not recommended as a prophylactic, but is effective as a cure if you already have malarial symptoms. The chloroquine-based drug Malaraquin is widely marketed and cheap in Kenya but it's practically useless. Some pills give people mouth ulcers – you may want to be prepared with suitable remedies.

There is a growing interest in **homeopathic** anti-malarial treatments among travellers who are unable or unwilling to risk the side effects of standard prophylactics, but the claims of homeopathy are still hypothetical, and protection cannot be guaranteed.

It can't be overstressed that the best way to avoid malaria is to **avoid getting bitten**.

You can greatly reduce bites by sleeping under a **mosquito net** – they're not expensive – and burning **mosquito coils** (readily available in Kenya) for a peaceful night. Don't use Cock Brand or Lion, which are said to contain DDT and are banned in many countries. If you're carrying your own mosquito net, it's worth impregnating it with pyrethrum or Deet (see below).

Female *Anopheles* mosquitoes – the aggressors – prefer to bite in the evening. They can be distinguished from other mosquitoes by their rather eager, head-down position. After dark, always cover your exposed parts with something strong. Deet (the insecticide diethyltoluamide) works well – look for a product with at least fifty percent concentration, such as Nomad Neet Deet. The idea of soaking wrist and ankle "sweat bands" (bought from a sports shop) with Deet seems a good one, but it's fiddly in practice; the stuff gets everywhere and corrodes most artificial materials, especially plastic. If you don't like all this synthetic protection, there are now some good, natural alternatives: a particularly effective, pyrethrum-based formulation, not tested on animals, is X-Gnat skin gel (X-Gnat Laboratories, Cumbernauld, Scotland). Strangely, one of the most effective mosquito repellents is said to be Avon "Skin-so-soft" bath oil – not that they market it as such; try the "Lightbouquet" version. Some people swear by the effects of vitamin B tablets in deterring mosquitoes.

In Nairobi and the highlands, the malaria risk is low or non-existent, but you should under no circumstances break your course of pills as it's vital to keep your parasite-fighting level as high as possible. On the coast, where mosquito bites are assured, the malaria situation is still quite serious and chloroquine is reckoned to be ineffective.

OTHER DISEASES

Bilharzia is a dangerous disease. The usual recommendation is never to swim in, wash with, or even touch, lake water that can't be vouched for. In fact, while various lakes and rivers harbour the disease – in places – the only inland water you would probably want to swim in is Lake Turkana or Lake Naivasha, both of which are bilharzia-free.

Bilharzia, the medical name of which is **schistosomiasis**, comes from tiny flukes (the schistosomes) that live in freshwater snails and which, as part of their life cycle, leave their hosts and burrow into animal (or human) skin to multiply in the blood-stream. The snails only favour stagnant water and the chances of picking up bilharzia are small. Of course, if you feel major fatigue and pass blood – the first symptoms – see a doctor: it's curable.

The only other real likelihood of your encountering a serious disease is if it's **sexually transmitted**. Venereal diseases are widespread, particularly in the larger towns, and the **HIV virus** which can cause AIDS is alarmingly prevalent and spreading all the time (see p.71). It's very easily passed between people suffering relatively minor, but ulcerous, sexually transmitted diseases, and the very high prevalence of these is thought to account for the high incidence of heterosexually transmitted HIV.

WATER AND BUGS

Until a few years ago, most visitors to Kenya drank **tap water**, or, in doubtful cases, boiled

MEDICINE BAG

There's no need to take a mass of drugs and remedies you'll probably never use. Various items, however, are immensely useful, especially on a long trip, and well worth buying in advance.

On a local level, if you're interested in herbal and other natural remedies, you'll find a wealth of examples in markets, as well as traditional doctors (you'll find them under "Herbalists" in the *Yellow Pages*, or just ask around). Intuition, common sense and persistent enquiries are all you need to judge whether they're worth trying.

Aspirin or paracetamol For pain and fever relief.

Iodine tincture (with dropper) or water purifying (chlorine) tablets Chlorine tastes horrific; iodine is pleasant in comparison, much cheaper, and can also be used to disinfect wounds instead of alcohol. Some people are allergic to chlorine, others to iodine (especially if seafood gets to you). Neither are recommended for long-term use. Murky water must be filtered first through fine muslin.

Anti-malaria tablets Enough for prophylactic use plus several courses of Fansidar and/or quinine tablets in case of attack.

Codeine phosphate This is the preferable emergency anti-diarrhoeal pill but is on prescription only. Some GPs may oblige. Immodium is also useful.

Antibiotics Ciproxin or Bactrim are good in a lower bowel crisis. Amoxil (amoxicillin) is a broad spectrum antibacterial drug useful against many infections. Flagyl (metronizadole) is the recommended treatment for giardia and amoebic

dysentery. None should be used unless you cannot see a doctor.

Antihistamine cream To treat insect bites: best applied immediately after being bitten.

Zinc oxide powder Useful anti-fungal powder for sweaty crevices.

Antiseptic cream Cicatrin and Bacitracin are good, but creams invariably squeeze out sooner or later so avoid metal tubes. Bright red or purple mercurochrome liquid, or iodine, dries wounds.

Alcohol swabs Medi-swabs are invaluable for cleaning wounds, insect bites and infections.

Sticking plaster, steri-strip wound closures, sterile gauze dressing, micropore tape You don't need much of this stuff. If you use it up, supplies can be replenished in any pharmacy.

Lip-salve/chapstick Invaluable for dry lips.

Thermometer Very useful. Ideally you'll be 37°C. A Feverscan forehead thermometer is unbreakable and gives a ready reckoning (from pharmacists).

Lens solution If you wear contact lenses you'll need a good supply of solution.

GENERAL HEALTH TIPS

Many people get occasional **heat rashes**, especially at first on the coast. A warm shower, to open the pores, and cotton clothes should help. And, on the subject of heat, it's important not to overdose on **sunshine** in the first week or two. The powerful heat and bright light can mess up your system. A hat and sunglasses are strongly recommended.

Some people **sweat** heavily and lose a lot of salt. If this applies to you, sprinkle extra salt on your food. Salt tablets are a waste of money but you do need to keep a healthy salt balance.

Papaya (pawpaw) – if you like it – can be eaten as a kind of tonic. The fruit contains excellent supplies of invigorating minerals and vitamins, and is reckoned to help the healing process and to aid digestion. Papaya seeds, which taste like watercress, are good for you, too. If you're not wild about lowland papayas, try the smaller and much more fragrant **mountain** variety.

If you're going to be on the road for a long time, it may be worth considering taking some **vitamin tablets** with you.

water. Then someone hit on the idea of bottling spring water and making it the most expensive soft drink in the country. In most places (Nairobi and most highlands towns), the tap water can be drunk and is considered pure (it is, in any case, the same water that fills the majority of so-called mineral water bottles). But since bad water is the most likely cause of **diarrhoea**, you should be fairly cautious about drinking rain- or well-water if you can't get clean tap water. Endless cups of super-heated *chai* are the obvious solution, if your teeth can stand it. It can't do any harm, except to your purse, to drink bottled water only – it costs Ksh40–50 per litre – but it can mean you don't drink enough, especially on long, hot journeys.

"TRAVELLER'S HEALTH"

Edited and regularly updated by Richard Dawood, *Traveller's Health* (OUP/Viking Penguin) is a sane, detailed and well-written guide, with something for just about every imaginable symptom.

In truth, serious **stomach upsets** don't afflict a large proportion of travellers. If you're only staying a short time, it makes sense to be very scrupu-

lous: purifying your drinking water with tablets or, better, iodine (six drops per litre of water, then wait for half an hour), or boiling it for thirty minutes kills most things. For longer stays, think of **re-educating your stomach** rather than fortifying it; it's virtually impossible to travel around the country without exposing yourself to strange bugs from time to time. Take it easy at first, don't overdo the fruit (and wash it in clean water), don't keep food too long, and be very wary of salads served in cheap restaurants.

Should you have a **serious attack**, 24 hours of sweet, black tea and nothing else may rinse it out. The important thing is to replace your lost fluids. If you feel the need, you can make up a **rehydration mix** with four heaped teaspoons of sugar or honey and half a teaspoon of salt in a litre of water. Flat Coca Cola is quite a good tonic; avoid coffee, strong fruit juice, and alcohol. If it seems to be getting worse – or if you have to travel a long distance – any chemist should have name brand anti-diarrhoea remedies. These – Immodium, Lomotil, Codeine phosphate and so on – shouldn't be overused. Stay right away from the popular Kaomycin, which isn't particularly safe to use and can even encourage diarrhoea. And avoid

HOSPITALS

If you need serious treatment in Kenya, you'll discover a frightening lack of well-equipped **hospitals** and drugs, and in most you're routinely expected to bribe for treatment, and also pay for syringes, plastic gloves, cotton wool, drugs and other medical equipment (the US Embassy bombing in Nairobi emptied a year's already stretched medical supplies in a matter of days). The Consolata

Sisters' hospitals – the Nazareth Hospital on Riara Ridge, outside Nairobi (☎02/335684), and another in Nyeri (☎0171/72032) – are reassuring exceptions. Nairobi itself is fairly well provided: the Nairobi Hospital in Argwings Kodhek Road is reasonably good (☎02/722160). We've mentioned the best local hospitals throughout the text in the "Listings" sections.

jumping for antibiotics at the first sign of trouble: they annihilate what's nicely known as your "gut flora" (most of which you want to keep) and will not work on viruses. Most upsets resolve themselves. If you continue to feel bad, you should seek a doctor.

INJURIES AND ATTACKS

Take more care than usual over minor **cuts and scrapes**. In the tropics, the most trivial scratch can quickly become a throbbing infection if you ignore it. Take a small tube of antiseptic with you, or apply alcohol or iodine.

Otherwise, there are all sorts of potential bites, stings and rashes which rarely, if ever, materialize. **Dogs** are usually sad and skulking, posing little threat. **Scorpions and spiders** abound but are hardly ever seen unless you deliberately turn over rocks or logs: scorpion stings are painful but almost never fatal, while spiders are

mostly quite harmless. **Snakes** are common but, again, the vast majority are harmless. To see one at all, you'd need to search stealthily; walk heavily and they obligingly disappear.

TEETH

Get a thorough **dental check-up** before leaving home and take extra care of your teeth while in Kenya. Stringy meat, acid fruit and sugary tea are some of the hazards. You might start using a freshly cut "toothbrush twig" (*msuake*), as local people do. Some varieties contain a plaque-destroying enzyme; you can buy them at markets.

If you lose a filling and aren't inclined to see a dentist in Kenya, try and get hold of some *gutta-percha* – a natural, rubbery substance – available from some pharmacists, or from your dentist. You heat it and then pack it in the hole as a temporary filling. Using chewing gum is a bad idea.

INSURANCE

Insurance, in the light of all the medical possibilities, is too important to ignore. Before you purchase special travel insurance, whether for medical or property mishaps, check to see that you won't duplicate the coverage of any existing plans which you may have or be covered by. Travel facilities paid for with credit cards are routinely insured, but this won't help you if your camera is stolen or your jeep is rammed by a buffalo.

Home insurance may cover theft or loss of documents, money and valuables while overseas, though exact conditions and maximum amounts

vary from company to company. Students may even be covered by their parents' policies. Travel insurance policies usually offer only limited cover for the loss of valuables such as cameras, jewellery and watches (typically £250–£350 in total, with a maximum of £150–£250 per item; a camera, including lenses, counts as one item).

You should, however, be most interested and concerned about insuring your **health** and being certain that if you have to spend time in hospital, or even have to be repatriated, you'll be covered.

BRITAIN AND IRELAND

Premiums among **British** insurers vary widely – from the very reasonable ones, offered primarily through student and youth travel agencies (though available to anyone), to ones so expensive that the cost for anything more than two months of coverage will probably equal the cost of the worst possible combination of disasters. You should note also that few – if any – insurers will arrange on-the-spot payments in the event of a major expense or loss; you will usually be reimbursed only after going home.

ISIS travel insurance, available through branches of STA Travel or Endsleigh (in London, 71 Old Brompton Rd, SW7 3JS, ☎0171/589 6783;

or 97–107 Southampton Row, WC1, ☎0171/436 4451) is one of the cheapest and best available in Britain. A fee of £42–50 per month will cover you against all sorts of calamities as well as lost baggage, flight cancellations and hospital charges. You might also contact Suretravel, The Pavilion, Kiln Park Business Centre, Kiln Lane, Epsom, Surrey KT17 1JG (☎01372/749191). Their insurance cover (sold direct or through travel agents) covers risks like watersports that many other insurers don't as a rule. If you plan to take several trips over the course of a year it would make sense to consider an annual or multi-trip policy: you could try Worldwide Travel Insurance Services, PO Box 99, Elm Lane Offices, Elm Lane, Tonbridge, Kent TN10 3XS (☎01732-773366), who, again, cover you for watersports.

If you need to **claim**, you must have a police report in the case of theft or loss, and supporting evidence in the case of hospital and medication bills. Keep photocopies of it all and don't allow months to elapse before informing the insurer.

In **Ireland**, travel insurance is best obtained through a travel specialist such as USIT (see box on p.5), with policies costing from £43 for a month. Discounts are offered to students of any age and anyone under 26.

USA AND CANADA

American and Canadian holders of **ISIC** cards (which cost $18 with valid youth/student ID) are entitled to $3000 worth of basic sickness and accident coverage and sixty days ($100 a day) of hospital in-patient benefits for the period during which the card is valid. University **students** will also often find that their student health coverage extends for one term beyond the date of last enrolment. Bank and charge **accounts** (particularly American Express) will also often have certain levels of medical or other insurance included.

Canadians are usually covered for medical expenses by their provincial health plans (but may only be reimbursed after the fact).

Only after exhausting these possibilities might you want to contact a specialist travel insurance firm; your travel agent can usually recommend one. Companies to consider include: ISIS, sold by STA Travel (☎1-800/777-0112), with policies for $80–105 for a month (depending on level of coverage); Travel Guard, 1145 Clark St, Stevens Point, WI 54481 (☎1-800/826-1300 or 715/345-0505), who offer cover for a premium of $69 on a $1000

trip or $109 on a $2000 trip; and Access America, 600 Third Ave, New York, NY 10163 (☎1-800/284-8300 or 212/949-5960), who provide a deluxe plan at similar prices with a daily rate of $2.50 per day for trips of over 31 days.

A most important thing to keep in mind – and a major disappointment to would-be claimants – is that nearly all of the currently available policies do not insure against **theft**. North American travel policies apply only to items **lost** from, or **damaged** in, the custody of an identifiable, responsible third party, such as a hotel porter, airline, luggage consignment and so on. Even in these cases you still have to contact the local police to have a complete **report** made out for your insurer to process the claim.

AUSTRALIA AND NEW ZEALAND

In **Australia and New Zealand**, travel insurance is put together by the airlines and travel agent groups in conjunction with insurance companies. They are all comparable in premium (around A$190/NZ$220 for one month, A$260/NZ$300 for two months and A$330/NZ$400 for three months); most adventure sports are covered, but always check your policy. Companies worth contacting include: UTAG, 122 Walker St, North Sydney (☎02/9956 8399, toll-free 1800/809 462); Cover-More, Level 9, 32 Walker St, North Sydney (☎02/9202 8000, toll-free 1800/251 881); and Ready Plan, 141–147 Walker St, Dandenong, Victoria (☎1300/555 017), or through STA Travel; in New Zealand, 10th Floor, 63 Albert St, Auckland (☎09/379 3208).

FLYING DOCTORS

Kenya's flying doctor **Air Ambulance** service (which also operates in Tanzania) offers free evacuation by air to a medical centre – very reassuring if you'll be spending time out in the wilds. Annual tourist membership costs $50 per person. The income goes back into the service and the African Medical Research Foundation (AMREF) behind it. You can contact them in advance (PO Box 30125 Nairobi; membership/information: ☎02/501301 or 500508, fax 502699; 24-hour emergency: ☎02/501280 or 602492, fax 336886) or buy their insurance on arrival: they have an office at Wilson Airport, from where most of their rescue missions set out. Similar services are offered by AAR Health Services (☎02/717375–6) and ICAA (☎02/604945, 503755, fax 604920), both in Nairobi.

MAPS AND ADVANCE INFORMATION

Kenya Tourist Offices abroad tend to be thin on useful maps and information (the Ministry of Tourism relies on the private sector to promote Kenya), but they are always worth visiting if you're nearby. Try to buy maps in advance – with the exception of the inexpensive Kenya Survey maps, they're usually cheaper.

If you're going to Kenya for some time, there's a growing list of **libraries**, **resource centres** and **journals** which can give you some insight into the country before you touch down.

In **Nairobi**, there's a good selection of maps at the **Public Map Office** (see "Nairobi Listings" for details on how to obtain the Survey maps, which you might want to do months in advance)

and it's really worth getting hold of the Survey of Kenya park maps before taking off for the wilds: with the aid of the numbered junctions, you can actually find your way around. At the park gates they're usually either out of stock or twice the price. The best maps for each national park are mentioned at the start of the relevant sections.

LIBRARIES AND RESOURCE CENTRES IN LONDON

Africa Centre, 38 King St, London WC2E 8JT (☎0171/836 1973). Office and reading room open Mon–Fri 9.30am–5.30pm. Britain's best independent charity institute for African affairs, open to all: reading room with magazines and newspapers, exhibitions, music, theatre, cinema, language teaching (good Swahili classes), bar and restaurant open all week. A good place to meet people.

Commonwealth Institute, Kensington High St, London W8 6NQ (☎0171/603 4535). Large centre offering library and resource services, shop, exhibitions, workshops. Performance venue.

Royal Geographical Society, 1 Kensington Gore, London SW7 2AR (☎0171/581 2057). Helpful Expedition Advisory Service provides a wealth of information, including maps and technical guides.

School of Oriental and African Studies Library, Thornhaugh St, Russell Square, London WC1H 0XG (☎0171/637 2388). A vast collection of books, journals and maps in a modern building. Day visits are allowed but membership to borrow is expensive and requires a reference.

KENYA TOURIST OFFICES ABROAD

CANADA: 415 Laurier Ave East, Ottawa, Ontario K1N 6RY (☎613/563-1773).

FRANCE: 5 rue Volney, Paris F-75002 (☎01.42.60.66.88, fax 42.61.18.84).

GERMANY: Neue Mainzer Strasse 22, D-60311 Frankfurt (☎69/23 20 17, fax 69/23 92 39).

HONG KONG: 1309 Liu Chong Hing Bak Building, 24 Des Voeux Rd, Central GPO Box 5280, Hong Kong (☎523 6053).

ITALY: c/o Kenya Embassy, Via Archmede 0097 (☎06/808 2714, fax 808 2707).

JAPAN: RM 216 Yurakucho Building, 1-10 Yurakucho, 1-Chome, Chiyoda-Ku, Tokyo (☎3/214 4595).

SOUTH AFRICA: 155 Fifth St 2196, Sandton, PO Box 652819, Benmore 2010 (☎011/784-8196, fax 784-8198).

SWEDEN: PO Box 7694, 10395 Stockholm (☎08/240 445, fax 200 030).

SWITZERLAND: Bleicherweg 30, Postfach 770, CH-8039 Zurich (☎1/202 22 44, fax 1/202 22 56).

UNITED KINGDOM: 25 Brook's Mews, Mayfair, London, W1Y 1LF (☎0171/355 3144, fax 495 8656).

USA: 424 Madison Ave, New York, NY 10017 (☎212/486-1300, fax 212/688-0911); 9150 Wilshire Blvd, Suite 160, Beverly Hills, CA 90212 (☎310/274-6635, fax 310/859-7010).

MAP AND TRAVEL BOOK SUPPLIERS

UK

Africa Bookcentre, 38 King St, London WC2E 8JT (☎0171/240 6649). Located in the Africa Centre, Mon–Sat 10am–6pm, Thurs 10am–7pm. A very wide selection of books from and about the continent, with an emphasis on African writers and academic works.

Daunt Books for Travellers, 83 Marylebone High St, W1M 3DE (☎0171/224 2295). Huge selection of guides and maps, plus history and novels.

Nomad Books, 781 Fulham Rd, London SW6 5HA (☎0171/736 4000). Small, friendly travel book specialist.

John Smith and Sons, 57–61 St Vincent St, Glasgow, G2 5TB (☎0141/221 7472, *www.john-smith.co.uk*). Specialist map department in long-established booksellers; full range of foreign maps; mail order service.

Stanford's, 12–14 Long Acre, Covent Garden, London WC2E 9LP (☎0171/836 1321; also mail order *sales@stanfords.co.uk*); 52 Grosvenor Gardens, London SW1W 0AG; 156 Regent St, London W1R 5TA. One of the world's best map and guidebook suppliers.

The Travel Bookshop, 13 Blenheim Crescent, London W11 2EE (☎0171/2295260, *www.thetravelbookshop.co.uk*). The oldest travel bookshop in London, with a good selection of secondhand classics and old travelogues.

USA

The Complete Traveler Bookstore, 199 Madison Ave, New York, NY 10016 (☎212/685-9007); 3207 Filmore St, San Francisco, CA 92123 (☎415/923-1511).

Forsyth Travel Library, 9154 W 57th St, Shawnee Mission, KS 66201 (☎1-800/367-7984).

Latitudes Map & Travel Store, 4811 Excelsior Blvd, St Louis Park, Minneapolis, MN 55416 (☎612/927-9061).

Map Link, 30 S La Petera Lane, Unit 5, Santa Barbara, CA 93117 (☎805/692-6777).

Oceanie Afrique-Noire Books (OAN), 15 W 39th St, second floor, New York, NY 10018 (☎212/840-8844). Bookshop specializing in African art and culture.

Phileas Fogg's Books & Maps, 87 Stanford Shopping Center, Palo Alto, CA 94304 (☎1-800/233-FOGG in California; ☎1-800/533-FOGG elsewhere in US).

Rand McNally, 444 N Michigan Ave, Chicago, IL 60611 (☎312/321-1751); 150 E 52nd St, New York, NY 10022 (☎212/758-7488); 595 Market St, San Francisco, CA 94105 (☎415/777-3131); 7988 Tysons Corner Center, McLean, VA 22102 (☎703/556-8688). For other locations, or for maps by mail order, call ☎1-800/333-0136 (ext 2111).

The Savvy Traveller, 310 S Michigan St, Chicago, IL 60602 (312/913-9800).

Travel Books & Language Center, 4931 Cordell Ave, Bethesda, MD 20814 (☎1-800/220-2665).

CANADA

Open Air Books & Maps, 25 Toronto St, Toronto, M5C 2R1 (☎416/363-0719).

Ulysses Travel Bookshop, 4176 St-Denis, Montréal (☎514/843-9447).

World Wide Books and Maps, 736 Granville St, Vancouver, BC V6Z 1E4 (☎604/687-3320).

AUSTRALIA AND NEW ZEALAND

Mapland, 372 Little Burke St, Melbourne (☎03/9670 4383).

The Map Shop, 16a Peel St, Adelaide (☎08/8231 2033).

Perth Map Centre, 884 Hay St, Perth (☎08/9322 5733).

Specialty Maps, 58 Albert St, Auckland (☎09/307 2217).

Travel Bookshop, Shop 3, 175 Liverpool St, Sydney (☎02/9261 8200).

Worldwide Maps and Guides, 187 George St, Brisbane (☎07/3221 4330).

MAPS

You'd do well to buy a good, large-scale **map of Kenya** before leaving, possibly two if you're planning to head off on less trodden roads (none of the maps below are completely accurate). Other, locally useful maps are mentioned in passing through the guide.

Bartholomew This offering makes all the roads look the same so can't be recommended as a travelling companion.

Macmillan Clear and fairly tough, but it could be more detailed, though it has Nairobi and Mombasa plans on the reverse. Macmillan also does park maps for Amboseli, Tsavo and Maasai Mara, but these are now well overdue for updating.

Nelles Verlag German, but published in English, and detailed (though poor on minor road numbers and missing various highways built in the last ten years). Includes a good chunk of Northern Tanzania and some inserts, together with mostly accurate annotations.

New Holland Globetrotter Travel Map Very clear, and detailed enough for most purposes but not for off-the-beaten-track adventuring; also published in atlas form with large-scale maps of tourist areas.

Shell/Marco Polo The best of the lot, largely up to date and easy to read, at 1:1,000,000, with road surfaces clearly distinguished (if not always correctly), and plenty of topographical detail (hill peaks, obscure wells, dunes and so on).

If you're doing more in Africa than visiting Kenya alone, you probably want one or more of the **Michelin** series, nos. 953, 954 or 955, still the best all-purpose travel maps for Africa. Kenya comes out small at this scale but with surprising detail.

MAGAZINES AND PERIODICALS

Good Africa-centred **magazines**, worth checking through for news before you go, and not likely to be available once you're there, include the following:

Africa Confidential, Miramoor Publications, 73 Farringdon Rd, London EC1M 3JB (☎0171/831 3511). Fortnightly eight-page newsletter with solid inside info on politics and other matters. Subscription only. Not to be taken into Kenya.

African Business, IC Publications, 7 Coldbath Square, London EC1R 4LQ (☎0171/713 7711). Good general coverage.

BBC Focus on Africa, Bush House, PO Box 76, Strand, London WC2B 4PH (☎0171/379 0519 or 257 2906). News, general-interest features, and information from the BBC World Service.

New African, IC Publications, 7 Coldbath Square, London EC1R 4LQ (☎0171/713 7711). Another in the IC stable, this is a news and lifestyle magazine after the style of the French *Jeune Afrique*, with quarterly special supplements.

Safara, Goldcity Communications, suite F11, Shakespeare Business Centre, 245a Coldharbour Lane, London SW9 8RR (☎0171/737 5933). Quarterly round-up of news aimed at those with business interests in Africa.

KENYA ONLINE

There are two main Internet services in Kenya – Africaonline and Form-net – and a number of businesses in the travel industry are already using email. There are also several Internet cafés in Nairobi, and a number of small weblink offices along the coast. As for what you can learn about Kenya from surfing the Worldwide Web, the picture is not a very exciting one. Nevertheless, if you have Internet access, it's well worth clicking away at the Web sites listed below. Also look at two newsgroups, **rec.travel.africa** and **soc.culture.kenya**, which are genuinely useful information forums and good sources for new Web sites.

www.africaonline.co.ke/africaonline/index.html
Nicely packaged in the USA, but with a slightly official feel ("Kenya is a stable and peaceful country . . ."). Excellent music info.

www.africaonline.co.ke/africaonline/covermusic.html
Excellent introduction to Kenyan pop music and some of the current clubs and bands.

www.africa.u-shizuoka-ken.ac.jp
Lovingly put together "haiku ethnography" by Japanese friends of the Samburu. Great pictures of daily life and ritual, plus downloadable sounds, music and essays.

blissites.com/kenya/
Largely still under construction, this could develop into an excellent cultural site, with long pieces on Kenya's people, and pleasing oddities like practical advice on how to make traditional musical instruments.

www.bwanazulia.com/kenya
Practical stuff with good links to cultural and tourist sites.

www.citynet.com:80/countries/kenya
Practicalities and links.

www.fco.gov.uk/travel/countryadvice.asp
British Foreign Office latest advice. Never to be ignored, but always inadequate.

www.kenyaweb.com/history/history.html
Succinct but interesting information on Kenya's people.

www.lawrence.edu/~bradleyc/kenya.html
Great for information and downloads of pictures and sounds from western Kenya as well as sobering updates on politics and AIDS, plus dozens of links.

www.lclark.edu/~soan/alicia/rebensdorf.101.html
Top marks for totally arcane PhD research: "Exploring appropriations of Hip-Hop Culture in the Internet and Nairobi".

www.rcbowen.com/kenya/
Tends to be a bit out of date and concentrates on facts and figures rather than anything really exciting, but has useful information. Its newsgroup (*rcbowen.com/kenya/newsgroup*) is lively enough, with debates on circumcision, politics and the environment, and also seems to attract lonely hearts.

www.sas.upenn.edu/African_Studies/Country_Specific/Kenya.html-links
Links site maintained by the Norwegian Council for Africa.

www.spidergraphics.com/khr/khrdef.html
A quick course in the current condition of human rights in Kenya, but somewhat directionless since the release of high profile prisoner of conscience Koigi wa Wamwere. Links to Amnesty and others.

GETTING AROUND

A quick reference round-up of regional travel details is given at the end of each chapter. Details refer both to routes within the chapter and to routes from towns covered in the chapter to places in other chapters. Hence, for example, details of getting to the coast are covered in the Nairobi chapter. Bus and train telephone booking numbers are also given.

BUSES, MATATUS AND TAXIS

There's a whole range of vehicles on Kenya's roads. Alongside the flashy "**video coaches**" tearing up one or two of the main highways, you'll find smaller "**country bus**" companies operating a single battered Leyland. In towns of any size, a whole crowd of **minibuses**, **pick-up vans** and **Peugeot taxis** hustle for business constantly.

Fares vary a great deal according to the competition and the condition of the road. There is also great variation in fares between the speed and comfort of a Peugeot 504 station wagon and the grinding progress of a clapped-out country bus. But fares in the latter type of vehicle can still be little more than Ksh1 per kilometre and shouldn't be above Ksh3 per kilometre in a Peugeot except on short routes. This means that most journeys of up to a day in length will cost under Ksh500 ($8.80) and quite often half this. Rarely will anyone attempt to charge you more than the going rate. Baggage charges should not normally be levied unless you're transporting commercial goods, though enough touts will try and convince you otherwise: if you get stuck, talk to other passengers (away from the touts, who will otherwise intervene in Swahili and bribe the passenger) to find out how much they paid – it should never be more than half your fare.

It is worth considering your general **direction** through the trip and which side will be shadier. This is especially important on dirt roads when the combination of a slow, bumpy ride, dust and fierce sun through closed windows can be horrible.

Lastly, if you feel unsafe (*matatus* are notoriously dangerous), don't hesitate to ask to get out of the vehicle and demand a partial refund – which will be forthcoming.

URBAN TRANSPORT

Nairobi and Mombasa have the municipally run **Kenya Bus Services** (KBS) and city **taxis**. The taxis are about the only means of getting around late at night, but always settle on a fare before getting in because the meters hardly ever work. Taxis around town are usually between Ksh100–200, though drivers will invariably try to rip you off – haggle hard, and if you get nowhere, try another driver.

BUSES

Ordinary **buses** cover the whole country, getting you close to almost anywhere. Some, on the main runs between Nairobi and Mombasa, and to a lesser extent the west, are fast (and potentially dangerous), comfortable and keep to schedules: you generally need to **reserve** seats on these a day in advance. The large companies – in particular Akamba Public Road Services – have ticket offices near the bus stations in most towns, where they list their routes and prices. But their parking bays are rarely marked and there are no published timetables. The easiest procedure is to mention your destination to a few people at the bus park and then check out the torrent of offers. Keep asking – it's virtually impossible to get on the wrong bus. Once you've acquired a seat, the wait can be almost a pleasure if you're in no hurry, as you watch the throng outside and field a continuous stream of vendors proffering wares through the window. (If you want something, ask one of them to get it for you; there'll be a tiny mark-up.)

MATATUS AND SHARED TAXIS

Public vehicles at the smaller end of the spectrum have a gruesome safety record and their drivers, on the whole, a breathtaking lack of road sense; this is especially true of **matatus** – usually white Nissan minibuses along main routes, or pick-up vans fitted with wooden benches and a canvas roof for rural trips. The Nissans are especially dangerous: try to sit at the back (to avoid too graphic a view of blind overtaking), and it's a good idea to wear sunglasses if your face is near a front window – they sometimes shatter.

Some of the *matatus* are clearly falling apart: they break down often and travel terrifyingly fast when they're able to. But on occasions they can be an enjoyable way of getting about, giving you close contact (literally) with local people, and some hilarious encounters. They are also often the most convenient and sometimes only means of transport to smaller places off the main roads, and they're cheap – a trip within town will rarely cost you more than Ksh20–30, and even the longest journey should not cost you more than around Ksh300–400. You should not be charged for any baggage, though people will try.

Always choose a vehicle that's full and about to leave or you'll have to wait inside until they are ready to go – sometimes for hours. Beware of being used as bait by the driver to encourage passengers to choose his car, and equally of a driver filling his car with young touts pretending to be passengers (spot them by the newspapers and lack of luggage), who mysteriously disappear when you've bought a ticket. Competition is intense and people will lie unashamedly to persuade you the vehicle is going "just now".

Peugeot taxis operate mainly from Nairobi to the highlands and the west, are faster and more expensive than *matatus* (so not for the faint hearted), and usually drive directly from one point to another with a full complement of passengers. This should consist of one passenger in the front (who sometimes pays a supplement), four in the middle and three in the back, which is only marginally less uncomfortable than *matatus*. Any more and they're overloaded and will be stopped by the police all along the route, paying in bribes any extra fares they may have collected.

In particular, don't hand over any money before you set off; or, if the taxi does get going, wait until you've left town. This isn't a question of being ripped off (though discreetly noting the licence plate of the vehicle is never a bad idea), but too often the first departure is just a cruise around town rounding up passengers and buying petrol (with your money) and then back to square one. If your destination doesn't lie on a standard shared taxi route, or if you don't want to wait for a car to fill up (or, indeed, if you just want to travel in style), drivers will happily negotiate a price for the rental of their whole car. This will normally be the same as the sum total of the fares they would receive from a full complement of paying passengers over an equivalent distance.

TRAINS

In the wake of a catastrophic train crash in March 1999 along the Nairobi–Mombasa line, possibly caused by brake failure, the future of passenger services on Kenya Railways was for a time uncertain. The **railways** have been underfunded (or funds have been siphoned off) for years, with the result that only four lines remain: Nairobi to Mombasa, Nairobi to Kisumu (both overnight), and two fantastically slow branch lines – Voi to Taveta, and Kisumu to Butere. There are no longer any connections into Tanzania or Uganda (and not much remaining of their rail services either).

The main draw for travellers is the overnight **Nairobi–Mombasa** run via Voi, which leaves in either direction at 7pm each day, to arrive anytime between 8am and 10am the following morning. Frustrating though the (almost routine) delays are, they at least mean you are likely to have at least a couple of hours of morning light to watch the passing scene: approaching Nairobi, the animals on the Athi Plains; approaching Mombasa, the sultry crawl down from the Maungu Plains to the ocean.

It's important to **make reservations**, especially if you want a first-class compartment. While it may be fine to leave this until a couple of hours before departure during the low season, it's advisable to reserve well in advance if you plan to travel during the busy Christmas and New Year period when trains are often full. Ticket offices at the stations in Mombasa and Nairobi are open mornings and afternoons, and will take reservations weeks ahead. Travel agents will usually do the work for you, sometimes for a fairly hefty supplement. A number of overseas agents will handle first-class train reservations, too, though you can expect to pay a little more.

To travel **first class**, you have to take a private two-berth compartment. **Second-class** compartments are shared by four people and are single-sex, though, with the consent of the occupants, this can sometimes be disregarded. The **third-class** carriages have seats rather than bunks and are packed.

Fares for Nairobi–Mombasa are Ksh3000 first-class, Ksh2100 second-class and Ksh300 third-class (all one-way). You can pay by credit card at either end, but there's a surcharge. The first- and second-class fares include reserved berth number, pre-paid dinner, breakfast and bedding vouchers: you have to wait at the sign board at either station for your name to be pinned up with the relevant number, and also need to get one of the white-suited attendants to give you your dinner voucher (for one of four sittings, all rushed). Both dinner and breakfast are hearty cooked meals, and eating in the dining car is an experience in itself, but don't expect *haute cuisine*. Wine, beer and sodas cost extra. If you buy from Kenya Railways direct you can elect to pay just for your berth. Note that you can't normally reserve Mombasa–Nairobi berths in Nairobi (and vice versa).

The other main line is the run from **Nairobi to Kisumu** via Nakuru (6pm daily in either direction, arriving between 7.15am and 10am), which is now third-class only (Ksh150). From Kisumu, a small and tortuously slow **branch line** runs north to Butere. Another branch line heads off to the Tanzanian border at Taveta from Voi (on the main Nairobi–Mombasa line), leaving four times a week at 5am (5hr; second-class Ksh180, third-class Ksh60), returning the same day. There are currently no connections into Tanzania or Uganda, whose railways are in an equally parlous state.

Lastly, there's a small branch line up from Lake Magadi to Konza on the Nairobi–Mombasa line, operated by the Magadi Soda Company. There are no regular passenger services, so it's a matter of arranging things informally with staff. Other lines still marked on most maps no longer have passenger services (notably Eldoret, Kitale, Nanyuki, Nyeri and Nyahururu).

PLANES

Kenya has a number of reasonably priced **internal air services**, and it's well worth seeing the country from the eagle's point of view at least once: the flight from Lamu to Malindi/Mombasa is an especially exotic and exhilarating one over reefs and jungle. There are details at the end of each chapter and in the relevant "Moving on" sections. Occasionally, you can pick up non-scheduled flights at Nairobi's Wilson Airport to towns in the northern deserts, for example – and you might even hitch a ride if you're persuasive.

Baggage allowances on internal flights, apart from Kenya Airways, are usually under 20kg and may be as little as 10kg. Fortunately the excess baggage charges are nominal. There is an airport tax of Ksh100 on all domestic flights, usually included in the fare.

Lastly, note that ordinary **connecting times** shouldn't be relied on if you're flying to catch an international departure. Many of the cheaper flight tickets to Europe cannot be endorsed to another airline if you miss your flight, and domestic services are often delayed.

FERRIES

On the coast, the only regular **ferries** of any importance are those connecting the islands of the Lamu archipelago and sporadic services between Mombasa and Zanzibar. On Lake Victoria, which used to have a network of steamer routes, an invasion of water hyacinth – which snarls up propellers and even small canoes – has put paid to the regular ferries operated by Kenya Railways to a few islands near Kisumu, so it's a matter of catching local "*matatu*" boats. Also suspended is the international passenger steamer service between Mwanza (Tanzania), Kisumu (Kenya) and Port Bell (Uganda). Some commercial vessels will also take passengers across the lake, weed permitting.

HITCHING

This is how the majority of rural people get around – by **waving down a vehicle** – but they invariably pay, whether it's a bus, a *matatu*, a lorry or a private vehicle with a spare place. Private vehicles, except on the main Kisumu–Nairobi–Mombasa artery and one or two through routes, are comparatively rare and usually full. Because of the cheapness of buses, travellers don't try it much, but hitching can be a good change of pace, enabling you to cover distances fast and usually in safety. Along the coast, where there are relatively fewer *matatus* and more private cars, it's often easy. More calculatingly, if you're on a low budget, hitching rides with private

cars can throw you in with Asians and Europeans, often resulting in opportunities to visit national parks and reserves.

Hitching **techniques** need to be fairly exuberant; a modest thumb is more likely to be interpreted as a friendly, or even rude, gesture than a request for a lift. Beckon the driver to stop with your palm. And if you can't afford to pay, say so right away; generosity will often provide you a lift anyway.

CAR RENTAL AND DRIVING

Renting a car has advantages over any other means of transport, which makes it seriously worth considering for a week or two. All the parks and reserves (except Saiwa Swamp) are open to private and rented vehicles (as well as organized tours), and there's a lot to be said for the freedom of choice that having your own wheels gives you. Unless there are more than two of you, though, it won't save you money over one of the cheaper camping safaris. You're also required to leave a hefty deposit, roughly equivalent to the anticipated bill. Credit cards are useful for this.

CHOOSING A VEHICLE

Four-wheel-drive (4WD) **Suzuki jeeps** are the most widely available vehicles and they make ideal safari transport: light, rugged and capable of amazing feats of negotiation. Don't expect them to top more than their legal limit of 80kph (50mph), however, and beware their notorious tendency to fall over on bends or on the dangerously sloping gravel hard shoulders that line many Kenyan roads. They also tend to stall on exceptionally steep inclines on rocks or boulders. Long-wheel-base Suzukis, with luggage space behind the rear seats, three doors and enough room for four, or five at a pinch, are more stable and easier to drive. It would be wise to avoid driving the flashier four-wheel drives like Mitsubishi Pajeros and Freelanders: they are much in demand in Somalia and there's a risk of hijack. They're also much less controllable on mud than the Suzukis.

Petrol (gasoline) costs about Ksh40 per litre (40p or 66¢), which is about $2.50 per US gallon. You should get 12–15km per litre out of a Suzuki (which holds about 38 litres). That's around 33mpg (US) or 38mpg (imperial). It's not difficult to run out of petrol, so keep topping up. All towns and villages (except the very smallest) have petrol for sale, but if you're intending to do a lot of driving in a remote area you should definitely carry spare fuel in cans. If you plan to pay by credit card, check that you can use it: some places only accept Kenyan-issued plastic. Note, too, that cheating at petrol stations is increasingly common. Check the gauge is set to zero and anticipate how many litres your tank will need.

Renting a car is often cheaper by the week if you do enough kilometres, and many firms are prepared to negotiate a little as well, especially off season. Reckon on driving an average of 1000km per week (around 600–700 miles).

There are one or two car-rental places in the smaller towns and along the coast but the only real choice is in Nairobi and Mombasa. The minimum age is usually 23, sometimes 25. Foreign driving licences are accepted for up to three months; you're supposed to have them validated at a provincial headquarters, but few people seem to bother. Check the insurance details and always pay the daily **collision damage waiver (CDW)** premium, sometimes included in the price: even a small bump could be very costly otherwise. **Theft protection waiver (TPW)** should also be taken. However, even with these, you'll still be liable for **excess liability**, usually averaging $200–500, exceptionally as low as $75–100, and sometimes an astronomical $2500 (avoid these companies). Lastly, always check whether VAT (sixteen percent) has to be added to the cost. A comparative run-down of various company's charges is included under the Nairobi safari plans section on p.132.

Don't automatically assume the vehicle is roadworthy: have a good look at the engine and tyres, and don't set off without checking the spare (preferably two) and making sure you have a few vital tools. Ideally, always carry a tow rope, spare water and fuel. You might also take a spare fan belt, brake pads, and brake fluid.

Four-wheel drive (4WD) is always useful but, except in mountainous areas and on some of the marginal dirt roads during periods of heavy rain, not essential. High clearance, however, is, thanks to the dire state of many roads, even in dry weather. However, few, if any agencies will hire out non-4WD vehicles for use in the parks, and most park rangers will turn away such cars at the gate, regardless of season. This does depend on the park: Maasai Mara and the mountain parks (Mount Elgon, Mount Kenya and the Aberdares) are the most safety-minded.

DRIVING IN KENYA

A **useful book** for driving around Kenya, which has some good routes and lots of useful detail, is *On Safari* by Phillippe Oberlé (widely available in Kenya; about Ksh700).

When **driving**, beware of unexpected rocks, ditches and potholes – and animals and people – on the road: it's accepted practice to honk your horn stridently to warn pedestrians. Kenya drives on the left, though in reality vehicles keep to the best part of the road until they have to pass each other.

Driving-test examiners aren't incorruptible and Kenya's **accident statistics** are horrifying. Counting the casualties is a national obsession: there was recently a campaign – which miserably failed – to keep the annual death toll below 2000 (it's currently around 3000). Police records currently suggest that an average of eight to nine people die on Kenya's roads every day. To put some perspective on this, there are 48,000 road deaths per year in the USA, but also ten times as many people and umpteen times as many vehicles, and only a small fraction of Kenya's population regularly use vehicles or go near busy roads.

Beware of "**speed bumps**". Occasionally you'll see a sign like "Rumble strips ahead", but more usually the first you'll know of them is when your head hits the roof. They are found both in rural areas, wherever a busy road has been built through a village, and on the roads in and out of nearly every large town. Since they cause such destruction and render vehicles unsafe, it seems likely they are responsible for more lives lost than saved.

On the question of **driving etiquette**, it's common practice to flash oncoming vehicles, especially if they're leaving you little room or the headlights are blinding you, and to signal right to indicate your width and deter drivers behind you from overtaking. You may find both practices disconcerting at first. Left-hand signals are used to say "Please overtake" but you shouldn't assume the driver in front can really see. In fact, never assume anything about other drivers.

Driving at night is to be avoided, especially in a Suzuki, as its lights are hopeless (though remember if you've been off the road and you can't seem to see 10m in front, your headlamps may be caked in mud). Be especially careful when passing heavy vehicles, and even more so when passing lorries groaning uphill: sometimes a line of them churning out diesel fumes can cut off your visibility without warning – extremely dangerous on a narrow mountain road. If you're driving in a city at night (especially Nairobi and Mombasa), the local advice is to keep your doors locked and windows rolled up to avoid grab-and-run incidents at traffic lights or in heavy traffic. You may feel safer doing this during the day, too. Incidentally, **car-jackings** are common in Nairobi and in remote parts of the northeast. However, tourists and hire cars are generally not a target, at least not unless you're in a flashy, high-powered cruiser. The puny Suzuki jeeps are quite the safest in this respect.

On most of the main paved highways you can make good time, but as soon as you leave them, **journey times** are very unpredictable. We've tried to give some idea of road conditions in various places throughout the book, but they can change radically in half a year. The north and highland regions are the worst, particularly during periods of heavy rain when districts may become virtually cut off. In 1993, a study funded by the World Bank concluded that the increase in vehicle operation costs (due to wear on vehicles, wasted petrol on tortuous routes and so on) resulting from the disrepair of many of Kenya's roads totalled three times the country's shortfall in road maintenance expenditure. True to form, next to nothing has been done since then, to spectacular effect during the 1997–98 El Niño rains which washed away a good portion of the main Mombasa to Nairobi road as well as dozens of others.

Signposting in Kenya, while generally useful, is haphazard – especially on dirt roads. If a junction appears to lack a sign, it's assumed you'll keep to the busiest track.

Should you have the misfortune to have a **breakdown** on the road, or an **accident**, the first thing to do is pile bundles of sticks or foliage 50m or so behind and in front of the car. These are the universally recognized "red warning triangles" of Africa, and their placing is always scrupulously observed (as is the wedging of a stone behind at least one wheel). When you have a puncture, as you will, get it mended straight away – it costs very little (Ksh50–60) and can be done almost anywhere there are vehicles. Local mechanics are usually very good and can apply creative ingenuity to the most disastrous situations. But spare parts, tools and proper equipment are rare off the main routes. Always settle on a price before the work begins. And beware of scams and con-artists: the "oil leak" under your parked car still catches many people out (see p.240).

Parking in towns, you should obviously never leave your vehicle with anything of value in it. That said, finding somewhere to park is rarely a problem, even in Nairobi or Mombasa. There are parking meters in Mombasa and over-eager traffic wardens in Nairobi from whom you can buy a

---

BOOKING CAR RENTAL IN ADVANCE

It's quite easy to **book a vehicle** before you even set foot in Kenya, pay for it at home, then pick it up when you arrive. It costs very much more to do this than tracking down a good deal locally – and prices are extremely variable – but if time is short (or money no object) you may find it preferable.

UK
Avis ☎0181/848 8733
Europcar ☎0345/222525
Hertz ☎0181/679 1799

IRELAND
Avis ☎01232/240404
Europcar ☎01232/450904 or 423444
Hertz ☎01/660-2255

US AND CANADA
Avis ☎1-800/331-1084
Hertz in US ☎1-800/654-3001; in Canada ☎1-800/263-0600
National ☎1-800/CAR-RENT

AUSTRALIA
Avis ☎1800/225 533
Budget ☎13 2727
Hertz ☎13 3039

NEW ZEALAND
Avis ☎09/526 2847; toll-free ☎0800/655 111
Budget ☎09/375 2222; toll-free ☎0800/652 227
Hertz ☎09/367 6350; toll-free ☎0800/655 955

ticket for the day (Ksh50). If you don't, you car will either be clamped or towed away (find it at City Hall – the fines are around Ksh750).

Being **stopped by the police** – even when they can see you're likely to be a tourist – is becoming increasingly common: one or two regular checkpoints are mentioned in the text. Checkpoints are generally marked by low strips of spikes across the road with just enough room to slalom round. You should always stop if signalled. The usual reason given is that you were speeding (and they do indeed have one or two radar traps), but that is not why they stop cars. Don't reach into your purse: apologize; agree that it's a pity you will have to go to court; and wait to be sent on your way with a caution (court appearances are just work for all concerned). It's worth knowing that you may be asked to produce evidence that your rented car has a **PSV licence** as a "passenger service vehicle". You should have a windscreen sticker for this as well as the letters "PSV" written somewhere on the body, and you're strongly advised to check it out with the company before you leave.

BUYING A SECONDHAND CAR

Lastly, if you're going to be in Kenya for some time, or you're planning to travel more widely, **buying** a secondhand vehicle in Nairobi, though prices are inflated, is a realistic possibility if you're confident about engines. Rental companies sometimes have vehicles to dispose of, and the *Nation* and *Standard* carry lots of ads. The Sarit Centre in Nairobi has a weekly used-car sale, on Sunday mornings, and you can sell back fairly easily in Nairobi.

CYCLING

Kenya's climate and varied terrain make it challenging **bicycling** country. If it appeals to you – whether you're a lycra-laminated pro or just use a bike once in a while – it's one of the best ways of getting around. With a bike, given time and average determination, you can get to parts of the country that would be hard to visit by any other means except perhaps on foot, and of course people will treat you in a completely different way – as a traveller rather than a "tourist". And what would take several days to hike can be cycled in a matter of hours. It's also one way you'll get to see wildlife outside the confines of the game parks. For details about inclusive cycling tours see p.9. Most towns have bicycle shops which sell

both mountain bikes and the trusty Indian three-speed roadsters – we've mentioned some of these in the Mombasa and Nairobi "Listings" sections.

PRACTICAL CONSIDERATIONS

Whatever you take – and a mountain bike is certainly best – it will need low gears and strongly built wheels and you should have some essential **spare parts**. If you have a sympathetic local bike shop, you might consider leaving a deposit with them so they could send you spare parts if and when necessary. A combination of fax and courier service could get them to you in a couple of days.

If you're taking a bike with you, then you'll probably want to carry your gear in **panniers**. These are fiendishly inconvenient when not attached to the bike, however, and you might consider sacrificing ideal load-bearing and streamlining technology for a backpack you can lash down on the rear carrier. An arrangement like this is probably what you'll have to do if you buy a bike in Kenya. With light wood, or the kind of cane used to make cane furniture, plus lashings of inner tube rubber strips, you can create your own highly unaerodynamic **carrier**, with room for a box of food and a gallon of water underneath.

With a bike from home, take a battery **lighting system** – it's surprising how often you'll need it. The front light doubles as a torch and getting the large-sized U2 batteries is no problem. Also take a **U-bolt cycle lock**. In situations where you have to lock the bike, you'll always find something to lock it to. Out in the bush it's less important. Local bikes can be locked with a padlock and chain in a length of hosepipe which you can buy and fix up in any market.

Cycling won't restrict your travel options. Buses and *matatus* with roof-racks will always carry bicycles for about half-fare – even if flagged down at the roadside – and trucks will often give a lift. The trains take bikes, too, at a low fixed fare. You need to consider the **seasons** however; you won't make much progress on dirt roads during the rains when chain sets and brakes become totally jammed with sticky mud. Obviously, you also need to be cautious when cycling on **main roads**. A mirror is essential, and, if the pavement is broken at the edge, give yourself plenty of space and be ready to leave the road if necessary. That said, cycle tourists are still a novelty in Kenya: drivers often slow down to look and you'll rarely be run off the road.

OUTDOOR ACTIVITIES

Kenya is a country with huge untapped potential for outdoor activities. Safaris are covered in a separate section further on. The following brief notes suggest the possibilities for walking, riding, fishing, golf, diving, climbing and rafting. Cycling is covered in the previous section and under "Getting there from Britain and Ireland" (see p.3).

WALKING

Walking, if you have plenty of time and the relevant Survey of Kenya maps (see p.36 for details on how to obtain them), is highly recommended and gives you unparalleled contact with local people. In isolated parts, it's often preferable to waiting for a lift, while in the Aberdares, Mau and Cherangani ranges, and on Mounts Kenya and Elgon, it's the only practical way of moving away from the main tracks. You will sometimes come across animals out in the bush, but buffalo and elephant, unless solitary or with young, usually move off. Don't ignore the dangers, however, and stay alert. *Mountain Walking in Kenya*, by David Else (McCarta, UK) is a useful book. For hill and mountain hiking, *The Mountains of Kenya: A Walker's Guide*, by Paul Clarke (Mountain Club of Kenya, PO Box 45741 Nairobi; 1989) is also recommended, with step-by-step route details for almost one hundred hills and mountains. For walking you'll need to carry several litres of water much of the time, especially in lower, drier regions.

Before plunging off into the bush, though, you might prefer to go on an organized walking safari, at least as a starter. Walking safaris are offered by a number of safari companies in Nairobi (see p.136).

RIDING

There are good **riding opportunities** in the Central Highlands and an active equestrian community in Nairobi. Safaris Unlimited (see p.137) offer riding safaris near the Maasai Mara National Reserve. **Camel safaris** are popular too, though the best operators to contact tend to change from year to year. Contact any of the addresses under "Special Activity Safaris" on p.136.

FISHING

Many of the highlands' streams are well stocked with **trout**, which were imported early this century by the settlers. A few local fishing associations are still active and the usual rules about seasons and licences apply. *Naro Moru River Lodge* and the *Izaac Walton Inn* in Embu offer rods for hire. The Fisheries Department headquarters, next to the National Museum in Nairobi, can supply details. For **lake fishing**, it's possible to rent rods and boats at lakes Baringo, Naivasha and Turkana, and there are luxury fishing lodges on Rusinga, Mfangano and Takawiri islands on Lake Victoria. The **Indian Ocean** offers excellent sport fishing opportunities: enthusiasts have the chance to land an impressive tally of species including sailfish, marlin, swordfish, barracuda and shark.

Kenya's superb stretch of off-shore coral reef, with its deepwater drop-offs and predictable northerly currents, is ideal for near-shore angling. Watamu, Malindi and the resorts around Mombasa are the most popular centres for ocean fishing.

GOLF

Kenya has almost forty **golf clubs**, mostly patronized by the European and Asian communities, notably around the old colonial centres of Nairobi, Naivasha, Thika, Nanyuki and Nyeri in the central highlands, and Kisumu and Kitale in the west. There are also a number on the coast, and – incontestably the most bizarre – on the scorched moonscape shore of Lake Magadi. Green fees vary widely, usually from about US$110 per person per day. Details for all of these from the Kenya Golf Union, PO Box 49609 Nairobi (☎02/763898, fax 765118, *www.kgu.or.ke*). For organized upmarket golfing **safaris**, contact Tobs Golf Safaris Ltd, PO Box 20146 Nairobi (☎02/721722 or 727790, fax 722015, *tobsgolf@form-net.com*).

DIVING

Kenya's coastal waters are warm all year round so it's possible to **dive** without a wetsuit. Most of the diving bases are located at Malindi, Watamu or on the coast south of Mombasa;

Diani Beach is probably the most popular area. There are centres here which will provide training to PADI leader level (for details see Chapter Six). For underwater photographers, in particular, the immense coral reef is a major draw – the landscape is spectacularly varied, with shallow coral gardens and blue-water drop-offs sinking as deep as 200m, and, as there are few rivers to bring down sediment, visibility is generally excellent. *The Dive Sites of Kenya and Tanzania*, by Anton Koornhof (New Holland, London 1997) is highly recommended, and also covers sites suitable for snorkelling.

CLIMBING

Apart from **Mount Kenya**, there are climbing opportunities at all grades in the **Aberdares**, **Cheranganis**, **Mathews Range**, **Hell's Gate** and **Rift Valley volcanoes** – including Longonot and Suswa. Mount Elgon is also possible, but its sensitive location on the border with Uganda (prime cattle-rustling land) means a wearying paperchase before you start (begin at Kenya Wildlife Service headquarters in Nairobi; see p.148). If you have time to get acquainted with it, the Mountain Club of Kenya (PO Box 45741 Nairobi; club house at Wilson Airport; club night Tues 8pm; ☎02/501747) is a good source of advice and **contacts**, not just for climbing, but for outdoor pursuits in general. If you intend to do any serious climbing in the country, you should make early contact in writing. Don't expect them to answer detailed route questions, however; leave that until you arrive. If you want to go climbing with a guide, safari companies in Nairobi offer everything from a simple hike to technical ascents of Batian and Nelion (see p.136).

RAFTING

Both the **Tana** and **Athi** rivers have sections which can be rafted when they're in spate. Approximate dates are November 1 to March 15 and April 15 to August 31. Savage Wilderness Safaris is the main operator (see p.137), and most trips are for one day only.

ACCOMMODATION

Accommodation in Kenya exhibits a fine diversity, ranging from campsites and local lodging houses for $3–5 a night to genuinely excellent, luxury hotels costing fifty or a hundred times as much. Beds can also be found in "tented camps" and "tree hotels" at the expensive end of the spectrum, and bandas and a clutch of youth hostels at the budget end.

BOARDING AND LODGING

In any town, down to the very smallest, you'll always find **Boarding & Lodgings** (for which we've coined the abbreviation "B&Ls"). These can vary from a mud shack with water from the well, to a little multi-storey building of self-contained rooms ("s/c") with washing facilities, a bar and restaurant. B&Ls tend to be noisy; they're sometimes rather airless and often double unofficially as brothels, but the better ones are clean and comfortable. To those unaccustomed to budget travel, they can nonetheless come as something of a shock.

Prices of rooms aren't always a good indication of the standard, though you should rarely have to pay more than Ksh600 for a double (Ksh400 for a single), often much less. Always try to bargain for a good price. It's worth checking several places, testing the hot water (if any) as well as cold (buckets in the bathrooms mean it has to be carried up and chances are it'll be cloudy) and asking to see the toilets; you won't cause offence by saying no thanks. Bringing toilet paper, and a towel and soap is a good idea. And if the place seems noisy in the afternoon, it will probably become cacophonous during the night, so ask for a room away from the source of the din. This applies especially to Wednesday, Friday and Saturday nights, when most discos operate.

Security is also an important factor: obviously, the more the establishment relies on its bar for income, the less guarantees you have. You can leave valuables with the owner, though you'll need to use your judgement. Leaving valuables in rooms is usually safe enough, especially if things are not left lying around too temptingly – better still, if they allow you, would be to take you key with you.

Boarding & Lodgings are covered in detail through the regional chapters; there's nearly always at least one good example in every town.

If you're driving, some lodgings have lock-up yards where you can park – helpful in avoiding mysteriously deflated tyres and lost wing-mirrors and wipers. Obviously, don't leave anything inside a car overnight, or even during the day.

HOTEL RESERVATIONS

Local addresses and telephone numbers for most hotels are included in the guide. Many are part of chains or management groups; rooms can be reserved by phoning or writing to the head offices. Some chains don't have overseas offices, but travel agents will often make the reservations.

ALLIANCE HOTELS
Small, highly rated group with very pleasant package-tour hotels, noted for their good food and experienced management.
Kenya: College House, University Way, PO Box 49839 Nairobi (☎02/337501 or 337508, fax 219212) or c/o Safari Beach Hotel, Diani, PO Box 90690 Mombasa (☎0127/2726, fax 2357, *alliance@africaonline.co.ke*).

Lodges
Naro Moru River Lodge, Naro Moru, Mount Kenya
Coast
Africana Sea Lodge, Diani Beach
Jadini Beach Hotel, Diani Beach
Safari Beach Hotel, Diani Beach

BLOCK HOTELS
Generally good, sometimes excellent, package-tour establishments, popular with Kenya residents too.
Kenya: Block House, Lusaka Rd, off Uhuru Highway, PO Box 40075 Nairobi (☎02/540780, fax 540821, *www.blockafrica.com* or *www.blockhotels.com*).

Lodges and tented camps
Keekorok Lodge, Maasai Mara National Reserve
Lake Baringo Club, Lake Baringo
Lake Naivasha Country Club, Lake Naivasha
Larsens Tented Camp, Samburu National Reserve
Ol Tukai Lodge, Amboseli National Park
Outspan Hotel, Nyeri
Samburu Lodge, Samburu National Reserve
Shimba Hills Lodge, Shimba Hills National Park
Treetops, Aberdares National Park
Nairobi
Landmark Hotel, Westlands
Coast
Indian Ocean Beach Club, Diani Beach
Nyali Beach Hotel, Mombasa

BUSH HOMES OF EAST AFRICA
The marketing company for over a dozen small, very exclusive privately-owned tented camps and ranch houses in less accessible corners of Kenya (guests usually arrive by air). Around $500 for two people.
Kenya: PO Box 56923 Nairobi (☎02/571647, 571649 or 571661, fax 571665, *bushhome@africaonline.co.ke*).

Inland
Wilderness Trails, Lewa Downs, Laikipia
Ol Malo, Laikipia
Rekero, outside Maasai Mara National Reserve
Patrick's Camp, Solio Estate, Laikipia
Kitich Camp, Mathews Mountain Range, northern Kenya
Sirata Siruwa, Melepo Hills, west of Amboseli National Park
Deloraine, Rift Valley
Lokitela Farm, Mount Elgon
Coast
Tana Delta Camp, Tana River (access from Malindi)
Takaungu House, Takaungu
Al Qasr, Kilifi

CONSERVATION CORPORATION OF EAST AFRICA
Small, exclusive group.
Kenya: c/o *Mayfair Court Hotel*, Msapo Close, off Parklands Rd, PO Box 74957 Nairobi (☎02/750298, 750780 or 750813, fax 750512, 746826, *conscorp@africaonline.co.ke*).
Europe: Dublin (☎+353 1662 3222, fax +353 1662 9138).
USA: Miami (☎+305 373 9922, fax +305 372 9297).

Lodges and tented camps
Kichwa Tembo, Maasai Mara National Reserve
Siana Springs Tented Camp, Maasai Mara National Reserve
Nairobi
Mayfair Court Hotel

GOVERNORS' CAMPS
Expensive and not as exclusive as they pretend.

Kenya: Musiara Ltd, 3rd floor, International House, Mama Ngina St, PO Box 48217 Nairobi (☎02/331871, 336169 or 337344, fax 726427, *govscamp@africaonline.co.ke*).

Lodges and tented camps

Governors' Camp, Maasai Mara National Reserve

Governors' Paradise Camp, Maasai Mara National Reserve

Governors' Private Camp, Maasai Mara National Reserve

Little Governors' Camp, Maasai Mara National Reserve

Loldia House, Lake Naivasha

Mfangano Island Camp, Lake Victoria

KENYA SAFARI LODGES & HOTELS

Rump of the collapsed *AT&H* chain, but may expand in future. The three present properties are old (1970s) but well-maintained and superbly positioned package-tour places.

Kenya: *Mombasa Beach Hotel*, PO Box 90414 Mombasa (☎011/471861-5, fax 472970).

Ngulia Safari Lodge, Tsavo West National Park

Voi Safari Lodge, Tsavo East National Park

Mombasa Beach Hotel, North Coast

KILIMANJARO SAFARI CLUB

Mid-range lodges covering the main game parks of Tsavo East and Amboseli.

Kenya: 3rd floor, IPS House, Kimathi St, PO Box 30139 Nairobi (☎02/227136, fax 219982, *ksc@africaonline.co.ke*).

Lodges

Amboseli Lodge, Amboseli National Park

Aruba Dam Lodge, Tsavo East National Park (opening end-2000)

Kilimanjaro Buffalo Lodge, near Amboseli National Park

Kimana Lodge, between Amboseli and Tsavo West

Tsavo Inn, Mtito Andei, Mombasa Highway

Tsavo Safari Camp, Tsavo East National Park

LONRHO HOTELS

Busy upmarket package tour refuges, with excellent standards across the board.

Kenya: *Norfolk Hotel*, Harry Thuku Rd, PO Box 58581 Nairobi (☎02/216940, fax 216796, *lonhotsm@form-net.com*).

UK: Oakslade, Hatton, Warwick, CV35 7LH (☎01926/844034, fax fax 844035, *lha-uk@dial.pipex.com*).

USA: 620 Longview, Longboat Key, Florida 34228 (☎(1-941) 387-0301, fax (1-941) 387-0028; toll free 800-845-3692, *www.lonrhohotels.com*).

Lodges and tented camps

Aberdare Country Club, Mweiga, north of Nyeri

The Ark, Aberdares National Park

Mara Safari Club, Maasai Mara National Reserve

Mount Kenya Safari Club, Nanyuki/Mount Kenya

Ol Pejeta Ranch House, Laikipia, near Nanyuki

Sweetwaters Tented Camp, Laikipia, near Nanyuki

Nairobi

Norfolk

MSAFIRI INNS

A group formed to look after some of the Kenya Tourist Development Corporation's less successful hotels. Standards vary, but the lodges, at least, are in fine locations.

Kenya: 11th floor, Utalii House, Uhuru Highway, PO Box 42013 Nairobi (☎02/330820, 229751 or 222661, fax 227815).

Lodges

Marsabit Lodge, Marsabit (currently closed)

Mount Elgon Lodge, Mount Elgon

Town hotels

Golf Hotel, Kakamega

Izaac Walton Inn, Embu, Mount Kenya

Tea Hotel, Kericho

PRESTIGE HOTELS

Kenya: 1st Floor, Chancery Building, Valley Rd, PO Box 74888 Nairobi (☎02/716457 or 716628, fax 716459, *prestigehotels@form-net.com*).

Europe: c/o International Marketing Concepts, rue Bermont 4, 1204 Geneva, Switzerland (☎22/312 4611, fax 22/312 4620).

Lodges and tented camps

Mara Intrepids Club, Maasai Mara National Reserve

Samburu Intrepids Club, Samburu National Reserve

Kipungani Bay, Lamu

Ziwani Tented Camp, Tsavo West National Park

Continued overleaf...

HOTEL RESERVATIONS (CONTINUED)

Hotels
Silver Beach Hotel, Mombasa
Silver Star Hotel, Mombasa

SAROVA HOTELS
Mostly high quality and good service at competitive (for the luxury level) prices (*www.sarovahotels.com*).
Kenya: *Panafric Hotel*, PO Box 72493 Nairobi (☎02/713333, fax 715566, *reservations@sarova.co.ke*).
USA: ☎1-410 563 6331, fax 563 6323.

Lodges and tented camps
Sarova Lion Hill Lodge, Lake Nakuru National Park
Sarova Mara Camp, Maasai Mara National Reserve
Sarova Shaba Lodge, Shaba National Reserve
Nairobi
The Stanley
Hotel Ambassadeur
Panafric Hotel
Coast
Whitesands Hotel, Mombasa North Coast

SAVANNAH CAMPS AND LODGES
Small upmarket camps and lodges in less frequented corners, mostly on private land. These are some of Kenya's most delightful lodges, and most have great bird-watching interest.
Kenya: 11th floor, Fedha Towers, Standard St, PO Box 48019 Nairobi (☎02/331191 or 335935, fax 330698, *www.savannahcamps.com*).

Lodges and tented camps
Delamere's Camp, Soysambu Wildlife Sanctuary, Lake Elmenteita

Galla Camp, Taita/Rukinga Ranches, near Tsavo East
Indian Ocean Lodge, Malindi
Lerai Tented Camp, Lewa Downs Conservancy
Mara River Camp, Maasai Mara National Reserve
Sangare Ranch, Aberdares National Park
Private Luxury Mobile Camp, anywhere you like in Kenya

SERENA HOTELS
Some of Kenya's (and Tanzania's) most comfortable and well-managed hotels, combining strong architectural themes with harmonious local blending. Mostly recommended.
Kenya: 4th floor, Williamson House, 4th Ngong Ave, PO Box 48690 Nairobi (☎02/710511, fax 718100; reservations ☎02/711077–8, fax 718103, *mktg@serena.co.ke*; reservations in Mombasa ☎011/220732, fax 220705).
Tanzania: 6th floor, AICC Ngorongoro Wing, PO Box 2551 Arusha (☎057/4058 or 6304, fax 4155, *www.serenahotels.com*.).

Lodges
Amboseli Serena Safari Lodge, Amboseli National Park
Mara Serena Safari Lodge, Maasai Mara National Reserve
Mountain Lodge, Mount Kenya
Samburu Serena Safari Lodge, Samburu National Reserve
Nairobi
Nairobi Serena Hotel
Coast
Mombasa Serena Beach Hotel, Mombasa North Coast

HOTELS AND LODGES

More **expensive hotels** are a variable commodity. At the top end of the range are the big tourist establishments, many in one of the country's four or five chains. In the game parks, they are known as **lodges**. Some establishments are extremely good value: a night in a good hotel can be tremendously fortifying if you're usually roughing it. Others are shabby and overpriced, so check carefully before splurging. If possible you should try to reserve the more popular establishments in advance (see the box on p.48), especially for the busiest season from December to February.

As a rule, expect to pay anything from Ksh800 to Ksh3000 for a decent double or twin room in a **town hotel**, with attached bathroom (self-contained, or "s/c") electricity, hot water and breakfast included. Singles usually cost around seventy percent of a double. Out of the towns and on the coast, hotels and lodges in the top price brackets are normally quoted in dollars and on a half- or full-board basis, and prices can go right into orbit ($80–300 is usual, with the exceptions reaching over $1000 for a double). Most of these hotels cut their prices in the low season, April–June, and many have much lower rates for Kenyan residents (sometimes citizens) which you might get if you're convincing.

Between the hotels featured in the glossy brochures and the cheap lodging-houses, come all the **medium-priced**, middle-class places. Some of them were once slightly grand, others are old settlers' haunts that don't fit modern Kenya, and some newer ones cater for the black middle class. A few are fine – delightfully decrepit or bristlingly smart and efficient. Most are boozy and uninteresting; it adds more colour to your travels to mix the cheapest lodgings with the occasional night of luxury.

COTTAGES, VILLAS AND HOMESTAYS

Increasingly, it's possible to book **self-catering apartments**, **villas** or **cottages**, especially on the coast. Kenya Villas, Westminster House, Kenyatta Ave, Nairobi (PO Box 57046; ☎02/338041, fax 338072), and Holiday Homes Ltd, ABC Place, Waiyaki Way, Westlands (PO Box 10723; ☎02/444052, fax 444053), are agents for a wide range of holiday homes. Try writing, but they may need a phone call. Another style of accommodation on the increase is **homestays** – inclusive accommodation in a (usually Anglo-Kenyan) household in the countryside. Meals and drinks are generally part of the package, and excursions and safaris with generous helpings of local insight, or occasionally prejudice, are optional. Let's Go Travel (address p.142) have details of some.

YOUTH HOSTELS

Disappointingly, only three **youth hostels** are affiliated to the International Youth Hostel Association (IYHA) – Nairobi, Nanyuki and Mount Kenya. Non-members normally have to join the association first (Ksh540), though this can be done by buying Ksh90 "stamps" on each of your first six overnights, which then qualifies you for international membership. The hostels can be booked from outside Kenya through the IYHA, or in Kenya through KYHA (Nairobi Youth Hostel), Ralph Bunche Road, PO Box 48661 Nairobi (☎02/723012, fax 724862).

There are **YMCAs** and **YWCAs** in Kisumu, Nairobi and Mombasa, and church-run hostels and dormitories in a number of small towns including Kikambala, Makindu, Maralal and Nanyuki. In these, the atmosphere can be a cloying contrast to the sleazier lodging-houses.

CAMPING

While a **tent** is dead weight whenever you sleep in a hotel, Kenya has enough campsites to make it worthwhile carrying one, and camping rough is very often a viable option, too. Bring the lightest tent you can afford or consider **making your own**. A few weekends with a sewing machine, rip-stop nylon and some netting should see the job done: make a scale model in paper first, and test the tent under wet conditions before taking it to Kenya. Camping in the rain doesn't make much sense (whatever the protection, you're likely to get wet); the main point of a tent is to keep insects out, but it's still good to be protected against unexpected showers. Nylon netting with a sewn-in groundsheet is the basic tent. A rip-stop nylon fly sheet adds privacy. Outside poles back and front can be used for guys and tension, but you'll probably resort to trees if there are any.

CAMPSITES AND CAMPING ROUGH

Campsites, wherever they exist, are mentioned in the main body of the guide. Those in the parks are usually very cheap and equally basic. The mysterious "special campsites" in a number of parks, are, in reality, simply restricted sites which you can reserve on an exclusive basis for private use – and they cost a lot more. Some of them are especially attractive – so they draw film crews and the like – but they are all quite devoid of facilities. To book them, either write to the warden or visit/write to Special Campsite Reservations, Kenya Wildlife Service, Langata Rd, PO Box 40241 Nairobi (☎02/501081–2, fax 505866 or 501752, *kws@africaonline.co.ke*): this office is one of those right by Nairobi National Park main gate. On top of the flat advance booking fee of Ksh5000, you have to pay daily camping charges at the prevailing rates (see box on p.63).

A handful of privately owned sites have more in the way of facilities. In rural areas, hotels are often amenable if you ask to camp discreetly in their grounds.

Camping rough depends on whether you can find a suitable space. In the more heavily populated and farmed highland districts, you should ask someone before pitching in an empty spot. Out in the wilds, hard or thorny ground is likely to be the only obstacle (a foam sleeping-mat is a good idea if you don't mind the bulk). During the dry seasons, you'll rarely have trouble finding wood for a fire so a stove is optional, but don't burn more fuel than you need. You're not allowed to collect firewood in the mountain parks. Camping gas cartridges and packaged, dried food is available in variety in Nairobi, but the easiest and cheapest camping food is *ugali* (see "Eating and Drinking" below), flavoured with curry powder or sauce mixes if you like.

SAFETY

Camping out is generally pretty safe, although in populated areas you should ask beforehand. Be aware also of areas where there are ethnic tensions (these are mentioned in the text), or where cattle-rustling is prevalent. A fire may worry local people and delegations armed with *pangas* sometimes turn up to see who you are, and might want to stay and chat. Camping right by the road, in dried-out river beds, or on trails used by animals going to water, however, is unwise.

On the subject of **animals**, if you're way out in the bush, lions and hyenas are very occasionally curious of fires, but will never attack you unless provoked. More dangerous are **buffalo**, which you should steer well clear of (especially old solitary males), and lake- or river-side **hippo**, who will attack if they fear that you're blocking their route back to water.

An important exception to the safety of rough camping is the Indian Ocean coast. Almost anywhere between Malindi and the Tanzanian border, **sleeping out on the beaches** should be counted as an invitation to robbery. North of Malindi, there are fewer tourists and the risks are correspondingly reduced, although the region is prone to banditry which sometimes makes getting to the beaches a more risky business.

EATING AND DRINKING

Not surprisingly, perhaps, Kenya has no great national dishes: the living standards of the majority of people don't allow for frills and food is generally plain and filling. Eating out is not a Kenyan tradition. Still, in the most basic local restaurant, decent meals can be had for less than Ksh100 (£1/$1.60). For fancier meals in touristy places, expect to pay up to Ksh1000 (£10/$16) – rarely more – for a large meal of international-style dishes. For culinary culture, only the coast's long association with Indian Ocean trade has produced distinctive regional cooking, where rice and fish, flavoured with coconut, tamarind and exotic spices, are the dominant ingredients.

HOME-STYLE COOKING

If meals are unlikely to be a lasting memory, at least you'll never go hungry. In any **hoteli** (a small restaurant, not a hotel), there's always a number of predictable dishes intended to fill you up at the least cost. Potatoes, rice and especially *ugali* (a stiff, cornmeal porridge) are the national staples, eaten with chicken, goat, beef, or vegetable stew, various kinds of spinach, beans or sometimes fish. Portions are usually gigantic: half-portions (ask for *nusu*) aren't much smaller. But even in small towns, more and more **cafés** are appearing where most of the menu is fried – eggs, sausages, chips, fish, chicken and burgers.

Snacks, which can easily become meals, include samosas, chapatis, miniature kebabs, roasted corncobs, *mandaazi* and "egg-bread".

Mandaazi – sweet, puffy, deep-fried dough cakes – are made before breakfast and served until evening time, when they've become cold and solid. Egg-bread (misleadingly translated from the Swahili *mkate mayai*) is a light wheat-flour "pancake" wrapped around fried eggs and minced meat, usually cooked on a huge griddle. While you won't find it everywhere, it's a delicious Kenyan response to the creeping burger menace.

The standard blow-out feast for most Kenyans is a huge pile of **nyama choma** (roast meat). *Nyama choma* is usually eaten at a purpose-built *nyama choma* bar, with beer and music (live or on a jukebox) the standard accompaniment and *ugali* and spinach optional. You go to the kitchen and order by weight (half a kilo is plenty) direct from the butcher's hook or out of the fridge. There's usually a choice of goat, beef or mutton. After roasting, the meat is brought to your table on a wooden platter and chopped to bite-size with a sharp knife. *Kuku choma* is roast chicken.

BREAKFAST

The first meal of the day varies widely. Stock *hoteli* fare consists of a cup of sweet **chai** and a doorstep of white bread, thickly spread with margarine (on both sides *and* the edges). At the other extreme, if you're staying in a **luxury hotel** or lodge, breakfast is usually a lavish acreage of hot and cold buffets that you can't possibly do justice to. In the average **mid-priced hotel**, you'll get "full breakfast", like something from an English B&B – greasy sausage, bacon, eggs and baked beans, with instant coffee (in a pot) and soggy toast.

RESTAURANT MEALS

Indian restaurants in the larger towns – notably Nairobi and Mombasa – are generally excellent (locally, there's often a strong Indian influence in *hoteli* food as well), with *dal* lunches a good stand-by and much fancier regional dishes widely available too.

When you splurge, apart from eating Indian, it will usually be in hotel restaurants, with food often very similar to what you might be served in a restaurant at home. It will rarely cost more than Ksh1000 a head, though there's a handful of classy establishments in Nairobi, Mombasa and Diani Beach which take delight in charging, for Kenya, outrageous prices for lavish meals – up to Ksh2500 – generally with some justification.

Kenya's **seafood** and **meat** are renowned and they are the basis of most serious meals. Game meat is a bit of a Kenyan speciality, supposedly farmed on ranches, though there is a fair amount of illegal poaching still going on to supply the trade. Giraffe, zebra, impala, crocodile and ostrich all regularly appear at various restaurants, and often on a weekly basis in hotel buffets. Gazelle and impala is especially good, as is zebra; not the horse meat you might imagine.

The lodges usually have buffet lunches at about Ksh500–1200, which can be great value if you're really hungry, with table-loads of salads and cold meat. Among Kenya's exotic cuisines, you'll find Italian restaurants and pizzerias, various Chinese cuisines, and French, Japanese, Korean, and even Thai food.

VEGETARIANS AND FRUIT

If you're a **vegetarian** staying in tourist-class hotels, you should have no problems, as there's usually a meat-free pasta dish, or else the usual omelettes. Vegetarians on a strict budget don't have an easy time because meat is the conventional focus of any kind of special meal – in other words, any meal not eaten at home – and *hotelis* seldom have much else to accompany the starch. Even vegetable stew is normally cooked in meat gravy. Nor are salads and green vegetables served much in the cheaper *hotelis* (and if they are, make sure they're fresh). Eggs, at least, can be had almost anywhere, and fresh milk is distributed widely in wax paper tetra-packs as well as UHT or fresh in thin plastic packs. With bread and tinned margarine, two more staples available everywhere, you won't starve. Look out for **Indian vegetarian restaurants** where you can often eat remarkably well at a very low cost.

Fruit, of course, is the main delight, whether you eat meat or not. Bananas, avocados, papayas and pineapples are in the markets all year, mangoes and citrus fruits more seasonally. Look out for passion fruit (the familiar shrivelled brown variety, and the sweeter and less acidic smooth yellow ones), cape gooseberries, custard apples and guavas – all highly distinctive and delicious. On the coast, roasted cashew **nuts** are cheap, especially at Kilifi where they're grown and processed (never buy any with dark marks on them), while coconuts are filling and nutritious, going through several satisfying changes of condition (all edible) before becoming the familiar hard brown nuts.

MENU AND FOOD TERMS

The lists below should be adequate for translating most Swahili menus and explaining what you want. Spelling may vary: see "Language" in Contexts.

Basics

Food	*Chakula*	Spoon	*Kijiko*	Pepper	*Piripiri*	Egg/Eggs	*Yai/Mayai*
Water,	*Maji*	Knife	*Kisu*	Bread	*Mkate*	Fish	*Samaki*
juice		Fork	*Uma*	Butter,	*Siagi*	Meat	*Nyama*
Ice	*Barafu*	Bottle	*Chupa*	margarine		Vegetables	*Mboga*
Table	*Meza*	Bill	*Hesabu*	Sugar	*Sukari*	Sauce	*Mchuzi*
Plate	*Sahani*	Salt	*Chumvi*	Milk	*Maziwa*	Fruit	*Matunda*

Snacks

Chapati	Unleavened, flat wheat bread, baked on a hot plate or in an oven (*tandoor*)
Keki	Cake
Kitumbuo	Deep-fried rice bread
Mandaazi	Deep-fried sweet dough, sometimes flavoured with spices, known as *mahamri* on the coast
Maziwalala	Yogurt
Mkate Mayai	"Egg-bread": soft thin dough wrapped around fried egg and minced meat
Samosa	Deep-fried triangular case of chopped meat and vegetables
Tosti/Slice	Slice of bread
Halwa	Sweetmeat; Turkish delight

Dishes

Irio/Kienyeji	Potato, cabbage and beans mashed together (Mount Kenya region)
Kima	Mince
Matoke	Mashed plantain
Mboga	Vegetables: usually potatoes, carrots and onions in meaty gravy
Mchele	Plain white rice
Michicha	Spinach cooked with onions and tomatoes
Pilau	Rice with spices and meat
Sukuma wiki	Green leaves boiled, usually a kind of spinach
Ugali/Sima	Cornmeal boiled to a solid porridge with water, occasionally milk; yellow *ugali* is considered inferior to white but is more nutritious
Uji	Porridge or gruel made of millet; good for chilly mornings
Wali	Rice with added fat and spices; almost *pilau*

DRINK

The national beverage is **chai** – tea. Universally drunk at breakfast and as a pick-me-up at any time, it's a weird variant on the classic British brew: milk, water, lots of sugar and tea leaves, brought to the boil in a kettle and served scalding hot. It must eventually do diabolical dental damage but it's curiously addictive and very reviving. Instant **coffee** – fresh is rare – is normally available in *hotelis* as well, but it's expensive (ironically, in Kenya), so not as popular as tea.

Soft drinks ("sodas") are usually very cheap, and crates of Coke, Fanta and Sprite find their way to the wildest corners of the country where, uncooled, they're pretty disgusting. Krest, a bitter lemon, is a lot more pleasant. Krest also make a ginger ale but it's watery and insipid; instead go for Stoney Tangawizi (*tangawizi* means ginger) which has more of a punch. Sometimes you can get Vimto, which is supposed to do you some good, and occasionally plain soda water, which can't do you any harm. There are fresh **fruit juices** available in the towns, especially on the coast (Lamu is fruit juice heaven). Passionfruit, the cheapest, is excellent, though nowadays it's likely to be watered-down concentrate. Some places serve a variety: you'll sometimes find carrot juice and even tiger milk – from tiger (*chufa*) nuts.

Ordinary bottled **mineral or spring water** is expensive and only available in large towns or major hotels. Mains water (see "Water and Bugs",

Meat

Kuku	Chicken		*Ngombe*	Beef
Mushkaki	Kebab–small pieces of grilled, marinated meat on or off the skewer		*Nguruwe*	Pork
			Steki	Steak, grilled meat
			Mbuzi	Mutton, goat meat

Terms

Choma	Roast (*nyama choma* – roast meat – is the food for parties and celebrations)	*Chemka*	Boiled	*Baridi*	Cold
		Kaanga	Fried	*Nusu*	Half
		Moto	Hot	*Ingine*	More, another

Fruit

Limau	Lime	*Matopetope*	Custard apples	*Papai*	Papaya/ Pawpaw
Machungwa	Oranges	*Nanasi*	Pineapple		
Madafu	Green coconuts	*Nazi*	Coconuts	*Parachichi*	Avocado
Maembe	Mangoes	*Ndimu*	Lemon	*Pera*	Guava
Mastafeli	Soursops	*Ndizi*	Bananas	*Sandara*	Mandarins

Vegetables

Maharagwe	Red kidney beans, often cooked with coconut	*Muhogo*	Cassava
		Ndizi	Bananas or plantains (often served with meat dishes)
Mahindi	Corn		
Mbaazi	Pigeon peas, small beans	*Nyanya*	Tomatoes (also means grandmother)
Mtama	Millet (made into a gruel for breakfast)	*Viazi*	Potatoes
		Vitunguu	Onions

Drinks

Chai, chai kavu, chai strungi	Tea, black tea, strongly spiced tea	*Kahawa*	Coffee
		Bia	Beer
Maziwalala	Fermented milk/almost-yogurt (literally "sleeping milk")	*Pombe*	Home-brewed "beer"
		Soda	What else?
		Tembo	Coconut palm wine

p.31) is usually quite drinkable, but it's best to take heed if your hotel or lodge advises against it.

BEER

Kenyan **lager beer** is generally good, and prices vary according to where you drink it: from around Ksh45 in local dives up to Ksh150 in posher establishments. Of the normal beers, Tusker, White Cap, Pilsner (a little stronger) and the South African Castle Lager are the main brands, sold in half-litre bottles, or in one-third-litre sizes at fancier establishments and hotel bars. White Cap seems to be the old colonials' brew and Tusker is certainly the biggest seller, though the aggressively marketed Castle Lager may make inroads there. A recent addition is Pilsner Ice, in third-litre

bottles, which promises Kenyan men – somewhat unconvincingly – of their ability to stagger back home without reeking of stale beer. There are also two **stouts**: a head-thumping version of Guinness at over seven percent, and Castle Milk Stout, a milder competitor.

There are two points of **beer etiquette** worth remembering. Firstly, never take your bottle out of the bar (bottles carry deposits and this is considered theft – surprisingly ugly misunderstandings can ensue). Secondly, in small places out of the cities (especially in western Kenya), men buy each other beers and accumulate them on the table in a display of mutual generosity. When he's drunk enough, each customer takes his unopened presents back to the bar and stores them for the next day.

OTHER ALCOHOLIC DRINKS

Kenya Cane (white rum) and **Kenya Gold** (a gooey, coffee-flavoured liqueur) deserve a try perhaps, but they are expensive and nothing special.

More interesting is **papaya wine**, Kenya's desperate solution to its shortage of vineyards. This – ostensibly in medium or dry, white and rosé – is certainly an acquired taste, but it's one you might acquire quickly: the stuff is potent and much cheaper than imported wine. A whole range of fruity wines has recently appeared, including passion and mango. But there are now several quite drinkable **white wines** made from Kenyan grapes – notably the products of Naivasha Wineries – and reasonably priced South African wine is widely available.

You won't often find **cocktails** except in more expensive hotels and restaurants. One Kenyan mix to try, cautiously, is a *dawa* ("medicine") – vodka, white rum, honey and lime juice.

There's a battery of laws against **home brewing** and **distilling** – perhaps because of the loss of revenue in taxes on legal booze – but these are central aspects of Kenyan culture and they go on, despite the litany of wife-beatings and deaths (through poisoning) which result. You can sample **pombe** (beer) under many different names all over the country. It is as varied in taste and colour as its ingredients: basically fermented sugar and millet or banana, with herbs and roots for flavouring. The results are frothy and deceptively strong.

On the coast, where the coconuts grow, merely lopping off the growing shoot produces a naturally fermented **palm wine** (*tembo*), which is indisputably Kenya's finest contribution to the art of self-intoxication. Though there's usually a furtive discretion about *pombe* or *tembo* sessions, nobody ever seems to get busted.

Not so with spirits. Think twice before accepting a mug of **chang'aa**. It's treacherous firewater, and is also frequently contaminated, regularly killing drinking parties en masse, and filling a niche in the Kenyan press currently taken by crack cocaine in the West. Sentences for distilling and possessing *chang'aa* are harsh, and police (or self-styled vigilante) raids common.

THE MEDIA

English tends to predominate over Swahili in public life; higher education and parliament get by almost exclusively on it, and the media use it heavily.

RADIO AND TV

KBC radio has three services, broadcasting in English, Swahili and vernacular languages, as well as an FM station, Metropolitan FM, competing with the independent Capital FM (which also broadcasts World Service programmes in English, Swahili and Somali). If its newspapers are anything to go by, the new Nation Radio (96.4FM; due to begin transmission shortly after the time of writing) should be worth listening to, if the government don't revoke their licence again. The BBC World Service is on shortwave kHz 6005, 11860 and 11940, and in Nairobi on 93.7FM. Voice of America can also be picked up on shortwave.

Kenyan **television**, much of it imported, is in English and Swahili. There are two main channels, the stuffy and hesitant KBC (which used to carry BBC's World Service TV until it pulled out over government censorship; the station is now apparently making moves to distance itself from the establishment) and the upbeat, CNN-dominated KTN (urban areas only), which also carries a lot of CNN and the South African "Channel O" music channel after midnight. KBC also operates a pay channel, KBC2, which is run in conjunction with South Africa's M-NET. Nation Group are currently battling in the courts to have their broadcasting license given back to them – look out for their East African Television Network.

THE PRESS

Kenya, like Britain, is a nation absorbed in its press. Despite continued suppression (and blatant threats to curb their freedoms from KANU party bigwigs), the Kenyan **press** has enjoyed a renaissance since the unbanning of the opposition in 1992 and there are many magazines and occasional papers, all of which carry interesting articles from time to time and often surprise their readers with their outspokenness.

The leading quality daily is the *Daily Nation* (and *Sunday Nation*), part-owned by the Aga Khan

(45 percent; the remaining 55 percent by share-holders), which has meaty news coverage (international, too, as well as European football results), a daring editorial line, and a letters page full of insights into Kenyan life. Its main competitor, the *East African Standard*, is dull and light-weight in comparison. The *Kenya Times* is a stodgy KANU organ partly owned by Britain's Mirror Group Newspapers. The Nation Group also publishes the excellent and highly recommended *The East African* on Mondays, a relatively weighty, conservatively styled round-up of the week's news in Kenya, Uganda and Tanzania, shot through with an admirable measure of justified cynicism. Its own reporting is consistently incisive, intelligent and thought-provoking, and it also carries the cream of the foreign press news features. Another weekly worth trying is *The People*, whose logo "Fair, Frank and Fearless" is about right, and which verges on the scurrilous. All are available from street vendors.

Other papers, *Taifa Leo* and *Kenya Leo*, are in Swahili. The *Weekly Review* is always worth picking up (as are *Society*, *Law* and *Finance* – if you can find any copies that haven't been confiscated for one crime of the pen or another). In similar vein, *Kenya Confidential* (on blue paper) seems to get delivered straight to the government pulping plant; it features painfully detailed exposés on corruption and the manifold misdeeds of Kenyan politicians. Its editor really should consider moving his office to Nairobi prison, as he

gets thrown in there with alarming frequency (the last time for an article headed "The Kenya Police: A monstrous disaster").

Drum and *Presence* (a women's magazine) are two lifestyle magazines that are usually available.

NEWSPAPERS ONLINE

The Nation is at *www.nation.co.ke* or *www.nationaudio.com*.

The East African is at *www.nation.co.ke/eastafrican*.

The regional weekly **Coastweek** is at both *www.africaonline.co.ke/coastwk* and *www.net2000.com/coastwk*.

Of the **foreign press**, the *Daily Telegraph* gets to all sorts of settler-ish bastions. British Sunday and daily papers (such as the *Times*, *Express* and *Mail* and more occasionally *The Guardian*) and the *International Herald Tribune* can usually be found in Nairobi or, a few days old, at one or two stores around the country. They tend, however, to be unavailable when Kenya's internal affairs make international news. British tabloids are usually available, several days late.

Time and *Newsweek* are hawked widely and, together with old *National Geographic*s and copies of *The Economist*, filter through many hands before reaching the secondhand booksellers.

POST AND TELEPHONES

Keeping in touch by mail and telephone is generally easy, if not fantastically reliable. Mail takes a few days to Europe and perhaps ten days to North America, Australia and New Zealand; times from these places to Kenya are slightly longer, and things go missing frequently enough – keep photocopies of letters you don't want to lose, and don't send valuables. Kenya's telephone system is improving, though lines are often busy, and it's one of the most expensive in the world.

RECEIVING AND SENDING MAIL

Poste restante is free, and fairly reliable in Nairobi, Mombasa, Malindi and Lamu. Have your family name marked clearly but look under any combination of initials and be ready to show your passport. Smaller post offices will also hold mail but your correspondent should mark the letter "To Be Collected". Parcels can be received, too, but expect to haggle over import-duty payment when they're opened. Ask the sender to mark packages "Contents To Be Re-exported From Kenya".

When posting things home, out of Kenya, air-mail packages are expensive but **surface mail** (up to a maximum of 20kg) is good value, reliable and worth considering if you've accumulated things on your travels. Parcels must be no more than 105cm long and the sum of the three sides less than 200cm, and must be wrapped in brown paper and tied with string. They are usually examined in advance, so everything has to be checked, in the post office, before you wrap it. Cheaper still is to get yourself and the parcel to the British Airways cargo counter at Jomo Kenyatta International Airport in Nairobi (p.142); BA can send it to any airport in Europe for $3.50 a kilo – rapid and efficient to London, but can take weeks to anywhere else.

Stamps can be bought only at post offices and large hotels. There are main post offices in all the towns and, except in the far north, sub-post offices throughout the rural areas. Prepaid "**aero-grams**" are the cheapest way of writing home, but they tend to sell out quickly. If you want speedy delivery, pay a little extra for express. The internal service, like the international one, is steadily getting less efficient and things do go missing.

ADDRESSES IN KENYA

All addresses in Kenya have a post office box number except out in the sticks, where some are just given as "Private Bag", or "PO", followed by the location of the post office. There's no home delivery service. In large towns, business and office addresses are usually identified by the "House" or "Building" in which they're situated.

TELEPHONES

The local **telephone service** is generally depend-able and inexpensive; not so long distance, which gets close to international rates. Outside the big towns, you can spend a long time waiting for a connection or passing the time of day with the operator. Phonecards (see below) are a help, if you find any (they're perennially out of stock).

To make **local telephone calls** from a call box you need a good handful of Ksh1, 5 and 10 coins. When you pick up any pay phone you'll hear a sustained tone and, in the background, a series of beeps. After five beeps you dial (you can dial before that, but you might lose your money). Use the area code or dial 900 for the operator.

The easiest and most economical way to make an **international** call is to dial direct from a **cardphone** (found outside Extelcoms in Nairobi and outside post offices in most large towns). The prepaid, credit-card-sized plastic phonecards used in them can in theory be bought at news-stands as well as at post offices, but are rarely available. Cardphones are also useful for using a **charge card** from your own telephone company (they don't take ordinary credit cards). You dial ☎0800/44 for the UK or ☎0800/10 for the USA or Canada and get through to an international oper-ator in your country. The operator should be able to tell you how much the call – debited to your account – will cost; the Kenyan telecom people have no idea.

In the absence of a cardphone it's possible to make operator-assisted international calls from a main post office ("station-to-station"). **Charges** are about £9 ($15) for three minutes to Europe, more to North America. Shorter calls are now possible, but cost more per minute (about £5/$8.30). When you ask for a station-to-station connection, you pre-pay for a specified number of minutes, and you get your money back if you fail to get through, but not if the conversation ends up taking less time than you expected, for example if you get through to an answerphone. If you want more minutes you have to specify how many – all very user-unfriendly. You shouldn't have a prob-lem making a connection to the UK, but be pre-pared for long waits to other countries.

Reverse-charge (collect) calls can also be made, but not from call boxes. Three minutes' worth costs about £13 ($20). It works out cheaper overall if you call your correspondent briefly and ask them to call you back at a hotel.

Larger post offices have **fax** machines – the international rate is around £6 ($9) per page – or you can use a private fax bureau, where the rate will sometimes be cheaper. Charges for receiving faxes, however, are nominal. **Post office** opening hours are usually 8am–5pm on weekdays; larger ones are open on Saturday mornings. Otherwise, you can usually phone from large hotels, but you can pay well over twice the price for this facility.

INTERNATIONAL DIRECT DIALLING CODES

Kenya's international dialling code is 254. Then dial the number omitting the first 0 from the area code. If you have to be connected by the operator, call your own international operator and quote the exchange and number.

Calling out of Kenya, dial 001 then:

Australia 61	**Germany 49**	**Netherlands 31**	**UK 44**
Canada 1	**Ireland 353**	**New Zealand 64**	**USA 1**

For international operator service and directory enquiries call 0196.
If you have a problem with a line, call 980.
Kenya is **3hr ahead of GMT** (2hr ahead of British Summer Time).
4am New York=9 or 10am London=noon Kenya=7pm Sydney=9pm New Zealand.

BUYING ARTS AND CRAFTS

What constitutes something worth buying is really up to you. Sculptures and carvings in wood and soapstone (*kisii-stone*) are cheap and ubiquitous. The most striking carvings are in the dramatically vertical and delicate makonde style (after the Makonde people of Mozambique and Tanzania), ostensibly carved in ebony, but in Kenya usually made of blackened rosewood or something similar. This shouldn't deter you: it saves on ebony forests' stocks and looks just as wonderful on your mantelpiece.

The familiar **sisal baskets** (*chondo*, or *vyondo* in the plural) come in a huge variety of patterns and can be made from cheap nylon string as well as sisal and, much more rarely, baobab bark twine, with beads woven in. They're all light, and functional.

Beadwork (*ushanga*, *mkufu*) and **tribal regalia** – weapons, shields, drums (*ngoma*), musical instruments, stools, headrests and metal jewellery – are common as well, but much more expensive when authentically used rather than made for the tourist industry.

Masks are mostly imported from west and central Africa (they're not a feature of traditional Kenyan art) and by no means sure to be old or "authentic" no matter how much congealed cow dung appears to fill the crevices.

Textiles, notably a profusion of printed women's wraps in cotton – **kanga** – and heavier-weave men's loincloths – **kikoi/vikoi** – are really good buys on the coast, and older ones repre-

sent collectable items worth seeking out. *Kangas* are always sold in pairs and are printed with intriguing Swahili proverbs. They're usually found to have been manufactured in the Far East.

Whether or not you have children or are buying presents for kids, the **toys** you can come across from time to time are highly recommended souvenirs. Most worthwhile are the beautifully fashioned, and sometimes large and intricate, wire buses, cars and lorries, fitted with stick-up steering wheels, that lucky boys in rural areas get given by older brothers and uncles. These are rarely for sale, but you might commission one, if you have time (Kariokor market in Nairobi is the place for this). More widely available are various push-along bikes, birds and monkeys, and pottery *matatus*, these latter for the tourist market.

Other local specialities are mentioned through the guide. In the end, what you take home is going to depend partly on how much you can carry. It's easy, with attractive items and low prices, to get quite carried away, but carvings (especially ebony *makonde*) and soapstone are extremely heavy.

Ivory, incidentally, carved or otherwise, and in any quantity, is strictly illegal. Most countries have banned all ivory imports. It will be seized and, in many countries, the carrier is subject to a heavy fine.

BARGAINING

Bargaining is an important skill to acquire. Every time you pay an unreasonable price for goods or services, you contribute to local inflation. You're expected to knock most negotiable prices down by at least half: souvenirs are sometimes offered at first prices ten times what the vendor is prepared to accept. You can avoid the silly first prices by having a chat first and establishing your streetwise credentials. The bluffing on both sides is part of the fun; don't be shy of making a big scene. Where prices are marked, they are generally fixed – which you'll quickly discover if you walk out and aren't called back. Once you get into it, you'll rarely end up paying more than the going rate for food, transport or accommodation.

FESTIVALS AND HOLIDAYS

Both Christian and Muslim holidays are observed, as well as secular national holidays. Local seasonal and cyclical events, peculiar to particular ethnic groups, are less well advertised.

CAR RALLIES

The only regular national event that gets much international attention is the three-day **Safari Rally**, in late February or early March. From the beginning of the year, the Kenyan papers wax eloquent about this "toughest motor rally in the world", the teams and drivers who will be entering, and the cost of their preparations. Asian and European entrants predominate; while the whole country seems gripped with rally fever, the costs are prohibitive for most Kenyans and no African driver has yet won. Unless you're a rally buff, however, it's really nothing to get excited about: the route has become monotonous of late, invariably starting with a one-day "special" show stage around Nairobi, followed by two days south and west of the capital in Maasai-land. Information can be had from the Automobile Association at their Hurlingham headquarters in Nairobi (PO Box 40087; ☎02/720382). If you're into this kind of thing, look out also for the **Caltex Equator Rally**, which takes place in

early October, and the annual **Rhino Charge** rally in the Rift valley, which is a ten-hour spin across tough, unmarked terrain to find checkpoints. Information and advance booking (you can get in as part of a safari) from Rafiki (fax 884238, *safarico@arcc.or.ke*).

AGRICULTURAL SHOWS

The annual **agricultural shows** put on by the Agricultural Society of Kenya (ASK) are lively, revealing occasions, borrowing a lot from the British farming show tradition, but infused with Kenyan style. As well as stock and produce competitions, and the usual beer and snack tents, there are often some less expected booths: women's groups, family planning, beekeeping, soil conservation, herbalism. Large towns have an ASK fairground (sometimes reasonable places to camp, incidentally) and the shows happen at roughly the same time each year. Many smaller towns have annual district shows as well.

PUBLIC HOLIDAYS

Public holidays, when all official doors are closed, are: Christmas Day and Boxing Day (December 26), New Year's Day, Good Friday and Easter Monday, May 1 (Labour Day), June 1 (Madaraka Day, celebrating the granting of self-government in 1960), October 10 (Moi Day), October 20 (Kenyatta Day, the anniversary of his imprisonment) and December 12 (Jamhuri Day, or Independence Day).

ASK SHOWS

Eldoret	Late Feb
Nanyuki	First week in May
Meru	Early June
Nakuru	Early July
Kisii	Mid-July
Garissa	Third week in July
Kisumu	First week in Aug
Embu	Second week in Aug
Mombasa	Last week in Aug
Nyeri	Early Sept
Nairobi	First week in Oct
Kitale	First week in Nov
Kakamega	Last week in Nov

ISLAM FESTIVALS: APPROXIMATE DATES			
Beginning of Ramadan (1st Ramadan)	9 Dec 99	16 Nov 2000	6 Nov 2001
Id ul Fitr/Id al-Saghir (1st Shawwal)	8 Jan 2000	17 Jan 2001	5 Dec 2001
Tabaski/Id al-Kabir (10th Dhu'l Hijja)	16 March 2000	5 March 2001	22 March 2002
New Year's Day (1st Moharem)	4 April 2000	24 March 2001	10 April 2002
Ashoura (10th Moharem)	13 April 2000	4 April 2001	19 April 2002
Maulidi/Mouloud (12th Rabia I)	13 May 2000	4 May 2001	19 May 2002

THE ISLAMIC CALENDAR

On the coast, throughout the northeast, and in Muslim communities everywhere, the lunar **Islamic calendar** is followed, parallel to the Gregorian one. The Muslim year has 354 days, with 355 days eleven times every thirty years, so dates recede against the Western calendar by an average of eleven days each year. Only the month of fasting called **Ramadan**, and Id ul Fitr – the feast of relief at the end of it which begins on the first sighting of the new moon – will have much effect on your travels. During Ramadan, most stores and *hotelis* are closed through the daylight hours in smaller towns in Islamic districts. Public transport and official business continue as usual. **Maulidi**, the celebration of the prophet's birthday, is worth catching if you're on the coast at the right time, especially if you'll be in Lamu.

DANCE, MUSIC, THEATRE AND SPORTS

Kenya's espousal of Western values has belittled much traditional culture, so only in remote areas are you likely to come across traditional dancing and drumming which doesn't somehow involve you as a paying audience. If you're patient and reasonably adventurous in your travels, however, you'll be able to witness something more authentic sooner or later – though most likely only by accident or if you stay somewhere off the beaten track long enough to make friends. Kenyan popular music, gospel, and spectator sports are more accessible. For more information on the Nairobi arts scene, see "Cultural venues and art galleries" on p.115.

DANCE

Best known are **Maasai** and **Samburu dancing**: hypnotic swaying and military displays of effortless leaping. Similar dance forms occur widely among other non-agricultural peoples. Foremost among exponents of drumming are the Mijikenda on the coast (the Akamba have sadly all but forgotten the art). **Mijikenda** dance troupes (notably from the Giriama people) perform up and down the coast at tourist venues. As with the Maasai dancing, it's better to ignore any purist misgivings you might have about the authenticity of such performances and enjoy them as distinctive and exuberant entertainments in their own right.

MUSIC

As for **popular music**, apart from what your ears pick up on the street and in buses (often amazingly loud), the live spectacle is limited to Nairobi, coastal entertainment spots, and a fair scattering of up-country discos and "country clubs". The indigenous music scene seems overshadowed by foreign influences: British and American soul and jazz-funk, reggae (especially in the sacred image of Bob Marley) and a vigorous contribution from Congo predominating on radio and in record shops. Congolese music has had a pervasive influence on local sounds, too. The guide to the **Nairobi club and music scene** (p.128) includes a detailed rundown on where to hear the home-grown product. The article in Contexts (p.668–683) at the end of the book gives a condensed history of music in Kenya and a current discography.

If you're lucky enough to be invited to a coastal Swahili wedding with all the trimmings, a **tarabu** band may be playing. *Tarabu* (or Taarab) music, especially the older music (modern *tarabu* relies heavily on synthesizers) is hauntingly beautiful, an effervescent blend of African, Arabic and Indian musical influences. Steady drumbeat, tambourines, accordions, an instrument called the *udi* – like a lute – and plaintive Swahili lyrics are the traditional components, while electric guitars, fiddles and microphones are modern additions.

THEATRE AND FILM

Theatrical performances are effectively limited to one or two semi-professional clubs in Nairobi and Mombasa and a handful of up-country amateur dramatic groups. African actors and scripts tend to be rare but things are improving, at least in Nairobi, where there are a number of groups performing in English.

Indigenous theatre was dealt a severe blow in 1978 when the innovative Kamiriithu Community Education and Cultural Centre in Limuru put on a Kikuyu language play by Ngugi wa Thiongo and Ngugi wa Mirii (*I Will Marry When I Want*), which, after seven weeks of playing to packed houses, was banned. The authorities mistrusted the play's power to mobilize peo-ple and question the status quo in Kikuyu rather than English; Ngugi wa Thiongo was detained without trial for a year as a result. In such a climate – which doesn't appear to have altered much – the notion of popular, issue-raising theatre gets automatically labelled as subversive and hasn't much hope of emerging again. Kamiriithu's brief but spectacular success only shows the potential.

Cinema in Kenya revolves almost entirely around imports. The big towns have cinemas and a few drive-ins, while smaller towns may have one cinema with the occasional screening. American and Indian box-office hits are the staple fodder.

SPORTS

Sports received encouragement from Kenya's much-vaunted – if financially disastrous – hosting of the 1987 All Africa Games. The country's Olympic successes are indisputable, with a regular clutch of gold and silver in the track events. Kenya's athletes are the continent's leaders and the country's long-distance runners are the best in the world, with Moses Kiptanui, from Kapcherop in the Cherangani Hills, the most dazzling recent record-breaker.

Kenya has possibly the most successful athletics training school in the world in St Patrick's High School, Iten, in the Rift Valley. You'll also find evidence of keen amateur involvement – joggers, martial arts tourneys and road cyclists in training.

Soccer is wildly popular. Kenya was to have hosted the Nations Cup finals in early 1996 and it was a major disappointment when they had to pull out due to insufficient funds. The national team, Harambee Stars, wins the East and Central Africa Challenge Cup frequently and, in the Premier League, Nairobi's AFC Leopards and Gor Mahia rank with the best clubs on the continent. Crowds are pretty well behaved, perhaps because forking out for the modest gate fee precludes getting drunk as well.

NATIONAL PARKS AND RESERVES

The national parks are administered by the Kenya Wildlife Service (KWS) in Nairobi as total sanctuaries where human habitation (apart from the tourist lodges) is prohibited. Things seem to be gradually changing, however, as the benefits of readmitting traditional pastoralists begin to be appreciated (humans and wildlife lived in equilibrium before the British arrived). National reserves, run by local councils, tend to be less strict on the question of human encroachment. Parks and reserves are not fenced in (except Nakuru National Park, parts of the Aberdares and the north side of Nairobi National Park), and the animals are free to come and go, but they tend to stay within the boundaries, especially in the dry seasons when cattle outside compete for water.

Most parks and reserves are open to private visits (though it's worth noting that foreign-registered commercial overland vehicles are not allowed in); the exceptions are the upper reaches of Mount Elgon, and a number of places in the northeast, where for reasons of security (banditry is widespread) you need explicit written permission from KWS. A few parks have been heavily developed for tourism with graded tracks, signposts, lodges and the rest, but none has any kind of bus service at the gate for people without their own transport. The largest and most frequently visited are covered in depth in Chapter Five. An introduction to the main game parks, giving you some idea of what to expect from them and the best times to visit, is given on p.356. Details about smaller and lesser-known parks and reserves, some of which can be visited on foot, are included in the rest of the guide.

ENTRY FEES

Park entry fees are charged per person per day (or 24 hours, so you only pay for one day if you arrive in the afternoon, stay overnight and leave at midday). Prices are fixed in dollars, though you can also pay in shillings, at a bad rate. You pay in advance at the park gate, though in practice it's possible to pay for extra days on leaving if you've stayed longer than you originally intended. To qualify for the student rates, you need a **student card** (ISIC). Fees vary according to the popularity of the park: the Aberdares, Amboseli and Lake Nakuru cost $27 ($10 children/students), Tsavo East and West cost $23 ($8 children/students), Nairobi, Shimba Hills and Meru cost $20 ($5 children, $10 students), Mount Kenya charges $10 ($5 children/students), and other parks $15 ($5 children/students). The marine parks are very cheap ($5, or $2 children/students). If you want to camp, you have to stay in a recognized campsite and pay extra ($2–15, depending on the park and whether it's a "special" campsite). Details of these are given in the text.

Kenyan citizens and resident expatriates are eligible for massively reduced rates (you won't pay more than Ksh250). If you qualify, you must have ID to prove this, and KWS is now very strict about enforcing the regulation. If you don't

qualify, it is strongly recommended that you pay the proper fee and get the right receipt. KWS, and thus the future of Kenya's national parks, depends heavily on gate money: if you defraud them, you're conspiring in the destruction of Kenya's wildlife. High as they are compared to residents' rates, the fees are a small price to pay.

For residents, there's a special one-year **"National Parks Pass"** (Ksh6600 per adult or Ksh11,000 per couple; Ksh1000 per child under sixteen). The pass allows you and your vehicle unlimited access to KWS national parks and reserves, excluding the Maasai Mara and the Samburu complex. You can get the pass in person from the licensing section at the parks headquarters on Langata Road in Nairobi (Mon–Fri 8.30am–noon & 2–3.30pm), or you can contact them at PO Box 40241 Nairobi; ☎02/501081 or 506671 or 602345.

Vehicles of less than six seats are charged at Ksh200 per day, 6–12 seats Ksh500, 13–24 seats Ksh1000. A **guide service** costs, per person per guide, Ksh500 for a day, Ksh300 for half a day (4hr). Prices, gate opening times, regulations and information on maps are given at the start of the relevant sections in the guide.

ON SAFARI

Harassment of **animals** disturbs feeding, breeding and reproductive cycles. Too many vehicles surrounding wildlife is not only unpleasant for you, but will also distress the animals. Be quiet when viewing, ask the driver to switch off the engine and keep a minimum distance of 20m. Don't, under any circumstance, get out of your vehicle. And do not feed animals, as it upsets their diet and leads to unnecessary dependence on humans. Habituated baboons especially can become violent if refused handouts. Cheetah only hunt during the day and if surrounded by vehicles will be deprived of a meal.

Off-road driving causes irreparable damage to the vegetation. Ask your driver to stay on the designated tracks (even if it means you won't get the best photograph), as he is only doing what he thinks the client wants.

If you **smoke** while on safari, tip all ash in an ashtray. Carelessly discarded cigarettes start numerous unnecessary bush fires every year, which cause great damage to vegetation and wildlife.

CAMPING SAFARIS

Once in Kenya, choosing a safari company to spend your money on can be fairly hit or miss. Unless you have the luxury of a long stay, your choice will probably be limited by the time available. Remember, though, that you may be able to use this to your advantage; if you ask, many companies are willing to discount a trip in order to fill unsold seats if you're buying at the last minute. Some outfits will also give student discounts if you ask. In fact, any angle you can use to get a good deal, you should use.

This is not to recommend the very cheapest outfits: as the competition in Nairobi becomes more cut-throat, some budget camping operators, not all of them licensed (and none of them included in our listings on p.135), are pushing safaris at the very bottom of the market in a **price war** which completely undercuts the legitimate firms. Any safari which is offered at much less than £40 ($60) per day is likely to be cutting corners. The easiest way for disreputable operators to cut costs is to avoid paying park entry fees. Give these fly-by-night companies a miss.

A number of **recommended operators** are given in the Nairobi account on p.135 but it's notoriously difficult to find a company that's absolutely consistent (if they're a member of KATO – see below – that's a good sign, and at least you have somewhere to complain to). Group relations among the passengers can assume surprising significance in a very short time and other unpredictables such as weather, illness and visibility of animals all contribute to the degree of success of the trip. More controllable factors, like breakdowns, food, camping equipment and competence of the drivers and tour leaders, really determine reputations. The companies we've listed all have pretty good records and get regularly mentioned in readers' letters, but even they turn up the occasional duff trip. Give them a try unless an alternative sounds especially good. The Nairobi grapevine is probably your most reliable guide on this.

If anything goes wrong, reputable companies will do their best to compensate on the spot (an extra day if you broke down, a night in a lodge if you didn't make it to a campsite, partial refunds without demur). But, these days, there's a great deal of competition and corners do get cut. If your grievance is unresolved, you might want to contact the Kenya Association of Tour Operators (KATO), PO Box 48461, 5th Floor, Jubilee Insurance Exchange Building, Mama Ngina St, Nairobi (☎02/225570, fax 218402, *kato@ africaonline.co.ke*), who can intercede with their members.

When going on a camping safari (or any safari for that matter), it's important not to take a passive attitude to the trip. Although some of the itinerary may be fixed, it's not all cast in stone, and daily routines may be altered to suit the clients easily enough if you ask. It's common on camping safaris, for example, to spend the hot part of the day at the campsite. While some are shady and pleasant, that's not always the case, and, where there are lodges with swimming pools, cold beer and the rest, there's no reason not to spend a few hours in comfort. Similarly, if you want to go on an early game drive, don't be afraid to suggest you skip breakfast, or take sandwiches. In too many companies, interpretations of what customers want are passed from management to drivers and cooks and rarely questioned.

As long as they know there will be reasonable **tips** at the end of the trip, most staff will go out of their way to help. Tipping on budget trips, howev-

er, can often cause days of argument and misunderstanding between the clients, who are usually expected to organize themselves to give collective gratuities on the last day. Good companies make suggestions in their briefing packs. Something like Ksh1000–1500 per employee per week from the whole group is not excessive and would still be greatly appreciated (bear in mind that the average teacher earns around Ksh8000 a month).

PHOTOGRAPHY

Kenya is immensely photogenic and with any kind of camera you'll get beautiful pictures. If you take photography seriously, you'll probably want a single-lens reflex (SLR) camera and two or three lenses, but remember, these are heavy, relatively fragile and eminently stealable. Except in the game parks (where some kind of telephoto is essential if you want pictures of animals rather than savannah), you don't really need cumbersome lenses. It's often easier and less intrusive to take a small compact and keep your money for extra film.

Whatever you decide to take, **insure** the camera (if ordinary travel insurance won't cover it, check the insurers who advertise in photo magazines) and make sure you have a dust-proof bag to keep it in, as film gets scratched otherwise. Take spare **batteries** – they can be outrageously expensive in Nairobi, and flashy hyper-automated cameras are completely useless without juice (SLRs in contrast will usually work without a battery, it's just the light meter that goes dead). **Film** is no longer especially expensive, but try to bring all you'll need just the same, particularly if you use colour transparency film or black and white. Try to keep it cool by stuffing it inside a sleeping bag, or wrapping it in newspaper. If you're away for some time, posting film home seems a good idea but is still risky, even if registered: better to leave it with a reliable hotel or friend in Nairobi or Mombasa. Processing in Kenya has improved with the introduction of automatic machines (four-hour service is not uncommon), and is not particularly expensive, but be aware that even machines can screw up your film, especially when mounting slides. A few places in Nairobi have a decent enough reputation (see p.149).

SUBJECTS

As for subjects, **animal photography** is a question of patience and not taking endless pictures of nothing happening: if you can't get close enough, don't waste your film. While taking photos, try keeping both eyes open, and, in a vehicle, always turn off the engine.

The question of **photographing people** is more prickly. Every two seconds, somebody in Kenya has their photo taken by a tourist – and they're getting pretty fed up with it. But in fact, most people are amazingly tolerant of the camera's harassment. The Maasai and Samburu – Kenya's most colourful and photographed people – are usually prepared to do a deal (at monopoly prices), and in some places you'll even find professional posers making a living at the roadside. If you're motivated to take a lot of pictures of people, you might seriously consider lugging along a Polaroid camera and as much film as you can muster – most people will be very pleased to have a snap. Or you could have a lot of photos of you and your family printed up with your address on the back, which should at least raise a few laughs when you try the exchange.

One thing is certain: if you won't accept that some kind of **interaction and exchange** are warranted, you won't get many pictures. Taking the subject's name and address and sending a print when you get home is an option that some people prefer, but it is decreasingly popular with subjects who look on the photo call as work and have fixed the rates they're prepared to accept. Blithely aiming at strangers won't make you any friends and it may well get you into trouble.

On the subject of sensitivity, it's a bad idea to take pictures of anything that could be construed as strategic, including any military or police building, prisons, airports, harbours, bridges and His Excellency the President.

TECHNICAL BUSINESS

Getting (slightly) **technical**, use skylight or UV filters to block haze and protect your lens and yellow filters for dramatic black and white shots. Take several speeds of film (don't let anyone tell you it's unnecessary to have fast film) in rolls of twenty, so you don't get stuck at the wrong speed too long. And, if you feel it's worth taking a camera bag of lenses for your SLR, then it really makes no sense not to take two camera bodies as well – less lens changing, more film speeds available, and you could shoot the same subject in (say) fast black and white and slow, fine-grain colour.

Early morning and late afternoon are the best times for photography. At midday, with the sun almost directly overhead, the light is flat and everything is lost in a formless glare. In the morning and evening, the contrast between light and shade can be huge, so be careful to expose for the subject and not the general scene. And remember, as you negotiate for your next Maasai masterpiece, that black skin usually needs a little more exposure (think of people as always back-lit); a half stop is normally enough. The **rainy seasons** are rewarding, especially when the first rains break: months of dust are settled, greenery sprouts in a few hours, the country has a lush, bold sheen, and the sky is magnificent.

THE ENVIRONMENT AND ETHICAL TOURISM

Tourism may soon become the world's largest industry. It can play an important part in maintaining indigenous cultures, and also provides an invaluable source of foreign currency for many African countries. Although there are many benefits, there are also some irreversible and detrimental consequences.

Tourism's growth in Kenya has been spectacular, from 36,000 visitors in 1955 to 863,000 in 1994. It has been a boon for the economy, but with serious and potentially disruptive effects environmentally, socially, culturally, and economically. Environmental and land degradation as a direct consequence of tourists is evident in Maasai Mara, Samburu and Amboseli, as well as on the beaches.

Local issues have been covered throughout this book. If you're at all concerned about the impact of tourism or environmental matters, get in touch with the organizations mentioned in the text, or the ones listed below. Read also the boxes "Responsible snorkelling, diving and fishing" (p.410) for the coast, and "Environmental concerns" for information on game parks (p.358).

FORESTS AND LAND-GRABBING

The rate of clearance of Kenya's remaining areas of **indigenous forest** is alarming, worsening the problem of soil erosion, and the consequent siltation of lakes, rivers and estuaries. As corruption

becomes more and more entrenched among the ruling classes, there seems little hope of putting an end to the illegal "land grabbing" that grabbed the headlines for much of 1998 and 1999. Most controversial was the discovery that large parts of Nairobi's Karura Forest had been illegally allotted to and cleared by private developers to build luxury residential estates. Even the Forest Department was issued with a notice to vacate the forest that they were supposedly protecting. Countless demonstrations, legal moves and protests later, the government remains strangely silent over the whole affair.

Also seriously threatened are Kakamega Forest (p.327), parts of Mount Kenya Forest with its near extinct camphor plant, the coastal mangroves, and Arabuko-Sokoke Forest (p.488).

CONTACTS

More organizations are mentioned in the "Listings" section under Nairobi (p.146).

CERT, the Campaign for Environmentally Responsible Tourism, PO Box 4246, London SE21 7ZE. Lobbies to educate tour operators and tourists in a sensitive approach to travel, focusing on immediate practical ways in which the environment can be protected.

East African Wildlife Society, PO Box 20110 Nairobi (☎02/574145, fax 570335, *eawls@elci. sasa.unon.org*). This influential body was strongly involved in the movement to ban the ivory trade (achieved in 1989, but now under threat again), and remains active in other areas, recently concerning itself with forest protection and the plight of the endangered hirola antelope. Individual membership entitles you to an annual subscription to their excellent magazine *Swara*, and costs £35 (£45 airmail) in the UK, $50 in the US.

Friends of Conservation, PO Box 74901 Nairobi (☎02/339537 or 02/243976); Sloane Square House, Holbein Place, London SW1W 8NS, (☎0171/730 7904); 1520 Kensington Rd, Oakbrook, Illinois, IL 60521 (☎708 954 3388). An international organization working to stop the

threats facing East and southern African wildlife and habitat. The organization's objectives include wildlife monitoring programmes, anti-poaching support, recreation of habitat, rhino translocation and veterinarian support, and education of both indigenous peoples and visitors.

Tourism Concern, Southlands College, Wimbledon Parkside, London SW19 5NN. Campaigns for the rights of local people to be consulted in tourist developments affecting their lives. They produce a quarterly magazine of news and articles.

TROUBLE

There are still places in Kenya where you can leave an unattended tent for the day and find it untouched when you return in the evening. And there are a few spots where walking alone after dark is almost guaranteed to get you mugged. As a general rule, though, you have a far higher chance of being a victim in touristy areas. It's only fair to point out that the number of "attack on tourist" stories that appear in the world press is not unconnected with the hundreds of thousands of tourists who pass through, and the hundreds of journalists based in Africa's most comfortable city – Nairobi.

AVOIDANCE

After arriving by air for the first time, an incredible number of people get robbed during their first day or two in **Nairobi**, perhaps because, with pallid

skin, and possibly new luggage and clean shoes, they stick out a mile. You should at first be acutely conscious of your belongings: never leave anything unguarded even for fifteen seconds, never take out cameras or other valuables unless absolutely necessary, and be careful of where you walk, at least until you've dropped off your luggage and you're settled in somewhere. It's hard not to look like a tourist, but try to dress like a local – short-sleeved shirt, slacks or skirt and sunglasses – and try not to wear anything brand new. Sunglasses make avoiding unwanted eye contact easier. Most importantly, don't carry a bag, particularly not the little daypack over your shoulder which will virtually identify you as a tourist. See also the section on security in the Nairobi chapter (p.85).

The only substantial risks outside Nairobi are down at the coast (where valuables often disappear from the beach or occasionally get grabbed), in the other big towns (Nakuru and, to a lesser extent, Kisumu), and in some of the game parks – Samburu and Maasai Mara have had a number of incidents in recent years.

If you're **driving**, it's never a good idea to leave even a locked car unguarded if it has anything of value in it. In towns, there's usually someone who will volunteer to guard it for you for a tip (Ksh10 or Ksh20 is enough).

Doping scams seem to be on the rise at present, with operators on different public transport routes managing to drug tourists and relieve them of their belongings. Be very wary of accepting any food or drink on public transport.

All of this isn't meant to induce paranoia. But if you flaunt the trappings of wealth where there's

TROUBLE FROM MISUNDERSTANDINGS

It's very easy to fall prey to misunderstandings in your relations with people (usually boys and young men) who offer their services as guides, helpers or "facilitators" of any kind. You should absolutely never assume anything is being done out of simple kindness. It may well be, but, if it isn't, you must expect to pay something. If you have any suspicion, it's invariably best to confront the matter head on at an early stage and either apologize for the offence caused by the suggestion, or agree a price. What you must never do, as when bargaining, is enter into an unspoken contract and then break it by refusing to pay for the service. If you're being bugged by someone whose help you don't need, just let them know you can't pay anything for their trouble. It may not make you a friend, but it always works and it's better than a row and recriminations.

urban poverty, somebody will want to remove them. There's always less risk in leaving your valuables in a locked hotel room or – judiciously – with the management, than in taking them with you. Don't wear dangling earrings or any kind of chain or necklace, and even a cheap wrist watch is tempting. If you clearly have nothing on you, you're unlikely to feel, or be, threatened. In Nairobi, the rush hour at dusk is probably the worst time, but it's a good idea to be alert getting off a night bus early in the morning, too. It's also worth tuning into the monthly cycle of poverty and wealth among urban Kenyans; there are always more pickpockets about at the end of the month, when people are carrying their pay packet.

When you have to **carry money**, put it in several places if possible: a money belt tucked into your trousers or skirt is invisible and thus usually secure for travellers' cheques, passport and large amounts of cash. Put the rest – what you'll need for your day/walk/night out – in a pocket or somewhere more accessible: somewhat perversely, you're safer with at least some money to hand, as few muggers will believe you have nothing on you.

CONS AND SCAMS

Approaches in the street from "schoolboys" with sponsorship forms (only primary education is free, and even then, books, uniforms, even furniture have to be bought) and from "refugees" with long stories are not uncommon and probably best shrugged off. Some, unfortunately, may be genuine.

One scam, almost "traditional" by now and surprisingly successful to judge by the number of tourists who fall for it, relies entirely on people's belief in the paranoid republic. It involves an approach by a "student", followed by a request for a small sum of money. As you leave with a sigh of relief, a group of heavies surround you and claim to be undercover police, interested in the discussion you've been having with that "subversive", or "Sudanese terrorist", or whoever, and the funds you provided him. A large fine is demanded. You can tell them to go to hell, or suggest you all go to the police station. Such aggressions are never the real thing.

A treat for Nairobi motorists is a small boy popping up and slapping you in the face as you get out after parking. As you make to go after him in outrage, his friends grab what they can from the car. Other car tricks are described in the "Car Rental and Driving" section on p.41 and in the sections on Nakuru and Isiolo – where they seem most popular.

Lastly, an old one that still catches people out: if you're grabbed by a man who has just picked up a wad of money in the street and seems oddly willing to share it with you in a convenient nearby alley, you'll know you're about to be robbed.

MUGGINGS

If you get **mugged**, the usual rule applies: don't resist; knives and guns are occasionally carried. It will be over in an instant and you're unlikely to be hurt. But the hassles, and worse, that gather when you try to do anything about it make it imperative not to let it happen in the first place. Thieves caught red-handed are usually mobbed – often killed – so when you shout "Thief!" ("*Mwizi!*" in Swahili), be ready to intercede once you've retrieved your belongings.

Usually you'll have no chance to catch the thief, and the first reaction is to go to the **police**. Unless you've lost a lot of money (and cash is virtually irretrievable) or irreplaceable property, however, think twice about doing this. They rarely do something for nothing – even stamping an insurance form will probably cost you – and secondly you should consider the ramifications if you and they set off to try and catch the culprits. This kind of scenario, with you in the back of a police car expected to point out the thief in the crowds, is a complete waste of time. And, whatever you do, never agree to act as a decoy in the hope that the same thing will happen again in front of a police ambush. Police shootings take place all the time and you may prefer not to be the cause of a cold-blooded murder.

If you have to visit the police in Nairobi, go to the main police station (marked on the map), not any of the smaller posts and offices.

DEALING WITH THE POLICE

Kenyan police are probably no worse than most other police forces around the world. Stories do sometimes get recounted of extraordinary **kindness** at times of trouble and of occasional bursts of **efficiency** that would do credit to any police force. But, badly educated and poorly paid as the police mostly are, you would be wise to steer clear as far as possible. If you have **official business** with the police, then politeness, smiles and handshakes always help. If you're expected to give a bribe – *chai* is the usual word for it, which means "tea" – wait for it to be hinted at and haggle over it as you would any payment; the equivalent of a dollar or so is often enough to oil small wheels. Be aware, of course, that bribery is illegal, no matter what the behaviour of Kenyan politicians – if you know you've done nothing wrong and are not in a rush, refusing a bribe will only cost a short delay until the policeman gives up on you and tries another potential source of income.

In **unofficial dealings**, the police, especially in remote outposts, can go out of their way to help you with food, transport or accommodation. Try to reciprocate. Police salaries are low – no more than a few thousand shillings a month – and they rely on unofficial income to get by. Only a brand new police force and realistic salaries could alter a situation which is now entrenched.

Common ways of exciting police interest are staggering around a city late at night, and drug possession. The first needs lots of humble pie and nothing more, the latter carries a mandatory eight-year prison sentence, though you may be lucky and be given a large fine and deportation – but don't expect to buy yourself out of this kind of trouble. Driving offences are less serious, though being stopped at the fairly frequent road checkpoints is becoming increasingly common, with the sole purpose of finding fault to elicit a bribe. Insist on a receipt before handing over any money – if he refuses, you can talk yourself out of it. It's worth knowing that some forces have speed-trap radar equipment which they set up outside towns: drive with caution as speed limits are often vague.

UNSEEMLY BEHAVIOUR

Be warned that failure to observe the following points of **Kenyan etiquette** can get you arrested or put you in a position where you may be obliged to pay a bribe. Stand in cinemas and on other occasions when the national anthem is playing. Stand still when the national flag is being raised or lowered in your field of view. Don't take photos of the flag or His Excellency the President (often seen on state occasions in Nairobi). Pull off the road completely when scores of motorcycle outriders appear, then get out and stand by your vehicle (for it is he). Never tear up a banknote, of any denomination. And don't urinate in public.

WOMEN'S KENYA

Machismo, in its fully fledged Latin varieties, is rare in Kenya and male egos are usually softened by reserves of humour. Women's groups flourish across the country, but are concerned more with improvement of incomes, education, health and nutrition than social or political emancipation, though this is changing.

SEXUAL HARASSMENT

Women, whether travelling alone or together, may come across occasional **persistent hasslers** but seldom much worse. Universal rules apply: if you suspect ulterior motives, turn down all offers and stonily refuse to converse, though you needn't fear expressing your anger if that's how you feel. You will, eventually, be left alone. Really obnoxious individuals are usually on their own, fortunately. These tactics are hardly necessary except on the coast, and then particularly in **Lamu**. Avoid walking alone down beach access roads north or south of Mombasa, however, as there's a danger of violent robbery for either sex.

Blonde women suffer more, though cutting your hair short or dyeing it seem drastic and rather prejudicial steps. There is already enough discouragement in the world to women wanting to travel without the company of men – and Kenya is probably easier in this respect than most countries.

For a book packed with anecdotes, information and encouragement, get the Rough Guide special, *Women Travel*.

BROADER ISSUES

In 1985, when Nairobi hosted the International Women's Decade Conference, Kenya's **women's movement** was still embryonic. Ten years on, the fourth UN World Conference on Women, held in Beijing in 1995, gave fresh incentive to women's groups throughout Kenya to work together to improve women's status and conditions. Women are becoming increasingly vocal in their call for political representation at local and national levels. The Maendeleo ya Wanawake Organization (MYWO) is seen as the national network best equipped to implement issues tackled in Beijing, although its unquestioningly pro-government stance softens its sting somewhat. Having started to help women at a very basic level forty years ago, MYWO now encourages economic independence and, as annual membership costs only Ksh20, almost every woman in Kenya can belong. The umbrella group teaches basic literacy, family planning and nutrition and is working hard to abolish the practices of ritual female genital mutilation, "female circumcision". Kenya, tragically, is still used as something of a contraceptive testing ground, with less stringent rules on over-the-counter drugs than many countries; Depo-provera, high-level oestrogen pills and the Dalkon shield have all been foisted on Kenyan women.

For more information and contacts, get in touch with MYWO (see Nairobi "Listings", p.153), or the much more independent National Council of Women of Kenya, headed by the admirable Professor Wangari Maathai, a ceaseless campaigner for women's rights, and also the founder of the Greenbelt Movement, who plant more trees in a year than the government has in a decade, and is currently engaged in a campaign to revoke illegal forest land allocation at Karura in Nairobi (during which Maathai was hospitalized by the security forces). You might also try writing to the Pan-African Women's Trade Union, PO Box 61068 Nairobi, or contact the Forum for African Women's Education, which has a good library.

SEXUAL ATTITUDES

Sexual mores in Kenya are refreshingly hedonistic and uncluttered, nor is prostitution the rigid, secretive transaction of the West. Unfortunately, sexually transmitted diseases, including the HIV virus, are rife. Kenyans are waking up to this reality, but you should be aware of the very real risks should you accept a proposition. Various surveys have revealed that anything from one in four to nine out of ten Nairobi and Mombasa prostitutes are HIV positive, and the government itself estimated in 1998 that eight percent of the entire population were HIV-positive: the real figure is possibly much more. Four out of five deaths among 25 to 35 year olds are AIDS-related. It goes without saying that casual sex without a condom is a deadly gamble and you should assume any sexual contact to be HIV positive.

Despite this, female **prostitution** flourishes enthusiastically everywhere and a remarkable number of the cheaper hotels double as brothels, or at least willingly rent their rooms by the hour. Gigolos and male prostitutes – far fewer – are limited mostly to Nairobi and the coast.

Among tourists, enough arrive expecting sexual adventures to make flirtatious pestering a fairly constant part of the scene, irritating or amusing as it strikes you. And if you're a woman looking for a holiday affair, Lamu seems to be the place.

As for attitudes to **gay life**, they're rather hard to pin down. While there is no gay scene as such, male homosexuality is an accepted undercurrent on the coast, where it finds most room for expression in Lamu, and to a small extent in Nairobi. The Lake Victoria region has a fairly relaxed attitude, too, as well as the country's highest incidence of AIDS. _Msenge_ is Swahili for gay man. Elsewhere, homosexuality _seems_ scarce enough not to be an issue. On the statute books, however, it remains illegal.

PEOPLE AND LANGUAGES

Whether called peoples, ethnic groups or tribes (the term still used officially and in casual conversation), Kenyans have a multiplicity of racial and cultural origins. Distinctions would be simple if similarities in physical appearance were shared by those who speak the same language and share a common culture. But "tribes" have never been closed units, and appearance, speech and culture have always overlapped. Families, for instance, often contain members of different tribes, though tradition still dictates whether an individual's "tribe" is determined through their father's line, or through their mother's brother's line.

In the last fifty years, tribal identities have broken down as broader class, political and national ones have emerged. However, a worrying recent development, spurred on by the chaotic general elections of 1992 and 1997, has been the organizing and splitting of political parties along tribal lines, at the same time as an upsurge in ethnic violence. Although small on an African scale, the killings and attacks, mostly in remoter parts of the Rift Valley, pose a much greater problem nationally – the potential disintegration of the nation.

The most enduring ethnic distinction is language. A person's **"mother tongue"** is still important as an index of social identity and a tribe is best defined as people sharing a common first language. But, in the towns and among affluent families, language is increasingly unimportant. Many people speak three languages (their own,

AFRICAN LANGUAGE GROUPS IN KENYA

This, broadly, is the breakdown of Kenya's language groups into separate ethnic identities. You'll find variations on these spellings, and inconsistencies in the use of prefixes (ie Kamba instead of Akamba, Agikuyu instead of Kikuyu, and so on).

BANTU-SPEAKING

Western Bantu: Luhya, Gusii, Kuria.

Central Bantu: Akamba, Kikuyu, Embu, Meru, Mbere, Tharaka.

Coastal Bantu: Swahili, Mijikenda, Segeju, Pokomo, Taita, Taveta.

NILOTIC-SPEAKING

Lake-River Nilotic: Luo.

Plains Nilotic: Maasai and Samburu (Maa-speakers), Turkana, Teso, Njemps, Elmolo.

Highland Nilotic: Kalenjin group including Nandi, Marakwet, Pokot, Tugen, Kipsigis, Elkony.

CUSHITIC-SPEAKING

Southern Cushitic: Boni.

Eastern Cushitic: Somali, Rendille, Orma, Boran, Gabbra ("Oromo" is often used to describe all these language groups except the Somali).

Swahili and English) or even four if they have mixed parentage. And for a few, English has become a first language.

There are pieces throughout the book on aspects of the history and cultures of the main language groups in each region.

NAMES AND GROUPS

Books continue to use various unwieldy terms: **Bantu** and **Nilotic** are language groups (like Indo-European or Semitic) and, restricted to a linguistic sense, are fair enough. But Hamitic, which still pops up occasionally, is almost meaningless and hedged with racist overtones. "Hamitic influence" has been credited with many technological, social and political innovations in the past. The Biblical origins of the word give it away: it reflects the early European presumption that lighter-skinned people with thinner lips and straighter noses were more intelligent than other Africans. The origins of these people in northeast Africa and their implied association with the well-springs of Mediterranean civilization were further "evidence" of this. The term "Nilo-hamitic" (often used to refer to the Maasai and other pastoralists admired by the Europeans) just confuses the issue further; it implies the cross-cutting cultural, linguistic and racial overlays that most Kenyans have inherited, without abandoning the idea of racially superior influences from the north.

Biologically, of course, Negroid inheritance predominates among Africans, with Caucasoid elements clear enough in many regions. But physiology doesn't have much to do with language or culture. Travelling around Kenya, you become aware of just how far off the mark the old racist doctrines really were.

Apart from the African majority, who make up about 99 percent of the population, Kenya has a considerable and diverse **Asian** population – perhaps over 100,000 – most of whom live in Nairobi, Mombasa, Kisumu and Nakuru. Descendants in part of the labourers brought over to build the railway, they also number many whose parents and grandparents came in its wake, to trade and set up businesses. And some families, notably on the coast, have lived in Kenya for centuries. Predominantly Punjabi and Gujerati speakers from northwest India and Pakistan, they are overwhelmingly dominant in business. There's a dispersed Christian Goan community, too, identified by their Portuguese surnames, who tend to have less formalized relations with other Kenyans. And a persistent, but diminishing **Arab**-speaking community remains on the coast.

Lastly, there are still an estimated ten thousand **European** residents – a surprisingly motley crew from British ex-servicemen to Italian aristocrats – scattered through the highlands, and the rest of the country, some four thousand of whom hold Kenya citizenship. Some maintain a scaled-down version of the old planter's life, and a few still hold senior civil service positions. Increasingly, though, the community is turning to the tourist industry for a firmer future – and a life beyond Kenya if necessary.

RELIGION AND ETIQUETTE

In the matter of religion, the majority of "up-country" Kenyans have converted to Christianity, with most people on the coast professing Islam. Indigenous religion is rapidly disappearing, but it holds on in remoter areas.

Varieties of **Catholicism** and **Protestantism** are dominant in the highlands and westwards, and are increasingly pervasive elsewhere. In the Rift Valley and the far west, especially towards Lake Victoria, there are many minor **Christian sects** and churches – over a thousand denominations – often based around the teaching of local prophets and preachers.

Broad-based, non-fundamentalist **Sunni Islam** dominates the coast and the northeast, and is in the ascendant throughout the country. Many towns have several mosques (or dozens on the coast), but one usually serves as the focal **Friday mosque** for the whole community. Shiite fundamentalism was previously almost unknown among African believers, but the Islamic Party of Kenya (IPK) has some vocal fundamentalist campaigners among its supporters. The Aga Khan's **Ismaili** sect is an influential Asian constituency with powerful business interests. **Hindu** and **Sikh** temples are found in most large towns, and there are adherents of **Jainism** and the **Bahai** faith, too.

Indigenous religion (mostly based around the idea of a supreme god and intercession between the living and the spirit worlds by deceased ancestors) survives as an inclusive belief system only in the remotest areas of northern Kenya, among the remaining Okiek (or Ndorobo) hunter-gatherers in a very few forests, and among pastoralists like the Maasai. But while it is continually under threat from Christian missionaries, its influence over the lives of many nominally Christian or Muslim Kenyans remains powerful.

ETIQUETTE

Islamic moral strictures tend to be generously interpreted. On the coast, it's always best to **dress** in loose-fitting long sleeves and skirts or trousers in the towns, but shorts and T-shirts won't get you into trouble: people are far too polite to admonish strangers. Malindi, in particular, is very relaxed. Lamu calls more for *kikoi* and *kanga* wraps for both sexes and, because it's so small, more consideration for local feelings. Suitably dressed and hatted men, and often women, can enter **mosques**. Few are very grand, however, and you rarely miss much by staying outside.

DIRECTORY

Beggars are fairly common in the touristy parts of Nairobi and Mombasa. Most are visibly destitute; many are cripples, lepers or homeless mothers with children. Some have regular pitches, others keep on the move. They are harassed by police and often rounded up. Kenyans often give to the same beggar on a regular basis and, of course, alms-giving is a requirement of Islam believed to benefit the donor. The hundreds of glue-sniffing boys are a sad development of recent years in most cities and big towns. They're responsible for much of the cities' petty crime – and often pay a swift, final price.

Books Less than fifty percent of Kenyans are literate but books and reading material have a high profile. Bookstores in Nairobi, Mombasa and in the tourist hotels have imported paperback selections. Locally printed books are sometimes very cheap, and provide insights into Kenyan life you wouldn't otherwise find. Secondhand book stalls are often worth looking at, too. Or ask other travellers: bring one book and keep exchanging. For suggestions on reading matter, see p.648 of Contexts.

Clothes Particularly if you're only coming for a short stay, it's important to bring what you need to be comfortable. Take loose cotton clothes, comfortable flip-flops (or suede shoes or boots for the highlands), plus at least one really warm sweater or, better still, a soft-lined jacket with pockets. (See the "Mount Kenya" section for advice on what you need at high altitudes.) And, even if you're on a shoestring, take some nicer clothes to wear in lodges: access is often difficult for the ragged.

Contraceptives Condoms are available from town pharmacies and supermarkets. Family planning clinics in most main towns are helpful (see Nairobi and Mombasa "Listings") and will sometimes provide them and – with a prescription – oral contraceptives, free or for a small charge. But it's far wiser to bring all you'll need.

Departure tax When leaving Kenya by air there's a departure tax equivalent to US$20, payable in foreign currency or Kenyan shillings (around Ksh1200 at the current rate of exchange), which most airlines now include in their fare (ask when buying your ticket). If you don't have the right money, change will be given only in Kenyan shillings. Departure tax on domestic flights is Ksh100, again mostly included in the airfare. Neither kind of departure tax is payable for infants.

Drugs Grass (*bhangi*) is widely cultivated and smoked and is remarkably cheap. Officially illegal (eight years is the statutory sentence for possession with no option of a fine; buying or selling carries a twenty-year sentence), the authorities do make some effort to control it. Use and attitudes vary considerably but you should be very discreet if you're going to indulge. Official busts result in a shakedown by the police, a heavy fine and deportation at the very least. Your embassy will not be sympathetic. Anything harder than marijuana is rarely sold and will get you in worse trouble if you're caught. *Miraa* (or *qat*), a mild herbal stimulant chewed for ages and then spat out, is legal and widely available, especially in Nairobi,

Mombasa and in the north. It's traditionally used by people in drought-prone areas, as it suppresses hunger. It also keeps you awake all night, and so is favoured by East African lorry drivers. Local police chiefs sometimes order crackdowns on its transport.

Electricity Kenya's electricity supply is usually reliable and, like Britain's, uses square, three-pin plugs on 220–240V (the exceptions are Kisii and some older buildings, which use large round two-pin plugs). Only fancier hotels have outlets or shaver points in the rooms.

Emergencies For police, fire and ambulance dial ☎999. They take ages to arrive.

Gifts Ballpoint pens and postcards are about the only small items worth taking and can always be given to children, but they encourage begging if just handed out of a truck or minibus window. Off the beaten track, these gifts will be appreciated by many adults, too, though few people will have an exaggerated idea of their real value. If you'll be travelling or staying for some time and really want to prepare, get a large batch of photos of you and your family with your address on the back. You'll get lots of mail.

"Kenya" or "Keenya"? Although you'll hear "Kenya" most of the time, the second pronunciation is still used, and not exclusively by old colonials. It seems that the colonial pronunciation was closer to the original name of the mountain, Kirinyaga. This was early on shortened to Kinya and spelt "Kenya" (with affinity to English "key"). With the arrival of modern African orthography, this spelling came to be pronounced with a short "e", and when Kenyatta became president the coincidence of his name was exploited.

Laundry There are virtually no launderettes/laundromats in Kenya and it's usually easiest to wash your own clothes: you can buy packets of Omo soap powder, and things dry fast. Beware of New Blue Omo – it's very strong and wrecks clothes if you use it for long. Otherwise, there's often someone wherever you're staying who will be prepared to negotiate a laundry charge. Don't spread clothes on the ground to dry: they might be infested by the tumbu fly, which lays its eggs in them for the larvae to hatch and burrow into your skin.

Opening hours Standard opening hours, where there are any, follow familiar patterns: in larger towns, the major stores and tourist services will be open from 8am to 5 or 6pm, offices and museums at similar times, though offices will often break for lunch. Banks and post offices are generally open Monday to Friday and sometimes Saturday mornings. In rural areas and out in the bush, small shops can be open at almost any hour, and may double as *hotelis* or *chai* kiosks.

Place names Place names all over Africa (not just Kenya) are remarkably confusing to outsiders. In some parts every town or village seems to have a name starting with the same syllable. In the Kenya highlands, you'll find Kiambu, Kikuyu, Kiganjo, Kiserian, Kinangop etc. Further west you confront Kaptagat, Kapsabet, Kabarnet, Kapsowar . . . As soon as you detect a problem like this, just get into the habit of "de-stressing" the first syllable and remember the second. A more practical problem all over rural Kenya is the vague use of names to denote a whole district and, at the same time, its nucleus, be it a small town, a village, or just a cluster of corrugated iron shops and bars. Sometimes there'll be two such focuses. They often move in a matter of a few years, so what looks like a junction town on the map turns out to be away from the road, or in a different place altogether. Ask for the "shopping centre" and you'll usually find the local hive of activity and the place with the name you were looking for.

Receipts Petty bureaucracy is deeply engrained in Kenya and you will often be given a hand-written receipt after making the most elementary purchase. If you have cause to doubt that the sum you're being asked to pay is officially sanctioned, however - for example, an obscure entrance fee, or a fee for a guide, or in cases where police try to impose an on-the-spot fine - just ask for a receipt and this will often clarify matters.

Snorkelling If you plan to do a fair bit of goggling, try to bring your own mask and snorkel. They aren't highly expensive, or particularly heavy, and you'll benefit from having equipment that fits and works, and save money you'd otherwise spend renting it. Don't forget that although certain parts of the coast have exceptional stretches of reef, you can have a rewarding dip under the waves almost anywhere.

Student cards If you qualify, get hold of an International Student Identity Card (ISIC) from student unions or student/youth travel agents. In Kenya, it's no passport to automatic cheap deals, but it can be worth showing for discounted park and museum entry fees. Note that only American ISIC cards provide automatic basic insurance cover for their holders.

Tampons Available in town chemists but expensive, so bring supplies.

Time Kenya is three hours ahead of Greenwich Mean Time all year round, which means two hours ahead of Britain during the summer, eight hours ahead of Eastern Standard Time, and seven hours behind Sydney. With slight variations east and west, it gets light at 6am and dark at 6pm. If you're learning Swahili, remember that "Swahili time" runs from dawn to dusk to dawn rather than midnight to midday to midnight. 7am and 7pm are both *saa moja* (one o'clock) while midnight and midday are *saa sita* (six o'clock). It's not as confusing as it first sounds – just add or subtract six hours to work out Swahili time (or read the opposite side of your watch). People and things are usually late in Kenya. That said, if you try to anticipate, you're generally caught out. Trains nearly always leave right on time; buses often have punctual departures as well. In more remote areas though, if a driver tells you he's going somewhere "today", it doesn't necessarily mean he expects to arrive today . . .

Tipping If you're staying in tourist-class establishments, and travelling a lot, you will often have to tip staff. In expensive hotels, Ksh100 wouldn't be out of place for portering a lot of luggage, but coins are usually adequate, or small notes at the most. For most small services, Ksh20 is more than adequate. With the peculiar, upside-down logic of the world of service industries, in the very humblest establishments, tipping is not the custom. Note that on safaris, tips are considered almost part of the pay and you're expected to shell out at the end of the trip (see p.65).

Toilets Carry toilet paper – which you can buy in most places – as few cheap hotels provide it. Town public toilets (*Wanawake* = Women; *Wanaume* = Men) are invariably disgusting, as are those in cheaper B&Ls. Public buildings and hotels are unlikely to turn you away if you ask.

Weddings Many of the coastal hotels and a few game lodges will lay it on thick if that's what you really want – garlands of flowers, gospel choirs, "complimentary" cakes and tributes, tree-planting ceremonies ("If it dies, we shall plant another") and so on. The whole experience can feel rather conveyor-belt-driven (you may be just one of half a dozen happy couples getting hitched on the same day at your dream resort hotel), and you might find that being gawped at by holidaymakers in swimming togs as you say "I do" doesn't do

THINGS TO TAKE

In no particular order, and not all essential:

• **Binoculars** (the small, fold-up ones) are invaluable for game watching. Without them you'll miss half the action. Take a pair for each person.

• **Sunglasses** are a health precaution worth bringing even if you're not used to them, and they're expensive to buy in Kenya.

• **Plastic bags** are invaluable: large bin-liner bags to keep dust off clothes, small resealable ones to protect cameras and film.

• Take a multipurpose **penknife**, a **torch**, an **alarm clock** (handy for pre-dawn starts) and a **padlock** – vital in lodgings where doors don't lock.

• **Camping gas stoves** are light and useful even if you're not camping. The cylinders can be bought in Nairobi (see "Listings", p.146) and in a number of other places.

• A tube of **ant-killer** comes in handy if you're camping, particularly on the coast.

• Down on the coast, too, **plastic sandals** are best for walking on the reef; you can buy them cheaply in Kenya.

• You might want to take your own **flip-flops/thongs** for cheap hotel bathrooms (though a pair is often provided).

• **Earplugs** are a help in some lodgings if you're a light sleeper.

• A **sheet sleeping bag** (sew up a sheet) is essential for low-budget travel.

• If you shave, bring disposable **razors**.

For driving around the parks and hiking, a **compass** is immensely useful.

---

much for the solemnity of the occasion. Choose your venue carefully.

Work Unless you've lined up a job or voluntary work before leaving for Kenya, you have little chance of getting employment. Wages are extremely low – for university lecturers, for example, they start at not much more than the equivalent of £150 ($225) per month, whilst school teachers earn about £80 ($145) – and there's serious unemployment in the towns. Particular skills are sometimes in demand – mechanics at game park lodges, for example – but the employer will need good connections to arrange the required papers. It's illegal to obtain income in Kenya while staying on a visitor's pass. You may be able to find work on a voluntary work camp, however: see p.9

PART TWO

THE

GUIDE

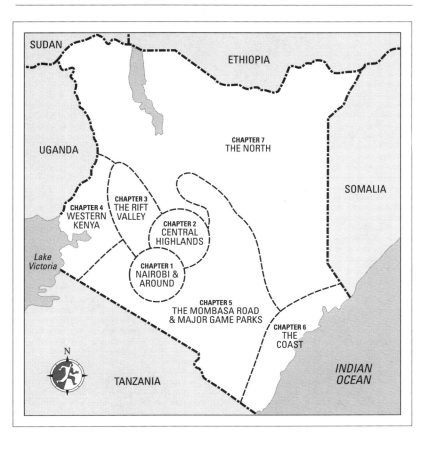

NAIROBI AND AROUND

E asily the largest city in East Africa, **NAIROBI** is also the youngest, the most modern, the fastest growing, the largest and, at 1700m, the highest. The superlatives could go on forever. "City in the sun", runs one tour brochure sobriquet, "City of flowers", another. Less enchanted visitors growl "Nairobbery". The city catches your attention at least. This is no tropical backwater.

Most roads, particularly paved ones, lead to Nairobi and, like it or not, you're bound to spend some time here. But walking down Kenyatta Avenue at rush hour, or up Tom Mboya Street after dark, when the security men armed with whips and clubs cluster around their fires on the pavement, it's perhaps easy to forget how quickly you can leave the city and be in the bush. Apart from being the **safari** capital of the world,

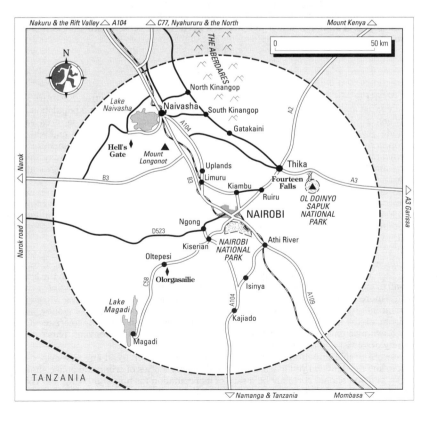

ACCOMMODATION PRICE CODES

Rates for a standard double or twin room. For a full explanation of these rates, see p.47.

① Under Ksh500	(under approx £5/$8)	⑥ Ksh6000–9000	(£60–90/$96–144)*
② Ksh500–1000	(£5–10/$8–16)	⑦ Ksh9000–12,000	(£90–120/$144–192)*
③ Ksh1000–2000	(£10–20/$16–32)	⑧ Ksh12,000–16,000	(£120–£160/$192–256)*
④ Ksh2000–4000	(£20–40/$32–64)	⑨ Over Ksh16,000	(over £160/$256)*
⑤ Ksh4000–6000	(£40–60/$64–96)	* = *usually priced in dollars*	

Nairobi is an excellent **base for travel**, just nine hours by road to the coast, or an overnight train journey, about the same time to the far west, and just a couple of hours northwest to the great trough of the Rift Valley or north to the slopes of Mount Kenya.

For **shorter trips**, worthwhile destinations, covered at the end of this chapter, lie all around, with the first and closest target **Nairobi National Park**, a wild attraction where you'd expect to find suburbs. **Lake Naivasha** to the northwest and **Lake Magadi**, south, are two utterly different Rift Valley lakes, each just a few hours away from the capital – a day trip by car, two or three days if hitching or taking the bus. The prehistoric site of **Olorgasailie** is on the way to Magadi. If you're looking for greener and cooler destinations, an interesting hiking (or biking) route runs from **North Kinangop to Thika**. For loftier heights turn north to the central highlands (Chapter Two).

NAIROBI

NAIROBI is one of Africa's major cities: the UN's fourth "World Centre", East Africa's commercial and aid hub, and a significant capital in its own right, with a population of between a million and a half and three million, depending on how big an area you include. As a traveller, your first impressions are likely to depend on how – and where – you arrive. Coming here overland, some time resting up among the fleshpots can seem a pleasant proposition. Newly arrived by air from Europe, though, you may wonder – amid the rash of signs for *California Cookies*, *Wimpy* and *Oriental Massage* – just how far you've travelled. Nairobi, just a century-old in 1999, has real claims to Western-style sophistication but, as you'll soon find, it lacks a convincing heart, at least in those terms. Apart from some lively musical attractions – some of East Africa's busiest **clubs** and best **bands** – there's little here of magnetic appeal, and most travellers stay long enough only to take stock, make some travel arrangements and maybe visit the **National Museum**, before moving on.

If you're interested in getting to know the real Kenya, though, Nairobi is as compelling a place as any and displays enormous vitality and buzz. The controlling ethos is commerce rather than community, and there's an almost wilful superficiality in the free-for-all of commuters, shoppers, police, hustlers and tourists. It's hard to imagine a city with a more fascinating variety of people, and almost all of them newcomers. Most are immigrants from rural areas, drawn to the presence and opportunities of money, and Nairobi, on the surface at least, seems to accept everyone with complete tolerance. On any downtown pavement you can see a complete cross-section of Kenyans, plus every variety of tourist and refugees from many African countries.

Nairobi's rapid growth inevitably has a downside however (read any newspaper or talk to any resident and you'll hear some jaw-dropping stories of crime and police shootings), and you should certainly be aware of its reputation for **bag-snatching** and **robbery**, frequently directed at new tourist arrivals (see the box on security on p.85). If you plan to stay for any length of time, learn the art of survival; with the right attitude, you're unlikely to have problems. For the few days that most people spend in Nairobi – if initial misgivings can be overcome – it's a stimulating city.

Some history

Nairobi came into being in May 1899, an artificial settlement created by Europeans at Mile 327 of the East African railway line, then being systematically forged from Mombasa on the coast to Kampala, now the Ugandan capital. It was initially a supply depot, switching yard and campsite for the thousands of Indian labourers employed by the British. Its site, bleak and swampy, was simply the spot where operations came to a halt while the engineers figured out their next move, namely getting the line up the steep slopes that lay ahead. The name came from the local Maasai word for the area, *enkare nyarobi*, "the place of cold water", though the spot itself was originally called *Nakusontelon*, "Beginning of all Beauty".

Unexpectedly, the unplanned **settlement** took root. A few years later it was totally rebuilt after an outbreak of plague and the burning of the original town compound. By 1907, it was so firmly established that the colonists took it as the capital of the newly formed "British East Africa" (BEA). Europeans, encouraged by the authorities, settled in large numbers, while Africans were forced into employment by tax demands (without representation) or onto specially created **reserves** – the Maasai to the Southern Reserve and the Kikuyu to their own reserve in the highlands.

The capital, lacking development from any established community, was somewhat characterless – and remains so. The **original centre** retains an Asian influence in its older buildings, but today it is shot through with glassy, high-rise blocks. Surrounding the commercial hub is a vast area of **suburbs**: wealthiest in the west and north, increasingly poor to the south and especially east, where they become, in part, out-and-out slums.

Names of these suburbs – Parklands, Lavington, Eastleigh, Shauri Moyo, among others – reflect the jumble of African, Asian and European elements in Nairobi's population, none of whom were local. The term "Nairobian" isn't in circulation because it would scarcely apply to anyone. Although it has a predominance of Kikuyu, the city is not the preserve of a single ethnic group, nor is it built on any distinctively tribal land. Standing as it does at the meeting point of Maasai, Kikuyu and Kamba territories, its choice as capital, accidental though it may have been (Kikuyu **Limuru** and Kamba **Machakos** were also considered), was a fortunate one for the future of the country.

DRIVING IN NAIROBI

Driving in **Nairobi** can be a nerve-wracking experience for inexperienced or nervous drivers, though you do tend to get used to things after a few days. The main things to watch out for are *matatus*, which stop as suddenly as they lurch back into the fray, and roundabouts. These labour under "priority traffic" regulations, which in theory means cars already on the roundabout have priority, but in practice means chaos as no-one is terribly keen to cede right of way. Always stay in lane. If you're worried, you should pick up the car at the airport, which gives you time to get used to the car and the traffic before joining the city centre fray.

Parking in central Nairobi can be difficult during business hours, though there's usually space at the car park at the west end of Kenyatta Avenue by Uhuru Highway. The old parking meters literally got the chop, so you're now supposed to find a NCC traffic warden, dressed in yellow, to pay your Ksh50 daily fee to (if you don't, you risk have your car towed away).

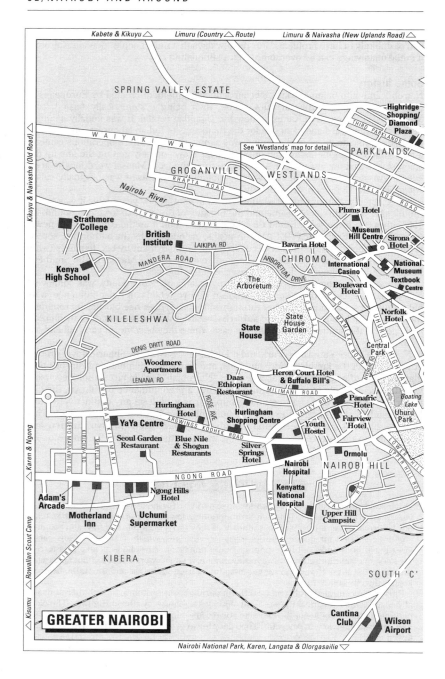

GREATER NAIROBI

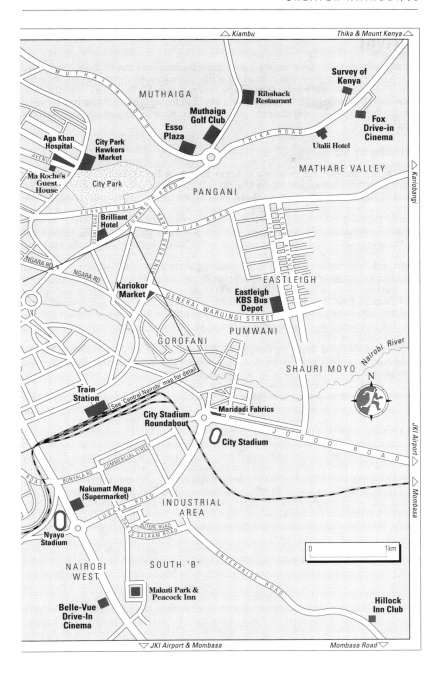

Arrival

Getting into central Nairobi presents few problems, and, once you're there, you'll have little trouble finding your way around. The city has widespread suburbs but its inner area is relatively small: a triangle of stores, offices and public buildings, with the train station on the southern flank and the main bus stations on the east. Note that if you're arriving on a Sunday, it will all seem strangely quiet: most shops and many restaurants are closed.

Arriving by air

Arriving by air, you'll find yourself at **Jomo Kenyatta International Airport**, 15km out of town to the southeast off the Mombasa highway. Arrivals are normally straightforward, but do beware of **pickpockets**, even inside customs. The **visa desk** is to the right of passport control – obtaining one, if you haven't already done so, should be a simple, form-filling formality – (payment in dollars or sterling cash only). Once through passport control, check your **luggage** is intact as soon as you get it off the carousel. If anything appears to be missing go straight to the "Lost Luggage" desk before passing through customs. For customs advice, see p.24. If at any stage someone asks you for a **bribe**, refuse tactfully, pointing out the many signs on the walls concerning the heavy penalties for attempted bribery and corruption. If you really get stuck, kicking up a loud fuss and demanding to see the airport manager usually works. Whilst still in baggage reclaim, take the time to get your luggage in order, hiding cameras, small handbags and other valuables – you'll have rather less privacy to do so in the main arrivals hall. It'd be wise, also, to have decided where you want to go, and how, before facing the taxi touts outside.

There's a **24-hour bank** (in theory) inside customs, and another exchange bureau in the main hall, both with Visa card cash dispensers. Both refuse travellers' cheques from time to time, so you'd be safer bringing some cash. Examine the receipt and your money carefully – there have been reports of rip-offs. Safer still would be to change some shillings at your airport of departure, though the rate is invariably worse. Also inside customs is a **duty-free shop**, which you're free to use on arrival. The airport has an office of the **Flying Doctors** organization, where you can buy their special brand of life-saving insurance if you expect to be out in the wilds a lot. The *Simba Restaurant* at the top of the arrivals building is surprisingly good and reasonably priced.

Invariably, hordes of **taxi** touts assail you once you are through customs. You need not be alarmed by this – just ignore them and walk straight to the waiting cabs lined up outside, or else to the Kenatco office – but if you'd prefer to be met, try contacting Let's Go Travel (address on p.142). For the London-style cabs there's a fixed price to the city centre, currently around Ksh1000, depending on which hotel you want to go to. Other taxis to the city centre should be less than this – they don't have meters, so bargain firmly. Don't be afraid to ask several drivers their price. Given that even a good fare is a rip-off, tipping is not necessary.

The local KBS Stagecoach **bus #34** operates roughly every twenty minutes (6.15am–8.30pm) and costs just Ksh30. It enters the city through the eastern suburbs (rather than running straight up the proud artery of Uhuru Highway) and stops at the central KBS bus station on Mfangano Street before continuing to the youth hostel on Nairobi Hill. (See the warning about robbery on the #34 bus in the box opposite)

You will be obliged to take a taxi if your plane arrives **late at night** – Air France, British Airways, Cameroon Airlines, Emirates, Kenya Airways, KLM, Olympic, Pakistan and Sabena have such flights. You may well feel intimidated by a night-time first contact with central Nairobi and you'll find many of the cheapest hotels are already

SECURITY

First read the "Trouble" section in Basics, p.67.

An alarming number of new arrivals have to deal with a **robbery** in their first day or two in Nairobi, before they've adjusted to the city's pace and ways. Despite the fact that it usually carries armed undercover police, a lot of people used to get ripped off within an hour of arriving on the **#34 bus** from the airport. Victims get distracted in conversation or jostled, or have their hands grabbed and shaken by strangers. It's no joke and the best way to avoid losing wads of newly changed shillings is to secrete them all out of harm's way before you go anywhere near the bus, and likewise cameras or any other precious hand luggage you had on the plane. If anything starts to happen, make a lot of noise – it's no time to be shy. Sometimes it's enough just to clock the thieves – often young – and let them know you've seen them, which, surprisingly enough, usually stops them, and you can all have a (nervous) laugh.

Once in town, you should take exaggerated care of your valuables to avoid being victimized: stash away cameras, wristwatches and jewellery; tuck your money belt inside your trousers/skirt; keep nothing of value in breast-pockets; and ensure that luggage zips and pockets are closed. It also helps to memorize any route you're walking, as lost-looking tourists are the easiest target of all. Keep your hands out of reach and be – rationally – suspicious of everyone until you've caught your breath. It doesn't take long. Every rural Kenyan coming to the city for the first time goes through exactly the same process, and many are considerably less streetwise than you, having never been in a city before. As suggested in Basics (p.67), dressing like a local expatriate and not carrying a bag will help you avoid ninety percent of unwanted approaches.

The ubiquitous glue-sniffing **street children** are no problem bar very occasional petty thieving: giving food is better for them than money, but even so some charitable organizations advise against hand-outs as they might encourage others onto the street. If you're driving, keep the windows rolled up at dusk and at night, especially at traffic lights.

Beware of the fact that certain areas have acquired **local notoriety** and the carrying of knives and guns is on the increase. Most areas are fine in daylight, but you should not walk anywhere outside the commercial centre at night unless you're really clued in. If you head out from the centre to poorer districts there seems to be less of a threat. Be especially wary in the following areas, which are all parts of the city where tourist pickings are fairly rich – and there are always a few who haven't read a guidebook:

River Road district, which in practical terms means anything east of Moi Avenue, and indeed sometimes including the avenue. If you feel streetwise and have little to lose, then the area poses little threat, though there are exceptions of course, notably Eastleigh and Kariobangi. However, if you're even slightly anxious or have any valuables or bags with you, do *not* walk there – take a taxi or an *askari* (security guard), at least until you know your way around. Walking at night is just asking for trouble.

Uhuru Highway, **Uhuru** and **Central parks** are fine during the day but prime muggers' territory at night, with occasional shootings.

The area west of Uhuru Highway from the **Serena Hotel** to the **Youth Hostel** is unsafe at night.

The area near the **Museum** and **Casino** is extremely dangerous at night.

By day, the area between **Kenyatta Avenue** and **University Way**, especially around the **City Market**, is prone to con-merchants and occasional snatch-and-run robberies.

All **main bus** and **matatu stations**. These chaotic places are the ideal stage for pickpockets and snatch-and-run robberies. Do not accept food, drinks, candies or cigarettes from strangers, as doping is common.

Lastly, if you're an American worried about the effect of the 1998 US Embassy terrorist bombing, don't be – Kenyans of all creeds coped with the aftermath with remarkable fortitude, compassion and equanimity. Although tribalism is getting to be a problem in more remote parts of the country, religion has never been a divisive issue, and Americans have never been treated differently from other *wazungu* (white people).

closed before midnight. An obvious alternative is simply to curl up in a corner of the arrivals hall (there are police and soldiers) until morning. Remember, though, this isn't a large airport: comforts and even basic facilities are limited and dossing in a corner is barely tolerated. Watch out with your bags, too.

Arriving by train

Arriving by overnight train, either from Mombasa or western Kenya, you'll find yourself virtually in the city centre. From the **train station** (watch out for taxi drivers and porters who will more or less kidnap your luggage if you let them), just walk straight out through the station concourse and follow Moi Avenue into town. The only real attention you'll attract is from **safari touts** (see "Safari Operators", p.134) – they're persistent but friendly enough, and useful if you need an escort to one of the cheaper River Road addresses; a small tip (say Ksh50) would be appreciated. If you're worried about wandering about with your bags, there are two **left luggage** facilities at the station.

Arriving by bus and matatu

Most **bus companies** have their booking offices or parking areas in the River Road district, just a short walk from the city centre. Many of the *matatu* stages are here, too. If you've been following the map and know where you are, however, you can generally ask to be dropped off anywhere along the route into town. All the bus company terminals are marked on the map on pp.88–89, and the main bus and *matatu* routes and their terminals are listed in the box on p.90.

Orientation and city transport

The triangle of **central Nairobi** divides into three principal districts bisected by the main thoroughfares of **Kenyatta Avenue** and **Moi Avenue**.

The grandest and most formal part of town is the area around **City Square**, in the southwest. This square kilometre is Nairobi's heart: government buildings, banks and offices (most of them housed in commercial buildings with names like Jubilee Insurance House and Lonrho House) merge to the north and east with upmarket shopping streets and luxury hotels. The area's big landmarks are the extraordinary **Kenyatta International Conference Centre**, with its huge cylindrical tower and artichoke-shaped conference centre, the blue-glass skyscraper of **Lonrho House**, and the bizarre zebra-striped "legs" of the **Nation Centre**, all visible from points miles outside the city. To the south of this area, towards the train station, looms the bombed-out shell of the **Cooperative Bank House** skyscraper (see the box on p.106).

North of Kenyatta Avenue, there's a shift to smaller scale and lesser finance. The **City Market** is here, surrounded by a denser district of shops, restaurants and hotels. The **Jeevanjee Gardens** are a welcome patch of greenery (though avoid walking through after dark), and a little further north is the university district and Nairobi's oldest establishment, *The Norfolk Hotel*, contemporary with the original rebuilding of the city.

East of Moi Avenue, the character changes more radically. Here, and down towards the reeking Nairobi River, is the relatively poor, inner-city district identified with **River Road**, its main thoroughfare. The River Road quarter is where most long-distance buses and *matatus* start and terminate, and where you'll find the capital's cheapest restaurants and hotels, as well as the highest concentration of African-owned businesses. It is also a somewhat notorious area, with a traditional concentration of sharks and pickpockets (see "Security" box). Some unwary *wazungu* consider themselves likely victims here; you can meet European residents who work five minutes' walk away and in all their years in Nairobi have never been to this part of town.

Getting around central Nairobi is straightforward. By day, most visitors **walk**; by night, they take a **taxi**. Unless you're only here for a day or two, though, it's certainly worth getting to know the city's **public transport** systems.

Taxis

While Nairobi's **taxis** are overpriced by Kenyan standards, at night, when certain parts of the city are definitely not recommended for pedestrians, you'll almost certainly want to make use of them. Grey, London-style taxi cabs (Kenya Taxi Cabs Association; ☎02/215352) crowd around key spots in the city – notably outside the *Hilton Hotel* and *680 Hotel* – and have pretty fixed prices, with the current bottom-line fare for any trip in the city centre well known by all (the cheapest ride isn't likely to be less than around Ksh250). Another reliable company is the 24-hour Kenatco, who have their office at Uchumi House on Aga Khan Walk (☎02/225123, 338611 or 230771–2), and a branch at Jomo Kenyatta International Airport (☎02/824248 or 822356). It's really only possible to bargain with the private drivers, who drive sometimes astonishingly battered cars: you'll find them angling for business on Mama Ngina Street, Kimathi Street outside the *Oakwood Hotel*, and at the junction of Standard Street and Muindi Mbingu Street, by the *680 Hotel*.

Tuk-tuks, motorized rickshaws, are also now available at certain places in the city centre and cost a little less than regular taxis. Bargain hard.

Buses and matatus

The **public transport** – buses and *matatus* – used by the ordinary people (the *wananchi*) of Nairobi will save you money on getting around, certainly for longer trips out of the city centre, but it takes some figuring out. The KBS Stagecoach **buses** (they may change name soon) roar around Nairobi all day, usually packed far beyond capacity. They're cheap (Ksh10–30) and very unpredictable. Buses are numbered but bus stops aren't and routes change frequently. **Matatus** can be slightly easier. They tend to take the same routes as buses and often display the same route numbers. They're generally faster if more dangerous, and packed far beyond comfort, though bad accidents rarely happen in the city. The confusion in Nairobi is occasionally exacerbated by *matatus* going on strike, or by clumsy police sweeps in which *matatu* and bus drivers are "netted" for overloading their vehicles, playing loud music or, latterly, not carrying the new "Good Conduct" ID cards, leaving their passengers stranded – usually at rush hour when they cause maximum chaos. The "stages" (terminuses) are scattered throughout River Road district. The more helpful bus and *matatu* routes, and where to board them, are listed in the box on p.90.

Accommodation

Finding **accommodation** in Nairobi isn't difficult. There's loads of choice, and hotels are rarely full even during the peak season. The main question is which area fits your needs: the city lacks a long-established focus, so travellers end up congregating at a number of different spots determined by budget and requirements. The following listings are arranged by approximate location: they are all keyed, or named, on the maps (key numbers refer to hotels marked on the "Commercial Centre and River

△ The Norfolk Hotel   △ Parklands

N

University

Windsor House ❶

Nairobi Safari Club

❷ ❸

Anniversary Towers

College House

Ⓕ Uchumi Supermarket

Ⓖ

Jeevanjee Gardens

Meridian Court Hotel

Khoja Mosque

Maendeleo House

Hollywood Nightclub Ⓚ

Garden Plaza

Kalyan House

French Cultural Centre

Unafric House

Ⓝ

Barclays Bank

Atul's

Caltex

Kenindia House

Nyati House

Loita House

Ⓜ ❹ ❸

Crafts Market ❺

McMillan Library

STANBIC Bank Building

Utalii House

Jamia Mosque

Cameo Cinema

Grand Regency Hotel

Ⓑ

Arrow House

New Florida Nightclub

Postbank House

City Market

African Heritage

ICEA Building

Pan-African Insurance Building

Barclays Plaza

Ⓔ

Kobil

Gilfillan House

Barclays Bank

Simmers

Ⓗ

Rehani House

Nakumatt (supermarket)

Phoenix House

Hamilton House

Ⓟ

Ⓑ BP

Fedha Towers

Ⓞ

KCB

Six-Eighty Hotel

Ⓥ

❶ Hotel keyed in text

Ⓐ Restaurant keyed in text

Ⓦ

Ⓧ

Let's Go Travel

Bruce House

UTC Building

New GPO

Club le Balafon

City Hall

Nyayo House

Holy Family Cathedral

City Square

Garden Square Club

Hotel Intercontinental

Ⓜ	20th Century Plaza
Ⓔ	Chester House
Ⓑ	Cianda House
Ⓗ	City House
Ⓘ	Corner House
Ⓓ	HFCK Building
Ⓞ	Jubilee Insurance House
Ⓙ	KCS House
Ⓠ	Kenya Cinema Plaza
Ⓖ	Lonrho House
Ⓒ	Old Mutual Building
Ⓝ	Prudential Assurance Building
Ⓕ	Rehema House
Ⓟ	Stewart Building
Ⓚ	Vedic House
Ⓐ	Victor House
Ⓛ	Jubilee Exchange House

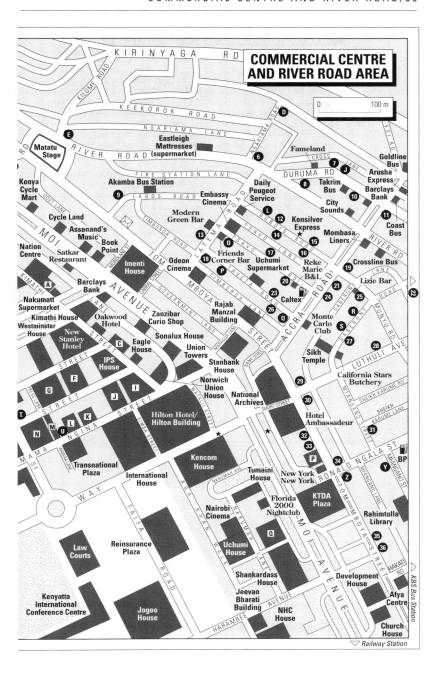

COMMERCIAL CENTRE AND RIVER ROAD AREA

0   100 m

KIRINYAGA RD

KILOME ROAD

KEEKOROK ROAD

NGARIAMA LANE

RIVER ROAD

E

Matatu Stage

D

Eastleigh Mattresses (supermarket)

6

Fameland

CROSS

7 **J**

Goldline Bus

DURUMA RD

8

Takrim Bus

Arusha Express

Barclays Bank

FIRE STATION LANE

Akamba Bus Station

9

LAGOS ROAD

Embassy Cinema

Daily Peugeot Service

City Sounds

10

11

Coast Bus

Kenya Cycle Mart

GOVT LANE

Modern Green Bar

L

D

12

Kensilver Express

15

Mombasa Liners

RIVER RD

Cycle Land

TSAVO LANE

Assanand's Music

Book Point

13

14

O

17

16

Reke Marie B&L

MOI AVENUE

Nation Centre

Satkar Restaurant

Imenti House

Odeon Cinema

18

Friends Corner Bar

Uchumi Supermarket

19

Crossline Bus

KIMATHI

Barclays Bank

A

TOM MBOYA STREET

P

TAVETA LANE

20

21

Lizie Bar

22

Nakumatt Supermarket

Oakwood Hotel

Zanzibar Curio Shop

GOVERNMENT ROAD

Rajab Manzal Building

23

26

Caltex

24

25

R

Kimathi House

Westminster House

New Stanley Hotel

C

Eagle House

Sonalux House

Union Towers

Q

Monte Carlo Club

S

27

28

IPS House

F

Stanbank House

MARADU LANE

BANK STREET

ACCRA ROAD

Sikh Temple

GABERONE ROAD

LUTHULI AVE

G

I

Norwich Union House

National Archives

29

California Stars Butchery

SHEIKH KARUME RD

T

J

L **K**

N **M** **U**

NGINA STREET

WABERA LANE

STANDARD STREET

Hilton Hotel/ Hilton Building

SHORT STREET

30

Hotel Ambassadeur

SHEIKH KARUME LANE

31

MFANGANO STREET

MAMA NGINA ST

Transnational Plaza

International House

SIMBA STREET

AGA KHAN WALK

Kencom House

MARUMAR AVE

Tumaini House

32

33

P

New York New York

RONALD NGALA ST

34

Z

Y

MANGANO ST

BP

WAY

TAIFA ROAD

Nairobi Cinema

Florida 2000 Nightclub

Q

KTDA Plaza

MOI AVENUE

MBOYA STREET

Rahimtulla Library

35

36

Law Courts

Reinsurance Plaza

Uchumi House

Development House

HAKATI RD

Kenyatta International Conference Centre

Jogoo House

Shankardass House

Jeevan Bharati Building

HARAMBEE AVENUE

NHC House

Afya Centre

Church House

△ KBS Bus Station

▽ Railway Station

NAIROBI BUS AND MATATU ROUTES

For national bus, *matatu* and train services, see the "Moving on from Nairobi" section on pp.138–146).

Local buses are run by KBS Stagecoach, who have their main bus station in the eastern corner of River Road district, between Ronald Ngala, Mfangano and Uyoma streets, beside the bizarre-looking Siri Guru Singh Sabha Temple. This is also a major stage for *matatus*. Other bus and *matatu* stops include: outside the **Ambassadeur** hotel on Moi Avenue (mainly eastbound); outside the **Kencom** building facing the *Hilton* on City Hall Way and also outside the almost finished **GPO** tower on Kenyatta Avenue (mainly westbound); the **train station** end of Moi Avenue (west and southwest); and **Latema Road** (north and northeast).

1 (bus/*matatu*) Ngong Road, Dagoretti Corner; from new GPO.

2 (bus/*matatu*) Ngong Road, Dagoretti Corner, Kikuyu town; from KBS bus station or new GPO.

3 (bus/*matatu*) Ngong Road, Adam's Arcade, Dagoretti Corner; from new GPO.

4 (bus) Ngong Road, Adam's Arcade, Dagoretti Corner; from Kencom or new GPO.

4 (bus) Kariokor market, General Waruinge Road, Eastleigh; from *Ambassadeur*.

6 (bus) Kariokor market and Eastleigh; from Accra Road or Tom Mboya Street.

8 (*matatu*) Kenyatta National Hospital, Kibera; from railway stage.

9 (*matatu*) Eastleigh; from corner Accra Road/Tom Mboya Street.

11 (*matatu*) City Park, Parklands; from Tom Mboya Street by *Mayur* restaurant.

15 (*matatu*) Langata Road (National Park, Wilson Airport); from Mfangano Street/Ronald Ngala Street.

17B (*matatu*) Thika Road, Kasarani; from KBS bus station.

18 (bus) Kenyatta National Hospital; from new GPO.

20 (bus) Kenyatta National Hospital; from new GPO.

21 (bus) National Museum, Westlands; from Kencom.

21 (bus) City Stadium roundabout, Jogoo Road; from *Ambassadeur*.

23 (bus) National Museum; Westlands; from Kencom.

24 (bus/*matatu*) Langata Road, Bogoni Road, Karen; from Mfangano Street/Hakati Road or new GPO.

25 (*matatu*) Murang'a Road, Thika Road; from Odeon Cinema Latema Road, or Koinange Street.

28 (bus) Eastleigh, Kariobangi; from *Ambassadeur*.

30 (*matatu*) Murang'a Road, Westlands; from KBS bus station.

31 (bus) Kariobangi; from *Ambassadeur*.

31 (bus/*matatu*) Langata Road (National Park, Wilson Airport); from new GPO.

32 (*matatu*) Kariokor market; Eastleigh; from corner Accra Road/Taveta Road.

34 (bus) Jogoo Road, Jomo Kenyatta International Airport; from *Ambassadeur* and KBS bus station.

34 (bus) Youth Hostel, Langata Road, Wilson Airport; from Kencom and KBS bus station.

36 (bus) Jogoo Road, Kariobangi South; from *Ambassadeur* and KBS bus station.

37 (bus) Jogoo Road, Kariobangi South; from *Ambassadeur*.

38 (*matatu*) Jogoo Road, Kariobangi South; from KBS bus station.

Road area" map, p.88). If you're arriving in town very early, beware that most places won't allow you to take a room before 10am. If you're travelling by rented car and concerned about safe parking, don't panic: the city council and most hotels employ *askaris* (security guards), who can be persuaded to up their workload for a modest tip (failure to do so may mysteriously deflate your tyres, or worse). Most top-of-the-range places have guarded or enclosed parking anyway. Naturally, leave nothing in, or attached to, the vehicle. To help you aim straight for the best places, the ones in the

39 (*matatu*) Jogoo Road, Kariobangi South; from KBS bus station.

40 (bus) Kariokor, Kariobangi; from *Ambassadeur*.

40 (*matatu*) Thika; from BP station on Ronald Ngala Street.

41 (bus) Valley Road (Youth Hostel), Argwings Kodhek Road; from new GPO.

42 (*matatu*) Kariokor market, Eastleigh; from corner Accra Road/Tsavo Road.

42 (bus) Kibera; from Kencom or KBS bus station.

44A (*matatu*) Ngumba Estate, Thika Road; from KBS bus station.

45 (bus) Thika Road (Moi Sports Centre); from Kencom.

46 (*matatu*) Valley Road, Argwings Kodhek Road; from railway stage and new GPO.

46 or 46B (bus) Valley Road, Argwings Kodhek Road, Gitanga Road; from Kencom.

46 or 46B (bus) Kariokor market; from *Ambassadeur*.

48 (*matatu*) Arboretum; from Odeon cinema, Latema Road.

61B (bus) Kenyatta National Hospital; from new GPO.

100 (*matatu*) Kiambu Road, Kiambu; from KBS bus station.

102 (bus/*matatu*) Ngong Road, Dagoretti Corner, Kikuyu town; from KBS bus station.

103 (bus) Ngong Road, Dagoretti Corner, Kikuyu town; from KBS bus station.

104 (*matatu*) Westlands; from KBS bus station.

108 (bus) Murang'a Road; Muthaiga Road; Limuru Road; from KBS bus station.

110 (*matatu*) Kitengela, Athi River (Chapter Five); from KBS bus station (hourly).

111 (bus) Ngong Road, Dagoretti Corner, Karen, Ngong, Kiserian; from KBS bus station.

114 (*matatu*) Limuru; from Jamia Mosque (Kigali Road) or outside Mayur on Tom Mboya Street.

115 (*matatu*) Kikuyu town; from railway stage.

119 (bus) National Museum, Westlands, Peponi Road, Wangige; from KBS bus station.

125 (*matatu*) Langata Road, Magadi Road, Kiserian; from KBS bus station.

126 (bus) Langata Road, then either to Karen or Kiserian along Magadi Road; from KBS bus station.

137 (bus) Thika Road; from KBS bus depot in Eastleigh.

137 (*matatu*) Thika Road; from Koinange Street.

145 (bus) Thika Road (Moi Sports Centre); from Kencom.

145 (*matatu*) Thika Road (Moi Sports Centre) to Ruiru via Githurai; from KBS bus station.

160 (*matatu*) Thika Road (Moi Sports Centre) to Ruiru via Githurai; from KBS bus station.

237 (*matatu*) Thika; from Kencom. Other Thika *matatus* from corner BP station on Ronald Ngala Street.

Un-numbered:

to Enterprise Road, marked "Industrial Area/Hillock"; from Afya Centre, Tom Mboya Street.

to Limuru; from outside *Mayur* restaurant, Tom Mboya Street.

to Parklands and Highridge, marked "Parklands/Aga Khan"; from Latema Road, facing *Iqbal Hotel*, or from along Tom Mboya Street.

following shortlist meet with near-universal approval: *Iqbal* and *Planet Safari* (low-budget, popular with travellers, River Road district); the YMCA (cheap, out-of-centre meeting place with a pool, popular with travellers); *Fairview* (peaceful mid-range out-of-centre hotel, great for families); *Boulevard* (reliable mid-range out-of-centre base); *Oakwood* (reliable mid-range city centre base); *The Stanley* and *Grand Regency* (excellent value in the luxury range); and *Safari Park* (totally Kenya-proof luxury resort out of town).

East Nairobi

The very cheapest lodgings are around **River Road**, the main drag through the city centre's poorest quarter – although in recent years, a number of more expensive hotels have been built here. Despite the constant worry about safety, River Road is the city's most stimulating and animated area, and offers a plunge into a world which would pass you by if you stayed in the city centre or out in the suburbs. The cheapest places generally double as rowdy bars and nightclubs (not for women alone), and are neither terribly clean nor secure. Should a modicum of hygiene and perhaps s/c facilities be important to you, you're looking at between Ksh600–1000 for a double room. In several of those listed below you can expect to run into other travellers. If you're genuinely broke, try the welcoming **Sikh Temple** on Gaberone Road ("Commercial Centre and River Road area" map, p.88): overnights and meals are free, though you're expected to leave a donation.

River Road area: cheap lodgings

Al Mansura B&L (25), Munyu Rd (PO Box 22020; ☎02/336338). Cheapest of the cheap, pleasantly characterful and friendly, though if you're single you may have to share. There are no iron gates to pass, but the place appears secure enough and, being Muslim-run, this is almost the only establishment on Munyu Rd which doesn't have a bar. The restaurant downstairs, through which you pass, is simple and good, the smell and smoke drifting up to the rooms more of a bonus than a drawback. ①.

Cana Lodge Hotel (10), Duruma Rd (PO Box 41237; ☎02/217254). Small, clean s/c rooms (with phones) and good security, if a slightly desultory atmosphere. Quieter rooms are at the rear. Hot water mornings and evenings. A good first base in Nairobi, with clean sheets daily and good breakfasts. B&B ②.

Danika Lodge (15), Dubois Rd (PO Box 12840; ☎02/230687). Very secure (the gate is locked at all times) and friendly, quieter than most, with clean and breezy s/c rooms, hot water 24 hours, and the rare luxury of mosquito nets. Good laundry service. Recommended. ②.

Destiny Hotel (7), Duruma Rd (PO Box 72780; ☎02/253123-6). Built in 1996, this four-storey block offers good value and is conscientiously run, with clean, airy s/c rooms and hot showers (telephones are due to be installed). There's a laundry service, and a bar and restaurant are planned. B&B ②.

Dolat Hotel (31), Mfangano St (PO Box 45613; ☎02/222797). Clean, friendly, spacious, with hot water and, though not fancy, excellent value. One of the best of the cheapies (breakfast not included), and there's a safe lock-up for luggage when you're on safari (Ksh30/day). ②.

Evamay Lodge (8), River Rd at the junction with Duruma Rd (PO Box 16000; ☎02/216218). Very good value for the price with clean s/c rooms, with phones and nets, and good security. ②.

Hotel Gloria (34), Duke House, corner Ronald Ngala St and Tom Mboya St (PO Box 10345; ☎02/228916). An overpriced and only slightly better-than-basic B&L, with grubby rooms (s/c with nets and baths, but erratic hot water), and "enough security". Not noticeably welcoming, and it's on a noisy, hustly corner. B&B ②.

Iqbal Hotel (18), Latema Rd (PO Box 11256; ☎02/220914, fax 332498). Still Number One in the budget travellers' popularity stakes, although standards keep on sliding and it's not usually the friendliest of places. The rooms are basic and none-too-clean, but the main advantage is the opportunity to meet other travellers. Rooms are secure (no "guests" allowed, either), but aren't s/c and those at the front overlooking the *matatu* stand are noisy. Features are temperamental hot water, a

---

DRINKING WATER

Nairobi's heavily chlorinated **tap water** is generally safe to drink. The only times where caution is advised is when staying in cheap and insalubrious lodgings, or during particularly heavy rain, when the system gets overloaded. A cholera epidemic in December 1997 affected Korogocho slum, and came after exceptionally severe flooding across the whole of the country. See also "Water and bugs" on p.31.

cheap laundry service, a lock-up store, a pushy safari booking office and a noticeboard. There's a café upstairs (no food) with a breezy terrace for residents. It's often full, so book in advance. Singles same price as doubles. ①.

Mercury Hotel (36), Tom Mboya St. Next door and similar to the *Princess Hotel* (see below), but cheaper and not as well furnished. ①.

New Kenya Lodge (6), River Rd at the top of Latema Rd (PO Box 43444; ☎02/222202). Like the *Iqbal*, a long-established backpackers' haunt with a popular communal area, though altogether earthier. Friendly, cheap and unhygienic, with little or no hot water, and uncertain security ; don't come here if you've much to lose; we've received persistent reports of thefts from bags left unattended in rooms and in storage. They also organize cheapish safaris (around $50 per day) which, by all accounts, are perfectly reasonable. There's also a book exchange. The "annexe" on Duruma Rd (☎02/338348) is even less tempting (though breakfast is thrown in). ①.

New Swanga Lodge (11), Duruma Rd (PO Box 46387; ☎02/213777 or 213827). The rooms here, though not large, are comfortable and s/c (with telephones), secured behind spectacular, time-consuming, triple locks. Clean sheets daily. Good value, though hardly quiet. Often full. B&B ②.

North Eastern B&L (16), Dubois Rd (☎02/222554). Basic rooms tucked away like a rabbit warren, the main draw being that it's popular with traders from Cameroon, Senegal and elsewhere in Africa, which makes for some interesting encounters. Not s/c. Reasonable security (the stairway gates are locked at night). ①.

Planet Safari, 9th floor, Sonalux House, Moi Ave (PO Box 79347; ☎02/229799, fax 211899, *planet@africaonline.co.ke*). Just out of River Road district, this is the oddest place in Nairobi – and very popular with backpackers – with two rooms (and fifty bunks planned), and six tents pitched on the roof. There's a grubby communal kitchen, and a safari booking office for its captive market (you can stay free for up to three days if you take them up on a trip). Elevator to 5th floor, then stairs. Security appears reasonable, despite some off-putting hangers-on. ①.

Princess Hotel (35), Tom Mboya St (☎02/214640). Very busy, local establishment with bars on all floors. It's Nairobi's main gay rendezvous (rooms by the hour), and much cheaper if you're a couple. Basic but adequate, and it fills up quickly. ②.

Safety Line B&L (formerly Safe Life) (12), Dubois Rd (PO Box 33915; ☎02/221578). Despite its bizarre name, this doesn't appear to be terribly safe, despite iron gates – the hangers-on inside are the ones to watch out for. The rooms (not s/c) are very basic, with filthy floors and windows. ①.

Sirikwa Lodge (19), Munyu Rd, at the corner with Accra Rd (☎02/226687 or 333838). Reasonable s/c rooms accessed over a cheerfully blaring music shop, and great for observing the chaos at the Accra Rd *matatu* stages. 24-hour hot water, and secure basement parking. Often full. B&B ②.

Sunrise Lodge (13), Latema Rd (PO Box 48224; ☎02/330362). Small, reasonably secure, but not terribly hygienic and lacks running water. Some rooms are exceptionally noisy due to its location next to the *Modern Green Bar*. Don't dawdle after dark in the alley between them or you'll get mugged. ②.

River Road area: pricier lodgings and mid-range hotels

Abbey Hotel (27), Gaberone Rd (PO Box 75260; ☎02/243256 or 241562). A noisy, boozy place, rather expensive nowadays, but the rooms have nets and are mostly clean and fresh, with tiled bathrooms (hot showers). Unlovely but adequate. ③.

Hotel Accra and Fitness Club (24), Accra Rd (PO Box 75862; ☎02/215698). Overpriced for a basic B&L, with small, superficially s/c single rooms (no toilet paper or toilet seats), but perhaps worth it for a night's clubbing in the wild neighbourhood. Sweat out your hangover in its unlikely sauna and steam room (Ksh300), with or without a massage (also Ksh300), or punish yourself in their gym (Ksh100). There's *nyama choma* on the second floor. ③.

Hotel Africana (14), Dubois Rd (PO Box 47827; ☎02/220654, fax 331886). Clean linoleum-floored s/c rooms with telephones and hot water. The single beds are tiny. There's a café downstairs. Recommended if you want to be near the Latema Road area but need a little more comfort, though not as smart as it was. There's better, but it's perfectly adequate at the price. B&B ②.

Hotel Dama (28), Luthuli Ave (PO Box 48031; ☎02/221738). An impressive facade conceals the same old stuff within: small, far from spotless s/c rooms, but good security. They sometimes have (loud) discos downstairs. ③.

Diplomat Hotel (33) Tom Mboya St (PO Box 30777; ☎02/245050, fax 220475). Fifty large, well-kept s/c rooms (showers) with telephones, and there's lift access. The price needs bargaining down by at least a third. ④.

Hotel Emmaccra (21), Accra Rd (PO Box 28172; ☎02/242609). Friendly, with good security and nets over the beds, but the rooms are small and dirty. *Nyama choma* available from the bar downstairs; rooms with windows on the street side are quieter (relatively speaking, of course). They're happy to store bags while you go off up country. B&B ②.

Eureka Highrise Hotel (32), Tom Mboya St (PO box 28229; ☎02/228935). Three floors up. Slightly overpriced, but with large, clean s/c rooms with hot water for the showers, good security and a calm, vaguely Christian atmosphere. ③.

Grand Holiday Hotel (20), Tsavo Rd (PO Box 69343; ☎02/330704 or 211372, fax 243851). Grand is hardly the word. Rather spartan rooms with cheap and mangy mattresses, though the more expensive suites (also ③) have enormous beds, as well as TVs. Tall people beware: the staircase lintels are low. It has a calm, almost posh first-floor restaurant, complete with fish tank. Acceptable at this range, but there's better. ③.

Hotel Greton (17), Tsavo Rd (PO Box 55909; ☎02/242891, fax 242892). Rather small rooms, but they have phones and it's friendly, with good security and attentive management. A clean, pleasant, value-for-money hotel. Recommended. B&B ③.

Marble Arch Hotel (9), Lagos Rd (PO Box 12224; ☎02/245720 or 245656, fax 245724). Totally out of keeping with the generally slummy surrounding accommodation: the plushest of the area's hotels, and it even won an architectural design award. The coffee shop, bar and restaurant are replete with polished marble, brass fixtures and tacky fountains. Rooms are of a similar standard: wall-to-wall carpet, direct-dial phone, bath, video, TV and "piped music". ⑤.

Oriental Palace Hotel (23), Taveta Rd (PO Box 72237; ☎02/217600–3, fax 212335). One of the best-appointed hotels in the district: all 106 rooms here have TV (with in-house video), direct-dial phones, and – fortunately – ceiling fans (the *Little India* restaurant on the ground floor generates a ubiquitous curry atmosphere). Overpriced however, especially for the location – you can get much better in the city centre for about the same. B&B ⑤.

Sagret Hotel (22), River Rd (PO Box 18324; ☎02/333395). Comfortable and efficiently managed, very clean and very secure, but very loud and too expensive.

> Stop press: the *Sagret* was closed by the police in May 1999. It's not clear if, or when, it will reopen.

Hotel Salama (29), corner of Luthuli Ave and Tom Mboya St (PO Box 28675; ☎02/225898, fax 718667). Characterful and seemingly family run, despite the "massage" service offered by a permanent guest. The rooms themselves (all s/c) are clean and come with nets. B&B ③.

Samagat Hotel (26), Taveta Rd (PO Box 10027; ☎02/220604). A nine-storey former apartment block (lift access). Spacious s/c rooms, upper ones with views over the commercial district's highrises, with kitchen areas but no cooking equipment. There's a ninth-floor dining/TV-room. Good value. Lower end of price bracket. B&B ③.

Solace Hotel (30), Tom Mboya St (PO Box 48867; ☎02/331277). The corridors and stairs here are tatty, but the rooms themselves very decent: clean, with telephones and nets, and reliable hot water to fill the baths. One of the better mid-range choices. ③.

West of Moi Avenue

The following listings cover the more monied parts of the city, roughly north as far as the museum and west as far as Central and Uhuru Parks. There are a number of **medium-priced places** on the west side of Moi Avenue up near Jeevanjee Gardens and City Market. For the faint-hearted, this may be a better prospect than the River Road area – quieter and possibly safer (at least more salubrious).

West of Moi Avenue: mid-range hotels

Hotel County, County Lane, off Haile Selassie Ave (PO Box 41924; ☎02/226190 or 220390, fax 213889, *aladins@africaonline.co.ke*). A very reasonable, functional block and quieter than most: the first hotel from the airport, close to the railway museum, but relatively far from the main shopping streets. Popular with African businessmen, and offers email services. Good value. ④.

Down Town Hotel (4), Moktar Daddah St (PO Box 9160; ☎02/337591, fax 338581). Just down from the *Terminal*, and not as loud, but nonetheless overpriced in comparison. Rooms are smaller and not especially clean, lack nets, and the hustly atmosphere doesn't feel at all safe. Bed only. ③.

Hotel Embassy (5), Tubman Rd, right behind the City Market (PO Box 47247; ☎02/224087, fax 224534). Scruffy but clean and quite decent, with ancient telephones lovingly preserved in some rooms (they don't all work) and a nice restaurant, but be wary of leaving valuables in the rooms. ③.

Parkside Hotel (2), Monrovia St (PO Box 53104; ☎02/214156, fax 334681). Facing Jeevanjee Gardens, large, secure, reasonably quiet and pleasant with airy s/c rooms, hot water and telephones, but slightly overpriced, and not as glossy as its brochures. The restaurant is nothing special, and breakfast varies in quality. B&B ③.

Suncourt Inn (1), University Way (PO Box 51454; ☎02/221418, fax 217500). Seems a touch expensive but it's not at all bad, and totally unpatronized by tourists – plus the phones work. Its quirky *Wisemen's Corner* is a businessmen's bar. The cheaper carpetless rooms are better value. B&B ④.

Hotel Terminal (3), Moktar Daddah St (☎02/228817, fax 220075). A long-time backpackers' favourite, with large, clean, well-kept rooms, all with nets, telephones and hot showers. No guests after 7pm. Good value compared to other city centre places, and would be recommended if it wasn't for the rowdy bar-restaurant downstairs: for the profoundly deaf. Room only. ③.

West of Moi Avenue: upmarket and luxury hotels

Central Nairobi has over twenty **luxury places** and many more trailing close behind. They all take credit cards. All the following are marked on the "Central Nairobi" map on p.102, unless stated.

Hotel Ambassadeur, Moi Ave (PO Box 30399; ☎02/336803, fax 336860; reservations through Sarova, p.50). A modern, adequate, if rather tired international-style hotel, lagging miles behind Sarova's usual standards, but it's cheap. The staff are helpful, and the rooms are large and bright if unspectacular, but it's surprisingly noisy: if possible get a double-glazed, top-floor room, but even these are no match for determined *matatu* horns and night-time River Road discos. The two bars are calm, and there's a very pleasant coffee house and restaurant on the ground floor, though its food sometimes takes a dive. Guests can use *The Panafric*'s pool. Rates open to discussion. B&B ⑤.

Boulevard Hotel, Harry Thuku Rd ("Greater Nairobi" map, p.82), right by the museum (PO Box 42831; ☎02/227567–9, 337221, fax 334071, *hotelboulevard@form-net.com*). Perhaps the best mid-range address in the city – functional rather than extravagant, well cared for, in a pleasant garden setting and with a good pool (though unfortunately it's on the traffic side of the building), tennis court, TVs in all rooms and ample parking. To overcome Uhuru Highway's noise, get a room at the back in the middle, overlooking the garden. Uhuru Highway is prone to muggings at night. Buses #21, #23 and #119, *matatu* #104. Room only ⑤.

Grand Regency, off Loita St (PO Box 57549; ☎02/211199, fax 217120, *grandregency@form-net.com*). Built in 1994, a successful example of modern technology melded to architectural ambition. The interior is gobsmacking to say the least: built around a cool marble-clad atrium, three glass and gold-lacquer lifts glide up and down one side to the rooms. The more expensive rooms have balconies opening onto the atrium. Service is efficient, the clientele mostly businessmen. There's also an expensive pool and health club (Ksh950). ⑧–⑨.

Hilton Hotel, Mama Ngina St (PO Box 30624; reservations ☎02/334000, fax 339462, *hilton@africaonline.co.ke*). The cylindrical tower is unmistakable, and the lobby impressive, but otherwise an average example of the species, somewhat impersonal and catering mainly for expense accounts. Rooms get better the higher you go; but the "rooftop pool" is down at second-floor level and rather overshadowed. Also offers a health club, jacuzzi, sauna and steam bath, as well as four restaurants, but nonetheless overpriced compared to *The Stanley*. Room only ⑧.

Hotel Inter-Continental, City Hall Way (PO Box 30533; ☎02/261000, fax 210675, *www.interconti.com*). Thirty years old and not as good value as its competitors, but still fairly palatial if you're not a regular in such places. It has some surprisingly secluded corners in the grounds, and many amenities (including a heated pool, health club, casino and a good Mediterranean restaurant, *Le Mistral*). Disabled facilities, and they can pick you up or drop you at the airport. Room only ⑧.

Meridian Court Hotel, Murang'a Rd, off the top of River Rd (PO Box 30278; ☎02/333916, fax 333658). Grim position hemmed in by bad drivers and exhaust emissions, but no matter: the *Meridian* is well-run and friendly, and offers excellent value for its facilities. All rooms have bath, fridge, a safe, satellite TV and kitchenette (but no cooking facilities), whilst amenities include a rooftop pool (Ksh100 for non-guests) and bar, sauna, 24-hour room service, and two good restaurants; the *Khyber* and the *Mandarin* (see "Eating and drinking", p.116). Underground parking. Room only ④.

Nairobi Safari Club, University Way (PO Box 43564; ☎02/251333, fax 224625, *nsclub@africaon-line.co.ke*). A prestigious address but not as exclusive as you might imagine, despite the copy of the club's bye-laws issued to you at reception and the astronomical rates. It's a twelve-storey block, ill-placed on the loud and fume-filled University Way, but with good service, and seems gradually to be moving away from its suffocatingly pompous club atmosphere. Rooms are well-equipped suites, the quieter ones higher up, but it's still ridiculously overpriced, and even use of the small pool and health club costs extra. Room only ⑧.

Norfolk Hotel, Harry Thuku Rd (PO Box 40064; ☎02/250900, fax 336742; reservations through Lonrho, p.49). Nairobi's oldest and most historic lodgings, built in 1930s mock-Edwardian style. It was and remains the traditional haunt of visiting celebrities. Elspeth Huxley once noted the possibility of having "an Italian Count or an Austrian Baron thrown through the window on to your bed in the middle of the night". Still recommended on the whole, but much too expensive for the facilities on offer, limited to a pool, expensive shop, health club and sauna, and a few old cars and rickshaws in the courtyard. The newer accommodation blocks have also cluttered up the grounds somewhat. Room only ⑨.

Oakwood Hotel, Kimathi St (PO Box 40683; ☎02/220592, fax 332170, *madahold@form-net.com*). An older, two-storey hotel, and an endearing oddity lost amidst the skyscrapers rising all around: all wood panelling, dodgy telephones and TVs, and a great antique elevator which still works. The location is as central as you can get, with good large rooms and excellent bathrooms (hot water and real baths), and there's good security. Popular with aid workers as well as tourists, it also has a pleasant first floor bar overlooking the touristy *Thorn Tree Café*. Wed, Fri and Sat nights can be noisy due to *Jax Invitations* disco next door, but it remains good value compared to other city-centre hotels. B&B ④.

Serena Hotel, Nyerere Rd, off Kenyatta Ave (PO Box 46302; ☎02/725111, fax 725184, *nairobi@ser-ena.co.ke*; reservations through Serena, p.50). One of the "Leading Hotels of the World": highly polished and sumptuous. Impeccable rooms, first-class service, a calming atmosphere and exceptional if expensive food ($25–28 per meal). Amenities include a health club, pool and shops. Unfortunately the location, fronting onto Central Park, is dangerous at night. The real muggers, however, are at the reception: it's way overpriced. Room only ⑨.

680 (Six-Eighty) Hotel, corner of Kenyatta Ave and Muindi Mbingu St (PO Box 43436; ☎02/332680, fax 332908). Soulless 340-room 1970s towerblock, right in the heart of the city, but comparatively cheap. Safe underground parking and convenient for shopping. Guests can use the *Boulevard's* pool. Room only ⑤.

The Stanley Hotel (formerly *New Stanley*), corner of Kimathi St and Kenyatta Ave (PO Box 30680; ☎02/228830, 333233, fax 229388, *www.sarovahotels.com*; reservations through Sarova, p.50). Complete with its famous *Thorn Tree Café* rendezvous, this is the best upmarket choice, and as central as you can get. Originally an Edwardian structure, with touches of Art Deco, it's a popular downtown base for tourists and businessmen alike. The period decor isn't overdone, service friendly and efficient, and the rooms themselves equipped with satellite TV, minibars and essential double glazing. They have specially designed rooms for disabled. Facilities include a modern gym, sauna and steam room, and a pleasant heated rooftop pool and bar. Courtesy bus to the airport. Room only ⑦ low, ⑧ high.

Accommodation out of central Nairobi

Most of Nairobi's better value mid- and upper-range hotels are located out of the city centre, both in the relatively affluent **suburbs** of Westlands and Parklands which are also the main focus for more sophisticated night-time bars and clubs, and along the main roads radiating out of the city. Two of the main focuses for budget travellers, the youth hostel and *Ma Roche's Guest House* (see "Greater Nairobi" map, p.82), are a short journey away from the city centre in the suburbs, and both have their devotees, while the excellent **YMCA** is within walking distance.

Camping and hostels

Central YMCA ("Central Nairobi" map, p.102), State House Rd, 300m from Uhuru Highway (PO Box 30330; ☎02/724066, 724070, fax 728825, *kenyaymca@connect.co.ke*). This is an excellent place popular with travellers not quite on a shoestring budget. It's well equipped, with a choice of dorms and s/c rooms (③), and isn't markedly different from a modest hotel. There's well-priced if average food, a guarded parking lot, but the clincher is the excellent pool (Ksh40 for day visitors). And no, you don't have to be Christian or male. Open 24 hours; no alcohol (or drunks) allowed. Dorm rates from Ksh580 per person.

Ma Roche's Guest House ("Greater Nairobi" map, p.82), Third Parklands Ave, opposite the Aga Khan Hospital admissions (☎02/562452). A private home, in the predominantly Asian suburb of Parklands. Take a bed either in one of the cabins or in Mrs Roche's bungalow, camp in the garden, or sleep on the verandah. Popular with worn-out overlanders and travellers who really loathe Nairobi. Fall into either category and you should love it. It is a good place to meet people and it's often possible to fix up shared arrangements to drive to the game parks or head on through Africa – use the notice board. There's also a laundry and a convenient lock-up store to leave surplus gear while you travel, but there's no *askari* – don't leave valuables in your tent. Take a *matatu* #11, or one from Latema Rd, opposite the *Iqbal*, asking for "Aga Khan". Ksh300 per person.

Nairobi Park Services Campsite ("Nairobi outskirts" map, p.154), Magadi Rd, off Langata Rd just past Langata Gate (PO Box 54867; ☎ & fax 890325, *brendan_black@hotmail.com*). The newest and best-equipped campsite, popular with overland trucks, with some dorm beds too (*bandas* are planned). The site is secure, and the bar is good for soaking up to fellow *wazungu*. There's food available, and cable TV in the bar. *Matatu* #125 or bus #126. Camping Ksh200 per person (tent hire Ksh60 per person/night), Ksh200 per vehicle; beds in the dorm Ksh300 per person.

Nairobi Youth Hostel ("Greater Nairobi" map, p.82), Ralphe Bunche Rd, near Nairobi Hospital (PO Box 48661; ☎02/721765, fax 724862). A gentle introduction to the city, and full most of the time, but second best to the YMCA. Not having a IYHF card isn't a problem, as you can pay a daily Ksh90 fee for a stamp, which after six nights (Ksh540) converts to annual international membership. The small compound can get claustrophobic, though, and it's a bad idea to walk into (or back from) town after dark. Still, there are lots of other hostellers to talk to, it also has a few two- and four-bed rooms, and there's a s/c flat (③) available too. Usual YH rules apply, including a (lax) ban on booze. Many buses and *matatus*, including #34, #41 and #46 pass by one end or the other of Ralphe Bunche Rd. Ksh380–480 per person.

Rowallan Scout Camp ("Nairobi outskirts" map, p.154), off Kibera Drive, south of Jamhuri Park (PO Box 41422; ☎02/573799). Set deep in the Ngong Rd forest, the Kenya Scouts Association have the best campsite location in Nairobi, with richly overgrown vegetation, plenty of shade, a myriad forest tracks for walks (great for bird-watching), and even a few caves around. You're best bringing your own tent (Ksh100 per person; tent hire Ksh200 per night), as the *bandas* and dorms are filthy and close to collapse. Things aren't helped by the squalid pit latrines and showers, but despite all this it's a beautiful place. You can buy firewood for the outdoor kitchen, and limited supplies from the *duka*. There's a fridge for sodas, and a large, rather green, swimming pool. The huge site is patrolled by police officers and *askaris*, but leave valuables with the helpful warden. Incidentally, you don't have to be boy scout or girl guide. Get there either from Ngong road (a two-kilometre walk down Kibera Drive), or on #42 bus or #8 *matatu* to Kibera, from where it's a ten-minute walk along the tarmac downhill to the forest's edge, with a signposted left 300m further on.

Upper Hill Campsite ("Greater Nairobi" map, p.82), Menengai Rd, off Hospital Rd (☎02/720290, fax 723788). A newish campsite, already well discovered by the overland trucks, with beds in dorms (Ksh250 per person) and clean double rooms (②) also available. Hot showers, kitchen, a bar, restaurant and relaxed atmosphere; cheap tent hire is possible. Good security. Take *matatu* #8, or bus #18 or 20 to Nairobi hospital.

Wildlife Clubs of Kenya Hostel ("Nairobi outskirts" map, p.154), Langata Rd in Nairobi South "C", next to the Bomas of Kenya (☎02/891904). A rather wild overgrown site, popular with locals, with dormitory-style rooms (Ksh300 per person) and decent facilities. Bus/*matatu* #24, #34, #125 or #126.

Westlands and Parklands hotels

The following hotels are on the "Westlands" map unless stated. Buses/*matatus* #21, #23, #30, #104 and #119 go to Westlands. For Parklands (adjacent to Westlands), catch a *matatu* on Latema Road. Both areas are relatively safe for walking around with luggage during the day.

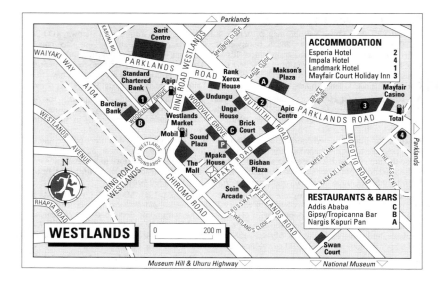

Bavaria Hotel ("Greater Nairobi" map, p.82), Chiromo Rd, Westlands (PO Box 31153; ☎02/741132 or 747394). A *nyama choma*-joint-cum-hotel setup, common "up-country" but unusual for Nairobi, just up from the *International Casino*. The rooms are nothing flash, but there's a beer garden, a sauna (for a steaming Ksh600/hour), 24-hour bar (loud discos Wed, Fri & Sat), Indian/Chinese restaurant, a swimming pool (Ksh100 for non-guests) and safe parking. Room only ③.

Esperia Hotel, Muthithi Rd, Westlands (PO Box 14642; ☎02/742818, fax 746214). In a tatty colonial-era administration building, with adequate linoleum-floored rooms with showers, telephones and safe parking. There's an equally dilapidated bar outside. B&B ③.

Impala Hotel, Parklands Rd, Parklands (PO Box 14144; ☎02/742346–7, fax 743258). Not at all touristy, with reasonably priced rooms, good parking and a shaded, leafy bar. ③.

Landmark Hotel, Waiyaki Way, Westlands (PO Box 14287; ☎02/448713, fax 448977, *landmark@africaonline.co.ke*; reservations through Block, p.48). After a bad decline, the former *Jacaranda* reopened in 1996 after a $2.5 million refit. The rooms are a bit small, but all have satellite TV and fans, but the building itself remains charmless, its lawns surrounded by tall fences. Service varies between middling and excellent, and there's a nice pool. Be careful when walking in the vicinity at night. B&B ⑥.

Mayfair Court Holiday Inn, Parklands Rd (PO Box 66807; ☎02/740920–1, fax 748823, *mayfair@africaonline.co.ke*). Classy modern hotel in pastiche Edwardian and Art Nouveau styles (the original structure was a 1930s hotel), with small tropical gardens, and a bar which attracts the weekend *wazungu* crowd. It's rather business-oriented, but efficiently run and has good disabled access with some specially designed rooms. There's also a pool, the obligatory fitness centre and sauna, and adjacent *Mayfair Casino*. Excellent value in its class. B&B ⑦.

Plums Hotel ("Greater Nairobi" map, p.82), Ojijo Rd, Parklands (PO Box 40747; ☎02/745222–3). Pleasant establishment near the museum, with good car security if you're driving, plus an attached *nyama choma* joint playing Kikuyu and *zilizopendwa* oldies weekends (ie it can get loud). ②.

Out-of-centre hotels

Fairview Hotel ("Greater Nairobi" map, p.82), Bishops Rd (PO Box 40842; ☎02/723211, fax 721320, *reserv@fairviewkenya.com*). A peaceful, rambling country-style place with pleasant grounds (great bird-watching), and a wide variety of accommodation. All rooms have nets and TVs, some have baths, and the deluxe doubles are excellent. Family rooms have bunk beds for kids, but some of the standard rooms are dull and not much better than a decent B&L. Moreover, if you don't look the part the atmosphere can feel stuffy, and they can be awkward about letting you see rooms. Good meals, though, and it's popular with families, so reserve ahead. Bus/*matatu* #1, #2, #3, #4, #41, #46 or #111 to 3rd Ngong Ave, then a three-minute walk. B&B ⑤.

Giraffe Manor ("Nairobi outskirts" map, p.154), Koitobos Rd, adjacent to the AFEW Giraffe Centre, Langata (☎02/891078, fax 890949). If you have serious money to burn, this place rises neck and shoulders above the rest: a wonderfully eccentric set-up in a Scottish-style manor house in the grounds of AFEW Giraffe Centre whose quadrupedal inmates like to share your breakfast through the first-floor dining room windows. It's extremely exclusive, expensive ($480 double including drinks), and bookings are by prior arrangement only. Profits go to the centre; closed April. Take a taxi to get there. FB ⑨.

Hurlingham Hotel ("Greater Nairobi" map, p.82), Argwings Kodhek Rd (PO Box 43158; ☎02/721920, fax 726691). A pre-war feeling lingers here which some find charming, others gloomy. Most people enjoy it, though, especially for the excellent cooking, with touches like wholemeal bread. However, most of the seventeen rooms are long overdue for a revamp, and some mattresses badly need replacing – inexcusable at the price. Check the rooms before paying. Prices bargainable. B&B ③.

Kentmere Club (off the top of "Nairobi outskirts" map, p.154), Limuru Rd, Tigoni (PO Box 39508; ☎0154/41053, fax 40692). Situated 16km north of Nairobi amidst the tea and coffee plantations of the Tigoni highlands, *Kentmere* is a small and friendly country inn, pretty much what you might find in the Cotswolds in England, all wooden beams and wooden "slate" roofs. It has sixteen s/c rooms in cottages with beautiful gardens and cosy fireplaces, and a good restaurant which uses mostly locally-grown ingredients. Ten minutes drive away is the Limuru Country Club with its golf course and swimming pool. *Matatu* #114 or one from outside *Mayur* restaurant on Tom Mboya St. HB ⑤.

Ngong Hills Hotel ("Greater Nairobi" map, p.82), Ngong Rd (PO Box 40485; ☎02/566684, fax 571750). Helpful mainly if you fancy boogying the night away at the hotel's popular live music venue (see p.130) or around the jumping nightspots of Dagoretti Corner and Ngong Rd, and don't want the hassle of getting back in the wee hours. The ambience is relaxed, and the s/c rooms – off prison-like corridors – are good, with carpets, nets, telephones and proper baths: the green pool is more inviting after a few beers. Bus/*matatu* #1, #2, #3, #4, #102, #103 or #111. B&B ④.

Panafric Hotel ("Greater Nairobi" map, p.82), Kenyatta Ave, Nairobi Hill (PO Box 30486; ☎02/720822, fax 726356, 721878; reservations through *Sarova*, p.50). 500m up the hill west of Uhuru Park, with views over the city. Potentially a good uptown option, but this 1965 concrete block is generally uninspiring and in need of zest (and renovation), despite the refreshing pool and satellite TV. Its *Flame Tree* restaurant has garnered a solid reputation for high quality. Bus/*matatu* #1 to #4, #34, #41, #46 or #111. Room only ⑥.

Pathway Hotel ("Nairobi outskirts" map, p.154), Ngong Rd, opposite the racecourse (PO Box 54803; ☎02/577545). A new and well-priced place over a mellow bar (fear of neighbours' complaints keeps the volume down and the pace slow – as yet), with good s/c rooms and hot water. Like the Ngong Hills Hotel, a reliable base for exploring the nightlife around Dagoretti Corner and the Ngong Rd. Bus/*matatu* #1 to #4, #102, #103 or #111. ②.

Safari Park Hotel (Nairobi outskirts" map, p.154), Thika Rd, 14km from town (PO Box 45038; ☎02/802493, fax 802477, *safariht@arcc.or.ke*; reservations at Kimathi House, Kimathi St, ☎02/216070, fax 217677). A huge, purpose-built "inland resort", offering a wholly sanitized vision of "Real Africa". Although far out of town (there's a regular shuttle bus), it's an attractive base for an upmarket stay, with a large expanse of landscaped gardens, a massive freeform swimming pool, health club, tennis courts, four-poster beds in all rooms, seven excellent and remarkably affordable restaurants, a discotheque, piano bar, horse riding, and faultless service. Everything you could wish for, and certainly should expect at this price. There's also a casino, should you have any money left over. Bus/*matatu* #45, #137, #145, #160 or #237. Room only ⑧–⑨.

Silver Springs Hotel ("Greater Nairobi" map, p.82), Valley Rd/Argwings Kodhek Rd (PO Box 61362; ☎02/722451–6, fax 720545). A large and rather grey establishment overlooking the hospital (it reeks of antiseptic), with comfortable rooms, pool, health club and massage, but it lacks the class of its competitors. Safe parking. #41 or #46 bus. B&B ⑤.

Simbayo House ("Nairobi outskirts" map, p.154), Bogoni East Rd, two compounds down from Utamaduni crafts centre (PO Box 15110; ☎02/890921, fax 890462). This is an American-owned homestay run by the same people as the *Jikoni* restaurant at Utamaduni. There are three rooms available (one s/c), each with verandah looking out onto gardens. Singles half price. Bus/*matatu* #24. B&B ④, FB ⑤ (including lunch at *Jikoni*).

Utalii Hotel ("Greater Nairobi" map, p.82), Thika Rd, 6km from town (PO Box 31067; ☎02/802540-7, fax 803094, *utalii@form-net.com*). This offers something different, with unbeatable standards. It's run by the Utalii College, Kenya's college of tourism, so you get impeccable, if slightly hesitant, service. Rooms have TVs. Amenities include a large outdoor heated pool, tennis courts, and an astonishingly good restaurant (Tues Kenyan buffet lunches; Sat evening poolside BBQ; Sun buffet lunch). Facing it, across the banana tops, sprawls one of Nairobi's worst slums, Mathare Valley. Courtesy bus to city centre, or bus/*matatu* #45, #137, #145, #160 or #237. B&B ⑤.

Whistling Thorns (see chapter map on p.79 for the Kiserian–Isinya road), 35km south of Nairobi off the Magadi Rd: turn left after Kiserian (22km) onto the D523 to Isinya for 13km (PO Box 51512; ☎ & fax 02/350720, *speccampsaf@thorntree.org*). Overlooking the Ngong Hills and the plains south of Nairobi National Park, this place offers homely two-bedroomed cottages and a swimming pool, and the option of walks, cycling (Ksh400 per half-day) and horse-riding (Ksh1000 per hour). Also open daily for food (pizzas and grilled wildebeest). You can camp there too. Very good value if getting out here isn't a problem (bus #126 or *matatu* #125 to Kiserian, then potluck with *matatus* headed for Isinya). Credit cards accepted. B&B ④.

Windsor Golf & Country Club ("Nairobi outskirts" map, p.154), off Kigwa Rd, Ridgeways, 15km north of the city (PO Box 45587; ☎02/862300, fax 802322, *windsor@users.africaonline.co.ke*). An absurdity: built in 1992, this golfers' resort complex has been styled and fitted entirely in mock-Victorian and Georgian style, complete with landscaped gardens, copper-plate clock tower, gazebos, and even designer creaking floorboards. It's superbly run, with services and amenities second to none. Situated on an old coffee plantation, the conversion to golfer's paradise has been done to a tee: most rooms look out over the manicured course, complete with lakes and bunkers. Facilities include an outdoor heated pool, health club with steam room and massage, tennis and squash courts, a croquet lawn, fishing and riding, and there's a resident ornithologist. Accommodation ranges from rooms and suites to some lovely twin cottages ($570). Take a taxi. Bed only. ⑧–⑨.

Long stays

For long stays in Nairobi, cheap **flats, rooms and studios** are advertised in the classified columns of the *Nation* and the *Standard*. Otherwise contact an apartment agency (Westlands is probably the most promising area), or there's a very useful noticeboard at the supermarket in Karen. Remember, if the place has no *askari* (security guard), the danger of burglary is very real. If your stay is more temporary, the YWCA is your best bet.

Apartments ("Greater Nairobi" map, p.82), Rose Ave, off Lenana Rd, three blocks from the Yaya Centre (PO Box 74381; ☎02/724080, fax 720721, *woodmere@net2000ke.com*; bus/*matatu* #46 to Yaya Centre). A little bit out of the way: well-guarded premises, small pool, sauna and "garden" and space for kids. Accommodation ranges from small serviced studios with tiny kitchen and "loft" sleeping to spacious one and two bedroom apartments. From about $50 per night, with cheaper weekly and monthly rates.

Heron Court Apartment Hotel ("Greater Nairobi" map, p.82), Milimani Rd (PO Box 41848; ☎02/720740-3, fax 721698). Much used by volunteers and their kin, and fine (if a little moth-eaten) especially if self-catering appeals. Reasonable rooms or studio apartments. There's a bleach-filled pool and the dubious benefit of *Buffalo Bill's*, a seedy pick-up bar, which can be rather noisy at night but is kept separate from the hotel itself. Bus/*matatu* #1, #2, #3, #4, #34, #41, #46 or #111 to *Panafric*, then a five-minute walk up Milimani Rd. Monthly rates Ksh19,500 double (per night ③).

Nairobi Protea Apartments, Yaya Centre ("Greater Nairobi" map, p.82), Argwings Kodhek Rd (PO Box 76377; ☎02/713360, fax 561902, *protea@africaonline.co.ke*). Currently the top luxury option for long stays, with fully furnished and serviced apartments (one to four bedrooms) including kitchens and satellite TV. Amenities include an Olympic-sized pool and two floodlit tennis courts (with resident coach). Safe parking. Bus #41 or #46. One-bedroom $1700 per month, two-bedrooms $1890/month.

New Fairview, Bishops Rd (same management and details as *Fairview Hotel*, p.98). Three-room flats available for three-month stays or longer at Ksh72,000 per flat per month.

YWCA ("Central Nairobi" map, p.82), Mamlaka Rd, off Nyerere Ave, just west of Central Park (PO Box 40710; ☎02/724699). Best value for men as well as women (and couples can share). Rates for room only are in the order of Ksh7000 per month for a double room with washbasin, or about Ksh5000 per month for a single. There are flatlets for about Ksh9000. Write well in advance to reserve.

Around central Nairobi

Kenyatta Avenue is the obvious place to start looking around Central Nairobi. A good initial overview of it – and lots else besides – can be had from the vertigo-inducing, glass-walled lifts in the **ICEA building**, on the northwest corner of Wabera Street. If the guards at the bottom need an excuse, tell them you're visiting the Japanese Embassy on the fifteenth floor; they may even be persuaded to escort you onto the roof. Tipping (Ksh20–50) might be helpful.

Kenyatta Avenue

Kenyatta Avenue was originally designed to allow a twelve-oxen team to make a full turn, even though livestock is nowadays longer permitted within the city limits. Broad, multi-laned and planted with flowering trees and shrubs, it remains (along with the Kenyatta Conference Centre) the capital's favourite tourist image. The avenue is smartest – and most touristy – on its south side, with would-be moneychangers, itinerant souvenir hawkers and safari touts assailing you from every direction, and wily shoeshiners inspecting each passing pair of feet from their stands (who given half a chance will glob some wax on your shoes and then insist on having to clean it off!). The focus of the avenue's eastern end is the *Stanley Hotel*'s **Thorn Tree Café**, diagonally opposite Nakumatt supermarket on the corner of Kimathi Street. The *Thorn Tree* is Nairobi's one proper pavement café and, despite its prices and largely *wazungu* and rich businessman clientele, an enduring meeting place. The thorn tree in question was cut down in 1997 and replaced with a new sapling in December 1998. There used to be a message board nailed to the tree, which has yet to be reincarnated.

At the other end of Kenyatta Avenue is the almost complete skyscraper of the **General Post Office** (GPO) on the left and, just before it, **Koinange Street**, named after the Kikuyu Senior Chief Koinange of the colonial era. The peculiar caged **Galton-Fenzi Memorial**, just here on the left, is a monument to the man who founded, of all things, the Nairobi branch of the Automobile Association. Fenzi was also the first motorist to drive from Nairobi to Mombasa, back in 1926 when there was only a dirt track.

City Square and Parliament

Head down Koinange Street and on to Kaunda Street, passing the *Inter-Continental* on your right and, crossing City Hall Way, you enter **City Square**. Jomo Kenyatta's statue sits benevolently, mace in hand, on the far side of the wide, flagstoned court; his mausoleum, with flickering eternal flames, is on the right as you approach the Parliament building. When the flags are out for a conference it all looks very bright and confident.

The legend over the main doors of Kenya's **Parliament** reads: "For a Just Society and the Fair Government of Men". With the government forced by both national and international pressures to allow greater democracy and accountability in its business, the motto seems finally to be losing its edge of irony. Parliament is open to the public: talk to the guards at the gate, who will tell you when the next session is taking place (usually Wed & Thurs at 2.30pm; it's in recess mid-July to mid-October) or, when it's not in session, how to get a tour of the building. If you're assigned a guide make sure both parties are clear about how much you'll pay. To sit in the public gallery you must first register

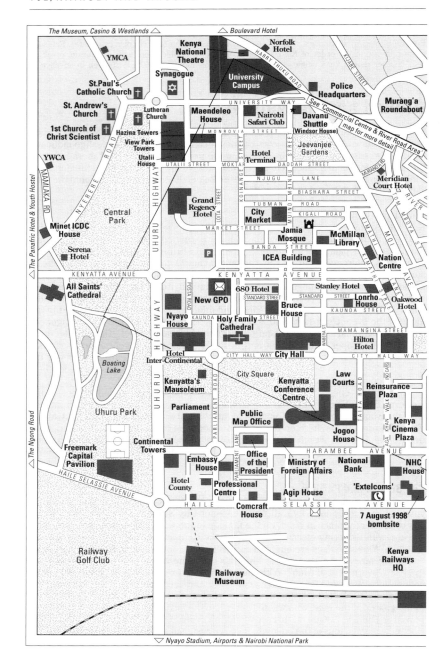

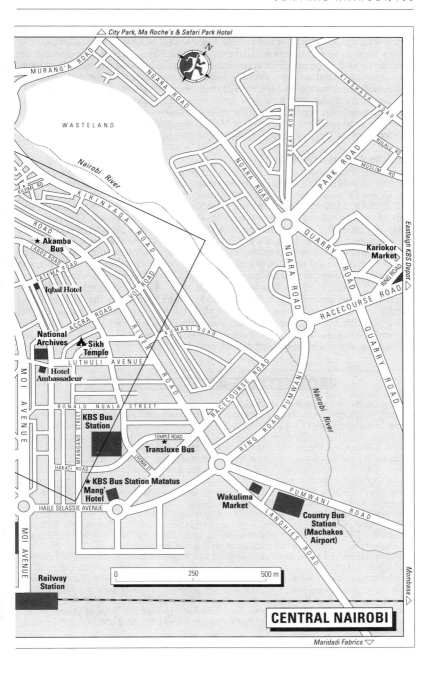

City Park, Ma Roche's & Safari Park Hotel

N

MURANG'A ROAD

NGARA ROAD

WASTELAND

Nairobi River

KINSHASA ROAD

DESAI ROAD

PARK ROAD

KULALU RD

MUSLIM RD

KILOME RD

KIRINYAGA ROAD

ROAD

★ Akamba Bus

LAGOS ROAD

LATEMA

VOI ROAD

NGARA ROAD

QUARRY

Eastleigh KBS Depot

Kariokor Market

RING ROAD

■ Iqbal Hotel

ACCRA ROAD

KUMASI ROAD

RIVER ROAD

RACECOURSE ROAD

QUARRY ROAD

National Archives

♦ Sikh Temple

LUTHULI AVENUE

■ Hotel Ambassadeur

RONALD NGALA STREET

MFANGANO STREET

RACECOURSE ROAD

RING ROAD PUMWANI

Nairobi River

MOI AVENUE

KBS Bus Station

TEMPLE ROAD

★ Transluxe Bus

DUKAS ST

HAKATI ROAD

★ KBS Bus Station Matatus

Mang' Hotel

HAILE SELASSIE AVENUE

Wakulima Market

PUMWANI ROAD

Country Bus Station (Machakos Airport)

LANDHIES ROAD

MOI AVENUE

0   250   500 m

Railway Station

Mombasa

CENTRAL NAIROBI

Maridadi Fabrics

at the gatehouse on the corner of Parliament Road and Harambee Avenue, leaving all your belongings with the attendant outside. Once seated, be on your best behaviour. The gallery tends to be full of very well-behaved schoolchildren – which of course is more than can be said of the members of parliament. With the admission of opposition members since 1992, and an even stronger opposition presence after the 1997 elections (opposition and government MPs are almost perfectly balanced), proceedings are livelier now than perhaps they have ever been, with a host of contentious motions being openly debated concerning corruption, ethnic violence and even, in October 1998, a failed vote of no-confidence in President Moi's government. Try to get hold of a copy of the Orders of the Day: there may be a juicy question or two worth anticipating.

Kenyatta Conference Centre

From Parliament, walking down Harambee Avenue along the shady pavement, you come to Nairobi's pride and joy – the **Kenyatta International Conference Centre** (KICC) and its tall brother, "KANU tower", the ruling party headquarters (all enquiries ☎02/332383). This, for a long time the tallest building in Kenya, is capped by a milehigh formerly-revolving restaurant (a mile above sea level that is). Confusion has always arisen on the ground floor about whether anyone was allowed up to the 28th. The restaurant has closed, but it's worth making an effort to get as high as possible; if you talk to the security staff in the foyer, assent is usually given for ascent partly because it has become accepted practice to tip the guards who come with you (a mean Ksh200 is the going rate, though nothing's fixed). The view of Nairobi is without equal and a firm reminder of the vastness of Africa. Just 4km to the south, you see the Mombasa Road leave the suburbs behind and take off across the yellow plains. Northwards, hills of coffee – and, at higher altitudes, tea – roll into the distance. If you pick a good day in December or January you really can see Mount Kenya in one direction and Kilimanjaro in the other. Immediately below, the traffic swarms – and Jogoo House is suddenly seen to be built remarkably like a Roman villa.

SABA SABA AND THE TREES OF PEACE

The months preceding the December 1997 **general elections** were fraught with violence. It all began on the July 7, already nick-named Saba Saba Day ("seven-seven day", from the anniversary of a brutal crackdown on a pro-democracy demonstration on July 7, 1990), when history repeated itself. A rally in central Nairobi degenerated into running battles with police, whose brutality was widely reported on Kenyan and international TV; this in turn led to nationwide riots in which thirteen people were killed. Police, chanting *Uua! Uua!* (Kiswahili for "kill") stormed an examination room at Nairobi University and beat up students, others stormed the Anglican Cathedral – a focal point of the pro-reform movement – where many people had taken refuge, while on the streets police dragged passengers out of taxis and beat them up, and TV news bulletins carried pictures of women with their babies strapped to their backs being attacked by policemen.

The effect of all this, together with the spiralling violence of the following months, was to shatter Kenya's previously peaceful international image, and indirectly led to the suspension of an IMF loan to the country, as well as the virtual collapse of Kenya's tourist industry. Hemmed in on all sides, President Moi finally acceded to the demonstrators' demands and promised to institute a set of reformist measures, including the unbanning of Richard Leakey's Safina party, just before the election. A poignant memorial to the bloody events that led to this, as well as to the August 7, 1998 terrorist bombing at the downtown American Embassy, can be seen at the roadside verge of Uhuru Park at Kenyatta Avenue, where a dozen saplings have been planted as "Trees of Peace", each bearing a simple wooden cross bearing the name of a victim, and the words "Saba Saba" or "August 7".

National Archives

Straight down Harambee Avenue, cut across Moi Avenue and up to the **National Archives** (Mon–Fri 8am–4pm, Sat 8am–12.30pm; PO Box 49210; ☎02/228959 ext 211, fax 228027, *knarchives@form-net.com*). Housed in the striking old Bank of India building on the bend of Moi Avenue across from the *Hilton*, they amount to a **museum/art gallery** in the heart of the city, which few visitors to Nairobi seem to know about; entry is free and a look around takes an hour or so.

The ground floor is a public gallery with Joseph Murumbi's (briefly vice-president under Kenyatta) oddball collection of paintings dominating the walls. The collection, sold to the government in 1966, ranges from uninteresting dabbles to some beautiful drawings and striking collages, but in a city that's not exactly cluttered with art collections, it does deserve a look. In the centre of the floor there's also a delightfully jumbled collection of African ethnographia – musical instruments, masks, weapons, domestic artefacts: the Senufo masks and figures from the Ivory Coast are especially impressive.

The second floor houses a **photographic exhibition** of the struggle for **Independence** – compelling not just for its content but because this is almost the only public place in the country where Kenyans can be reminded of the period in their history euphemistically called "The Emergency". There's also a collection of black-and-white press **photos**, highly revealing as a record of the early part of Daniel Arap Moi's presidency, with foreign tours figuring prominently. Also here are a number of fascinating portraits of tribal elders, mostly from the colonial era. If you're around on a Saturday, there are free 10am screenings of films relating to culture, politics or wildlife. The actual archives themselves (mainly books, papers and correspondence, and some recordings) are closed to the general public, though if you're interested you can pay a small fee (just Ksh50) for a year's membership.

The Jamia Mosque

The **Jamia Mosque** stands near the City Market. The ornate green-and-white exterior contrasts strikingly with the simple interior, where the large central dome appears far larger from beneath than it does from the courtyard outside. Although most Kenyan towns now have at least one mosque, often financed by Saudi Arabia, few are as large or as beautiful as the Jamia, which is currently being enlarged. It is highly unlikely that non-Muslims will be allowed in, although polite requests, a genuine interest in Islam, and the usual modesty of attire (limbs covered, feet washed and unshod) may help. So for an alternative, bird's-eye view of the mosque, the top of the ICEA building is (again) a good vantage point.

The museums and parks

Covered here are the handful of **parks** and **museums** in Nairobi itself. Nairobi National Park gets separate coverage in the "Nairobi Province" section later in this chapter (see p.153), as do the Bomas of Kenya, the Karen Blixen Museum and the Langata Giraffe Centre. Unless you have your own wheels you may be better off joining a tour for them. The following sites, however, are all easily walkable.

The Railway Museum

Station Road; daily 8.30am–5pm; Ksh200, children Ksh150; free guides.

Now privately run, Nairobi's **Railway Museum** is a natural draw for rail fans and of more than passing interest for anyone else. It's signposted, ten minutes' walk from the station, but be careful, as there was a rash of grab-and-run robberies down here a few years back.

THE US EMBASSY BOMBING AUGUST 7, 1998

It was a Friday morning just like any other, and the Nairobi rush hour was getting into its habitually chaotic swing. As usual, the roundabout next to the **US Embassy** at the junction of Moi and Haile Selassie avenues was packed with vehicles, and the streets were full of people. On Haile Selassie Avenue, a yellow Mitsubishi van made its way into the parking bay at the rear of the embassy.

Some witnesses say that a gunfight ensued, others that a hand-grenade was hurled at the embassy's guards. Whatever, moments later, the van's cargo of 800kg of TNT exploded, gouging a deep crater in the ground, setting fire to the asphalt and propelling the vehicle 10m into the air, where it remained stuck to the side of the embassy in a cloud of black smoke and flame. The force of the explosion was so intense that it was felt over 10km away. In the embassy itself – the intended terrorists' target – some forty people perished – twelve of them Americans – despite the reinforced concrete walls. The brunt of the blast, however, was borne by the adjacent four-storey Ufundi Cooperative House, a commercial building that also housed a secretarial and computer college. It was reduced to a mound of burning rubble. Next to it, the 22-storey Cooperative Bank House skyscraper had black smoke pouring out from its shattered windows. Some office workers were decapitated by flying debris, others were sucked out of the windows by the shock wave, along with filing cabinets, papers, chairs and desks. Altogether, some forty buildings within a 150-metre radius were seriously damaged by the blast. In the packed streets below, thousands of people were showered with flying glass and masonry, as were the buses and cars that were snared up at the roundabout. In their panic, many fled the city on any transport they could find, believing that World War III had started, or that a coup was underway. But many more, even some of the injured, gathered their wits and started to help with the rescue operation.

A few minutes later, a second car bomb exploded outside the US Embassy in Tanzania's capital, Dar es Salaam, killing eleven people. In Kenya, the final toll stood at 263 dead and over 5000 injured, almost all of them Kenyans. Sixty people lost their eyesight, many more were partially blinded, and the material damage was estimated at around $500 million. The Americans were quick to blame Osman bin Laden, the Saudi millionaire dissident based in Afghanistan, for the attack, and promptly retaliated by bombing a suspected chemical weapons factory in Sudan and bin Laden's alleged terrorist training base in Afghanistan. The country was plunged into confusion, mourning and grief: why had the terrorists chosen Kenya, which had no quarrel with either the USA or Islam? The answer appears to have been a lethal combination of lax security both at the embassy and at the Tanzanian border (over which the explosives were apparently smuggled), the embassy's central and exposed location, the proximity of the international press corps in East Africa, the United States' covert activities in Sudan, and the fact that Nairobi had been America's second largest CIA and FBI base in Africa.

The mindless cruelty and barbarism of this act was symbolized by what happened to Rose Wanjiku, a tea-lady in one of the Ufundi House offices. After the building collapsed, she remained buried alive for five days as rescuers, including a special unit of Israeli soldiers, worked desperately around the clock in their effort to save her and others. She had communicated constantly with them from beneath the rubble, but died half a day before she was reached. The tragic futility of her struggle for life touched millions across the world, and in Kenya, the long-stemmed rose became the symbol of the bomb blast victims. The National Memorial Service held two weeks after the outrage included Hindu and Muslim speakers, and the papers were full of praise for all Kenyans, whatever their religion or tribe, for having helped rescue victims in the immediate aftermath.

The site of the explosion itself, a few metres from the fenced-in pile of rubble which is all that remains of Ufundi House, has become a site of pilgrimage where, every day, individuals, groups and delegations lay tributes of long-stemmed roses and other flowers. Others just stand in silence, with the gaping hulk of the ruined Cooperative Bank House looming over them in mute response.

The main hall contains a mass of memorabilia: photos of early stations, of the "Lunatic Express" East African Railway from Mombasa to Kampala being built, and the engineering feats involved in getting the carriages up and down the escarpment, and strange pieces of hardware, such as the game-viewing seat mounted at the front of the train. Passengers who risked this perch were reminded that "The High Commissioner will not be liable for personal injury (fatal or otherwise)". In the museum annexe, the motorized bicycle inspection trolley is quite a sight but, as the write-up explains, the experiment in the 1950s "was not really successful", as the wheels kept slipping off the rail.

The engines

Outside, exposed to the elements, is the museum's collection of old **locomotives**, most of them built in England. You can clamber inside any of the cabs to play with the massive levers and switches. The restriction of forward visibility on some of the engines seems incredible: the driver of the *Karamoja Express* couldn't have had any idea what was in front of him while steaming down a straight line. If it all fills you with nostalgic delight, you should also note that Nairobi and Mombasa stations both have locomotive graveyards which, with enthusiastic persistence, you should be able to look around. There are plans to renovate some of the old steam locos, and to have trips hauled by them.

Lions figure prominently in the early history of the Uganda Railway: look in the shed for first-class coach no. 12 to learn the story of Superintendent C. H. Ryall. During the hunt for the "Maneaters of Tsavo" in 1898, Ryall had readied his gun one evening, settled down in the carriage and offered himself as bait. Somehow he nodded off . . . He was dragged from this carriage and devoured while colleagues sat frozen in horror. The coach, together with the repainted loco no. 301, took part in the filming of *Out of Africa* at Kajiado.

The National Museum

Daily 9.30am–6pm (tends to close at 5.30pm); adults Ksh200, children/students Ksh100; guides (free) available on request; National Museums of Kenya: PO Box 40658; ☎02/742131-4, fax 741424, www.museums.or.ke.

The **National Museum** is probably the city's prime sightseeing attraction but surprisingly few travellers make the small effort to get to it. However, it's the best possible prelude to any tour around the country, and only about a thirty-minute walk from Kenyatta Avenue – and only a few minutes by taxi or bus #21, #23 or #119. Allow yourself a morning or afternoon to look around. If museum fatigue hits you, the pleasant *Café Bustani* is open daily until 6pm, and does self-services lunches.

Natural history and geology

The museum's most extensive collections are **ornithological**, with most of Kenya's thousand-plus species of birds represented. Kenya's birdlife usually makes a strong impression, even on non-bird-watchers. Look out for the various species of hornbills, turacos and rollers, and for the extraordinary standard-wing nightjar, which frequently has people doing a double-take the first time they see it fluttering low over a swimming pool at dusk in its hunt for insects. There's also a multitude of stuffed game heads, dioramas of Kenyan mammals in the large mammal room (currently amusingly displayed in Noah's Ark), casts of fish, even a whale skeleton, as well as the skeleton and a fibreglass replica of Ahmed, the famous elephant from Marsabit.

Especially useful if you're going anywhere near the Rift Valley, the **Geology Gallery** is a mine of information on plate tectonics and the life-cycle of volcanoes, with a good collection of rocks and minerals which you may see on your travels.

Gallery of Contemporary East African Art

On the second floor, next to the birds, the **Gallery of Contemporary East African Art** is an exhibition space and **showroom** for principally Kenyan, Tanzanian and Ugandan artists to display their work and wares. Everything is for sale and the gallery, although non-profit-making, takes a commission from what's sold and ploughs this back into running the place, and into acquiring work for the museum's own, long-planned Modern Art Gallery.

Human prehistory

The special interest of Nairobi's museum lies in the cultural, human and quasi-human exhibits. The **Prehistory Gallery**, where the palaeontology exhibits are housed, has walls disguised with stunning reproductions of a series of Tanzanian rock paintings. Ahead, on the floor, is a cast of wide-splayed, human-looking footprints – the small pair following in the prints of the larger one – which were discovered at Laetoli in Tanzania. They belong, almost certainly, to *Homo erectus*, believed to be the direct ancestor of our own species. The prints were squeezed into the mud about 1,500,000 years ago. Down the hall, eerily life-sized reconstructions of a family of *Homo erectus* (rather like a scene from *Planet of the Apes*) wolfing down an antelope carcass, as well as other dioramas of the more primitive (and ultimately unsuccessful) australopithecines, bring the story of human evolution vividly to life.

There's a separate display telling the story of the Lake Turkana **Koobi Fora excavations** – "The Origins of Man in Kenya" – on the ground floor to the right of the Prehistory Gallery entrance.

Ethnography and history

In contrast, the rather dry second-floor cases of **ethnographic** exhibits aren't awfully illuminating, though you can piece a lot of information together if you've the time. However, they contain some fascinating odds and ends – don't miss the Maasai ear-stretching devices, and the "divining sandals" made of elephant hide tanned in dung and urine. If you're planning on travelling through any of the areas inhabited by pastoral peoples (especially Pokot, Samburu, Maasai or Turkana), then seeing some old and authentic handicrafts beforehand is a good idea. This will also be a big help when you find yourself faced with, for example, an urgent vendor offering you a dozen different carved headrests – not an uncommon experience. The collections indicate the tremendous diversity of Kenya's cultures, a quality impressively evoked by Joy Adamson's series of ethnic portraits mounted on the walls, commissioned by the colonial government and now an impressive record of, in many cases, already vanished cultures. Her beautiful **botanical paintings** are displayed downstairs by the main entrance.

Finally, in the **Lamu Gallery** on the main floor, the once excellent exhibition "The Kenya Coast 9th–19th Century", is now sadly depleted and looks to all appearances as though it has been ransacked.

If you want to keep abreast of developments in Kenya's museums and on-going ethnological and archaeological research, contact the **Kenya Museum Society** (PO Box 40658; ☎02/750136 or 742131–4 ext 289, *kms@africaonline.co.ke*), who are based in the museum grounds. As well as publishing the excellent annual journal *Kenya Past and Present*, they organize an annual two-week "Know Kenya Course" (Ksh4500), including lectures, films and fieldtrips on Kenyan natural history, prehistory, ethnography, wildlife and conservation, and traditional medicine, towards the end of October to early November. Individual morning lectures can be attended in that period for Ksh500. They also organize an Arts Festival around March which promotes local artists. For research contacts and more on environmental matters, see the "Nairobi listings" section on pp.146–153.

The Snake Park and Aquarium

Same prices and times as the National Museum.

Opposite the museum and going downhill (in both senses of the word) is the **Snake Park**. It's only fair to say that you'd have to be very enthusiastic about reptiles to find this interesting, and very insensitive to find it enjoyable. Exhibits take in East African and American snakes, a crocodile or two, some murky terrapins, emaciated monitor lizards and boring fish tanks. There are much better (and cheaper) snake parks on the coast. There are plans to start a nature walk in the grounds, which would at least provide a nice picnic site.

The city's parks

A colour map of Nairobi suggests a multitude of cool green spaces around the city. The two remaining **forests** – Ngong Road in the west and Karura in the north – are currently battlegrounds between environmentalists and those who have illegally expropriated these public lands for private development amid a morass of corruption and government inaction. **Karura Forest** is especially under threat, and there have been several violent confrontations between protesters and the security personnel guarding the illegal plots (to find out more, contact the Greenbelt Movement, Adams Arcade, Ngong Road; PO Box 67545 Nairobi; ☎02/603867 or 571223). **Ngong Road Forest** is presently much calmer, but don't visit unless you're with someone who knows the area well – you're a long way from help. Much more accessible is the **Arboretum** (gates close at dusk), northwest of Uhuru Park on Arboretum Road (*matatu* #48). Somewhat overgrown, almost jungly in parts, it's a lovely place to wander or picnic, and, of course, a must if you're botanically inclined: there are over 200 varieties of tree alone, and even the odd monkey. There are security notices everywhere, so don't take any valuables. You may be reassured – or unnerved – by the officious plain clothes policemen who stalk the glades (it backs onto State House). On the last Monday of each month there is a guided walk; be at the gate by 9.30am if you're interested.

BIRD-WATCHING IN NAIROBI

Bird-watching need not be exclusively a bush pursuit. For any visitor staying in central Nairobi, an impressive sight during the early morning and late evening is that of groups of **black kites** circling over the city as they move between feeding and roosting sites; amongst these are **pied crows**, readily identified black-and-white birds. **Marabou storks**, **sacred ibises** and **silvery-cheeked hornbills** can sometimes be seen flying over the city, while flocks of **red-winged starlings** call noisily from office buildings.

The leafier areas of the city are likely to produce even more birds. The gardens adjacent to the National Museum are an interesting and relatively safe area to start birdwatching. Here, keen birdwatchers may encounter the **cinnamon-chested bee eater**, a common, small, green bee eater found in open areas with scattered bushes. The plants and flowering shrubs outside the front steps of the museum provide excellent opportunities to observe **sunbirds**: several species, including variable and Hunter's sunbirds can be seen here. Another bird of the gardens is the **African paradise monarch**, a species of flycatcher. In breeding plumage, the rufous males have long tail streamers, which trail behind them like ribbons, as they flit from tree to tree.

Nature Kenya (formerly the East Africa Natural History Society) organizes bird walks from the National Museum every Wednesday morning at 8.45am. They usually proceed to another part of Nairobi. Longer trips are also held at least once a month. For more information, contact Nature Kenya at the museum (PO Box 44486; ☎02/749957 or 02/741049).

Otherwise, Nairobi's **parks** aren't always very inviting, but several are pleasant places to retreat to for a while. Biggest and best is **City Park** in the north, a half-hour stroll from the National Museum down Forest Road and Limuru Road, or by bus #19 from the *Iqbal*. City Park has a wealth of tropical trees and birdlife, several troops of vervet monkeys, a small stream with wooden bridges, gravel paths, shady lawns, and, on weekends, families everywhere. During the week it's delightful, though not for women alone. And as usual, hang onto your possessions. And if you're a couple, beware of a recent, apparently 100 percent legal **scam** operated by police: they've made a habit of surprising kissing or canoodling couples, and then promptly charging them with "indecent behaviour in public", referring the unfortunate lovers to the Laws of Kenya: The Penal Code, Chapter 63, Article 182. Around Ksh200 should be enough to pay them off.

Uhuru and **Central** parks, on the western side of Uhuru Highway, have the city's worst reputation for muggings, particularly after dark. They're unfenced and never closed but to walk across either park after 6pm is, to put it mildly, asking for trouble. There are rowing boats for hire in the small murky lake in Uhuru Park, which are very popular at weekends and holidays.

In a more reputable part of the city (though a night walk even here would be foolish), try **Jeevanjee Gardens**, especially during a weekday lunchtime when you can picnic on a bench and chat with the office workers who aren't thronging the nearby restaurants. You can listen, too, to the preachers who have made Jeevanjee their church and the bemused picnickers their congregation. The park contains a curiously small statue, just about recognizable, of Queen Victoria, presented to Nairobi by nineteenth-century business tycoon A. M. Jeevanjee, founder of the *Standard* newspaper.

Markets and shopping

It doesn't take long to realize that commerce is Nairobi's *raison d'être*. Disappointingly perhaps, the form which trade takes here is not always very exotic. But Nairobi is the best place in East Africa to buy **handicrafts**, with the widest (if not the cheapest) selection and the best facilities for posting the stuff home. The city also has some lavish **produce markets**, enjoyable even if you only want to browse.

Bargaining is expected at all Nairobi's markets and most shops, with the exception of supermarkets and stores selling imported goods. Be aware, however, that the "last price" will vary seasonally and can sky-rocket when a major conference hits town.

Produce markets and food

It doesn't offer the city's lowest prices, but for a colourful and high-quality range of fruits and vegetables, the **City Market** (closes Sun at 1pm) is the obvious target (beware of bag-snatching in the area). If you're buying, the best-value stalls are in the outside aisle flanking the main hall on the right. Fish and meat are on either side of the main building, and the supermarket at the entrance has a good variety of Kenyan cheeses. The other large produce markets are the **Wakulima** (farmers) market, also known simply as "Marikiti", a cavernous and dank hall at the bottom of River Road, just before the country bus station (fruit and vegetables are pretty cheap here), and the excellent if totally chaotic open-air **Kariokor market** at the north end of Racecourse Road at the junction with General Waruingi Street. There's a smaller, less hassly produce market at the corner of Woodvale Grove and Ring Road Westlands in Westlands (daily 6am–6pm).

There are usually dozens of children and young women selling a few oranges, mangoes, whatever, on street corners. Blink, and they may be gone, tipped off that city *askaris* are about to "swoop". So buy from them while you have the chance.

There are **supermarkets** and groceries all over the city. Branches of **Uchumi** (Aga Khan Walk; Kimathi House, Kimathi Street; Market Street; Nkrumah Avenue; Taveta Lane) and **Nakumatt** (Kenyatta Avenue at Kimathi Street; Kenyatta Avenue between Wabera Street and Muindi Mbingu Street) are both open Mon–Sat 8.30am–8.30pm and Sun 10am–7pm. They're also good for camping supplies, sleeping bags, and have general household goods and stationery. Samaki & Tilley, on Kaunda Street, are first-class **butchers** and **fishmongers**; there's a good **cheese shop** in the YaYa Centre in Hurlingham, and a number of excellent delicatessens in Lenana Forest Centre on Ngong Road and in most of Westlands' many malls (see "Shopping malls" on p.114). For a good cheap selection of Kenyan and South African **wines**, try Joles Ltd at Hamilton House on Kaunda Street. An excellent **bakery**, with daily supplies of fresh rye and wholemeal bread, is Oscarsson's in 20th Century Plaza, Mama Ngina Street (there's another branch at Rank Xerox House in Westlands).

Crafts

For the exhausting business of buying **crafts and curios**, it's advisable to decide what you want before stepping into a shop or looking at a stall. At some of the more pretentious places you can browse for ages undisturbed, but at the cheaper outlets dilly-dallying is not encouraged and the pressure may be on to part with your money. To browse and to establish comparative values, pay a visit to the excellent Zanzibar Curio Shop on Moi Avenue, which has a huge range of stuff at fixed and very reasonable prices. With the exception of some antique sculptures, masks and xylophones, you'd be hard-pressed to match its prices by bargaining anywhere else.

Curio shops and hawkers

Elsewhere, there are dozens of **curio shops** and, depending on any number of factors, you might get a good deal at almost any of them: never accept their first price – you're subject to "*wazungu* rates", so bargain hard. The more upmarket ones are clustered on Standard, Kaunda and Mama Ngina streets. Apart from the Zanzibar Curio Shop, African Heritage on Banda Street (also open Sun 11am–4pm) is the main lure, and has some beautiful things (including great musical instruments like thumb pianos and lyres), but mostly at absurdly inflated prices. If you're mobile, there's a much bigger selection at its branch at Libra House on the Mombasa Road, on the way to JKI Airport (same hours), which also has a pleasant café and salad bar. It's the largest curio shop in Kenya, with eager suppliers in many parts of Africa. There's also the good Arki Ethiopian Curio Centre in Barclays Plaza, just the place for Coptic crosses (they also have advice on travel to Ethiopia).

You'll find lots more curio shops in the streets around the **City Market** (beware of bag-snatching in and around it), mostly overpriced and stubbornly unresponsive to substantial bargaining. Clearly, however, the cheaper prices will usually be at places where they don't have to pay a shop rent – **street stands** and **market booths** – though these are currently an almost extinct species, constantly being harassed and demolished by the city council. The more permanent booths in the enclosure at the back of the City Market off Koinange Street are an obvious choice, especially for soapstone, batiks and basketwork, but the whole area is something of a tourist trap, and while you'll probably find what you're looking for, you're unlikely to knock it down to a good price (some people report good deals by offering clothes in exchange).

For **traditional fabrics and clothes** such as *kikois* and *kangas*, there are around a dozen shops to browse through along Biashara Street: of these, Haria's Stamp Shop has an excellent and very reasonably priced range (prices around Ksh200–600 per metre). The **traditional masks** you'll see everywhere are imported from elsewhere. Only a handful of Kenyan tribes make masks, the Kikuyu being the best known, and these are exceedingly rare. Mount Kenya Sundries, Vedic House, Mama Ngina Street, have one of the best selections from West and Central Africa, albeit mostly reproductions, and are knowledgeable about their varied significance and use in ritual. For more masks, batiks and outstanding **beads**, a wonderful if expensive place is Kenafro Antiques & Crafts, Olympic House, at the corner of Tubman and Koinange streets, but you'll need to have honed your haggling skills to ruthless perfection.

Buying curios from **strolling vendors** is generally unwise but can occasionally turn up a good deal if you're skilled at bargaining and the vendor's desperate. Furthermore, while you're being distracted on one side, you may be being ripped off on the other. If you're not interested, say *Sitaki biashara* – "I don't want to do business". Steer well clear of the **elephant-hair bracelets**. Although it's unlikely that they really are made from pachyderm (unless they're from Tanzania, where protection orders are less widely enforced), the vendors are quite perversely adamant about their origin – collected, they say, not poached. One bracelet salesmen claimed: "We follow the animal softly and when it goes to sleep we sneak up quietly and cut off the tail hair with scissors." Another, hardly more plausible, vouchsafed: "We follow the animal until it goes to sleep, then all the hairs fall out and we collect them in the morning when it has gone away." In fact, most are made either from plastic, tree root fibres or "captured" telephone lines: one resident pleaded with us to mention this, as they were fed up with their line going dead.

Community craft centres

Nairobi has a number of craft shops with charitable status, or based on development or self-help projects. Although sometimes a little expensive – and you can't bargain – they are worthy of support, and often have unusual and well-made stock (some of which finds its way into the Christmas charity catalogues overseas). Some are a little way out of town, but well worth making special journeys to visit – good tonics if you're suffering from curio shop fatigue.

Kamili Designs, Langata Rd, Karen (Mon–Fri 9am–4.30pm; bus/*matatu* #24, #111, or some #126; ☎02/822313). This is a textile workshop, selling locally designed, hand-printed fabrics. The designs are typically bold and colourful, available both by the metre and in cushions, bedspreads and the like.

Kazuri Beads & Pottery Centre, Mbagathi Ridge, Karen (workshops Mon–Fri 8am–4.30pm, Sat 8am–noon; shop Mon–Sat 8am–4.30pm, Sun 11am–4.30pm; bus/*matatu* #24, #111, or some #126; ☎02/882362). Kazuri, which means "small and beautiful", employs nearly a hundred formerly destitute women, who make an extraordinary variety of handmade jewellery and beads, principally ceramic, and there's also a pottery showroom. You can watch the whole process from shaping and colouring to firing. It's expensive, but the stuff is lovely. They also have outlets at African Heritage.

Maridadi Fabrics, City Stadium roundabout, Landhies/Jogoo Rd (Mon–Fri 8am–5pm; buses #21, #34 or #36; ☎02/554288). Church-based, like Undugu (see below), Maridadi was created in 1966 as an income-generating community project for women in one of Nairobi's oldest slum areas – Pumwani and Shauri Moyo. The main workshop is a delight if you're into making your own clothes. A large screen-printing workshop (on view from the visitors' gallery) produces the wide range of prints for sale in the shop; the bark cloth prints are especially appealing. Bark cloth, a natural weave obtained from beneath the outer bark of certain trees, is soaked, stretched, hammered before use, and was used for clothing by many East African peoples until the end of the nineteenth century. In the district around the Maridadi workshop, there's a huge diversity of enterprises, with two distinctive market areas – Gikomba (clothes) and Landhies Mawe (scrap metal processing) – both recommended. The latter is deafeningly unmistakable, the place to go to get that handmade tin suitcase. Be careful in either area.

Mikono Craft Shop, opposite Ratna Fitness Studio, Gitanga Rd, Kawangware, just north of Dagoretti Corner (☎02/577498; bus #46 or #46B). The outlet of the Jesuit Refugee Service, with well made work (especially beautiful patchwork textiles) from Somalis, Sudanese and, particularly these days, Rwandans.

Ormolu, Chyulu Rd, off Haile Selassie Ave, where it joins Ngong Rd (☎02/727484 or 725366, fax 728283; any Ngong Rd bus or #18 or #61B). An outlet for naturally dyed sisal baskets and mats woven by rural women.

Spinner's Web, 2nd floor, Viking House, Waiyaki Way, Westlands (☎02/440882; any Westlands bus/*matatu*). A large shop, with a Germanic influence, selling a lot of good stuff – crafts, textiles, woollen goods and jewellery, much of it made by self-help groups and individuals, including Meru's Makena Textile Workshop.

Terra Pottery Centre, opposite War Cemetery, Ngong Rd (☎02/567636; any Ngong Rd bus). A pottery shop with a difference: they encourage you to try your hand at casting and turning.

Undugu, Woodvale Grove, Westlands, opposite Westlands produce market (Mon–Fri 8.30am–5pm; any Westlands bus/*matatu*, ☎02/443525). This is the Undugu (fraternity) society's retail outlet, helping raise funds for an expanding list of development and community self-help programmes, notably for the homeless and jobless, young men in particular. With its roots in the church, Undugu is the most vigorous society of its kind in the country and, by promoting co-operation, goes some way to patching up the worst effects of the struggle for existence in Nairobi. The shop sells a good selection of well-priced, high-quality crafts with some more unusual items, such as Ethiopian jewellery, basketwork, and crafts from Congo, Somalia, Tanzania and Uganda. A free booklet about the Undugu society is available and you may be able to have a look around the workshops. They also organize regular guided visits to their slum projects.

Utamaduni Crafts Centre, Bogoni East Rd, between the Ostrich Park and Giraffe Sanctuary, Langata (daily 10am–6pm; bus/*matatu* #24; ☎02/890464). Eighteen individual craft shops in one large house, opened by Richard Leakey in 1991 (a portion of the profits go to the Kenya Wildlife Service). It has everything you might want, much of it made on site or from street-kid projects; quality and prices are high. The attached *Jikoni* restaurant (see p.119) is one of Nairobi's best.

The Maasai Market

If you're after Maasai traditional and tourist gear, the **Maasai Market** (Tues 9am–3pm) is a hot recommendation, also known as "Globe Cinema: or "Tuesday" market. Anything from twenty to fifty Maasai women display their wares on the waste ground beside the roundabout connecting Murang'a Road and Kijabe Street (past the *Meridian Court Hotel*). Assuming that they don't get evicted (as they were from all their previous sites), you'll find prices here well below those in any tourist mart, or even in the Narok/Mara area, with especially good deals on the simpler designs of beaded jewellery, and also on baskets and gourds. You can bargain to as little as ten percent of the sort of prices marked in fancy curio stores, if you've the time and energy. Often, items like nail varnish and cheap watches are helpful for bargaining. However, the market now also attracts rather more aggressive male vendors, which can make for an unpleasant shock early on in a trip. Be sure to buy from a stall rather than them.

If you miss this market, there's a much smaller, "civilized" Maasai crafts market held inside the National Theatre on Harry Thuku Road, opposite the Norfolk Hotel, every Thursday (7am–6pm).

Kariokor Market

A real artisans' market is **Kariokor Market**, between Racecourse Road and Ring Road (bus/*matatu* #4, #6, #7, #14, #30, #32, #40, #42, or #46/46B). This is without question *the* place in Nairobi to buy **sisal baskets** (*vyondo*). Inside and outside the market there are thousands of baskets available, and since many are made here, you can buy just the basket without the leather pieces or straps which raise the price. Long sisal straps can be bought separately for a few shillings. *Vyondo* come in sisal, coloured with natural or artificial dyes, in garish plastic, or in cord manufactured from the bark of the baobab tree. Some of these last baskets are truly exquisite, occasionally quite old, with tiny beads included in the tight weave.

Kariokor (named after the despised wartime "Carrier Corps") is closer to an oriental bazaar than most markets in Kenya, with permanent booths for the traders. Inside, there's as much manufacture and finishing going on as selling – sisal weavers, leather workers, makers of tyre-rubber sandals ("5000-mile shoes", about Ksh100 a pair and surprisingly comfortable), carpenters, toy-makers, tailors, hairdressers, and a row of good, very cheap, amazingly clean eateries, popular at lunchtime with local workers. A number of booths sell vaguely pharmaceutical oddities – snuff, remedies, charms, amulets and so on – where you can pick up anything from feathers to snakeskin. Outside, you'll find the odd African literary gem on the second-hand bookstalls.

General merchandise, clothes, shoes and toys

For everyday **general merchandise stores**, the eastern part of the City Market district is the most worthwhile area. **Biashara Street** (*biashara* means commerce) is the street for fabrics and the best place to buy tents and mosquito nets (see "Listings" on p.146). For cheap and not-so-cheap imports, the hangar-like Freemark Pavilion in south **Uhuru Park** has hundreds of stalls. There used to be a thriving black market trade on **Tubman Road** and **Kigali Road**, but these were brutally cleared away by city council *askaris* in 1997–98, presumably to make way for another high-rise or car park. The upper part of Moi Avenue is Nairobi's busiest ordinary shopping street, all colonnaded shop-fronts and antiquated name-boards, fun to wander past. You'll find clothes shops all over, with high-fashion outlets on Standard and Kaunda streets, and more down-to-earth gear on Kenyatta Avenue, Moi Avenue and Kimathi Street. Abdulla Fazal in the Jubilee Exchange House on Mama Ngina Street has a good selection of locally made clothes. Good value **footwear** is available from the African Boot Co, on Moi Avenue opposite Bookpoint, and even cheaper footwear at Miniprice Footwear Supermarket on River Road, by the *Bull Café*. If you're buying **toys**, the best items are locally made wire-and-fabric confections – cars, bicycles, flapping birds – which are sometimes beautiful works of art. Scouring the out-of-centre markets will find you some, but the best are usually made at home for sons and nephews and not for sale. The best general toy shop, full of standard imports, is Hobby Centre on Kaunda Street in the Jubilee Insurance House.

Shopping malls

Nairobi now has the dubious distinction of having more **shopping malls** than any other African city, barring those in South Africa – over twenty – providing a hassle-free environment for getting on with ordinary shopping and office business. You'll find most of them stuffed into more affluent suburbs like Westlands and Parklands. They cater to the expatriate and more affluent Kenyan markets and many include banks, travel agents, specialist food suppliers and an assortment of cafés and restaurants. If you have a young family, they're very useful. The following is a selection:

Esso Plaza, Muthaiga Rd, Muthaiga. This boasts a good health-food shop, a bagel bakery and the tacky *Celebrities Nightclub*.

Lenana Forest Centre, half a kilometre before the racecourse on Ngong Rd. Notable for a number of great delicatessens and French-style *charcuteries*.

The Mall, Westlands (buses #21, #25, #29, #30 and many others). Shops and offices includes a branch Let's Go Travel, a sports shop, a French bakery, ice-cream parlour, a 7/11-style convenience store and numerous fashion and clothing stores.

Sarit Centre, Westlands (buses as for The Mall). A big, established complex, with over sixty shops and offices, including a dry cleaner, a health-food shop, a watch repairer, a post office and a large new branch of the Textbook Centre.

Yaya Centre, Argwings Kodhek Rd, Hurlingham (bus/*matatu* #41, #46/46B or #56). Escalators, fountains and all. There's a good cheese shop here, a useful newsagent with a wide selection of mainly British magazines, a bookshop, supermarket, health-food shop, French bakery, post office, chemist, and a useful "for sale" notice board.

Cultural venues and art galleries

After years of stagnation, the Nairobi arts scene seems finally to be finding a rhythm of its own, independent of the tourist market which had previously driven much of it. The last few years have seen a very positive and encouraging proliferation of arts and cultural activities which, though still modest by international standards, are infectiously energetic and stimulating, and well worth discovering: you'll learn much.

The new **Mzizi Arts Center**, 6th floor, Sonalux House, Moi Avenue (PO Box 48955; ☎02/245364, or 02/792469 after hours; fax 245366, 215905 or 785494, *sanaa@insightkenya.com*) is the first port of call, and has become the scene's main focus, with a dedicated nucleus of writers, artists and musicians staging exhibitions, concerts, happenings, and innovative theatrical productions often by young Kenyan playwrights. Their offices, though cramped and far from ideal (they'd like to move if they get funding), are a hive of activity and a great source of information and contacts, and also contain an impromptu gallery of modern art and sculpture. Mzizi also publish the fortnightly *Sanaa* freesheet, carrying arts and food reviews, news articles and general information: you can pick up a copy at their office, or at Kenya Cinema on Moi Avenue, the Japanese and French cultural centres, British Council and Goethe-Institut (addresses below), or at the Professional Centre theatre (see "Stage" on p.124). Annual membership of their Nyungu Cultural Club (Ksh4500, or for Ksh2000 students) gives you discounts and free entry on some performances, but is more a way of supporting their activities: the club organizes highly recommended monthly "Sigana" performances (Ksh300) at the centre which combine narration, song, music, dance, chant, ritual, mask, movement, banter and praise poetry.

The two other central places which you might not otherwise notice are the **French Cultural** and **Cooperation Centre** in the Maison Française (PO Box 49415; ☎02/336263, fax 336253), and the **Goethe-Institut** in Maendeleo House (PO Box 49468; ☎02/224640, fax 340770), both at the top of Loita Street near Uhuru Highway. The Goethe-Institut puts on art exhibitions and concerts, both German and Kenyan, and has a monthly programme of subtitled German films. The French Cultural Centre has an equally dynamic programme, offering a space for Kenyan dance and theatre as well as staging events and activities derived from France. Long the most active cultural and intellectual forums in Nairobi, they're well worth checking out during your stay. Other similar venues, with less frequent events, include the British Council, ICEA Building, Kenyatta Avenue (☎02/334855, fax 02/334854); the Italian Cultural Institute, Prudential Building, Wabera Street (☎02/340966); and the Japan African Culture Interchange, Kamburu Drive (☎02/566262). See also the section "Film, theatre and casinos" pp.123–125.

As to permanent exhibition spaces, most of the "galleries" scattered around the central business district are commercial and entirely tourist-orientated, heavy on batiks, *makonde* wood sculpture and paintings of the elephants-in-a-dustbowl school. The only **art galleries** deserving the name (other than the National Archives, p.105) are **Gallery Watatu** at Lonrho House on Standard Street (Mon–Sat 9am–6pm, Sun 10am–5pm; PO Box 41855; ☎02/228737, 225666), and the **Paa Ya Paa Arts Centre**, way out of town on Ridgeways Road, off Kiambu Road, Ridgeways (☎02/512421, *stern-jm@maf.org*; see "Nairobi outskirts" map on p.154). Gallery Watatu is dedicated to the development and promotion of contemporary African art, mostly painting – exhibitions change monthly, and they've stacks of work for sale at the back. It is also the venue for occasional "alternative" events. If you're at all artistically minded, missing Paa Ya Paa ("the Antelope Rises") would be a great shame. Begun in 1965, this suffered a disastrous fire in 1997 which gutted most of its galleries and destroyed countless paintings and sculptures. As the undaunted and ever-charming Njau family say: "the love we were shown after the fire was amazing and helped us back on our feet." Starting over more or less from scratch, the idea is now to create an artistic space where performers, artists and poets can meet, work, exhibit, live and be inspired. Mrs Njau teaches piano, and plays in the "Bush Bach" ensemble, an eclectic fusion of classical piano and African drum rhythms. There's usually an artist or two in residence, occasional workshops, and many paintings hung or propped up all over the place (some for sale) as well as a few sculptures which survived the fire. Set in overgrown woodland and banana trees, the clutter is wonderfully soothing, as is the informal atmosphere. Essentially, it's up to you to suggest what you'd like to do. Get to Ridgeways Road by #100 *matatu*, and walk for five minutes, turning left after Ridgeways Supermarket.

Eating and drinking

Nairobi has no shortage of **eating places**. Their diversity is one of the city's best points and eating out is an evening pastime which never dulls. Admittedly, African food is generally not highlighted in the more expensive restaurants. What stands out in these places, gastronomically speaking, is a range of Asian and European food, and spectacular quantities of meat.

This bias isn't really a problem. You can save money *and* eat African and Asian food in hundreds of unpretentious places, though to catch the cheap eats you'll have to go out early: by 8pm most of the bargain restaurants have finished the day's food. And if you want a burger or a pizza or a huge steak or totally vegetarian salad, it's all available.

With some exceptions, the following listings are restricted to the city centre; but Nairobi, including the suburbs, has hundreds of restaurants with new ones opening every month. **Westlands**, in particular, is a culinary growth area, with every street and shopping mall containing a handful (we've mentioned a few of the best).

Breakfasts

Get up for breakfast. It's the only time of the day to really enjoy *mandaazi* and *chai*. You can get fried eggs, sausages and bread in many cheap places, too (look for Swahili menus saying something like *Mayai kukaanga* or sometimes "Eggs fly"). None of it is healthy, or aims to do anything but inject you with hot calories, but it tastes good.

You can get an excellent **continental breakfast** at the *Goldstar Restaurant* (see p.118). For something more hearty, most of the *hotelis* around River Road serve up stacks of well-prepared eggs, sausages, beans and toast. The big hotels do lavish breakfast **buffets**, and, if you wake up in a certain frame of mind, you might go down to the *Hilton Hotel* for theirs: it's pretty highly rated. Alternatively, both the *Meridian Court's* and the *Ambassadeur's* are also good, and cheaper (around Ksh300). For something simpler, all the cafés and snack bars listed below cater for early-birds, as do *Pasara* and *Calypso* (see "Salads", p.123).

FINDING RESTAURANTS ON OUR MAPS

To avoid cluttering up the "Commercial Centre and River Road area" map on p.88, we've omitted those **restaurants** located in commercial buildings which are already marked on the map (eg *Supermac* in Kimathi House). Those not in commercial buildings have been keyed using letters. Restaurants located out of the centre on other maps are noted accordingly, together with directions on how to get there by bus or *matatu* (the relevant stops are listed in the box on p.90).

STREET FOOD

Strictly speaking, **street food** is limited to **roasted corncobs** (which are so tough and take so long to eat you'll feel you've had a whole meal) and **fruit**. But places like the shacks near the Country Bus Station can fill you up with tea and *mandaazi* for next to nothing. On Haile Selassie Avenue by the Agip Garage, women cook up *githeri* which you eat squatting down on the pavement. The best place, though, is **Kariokor Market**, which has an enclosure containing dozens of *chai, ugali* and *nyama choma* joints vying for business; the meat and fish all totally fresh and sizzling outside on charcoal grills, as reggae music blares: prime rump steak, brains or sweetmeats, it's all there, and if you're thirsty, several dodgy bars oblige. It's a great little place.

Cheap eateries and snacks

The **River Road area** has all the very cheap places with one *hoteli* (cheap restaurant) after another on most streets, most dishing up standard fare of chips or *ugali* with fish or fried chicken. At any of the following you should be able to eat hugely for Ksh200, often for much less. The following are all found on the "Commercial Centre and River Road area" map, p.88.

Ali Baba (A), Murang'a Rd, opposite *Meridian Court Hotel*. Superficially Lebanese (some kebabs, falafel and kibbé), but popular mainly for its filling lunchtime mini-buffets (Ksh280).

Al Mansura B&L (25), Munyu Rd (open from 6am). Good for *mandaazi* and *chai* breakfasts, and simple but tasty standard Kenyan fare at other times (*ugali*, stews, and goat-meat *nyama choma*).

Benrose (R), Gaberone Rd. Busy, bustling and *fast* food. Gorgeous *chai* and samosas.

City Fry's (C), Murang'a Rd. Excellent stand'n'eat fish'n'chip shop.

Fameland, Duruma Rd. Good solid meals (notably *nyama choma* with *ugali*) with excellent music, sometimes live, in this unusually good "day and night club".

Ismailia's (I), River Rd. Very inexpensive, welcoming and comfortable, with a good vegetarian selection.

Kenchic Inn (K), corner of Moktar Daddah St/Muindi Mbingu St. No-frills halal fish and chicken bar, busier than most and therefore fresher.

Malindi Dishes (S), Gaberone Rd. Mainly snacks – less intimate than *Benrose*, more like a cafeteria but still welcoming.

Paris Metro (Y), Mfangano St. Yes, there is a reason – the tiled vault inside is supposed to resemble a metro station, but apart from that it's entirely on the other side of the channel: chips, fried chicken, sausages and occasionally fish to take away.

Pre Area Eating House (J), Duruma Rd. Snacks, stews and booze: great for breakfast the night after.

Reata Fish & Chips (Q), corner of Taveta and Accra Rd. A renowned purveyor.

Supermac, Kimathi House, Kimathi St, next to the *Oakwood Hotel*. Quality this ain't, but it is one of the cheapest places in the city centre: feast on fluorescent mushy peas, chips and soggy burgers.

Sunrise Lodge (13), Latema Rd, across from the *Iqbal Hotel*. Standard *hoteli* fare in a reasonably bright, workaday atmosphere. Take a table at the front and watch street life on Latema Rd.

Sun Sweet Centre (D), Ngariama Rd. Vegetarian Indian place, bright and appetizing, with tempting sweets and – for once – open till late.

Swara, Imenti House, Tom Mboya St (daily 7.30am–10pm). Cheap and reliable for proper meals (steaks, fish, stews; meals around Ksh200), with good service in a slightly tattered dining room full of velvet-upholstered chairs and dusty textile lampshades. Popular with office workers.

Zaïqa New Flora (O), Tsavo Rd. Used to be extremely popular among locals and travellers alike for very good budget meals with tandoori bread, but the sometimes terrible service is a drawback. The dining room upstairs is more refined. Open for lunch and early dinner.

Cafés, fast food joints and ice-cream parlours

You'll find most cafés and snack bars as well as a rash of McDonald's-style fast food joints (at Stateside prices) situated in the upmarket business district **north of City Hall Square**. Most are closed on Sundays after lunch. Passion juice is widely advertised these days, but check whether it's fresh or factory-pressed or, worse, just syrup and water. All the following are on the "Commercial Centre and River Road area" map, p.88.

Bel Canto, Bruce House, Standard St, opposite *Akasaka*. Not exactly gastronomic heaven, but filling and relatively cheap by city-centre standards (meals around Ksh300, cheaper snacks).

Coffee House (U), Mama Ngina St (closed Sat pm & Sun). The Kenya Coffee Board's café, and the best cup in town. Faded murals on the walls hark back to a not-so-distant era of African coffee estate labourers, white overseers and continental café loungers. You can buy the house blends by the kilo for something like a quarter of what you'd pay at home (call in before flying home).

Express Bakery (V), Standard St, next to Let's Go Travel. Always crowded at lunchtime but otherwise a good place to sit and recoup your energy.

Goldstar (M), corner of Koinange and Moktar Daddah streets (Mon–Sat 7am–10pm, Sun 7am–3pm). Does excellent breakfasts and cheap filling meals at other times.

Hooters, Hamilton House, Kauna St. Very smart, chrome and wood café verging on fast-food joint (milk shakes, burgers, pizzas), with music videos on the monitors. Overpriced to keep out the rabble, and good service.

K&A Coffee House (W), corner of Standard St and Koinange St. Next door to K&A supermarket, a simple little cafeteria with good *brioches* and coffee. Also good for breakfast and lunch.

Kahawa Coffee House, Fedha Towers, Kaunda St. Crowded, notably upmarket, and great for breakfast – fried eggs, milkshakes, excellent samosas and iced tea.

Kencake Coffee Shop, Jubilee Exchange House, Kaunda St. Good for ice-creams.

Nandos, Union Towers, corner of Mama Ngina St and Moi Ave. Three fast-food emporia in one: pizzas, Portuguese snacks, and fried chicken, with a large and spotless dining room upstairs overlooking the busy junction. Same prices as European equivalents, but still busy. Free drinking water. There's also a branch next door to the *New Florida* nightclub on Koinange St.

Perida Café (L), Dubois Rd. An oddity for River Road district: freshly-made Viennese rolls, custard pastries and Black Forest gateau.

Plaza Café, lower ground floor, Barclays Plaza (closed Sun). Spotless and swish café in the similar mall, with good fast food, decent cappuccinos, espressos and Irish coffees.

Sno-Cream (G), corner of Koinange St and Monrovia St (daily until 9.30pm). Rather run down but still the best parlour in town, especially after a hot day's walkabout, with amusing retro decor depicting various ice cream fantasies – most of them available.

Steers (H) & **(Z)**, branches at Muindi Mbingu St (opposite Jeevanjee Gardens), and at the junction of Tom Mboya St and Ronald Ngala streets (both to 9pm). Also at the Apic Centre in Westlands. Halal meets *McDonald's*, yet this potential powder-keg mismatch works surprisingly well. The Islamic South African fast-food chain's first venture into Kenya offers the usual junk food, plus toasted sandwiches, salads, milk shakes, juices (try the passion) and great toffee ice-cream.

Restaurants

The following listings are mostly for more upmarket eating houses, at some of which it's a good idea to reserve a table (many are closed one day a week, often Sun or Tues, and most are closed 2.30–6.30pm). Prices, without drinks, should normally work out at around Ksh400–500 a head, though you can certainly eat more cheaply at several of the curry houses. In the more international league, specializing mainly in meat, prices are higher (say Ksh500–800 a head) and you'll pay up to Ksh1500 at fancy establishments. The city has famously good beef and other fleshy delights so, if you enjoy it, indulge while you're here, as the rest of the country is much less well endowed. All are either marked on the maps noted or can be found in relation to the buildings they're in. You can get to **Westlands** by bus or *matatu* #21, #23, #30, #104 or #119.

"African", Ethiopian and Swahili

Many hotel restaurants offer an "African night" or lunchtime buffet once a week. These include Tuesday nights at the *Fairview, Utalii Hotel*, and *Nairobi Safari Club*, Tuesday lunches at the *Green Corner Restaurant* (see "live music venues"), Wednesday evenings at the *Stanley Hotel*, and Friday evenings at *Hotel Inter-Continental*. The *Suncourt Inn* and the *Solace Hotel* both do weekday lunchtime buffets, and the *Hilton* has an eat-all-you-can *nyama choma* barbecue every lunchtime at its poolside restaurant for Ksh795, with live music Sundays.

Addis Ababa Ethiopian Restaurant ("Westlands" map, p.98), Woodvale Place, Woodvale Grove (☎02/447321). More upmarket Ethiopian, with attentive service, fantastic food, and occasional live entertainment.

Beneve (X) ("Commercial Centre and River Road area" map, p.88), corner of Koinange St and Standard St (lunchtimes only). Off putting from the outside, but clean within. This is a cheap self-service joint popular with office workers, serving well-made Kenyan dishes: fried or stewed tilapia fish, *ugali* and beef stew, *sukuma wiki* and other greens. Under Ksh200.

Blue Nile Ethiopian Restaurant ("Greater Nairobi" map, p.82), Argwings Kodhek Rd, Hurlingham (no phone; daily; buses #41, #46/46B or #56). Very pleasant, laid-back place, with a good range and a helpful "mix dish" where you can try everything out for Ksh280. Try their *tej* (a mead-like Ethiopian honey beer). Steer clear if you don't like chilli.

Daas Ethiopian Restaurant ("Greater Nairobi" map, p.82), Lenana Rd, near the Chinese and Nigerian embassies (☎02/712106; daily; *matatu* #46 to Argwings Kodhek/Woodlands Rd, then walk 200m up Woodlands and turn right). A bit of a revelation if you thought you'd eaten traditional African food. The basic staple *njera* "bread" does take some getting used to, but the spicy overall effect of *doro wat* (chicken in a spicy sauce; *wat* means sauce) or *anye* (spinach, cheese and spices), washed down with copious quantities of *tej*, is a fine culinary experience. Food is cooked on your own table's *jiko* (stove). A little costly, but recommended.

Garden Square Restaurant ("Commercial Centre and River Road area" map, p.88), Garden Square, City Hall Way (☎02/226474). Relaxed spacious place, which used to have live bands (and may again in future). Cheap African buffets lunchtimes, sometimes evenings. Safe parking.

Illiki Coffee House, at the *Ambassadeur Hotel* ("Commercial Centre and River Road area" map, p.88). Pleasant Lamu-style decor on the ground floor, with a small selection of quasi-traditional Kenyan dishes: try the Maasai *mshikaki*. Also good for breakfast.

Jikoni, Utamaduni Crafts Centre ("Nairobi outskirts" map, p.154), Bogoni East Rd, Langata (daily 10am–6pm; bus/*matatu* #24; ☎02/890921). Difficult to categorize, but no matter: calm, relaxed and classy, this is one of the best in Nairobi, with an excellent selection of mouth-watering delicacies from both Africa and the USA: the Zanzibari red snapper and coconut soup is wonderful, as is the rich chewy fudge brownie for dessert. Good fresh salads, take-away pizzas and a vegetarian selection, too, and the prices are surprisingly reasonable. Weekend BBQs.

Makuti Park ("Greater Nairobi" map, p.82), South B Shopping Centre, Mchumbi Rd, South "B" (☎02/558012; *matatus* from railway stage to South "B"). Mellow and entirely free of touristy panderings, this famous music venue has recently started concentrating on Kenyan food: simple, cheap and very traditional, including dried meat (*aliya*), fire-dried meat (*athola*), liver, *kienyeji* and coastal Swahili dishes. There's also a children's "fun corner".

Simmers ("Commercial Centre and River Road area" map, p.88), corner Kenyatta Ave, Muindi Mbingu St and Standard St (daily 7am–midnight). Large and laid-back, central Nairobi's only *nyama choma*-style joint (and so very popular), with an "African buffet" for Ksh350, and a live band (Destinée) Sunday lunchtime. Discos Wed, Fri & Sat nights.

Chinese, Thai and Korean

The following are closed Sat unless stated: ring to check.

Bangkok Restaurant, Rank Xerox House ("Westlands" map, p.98), Parklands Rd (☎02/751311). Expensive – fine, as long as you don't expect it to taste like real Thai.

China Jiangsu, Soin Arcade ("Westlands" map, p.98), Westlands Rd (☎02/446700). This has all the authentic dishes including jellyfish, shark's fin and green onion pancakes as well as the old sweet and sour favourites. Reasonably priced.

Hong Kong (F) ("Commercial Centre and River Road area" map, p.88), Kenya House, Koinange St (☎02/228612; closed Mon). Excellent Cantonese, related to the *Hong Kong* in Mombasa, though not particularly friendly.

Little China, Rank Xerox House ("Westlands" map, p.98), Muthithi Rd (daily to 10pm). Chinese take-away, under Ksh500 a head, can deliver around Westlands.

Meridian Mandarin, 5th floor, *Meridian Court Hotel* ("Commercial Centre and River Road area" map, p.88; ☎02/333916). Usual high quality with a very affordable "business lunch" for around Ksh320.

Pagoda, 1st floor, Shankardass House ("Commercial Centre and River Road area" map, p.88), Moi Ave (☎02/338205; daily). Highly recommended Szechuan cooking, but pricy.

Rickshaw Chinese Restaurant, 1st floor, Fedha Towers ("Commercial Centre and River Road area" map, p.88), Kaunda St (☎02/223604). A pleasant Cantonese restaurant with good service and not unduly expensive. The food's nothing special, though. Open daily.

Seoul Garden Restaurant ("Greater Nairobi" map, p.82), Kamburu Rd, off Ngong Rd (☎02/720292; Ngong Rd *matatus*). Tasty Korean barbecued meat, with good salads and vegetables. Around Ksh800.

Siam Thai, 1st floor, Unga House ("Westlands" map, p.98), Muthithi Rd (☎02/751727). Run by an Indian family in love with Thai food, and it shows – it's probably the best of Nairobi's three Thai restaurants, despite its uninspired decor. The use of herbs and spices is subtle and sometimes unusual: try the tangy *Tom Yam Goong* soup (with lemon grass and coriander), spare ribs (plenty of garlic), or *Larb Gai*: spiced minced chicken with onions, mint leaves and lemon grass. Food around Ksh750, cheaper lunchtime set menus under Ksh600. Licensed and open daily.

Silver Sun (N) ("Commercial Centre and River Road area" map, p.88), Loita St, opposite Kenindia House (☎02/330858). Good Szechuan and a reasonable selection of Thai dishes. Expensive in the evenings but a bargain at lunchtime.

Tin Tin, Kenyatta Conference Centre ("Central Nairobi" map, p.102), entrance off Harambee Ave (☎02/229093). Heavy on the monosodium glutamate, with cheapish business lunches (around Ksh500) but severely overpriced à la carte at other times. Good service, awful muzak.

Winners Pavilion, at *Safari Park Hotel* ("Nairobi outskirts" map, p.154), 14km up Thika Rd (☎02/802493–7; taxi costs Ksh800, or bus/*matatu* #45, #137, #145, #160, #237). One of seven equally good restaurants in the vast Thika Road complex, with surprisingly affordable Szechuan cuisine.

French

Alan Bobbe's Bistro, Cianda House ("Commercial Centre and River Road area" map, p.88), Koinange St (☎02/224945 or 226027; Sat dinner only, Sun closed). The manicured poodle logo says it all: a welcome touch of humorous absurdity, with your first impression of high camp pretentiousness soon belied by the genuine interest in seriously good food. And the sheep's brains are actually quite nice. One of the oldest restaurants in the city (since 1962); still devoutly French and devotedly patronized. Around Ksh1200 for dinner with wine is normal, but you'd pay four times more in a European equivalent. Lunchtimes are a deal cheaper (around Ksh650). Recommended.

The Claremont, at the *Lord Errol*, the Village Market ("Nairobi outskirts" map, p.154), off Limuru Rd (weekends only; *matatu* #108, #114 and others to Limuru, get off at the "Village Market"; ☎02/521308). The better of the two restaurants here (the other is the *Conservatory*, open daily), dominated by a hexagonal stained glass ceiling featuring two women, one black, the other white. A roaring fireplace, candles and heavy silver cutlery complete the scene. Ostentatious, but pulled off with grace, style and panache. Both food and service are excellent, and there's a fine selection of imported wines to go with the classic French menu (snails, and even rock lobster, cooked with wine, mushrooms, mustard and cream, and served in its shell). The bill, presented on a silver platter, is bound to be hefty (Ksh2200–5000, including wine).

Zéphyr, 1st floor, Rank Xerox House ("Westlands" map, p.98), Parklands Rd (closed Mon & Sun dinner; ☎02/750055). A shade cheaper than *Alan Bobbé's* and still cordon bleu, with a Japanese chef who does some tasty hybrid cooking. Strong on seafood. Under Ksh1000.

Greek

Kebabish Centre, Highridge Shopping/Diamond Plaza ("Greater Nairobi" map, p.82), 3rd Parklands Ave (*matatu* from Latema Rd opposite the *Iqbal* to "Aga Khan"). Just the place for a Saturday night kebab before throwing back the beers.

Indian

Anghiti, New Rehema House (off the "Westlands" map, p.98), Rhapta Rd (☎02/441258). The decor is a bit stark, but this newcomer is, along with the *Haandi*, Westland's leading subcontinental gastronomic experience. The *anghiti* is a traditional Indian clay stove which apparently keeps the aroma of foods cooked in it. The speciality is *Raan Anghiti*, whole mutton leg marinated overnight in garlic, ginger, vinegar and chillies before being baked. No beef or pork.

Cheers Bhajia Hotel, under the *New Kenya Lodge* ((6); "Commercial Centre and River Road area" map, p.88), River Rd. Popular south Indian vegetarian: huge meals and small bills.

Curry Pot (B) ("Commercial Centre and River Road area" map, p.88), Monrovia St (☎02/251403; daily). Cheap and always busy, serving mainly chicken and tandoori.

Haandi, The Mall ("Westlands" map, p.98), Westlands (☎02/448294). Generally considered Nairobi's best (north) Indian restaurant, if a little expensive (Ksh1000 per head), specializing in masalas. Skip breakfast to make room.

Khyber, at *Meridian Court Hotel* ("Commercial Centre and River Road area" map, p.88), Murang'a Rd. Excellent and very reasonably priced Mughlai cuisine, with good lunchtime set menus (around Ksh300).

Mayur/Supreme Hotel (E) ("Commercial Centre and River Road area" map, p.88), corner of Keekorok Rd and Ngariama Lane (daily noon–2.30pm & 7–9.30pm; ☎02/225241 or 331586). South Indian, and the only certified vegetarian restaurant in the city centre, and so delicious and well presented that to miss eating at the *Mayur* would be a shame. The eat-as-much-as-you-like buffet upstairs (lunch Ksh260, dinner Ksh280 – an absolute bargain, even with a large tip expected) is worth starving all day for. Downstairs, there's a less lavish choice, and you have to put up with maddeningly chirpy *muzak*, but they have substantially the same dishes, and also a good selection of sweets by the kilo. Takeaway also available. The only downside is the rather somnolent atmosphere.

Minar, Stanbic Bank Building ("Commercial Centre and River Road area" map, p.88), Banda St (☎02/330168). Slick, north Indian *Mughlai* with a light Middle Eastern influence, such as kebabs, and a touch of Goan, too, and a first-class reputation. Alcohol available. An à la carte splash costs around Ksh700, and there's a lunchtime buffet for Ksh470. There's a branch in the Yaya Centre, Hurlingham (☎02/561676), with occasional Bhangra nights. Open daily. Recommended.

Nargis Kapuri Pan ("Westlands" map, p.98), next to "Global Museum" Yoga Centre, Parklands Rd. Small cheap meals, mainly in chicken tikka, kebabs and takeaway. Pleasant tables outside, and some colourful child-sized tables and chairs. Safe parking. Daily 1–3pm & 6–10pm.

Slush's Happy Eater, Kalyan House ("Commercial Centre and River Road area" map, pp.88–89), Tubman Rd (☎02/220745; daily). Indian vegetarian, with a good variety of snacks and takeaways. There's also a branch in Diamond Plaza, Parklands ("Greater Nairobi" map, p.82).

Taj (P) ("Commercial Centre and River Road area" map, p.88), Taveta Rd. Very cheap and filling; good birianis. Open daily.

Top of the Town, 2nd floor, Hamilton House ("Commercial Centre and River Road area" map, p.88), corner of Wabera and Kaunda St. One of the few places open late, combining Indian and Chinese food with a live but none-too-exciting band. Moderately priced. Evenings only from 9.30pm.

Italian

Bon Appetit, City Hall ("Commercial Centre and River Road area" map, p.88), Mama Ngina/Wabera St (☎02/217851). In the City Hall garden courtyard. By no means exclusively Italian, and not the greatest cuisine, but wholesome, plentiful and pleasantly relaxing. Mon–Sat 7am–10pm, Sun 7am–3pm.

La Galleria, at the *International Casino* ("Greater Nairobi" map, p.82), Westlands Rd, off Museum Hill (bus #21, #23 or #119; ☎02/744474). Likes to consider itself classy, and is pleasant enough, but the *Toona Tree* in the same complex is much nicer. Mon–Fri lunch and dinner, Sat lunch only, closed Sun.

La Scala Pizzeria, Phoenix House Arcade ("Commercial Centre and River Road area" map, p.88), Standard St/Kenyatta Ave (☎02/332130). Much cheaper than *Trattoria*, with a simple, uncluttered interior. Pizzas are inexpensive (under Ksh200), small but perfectly formed, salads are large and fresh. Good service, and the lunchtime specials are a bargain. Daily until midnight. Recommended.

Toona Tree, at the *International Casino* ("Greater Nairobi" map, p.82), Westlands Rd, off Museum Hill (☎02/744477; daily; bus #21, #23 or #119). Very pleasant above-ground, open-air place, set among the boughs of the eponymous tree, and majoring on seafood. Playground for kids. Regular live music.

Trattoria (T) ("Commercial Centre and River Road area" map, p.88), corner of Wabera St and Kaunda St (☎02/340855). Growing more pretentious with age, this still gets enthusiastic notices from low-budget travellers having a splurge, though it's sometimes too busy for its own good (at lunchtime, full meals only). The pasta dishes and pizzas are the real thing and the cakes and ice cream – when they come – magnificent. No credit cards. Daily until midnight.

Japanese

Akasaka, Six-Eighty Hotel Building ("Commercial Centre and River Road area" map, p.88), Standard St (☎02/220299). Without doubt one of Nairobi's best restaurants, with its uncluttered Zen-like interior, impeccable service and food. Its "lunchboxes" at around Ksh500 are good value, especially *sashimi* (raw fish). Highly recommended. Closed Sun.

Chiyo, at *Safari Park Hotel* ("Nairobi outskirts" map, p.154), 14km up Thika Rd (taxi costs Ksh800, or bus/*matatu* #45, #137, #145, #160, #237; ☎02/802493–7). Blend steel tables, Chef Song and his minions, several cleavers and a slightly unreal atmosphere, and you get perfect *teppanyaki*-style Japanese food (whatever that is). It's surprisingly good value, although the taxi there and back (about Ksh800 one way) will add to the night's folly.

Shogun ("Greater Nairobi" map, p.82), Argwings Kodhek Rd, behind the *Blue Nile* restaurant, Hurlingham (☎02/716080; closed Sun lunch; buses #41, 46/46B or 56). Similarly excellent, slightly less formal than *Akasaka* and slightly cheaper (evening meals from Ksh750), though dreadful muzak does rather spoil the atmosphere. Their *sushi* is excellent. A huge range of dishes. Reservations advisable for traditional Japanese "rooms". Recommended.

Mainly fish

Stavrose, Mezzanine floor, Postbank House ("Commercial Centre and River Road area" map, p.88), Market Lane (☎02/335107 or 728157). A little-known posh fish restaurant, famed among those in the know for its tilapia fish, cooked any way you want it. They also do good salads. Expensive.

Tamarind, National Bank Building ("Central Nairobi" map, p.102), Harambee Ave, between Extelcoms and the bombed Cooperative Bank House (☎02/338959, fax 724734). If you can cope with the location next to the August 7 bomb site, this is Nairobi's largest, best and most expensive seafood restaurant. Highly rated. Reservations essential. Daily Mon–Sat, Sun dinner only.

Mainly meat

Angus Steak House, Uchumi House ("Commercial Centre and River Road area" map, p.88), Aga Khan Walk (☎02/339295 or 224306). Excellent steaks, salad bar and beer for around Ksh350.

Carnivore ("Nairobi outskirts" map, p.154), Langata Rd towards the National Park entrance (☎02/501775, fax 501739, *tamcnv@africaonline.co.ke*; buses/*matatus* #15, #24, #31, #34, #125, #126 all pass the entrance road, from where it's a one-kilometre walk – overall much easier by taxi). Grossly named and yes, there is a connection – endless supplies of the fauna you thought was carefully protected, served charcoal-grilled. The game meat comes largely from private farms, so they say. The all-you-can-eat menu (lunch Ksh885, dinner Ksh985) includes impala, giraffe, zebra, ostrich, crocodile, although midweek fare is heavier on less exotic sausages and chicken wing. A meal here has become part of every package itinerary and it's often tacked onto the tour outfits' excursions to Nairobi National Park. It's touristy – with discos at the end of the week and at weekends in the adjoining *Simba Saloon* – but very few people seem to dislike it. There is good a vegetarian buffet, too, and on Saturday afternoons you can get rid of the kids at their Funland which features fairground, donkey and camel rides, games, magic shows, face-painting – enough to keep them happy for a few hours. It's debatable whether the nearby 500-metre Grand-Prix Karting circuit (Wed–Sun; ☎02/501758) aids or hinders digestion. See also "Live music venues", p.128. Daily noon–3pm & 7–10.30pm.

Nyama Choma Ranch, at *Safari Park Hotel* ("Nairobi outskirts" map, p.154), 14km up Thika Rd (☎02/802561; taxi costs Ksh800, or bus/*matatu* #45, #137, #145, #160, #237). At once classy and tacky, with perfectly grilled food served an assortment of dancers and wildlife videos to keep you entertained. Better value than *Carnivore*, but you'll need a taxi to get back at night.

Porterhouse, KCS House ("Commercial Centre and River Road area" map, p.88), Mama Ngina St (☎02/221829). Great steaks any way you want them.

Professional Centre Restaurant ("Central Nairobi" map, p.102), Parliament Rd (☎02/220014; closed Sun). Wide choice of well-prepared steaks, as well as a number of decent vegetarian dishes. In the same building as the Phoenix Players (see "Film, theatre and casinos").

Red Bull, 1st floor, Transnational Plaza ("Commercial Centre and River Road area" map, p.88), Mama Ngina St (☎02/228045). A very 1970s German/Swiss "theme" restaurant, now aiming more upmarket. Wonderful steaks, game meat, seafood and vegetarian selection. Dinner only Sat & Sun.

Rib Shack ("Greater Nairobi" map, p.82), 1km up Kiambu Rd, Muthaiga North (☎02/512439; get there by taxi or *matatu* #100). An upmarket *nyama choma* joint (and disco palace at night; see below), cheaper than *Carnivore*, and there's a play area to dump your kids in.

Salads

Calypso, Bruce House ("Commercial Centre and River Road area" map, p.88), entry from Standard St or Kaunda St (☎02/501519). Full of smart young business types. Pancakes and waffles, and a fresh salad buffet. Mon–Sat 8am–5pm

Pasara, 2nd Mezzanine floor, Lonrho House ("Commercial Centre and River Road area" map, p.88), Standard St (☎02/338247). Delicious lunches, including sandwiches, muffins and pancakes. Mon–Fri.

Zanzebar, 5th floor, Kenya Cinema Plaza ("Commercial Centre and River Road area" map, p.88), Moi Ave (☎02/222568). Quiet, lunchtime getaway with an economical salad buffet and KTN television and soft rock in the background. Famous for its "twelve-inch hot dogs". Lively bar in the evening and sometimes live bands. Daily.

Film, theatre and casinos

Nairobi has twelve **cinemas**, including two drive-ins. **Theatre** in the city is gradually improving, with a number of active stage venues and a dedicated local acting community.

Screen

The twin-screen 20th Century on Mama Ngina Street (☎02/338070; two screens), the Nairobi, in Uchumi House, Nkrumah Lane just off Harambee Avenue (☎02/241614 or 338058), and the Kenya Cinema on Moi Avenue (☎02/226982; two screens) screen fairly recent mainstream releases – usually blockbusters or award winners – when they can get them. Other movie theatres tend to show kung fu, vintage James Bond, old Westerns and, of course, Hindi and Punjabi movies which you don't need to understand to enjoy – the Fox Drive-In on the Thika Road (☎02/802293) and the Belle-Vue Drive-In (☎02/505779) on the Mombasa Road have gone over pretty well exclusively to the genre. The Embassy (☎02/225385) and the Odeon (☎02/222030), both on Latema Road near the *Iqbal Hotel*, are cheap fleapit dives with dire sound and film quality, and actually much more fun than the blander upmarket screens. Weekend matinees here are packed. The Cameo on Kenyatta Avenue (☎02/226843) is leaning more and more towards soft porn, and has a rowdy pool room and bar upstairs. Seats in the mainstream cinemas cost up to Ksh160, and around Ksh60 in the dives. Daily programmes can be found in the *Nation* and the *Standard* newspapers (the *Nation*'s two-line resumés are often more entertaining than the movie in question).

Stage

The small theatre at the **Professional Centre**, at the end of Parliament Road (Mon–Fri 10am–5pm; box office and enquiries ☎02/225506), has now assumed the old Donovan Maule Theatre's mantle as Nairobi's leading playhouse, and is highly recommended. Its energetic repertory company, the **Phoenix Players** (formed in 1948), stage contemporary works by Kenyan or foreign playwrights, or sometimes perform classics adapted for Kenya. Their productions, especially in the increasingly less self-censoring climate of the 1990s, are always worth catching and sometimes excellent: they have some fine actors and superb singers, and the centre is a pleasant, intimate venue.

Under the dynamic directorship of Agatha Ndambuki, the **Kenya National Theatre** in Harry Thuku Road (☎02/220536), opposite the *Norfolk*, gives considerable emphasis to Kenyan drama and African theatre in general – though with a less hectic schedule than the Phoenix Players.

You should also see what's going on at the University (they often have festivals of African and Caribbean theatre performed in the Education Department Lecture Theatre), and if you're around at the beginning of November, check out the **Kenya Music Festival** at the Kenyatta International Conference Theatre, heavy on choirs but with a lot of other fascinating song and dance. Otherwise, see if the **Serekasi Players** are doing anything in the basement of the conference centre; check out the productions of the **Miujiza Players** at the Rahimtulla Trust Library Theatre in Mfangano Street (☎02/210363), and enquire about the **Tamduni Players**, a long-established group run by a Gambian woman, Janet Young, who do occasional productions.

If you're interested in the state of the theatre in Kenya, the **French Cultural & Cooperation Centre** (Maison Française), the **Goethe-Institut**, **Paa Ya Paa** or even **Gallery Watatu** (details for all on p.115), may be able to tell you more, and the first two sometimes host productions. The *Standard's* Thursday edition and the Friday and Saturday *Nation* carry theatre pages.

Casinos

There are more than enough places in Nairobi in which to unburden yourself of your money. One place that draws fair numbers of tourists is the **International Casino** (☎02/742620; bus #21, #23 or #119) on Westlands Road off Museum Hill, close to the *Hotel Boulevard* and museum. The complex consists of the main gaming room itself (main entrance off Chiromo Road; open from 9pm weekdays, 4pm weekends; smart casual dress code; nominal entrance fee), a couple of restaurants (see *Toona Tree* and *La Galleria* on pp.121–122), a slot machine hall, the *Lucky Strike* – a bit of a dive but the view is good – and a private member's club (*Galileo's*, basically just a disco). Beware that the whole area around the casino is dodgy – and extremely unsafe after dark – with clusters of prostitutes and drug-hawkers to waylay you and opportunities for being mugged for your winnings.

Other options include the plush *Mayfair Casino*, next to the *Mayfair Court Hotel* (Sat–Thurs noon–3am, Fri all night), the *Florida Casino* on Loita Lane (tables daily 6pm–6am; slot machines and restaurant daily noon–4am; 24-hour cafeteria), and the rather classier *Casino Paradise* at the *Safari Park Hotel*, sumptuous in every respect (no minimum bet, and it stays open, obligingly, until the last bankruptcy), but rather too far to walk back from if you're penniless. Lower down the social gambler's scale are a number of **bingo halls** that have recently appeared in the city centre, complete with nasally-intoning callers and slot machines (usual prices are around Ksh500 for five bingo cards, entrance is free): try *Slots of Luck* under the *Oakwood Hotel* in Kimathi Street, or the flashier *Savoy Casino*, above *New York New York* disco in Accra House, at the junction of Tom Mboya Street and Accra Road. Both are currently open 24 hours, despite a number of armed raids.

Nightlife and music

With the limited range of cultural activities available, it's not surprising that **drinking and dancing** are what a night out in Nairobi is usually about. Entrance fees are low by international standards and prices for drinks are much the same as you'll pay in similar establishments elsewhere in the country. Be warned, however, that, male or female, if you're not accompanied by a partner of the opposite sex, you soon will be.

Bars

Although things are gradually getting livelier, central Nairobi is still a bit of a dead loss at night if you just want a **drink**, as most people tend to head off towards **Westlands** for its sleeker, more upmarket bars, or else pack into a number of sweaty discos. The great exception for city centre revelling is the **River Road area**, where, suitably stripped down (to the clothes on your back and a little cash), you can venture out to the land of "**Day & Night Clubs**" (see p.126). The district vibrates from dawn to dusk and back to dawn again with the sound of beery mayhem and jukeboxes – if you like the sound of it, you might consider taking a room nearby to avoid the hassle of getting back.

Ambassadeur Hotel, Moi Ave. Popular with businessmen, and largely hassle-free (the prostitutes limit their advances to waving at you).

Buffalo Bill's, Milimani Rd, by the *Heron Court Hotel* (take a taxi if you're not staying up Nairobi Hill). A famous and remarkably seedy joint ("What are you here for if you just want a drink?!") – a cowboy theme bar with a waiting woman in every "covered wagon" drinking booth. Noisy and high-spirited at night, the tone is much gentler by day, with good cheap food (the "hangover plate" is recommended) and occasional live jazz on Saturday and Sunday afternoons. The bar closes at 11.30pm, when the prostitutes head off downtown to either of the *Florida* nightclubs.

Dodi's Food and Drink, Kenya Cinema Plaza, Moi Ave. Nice place, shame about the name: a bright and laid back two-level bar overlooking the fun and games and occasional preachers on Moi Ave. Closes around 10pm.

Gipsy Bar (aka *Tropicanna*; ☎02/440964), Woodvale Grove, Westlands. Near the *Landmark Hotel*, this is currently the most popular upmarket late-night choice, if a little cliquey. It serves tapas and remains open to the early hours.

Hurlingham Hotel, Argwings Kodhek Rd. This hosts an international working crowd and has darts, but closes at 10pm and can be a bit snooty.

Jockey Club, *Hilton Hotel*, City Hall Way, next to Egyptair. This has a more traditional pubby feel, but is predictably rather bland.

Mayfair Court Hotel, Parklands Rd. This is where the Friday night *wazungu* crowd moved to when the *Norfolk*'s prices went up. Open to the early hours.

Norfolk Hotel. Sooner or later, a people-watching drink or a snack at the *Norfolk*'s *Lord Delamere Terrace* bar is a must, though at times it can feel like a pub in the City of London. It does, however, offer the full range of Tusker beers, and the snacks aren't as expensive as you might expect.

Thorn Tree Café, at the *Stanley Hotel*, Kimathi St. Hard to avoid, as it's in the thick of the worst zone for tourist hustling, so a welcome if almost wholly *wazungu* refuge, and a handy meeting place. Snacks (excepting its terrible pizzas) are good but overpriced. There's a cheesy band in the evenings. Closes around 11pm.

Zanzebar, 5th floor, Kenya Cinema Plaza, Moi Ave. A pleasant place to down the beers (or cocktails) in the afternoons or evenings, before it gets disco-feverish. See also "Disco Palaces", p.127.

Local dives – River Road district

On **Latema Road**, people contort themselves just to get into the *Modern Green Day and Night Club*. Here, entrance is free, cold beer is not the fashion – though you can get it, from the barman in his security cage – and the floor show is you and the rest of the customers. Just why the place is so popular is hard to say. For the girls it's partly because of the steady trickle of potential customers from the *Iqbal* and other lodgings nearby – it's amazing how many *wazungu* are still prepared to play with HIV. For some of the men it's a place to chew *miraa* all night for the price of a soda. From the outside, with the usual arguments and hustle going on in the doorway, it might appear a place to avoid, but squeeze inside, drink a beer or two, and soak up the elevated (and very relaxed) atmosphere. People make friends quickly here, though having a conversation over the racket of the throng and the din of the jukebox is exhausting.

If you can't take the pace, try the *New Congoni Day and Night Club* on River Road, off Luthuli Avenue (see "Reggae Discos" opposite), and the excellent *Fameland* on Duruma Road (great music and food). *Habari Day & Night Club*, on Luthuli Avenue, and *Lizie Bar* at the corner of Gaberone Lane and Munyu Road, are both raucous and cheap like the *Modern Green* but minus the hustling young women. *Reke Marie B&L* on Munyu Road is funnier and full of drunken old men, whilst *Friends Corner*, on the corner of Latema and Tsavo roads, one block up from the *Iqbal*, is also a favourite spot for a drink, although the toilets are horrible: the atmosphere is a characterful mixture of card-playing old-timers and more youthful faces making eyes – it's easy to make friends here. Also worth a mention is the *California Stars Butchery* on Gaberone Road, actually a bar and *nyama choma* joint, with tables out on the street opposite the Sikh Temple. There's nothing to keep you from checking out dozens of others – plenty of people do: for a place to start, try **Munyu Road**, which has more bars and clubs per hundred metres than any other place in Kenya.

> Stop press: a number of these local dives were **closed down** by the police in 1999, including the *Modern Green* and *Friends Corner*. It is not clear if, or when, they'll open again.

Local dives – Dagoretti Corner

Aside from the city centre clubs and the fairly touristy places which draw their custom from a wide area, there are plenty of other nightspots catering for a more local clientele in the outlying communities. Reputations change rapidly enough depending on the state of the neighbourhood and the security situation – asking around River Road's clubs will fill you in pretty quickly about what's in (and safe) and what's not. Currently one of the livelier of such communities, musically or otherwise, is **Dagoretti Corner**. Although only a fifteen-minute bus ride from town, it has a completely different look and feel from the modern centre.

Quite a number of bars in and around Dagoretti Corner, at the junction of Ngong Road and Naivasha Road, feature **live music** (another reason to think of staying out there), if not necessarily on a regular weekly schedule. Check out the four-storey *Matigari Bar*, hard to miss as it's painted top to toe with a Guinness ad, between Ngong and Naivasha roads, which sometimes features bands and is an interesting enough place the rest of the time. Heading back to town along Ngong Road, other choices include the **Impala Club**, **Motherland Inn** and *Ngong Hills Hotel* (again, all covered below), all of which feature fairly regular live music. The best disco at Dagoretti Corner is currently the *Holiday Inn* on Ngong Road past the junction with Naivasha Road, which is wildly packed at weekends with not a *mzungu* in sight. Buses and *matatus* #1, #2, #3, #4, #102, #103 and #111 run along Ngong Road to Dagoretti Corner.

Discos

Reggae is the popular staple sound of the **cheap discos**, often not much more than "Day & Night Clubs". The government's anti-rasta drive of the early-1990s fizzled out and reggae music is back on the airwaves and in the street. Nairobi also has a scattering of **disco palaces** complete with flashy interiors and the latest dance hits from Europe and America, as well as more danceable tunes from Congo. If this style appeals, try one of the established places below (or *Carnivore*, see p.122). In the glitzy places, men usually pay more than women, around Ksh100–300 as against Ksh50–100. In the rootsier discos, entrance is free or very cheap.

Reggae discos

Hollywood ("Commercial Centre and River Road area" map, p.88), Moktar Daddah St (☎02/27949). This is mostly a drinking club, with dancing something its regulars do to keep from falling asleep. Jah'mbo Soul have their residency here, though the action closes early. Wed–Sun; live reggae on Sunday.

Monte Carlo Club ("Commercial Centre and River Road area" map, p.88), Accra Rd (☎02/223181). A cavernous place with a good atmosphere and music ("No weapons or *miraa*", say the signs). Lone women should be OK. Daily till dawn; reggae disco Wednesday from 8pm, Saturday from 4pm, Sunday from 2pm; Ksh100.

New Congoni Day & Night Club ("Commercial Centre and River Road area" map, p.88), River Rd, off Luthuli Ave (☎02/331789). Unpredictable live music, predictably smelly toilets. Reggae discos on Sunday afternoons.

Disco palaces

The big **discos** all put on floor shows for those who stay late enough – gyrating trios, limbo dancing and all – but except for the once-weekly "African Nites", don't come expecting any startling African musical revelations: you're more likely to hear Madonna, Abba, Sade and the Bee Gees.

CENTRAL NAIROBI
These are all on the "Commercial Centre and River Road area" map on p.88.

Club Le Balafon, Kaunda St (☎02/230794). Slushy, saccharine "snack bar and dancing"; oddly enough, still popular. Strong on Congolese dance at weekends. Daily 5.30pm–dawn.

Dolce Club, Cianda House, Koinange St (☎02/218298). Slick and smooth soukous and soul for a glitzy crowd; deafening sound system.

Florida 2000, 1st floor, Commerce House, Moi Ave near the Kenya Cinema (☎02/229036). The red-and-black themed *New Florida*'s sister attracts similar clients and offers equally unambiguous entertainment, pumped up with what they call "most exotic floor shows" (nightly 1am). For the local ladies, this means grabbing drunken *wazungu* on the razzle. Wildly popular, and its Sunday afternoon disco is *the* place to keep on swinging if sleep has somehow eluded you. Daily.

Jax Invitation, 1st floor, Old Mutual Building, Kimathi St. Rather dark and unexceptional except on pay days and holidays. Loud discos Wednesday, Friday and Saturday, majoring on shrink-wrapped soul with only a sprinkling of Lingala, and 1980s numbers you hoped never to hear again (remember Rick Astley?).

L'Ora Blue, Corner House, Kimathi St (☎02/218953; closed Sun). A brand-new, rather smart dinner-dance place, appealing to grown-up, upmarket smoochers rather than disco freaks. Cabarets some nights. Judging by the lack of clientele, this may very well turn into something else.

New Florida, Chai House, Koinange St (☎02/334870). Irresistible for its tackiness (with matching floorshows), this big orange mushroom of a building above the Total filling station is always full of hookers and rather desperate-looking business types, but the atmosphere is merely steamy, not heavy. To go with the lager, there's a traditional English restaurant (ie Chinese). Reggae on Wednesday.

New York New York, Savoy Building, junction of Tom Mboya St and Moi Ave (☎02/252844). Brand new and already massively popular, connected with the Savoy bingo and casino, cashing in on the rekindled interest in retro 1980s disco with a touch of techno. There's a nightly 1am cabaret, occasional events like beauty contests, and Sunday afternoon jam contests. Daily 9pm–6am.

Zanzebar, 5th floor, Kenya Cinema Plaza, Moi Ave (☎02/222568). Very swish pinewood and neon club full of trendy types. Tuesday and Thursday are karaoke; Wednesday soul (of the diva sort); Friday disco till dawn, Saturday is turning over to *ndombolo*, sometimes live, and Sunday has a mixture of everything. Daily; free except Fri, Ksh100.

OUT OF TOWN
These are all on the "Nairobi outskirts" map on p.154.

The Barn, Ngong Racecourse (buses/*matatus* #1, #2, #3, #4, #102, #103 and #111). Considered by many to be the best disco at the moment, with a relaxed club atmosphere. No gimmicks: it's popular simply for being popular, which makes for a good night out. Safe parking and good security.

Beauty and the Beast, Thika Rd, Ruaraka, 2km before *Safari Park Hotel*, next to *Roasters Inn* (bus/*matatu* #45, #137, #145, #160 or #237). Top prize for ikkiest name. Another new place way out of town, boasting a terrific system. It's massive, easily accommodating a couple of thousand sweaty pairs of boogy shoes, and has pool tables if you fancy smacking a few balls around.

Chocolate City at *Safari Park Hotel*, 14km up Thika road (bus/*matatu* #45, #137, #145, #160 or #237). Smooth tunes, perfect lighting and sound system, but too much moneyed cool to get close to melting cocoa butter. Get a taxi back.

Psy's, off Langata Rd, opposite the turning for *Carnivore* (buses/*matatus* #15, #24, #31, #34, #125 or #126). New dancey place attracting migratory birds from the *Carnivore*'s *Simba Saloon*. Wednesday, Friday and Saturday are the main nights, with Friday attracting the flocks disenchanted with rap's inroads at *Simba Saloon*'s "Soul Nite".

Rhino Club, at *Park Place Hotel*, Magadi Rd (☎02/890456; *matatu* #125 or bus #126). Relaxed and unhustly, and fine for lone women.

Sahara City, Mombasa Highway (☎02/822933; *matatu* #110). Arguably Nairobi's top disco with the best sound system – an excellent place for dance freaks, with the best DJ working Wednesday–Sunday. Few *wazungu*, no tourists and plenty of young affluent Asians dancing *mujurrah*.

Swamp Village Park Inn, Kikuyu Rd, Siruta (☎02/571361; *matatus* #2 and #102). A thorough convert to the Congolese *ndombolo* invasion, which is featured Saturday–Sunday, together with tempting extras like beer-drinking competitions, dance contests and hair beauty shows. There are also occasional live acts.

Live-music venues

Given the volatile nature of the music business in Kenya, **venues** and **bands** change at a moment's notice. Although there are a few downtown music places, much of Nairobi's live music action takes place on the perimeter of the city. The following listings include all the places that have been around for some time, plus the latest information on new ones. In addition, you might check out Friday's and Saturday's *Daily Nation* for announcements of one-off gigs. **Starting times** vary considerably for all the clubs. On weekdays, 7.30 or 8pm wouldn't be too early, while weekend warm-ups usually begin around 9–10pm, and some may not get really rolling until midnight. But don't judge any band by their first hour: many run through some pretty dreadful warm-up material to begin with. Remember, too, that many clubs have **Sunday afternoon "jam sessions"** that can be just as lively as the evening shows, and often include acrobats, jugglers, magicians or comedians as well – excellent for families, too, and convenient if you don't want to be taxiing around the city late at night.

City centre
The following are on the "Commercial Centre and River Road area" map on p.88, unless otherwise stated.

African Heritage, Banda St (☎02/333157). Easy-going, informal, weekend afternoon mixes of reggae, soukous and more traditional music. Sat & Sun 1–5pm.

NAIROBI BANDS

The big names to watch out for are the Tanzanian group **Les Wanyika** (*Watering Point Club*) and their "cousins", the **Mavalo Kings**, the **Maroon Commandos** (if they're still around, make a beeline for their gigs), **Super Mazembe**, **Juma Toto & Toddy Nationale**, **Matata Five** (*Motherland* on Ngong Road), **Tshackatumba** (a mix of Congolese and Kenyan musicians), the **Seiko System Band** (playing a fusion of *benga* and rumba), rumba from **Bilenge Musica d'Afrique**, **Golden Souls Band** (featuring fantastic sax players Twahir Mohamed and Rama Athumani), *benga* man **Aziz Abdi**, and number-one female *benga* singer **Queen Jane**.

Possibly less interesting sounds come from the voices and instruments of a clutch of tourist and international-style pop and rock bands – **Them Mushrooms** (*Splash!*), the **Pressmen** (*Hard Rock Café*), **Tangerine Fusion** and **Hakuna Wafungwa**.

Since 1994 there's been a huge **gospel** trend in Nairobi. You're bound to hear of some of the following artists: **Mary Atieno**, **Augustus Baraza**, **Wilson Majale**, **Joseph Mwaura** and **Kimani Thomas**. The best-known name is that of **Joseph Kamaru** who renounced raunchy Kikuyu folk-pop for the word of the Lord and depressed millions of fans.

RECORDS AND CASSETTES

Pirated cassettes may seem a good deal at under Ksh100 (originals cost Ksh150) but quality and durability are so bad they're practically worthless. Identify them by the lack of labels on the cassette itself. For CDs and tapes, try Assanand's and Musikland on Moi Avenue or, better still, any of a host of shops and stalls on and around River Road and Accra Road.

Arturo's Restaurant, Tumaini House, Moi Ave (☎02/226940). Not exactly a restaurant (though the food's OK) and not really Italian, but its first-floor verandah has live music (could be anything: Congolese, Kikuyu, Luo) on Wed, Fri and Sat nights. Very danceable, very local and entrance is free.

Fameland Club (10), Duruma Rd, River Road district (☎02/248000) – live bands and good DJs weekends in this "elegant and cosy joint". Thursdays are African night discos, with plenty of hip-gyrating rhythms to grind to. Don't walk around here unaccompanied.

Freemark Capital Centre ("Central Nairobi" map, p.102), Uhuru Park. An odd, hangar-like venue, where the quality of live shows can be erratic, though recent acts have included Bora Bora and Princess Faridah, "the queen of chakacha". The area is dangerous at night – take a taxi.

Green Corner Restaurant, Tumaini House, Nkrumah Rd (☎02/335243). The "Cactus Bar" here is handy to fill a dull night but nothing special in itself: there's the obligatory Wed ladies' night, a busy "Friday Jam" (DJs), and karaoke on Sat.

Hard Rock Café, Mezzanine 2, Barclays Plaza (☎02/220802). Average, overpriced food with silly names, daft cocktails, and old Chevrolets lunging in through the ceiling. The Pressmen have a residency on Wed, Fri and Sat (see box on "Nairobi Bands"). There's a cybercafé here too. Daily 9am–2am; free.

Mang' Hotel ("Central Nairobi" map, p.102), Haile Selassie Ave (☎02/224090). An exuberant local venue where soukous and Lingala still reign. Mpingo Band play Wed & Fri from 6pm; there's a disco on other nights and more live soukous after midnight.

Terrace Hotel, Ronald Ngala St, River Road district. *Nyama choma* settles your centre of gravity before gyrating to Congolese *ndombolo* provided by Lisanga Musica band. Rooms available.

Suburban and out of town

Almost all of the following double as *nyama choma* joints. Except when noted, all can be found on the "Nairobi outskirts" map on p.154.

Calabash Bezique, 20km down Thika Rd at Kahawa Sukari, opposite Kenyatta University (☎02/811084; bus/*matatu* #137 or #237). A large 24-hour *nyama choma* place with studenty discos Thurs–Sat and occasional live bands – phone in advance for details.

Cantina Club ("Greater Nairobi" map, p.82), Wilson Airport entrance, Langata Rd (☎02/506085; buses/*matatus* #15, #24, #31, #34, #125 or #126: get off at the BP station). No tourist panderings here – this is an old African club with *nyama choma*, a great record archive and a big following of devoted locals. The *Cantina* attracts a slightly older crowd that keeps the atmosphere both boisterous and mellow at the same time – and it's pleasantly spacious and airy. Daily 24hr.

City Cabanas, Mombasa Highway 3km before the airport turning (☎02/824800–2 or 820993-7; *matatu* #110). A massive entertainments complex rapidly becoming one of the prime venues for visiting international stars (including Congolese *ndombolo* dancesters Koffi Olomide and Le General Defao), as well a lot of the home-grown talent – look in the press for details. Big name tickets around Ksh800.

Hillock Inn ("Greater Nairobi" map, p.82), Enterprise Rd near the Ngong River bridge (☎02/544819 or 545668). In the unlovely Industrial Area, this is a long-established venue, with *nyama choma*, several bars, tacky fountains and "Intelligent Band" resident Wednesday, Friday and Saturday (6pm to past midnight), and Sunday afternoons. They have some s/c rooms available (①–②) if you feel less than clever for the taxi ride back (Ksh800). Get there on a *matatu* for "Industrial area/Hillock" outside the Afya Centre, Tom Mboya St.

Impala Club, Ngong Rd (☎02/565684; buses/*matatus* #1, #2, #3, #4, #102, #103 and #111), has occasional live acts, especially Friday & Saturday nights.

The Jazz Bar, 2nd floor, Yaya Centre ("Greater Nairobi" map, p.82), Hurlingham (☎02/711473; bus #41 or #46). A sadly pretentious (and expensive) piano bar rather than the jumpin' jazz joint Nairobi really needs. Still, it hosts smooth US jazz artists from time to time – ring, or check press for details. Daily 10am till late.

JKA Resorts Club, Mombasa Highway, just beyond the airport turn-off from Nairobi (☎02/822066; *matatu* #110). Although some way out of town and a little difficult to get to, *JKA Resorts* usually features a regular band on Friday and Saturday nights and Sunday afternoons into the evening. Watch the papers, too, for announcements of special events often coinciding with holidays. The club area has a pleasant, garden setting and, at cooler times of the year, they light fires in hearths on either side of the dance floor. Given taxi fares these days, an overnight at the *JKA Hotel* attached to the club, while not very cheap, might be worth considering.

Makuti Park ("Greater Nairobi" map, p.82), Nairobi South "B" Shopping Centre (☎02/545957; *matatus* from railway stage to South "B"). Recently renovated, a reliable mellow place for live music (generally Fri–Sun, sometimes midweek). There's also comedy – look up the listings in Saturday's *Nation* newspaper, and good cheap Kenyan food. Sunday afternoons are for the family, with shows, face-painting, acrobats and stalls.

Motherland Inn ("Greater Nairobi" map, p.82), Ngong Rd (opposite Menelik Rd; buses/*matatus* #1, #2, #3, #4, #102, #103 and #111). Matata Five Band play here regularly.

Ngong Hills Hotel ("Greater Nairobi" map, p.82), Ngong Rd (☎02/566677; buses/*matatus* #1, #2, #3, #4, #102, #103 and #111). Currently one of the best venues, very popular, and with few *wazungu*, this hotel has Orchestra Malembe Stars resident on Wednesday, Friday and Saturday nights (8pm–3am), and Sunday afternoons (2–8pm). The atmosphere is not at all intimidating and the bands (Kenya's coolest, Tanzania's hottest and some Lingala) uniformly excellent. Sunday afternoons host a very laid-back jam session, complete with dancers, acrobats, tight-rope walkers and *nyama choma* by the green pool to drown your hangover in. Ideal for kids. Ample parking.

Peacock Inn ("Greater Nairobi" map, p.82), Dai Dai Rd, Nairobi South "B" Shopping Centre (☎02/552639; *matatus* from railway stage). On Fridays this is well worth checking out for occasional visits by Tanzanian bands, including Arusha's Ngamiani Band.

Roasters Inn, Thika Rd, Ruaraka, 2km before *Safari Park Hotel* (☎02/861000; bus/*matatu* #45, #137, #145, #160 or #237). Opposite Kenya Breweries, this place is best combined with a night out at the nearby *Beauty and the Beast* mega discotheque. *Roasters* hosts the resident Forvics Band (playing "oldies") as well as cabaret. Wednesday, Friday and Saturday are the main nights. Take a taxi.

Rib Shack ("Greater Nairobi" map, p.82), 1km up Kiambu Rd, Muthaiga north (☎02/512439; *matatu* #100). An upmarket *nyama choma* joint featuring Wamilika and the Ruiru Youngstars live every Wednesday (basically jazz-funk), and pure disco-trash Friday–Sunday am. Cheaper than *Carnivore*, but it's miles out. Take a taxi back.

Shade Hotel, Ngong Rd, Karen (☎02/882298; bus/*matatu* # 24, #111 or sometimes #126). A variety of live acts: music, dancers, acrobats, drummers and comedians, and of course *nyama choma*.

Simba Saloon, at *Carnivore Restaurant* (see above) (☎02/501779). A successful meld of live music and disco in a pleasant, outdoor environment (see p.122 for the restaurant write-up). Wednesday nights are rock (till 2am; free before 9pm); Thursday is live jazz or rave (6pm–midnight; free before 9pm); Friday is "Africa Nite" with a band called Simba Ngoma; Saturday disco party night (smoochy African and US crooners; 6pm till dawn); and Sunday is Simba Soul (6pm till 2am; free till 9pm). Visiting big-name groups sometimes take the Sunday afternoon slot. Look out for occasional comedy (in English as well as Swahili) on Tuesdays. No music Mon or Tues.

Sirona Hotel ("Greater Nairobi" map, p.82), Keiyo Rd, off Forest Rd, Parklands (☎02/742730; bus #108 to Parklands Roundabout). Within easy striking distance if you're staying at *Ma Roche's*. Sunday afternoons have featured the reggae sounds of Mpendo Moja, but don't walk here at night.

Splash!, 300m from *Carnivore* (see p.122; ☎02/603777). Live music Friday nights, and you can still go swimming. Them Mushrooms (see "Nairobi Bands" box on p.129) are the resident band. Plans to expand into an enormous amusement complex. Ksh150.

Sportsview Hotel, Thika Rd, Kasarani, near the Moi Sports Complex (☎02/861648; bus/*matatu* #17B, #45, #137, #145, #160 or #237, plus 1.5km walk). Another outsize *nyama choma* joint which occasionally books some interesting groups. Currently resident (Sundays only) are the please-all Metro Band, which entertain the crowds along with jugglers, magicians and comedians. There are horse rides and a playground for the kids. Friday and Saturday nights have discos, the rest of the time it's a mellow *nyama choma* place.

Watering Point Club, Ngong Rd, Dagoretti Corner (buses/*matatus* #1, #2, #3, #4, #102, #103 and #111). Unassuming *nyama choma* joint from the outside, some of East Africa's hottest sounds within. Currently resident are Tanzanian transplants Les Wanyika – ecstatic stuff, with John Ngereza on lead guitar and Professor Omari on rhythm. The crowd here is always happy and relaxed, and they're usually a more mature gathering than the usual clubbers. Not to be missed.

Wida Highway Motel, Naivasha Rd, Kikuyu (☎0154/32813; bus/*matatu* #2 or #102). Two parts, one is beer and *nyama choma* garden with live music (especially Fri), the other is the disco Groove Syde (soul and R&B Saturday). The live music is mainly local bands with the odd rowdy beauty contest thrown in for fun. Saturday and Sunday afternoons have family-oriented shows, with R&B disco, some gospel, acrobats and comedy.

Safari transport and travel planning

Nairobi is the travel hub of Africa, with a mass of opportunities for **safaris** around Kenya, and good facilities for making **travel arrangements** across the continent – and more or less anywhere else in the world. There are literally hundreds of safari operators, car rental outlets and travel agents. The following summaries aim to make sense of the whole business and pick out some recommended firms. Public transport and flight details are given in the "Moving on from Nairobi" section on p.138. If you want to make simple hotel and lodge reservations, either do it through a travel agent (see "Nairobi listings", or contact the hotel reservation services in person (addresses and hotel lists on p.48). If you fancy **camping** but don't have a tent, see "Camping equipment" in the Nairobi listings on p.146. Most of the commercial buildings which house the offices in the following listings are marked on our "Commercial Centre and River Road area" map on p.88.

Cycling

Before making any bookings, one option you might not have considered is **cycling** (see p.43). Although the big game parks will still be out of your reach, several of the smaller parks will let you in (Hell's Gate at Naivasha, Lake Bogoria Reserve, Kakamega Forest) and much wonderful cycling country is explorable. The cheapest Chinese and Indian three-speed machines are widely available, as well as large numbers of cheap mountain bikes (from around Ksh5500) and a few lightweight models with good specification – even front fork suspension. These can be good value, but you'll have trouble reselling. For **bicycle rental**, contact Bike Treks (see "Special activity safaris, p.136): it costs Ksh1000 per day, but they prefer you to use them for longer treks to reduce the risk of theft in Nairobi.

Cycle Land, Moi Ave (☎02/223955). Good range in stock, including some quality mountain bike imports.

Cycle Mart & Exchange Ltd, Kijabe St (☎02/223459). Good stock and spares, bargaining should be possible.

Gitonga Cycle Dealers, OTC Building, Landhies Rd (☎02/253022). Beyond the Country Bus Station.

Kenya Cycle Mart, Moi Ave (☎02/223417). A traditional cycle store.

Sadar Singh Vohra Ltd, River Rd, next to Evamay Lodge (☎02/222715). One of the cheaper outlets with reasonable eighteen-speed mountain bikes for Ksh12,000. Spares for all specs.

Westlands Cycle Mart, Old Uchumi Building, opposite The Mall, Westlands (☎02/448055). The best place to resell your bike (or try the Sun morning second-hand vehicle market along Parklands Rd).

Cars and rental

First read the section on "Car rental and driving" in Basics (see p.41). The minimum age is usually 23 and, remember, you'll need to pay a deposit (easiest by credit card)

CAR RENTAL COMPANIES

The prices quoted below are daily rates for a 4WD Suzuki Sierra (or Maruti), and 4WD Mitsubishi Pajero, which were current in 1999. The prices include Collision Damage Waiver (CDW) and Theft Protection Waiver (TPW) for a car rented over a week with unlimited mileage (or 100km/day if not available). Note that out of high season, all companies should be amenable to bargaining. Incidentally, you won't necessarily get good service or a good deal from the multinationals – all are franchises, and many have become complacent.

Avis, College House, University Way (PO Box 49795; ☎02/336794, fax 339111). Slow service and sky-high rates makes this one to avoid. No Suzukis; their nearest equivalent is the more upmarket Daihatsu Feroza: Daihatsu Ksh9280 (unlimited); Pajero Ksh13,800 (100km/day); liability Ksh40,000.

Budget/Payless, Hilton Building, Simba Street (PO Box 49713; ☎02/223581–2, airport ☎02/822370, fax 223584, *payless@form-net.com*). Not especially reliable, some dud vehicles, and lacks the back up you'd expect from an international player. Suzuki Ksh5350 (unlimited); Pajero Ksh10,810 (unlimited); liability Ksh50,000.

Central, ground floor, Fedha Towers, Standard Street (PO Box 49439; ☎02/222888, fax 339666). The only local company to concentrate solely on car hire, and it shows: cars are in good condition, service is helpful and it's cheaper than the rest. Recommended. Suzuki Ksh4410 (100km/day); Pajero Ksh8468 (100km/day); liability Ksh2000.

Concorde, Agip Garage, Waiyaki Way, Westlands (PO Box 25053; ☎02/448953, fax 448135). Calm and efficient, but they don't do unlimited mileage (so more expensive if you're planning long drives). Suzuki Ksh4600 (100km/day); Pajero Ksh8570 (100km/day); liability Ksh20,000 (Suzuki), Ksh50,000 (Pajero).

Crossways, Banda Street (PO Box 10228; ☎02/220848); Standard Street (☎02/223949, fax 214372). Average service with no bad reports. Suzuki Ksh4800 (110km/day); Pajero Ksh9000 (110km/day); liability Ksh60,000.

Eurodollar Kenya, Woodvale Grove, Westlands (PO Box 64010; ☎02/440333, fax 552857; airport ☎02/432069, *natcarnb@africaonline.co.ke*). Will readily give discounts (not surprising seeing their rates), very expensive liability if you crash. No Suzukis; Pajero Ksh12,490 (unlimited); liability Ksh100,000.

Europcar, Express Travel Group, Bruce House, Standard Street (PO Box 40433; ☎02/334722–7, fax 334825, *expressk@africaonline.co.ke*). Reliable but ridiculously expensive. Suzuki Ksh7600 (unlimited); Pajero Ksh18,560 (unlimited); liability Ksh70,000.

plus extra for insurance; expect to pay between $70 and $90 per day all-in for a short-wheelbase 4WD Suzuki jeep (either the Sierra or the upgraded 1300cc Maruti Gypsy), the most useful vehicle for the parks. Prices vary greatly, with some quoted in Kenya shillings, though most in dollars. Shop around for the best deals (making sure you're quoted the inclusive price, including the minimum daily mileage) and try to negotiate as you might with any purchase, bearing in mind the season and how long you're renting: this is easier with independent companies than the big-name franchises. However, the big names are much better insured for damage and collision while some of the independent companies may leave you liable for up to an $2500 **excess liability** in the event of an accident. July and August, and Christmas, are busy times, so you might book ahead.

Don't assume your vehicle is roadworthy; the best companies sometimes send out vehicles in a terrible state. Check it as carefully as you can. You are, of course, responsible for any ongoing **repair and maintenance work** that needs doing while you're renting the vehicle (see the next section), but keep any receipts as the company should reimburse you. The commonest requirement is for a new tyre. Try to get a list

Habib's Tours & Travel, Agip House, Haile Selassie Avenue (PO Box 48095; ☎02/220463, fax 220985, *habibtours@attmail.com*). Agents only, and expensive if you crash. Suzuki $90 (100km/day); Pajero $180 (100km/day); liability $1000.

Hertz/UTC, corner of Kaunda Street and Muindi Mbingu Street (☎02/331960, fax 216871; airport ☎02/822339, *utcn@africaonline.co.ke*). Reliable, with good accident back-up and customer care, but extremely expensive and no Suzukis. Pajero $267 (unlimited); liability $1340.

Kenia Tours and Safaris, 4th Floor, Jubilee Insurance House, Kaunda/Wabera Street (PO Box 19730; ☎02/223699, out of hours ☎02/444572, fax 217671, *kenia@africaonline.co.ke*). No longer has its own fleet, but can arrange good deals with other operators to suit your pocket.

Let's Go Travel, Caxton House, Standard Street (PO Box 60342; ☎02/340331, fax 336890). Reliable, but not all cars are theirs. The excess liability is low. Suzuki Ksh5310–5420 (unlimited); Pajero Ksh11,350–12,150 (unlimited); liability Ksh7000.

Pola's Car Hire, 1st floor, NCM House, Tom Mboya Street (PO Box 31532; ☎02/334207, fax 337933). Much cheaper than the competition, so check the car and conditions carefully. Suzuki Ksh3500 (170km/day); liability 50,000. Suzuki Ksh5310–5420 (unlimited); Pajero Ksh11,350–12,150 (unlimited); liability Ksh7000.

Rasuls, Butere Road, Industrial Area (taxi to Mater Misericordiae Hospital; PO Box 18172; ☎02/558234, fax 540341). Friendly and reliable, but they have sold their Suzukis, and they don't do unlimited mileage (which makes it cheap if you only need to drive small distances). Pajero (old model) Ksh6600 (100km/day); Pajero (new model) Ksh9400 (100km/day); liability Ksh80,000.

Southern Cross Safaris, Stanley Hotel, Standard Street (PO Box 56707; ☎02/225255, fax 216553, *sxsnbo@africaonline.co.ke*). Long-standing company, expensive daily rates but the advantage of incredibly low excess liability: great for peace of mind. Suzuki $105 (unlimited); Pajero $235 (unlimited); liability $75.

Suntrek Tours & Travel, Swan Court, off Muthithi Road, Westlands (PO Box 48146; ☎02/751349, 744767, fax 742055, *suntrek@form-net.com*). Good value and generally reliable, with good back up. Suzuki Ksh4450 (100km/day); Pajero by special arrangement; liability Ksh40,000.

Venture Africa, 3rd floor, City House, corner of Standard Street and Wabera Street (PO Box 8699; ☎02/219511, fax 219263, *ventureafrica@form-net.com*). Upstart safari firm also renting cars – cheap and no bad reports. Suzuki Ksh4020 (145km/day); liability Ksh40,000.

of recommended service stations from the rental company: to avoid bogus repairs some of them will insist you use certain garages. Always bargain hard before work begins.

Buying cars and repairs

If you're looking to **buy** a vehicle in Kenya, scan the classified ads in the papers or visit the stretch of Langata Road opposite Nyayo National Stadium on a Sunday morning, when there's a regular second-hand vehicle sale. You're only likely to need work done in Nairobi itself if you're travelling in Africa in your own vehicle. For **repairs**, the Undugu Society workshop, near Maridadi Fabrics by the city stadium roundabout (☎02/755631), is reliable. The following also come recommended for serious repair work.

Aquva Fabricators, Baricho Rd, off Bunyala Rd, Industrial Area (PO Box 48641; ☎02/557360, 552380).

Dash Engineering Works, corner of Munyu Rd and Luthuli Ave (PO Box 10798; ☎02/227050, 224798).

Chartering a plane

Details of domestic flights out of Nairobi are given on p.142; see also Classic Aerial Safaris below. If you're in the market to **charter** a light aircraft, a couple of dozen small operators, mostly based at Wilson Airport (☎02/501941–3), will oblige. It's not as outrageously expensive as you might assume and the opportunities for photography and just seeing the country are without equal. The current standard rate for a Cessna 182 (two passengers) is around $1.50 per mile (1.6km) – the minimum mileage is usually 500 miles (or three hours' flying) for $750 – though that takes you a very long way. You shouldn't be charged for *démarrage* (the plane parked on the ground) if you're coming back the same day.

Boskovic Air Charters Ltd, Wilson Airport (PO Box 45646; ☎02/501210, fax 609619).

East African Air Charters, Wilson Airport (PO Box 42730; ☎02/504731, fax 502358).

Safari operators

You can pick up plenty of leaflets about safaris from touts, or at any travel agent or ticket-booking company. Armed to the teeth with brochures and anxious to take you to operators' offices, **touts** are by no means a bad thing, as they often work for several companies and their commission is never added to the price you pay. Indeed, some are very knowledgeable and will be able to advise you relatively truthfully about which companies are currently good for what.

The best of the **travel agents** are reputable (see under "Travel agents and airline bookings", p.142), but it's always a good idea to meet the company you're travelling with in advance and to try to ensure that it is that company and not you who is paying the agent their commission. You should also check whether the advertised safari is actually run by the company in question, as the practice of one company subcontracting a safari to another is quite common, especially in low season, and gives you less redress if things go wrong. This is especially important for safaris to **Tanzania** and **Uganda** – ensure that the company has at least an office in the relevant country. For a copy of the operator's code of conduct, as well as a list of companies which adhere to the code, contact the **Kenya Association of Tour Operators (KATO)**, 5th floor, Jubilee Exchange House, Mama Ngina Street (PO Box 48461; ☎02/225570, fax 218402, *kato@africaonline.co.ke*). They should also be able to advise you on the reputation of a company you're considering going with. Whatever the price you pay, you should also make allowance for **tipping** at the end of the journey (read the section on "Camping Safaris" in Basics, p.64).

The following listings are classified broadly – several operators could be put into more than one bracket. All are members of KATO unless otherwise stated. Note that if you're a student, you should get a reduction on park entry fees.

Camping safaris

First, read the section on "Camping Safaris" in Basics (p.64). Every other shop seems to belong to a safari outfit and it's obviously impossible to mention more than a few. With so much to go wrong, spotless reputations are hard to maintain but the following, who run most of their **camping trips** by truck or minibus, are good value and only rarely come in for criticism.

Gametrackers, 1st Floor, Kenya Cinema Plaza, Moi Ave (PO Box 62042; ☎02/338927, fax 330903, *www.gametrackers.com*). Popular and consistently good operator with some twenty tours, including – apart from game safaris – cycling, camel treks, Aberdares walking and Mount Kenya climbs, as well as trips further afield (they have branches in Tanzania and Uganda). Around $60–80 per day and up. They run an excellent eight-day Turkana safari via Samburu National Reserve, Marsabit National Park and the Chalbi Desert, which is highly recommended ($480).

Guerba Kenya, 1st floor, International House, Mama Ngina St (PO Box 43935; ☎ & fax 890182, *www.gorp.com/guerba/*). The Kenyan arm of the respected Africa overland specialists, primarily dealing with their overseas clients but also offering safaris to walk-in customers, usually on a small commission.

Habib's Tours & Travel, Agip House, Haile Selassie Ave (PO Box 48095; ☎02/220463, fax 220985, *habibtours@attmail.com*). Pricier than most but reliable and long-established, specializing in tailor-made safaris and packages to suit most price ranges (aided by discount deals with many hotels). From $70 per day for camping safaris, and $110 upwards for the same in lodges or hotels.

Kenia Tours and Safaris, 4th Floor, Jubilee Insurance House, Kaunda/Wabera St (PO Box 19730; ☎02/223699, out of hours ☎02/444572, fax 217671,*www.gorp.com/kenia*). Proficient and generally reliable general Kenya camping safaris specialist, keenly priced and conscientious. $70–80 per day for camping safaris, $95–100 for lodge safaris, discounts in low season.

Let's Go Travel, Caxton House, Standard St (PO Box 60342; ☎02/340331, fax 336890; *www.letsgosafari.com*; *www.kenya-direct.com/letsgo*). Apart from acting as agents, Let's Go also run their own well-organized budget camping safaris, from $85–100 per day. Lodge safaris are $130–170 per day depending on season and group size. They're one of the few companies to have offices in both Tanzania and Uganda who run their trips in those countries.

Safari Camp Services, lower ground floor, Barclays Plaza, Loita St (PO Box 44801; ☎02/228936, 330130, or after hours ☎02/891348, fax 212160,*www.kenyaweb.com/safari-camp*). For over twenty years the operators of the original "Turkana Bus" (a converted Mercedes lorry; $450 for 7 days) and also of a "Wildlife Bus" trip ($578 for 7 days) emulated by many others. Their customer service and experience is second to none, and their limited number of tried and tested safaris keeps standards up and prices fairly well down; the combined Turkana Bus and Camel Trek in the Matthew's Range and Lake Turkana should be brilliant ($910 for 13/14 days). No-frills safaris $60–70 per day; more comfortable, less streamlined, small-group camping safaris, around $150 per day.

Safari Seekers, 5th floor, Jubilee Exchange House, Kaunda St (PO Box 32834; ☎02/226206, fax 334585, *www.kenyaweb.com/safari-seekers*). General operator, offering mountain bike safaris in cooperation with an American company, Paradise Bicycle Tours. From $70–80 per day.

Scenic Safaris, Biashara St (PO Box 49188; ☎02/226525, fax 225833; *scenic@nbnet.co.ke*). Wide range of shorter trips and reasonably priced lodge safaris. Camping from around $60 per day; lodges from $150 per day.

Twiga Tours, 4th floor, Victor House, Kimathi St (PO Box 14365; ☎02/337332, 211750, fax 337330, *www.twiga-tours.com*). A relative newcomer with tailor-made tours for as few as two people from $90–$100 per person per day.

Venture Africa, 3rd floor, City House, corner of Standard St and Wabera St (PO Box 8696; ☎02/219511, fax 219263,*www.venture-africa.com*). Relatively new operator with no bad reports. Camping safaris from $70 per day, lodge safaris between $100–200 a day.

Lodge and homestay safaris

The following are all pretty conscientious and helpful operators, catering for those who appreciate their wildlife taken with more than a modicum of luxury. Most have discounted deals with hotel chains (see p.48 for a list of these), which means that their more popular trips are generally better value than less frequently run ones. If you don't mind the effort of driving, hiring a car and booking accommodation yourself shouldn't work out much more expensive, but read our hotel and lodge reviews first. All also run half- and full-day trips in and around Nairobi for $35–80.

Let's Go Travel. See p.142.

Pollman's Tours & Safaris, Pollman's House, Mombasa Rd (PO Box 84198; ☎02/533140, fax 544544). One of the largest operators, running to all the major parks, though decidedly package-tour in feel (travelling in "convoy" with four or five other Pollman's minibuses isn't unusual). Around $380 for three nights. Popular with German visitors.

Rhino Safaris, Hilton Building, Simba St (PO Box 48023; ☎02/332372–3, fax 338427, *rhinosafarisnbo@form-net.com*). Highly regarded and long-established firm, founded in 1970, specializing in scheduled lodge, homestay and flying safaris. Customer service is second to none, and they're happy to tailor itineraries to individual needs. Prices start from around $390 for a three day/two night Mara trip, to over $1000 for a six-night tour covering Samburu, the Aberdares, Lake Nakuru, and Maasai Mara or Amboseli. They have offices in Mombasa and Arusha in Tanzania.

Somak Travel, 8th floor, Corner House, Mama Ngina St (PO Box 48495; ☎02/330285, fax 218954, *somak@form-net.com*). Well-regarded, offering a range of scheduled departures for all the main parks.

Southern Cross Safaris, *Stanley Hotel*, Standard St (PO Box 56707; ☎02/225255, 336570, fax 25345, *www.kenya-direct.com/southerncross*). Reliable and long-established mid-range operator specializing in overnights in lodges and luxury tented camps rather than basic camping safaris, including visits to private wildlife sanctuaries as well as the national parks. Fine if you like everything taken care of and are happy to pay for it, but otherwise expensive compared to a DIY combination of car hire and self-booked nights. They have an office in Mombasa, and operate their own vehicles in Tanzania.

Suntrek Tours & Travel, Swan Court, off Muthithi Rd, Westlands (PO Box 48146; ☎02/751349, 744767, fax 742055, *suntrek@form-net.com*). Long-established quality outfit happy to tailor itineraries and accommodation style to your needs. Standard trips cover all the major game parks and use reliable lodges. Recommended, if you're short on time, are their five- or six-night trips which cover a combination of different parks and scenery, for example Tsavo West, Amboseli, the Aberdares, Lake Nakuru and Maasai Mara national parks. Lack of regularly scheduled departures means you're unlikely to have other tourists on the same safari, although this makes things more expensive if there are only two of you. They also run trips into Tanzania. From $165–185 per night.

Tour Africa Safaris, 7th floor, Rehani House, corner Kenyatta Ave and Koinange St (PO Box 34187; ☎02/336767, fax 338271, *www.tourafrica-safaris.com*). Well-run and very competent travel agency, which also runs its own tailor-made lodge safaris (its camping safaris are arranged through other companies). A five-day jaunt in high-class lodges costs between $600–800. They also arrange safaris in Tanzania, including the lesser-known national parks, from $90–120 per day camping, or $150–180 in lodges.

Special activity safaris

The following are recommended because they offer unusual, if normally much more expensive, trips – notably safaris on foot (sometimes using pack animals), by bicycle (usually with vehicle back-up), on horseback or camel. Those that don't have walk-in addresses are usually small companies: enquire and book with a large agent like Let's Go Travel (see above). For information on balloon "safaris", see p.397.

Bateleur Safaris, Ndorobo Rd, Langata (PO Box 42562; ☎02/890454, fax 891007). Specialists in walking safaris for ornithologists.

Bike Treks, Kabete Gardens, behind Sarit Centre, off Karuna Rd, Westlands (PO Box 14237; ☎02/446371, fax 442439, *biktreks@form-net.com*). Truly adventurous trips, tailor-made, with vehicle back-up, led by a veteran mountain-bike enthusiast; the trans-Mara ride during the wildebeest migration is quite something. Minimum three people for guaranteed departures. They can also arrange trekking and mountain-climbing trips. $95–100 per day.

Camel Trek (information and bookings through Savannah Camps & Lodges, p.50. An established company (founded 1979) offering upmarket camel safaris around Isiolo district (Lewa Downs, and the Ewaso Nyiro River near Samburu). The basic trip is three or five nights (from Ksh23,500 including pick-up from Isiolo), which can be extended to several weeks into the Suguta Valley and Lake Turkana, if the idea of trekking through Kenya's hottest region doesn't melt your resolve. Incidentally, most people find walking alongside the camels (four to five hours a day) much more comfortable, though you're free to jump on if you wish. May be closed March to July and mid-Oct to mid-Dec (rains).

Desert Rose Camels (information and bookings c/o Safari Camp Services, see above). Expertly guided and flexible camel (or horseback) expeditions in and around the Matthews, Ndoto and Nyiru mountain ranges of Samburu district. Don't come expecting total comfort, but it is a wonderful experience, with plenty of contact with local people. The only, rather minor and unusual, gripe might be the overly romantic view that your hosts have of the tribespeople. Rates vary according to length of safari and number of people participating. $170–210 per person per day. They also run the exquisite *Desert Rose Lodge*, between Baragoi and South Horr (see p.567).

East African Ornithological Safaris (☎02/331191 or 222075, fax 330698 or 216528, *eaos@africaonline.co.ke*). By no means the cheapest safaris, but with years of experience in bird-watching. It costs $3000 all-in, including accommodation at well-selected lodges and tented camps (and at most of the related Savannah Camps & Lodges chain, p.50).

Ewaso River Camel Hikes (bookings via Southern Cross Safaris, see above). Based near Loisaba, 2hrs northeast from Rumuruti in Laikipia on the Ewaso Nyiro River. Camel-assisted walks at $205 per person per day, or just camel hire ($35 per camel) if you've got your own wheels to get there (the nearby *Colcheccio Lodge* is one of Kenya's priciest).

Hiking & Cycling Kenya, 2nd Floor, Arrow House, Koinange St (PO Box 39439; ☎02/218336–8, fax 224212, *hiking@africaonline.co.ke*). Half a dozen tours concentrating on walking, with a ten-day, vehicle-assisted Ngong–Mara–Bogoria cycle trip at about $700.

Naturetrek Adventure Safaris, no walk-in office (PO Box 70933; ☎02/780466). Specialists in walking safaris, notable for a seven-day walk in the Rift Valley and Loita Hills on the Tanzanian border, and a thirteen-day jaunt in Tanzania itself encompassing Mount Meru, lakes Manyara and Natron, and Ngorongoro. From $200 per day. Not in KATO.

Safaris Unlimited Ltd, 328 Langata Rd (PO Box 24181; ☎02/890435, fax 891113, *www.safarisunlimited.com*). Specialists in horseback safaris, covering the Aberdares, Samburu, the Rift Valley and Maasai Mara. Exclusive and expensive: trips cost around $300–500 per person per day, depending on the length of the trip and group size. They also run Longonot Ranch House in Naivasha (p.169).

Savage Wilderness Safaris, no walk-in office (PO Box 44827; ☎02/521590, *whitewater@thorntree.org*, may change to *.com*). Excellent if naturally risky programme of technical climbing and walking trips on Mount Kenya, "white-water" rafting, and walking safaris in the Chyulu and Loita Hills. One-day rafting from $95. Other trips $100 per day and up depending on numbers. Not in KATO, but in Kenya Professional Safari Guides Association.

Tropical Ice, Suite 8, 1st floor, Muthaiga Shopping Centre, Muthaiga Rd (PO Box 57341; ☎02/740811, fax 740826, *tropice@africaonline.co.ke*). Upmarket walking safaris along the Galana river for $160 per day. Not in KATO.

Yare Safaris, Union Towers, Moi Ave (PO Box 63006; ☎ & fax 214099, *www.iconnect.co.ke/~travelkenya/*). One of the leaders in North Kenyan safaris, they offer various off-beat tours and camel treks in the Samburu district from their base in Maralal (see p.562). A seven-day camel safari, with transfer from Nairobi, costs $495 per person.

Upmarket safaris

If you can afford it, the **expensive safari outfits** are mostly operated to very high standards. They often depend heavily on reputations passed by word of mouth among clients and overseas operators. The following firms will give good return for your money if you are in the $300–1000 per day league and want something special. At this level, what you do is entirely "tailor-made" – in other words, it's largely up to you. Transport is usually by land cruiser, accommodation is in luxury lodges or pre-set private campsites and leader/tour guides tend to be white hunter types who know the ground well and their clients' requirements even better.

Abercrombie & Kent, Bruce House, Standard St (PO Box 59749; ☎02/334955, fax 215752, *www.abercrombiekent.com*).

Cheli & Peacock (PO Box 39806; ☎0154/22551–2, fax 0154/22553, *www.chelipeacock.com*).

East African Wildlife Safaris, Titan Aviation, Wilson Airport (PO Box 43747; ☎02/605661, 605350, fax 605622, *www.kenyaweb.com/eaws*).

Glen Cottar Safaris, 60 Forest Lane, Karen (PO Box 44191; ☎02/884508, fax 882234, *cottars@form-net.com*).

Ker & Downey Safaris, Busia/Enterprise Rd, Industrial Area (PO Box 41822; ☎02/556466, fax 552378, *kerdowneykenya@form-net.com*).

Richard Bonham Safaris, Nandi Rd, Karen (PO Box 24133; ☎02/882521, fax 882728, *bonham.luke@swiftkenya.com*).

Tor Allan Safaris, 80 Bogani East Rd (PO Box 15114; ☎02/891190, fax 890142, *torallan@africaonline.co.ke*).

Moving on from Nairobi

Getting out of Nairobi by public transport is normally a fairly haphazard business. The following is intended to lend a degree of structure to a chaotic scene, but to make it comprehensive would be a never-ending task. If in doubt, ask. You'll always get where you want to, somehow. There are details about international and domestic flights, airline booking offices and procedure at Jomo Kenyatta International Airport at the end of this section.

By matatu

If you decide to take a mini-bus **matatu** out of Nairobi, you'll find that vehicles for different destinations congregate in different areas of town, the most useful of which are listed here. Be warned, however, that their locations change fairly frequently – ask around, and remember, the suicidal reputation attached to *matatus* is by no means entirely the result of paranoia. *Matatus* to Nakuru, Naivasha and Thika have a particularly bad reputation. See also p.39 in "Basics". *Matatu* routes within Nairobi are listed in the box opposite, together with local bus routes.

Buses and express shared taxis

Slower, cheaper and generally safer than *matatus* are the **bus services** which cover almost all of Kenya. The smaller companies operate out of the Country Bus Station (aka "Machakos Airport"), 1.5km east of the city centre just past Wakulima market, between Pumwani Road and Landhies Road (bus #4, #18 or #28 from the *Ambassadeur*). The larger companies have booking offices in various locations around River Road (see box on p.140), from where most of their services operate. Most services will sell seats to towns on the way, when space permits. Seats should, if possible, be reserved in advance at the bus offices. **Shared taxis**, usually Peugeot station wagons, are faster and cost roughly twice as much, and cover all the main towns in the centre and west of the country (chapters two, three and four). They're best caught early in the morning (around 8am) on Accra Road, each displaying

---

MATATUS

Chapter One: Around Nairobi
Naivasha (1hr; Ksh110), Nyamakima Bar, Duruma Road; Thika (40min; Ksh40–50), Ronald Ngala Street by the BP station, or Koinange Street by *New Florida*.

Chapter Two: The Central Highlands
Embu (2hr–2hr 30min; Ksh200), Accra Road between River Road and Duruma Road; Karatina (2hr; Ksh160), Accra Road/River Road, opposite *Crossline*; Meru (4hr 30min; Ksh270), Accra Road between River Road and Tsavo Road; Mwea (5hr 30min; Ksh170), Accra Road between River Road and Tsavo Road; Nanyuki (4hr; Ksh200), Accra Road between River Road and Tsavo Road; Nyahururu (Ksh200), Latema Road; Nyeri (3hr; Ksh160), Accra Road/River Road, opposite *Crossline*.

Chapter Three: The Rift Valley
Gilgil (90min; Ksh220), Nyamakima Bar, Duruma Road; Nakuru (2hr; Ksh180), Nyamakima Bar, Duruma Road.

Chapter Four: Western Kenya
Eldoret (4hr; Ksh330), Nyamakima Bar, Duruma Road; Kitale (5–7hr; Ksh430), Nyamakima Bar, Duruma Road.

Chapter Five: The Mombasa Road and major game parks
Kajiado (90min; Ksh100), Ronald Ngala Street; Machakos (1hr; Ksh100), the car park just north of Country Bus Station; Namanga (3hr; Ksh180), Ronald Ngala Street; Narok (2hr 30min; Ksh200), Nyamakima Bar, Duruma Road.

Chapter Six: The coast
There are no direct *matatus* to the coast.

Chapter Seven: The north
Isiolo (5hr 30min–6hr; Ksh250), Accra Road between River Road and Tsavo Road.

---

boards with their destinations. Addresses and phone numbers for all bus and shared-taxi companies mentioned are given below.

First, a couple of **warnings** about buses and bus stations: drugging of food, drink, cigarettes and chewing gum is not uncommon – do not accept such gifts, even at the risk of giving offence, nor leave your own stuff unattended. Secondly, as the most useful services often leave at night, getting to the bus station can be a problem (though the buses themselves are considered safe). Needless to say, walking unaccompanied with your luggage at night is the height of folly – take a taxi, hire an *askari* escort from your hotel, or else catch a daytime service.

By train

The **train station** (☎02/221211 ext 2700 or 2701) is at the south end of Moi Avenue, beyond the bustle and confusion of the railway *matatu* stage. There's a safe **left luggage service** here if you want to dump your bags (Ksh150 per item per day). See Basics on p.40 for advance booking details.

To Mombasa: daily at 7pm, arriving at 8.05am (calling at Voi around 4.30am for the connection to Taveta): 1st class Ksh3000; 2nd class Ksh2100; 3rd class Ksh300.

To Kisumu: daily at 6pm, arriving at 7.10am via Naivasha (9pm) and Nakuru (10.50pm). Third class only, Ksh150.

It may be worth enquiring whether passenger services to Kitale via Eldoret, to Moshi (via Voi) and to Kampala (via Kisumu) have been reinstated.

BUS SERVICES

Chapter One: Around Nairobi

For services within this chapter, head for the mêlée of the Country Bus Station. A continual stream of buses leaves for Thika and destinations in Kiambu district. Many call at Naivasha en route for points west, but ensure that the bus actually goes into town (Moi Avenue) instead of dropping you at the flyover 1.5km out. Akamba's services for Olorgasailie and Magadi leave from their Lagos Road office at 1pm and 3pm.

Chapter Two: The Central Highlands

The most frequent runs are provided by Sunbird Services, with almost hourly departures to Maua via Embu (Ksh120), Chogoria and Meru (Ksh200). Kensilver runs comfortable 25-seater mini-buses to Meru. Akamba cover all the main destinations, usually only once or twice a day. You'll find smaller companies at the Country Bus Station for Murang'a (Ksh80), Nanyuki (Ksh170) and Nyeri (Ksh140). Eastern Express continues on up to Isiolo (Chapter Seven), but has a dangerous reputation. Arusha Express have a service to Nanyuki and Nyeri. KBS Stagecoach service #231/233 at 7am and 9pm runs to Embu, Meru and Maua.

Chapter Three: The Rift Valley

The majority of passengers for Nakuru travel by *matatu* or Peugeot, though there are buses for Nakuru (Ksh130) from the Country Bus Station. The Peugeot 504 station wagons hang out in the Duruma/Accra roads area. Nakuru is also covered by most westbound (Chapter Four) services, but check before buying tickets that the bus actually stops inside the town – otherwise you may have a long walk in.

Chapter Four: Western Kenya

Akamba, Transluxe and KBS Stagecoach are the main companies, with several daily and overnight departures to most locations. Other buses leave from the Country Bus Station for Busia (Ksh500), Kakamega (Ksh400), Kericho (Ksh250), and Kisumu (Ksh300): you'll catch most of them between 7–8am and 8–9.30pm. Eldoret Express have frequent runs to Eldoret (Ksh250) and Kitale (Ksh350) from the Country Bus Station. Faster and roughly twice as expensive (ie Ksh600-800) are the Peugeot shared-taxis, which cover most of the region: Bungoma; Busia; Eldoret; Kakamega; Kericho; Kisii; Kisumu; Kitale; Luanda; Malaba; Mumias; Siaya; Vihiga; Webuye. Services depart early in the morning from Accra Road or Dubois Road.

Chapter Five: The Mombasa Road and major game parks

Regular services from the Country Bus Station to Machakos (Ksh60) and Kitui (Ksh150).

Chapter Six: The coast

Competition is fierce over the Nairobi–Mombasa route, with reputations tarnished all round and accidents not uncommon. Safest of the lot are Akamba. Coast Bus and Mombasa Liners have newish coaches. Avoid Tawfiq. Malindi Bus, who have more daily runs than any other company, are pretty reckless too. Crossline's twice-daily minibus is extremely fast, whilst Goldline's fleet is astonishingly rickety. Most companies run at least two day buses and one at night. It's hard to decide which is worse – arriving after dark or driving all night (accidents generally occur in daylight, but the occasional hijackings and shootings usually happen at night).

Chapter Seven: The north

Mwingi Coach and Garissa Express run via Kitui to Garissa (Ksh300) and Hola (Ksh450) from the Eastleigh KBS depot on General Waruinge Street, travelling in convoy from Mwingi. Runs are currently scheduled at 7am and 8am on Mon, Wed, Fri & Sun. There are no onward services from Garissa at present other than Hola, although you may find connections to Wajir and Garsen (for Lamu and Malindi) should security improve. The rest of the north is equally ill-served, with the northernmost limits of bus services being Isiolo (Ksh250–300; Akamba and Eastern Express, both daily), Maralal (Goldline) and Kitale (Eldoret Express and Akamba).

Tanzania
Apart from regular public buses run by Arusha Express to Arusha (Ksh1000) and Takrim/Taqwa (Duruma Road) to Dar es Salaam (2 daily) and Mwanza (daily), more comfortable (and expensive, around $30–35) coaches to Arusha and Moshi are operated by Davanu Shuttle (2 daily) and Riverside (2 daily; bookings through Tour Africa Safaris, p.142).

Uganda
Malaba is served by buses from the Country Bus Station (Ksh550). Akamba run both day and night services via Busia to Kampala (Ksh950 standard, Ksh1800 in comfier seats), as do some of the Peugeot companies. Jaguar Shuttle Services have the most comfortable coaches (Ksh2000; they're at Gilfillan House, Kenyatta Avenue – or book through a travel agent).

BUS COMPANIES
The following terminals and offices are marked on either the "Commercial Centre and River Road area" or "Central Nairobi" maps. Companies not listed below operate from the Country Bus Station ("Machakos Airport").

Akamba Bus, Lagos Road (☎02/340430 or 221779). Most services go from outside the office, with some from the Country Bus Station. The largest long-distance operator, with a relatively safe reputation. It's more comfortable vehicles operate at night.

Arusha Express, Cross Road/River Road (☎02/212083 or 338322). Safe reputation.

Coast Bus, Accra/Duruma Road (☎02/214819).

Crossline, River Road (☎02/245358).

Cross Road Travellers, Cross Road (turn right at the top of Accra Road) (☎02/331531). Peugeot shared-taxis.

Daily Peugeot Service (DPS), Dubois Road (☎02/242824). Run Peugeots north and west.

Davanu Shuttle, Windsor House, University Way (☎02/222002).

Eastern Express (no phone). From the Country Bus Station.

Garissa Express (Garex), opposite Eastleigh KBS depot, General Waruinge Street (☎02/764998-9).

Goldline, top of Accra Road/Cross Road (☎02/225279 or 221963).

KBS Stagecoach, KBS bus station, Mfangano Street (☎02/246047).

Kensilver Express, Dubois Road (☎02/221839 or 240218).

Malindi Bus, Duruma/Kumasi Road (☎02/229662).

Mombasa Liners, Accra/River Road (☎02/241564).

Mwingi Coach, opposite Eastleigh KBS depot, General Waruinge Street (☎02/765763).

Sunbird Services (no phone). From the Country Bus Station.

Transluxe, Opposite OTC (behind the KBS bus station), Temple Road (☎02/220059).

By plane: Jomo Kenyatta International Airport

International flights and **internal Kenya Airways** services leave from Jomo Kenyatta International Airport, 15km southeast of the city on the Mombasa road (flight arrivals and departures information on ☎02/822111 or 822206). Remember to **reconfirm** your flight reservations and also try to check that the plane is scheduled to arrive on time (addresses and telephone numbers on p.144). To get to the airport, take the KBS Stagecoach #34 bus (Ksh20 from the Ambassadeur Hotel, Ksh30 from the Youth Hostel; every 20min from around 6am to 8pm). See the warning in the "Security" box on p.85 about robbery on the #34 bus. After 8pm you'll have to get a taxi; all hotels will arrange this, or contact one of the companies listed on p.152. The ride is generally cheaper than on the way in, costing around Ksh600–800 if you pick one up on the street. Don't forget the $20 airport departure tax if you're flying out of Kenya, which can also be paid in shillings. You are allowed to take up to Ksh100,000 out of the country so long as you've kept the exchange receipts.

    Timetables: Bunson Travel Group publish a free comprehensive timetable of all scheduled national and international flights from Nairobi; Let's Go Travel have a handy list of flights within Kenya and for Zanzibar: addresses for both below. The *Nation* publishes a timetable of flights in and out of JKI every Friday.

Kenya Airways flights from JKI airport

To Mombasa: at least 8 daily non-stop from 7am to 8pm, extra weekend and high-season flights (1hr–1hr 15min; $85 single).

To Malindi: 2 daily, non-stop (1hr 10min; $85 single Kenya Airways; Ksh8400 African Express).

To Kisumu: 1 or 2 daily (1hr; $47 single).

To Zanzibar: 3 weekly (1hr 10min; $141 single; much cheaper from Mombasa).

Always check-in with time to spare – overbookings are commonplace.

Discounted international tickets

Flights to **African destinations** are rarely discounted; for these, visit Ethiopian Airlines, which has the best network (see box on p.145), or the national carrier of your

---

TRAVEL AGENTS AND AIRLINE BOOKINGS

Reputable general travel agents include:

Bunson Travel Service, Pan Africa House, Standard Street (PO Box 45456; ☎02/337712, fax 214120, *bunson@africaonline.co.ke*), one of the longest-established travel agents in Kenya, handling flight bookings, train reservations, safaris, car hire, and discounted hotel bookings.

Let's Go Travel, Caxton House, Standard Street (PO Box 60342; ☎02/340331, fax 336890, *www.kenya-direct.com/letsgo*). Branches in Karen shopping centre (☎02/882505, fax 882172) – and The Mall, Westlands (☎02/441030, fax 441690). Kenya's most useful independent agent/operator, Let's Go are outstanding, providing complete lists of hotel tariffs and helpful, not pushy, advice on just about everything, including international flights. They are the sole agents for a large number of homestay and ranch-house sites throughout Kenya, and also offer some specially negotiated deals on some of the more expensive hotels.

Tour Africa Safaris, 7th floor, Rehani House, corner Kenyatta Avenue and Koinange Street (PO Box 34187; ☎02/336767, fax 338271, *www.tourafrica-safaris.com*) are helpful and efficient, and offer much the same in addition to consolidated airline tickets and Tanzanian bookings.

destination. If you're thinking of flying to **Zanzibar** (3 weekly on Air Tanzania, $141 one-way), consider flying out from Mombasa, which is much cheaper ($64 one-way). For **flights to Europe and Asia** (there are no direct flights to the Americas or Australasia), you might visit some or all of the following discounted ticket agencies, though you'll only find the cheapest seat by checking them out one by one. The best deal, however, is invariably much more expensive than the same seat bought in Europe. Seats are purchased by the shops at the airline's unofficially discounted rate, so variations depend on the shops' mark-ups. Fares tend to be lowest if you book in a group. The cheapest seats to Europe tend to be with Egyptair, Gulf Air and Olympic.

Bankco Tours & Travel, 1st floor, Mulji Jetha Mansion, Latema/Lagos Rd (PO Box 11536; ☎02/336144, fax 331874).

Crocodile Travel, Stewart Building, Ronald Ngala/Tom Mboya St (PO Box 20380; ☎02/335250).

Haidery Tours & Travel, 1st floor, Impala House, Tom Mboya St (PO Box 45728; ☎02/335256, fax 211949).

Hanzuwan El-Kindy Tours & Travel, Dubois Rd (PO Box 49266; ☎02/227387).

Kambo Travel, Tom Mboya St, opposite Latema Rd (PO Box 41819; ☎02/228131, fax 228734).

Prince Safaris, Ground floor, Kenyatta International Conference Centre (PO Box 51096; ☎02/219499, fax 217692).

Trade & Travel Ltd, Monrovia St, opposite Jeevanjee Gardens (PO Box 11392; ☎02/227575, fax 228710).

By plane: Wilson Airport

Wilson Airport has regular **scheduled services** within Kenya (and to the Kilimanjaro region in Tanzania), and unscheduled flights into Somalia and the Democratic Republic of Congo (ex-Zaïre), both embroiled in bitter civil wars at present. Get to the airport on bus or *matatu* #15, #24, #31, #34, #125 or #126, alighting at the BP station (it's on your left). Note that several internal operators have only a 10kg baggage allowance, although a blind eye is sometimes turned. In any case, excess baggage isn't usually charged too highly ($1/kg is normal). Internal flights are subject to a Ksh100 departure tax. If you're in the market for **chartering a plane**, see p.134.

Scheduled flights from Wilson Airport

Amboseli Lodges: Airkenya, daily 7.30am (roughly 45min depending on lodge; $135 return).

Kilimanjaro (Tanzania): Airkenya, daily except Mon & Thurs 10.30am (1hr 25min; $135 single).

Kiwaiyu: Airkenya, daily 1.15pm (1hr 45min; $182 single).

Lamu (Manda Island): Airkenya and Kenya Airways, daily 1.15pm (1hr 45min; $130–187 single).

Lokichokio: Aircraft Leasing Services, Mon, Tues, Wed & Sat 11am (1hr 45min; $245 single).

Maasai Mara Lodges: Airkenya, daily 10am and 3pm; Aircraft Leasing Services daily 10am and 2.45pm (roughly 45min depending on lodge; $165 return).

Malindi: Airkenya, via Mombasa: Tues 8am, Fri 8am & 5pm; direct Sun 3.15pm (1hr 15min–1hr 55min; Ksh5385–8885 single).

Mandera: Blue Bird Aviation, Wed & Sat 1pm (3hr; single Ksh13,650, return Ksh20,800).

Mombasa: Airkenya, Mon–Sat 8am & 3.15pm (1hr 15min; Ksh5385-8885 single).

Mwanza (Tanzania): Eagle Aviation, Mon & Fri 9am (1hr 30min; $185 single).

Nanyuki: Airkenya, daily 9.15am (45min; $124 return).

Samburu (& Lewa Downs): Airkenya, daily 9.15am via Nanyuki (1hr 35min; 1hr 5min to Lewa Downs; $195 return).

Wajir: Blue Bird Aviation, Wed & Sat 1pm (1hr 30min; single Ksh10,000, return Ksh14,625).

AIRLINE OFFICES

Most airline offices are open Mon–Fri 8am or 8.30am–1pm & 2–4.30pm or 5pm, and Sat 8.30am–1pm. The following operate flights:

INTERNAL CARRIERS
(most at Wilson Airport, Langata Road)
Aircraft Leasing Services (☎02/500156)
Airkenya (☎02/501421–3; bookings ☎02/607750, fax 500845)
Blue Bird Aviation (☎02/602338)
Eagle Aviation (☎02/606015–6, fax 606017)
East African Air Charters (☎02/504731, fax 502358)
Fuf Aviation (☎02/505541)
Sarman Aviation (☎02/606416)
Trackmark (☎02/501263, fax 504907)

INTERNATIONAL CARRIERS
Note: Kenya Airways operates jointly with Ethiopian Airlines and Air France.
Aero Zambia, ground floor, International House, Mama Ngina Street (☎02/246519, fax 246523)
Air France, 2nd floor, International House, Mama Ngina Street (☎02/217501, fax 217517)
Air India, 3rd floor, Jeevan Bharati Building, Harambee Avenue (☎02/334788, fax 340582)
Air Madagascar, 1st floor, Hilton Building, City Hall Way (☎02/225286, fax 252347)
Air Malawi, Hilton Hotel Arcade, City Hall Way (☎02/333683, fax 340212)
Air Mauritius, mezzanine, International House, Mama Ngina Street (☎02/229166, fax 221006)
Air Seychelles, Archer's Tours & Travels, ground floor, Lonrho House, Standard Street (☎02/224361–2, fax 212656)
Air Tanzania, ground floor, Chester House, Koinange Street (☎02/336224, fax 214936)
Air Zimbabwe, ground floor, Chester House, Koinange Street (☎02/339524, fax 331983)
Alitalia, Archer's Tours & Travels, ground floor, Lonrho House, Standard Street (☎02/224361–2, fax 212656)
Aeroflot, Corner House, Mama Ngina Street (☎02/220746, fax 212213)
Balkan Bulgarian Airlines, 2nd floor, Royal Card Centre, Mpaka Road, Westlands (☎02/445900)
British Airways, International House, Mama Ngina Street (☎02/334440, fax 217437)
Cameroon Airlines, 9th floor, Rehani House, Kenyatta Avenue (☎02/224827, fax 219677)
Egyptair, Hilton Building, City Hall Way (☎02/226821, fax 213198)
El Al Israel Airlines, 9th floor, KCS House, Mama Ngina Street (☎02/228123, fax 212318)

Other flights from Wilson Airport

There are about a dozen commercial and NGO aviation companies who may also take passengers; all have offices at Wilson Airport. Some flights are advertised in the *Nation* and *The People*. Note that flights to the northeast and Somalia are "*miraa* flights", transporting the green leaves to its traditional consumers before they dry out and lose their efficacy, so your fare will be the equivalent of the amount of the drug you've left on the runway. These flights are often overloaded, and crashes are not infrequent.

Emirates, 20th floor, View Park Towers, Loita Street (☎02/822331)

Ethiopian Airlines, Bruce House, Muindi Mbingu Street (☎02/330837, fax 211986 or 219007)

Gulf Air, ground floor, International House, Mama Ngina Street (☎02/241123, fax 822399)

Kenya Airways, 5th floor, Barclays Plaza, Loita Street (☎02/229291, fax 336252)

KLM, 12th floor, Fedha Towers, corner of Muindi Mbingu Street and Standard Street (☎02/332673–7, fax 332788)

Olympic Airlines, 12th floor, Ambank House, University Way (☎02/338026, fax 338441)

Pakistan International Airlines, ICEA Building, Banda Street/Kenyatta Avenue (☎02/333901, fax 218706)

Royal Swazi National Airways, 4th floor, KCS House, Mama Ngina Street (☎02/210670)

Sabena, 11th floor, Ambank House, University Way (☎02/241212, fax 215508)

Saudi Arabian Airlines, mezzanine II, Anniversary Towers, University Way (☎02/230337, fax 337565)

South African Airways, 1st floor, Lonrho House, Kaunda Street (☎02/227486, fax 227488)

Swissair, Ambank House, University Way (☎02/250288, fax 256569)

Uganda Airlines, 1st floor, Uganda House, Kenyatta Avenue (☎02/221354, fax 214744)

AIRLINES WITH NO KENYA FLIGHTS THAT MAINTAIN RESERVATIONS AND ENQUIRIES OFFICES:

Aeroflot, Corner House, Mama Ngina Street (☎02/220746, fax 212213)

Air Botswana, Hilton Building, Mama Ngina Street (☎02/331648, fax 212041)

Air Canada, 6th floor, Lonrho House, Standard Street (☎02/218776, fax 212871)

Air Gabon, Archer's Tours & Travels, ground floor, Lonrho House, Standard Street (☎02/224361-2, fax 212656)

Air Namibia, Hilton Building, Mama Ngina Street (☎02/331648, fax 212041)

Air Zaïre, 1st floor, Consolidated House, Koinange Street (☎02/230142, fax 217412)

American Airlines, 2nd floor, 20th Century Plaza, Mama Ngina Street (☎02/242557, fax 212871)

Austrian Airlines, Hilton Building, Mama Ngina Street (☎02/331648, fax 338969)

Cathay Pacific Airways, Lonrho House, Standard Street (☎02/230235, fax 212871)

Iberia, Hilton Building, Mama Ngina Street (☎02/331648, fax 212041)

Japan Airlines, International House, Mama Ngina Street (☎02/220591, fax 333277)

Lufthansa, 9th floor, Ambank House, University Way (☎02/335819, fax 222161)

Nigeria Airways, Hilton Building, Mama Ngina Street (☎02/822026)

Qantas, ground floor, Rehema House, Kaunda Street (☎02/213321, fax 216871)

Sudan Airways, UTC Building, General Kago Street (☎02/822265, 225129)

VARIG Brazilian Airlines, Hilton Building, Mama Ngina Street (☎02/220961, fax 338916)

To the coast (Lamu, Mombasa, Malindi and Zanzibar): Eagle Aviation (☎02/606015–6, fax 606017).

To Tsavo West: East African Air Charters (☎02/504731, fax 502358).

To the northwest (Lokichokio): Trackmark (☎02/501263, fax 504907).

To the northeast (Mandera, Wajir, Liboi, Dadaalo): Fuf Aviation (☎02/505541); Sarman Aviation (☎02/606416).

To Somalia (Mogadishu): Blue Bird Aviation (☎02/602338); Prestige Air (☎02/501211).

To Democratic Republic of Congo: Aim Air (☎02/602300); Boskovic (☎02/501210, fax 505964).

Hitch-hiking

Here are some **jumping-off points** to get you started:

To Naivasha and beyond: take bus/*matatu* #2, #102, #103 or #115 as far as the "Kikuyu flyover".

To Thika and beyond: take bus/*matatu* #17B, #25, #45, #137, #145, #160, #237 as far as Kenya Breweries.

Listings

Air ambulance If you're worried about medical evacuation from the wilds, contact: AAR Health Services (☎02/717375–6); or the Flying Doctors Service (Amref) (☎02/501280, 602492, fax 336886).

Airlines and ticket agencies See p.144 and p.142 respectively.

American Express, Express Travel Group, Bruce House, Standard St (PO Box 40433), is the main walk-in office (☎02/334722, fax 334825). All the usual services and they'll hold card-holders' mail.

Artists' materials Sciencescope, Victor House, by the Nation Centre, Kimathi St (☎02/210741 or 447920), is the place for professional oils, acrylics, pastels, paper etc. They have a branch at the Yaya Centre, Hurlingham.

Automobile Association ☎02/714212, 724378 or 712809.

Banks There are branches of Barclays everywhere, most with ATM cash machines and efficient, helpful service, but only Standard Chartered Bank, which also has ATMs, has more abysmal exchange rates. The best bank rates are offered by Stanbic Bank, Stanbic Bank Building, Kenyatta Ave. Good rates are also offered by African Banking Corporation (ABC), Koinange St, and also at Woodvale Grove, Westlands. The best rates are posted by the numerous competing forex bureaux found throughout the city, whose rates differ only by one percent or so. Many of them are little more than a desk and armed *askari* guard; some don't accept travellers' cheques (or require your proof of purchase), others refuse plastic, but their service is usually fast. If you're worried security-wise about being seen to change money, the Commercial Bank of Africa inside the *Hilton Hotel* (Mon–Fri 1–8pm, Sat 8am–8pm) is out of sight, but has bad rates. There are no banks open on Sundays except the exchange bureaux at the airport, though the larger hotels may oblige with their facilities. Western Union Transfers are received by Postbank, Postbank House, Market Lane (☎02/229551, fax 210593; Mon–Fri 8.30am–4pm, Sat 8.30–11am). For details of bank charges and using plastic in ATMs, see p.25.

Bicycles See p.43.

Blood tests See "Doctors".

Books Good downtown bookshops, carrying wide selections of coffee-table books, maps of Kenya and the major game parks, and imported paperbacks, include: Westland Sundries/Nation Bookshop, Kenyatta Ave (entrance also from the *Stanley Hotel*); Bookpoint, Loans House, Moi Ave; Premier Bookshop, corner of Tom Mboya St and Ronald Ngala St (who have the widest range of maps); Prestige, Prudential Assurance Building, Mama Ngina St (also open Sun 9.30am–12.30pm); and Primrose Sundries, 20th Century Plaza, Mama Ngina St. The Textbook Centre, Kijabe St (☎02/330340–5, fax 225779) behind the *Norfolk Hotel*, with an excellent branch at the Sarit Centre, Westlands (☎02/747405), also has a good choice, as well as stationery and artists' materials. In River Road district, you'll find a cluster of bookshops at and around the junction of Lagos Rd and Latema Rd. For a good second-hand selection, try Prestige, or the Book Stop, Yaya Centre, Hurlingham. East African Educational Publishers have their sales office on Kijabe St (☎02/222144).

Buses and matatus See pp.139–140 for national services, and the box on p.90 for local ones.

Camping gas Available at a number of places including Nakumatt for about Ksh70 a cartridge. It's twice the price anywhere else in Kenya.

Camping equipment Atul's, Biashara St (Mon–Fri 9am–1pm & 2.30–5.30pm, Sat 9am–3pm; PO Box 43202; ☎02/228064), is the only place where you can rent outdoor equipment – especially useful if you're going to Mount Kenya – but the prices can seem excessive to budget travellers (for example, tent rental from Ksh320 per day). They are also fully equipped for repair jobs, and sell equipment too. On the same street but on the other side of Muindi Mbingu St, Kenya Canvas Ltd

(Mon–Fri 8am–5pm, Sat 8am–1pm; PO Box 45688; ☎02/333509) sells tents (from Ksh9000), mosquito nets (Ksh375) and other equipment. Much cheaper than either for basic tents (from Ksh4000), sleeping bags (Ksh3000 and up), kipmats (Ksh800), cooking stoves and gas bottles is the Nakumatt Centrepoint supermarket on Kenyatta Ave, between Koinange St and Muindi Mbuingi St (Mon–Sat 8.30am–8.30pm, Sun 10am–7pm).

Cars and car rental See p.41 and p.44.

Chartering a plane See p.134.

Contraceptives Oral contraceptives are available from the Family Planning Clinic, 5th Floor, Phoenix House, Standard St (☎02/335775). Condoms are sold in any supermarket or pharmacy.

Doctors Recommended are: Dr R. Kaushal in Westlands (☎02/441176 or 582040) and Dr Sheth, Sarit Centre, Westlands. Alternatively, ask your embassy for a list. For blood tests, Nairobi Laboratories Ltd, Pioneer House, Moi Ave (☎02/331954), are very good. A malaria check costs about Ksh600. If you prefer homeopathic treatment, consult Dr R. J. S. Panesar, Diamond Plaza, High Ridge, near *Mrs Roche's Guest House* (☎02/746772). A recommended chiropractor is Dr Thomas Adagala, mornings downtown at 1st floor, APDC House, Lagos Rd (☎02/330782), afternoons at Vanga Rd, Lavington (☎02/560078).

Ecology and conservation (see also "Kenya Wildlife Service") The influential East African Wildlife Society (PO Box 20110; ☎02/574145, fax 570335; *eawls@elci.sasa.unon.org*) was strongly involved in the movement to ban the ivory trade (achieved 1989), and remains active in other areas, recently concerning itself with raising awareness about forest and mangrove protection, and the plight of the endangered hirola antelope. Individual membership, which entitles you to annual subscription of their quarterly magazine *Swara* and use of their library, costs £35 (£45 airmail) in the UK, $50 in the US. In similar vein, the Friends of Conservation (Kenya: PO Box 74901 Nairobi, ☎02/339537 or 243976, fax 332106; UK: 1st floor, 22 Chapter St, London SW1P 4NP ☎0171/559 4790, fax 0171/559 4792; USA: 1520 Kensington Rd, Suite 201, Oak Brook, IL 60521 ☎630/954 3388, fax 954 1016) concerns itself with raising awareness of the detrimental consequences of tourism in East and Southern Africa. In return for membership (£10/$15 student/senior citizen; £15/$25 and up for adults), you receive their newsletter, *Survivor*. The Friends of Nairobi National Park (PO Box 42976; ☎02/500622 ext 18, fax 505866; *wildnetafrica.co.za/wildlifeorgs/fon/*) strive to keep the migratory routes to the park open, and aim to raise awareness among Nairobi citizens about the park. Members (adults $25, students $5, families $50) receive a monthly newsletter. The Kenya Forests Working Group (KFWG) is concerned with conserving and managing Kenya's forests, and have a "Forest Hotline" for up-to-date information on current issues (☎ & fax 02/571335). More practical work is being done by the Greenbelt Movement (Adams Arcade, Ngong Rd; PO Box 67545 Nairobi; ☎02/603867 or 571223) to stop the illegal expropriation and development of public land, notably the controversial Karura Forest development saga. Cynthia Moss's African Wildlife Foundation, which has a long-running study of Amboseli's elephants and produces many films on the subject, is contactable on ☎02/710367 or 710369–70.

Email and Internet services The cheapest email and Internet access is provided by Win.World, 7th floor, Standard Building, Standard St (*win.world@nbnet.co.ke*; Ksh50 to send, Ksh40 to receive emails; or Ksh1500 monthly membership which entitles you to 15min daily Internet access). Other places include: the *Hilton*'s business centre, 2nd floor, *Hilton Hotel* (Mon–Fri 7am–8pm, Sat 8am–4pm, *hilton@africaonline.co.ke*; emails Ksh70 to receive; Internet Ksh500 per 30min); Cyber Safaris at *Simmers Restaurant*, corner of Kenyatta Ave and Muindi Mbingu St (emails Ksh100 per 15min; Internet Ksh400 per hr); *Cybervore Internet Café* at *Carnivore* (Mon–Fri 10.30am–11pm, Sat–Sun 11am–11pm; email/Internet Ksh150 per 15min; Ksh10 per page printed); *Galexon*, lower ground floor, Kimathi House, Kimathi St (8am–7pm Mon–Sat; email Ksh100 to send, Ksh40 to receive; Internet Ksh500 per hr); and *Cyberc@fe*, Bruce House, Kaunda St (Mon–Fri 8.15am–6pm, Sat 8.15am–1.30pm, *cybercafe@insightkenya.com*; email Ksh65 to send/receive; Internet Ksh300 per hr).

Flight information ☎02/822111 or 822206 at Jomo Kenyatta Airport. Full information on flights, airlines and bookings on p.142–145.

Football (soccer) Nyayo Stadium, at the junction of Uhuru Highway and Langata Rd. Seats cost Ksh60–120. Highly recommended, whether you're a regular fan or not, but especially for international matches (these may be played at Moi International Stadium on the Thika Rd). Getting back to the town centre afterwards by public transport can be a problem.

Freight Air freight is cheaper than sea freight except for very large items. All companies charge the same per kilo rates (currently $5.32 per kg, with discounts for certain items like books), but shop around for the lowest handling charges. Federal Express, Bruce House, Standard St (PO Box 49707; ☎02/240106 or 240138, fax 211307) are reliable and charge a minimum fee of $80 which is less than most. Alternatively, much cheaper is simply to bypass the middlemen and send your parcels direct from the British Airways cargo counter at Kenyatta International Airport's international departures lounge (☎02/822172–5; currently $3.50 per kg for any airport in Europe, no handling charges). See also "Post and parcel couriers".

Golf clubs Bookings for all the following can be done through Tobs Golf Safaris Ltd (PO Box 20146; ☎02/721722, 727790, fax 722015, *tobsgolf@form-net.com*). Windsor Golf & Country Club, Kigwa Rd, 15km north of the city (☎02/862300) has the best location, in rich lake- and woodland teeming with Sykes monkeys. The 6751-yard par 72 course, with a long 640-yard 5th, is reckoned the most challenging, and there's a resident pro, too. On Muchai Drive, the Royal Nairobi Golf Club's 7021-yard par 72 course is easier, with a cultivated landscape and views of the Ngong Hills (☎02/725769). Muthaiga Golf Club (☎02/762414) on Muthaiga Rd, has its 6676-yard par 72 on the edge of Karura forest (currently under threat from illegal development). It boasts a variety of indigenous trees and flowering shrubs, has fast greens, and hosts the Kenya Open. Other clubs include the pretty and very colonial Karen Golf & Country Club (☎02/882801) with a 6893-yard par 72, next to the Blixen Museum; and Limuru Country Club's 6519-yard par 71, in tea country, whose altitude (2130m) provides the rainfall to keep the turf green year-round.

Guides Guides for almost anywhere in Kenya can be arranged through Utalii College, Kenya's college for tourist-oriented trades, though it would be advisable to contact them well in advance (PO Box 31052; ☎02/802540–7).

Hairdressers and barbers. Very cheap, no-fuss men's cuts at Boston's, Uganda House Arcade, Kenyatta Ave/Standard St. Manes Unisex Hair Salon, mezzanine floor, Avenue House, Kenyatta Ave, offers bonding weaves, spiral rolls, pedicure, false nails and pussycat, among other mysterious delights.

Health foods Healthier Options, Soin Arcade, Westlands Rd, Westlands. Good range of imported health foods and remedies.

Horse racing Frequent buses on race days (usually Sun) to Ngong Rd Race Course from the KBS bus station.

Horse riding Arifa Riding School, Marula Lane, Karen (☎02/882937), offers lessons and hire. Kitengela Polo Club, Karen (☎02/882782), also has lessons, "game drives", picnic rides and, of course, polo.

Hospitals The Kenyatta National Hospital, Argwings Kodhek Rd (☎02/726300) is the main public hospital for accidents and emergencies, and did miraculous work in the aftermath of the August 7 US Embassy bombing. It's adequate for non-life-threatening problems but under-staffed and under-funded. You may have to wait your turn. The private Consolata Sisters' Nazareth Hospital (☎02/335684), on Riara Ridge Rd, near Limuru, about 25km from Nairobi (bus #117 from bus station), charges reasonable rates and is recommended if you need to be in for some time (assuming you have any choice in the matter). Another private place with a good reputation is the Aga Khan Hospital in Third Parklands Ave (PO Box 30270; ☎02/740000). For emergencies, dial ☎999 (free calls).

Kenya Wildlife Service (KWS) This is Kenya's National Parks organization, who are in charge of their day-to-day running and security, as well as liaison with local communities. Contacting them is essential if you plan to visit the more remote parks and reserves, or have specialist requests or queries. They are also the only body to give (hard to get) official clearance for entering parks and zones where security is a concern (notably Mount Elgon, and all the parks and reserves in Northeastern Province): KWS Headquarters, Langata Rd, Nairobi National Park Main Gate (PO Box 40241; ☎02/501081–2, fax 505866 or 501752, *kws@africaonline.co.ke*).

Language schools Trans Africa Language Services, Joseph Kangethe Rd, Adam's Arcade, off Ngong Rd (PO Box 21394; ☎02/561160), offer Kiswahili courses individually and in groups. Other languages are also available. A similar service is offered by Makioki Language Services, Kijabi St (☎02/242330). Nairobi Cultural Institute, Ngong Rd (☎02/569205) runs Kiswahili courses. For private teaching, check the notice board at Gallery Watatu.

Laundry There are two laundries in Nairobi, Mbuni Dry Cleaners in Westlands at the corner of Chiromo and Mpaka roads, the other one – better and more expensive – is Niki's in Hurlingham Plaza, Hurlingham, Argwings Kodhek Rd (☎02/715387). Laundry may be left with the staff to wash and iron for later collection. There are plenty of dry-cleaners: Pearl branches are everywhere and cheap, whilst the equally ubiquitous White Rose is more expensive but has an express service. Hotels and lodgings will always do washing for you at prices appropriate to the room charges. Some indeed will insist you don't wash your own.

Left luggage Bags can be left safely at either of the two left-luggage offices at the train station: there are lockers at the side of the 1st/2nd class entrance (daily except Sun 6.30am–noon & 2–6.30pm; Ksh150 per item), whilst larger bags can be left at the third-class hall (daily 7.30am–7.30pm; Ksh300 per item). Given the expense, consider leaving bags in the care of your hotel, if you think you can trust them. There is no left-luggage facility at the airport.

Libraries The British Council, ICEA Building, Kenyatta Ave (Tues–Fri 10am–5pm, Sat 9am–noon; ☎02/334855), has British newspapers and magazines, in addition to videos for rent, and film/video screenings on Tues and Thurs at 5.30pm. The McMillan Memorial Library, Banda St (Mon–Fri 9am–5pm, Sat 9.30am–1pm; free; ☎02/224281 ext 2253), is the main public library, with a good "Africana" reading room (Ksh100 for a week's use). For serious research, the British Institute in Eastern Africa, 3km northwest of town at Laikipia Rd (off Arboretum Drive), Kileleshwa (PO Box 30710; ☎02/43721 or 43330, fax 43365, *britinst@insightkenya.com*) is excellent, with a comprehensive collection of books, academic journals, off-prints and theses: membership costs Ksh500 for residents, £12.50 for non-residents, for which you also receive the annual journal *Azania*. Also good for research is the reading room in the National Archives, Moi Ave (see p.105), whose annual membership is a paltry Ksh50. There are also small research libraries at the university's Department for African Studies, based in the National Museum compound, and at the National Museum itself, jointly run with the East Africa Natural History Society.

Maps Game park maps published by the Survey of Kenya (some of which are over a decade out of date), and maps of Nairobi and environs, are available from bookshops; so, too, are the city-wide *A–Z of Nairobi* (Kenway Publications; somewhat out of date, too) and general maps of Kenya. For Survey of Kenya covering other parts of the country, the procedure is complicated to say the least: you first visit the Public Map Office, Harambee Ave (just west of the Conference Centre), to find out which of the sheets you want are available, and note their numbers (they sell all the game park maps, too). Then you go to the Survey of Kenya offices (PO Box 30046) out on the Thika road (see "Greater Nairobi map", p.82) where you make a formal written request stating which sheets you want, why ("I am a tourist wishing to visit. . ."), and leaving your address. They will, eventually, get back to you, with an authorization to buy the maps. You might want to do all this before even reaching Kenya, though in fact some of the supposedly "sensitive" maps are available to order through stockists in Europe and America. The British Ordnance Survey is one such agent.

Newspapers and magazines Foreign papers such as the *International Herald Tribune* are available from several newsstands around Kenyatta Ave, as are *Newsweek* and *Time*, and most of the British dailies and Sundays. Most of the bookshops stock magazines. The best Kenyan daily is the *Nation*. *The People* on Fridays and the *East African* on Mondays are also good.

Notice boards The best-known was at the *Thorn Tree Café* at the *Stanley Hotel*, but this disappeared after the eponymous tree was cut down in early 1998. A replacement was planted in December 1998, and hopefully will sprout a new board. The *Iqbal's* notice board is probably the best in town for budget travellers. *Ma Roche's* also has a budget-oriented notice board, as does the youth hostel. The *Fairview Hotel* has a slightly more upmarket notice board, used by travellers. The Yaya Centre in Hurlingham (vehicles for sale, houses for rent and so on) is likely to be of more interest to long-term visitors.

Opticians All your needs, including contact lenses and solutions, at Eye Masters Ltd, Kenya Cinema Plaza, Moi Ave (Mon–Fri 7.30am–6pm, Sat 9am–2pm; ☎02/222601).

Ornithology The Museum Ornithology Society organizes bird walks or bird drives around Nairobi. Enthusiastic non-members are welcome if they make a donation. Meet at the museum on Wed at 8.30am.

Passport photos Five-minute passport photo service at Studio One, corner of Moi/Nkrumah avenues, and at Custom Color, Kaunda St. There's a "Photo-Me" at Vedic House on Mama Ngina St.

Pharmacy Kam Pharmacy, Mpaka Rd, Westlands (☎02/443776). There's also a chemist in the *Hilton* (Mon–Fri 9am–6pm, Sun 9am–1.30pm).

.**Photocopying** Numerous places throughout Nairobi, the largest being Mita Copier Centre on Muindi Mbingu St/Kaunda St.

Photography For camera repairs, try Camera Clinic, Biashara St (☎02/222492). Buying a camera is approximately twice as expensive as in Europe. Instead, check Nairobi notice boards (see under

EMBASSIES, HIGH COMMISSIONS AND CONSULATES

In addition to the following, Nairobi has a number of other Latin American and Asian embassies.

Algeria, 4th floor, Comcraft House, Haile Selassie Avenue (PO Box 53902; ☎02/213864–6, fax 217477)

Australia, ICIPE House, Riverside Drive, off Chiromo Road (PO Box 47718; ☎02/445034–9, fax 444617)

Austria, 2nd floor, City House, Standard/Wabera Street (PO Box 30560; ☎02/228281–2, fax 331792)

Belgium, Muthaiga/Lumuru Road, Parklands (PO Box 30461; ☎02/741564–7, fax 741568)

Burundi, 14th floor, Development House, Moi Avenue (PO Box 44439; ☎02/335973 or ☎ & fax 219005)

Canada, 6th floor, Comcraft House, Haile Selassie Avenue (PO Box 30481; ☎02/214804, after hours 02/214804, fax 226987)

China, Woodlands Road, off State House Road, Hurlingham (PO Box 30508; ☎02/722559, fax 726402)

Congo, 12th floor, Electricity House, Harambee Avenue (PO Box 48106; ☎02/229771-2)

Cyprus, 5th floor, Eagle House, Kimathi Street (PO Box 30739; ☎02/220881, fax 331232)

Czech Republic, Embassy House, Harambee Avenue (PO Box 30204; ☎02/210494 or 223448)

Denmark, 11th floor, HFCK Building, Kenyatta Avenue/Koinange Street (PO Box 40412; ☎02/331088–90, fax 331492)

Djibouti, 2nd floor, Comcraft House, Haile Selassie Avenue (PO Box 59528; ☎02/48089, fax 339633)

Egypt, 7th floor, Harambee Plaza, Uhuru Highway/Haile Selassie Avenue (PO Box 30285; ☎02/250764 or 225992, fax 211560)

Eritrea, 2nd floor, New Rehema House, Rhapta Road (PO Box 38651; ☎02/443163, fax 443165)

Ethiopia, State House Avenue, Nairobi Hill (PO Box 45198; ☎02/723027, fax 723401)

Finland, 2nd floor, International House, Mama Ngina Street (PO Box 30379; ☎02/334777, fax 335986)

France, 9th floor, Barclays Plaza, Loita Street (PO Box 41784; ☎02/339978, fax 339421)

Germany, 8th floor, Williamson House, 4th Ngong Avenue (PO Box 30180; ☎02/712527–8, fax 714886)

Greece, 13th B floor, Nation Centre, Kimathi Street (PO Box 30543; ☎02/340722, fax 216044)

Hungary, Ole Odume Road, off Argwings Kodhek Road (PO Box 61146; ☎02/560060 or 226915)

Iceland, Bendera Lane, off Spring Valley Road PO Box 45000; ☎ & fax 521487)

India, 2nd floor, Jeevan Bharati Building, Harambee Avenue (PO Box 30074; ☎02/222566–7, fax 334167)

Indonesia, 3rd floor, Utalii House, Uhuru Highway (PO Box 48868; ☎02/215848, fax 340721)

Ireland, 5th floor, Waumini House, Chiromo Road (☎02/444367 or 571635)

Israel, Bishops Road (PO Box 30354; ☎02/724021–2, fax 715966)

Italy, 9th floor, International House, Mama Ngina Street (PO Box 30107; ☎02/337777, fax 337056)

Ivory Coast, Standard Street (☎02/220179 or 220864)

Japan, 15th floor, ICEA Building, Kenyatta Avenue (PO Box 60202; ☎02/332955-8, fax 216530)

Lebanon, 9th floor, Maendeleo House, Monrovia Street (PO Box 55303; ☎02/229981-3, fax 340944)

Luxembourg, 8th floor, International House, Mama Ngina Street (PO Box 30610; ☎02/224318, fax 229938)

Madagascar, 1st floor, Hilton Building, Mama Ngina Street (PO Box 41723; ☎02/225286 or 226494)

Malawi, Mvuli Road/Church Road, off Waiyaki Way, Westlands (PO Box 30453; ☎02/440568–9)

Morocco, 3rd floor, Diamond Trust House, Moi Avenue (PO Box 61098; ☎02/222264, fax 222364)

Mozambique, HFCK Building, Kenyatta Avenue/Koinange Street (☎02/222446 or 221979)

Netherlands, 6th floor, Uchumi House, Nkrumah Avenue (PO Box 41537; ☎02/332420, fax 339155)

New Zealand, 3rd floor, Minet ICDC House, Mamlaka Road (PO Box 47383; ☎02/722467)

Nigeria, Lenana Road, Hurlingham (PO Box 30516; ☎02/564116-8, fax 562776)

Norway, 8th floor, HFCK Building, Kenyatta Avenue (PO Box 46363; ☎02/337121-2, fax 216009)

Pakistan, Church Road, off Rhapta Road, Westlands (PO Box 30045; ☎02/443911-2, fax 446507)

Poland, Kabarnet Road, off Ngong Road, Woodley (PO Box 30086; ☎02/566288, fax 727701)

Portugal, 10th floor, Reinsurance Plaza, Taifa Road (PO Box 34020; ☎02/338990, fax 214711)

Russia, next to Army HQ, Lenana Road (PO Box 30049; ☎02/728700, fax 721888)

Rwanda, 12th floor, International House, Mama Ngina Street (PO Box 48579; ☎02/240563 or 212345, fax 336365)

Saudi Arabia, Muthaiga Road (PO Box 58297; ☎02/762781-4, fax 760939)

Seychelles, 7th floor, Agip House, Waiyaki Way (PO Box 20400; ☎02/441150 or 445599)

Slovakia, Milimani Road (☎02/721896–7)

Somalia, 5th floor, International House, Mama Ngina Street (PO Box 30769; ☎02/580165 or 581683)

South Africa, 17th floor, Lonrho House, Standard Street (PO Box 42441; ☎02/215616–8, fax 223687)

Spain, 5th floor, Bruce House, Standard Street (PO Box 45503; ☎02/335711)

Sudan, 7th floor, Minet ICDC House, Mamlaka Road (PO Box 74059; ☎02/720883, fax 721015)

Swaziland, 3rd floor, Transnational Plaza, Mama Ngina Street (PO Box 41887; ☎02/339231–3, fax 330540)

Sweden, 10th floor, International House, Mama Ngina Street (PO Box 30600; ☎02/229042–45, fax 218908)

Switzerland, 7th floor, International House, Mama Ngina Street (PO Box 30752; ☎02/228735–6, fax 217388)

Tanzania, 5th floor, Continental Towers, Uhuru Highway/Harambee Avenue (PO Box 47790; ☎02/331104, fax 218269)

Uganda, 5th floor, Uganda House, Kenyatta Avenue (PO Box 60853; ☎02/330801)

United Kingdom, Upper Hill Road, off Haile Selassie Avenue (PO Box 30465; ☎02/719107 or 719082, fax 719112, *consular@nairobi.mail.fco.gov.uk*)

USA: since the August 1998 bombing, temporarily based at the US AID building, The Crescent, Parklands (PO Box 30137; ☎02/751613, fax 743203 or 749590 or 749892). Travellers are encouraged to register with the Embassy by fax.

Yemen, Ngong/Kabarnet Road (PO Box 44642; ☎02/574646 or 564517, fax 561071)

Zambia, Nyerere Road (PO Box 48741; ☎02/724796, fax 718494)

Zimbabwe, 6th floor, Minet ICDC House, Mamlaka Road (PO Box 30806; ☎02/721049, fax 726503)

"Notice boards"). For batteries and to rent cameras and binoculars, the main outlet is Elite Camera House, Kimathi St, south of Kenyatta, but they are not recommended for repairs. Expo Camera, Esso House, Mama Ngina St (next to the Kenya Coffee Board), offer a fast, reliable service for prints and slides and also do good repairs. Any branch of Colorama is likely to be reliable, and there's an efficient one-hour service (2hr for slides) from Spectrum Colour Lab at Rehema House on Standard St.

Postal services Until the new GPO on Kenyatta Ave is opened, poste restante and everything else is at the City Square Post Office on Haile Selassie Ave by the pedestrian footbridge (Mon–Fri 8.30am–5pm, Sat 9am–noon). Letters normally take under a week to arrive from Europe, although 3–4 weeks is not unheard of, and too many things simply never arrive. The parcels office is upstairs (open for posting Mon–Fri 8am–5pm, Sat 9am–noon; open for collecting Mon–Fri 8am–1pm & 2–5pm). Parcels from home can be addressed to you at poste restante: you'll get a note from the Parcels Section. There are smaller branch offices on Moi Ave opposite Tubman Rd, and another nearby on Tom Mboya St. Alternatively, one of the larger hotels may oblige by selling you stamps.

Post and parcel couriers If you have valuable items to send home contact: DHL, Longonot Place, Kijabe St (PO Box 67577; ☎02/223063, fax 339850); TNT Express Worldwide, Kiambere Rd (PO Box 41520; ☎02/723554, fax 723077; UPS, Fedha Towers, Kaunda St (PO Box 46586; ☎02/252200, fax 252201); or EMS Speedpost on Posta Rd. See also "Freight".

Sports and health clubs (see also "Golf clubs"). The *Norfolk Hotel* sells one-month membership (under $50) of its health club, which includes use of its heated pool and gym, and aerobics. The *Serena Hotel* has a similar deal, which includes its unheated pool and multigym. The Nairobi Safari Club's facilities are ridiculously expensive, as are the *Grand Regency*'s. Much more fun than any of these is Grand-Prix Karting, next to *Carnivore*, with its 500-metre circuit (Wed–Sun; ☎02/501758). There's indoor bowling at the Cosmic Bowling & Pool Centre in Sound Plaza, Woodvale Grove, Westlands.

Swimming pools One of the best pools is at *Hotel Boulevard*, a nice setting with delightful water and better value than the *Norfolk*'s. For the genuinely skint, *Heron Court Hotel* charges a mere Ksh40 for its pool, and the excellent one at the YMCA on the west side of Uhuru Highway costs Ksh40. The pool at the *Panafric* is handy if you're staying at the youth hostel; the pool at *Silver Springs Hotel*, Valley Rd, behind the hostel, is even better. A day by an ordinary pool usually costs around Ksh100–200. If you're staying at *Ma Roche's*, you should certainly check out the modern sports complex behind the Aga Khan Hospital – fantastic pool, diving board, lounging area, snooker rooms, gym and team-sport pitches and courts all for about Ksh60 a day. More central are the pools at the *Stanley Hotel* (including jacuzzi and steam room), *Meridian Court Hotel*, and *Hotel Inter-Continental* (use of the steam room, jacuzzi and sauna for Ksh600, though you stay as long as you like). *Safari Park Hotel*'s pool is unfortunately for residents only. For real water-babies, a trip to *Carnivore*'s Splash! water park is a must – waterslides, fountains, ecstatic children and sometimes a disco at night.

Taxis Kenatco, Uchumi House, Aga Khan Walk (☎02/225123, 338611, 230771–2; JKA airport branch ☎02/824248 or 822356) is reliable and open 24 hours (airport Ksh1000). Discount Travel, ground floor, 20th Century Plaza, Mama Ngina St (☎02/251203), runs to the airport for Ksh900.

Telephone and faxes (see also email and Internet services, and read the details in Basics on p.58). The main place is the official Extelcoms on Haile Selassie Ave, next to the gaping hulk of the bombed Cooperative Bank Building. There are two entrances: the one on the left is for calls within Kenya (open 24 hours); the one on the right is for international calls (daily 7am–midnight): calls are made through an operator – you fill in a form stating how many minutes you'd like (currently Ksh540 per minute to Europe, or three minutes for Ksh930, then wait for the call to be put through (sometimes immediate, sometimes takes hours). Lines are less busy at weekends. It's easier, if they haven't run out, to buy a phone card (Ksh200 & Ksh500) to use the blue IDD card phones outside the building (or in the Kenyatta International Conference Centre), but the largest card will only last you a couple of minutes. Note that card phones elsewhere in the city are for national calls only. If all else fails, you can make calls from large hotels: you pay through the nose for this (Ksh1500 and up for 3min) but at least you can talk in peace. Faxes can be sent and received at Extelcoms (fax 330170; Ksh403 to send a page worldwide, Ksh28 to receive); but much cheaper is Win.World, 7th floor, Standard Building, Standard St (Ksh170 per page worldwide). As the Internet develops in Kenya, there should be many more such places in future. Hotels will receive faxes for a small fee (usually around Ksh50 per page).

Tourist information Nairobi has no official tourist information service – a lamentable state of affairs. The free and widely circulated monthly *What's On in Kenya* is always worth a glance. If you can't find a copy, ask at the Nation Centre, Kimathi St. The *Standard* and *Nation* newspapers are a useful source of current information and special offers.

Train services See p.86 for arriving, and p.139 for information on departures.

Vaccinations Cholera, yellow fever, typhoid and hepatitis jabs can be obtained from City Hall, City Hall Way, or from Dr C.S. Sheth, Sarit Centre, Westlands, who can also advise about malaria.

Visitors' passes/visas Visitor's pass extensions (up to six months in all) can be obtained at Nyayo House, Posta Rd, behind the GPO (Mon–Fri 8.30am–12.30pm & 2–3.30pm; ☎02/332110). This is usually done while you wait. Do not go there if you have overstayed your permit (see p.23).

Women's movement The Maendeleo ya Wanawake ("Women's Progress") organization has its main office in Maendeleo House on Monrovia St (PO Box 44412; ☎02/222095, fax 225390). Founded in 1952, the MYWO also has a shop on Muindi Mbingu St, selling crafts without the middle men. The Forum for African Women Educationalists (FAWE), established in 1992, aims to improve girls' and women's education (PO Box 53168; ☎02/226590, fax 210709).

Worship As well as large numbers of mosques and temples, Nairobi has a number of churches, two cathedrals, and a synagogue (all on the "Central Nairobi" map, p.102). The synagogue has services at 6.30pm on Friday and 8am on Saturday and the rabbi is delighted to see visitors. The four main churches are located in the northwest of the city centre (near the synagogue) and the area is a lively focus for Christians on Sunday mornings. All Saint's Cathedral, a beautiful church behind Uhuru Park, has often been a gathering point for peaceful opposition protest to the government (services in English Sun 7.15am, 9.30am, 11am & 6.30pm; Tues 1.15pm, Wed 7.30am; Thurs 11am), and was last stormed by riot police in July 1997.

NAIROBI PROVINCE

Nairobi Province stretches way beyond the city suburbs, taking in an area of some 690 square kilometres (270 square miles) ranging from agricultural and ranching land to jungle and national park.

For visitors, most of the interest lies to the **south**, in the predominantly Maasai land that begins with **Nairobi National Park** and includes the watershed ridge of the **Ngong Hills**. It's a striking landscape, vividly described in Karen Blixen's *Out of Africa*.

North of the city, the land is also distinctive: narrow valleys twisting down from the Kinangop plateau, some still filled with jungle and, it's said, leopards. In spite of that, the steep slopes here are high-value real estate, in the process of development as exclusive suburbs, planted with shady gardens and festooned with security signs. To the **west**, the railway cuts through largely Kikuyu farmland, densely cultivated with corn, bananas and the cash crop insecticide plant, pyrethrum. **East**, beyond the shanty suburb of Dandora, are the wide Athi plains, which are mostly ranching country.

Nairobi National Park

Daily 6am–7pm, no entry after 6.15pm; $20 (plans afoot to halve this); 30kph speed limit. Warden PO Box 42076 (☎02/500627, fax 505866). Maps: the best is the KWS one sold at the Main Gate (1997); otherwise, Survey of Kenya SK71 (1990) has loads of detail, but is a little out of date.

If you don't think you'll be able to see any of the big Kenyan game reserves, try at least to spend a morning or afternoon in Nairobi's own **National Park**. Despite the hype, it really is remarkable that this 113-square-kilometre patch of plains and woodland should exist almost uncorrupted – complete with more than eighty species of large mammals – literally within earshot of the downtown traffic. The park has no elephants but this is a small deficiency among a surprisingly high concentration of animals. For all the low-flying planes and lines of tourist minibuses, you have a greater chance of witnessing a kill here than in any of the other parks. Kenya residents use the park as a route from Karen and Langata to the Jomo Kenyatta International Airport – it does make a pleasant way of leaving the country if you can work it into your flight times.

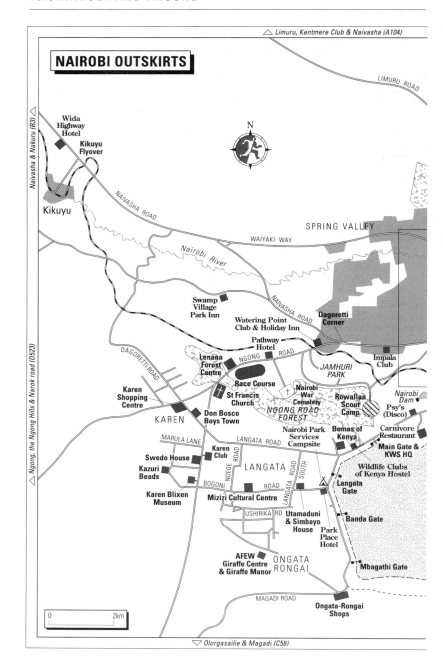

△ Limuru, Kentmere Club & Naivasha (A104)

NAIROBI OUTSKIRTS

LIMURU ROAD

Naivasha & Nakuru (B3) △

Wida Highway Hotel

Kikuyu Flyover

NAIVASHA ROAD

Kikuyu

SPRING VALLEY

WAIYAKI WAY

Nairobi River

NAIVASHA ROAD

Swamp Village Park Inn

Watering Point Club & Holiday Inn

Dagoretti Corner

Pathway Hotel

Impala Club

DAGORETTI ROAD

Lenana Forest Centre

NGONG ROAD

JAMHURI PARK

△ Ngong, the Ngong Hills & Narok road (D523)

Karen Shopping Centre

Race Course

Nairobi War Cemetery

Rowallan Scout Camp

Nairobi Dam

St Francis Church

NGONG ROAD FOREST

Psy's (Disco)

KAREN

Don Bosco Boys Town

Nairobi Park Services Campsite

Bomas of Kenya

Carnivore Restaurant

MARULA LANE

LANGATA ROAD

Main Gate & KWS HQ

Swedo House

Karen Club

NDEGE ROAD

LANGATA

LANGATA ROAD SOUTH

Wildlife Clubs of Kenya Hostel

Kazuri Beads

BOGONI ROAD

Langata Gate

Karen Blixen Museum

Mizizi Cultural Centre

USHIRIKA RD

Utamaduni & Simbayo House

Banda Gate

Park Place Hotel

AFEW Giraffe Centre & Giraffe Manor

ONGATA RONGAI

Mbagathi Gate

MAGADI ROAD

Ongata-Rongai Shops

0   2km

▽ Olorgasailie & Magadi (C58)

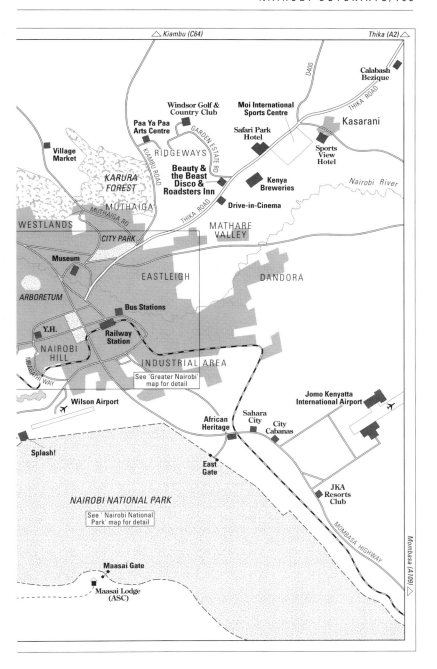

Getting there

The first hours of the day are always best for game-watching. Without your own transport, the cheapest and most adventurous way in is to **hitch a ride** at the main gate. This is probably easiest on a Saturday or Sunday morning, when Kenyans are most likely to visit. The weekends are also by far the busiest time; during the week you'll find it very quiet. Take bus #126 at 5.40am from Nairobi's KBS bus station to the main gate, or after that time any bus or *matatu* which goes down Langata Road (see list on p.90).

Alternatively, you should be able to swing a good deal on a **rental car** for a single day – you won't need anything more than a saloon car and kilometre charges won't amount to much. You could compare the cost with that of hiring a taxi for a few hours; if you do that, be dead sure of what you'll get for the agreed price – petrol will cost you.

Lastly, most of the safari shops in town sell three- to four-hour **trips around the park** for around \$40–75. The only operator with regularly scheduled trips is the United Touring Co (UTC), Fedha Towers, Muindi Mbingu Street (PO Box 42196; ☎02/331960, fax 331422, *utcn@attmail.co.ke*), charging \$75 excluding lunch. The problem with organized tours is that they normally leave at 10am and 2pm, which are not ideal times – though late afternoon is better than midday. A trip like this doesn't guarantee anything, but your chances of sighting most of the animals are high. Note that open-topped minibuses provide better vantage points than cars.

If you're looking for a spot to **picnic**, go a couple of kilometres into the park to the first fork: there's a shady site on the left, beside a raised mound of elephant tusk ash, publicly burned in 1989 by President Moi to mark the start of a major (and astonishingly successful) offensive on ivory poaching and smuggling, led by the director of the Kenya Wildlife Service, Dr Richard Leakey.

Seeing the animals

Ask any ranger on arrival and you'll get the day's results, "Number 13 for a cheetah; two rhinos at 6; lions at number 4 . . .", the numbers referring to the road junctions, marked on every map of the park.

Alternatively, just follow your nose. If you're driving around independently, go to the western end, near the main entrance, where most of the woodland is concentrated. This is where you are most likely to see giraffe and, just after dawn, if you're very lucky, a leopard – back perhaps from a nocturnal foray into Langata, hunting for guard dogs (apparently quite a problem). The highest point here, known as **Impala Hill**, is also a **picnic site** (with toilets) and a good spot from which to scan the park with binoculars, but **lions**, usually found in more open country, are more easily located by checking with the rangers at the gate. There are a few families of **cheetahs** in the park, though you have to be lucky, and seasonal long grass will make seeing them very difficult. It's not that difficult to see some of the park's **rhinos**, however, most often found in the forest glades in the west.

Several of the park's seasonal streams are dammed to regulate the water supply: in the dry season, these **dams** – all located on the northern side of the park where the streams come down off the Embakasi plain – draw the heaviest concentrations of animals. Many of the herds cross the Mbagathi every year and disperse across the Athi plains as the rains improve the pasture, returning to the park during the drought. Before 1946, when the park was opened, only the physical barrier of Nairobi itself diverted the northward migration. The erection of fences along the park's northern perimeter has changed that, but the occasional lion still finds its way up as far as the suburb of Karen.

Birdlife in the park is staggering – a count of more than four hundred species. Enthusiasts won't need priming, and will see rarities from European latitudes as well as the exotics. Even if you're fresh off the plane and ornithologically illiterate, the first glimpses of ostrich, secretary bird, crowned crane and the outlandishly hideous marabou stork never fail to impress.

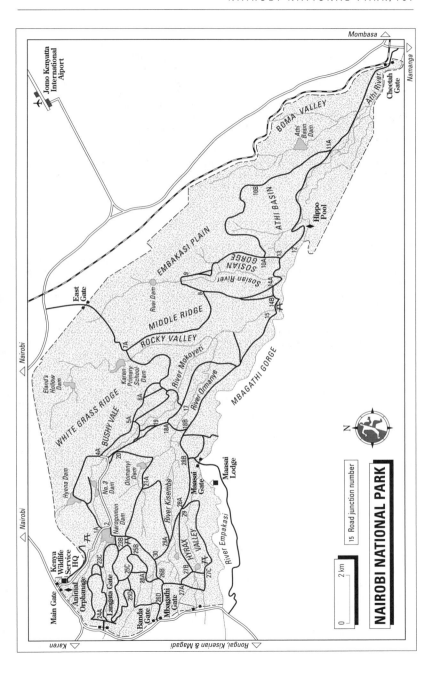

NAIROBI NATIONAL PARK

15 Road junction number

0 2 km

Although the western end has the best cross-section of wildlife, there are two gates out onto the Mombasa road in the east, so you don't have to retrace your route. The lovely **Mokoyeti picnic site** (junction 14B) is near the "Leopard Cliffs" (junction 15), en route to Cheetah Gate near Athi River (p.372). This route gives you a chance to drive through the open savannah country favoured by **zebra** and **antelope**. There are large herds of introduced **buffalo** which you can see – they're hard to miss – out here and almost anywhere in the park. **Hippos** can usually be viewed at a pretty pool at confluence of the Mbagathi and Athi rivers in the east (junction 12), beyond the Leopard Cliffs, which has the added attraction of a **nature trail** and **picnic site** where you can leave the car and disappear into the thickets for closer communion with nature (there's an armed ranger on guard until around 5.30pm). As you're wandering, look out for crocodiles in the river (to an untrained eye little different from submerged logs), and monkeys in the bushes. The Mbagathi/Athi forms the southern boundary of the park and is its only permanent river. It's fringed with the yellow acacias that early explorers and settlers dubbed "fever trees" because they seemed to grow in the areas where fever (malaria) was most common. Their notions were doubtless encouraged by the sight of the gravity-defying marabou storks and vultures commonly seen sitting on the highest branches.

Mini Animal Orphanage and David Sheldrick Wildlife Trust

If you're fed up with seeing animals only from a distance, the **Mini Animal Orphanage** (daily 8am–6.30pm; $5) by the park's Main Gate is moderately interesting, and mainly intended for children. Here, a motley and shifting collection of waifs and strays, protected from nature, have for some years been allowed to regain strength before being released. That anyway was the idea, though many of the inmates seem to be established residents and it appears doubtful whether "this orphanage is not a zoo", as the sign claims. At least it's a zoo with a difference: there are as many wild monkeys outside the cages as in them. Probably better (it hadn't opened at the time of writing), is the Nairobi Safari Walk, on the right of the Main Gate before entering the park. This is the site of the old Animal Orphanage, and it promises to be "more intimate and natural than a zoo". There's also a gift shop at the gate, and the very pleasant self-serve *Sebastian's Café* (breakfasts, sandwiches, burgers, and *ugali* with stew).

More seriously, the **David Sheldrick Wildlife Trust** elephant and rhino orphanage (daily 11am–noon ☎02/890053 or 891996), has recently re-opened after having been closed to the public for many years: they had been besieged by visitors which hindered their delicate hand-rearing work. The centre is run by Daphne Sheldrick in memory of her husband, the anti-poaching warden of Tsavo National Park. Ringing beforehand is absolutely essential, both to check whether they're open and to get directions (it's usually accessible through the closed-to-the-public Maintenance Gate on Magadi Road). The trust is run on a voluntary basis, so entry is by donation.

The Bomas of Kenya

Forest Edge Road, at the junction with Langata and Magadi Road, 1km past National Park Main Gate; from city centre, bus/matatu #15, #125 or #126; performances Mon–Fri 2.30–4pm, Sat, Sun & holidays 3.30–5.15pm; Ksh600, students/children Ksh300 (PO Box 40689; ☎02/891801–2).

The **Bomas of Kenya** were originally an attempt to create a living museum of indigenous Kenyan life, with a display of eleven traditional homesteads (*bomas*) and an emphasis on regional dances. Unfortunately the place has always had a heavily touristy feel, not helped by its huge indoor amphitheatre where the dances are performed. Its vitality is channelled mainly into souvenir-selling. The homesteads (a guided tour is included in the price), representing the architectural styles of Kenya's people, are for the most part sadly unkempt. Even so, if you're looking to fill an afternoon, or you want a change from the National Park, they can be enjoyable enough, particularly on weekends when they're crowded and a disco follows the dance show.

Surprisingly, perhaps, the dances are not performed by the appropriate Kenyan nationalities; instead, the **Harambee Dancers** do fast costume changes between acts and present the nation's traditional repertoire as professionals rather than participants. If the sound system were good, the acoustics bearable and the whole place less of an amphitheatre, the impression would undoubtedly be better, but at least you do get a very comprehensive taste of Kenyan dance styles, from the mesmeric jumps and sinuous movements of the Maa-speaking peoples to the wild acrobatics of some of the Mijikenda dances. But this is definitely a theme park, not a living museum.

AFEW Giraffe Centre

Koitobos Road, 3km off Langata Road (signposted); daily 10am–5.30pm; adults Ksh250, children Ksh150 (PO Box 15124; ☎02/891658, fax 890973).

Although promoted as a children's outing, the **AFEW Giraffe Centre**, run by the African Fund for Endangered Wildlife, has serious intentions: it has successfully boosted the population of the rare Rothschild's giraffe and educates children about conservation. The original nucleus of giraffes here came from the wild herd near Soy (p.309). You'll get some great mug shots from the giraffe-level observation tower, where they push their huge heads through to be fed by pellets offered by the visitors. Try to go in the morning or on a dull day as afternoon shots into the sun can be tricky. There are various other animals around, including a number of tame warthogs (the original one, named after Walter Cronkite, fell to poachers; his life story is told in a book at the gift shop). There's also a tea house. If you really like it here, and have money to burn, you can stay overnight at the wonderful, Scottish-style **Giraffe Manor** (p.99).

Mizizi Cultural Centre

Bogoni Road, halfway between Langata and Karen; take the #24 bus or matatu from outside the GPO on Kenyatta Avenue; PO Box 52283; daily 9am–5.30pm; Ksh300, children Ksh150; ☎02/891050 (Mr. Kamau).

Mizizi means "roots of culture", and the venture is aimed at the preservation and propagation of traditional cultures as expressed through dance, music, handicrafts, foods and architecture, intended not so much for tourists (as the Bomas of Kenya plainly are) but for Kenyans themselves, particularly as a place where schoolchildren can learn about their nation's rich tribal heritage. It's a noble idea, but unfortunately lack of funds has brought its plans to a standstill. It no longer has any guaranteed daily performances or musicians on hand, and seems to function more as a laid-back sort of bar, but it's still worth ringing them a day or two in advance to check whether there will be anything happening, like hands-on workshops or performances for children.

Karen

Until recently, **KAREN** was the quintessential white suburb – five-acre plots spaciously set on eucalyptus-lined avenues amid fields grazed by ponies. But, whilst African homes are few, their number is steadily increasing as the middle classes become more affluent and move out of Nairobi itself. The Karen shopping centre, at the crossroads of Langata and Ngong roads, includes the mock-Tudor *Horseman Restaurant*, branches of Barclays and Standard Chartered banks, both with ATMs, a forex bureau with better rates, and an arty riding-tack and gift shop. Still separated from Nairobi by a dwindling patch of dense, bird-filled woodland – the Ngong Road Forest – Karen is a reminder of how completely the settlers visualized and created little Europes for themselves. In Karen you could almost be in the English shires – or, for that matter, northern California.

The *Horseman Restaurant* (daily to 11pm; ☎02/882782) is certainly worth a visit, with several separate speciality kitchens (including Mongolian, fondue and pub-style) and a wide choice of game meat. The food is fresh and imaginative: Zanzibari fish and coconut soup is well worth trying, as is "Beach and Bush" (crab claws, green bananas, *ugali* in coconut, and medallions of Thomson's gazelle). They have real Italian ice cream, too.

On the way to Karen, if you're driving the more direct way from the city, along Ngong Road, you pass **Jamhuri Park** (the Agricultural Society of Kenya showground, see p.60), the **Nairobi War Cemetery** and the **Racecourse**. The World War II cemetery is a peaceful and dignified place, set far back from the busy road among shady trees, with pink stone and carefully tended lawns.

Buses to Karen include the #111 (fast) and the interminable #24 from the KBS bus station. *Matatus* also run the route.

Karen Blixen Museum and Swedo House

Bus #24 can drop you at the **Karen Blixen National Museum**, Karen Road (daily 9.30am–6pm; Ksh200, children Ksh100), the house where much of the action of Karen Blixen's *Out of Africa* took place. The epitome of colonial Africa, the Danish government presented it to Kenya as an Uhuru gift along with the agricultural college built in the grounds. It's a beautiful, well-proportioned house with square, wood-panelled rooms; the restoration of its original appearance and furnishings has evidently been very thorough. A guided tour is included in the price but can be somewhat rushed, especially at weekends, and there's no guarantee that they'll let you wander around on your own, which is unfortunate.

On weekends, too, you may be suffocated by Mozart and tour groups complaining about how little Denys Finch Hatton resembles Robert Redford, but come during the week and it's more peaceful. The gardens, laid out as in former times, are delightful. If you're a true fan, you can come on an organized tour from town (around $45–70) – often including the *Giraffe Manor*.

The fake-1920s Nairobi that was built nearby for the shooting of *Out of Africa* would have been a more magnetic attraction than the museum house. Strangely, political dictates ensured its demolition once the film crews left. Just up the road towards Karen *dukas* is **Swedo House**, an old Swedish coffee plantation manager's residence, built in 1912 and stuffed with archetypal colonial memorabilia and fittings, but which is usually closed to the public. The grounds are delightful, and there's a bar and restaurant here: the *Karen Blixen Coffee Garden* (daily 9.30am–11pm), with tables in the gardens under the trees. The food is variable, but the Sunday buffet lunch (Ksh700) remains popular. There's also a craft shop, although much better local handicrafts can be bought at the nearby **Kazuri Bead Centre**, behind Hillcrest School (see p.112 for more details). Incidentally, the suburb was not named after Karen Blixen (who went by the name Tania von Blixen when in Kenya) as is popularly supposed, but her cousin, Karen Melchior, whose father was the chairman of the Karen Coffee Company Ltd.

The Ngong Hills

Ngong village, the jumping-off point for the **Ngong Hills** ahead, is 8km past Karen *dukas* (bus #111 every 30min, every 20min at weekends; sometimes bus #126, but you might have to change at Kiserian). If you have the chance, stop on the way at **Bulbul** and take a look at the pretty mosque of this largely Muslim village. As often happened in Kenya, Islam spread through the settlement of discharged troops from other British-ruled territories – this time Sudanese Nubia. Ngong itself is basically just a small junction town with limited shops and services and the rough D523 road trailing out to the right towards the Maasai Mara.

The hills are revered by the Maasai, who have several traditional explanations of how they were formed. The best known says that a giant, stumbling north with his head in the clouds, tripped on Kilimanjaro. Thundering to the ground, his hand squeezed the earth into the Ngongs' familiar, knuckled outline. An even more momentous story explains the Ngongs as the bits of earth left under God's fingernails after he'd finished creating.

The walk along their sharp spine was once a popular day's hike and picnic outing. The views, of Nairobi on one side and the Rift Valley on the other, are magnificent, and the forested slopes are still inhabited by buffalo and antelope. Unfortunately, the number of attacks and robberies of unwary walkers has discouraged people, Kenyans included, and the north side is considered especially dangerous. The route up from the village is now patrolled by police most of the time. Check things out at Ngong police station, where they'll usually provide you with an escort. Women travelling without men are, as usual, at a disadvantage. All this is a great pity as the walk, even simply up to the radio relay station above Ngong village, is a fine one.

With a car (4WD if it's been raining), you can get to the summit, **Point Lamwia** (2459m), which offers 360 degrees of view. Down on the lower ridges, almost due east of the highest point, is the **Finch Memorial**, Karen Blixen's tribute to the man who took her flying. It's on privately owned land and there's a Ksh100 entrance fee.

BEYOND NAIROBI

Once they decide to leave Nairobi, many travellers overlook the attractions of the surrounding area. **Naivasha**, a strange and lovely Rift Valley lake, is the most obvious example: a highly recommended first staging post, with birdlife and hikes enough to keep you busy for several days. On from here (a short bus ride) is the wilder and more beautiful country around **Kinangop** – again, rewarding for walkers.

To the south, in Maasai land, **Lake Magadi**, a soda lake, is a harsh, fiercely hot place, virtually ignored by Nairobi. If you're driving, this is a possible day's excursion from the capital, including time out to see the prehistoric site at **Olorgasailie** on the way. **Thika**, to the east, has little of the romance of its name, but **Fourteen Falls** and **Ol Doinyo Sapuk National Park** nearby are worth the short drive.

Lake Naivasha and around

Naivasha, like so many Kenyan place names, is a corruption of a local (Maasai) name *E-na-iposha* (heaving waters), a pronunciation still used by Maa speakers you'll meet in the vicinity. The grassy shores of the lake were traditional Maasai grazing land for centuries, prior to its "discovery" by Joseph Thomson in 1884. Before the nineteenth century was out, however, the "glimmering many-isled expanse" had seen the arrival, with the railway, of the first European settlers. Soon after, the Maasai *laibon* Ole Gilisho, whom the British had appointed chief of the Naivasha Maasai, was persuaded to sign an agreement ceding his people's grazing rights all around the lake – and the country houses and ranches went up. Today the Maasai are back, though very much as outsiders, either disputing grazing rights with the many European landowners still left here, or as workers on the vast horticultural farms, which export the bulk of fresh flowers sold in the UK.

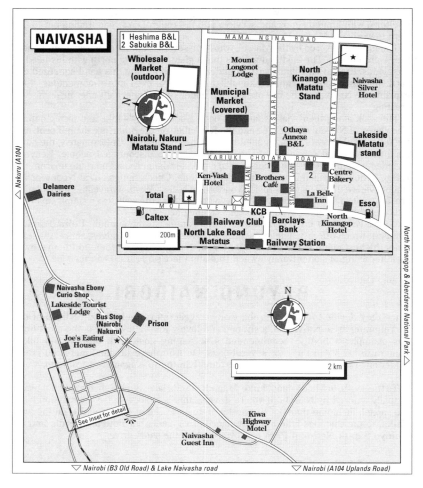

NAIVASHA

1 Heshima B&L
2 Sabukia B&L

Wholesale Market (outdoor)

Mount Longonot Lodge

North Kinangop Matatu Stand

Naivasha Silver Hotel

MAMA NGINA ROAD

Municipal Market (covered)

BIASHARA ROAD

KENYATTA AVENUE

Othaya Annexe B&L

Lakeside Matatu stand

Nairobi, Nakuru Matatu Stand

KARIUKI CHOTARA ROAD

N

Ken-Vash Hotel

POSTA LANE

1
Brothers Café

STATION LANE

2

Centre Bakery

La Belle Inn

Total

MOI AVENUE

Caltex

KCB

Barclays Bank

Esso

North Kinangop Hotel

Railway Club
North Lake Road Matatus

Railway Station

0   200m

Delamere Dairies

△ Nakuru (A104)

North Kinangop & Aberdares National Park △

Naivasha Ebony Curio Shop

Lakeside Tourist Lodge

Bus Stop (Nairobi, Nakuru)

Prison

N

Joe's Eating House

See inset for detail

0   2 km

Kiwa Highway Motel

Naivasha Guest Inn

▽ *Nairobi (B3 Old Road) & Lake Naivasha road*   ▽ *Nairobi (A104 Uplands Road)*

The lake, a slightly forbidding but highly picturesque waterscape with its purple mountain backdrop and floating islands of papyrus and water hyacinth, has some curious physical characteristics. It is fresh water – Lake Baringo is the only other example in the Rift – and the water level has always been prone to mysterious fluctuations. It dropped massively in the 1980s (partly the unmysterious result of farmers to the north taking off some of the Thurusha River's inflow to irrigate their crops) though the shore has not receded enough to regain the areas that were cultivated in the 1950s when the lake was half its present size. Even though the lake level increased in 1998 following the El Niño floods, the outer edge of the fringing band of papyrus marks the shoreline the settlers knew and you can still see fence posts sticking up.

Perhaps of more immediate and visible interest is the lake's **wildlife**, especially its protected **hippo** population. The dull earth tremors you sometimes feel if you're camping add considerably to the already exciting African night. Despite their bulk, hippos seem to be remarkably sensitive creatures, and they must be able to see in the dark, too, for nary a guy-line is twanged. Both *Fisherman's Camp* and *Fish Eagle Inn* receive occasional nocturnal visits, especially now that the waters have risen to cover the ditches dug to keep them out (apparently a drunken German tourist once went looking for hippos at 4am, and found them with tragic consequence). By day, you can occasionally see **giraffes**, floating blithely through the trees, taking barbed wire and gates in their stride. Naivasha has extraordinary **birdlife** too: all kinds, from the grotesque marabou storks to pet shop lovebirds in pairs, doves cooing in the woods and splendid fish eagles, whose mournful cries fill the air like seagulls. These, and the area's climate, with a light breeze always drifting through the acacias, make Naivasha a hard place to beat as a first stop out from Nairobi.

Naivasha town

All told, **NAIVASHA** town has little to offer as a place to stay: unless you arrive late in the day, you may as well head straight on down to the lake once you've done the shopping. Sadly, coming by **train** isn't up to much scenically, as both the Nairobi and Kisumu services travel through the night (arriving at around 9pm from Nairobi, or 5am from Kisumu). It's now third-class only, barely more comfortable (and much slower) than catching a bus, and the colonial dining carriage is no more. Coming from Nairobi on the **B3 old road** (recently resurfaced), you could ask to be dropped off at the lake road turning. If you're hitching or coming by bus or *matatu*, you may arrive on the **A104 Uplands road** and might be dropped inconveniently at the top junction, 1.5km uphill behind the town. It's possible to catch a *matatu* or bus straight down to the lake, but if you plan to spend any time in the area, you should go into the town of Naivasha first to stock up on essentials. Most travellers tend to do their own cooking and there's a much wider choice of supplies in town than at the lake itself. For **food supplies**, the fruit stalls on the main road are good, though there is more choice at the covered market. The oddly named Naivasha Mattresses Supermarket, at the upper end of Biashara Road, is cheaper and has more variety than the Multiline Supermarket. There's good lake fish at the kiosk opposite *La Belle Inn* and, if you're driving, super-fresh milk and yoghurts at Delamere Dairies, 3km north on the Nakuru road. There's a **post office** on Moi Avenue (Mon–Fri 8am–1pm & 2–5pm, Sat 9am–noon) and two **banks:** Barclays (with an ATM) and KCB, both on Moi Avenue (both Mon–Fri 9am–3pm, Sat 9–11am).

Accommodation

If you do **stay in town**, there's one favourite old hotel, the *La Belle Inn*, and numerous lodgings ranging from the quite decent to the unspeakable.

Heshima B&L, Kariuki Chotara Rd (PO Box 1141; ☎0311/20631). Not as cheap as it was, though the rooms at the top are nice and the café is popular with Congolese music fans. They also run the *Waboko Hotel* on Moi Ave. ②.

Ken-Vash Hotel, Posta Lane (PO Box 211; ☎0311/30049, fax 0311/30084). Naivasha's biggest hotel (61 rooms), with impersonal but efficient service, and reasonably quiet. Excellent rooms, safe parking. ③.

La Belle Inn, Moi Ave (PO Box 532; ☎0311/21007, fax 0311/21119). A popular old staging post on the main street through town, with a variety of rooms (due to be rebuilt) and a generally reliable restaurant, serving great fried breakfasts. They may have one or two cheaper non-s/c rooms still available. B&B ④.

Lakeside Tourist Lodge, Moi Ave (PO Box 894; ☎0311/30267 or 20856, fax 0311/30268). Spacious new construction just off the Nairobi–Nakuru road. Good rooms, good food (especially their "African buffet") and efficient service, but unfortunately no lakeside views. ③.

Mount Longonot Lodge, Biashara St (PO Box 19; ☎0311/21026). Next to Naivasha Mattresses, with an indifferent front restaurant, though the twenty s/c double rooms round the back are a pleasant surprise. All rooms have nets and comfy wicker chairs. ②.

Naivasha Guest Inn, Kenyatta Ave, 2km from the town centre (PO Box 491; ☎0311/20712). A well-kept joint to collapse into if you've just been dropped at the junction. Reasonable rooms (all s/c) with a nice terrace-bar-restaurant. Secure parking. ①.

Naivasha Silver Hotel, Kenyatta Ave (PO Box 999; ☎0311/20580). One step up from a regular B&L, with some quite nice rooms. ②.

Othaya Annexe B&L, Kariuki Chotara Rd (PO Box 651; ☎0311/20770). Cheap and cheerful but not too clean; the s/c rooms have a large bed and a set price for a single or a couple. There's a good *hoteli* downstairs and a bakery on the premises. ①.

Sabukia B&L, Kariuki Chotara Rd (PO Box 433). Very basic establishment in a yellow building, wearily welcoming or utterly squalid, depending on your sensibilities. ①.

Eating and drinking

There's a whole clutch of cheap, local **places to eat** at on the western end of Moi Avenue around the Caltex and Total gas stations, the best of which is the delightful *Joe's Eating House*, with good *ugali*, meat stew and chapati, accompanied by singing in the kitchen and chickens pecking at your toes. Of the places listed below, don't miss *La Belle Inn* and, if you're driving, call in at the *Kiwa Highway Motel* above town on the Nakuru–Nairobi road.

Brothers Café, Station Lane. Long-established and good value – with music.

Centre Bakery, Kariuki Chotara Rd. Naivasha's main bread shop (though *La Belle Inn* caters for more esoteric tastes). Open till midnight.

Kiwa Highway Motel, A104 Highway, near the top junction (☎0311/20839). A windblown *nyama choma* joint, fairly expensive except for beef at Ksh150 a kilo. There's also a bar and disco.

La Belle Inn, Moi Ave (see "Accommodation", p.163). Recommended dishes include barbecued tilapia, spiced Louisiana crayfish and Naivasha bisque (lakefish soup); they have a wide choice for vegetarians (easily the best in town) and a nice line in pizzas and real croissants. They also sell choice picnic supplies (the "lunchbox" costs Ksh300), honey and capers.

North Kinangop Hotel, Moi Ave. Inexpensive fish and chips and amazingly filling *mandaazi*.

Nightlife

Music is inescapable in Naivasha, as almost all the B&Ls double as café-bars which bounce along on the infectious rhythms of Congolese and South African sounds. Venues tend to have a short lifespan, though, so ask around for the latest. Among the established **clubs**, the *Salama Bar and Hotel* on Moi Avenue, opposite the station, is perhaps the liveliest; it also has cheap rooms, should the night's revelry prove too much. It might also be worth checking out the *A to Z Nightclub* on Kariuki Chotara Road. The *Railway Club* by the station (☎0311/20552) has live bands Thursday to Sunday evenings (closing time 3am). Otherwise, the Golf Club (north up Moi Avenue) is an almost exclusively white meat market, its "members only" rule applied only to locals.

Lake Naivasha

The fast new lakeside road has brought thousands of migrant workers to the **farming estates**, where they grow string beans, mangetout and flowers, all exported by air to European supermarkets. Great stretches of acacia scrub have been cleared since the late 1980s to make way for the expansion of the farms, and ugly lines of squalid field-hand housing have sprouted in the dust between the plantations. Passing through this scene of ragged-clothed backs stooping between the rows – with rambling country houses in the background – it's difficult to ignore the images of American slavery that

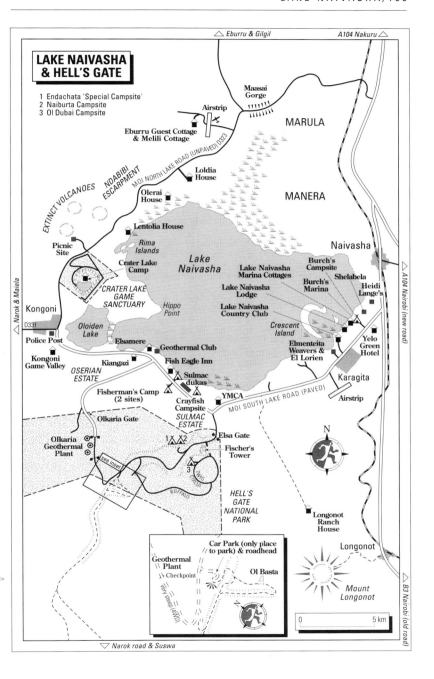

LAKE NAIVASHA & HELL'S GATE

1 Endachata 'Special Campsite'
2 Naiburta Campsite
3 Ol Dubai Campsite

repeatedly spring to mind. There are always people looking for work, of course (there seems to be little disapproval of the development), and there's a fair scattering of Europeans of very modest means eking out a living between the landowners. But the scale of the distinction between rich and poor is brutally apparent all the same. Happily, there are still patches of relatively undisturbed bush and the lakeshore remains a magnet for savannah game – zebra, giraffe and waterbuck congregate in certain areas, such as Crescent Island.

THE THORNS OF THE ROSE

Covering a large part of the land around the lake, the ecological consequences of Naivasha's multi-million dollar **horticultural industry** are causing mounting concern among environmentalists, worried not only about the lake's fluctuating levels, but also the use of **pesticides**, especially by the big flower combines, which adversely affects wildlife. Until the exceptional 1997 rains raised the lake levels, thereby diluting the pollutants, the **fish eagle** had been especially badly affected, and had not bred successfully at the lake for many years: either the hatchlings were too weak, or their eggs had shells so thin that they broke before the birds were fully developed. Especially disturbing is the continued use of the highly toxic pesticide **methyl bromide**, of which some 300 tonnes are sprayed annually onto Naivasha's flowers and crops. Inevitably, some of this finds its way into the lake, with as yet unknown effects. Banned in some countries, the chemical is also a major ozone-layer-depleter, with ten percent of losses attributed to its use worldwide. It is also very powerful, killing almost everything in the soil, including insects vital to replenishing nutrients, which means that yet more fertilizer has to be applied to make anything grow, which in turn means more nitrates leaching into the lake which reduces oxygen levels. On top of all this, the **Louisiana crayfish**, which were introduced in the 1960s for commercial fishing, have proved to be an ecological disaster and are steadily eating their way through the lake's flora, which other fish species depend on for both food and breeding sites. To those who argue that the lake "can take it", the disastrous effects of unchecked industry on a lake's ecology can already be seen at Nakuru (see box on p.248). There's also some water hyacinth (see p.274 for its effect on Lake Victoria), although it doesn't seem to be posing a problem in Naivasha as yet.

Despite promises by the new Kenya Flower Council growers association (which includes the massive Sulmac and Homegrown combines) to "grow flowers in such a manner as to safeguard the environment", the cynics remain unfazed, the use of methyl bromide continues undiminished and many workers are still not using adequate protective gear when handling chemicals. Some growers have built illegal dykes to "reclaim" land from the lake, shrinking the lake's surface and reducing the water level, thereby further increasing the lake's concentration of man-made chemicals. The cavalier attitude of certain growers was exemplified in another way in August 1998, when an outbreak of **dysentery** killed 28 workers.

Some companies, however, finally appear to be waking up to their responsibilities: Homegrown, who export over 50 million flower stems to the UK each year, pay their workers a handsome $1200 annually, about five times the Kenyan average, whilst Oserian, the largest rose producer in Africa, has undertaken not to cultivate within 1km of the lake to avoid run-off (and possible future legal action), and has in common with other producers instituted extensive health checks on its workers dealing with pesticides.

Sadly, with so much money at play, the radical change which is necessary appears unlikely: despite the environmental organization Earthwatch succeeding in getting Naivasha listed as a Ramsar Site – a wetland of internationally-recognized ecological importance, which in theory obliges both government and local inhabitants to preserve the lake – the long-term future seems far from being a bed of roses.

To **get to the lake** from Naivasha town, there's easily hitchable traffic, a regular shuttle of *matatus*, and a bus every hour or so (with regular 8am and 1pm return departures from *Fisherman's Camp*; see below).

Lakeshore accommodation

There's a wide variety of accommodation along **Moi South Lake Road** – everything from frugal *bandas* or camping to stately hotels and homestays. For these places, the number of kilometres (in brackets) refers to the distance from the lake road junction with the main Nairobi road (which is 3km from Naivasha town itself). Places to stay off **Moi North Lake Road** are generally more difficult to get to, as the road is unsurfaced – full directions are given in the listings where appropriate.

BUDGET AND MID-RANGE ACCOMMODATION AND CAMPING

Burch's Marina (2.3km; PO Box 40; ☎0311/21010). You can camp here, or stay in traditional *rondavels* (basic round houses with enclosed verandahs in a field), in square *bandas*, or in more expensive, if still basic, four-bed s/c cottages. The main attraction is the peaceful nature of the place: no noise after 9pm, you have to book in advance (allow two weeks for weekends), and you pay extra for bedding if you don't bring your own (gas stove, pots and pans are included if you rent bedding for the cottages). It's cheap, though. Hot showers are available and farm produce for sale. *Rondavels/bandas/*camping ①; four-bed cottage ③.

Crayfish Campsite (17km; PO Box 176; ☎0311/20239). A new campsite ten minutes from the lake, and cheap, but little more than a small field and bar, which can get noisy and is frequented by "better paid locals", according to the manager. There's not much security, either, but it's cheap (and you can hire a tent for Ksh200), there's hot water, and the usual eight-seat boat rides are offered (Ksh2000 per hour). Ksh150 per person.

Lake Naivasha Marina Cottages (2.8km; bookings: PO Box 59310 Nairobi; ☎02/747030, fax 747098). Good, simple but clean cottages, each with two double beds, ideal for families. All cottages s/c, with hot showers and electricity. Cooking facilities available for Ksh200. They also have a campsite (Ksh200 per person, tents for hire Ksh900–1200). Boats for hire (Ksh1000 per hour for an eight-seat boat; Ksh800 to Crescent Island). There's a reasonable restaurant in the old ranch house. Five minutes from the lake. Cottage ④.

Fish Eagle Inn (19.3km, entrance beside *Fisherman's Camp*; PO Box 1554; ☎0311/30306, fax 0311/21158). An unusual and pleasant if slightly overpriced restaurant/*banda*/campsite/health club complex. Calmer and more dignified than *Fisherman's Camp*, you can also camp here (Ksh150; no tent hire), kip in a dorm ($6 per person), or stay in a variety of dull if well-equipped *bandas* (with nets, hot water and spotless toilets); doubles are tiny, but the more expensive "suites" are cosier. The restaurant is good, and there's a fully-equipped gym (as well as sauna, steam room and outdoor pool; around Ksh600–700 extra per day for their use). Mountain bikes for rent. B&B ④, HB ⑤.

Fisherman's Camp (19.3km; PO Box 79; ☎0311/30088; reservations through Let's Go Travel, p.142). This favourite budget hideaway consists of two areas. *Bottom Camp* has the best camping site in Naivasha, right by the water's edge, and is shaded by tall, beautiful fever trees. There's a choice of camping (Ksh200 per person; tent hire Ksh200 per person); four s/c, if rather dingy *bandas* (③); and a "Youth Hostel" consisting of seven very basic dormitories, each with four narrow bunk beds, sometimes occupied by British soldiers on "jungle training" (Ksh300 per person). *Top Camp* (☎0311/30276) has seven further *bandas* and one cottage (③), overlooking the lake but high above the road. Five of the *Top Camp bandas* offer basic shelter only (②), with open cooking on charcoal *jikos* outside and bedding available (extra), while two also have hot water showers and toilets, suitable for small families (②). The bar at *Bottom Camp* has limited food, as does nearby *Watalii Kiosk* (see "Shopping and services" below). Some people find the sometimes beery white Kenyan atmosphere at *Bottom Camp* off-putting; others love it. Rowing boats and bicycles (Ksh250–500) are for hire, and there's parascending (Ksh1500 for 15min) and water-skiing (Ksh800 for 15 min).

Yelo Green Hotel (0.8km; PO Box 561; ☎ & fax 0311/30269). Far from the lake itself, and a little tatty but quite acceptable chalet-style *bandas* (all s/c with hot water), set in lovely bougainvillaea-filled gardens. The owners are charming and helpful, and there's a restaurant and bar (popular with locals at weekends). Great Rift Lakes Bikes and Tents is 1km down the road. However, room prices are a little over the odds. They also have a campsite (Ksh150 per person). B&B ③.

YMCA (15.1km; PO Box 1006; ☎0311/30396). The idyllic, rural ambience the YMCA once had has been progressively nibbled away as the farms press in on all sides and the lake recedes – it's now a ten-minute walk away. The "Y" is still one of the lake's cheapest (and friendliest) places to stay – either camping in what's left of the acacia grove (Ksh150 per person; tents hired for Ksh200), staying in a dorm (for which you need bedding), or renting one of the spartan *bandas* – and certainly the easiest base if you're planning an early-morning hike into Hell's Gate National Park, as the Elsa Gate is just up the road. Firewood, eggs, lake fish and milk are sporadically available, but the shop has almost nothing. There's hot water, boat hire (Ksh2000 for an eight-seater) and food can be cooked to order. ①.

HOTELS AND LODGES

Lake Naivasha Country Club (3.8km; PO Box 15; ☎0311/21004, 21160, fax 0311/21161; reservations through Block, p.48). The best hotel on the lake (still usually known as the *Lake Hotel*), and, despite the expense, still an excellent alternative base to Nairobi, with magnificent gardens and bird-watching opportunities (and fish-eagle-eyed guides), good facilities (including a chilly swimming pool) and a lounge evocative of the old colonial days between 1937 and 1950, when flying-boats used to land on the lake en route between London and South Africa, and the passengers stayed here. It's suitable for children (small adventure playground and huge lawns) and visitors with disabilities (all ground-floor rooms; a few steps up to the dining room), but the generally old-fashioned rooms vary considerably from adequate to luxurious, so don't be afraid to ask. For casual visitors – usually attracted by the sumptuous lunchtime buffets in the garden (Ksh900) – there's an additional Ksh100 entry fee. There are bicycles for hire (Ksh200 per hour or Ksh800 per day), massages, bird walks (Ksh300), boat rides (Ksh3200 per hour for a seven-seat boat) and one-hour trips by Cessna aircraft (Ksh12,000). There's a money exchange facility, with the usual bad rates. No B&B. FB ⑥ low, ⑧ high.

Lake Naivasha Lodge, formerly *Lake Naivasha Holiday Villas* (3.5km; PO Box 685; ☎0311/30298, fax 0311/21156; reservations in Nairobi at Arrow House, Koinange St; PO Box 70559; ☎02/224998, fax 212405). A lovely place in uncluttered, airy style with twelve spacious double rooms, s/c and spotless, some with private verandah overlooking the enormous gardens. Boat trips offered (Ksh2500 for an eight-seat boat for an hour; Ksh540 to Crescent Island). Ten-minute walk to the lakeshore through pleasant grounds. Secure parking. B&B is good value, half-board or full-board less so, though they're convenient. HB ⑤, B&B ④.

Crater Lake Camp (reservations through Southern Cross Safaris, p.136). A recently completed luxury tented lodge inside the crater overlooking the green lake and game sanctuary (see "Green Crater Lake" on p.172). Superb views from the ten secluded, yellow-acacia-shaded, *bandas* (or from a specially-built "raft" for bird-watching), and nice touches like its china dinner service and silverware. You can also just drop in for lunch ($20). The price includes night game drives and escorted walks. No access for the disabled. FB ⑨.

RANCHES, COTTAGES AND HOMESTAYS

For the ideal antidote to Nairobi, a number of extremely luxurious ranch and farmhouses lie dotted around the lake, as well as a couple of idyllically situated cottages, these being well within the reach of even the lowliest budget. Reservations are handled by Let's Go Travel in Nairobi (see p.142) unless otherwise stated.

Eburru Guest Cottage. Formerly known as *Mayers Soyet*, this is part of the as yet undeveloped "Green Park Development", in beautiful walking country (beware of buffalo). Two double bedrooms in a basic but fully s/c cottage with gorgeous views over the lake and Mount Longonot. Part of its charm is its inaccessibility – bring all your food (a kitchen/lounge is at your disposal). Water is provided. *Matatus* run twice daily (once on Sundays) from Moi Ave in Naivasha, leaving you with a two-kilometre walk from Green Park Development gate; taxis Ksh700–1000. Hitching a ride on a *shamba* vehicle is also possible: ask at *La Belle Inn*. If you're making your own way here, see *Melili Cottage* below. ③.

Elsamere (22.1km; PO Box 1497; ☎0311/21055, fax 0311/21074, *elsa@africaonline.co.ke*). Joy Adamson's former home, open to the public as a conservation centre (see p.171), offers comfortable and very peaceful rooms in cottages, each with verandahs facing towards the lake. The grounds are beautiful, too, but they don't put up children under seven years old unless by prior arrangement, and they can be a bit snooty if you don't fit their picture of an ideal guest: they don't like the house to be treated as a hotel, and prefer a measure of enthusiasm for the lady and her works, or at least for natural history. Reservations advisable. FB only, ⑤.

Kiangazi (25.5km; PO Box 719; ☎0311/21052, fax 0311/21059). A very personable homestay as guests of the family in a separate guest house, with a large verandah overlooking the valley. Three artificial pools (two for buffalo, zebra and antelope, the other for you to swim in) provide entertainment, and game drives (both day and night) are included in the price. The food is superb and served with excellent wines. FB ⑨.

Kongoni Game Valley (28.5km; PO Box 15026 Nairobi; ☎02/890184, fax 890096). The plushest homestay in Naivasha, though not exactly the most tasteful: an enormous, overly modernized ranch house built by the Count and Countess de Perigny at the turn of the century. FB ⑨.

Lentolia House (Moi North Lake Rd; queries to Abigail Allison, ☎0311/30277). Located 2km beyond Crater Lake Game Sanctuary, coming from Kongoni, then right for 2–3km. A delightful Edwardian house with an Italian-style central patio for rent in its entirety – it's very good value. Graceful and spacious, it comes with a large expanse of farmland. There are two double and four twin bedrooms. Kitchen staff are included in the price, but bring your own drinking water. Vegetables and diary produce is usually available. Ask the staff to heat water for baths. Electricity 6pm–11pm only. ⑥.

Loldia House (Moi North Lake Rd; Rick Hopcraft, PO Box 199; ☎0311/30024). Naivasha's oldest stone house, built in the 1940s by Italian POWs, with delightful period charm. Sweeping views of Mount Longonot over the grassy lawn, a grand piano in the lounge and a claw-foot bathtub in the master bedroom. There's a small guest cottage nearby. Horse rides through herds of cattle and a flock of farmed ostriches can be arranged. For all that, way overpriced. FB ⑨.

Longonot Ranch House (10.5km, then left 8km up a rough track signposted "Kedong Ranch"; reservations at Safaris Unlimited, 328 Langata Rd, Nairobi; PO Box 24181; ☎02/891168, 890435, fax 891113, *safunlim@africaonline.co.ke*). A traditional long ranch house (six double en-suite bedrooms), complete with full staff. Built by Martha Gellhorn, journalist and one-time wife of Ernest Hemingway, atop a hillock under the shadow of Mount Longonot, the attractions are manifold: stunning scenery, lots of wildlife (escorted game walks and night game drives available), stables and horse riding ($15 per hour). Reservations essential. FB ⑧–⑨.

Melili Cottage. Next to *Eburru Guest Cottage* and similarly delightful. Ideal for families (sleeps four) but bring your own food, sheets and towels. If you're driving to either cottage, turn left 13km north of Naivasha on to Moi North Lake Rd (unsurfaced and in places badly pitted). Turn right immediately, then left 3km further on, and then follow the road up through "Maasai Gorge". Ignore the turn-off to Gilgil and take the next right. Pass the barrier, go over the airstrip and turn left at a reflective arrow, 100m past *Eburru Cottage*. ④.

Olerai House. Four kilometres past the "Green Park" turn-off is the former home of Iain and Oria Douglas-Hamilton, who were involved in the struggle to ban the ivory trade (they still live on the estate). Six s/c double bedrooms in guest houses surrounding the main, flower-covered house; breakfast and lunch are served under fever trees from a long dug-out boat. Excursions, walks and boat rides are included in the price, which even so is hugely expensive at $640 a double. ⑨.

Eating, drinking and shopping

The number of kilometres (in brackets) refers to the distance along South Lake Road from the lake road junction with the main Nairobi road (which is 3km from Naivasha town itself). As well as the following places, you can also drop-in for meals and drinks at *Fish Eagle Inn, Fisherman's Camp, Lake Naivasha Country Club, Lake Naivasha Lodge*, and the *Yelo Green Hotel. Crayfish Campsite* has a bar.

Heidi Lange's, (0km, at the junction of the Nairobi road and Moi Lake Road South. There's a small sign). This is where German-born artist Heidi Lange sells her batik seconds (very slight flaws): prices range from Ksh100 to Ksh1000.

Shelabela House (2km, turn right at the signpost for Bee's Garden Farm; PO Box 108; ☎0311/20462, fax 0311/21389). A swanky new hippyish gift shop, with supposedly antique tribal arts, a selection of textiles, and local medicinal and culinary herbs for sale. They also offer "Aura Soma Colour Therapy".

The Campbell Clause Gallery (3.3km; ☎0311/20681). A new galley/giftshop with a currently small selection of crafts and artworks (the bronze Maasai warriors are rather good), well worth poking a look if you're around that way.

Great Rift Lakes Bikes and Tents (3.5km; opposite the turning for *Lake Naivasha Lodge*; ☎0311/20514, fax 0311/21116). Two kiosks, one selling drinks and snacks at low prices, the other renting out bicycles (Ksh500 per day) and a variety of modern tents (Ksh500–800 for 24 hours). They also offer biking trips to Crescent Island, along a narrow causeway from private farmland.

Elmenteita Weavers & El Lorien (4.3km, and 800m along the signposted track). Two good browsing places. *El Lorien* (9am–5pm, closed Wed; ☎0311/21062) sells fresh vegetables and Naivasha wine (Ksh200–400 a bottle), with singing women working in the back, but the main draw is Elmenteita Weavers (Mon–Sat 9am–5.30pm, Sun 9am–5pm; PO Box 85; ☎0311/30115, fax 740721), a high quality and very friendly weaving shop, with looms behind the showroom. Carpets and rugs, sweaters (some superb), *kangas* and *kikois* compete with various other bought-in crafts. Justifiably expensive. Credit cards accepted.

Karagita Village (4.5km). A little adobe and tin-plate village of flower-farm workers, immigrants and victims of ethnic strife elsewhere in the Rift, but very friendly if you take a genuine interest in the people and their way of life. This is not a tourist attraction (and no white ex-colonial Naivashan has ever even set foot there), despite the roadside souvenir stalls, and intrusive photography will not be welcome. The black-and-white *Punda Bar*, at the start of the village, is a friendly place to hang out.

"Sulmac" dukas (17.6km). *Sulmac* (near *Fisherman's Camp*) is one of the biggest flower planta-tions in the area, employing over 4000 people. Near the main entrance, there's a small shopping cen-tre where you can eat for next to nothing. Newspapers are on sale in the morning by the farm gate and, 500m further west, you'll usually find a gathering of ladies selling the produce from their small vegetable plots. If there was any land free, this would undoubtedly evolve into a small town. It's the main south lake transport focus, though a bus goes on as far as *Fisherman's Camp* and then back to Naivasha town around 8am and 1pm every day.

Watalii Kiosk (19.4km; PO Box 785; ☎0311/21327). Watalii Kiosk, on the road to Hell's Gate, is run by an energetic local councillor. Here you can rent bikes (Ksh420 a day, including a soft drink), stock up on supplies, or collapse in the speakeasy he set up for locals (pineapple wine Ksh10 a glass). There's also cheap food, but order early. The owner is a font of information and also orga-nizes safaris, including speciality tours of tea, coffee, flower and barley (beer) cultivation processes. He also offers homestays (Ksh500) and a laundry service. If he manages to buy a Land Rover, he may even pick you up from Nairobi airport.

Geothermal Club (21.8km). A gem of a place owned by *La Belle Inn* (see p.163), with some of the best views over the lake. Entrance is free, and a day's use of the pool costs Ksh100. Excellent English breakfasts and gastronomic African dishes for lunch and dinner. Very relaxed, and drinks are cheap. Recommended.

Getting around

It's possible to go **out in a boat** at most of the lakeshore establishments. *Burch's*, the *Lake Hotel* and *Fisherman's Camp* all have various vessels. *Fisherman's Camp* has a fast motorboat at about Ksh1750 per hour and a half-speed one for Ksh1000 (both take up to eight passengers). You need an hour in the fast boat to get over to the main concen-tration of hippos and back. Splashing along the papyrus-fringed shore just after the sun has come up, drifting among the pelicans and past other people's back gardens, is a rare pleasure – though large areas are now filled with a rank growth of weed and lily-pads which makes it an exhausting one too. With luck (and a rod), you'll catch a tilapia.

Bicycles are a good way of exploring the lakeshore, and particularly for getting around Hell's Gate National Park: both *Fisherman's Camp* and Watalii Kiosk (see above) rent out bikes, and both have good photocopied sketch maps of the lake and Hell's Gate. Other bike rental places include Great Rift Lakes Bikes and Tents, *Fish Eagle Lodge*, and *Lake Naivasha Country Club*. Incidentally, by all means give lifts if you're cycling – the locals, understandably, find it hilarious that *wazungu* should shed sweat for them, and it's a great way of making friends on equal terms. For Hell's Gate, you're better off enter-ing by Olkaria Gate, which makes for an easier downhill ride to Elsa Gate.

Circumnavigating the lake **by road** is difficult unless you have wheels. With a vehi-cle, you soon reach the 30km mark and hit the dust and potholes which were the noto-

---

LAKE DANGERS

Beware, out on Naivasha. The possibility that underground springs may feed the lake, its location on the floor of the Rift Valley, and its shallowness, all combine to produce notoriously fast changes of mood and weather: grey and placid one minute, suddenly green and choppy with whitecaps the next. Watch out, too, for hippos, which can overturn a small boat easily enough if frightened or harassed. Naivasha shouldn't be underestimated, as boating mishaps are all too common, but swimming, when the hippos are distant, is said to be safe enough and bilharzia is not present.

---

rious condition of the whole lake road until a few years back; there's 35km of this (between an hour and two hours' worth) before you reach the Naivasha–Nakuru highway at a point 9km north of Naivasha. If you're hitching or using public transport, you'll find very few vehicles have reason to go beyond Kongoni Village and it's not really worth trying to go the whole way.

Just over 6km from the lake road junction is the base of Air Naivasha (Kamuta Ltd/Simpson Safaris, PO Box 411; ☎0311/30091), with a three-passenger Cessna 182 that's available, usually at short notice, for **charter flights** anywhere in Kenya, at $150 per hour (in which time it flies 200 straight kilometres). More realistically for most people, they do wonderful, highly recommended **short flights** around Lake Naivasha and over Hell's Gate ($25 per person for 30min). They also do day trips to the Maasai Mara which, at around $200 each for three people, are much better value than the one-hour balloon rides down there. Simpson Safaris also run tailor-made **camping safaris** by land cruiser that start from about $90 per person per day.

Exploring on foot can also be very pleasant. From *Fisherman's Camp*, it's worth walking up to the superb viewpoint overlooking **Small Lake**, and visiting *Elsamere* (see below).

Elsamere and the Environmental Education Centre

Moi South Lake Road, 22.1km; PO Box 1497; ☎ & fax 0311/21247; daily 3–6pm; Ksh200.
Elsamere, former home of the naturalist and painter Joy Adamson, is now a conservation centre, open to the public in the afternoons: there's a video (which you don't have to watch), followed by a copious and civilized afternoon tea on the lawn (Ksh300). It you really like the place, you can take lunch (Ksh600) or dinner (Ksh800) here, though you need to book ahead: it's unlicensed, but you can bring your own wine for dinner. If the house is somewhat shrine-like, the garden is a fine place to while away a couple of hours with a pair of binoculars: a troop of colobus monkeys (normally found only in moist forests) can be seen in the acacias around the grounds.

Elsamere, and the neighbouring **Environmental Education Centre**, is the focus for the Naivasha region's environmental issues, with regular seminars and the involvement of Leicester University in England and the Earthwatch organization.

Crescent Island Game Sanctuary

A very popular short trip is a visit to the **Crescent Island Game Sanctuary**. The "crescent" is the outer rim of a volcanic crater which forms a deep bay, the deepest part of the lake. The island is attached to the shore by a narrow causeway on the private land of Sanctuary Farm (about 6km from the lake road junction), but don't try to enter there; go instead to Lake Naivasha Country Club and ask at the reception desk about a **boat**. The fixed price is Ksh500 (plus Ksh200 entrance) and you have to state at what time you wish to be picked up – if you miss the boat, you'll be charged for the cost of a search party. The boatmen are most obliging, and will detour to show you the hippos and giant kingfisher. Once there, you're free to wander as you will. At first you may think there's nothing there, but the island, barely two square kilometres, is home to hundreds of species of birds as well as gazelle, giraffe, waterbuck (caution – they can be dangerous) and some startlingly large, though harmless, pythons. **Horse riding** is available at Sanctuary Farm, at about $6 per hour.

Green Crater Lake – Lake Songasoi

Now that people are visiting it, the once-mysterious (because rarely visited) **Green Crater Lake** is a straightforward target for a short trip – preferably with a vehicle, as it's 17km past Fisherman's Camp and 6km beyond the end of the tarmac and reliable transport. There is one *matatu* daily, leaving Crater Lake at 9am, returning towards 4pm (it leaves Naivasha at 3pm), which is really only of use if you're camping or staying at the *bandas* by the lake. A proper **game sanctuary** has been set up all round the crater, with entrance fees (currently just Ksh100, and Ksh50 extra if you bring a car), and there's an exclusive tented lodge in the crater itself (see p.168). In the sanctuary there are various tracks you can take, though the one to the crater rim is only for hikers or 4WD vehicles. You'll see a fair amount of plains game if you follow the perimeter fence: there are plenty of buffalo in the sanctuary, so exercise caution.

The brilliant, jade lake is quite breathtaking, in a small way: the Maasai consider its deep alkaline waters good for sick cattle, but it's also a favourite place for them, with sacred associations. From the main viewpoint on the west rim, it's possible to scramble up for ten minutes to the highest point. There are not many places where you can get down to the crater floor but the easiest are on the south side.

Hell's Gate National Park

Daily dawn to dusk; $15, students/children $5; $8 to camp, $10 at "special" campsites. Warden PO Box 234 Naivasha (☎0311/20510, fax 0311/20577); Map: Survey of Kenya "Hell's Gate National Park" at 10cm:1.25km (1993).The road to the park at Olkaria Gate, 21.5km from the lake road junction, is tarred all the way (5km) through the geothermal area, but there's a very steep descent to the gorge and roadhead at the end.

The best expedition in the Naivasha area is the hike through the Njorowa gorge – **Hell's Gate**. This is a spectacular and exciting area, the gorge's red cliffs and undulating expanse of grassland providing one of the few remaining places in Kenya where you can walk among the **herds of plains game** without having to go a long way off the beaten track. Buffalo, zebra, eland, hartebeest, Thomson's gazelle and baboons are all usually seen; lions and leopards hardly ever, but you might just see a cheetah, and you'll certainly come across their footprints if you scan the trail. There are servals, one of the most delicate cats, and, high on the cliffs, small numbers of klipspringer ("cliffjumper") antelope. Njorowa is a fairly small area and the quantity of wildlife varies seasonally. The gorge is occasionally rather empty of animals.

The main entrance road to Hell's Gate is just south of the YMCA, but the Elsa Gate is a further 1.5km along this track. If you're wheel-less you should ideally get there as early as possible in the day: it's about 25km to the roadhead and back and, while a fair number of vehicles visit at weekends, there are far fewer during the week, making your chances of a lift somewhat slim. The best time to arrive is dawn, when most animals are about. Try at any cost to avoid the midday hours, as the heat away from the cooling lake is intense. You'll need to carry plenty of water and some food (the only place to buy anything in the park is a simple staff kiosk in the Olkaria Geothermal Area).

There are also several **campsites** in the park if you want to stay overnight, with picnic benches and shower stands but no water or toilets (the rangers at Elsa Gate have a tap). The nicest camping is at the shady and superbly sited *Ol Dubai* campsite on the clifftop south of Fischer's Tower. *Nairburta* and *Endachata* campsites (the latter a more expensive "special campsite") are across the gorge on the northern cliffs (see map "Lake Naivasha & Hell's Gate", p.165).

The upper gorge

From Elsa Gate, take a look first at the rock known as **Fischer's Tower**, after the German explorer who arrived at Lake Naivasha via Hell's Gate. The rock is a volcanic plug – the hard lava remaining from an ancient volcano after the cone itself has been eroded away. It's now the home of a colony of very astute rock hyraxes ("dassies"), which look like large, shaggy guinea pigs and expect to be fed.

Continuing through the gorge along the main track, more and more animals are visible on the slopes leading up to the sheer cliffs. Ornithologists probably don't need reminding that at least one pair of rare **lammergeier eagles** used to nest on the cliffs. But they haven't been reliably seen since 1984 – report any sightings to a ranger. More obvious are the secretary birds: these you'll always see, mincing carefully through the grass at a safe distance.

If you're driving or on a mountain bike, you can take the longer Twiga and Buffalo Circuits. Twiga climbs up to the left from just inside Elsa Gate before you reach Fischer's Tower and then Buffalo Circuit ploughs through thick bush (don't go anywhere near the buffaloes, though, as they can be extremely unpredictable and dangerous). These tracks are insanely dusty but, when the dust clears, the views out over Hell's Gate and across to the Aberdares range are magnificent.

Hell's Gate is somehow a very authentic-looking part of East Africa. Its colours and acoustics give it a distinct sense of place. It has been used several times as a film location, most recently for that stirring epic *Sheena – Queen of the Jungle* (a number of fibreglass rocks still litter the deep part of the gorge). Hell's Gate's more enduring significance is as the one-time outlet for the prehistoric freshwater lake that stretched from here to Nakuru and, it's believed, would have supported early human communities on its shores.

The lower gorge

At the southern end of the gorge (12km from the entrance), a second rock tower – **Ol Basta** – marks its transition into tangled ravine. Here, there's a car park where, if you're driving and want to get out, you'll have to continue on foot, as there's nowhere to park on the narrow, rocky track that follows the gorge to the south for a short distance. The nearby "Interpretation Centre" is now a **viewpoint**, a good place to picnic and to shelter from rain or sun. The best move you can make from this **roadhead** is to cross the gorge and follow the "Nature Trail" round the north side of Ol Basta. There's nothing nature trail about it but it's easy enough to follow as far as the rock tower where most people turn back.

If you want to **hike in the ravine**, from Ol Basta the trail becomes more indistinct and it's quite easy to lose your way until you turn down into the head of the ravine itself. Beware of suggestions that there's a path around the south side of Ol Basta, directly above the eastern branch of the ravine: there is not, and trying to prove otherwise is dangerous. Equally dodgy is the very steep way down into the ravine just south of the gorge crossing, near the car park. You need tough walking shoes for this and shouldn't attempt it alone. Once down on the ravine floor, you've a one-hour walk or thereabouts southwards to the point where you can climb up to the road on the west side again. Watch out for unexpected slippery surfaces and seek advice if it's been raining, as flash floods sometimes rip through the ravine. It's a tough, exhilarating and realistic hike that most people should be able to do quite easily.

If you've come equipped for a night out, you can press on, to emerge after a further (and difficult) 12km at the end of the canyon – still 15km short of the Narok road. For orientation, aim for **Mount Suswa** – itself an area of great exploring interest, only properly documented in the last few years.

Otherwise, either turn back and retrace your path to Elsa Gate, or else climb up towards the noise and steam of Olkaria geothermal station. Here on the cliff-top you can look out over the gorge and a Maasai *enkang* below, with your back to the first productive **geothermal installation** in Africa. The underground temperature of the super-heated, pressurized water is up to 304°C, one of the hottest sources in the world, and the station is eventually expected to supply half of Kenya's energy requirements. Surprisingly, although the whole complex is working at full tilt, the impact on the local environment appears to be small, and it certainly doesn't spoil the landscape until you're in the complex itself.

Heading for the main buildings through the scrub, and the maze of pipes and hissing steam jets, you meet a perfect new **tarmac road**: from here, you shouldn't have any problem getting a ride with plant workers down to the lake road at a point 2km past *Fisherman's Camp*. The road emerges near the Oserian farm where they produce carnations. If you hike it, allow about three hours to complete this section. There are fine views of Small and Green Crater Lakes.

Mount Longonot

Daily dawn to dusk; $15, students/children $5; $2 to camp.

Especially when the weather's right (most likely January–March and July–October), **Mount Longonot** is worth climbing for the fabulous views in every direction as you circle the rim. Don't try to make the ascent from the lake road or Hell's Gate, however – it's further and steeper than it looks, and is covered in dense bush on its north slopes, frequented by buffalo. Moreover it's a national park and you have to do things the right way. Head for Longonot village on the old Nairobi road.

If you're **driving**, there's a road that leads the 6–7km from just southeast of the level crossing by the main road to the base of the mountain, and you can leave your car there safely and get a drink. There's only one straightforward route up to the crater rim, and you may be escorted by Kenya Wildlife Service rangers. For **overnight stays** on the mountain, special permission may be needed from the warden and you need a tent; there are no official campsites. In the village, *Jogoo Bar B&L* is right by the train station – very cheap and basic, but friendly.

Up the mountain

Longonot's name comes from the Maasai *oloonong'ot*, "mountain of many spurs" or "steep ridges", and you soon find out why. The cone is composed of very soft volcanic deposits that have eroded into deep gulches and narrow ridges. The **hike to the rim** takes about an hour. At the top you can collapse (the last section is rather steep), and look back over the Rift Valley on one side and the enormous, silent crater on the other. Joseph Thomson, the first *mzungu* up here, was overcome:

> *The scene was of such an astounding character that I was completely fascinated, and felt under an almost irresistible impulse madly to plunge into the fearful chasm. So overpowering was this feeling that I had to withdraw myself from the side of the pit.*

If you feel the same urge, you can now walk, or scramble, down a steep **crater path**; you turn left from the gravelly landing on the rim and find the path after about ten minutes' walk. Exciting encounters with buffalo on the crater floor aren't uncommon: a 1937 guidebook observes that "any attempt to descend into the crater is accompanied by hazard".

The walk **around the crater rim** is what most climbers do. The anti-clockwise route is easier because the climb to the summit on the western side is quicker and steep sections more negotiable. It doesn't look far, but allow two to three hours. Much of the path is over crumbly volcanic tufa and has been worn, by a combination of walkers and rain, into a channel so deep and narrow that it's almost impossible to put one foot in front of the other.

Until recently, Longonot's crater was famous for its steam jets (the volcano is classed as "senile", not "extinct"). Although their vents, like pockmarks, are still visible in several places around the rim and on the crater walls, their emissions of steam have decreased since the Olkaria plant went on line, though the hot-air thermals are said to be still sufficient to deflect light aircraft. Another rumour is the existence of a tunnel running from the inside base of the crater on the south side and out onto the plain beyond.

From Kinangop to Thika

If you're serious about hiking, mountain-biking, or fairly adventurous expeditionary driving, the route from **North Kinangop to Thika** is a dramatic and attractive one. It cuts up from the Rift Valley and right over the southern flank of the Nyandarua (Aberdare) range – still, in large part, virgin mountain rainforest.

The approach from Naivasha is quite straightforward, as frequent *matatus* make the journey up to North Kinangop. Routine though it may be, this part of the journey is still spectacular. The road climbs constantly towards the **Kinangop Plateau**, with the Rift Valley and Lake Naivasha way below. The land hereabouts is Kikuyu farming country, once widely settled by Europeans, who were lured by the wide open moors, rocky outcrops and gushing streams. Sheep and cattle graze everywhere. If you're doing this under your own steam, follow the route description for getting up to Aberdares National Park given on p.218, turning right or straight ahead rather than left when you reach the end of the fourteen-kilometre stretch of reasonably intact tarmac.

North Kinangop is nowadays a rather isolated rural community, a village of big rubber boots and raggy sweaters (it can freeze here at night), whose road becomes nearly impassable during the long rains. Transport onwards from here outside the rainy season, though, is usually little problem – at least as far as South Kinangop. Tractors will pick you up and there are a few old lorries, too, trundling around. **South Kinangop** (also known as **Njabini**) is livelier than its northern counterpart, a small trading centre with a paved road straight to Naivasha (look out for the quaint, red-tiled colonial buildings which are now a Caltex station). You can also get *matatus* direct to South Kinangop from Naivasha. If you get stuck in South Kinangop, give the *Gimwa Rest Lodge* a try at the Thika end of town – clean, very inexpensive s/c rooms and good hot showers.

Beyond here – heading towards Thika – you're pretty much down to walking. A *murram* road (the C67) does continue, but there's very little traffic as it switchbacks in descent, across a series of streams flowing south from the Aberdares to the Chania River. The road follows the river, with tremendous scenic variation, though almost always through forest – sometimes wild, sometimes conifer plantation. But after the turn-off (left) for **Kimakia forest station**, the occasional *shambas* and all signs of habitation stop completely: from here down, the forest is untouched mountain jungle, trees with huge dark green leaves, birds shrieking in alarm, the crashing of colobus monkeys, chameleons wobbling across the road and even tell-tale elephant dung. In the wrong season the road becomes an appalling quagmire, really just for tractors (though you don't see many), but on foot, or even by mountain bike, there's no danger of getting stuck.

You reach tarmac and human population again at **Gatakaini**, and, just before you do, there's the very pleasant *Kimakia Fishing Camp* (*bandas*, toilets and running water), unsupervised but a good place to spend the night with your own tent. The camp is run by the Fisheries Department (contact the Naivasha Senior Fisheries Officer on ☎0311/20505). At Gatakaini you can also find *matatus* and buses to get you down to the relative metropolis of Thika. Irritatingly, towards evening public transport thins out and the country bus may leave you stranded at Gatura. If you have no luck hitching, give the excellent, but no longer appropriately named, *Tarmac End Inn* a try: a clean B&L with hot water, well inside the ① bracket.

South Kinangop to Gatakaini is a thirty-kilometre stretch, taking seven to eight hours on foot. It's also a great mountain-bike trip. It proves, again, how many exhilarating areas there are close to Nairobi – and how many more there must be.

Thika and nearby

Despite the literary connections (Elspeth Huxley's *The Flame Trees of Thika*), **THIKA** is a dull little town – suitably humdrum if you've just arrived from the wilds of the Kinangop or Garissa – not even redeemed by the profusion of flame trees you might expect. These days it's essentially a satellite town of Nairobi.

Pineapples, introduced in 1905, are Thika's contemporary claim to fame. Thousands of acres flourish here, easily confused with the sisal that is also grown in the area. Until 1968, most of the valuable export crop was produced on *shambas*; since then Del Monte has held the lion's share of the plantations.

Thika is off the tourist route – or at least the main road to Mount Kenya (*matatu* route #237 from the Kencom Building in Nairobi, or others from the BP station on Ronald Ngala Street) – but it's noticeably cheaper than Nairobi and a laid-back, friendly sort of place. There's a Standard Chartered **bank** with an ATM if you need money. If you stay, the best-value **accommodation** is *New Fulila Hotel*, Uhuru Street (PO Box 1161; ☎0151/21840; ①) which has clean s/c rooms. Other slightly more expensive possibilities include *December Hotel*, Commercial Street (PO Box 156; ☎0151/22140; ②), whose enormous rooms are clean and have telephones (ask for s/c), though hot water is erratic, and *White Line Hotel*, Stadium Road (PO Box 290; ☎0151/22857; ①), which is fairly acceptable and has a lively bar, but only non-s/c singles. Two kilometres south of town, the *Thika Inn* (PO Box 4020; ☎0151/31590; ③) has s/c bedrooms with nets and phones for those overcome by the pulse of the adjacent *Vybestar* nightclub (see below).

The **upmarket choice**, out of town on the Nairobi–Muranga'a road is *Blue Posts Hotel* (PO Box 42; ☎ & fax0151/22241 22589; ③), which is older than the town itself, dating from 1908. Although you might expect a certain quaint shabbiness, the old place has been refurbished and rooms in the Chania Wing are excellent: en suite with balconies overlooking lush gardens, with glimpses of the Chania Falls. Its restaurant has a sweeping view of the falls, and tea with pastries costs only Ksh120. The *Blue Posts'* grounds contain both the Chania Falls and the Thika Falls – with a five-minute walk between the two. The hotel makes a good stop-off on the road to Murang'a or Nyeri – the food is good, and the terrace is very pleasant for a drink overlooking the garden and Chania Falls. The toilets are clean, and parking is safe.

Restaurants in town include the relatively swish (and expensive) *Prismos Hotel*, MTC Building, Uhuru Street, the *New Fulila*'s bar-restaurant, which is a deal cheaper, *Macuast Restaurant* for fish and chips, and good local eats at *Golden Plate* and *Thika Central Restaurant*. Outclassing them all is the restaurant at the *Blue Posts*, and the *nyama choma* enclosure at *Thika Inn* (see above). For a decent cup of **coffee** (the plantations around Thika are the nearest to Nairobi), the *December Hotel* has a great Parisian-style pavement café which was opened by Kenyatta himself in December 1970. For your own supplies, Safeway **supermarket** is at Thika Arcade, and Kangari Central

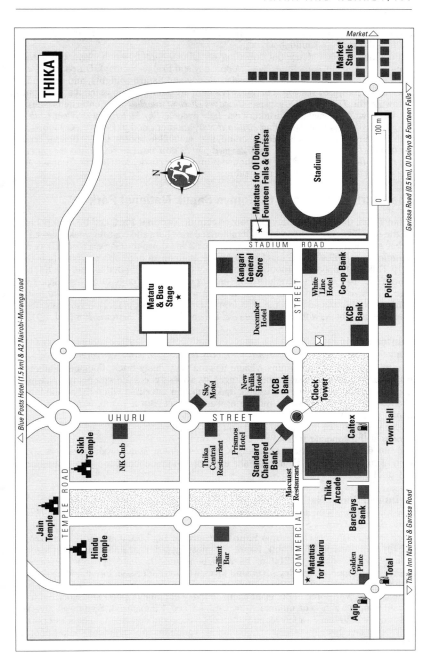

THIKA

Market Stalls

Market △

Stadium

Matatus for Ol Doinyo, Fourteen Falls & Garissa

Matatu & Bus Stage ★

STADIUM ROAD

Kangari General Store

December Hotel

White Line Hotel

Co-op Bank

KCB Bank

Police

N

△ *Blue Posts Hotel (1.5 km) & A2 Nairobi-Muranga road*

Sky Motel

New Fulila Hotel

KCB Bank

Clock Tower

UHURU STREET

Sikh Temple

NK Club

Thika Central Restaurant

Prismos Hotel

Standard Chartered Bank

Macuast Restaurant

Caltex

Town Hall

TEMPLE ROAD

Jain Temple

Hindu Temple

Brilliant Bar

Thika Arcade

Barclays Bank

COMMERCIAL

★ Matatus for Nakuru

Golden Plate

Total

Agip

▽ *Thika Inn Nairobi & Garissa Road*

Garissa Road (0.5 km), Ol Doinyo & Fourteen Falls ▽

0   100 m

Store is off the top of Stadium Road; the **market** is east of town, past the thriving street stalls at the stadium roundabout.

Foot-tappers should try out *NK Club* on Uhuru Street, which plays **Congolese music** and **reggae**, sometimes live (Wednesday and Friday–Sunday). **Disco** freaks can head for the *Vybestar Club* on Wednesday, Friday and Saturday nights, and on Sunday afternoons for a jam session (currently resident are Ruiru Young Star); it's 2km south of town at the *Thika Inn*. Otherwise, *Cascades Disco* at the *Blue Posts* entertains Nairobi clubbers, whilst heavy-duty drinkers can fade away at *Sky Motel Day & Night Club* or the decidedly less than sparkling *Brilliant Bar*, another good place to meet inebriated locals. More dignified clubbing can be had at Thika Sports Club, Bendor Road (☎0151/21101, or 31088) with its 6724-yard par 72 **golf course** set amidst the pineapple and coffee plantations. The clubhouse is unusually rustic, with a large fireplace and wooden beams running along the ceiling.

The Fourteen Falls and Ol Doinyo Sapuk National Park

From Thika, the trip out to tiny **Ol Doinyo Sapuk National Park** and **Fourteen Falls** on the Athi River is a popular one with motorized travellers and Nairobi weekenders. For either site, head for Kilima Mbogo village, some 22km down the Garissa road. There are *matatus* from Thika's "U Shops" stage by the stadium to here. *Munje Hotel* (PO Box 1510 Thika; ①) may have rooms, which at any rate should be better than the tumbledown *Hotel 14 Falls*. If you're lucky, the *matatu* might carry on to Ol Doinyo Sapuk village ("Doinyo"), 2.5km off to the right down a dirt track, which passes close to the entrance to the falls and is some 2km from the national park gate. Doinyo village itself is surprisingly busy, with dozens of *dukas*, bars and the basic *Bestland Inn* B&L (①).

Fourteen Falls
Daily 9am–5pm; Ksh100, children Ksh50, vehicles Ksh120, cameras Ksh50.

Ten minutes' walk from Doinyo village down a very dusty track, Fourteen Falls is a broad cascade of white water which plunges 30m over a precipice with many lips, which give rise to the name. They're especially spectacular after rain when they flood into a single, genuinely impressive thundering red cataract. But a vague, obnoxious smell hangs in the air, presumably caused by effluent from Thika's emerging industries. There are no hotels hereabouts, but you can **camp** or stay in spartan but dirt-cheap *bandas* at the council-run *14 Falls Campsite* on the Athi River, for which you theoretically need YHA membership (camping Ksh25 per person; *bandas* Ksh70 per person). A rash of robberies at the Fourteen Falls explains the presence of two policemen every day until 5pm.

Ol Doinyo Sapuk National Park
Daily 6am–6pm; $15, students/children $5; $2 to camp. Warden PO Box 1514 Thika. Map: Survey of Kenya SK113, 1990.

Seen from a distance, **Ol Doinyo Sapuk** (Maasai for Big Mountain), or Kilima Mbogo (Kikuyu for Buffalo Mountain), is not the most inspiring of hulks, nor is it high in Kenyan terms, rising to 2146m. Its attractions only become apparent when you approach the gate, as the dry scrubland gives way to redder soil, forest and cooler air. The national park encloses the entirety of the mountain. Surrounding the summit is a primal forest with some of the giant plants, notably the lobelia *giberroa*, associated with the Afro-alpine zones of mounts Kenya, Elgon and Kilimanjaro. Birdlife is diverse, though the mammals – a few leopard, buffalo, Sykes' and colobus monkeys and porcupines – makes themselves scarce in the thick vegetation. Watch out for snakes, too. At the 7km mark, you come to the grave of Sir William Northrup MacMillan, the fattest of famous settlers, whose intended burial place on the summit had to be abandoned when the modified tractor-hearse's clutch burned out. He rests here with his wife, maid and dog. Views from here are tremendous and you're not likely to get further in a vehicle, even with four-wheel drive, because the final couple of kilometres of track is particularly bad. Between the MacMillans' graves and just below the summit the track winds through dense forest cover. If you make it to the top, the 360-degree panorama over a huge oxbow in the Athi River, Thika's pineapple fields and mounts Kenya and Kilimanjaro can be wonderful in December and January, when the air is really clear.

The **national park gate** is reached by crossing the Athi river, then taking a (signposted) right turn at the end of Kilima Mbogo village. The gate is 3km further on, and is the only place where you're allowed to camp (park fees are payable, as it's just inside the gate). Long prohibited for security reasons (large numbers of buffalo, and sporadic incidents of banditry up to 1997), **walking** the 9km to the summit is now possible, so long as you take an armed ranger along with you (Ksh300 per person for half a day, Ksh500 per person for a whole day). Most people drive up the summit, which is rough going but usually feasible in 4WD. You'll probably catch a ride if you wait at the gate, especially on a weekend.

Olorgasailie and Lake Magadi

The journey to the prehistoric site at **Olorgasailie** and the dramatic salt lake of **Magadi** takes you instantly out of the commotion of Nairobi and down into a hot, sparsely inhabited part of the Rift Valley. There should be two **matatus** from Nairobi leaving in the early afternoon (best caught in Kiserian); alternatively, the Akamba **bus** (1pm & 3pm; 3hr) is cheap, and the Maasai, who invade it *en masse* at Kiserian, are lovely company.

KISERIAN is your chance to buy last-minute provisions, as further south there's almost no food available; if you decide to stay in Kiserian, *Kituo Bar* is a basic **B&L** at the eastern end of the market square, with good *nyama choma* and a first-floor balcony overlooking the wonderful commotion of the market. Accommodation in a different class can be found at *Whistling Thorns*, 13km east of Kiserian on the newly tarmacked Isinya road (see p.100 for details). You should be able to catch a *matatu* from Kiserian. There is also a surprisingly good **restaurant** in the *Makena Village Inn*, a couple of kilometres back to Nairobi on the main road. At the south end of Kiserian, *Tenco Hill Resort* offers odd live music weekends, including "Retired General" and his one-man band.

The scenery opens out dramatically as you skirt the southern flank of the Ngong Hills and descend steeply down the escarpment. Try to get a front seat, as giraffe and other animals are often seen. If you're travelling under your own steam, there's a pleasant picnic site at *Olepolos Country Club*, 12km after Kiserian. At Olepolos itself, there are a number of *nyama choma* joints, a good bar with chairs on the roadside under some trees, and entirely Maasai clientele.

Olorgasailie

Daily dawn to dusk; Ksh200.

Olorgasailie Prehistoric Site (1.5km from the main road) is signposted 3km after **Oltepesi**. You need to bring all requirements apart from water (ie food and bedding). The **accommodation** and **museum** are just above the excavations on a ridge overlooking what was once a wide, shallow lake. There are double *bandas*; you can make reservations in advance through the Director's Office at the National Museum in Nairobi (☎02/742131–4; ①) to be sure of beds, but it's rarely necessary – or you can camp. Do-it-yourself showers and free firewood are also available. Olorgasailie is a peaceful place to stay, while the **guided tour** around the excavations (included in the entrance charge) is not to be missed. A group from the Los Angeles County Museum and Smithsonian Institute refurbished the displays in 1994, and the site itself is endowed with numerous pathways, catwalks and informative signs.

The hand axe site

Between 400,000 and 500,000 years ago, the lakeshore was inhabited by "people", probably *Homo erectus*, of the **Acheulian culture** (after Street Acheul in France, where it was first discovered). They made a range of identifiable stone tools: cleavers for skinning animals; round balls for crushing bones, perhaps for hurling or possibly tied to vines to be used, à la gaucho, as *bolas*; and heavy hand axes, for which the culture is best known, but for which, as Richard Leakey writes, "embarrassingly, no-one can think of a good use". The guides tell you they were used for chopping meat and digging. This seems reasonable but some are very large, while hundreds of others (particularly at the so-called factory site) seem far too small, the theory being that they were made by children practising. The great thing about places like Olorgasailie is that the answers are not cut and dried, and there's plenty of room for the imagination to construct scenarios of how it might have been.

Mary and Louis Leakey's team did most of the unearthing here in the 1940s. Thousands of the stone tools they found have been left undisturbed, *in situ*, under protective roofs. Maybe the most impressive find is the fossilized leg bone of a gigantic extinct elephant, dwarfing a similar bone from a modern elephant placed next to it. It was long hoped that human remains would also be uncovered at Olorgasailie, but despite extensive digging none have been found – more scope for speculation.

Staying on

Although you could conceivably look around the site before the next bus passes two hours later, and then ride down to Magadi, it's much better to give yourself a day and a night. Sitting in the shade of the open-sided picnic *bandas* with a pair of binoculars and looking out over what used to be the lake can yield some rewarding animal-watching, especially in the brief dusk. Go for a walk out past the excavations towards the gorge and you'll see more: gerenuk, duiker, giraffe, eland and baboons.

Contacts with Maasai are good here, too. If you'd like to take pictures, food is a more acceptable payment than money. There's usually also some jewellery for sale. And if you're enchanted with the peace and presence of Olorgasailie, and stay longer than you'd anticipated, you can cultivate further friendships – and collect some scant **provisions** – at the cluster of desolate *dukas* at Oltepesi, 3km back along the Nairobi road, where they also have warm beer and soft drinks.

Lake Magadi and west to the Nguruman escarpment

Heading south and descending, **Lake Magadi** is a vast shallow pool of soda, a sludge of alkaline water and crystal trona deposits lying in a Rift Valley depression 1000m below Nairobi. This is one of the hottest places in the country. On a barren spit of land jutting out across the multicoloured soda, the Magadi Soda Company, until 1991 an ICI interest, has built the very model of a company town. Everything you see, apart from the homes of a few Maasai on the shore and a few *dukas* and places to eat in town, is owned and run by the corporation. You pass a company police barrier where you sign in and enter over a causeway, past surreal pink salt ponds. Now on company territory, a sign advises visitors that "it is dangerous to walk across the lake surface", just in case you were wondering. Note that some of the company police are touchy about you taking photos of the factory installations.

Despite this, the atmosphere here, somewhat surprisingly because of the nature of the work and harshness of the environment, is relaxed and welcoming. By comparison with the rest of Kenya, the company pays high wages; people tend to get drunk a lot, and accommodation and services are free.

Practicalities

Having arrived, you might wonder how you'll fill the time until the bus leaves for Nairobi the next morning. Behind the police station, which stands on the highest point of the peninsula, the lake glows unnaturally in the afternoon sun. Looking the other way (to the west), the road to the left leads to the "European" end of town, where a dozen or so managers live and where there's a strange, barren golf course; to your right, the town slopes gently down to a crusty shore where most of the Kenyan employees live. There's a Barclays Bank here with spectacularly unhelpful hours (Wed 11am–2pm – and you can't even bank on that). There is also a thriving **daily market**, although choice is limited. *Oguts Hotel & Bakery* serves cheap and filling **meals**, and for a drink (you'll be refused entry at all three staff "clubs"), try the madhouse *Maasai Bar*, opposite the mosque.

The company has built blocks of apartments, a church, a mosque and schools and, with a touch of inspiration, a large, glittering **swimming pool**. The sign says "for residents only" but a beetroot face and rolling eyes should convince them otherwise. The poolside bar and *nyama choma* kiosk are popular in the evenings and, on weekends, there are even a few picnickers from Nairobi. Magadi has one **hotel** opposite the hospital, the *Lower Guesthouse* (PO Box 8; ☎0303/33000–8 ext 278 or 33278 out of hours; ②) which officially isn't open to tourists, so a measure of tactful persistence might be needed. You can pitch a tent almost anywhere south of the township – though the utterly bizarre golf course (actually a rock- and thorn-strewn wasteland with not a blade of grass in sight) has two equally bizarre "Keep Off" signs. Anywhere here is baking hot during the day and a favourite haunt for baboons – but it's likely you'll be invited home by employees anyway.

The lake

Many visitors come to Magadi specifically for its **birdlife**. There's a wealth of avifauna here including, usually, large numbers of flamingos at the southern end of the lake. At this end, there are also freshwater swamps which attract many species.

The **lake** itself is fascinating to walk across (on the causeways: in practice only the inlet between Magadi and the eastern shore). On the eastern side, where you first arrive, you can watch the sweepers in rubber boots shovelling the by-product, sodium chloride (common salt), into ridges on the technicolour "fields". Sodium chloride crystallizes on top of the sodium carbonate (the "soda") and is loaded on to tractor-drawn trailers and taken away to be purified for human and animal consumption.

But the company is primarily concerned with extracting the soda. Magadi is the second largest source of sodium carbonate in the world, after the Salton Sea in the USA, and the company's investment here is guaranteed – hot springs gush out of the earth's crust to provide an inexhaustible supply of briney water for evaporation. The dried soda is exported, first by rail to Mombasa via Kajiado and Konza, thence, much of it, to Japan. Magadi soda, used principally for glass-making, is Kenya's most valuable mineral resource. But, despite the "high" wages, you wonder how anyone can be persuaded to work in this lurid inferno: the first rains here are usually "phantom rain", the ground so hot that the raindrops evaporate before hitting the surface. It's important to wear sunglasses and a hat while out in the sun, and bring plenty of water.

Across from the town, on the western shore, Maasai will sell you *pombe* made from a base of roots and herbs, and fermented with honey. It's a lot cheaper than beer, and stronger, too. Asked if there was another name apart from the generic *pombe* they said, "We just call it Ups". Drinking it in the middle of the day is not advisable.

Onwards from Magadi

Returning to Nairobi from Magadi, the *matatu* leaves at 5am and the **buses** at 6am and 7am, or you could ask about hitching a ride on the **train** to Kajiado (on the main Kenya–Tanzania highway) or to Konza and Mombasa if you're headed that way. There's supposed to be a passenger service on Wednesday, usually leaving late afternoon – though you're advised to arrive early.

With your own vehicle (or Ksh500 to rent a company car if you meet a worker with a day to spare – it's the worker, not you, who can rent the car), you can drive on from the town, across the lake to the **hot springs** on the western side. Check the map in the police station first.

From the hot springs, you can drive to the Ewaso Ngiro River at the foot of the Ol Choroi plateau, also known as the **Nguruman Escarpment**. By the river there's a game warden's camp, near to which you may be able to pitch a tent. There is, however, no guarantee of this; the whole Ol Choroi area is private land, leased off the Elangata Enkutoko Group Ranch which is formed of the district's Maasai clans. The lessees have plans to encourage Maasai involvement in tourism initiatives, but some of the few travellers and overland trucks that have visited this spot in recent years have left rubbish, damaged the vegetation and lit fires in unsuitable places, causing resentment among local people. They get few visitors here and, in theory it's a good place to meet untouched Kenya, but you should be extremely sensitive to local feelings. Don't tamper with, or drive around, locked gates. And forget about trying to four-wheel-drive it up the rough track beyond the river, over the escarpment and on to the Mara. People have done that in the past, but the whole area is privately owned Maasai land and, for the moment at least, not accessible.

For **Travel Details** for this chapter, see pp.138–146.

CHAPTER TWO

THE CENTRAL HIGHLANDS

A s the political and economic heartland of the country, the **Central Highlands** stand at the focal point of Kenyan history. Mount Kenya, Africa's second highest peak, gave the colonial nation its name, and the majority of British and European settlers carved their farms from the countryside around it. Later, and as a direct consequence, it was this region which saw the development of organized anti-colonial resistance culminating in Mau Mau.

Until Independence, the fertile highland soils ("A more charming region is not to be found in all Africa," thought Joseph Thomson, exploring in the 1880s) were reserved largely for Europeans and considered, in Governor Eliot's breathtaking phrase, "White Man's Country". The **Kikuyu peoples** (Kikuyu, Meru and Embu) were skilled farmers and herders who had held the land for centuries before the Europeans arrived. They were at first mystified to find themselves "squatters" on land whose ownership, in the sense of exclusive right, had never been an issue in traditional society. They were certainly not alone in losing land, but, by supplying most of the fighters for the Land and Freedom Army (see Contexts p.610), they were placed

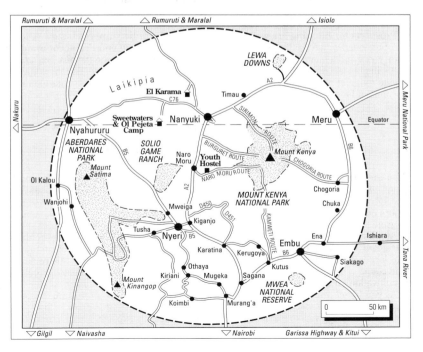

ACCOMMODATION PRICE CODES

Rates for a standard double or twin room. For a full explanation of these rates, see p.47.

① Under Ksh500	(under approx £5/$8)	⑥ Ksh6000–9000	(£60–90/$96–144)*
② Ksh500–1000	(£5–10/$8–16)	⑦ Ksh9000–12,000	(£90–120/$144–192)*
③ Ksh1000–2000	(£10–20/$16–32)	⑧ Ksh12,000–16,000	(£120–£160/$192–256)*
④ Ksh2000–4000	(£20–40/$32–64)	⑨ Over Ksh16,000	(over £160/$256)*
⑤ Ksh4000–6000	(£40–60/$64–96)	* = *usually priced in dollars*	

---

squarely in the political limelight. In return, they have received a large proportion of what Kenyans call the "Fruits of Independence".

Today most of the land is in African hands again, and it supports the country's highest rural population. There is intensive farming on almost all the lower slopes, as well as much of the higher ground, beneath the **national parks** of **Mount Kenya** and the **Aberdares**.

There are considerable rewards in travel through the Highlands. Above all, if you're into hiking, there's the ascent of Mount Kenya. And, while hikes lower down and in the Aberdare range are easier, they are scarcely less dramatic, with the bonus of a chance to see some of the highland **wildlife**. The mountain streams are full of the trout that were introduced early this century, and most tourist lodges will rent out **fishing** tackle even if you're not staying there. Nor is travel itself ever dull in the Highlands, where the range of scenery is a spectacular draw in its own right: primary-coloured **jungle** and **shambas**, pale, windswept **moors**, and dense **conifer plantations**, all with a mountain backdrop. People everywhere are friendly and quick to strike up a conversation, the towns are animated and markets colourfully chaotic.

Prospects for **hitching** are well above average, but **public transport** is good, too, and bus journeys invariably packed with interest and amusement. For **accommodation**, you'll find a handful of tourist hotels and lodges – including the famous *Treetops* – that will give fair return for your cash if you're in the mood to splurge. But there's also a wide range of reasonably priced lodgings. *Hotelis* are plentiful and serve gargantuan portions of food.

AROUND MOUNT KENYA: THE KIRINYAGA RING ROAD

After the main game-viewing areas and the coast, this natural **circuit** is one of the most travelled in Kenya. Not that it's overcrowded, or even really touristy (such places are few indeed up-country), but there are always a few safari minibuses to be seen somewhere on the road and other signs that the whole tourist industry up here is beginning to grow.

At present, the whole region is wonderfully untouched by anything much more than the steady encroachment of *shambas* up the ridges and the burgeoning of small towns into larger ones. Apart from the high forests, moors and peaks, little of this remains wild country, but the Kikuyu, Meru and Embu have created an extraordinary spectacle of cultivation on the steep slopes, gashed by the road to reveal brilliant red earth.

As you travel, you're also aware of the looming presence of **the mountain**. Its twin peaks are normally obscured by clouds, but early in the morning and just before sunset, the shroud can vanish suddenly, leaving them magically exposed for a few minutes. With a base 80km across, Mount Kenya is one of the largest free-standing volcanic

THE KIKUYU PEOPLES: SOME BACKGROUND

The ancestors of the **Kikuyu** migrated to this region over successive generations between the sixteenth and eighteenth centuries, from somewhere northeast of Mount Kenya. Stories describe how they found various hunter-gatherer peoples already living in the region they now occupy: the **Gumba** on the plains and the **Athi** in the forests. A great deal of intermarriage, trade and adoption took place; the newcomers cleared the forests and planted crops, giving the hunters gifts of livestock, honey, or wives in return for using the land. As this Bantu-speaking, cultivating, livestock-keeping culture expanded and consolidated in the Highlands, the indigenous peoples gradually lost their old identities.

Between the Kikuyu and the **Maasai**, relations were less easy. They both placed (and still place) high value on the ownership of cattle, the Maasai depending entirely on livestock. During bad droughts, Maasai might raid their Kikuyu neighbours' herds, with retaliation at a later date being almost inevitable. But such **intertribal warfare** often had long-term benefits, as ancient debts were forever being renegotiated and paid off by both sides, thus sustaining the relationship. There was lively trade and **intermarriage** between the two peoples, and married Kikuyu women enjoyed a special immunity enabling them to organize trading expeditions deep into Maasai-land, often with the help of a *hinga*, a Kikuyu of Maasai descent, to oil the wheels.

As well as these economic and social relations, the Kikuyu had, in the past, close **cultural affinities** with the Maasai. Many visitors are surprised when they first see the evidence of this – for example, in traditional dress styles – in museums or old photos. Like the Maasai, the Kikuyu advanced in status as they grew older, through named age-sets, with appropriate rituals at each stage. Age is still an important social index: a Kikuyu who discovers you're both the same age is likely to say "We're age mates then!"

Circumcision, of young men and women, still marks the important transition into adulthood for most Kikuyu, though "female circumcision" (clitoridectomy) is illegal and performed less and less. In the past, the operations were accompanied by changes in dress and ornament. Once circumcised, boys could grow their hair long and dye it with ochre in the style of Maasai warriors (in fact, the Maasai got their ochre from the Kikuyu, so it may really be the other way around). They also wore stacks of glass beads around their necks, metal rings on their legs and arms, and pulled their ear lobes out with heavy weights and ear plugs. Women wore a similar collection of ornaments and, between initiation and marriage, a headband of beads and discs, still worn today by most Maasai women.

Traditionally the Kikuyu had no centralized **authority**, no tribal or clan chiefs: "chiefs" were only installed by the colonial administration. When disputes had to be settled or far-reaching decisions made, the elders of a district would meet as a council, usually with a little persuasion in the form of meat or beer from the people summoning them, and the matter would be cleared up in public, with a party to follow. After their deaths, elders – as ancestors – continued to be respected and consulted.

Although Christianity has altered the picture in the last few decades, many churchgoers still believe strongly in an **ancestor world** where the dead have powers for good and bad over their living descendants because of their closeness to *Ngai* or *Mwininyaga* (God). The Kikuyu traditionally believed that *Ngai*'s most likely abode, or at least his frequent resting place, was **Kirinyaga** (Place of Brightness), Mount Kenya. Accordingly, they tried to build their houses with the door always looking out towards the mountain; hence the title of Jomo Kenyatta's book, *Facing Mount Kenya*.

Today the Kikuyu remain in the forefront of Kenyan development. Despite entrenched nepotism and a growing poverty gap, they are accorded grudging respect as successful business people and formidable politicians – though their political power at national level has been much eroded in recent years and is only starting to return with the legalization of political opposition. There is considerable political rivalry between the **Kiambu Kikuyu** of the tea- and coffee-growing district north of Nairobi (Jomo Kenyatta's district and now a Democratic Party stronghold), and the **Nyeri Kikuyu**, who rely on a more mixed economy and where there is more support for the FORD Asili and FORD Kenya parties.

cones in the world, and the peaks – when you can see them from the road – are always distant. To the east and south, the mountain slopes steeply away to the broad expanse of Ukambani (Akambaland) and the Tana River basin. Westward, it drops more gently to the rolling uplands of Laikipia, drier than the east and for the most part treeless.

Getting here is an easy trip from Nairobi up a busy road: if you're not driving, either buy a bus ticket from Nairobi direct to any of the towns in this section, or make **Thika** (p.176) or **Murang'a** a first destination before heading clockwise or anti-clockwise around the mountain. **Naro Moru**, the usual base for climbing Mount Kenya, lies on the west side some 25km south of **Nanyuki**, an alternative base for a climb from the north. On the eastern slopes, **Chogoria**, between **Meru** and **Embu**, offers arguably the finest route up the mountain.

Murang'a

Leaving Thika behind, **MURANG'A** is the first town of any size you come to. Established as the administrative outpost of **Fort Hall** in 1900, it has since come to be thought of as the "Kikuyu Homeland" because of its proximity to *Mukuruwe wa Nyagathanga*, the "Garden of Eden of the Kikuyu". Here, in Kikuyu mythology, God made husbands for the nine daughters of Gikuyu and Mumbi, spiritual ancestors of all the Kikuyu people. The husbands, who became the ancestors of the nine Kikuyu clans, were found by Gikuyu under a large fig tree. Take a *matatu* to **Mugeka** and walk from there to Gakuyu village if you'd like to see the site; plans for a museum here are, as yet, still only plans, and the original *mukuruwe* (fig tree) disappeared long ago.

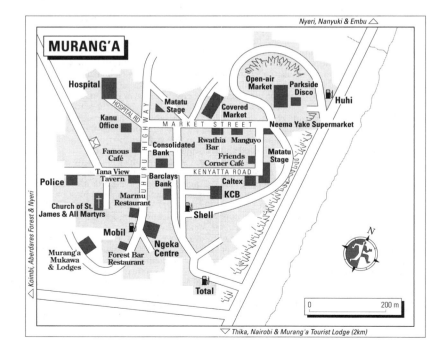

Fort Hall was never a settlers' town. The district was outside the zone earmarked for white colonization and most of it comprised the "Kikuyu reserve". Richard Meinertzhagen, an officer in the King's African Rifles posted here in 1902, found the time (when not shooting animals – or people) to write:

If white settlement really takes hold in this country it is bound to do so at the expense of the Kikuyu who own the best land, and I foresee much trouble.

Kenya Diary (Kenway Publications, Kenya 1989)

That said, Meinertzhagen helped put down some of this trouble, launching "punitive expeditions" from Fort Hall with his African troops.

There's even a bit of sightseeing. In the **CPK Cathedral** (formerly the Church of St James and All Martyrs) hangs an unusual *Life of Christ* mural sequence by the Tanzanian artist Elimo Njau. It depicts the Nativity, Baptism, Last Supper, Gethsemane and Crucifixion of an African Christ in an African landscape. The murals were painted in 1955, the year the church was founded by the Archbishop of Canterbury, as a memorial to the thousands of Kikuyu victims of Mau Mau attacks.

Practicalities

At the beginning of this century, Fort Hall consisted of "two grass huts within a stone wall and a ditch". Present-day Murang'a, perched above the busy main road, remains small and is strewn with litter, but there are a number of decent, basic hotels on the steep hillside if you feel like staying – and it's a happy enough place, bustling energetically. Recommended **lodgings** are *Murang'a Mukawa & Lodges* on Uhuru Highway (PO Box 207 Maragua; ☎0156/22542; B&B ③), large and clean with a somnolent bar-restaurant, but no nets in the bedrooms, and *Murang'a Tourist Lodge*, 2km down the Thika road (PO Box 52; ☎0156/22120; ②), similar to the *Mukawa* with airier rooms and nets, but breakfast costs extra. *Rwathia Bar* on Market Street (PO Box 243; ☎0156/22527; ①) is very basic but clean with a pleasant courtyard, and is the best of three adjacent day-and-night club lodgings; the *Manguyo* next door also has rooms and does good *kienyeji*. You might also try the *Forest Bar Restaurant*, 200m up Uhuru Highway from *Murang'a Mukawa* (PO Box 382; ①).

There's no shortage of **hotelis** either. *Famous Café* on Uhuru Highway has great samosas, *Marmu Restaurant* on the same street has a good range of snacks, and the *Tana View Tavern* at the corner of Uhuru and Kenyatta Road is recommended not only for its fine balcony but for its lightly curried rabbit dishes (Ksh100 with chips), a strange delicacy introduced to a sceptical Murang'a (rabbit meat was previously seen as children's food) by the *Tavern*'s congenial proprietor. Nankas Bakery is in Ngeka Centre above the Co-op Bank, spicy *chai* is served at the zebra-striped *Friends' Corner Café* by the *matatu* stage, and there's the Neema Yake **supermarket** at the east end of Market Street. There's one **nightclub** in the form of *Parkside Disco* (busy Friday and Saturday nights and Sunday lunch), near the open-air market. Barclays Bank has an ATM.

Onwards from Murang'a

There are three onward travel options from Murang'a: clockwise around Mount Kenya via Karatina and Naro Moru (see below); anti-clockwise around the mountain via Embu (see p.214); or up to Nyeri and the Aberdares (p.217). Nyeri, a few kilometres off the Mount Kenya circuit, is a recommended detour and one which most public transport on the ring road will include.

Routes west into the Aberdare range

If you want to get up into the **Aberdare forest**, take one of the two minor roads leading out of Murang'a to the west. They join at Kiriani and dip north to Nyeri via Othaya. If you have all day to dawdle, either of them would make a nice, circuitously backwoods route to Nyeri. *Matatu* availability may determine which you take. If you have your own wheels, the longer of the two, via Koimbi, takes you past the start of a rough, snaking, high-altitude track which climbs as far as Tusha, just 10km from the Aberdare National Park's Kiandongoro Gate, one of the two park entrances above Nyeri.

Towards Mount Kenya: Sagana, Karatina and Mountain Lodge

Heading north, **SAGANA** lies at the junction for Thika, Nyeri and Embu, but has little to recommend it apart from some basic accommodation options: the pleasant *Sagana Country Hotel* (PO Box 25 Sagana; ☎0163/46229; ②), on the Nairobi road 500m before junction has singles only, with good solid meals, bar and tables outside under some trees. In town, try *Central Star B&L* (①), or the more modern *Hotel Chakaka* (①) at the western (Murang'a) end. If you're **camping**, you can stay for free at *Savage Wilderness*' **river rafting** base a few kilometres before Sagana (coming from Nairobi), signposted on the left. A day's river rafting here costs $95 (more details on p.46).

If you pass through the feverish commercial centre of **KARATINA** on a Monday or Wednesday, stop to have a look around the market: it's one of East Africa's biggest cattle and produce sales. There are several **lodgings** in town, including the reasonable *Karatina Tourist Lodge* (Private Bag, Karatina; ☎0171/71522, fax 72520; ③) which has safe parking. Cheaper options include the clean *New Mugi Motherland Hotel 1995* (no phone; ①), the more lively *Three-in-One Hotel* (PO Box 768; ☎0171/72316; ②), and *Ibis Hotel* (PO Box 240; ☎0171/72777, fax 72777; ②) opposite Agip. **Camping** is possible at *Wajee Campsite* (PO Box 148 Nyeri; ☎0171/60359) – turn off the main road 2km north of town onto the Gakonya road. There's good filling **food** at *Samaria Hotel* at the north end, and at *Karatina Express Café* by the railway, with its shaded terrace and smooth service. The main **nightspot** in town is *Galaxy Club*, with soul on Friday and Saturday nights, and the obligatory Sunday jam session.

Karatina is also the base for **Mountain Lodge** (PO Box 123 Kiganjo; ☎ & fax 0171/30785; reservations through Serena, p.50; HB ⑧–⑨), the most accessible of Kenya's three highland tree-hotels (the other two being *Treetops* and *The Ark*) and the only one on the slopes of Mount Kenya. The lodge is set at an altitude of 2200m, about 30km from Karatina, mostly along good tarmac (the President's Sagana State Lodge is also up this way so be discreet with your camera): the signposted turning is just on the Nairobi side of town. Alternatively, if you're coming from the west, leave the Mount Kenya ring road at Nyeri Station (4km north of Kiganjo), and follow the signposted but badly pot-holed road up for about 20km. Alternatively, a taxi from either Nyeri or Karatina shouldn't cost more than Ksh1500.

Mountain Lodge has consistently good **game-viewing** over the floodlit water hole, and larger rooms than either of its competitors. The rooms have private bathrooms and balconies and there's good food. You can stay up all night, with continuous supplies of tea and coffee on hand. Or you can be choosy about your animal-watching, tick off what you're interested in being woken to see, and then slumber through the herds of buffalo and antelope. They wake you at 6am in any case.

Towards Mount Kenya: Castle Forest Lodge

From Murang'a, a different kind of Mount Kenya accommodation is easily accessible. **Castle Forest Lodge**, nestling in the forest on the southern slopes of the mountain, is a private home, reputedly built for British royalty before World War I. Large, comfortable rooms and several cottages in the grounds can be reserved in advance (PO Box

564 Kerugoya; reservations through 3rd floor, Arrow House, Koinange St, Nairobi, PO Box 70460; ☎02/212387, fax 214020, or via Let's Go Travel in Nairobi, see p.142; ③ low, ④ high), but it's not normally necessary. Meals are available to order and, in between sleeping and eating, you can walk in the woods, sit by the waterfalls of the Karute stream, or fish in it for trout. The only problem, if you don't have transport, is access. *Castle Forest* is about 50km from Murang'a, via Sagana and Kutus on the B6. From Kutus, head east on the B6 for just 400m, then turn left on the tarmac D458 and, after about 6km, at Rukenya, turn right onto a *murram* track. Fifteen kilometres up here you reach the Mount Kenya forest boundary gate, *Thiba Fishing Camp*, and, 5km further, the house.

If you're keen to try an unusual approach to the summit of Mount Kenya, the seldom-used **Kamweti route** begins at the roadhead, eight steep kilometres north of *Castle Forest*. The managers at the house should be able to advise on guides and porters, though you'll most likely have to arrive fully equipped.

North to Naro Moru

Continuing up the A2 from Karatina, passing the turning to Nyeri (see p.222), and then going through Kiganjo (a second road turns left to Nyeri here and then one to the right to *Mountain Lodge*) you emerge from the folded landscape of Kikuyu cultivation onto a high, windswept plain. Here, you're crossing one of the great animal migration routes, severed by human population pressure over the last eighty years. Until 1948, when the two mountain parks were created, every few years used to see the mass migration of **elephants** from one side to the other. In 1903, a herd estimated at seven hundred animals was seen wending across the open country from Mount Kenya to the Aberdares. When the parks were opened, it was decided to keep the elephants away from the crowded farmlands in between, so an eight-kilometre ditch was dug across their route.

Naro Moru

The road climbs gently and steadily to **NARO MORU**, which stands on the watershed between the Tana and the Ewaso Nyiro river basins. The most straightforward **base** for climbing **Mount Kenya**, or simply exploring the mountain forests lower down, Naro Moru is nondescript, built around its now disused railway station. There's a post office (Mon–Fri 8am–1pm & 2–5pm) but no bank and not a lot in the food department, either, though things are improving. If you plan to spend several days on the mountain, buy any special food you want in Nairobi. Naro Moru's offerings are strictly in the bread and milk, *karanga na chapati*, line.

There are several **cheap accommodation** options should you need a room at the end of the day. Besides the ominous-sounding *Silent Lodge* (①), and the fresh and reasonable *Naro Moru Hotel '86* (①), complete with *Kirinyaga*-viewing balcony, there's the much improved and recommended *'82 Lodge* (①), with s/c rooms, and *Mountain View Hotel* (☎0176/62088; ②) also with a balcony. Out of town, there's a clutch of alternatives. Cheapest and closest is the rather exposed **campsite** (Ksh200 per person), with its freezing showers and pretty expensive firewood, which is to be found at *Naro Moru River Lodge* (about 2km north of town and signposted). With the B&Ls in town, there's not really much point in paying over the odds for a hard bunk in one of the bunkhouses.

There are two more expensive options, too. **Naro Moru River Lodge** itself (PO Box 18 Naro Moru; ☎0176/62212, fax 62211; reservations through Alliance, p.48; HB from ④ low, ⑤ high; self-catering cottages ④) is the only place where you can indulge yourself if you're feeling in need of creature comforts, and is very good value given its facilities. It has a welcoming log-fire atmosphere, pretty gardens, a trout stream with nature trail and good bird-watching. A blissful sauna, a heated pool facing the mountain, and horseback rides complete the picture. It tends to be full of upmarket mountain-climbing package clients and has an expensive but well-stocked equipment-rental shop. Kids' rates are, for a change, substantially cheaper (20 percent of the adult rate). If it wasn't for everything being overpriced, a good alternative to Naro Moru as a west-side base would be *Mountain Rock Bantu Lodge*, about 8km north of Naro Moru (PO Box 333 Nanyuki; ☎0176/62625, fax 62051, *mtnrock@form-net.com*). The entrance can't be missed, as it's marked by two enormous painted Kikuyu figures carved out of tree trunks and flamboyantly painted, but the difference between "resident" and "non-resident" rates is unjustified. If money's no object, they have fairly decent **rooms** (B&B from ⑤) with log fires, tented accommodation (from ④), and a restaurant and bar. You can **camp** in the grounds ($6 per person; tent hire $13–22, or $23–39 with bedding, which is just daft), and there's a small water hole in the back garden that attracts elephants once in a blue moon. There's **horse riding**, too ($20–25 for 2hr), though the limited tack needs careful checking, and ask about fodder and water before galloping off. You can also do expensive escorted walks through the forest in the vicinity of the lodge.

The youth hostel and the road to the gate

The **youth hostel** site lies about 9km up the well-signposted track to Mount Kenya's Naro Moru Gate. You may get a lift up from the main road; otherwise break your walk with a *chai* at the *Kariaku Restaurant*. The hostel itself (PO Box 274 Naro Moru; ☎0176/62414, fax 62078; Ksh400) is excellent and friendly, housed in a rebuilt farmhouse (the last incarnation burned down when a cooking cylinder exploded); it's a popular travellers' meeting place. The dorms are basic and comfortable, with hot showers and a well-equipped kitchen, and camping is welcomed in the grounds. They also have equipment for rent, at prices a good deal cheaper than the *Naro Moru River Lodge*.

If you're alone, and on a budget, the youth hostel is undoubtedly the best place to team up with others for the ascent (campers with their own vehicles tend to use the more expensive set-up at *Naro Moru River Lodge*). Three little *dukas* up the track, a kilometre or so beyond the youth hostel, sell one or two vital commodities, but they're very basic indeed.

Mount Kenya National Park

$10 per person daily, $5 students/children; camping $2 per night. Entry allowed on foot; minimum group two people. Warden: PO Box 69 Naro Moru; ☎0171/21575.

An extinct volcano, some three and a half million years old, with jagged peaks rising to 5200m, **Mount Kenya** is Africa's second highest mountain. Its heart is actually the remains of a gigantic volcanic plug – the mountain stood at over 7200m above sea level about a million years ago – from which most of the outpourings of lava and ash have eroded away by glacial action to create the distinctive silhouette. These peaks are permanently iced with snow and glaciers, while, on the upper slopes, the combination of altitude and a position astride the equator results in forms of **vegetation** that only exist here and at a few other lofty points in East Africa. Seemingly designed by some 1950s science fiction writer, it's hard to believe the "water-holding cabbage", "ostrich plume plant" or "giant groundsel" when you first see them. Mount Kenya is unexpectedly different and, unless your time is very limited, too good to miss.

Europe first heard about the mountain when the missionary Krapf saw it in 1849, but his stories of snow on the equator were not taken seriously. It was only in 1883 that the young Scottish traveller, Joseph Thomson, confirmed its existence to the Western world. The Kikuyu, Maasai and other peoples living in the vicinity had venerated the mountain for centuries: park rangers still occasionally report finding elderly Kikuyu high up on the moorlands, drawn by the presence of *Ngai*, whose dwelling place this is. It's not known, however, whether anyone had actually scaled the peaks before Sir Halford Mackinder reached the highest, Batian, in 1899. Another thirty years passed before Nelion (10m lower but a tougher climb) was conquered. Both are named after nineteenth-century Maasai *laibon* or ritual leaders.

Climbing Mount Kenya: the practicalities

There are **four main routes**. The **Naro Moru trail** provides the shortest and steepest way to the top. The **Burguret** and **Sirimon trails** from the northwest are less well trodden: Sirimon has a reputation for lots of wildlife, while Burguret passes through a long stretch of dense forest. The fourth, the **Chogoria trail**, is a beautiful but much longer ascent up the eastern flank of the mountain.

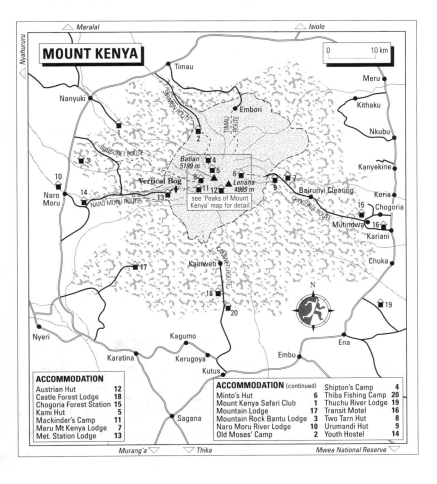

MOUNT KENYA

ACCOMMODATION

Austrian Hut	12
Castle Forest Lodge	18
Chogoria Forest Station	15
Kami Hut	5
Mackinder's Camp	11
Meru Mt Kenya Lodge	7
Met. Station Lodge	13

ACCOMMODATION (continued)

Minto's Hut	6	Shipton's Camp	4
Mount Kenya Safari Club	1	Thiba Fishing Camp	20
Mountain Lodge	17	Thuchu River Lodge	19
Mountain Rock Bantu Lodge	3	Transit Motel	16
Naro Moru River Lodge	10	Two Tarn Hut	8
Old Moses' Camp	2	Urumandi Hut	9
		Youth Hostel	14

Batian (5199m) and **Nelion** (5188m) are accessible only to experienced, fully equipped mountaineers – they look almost vertical – and the easiest route is Grade IV, making them a lot more testing than most of the routes up the Matterhorn. If you want to climb these peaks, you should join the Mountain Club of Kenya (PO Box 45741 Nairobi; ☎02/501747; their clubhouse is at Wilson Airport, bus #34). They will not only put you in touch with the right people but also give you reductions on hut fees.

On the question of **cost**, climbing Mount Kenya is an expensive business. A DIY four-day trek for two people, excluding guides or porters, costs anything between Ksh6000 and Ksh11,000 (including park fees, overnights, food, and transport to the roadhead, not including any additional equipment and tent rental). The cost of one porter/guide for this period would add anything between Ksh2000–4500 to the tally, whilst an organized trek easily costs over $100 a day. The park itself operates a sign-in/sign-out system, and you pay fees on entry for your anticipated stay. It's a bad idea to try to evade the exit gate on departure: they will go looking for you and eventually organize an air search if you don't show up. Stories circulate of people being pursued to Nairobi and beyond for non-payment of huge rescue service bills.

If you need to **change money**, do so in Nairobi or in the big ring-road towns of Nyeri, Nanyuki, Meru, Embu or Karatina – Chogoria has no exchange facilities (Chuka town is the nearest), and neither has Naro Moru.

Location and climate

Anyone who is reasonably fit can have a crack at **Point Lenana** (4986m), but this climb has somehow acquired the reputation of being fairly easy, and lots of people set off up the mountain quite unprepared for high-altitude living – indeed, some 25 percent of attempts fail for this reason. If you try it, forget you're on the equator. Over about 4000m, the mountain is **freezing cold**, foggy and windy – wickedly so after dark; the air is thin, and it rains or snows, at least briefly, almost daily, though most precipitation comes at night. Mount Kenya's **weather** is notoriously unpredictable. Even during the rainy seasons, there are days when it's fairly clear, but driving up the muddy roads to the park gates may be nearly impossible, and if it's really bad, you probably won't be allowed in anyway. The most **reliable months** are February and August, although January and most of July can be fine, too.

Preparations

Above all, it's essential to have a **really warm sleeping bag**, four-season at the very least, ideally with an additional liner and/or Gore-tex bivouac bag. One **thick sweater** at the very least (better still, several thinner ones), and either a **windproof jacket** or a down- or fibre-filled one are absolutely necessary. A **change of footwear** is pretty much essential, too, as you're bound to have wet feet by the end of each day. **Gloves** and a **balaclava** or **woolly hat** are also handy. A light cagoule or anorak is good to have, as is a set or two of thermal underwear for the often shivering nights. Out of sea-

---

KEEPING MOUNT KENYA CLEAN

The Kikuyu and other tribes venerated Mount Kenya – *Kirinyaga* – as the dwelling place of the supreme God, *Ngai*. If you went beyond the peaks, some thought, you would find him. Medicine men and diviners routinely trekked up the mountain to seek his guidance, miraculous cures, or simply inspiration. Nowadays, it's mainly tourists who retread their steps: some 15,000 each year. Few of them, it seems, particularly respect, never mind venerate, the old mountain God: several dozen tonnes of rubbish are left on its sides every year, only part of which is removed (mainly by boy scouts and other voluntary groups). Please take your trash down with you.

son (that is, most of the year), an **emergency foil blanket** is advisable and weighs and packs down to next to nothing. Another prerequisite is a **stove**, as you'll be miserable without regular hot fluids: firewood is not available and cannot be collected once you enter the park. For **food**, dehydrated soup and chocolate are perhaps the most useful. Remember, excess baggage can be left for about Ksh60 a day at *Naro Moru River Lodge*, so take only what you'll need. Here you can also purchase a packaged mountain climb, all inclusive (PO Box 18 Naro Moru; ☎0176/62212).

The *River Lodge* has a **rental** shop where you can get just about anything, at prices that may make you wish you'd simply bought it in Nairobi (see under "Camping equipment rental" in the Nairobi Listings, p.146); the youth hostel has a limited range of items for rent. Be cautious of anyone who approaches you offering to rent out gear.

If you are travelling alone and don't meet a suitable companion (you must be in a group of two or more to make the climb), it's possible to hire a **guide or porter** at the *Naro Moru River Lodge* in Naro Moru, at *Mountain Rock Bantu Lodge* 8km north of Naro Moru, at *Cousin Café* or *Nanyuki River Lodge* in Nanyuki, at the *Transit Motel* in Chogoria, or at the youth hostel up the Naro Moru route (the latter is the best place to find someone much more cheaply). Expect to pay up to Ksh850 per day for a guide, Ksh500 for a porter, Ksh600 for a cook (plus all their park fees – Ksh250 per day), but insist on a written agreement showing the wages, the number of days, who's providing the food – everything. If they ask for more (as they tend to do in Chogoria), they're trying to rip you off. You shouldn't pay the full fee until the trip is finished; nor should you entirely rely on your guide to make every necessary preparation. Incidentally, any guide now needs to possess an **official KWS guiding permit** – ask to see it, and don't be fobbed off with local guiding association cards – it isn't enough. Note that you're not likely to find a guide up at the park gates.

For a quick taste of the mountain, you can fix up a **day hike** to *Mackinder's Camp*, inclusive of lifts up to the gate and back down again, for around $35 (plus park fees), through one of the caretakers of the youth hostel.

Mountain health

While good physical fitness certainly won't hinder your climb, the ascent itself is mostly just a steep hike, if rough underfoot in parts. It is the altitude rather than the climb itself that may prevent you from reaching the top. Much more germane than the training programmes that some people embark on is giving yourself enough time to acclimatize, so your body has a chance to produce extra oxygen-carrying red blood cells. Above 4000m, you are likely to notice the **effects of altitude**, and the speed of your climb is critical. Physical symptoms are unpredictable; they vary between individuals, and appear to be unrelated to how fit you are – indeed, fit young males often suffer the most acute symptoms. Breathlessness, nausea, disorientation and even slurred speech are all possible, and headaches are fairly normal at first, especially at night. All this can be largely avoided by taking your time over the trek, as minor symptoms gradually disappear. You may consider bringing a tent for this reason, to avoid the sometimes rapid climbs between huts. Do not attempt to climb from the base of the mountain (that is, from the ring road) to Point Lenana in less than 72 hours; if you've just arrived in Kenya, allow five days for the ascent. Giving yourself a week for the whole trip is a good idea. Keeping your **fluid intake** as high as possible will also help (three to five litres a day is recommended) and it's best to avoid alcohol. If someone in your group shows signs of being seriously tired and weak, stay at that altitude. Should the symptoms develop into unsteadiness on the feet and drowsiness, **descend immediately**, whatever the circumstances. The effects of altitude are remarkable – especially on bodies tuned only to sea level – and can quickly become very dangerous. Every year, dozens of climbers are struck by pulmonary oedema (when water collects in the lungs), accounting for almost half the cases worldwide.

You may find Ibuprofen works against headaches and that Diamox is helpful against the general effects of altitude.

Accommodation on the mountain

Taking a **tent** is, outside the months of February or August, almost essential because the only other **accommodation** on the mountain is a handful of very basic cabins and mountain huts, which can become so cold at night as to threaten hypothermia and rob you of a night's much-needed sleep. For the Naro Moru route, bunks at the *Meteorological Station Lodge* and *Mackinder's Camp* (also known as *Teleki Valley Lodge*) are supposed to be reserved at *Naro Maru River Lodge*, though unless you want to be sure of a bed, in practice there's no problem simply turning up and paying there. If you have a tent, you can **camp** anywhere in the park, the only practical advantage of the campsites at the *Met Station* (3048m) and *Mackinder's* (4328m), and various other designated campsites on the mountain, being water pipes and "long drop" toilets. Most water on the mountain is reckoned to be safe to drink (exceptions are noted) and you're never far from it.

The *Meteorological Station bandas* ($8 per person) are good, but often burgled by monkeys. *Mackinder's Camp* ($11 per person for a bed in a concrete cell) has an informal alternative in the shape of the *Rangers' Cabin* nearby, with negotiable rates usually costing you about half the *Mackinder's Camp* price. Camping is allowed here and it's altogether a friendlier place to huddle than *Mackinder's*, with a fire burning most nights. Porters around *Mackinder's* will cook up a huge meal (given sufficient notice) for $4–5.

On the Chogoria and Sirimon routes there are several other basic **bunkhouses** and **cabins**, some permanently staffed (details follow under each route). The best accommodation on the mountain is the *Meru Mount Kenya Lodge* self-service *bandas* on the Chogoria route.

Also available are the small, bare **huts** built by the Mountain Club of Kenya, which normally have four walls, a roof, bunks, and nothing else (free; the wardens at the gates used to collect fees but recently washed their hands of the affair given the deplorable state of the huts – details are given under the relevant routes). These are located near the peaks, thus making it possible to spend a day or two around the high tarns and glaciers before returning to the base of *Mackinder's Camp* (warmer and more oxygen). *Top Hut*, next to *Austrian Hut*, is reserved for MCK members. The huts have no facilities or staff – you must be entirely self-sufficient. Their foam mattresses disappeared long ago (presumably burned to warm the frost-bitten nights), and a closed-cell bedroll is essential.

The Naro Moru route

From the main A2 road to the *Meteorological Station*, where the drivable earth road ends, is a 26-kilometre haul; even from the youth hostel (p.190) it's at least a five-hour walk. *Naro Moru River Lodge* will taxi you up here – for an extortionate price – or you may be lucky and get a lift, but a completely free ride would be a miracle.

Some 9km from the youth hostel, you come to the airstrip, the **park gate and HQ**, and usually three or four gigantic buffalo chewing the cud on the lawn. Entry is the usual $10 national park fee if you're going in for the day. Porters pay the residents' rate, and student card holders pay half-price. Don't overestimate; there are no refunds. From the gate, you leave the conifer plantations and occasional *shambas* behind as the road twists and climbs through shaggy forest into a zone of colossal **bamboo**. Look out for elephant and particularly **buffalo** if you walk this stretch, though you'll more often see their droppings and footprints. If you find buffalo on the path, you're supposed to lob stones at them – and they're supposed to move out of the way. Much safer is the tried and trusted retreat-steadily-without-keeping-your-eyes-off-them-until-they've-gone

---

GUIDEBOOKS AND MAPS

The **topographical map**, *Mount Kenya 1:50,000 Map and Guide* by Andrew Wielochowski and Mark Savage (available from Executive Wilderness Programmes, 32 Seamill Park Crescent, Worthing, BN11 2PN, UK; also available in Kenya) covers just the mountain itself at 1cm:500m and includes a detailed rundown on the huts and technical information for scalers of Nelion and Batian.

If you're a **climbing** enthusiast, you'll want to get hold of the Mountain Club of Kenya's *Guide Book to Mount Kenya and Kilimanjaro* or the *East Africa International Mountain Guide* by Andrew Wielochowski (West Col Productions, 1 Meadow Close, Goring, Reading, Berks, RG8 9AA, UK; also available in Kenya), which is adequate on the technical ascents.

Trekking in East Africa by David Else (Lonely Planet) is a usefully detailed, general companion.

As for **maps**, don't expect to find any in the Naro Moru area or at any of the park gates. The recent *Tourist Map of Mount Kenya National Park and Environs* (Ordnance Survey, through regular stockists) is an updated version of an excellent Survey of Kenya map. At 1cm:1.25km, it provides a very useful – and visually pleasing – overview of the whole district, showing all the routes, the region around the base and most of the ring road. It's frankly not much use for the final ascent, however.

There's also a quite user-friendly, small Survey of Kenya topographical map of the **peak area** at 1cm:250m that's worth getting hold of in Nairobi if you're intending to walk around the peaks.

---

approach: more people are killed by buffalo than by another other wild animal in Kenya.

The final 3km to the *Met Station* is a series of steep hairpins usually drivable only in a 4WD. You start to get some magnificent views out over the plains from up here, while right under your nose you may find a three-horned **chameleon**, stalking cautiously through the foliage like a miniature dinosaur. The high forest is its favourite habitat. **Black panthers** – the melanistic form of the leopard found at high altitudes – can also be seen in this habitat, and the latest local denizen was a lion, who walked into a tent at the *Met Station* and made off with a duvet jacket.

With an early start, it's quite possible to reach *Mackinder's* (4175m) in one day, but unless you're already acclimatized, you'll probably feel well below par by the time you get there. It is far better to take it easy and get used to the *Met Station's* 3050-metre altitude; perhaps stroll a little higher or, if you have a tent, climb an hour or so up to the tree line and camp there. Ready-erected tents can be hired at the *Met Station* if you can't afford the *bandas* (though, after the lion incident there was no camping for some months). The mountain's weather is another good reason to stop here: after midday, it often gets foul, and the infamous vertical bog is no fun at all in heavy drizzle and twenty-metre visibility.

Up the Teleki Valley

An early start from the *Met Station* the next morning should see you to *Mackinder's* by lunchtime, before the clouds start to thicken up. In fair weather, the **vertical bog** is not as daunting as it sounds: you keep to the left of the red-and-white marker posts where it isn't as wet. In wet conditions, however, it can be ghastly, as the rosette plants hold just enough freezing water to be able to reach certain parts in a bracing manner whenever you slip. As you reach the bog, you enter another vegetation zone, that of **giant heather**. Beyond and above the bog, the path follows a ridge high above the **Teleki Valley** with the peaks straight ahead, rising brilliantly over a landscape that seems to have nothing in common with the hazy plains below.

MOUNT KENYA'S HIGH ALTITUDE FLORA

The mountain's **vegetation** is zoned by altitude. Above about 2000m, *shambas* and coniferous plantations cease and the original, dense cloud forest takes over, with the best and broadest stands on the mountain's southern and eastern, rain-facing slopes.

As you gain altitude (2400m), forest gives way to giant bamboo, with clumps up to 20m high. The bamboo, a member of the grass family, appears impenetrable, but dark-walled passages are kept open by elephants and buffalo. Again, the best bamboo areas are to the south, while on the dry, northern slopes, there's very little of it.

Above the bamboo (2800m) you come into more open country of scattered, twisted *Hagena* and St John's Wort trees (*Hypericum*), and then the tree line (3000m) and the start of the peculiar, Afro-Alpine moorlands. Above about 3300m you reach the land of the giants – giant heather, giant groundsel, giant lobelia. Identities are confusing: the cabbages on stumps and the larger candelabra-like "trees" are the same species – giant groundsel or tree senecio – an intermediate stage of which has a sheaf of yellow flowers. They are slow growers and, for such weedy-looking vegetables, they may be extraordinarily old – up to two hundred years. The tall, fluffy, less abundant plants are a species of giant lobelia discovered by the explorer Teleki and found only on Mount Kenya. The name plaque below one of these (there's a little nature trail along the ridge above the Naro Moru stream) calls it an "Ostrich plume plant" (*Lobelia telekii*), and it is the only plant that could fairly be described as cuddly. The furriness which gives it such an animal quality acts as insulation for the delicate flowers.

For **Mackinder's Camp**, you follow the contours across the valley side and jump, or cross by stepping stones, over the snowmelt Northern Naro Moru stream. The camp, virtually at the head of Teleki Valley, is a long stone and concrete bunkhouse with dishevelled tents tacked into the icy ground around it. Certainly no hotel, it does at least provide some warmth and the company of others: climbers, Kikuyu guides and porters. **Batian** and **Nelion** tower magnificently over the valley, with a third pinnacle, **Point John**, even closer. There's usually a fresh icing of snow every morning but early sunlight melts most of it by midday.

Point Lenana

If you want to climb straight to **Point Lenana**, you're likely to find at least one group leaving early the following morning (say around 3am) with a guide, though it's not that difficult to find your own way up, especially if there's a moon. Leaving this early allows you to get to the top by dawn for a fabulous view (sometimes) from northern Kenya on one side to Kilimanjaro on the other. It's not advisable to rush into this final ascent, however. For most people, day three is better spent getting acclimatized in the Teleki Valley, making the climb to Point Lenana the next morning. And note: spending your third night on the mountain at *Austrian Hut*, just below Point Lenana, is a bad idea. Not only is *Austrian* in a disgusting state, but sleeping unacclimatized at high altitude is literally a nightmare.

Trekking around the peaks

Though most people head straight up to Point Lenana, trekking round **the peaks** is really a far more exhilarating experience, with the added chance to explore some of the tarns and glacial valleys on the north side. It's supposed to be easier to do this anticlockwise in two or three days. If you want to do it in one, however, set off clockwise from *Mackinder's* via *Two Tarn Hut* by **Hut Tarn**, set in a glorious and eerily silent col beneath the glaciers and scree. The walk from here round to Point Lenana is very much a switchback affair but, as long as the mists stay away, the scenery is fairy-tale.

If you're fairly fit and acclimatized, it should take eight to ten hours. *Kami Hut*, on the north side of the peaks, and *Austrian Hut* (as well as *Two Tarn*), are suitable night stops, though, again, you may not get much sleep, particularly at *Austrian Hut*, which is the highest.

Incidentally, your nights up in the mountain huts will normally be shared with large numbers of persistent **rodents** which you won't see until it's too late. Remember to isolate your food from them by suspending it from the roof. The familiar diurnal scavengers that you'll see are **rock hyraxes**, which are especially tame at *Mackinder's Camp*: the welfare service provided to them by tourists preserves elderly specimens long past their natural life span. Hyraxes are not rodents: the anatomy of their feet indicates they share a distant ancestry with elephants. You're likely to come across other animals at quite high altitudes, too, notably the **duiker antelope** on the moorlands.

The descent doesn't take long. You can do so in one day, right to Naro Moru or further, assuming you've left your vehicle at the *Met Station*, or else manage to find a lift. Rather than retrace your steps to Naro Moru, a more exhilarating and less frequently used alternative is to descend by one of the other routes: the Chogoria trail, for example. This would mean taking all your gear up with you, as well as extra food.

The Chogoria route

The **Chogoria trail** is scenically far superior to any of the others, and it's become more popular now that the road around the east side of the mountain has been paved. It is also the longest route, requiring good shoes and probably a plentiful supply of blister pads. A tent is preferable for the trek beyond the park gate. From the eastern side, the hike to the top can be done in three days, but it's easier to allow four or five if you're setting out from Nairobi.

Up to the park entrance

The hustly and not especially friendly village of **CHOGORIA** is your first target (Akamba, Kensilver and Sunbird Services have regular buses from Nairobi – the journey takes 4–6 hours – which pass the Chogoria turn-off en route to Meru, leaving you with a three-kilometre walk). The *Transit Motel*, 3km south of Chogoria centre at Karaa Market (PO Box 190 Chogoria; ☎0166/22096; B&B ②) is by far the best of several **lodgings**, with reasonable self-contained rooms, most with a balcony but no nets, and a restaurant of sorts – alight at Kariani stage a few kilometres before the Chogoria turn-off, which leaves you with a 1.5-kilometre walk. *Chogoria Cool Inn* (☎0166/22355; ①, but prone to overcharging) is in the village itself and considerably cheaper, but very basic (sometimes no water at all) and overrun with irritating guides and touts. *Chogoria Guest House* (①) is much the same. The *Motherland Hotel* has good basic food; for an antiseptic contrast, *Lenana Restaurant*, in the Presbyterian Mission Hospital, has cheap snacks in a linoleum-lined hall. The branch of Barclays here doesn't change money (Chuka is the nearest place).

There are a number of porter/guide associations in Chogoria, most of whose members are extremely pushy. The most reliable association (but also the most expensive) is Mount Kenya Chogoria Guides & Porters (PO Box 114), based at the *Transit Motel*. Their usual (bargainable) rates are Ksh400 a day for a porter, and Ksh600–750 a day for a porter-guide (remember, if you're alone you must have one to be allowed to stay in the park overnight, and he needs to possess an official KWS guiding permit). From the hamlet of Mutindwa, 4km up the mountain, it's about 26km to the park gate. On weekends, you may stand a better than average chance of getting a lift.

Otherwise, you could **rent transport** at the *Transit Motel* or elsewhere in Chogoria. There are a number of options, with prices depending on the state of the track: halfway to the park gate (15km drive, 15km walk; up to Ksh500); two-thirds (20km drive to

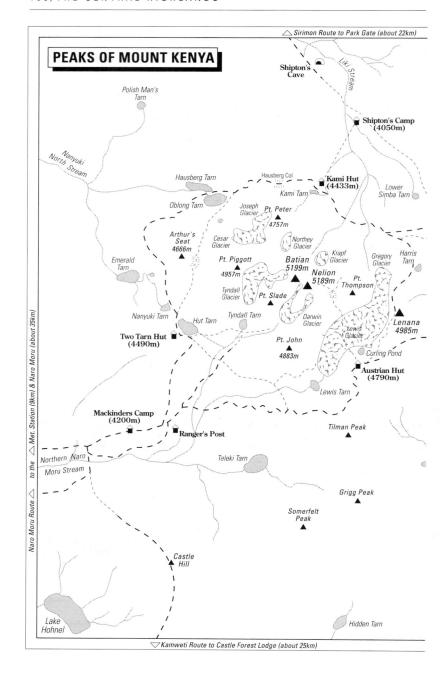

PEAKS OF MOUNT KENYA

△ Sirimon Route to Park Gate (about 22km)

Liki Stream

Shipton's Cave

Shipton's Camp (4050m)

Polish Man's Tarn

Nanyuki North Stream

Hausberg Tarn

Hausberg Col

Kami Hut (4433m)

Kami Tarn

Lower Simba Tarn

Oblong Tarn

Joseph Glacier

Pt. Peter 4757m

Arthur's Seat 4666m

Cesar Glacier

Northey Glacier

Krapf Glacier

Gregory Glacier

Harris Tarn

Emerald Tarn

Pt. Piggott 4957m

Batian 5199m

Nelion 5189m

Pt. Thompson

Tyndall Glacier

Pt. Slade

Nanyuki Tarn

Hut Tarn

Tyndall Tarn

Darwin Glacier

Lenana 4985m

Lewis Glacier

Two Tarn Hut (4490m)

Pt. John 4883m

Curling Pond

Austrian Hut (4790m)

Lewis Tarn

Mackinders Camp (4200m)

Ranger's Post

Tilman Peak

Northern Naro Moru Stream

Teleki Tarn

Grigg Peak

Somerfelt Peak

Castle Hill

Lake Hohnel

Hidden Tarn

to the △ Met. Station (9km) & Naro Moru (about 35km)

Naro Moru Route △

▽ Kamweti Route to Castle Forest Lodge (about 25km)

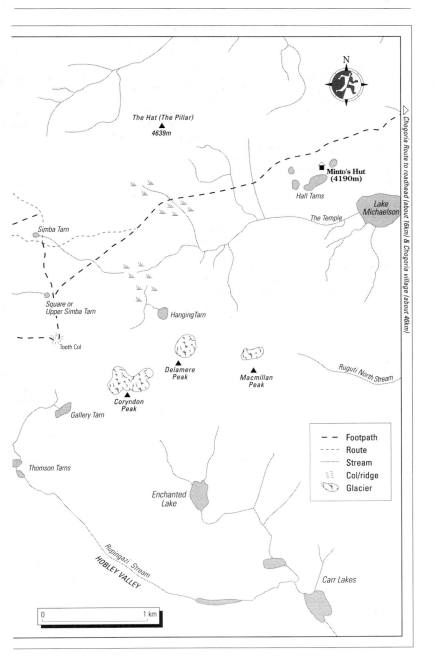

Bairunyi Clearing, 10km walk; up to Ksh2000); to the park gate (30km; Ksh3000–4000); or to the roadhead, some 7km further (Ksh4000). It's a good idea not to pay (at least not everything) until reaching the destination – a feat that for most of the year is by no means guaranteed because of the weather. You may prefer to walk up, in any case, because it gives you a chance to acclimatize, though the tsetse flies in the bamboo forest can make for a miserable time. If you get a lift up early in the day, do avoid climbing any higher before stopping for the night.

Walking up from **Mutindwa**, there's a good campsite after just a couple of kilometres at the **Chogoria Forest Station**, with firewood available. Exciting, dense rain forest follows, where you're likely to see colobus monkeys, spotted hyena, buffalo and numerous elephant droppings. Before, during and after the rains, though, you'll probably be more occupied with fending off swarms of hungry tsetse fly, which isn't much fun and runs the (slight) risk of sleeping sickness. The next available campsite is the only clearing in the forest, at a place called **Bairunyi Clearing**, 14km further up the track (no water). The National Park's **Chogoria Gate** is 8km further up the increasingly steep and rough track (4WD vital, and not always enough), flanked by giant, creaking bamboo forest. If you arrive late in the day and are not going beyond the roadhead (7km on – the actual boundary of the National Park), the rangers may waive park fees for that day, but be sure to keep receipts for the fees you pay to satisfy the rangers at whichever gate you exit from.

The park entrance and roadhead

The best **place to stay** is the very good and wonderfully sited *Meru Mount Kenya Lodge*, a group of self-service *bandas* just before the gate (no park fees payable), run by the district council (it may be worth booking in advance through Let's Go Travel in Nairobi, see p.142; Ksh1050 per person). They have a spartan shop that sells beer, and blissful wood fires in each *banda*. They're often visited by buffaloes, and you can sometimes see elephants at the nearby water holes, visible from the ridge of the hill behind the *bandas*.

Assuming you're not staying in the *bandas*, but it's time to stop for the day, you might as well stay put by the gate with your tent (if you have a tent), or go on to *Parklands Campsite*, twenty minutes' walk away, with toilets and, usually, water (stay on the main track for 500m then fork left: keep a look out, the turning is easily missed). Alternatively, follow the main track up from the park gate and you'll come to a "special campsite" with running water and toilet. This is a beautiful place to camp, but has special fees (reservable through the warden; $10 per person).

The nearest **mountain hut** is reached by branching left off the main track (it's well signposted) and continuing past *Parklands Campsite*: the uninviting *Urumandi Hut* is an hour's walk up the track. It's long overdue for a refit, only retains three unbroken beds and, like all the MCK huts, has lost its complement of mattresses. There's water from the ravine nearby. The neighbouring *Urumandi Campsite* is equally unprepossessing – little more than an overgrown swamp and a derelict shed.

Both the main track and the side branch eventually meet up at the **roadhead**, 6km further on. The side branch, via Urumandi, is the more interesting walk, but tougher on vehicles. The roadhead, with a small parking area, is on the north side of the Nithi stream and there's a very pleasant **campsite** here, with good stream water.

There are good walks round about, useful for acclimatizing to this three-thousand-plus-metres altitude. Short scrambles from the roadhead take you to the four sets of **Nithi Falls**, while longer walks (3–6hr round trip) take you north to **Mugi Hill**, **Lake Ellis** and the flat-topped peak Kilingo – the **Giant's Billiard Table**.

On the mountain

From the roadhead, all wheels are abandoned as you slog on foot up to *Minto's Hut*, a six-hour (9hr from *Meru Mount Kenya Lodge*) stint away in the high moorlands. The route tracks along the axis of an ascending ridge, then flattens onto the rim of the spectacular **Gorges Valley**, carved deep by glaciation. There are unobstructed and encouraging views up to the peaks as you hug the contours of the valley wall.

Minto's Hut, like *Mackinder's* on the west side of the mountain, is three to five hours from Point Lenana. Situated by the four small "Hall Tarns", it's perched above the larger Lake Michaelson at the head of the valley below – a very beautiful place, inspiringly set off by giant groundsel, lobelia plants and weird volcanic formations inhabited by rock hyraxes. "The Temple", a short walk away, is right above Lake Michaelson. Unfortunately, the hut itself is one of the worst: slummy, freezing cold at night and wet in the morning; the available tarn water is not pure. Beware: boiling it at this altitude will not kill the bugs so you should use purifying tablets or iodine.

In the morning, assuming you didn't freeze to death, you have two options. The first is to head up to the ridge west of *Minto's* and follow it, through pretty scenery, to **Simba Tarn**, below Simba Col. From there, head due south around the peaks and past little **Square Tarn** before turning right to follow the contours for a tough kilometre to the so-called **Curling Pond** (matches have been held on the ice here) and *Austrian Hut*. Note, if you're thinking of a short cut straight up to Square Tarn, it's very steep.

Alternatively, from *Minto's* make for the base of the ridge extending east from Point Lenana, then tackle the cruel scree slope to the south for a ninety-minute scramble up to a saddle followed by a straight drop to the head of the **Hobley Valley** with its two tarns. From here, it's just an hour across to the base of Lenana Ridge, behind which, again, is *Austrian Hut*. Mercifully, whichever route you choose, this day's hike is a short one and at this altitude (over 4000m), you'll be glad to spend the rest of the day at one of the huts, recuperating for the final ascent. Considering the altitude, a safer and probably more comfortable option would be to spend a second night, acclimatizing, at the base of Simba Tarn (tent only), followed by a pre-dawn assault on Point Lenana.

After the climb to Lenana, you have a ninety-minute **descent** from *Austrian Hut* along the edge of Lewis Glacier, tracking back and forth over miserable scree, to the Teleki tarn at the head of the Naro Moru stream. *Mackinder's*, and the scent of civilization, is just an hour away down the valley. But if you can resist that lure, and it is still early in the day, *and* if you have enough food and water, you can continue around the west side of the peaks to Hut Tarn, then up and down over the ridges to *Kami Hut*, at the head of the Sirimon route on the north side.

If you want to do it, and you feel acclimatized, there's no problem making it from *Minto's* to Point Lenana and on down to the *Met Station* in one day.

The Sirimon route

The **Sirimon route** leads up from the Mount Kenya ring road some 14km east of Nanyuki. It has certain advantages: throughout the year it's relatively drier than the others, the scenery is more open, and it's renowned for wildlife. *Mountain Rock Bantu Lodge* specializes in inclusive three- or four-day **guided tours** up to Point Lenana using this route, and the *Naro Moru River Lodge* also offers trips up this way. Prices are around $345 per person (4 days) in a group of four, or $405 per person if there are two of you, including transport to and from the base of the trail, all food and equipment, and a last night at *Mountain Rock Bantu Lodge*. Park fees are an additional expense. Much cheaper, if you're just looking for a guide, is to enquire at the *Cousin Café* in Nanyuki (see p.203), or else at *Nanyuki River Lodge*.

Unpackaged walking on this route is fine if you're in a small group, but you're much less likely to find company up here than on the Chogoria or very busy Naro Moru routes as there isn't any real "base town" to start from excepting a huddle of *dukas* on the ring road, 9km from the park gate. The route climbs over the northern moorlands, giving superb views on the way of the main peaks as well as the twin "lesser" peaks of Terere and Sendeyo (4714m and 4704m), which have small glaciers of their own.

Mountain accommodation on the way consists of *Old Moses Camp* (3300m, at the roadhead, 4WD access only; $10, $8 students/children) and *Shipton's Camp* **bunkhouses** (4200m; $12, $10 students/children), both of which are bookable at *Mountain Rock Bantu Lodge*, though you can also simply pay on arrival for a nominal mark-up. There are also plans for a sixty-bed "eco-lodge" near the gate (the facilities manager at KWS in Nairobi, p.148, should have the details).

The Burguret route

Mountain Rock Bantu Lodge's preferred route used to follow the **Burguret River** up from the hotel through thick bamboo forest and moorland, but this is now mostly overgrown and hard to follow without a guide (available at *Mountain Rock* for Ksh850 per day, excluding the guide's park fees). A 4WD vehicle can drive up to 3000m on this route and it terminates at *Two Tarn Hut* behind Teleki Valley. En route, it passes a clutch of caves described as a "Mau Mau conference centre". *Mountain Rock* still offers four-hour trips to the caves, including some waterfall hiking, for $6–7 per person, depending on group size, or the same on mountain bikes ($18–33 per person).

Other routes

The four trails described here represent only the most obvious and well-trodden of the mountain's hiking possibilities. All ground above 3200m is within the boundaries of the National Park, and, with time and sufficient food (and money to pay park fees), you could hike the moors and highland zone for weeks. On the north side, a very rarely used route leads up from Timau through dense forest, for which a guide, a good map and accurate orienteering skills are essential. The southern flanks of the mountain seem to have largely escaped the notice of hikers, but there are several forest stations in the vicinity of Embu and plenty of scope for exploration – the Kamweti route is a possibility (see p.189). Most of the southern slopes were a designated "Kikuyu reserve" during the colonial period, so few European climbers created routes up here. A **warning**: hiking in the forests, though feasible, is absolutely not advised unless you're with a guide; it's easy to get hopelessly lost, as a number of apocryphal tales circulating tell. Hyena and other hungry or bad-tempered beasts abound, and without serious jungle or rainforest experience, you're asking for trouble.

Over the equator: Nanyuki and around

North of Naro Moru, the El Niño-damaged A2 now rattles and lurches over fantastically deep potholes across the yellow-and-grey downs, scattered with stands of tall gum trees, roamed by cattle and overflown by brilliant blue roller birds, before dropping to the equator and Nanyuki. You might be forgiven for expecting something momentous to take place at **the equator**, but there's no "crossing of the line ceremony" here. Still, if you have any control over your transport, you'd have to be pretty cool just to breeze by.

There's a sprouting of several signs ("This sign is on the Equator"), and, in case there was any doubt, a veritable bazaar of souvenir stalls with salesmen who will go to absurd lengths to entice you ("Hey guy! Want cocaine?"). What they actually offer is all the usual beadwork, carvings, soapstone and bangles at the sorts of prices you'd expect. There's even an "Equator Professor" who'll demonstrate the Coriolis effect of the earth's rotation using a bucket of water and a matchstick (aided by sleight of hand

– the effect is too weak to have an effect over the 10m or so the professor uses): in the northern hemisphere water gurgles through a plug hole in an anticlockwise direction, whereas in the southern hemisphere it flows out clockwise. The demonstration is free, the "certificate" comes for a fee.

The town centre is just 1.5km down the road, so you could reasonably ask to be dropped at the equator and then walk in.

Nanyuki

NANYUKI has the dual distinction of being Kenya's air force town (a base which has had a lot of attention lavished on it in recent years) as well as playing host to the British Army's training and operations centre. For long an affluent place, the El Niño floods turned Nanyuki's once pristine streets into a series of potholes, and at the same time the town saw an influx of refugees fleeing the **ethnic violence** in Laikipia district between Kalenjin and Kikuyu: they're housed in the slums to the west of town. The hope is that the ongoing (1998–99) **Laikipia peace talks** might enable them to return to their original villages and *shambas*.

Nevertheless, Nanyuki remains in atmosphere very much a country town, and is oddly charming despite its increasing poverty. A wide, tree-lined main street and the mild climate lent by its altitude of 2000m bestow an unfamiliar, cool spaciousness that seems to reinforce its oddly colonial character. Shops lining the main road include the Settlers Store (since 1938), the Modern Sanitary Stores (which sells camping gas), and United Stores with its pile of *Daily Telegraphs*.

The first party of settlers arrived in the district in 1907 to find "several old Maasai *manyattas*, a great deal of game and nothing else"; Nanyuki is still something of a set-

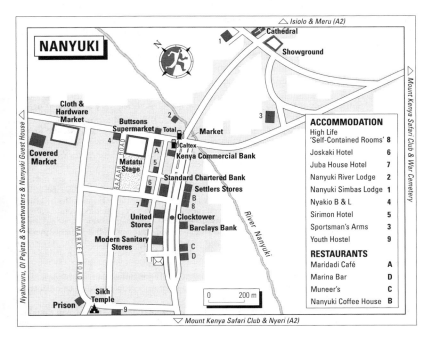

tlers' town and European locals are always around. The animals, sadly, are not. Although you may see a few grazers on the plains, the vast herds of zebra that once roamed the banks of the *Ngare Nanyuki* (Maasai – Red River) were decimated by hunters seeking hides, by others seeking meat (particularly during World War II, when 80,000 Italian prisoners of war were fed a pound each day), but most of all by ranchers protecting their pastures. As the zebra herds dwindled, so the lions became a greater threat to livestock; they retreated – under fire – to the mountain forests and moors. And the rhinos just disappeared, almost to the brink of extinction (see Solio Ranch on p.227).

Practicalities

If you're passing through Nanyuki, wholesome **food** is available at the *Maridadi Café*. Good snacks and occasionally great curries are to be had at *Muneera's Restaurant*; *Mother's Choice Café*, next door, has sweet cakes and sausages. For a lively **drink**, try the *Marina Bar & Restaurant* opposite the post office, a popular hangout for tourists and soldiers (unfortunately you may meet with some verbal abuse while in Nanyuki, presumably on account of the British base and most likely if you are – or might be mistaken for – an off-duty serviceman). *Nanyuki Coffee House* is a great old timers' place (serving both coffee and beer), wonderful in the low afternoon sun. Next door is *High Life Day and Night Club* which, not surprisingly, attracts all the low life. For **money-changing** in town, the best bet is the KCB (bureau de change open Mon–Fri 9am–3pm, Sat 9–11am). Standard Chartered has an ATM. If you're looking for a **guide** for the Sirimon route up Mount Kenya, try first the *Cousin Café* next to *Marina Bar & Restaurant*, or else the boys down at *Nanyuki River Lodge*.

If you have time before leaving, pay a visit to the **Nanyuki Spinners and Weavers** workshop, located about 1km down the Nyahururu road on the left, opposite the District Hospital (closed Sun). This women's group provides the *Spinners' Web* shop in Nairobi with rugs and other articles woven on hand looms, which you can buy here at reduced prices. There's also astonishingly ambrosial **wild honey** from the *dukas* a kilometre or so east of the last police barrier, on the road to Meru.

For **overnight stays**, you have a number of options, including **camping** at the *Sportsman's Arms*, or one of the places listed below.

ACCOMMODATION

High Life "Self-contained Rooms" (no phone). Basic but tolerable and very economical. ①.

Joskaki Hotel, Bazaar St (PO Box 228; ☎0176/22820, fax 32912). Good s/c rooms, and recommended for its generally excellent food and rooftop views of the town and Mount Kenya. Unfortunately, it's a vast, corridor-riddled warren and can be indescribably noisy when the bar is open all night, or there's a disco. A copy of the *Rough Guide* may get you a discount. ②.

Juba House Hotel (PO Box 504; no phone). A basic central stand-by, with a lively bar. ①.

Mount Kenya Safari Club, about 8km southeast of Nanyuki, accessible either from just north of the *New Silverbeck*, or from the north side of town (PO Box 35 Nanyuki; ☎0176/22960, fax 22754; reservations through Lonrho, see p.49). Founded by Hollywood star William Holden, the heights of equatorial comfort are reached here – magnificent meals, slick service, and kinky round baths in the cottages. If you're mobile it's fun to call in anyway (Ksh350 daily membership including use of the pool): a range of activities in and around the hotel – including tennis, riding, fishing, gyms, a bowling green, heated pool and an animal orphanage – all fill the day very pleasantly. And if you ever dreamed of golf on the equator, what they term a "brutal" nine-hole course obliges. For all this, however, it's massively overpriced. ⑨.

Nanyuki Guest House (PO Box 211 Meru; ☎0176/22822). Ten minutes' walk out of town along the Nyahururu road. The prison-like exterior belies a good atmosphere, helpful manager and probably the cheapest self-contained rooms in the country. ①.

Nanyuki River Lodge (PO Box 101; ☎0176/32523). Reasonable rooms and a pool, and would be good value if it wasn't for the hustly touts and curio peddlers at the entrance and the uncertain security (its rowdy bar appears to be the mainstay these days). The guides have their own porters' association for Mount Kenya with reasonable rates (porter-guide Ksh600 per day) for tackling the Sirimon Route, although their all-in package prices are as expensive as any ($323 per person for a four-day jaunt for two, $278 in a group of four). ②.

Nanyuki Simbas Lodge (PO Box 211; ☎0176/22556). A peaceful place and actually quite pleasant despite the barrack-like motel rooms. Safe parking, and a reasonable restaurant. Currently much better, if more expensive, than *Nanyuki River Lodge*. ③.

Nyakio B&L, Bazaar Rd (PO Box 179; ☎0176/22505). Good s/c rooms, and a lively atmosphere thanks to the busy bar downstairs. ②.

Sirimon Hotel, Biashara St (PO Box 326; ☎0176/32344). The tour drivers' favourite digs – sleazy but amiable, with clean rooms, excellent hot showers, and a video cinema (admission Ksh20). Slightly cheaper than the *Joskaki* and *Juba*. ①.

Sportsman's Arms (PO Box 3; ☎0176/32347–8, fax 22895). An old establishment, which used to be the base for visits to the *Secret Valley* (a *Treetops*-type establishment) until that burned down in 1981. Letters and photos smother the walls, reminders of the good old days. There's a wide choice of accommodation, from slightly dilapidated s/c wooden cottages, rooms in a new wing, and even newer cottages. The rooms and newer cottages are better equipped, and there's a sauna, jacuzzi and pool (Ksh100 for each for non-residents). The disco and jumping *nyama choma* joint at weekends might make sleeping difficult. B&B. Rooms and old cottages ④; new cottages ⑤.

Youth Hostel at Emmanuel Parish Centre, Market Rd, near the post office (PO Box 279; ☎0176/22112; not IYHA-affiliated). A friendly place, with very cheap beds in single and double rooms. Accommodation is clean but cramped and very spartan, and makes no concessions to privacy – unless you're the only guest, of course, in which case it's not a problem. The toilets are a hazard. ①.

Moving on: Laikipia

Laikipia District is a vast plateau northwest of Mount Kenya, about the size of Wales, encompassing much of the transitional lands between the well-watered central highlands to the south and the semi-desert grazing steppe of the Samburu in the north. It also straddles the disputed division between the Kikuyu people in the east and the Kalenjin to the west.

On the face of it, Laikipia is not an obvious tourist destination: the land is generally flat (between 1800m and 2100m), and not terribly spectacular (unless the sky clears enough to give views of Mount Kenya to the southeast), and the few roads that do cross it are uniformly awful, often impassable in the rains. Laikipia also became notorious in the run-up to the 1997 general elections, when **ethnic violence** between Kalenjin and Kikuyus swept the district, leaving several hundred dead and tens of thousands homeless. The killings continued into early 1998, but have since ceased, and it's hoped that the ongoing **Laikipia peace talks** in Nanyuki may bring a solution to this age-old enmity.

For all this, however, Laikipia is also one of the most underrated places to see **wildlife** outside the confines of the national parks. Thanks mainly to its isolation, the district contains a wealth of endangered species: some 2000 **elephant** still undertake a seasonal migration from Laikipia north into the Samburu rangelands during the long rains, and the district also supports an estimated 25 percent of the world's remaining population of **Grevy's zebra**, which is fast disappearing in its other habitats in Ethiopia and Somalia. Laikipia is the best place to see **black rhino** (see also Solio Ranch on p.227), whose world population today is barely 2000, five hundred of them in Kenya. They are grouped in five heavily-guarded sanctuaries, set-up by cattle farmers as part of an experiment in integrated ranching, and latterly also for tourism. As browsers, the rhinos don't interfere with cattle pasture, and do well in the same environment so long as the bush isn't cleared.

GETTING THERE AND AROUND

If you're **heading to Nyahururu**, beware of the unpaved C76 road. The El Niño rains have made it even more fiendish than it was before (it was terrible then), even in the

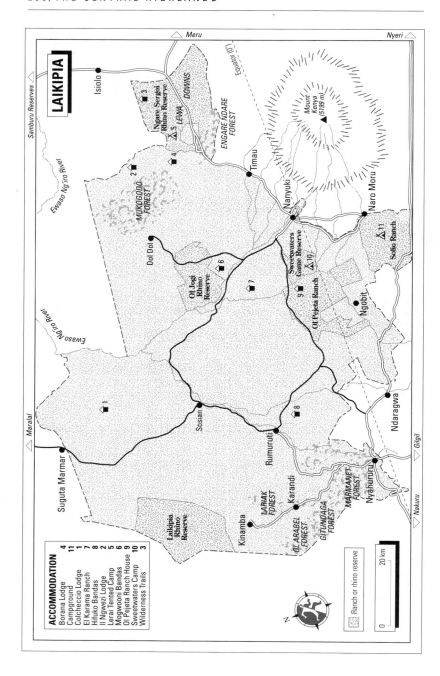

LAIKIPIA

ACCOMMODATION

Borana Lodge	4
Campground	11
Colcheccio Lodge	1
El Karama Ranch	7
Hituko Bandas	8
Il Ngwezi Lodge	2
Lerai Tented Camp	5
Mogwooni Bandas	6
Ol Pejeta Ranch House	9
Sweetwaters Camp	10
Wilderness Trails	3

Ranch or rhino reserve

20 km

dry season, and in periods of heavy rain vehicles get stuck along it for days on end. Despite the setbacks, it's a good road for wildlife-spotting: you've every chance of seeing giraffe, gazelle and even elephant if you set off early. There's no public transport along this route, so your own 4WD is essential, though you might be lucky and catch a lift with a rancher in Nanyuki: ask at the *Sportsman's Arms*.

For **day-trips** (again, under your own steam), **Ol Pejeta Ranch** is the place to aim for, which contains one of Laikipia's biggest concentrations of wildlife, again including black rhinos. The ranch covers some 400 square kilometres, nearly a quarter of which is given over to a rhino sanctuary – **Sweetwaters Game Reserve** ($16 entry per person) – one inmate of which, "Morani", is tame enough to be approached very closely. There's also a **chimpanzee sanctuary** here, with animals from the Jane Goodall Institute in Burundi (chimps aren't otherwise found in Kenya). To get there, the easiest way is to take the fifteen-kilometre track (all-weather in theory) which starts south of Nyahururu by the equator; otherwise, take the left (signposted) fork on the Nyahururu road 10km after Nanyuki, and continue along the abysmally muddy track (impassable during the rains) for 19km. For more information, contact The Sweetwaters Trust, c/o Ol Pejeta Ranching, PO Box 167 Nanyuki.

For the more adventurous, **luxury camel safaris** in the district are offered by Camel Trek (see p.137), Ewaso River Camel Hikes (p.137), and Northern Frontier Ventures (fax 02/447310).

RANCHES AND ACCOMMODATION

With only few exceptions, **accommodation** in Laikipia is for the well-heeled only, and requires your own transport (there are no *matatus* or buses), although all places can arrange for you to be picked up from Nanyuki (at additional cost). Most guests fly in (contact Tropic Air Ltd, PO Box 161 Nanyuki; ☎0176/32890–1; fax 32787, *tropicair@kenyaonline.com*). Many **game ranches** have opened their doors to guests, and combine a quasi-colonial welcome and atmosphere with all-inclusive game drives and visits to the rhino sanctuaries. Other options, covered elsewhere in this book, are *Solio Game Ranch* near Nyeri (p.227), *Colcheccio Lodge* north of Rumuruti (p.558), and the *Lewa Downs Conservation Centre* on the road to Isiolo (p.209). You can book all of the following at Let's Go Travel in Nairobi (p.142), usually with a discount thrown in:

Borana Lodge, between Mukogodo and Engare Ndare forests (reservations through Tandala Ltd, PO Box 24397 Nairobi; ☎02/568804, fax 564945, *royal.africasaf@commsol.sprint.com*). Worth a mention only for being one of Kenya's costliest options: surrounded by a private commercial "conservation" ranch, this has six cedar, thatch and stone cottages and offers day and night game drives, visits to a rhino reserve, entertainment at a nearby water hole and horse riding, all for a gigantic $580 per person per day. Booking via Let's Go Travel knocks it down to a mere $720 for a double (plus $30 per person admission to the ranch). ⑨.

El Karama Ranch, 42km northwest of Nanyuki off the track to Maralal (PO Box 172 Nanyuki; reservations through Let's Go Travel in Nairobi, address p.142). From Nanyuki, fork right after 9km, continue for 23km, then turn left at the signboard "Ol Jogi – No Shooting" for 10km. Hats off to these guys – the guardian angels of budget travellers. An exceptionally nice set-up on the banks of the Ewaso Nyiro river, and highly recommended if you have a way to get to it. You're welcome to pitch your tent, and they provide a small amount of cheap farmhouse and self-service *banda* accommodation (bring food and drinking water), game rides on horseback (Ksh1500 per person) and escorted wildlife walks (Ksh300 per person). ③.

Mogwooni Bandas, 30km from Nanyuki (reservations through Cape Chestnut Ltd; ☎0176/32526, fax 32208). On a commercial cattle and sheep ranch on the bank of the Nanyuki River. Activities include horse riding, tennis, and plenty of walking. ③.

Ol Pejeta Ranch House, 7km beyond *Sweetwaters* (PO Box 763 Nanyuki; ☎0176/23414; reservations through Lonrho, p.49). More expensive than *Sweetwaters*, this has long been a hideaway for the rich and famous, and is a genuinely classy option. There are only six bedrooms, lots of semi-tame giraffe poking around the gardens, two swimming pools, a resident naturalist, and the same activities as for *Sweetwaters*. FB ⑨.

Sweetwaters Tented Camp, Ol Pejeta Ranch (PO Box 763 Nanyuki; ☎ & fax 0176/32409; reservations through Lonrho, p.49). Upmarket but good value when compared with similar set-ups in the national parks and reserves, this is a well laid-out tented camp popular with Kenya residents, especially families, with high-quality food and service. The lower tents are probably preferable to the ones set on stilts. It specializes in night game drives, and there's also a pool, and camel- and walking-safaris are offered. FB ⑥ low, ⑦–⑧ high, plus $58 per person for activities.

Moving on: east to Meru

Leaving Nanyuki eastwards, the ring road skirts closer to the mountain than at any other point in its circumference. The land here is extremely fertile, but is block-owned for the most part by large commercial estates – you'll see ordinary *wananchi* (peasants) cultivating the verges between the road and the estate fences to eke out a living.

After 14km, you come to the village of **TIMAU**, unremarkable but for two outstanding – if expensive – stopover possibilities. Prices at both are per person, which makes for good value if you're on your own. If you'd like a barbecued rainbow trout lunch on the way, call in at Kentrout trout farm, 3km to the right down a rough, sign-posted track from the village (4WD in rainy weather; PO Box 14 Timau; ☎ & fax 0176/41016, fax 41014). As well as their delicious lunchtime alfresco buffets (Ksh600), whose ingredients are grown (or bred) on the farm; they also have two wonderful, huge stone cottages for rent (all s/c), as well as three rooms in a rambling old ranch house. The gardens, river and indigenous forest are a delight, with plenty of birdlife and the crashing of colobus monkeys in the trees. **Camping** is possible on request, and if you show a copy of the *Rough Guide*, you'll get residents' rates (B&B ④–⑤, FB ⑤–⑥).

The other great draw is *Timau River Lodge*, 2km east from Timau, and 1km off to the right (PO Box 212 Timau; ☎0176/41230; B&B ③–④, FB ④–⑤). The living dream of a charming Afghani couple, the "lodge" (actually a varied collection of s/c log, mud and "underground" houses) has been planned, built and run on ecological principles: lighting is powered by sunlight and water-turbine, water heating uses energy-efficient wood boilers, and they've started a tree nursery to replace those used to build the houses. There's a tame ostrich that eats anything, an occasional visiting leopard, secluded waterfalls and river pools for bathing in, and a huge expanse of forest to get lost in. You can **camp** anywhere you like, or in a special campsite (Ksh200p per person which includes hot showers and other facilities; tent hire Ksh400). They also offer trail biking and horse riding. The accommodation itself is wonderful, and kids will adore the attic bedrooms in the largest houses. There's a communal cooking area with ancient Scottish cast iron ovens for self-catering.

After Timau, the scenery acquires a real grandeur, changing completely yet again before you reach Meru. The 70km from **Nanyuki to Meru** couldn't illustrate better the amazing variety of climate and landscape in Kenya. The road climbs steeply to almost 3000m, passing alternative routes to the peaks and giving unparalleled views of them in the early morning. But a spectacle you might not have guessed at is the panorama that spreads out to the north as the road drops once again: on a really clear day, after rain has settled the dust, this is devastatingly beautiful. Even on an average day, you can see as far as the dramatic mesa of **Ol Olokwe**, nearly 100km north in the desert. Isiolo (p.574) lies out there, too, first stop on the way to the northern wilderness.

LEWA DOWNS CONSERVATION CENTRE

A few kilometres down the Isiolo road, a signposted gate on the left takes you 8km along dirt track to the Lewa Downs Conservation Centre in the foothills of Mount Kenya. Still a working cattle ranch for the most part, it includes the electric-fenced **Ngare Sergoi Rhino Sanctuary**, currently containing around forty rhinos, both black and white. There are also some 250 seasonal elephant, and 300–400 Grevy's zebra, which account for a tenth of the world's remaining wild population.

This is conservation as a business: there's a $35 per person entrance fee ($20 children), which goes to the local Il Ngwesi Samburu group ranch, and the original Lewa homestead is now a conservation centre and gift shop. There's exceedingly pricy **accommodation** available in three cottages (reservations through Wilderness Trails, Bush Homes of East Africa, p.48; closed April, May & Nov; FB$530–580) in an atmosphere reminiscent of a comfortable 1930s English country house. The welcome is congenial, the cooking excellent, and the price includes games drives in an antiquated Land Rover to Lewa Swamp to see the rare sitatunga water antelope.

Also accessed through the ranch is the much lauded **Il Ngwesi Lodge** (bookings through Let's Go Travel, p.142; $395 for the entire lodge), a Samburu-owned and serviced eco-lodge, maintaining traditional use of land whilst encouraging the reintegration of wild animals. Profits go to Il Ngwesi group ranch members. There are four thatched *bandas* raised on stilts, water from a spring hauled by camel (even for filling the swimming pool), and solar power for lighting: a booking guarantees you'll get the place to yourself. It's self-catering, which means you provide food and it will be cooked for you. Camels are available for riding or walking trips, though visits to a nearby Samburu *manyatta* cost a mean $20 per person. Feedback from guests is mostly rapturous, though some find the whole set-up too tame. Most guests fly in to Nanyuki or Lewa and are picked up there.

The third accommodation option at Lewa Downs is **Lerai Tented Camp** (bookings through Savannah Camps & Lodges, p.50; FB $370 low, $440 high), which is in the Ngare Sergoi Rhino Sanctuary itself. The main lodge building is a thatched cedarwood cottage, with a lounge overlooking a floodlit waterhole where rhino, elephant and other animals come to drink. Accommodation is in eleven well-spaced luxury tents raised on lava-rock platforms stilts, and there are optional horseback safaris ($15 per hour).

Meru

Passing the Isiolo turn-off, the road to Meru suddenly plunges through verdant **jungle**, with glimpses through the trees of the **Nyambeni Hills** and the volcanic pimples dotting the plain. **Meru oak** is the commercial prize of this forested eastern side of the mountain, though judging by the number of active sawmills at the upper end of the town, supplies won't last much longer. The forest still comes almost to the town's edge, however, and paths lead off to cleared *shambas* where, for a year or two, just about anything will grow. The moist, jungly atmosphere around Meru, with wood smoke curling up against a background of dark forest, is very reminiscent of parts of West Africa (and the local Meru inhabitants are much darker-skinned than their neighbours) – a total change of mood after the dryish grasslands on the northwest side of the mountain.

Meru is, of course, the base for visits to **Meru National Park** (see p.403), but security there is still a concern, and there's still no accommodation, though plenty is planned.

Meru town

MERU town is strung out over 2–3km, the main road in from Nanyuki dropping steeply across the hillside to the town centre. It's an unusual place in an interesting location – there are great views from the upper (**Makutano**) half of town over the densely settled slopes – and well worth a stay.

Meru's municipal **market** is a large one and sells a wide range of goods – baskets, clothes, domestic utensils – as well as the agricultural produce of the district. This is cheap and excellent: they grow the best **custard apples** in Kenya here, and if you like *miraa*, you won't find bigger or better bunches anywhere. Also known as *qat* or *gatty*, **miraa** is a small tree whose bark contains a mild stimulant and appetite suppressant. The freshly plucked twigs and leaves are chewed with bubble gum and, though frequently denounced, it's legal in Kenya (although transporting it by road was recently banned). Meru district, where it grows wild but is also now cultivated, is the main source; northeastern Kenya is the biggest home market, and uncounted tons are exported to Somalia, Yemen and Djibouti. There's a trading corner devoted to *miraa* in the town centre, which also has lip-smacking roast yams and sugar cane by the yard. The outdoor market in Makutano seems reserved largely for small traders offering more, wonderful, cheap *shamba* produce.

The tiny but fascinating **Meru Museum** (PO Box 597; ☎0164/20482; daily 9am–6pm; Ksh200) is also a treat. It occupies the oldest stone building in town, a former District Commissioner's office, where you're likely to be the only visitor if it's not besieged by schoolchildren. Emphasis is on the traditional culture of the Meru people: small ethnographic exhibits, pick-up-and-feel blocks of fossilized wood, stone tools from the Lewa Downs prehistoric site and some woefully stuffed (and stinking) animals.

Outside there's a particularly good **herbal pharmacopoeia** – a collection of traditional medicinal plants growing in the garden, where you can see what a *miraa* bush looks like, among others. Nearby, a pool contains a mean-looking crocodile, turtles and tortoises, and several psychotically aggressive monkeys try to get at you through their cage bars beside the museum's star attraction (for the schoolkids at least): "Three-legged Bull". The **Meru homestead** is well presented and feels authentic – you get the impression someone actually lives here on the museum grounds, a feeling accentuated by the escape route in the perimeter fence for fleeing from invaders, which seems to

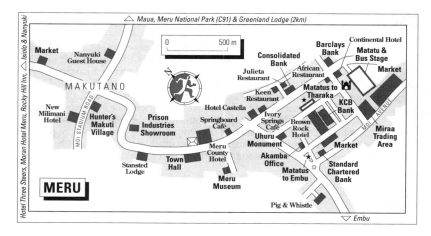

have the well-worn look of years of use. If you're really interested in the Meru people, ask at the museum about the **Njuri-Ncheke traditional courthouse**, approximately 9km north of Meru on the road to Maua, which was recently donated to the museum. The Njuri-Ncheke are a semi-secret society of elders sworn to preserve and uphold traditional cultural structures and religion, mainly through creating and enforcing traditional law and presiding over ceremonies and the administration of oaths. The museum may have a copy left of David Maitai Rimita's fascinating book on the Njuri-Ncheke (self-published, Meru 1988), which also covers Meru beliefs in supernatural spirits, witch-doctors, diviners and cosmology.

Practicalities

Meru is a hub for transport south, west and east. Numerous **bus** companies have their offices between the mosque and *miraa* trading area. The safest companies are Akamba (☎0164/20151), Kensilver (☎0164/30659), and KBS Stagecoach Express (☎0164/30186) for Nairobi, although chances are you'll end up on one of Sunbird Services' mangled wrecks; they have almost a dozen daily runs to the capital via Embu, and also run to Maua for Meru National Park (p.403). A helpful service is Arusha Express's twice-daily run to Malindi, and the daily Garissa Express (Garex) bus for Mombasa. As for **matatus**, most destinations are served from the main stage, with the exception of Embu (at the western end of Moi Avenue) and Tharaka, a little-visited district dominated by a series of dammed reservoirs on the Tana River, which is prone to bloody cattle raids and suffered an outbreak of cholera in September 1998. Of the banks, Standard Chartered and Barclays both have ATMs.

For **eating**, Meru will treat you well, at little expense. The most upmarket place, which isn't saying all that much, is the *Meru County Hotel*, with set lunches at Ksh420. *Ivory Springs Café* is the friendliest place and has excellent samosas and passion juice; the *Springboard Café*, opposite the KCB, does good snacks; and, opposite the cavernous *Continental Hotel* (a real drinkers' bar even for breakfast), is *African Restaurant*, a butchery and *nyama choma* joint. Also recommended for *nyama choma* is the zebra-striped *Keen Restaurant* on Moi Avenue, which is busier than most, whilst for chicken the place to head for is *Julieta*, next to Consolidated Bank. There's a fresh milk bar next to the KCB bank, and a supermarket – the Self-Choice – 2km up the Nanyuki road at the upper end of town.

If you fancy gyrating the night away, Makutano district is the centre for **nightlife**. Try the sweaty *Club Dimples* disco at the *New Milimani* hotel (Wednesday ladies' night, Thursday studenty, Friday and Saturday hip-hop and soul, Sunday jams; food available); the barn-like *Hunter's Makuti Village* dance hall, nearly opposite, which sometimes also has live bands; and weekend nights at the classier *Three Steers* (below). In town, try *Clouds* on Moi Avenue, with the usual Saturday night disco mayhem and a marathon Sunday dance which starts at 3pm.

In keeping with its market-town functions, Meru has no shortage of **accommodation**. If you have transport, there are a few places to consider even before you arrive.

LODGINGS ON THE NANYUKI AND MAUA ROADS

Greenland Holiday Resort, 4km from town on the Maua road (PO Box 2065; ☎0164/20409). A "country club" venture with flimsy and overpriced cabins, but the pool is worth dropping in for, if they ever get round to repairing the pump. They'll make good (tourist-priced) meals if you're passing through, and allow you to use the showers. Camping is usually possible, and there's live music on the last weekend of every month. ③.

Moran Hotel Meru, 7km out of town on the Nanyuki road (PO Box 1200; ☎0164/244387). Another "country club" which has clearly seen better times – there's a haunted feel about the empty smoke-filled dining rooms. The pool's pump has been broken for years, and it's rather damp, and over-priced. ③.

Nanyuki Guest House, some way out of town on the Maua road (PO Box 211; ☎0164/20677). Cheap, clean and very acceptable B&L. ①.

Rocky Hill Inn, some 8km out of town on the Nanyuki road (☎0164/41321). An ornate construction with chalets among pseudo-Japanese gardens; it has no proper water supply and is perhaps more a weekend *nyama choma* bar than anything else, but for all that it's endearingly weird (beware the "soup trees") and astonishingly cheap. ①.

LODGINGS IN TOWN

Brown Rock Hotel, overlooking Makutano stage and its market (PO Box 247; ☎0164/20247). A large, new establishment with cool rooms, though some are a little dark; the rooms up front or higher up are best. Hot water on request. ①–②.

Hotel Castella (PO Box 78; ☎0164/20873). Basic B&L. ①.

Continental Hotel & Bar (PO Box 133; ☎0164/30755). Barely more inviting than the *Castella*, rowdy and not at all continental, with beer for breakfast. ①.

Meru County Hotel (PO Box 1386; ☎0164/20432, fax 31264). The most modern of Meru's central options and fairly upmarket, with large, bright and breezy s/c balconied rooms (choice of baths or showers), a video lounge and reasonable restaurant. Well run and good value. B&B ③.

New Milimani Hotel, Moi Stadium Rd, Makutano (PO Box 9; ☎0164/20224). 2km back up the hill, but better than the *Stansted*. Rooms here are decent and s/c, and the menu long (specialities are curries and *kinyeji*, the Meru version of *irio*: order well in advance). It's also the cheapest place with safe parking in town. Lively and noisy on Wednesday, and non-stop Friday–Sunday, when there's the *Club Dimples* disco – but deserted during the week. B&B ②.

Pig and Whistle (PO Box 3160; ☎0164/31411 or 20574). Without doubt the best place in town and well worth the price. Well-appointed individual cottages (concrete or wood, though the latter can get damp), all with telephones and baths, set in pleasant, shaded grounds. The hotel lounges and bar are wooden, with creaking floorboards, and there's an inescapable atmosphere of decaying colonial languor. Affordable menu, and *nyama choma* joint in gardens. ③.

Stansted Lodge, just over 1km up the hill from the main *matatu* stage (PO Box 1337; ☎0164/20360). Some decent enough rooms, some not; some hot water, but generally overpriced, run-down and not particularly friendly. ②.

Hotel Three Steers, 2km along the Nanyuki road, Makutano (PO Box 155; ☎0164/30467, fax 20634). Large motel-type complex with good clean rooms (s/c with hot water and telephones), a *nyama choma* joint, two bars, and cheap Indian-influenced restaurant. Loud disco (sometimes with guest bands) Friday and Saturday. Enclosed parking. B&B ③.

Embu and district

From **Meru to Embu**, the new (regrettably fast, and dangerous if going by *matatu*) road swoops around the eastern slopes of Mount Kenya through brilliant, vibrant scenery. Five kilometres south of Meru you cross the **equator** once again. Hundreds of streams – run-off from luxuriant rainfall blown in by the southeast monsoon – cut deeply into the volcanic soil of this eastern flank. As a result, this side of the mountain has a much broader covering of jungle, which extends, *shambas* permitting, down to the level of the road and beyond. You plunge from one green and tan gorge to the next, and whether you enjoy the magnificent landscape or not depends on whether you dare take your eyes off the road. If you take an early-morning bus (slow, and considered safe), you can relax and admire. Sit on the right side for glimpses of snow-capped peaks, normally visible at this time of day.

Most public transport stops at **Chogoria**, a base for the eastern Mount Kenya ascent (see p.197), although if you're staying overnight you might consider continuing to the livelier (and friendlier) market town of **CHUKA**, which has a bank with exchange facilities and the *Kimwa Farmer's Hotel* (PO Box 794; ☎0166/30570; ②), which has recent-

LAMU: THE CROSS-COUNTRY ROUTE

From the Mount Kenya region, the obvious route to the coast is back to Nairobi, then down via Mombasa. It may be feasible, however, to strike out east from the Mount Kenya ring road and, using a combination of available public transport and foot-slogging, make for Mwingi, Garissa and Lamu. Beware, however, of getting yourself into unsafe territory: northeastern Kenya is full of people displaced by the Somali civil war. At the time of writing, Garissa and environs, and the Garissa–Lamu route were out of bounds. Read Chapter Seven, "The North", and seek local advice.

The easiest departure point on the ring road is the small centre of Ena, 16km northeast of Embu. Ena is at the junction of the new highway with the old "Mate road" (after Bernard Mate, a member of the Kenya's pre-Independence Legislative Council), the circuitous C92 that used to be the route around the eastern side of the mountain until the tarred highway was completed.

Buses and *matatus* run fairly frequently east along the C92 from Ena to Ishiara, which has a few B&Ls. On Mondays or Tuesdays there's a bus from Ishiara to Katse. Otherwise, from Ishiara, it's a three-hour walk to the new concrete bridge over the **Tana River**, where there's a *hoteli* and a tailor and not a lot else.

Another three hours' hike downstream on the right bank brings you to Konyu, where you shouldn't have trouble finding somewhere to put up for the night. The primary school may oblige: there are stunning views from here when the air is clear. You can now proceed by dirt road, but on foot, around the **hills east of Konyu** (first head north, then turn back south) to Katse (at least two days); or else try to find companions in Konyu to walk with you on a more direct (six-hour) **short-cut route** to Katse along a watercourse over the baobab-tufted hills (highest peak Mt Mumoni, 1747m). Katse has a pretty **lodging house** and a daily bus departure at 7am down to Mwingi, on the A3 Nairobi–Garissa highway – only a sixty-kilometre run but it takes hours. You should be able to get to Garissa the same evening and Lamu the next evening.

This is an interesting route to take, virtually unheard of, full of rewarding encounters and unexplored districts and wilderness. If you plan on walking much of the first part of the route, allow a week for the whole trip. Again, see Chapter Seven first.

ly added the busy *Party Point* disco (mainly *ndombolo* Friday–Sunday, and *nyama choma*), as well as bizarrely decorating its car park with a life-size model of an elephant and a fibreglass replica of Mount Kenya, complete with cascading waterfall. In order to climb Mount Kenya from Embu, you'll need to get yourself over to *Castle Forest Lodge* and the Kamweti route (see p.188).

Thuchi River Lodge

If you have independent transport, or don't mind walking the 3km from the main road, there's a charming **accommodation** option on this side of the mountain in the shape of *Thuchi River Lodge*, an establishment left over from the road-building exploits of the French company Kier, who constructed the road from Kangonde to Embu (PO Box 4 Runyenjes; ☎0161/62101; B&B ③). The place is peaceful and untouristy, with turkeys balancing badly on fence posts, occasional monkeys in the trees, and plenty of walking opportunities in the jungle-like forest. Electricity is sporadic and hot water is on request, but the accommodation itself is in simple but comfortable suites, complete with comfy old armchairs to sink into. It also has a pool (usually empty), bar, restaurant (mainly rubbery chicken), and even a squash court. Located a few hundred metres above the Thuchi River, it's exactly 27km south of Chogoria (29km north of Embu), then 3km east of the main road along the E652 track to nowhere.

Embu town

EMBU, like Meru, is situated at the bottom of a hill: at any rate, the town begins high and descends, with your expectations, to the centre. There's very little to get excited about here, and it's not obvious why it was chosen as the capital of Eastern Province. Certainly, without the apparatus of a provincial headquarters, Embu would amount to little. It does have a number of decent *hotelis*, though: *Rehema's Café*, a little way up the hill near the post office, is a busy **eating place**, well known for excellent spicy samosas, and the spotlessly clean, Somali-run *Zamzam Hotel* serves sweetly spiced pilau and *mataha* (rice, maize, beans, vegetables and potatoes all mashed together and eaten with beef). The *Arkland Hotel* is a good all-round bet, one step up from the usual eateries, popular and reliable. At weekends, *King's Restaurant* on the B6 Nairobi road, 1km out of town beside the Shell station, has local **live music**.

Accommodation

Should you need or want to spend the night here, there's plenty of choice in all ranges, though quality takes a nose-dive at the really cheap end.

Al-Aswad, town centre (PO Box 664; ☎0161/20679). Despite having a popular restaurant, this is dirty and has uncertain security (get a room with a lock). ①.

Highway Court Hotel, by the BP station in the centre (PO Box 354; ☎0161/20046, fax 30659). Newish four-storey block with s/c rooms all with nets, good security and safe parking, but not especially clean. It also has a rowdy first-floor disco and bar, so get a room at the top. B&B ②.

Izaac Walton Inn, at the top end of town on the way in from Meru (PO Box 1; ☎0161/20128–9, fax 30135). By far the best, with pleasant shaded gardens and a welcoming, vaguely colonial atmosphere, if a little overpriced. Rooms have a choice of baths or showers, and there's a guarded car park. You can get a very satisfying buffet breakfast here for Ksh350 (lunches and dinner cost Ksh600). B&B ④.

Kubu Kubu, 1km down the Kitui road (PO Box 180; ☎0161/20191). Small, clean and comfortable rooms, and a lively bar (*Jamaica*) playing blues and funk and serving cool fried chicken. ①.

New Rembo, 500m down the Kitui road (PO Box 934; ☎0161/20647). Slightly run-down and unwelcoming with singles only. ①.

Prime Hotel Embu, in the town centre (PO Box 1241; ☎0161/30692). The best of the central cheap options: rooms (s/c) are fresh, with nets, there's hot water daily and it has safe parking. It also has a quiet bar (with pool table) and good *nyama choma* (try the goat). B&B ②.

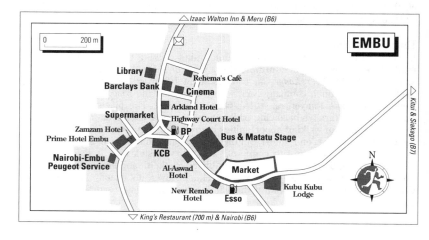

West of Embu: the Mwea rice scheme

The two-hour trip straight **back to Nairobi** via Makutano (at the junction for Nyeri; there are several decent B&Ls here if you get stuck) is covered by dozens of buses and *matatus* daily: Sunbird Services buses are fast and relatively safe; Akamba's twice-daily run is slower and safer still, as are Kensilver's 25-seaters.

Heading west, you begin to leave the red earth and lush vegetation of Mount Kenya behind as the land levels out into a series of intricately irrigated rice paddies, part of the **Mwea rice scheme**. Originally a resettlement area for landless farmers supported by Japanese NGOs and others, things turned sour in 1998–99, when the farmers began protesting against the National Irrigation Board, which, being the only body authorized to buy their rice crop, was accused of exploitation in paying them less than the open market rate for their crop. After eight months of boycotts, demonstrations, and sometimes bloody confrontations between farmers and police, the government finally acted by sacking the entire Irrigation Board. The underlying problem, however, remains unchanged, in that the land belongs not to the farmers but the government, making the farmers little more than tenants obliged to grow a crop which they cannot sell freely. If you get stuck around here, most of the roadside villages have basic **accommodation**, the best being the *Makuti Remera* at Wanguru (PO Box 191 Wanguru; ☎0163/48236; ①), with some reasonable non-s/c cottages, and a *nyama choma* bar with occasional live music.

South of Embu: the Kiangombe Hills and Mwea National Reserve

A more leisurely alternative to the main Nairobi road is to head southeast along the tarmacked but rarely driven B7, skirting the intriguing Kiangombe Hills and their main town, Siakago, then past Mwea National Reserve and the huge Tana reservoirs, before reaching the crossroads at Kangonde, with roads west to Thika (p.176), east to Garissa (p.594) or south along good *murram* to Kitui in Akambaland (p.341). Most **public transport** from Embu along this route goes to Thika, with only a few *matatus* bound for Kitui. If you're headed for Garissa, get off at Kangonde (no accommodation), where you'll have to try your luck hitching, or hope that one of the infrequent buses from Nairobi (Mon, Wed, Fri & Sun) has a spare seat – they pass by at around 10am.

Siakago and the Kiangombe Hills

The main centre of the **Kiangombe Hills**, Siakago, can be reached from Embu by *matatu* five or six times daily, in all conditions except the worst rains. The relatively modest altitudes (Kiangombe peak is 1804m) aren't enough to lure climbers – even those willing to go off the beaten track. But the unspoilt hills, upstaged by Mount Kenya, and ignored by tourists and travellers, are worth a visit if you have an interest in the region's mysterious folklore.

The hills are the home of the **Mbere**, related to the Kikuyu, Embu and Meru. The Mbere have a reputation in Kenya as possessors of magical powers. Some villages have elderly sages, **Arogi**, credited with terrifying abilities, though others – the **Ago** – have more beneficent gifts like the ability to foretell the future or find missing goats. Information is hard to come by; local people either laugh or look blank when directly questioned about such "unprogressive" activities. Numerous cups of tea and endless slices of bread and Blue Band Margarine elicited the story from one local man that a village called Uba-Riri was a place where the *Ago* were active, but he couldn't quite remember where it was, and if he had pointed the way, he explained, legend had it he would have lost the finger he pointed with. Yet the *Ago* do make their existence known at critical times, as in 1987 when their bush fires are said to have brought on the delayed rains.

And the forest rangers on the hills threaten poachers and illegal firewood-cutters with *Arogi* medicine to make their teeth fall out – witchcraft comes to the aid of conservation!

The identity of these "witches" – at best a hazy and mysterious one which people aren't in any hurry to talk about – is further confused by the supposed existence in the hills of a race of "**little red men**" whose diminutive size (estimated at 1.2m) and fleeting appearance and disappearance in the bush have led the odd, dreaming scientist to suppose that they might be australopithecine – ape-men hanging on into the twentieth century in their remote forest tracts. They, and the *Ago-Arogi*, may be just part of the "old people" mytho-history of central Kenya, which is at least partially based on the real, ancient and probably Cushitic-speaking peoples of two thousand or more years ago. Such, anyway, are the stories that might draw you from Embu. If you've ever entertained thoughts of seeing a Bigfoot, or a Yeti, or the Loch Ness Monster – and if you kept an eye open for Nandi bears near Eldoret (see p.305) – it's an interesting trip.

Siakago

There are two roads to **SIAKAGO**, either the signposted *murram* road 5km southeast of Embu on the B7 Kangonde road, which bumps along for some 23km, or along the better D467 *murram* road (11km) from Musonoke, further down the B7. Siakago is an unusually pleasant and relaxed one-street town, all deep red earth, green vegetation and colourfully painted shop fronts. There's a scattering of *hotelis* (usually combined with butcheries), a petrol station, two B&Ls, a market (main days Tues & Fri), and several mission churches set amid the huts and *shambas* on the outskirts. Siakago isn't a ki-Mbere word and its derivation is uncertain. It may well have derived from "Chicago", along with the group of American anthropologists who based themselves here in the 1930s and started the ape-men stories. The anthropologists were appalled at the **poverty** of the district, whose soil barely supports the population with corn and sorghum and sustains only the scrappiest *shambas* of cotton and tobacco as cash crops: their plan was to relocate the Mbere to better land, a recommendation fortunately never acted upon. The Mbere are still living a tenuous existence, but after the horrific famines and cholera outbreaks of the early 1980s, when the district's proximity to well-off Embu meant that they were largely overlooked, conditions have begun to improve.

In **practical terms**, the very cheap *Check Inn Bar*, 300m down the Embu road (PO Box 157 Siakago; ①) has basic accommodation and is a good base if you're going hiking. The somnolent bar is quite something, with every scrap of wall space covered with luridly imaginative religious murals ("No hiding place in this Wild Word – Go to Jesus"), and they can provide food given enough notice. The other B&L is the *Felana Bar & Restaurant* (①), 1km down the Embu road in a *shamba* with plenty of chickens and lazy cows. The rooms are s/c, and it promises to be "silent and clean".

The Kiangombe Hills

The Kiangombes rise behind Siakago town and look deceptively easy to **climb**. In fact, it's a stiff hike to the top. The main route approaches the summit area from the huts of the **forest rangers' station** beyond the village of Kune, 10km north of Siakago. You should pick up a **guide** at the forestry station, which usually has to be arranged the day before (or write or phone ahead to the Department of Environment and Natural Resources, Provincial Forest Officer, PO Box 2 Embu; ☎0161/20683 or 20601). Escorted, you can make it up to the peaks and down again in five or six hours, but it's better as a two-day trip, with a self-contained overnight camp in the hills. Out of Siakago, *dukas* are few and poorly stocked and there's no commercial accommodation.

There's no transport between Siakago and Kune, so you'll probably have to find your way on foot (unless you're driving), asking as you go. The walk should take about three hours. Once at the forestry station (thirty minutes' hike beyond Kune), ignore the vehicle track which winds into the hills; it's no longer used and soon becomes difficult to follow. Instead, use the **footpath** leading straight up from behind the huts. At any time but the end of the dry season, much of your way is likely to be impeded by thick vegetation. If you're alert to every photographic possibility, you'll find that concentrating on following the overgrown trail is tiresome – especially without a *panga* to trail-blaze with. As you climb, human population quickly thins out; this is red-people territory and traditionally feared by the Mbere.

About four hours' hiking from the forest station you reach the peaks area. From the **mountain meadows** just below the forested peaks you can look back over the lower hills and down to the hut- and *shamba*-specked plains beyond. With luck, Mount Kenya and the Aberdares can be seen poking through their respective cloudy wreaths. But you may need help from an *Ago*, as well as luck, to see one of the little red people.

The Mwea National Reserve
Daily fees $15, $5 students/children; $2 to camp.
There are three access routes to **Mwea National Reserve**, none of which have any form of public transport, so having your own wheels is really the only way, unless you're prepared to wait hours for a lift. The easiest access is on the east side from the B7 Embu–Kangonde road. At Machanga, 15km south of the D467 for Siakago, a signposted *murram* road heads off right for 11km, and is passable all year round. Further along the B7, on the south side of the hydro-electric Kamburu dam, another signposted road heads in 23km via Masinga Dam from just before the village of Kaewa: the first 11km are tarmac, the remaining 12km *murram* which is liable to be impassable in wet weather. One kilometre to the left at the end of the tarmac is the hilltop *Masinga Dam Resort* (bookings through Tana and Athi Rivers Development Authority, PO Box 47309 Nairobi; ☎02/535834–5; ④), overlooking the reservoir and Mount Kenya, which has a choice of rooms (prefab or stone-and-tile with better views), and the benefit of a pool and the off-chance of lifts with workers at the hydro-electric dam. You can have lunch or dinner here (under Ksh500), and they may finally repair their boat for trips out on the reservoir. Incidentally, swim in the reservoir at your own risk: the crocs have a mean reputation. Both Machanga and Kaewa are served by *matatus* and buses headed for Thika or Kitui. The third, and least frequented, route, branches off at **Wamumu** on the Embu–Thika road, but the 25km of dirt track can be very hard going.

Whichever way you get there, the reserve can be well worth the effort, especially if you have a tent: you can camp either by the main gate, which is not brilliant, or near the shore of the dam lake itself, which usually is. It's a beautiful, peaceful area with a wealth of ornithological interest and crocs and elephants often in evidence. The reserve is set to be fenced with electric wire over the next few years.

AROUND THE ABERDARES

The **Aberdare Range**, which peaks at 4001m, is less well known than Mount Kenya. The lower, eastern slopes have long been farmed by the Kikuyu (more recently by European tea and coffee planters), and the dense mountain forests covering the middle reaches are the habitat of leopard, bongo, buffalo and some six thousand elephant. Above about 3500m, lions and other open-country animals roam the cloudy moorlands. Melanistic forms – especially of leopard, but also of serval cat and even bushbuck – are also present.

The Kikuyu called these mountains *Nyandarua* ("drying hide", for their silhouette) long before Thomson in 1884 named them after Lord Aberdare, president of the Royal Geographical Society. In their bamboo thickets and tangled forests, **Kikuyu guerrillas** hid out for years in the 1950s, living off the jungle and surviving thanks to techniques learned under British officers during the Burma campaign in World War II, in which many of them had fought. Despite the manhunts through the forests and the bombing of hideouts, little damage was done to the natural habitat, and Aberdares National Park remains one of Kenya's most pristine forest reserves.

On the western side, the range drops away steeply to the Rift. It was here, in the high **Wanjohi Valley**, that a concentration of settlers in the 1920s and 1930s created the myth of **Happy Valley** out of their obsessive – and unsettled – lives. There's not much to see (or hear) these days. The old wheat and pyrethrum farms were subdivided after Independence and the valley's new settlers are more concerned with making their market gardens pay. The memories live on only among veteran *wazungu*.

The Kinangop plateau (p.175) was settled by Europeans, too, but the high forest and moorland here was declared **Aberdares National Park** in 1950. The park, which stretches 60km along the length of the peaks, with the "Salient" on the lower slopes reaching out east (access to the Salient only if you're staying at *The Ark* or *Treetops*), includes, like Mount Kenya National Park, the worst of the weather. Rainfall up here is high, often closing the Aberdares to vehicles in the wet season, although the "tree-hotel" game lodges – *The Ark* and *Treetops* – stay open all year. Somewhat inaccessible, the park is nevertheless close enough to Nairobi to be well worth the effort of getting to **Naivasha** or **Nyeri**, the usual bases. You'll find less transport **travelling** in the lower Aberdares than around Mount Kenya, but it's still relatively easy to get around, with regular bus and *matatu* services between the villages. Heading over the mountains and **through the park**, however, **hitching** is the sole, very uncertain, option if you don't have a vehicle. Determination can pay dividends, but you could wait for days. If you're going to try, it's suggested you stop at the *Outspan Hotel* in Nyeri and try to arrange a lift. If you tire of this, *matatu*-hop your way towards **Ruhuruini Gate**, deep in the forest, and try waiting at the gate itself. This, like **Matubio Gate** on the Naivasha side (which you could also probably reach in a half-day of lifts and walking) is friendly and helpful and would certainly allow you to camp.

Nyahururu, the other important town in the region, has **Thomson's Falls** as a postcard attraction, and is also the setting-off point for a wild cross-country journey to Lake Bogoria in the Rift Valley, 1500m below (Chapter Three). From here, too, begins one of the four routes into the northern deserts (Chapter Seven), in this case to Maralal and Loiyangalani on the eastern shore of Lake Turkana.

Aberdares National Park

Daily fees $27, $10 students/children; $8 to camp, $15 in "special" campsites. Entry on foot with permission of the warden: PO Box 22 Nyeri; ☎0171/55024 or Mweiga ☎24.

If you're **driving** into the park (which is the only really practicable way to do it, other than taking a trip by safari van), you need four-wheel drive – it can rain at any time and the route across the mountains is sometimes closed during heavy rains. It's also a very sensible idea to have two spare wheels.

Once you're in, it's a beautiful drive, with waterfalls and sensational views more than compensating for comparatively scarce **wildlife**: buffalo, elephants (and colobus monkeys lower down) are most often seen. For animals in quantity, and for any real chance of seeing rhinos, giant forest hog, or the Aberdares' prize inhabitant, the bongo antelope, you really have to spend a night at one of the two **game-viewing lodges**, *The Ark* or *Treetops* – expensive perhaps, but not an experience you're likely to forget.

There are several **accommodation** options in the high park, most easily accessed through the Kiandongoro Gate. The first, barely 2km inside the gate, is the self-help *Kiandongoro Fishing Lodge*, located on open moors above the Magura River. There are two stone-built, tin-roofed cottages, each with three separate bedrooms of two,

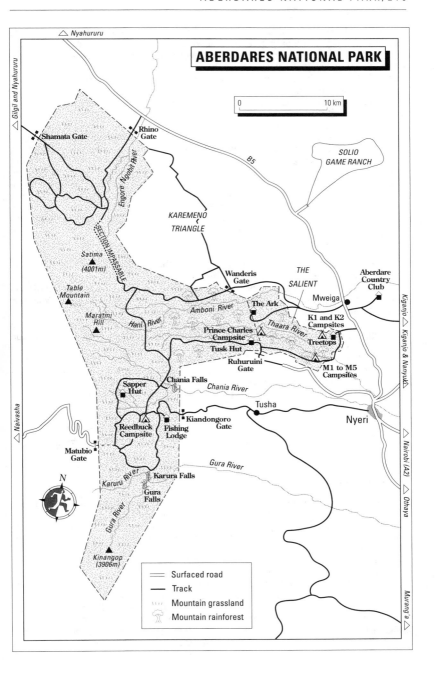

△ *Nyahururu*

ABERDARES NATIONAL PARK

0   10 km

SOLIO GAME RANCH

B5

■ Shamata Gate

■ Rhino Gate

Engore Ngobit River

△ *Gilgil and Nyahururu*

KAREMENO TRIANGLE

SECTION IMPASSABLE

▲ *Satima (4001m)*

▲ *Table Mountain*

▲ *Maratini Hill*

Hani River

Amboni River

Wanderis Gate

THE SALIENT

The Ark ■

Mweiga

Aberdare Country Club

△ *Kiganjo*

△ *Kiganjo & Nanyuki*

Prince Charles Campsite △

Thaara River

K1 and K2 Campsites ■

Tusk Hut

Treetops ■

Ruhuruini Gate

M1 to M5 Campsites △

Sapper Hut ■

Chania Falls ⬙

Chania River

Tusha

Nyeri

Reedbuck Campsite △

Fishing Lodge ■

■ **Kiandongoro Gate**

△ *Nairobi (A2)*

△ *Naivasha*

Matubio Gate ■

Karuru River

Gura River

⬙ **Karura Falls**

Gura Falls

△ *Ohaya*

N

▲ *Kinangop (3906m)*

═══ Surfaced road

——— Track

〃〃 Mountain grassland

🌳 Mountain rainforest

△ *Murang'a*

four and six beds. You book as much space as you need through the warden (or take a chance and pay at the park gate), and share the central open-fire cooking and eating area with other guests. You need to take everything with you except water – food, warm sleeping bags, firewood. Wood-fired boiler tanks outside will produce hot water. Sadly, rumours abound of its imminent closure – check at the park gates or with the authorities in Mweiga (PO Box 24). The other self-service option is *Sapper Hut* (reservations through Let's Go Travel in Nairobi, p.142; Ksh2000 for the hut; collect key from the *Fishing Lodge*), some 10km further west on a little tributary of the Chania river at around 3000m altitude. It consists of a wooden *banda* with a living room, double bedroom, fireplace, verandah and wood-fired boiler, but no shower, lamps, bedsheets or firewood, and only basic cooking facilities. Lower down (2300m), tucked into a glade surrounded by forest, there's the good *Tusk Camp*, 2km in from Ruhuruini Gate (reservations also through Let's Go). There are several wooden *bandas* here, an ill-equipped kitchen (bring pots, pans and cutlery), a pit latrine with one of Kenya's most regal views, and a caretaker to help you out: the catch is that you have to hire the entire place (Ksh5000) rather than just one *banda*. As for *Sapper Hut*, take bedding, towels, kerosene (for the lights), food and drinking water. Visits from here to the normally closed "Salient" sector of the park should be possible if you enquire first with the rangers at the gate; they used to levy a Ksh2000 fee for the admission key.

For **camping**, the basic *Reedbuck Campsite* near the *Fishing Lodge* is the only public site in the park; there are a number of "special campsites", but these are very expensive (Ksh5000 reservation fee, plus $15 per person per night), are equally bereft of facilities and were, in any case, closed until recently and may close again in future. Your last camping option is to be accompanied by an armed ranger.

The high moorlands have some exceptional **walking** and the three peaks – Satima (the highest) in the north, Kinangop in the south, and Kipipiri, an isolated cone outside the park above the Wanjohi Valley, in the west – can be climbed relatively easily, given good weather conditions: ask the Mountain Club of Kenya in Nairobi for details. Hiking in the park is allowed only with the approval of the warden, so apply in good time. You may be offered, or required to take, a guide (whom you'll have to pay). If you drive, it's usually permissible to wander a short distance from your car. The situation changes from time to time: over the years there have been a number of near-misses with several, apparently human-hungry, lions.

Road conditions vary considerably from one period of heavy rain to the next: you really need to check this with the rangers at the park gates. Surfaces are mostly red *murram*, though there are a few, very steep, rocky sections.

Through the park

The park splits into two different environments – the **high moorland and peaks** which form the park's main body, and the lower **Salient** to the east where the vegetation is dense rain forest and there is considerably more wildlife. The Salient slopes (location of *Treetops* and *The Ark*) are closed to casual visitors; all the earth access roads have locked barriers. You can get keys to these, in theory, from the warden in Mweiga, or possibly from the rangers at the eastern gates (but not from Matubio Gate in the west).

In the mid-1990s, the government pledged to establish a wholly enclosed **wildlife sanctuary** in this area, partly to protect the park's sixty black rhino (the largest indigenous population left in Kenya), but mainly to arrest the conflict between wildlife and humans, which most visibly manifested itself in the trashing of crops and homes fringing the park by "rogue" or "rampaging" elephants. To this end, the rangers are currently busy clearing a path on which to erect some 370km of electrified fence

(100km has already been erected). More information on the project can be obtained from Rhino Ark, PO Box 63410 Nairobi (☎02/749655, fax 748750 or 740721, *www.rhinoark.org*).

Unless you're planning several days of walking, fishing or camping, the most straightforward visit to the moorlands is to spend a day driving through from one side to the other between the main gates. There are two other eastern gates further from Nyeri (Wanderis and Kiandongoro) and two at the remote north end of the park (Shamata, accessible from Nyahururu, and Rhino Gate, from the B5 Nyeri–Nyahururu road), which has been earmarked for an eighty-bed **eco-lodge** (details from the facilities manager at KWS, see p.148), but there's no reliable route through the park from south to north, and the small circuit of tracks in the north is very rough. Driving via the park from Naivasha to Nyeri (or vice versa) is easy enough in good weather. If conditions are less than ideal, however, and you get stuck, you could be in for a long day – or a rather miserable night.

Naivasha to Matubio Gate

From Naivasha, follow the signs for the park via the Uplands road as if going to Nairobi, as far as the junction for Kinangop on the north side of town. From here, you climb about 14km, on reasonably intact tarmac, to another junction where the bad road begins. Go easy if you're driving: the cambered, rock-built surface is perfect for punctures. After another 5km or so you reach Kipipiri junction and, seasonally, a strange egret nesting colony in eleven conifers along the roadside.

At **Ndunyu Njeru** centre you pass the last chance of a puncture repair or petrol (fuel isn't always available) and the final stop of *matatus* up from Naivasha, before a few more kilometres of very bad surface. Finally the road runs out of reasons to continue except to the National Park itself – becoming a narrow, quite acceptable, tarmac switchback that is apparently forty years old – and climbs through the vegetation zones, with increasing evidence of elephants (dung everywhere), to pitch out finally through the highest extent of the forest to Matubio Gate, right on the threshold of the moorland. Along the last 7km there are some excellent views back over the climb and down to Lake Naivasha. Allow two to three hours to get this far.

Matubio Gate to Ruhuruini Gate

Allowing four hours from Matubio Gate to Ruhuruini Gate gives time enough, in good weather, for visits to the Chania Falls and the Karura Giant Falls.

Proper access to the top of the **Karura Falls** (there's no way down to the bottom) was only built in 1992, by the British Army's Royal Engineers, and they've created two superb, dizzy, timber viewpoints, one on each side, from which you can look across through dripping, Afro-Alpine vegetation, to the babbling, four-metre-wide Karuru stream as it plunges over the abyss, dropping nearly 300m in three stages. To the south, the distant veil of the **Gura Falls**, a kilometre or two across the yawning canyon, seems to make for a surfeit of dramatic beauty.

The much lower, sheer drop of the **Chania Falls** has old, rickety access walks and platforms (be very careful if they have not been replaced) and you can gaze from the top, or the bottom, and even contemplate a swim in the pool. It was in this vicinity in 1984 that an American tourist was badly mauled by a lion, an incident that so unnerved the park's authorities that they have only recently relaxed the rules on unaccompanied walking. This followed a controlled lion cull, aimed as much at public relations as at giving various herbivores (such as giant forest hog and bongo) a chance to rebuild their endangered populations. A cautionary sign by the path still warns about "wild animals", though there seems no reason to believe they favour this spot over any other.

Turning east, the 15km to **Ruhuruini Gate** descends in a breathtaking helter skelter through the cloud forest, with stunning views across the jungle-cloaked valleys. Once out of the gate, the road down to Nyeri is in good condition and you soon reach tarmac.

Nyeri and around

Self-styled capital of Kikuyuland – a title the Kikuyu of Kiambu might dispute – **NYERI** is, more prosaically, the administrative headquarters of Central Province and one of the liveliest, most chaotic and friendly highland towns. Another former British military camp, it emerged as a market town for European coffee growers in the hills and for settlers on the ranching and wheat farms further north. Located beneath the Aberdares, it was on the front line – as much as there was one – during the war for Independence. Of more specialist interest, Nyeri was also the last home of Robert Lord **Baden-Powell**, founder of the worldwide scouting movement, whose cryptically named Paxtu cottage, now a small museum (Ksh50), stands in the grounds of the *Outspan Hotel* and whose grave and memorial are to be found on the north side of town.

An active, and attractive, trading centre despite its fantastically broken-up streets, Nyeri nestles in the green hills where the broad vale between Mount Kenya and the Aberdares drops towards Nairobi. Tumultuous markets, scores of *dukas*, and even a few street entertainers playing on soda bottles and bottle tops, lend it an air of irrepressible commercialism. There are two branches of Barclays and a Standard Chartered, all with ATMs.

Cheap and mid-range lodgings

Nyeri's role as rural business centre and major transport crossroads means there are plenty of **cheap places to stay** in town, as well as the historical and upmarket *Outspan Hotel*.

RECENT HISTORY

The extraordinary density of **cultivation** in the tightly spaced *shambas* around Nyeri (maize, beans, potatoes, cassava, bananas, sugar cane, millet, squash and melons, tomatoes, citrus fruit, cabbages and carrots, as well as tea, coffee and macadamia nuts) is partly a hangover from white settlerdom, when a rapidly growing population was deprived of huge tracts of land and forced to cultivate intensively. Partly, too, it's the result of land consolidation: the "rationalization" of fragmented land holdings into unitary *shambas* that took place in the 1950s and turned people who had held traditional rights into deed-holding property owners. And partly it's the simple consequence of an excellent climate and soil plus a birth rate reckoned (like Kisii's, see p.295) to be one of the highest in the world.

There's no doubt that the **changes** which have taken place in Nyeri district have been some of the most profound and rapid anywhere in the country. Even the villages of Kikuyuland are nearly all innovations of the last forty years, the irreversible effects of the Emergency. Until then, the Kikuyu had mostly lived in scattered homesteads among their crops and herds. British security forces, unable to contain open revolt in the countryside, began the systematic internment of the whole Kikuyu population into fenced and guarded villages, forcing the guerrillas into the high forests. And the villages of today have mostly grown from such places.

On Nyeri's main street, Kimathi Way, is a cenotaph, unusual in the frankness of its inscription: "To the Memory of the Members of the Kikuyu Tribe who Died in the Fight for Freedom 1951–1957".

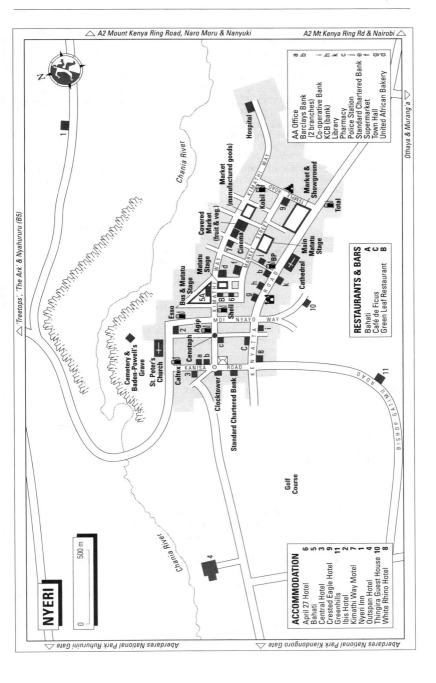

NYERI

0 ___ 500 m

△ *Treetops', The Ark' & Nyahururu (B5)*

△ A2 Mount Kenya Ring Road, Naro Moru & Nanyuki   A2 Mt Kenya Ring Rd & Nairobi △

Othaya & Murang'a ▽

Chania River

Hospital

Market (manufactured goods)

Market & Showground

Covered Market (fruit & veg.)

Kobil

Cinema

Total

BP

Main Matatu Stage

Matatu Stage

Bus & Matatu Stage

Cathedral

Esso

Agip

Shell

Cenotaph

Caltex

Cemetery & Baden-Powell's Grave

St. Peter's Church

KIMATHI WAY

KIMATHI ROAD

TEMPLE ROAD

MARKET STREET

MOI NYAYO WAY

KENYATTA ROAD

KANISA ROAD

BISHOP GATE ROAD

Clocktower

Standard Chartered Bank

Golf Course

Chania River

a AA Office
b Barclays Bank (2 branches)
i Co-operative Bank
h KCB (bank)
k Library
c Pharmacy
j Police Station
e Standard Chartered Bank
f Supermarket
g Town Hall
d United African Bakery

RESTAURANTS & BARS

Bahati   A
Café de Ficus   C
Green Leaf Restaurant   B

ACCOMMODATION

April 27 Hotel   6
Bahati   5
Central Hotel   3
Crested Eagle Hotel   9
Greenhills   11
Ibis Hotel   2
Kimathi Way Motel   7
Nyeri Inn   1
Outspan Hotel   4
Thingira Guest House   10
White Rhino Hotel   8

▽ Aberdares National Park Ruhuruini Gate

▽ Aberdares National Park Kiandongoro Gate

April 27 Hotel, off Kimathi Way (PO Box 316; ☎0171/2817). Very cheap, and with hot water, but get there early to be sure of a room. ①.

Bahati Restaurant & Lodging, Kimathi Way (PO Box 148; ☎0171/71491). Basic but clean B&L (not s/c), with a popular restaurant. ①.

Central Hotel, Kanisa Rd (PO Box 446; ☎0171/4233). Clean, cheap and friendly, with pleasant s/c rooms (some with balconies), and good breakfasts. Occasional weekend discos. Good value. B&B ②.

Crested Eagle Hotel (PO Box 12465; ☎0171/4933). A good high-rise with standard s/c rooms and safe parking, but it's expensive and the *Zebra Bar* makes things noisy up until midnight. ④.

Greenhills Hotel, Bishop Gatimu Rd, 1km south of town (PO Box 313; ☎0171/30604, fax 2199). The biggest hotel with the best facilities, *Outspan* excepted, close to the golf course with extensive gardens and lawns. There's a pool, sauna, two restaurants and bar, but it can be noisy on Wednesday, Friday and Saturday nights due to its popular discos. ④.

Greenleaf Restaurant (PO Box 2169; ☎0171/2126). Friendly and safe, with fairly decent s/c rooms with 24-hour hot water. The bar has great views over the street corner, and the restaurant is one of the best. Recommended. ①.

Ibis Hotel, Kanisa Rd (☎0171/4858 or 72777). Good budget choice, with large, clean s/c rooms with nets. ①.

Kimathi Way Motel (PO Box 2188; ☎0171/2799). A cheap lodging, with filling meals, but noisy (especially at weekends) and not terribly clean. ①.

Nyeri Inn, 3.2km down the Kiganjo road, 1.5km from the Nyahururu junction (PO Box 159; ☎0171/31092). A gem if you don't mind staying outside town. Set in calm, tree-shaded gardens (ideal for kids), its offers several large, airy two-bed cottages for rent, each s/c with baths and hot water. Its restaurant serves mainly chicken. No security problems. Recommended. B&B ②.

Thingira Guest House, off Kenyatta Rd (PO Box 221; ☎0171/4769). One of the nicest cheapies, close to the town centre but with none of its bustle. The management are friendly, rooms (s/c) are clean and have hot water. ②–③.

White Rhino Hotel, Kenyatta Rd (PO Box 30; ☎0171/30934). A laid-back atmosphere and *the* place for conscientious boozing. A crumbling colonial hotel, reasonable rooms, nice gardens. ③.

Eating, drinking and nightlife

Nyeri has a number of interesting **eating** options. It also has a **cheese** factory: lots of its produce is available locally. The main **nightspot** is *Club O Zone*, ideal for those fed up with smooth soul divas: look out for DJs Papa Kilosh, Charly and Pinka Pon. There are also discos at the *Green Hills Hotel*, where Sunday afternoons feature traditional dances, and the *White Rhino Hotel* is a popular place for whiling away an afternoon with a bottle or five.

Bahati Restaurant & Lodging, Kimathi Way. Known for its chicken cooked any way you want it so long as it's fried or stewed.

Café de Ficus, Kenyatta Rd. Consistently popular, shaded meeting place, with cheap snacks and more substantial meals.

Central Hotel, Kanisa Rd. Does good breakfasts.

Greenleaf Restaurant. This is surprisingly good, dishing up great trout and *nyama choma*. If the weather's OK, the first-floor terrace-bar, overlooking the commotion below, is fun too.

Nyeri Cinema. Beer garden and restaurant, *nyama choma*, and an ice cream parlour next to *Batian Tusker Bar*.

Nyeri Coffee House. Run by the Coffee Board of Kenya and serving a good brew.

Outspan Hotel (see above). This atmospheric pile welcomes day-visitors for its excellent (if expensive) buffet lunches, or for tea on the lawn and a swim in the pool (Ksh200). The hotel's *Kirinyaga Bar* is pleasant enough for a beer in the evening in civilized surroundings, but it's not overly stimulating.

Seremai Hotel. A decent, budget *hoteli*: the place to fuel up on *mandaazi*, or an enormous plateful of beans or stew with *ugali* for next to nothing.

Zebra Bar, at the *Crested Eagle Hotel*. A busy bar, open to midnight.

The Outspan Hotel

Two kilometres west of the clocktower off the Kiandongoro Gate Road (PO Box 24 Nyeri; ☎0171/2424–26, fax 2286; reservations through Block, p.48; B&B ⑥ low, ⑦ high), the *Outspan*, built in 1927, is the stately base for visits to *Treetops* (see below), where you check-in for lunch and are driven up in the afternoon. Set in beautiful gardens, with Mount Kenya rising behind, it offers more than enough reasons for staying here, too. The rooms vary in size, the larger ones being huge, with wonderful old baths, as well as more modern facilities (including satellite TV) in the new Chania Wing. There's a pool, and some good walks along the Chania River bank down on the fringes of the lovely gardens, though you have to go with a guard from the hotel (Ksh150, or Ksh300 for a bird walk). With the right approach, though, you might find yourself a lift over the Aberdares – but ask early in the day, when people would be setting off, rather than later. Adjacent to the hotel is Nyeri Sports Club with its 3316-yard **nine-hole golf course**, the second oldest in Kenya, founded in 1910. It's also possible to arrange **day-trips** to the **Aberdare National Park** from here, which work out cheaper the more people you go with.

The Aberdare Country Club

Situated 11km out on the Nyahururu Road near Mweiga, then 3km along a passable *murram* road (signposted), the luxuriously rural *Aberdare Country Club* (PO Box 449 Nyeri; ☎0171/55620, fax 55224, *ark@form-net.com*; ⑤ low, ⑦ high) is the base for *The Ark* "tree-hotel". Like the *Outspan*, it's an exceptionally nice and atmospheric place, dating from 1938, with rooms in stone cottages (room numbers 28 to 31 have the best views) and a wealth of things to do. For non-guests, the temporary membership fee (Monday–Thursday Ksh300, Friday–Sunday Ksh500) includes use of the pool, nine-hole golf course (clubs and caddie extra; local rules award six inches grace if the ball lands on animal droppings or rolls into an aardvark's hole), tennis courts, and a visit (on foot) to their game sanctuary with its comical warthogs, reticulated giraffe, zebra, eland, waterbuck, impala et al. They also organize very reasonable Aberdares game drives (Ksh1100 plus park entry), horse riding ($26pp for 1hr), and trips to Solio Game Ranch (Ksh6000 for a seven-seater vehicle, plus Ksh1600 per person entry fee; see below). Despite its popularity, it remains classy, and visitors are rarely disappointed.

The "tree-hotels"

For many visitors, a night in one of the two Aberdare "tree-hotels" is the stuff of dreams. Located in the park's otherwise inaccessible Salient area, the only visitors allowed in are guests of either *Treetops* or *The Ark* (on the lodge's own transport), which heightens the air of exclusivity since you cannot visit in advance to check them out. This multi-million-dollar industry is the closest you'll get on a package tour to "living bush", and the fact that both hotels are usually booked solid, and not just by safari-suited tour groups, affirms the attraction. Yet, having invested heavily for a night, both *Treetops* and *The Ark* can at first be a disappointment. After all the hype, you find yourself confined to the interior of a wooden building with a hundred or more fellow tourists, are shown to your tiny bedroom, and are then briefed on the animals you can hope to see and the things you're not allowed to do.It can all feel somewhat contrived.

But when the sun goes down and the floodlights come on, it's strange how quickly this is forgotten: the wildlife below draws everyone's attention and the cameras start clicking in earnest. Herds of heavyweights – elephant and buffalo especially – can be taken for granted, and the prospect of a night's sleepless vigil becomes magical, as even your cramped confines acquire a certain charm. Note that neither hotel permits flash photography, so bring enough 800ASA film (or faster) with you, as the ones sold in the hotel giftshops are unsurprisingly expensive.

TREETOPS
Reservations through Block, p.48. Minimum age 7 years (no child rates), except on occasional "children's nights"; FB ⑦ low, ⑨ high, including lunch at the Outspan Hotel. Aberdares National Park entry fees are extra ($27 each).

Perhaps Kenya's most famous hotel, **Treetops** was where Princess Elizabeth became Queen Elizabeth II, on the death of her father George VI, while she was staying in the original *Treetops* on the other side of the water hole. The original tree house was looted and burned down in 1955 by Mau Mau freedom-fighters: the present, much larger building is built on stilts among the trees. The lodge itself is tremendous fun, with growing branches of Cape chestnut twisting through the public rooms, and a dining room with trestle tables and polished benches. Intentionally like an officers' mess, it has something of the creaking atmosphere of a wooden ship. Last renovated in 1996, the bedrooms and shared facilities are nonetheless cramped. What you're paying for is the experience of *Treetops* – the opportunity to breathe the same air as the rich and famous. Photographs and letters framed on the varnished walls hark as far back as the 1930s and various royal and state visits.

During daylight hours, reality is never far below the surface. Through the forest, Kikuyu *shambas* and homesteads are visible in every direction and the main Nyeri road passes by just 3km away. The lodge is no longer *in* the forest, either: down by the **water hole**, a large area is now virtually bare – red dust and dead wood – the result of foliage destruction by elephants. One patch has even been fenced in to protect new plant growth. The problem, as always, is balancing tourist receipts with the needs of wildlife – which themselves conflict with those of farmers on the slopes nearby. Many of the animals which come to *Treetops* are lured by the **salt** which is spread beneath the viewing platform every afternoon before the visitors arrive. This draws large herds of elephant and buffalo, but only very few rhino, and in the long term it would seem to ensure the ruination of the environment around the lodge. It certainly discourages those animals that need plenty of cover. The curious **giant forest hog** sometimes turns up, but **leopards** are rarely seen and the large **bongo**, that "shy and elusive forest antelope", hasn't put in an appearance for many years – understandably.

THE ARK
Reservations through Lonrho, p.49. Minimum age 7 years (no child rates), except on occasional "children's nights"; FB ⑦ low, ⑨ high, including lunch at Aberdare Country Club. Aberdares National Park entry fees are extra ($27 each).

For better game viewing, **The Ark**, *Treetops'* upstart competitor, is set at a higher altitude, actually in the mountain forest. Here, they do on occasion see leopard (and, perhaps once a year, bongo), and there are almost guaranteed nightly sightings of elephant, rhino and buffalo. Transport from the *Aberdare Country Club* leaves daily at 2.30pm and 5pm, returning at 8am. You should try to get an afternoon nap: you'll be woken by buzzers through the night announcing the arrival of one of the "big five". The attraction for wildlife is the muddy pool and saltlick at the "prow" of the hotel, under the viewing terraces and next to a ground-level photographic hide. There's usually an animated scene here as the animals jostle for salt, and fights sometimes break out, especially when new-born calves are around. The accommodation has recently been comprehensively upgraded, but don't expect luxury: the rooms are still small, poky and dark.

Routes out of Nyeri

A signposted route leads **west**, past the *Outspan*, up into the Aberdares and the park's Kiandongoro gate in the high moorland. In the other direction, the road splits out of town, forking **south** to Murang'a via Othaya, or continuing **east** to the A2 Mount Kenya ring road and the quickest return route to Nairobi.

A fourth route takes you in a northwest direction heading out of town, splitting in two after 2km. Keep straight on if you want the A2 Mount Kenya ring road for Naro Moru and Nanyuki via Kiganjo.

Fork left and the road (the B5) sweeps past the track for the Ruhurini Gate in the forest of the Salient, then the unmarked tracks for *Treetops* and *The Ark* – with the turning for the *Aberdare Country Club* (p.225) between them, just before the hilltop centre of **Mweiga**. The highway continues, in excellent condition, across lonely, forested ridges and wide savannah to Nyahururu (Thomson's Falls), on the northern fringes of the Highlands.

Sangare Ranch

Near Mweiga you'll find Kenya's possibly most charming luxury tented camp, **Sangare Ranch** (reservations through *Savannah Camps & Lodges*, p.50; FB ⑨). Access is via the *Aberdare Country Club*, either by *matatu* to the signboard near Mweiga (leaving you with a three-kilometre walk), or by car or taxi. The ranch will pick you up in their own 4WD from the club. Located some 5km north of the club, the landscape and atmosphere could hardly be more different: the track winds up and down precarious forested ravines before emerging onto a fresh high plateau of scrub and meadow with a good view of Mount Kenya when the air is clear. There are only six tents, each with wood-heated showers and solar-powered light, sited on the east side of a small freshwater lake. The **birdlife** is the main draw, with black-headed herons squawking loudly in the trees over the tents, some migratory pelican, and glimpses of crowned eagle, accompanied by a fantastic chorus of frogs and toads throughout the night. There are usually some elephants and buffalo in the vicinity, as well as zebra, gazelle, hyena, colobus and Sykes' monkeys and the occasional leopard. The style is refreshingly informal, with superb farmhouse meals (cottage pie, treacle sponge pudding and the like) eaten in a small dining room with the manager and the camp's excellent botanical and wildlife guide. Horse-riding is possible, as are guided walks to a nearby cave used by the Mau Mau in the 1950s, and night walks in search of bats, bushbabies, mongoose and the apparently beautiful maned rat. If you have the money, it's highly recommended.

Solio Game Ranch

Continuing westwards along the B5 from Mweiga, the **Solio Game Ranch** (PO Box 2 Naro Moru; ☎02/763638 or locally ☎0171/420157, 420167, 420177, fax 55235; single entry fee of Ksh1600, children under 12 free; open all year unless very wet) lies a few kilometres further on off on the right. Privately run, Solio more or less single-handedly saved the Kenyan rhino population from extinction, by breeding them here for them to be subsequently translocated into the national parks and other Kenyan reserves. The figures speak for themselves: from an original population of 23 black rhino, there are now over 50; of the original 16 white rhino, imported from South Africa, the population now stands at over 70; and all of the relocated black rhinos, and most of the white, at Nakuru National Park's Rhino Sanctuary were bred here. Without 4WD, you can visit the ranch by hiring a vehicle and driver, or by joining a trip at the *Aberdare Country Club*. If you have your own wheels, the ranch provides maps, and a guide if there's one available (free). They have three basic campsites (water and firewood provided; Ksh400 per person). See also the section on Laikipia on p.205.

For a less conventional view of wildlife, the Gliding Club of Kenya operates from a field 2km south of Mweiga (contact Peter or Petra Allmendinger ☎ & fax 0171/2748, *gliding@africaonline.co.ke*; $50 for 10min), with two-seater aircraft and instructors available to introduce you to the sport.

Nyahururu (Thomson's Falls)

Like Nanyuki, **NYAHURURU** is almost on the equator, and it shares much of Nanyuki's character. It's high (at 2360m, Kenya's highest town), cool (in fact very cold on January and February mornings), and set on open savannah lands with patches of indigenous forest and plenty of coniferous plantation. Since the fast, B5 road to Nyeri was completed, Nyahururu has been less cut off, but still there's an air of slightly wild isolation about it. It's something of a frontier town for routes heading north to Lake Turkana and the desert: a tarred road goes out as far as Rumuruti and then the fun begins (see p.558). Other roads join Nyahururu with Nanyuki (the C76; an extremely

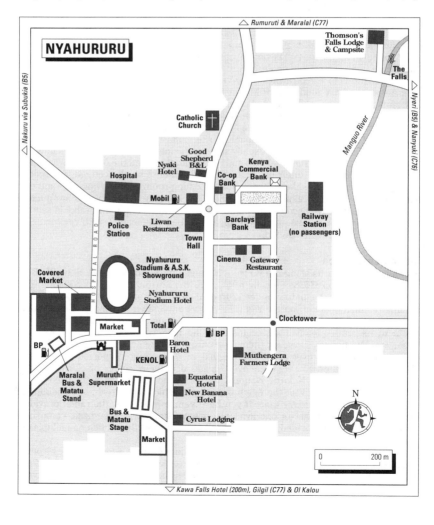

△ *Rumuruti & Maralal (C77)*

NYAHURURU

Thomson's Falls Lodge & Campsite

The Falls

◁ *Nakuru via Subukia (B5)*

▷ *Nyeri (B5) & Nanyuki (C76)*

Manguo River

Catholic Church

Good Shepherd B&L

Nyaki Hotel

Kenya Commercial Bank

Co-op Bank

Hospital

Mobil

Police Station

Liwan Restaurant

Town Hall

Barclays Bank

Railway Station (no passengers)

HOSPITAL ROAD

Nyahururu Stadium & A.S.K. Showground

Cinema

Gateway Restaurant

Covered Market

Nyahururu Stadium Hotel

Market

Total

BP

Clocktower

BP

Baron Hotel

Muthengera Farmers Lodge

KENOL

Maralal Bus & Matatu Stand

Muruthi Supermarket

Equatorial Hotel

New Banana Hotel

Bus & Matatu Stage

Cyrus Lodging

Market

N

0   200 m

▽ *Kawa Falls Hotel (200m), Gilgil (C77) & Ol Kalou*

bad road, but good for game viewing), Gilgil (p.234), and Nakuru and the remainder of the northern Rift Valley (p.254).

Joseph Thomson gave the town its original name when he named the nearby waterfall after his father in 1883. Many still call it "T Falls" – and not just the old settlers you might expect. Thomson's Falls was one of the last settler towns to be established. The first sign of urbanization was a hut built by the Narok Angling Club in the early 1920s to allow its members to fish for the newly introduced trout in the Ewaso Narok, Pesi and Equator rivers. In 1929, when the railway branch line arrived, the town began to take shape. The line has closed now, but the hotel built in 1931, *Thomson's Falls Lodge*, is still going strong, and Nyahururu remains an important market town – and not, in any sense, a tourist centre. Local people can react rather oddly to the presence of travellers in Nyahururu's lodging houses. If you're staying in town, be sensitive to the fact that some think you should stay in the lodge by the falls.

Thomson's Falls – and walks in the area

The falls themselves are pretty rather than spectacular – though they can be dramatic after heavy rain. They're a popular stop-off for tourists travelling between Samburu and Maasai Mara game reserves (fourteen minibuses at one time is nothing), and the lawns above the falls get crowded with picnickers from town at weekends. At such times, the souvenir sellers on the cliff edge can be a pain. When the crowds leave, they're good company, if you want it. The town council has long been trying to evict them, though apparently not for any aesthetic reason, but in order to make room for the planned tourist pavilion of a local political heavy.

The path leading down to the bottom of the 75-metre falls is somewhat dangerous, especially when wet. But certainly don't attempt to climb up again by any other route because the cliffs are extremely unstable. With several hours to spare, you can search for a longer **walk** down into the forested valley, following the Ewaso Narok River. If you want to try this, cross the bridge first, then look for a way downstream. The spray-laden trees are shaken periodically by troops of colobus monkeys and, as on Mount Kenya, three-horned chameleons are always around if you look hard. This area is also fruitful for ornithologists – recent sightings include a crowned eagle with a colobus monkey in its claws.

A much shorter stroll also takes you over the bridge and past the electricity sub-station, beyond which the first trail you come to leads to the top of a hill with a communications tower and a skeletal lookout post. Excellent views from here stretch south towards Ol Kalou and the marshy trough of Lake Ol Bolossat.

Another nearby stroll takes you in quest of the highest **hippos** in Kenya. Incredible as it seems, several hippos do live in the swampy area a kilometre or two back upriver above the falls. A kilometre from the turning off to the *Lodge* on the Nyeri road, you come to a small cluster of *dukas* on the right. Walk down towards the houses closest to town and, about 300m from the road, you emerge by a large lake. Immediately by the access path, the area is thick with reeds, but walk round the lake to the clump of trees and you can shin up one of these and select a natural observation platform. Sit and watch and you may see as many as six hippos.

Thomson's Falls Lodge

For **accommodation**, most people do head out to the touristy lodge (PO Box 38; ☎0365/22006, fax 32170; reservations in Nairobi on ☎02/221855; B&B ③–④), which – so long as you're content with nothing fancy – is good value, with its solid, highlands-farmhouse atmosphere and log fires in the rooms. Some have big old-fashioned baths, others rather more basic showers – ask to see a selection. Some details may annoy: service can be overbearing, there's often no hot water (you have to remind the staff to turn it on), and the food can be shamefully bad, so avoid half- or full-board. Alternatively, you can **camp** in the grounds, still within earshot of the falls. The campsite (Ksh300 per person; no tents for hire) is popular with budget safari groups. The price includes showers and ample firewood: again, you need to specifically ask for them.

Accommodation in town

If the rooms at the lodge are out of your price range and you don't have a tent, the next place down is something of a drop: the *Kawa Falls Hotel*, 400m past the end of the market on the Ol Kalou road (PO Box 985; ☎0365/32295, fax 32256; B&B ②), is the best of the rest, a friendly five-storey block with basic, if slightly damp and poky, s/c rooms, with safe parking, an airy first-floor bar, and it's away from the noise and hassling street kids in the centre. On the other side of town, an almost identical building houses the *Nyaki Hotel* (PO Box 214; ☎0365/22313; ③), overpriced apart from its cheap singles (Ksh200). Cheaper is the *Baron Hotel*, a "tourist-class" establishment right in the centre at the start of the Ol Kalou road (PO Box 423; 0365/32056; ②), but it suffers greatly from the loud *Equatorial Hotel* over the road and the *matatu* stage next door, the former jumping till 4am, the latter honking from 6am. Cheaper and much better if you don't mind the deeply religious atmosphere is the friendly and clean *Nyahururu Stadium Hotel* (PO Box 152; ☎0365/22608; ①) by the ASK showground, above the Karabui Gospel Music Store; it also has good security. The *Good Shepherd B&L*, in a traditional compound by the *Nyaki Hotel*, has singles only (①). Of the dozen or so other very basic B&Ls in town (all with noisy bars and uncertain security; ①), the least squalid are the *New Banana Hotel*, which has s/c singles only, *Equatorial Hotel*, also s/c and with a *nyama choma* joint and pool tables (and music most nights), and *Cyrus Lodging*. All are on the Ol Kalou road, opposite the *matatu* and market enclosure.

For **meals**, *Liwan Restaurant & Café* (☎0365/32613; closed Sun) is the best: clean, quiet and cheap, with a patio shaded by white bottle-brush trees. For fried tilapia, try *Gateway Restaurant* down the alley by the cinema, whilst *Muthengera Farmers Lodge* is recommended for chicken, a poultry replacement for its now sadly moribund bar. There's more meat at the *Nyaki Hotel*'s rooftop *nyama choma* joint and bar (order in advance); vegetarians should head for the *Cyrus*'s own restaurant, *Arafa*.

Whether eating out or not, the **market** is well worth a browse, especially on Saturdays. Find it anywhere west of the stadium – it sprawls out over most of the district, an indication of the town's rapid growth over the last decade or so.

For **action after dark**, check out the *Equator Hotel*'s **disco**, the cause of insomnia at the *Baron Hotel*, with reggae and soukous (sometimes live) to midnight, and soul divas on tape thereafter. For more action in the dark, the **cinema** has showings twice every evening, with an extra matinée on Sundays for those escaping church.

Onwards from Nyahururu

There are several buses and *matatus* each day down to Nyeri, or you could hitch from outside the *Lodge*. The road was built, for most of its length, along a new route, so villages are few; for the most part it either bucks up and down across forested valleys or soars across immense plains of swaying grass. It's a fast road not much used by heavy transport and still in relatively good condition.

Nyahururu's other transport connections are mentioned below in the Travel Details. Remember the unsurfaced road to Nanyuki can be treacherous in wet weather. For a spectacular change of scene, take the road down the **scarp** to Nakuru, via the Subukia valley, following the route to Lake Bogoria described in Chapter Three.

travel details

BUSES AND MATATUS

Around Mount Kenya

Unless you have a specific destination in mind, simply getting to the next town on the circuit is always easy, as there are frequent *matatus* from 6am to 6pm. Buses connect all the larger towns with each other, but run less frequently than *matatus*. **Nyeri** is something of an exception, where *matatus* all but monopolize the routes. **Nanyuki–Nyahururu**, **Nanyuki–Isiolo** and **Nyahururu-Nakuru** also have limited bus services. Eldoret Express run helpful daily buses to **Western Province**, from Nyeri via Nyahururu, Nakuru and Eldoret to Kitale. Nanyuki, Meru, Nyeri and Nyahururu all have at least one direct daily service to Nairobi, often more.

Around the Aberdares

From **Nyahururu to Nyeri** and vice versa, take the daily service between Nakuru and Nairobi, via the *east* side of the Aberdares.

To **Rumuruti** and **Maralal** (see Chapter Seven): two daily buses, but the last through bus leaves at 11am (5–6hr).

To **Gilgil**: frequent country bus and *matatu* runs; some go on to Nairobi.

To the coast: **Mombasa** is the only feasible destination, given the insecurity along the old route to **Lamu**. Arusha Express run daily from **Meru**, bypassing Nairobi. Other services invariably call at the capital.

TRAINS

There is no longer a passenger service to any town in this chapter.

FLIGHTS

Forget about flying **Nyeri–Nanyuki** no matter what the circumstances: the airstrips are so close together and so far from the towns they serve that you could drive the sixty-kilometre journey faster.

Nanyuki to: Maasai Mara (daily; 1hr 30min); Nairobi (daily; 50min); Nyeri (daily; 10min); Samburu Lodges (daily; 30min).

Nyeri to: Nanyuki (daily; 10min); Samburu (daily; 40min).

CHAPTER THREE

THE RIFT VALLEY

Kenya's **Great Rift Valley** is only part of a continental fault system that runs 6000km clean across Africa from Jordan to Mozambique. Perhaps Kenya's most important topographical feature, it is certainly one of the country's great distinguishing marks, a human and natural divide. As such, it has come to be seen as a monumental valley of teeming game and Maasai herders, a trough of grasslands older than mankind. This image is not entirely borne out by reality. The valley certainly is spectacular, a literal rift across the country, with all the stunning panoramas and gaunt escarpment backdrops you could wish for, and the plains animals are still abundant in places; nevertheless, much of the game has been dispersed by human population pressure onto the higher plateaus to the southwest, and most of the Maasai nowadays live further south.

At least the Rift Valley's **historical influence** cannot be diluted. People have trekked down it, generation after generation, over perhaps the last two or three thousand years, from the wetlands of southern Sudan and the Ethiopian highlands. Some of these immigrants were the forefathers of the **Maasai**, who dominated much of the valley and its surroundings for several centuries before the Europeans arrived. Until the beginning of this century, they lived on both sides, and the northern **Ilaikipiak** group were a constant threat to caravans coming up from the coast. With European settlement, they were forced from their former grazing grounds in the valley's turbulent bottleneck and confined to the "Southern Reserve" for much of the colonial era. Although many have now returned to the valley, and many towns retain their ancient Maa names, the Maasai are at their most conservative and traditional in southern Kenya, so more background is included in Chapter Five.

In practical terms, the part of the Rift Valley covered in this chapter offers several exceptional **lakes**, a couple of excellent fast roads, lots of spectacular twisting tracks, and some of the wildest country in central Kenya. (The southern regions of the Rift are covered in Chapter One and Chapter Five and the north – Turkana – in Chapter Seven.) If you're at all interested in wildlife, especially birds, you'll find it a source of endless fascination, with wonderful **nature reserves** at **lakes Nakuru** and **Bogoria**, and a freshwater ecosystem at **Baringo**.

Apart from **Nakuru** itself and the string of towns up the western escarpment – **Njoro**, **Elburgon** and **Molo** – the area covered in this chapter contains few places larger than a village: lodgings, strictly speaking, are scarce. Though there is usually

---

ACCOMMODATION PRICE CODES

Rates for a standard double or twin room. For a full explanation of these rates, see p.47.

① Under Ksh500	(under approx £5/$8)	⑥ Ksh6000–9000	(£60–90/$96–144)*
② Ksh500–1000	(£5–10/$8–16)	⑦ Ksh9000–12,000	(£90–120/$144–192)*
③ Ksh1000–2000	(£10–20/$16–32)	⑧ Ksh12,000–16,000	(£120–£160/$192–256)*
④ Ksh2000–4000	(£20–40/$32–64)	⑨ Over Ksh16,000	(over £160/$256)*
⑤ Ksh4000–6000	(£40–60/$64–96)	* = *usually priced in dollars*	

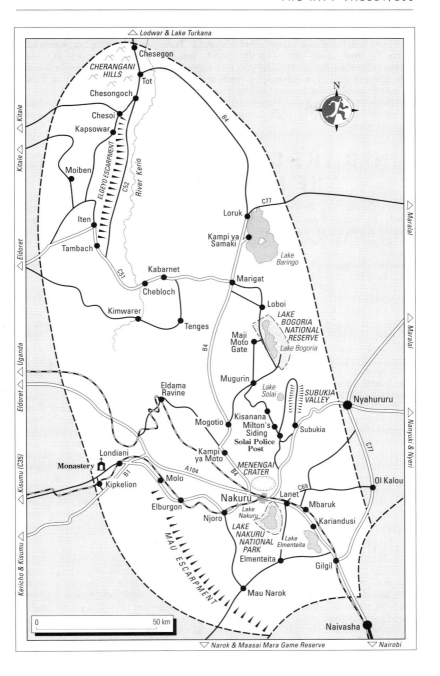

somewhere to lay your head, this is a region where a **tent** will be worth its extra weight, and good walking shoes are an added advantage. **Transport** in the higher, agricultural parts of the south is generally good, but northwards, or off the main Nakuru–Baringo–Kabarnet axis, you can expect long waits, next to no buses and infrequent *matatus*. For **drivers**, the roads are steadily improving in this region, thanks in part to presidential favours earned: the B4 up to Baringo is superb. Note that the northern Rift is lower – and consequently hotter – than most up-country regions, so be prepared for some very **high temperatures** and don't underestimate your **water** requirements.

INTO THE CENTRAL RIFT VALLEY: THE NAKURU DISTRICT

Many travellers' first view of the Rift Valley is from the souvenir-draped **A104 Uplands road**. This barrels through the forests north of Nairobi, crosses a broad, bleak plateau, then flirts with the precipice before following the contours of the slopes above Naivasha and dropping into the Rift. They sell rhubarb up here, as well as plums, carrots and potatoes. In the wet season, you can find yourself driving over a thick, white carpet of hailstones between gloomy conifer plantations. All this contrasts dramatically with the endless, dusty plains below. With binoculars, you can pick out herds of gazelle, Maasai with their cattle and, bizarrely, a satellite-tracking station near the grey cone of Mount Longonot.

The Uplands road is a good one to hitch on, and buses and *matatus* often use it, although the latter, especially Nissans, have some of the most reckless drivers in the country, which is quite something; remember to sit on the left for the best views. If you have a car of your own, you can stop at some of the stands on the roadside: small sheep-skins are often excellent value, but check they have been properly cured; the big woven grass baskets are also worthwhile and surprisingly cheap. Note that the last set of stands in the best location is also the most expensive. More seriously, if you are driving, treat this road as a continuous **black spot** – overtaking can be lethal.

The "**old road**", built by Italian POWs during World War II, runs parallel to and lower than the Uplands road; it's insanely bumpy and narrow and is only used by heavy goods vehicles which in theory are banned from the top road. Corresponding to its lower altitude, vegetation down here takes on a more Mediterranean aspect, candelabra euphorbia and spikey agave predominating. The little **chapel** before the Mai Mahiu junction for Narok, also Italian-built, seems fitting in this scene. Sadly neglected, it's more often used as a pit-stop picnic site.

Whichever road you use, you pass Naivasha and continue, on Kenya's contribution to the Trans-African Highway (a projected paved ribbon joining Lagos with Mombasa), into the central Rift Valley – and the area around lakes Elmenteita and Nakuru.

Gilgil, Elmenteita and Kariandusi

GILGIL – pronounced "Girgir" by many Kenyans – is as dull a town as you could expect to find anywhere: fragile-looking, dusty streets and *dukas* and, on the outskirts, the serried, pastel-coloured ranks of new housing for the hi-tech Gilgil Telecomms Industries workers, who assemble Zebra-brand computers among other things. If you're heading north towards Nyahururu and Maralal, you may well find yourself hitching or changing buses or *matatus* here. The pretty rooms and clean, threadbare beds at the cheap *Salama Lodge* (PO Box 721; ☎0367/2102; ①) can be safely recommended as probably

THE KALENJIN PEOPLES

In this part of the Rift Valley, the **Kalenjin** form the majority of the population. Their name, actually a recent adoption by a number of peoples speaking closely related languages, means "I tell you" in all of them. The principal Kalenjin are the Nandi, Terik, Tugen, Elgeyo, Elkony, Sabaot, Marakwet and Kipsigis, and more contentiously the Pokot. They are some of the earliest inhabitants of Kenya and probably absorbed the early bushmen or pygmy peoples who were here for hundreds of thousands of years before.

Primarily **farmers**, the Kalenjin have often adapted their economies to local circumstances. It is supposed that the first Kalenjin were herdsmen whose lifestyle has changed over the centuries. The pastoral **Pokot** group, who still spurn all kinds of cultivation and despise peoples who rely on anything but livestock, call the **Marakwet**, living against the western Rift escarpment, *Cheblong* (the Poor), for their lack of cattle.

The **Okiek** (Ndorobo) are another interesting clue to the past: these hunter-gatherers are a Kalenjin-speaking people, living in scattered groups in the forests of the high slopes flanking the Rift. Unlike most hunter-gatherers, they do very little gathering. Meat, and honey from their hives, are the traditional staples. They consider wild fruits and vegetables barely palatable, though cornmeal and gardening have been introduced, and they now keep some domestic animals too. They may be the descendants of Kalenjin forebears who lost (or ate) their herds: there are other groups in Kenya who live mostly by hunting – Ndorobo or Wanderoo – for whom such a background is very likely, and who are all gradually abandoning their old lifestyles and dislikes to the inexorable advance of "civilization".

Many of the mainstream Kalenjin played key roles in the founding of the Kenya African Democratic Union (KADU – now disbanded), but the most famous of their number in recent years has been President Moi, a **Tugen** from Baringo district. Coming from a small ethnic group, his presidency for years avoided the accusations of tribalism levelled so bitterly against Kenyatta, and he still devotes time to touring the country, holding *Harambee* meetings and spurring development. In the run-up to the 1992 elections, however, what had long been muttered about became increasingly obvious: the country was not being run for the benefit of all. The president's firm grip on the reins of power was being exercised through the Kalenjin-dominated civil service rather than the more ethnically mixed cabinet. This fact, coupled with the "ethnic cleansing" in the Rift Valley of non-Kalenjin by groups of surprisingly well-organized young men (widespread evictions from Rift Valley villages, the burning of compounds and several hundred people killed) fulfilled the president's own prophecy that multi-partyism would do nothing to harmonize tribal relations in the country. The same story repeated itself in the run-up to the 1997 elections, with Kikuyu the main victims, although the difference this time was that an enquiry was set up into the "tribal" conflicts in order to investigate cases and finger culprits for prosecution, including some high-up government officials accused of having organized and financed the clashes.

the best in town, which in Gilgil is not saying much. Otherwise, try *Sakima Silent Lodge* (no phone; ①) which isn't silent, or the *Mugoira B&L* (☎0367/5404; ①), cleaner, and with a slightly less raucous bar. Water supplies seem problematic, but in Gilgil maybe you should just count your blessings. The town has a post office (Mon–Fri 8am–1pm & 2–5pm), a bank and several car mechanics and petrol stations, but not much else. For details of a wonderful cycling or driving route around the area, see the box on p.237.

Gilgil War Cemetery

En route to Nyahururu – "T Falls" if it slips off the tongue more easily – you'll pass **Gilgil Commonwealth War Cemetery**. If you've a couple of hours to spare, walk the 2–3km out of town into the quiet, breezy savannah and have a look: it's a good place to stop for a picnic and some moments of contemplation before flagging down a vehicle.

There are about two hundred graves here from the East African campaign of World War II and from the War for Independence – "the Emergency" – in the 1950s. Whether by accident (which doesn't seem credible) or design, the African graves are all at the bottom of the slope, and record no personal details apart from name and rank. The graves of British soldiers are higher up and the stones inscribed with family messages. Most are from World War II, but there are also poignant reminders of lives lost between 1959 and 1962, after the British government's futile attempt to prevent the inevitable (see p.609). The fact that not a single freedom fighter is buried here demonstrates the ambivalent attitude of Kenyans to their struggle for *Uhuru*. The Gilgil cemetery, one of over forty in Kenya tended by the Commonwealth War Graves Commission, is lovingly maintained, one of the most meticulously kept in the country.

The road climbs past *Gilgil Country Club* on through moorland and conifer plantations around the resettlement zone of Ol Kalou, where some of the most violent Mau Mau attacks took place, and over the equator to Nyahururu (p.228), Kenya's highest town.

Lake Elmenteita

Beyond the turn for Gilgil, the fast road sweeps the eastern wall of the Rift Valley and pushes up high above **Lake Elmenteita**. It's a spectacular and primeval setting, framed by the broken caldera walls of several extinct volcanoes, which resemble a reclined human figure – the Maasai know these peaks as Elngiragata Olmorani (Sleeping Warrior); this name is ironically fitting, since the lake and its lands were expropriated from the Maasai at the start of the colonial period by Lord Delamere (the caldera is now also known as "Delamere's Nose"). You can get a good view from the big "parking lane" viewpoint – if you survive the rather desperate assaults from the curio sellers. This shallow soda lake, which shrivelled to a huge white salt pond as recently as 1985, is a good site for flamingos when Lake Nakuru is out of favour, and always good for pelican: there are an estimated 300 bird species in all. Like Lake Nakuru, Elmenteita has no outflow, and so its accumulated alkaline salts make it uninhabitable for all but one species of fish, *tilapia grahami*. The lake once had a herd of hippos, but the droughts pushed them back to Lake Naivasha and they seem unlikely ever to return.

There are two top-notch establishments offering **accommodation** on the lakeshore. *Delamere's Camp* (reservations through Savannah Camps & Lodges, address p.50; FB ⑨). A luxury tented camp within the private acacia-woodland **Soysambu Wildlife Sanctuary**, this is highly recommended for enthusiastic amateur naturalists and birdwatchers alike. To get there, turn right off the Naivasha–Nakuru road at the signpost for Kasambara, take the right fork immediately, and the entrance is 1km further on, followed by 2km of rough track. The price includes day and night game drives (and a possible poke around "Delamere's Nose") and as many, excellently guided, wildlife walks as you like (transport is also available). The setting is wonderful, with a lawn dropping down to the lakeshore (afternoon tea is taken there), and a spectacular view of the Sleeping Warrior and Mau Escarpment over the far side of the lake. Service is excellent, and there are even tame ostrich to feed. If you've really got money to burn, enquire about their treehouse accommodation, on the far side of the lake, which occasionally attracts leopard. The *Lake Elementeita Lodge* (PO Box 561 Nakuru; reservations through *Lake Nakuru Lodges*, 2nd floor, Arrow House, Koinange St, PO Box 70559 Nairobi; ☎02/212405, fax 227062; HB ⑤ low, ⑥ high; FB ⑥ low, ⑦ high). Much more affordable and less fancy than *Delamere's Camp*, this ranch-style lodge, built around the 1930s brick homestead of the cattle farmer Lord Cole, has equally jaw-dropping views, but the disadvantage of being some distance above the lake (a track leads down to it). There's a resident naturalist, a pool, and a very good restaurant. A hundred metres down the driveway from the main road is the **Ostrich Park Farm** (Ksh100), which provides amusing entertainment for kids.

Most of the land around the lake is part of the private (and fenced-in) Delamere Estate's Soysambu property. Its southeastern corner, however, is public land, accessible through *Lake Elementeita Lodge* (free entry; see below), and apparently also via a track from the viewpoint lay-by: clear it with anyone you come across down there. Around the once-lush shores are a number of prehistoric sites. **Gambles cave**, 10km southwest of Elmenteita village at Eburru, is the most famous; if you're an enthusiast, you can visit it by making arrangements ahead of time – ask first at the National Museum in Nairobi (see p.107).

Digs and mines: Kariandusi

For an easier shot of prehistory, try a visit to **Kariandusi**, with a surprising sideshow in the shape of a neighbouring diatomite mine. Kariandusi (signposted off the main A104 highway, 1.5km to the right or twenty minutes' walk; daily 8am–6pm; Ksh200, children Ksh100) is an **Acheulian site** characterized, like Olorgasailie (p.179), by heavy hand-axes and cleavers. The site is very small, consisting of just two excavated areas cleared

---

RIFT VALLEY SIDE TRACKS

Between Gilgil and Nakuru, if you're hiking – or driving or cycling with a few hours to spare – give the fast (but by no means smooth and occasionally unnerving) main A104 a miss and follow the tarmac **former route** which mostly runs parallel to the new road a few hundred metres off on the right-hand side. The old road, lightly potholed in parts, but quite negotiable, is almost unused by vehicles and serves as a rural footpath for people carrying firewood or cycling to the next hamlet.

You can join the old road at Gilgil by turning off the main highway at the junction 26.5km from Naivasha (Gilgil itself isn't signposted, though Gilgil Telecomms Industries and a host of schools and other places are). Go right through the quiet businesses and petrol stations of Gilgil and you arrive, 4km to the north of the town, at a fine viewpoint over Lake Elmenteita. Shortly after, on the right, you pass the obscure little **Church of Goodwill** – a settler's sentimental folly – still used on Sundays – in whose small grave-yard rest the remains of a few old colonials and military men.

Shortly after the church, you pass Kariandusi prehistoric site and, rounding a bend, the diatomite mine (both left). Between the two, by the crash barriers to the right, a pale-coloured, rocky, 4WD track leads, in 3km, up over the railway line to a stream. Here you can leave your vehicle and climb (guided by the usual retinue of boys) to a crystal-clear, **warm-water source** in the woods – known, blandly enough, as *maji moto* (meaning "hot water"). You can swim in the natural swimming pool – there are usually people about, washing clothes or bathing. Beyond the Kariandusi junction, the old road dries up and you have to rejoin the highway. You can get onto the quiet road again at the turning to "Mbaruk", 3km further on, then follow the railway to Lanet, a suburb of Nakuru.

If you want to take further time out and see a remote part of the Central Province highlands, take a right turn off the old road, 4km after the "Mbaruk" turning and follow the steep dirt road under the railway bridge and steeply up to the **Mbaruk Valley**. This is a beautiful road, rugged in parts (again, you're best off with 4WD) but with splendid compensation in the lush, forested cliffs across its far side. There's even a little **waterfall** 3km along the way, though it's easy to miss unless it's in spate. At the Ngorika cross-roads (tasty chapatis are provided at the *hoteli* on the corner) turn left and you hit the tarmac C69 after 6km, where, turning left again, you start to make a fine, looping descent to the Rift Valley floor, with distinctive flat-topped acacias between the sloping *shambas* and the glint of Lake Nakuru down in the distance.

To follow this route in the other direction, Nairobi-bound, take the left turning for the C69 immediately before the Lanet Esso petrol station, before you reach the railway bridge bend.

by Louis Leakey in 1928–31 and 1947, each displaying a scattered assortment of stone tools, many of them made of the black glassy volcanic rock, obsidian. The guide is knowledgeable, and there's a small **museum** too, which explains the formation of the Rift Valley, and has comparative skull specimens of our various distant ancestors.

Neither Kariandusi nor Olorgasailie have any signs of permanent habitation. This, and the fact that some 120,000 years ago Lake Elmenteita came right up to here, some 180m higher than its present level and contained fresh water, suggests that it attracted hunter gatherers who would wait by the water to catch animals coming to drink. Tools were made on the spot, and simply left for the next occasion, as the Acheulians had yet to invent receptacles to carry them in. As the lake levels fluctuated, many tools were covered by it, and as the waters receded again, were then carried by streams to their present concentrated clusters (some of the tools have been "rolled" by abrasive action, which supports this theory). Nothing much is known about the tool-makers themselves, apart from the fact that they obviously had a formidable grip. The most likely candidate is *Homo erectus*, an early hominid whose remains have been found at Olduvai Gorge in Tanzania alongside Acheulian artefacts, but the puzzle is that the site bears no evidence of fire, nor of combination tools (for example stone axes with wooden handles), nor of carrying receptacles, which *Homo erectus* is generally known for. This would suggest that the tool-makers were a primitive version of *Homo erectus*.

The diatomite industry

Right next door, just 800m from the highway, is a **diatomite mine** (Diatomite Industries, PO Box 32 Gilgil; ☎0367/2097), which is a fascinating complement to the prehistoric site. Diatomite is a light, white, crumbly rock composed of the compressed silica skeletons of microscopic sea organisms (diatoms). The Kikuyu used it as body paint (*karia andus*), and a "clean" variety of it is still eaten by pregnant women and sick children (it's full of calcium). It also makes an excellent filter and absorbs water like silica gel. Brewers use it for filtration and it makes an effective insecticide in grain silos by dehydrating the weevils without poisoning the grain.

The manager will gladly tell you more about diatomite, but the real excitement comes when you walk down into the mine itself: they're happy to receive visitors. A track spirals down the inside of a giant bowl, scooped out of the ground by pick and shovel over the last fifty years. Before digging stopped, they reached a level, about 50m down, where a high-grade, brilliant white diatomite is found. Here, a dozen or more **tunnels** dive into the cliffs to form a maze of ghostly subterranean passages, almost architectural in design and home to thousands of fluttering **bats**. The tunnels are wonderfully cool and vents keep the air circulating. You'll be assured that the structure of diatomite makes rock falls extremely unlikely, but a number of shored-up passageways may leave you unconvinced and glad to have along an accounts clerk – or some other conscripted employee – to guide you. You need a torch even though the light goes in a surprisingly long way, but you can't really get lost.

Mining is still carried out on a small scale, using picks and shovels, though the principal source is now an open-cast pit nearer Lake Elmenteita. The whole place has a somewhat archaic air about it, but an ancient, rusting kiln is periodically fired up to dry the diatomite for packing.

Nakuru and nearby sites

As you approach **NAKURU** along the main highway from Nairobi, the *shamba*- and conifer-cloaked mound directly ahead is the southern flank of Menengai crater, while to the left are the scrub-covered eastern heights of the Nakuru National Park.

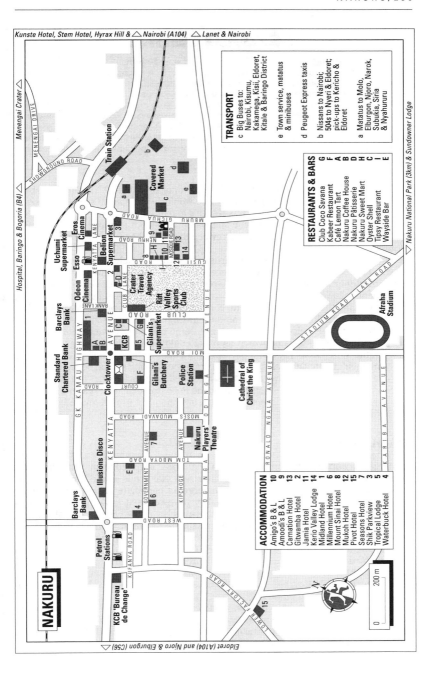

NAKURU

Kunste Hotel, Stem Hotel, Hyrax Hill & △ Nairobi (A104)   △ Lanet & Nairobi

△ Menengai Crater

△ Hospital, Baringo & Bogoria (B4)

SHOWGROUND ROAD

MENENGAI DRIVE

Train Station

Covered Market

Eros Cinema

Uchumi Supermarket

Belion Supermarket

Odeon Cinema

Esso

Barclays Bank

Standard Chartered Bank

Crater Travel Agency

Riff Valley Sports Club

Clocktower

Gilani's Supermarket

Illusions Disco

Gilani's Butchery

Police Station

Nakuru Players' Theatre

Barclays Bank

Petrol Stations

KCB 'Bureau de Change'

KENYATTA AVENUE

GK KAMAU HIGHWAY

KUFANYA ROAD

WEST ROAD

GOVERNMENT AVENUE

TOM MBOYA ROAD

KIPCHOGE

OGINGA ODINGA AVENUE

MOI ROAD

GUSII ROAD

MOSQUE ROAD

NEHRU ROAD

GICHUA ROAD

MBURU ROAD

CLUB ROAD

CLUB AVENUE

BANK LANE

KENYATTA LANE

COURT ROAD

MUDAVADI ROAD

MOSES ROAD

RONALD NGALA AVENUE

STADIUM ROAD / LAKE ROAD

KARIBA AVENUE

LOWER FACTORY ROAD

VICTORY ROAD

Cathedral of Christ the King

Afraha Stadium

▽ Nakuru National Park (3km) & Sundowner Lodge

△ Eldoret (A104) and Njoro & Elburgon (C56)

N

0   200 m

TRANSPORT

c Big Buses to: Nairobi, Kisumu, Kakamega, Kisii, Eldoret, Kitale & Baringo District

e Town service, matatus & minibuses

d Peugeot Express taxis

b Nissans to Nairobi; 504s to Nyeri & Eldoret; pick-ups to Kericho & Eldoret

a Matatus to Molo, Elburgon, Njoro, Narok, Subukia, Siria & Nyahururu

RESTAURANTS & BARS

Club Coco Savana	G
Kabeer Restaurant	F
Café Lemon Tart	A
Nakuru Coffee House	B
Nakuru Pâtisserie	D
Nakuru Sweet Mart	H
Oyster Shell	C
Tipsy Restaurant	I
Wayside Bar	E

ACCOMMODATION

Amigo's B & L	10
Amoodi's B & L	9
Carnation Hotel	13
Gitwamba Hotel	2
Jamia Hotel	11
Kerio Valley Lodge	14
Midland Hotel	1
Millennium Hotel	8
Mount Sinai Hotel	12
Mukoh Hotel	15
Pivot Hotel	7
Seasons Hotel	3
Shik Parkview	5
Tropical Lodge	4
Waterbuck Hotel	

ROADSIDE RIP-OFFS

A word of **warning**: if you're driving, beware of anyone around Nakuru telling you there's anything wrong with your car – this is the con-mechanic capital of Kenya. **Tricksters** hang around along the roadside either between Lanet and the town centre or between the town centre and the national park main gate, and have recently also been seen along the road to Eldoret. They work in teams, pointing one after another at your wheels as you drive past, or, if you stop anywhere, "discovering" oil dripping from your engine – anything to get you into their garage for a bogus repair job. Gangs have recently taken to placing large rocks across already badly pot-holed stretches of highway (especially between Nakuru and Eldoret), forcing you to slow right down: ignore their demands to stop.

Were it not for the fact that Nakuru is a major transport hub and has a national park even closer to its centre than Nairobi's, there would be no special reason to visit. A noisy, dusty and hustly town, Nakuru is Kenya's fourth largest city (though it projects a noticeably busier and more energetic image than Kisumu, the third); it is also capital of the enormous, sprawling Rift Valley Province that stretches from the Sudanese border to the slopes of Kilimanjaro.

Nakuru came into existence on the thrust of the Uganda railway and owed its early growth, at least in part, to **Lord Delamere**, the colony's most famous figure. In 1903, he acquired four hundred square kilometres of land on the lower slopes of the Mau escarpment, followed by two hundred more at Soysambu, on the other side of the lake. Eager to share the empty vistas with compatriots – though preferably with other Cheshire or Lancashire men – he promoted in England the mile-square plots being offered free by the Foreign Office. Eventually, some two hundred new settler families arrived and Nakuru – a name which as usual could mean various things, including "Place of the Waterbuck" (Swahili) and "Swirling Dust" or "Little Soda Lake" (Maasai) – became their country capital. It lies on the unprepossessing steppe between the lake and the flanks of Menengai crater. This desolate shelf has a nickname: "the place where the cows won't eat grass" (the pasture was found to be iron-deficient). Farmers near the town turned to the better prospects of pyrethrum, the plant used to make insecticide, as a cash crop.

Nakuru town

Still largely a workaday farmers' town, with unadorned old seed shops and veterinary paraphernalia much in evidence on the main street, Nakuru is a little Nairobi without the flashy veneer, its streets frequently undergoing ear-shattering repairs. Ongoing outbursts of ethnic violence in the Rift Valley have resulted in an influx of Kikuyu refugees from outlying parts of the province: it is, in many ways, more of a social barometer than Nairobi. The town can appear intimidating at first, especially if you arrive in the evening, and the beggars and street kids, many sniffing poppers and other solvents, are amongst the most pitiful you will ever see. Since it's a stone's throw from **Nakuru National Park**, equally close to the prehistoric settlement site at **Hyrax Hill** and the vast bowl of the **Menengai crater**, and the jumping-off point for trips down into the **northern Rift Valley**, you may find yourself passing through Nakuru more often than you'd like.

The town has some positive aspects, worth emphasizing if you're staying. The **market**, certainly, is animated and a pleasure to look around, though has its fair share of hassle. And there's a glimmer of charm still remaining in its colonnaded old streets and the **jacaranda**-brushed lined avenues at the edge of town.

Accommodation

The **train** and **bus/matatu stations** are packed together at the east end of town with **lodgings** all around: watch yourself at the bus and *matatu* enclosures, and if you need directions ask a driver or passenger. You're spoilt for choice for **cheap rooms**, with plenty of other places apart from the following found in the centre, though few of them stand out. A number of **mid-range hotels** are dotted about the western avenues, and are amazingly good value if you've just come from Nairobi. However, the sewers there can turn even the hardiest stomachs, and the distantly throbbing noise from the *Millennium Hotel* nightclub is also a nuisance. At the luxury end there's nothing at all in Nakuru: most of the thousands of tourists on their way to the park stay in one of the two lodges there.

If you're **camping**, either go to the National Park (see p.246) or try out the campsite about 7km up the B4 Baringo road, which provides great views of the town and the lake. It's well signposted and has clean long-drops and showers with hot water to order. There's another good campsite 17km back down the Nairobi road, a ten-minute walk off the road, and a similar distance from Lanet Gate, in the unlikely location of Greensteds School (☎0161/85224 or 85344). Turn off at the signs for the school and "The Battery Centre". There are good views, hot showers, a cheap bar filled with teachers on Fridays, and a bore hole which supplies drinking water. From the main road it's a ten-minute walk to the school gate.

CHEAP AND MID-RANGE LODGINGS

Amigo's B&L, Gusii Rd (PO Box 1461; ☎037/210170). This is one of the most popular cheapies, recently extended – a very basic secure lodging with a nice welcome, though rather dirty. The water, when there is any, is hot. ①–②.

Amoodi's B&L, Nehru Rd (PO Box 1731; ☎037/41939). A no-frills B&L with excellent security, plenty of hot water, clean toilets and the cheapest twin beds in town, in shoe-box rooms. ①.

Carnation Hotel, Mosque Rd, 1st floor (PO Box 1620; ☎037/43522). A large but well-run and attentive establishment – the best in the town centre and very fair value, and with a good restaurant. The waiters are keen to persuade you to go on a park trip. ③.

Gitwamba Hotel, Gusii Rd (PO Box 586; ☎037/40754). One of the best joints in this quarter of town, with light, clean and roomy s/c and non-s/c accommodation, though it's raucous on disco nights – Wednesday and Friday–Sunday – and there's a *matatu* stage opposite. Good cheap breakfasts. ①.

Kerio Valley Lodge, Gusii Rd (PO Box 2432; ☎037/41242). Simple non-s/c rooms in a quiet courtyard, and cheap. Hot water in the mornings. ①.

Mt Sinai Hotel, Gusii Rd (PO Box 238; ☎037/21779). Nakuru's best cheapie, opposite the coffinmakers. Great staff, good security and cool, functional rooms; restaurant down below. A tad overpriced. ②.

Mukoh Hotel, Gusii Rd (PO Box 238; ☎037/213516). Rather shambling place with 56 s/c and non-s/c rooms, those over the courtyard baptized daily by the Christco Fellowship gospel choir next door. Beds spotless, toilets less so. Overpriced. ②.

Pivot Hotel, Lower Factory Rd (PO Box 1369; ☎037/210226). Despite resembling a military hospital in every aspect, this is recommended: the rooms are shiny clean and have new mosquito nets. Go for rooms 1–15 to avoid the deafening disco din on some weekend nights. ②.

Seasons Hotel, Government Ave (PO Box 3163; ☎037/211986). Decent enough rooms – all self-contained – but dark and overpriced. ②.

Shik Parkview Hotel, Kenyatta Ave (PO Box 614; ☎037/212345 or 212346). Seventy-two rooms, clean and airy but on the small side. Separate bar and restaurant. The Nakuru Chess Club is resident upstairs (Wednesday and Friday 5pm, Sunday 2pm). ①.

Tropical Lodge, Moi Rd (PO Box 4193; ☎037/42608). A presentable, if rather gloomy, option with rooms big enough to swing several cats in and hot water morning and evening, but dirty bathrooms – wear the flip-flops they provide. ①.

Wayside Bar, Tom Mboya Rd (PO Box 1308; ☎037/215843). One of Nakuru's best music venues also has some s/c rooms, ideal after a night's cavorting, less so if you need a decent dose of shut-eye. ②.

MORE EXPENSIVE HOTELS

Kunste Hotel, 2.5 km down the Nairobi road (PO Box 1369; ☎037/212140). A good new hotel with sensibly priced rooms, but sometimes near deserted. They may allow camping. B&B ③.

Midland Hotel, GK Kamau Highway (PO Box 908; ☎037/212125, fax 44517). Long-established and good value – basically a huge pub with rooms, all of which are s/c and comfy, if a tad gloomy. The old wing (no TVs), refurbished in 1997, is much more pleasant. Two bars, both open until midnight. Good disabled access. B&B ③-④.

Stem Hotel, Nairobi road, close to the Nakuru National Park Lanet Gate, 8km from the town centre (PO Box 1076; ☎037/85391, fax 212332). Pleasant (in a functional, motel manner), with a small pool, gym, steam room and sauna (Ksh80–200 per hour), acceptable s/c rooms, and good Indian *Mughlai* food (try the biriani). They also provide transport into the National Park (Ksh5000 per minibus). They normally allow camping. However, the bar gets busy (and noisy) at weekends, and as with all highway motels, it's advisable to lock your door at night. B&B ④.

Sundowner Lodge, 1km down Kanu St off Lake Rd, in Langa Langa suburb (PO Box 561; ☎037/214216, fax 211204). Reasonable little place, run by the management of *Lake Nakuru Lodge*, but overpriced. Saturday's "Africa Nite" is a disco with traditional dancers and acrobats. B&B ④.

Waterbuck Hotel, West Rd (PO Box 3327; ☎037/215672, fax 214163). As the town centre's most prominent hotel this seems to be the current "upmarket" choice, although it looks like an army barracks. It does a respectable and very reasonably priced buffet lunch, and the breakfasts are huge, but the accommodation is overrated if cheap. It also has a new but rather dusty *nyama choma* joint round the back. Safe parking. ③.

Eating, drinking and entertainment

Finding good **meals** is getting easier in Nakuru: as a guide, older, more down-at-heel establishments are bunched towards the east end of town near the railway station, while the west end, especially along Kenyatta Avenue, tends to be more upmarket.

RESTAURANTS

Kabeer Restaurant, Government Ave. Very relaxing place for a substantial feed – Indian or Chinese as well as seafood – at around Ksh300; lunch curries Ksh240.

Nakuru Sweet Mart, Gusii Rd. A long-established Indian eatery which does an excellent and massive vegetarian *thali*, and a good range of breads. Very cheap.

Oyster Shell Restaurant, Club Rd/Kenyatta Ave, 1st floor. Magnificent dinners for under Ksh500, breakfast around Ksh200. Great service and atmosphere – real flowers and similar touches – although the dinner ambience can be marred by the *XTC Discotheque* upstairs.

Railway Station Restaurant. An utterly time-warped retreat, though service is very slow, rather like the trains. They used to silver-serve cornflakes and toast for breakfast, and still do immaculately served (though no less gastronomically uncreative) colonial repasts at lunch and dinner. Around Ksh200.

Tipsy Restaurant, Gusii Rd. Next door and similar to, but cheaper than, *Nakuru Sweet Mart*, and for the less hungry.

SNACKS AND BARS

Café Lemon Tart, Moi Rd. For snacks or breakfast this is hard to beat.

Jamia Hotel, Mosque Rd, next to the mosque. Nothing outstanding, but open 24 hours.

Millennium Hotel, Government Ave. Quite a pleasant beer garden and *nyama choma* joint – not a hotel – with thatched huts, wicker chairs and a wicked sound system.

Nakuru Coffee House, Moi Rd. A reliable venue for real coffee and a bite to eat.

Waterbuck Hotel, West Rd. A good snack menu all day, and a lively bar on Saturday nights.

FOOD SHOPPING

If you're passing through in your own car, check the Sita Supermarket for **food supplies**, at the Sita shopping centre a few kilometres east of the town centre on the

Nairobi road (the *Have More Restaurant* here is a good snack bar), or the shopping centre 4km west of town on the Kisumu road. The best supermarket in town is the main Uchumi on Kenyatta Lane, just off GK Kamau Highway (Mon–Sat 9.30am–8pm, Sun 9.30am–2pm). A smaller grocery is Gilani's on Club Road, while Gilani's Butchery on Moi Road has a good **cheese** counter where you can count on getting the cheap and excellent McLellan's Farmhouse brie-style rounds. *Nakuru Patisserie* on Club Lane has a wholesome selection of **bread** and baked bites. The main **produce market**, near the transport parks and railway station, has the full display of fruit and vegetables, but watch out for pickpockets and petty thieves.

ENTERTAINMENT AND NIGHTLIFE
Nakuru is surprisingly jumping when it comes to nightlife. The **nightspot** of the moment, eclipsing *Illusions Disco*, is *Club Coco Savana* on Club Road, open nightly (Ksh50–100), with a jam session on Sundays, a good restaurant next door, but nasty loos. Slightly less steamy are the famous weekend discos at the *Pivot Hotel* – their music is not at all bad – and the glitzy *XTC Discotheque*, above the *Oyster Shell Restaurant*. *Wayside Bar* on Tom Mboya Street is hot on Lingala and Kikuyu sounds, with its resident Kilimanjaro Sound Band and others at the weekends, and has a pleasant terrace bar and *nyama choma*. Also worth checking out for live bands are *Hotel Jams*, next to Afraha Stadium (especially Fridays), and **Club Sulwe** on Kenyatta Avenue. If you're in town for more than a day you may get the chance to see the Nakuru Players in action at their dour-looking **theatre** (☎037/40805) on Kipchoge Avenue. Of the two main **cinemas**, the *Odeon* and the *Eros*, both on GK Kamau Highway, the smaller *Eros* (screenings daily 6pm & 9pm, plus Saturday 3pm) is the more inviting.

Listings

Banks Scattered all over the town: there's a KCB with a "Bureau de Change" flagged on the western outskirts. All Mon–Fri 9am–3pm & Sat 9–11am; both Standard Chartered at Moi Rd, and Barclays on Kenyatta Ave, have ATMs.

Books Ereto Bookshop, Kenyatta Lane, has a good range of African writers.

Car repairs If you really do have a problem, try and find out exactly what it is before approaching the myriad workshops at the western ends of Government and Kipchoge avenues. Get quotes from several places before bringing your vehicle down. Hertz recommend CMC Motors Group (☎037/211875–7) or D.T. Dobie (☎037/211775–7), both on George Morara Ave.

Hair-braiding Try Penny Classic, next door to Eros Cinema on GK Kamau Highway (Mon–Sat 9am–6pm; ☎037/45985).

Medical clinic Nakuru Medical Clinics, by Barclays on Kenyatta Ave (☎037/214655), have a range of specialists.

Music If you want to beef up your cassette collection, there are a number of cassette shops on Nehru Rd.

Parking This can be something of a problem, with a high chance of break-ins, dripping-oil scams and the like. Whether you're staying the night or not, the best plan is to park in a guarded hotel parking area – absolutely essential if all your luggage is inside. A small tip for the *askari* is normally expected.

Pharmacy A proficient one is Medika Chemists, 1st floor Equator House, Kenyatta Lane, next door to Uchimi (☎037/214847).

Post office Moi Rd/Kenyatta Ave (Mon–Fri 8am–5.30pm & Sat 9am–noon), with good telephone and fax facilities, and an EMS express mail counter round the back.

Travel agents Crater Travel, Inder Singh Building, just off Kenyatta Ave (PO Box 2631; ☎037/214896, fax 215019), offers a full service for air ticketing, plus the usual range of (expensive) tour deals. Tayler's Travel, on Kenyatta Avenue itself (PO Box 527; ☎037/45806, fax 212912) has a reputation for reliable hotel bookings, but doesn't accept Visa cards. For general local arrangements, especially Nakuru National Park visits and other safaris, Blackbird Tours at the *Carnation*

Hotel (PO Box 4162; ☎037/45383, fax 210350) are friendly and competent: fees are generally per vehicle, and so work out cheaper if you can form a group, but they're open to discussion. Current going rates are Ksh3000 for the use of a four-seater Suzuki, including the driver-guide but excluding park fees, for 5–6hr, and Ksh5000 for the use of a seven-seater Nissan minibus. They're happy to pick you up from your hotel.

Moving on from Nakuru

Travel options **from Nakuru** are wide open. You're less than two hours from Nairobi – a journey as easy to hitch as any in the country. The train is inconsiderate of sightseeing and leaves at night, so the climb up the escarpment isn't an attraction.

Heading the other way, the **bus** lines all run regular and frequent services to Eldoret, Kisumu, Kitale, Kisii and other points west (Akamba Bus is safest; ☎037/213775–6). Alternatively, you can take the quieter road west, through the highland towns of Njoro, Elburgon and Molo, a route covered in this chapter on p.251. Southwards, you can get to Narok by **matatu** up the fantastic Mau escarpment (not a great distance, but allow the day to arrive). The most obvious destinations – in this chapter – are further north in the Rift Valley, around lakes Baringo and Bogoria especially, with at least two buses daily to Kampi ya Samaki at Lake Baringo and *matatus* making the run to Kabarnet in the hills to the west. There's also a lavishly scenic route to Nyahururu through the Subukia Valley, an ascent of the Rift that, for sheer grandeur, comes close to the Naivasha escarpment (daily bus and *matatu* runs). If you're driving, the turn-off 2.5km down the Nairobi road is not signposted – turn left at the Shell petrol station opposite *Kunste* hotel. A useful tip when entering Nakuru **bus station** from the railway station side is to go in via "Exit" to avoid the bevy of enthusiastic touts who hang around at "Entrance".

Menengai crater

Containing an enormous caldera, 12km across and nearly 500m deep in places, the extinct volcanic giant **Menengai** rises directly behind Nakuru, its sloping mass somehow not especially noticeable from the town. To reach it, head up Menengai Drive and take the fourth left turn (Crater Climb) through the modestly affluent suburbs above the town. Some 4.5km up the hill you come to a sign referring to a Campsite and Picnic Area, but no evidence of either. You could presumably camp by the trees here and get water from nearby houses, but you'd be ill-advised to leave your tent unattended and you should bring food. Half a kilometre away is a telecommunications tower: head for this then turn right, following the path through a fragrant forest of gum trees for twenty minutes, to a fire lookout tower on the bare cliff. From the top of this, the massive crater spreads out beneath you, a spectacular sea of bush-covered lava, its black waves frozen solid.

The crater was the site of a battle in which the Ilpurko Maasai defeated the Ilaikipiak, whom they considered upstarts disrespectful to Batian, the *laibon* (paramount chief) of the time after whom the highest peak of Mount Kenya was named. At intervals throughout the nineteenth century, these **Maasai civil wars** flared up over the issue of true Maasai identity: in this case, it was not simply a matter of honour but also of grazing rights in the Rift Valley, especially around Lake Naivasha and on the scarp slopes. The Ilpurko were herders, while the Ilaikipiak from the north grew crops as well. Both had been preparing for battle for some time and it is said that hundreds of Ilaikipiak *morani* were hurled over the crater rim to their deaths. The place retains a sinister reputation – even the normally fearless Maasai traditionally have it as the dwelling place of devils and other evil – and local people prefer not to go near the edge.

A century later, on the highest point of this windy crest, the Rotary Club erected one of their familiar hyperbolic signposts, laden with multiple pointers. Apart from informing you that Nairobi is 140km away and Rome 5997km in the opposite direction, it also points out that the crater wall is 2272m above sea level and its area some 90 square kilometres – the whole dramatic extent of which you can see. You'll get fantastic views over Lake Nakuru if you walk down the dirt road along the south side of the gum-tree plantation.

From Nakuru town centre it's about an eight-kilometre (three-hour) hike to the crater rim; on weekends, you might be lucky and get a lift, but there's no public transport. Taxis will take you of course. If you walk, you're best advised to go up in company.

Hyrax Hill

Hyrax Hill (daily 9.30am–6pm; Ksh200) is an easy target, 3.5km out of town, just to the left of the Nairobi road. *Matatus* bound for Lanet and Gilgil will drop you at the turn, then it's a two-kilometre walk to the small museum where you pay your fee. If you're driving, don't be misled by the sign next to the *Kunste Hotel* which appears to indicate a left turn here (the Subukia/Nyahururu road): it's about a kilometre further to the entrance track. The hill, named for the hyraxes which once scampered over it, has been a settlement site for at least three thousand years, and finds here date from the Neolithic period. It was discovered by Louis Leakey in 1926, excavated by Mary Leakey in 1937–38 and by others in 1965, 1973 and 1987. There's an excellent guide booklet (1983) on sale in the museum and a reprint of the paper in the journal *Azania* describing the most recent excavations. You can normally **camp** here, free or for a small fee (staff facilities only).

The Northeast Village

The path leading out to the right of the museum winds its way around the north side of the hill to an excavated pit dwelling, or at any rate a "sunken enclosure", with baulks left in place to show the depth of material that was removed during the digging. There are thirteen similar depressions in this **"Northeast Village"** (curiously named, as it is in the northwest) but it's uncertain exactly how they were used. They have yielded a tremendous quantity of pottery shards, tools made from flakes of obsidian and animal-bone fragments, but the absence of post-holes normally needed to support a roof suggests they may have been shelters for livestock rather than humans. Just as plausibly, a roof might have been added whenever needed, leaving no trace, and animals and people may have shared the shelters. The floor of the pit has been left exposed and is littered with stones and obsidian chips. Several reconstructed examples of the site's characteristic late Iron Age pottery (the Iron Age in Kenya essentially continued until the twentieth century) are displayed in the museum.

Excavations at Hollow F have discovered the floors of three oblong **houses**, facing onto the main pit, with rather frail foundations, suggesting a kind of lean-to or bender. This research, which included radiocarbon dating showing occupation of different hollows from something like 1100 to 1500 AD, led to the conjecture that the "village" had not all been occupied at the same time, but that pits and attached houses would be used for a number of seasons until uninhabitable, then abandoned for a newly built area nearby. Far from being a community, this could have been the home base of a single family, or even just an occasional encampment in the seasonal cycle.

It is believed the inhabitants would have been semi-nomadic Sirikwa- or Kalenjin-speaking herders. Today, Kalenjin-speakers mostly live further west, but they're associated with so-called pit-dwellings elsewhere (see "In Search of the Sirikwa Holes", p.268) and, in the case of Hyrax Hill, they may have been forced to flee by an expanding Maasai population from the north.

The fort and burial sites

Following the path towards the top of the hill, you come to an exposed **"fort"** facing out towards Nakuru, which consists of a circle of hefty boulders enclosing a flattened area.

Said to have been an Iron Age lookout post, there's no way of being certain what this actually was, nor even how old it might be, since no artefacts have been found. From the fort, you can scramble over the volcanic boulders – the whole hill is a tongue of Menengai's lava – to the summit, where you get a good view of the southern part of the site and the lake. Now several kilometres away, the lake once extended, probably as fresh water, right to the base of the hill and across much of the Rift Valley, turning Hyrax Hill into a peninsula or even an island.

A hundred metres down the hillside you come to more Iron Age pits and a **trench**. An extraordinary collection of bits and pieces was dug up here in 1974, including some eight thousand stone tools and six **Indian coins** between sixty and five hundred years old. Whether the oldest of these really implies the very early penetration of overseas foreigners into the interior or whether the coins were simply buried or smothered is unknown. Most likely they'd been handed down for generations and were either lost or hidden for safekeeping.

Nearby, in a fenced-in shelter, the massive stone slab which sealed a **Neolithic burial mound** has been removed to display part of a skull and some limb bones. The remains of a further nineteen Neolithic skeletons were discovered north of this, beneath a more recent Iron Age occupation area marked by the two stone circles (which were hut foundations). Nineteen Iron Age skeletons were also discovered, overlying the Neolithic graves, mostly of young men – possibly slain warriors – apparently buried unceremoniously or in a hurry, their skulls and limbs in tangled heaps.

These enigmatic graves have further, cultural implications: nine of the Neolithic skeletons are thought to be female and, unlike the male remains, they were found with accompanying **grave goods** in the form of domestic implements – dishes, pestles and flat mortars. The finds pose unanswerable questions. Certainly, many Kenyan peoples remember oral traditions of times when women were more socially and politically powerful than today: the female burials with grave goods might be evidence of this past. But the burials themselves are curious. The coincidence of nineteen skeletons at each level may be just that – coincidence. Or perhaps the Iron Age survivors who buried their young men knew about the ancient Neolithic graves beneath.

Neolithic recreation

For a less dramatic, but more accessible, impression of life at Hyrax Hill, the **Bau game**, cut into the rock just before you get back to the museum, is a delightfully fresh record. *Bau* is the Bantu name for a game of skill and – depending on the set of rules used – amazing complexity that has been played all over Africa for a very long time. Two people play, moving pieces (cowries, seeds or pebbles) from one hole to another to win. There are a number of these "boards" around the hill; the one near the museum is a particularly good example.

Lake Nakuru National Park

Admission $27, students/children $10; $8 to camp, $15 in a "special" campsite. No entry on foot. Warden: PO Box 439 Nakuru; ☎037/41605. Maps: Survey of Kenya Lake Nakuru National Park 1:30,000 (1994); Rowanya Enterprises Lake Nakuru National Park at 1cm: 500m (1990). You should be able to buy handy $2 colour maps at the gate, published by KWS.

Though not large – some 10km by 25km – **Lake Nakuru** is a beautiful park, the terra firma mostly under light **acacia forest**, well provided with tracks to a variety of hides and lookouts. It's also one of the easiest parks to visit, with or without a vehicle of your own. Towards the end of the dry season in March, the lake is often much smaller than the maps suggest, and, consequently, water birds are a greater distance from the park

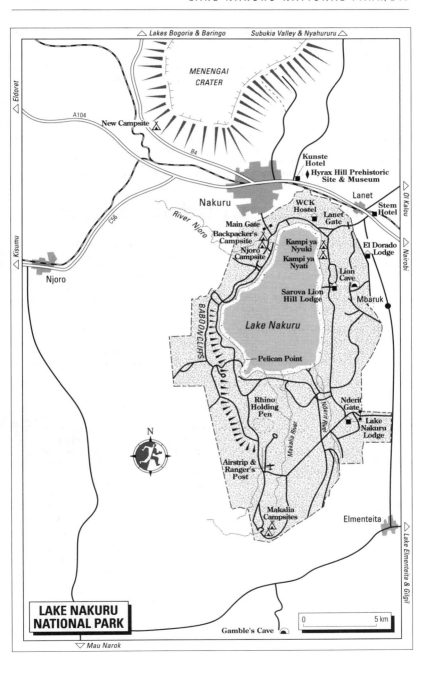

LAKE NAKURU
NATIONAL PARK

roads. The **northern side** of the park is commonly fairly busy with tour vehicles, but the **southern parts** are usually empty. A pleasure to drive around (it takes around three hours), its easy-to-follow topography means you really can't get lost or go far without arriving somewhere. And the contrast and apparent dislocation between the shallow soda lake with its primeval birds and the animated woodlands all around give it a very distinctive appeal.

Practicalities

The park has three gates. **Main Gate**, at the edge of Nakuru town, is also the park headquarters and has the main campsites nearby, plus a good, hand-painted map showing the most recent circuits, most of which are in fair condition. Entering through **Lanet Gate** gives the most direct access to the park's two **lodges** from Naivasha or

---

THE MYSTERY OF THE VANISHING FLAMINGOS

Despite their absence since autumn 1995 (excepting a few months at the end of 1997), Lake Nakuru has always been considered a flamingo lake *par excellence*; at one time, it was believed that up to **two million lesser flamingos** (perhaps one third of the world's population) were massing in the warm alkaline water to feed on the abundant blue-green algae cultivated by their own droppings. In addition, the lake was also home to a small population of the much rarer **greater flamingo** (whose world population is estimated at a mere 50,000): they're as tall as a small person and have less hooked beaks, with which they sift for small crustaceans and plankton, their heads underwater.

Like Lake Elmenteita, Nakuru has no outlet, meaning that its level fluctuates wildly. In 1962, it dried up almost completely, and in the late 1970s, a combination of increased rainfall and decreased evaporation lowered the lake's salinity and raised the water level. The flamingos began to disperse, some to Lakes Elmenteita, Magadi and Natron (the latter in Tanzania), some up to Turkana, but the majority to Lake Bogoria.

Since then, flamingos have been sporadically seen again in the surreal pink swarms that have become a photographic cliché, but the situation has become increasingly unpredictable of late, with the birds returning for two or three years then disappearing again. They were absent in late 1995, when the lake started drying up, and again almost completely in 1996. Water levels have since increased greatly due to the 1997–98 El Niño rains, with the result that the waters are now too fresh for the flamingos, and it may take a while before the waters re-establish sufficient salinity to entice them back. (In the meantime, you'll find a large part of the flock at Lake Bogoria, and a few others at Lake Elmenteita, Lake Magadi and at Lake Simbi on Lake Victoria.)

A great debate rages in the press about the causes of their disappearance and its detrimental effect on the tourist trade. Over the last twenty years, land use in the lake's catchment area has changed dramatically, with large areas of forest being converted to small farms, and Nakuru town has undergone rapid growth and industrialization. Pollution from the town's sewer effluent and industries is believed to be a major factor (Kenya Wildlife Service and the World Wide Fund for Nature built nine new "refuse chambers" for the town in 1996), as are water diversion, soil erosion (leading to siltation) and even sand-harvesting along the Njoro River. The introduction in 1962 of a hardy species of fish, *tilapia grahami* – partly to control mosquitoes – has encouraged large flocks of **white pelicans** in recent years and it's likely that their presence is another disruptive element (on Elmenteita a breeding colony of greater flamingos was forced off by the pelicans). The Nakuru Wildlife Trust has been studying the ecology of Rift Valley lakes since 1971 in an effort to find some of the answers, and the WWF now organizes educational trips to the park for local kids, as well as running a pilot scheme to monitor pollution from individual industries.

Nairobi and avoids the congestion of Nakuru town. It's not properly signposted, however. Before you reach the edge of town, the 1.5-kilometre track to the gate starts opposite the *Stem Hotel*; if you've crossed the railway bridge you've overshot. **Nderit Gate**, down in the southeast corner, is only useful if you're coming cross-country from Lake Naivasha or over the Mau escarpment from Narok.

Getting around

The most straightforward way to see the park if you don't have a vehicle is **by taxi**, especially as some of the taxi drivers around Nakuru town know the park well. The *Midland Hotel* is as good a place as any to track one down. This naturally works out cheaper for a group, but you'll probably want to reach an agreement with the driver before you're all present. Reckon on some stiff bargaining, then three hours at about $15 an hour, with park fees on top. Alternatively, contact Blackbird Tours at Caleb's Arcade in the *Carnation Hotel* (see Nakuru "Listings", p.243).

An alternative – though admittedly not always a very practical one – is to **hitch** at the **Main Gate**, about an hour's walk from the town centre. The rangers are usually sympathetic to low-budget travellers: they may help by asking drivers on your behalf, you'll have no park fees to pay unless you get a lift, and if you don't you can camp at the backpackers' campsite. You should expect to spend the night in the park once you get a ride, so be prepared for this.

If you're on foot and don't have a tent either, things look more difficult, but you could always stay the night at the cheap and cheerful *Florida Day & Night Club B&L* (①) right on the boundary between park and town. This won't give you a restful night, but you'll want to be up bright and early waiting for a lift in any case; there's the added bonus that you're bound to meet park staff here.

The best option has you **driving** around in your own vehicle and stopping where you choose: the park has a number of areas where you can walk and, of course, this gives you the option of staying, or eating, at the stylish **lodges** in the bush.

Accommodation

The park has two expensive lodges, a hostel and a few campsites; most people simply go on day visits, and stay in Nakuru town or elsewhere overnight.

Eldorado Lodge, on the eastern side past the turning to Lanet Gate (bookings through Let's Go Travel in Nairobi; p.142). Popular with Nairobi weekenders, this is actually more of a *nyama choma* joint: its breeze-block chalets aren't overly attractive but it's a good place to fix up a lift into the park. ⑤.

Lake Nakuru Lodge, PO Box 561, Nakuru (☎037/85446, fax 037/211204); Nairobi reservations through Lake Nakuru Lodges, 2nd floor, Arrow House, Koinange St, PO Box 70559 Nairobi (☎02/212405, fax 227062). Established lodge based around an old Delamere Estate house in shady gardens, with a pool ($5 for visitors) and uninterrupted views of the lake, though several kilometres from it. The *banda*-style rooms are on the small side and rather dark, though the new and much more expensive chalet suites, down a viewing platform/walkway, are first-class. The food is nothing special. FB ⑤–⑦ low, ⑦–⑧ high.

Sarova Lion Hill Lodge, 12km from the city centre, PO Box 7094 Nakuru (☎037/85455, fax 85212, reservations through Sarova, p.50). This is extremely comfortable, with a low-key atmosphere, helped along by friendly staff. There are good views from the very pleasant, chalet-style rooms stacked high above the main parts of the lodge, and the excellent meals (Ksh600) are slightly cheaper than at *Lake Nakuru Lodge*. Pool and sauna (Ksh300 for visitors); $90 per hr for game vehicle rental (up to nine people). FB low ⑥, high ⑦.

Wildlife Clubs of Kenya Hostel, on the northern side of the park (book through PO Box 33 Nakuru ☎037/212632). The only reasonably priced accommodation but somewhat run-down. The dorm beds (Ksh600 per person) and do-it-yourself catering arrangements seem just about adequate – the kitchen is well-equipped. You can also camp in the enclosed compound (same charge).

CAMPING

For accommodation under canvas, there's a specific **backpackers' campsite** (cold showers, high-level toilets, communal tap) on a pleasant grassy site under fine old yellow acacias, but beware the audacious vervet monkeys and baboons, who've taken to attacking campers and wrecking their tents. There are two other regular campsites in the park: **Njoro campsite**, a couple of kilometres down the west shore road and set back in the woods, and the somewhat elusive **Makalia campsites** in a wonderful location at the southern tip of the park, on either side of the stream of the same name and close to the waterfall. Very few organized tours come down this way, but should you feel isolated, you may be reassured to know there's a ranger station fairly close by.

There are also a couple of "**special campsites**" in the northeast part of the park – **Kampi ya Nyati** (Buffalo Camp) and **Kampi ya Nyuki** (Bee Camp). They are both located in clearings among the trees between the road and the open shore but the lighter and grassier *Nyuki* is the nicer of the two. Both have splendid "private" access to quiet vantage points on the shore through drivable tunnels of undergrowth. Bookings, as usual for special campsites, are supposed to be made in advance with the warden or through the National Parks headquarters at Nairobi National Park (see p.153).

Around the park

The **northern shores** of the lake are the most opened-up, with a busy route between the Main Gate and *Sarova Lion Hill Lodge*. The vegetation here is mostly lightly wooded acacia forest and, close to Nakuru town and its noise and pollution, this is the least interesting area for wildlife.

Heading clockwise, the main track runs through the woods, past the lodge and into an exotic-looking forest of candelabra **euphorbia** – great cactus-like trees up to 15m high. At the southern end of this zone you come into a spell of more open country, past the turning (left) up to *Lake Nakuru Lodge*, and one or two side tracks down to the mud and the lakeshore (right), and then the road turns west into the southern park's dense acacia jungle. This is where you may see a **leopard** and, if they overcome their shyness, one of the park's thirty-odd **black rhino**. Several kilometres further, the road opens again onto wider horizons with plenty of buffalo, waterbuck, impala and eland all around. This is also the most likely area for seeing the park's introduced **Rothschild's giraffe** herd, which numbers some sixty or seventy, in several groups. In fact, their introduction has been so successful that some are now being moved elsewhere to ease pressure on the park.

Down in this **southern part of the park**, take a northerly side track and you can circle around the southern savannah; opt for a southerly side track and you plunge into deep scrub and thicket – perfect rhino country. Eventually, heading south, you reach the electric boundary fence and the perimeter patrol track, which you can follow, east or west, back to the main circuit route.

The **west shore**, especially "pelican corner", has the best opportunities for seeing the **flamingos** in their dense, rose-coloured photogeneity. In places the road runs on what is virtually a causeway, past the lake's edge, with high cliffs rearing up behind. Photo conditions obviously depend on the time of day and the weather, but late afternoon usually produces the best results on this side of the lake: be careful not to overexpose – the most effective shots tend to be on the dark side.

Still heading clockwise, the main route leaves the shore and ploughs north, through **thick forest** with many high trees and dense undergrowth, back to the Main Gate.

Good **vantage points** around the lake include the northern **mud flats** (follow established tracks across the dry surface); the dead tree **watchtower** (northeast); *Kampi ya Nyuki* and *Kampi ya Nyati* campsites; *Lake Nakuru Lodge*, for a general view across unobstructed savannah; and the high "**baboon cliffs**" in the west.

LAKE NAKURU'S WILDLIFE

Fortunately, in view of the flamingos' here-today-gone-tomorrow caprice, there's a lot more to the lake's spectacle than the pink flocks. Its shores and surrounding woodlands are home to some four hundred other species of **birds** including, during the northern winter, many migratory European species.

There's a good number of **mammals** here as well. The lake isn't too briny for **hippos**: a herd of a dozen or more snort and splash by day and graze by night at the northern end. Nakuru has also become a popular venue for introduced species: there are **Rothschild's giraffe** from the wild herd near Kitale, and **lion** and secretive **leopard** from wherever they're causing a nuisance.

In the early 1990s, a number of **black rhinos** were relocated from Solio Game Ranch (p.227), and numbers are encouragingly increasing steadily year after year (present population 39, of which 17 were born in the park); ten **white rhinos** were donated by South Africa in 1994, and others were brought from Solio, bringing their number to 23. Electric fencing has been installed around the entire perimeter of the park – the only park in the country to be so enclosed – with the intention of maintaining a viable number of rhinos in one well-protected zone, secure from poachers. A huge investment, substantially from the World Wide Fund for Nature, has been expended on this major effort to save the rhino from extinction at a cost per beast – adding up to some £4000 per year – that is more than ten times the average income of the people on the other side of the fence.

You soon understand how Nakuru got its name (it is Swahili for "place of the waterbuck"): the park is **waterbuck** heaven. With only a handful of lions and small numbers of leopards to check their population, the shaggy, red-deer-sized beasts number several thousand and the herds (either bachelor groups or a buck and his harem) are large and exceptionally tame. **Impala**, too, are very numerous, though their lack of fear means you rarely witness the graceful flight of a herd vaulting through the bush.

The two other most often-seen mammals are **buffalo** – which you'll repeatedly mistake for rhinos until you get a look through binoculars – and **warthog**, scuttling nervously in singles and family parties everywhere you look.

Elephants are absent but you're likely to see **zebra**, **dikdik**, **ostrich** and **jackals** and, in the southern part of the park, **eland** and **Thomson's and Grant's gazelles**. More rarely you can encounter the odd **striped hyena** loping along the road in the eastern euphorbia forest at dawn, **reedbuck** down by the shore and **bushbuck** dashing briskly through the herbage. Along the eastern road, near *Lake Nakuru Lodge*, are several overtame **baboon troops** to be wary of.

The park is also renowned for its very large **pythons** – the patches of dense **woodland** in the southwest, between the lakeshore and the steep cliffs, are a favourite habitat. One of these huge snakes dammed up the Makalia stream a few years back, when it died of internal injuries after swallowing a gazelle.

Lastly, if you tire of the living spectacle, go looking for the **Lion Cave**, beneath Lion Hill ridge in the northeast: it's an excavated prehistoric rock shelter and rarely contains lions.

West of Nakuru: out of the Rift Valley

West of Nakuru, the A104 is a fast, busy, single-lane road, along which long-distance lorries and buses thunder by a top speed. It's hair-raising if you're driving yourself, and even more wearing on the nerves if you're travelling by *matatu*. The surface varies but it's generally good, the worst stretch running from Timboroa, some 90km west of Nakuru, for about twenty hilly, winding kilometres to Nabkoi. Beyond there it's mostly excellent.

If you're heading into western Kenya, there's a scenic and much quieter alternative to the main highway. This, the C56, climbs gently up to Njoro, Elburgon and Molo – in ascending order of altitude and size – before rejoining the Kisumu-bound fork of the main road (the B1).

Njoro

The turn-off (left) to Njoro and the Mau escarpment is 5km west of Nakuru, usually marked by the presence of a police roadblock: along with Laikipia district north of Nanyuki and Nyahururu, the Njoro and Molo areas were those worst affected by the inter-tribal clashes that have rocked the Rift Valley since the advent of multi-party politics in 1991. Violence erupted again just before the 1997 elections and continued well into 1998, leading to the deaths of several hundred people and the displacement of tens of thousands.

NJORO is the home town of **Egerton University** (main campus 5km out of town on the main road to Narok), whose other, equally remote, outpost is up the escarpment near Kinangop, north of Naivasha. The jacaranda-fringed main road runs straight past the "centre" of town – a great acreage of mud (or, at best, dust), backed by a humble row of *dukas* and *hotelis*. The only feature of note is the white and green mosque on the right, which broadcasts sermons and a noisy accompaniment from its congregation on Friday mornings – strange in this bleak highlands town. There are one or two very basic B&Ls, but nothing notable.

Beyond the Narok junction there's another and more soulful Njoro of wooden-colonnaded, tin-roofed, one-storey *dukas*. On this side of town are the post office and telephones (coin boxes only), a branch of the KCB bank and the Njoro Farmer's Petrol Station, a Shell garage. You emerge on the other side of town, past timber yards, into flat cereal country, with herds of dairy cattle and racehorses between the lines of gum trees and copses of acacia. Some 8km further along the C56 to Elburgon, past the junction for Menengai road, is the excellent **Kembu Campsite** (PO Box 23 Njoro; ☎037/61413 or 61583, *kembu@net2000ke.com*; Ksh300 per person), signposted on the left, which has farm produce for sale. The Nightingale family who run it also breed racehorses on their 900-acre farm; and you can rent mountain bikes.

Elburgon and Turi

ELBURGON is a good deal bigger than Njoro, and higher up. You're into seriously muddy, conifer country up here, the buildings, characteristically chalet-style, built of dark, weathered planks. In the centre, the town's second street branches off in a sea of mud (or dust) to the railway tracks and open-air market place. Down this street you'll find the post office, a branch of Barclays and several dirt-cheap B&Ls.

Elburgon is first and foremost a timber town, with logs and logging evident everywhere. Notice the little eating house near the tracks called *Wood Money Hotel*. It's wood money that gives Elburgon a degree of commercial prosperity and can be the only reason for the massive investment in the *Hotel Eel* (PO Box 36 Elburgon; ☎0363/31271 or 31471, fax 31477; ③). This oddly named **hotel** ("Eel" is an acronym) beats anything in Nakuru, although if you don't qualify as a Kenyan resident the rates are far higher than you'd expect in an up-country town. On offer are clean, comfortable rooms and cottages, secure parking, a disco at weekends and an adventure playground set in well-landscaped grounds. The **restaurant** serves good breakfasts and an imaginative choice of main meals (excellent steak with bacon and red wine). During the week the place has all the atmosphere of an out-of-season holiday camp, but things liven up at weekends and holidays, when discos, video shows and traditional dancing are laid on.

En route to Molo, **St Andrew's School** at **Turi** has a locally renowned **teachers' club** on Thursday nights and sometimes at weekends. You can have a meal and a few drinks and pass an evening in as wide a range of company as you're likely to find anywhere.

Molo and the Mau forest

West of Elburgon, the road winds and dips through the thick Mau forest for several kilometres, with glimpses of railway viaducts across the valleys, until it emerges, still higher up, among the cereals and pyrethrum fields at **MOLO**.

Molo straggles for several kilometres down into a broad valley across the rail tracks and up the other side on to Mau Summit Road, where you find post office, banks and several petrol stations with carefully tended floral forecourts. Head for the *Highlands Hotel* (PO Box 142 Molo; ☎0363/21192; ②), which is tremendous value for its huge, wood-floored rooms with log fires. Unfortunately it's extremely quiet, but the misty gardens are pleasant, and they have riding stables; the bar and dining room only wake up a little in the evenings as various long-term guests return from a day's work on local civil engineering projects. *Green Garden Lodge* (☎0363/21080; ②) is a plain but pleasant old place, decently kept up for no particular reason (there seem to be few, if any, guests). They offer 24-hour hot water and a cheap, tasty menu; sometimes they even have an old guitarist singing songs in the bar.

South of Molo, up into the **Mau forest**, a newly graded road runs to **Keringet** (where the huge old estate, once owned by Italians, and exhibiting all the most ostentatious trappings of colonial wealth, is gradually crumbling) and on to **Olenguerone**. From here, the road tunnels eerily through a forest of huge gum trees, traipsed by elephant and even rhino, to Bomet (see p.386). There are several daily *matatu* runs along this route from Molo.

The Kenya Wildlife Service has been trying for years to open up the mountain forest, like the Aberdares Park. There is some stubborn resistance however, not least from the forest's indigenous Okiek (Dorobo) hunter-gatherers, as well as from the loggers. There's more background on this area, and details of the Mau route to the Maasai Mara, on p.385.

Londiani and Kipkelion Monastery

West of Molo, there are two possible places to stay in the highlands, neither of them exactly routine receivers of visitors. The first, the *Kenya Forestry College Guest House* (②), is near **Londiani**, a small town off the B1 highway, 12km west of the straggling row of huts and *dukas* that marks the railway's highest (2650m) point – **Mau Summit**. Londiani is about 3km from the main road, with the odd *matatu* running there. For the *Guest House* you need to take the right turn a kilometre or so before the centre, signposted to "Ministry of Environment and Natural Resources . . .", and follow this narrower track, Forest Road, for 2km. Anyone around the new buildings should be able to direct you to the simply furnished bungalow guest house on the north side of the little campus: if in doubt ask to see the director. Although intended for the use of visiting academics and researchers, it's occasionally used by bird-watchers and passing hikers and is a peaceful, country retreat. The *Guest House* manager (reservations: PO Box 8 Londiani, or contact the District Forest Officer on ☎0361/64028 or 64005) is welcoming and flexible – you can self-cater or she can prepare meals. Camping is not normally permitted.

The Cistercian monastery

The second unusual target in the district is **Our Lady of Victoria Abbey**, a Cistercian Monastery between Londiani and **Kipkelion**. The area was formerly known by the Maasai as "Lumbwa", but Kipkelion ("Kif-*kel*-ion") is the original and much-preferred Kipsigis name. Founded in 1956, this is the only Cistercian monastery in Africa and, deep in this rural hill country, the tall cement-block church is a remarkable sight – focal point of a small but impressive community of Kenyan, Ugandan, Tanzanian, Danish, Dutch, English and Irish monks. They make a living from their dairy herd and chickens and run the only hospital in the area and an important school. Our Lady of Victoria (named after the lake rather than the queen) began as a Trappist monastery, with the silence and strict rules the reformist order stipulates, but later reverted to the rather less stringent code of the older Cistercian order. The brothers still talk only when necessary, but they are happy to receive people (men and women) on retreat and ordinary lay visitors in their guest rooms and dining room. One of the brothers is responsible for visitors and you're likely to receive a very warm, and surprisingly loquacious, welcome: it's hardly necessary to say there's no phone, but if you like the idea of silence and contemplation in a harmonious rural setting, write to let them know you're coming (PO Box 40 Kipkelion). You should obviously leave an appropriate donation.

The monastery is sited rather remotely north of the C35 backroad which leads beyond Londiani towards Kisumu. A few **matatus** service this road, but to get up to the monastery without your own vehicle you need luck in scoring a lift or several hours to walk it. The monastery is 11km up a rough track – signposted "Monastery Hospital" – from the small centre of **Baisheli** on the C35 (15km west of Londiani), and the track is rough, narrow and steep in parts, winding through intensively cultivated Kipsigis *shambas*. If you're approaching from the west, the easiest route to the monastery is via **Kipkelion station**, signposted off the main B1 highway, 25km east of Kericho. The road to Kipkelion station, 10km of good tarmac, gives out at the valley-floor station itself: to continue to the monastery you have a rocky, three-kilometre climb, then, turning right onto the C35, 6km to the track (left) up to the abbey. There's a "short cut" up to the monastery which is signposted ("Trappist", overwritten with "*Cistercian* Monastery 6km") just after you get onto the C35 – this track is often impassable. Note that none of the available maps of Kenya are any real guidance in this district: distances are significantly longer than they look.

THE NORTHERN RIFT

North of Nakuru, the Rift Valley drops away gently and, as the road descends, so temperatures rise, the landscape dries and human population becomes sparser. Not far from Nakuru or Nairobi, and no longer, necessarily, a difficult journey, this region has a bright, harsh beauty, quite different from the central Rift: its **lakes**, Bogoria and Baringo, both make alluring targets.

It's worth remembering also that this region offers three possible routes up to Lake Turkana (Chapter Seven), two of them joining with the Kitale–Lodwar road west of the lake, the third curving up to Maralal for the east side. Although public transport is virtually nonexistent and the roads pretty rough, the **Kerio Valley** route (see p.264) deserves a special recommendation if you're visiting the west side of Turkana.

Lake Bogoria National Reserve and around

Daily fees $15, $5 children/students; $2 to camp; access usually permitted on foot or bicycle. Warden: PO Box 64 Marigat; ☎037/40746. See the map opposite.

One of the least-visited lakes in the Rift Valley, **Lake Bogoria** is a sliver of saline water – unbelievably foul-tasting – entrenched beneath towering hills 60km north of Nakuru. With the increasing pollution of Lake Nakuru, Lake Bogoria has, since the early 1990s, become the adopted feeding ground of tens (at times hundreds) of thousands of **lesser flamingos**, whose population has been stable since 1995. The lakeshore itself is one of the few places where **greater kudu** antelope can easily be seen. But the reserve is

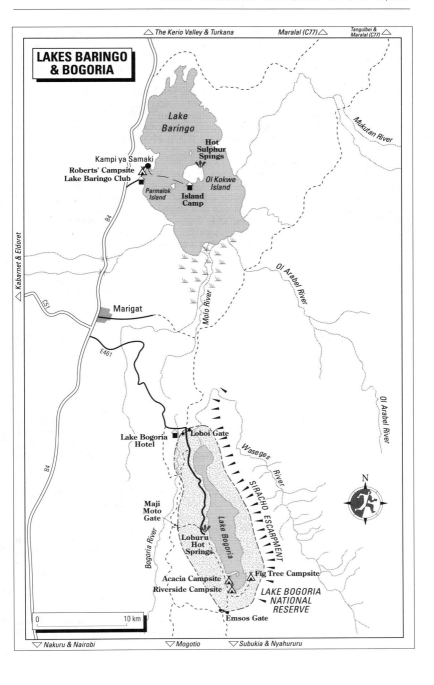

worth visiting as much for its physical spectacle as for the wildlife. It's largely a barren, baking wilderness of scrub and rocks, from which a series of furious **hot springs** erupts on the western shore and the bleak walls of the Siracho range rise sheer from the east. Even in the far north of the country there are few places so unremittingly severe.

Fortunately, the rigour of the landscape is relieved by three superb, shady **campsites**, one of which is nearly perfect. There are two **accommodation** options just outside the reserve's main Loboi Gate. The **warden** here (William Kimosop) is quite an authority on **birds** and, if he's free, will happily take you around, or accompany you in your vehicle (it's a good idea to try to arrange this in advance).

Main approaches and gates

The excellent B4 road running north from Nakuru to Baringo slices through a thinly populated region and carries little traffic – tortoises in the road present the greatest hazard to motorists speeding along the fast new tarmac. The road skirts to the west of Lake Bogoria by a margin of 20km, and, whilst there's a track cutting across at Mogotio, it's extremely rough going even by 4WD. Much easier, and quicker, is to continue on up the B4 to the signposted junction a few kilometres before Marigat. From here, a fast tarmac road takes you straight to the **Loboi Gate**, some 20km further on. There are infrequent *matatus* from Marigat to Loboi Gate (most leave Marigat around 3–5pm), or you could simply wait for a lift at the junction – it's a safe bet something suitable will pass within the hour. Returning to Marigat, *matatus* leave early at around 6–7am; some may continue down to Nakuru.

Sixteen kilometres from the junction, 3km before the Loboi Gate, the best feature of the *Lake Bogoria Hotel* (PO Box 208 Menengai West; ☎ & fax 037/40748; ⑦) is a sanitized **thermal pool**; it also has an ordinary, chlorinated "cold pool". A large stuffed lion dominates the lobby but even this does little to alleviate the blandness: it's really a town hotel in the bush and quite out of keeping with the area. Rooms and cottages are functional and taste-free, and way overpriced for non-Kenyans. The only alternative is the much more basic *Papyrus Inn* (PO Box 186 Marigat; ☎037/43279; ②), right by Loboi Gate. Toilets and showers are shared (hot water in buckets), but it's friendly and there's a large garden bar and restaurant, and an area set aside for **camping** (Ksh150). There's also the option of camping at the Loboi Gate, just outside the reserve – there's usually water here but you'll need your own stove or firewood and supplies. A rare treat for those without their own transport is that you are allowed into the reserve on foot, so long as there are at least two of you. In theory this is only permitted as far as the Loburu hot springs, although exceptions are made (and perhaps a ranger provided, for a fee) if you're heading for one of the three campsites further south.

Driving in from the south is shorter in terms of distance, but takes much longer on the rough roads; most vehicles visiting Bogoria come from Lake Baringo rather than directly from Nakuru. Using the main southern approach, the reserve is signposted (right) off the B4, 36km north of Nakuru at **Mogotio** (fill up on petrol here). Some 23km from this junction, shortly after **Mugurin**, you fork left for the western **Maji Moto Gate** (an incredibly rough 17km further, bringing you to the hot springs and tarmacked lakeshore road), or right/straight ahead for the southern **Emsos Gate** (an equally rough 13km, which brings you to the wooded part of the reserve). There's virtually no public transport, and note that with the currently high lake water level, Emsos Gate is something of a dead end, and you can't get to the hot springs either as the shoreline road lies underwater.

If you have a 4WD vehicle or are into hiking or mountain-biking, you might like to consider the **eastern cross-country approach** to Bogoria's Emsos Gate, described below.

Subukia and the cross-country route to Lake Bogoria

An adventurous alternative to taking the main road north to Bogoria from Nakuru is to approach the lake from the southeast, initially using the B5 tarmac route that ascends from the Rift Valley floor at Nakuru to the brim of the eastern escarpment at Nyahururu. Along the way there are several turnings, northwest, towards the lake. The tarmac portions of this trip can be made by country bus or *matatu* (there are several daily runs between Nyahururu and Nakuru via Subukia), but you should be prepared to **hike** the rest of the way down to Bogoria if necessary – a good two days.

Aside from the pleasure of tackling roads used by very few tourists, this route gives you a special feel for the Rift Valley's striking topography as it drops from one monumental block of land to another, with dramatic changes of climate and scenery. When you reach the plain at the bottom you've an indelible impression of the way the earth has split apart and sunk to form the Rift over the last twenty million years.

From Nakuru, it's a short trip, 14km, past Menengai crater (left) to the unsignposted fork for the police post at Solai (left, 14km, on rough dirt) and Nyahururu (right). The Nakuru–Nyahururu road is busy with *matatus* and buses; a fertile, rural backwater has been opened up since the route was hard-surfaced in the late 1980s. Beyond the fork you enter a steep, hilly landscape of Kikuyu *shambas*, increasingly interspersed with plots of tea bushes and pyrethrum.

From Nyahururu, the target is also the Solai police post: the early part of the route is particularly stimulating as it falls in a series of breathtaking steps over the fault lines until it reaches a high scarp above Subukia, where it hairpins its way steeply down to the valley. From the cool highlands around Nyahururu, you start to feel the heat building up: fields of sugar cane and bananas seem to grow before your eyes in the hothouse atmosphere and the earth takes on a rich, redolent smell.

The Subukia Valley and Lake Solai

The **Subukia Valley** was the Maasai's "Beautiful Place" (*Ol Momoi Sidai*) and its lush pastures their insurance against the failure of the grass up on the Laikipia plateau. But they were evicted in 1911 to the "Maasai Reserve" and the way was clear for the settler families. It's easy to see why they chose this high valley because, despite its isolation (even greater in the 1920s), it has a soft, arcadian beauty far removed from the windy plateaus above or the austere furnace of the Rift Valley floor below.

The village of **SUBUKIA** has a scattering of *hotelis* and *dukas*, and a Total filling station. Buses and *matatus* stop at this T-junction: there are one or two *matatus* to Solai police post (see "Down to Bogoria" on p.258).

If you have transport of your own and two or three hours to spare, or a couple of days to walk it, you can take a major **diversion** up the Subukia valley, then turn west and cut back south again, past small Lake Solai. To get started on this route, from the grubby junction at Subukia village where the main road passes, head north about 700m to an old T-junction signposted "Nakuru" (left) and "Lower Subukia" (right). Take the latter. The track, consisting of rough dirt and rocks, is easy to follow, but will clock up some 45km. Sources of food along the way are negligible, so you must be self-sufficient, and, although the road is being "improved" (made broader and more bone-shaking), there are few if any *matatus* along the way.

Lake Solai is a curiously isolated soda lake with a reedy shoreline grazed by cattle and a scattering of sisal plots. For many years it was a seasonal lake only, but it has been a permanent feature since the early 1980s. South of Lake Solai, the road climbs through scattered euphorbia and acacias to the junction (hard right) at **Solai police post** with its road sign ("Lake Hannington"), ancient but useful, and pretty mauve smudges of jacarandas. Lines of jacaranda streak the scenery at intervals all over this district; they border old driveways, evidence of the erstwhile community of **settlers**, nearly all of whom have left.

Down to Bogoria

The most **direct route** from Subukia village to Bogoria begins by climbing 4km out of the valley on the tarmac to Nakuru. A signposted right turn (or left if you've just come from Nakuru) goes over the hill past the curious apparition of **St Peter's** – a quaint Anglican church that looks as if it just flew in from England – and then 15km down to the Solai police post.

From here, the 50km to Bogoria is rough in many places, though normally quite negotiable in a 4WD vehicle (allow 3hr). Hitching, however, varies from slow to impossible from this point on and there is no public transport. If you're on foot or bicycle and still want to do it, check your emergency water and food supplies, tighten your bootlaces – or check your brakes – and set off west.

The road descends steeply to the Solai Valley with its disused railway line, which you cross at a place called **Milton's Siding**. When you reach the tracks, follow the road, parallel, to the right which runs for a kilometre and then turn sharp left to cross them. The road descends in a series of steps to a broad, flat valley with a sharp, right-hand bend up the hill on the far side, which it crosses to reach **Kisanana** – life-saving *chai* and a place to stop for the night if necessary, though there's no formal accommodation.

From Kisanana, you turn left at the old signpost and follow decent *murram* tracks for some 5km to a fork around some buildings. Here you head left and are soon pitching up a diabolical slope – rarely used by motor vehicles and by all appearances dynamited out of solid bedrock – which winds up and over a scrub-covered **hog's back ridge** for some 7km, eventually twisting north and dropping to better red *murram*, interspersed, strata-wise, with white, rocky stretches. You come to a crossroads (turn left), then after a few hundred metres a T-junction at a place of a few huts called **Mugurin** (turn right), where you may find a solitary *hoteli* open with good tea and chapatis. From here, you're within the compass of the lake, some 25km away. The road descends steadily now as you travel north – there's only the odd signpost but no danger of taking a wrong turn: if in doubt, head right.

Emsos Gate: practicalities

Hidden in its deep bowl, **Lake Bogoria** – when it is approached from Mugurin – is only visible when you're almost on top of it. The final stretch of the track leading down to the Emsos Gate is steep, rocky as well as being savagely beautiful, the landscape transformed into a strident dazzle of red and blue and splashes of green. The lake itself, a glistening pool of soapy blue and white, has a mirage of pink flamingos tinting its shores. During the middle hours of the day, the heat is relentless but the unparalleled **Fig Tree Campsite** is the incentive to make the trip: it's only forty minutes' walk from Emsos Gate and an absolute delight. Except, perhaps, if your visit coincides with a fresh covering of vegetation after the rains. Although this makes for an unusually verdant and picturesque scene, you'll also be welcomed by squads of determined tsetse flies. Note, if you're driving, that the road around the southern shore is very rocky and slow-going, and that access to *Fig Tree Campsite* is difficult for trucks and large vehicles as certain stretches are narrow and rock-bound.

Enquire with the rangers about heading down further to the thickly wooded shore at the south end (they might provide an escort, for a fee), and also check with them about **food**: a few basics are usually available near Emsos Gate to eke out your rations. **Water** is not a problem – a permanent, miniature brook, clear and sweet, runs right through the campsite and provides a natural jacuzzi. Less delightfully, the magnificent glade of giant fig trees which bathe the site in shade is a favourite haunt of baboons who gorge themselves day and night. In the fruiting season (December–February) you should be wary of camping directly beneath any concentrations of figs, for reasons which need no elaboration. Buffalo also graze near here and are not to be trifled with.

Getting around the lake

The **east shore road** has been quite impassable for years (a huge rock fall coupled with higher water levels), so there is no circuit round the lake. This also makes *Fig Tree Campsite* something of a dead end and, if you're down here and don't have your own vehicle, you may be in for a long wait before someone turns up to give you a lift out again. Your only option is to walk the 15km around to the Loburu hot springs on the western shore, passing *Riverside* and *Acacia Tree* campsites (neither currently have road access). If you're driving up this southern stretch, there's a river bed to negotiate before you reach the tarmac, for which 4WD is essential, and with the high lake level is not advisable unless you're with a ranger who knows the road. There are picnic sites near the hot springs and, although notices prohibit it, there seems little to prevent you from camping in the vicinity. The Bogoria Reserve **paved road** between the hot springs and the Loboi Gate is in excellent condition: by the hot springs is the junction for the dirt road out to the western, Maji Moto, gate, up a dreadfully steep, rocky incline (steely nerves and 4WD essential).

The Loburu hot springs

However you enter the reserve, you're bound to want to see the **hot springs**: a series of boiling water spouts on the shore. There's a drinks kiosk here, but no food. At present, the high lake level means that only one of the springs breaks the surface – the others signal their presence by the agitated green water above them, some steam and a strong smell. With normal water levels, they burst up from huge natural cauldrons of super-heated water not far below the surface and drain into steaming rivulets that cut through the crusty ground, continuously collapsing and reforming their courses down to the lake. Even at midday, when the sun glares like a furnace, clouds of steam drift across this infernal scene: tufts of grass tempt you to sit down and reward you with vicious spines, while, closer to the lakeshore, the macabre bleached skeletons of flamingos lie strewn in the sand (visions of them landing in the wrong pool), and, in the background, the dull thundering of the springs fills the air. It's like some water garden in Hell. It's also **dangerous**: picnickers sometimes think it's fun to boil eggs and heat tins of food in the pools, but the consequences of a slip can be messy and even fatal: over the years a number of people have slipped and died as a result. An *askari* has now been posted to watch out for visitors but if you scald yourself, help might still be a long time coming.

None of which should keep you from going. Although they hardly touch Yellowstone or Rotorua standards, "hot springs" is a tame appellation for this very impressive, terrifying and brilliantly photogenic phenomenon. And the **flamingos**, for some curious reason – possibly chemical – tend to flock in their greatest numbers to the shallows opposite the hot streams' debouchment (they appear to be immune to the heat). The Bogoria **fish eagles**, incidentally, have made a gruesome adjustment to their fierce, fishless environment: they prey on flamingos. Other birds to look out for include avocets, transitory pelican and migratory steppe eagles.

Wildlife, with the exception of the flamingos, makes itself scarce, most animals preferring the remote and presently inaccessible eastern shore: buffalo, hyenas, klipspringer, impala, dik dik, zebra, warthog and Grant's gazelle. The mild and nervous **greater kudu** formerly lived predominantly in the northeastern part of the reserve, but they have spread and multiplied significantly in recent years and they are now frequently seen in the more exposed western parts of the reserve. The kudu is a splendidly unmistakable, striped antelope; the bulls have long, spiral horns, shaggy dewlaps and enormous, spoon-like ears. Once widespread, the great rinderpest epidemics of the last century which took such a toll on cattle wiped out much of the kudu population too, leaving pockets only in the least favourable cattle country. Today, Bogoria is the most southerly part of the greater kudu's range in Kenya.

Lake Baringo

Roadblock operates 7am–7pm; adults Ksh200, students Ksh100, children Ksh50. Warden: PO Box 64 Marigat; ☎037/40746. See the map on p.255.

At one time a barely accessible retreat favoured by just a few weekenders, **Lake Baringo** now has a fine road from Nakuru, and another from Eldoret. At present, it remains a peaceful oasis in the dry-thorn country, rich in birdlife and with a captivating character entirely its own.

The lake is freshwater (Naivasha is the only other Rift Valley lake that's not saline), so its fish support **birds** less often seen – fish eagles, pelicans, cormorants and herons, for example – as well as quite a sizeable **crocodile** population. **Hippos** are common, too. Though you rarely see much more than ears and snout by day, they come ashore after dark, and on a moonlit night their presence can be unnervingly obvious; even in pitch darkness, they're too noisy to be ignored. The crocodiles are reckoned to be quite safe, too small to be dangerous, and rarely provoked by hunters as their skins are undersized – but if you're swimming, you might like to know that a supposed man-eater was shot in 1981.

The **Njemps** people of the lakeshore villages live by an unusual mixture of fishing and livestock herding, breaking the taboo on the eating of fish which is the norm among pastoralists. Speaking a dialect of Maa – the Maasai language – these fishermen paddle out in half-submerged dinghies made from saplings of the fibrous *ambatch* tree that grows in profusion at the southern end of the lake.

The lake itself is heavily silted with the red topsoil of the region, and it runs through a whole range of colours every day from yellow to coral to purple, according to the sun's position and the state of the sky. Years of drought had reduced it so that a broad swathe of grass and reeds grew between the water's edge and the lakeshore properties. In recent years there have been some heavy rains and lakeside acreage has been cut back once again by the advancing waters.

Baringo transport – and Marigat

Buses from Nakuru to **KAMPI YA SAMAKI**, the lake's only, and very small, town, run twice daily, but Nakuru *matatus* come up only as far as **Marigat**. From Eldoret, you can catch a bus at 10am for Kabarnet, and go by *matatu* from there to Marigat. From Marigat you can hitch or get a local *matatu* to the lake. Kampi ya Samaki is 2km from the main road, beyond the council-run **roadblock** where you pay your admission fee (make sure you get a receipt). Motor boats to **Ol Kokwe Island** (Ksh600) leave on request from *Island Camp*'s jetty on the north side of Kampi ya Samaki; otherwise, you'll have to bargain hard with the bevy of boat-trip touts (and pay an additional Ksh250 landing fee on the island).

Marigat
MARIGAT, by virtue of its location, ought to become the hub of the Baringo–Bogoria tourist circuit, but for now, at least, it's a bland, dust-blown little place where visitors are greeted with indifference. Urban development here follows what seems to be an unusual course, as among the tin shacks stands an impressive bright green and white **mosque**. With two tiers of large windows and a capacity that obviously exceeds the area's Muslim population, it dwarfs its humble wooden predecessor to the rear. Muslim Nubians from Eldama Ravine, working on the irrigation project south of Marigat, are supposed to have funded the building of this mosque. If you need **to stay** in Marigat, there are a couple of B&Ls on the main road near the junction with the B4, but they're

nothing special, so you might as well follow the sign at the junction to *Marigat Inn* (PO Box 58; no phone; B&B ③), 1500m off the main road on the eastern side of town. It's a pleasantly laid back, slightly decrepit sort of place, with distorted reggae daytime and an occasionally jumping music bar at night. The clean, s/c rooms with hot showers (and some non-s/c singles) are looked after by helpful staff. There's a small jungly garden, a shop selling essentials, and a friendly restaurant where the food, while not exactly cordon bleu, is more than edible.

Lakeside accommodation

Inexpensive accommodation at Lake Baringo is headed by the *Roberts' Campsite* (PO Box 1051 Nakuru; ☎0328/51403 10am–noon) in a large, acacia-shaded garden down on the lakeside beside *Lake Baringo Club*, with lots of space and great bird-watching, and a shop selling hand-printed *kangas*. Camping costs Ksh200 per person, firewood Ksh80. Alternatively, there are three good non-s/c *bandas* with electricity and bedding (Ksh500 per person; book ahead), and also a seven-bed cottage (from ④ for four people). If you want to cook, or for some reason prefer to shower separately from the campers, there's an adjacent, private kitchen/shower block that can be rented for Ksh500 per night. However, the shared toilets and bathrooms are far from clean, and sometimes lack toilet paper. There's no food, so bring your own supplies, and no boats, which means dealing with the touts outside the gates or elsewhere if you fancy a trip.

If you need somewhere cheaper, there are a number of basic B&Ls in **Kampi ya Samaki** (served by the "Lake Baringo Express" minibus from Nakuru until around 5pm). The best of them is the clean *Bahari Hotel Lodge*, on the left as you come in (PO Box 3; ☎0328/51408; ①), with a welcoming bar-restaurant. Ask for an upstairs room. Just before this, *Hippo Lodge* has reasonable rooms with mosquito nets (PO Box 74; ☎0328/51420; ①) – don't expect a quiet night here, as it's a tour-drivers' hangout, but it does have excellent food (order early from Alice). *Lake Breeze Hotel & Lodges* (PO Box 16; no ☎; ①–②) is better placed on the lakeside, with great views from the bar, and you can camp here too (Ksh200 per tent). The rooms are clean and have nets, but there's no hot water and its shared toilets are grubby, and lone women should steer clear. They've a jetty for boat trips, which they're pushy about you taking. Other places include the cheaper and more welcoming *Lake View Lodge* next door (PO Box 1; ☎0328/51413; ①), which is quiet and suitable for women (the young manageress knows her stuff), but the view, such as it is, is only dimly seen through the mosquito screens. The *Ushirika Lodge* opposite is the cheapest in town but only worth a try as a last resort (①).

Lake Baringo Club and Island Camp

In a totally different league, you're faced with a difficult choice from two very attractive places to stay, both offering substantial off-season and residents' reductions. And if this is not your sort of budget, it is still worth splashing out for cold drinks and a swim on a casual visit.

Lake Baringo Club (PO Box 40075 Nairobi; ☎0328/51402, fax 51401; reservations through Block, p.48). A sumptuous and unpretentious hotel, this is a regular stop on ornithological tours of Kenya: the lakeshore gardens are bursting with birds. Nurturing an interest in the natural environment is top of the agenda, with regular wildlife films and nightly audio-visuals to introduce guests to the local bird species. Children are made very welcome and will be round-eyed at the experience of encountering lake hippos at close range, coming to graze the well-watered lawns after dark (guards keep a careful watch). Reasonable entry fees are charged to casual visitors (Ksh100 weekdays, Ksh150 weekends), and these are deducted from your bill if you eat – and the meals are generally excellent (under Ksh1000 excluding drinks). For casual visitors, it's Ksh250 extra to use the small but irresistible swimming pool, and kids have badminton and table tennis to keep them amused. FB ⑥ low, ⑦ high.

Island Camp (mobile ☎071/374069, fax 882294; reservations through Let's Go Travel, p.142). Not as luxurious as some of Kenya's "tented camps", but who cares: the location is idyllic, on the southern tip of Ol Kokwe Island in the middle of the lake, dense with birdlife, as well as numerous varieties of lizard. There are 23 tents, each with expansive views over the lake, plus a small pool and bar. As well as from boat trips, you can go water-skiing, and there are guided walks on the island. The stepped nature of the site makes disabled access to the island impossible. The price includes motor boat transfer from their jetty 2km north of Kampi ya Samaki. For casual visitors, the transfer costs Ksh600 return in the lodge's boats, or you pay a Ksh250 per person "landing fee" if you come on another company's boat. FB ⑦–⑧.

Exploring the lake

Most **activities** tend to centre around *Lake Baringo Club* or *Island Camp*, both of which are pricey: boat trips around the shores (Ksh800–1500 for 1–2hr), water-skiing (Ksh1500 for 15min) and windsurfing ($15 per hour), camel rides (at *Lake Baringo Club*; Ksh350 for 30min), and visits to a nearby Njemps *enkang* (about $10). The headman here is paid a retainer and in return allows visitors to look around his compound and freely photograph his wives and children. The visit isn't a particularly comfortable one – you may feel obliged to buy some of the decorated gourds inscribed with planes and ostriches (among other motifs) which the women lay out – but your presence isn't resented.

There are, of course, cheaper ways of arranging excursions in the vicinity of the lake. There are at least four locally-run boat trip companies, each armed with a retinue of pushy young touts bad-mouthing the competition, who will all quote you the same starting price (currently Ksh1500 per hour for a boat which seats seven; if you are two or more, make sure you pay for the boat and not per person), which should be bargained

---

BIRD-WATCHING AT LAKE BARINGO

Baringo's 448 species of **birds** are one of its biggest draws, and even if you wouldn't know a superb starling from an ordinary one, the enthusiasm of others tends to be infectious, especially at *Lake Baringo Club*. The bird population rises and falls with the seasons (the dry season is the leanest time for bird-watching; many birds return with the rains) but the lakeshore resounds with birdsong (and frogs) at most times of year (try responding to some of the calls). It's surprisingly easy to get within close range of the birds – some species, such as the starlings and the white-bellied go-away bird, are positively brazen – so you'll find rapt amateur photographers lurking behind practically every bush.

Lake Baringo Club offers short, informal, morning or late-afternoon lecture **tours** with its resident ornithologist. Bird-watching by boat along the lake's reedy shore is best done in the morning, in combination with a visit to **Goliath Heronry** (known locally as Gibraltar), a rocky islet near Ol Kokwe Island where the birds breed, stopping over at the hot springs on Ol Kokwe itself. Afternoons can profitably be taken up on a trip out near the main road under some striking red cliffs, an utterly different habitat where, apart from hyraxes and baboons, you can see several species of hornbill, sometimes the massive nest of a hammerkop (wonderful-looking birds in flight, resembling miniature pterodactyls with their strange crests) and, with luck, the rare Verraux's eagle, a pair of which nest in the vicinity. Marabou storks are fed from the kitchens. You'll have a few dozen species pointed out to you in an hour. The world record "bird-watch" for 24 hours is 342 species – held by former Baringo ornithologist Terry Stevenson.

Of course you can organize your own bird-watching. There's some interesting bush just beyond the *Club* to the south (accessible by walking back along the road), where you should see some unusual species such as the white phase of the paradise flycatcher, a grey-headed bush shrike, violet wood hoopoe and various kingfishers. Hippos commonly graze here, too, even in daylight hours.

down. Share this between two or more, and even the starting price becomes excellent value. The local boatmen may not all be trained wildlife experts but most of them are practised at luring fish eagles by tossing them fresh fish; take your camera for spectacular close-ups as the birds swoop down for the bait.

Moving on from Baringo

Travelling **north of Baringo** is a hit-or-miss affair without your own wheels, so try to arrange something with mobile tourists. Otherwise you'll have to hitch: there's little transport either to Maralal or to Tot and Lodwar from here. If you're **driving**, there's the highly recommended and not too rough C77 from Lake Baringo towards Maralal (one day) or Samburu National Reserve (best done over two days). This route swings up from the lakeshore, leaving tarmac and tourism behind, and takes you into the rugged country of the Lerochi plateau, dotted with Tugen and Pokot settlements. With the right conditions, there are stunning views back over Baringo. You join the Rumuruti–Maralal *murram* road as far as Kisima, where you choose between a short journey to Maralal or some inspiring but wheel-shattering driving to Samburu (see p.348). There's **fuel** at Marigat, sometimes at Kampi ya Samaki (and normally at *Lake Baringo Club*), but none after that until Maralal or Archer's Post.

Returning to **Nakuru**, the first bus leaves Kampi ya Samaki at 6.30am, but Marigat is an easier departure point. You should find a local vehicle going there.

Kabarnet and the Kerio Valley

Many people make this trip in reverse order from Eldoret but, in either direction, it mirrors the journey down the eastern side of the Rift from Nyahururu, covered in the "Lake Bogoria" section. If you're setting out from Marigat, frequent *matatus* climb the first stage to **Kabarnet**, the road soaring and plunging through at times almost alpine scenery. From Kabarnet, you should be able to *matatu*-hop all the way to **Eldoret**. Leave early, as services tend to fill up towards afternoon, and you'd be lucky indeed to catch a lift at night.

Kabarnet

KABARNET, for all its piney preamble and the zippy new road cutting up the escarpment, is a major letdown. Its setting is superb, perched on the **Kamasia massif** – the slab of Rift country, also known as the Tugen Hills, that remained upstanding on the brink of the Kerio Valley when the rest of the Rift sank. But the town itself could hardly be more dull. Consisting of a small nucleus of *dukas* on the hillside, it has been considerably expanded in every direction in accordance with its designated function as capital of Baringo District. The result is a motley scattering of offices and civil servants' housing interspersed with wasteland; the planners must hope this will rapidly fill with enterprising businesses and workshops. President Moi's home town (he was born in Sacho, 30km away), Kabarnet is clearly earmarked for development, but is expanding in area faster than it's growing in significance. The **post office**, **supermarket** and covered **market** are about all that could interest you, and even then the market's selection is very limited.

Standing above it all, the faintly pompous *Kabarnet Hotel* (PO Box 109 Kabarnet; ☎0328/22094; ④) seems to be jumping the gun: it sometimes suffers from water shortages (so you can just dream about filling its baths) but it's worth a visit for its mountain views and above-average food (lunch costs Ksh450). There's also a swimming pool. The best alternative is *Hotel Sinkoro*, off the main road by the *matatu* stage (PO Box 256; ☎0328/22245; ②), with safe parking and a passable restaurant, but it's not cheap for what you get.

Across the Kerio Valley: Kabarnet to Iten

The quickest and easiest route across the valley is the paved C51 (the alternative Kabarnet–Tenges–Kimwarer road is described at the end of this section). The excitement of this route builds only after you leave Kabarnet and plunge into the **Kerio Valley**, a drop of 1000m in not much more than the same distance. You'll find pretty constant *matatu* traffic across the valley (and a daily bus from Kabarnet to Eldoret at 7am, returning at 10am); the road has magnificent views as it rolls through **Chebloch**, with its old bridge over the Kerio River. A right here will take you along a very rough 4WD road (forget it in rains) to **Lake Kammarok National Reserve**, 25km to the north along the Kerio Gorge. Back on the main Kabarbet–Iten route, the road then turns sharply up the **Tambach escarpment** on the western side of the Kerio Valley, passing the hamlets of Biretwo, Tambach and Kessup. A turn right just before Biretwo is the start of the lonely trans-valley route north to Tot (see below). Also before Biretwo, look out for the **Torok Falls**, looming high above to your left at the top of the Tambach escarpment, which are said to be worth a visit: count on a good half-day if you're hiking.

After a few more hairpins and a spectacular viewpoint (with obligatory curio and drinks stall), the road finally levels out at **ITEN**, a tiny grass-verged market town on the rim of the escarpment. Iten is the main centre this side of the Kerio Valley, with petrol, a KCB bank, a small market (handy for leather goods), and the basic *Gateway Guest House* (PO Box 563; no phone; ①). Iten is also home to the remarkable **St. Patrick's High School**, which must be the world's top school for long-distance runners. Any tourists who fancy themselves as athletes would be welcome to train with the kids there – just ask (and prepare to be humiliated). The school is just after the main shops of Iten, on the road north to Kapsowar. If you're **camping**, there's an idyllic site at the settlement of **Kessup**, 6km before Iten, signposted off on the right amidst a blaze of maize and banana *shambas*, in the evening shadow of imposing reddish-brown cliffs.

The main alternative to the C51 heads south from Kabarnet through Tenges and Kimwarer. To **Tenges**, a surfaced road twists spectacularly from Kabarnet along the spine of the Tugen Hills, with lovely views across the valley. You'll find some public transport to Tenges from Kabarnet, but very little when you turn right (west) for Kimwarer down in the valley. Whichever way you're heading in this region, if you have a **tent**, use it: there are loads of potential camping spots in spectacular countryside, and the locals are a pretty trustworthy lot. As ever, ask permission from the village headman if you plan to stay near a settlement or on cultivated land.

Kimwarer is the largest community in the Kerio Valley, a company town for the **fluorspar mine** at the head of the Kerio River. With nothing but bush, Kalenjin herders and the occasional party of honey-hunters round about, Kimwarer's tidy managerial villas and staff quarters come as a surprise, and "Fluorspar Primary School" looks positively progressive with its brilliant paint job and playground trees all neatly labelled with their Latin names. The town has grown rapidly in the last few years as plans for the production of a thousand tonnes a day of fluorspar have been realized. Fluorspar (calcium fluoride) is used in the manufacture of steel, aluminium, cement – and CFCs. If you're interested, arrangements can be made to visit the "rock crusher".

North up the Kerio Valley

If you want to **explore the Kerio valley** off the main Kabarnet–Iten C51 road, you'll notice a serious dearth of any kind of public transport. As usual, having your own 4WD vehicle is insurance against detours or setbacks on the rough tracks. Except during the heavy rains which usually fall in April–May (if local people are lucky), high clearance for rocks is more important than good traction.

Heading north from Biretwo (there's an alternative route along the Elgeyo Escarpment from Iten, described later), it's possible to **hitch** the length of the Kerio Valley to Tot, then skirt the northeastern fringes of the Cherangani Hills to emerge onto the main Kitale–Lodwar road near Marich Pass (see p.316), where there's accommodation and public transport to both Lodwar and Kitale. Most of the time, however, you'll probably be "footing" or waiting by the side of the road: no matter (as long as you have several days), for this road, following one of the country's most beautiful valleys, is worth a few blisters. Note however that you'll have to be pretty well self-sufficient: the villages along the way have no facilities for travellers, and only limited supplies. Climatic conditions are best in the few months of vivid greenery after the long rains – and fiercest in February and March, just before they break. Densely wooded and not much cultivated in the south, for most of the year the valley resonates with dry heat and the rattle of cicadas and crickets. The first 40km skirt the western edge of the new **Lake Kammarok National Reserve**, with its distinctive alkaline lake, but for the time being you can still hike everywhere. The section from Tot to the Marich Pass is covered below.

The Elgeyo Escarpment and Cherangani Hills

From Iten, head up north along the rough Kapsowar road, passing the villages of Singore and Bugar. Some 4km after Bugar, branch right to continue heading north via Chebiemit, Chebara and Cheptongei, where bearing right will bring you to Kapsowar and Chesoi. From Chesoi, you can walk or hitch (but don't count on seeing a vehicle, much less on its having space) the 25 breathtaking kilometres down to **Tot**, turning left halfway at **Chesongoch**. The rocky, almost perpendicular slopes are dotted with **Marakwet** homesteads, the huts unusual in being built of stone (there's a limitless supply up here), which gives them an ancient-looking permanence rarely seen in Kenyan rural architecture.

The Rift Valley is not short of astonishing vistas, but even here, few roads match the track down the **Elgeyo Escarpment** from Chesoi to Tot for precipitousness and sheer daring. A thousand metres below, spreading like a grey-green carpet into the haze, are the scrubby, bush-covered plains of Pokot and south Turkana. Dozens of tiny wisps of smoke from charcoal burners combine to smudge out the distant peaks of Mount Kenya to the southeast. Places where the trees grow thicker mark the passage of temperamental seasonal streams which flood and dry up with the rains: Pokot gold-panners still find enough gold in them to trade with anyone passing through. To add to this distinctive sense of place, the escarpment itself is the location of an ancient **irrigation system**, feeding water from the hills down to the lush cultivation at the foot of the scarp. Most easily approached on the returning leg of a trip to Turkana (make sure you've enough petrol), the Elgeyo Escarpment road is diabolical: too rocky for any kind of ordinary car and too steep for any but the most steel-nerved of drivers. It's a thrilling, gut-wrenching trip in a Land Rover – someone else's preferably – but think twice before driving *up* this road yourself: it is very, *very* steep and there's no fuel.

Take note: the northern reaches of the B4 along the foot of the Elgeyo Escarpment on the Trans-Nzoia/West Pokot border – especially around the village of Chesegon – were the scene of particularly brutal **ethnic clashes** in 1997 and 1998. Be aware also that until recently this part of the road was infamous for **armed hold-ups**: as usual, the only advice is to give in to their demands (you run a real risk of getting shot otherwise).

The Marakwet canals and Chesoi

Whatever the truth about their origins, **the waterworks** (see the box below) are undeniably impressive in scope, if not especially in appearance, stretching north–south for

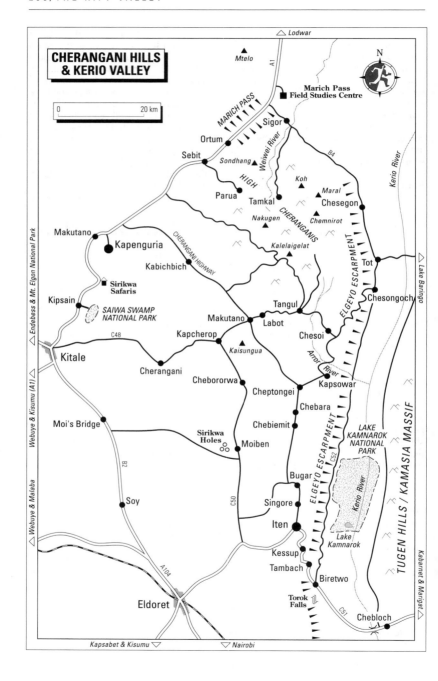

CHERANGANI HILLS
& KERIO VALLEY

THE MARAKWET IRRIGATION SYSTEM

The Marakwet may have arrived on these slopes as far back as a thousand years ago. Part of the broadly related Kalenjin group of peoples, they claim to have taken over the **irrigation system** on the escarpment from its previous users. They say the channels were there long before their own forefathers arrived, and it is possible the original irrigators were a mysterious group called the **Sirikwa**. These people have disappeared, or more likely been absorbed, and the only reminders of them are their name and a lot of curious **holes**, earthworks and cairns (see p.268) noticed by archeologists around the Kerio Valley and in other parts of western Kenya.

Marakwet elders still remember stories of a small people called the **Terngeng**, who may have lived in pits in the ground something like those at Hyrax Hill and Moiben. Other stories refer to tall, long-haired, bearded men who roamed the Rift Valley. Either or both of these groups might have been responsible for the building of the irrigation system, but neither sounds very agricultural; perhaps the Marakwet's claim to have inherited the system but not built it is just a way of saying how old it really is.

---

over 40km to divert water from the Cherangani Hills' gushing streams into a branching layout of furrows and aqueducts. Instead of plummeting straight into the Kerio River, the water gets neatly distributed along the escarpment, with complex, unwritten laws to ensure that each Marakwet sub-clan is fairly provided for. It's a system without parallel anywhere else in the country and the results, as you'll see along the base of the scarp, are spectacular. Indeed, for a considerable distance up the Kerio Valley, there's a band of intensive, luxuriant gardening: tiny *shambas* slotted back-to-back between the spurs and down towards the main river. Magnificent, richly flavoured bananas are on sale everywhere. Many of the irrigation channels now pass under the road, but a few still flow over it and a great deal of ongoing repair work is obviously needed to keep the streams flowing in the right direction.

The best place to see a good furrow is up near **CHESOI**, over the crest of the scarp. The land here buckles like a patchwork quilt, with the Cherangani Hills stretching west. "Chesoi canal" is a major water supply a couple of kilometres behind Chesoi centre, a metre-wide channel clinging to the hillside (ask someone to show you). In other places, the irrigation system has become almost a piped water supply, with hollow logs used as aqueducts, but this channel has been built with cement (which sells out everywhere as fast as it becomes available). Unfortunately, the water round about, diverted from the Arror River, tastes disgusting, even when boiled: it's a problem you encounter often in the Cheranganis.

There's nothing in Chesoi village itself – no water, no *hotelis* and certainly nowhere to stay – so stop down at the junction if you plan to overnight here. At least the people up here at the edge of the Cheranganis are delighted to meet strangers: as a start, go to the *Kosutany Hoteli* (a small *chai* shop), and ask if you can sleep on the floor. You could also **camp** easily, just about anywhere, if you can find a flat space – ask the landowner.

Onwards from Chesoi: walking in the Cheranganis

If you have the time and inclination, **walking in the Cheranganis** is exhilarating. The thickly forested hills are wild, hardly explored, and still home to bongo antelope. Higher up (Kamelogon peak on Mount Chemnirot is 3581m), they give onto mountain moorland and giant Afro-alpine vegetation: some superb hiking country where you're very unlikely to meet any others doing the same. A couple of days will see you over the southern ridges to Kapcherop on the so-called "Cherangani Highway", where you'll have no difficulty picking up transport west to Kitale or southeast into the Rift Valley.

For this route, you first climb through Chesoi village and past the mission for about ninety minutes through *shambas*; then there's an hour's walk through forest, mostly flat; ninety minutes of climbing through bamboo forest; and a further two hours though hilly pasturelands and woods before you reach **Tangul**. Tangul is a crossroads centre, a suitable stop for the night with a few *hotelis* and a morning and/or evening *matatu* run. From Tangul, routes lead: northwest to Kalelaigelat summit (motorable to the base in a couple of hours, but with no *matatus* and no water); north to the main Cherangani peaks (again motorable in 2–3hr or a day's walk); and south on a little-used road for two to three hours to **Labot** and – 5km further – **Makutano** (*not* the Makutano near Kapenguria). Labot has some *hotelis*; Makutano has none, but is on another significant crossroads. South of Makutano, a quiet motor road leads down through grassland, then forest to **Kapcherop** (home of Kenya's international athletics champion Moses Kiptanui) – about a three-hour walk. Note if you're driving that the Tangul–Chesoi part of this route is non-motorable and you can only drive to Tangul from the south or west.

If your hiking plans are more ambitious, get hold of the relevant Survey of Kenya 1:50m-scale maps (see p.37) and set off, suitably equipped, over the high central districts of the massif. There are several, relatively easily scaled peaks up here. *Mountain Walking in Kenya* by David Else (Robertson McCarta, UK) provides detailed guidance on certain routes.

Chesoi–Kapsowar–Eldoret

Altogether more straightforward as a continuation from Chesoi is the *murram* road **towards Eldoret**. To be sure of a *matatu* from Chesoi, you'll need to be up and ready by 6am; one or two other vehicles may come through later in the day but this transport can't be relied on. Alternatively, it's a fine and easy twenty-kilometre walk (mostly downhill) around the **highland spurs** to **Kapsowar**. Much of the time you'll seem to

---

IN SEARCH OF THE SIRIKWA HOLES

To seek out the **Sirikwa Holes** near Moiben purely for their own sake would require a certain degree of scholarly dedication, but if you're approaching the Cherangani Hills from the Iten–Eldoret road, or following the route out of the northern Kerio Valley from Kapsowar (with a good map), a visit does make an interesting diversion. Perhaps needless to say, it's a lot easier with your own wheels. *Matatus* run daily from Eldoret or Iten to Moiben (continuing on to Chebororwa on the edge of the Cheranganis); you might have to change at the junction where the *murram* road to Moiben leaves the paved C51. Occasional farm vehicles pass this way, but you could be in for a long wait.

The Sirikwa Holes are some 6km west of Moiben. From the crossroads by the upper primary school and chief's office, follow the dirt track past another school on the left and out into farmland. You may need to ask directions, first for Rany Moi Farm and then for the holes themselves – known locally as "Maasai holes" or "Maasai homes". Don't ask for "Sirikwa Holes", as Moiben is the main location of Sirikwa District and you'd probably be directed to the district offices.

The holes are a collection of depressions, some circular, about 10m across and a few metres deep, others a longer oval shape, all ringed by large stones. Some holes are alone, others are joined by passages dug a metre or so into the ground. They closely resemble the pit dwellings at Hyrax Hill near Nakuru. So far, the site is relatively undisturbed, except for gaps in the stone rings where the odd stone has been removed for building. But, as the pressure from local farms increases, it seems likely that these enigmatic remains will eventually be demolished and ploughed over.

be doubling back on yourself – Kapsowar and Chesoi are only 8km apart as the crow flies. Kapsowar's hospital makes it a local magnet and there's no problem finding onward transport from here.

Beyond Kapsowar, the road changes its mind less often and, after climbing again out of Kapsowar's valley through patches of **forest**, it emerges onto the Uasin Gishu plateau. Then it's all rolling ranch lands, wheat fields and stands of conifers and gum trees as far as Eldoret (p.304).

travel details

Nakuru is the whole region's travel hub. More local details are given in the appropriate sections. Peugeot taxis run from Nakuru to Nairobi constantly (90min).

BUSES

Nakuru to: Eldoret (3 daily; 4hr); Kampi ya Samaki (2 daily; 3hr); Kisumu (7 daily; 4hr 30min); Nairobi (16 daily; 3hr); Nyahururu (3 daily; 2hr).

MATATUS

Nakuru to: Mau escarpment towns (frequent; 1hr); Nairobi (frequent; 2hr 30min); Subukia (infrequent; 90min); Nyahururu (frequent; 2hr); Narok (daily; 4–7hr); Marigat (4–6 daily; 90min); Kabarnet (in frequent; 3hr); all over western Kenya.

TRAINS

Reservations can be made through Kenya Railways in Nakuru (☎037/212212–3).
Nakuru to:
Kisumu (daily 6–7hr); Nairobi (daily; 5hr 30min).

HITCHING

Nakuru to:
Nairobi. Stand on the road out of town just past the railway bridge. Walking further isn't very helpful.

Westwards Difficult, so take a *matatu* to get out of town and onto the right road, the A104.

Northwards OK as far as Kampi ya Samaki (Lake Baringo). The paved road stops at the end of the lake.

CHAPTER FOUR

WESTERN KENYA

L ike the tiers of a great amphitheatre, **western Kenya** slopes down to face the stage of Lake Victoria, away from Nairobi, the major game parks and the coast. Cut off by the high Rift wall of the **Mau and Elgeyo escarpments**, the western region of dense agriculture, rolling green valleys and pockets of thick jungle is one of the least-known parts of the country to travellers. Although more accessible than the far north, or even some of the big parks, it has been neglected by the safari operators – and that's all to the good. You can travel for days through lush landscapes from one busy market town to the next and rarely, if ever, meet other tourists or travellers.

It's not easy to see why it has been so ignored. Granted, the disastrous history of Uganda up until the late 1980s discouraged the through traffic that might otherwise have thrived. But there's a great deal more of intrinsic interest than the tourist literature's sparse coverage would suggest. What the west undeniably lacks are teeming herds of antelope and zebra, lions at the side of the road and narcissistic warriors in full regalia. What it does offer is a series of delightfully low-key, easily visited attractions. There are **national parks** at **Kakamega Forest**, a magnificent tract of equatorial rain forest bursting with species found nowhere else in Kenya; **Saiwa Swamp**, where pedestrians, for once, have the upper hand; and **Mount Elgon**, a volcano to rival Mount Kenya in everything but crowds. **Lake Victoria**, with the region's major town, **Kisumu**, on its shores, is a draw in its own right, dotted with out-of-the-way islands and populated by exceptionally friendly people.

Travel is generally easy: the region has a high population and many well-paved roads, so you'll rarely have long to wait for a bus or *matatu*, and driving is often a pleasure. If you're inclined to plan ahead, there *is* a vague circuit that begins in Kisumu (as this chapter does) and runs through **Kisii** (of Kisii-stone fame), Kericho, Eldoret, Kitale and Kakamega. You could easily do this in a couple of weeks – or a couple of months. But it's often more rewarding to let events dictate your next move: this area will repay your interest repeatedly if you take time to look around. Much of it, even the areas of intensive farming, is ravishingly beautiful: densely animated jungle near **Kakamega** and **Kitale**, regimented landscapes of tea bushes at **Kericho**, highland pastures and forests in the **Cherangani Hills**, and dank swamp and grasslands alive with birds by the lake.

There's almost no tourist infrastructure – the west has only a handful of hotels that could by any stretch of the imagination be described as luxurious – but there's no lack

---

ACCOMMODATION PRICE CODES

Rates for a standard double or twin room. For a full explanation of these rates, see p.47.

① Under Ksh500	(under approx £5/$8)	⑥ Ksh6000–9000	(£60–90/$96–144)*
② Ksh500–1000	(£5–10/$8–16)	⑦ Ksh9000–12,000	(£90–120/$144–192)*
③ Ksh1000–2000	(£10–20/$16–32)	⑧ Ksh12,000–16,000	(£120–£160/$192–256)*
④ Ksh2000–4000	(£20–40/$32–64)	⑨ Over Ksh16,000	(over £160/$256)*
⑤ Ksh4000–6000	(£40–60/$64–96)	* = *usually priced in dollars*	

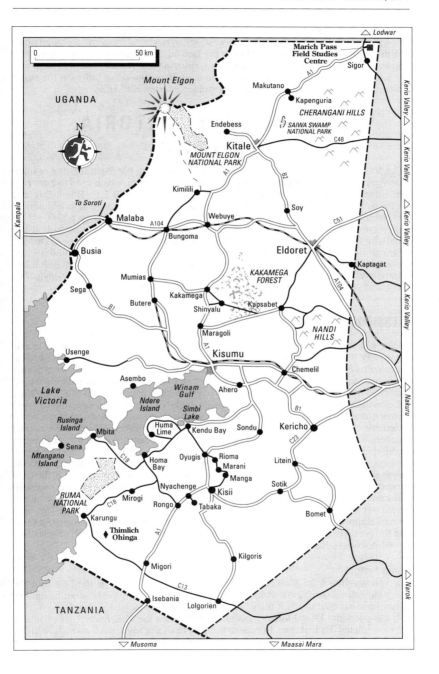

of good, modest **lodgings**. **Food** is as cheap as anywhere and generally excellent; most of Kenya's tea and sugar comes from the west, and agricultural concerns are paramount.

Ethnically, the region is dominated by the **Luo** on the lakeshore lowlands, but other important groups speak Kalenjin languages (principally the **Nandi** around Eldoret and the **Kipsigis** in the Kericho district) and there are Bantu-speaking **Luhya** in the sugar lands north of Kisumu and **Gusii** in the formidably fertile Kisii Hills.

AROUND LAKE VICTORIA: LUOLAND

Lake Victoria is the obvious place to make for in the west, but frustratingly few main roads get close to its shores. Most travellers arrive in Kisumu, which used to have regular motor ferries linking up with the Kenyan ports of Kendu Bay, Homa Bay and Mbita, as well as with Tanzania and Uganda, but these were suspended indefinitely in 1997 after the lake became infested with water hyacinth (see the box on p.274).

Kisumu itself offers only incidental lakes views: in order to get a good look at the lake, take the short trip out of town to **Hippo Point** and the fishing village of **Dunga**, or ask around at the port for *matatu*-boat services to nearby fishing villages and islands. If you really must mess about in a boat, the best place to head for is **Mbita**, which has regular *matatu*-boats to Mfangano Island, one of the least visited corners of Kenya, with the added attraction of some wonderful prehistoric **rock art**.

Kisumu

In the still, sultry atmosphere of **KISUMU**, the regional capital and Kenya's fourth largest city, the distinctive smell of the lake – not unpleasant – blows in on a vague breeze from central Africa, but the layout of the town turns its back on the water, focusing instead on its commercial centre and land links to the rest of Kenya. As a town with a sense of dignity as well as a sense of purpose, it has much more in common with Mombasa than with the hassle and grime of Nairobi or Nakuru. In the well-to-do residential district, well-guarded mansions are discreetly spaced along quiet, fragrant avenues and occasional expensive cars cruise the broad, colonnaded commercial streets. Even in the poorer quarters, it retains a great deal of character and tattered charm. The town went through a period of disintegration when the decline of lake traffic destroyed its status as a major port. Its fortunes were founded on the lucrative lake shipping business, funnelling goods between Kenya, Uganda and Tanzania, and the town suffered badly as a result of the East African Community's break-up. During the 1980s and early 1990s, the port was practically dormant, with little or no merchandise passing through and signs of dereliction everywhere – empty warehouses, broken windows, deserted dockworkers' houses. The commercial shipping services to Tanzania and Uganda have now resumed on a modest scale and the port sporadically buzzes with activity, but it will take a long stretch of sustained growth to restore Kisumu to its former affluence.

Some history

The **railway line** from Mombasa had been stretched out as far as the lake by 1901 (pleasing and reassuring the British public who, after so many years, were beginning to have serious doubts about the project ever reaching completion), but the first train only chugged into **Port Florence** station in 1903 when the Mau Escarpment viaducts were completed. By that time, European transport had already arrived at the lake in the form of a steamship brought up from Mombasa piece by portered piece, having

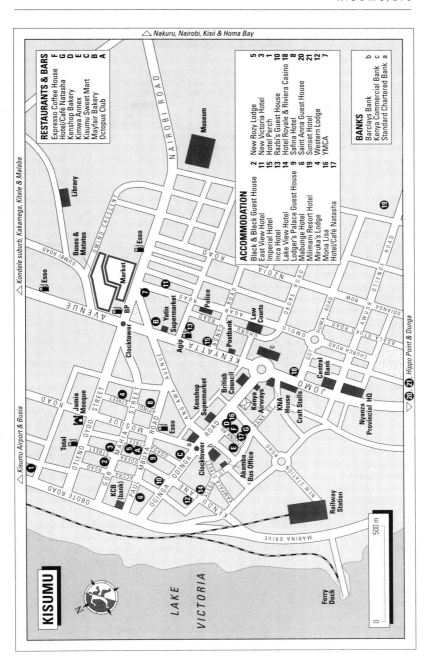

KISUMU

△ Nakuru, Nairobi, Kisii & Homa Bay

△ Kondele suburb, Kakamega, Kitale & Malaba

△ Kisumu Airport & Busia

▷ Hippo Point & Dunga

RESTAURANTS & BARS
Expresso Coffee House — F
Hotel/Café Natasha — G
Kenshop Bakery — D
Kimwa Annex — E
Kisumu Sweet Mart — C
Mayfair Bakery — B
Octopus Club — A

ACCOMMODATION
Black & Black Guest House — 2
East View Hotel — 11
Imperial Hotel — 15
Inca Hotel — 13
Lake View Hotel — 14
Lodger's Palace Guest House — 9
Mabunge Hotel — 6
Milimani Resort Hotel — 19
Mona Lisa — 4
Hotel/Café Natasha — 16
New Rozy Lodge — 5
New Victoria Hotel — 3
Hotel Perch — 1
Razbi's Guest House — 10
Hotel Royale & Riviera Casino — 18
Safina Hotel — 8
Saint Anna Guest House — 20
Sunset Hotel — 21
Western Lodge — 12
YMCA — 7

BANKS
Barclays Bank — b
Kenya Commercial Bank — c
Standard Chartered Bank — a

LAKE VICTORIA

LAKE VICTORIA

The westward view from Kisumu gives you little sense of the vastness of **Victoria Nyanza (Lake Victoria)**. The shores of the relatively narrow Winam Gulf curve gently to left and right, and it's difficult to grasp the fact that there's another 300km of water between the horizon and the opposite (Ugandan) shore, and an even greater distance south to Mwanza, the main Tanzanian port. Victoria, the second largest freshwater lake in the world (after Lake Superior), covers a total **area** of close on 70,000 square kilometres – more than twice the size of Wales – of which only a fraction belongs to Kenya.

Our knowledge of Lake Victoria is relatively recent. It was barely five centuries ago that the **Luo** first settled beside the vast equatorial lake they called **Ukerewe**, and the lake remained uncharted and virtually unknown outside Africa until well into the second half of the nineteenth century. Then, in the midst of the scramble to pinpoint the **source of the Nile**, the lake suddenly became a focus of attention.

To the nineteenth-century explorers, the search for the source of Africa's longest river was something of a crusade, and none was more obsessed with the pursuit of this geographical Holy Grail than the English adventurer **John Hanning Speke**. As soon as Speke set eyes upon Ukerewe in 1858, he was convinced that the long search was over, and he promptly renamed the lake in tribute to his sovereign, Queen Victoria. He returned to explore the area more comprehensively in 1860, and, in 1862, became the first European to sail the length of the Nile from Lake Victoria all the way to Cairo, famously confirming his discovery by cabling the Royal Geographical Society in London with the words "The Nile is settled". However, sceptics continued to counter that Lake Tanganyika was the true source, and it took a daring circumnavigation of Victoria, led by Stanley in 1875, to prove Speke right. Sadly, Speke didn't live to glory in the vindication – he was killed in a shooting accident in 1874.

Lake Victoria was of great strategic significance to the explorers but it was no paradise. **Bilharzia-carrying snails** flourished in the reeds around the lake's fringes, and the steamy shore was a fertile breeding ground for **malarial mosquitoes**. These hazards persist today. The Luo wash, swim and sail their vividly painted, dhow-like, mahogany canoes in and on Victoria Nyanza, but the danger of bilharzia is all too real. Instances of the disease are rare after brief contact with infected water, but for the visitor it's not worth the risk: take care if you're going fishing or boating on the lake, and don't even think about going swimming. Newer health scares surface from time to time: recently, scientists have speculated that the islands off the Ugandan shore may have served as hatcheries for HIV, the AIDS virus.

LAKE ECOLOGY

Lake Victoria is the largest lake in Africa, filling a shallow depression (no deeper than 80m) between the Western and Eastern Rift Valleys, yet is not part of the rift system. Interestingly, it contains nearly 200 different species of brilliantly coloured tropical **fish**, known as haplochromines or **cichlids** – all of them unique to the lake. Scientists, puzzling

steamed out from Scotland in 1895 (there's an obscure subplot to this story of European incursion: many of the ship's parts were evidently seized en route from the coast and recycled into Nandi ornamentation and weaponry: it was five years before a complete vessel could be assembled and launched on its maiden voyage across the lake to Port Bell in Uganda).

Kisumu was, by all accounts, a pretty disagreeable place in the early years. Apart from the endemic sleeping sickness, bilharzia, malaria and the nasty malarial complication known as "blackwater fever", the climate was sweltering and municipal hygiene primitive. But it quickly grew into an important administrative and military base and, with the consolidation of the colonies in the 1930s and 1940s, became a leading East African entrepôt and transport hub, attracting Asian investment on top of the businesses that had been set over how such a dazzling variety of species came to evolve in this largely uniform environment in the space of no more than a million years, have suggested that, at some stage in its history, the lake must have dried into a series of small lakes in which the fish evolved separately. Lake Victoria's cichlids are popular aquarium fish, and one of the commonest larger species, the tilapia, is a regional speciality, grilled or fried and eaten whole.

When, over the last couple of decades, the cichlid population seemed to be dwindling, accusing fingers were pointed at the new-fish-on-the-block, the **Nile perch**. Native to the Nile, but not to Lake Victoria, these carnivorous fish were introduced in the late 1950s to control mosquitoes, and established themselves extremely quickly. For the lake peoples they were a boon: they can grow to weigh as much as 250kg, and are both consumed locally and sold for export (in France Nile perch steaks are sold as *capitaine*). But the voraciousness of these fish began to send shock waves through the lake ecosystem, and ecologists were thrown into a panic by the prospect of the perch eating their way through the entire cichlid population and ultimately starving to death themselves. The expert verdict was that the murderous perch should be fished to extinction in order to save the other species, but the perch received a stay of execution when it was suggested that over-fishing using fine-meshed nets was even more of a threat to the cichlids than predation. The result has been a booming trade in Nile perch (catches are five times as high as in the 1970s), but with unfortunate consequences on traditional fish mongering and processing as the big boys move in with modern vessels and factories, their products mainly destined for European tables.

Over-fishing is in fact just one of a series of factors responsible for the **deterioration** of Lake Victoria and its shoreline. Oxygen levels in the lake appear to be falling, with the result that algae are proliferating and the fish population is under threat. The link to human population growth is a direct one – recent studies have estimated that over three million litres of human waste drains into the lake every day (the Swedish government is currently financing a study into the effects of pollution), while sand harvesting, overgrazing and clearance of lakeshore vegetation and forest for cultivation, releasing excess nutrients and silt into the lake, have all disturbed the fine ecological balance of the shore area. The building of the causeway from Mbita to Rusinga Island turned the Winam Gulf into a pond with only one outlet, inhibiting air circulation, with serious consequences for the local lake environment. A more sinister threat comes from the insidious **water hyacinth**, a native of Brazil which is believed to have arrived in the lake via Rwanda. This floating weed grows quickly around the lakeshore, blocking out the light and slowly choking the lake to death, as well as snaring up vessels. In Uganda, troops were mobilized to collect any plants they came across and treat any new areas of growth with weed-killing chemicals (which was stopped after an outcry by ecologists). Tanzania has been experimenting with weed-eating weevils, but Kenya, which has yet to take any decisive action beyond an abortive beetle-experiment (they weren't all that hungry) and researching the side-effects of a fungus which is said to kill only the weed, has suffered most. Since 1997, the ports of Homa Bay and Kendu Bay, and even Kisumu at times, have been strangled by a mile-wide cordon of the weed, which inhibits passage to all but the smallest canoes, with disastrous results for the local economy.

up at the railway terminus when the Indian labourers were laid off. Kisumu's rise seemed unstoppable until 1977, when the sudden collapse of the East African Community more or less overnight robbed the town of its *raison d'être*. The partial reformation of the community in 1996 has brightened prospects again, as have, ironically, the numerous wars and humanitarian catastrophies in other East African states: by 1999, the port was relatively busy, thanks largely to UN World Food Programme transit goods destined for Uganda, Burundi, Rwanda and now Congo. But a general air of stagnation and decay is evident all around: the huge molasses refinery, which would have given a much needed boost to the region's economy (still heavily reliant on sugar cane), has never been finished, and there's no immediate prospect of any progress. The lamentable catalogue of stalled initiatives also includes the Rice Mill, the Lake Basin Development Authority headquarters, and the fourteen-storey Nyanza Provincial headquarters construction project. The city's infrastructure itself, already barely adequate, is rapidly collapsing: apart from the obvious disintegration of road surfaces, only forty percent of the population has piped water (there are occasional outbreaks of cholera), the council is able to collect only thirty percent of garbage created (which explains its fantastically insalubrious side-alleys), and none of the city's fire engines work (they have to rely on the ones at the airport). As the crisis has deepened, employment has become scarcer and scarcer, skilled manpower has migrated to other towns, and the population has dropped to under 250,000. Kisumu is now officially the **worst-fed city** in Kenya, as well as being the poorest, with some 45 percent of the population living on less than $150 a year.

But the picture isn't entirely bleak. Kisumu does have considerable charm, and it's no small advantage to be one of the few up-country towns with real character (though the

---

THE LUO

The **Luo** are the third largest ethnic group and one of the most cohesive "tribes" in Kenya. Their language, Dholuo, is distinctive and closely resembles the Nuer and Dinka languages of southern Sudan, from where their ancestors migrated south at the end of the fifteenth century. They found the shore and hinterland of Lake Victoria only sparsely populated by hunter-gatherers, scattered with occasional clearings where Bantu-speaking farmers had settled over the previous centuries. Otherwise, the region was wild: untouched grasslands and tropical forest, dense with heavy concentrations of wildlife.

The Luo were swift invaders, driving their herds before them, always on the move, restless and acquisitive. They raided other groups' cattle incessantly, and, within a few decades, had forced the Bantu-speakers away from the lakeshore. Nevertheless, over the generations, **intermarriage** (essentially, the buying of wives) was common and the pastoral nomads were greatly influenced by their Bantu-speaking in-laws and neighbours, ancestors of the present-day Luhya and Gusii.

Early in the **colonial period**, the Luo benefited from some inspired, if dictatorial, leadership. They had inherited the institution of the *ruoth* (king or chief) from the original immigrants from Sudan. The *ruoth* of Gem, a location northwest of Kisumu, was Odera Akang'o, an ambitious and perceptive young man with an almost puritanical attitude to his duties. He had a private police force to inspect farms and report any idleness in his duties, and he regularly had his subjects beaten or fined for "unprogressive" behaviour. He introduced new crops and, under British protection, made himself quite a sizeable fortune. He was widely feared.

In 1915, the colonial government sent him, with two other chiefs, to Kampala; he returned full of admiration for the European education and health standards there, and ashamed of Gem and Luoland in general. Fired with enthusiasm, he applied his style of schooling and hygiene, bullying his subjects into sending their children to classes and keeping their shirts clean, while the British turned a blind eye. The results were rapid educational advances in Gem, which is still considered a progressive district today. Odera, unfortunately for him, was employed by the British to use his methods on the Teso people in Uganda, where they singularly failed. He was accused of corruption and sent into internal exile, where he died.

The Luo today are best known as fishermen but they also cultivate widely and still keep livestock. Culturally, they have remained surprisingly independent, and are one of the few Kenyan peoples who don't practise circumcision. Traditionally, children had six teeth knocked out from the lower jaw to mark their initiation into adulthood, but the operation is rarely carried out these days. **Christianity** has made spectacular inroads among the Luo, with an estimated ninety percent being believers, but doesn't so far seem to have destroyed the traditional culture quite as thoroughly as it has elsewhere: despite the ubiquity of Gospel, **traditional music**, especially the playing of the *nyatiti* lyre, is still very much alive and well worth seeking out.

slightly time-warped atmosphere of a place that's been treading water for over two decades may not be much comfort to its inhabitants). To anyone who's ever travelled in central Africa, Kisumu seems to have more in common with that region than with the rest of Kenya. It's a distinctly tranquil, easy-going town, the *manambas* in the bus station are unusually laid-back, and any anticipation of claustrophobia is quickly soothed by the spacious, shady layout. On Sunday evenings it seems the entire Asian community takes a constitutional along Oginga Odinga Avenue. The contrast with Nakuru is striking.

Arrival and accommodation

Kisumu is a natural base, excellently located for exploring western Kenya: half a day's travelling should get you to any of the centres detailed in this chapter. The **bus** and **train stations** are on opposite sides of town: the first is sited by the big junction of the Nairobi and Kakamega roads, the second down the hill in the port area. It is a good idea to install yourself soon after arriving, before starting any energetic wanderings, as it gets tremendously hot here. Try not to arrive on a Sunday: more than most towns, on the "day of rest" just about everything in Kisumu shuts down – even restaurants.

Accommodation

There's a wide choice of **places to stay**, with a good number of modest, mid-range hotels, though prices tend to be higher than usual. At the lower end, the B&Ls are mostly pretty basic, some verging on squalid. Temperature, humidity and mosquitoes will conspire to give you an uncomfortable night if you don't have a net or a fan (preferably both), so it's worth paying a little more for the few nights you may be in town. Unless you want to leave early, try not to stay near the mosque – morning prayer is loud-speakered at 5.30am. Note that *Dunga Refreshments*, formerly a good bet for a place to stay, with the option of camping, down by the lakeshore, has closed.

BOARDING & LODGINGS

Catherine Guest House (Dunga Catering College), Dunga, on the road to Hippo Point (PO Box 1364; ☎035/21302). Woe betide Kenyan tourism if this is the standard that students aspire to: rooms and towels are dirty, many nets have gaping holes, some showers don't work and there's a stagnant mosquito-infested pool round the back. B&B ②.

Lodgers Palace Guest House, Paul Mbuya Rd (PO Box 6234; no phone). Good breezy non-s/c rooms with nets, and friendly people. Bed only ②.

Mabunge Hotel, Paul Mbuya Rd (PO Box 1607; no phone). Not spotless but light and airy; there's a restaurant downstairs. ②.

Miruka's Lodge, Apindi St (PO Box 1717; ☎035/22131). Basic, dirt cheap, grubby rooms. Avoid the unspeakable *Nasim's* next door. ①.

Mona Lisa, Oginga Odinga Rd (PO Box 1435; ☎035/40843). Seedy at first glance, but really quite decent: s/c rooms with nets behind the long-established restaurant. ①.

New Rozy Lodge, Ogada St, next to the *Octopus Club* (PO Box 548; ☎035/41990). Someone's lost their rozy-tinted specs: dingy, unfriendly and overpriced. ②.

Razbi's Guest House, Oginga Odinga Rd (PO Box 1418; ☎035/41312). Run-down of late (it used to be a well-thought-of stand-by): basic, not terribly clean and disgusting toilets. One of the rooms has a lake view of sorts. ①.

Safina Hotel, Apindi St. A favourite divey hotel – cheap enough, but ask for a room away from where the cars pull up at night. Women travelling alone might find the atmosphere a little threatening. ①.

YMCA, off Ang'awa Ave (PO Box 1618; ☎035/43192). Offers rather bland good value but it's friendly and cheap, if erratically supplied with water. There's a canteen and it's also possible to camp here, though few people do. A few double rooms available (B&B ①). Ksh200 per person in four-bed dorms.

CHEAP HOTELS

Black & Black Guest House, Gor Mahia St (☎035/42571). Cheaper than the *New Victoria*, just up the hill, but tawdry in contrast, and don't expect your room to have mosquito nets or private facilities. ②.

East View Hotel, Omolo Agar Rd (PO Box 857; ☎035/41871). Reeking of hospital antiseptic, and consequently spotless, this place is handy if you've just crawled off the bus, but the atmosphere is about as lively as a morgue. Bizarrely, they don't allow you to see your room before you pay for it (you should insist). No bar, safe parking. B&B ②.

Inca Hotel, behind Agip, off Jomo Kenyatta Ave (PO Box 112; ☎035/40158). Large clean rooms in a four-storey block, no nets but sprayed nightly, all s/c with hot water and fans, and colour TVs. Two suites at the same price. The first floor bar is unusually quiet and laid-back. B&B ③.

Kimwa Grand Hotel, Kondele suburb, 3km along the Kakamega road (PO Box 2226; ☎035/43928 or 21412, fax 21718). Sixty good s/c rooms, the main attraction being the music in the attached club (see below). There's a good restaurant, too. Catch a *matatu* from the BP station on Kenyatta Ave. B&B ③.

Lake View Hotel, Alego St (PO Box 1216; ☎035/45055). No exceptional views, though with its corner position, it does offer some breeze. Fairly comfortable but overpriced. ②.

Hotel Natasha, Otuona Rd. Decent s/c rooms with hot water but there are better deals to be had elsewhere. ②.

New Victoria Hotel, Gor Mahia St (PO Box 276; ☎035/21067, 41007). Friendly and recently renovated, with clean s/c rooms with fans, AC and warm showers. Rooms 207–9 have lake views. The best by far in its price range. B&B ②.

Hotel Perch, corner of Mak'asembo Rd and Obote Rd (PO Box 1224; ☎035/22229 or 22313). "Discover the new broom in the region," enthuses the bizarre blurb. One of the better city-centre options, opposite the car mechanics' area, with 200 s/c rooms, all with fridges and self-adjusting "air-cushioned" beds, all soundproofed against the bar's "latest flavoured filtered music". ③.

Western Lodge, Kendu Lane (PO Box 1519; ☎035/42586). Relatively clean and secure (with a large locking cupboard in every room), it's a friendly place, and half the rooms have lake views. Unfortunately there's no food, and, when the nearby goods yard and port road are busy and the bar opposite turns the music up, it's noisy. ②.

MID-RANGE HOTELS

Imperial Hotel, Jomo Kenyatta Ave (PO Box 1866; ☎035/41455–7, fax 40345, *imperial-hotel@form-net.com*). The first choice for wealthy Kenyans, this seems determined to eclipse the opposition in terms of prices and flashiness. All rooms are AC, "deluxe" ones with satellite TV and mini-bars. The cocktail lounge has view over lake, as do some rooms. Outdoor café and pool, and forex for guests. B&B ④–⑤.

Milimani Resort Hotel, off Got Huma Rd (PO Box 2652; ☎035/23245, fax 23242). A brand new hotel in a secure compound in Kisumu's quiet residential district, with comfortable rooms (all with satellite TV) and self-catering apartments (lower end of ⑤). The staff are friendly and gracious and there are good views from the upper floors. Downstairs is a restaurant and lounge (no alcohol served); planned additions of cottages and a pool have been stuck in the pipeline for years. B&B ④.

Hotel Royale, Jomo Kenyatta Ave (PO Box 1690; ☎035/40924, fax 44644). Formerly a good place to meet people and still highly rated for its Wednesday evening Indian barbecue (Ksh350), it has now been overrun by a number of raffish bars and the *Riviera* casino and slot-machine parlour, which dominates the entrance. The rooms themselves aren't up to much considering the alternatives, though there is a (fairly green) swimming pool and some uncomfortable sunbeds and a disco Friday–Sunday. B&B ④.

Saint Anna Guest House, 3km south at Milimani (PO Box 19100; ☎035/44617). In the posh residential area (follow the signposts from the Central Bank building on Jomo Kenyatta Ave), a modest Christian-run two-storey hotel, with good large rooms and hot showers. Safe parking. B&B ③.

Sunset Hotel, Aput Lane, 2.5km out of town to the south (PO Box 215; ☎035/41100–4, fax 42445). Fronting on to the Impala Sanctuary (see below) and with a whiff of plasticky highlife, this ugly five-storey complex wouldn't be out of place in Spain. Fraying around the edges, the main draw remains the views of beautiful sunsets from every room (all have balconies), and the baths – with enough hot water to fill them. Well-tended gardens complete with a green swimming pool, monkeys and par-rots, and apparently the occasional nocturnal hippo. Ramps and lift access for the disabled. A taxi from town costs around Ksh250. ④–⑤.

The Town

The **market** by the bus station is the biggest and best in western Kenya, crammed with fruit and vegetables (including some oddities like breadfruit), and all the usual house-hold paraphernalia – pots and plates, reed brushes, wickerwork, and wooden spoons. It's an absorbing place to wander. The market is such a success that it has mushroomed out into the adjacent municipal park, much to the consternation of the local authorities. Three new market buildings were built in 1984 with a multi-million-shilling World Bank loan, but, convinced that high rents on the new buildings coupled with unequal com-petition from squatters would slash their profits, the traders have steadfastly refused to move, and the buildings are still empty, concrete white elephants for which nobody can think of a use. For more on shopping in Kisumu, see "Souvenirs and artefacts" in the "Kisumu Listings" on p.282.

The prayer calls from Kisumu's pastel green-and-white **Jamia mosque**, not far away down Otieno Oyoo Street, sound odd in this town, but Islam is well established here, and Mumias (see p.334) an important regional influence dating from well into the last century. The orthodox Shafi'ite mosque was built in 1919, though the women's section on the right was only finished in 1984. It currently has two imams, a Tanzanian and a Pakistani. Inside, the beautiful long mats are from Saudi Arabia.

Kisumu Museum

Foremost among the town's sights is **Kisumu Museum** (daily 8.30am–6pm; Ksh200). Engaging and ambitious, it is highly recommended, just a short walk east from the mar-ket. The single-roomed main gallery stands in a large garden with carefully labelled trees. Apart from the usual row of game heads around the walls, there are cases of "Mammals", "Primates", "Birds" (including two stray bats), "Amphibians and Reptiles", "Fish and Crustaceans from the Sea" and "Insects", all displayed with considerable flair and imagination. One of the prize exhibits is a 189kg Nile perch, caught near Siaya in 1978, its gruesomely embalmed body now marooned on sturdy plywood supports. Heavier perch have been landed since, but at the time this mighty fish was a record-breaker. Particularly good use has been made of old and moth-eaten exhibits from Nairobi's National Museum. A free-swinging vulture, for example, spins like a model aircraft over your head while, best of all, centre stage, a lion is caught in full, savage pounce, leaping onto the back of a hysterical wildebeest in the most action-packed piece of taxidermy you're ever likely to see.

The **ethnographic** exhibits are uncommonly illuminating, too. The Maasai aren't the only people who take blood from their cattle for food: Kalenjin peoples like the Nandi and the Kipsigis once did the same, and even the Luo lived mostly on cow's blood mixed with milk before they arrived at Lake Victoria and began to cultivate and fish. There's a good selection of **musical instruments**, including a fine *nyatiti* (a Luo lyre, the East African equivalent of the *kora*); it is the kind of thing crudely repro-duced in a hundred curio shops and now occasionally heard at African concerts abroad. And look out for the disembodied hands pumping the bellows in the metal-working display.

Railway enthusiasts may be interested in the small display of early twentieth-century photographs of the opening of the Port Florence terminus of the so-called Lunatic Line. The museum's other photographic display shows excavation work in progress at the remarkable Zimbabwe-like walled enclosures of the Thimlich Ohinga archeological site in South Nyanza (see p.288).

In separate halls from the main gallery are a disappointing **aquarium**, where you can see what your curried tilapia looked like before it left the lake, and a **snake house** with a fairly comprehensive collection of Kenyan species. Among them are venomous snakes from the Kakamega Forest and some unnervingly lethal-looking black mambas and forest cobras from the Kisumu area. Outside, a tortoise pen, a snake pit – one of the pythons was rescued from a hole beneath the tea counter at the bus station – and a croc pond are rather pointless extras. The crocodiles are fed on Mondays.

In the "**Traditional Luo Homestead**" you may come across the Kisumu Museum drama group rehearsing. An old Luo man used to live in the "First Wife's house", and would tell you in slow Swahili that this is how all the Luo used to live, and indeed how he himself was brought up. He seems to have gone to the ancestors, but the museum is good on guides and enthusiastic members of staff are often willing to show you around.

Walks around town: Dunga

For a pleasant walk out of town, you could head for Hippo Point and the Luo fishing village of **DUNGA**. From the vicinity of the *Sunset Hotel* you follow the main road – or the shoreline – south. Close by is the small **Impala Sanctuary** (daily 6am–6pm; free), which has a herd of 26 impala, and a few distressingly small cages containing a couple of bored leopards and some thoroughly depressed vervet monkeys. Worth a visit just for the chance to stretch your legs in the shade (accompanied by an armed warden, to protect not against wild beasts but "bad people").

The **Kisumu Yacht Club** along the lakeshore has seen far better days – to judge by the number of boats moored and the islands of floating water hyacinth – but it remains strictly members-only: the *askaris* will let you in and kindly turn you straight out again (though they can arrange boat trips; see "Listings", p.282). Five hundred metres further on you come to **Hippo Point**, where you can watch often riotous sunsets from the rock-strewn shore while being bitten senseless by clouds of merciless mosquitoes. Hippos are still seen here, and boatmen will offer to take you out to view them. There's a strong, warm breeze at dusk, and it's a curiously stifling sensation to sit by this giant body of water without a whiff of ozone in the air. Around the lake, Luo fishermen cast their lines from the shallows. If you take kids, heed the playground warning – "Children Playing at Their Own Risk" – in front of the various indescribable pieces of machinery.

Dunga village itself is some 2km further, on the headland, a picturesque settlement with Dunga Fishermen's Co-operative Society the main feature on the shore. If you'd like to spend a night with the **fishermen** on their boats, the co-op is the first place to ask, though you should expect some good-natured negotiations first.

Eating and drinking

Kisumu has a number of reasonable **places to eat** – except on Sundays, when chips are about all that's on offer, and most places are closed anyway. Eat early, as many places tend to close shortly after dusk. Fish is the commonest dish, but there are some tasty curries around, too. There are **supermarkets** at Mega Plaza (Nakumatt; where the post office is on Oginga Odinga Road), and on Kenyatta Avenue (Yatin).

Expresso Coffee House, Otuona Rd. A recommended volunteers' hangout with a long menu of fry-ups, juices and milk shakes, all of it actually available. Closed evenings.

Imperial Hotel. As well as a restaurant proper there's a barbecue terrace with good *nyama choma*.

Kenshop, Oginga Odinga Rd and Accra St. A good bakery.

Kimwa Annex Restaurant, Otuona Rd. A bright, clattery, self-catering canteen/bar open 24-hours with a reliable menu, popular with families and volunteers (especially for its pool tables). Good for cheap, filling plates of *kima* (mince) with rice or *githeri* (lentil stew).

Kimwa Garden Inn, KNA House, Jomo Kenyatta Ave. Like the *Annex*, a good and filling self-service joint.

Kisumu Sweet Mart, Oginga Odinga Rd. Reliable for really cold sodas, bhajias and other snacks.

Hotel Perch, corner of Mak'asembo Rd and Obote Rd. One of the few places for real African fare (try the *alia* dried meat), and filling Indian buffets Wednesday and Friday (Ksh400).

Mona Lisa Bakery, Oginga Odinga Rd. Highly rated for breakfast, but otherwise variable. Closes 6pm.

New Generation Café, Oginga Odinga Rd. Reliable if unexciting chicken and chips. Again.

Café Natasha, Otuona Rd. A bistro-style place with a young, relatively upmarket following; good for big plates of chicken or steak and chips. Also open Sunday after lunch.

Sunset Hotel. The buffet lunches here, at about Ksh450, are a real blow-out, and there's a nice bar with snacks overlooking the gardens.

Nightlife

If you make the effort, Kisumu more than rewards the enthusiastic, with ample opportunities for catching **live bands,** and sometimes even big-name stars. More run-of-the-mill **discos** are plentiful, too. At either kind of venue, you're now most likely to hear *ndombolo* – read the box below.

Apoc Complex, Nyamasaria (☎035/42181). Long synonymous with live *benga* – how long will it hold out against the tide from the other side of the lake? Beer hall and *nyama choma* too.

Beograda, near the bus station on Omino Crescent. They sometimes have live music in the evening, the group playing "until they get sick of it or sacked". Sounds just right for a long, hot night. They have rooms (①) if the side-effects of *ndombolo* get to you, but they're pretty dingy and otherwise not recommended.

Donna Club, Kondele suburb, 4km out on the Kakamega road. Home of the old vanguard, with a huge AC dancefloor – guitarists, live *benga* and Lingala, as yet unconquered by *ndombolo*. Happy hour 7–8pm.

Gatiba Bar, Kendu Lane. Loud music, thin crowds.

Kimwa Grand Hotel, Kondele suburb, 4km out on the Kakamega road. Excellent live music Friday–Sunday, currently hosting Congolese *ndombolo* group Amitie Musica. Family shows Sunday afternoons.

Lakers Country Club. Get a taxi. Big name Congolese bands and others, with Sunday family day and video shows.

Octopus/Bottoms Up Night Club, Ogada St (☎035/40835). A pick-up joint of the first order – but for an enjoyable night out, this is relaxed enough if you just want to mingle over a beer or two. The restaurant is often empty, but the disco is always lively, and the *Pirate's Den* roof terrace (with barbecue and dartboard) is a popular, breezy rendezvous point, albeit with dire service.

NDOMBOLO

Besides being known for bloody civil wars and dictators, the Congo (formerly Zaïre) has managed to establish and nurture an enviable reputation throughout Africa as the continent's dance music factory (one earful of any traditional stuff will tell you why). Whilst some Kenyans moan that the Congolese do little other than pinch and repackage their original ideas, the reverse seems very much the case. The most recent dance craze import is **ndombolo**, which has taken Kenya by storm and Kisumu in particular. Its chief exponents are Koffi Olomide and Le General Defao. Its invention is credited to Kinshasa street kids imitating the gait of chimpanzees, or, alternatively, to a parody of President Laurent Kabila's limping walk. Latterly, the dance has taken on something of a controversial sexual flavour, which led to its being banned in Limuru, north Nairobi, by the local chief, on the grounds of its "gyrations arousing the youth and forcing many to engage in unprotected sex".

Riviera Casino, at the *Hotel Royale*. Just in case Kisumu's lodgings haven't extracted your last shillings, the casino here opens from 8pm to late, and there are slot machines from midday on. The *Royale*'s restaurant itself is OK, with good food.

Show Breeze Club, Mamboleo. Live *ndombolo*, some *benga*, in fierce under-the-belt competition with *Lakers* for the big stars.

Town Hotel, 100m from the *Expresso Coffee House*. Good place to catch local bands.

Listings

Airlines Kenya Airways, Alpha House, Oginga Odinga Rd (PO Box 1427; ☎035/44055–6, fax 43339; airport ☎035/40125 ext 06).

Airport Kisumu Airport (☎035/21032/ 43900/41976).

Banks Standard Chartered, Barclays and KCB; all Mon–Fri 9am–3pm, Sat 9–11am. Barclays and Standard Chartered have ATMs. Post Bank, on Jomo Kenyatta Ave, is where you can be sent money via Western Union.

Boat trips The Kisumu Yacht Club can arrange boat trips on the lake, assuming the *askaris* let you in.

British Council, Oginga Odinga Rd (PO Box 454; ☎035/45004). The library is open Tues–Fri 10am–6pm, Sat 9.30am–1pm. British papers and magazines, occasional BBC news videos and films, and useful Survey of Kenya maps, showing Kisumu district, on the wall. There are also occasional theatre productions here.

Car rental National Car Rental, Jovena service station, Otieno Oyoo St (☎035/417427 or 21799) has small saloons for hire at around $85/day if rented over a week; try also Kisumu Tours & Travel near Barclays Bank (☎035/41910), but check the car carefully.

DHL agent Kisumu Travels Ltd, Oginga Odinga Rd, near Barclays.

Ferries All passenger ferries (run by Kenya Railways) are currently suspended due to the water hyacinth invasion. There used to be ferry services to Kendu Bay, Homa Bay, Mbita, Mfangano Island and Tanzania. For information, call ☎035/42211 ext. 242 (Control Office) or ext. 232 (Port Officer). Currently still operating are occasional *matatu*-boats (no fixed schedules), which sometimes run to ports in Tanzania and Uganda. Cargo ships may be prepared to take passengers across the lake, presently strongly inadvisable given the war in the Congo and ongoing ethnic tensions in Burundi and Rwanda. Ask at the docks for all boat enquiries.

Hospitals The main place is Nyanza Provincial General Hospital (☎035/44275–7); Aga Khan Hospital (☎035/43516, 43530, 43713) is the best private hospital. You can call an ambulance on ☎035/42074.

Immigration The Immigration Department (PO Box 1178; ☎035/45015), in a building behind Alpha House on Oginga Odinga St, opposite the British Council, is exceptionally helpful, stamping visa and visitor's pass extensions on the spot without objection. If you need a photo, there's a booth inside the entrance to the market.

Kisumu show Held in the first week of August.

Library Off Gumbi Rd, behind the bus and *matatu* station. Mon–Thurs 9.30am–6.30pm, Fri 9.30am–4.30pm, Sat 9am–1pm.

Pharmacies Open late are: Hillchem, Kilimani Shopping Centre (8am–10pm; ☎035/44604); and Winam Chemists, Kondele suburb, opposite MTC (7.30am–8pm; ☎035/44005).

Post office Mon–Fri 8am–5.30pm, Sat 9am–1pm. Poste restante available. If you want to make an international call through the operator, be prepared to wait. You're far better off buying a phonecard (if you can find one – they're forever out of stock) and queuing up to use the cardphone outside. Telex and fax services are also available.

Souvenirs and artefacts The row of craft stalls opposite the *Hotel Royale* is one of the region's best hunting grounds for souvenirs. The things to buy here (if you have space) are the heavy, three-legged Luo stools. The best are intricately inlaid with beads, and dark brown from repeated oiling. Also on offer are bangles, wooden carvings, and row upon row of soapstone knick-knacks. Soapstone (or Kisii-stone) is more expensive to buy in Kisumu than at source (Tabaka, near Kisii), but it's cheaper than in most places, and the craftsmen will carve designs to order. Pendeza Weavers

(PO Box 1786) is a worthwhile visit, about 3km out of town past the museum on the Nairobi road, past the chief's camp (on the right in the large field) and indicated by a small white sign on the right. Handwoven *kikois* here are as cheap as you'll find; they turn up later at Spinner's Web in Nairobi.

Swimming pools A swim at the *Sunset Hotel* is always a pleasure – non-residents pay Ksh100. You might also take a dip in the *Royale*'s pool. The *Imperial* has a less enticing, semi-indoor pool, surrounded by a very plain concrete terrace.

Taxis Kisumu Taxi Cab Service, Central Square (☎035/42198 daytime).

Moving on from Kisumu

Apart from boat connections (see "Listings"), Kisumu is very well connected to the rest of the country by **bus** and **matatu**. The main bus and *matatu* stage is on Gumbi Road, behind the BP station at the intersection of Kenyatta Avenue and Otieno Oyoo Street, from where you'll find services to more or less anywhere in Western Kenya, and to cities further afield like Nakuru and Mombasa (Coast Bus have overnight runs to Mombasa at 5pm and 6pm, taking over 14hr; avoid the deadly Tawfiq). Akamba have their office on Alego Street at the west end of the city (☎035/45076), with three buses daily to Nairobi (10am, 1pm & 8.30pm), and two for **Kampala** (noon & 1am; Ksh700–1000). Some other companies with Nairobi buses leave from the stage opposite. **Peugeots** for Nairobi leave from the BP station. If you're aiming for **Kakamega Forest**, buses and *matatus* run from the main stage to Kakamega town, from where it's possible to find transport to the forest (for details see p.325). **Trains** (third class only) run daily from the railway station to Nairobi (6pm; 12–13hr; Ksh200), and to Butere (8.45am; 3hr 10min; Ksh38).

Siaya district and the road to Uganda

Heading northwest out of Kisumu, down a broad avenue of flame trees, you pass the Sunni Muslim, Ismailia and Hindu cemeteries, then pass the golf club and emerge into the wide plains of **Siaya district**. Transport to the border town of Busia is fairly constant. The region is pleasantly rural but unremarkable; the one place on the road where you might want to stop for the night is the *Jera Inn* (PO Box 14 Sega; ☎0334/34118; ②), well signposted near **Sega**. This "country club" set-up has some rooms, food, discos (Wednesday, Friday, Saturday and Sunday) and a generally happy ambience that has brought it widespread fame in the district. The **rooms** – in fact very smart *bandas* – are self-contained and really good value.

USENGE (or Usengi), a short bus ride from Kisumu, is something of a diversion if you're en route to Uganda, but it's a useful target if you're planning an exploration of the district, and a town of precolonial historical significance in its own right. The nearby hill, Got Ramogi, is by tradition the site where the first Luo arrived at the lake from further north. It's not a hard climb to the top for a satisfying view over the island-dotted lake, the lagoon below (Lake Saru), and the land which the Luo fought for and eventually won from the Bantu-speakers at the end of the fifteenth century. Usenge itself is a pretty town with a causeway over the lake that connects with the Uganda road. Lodgings there are cheap.

Busia

BUSIA, on the Uganda border, is a surprisingly nice little town and a better place to cross than Malaba, the busier frontier post on the railway line further north. The formalities are straightforward enough. Busia consists of a line of shacks and bars on the Kenya side, with a similar line in Uganda. If you're staying the night, the optimistically named *Silent Lodge* is as cheap as they come, and sometimes even has warm water. Of much better standard is the *Farm View Hotel* on Hospital Road (PO Box 141; ☎0336/22470 or 22097; ③), with good s/c rooms, kids' play area, and "traditional" dancers and discos at weekends.

Whether you have a visa for Uganda or not (UK passport holders don't need one; Americans do), you're normally allowed to **cross the border** to look around on the Ugandan side. Unless you're desperate for a bottle of cheap whisky however, there's little point.

From Kisumu to Kisii

If you want it to be, the ride **from Kisumu to Kisii** can be a rapid transition along the main A1 highway from dusty or flooded plain (depending on the season) up into the ample, fecund hills of the Gusii. But there are various ornithological diversions along the way, if you're independently mobile or enthusiastic enough to make the effort with public transport and your own feet.

There's also a fine **alternative route** from Kisumu to Kisii, using the first-class paved **lakeshore road** from Katito (south of Ahero) to Kendu Bay (see p.293), and then taking the road to Oyugis back on the A1, just a short journey from Kisii. Except when the latter road is in very bad condition after heavy rain, the route takes barely longer than the direct approach.

Kisumu bird sanctuary

The swampland beyond Kisumu to the southeast is very rich in birdlife, and the first place worth investigating off the main A1 road is the **heronry** (Kisumu Bird Sanctuary; information from KWS District Warden, PO Box 1193 Kisumu; ☎035/21105) on the way to **Ahero**. From April to May, especially, this is the nesting site of hundreds of pairs of not just herons, but ibises, cormorants, egrets and storks, the dark and curiously scruffy open-bill stork included. Ornithologically world-famous, the sanctuary is a must if you're interested in birds.

To get there, take a right turn (south, towards the lake) around 7–8km from Kisumu (about 16km west of Ahero), to the school at **Orongo**, and from there branch left and follow the track for another 2–3km. Ask local people's advice, as the best sites and the easiest access to the colony move each year. The site is usually a good place to camp. This low-lying region between Kisumu and the western highlands is known as the **Kano plains** – disablingly hot, humid flatlands, swaying with sugar cane and rice fields, fertilized by occasional disastrous flooding.

There are a number of other breeding sites for herons and ibises beyond the sanctuary, some 20km from Kisumu, again to the right of the road in the marshy district southwest of Ahero.

Oyugis and the pelicanry

Climbing into Kisii district's round, picture-book hills, you arrive at the crossroads town of **OYUGIS**; like a number of other places, it was originally named after a local hero. Apart from the sprawling *matatu* stage, whose speeding vehicles presumably account for the battered state of the main street, and a few reasonable B&Ls – *Nyadendi's Palace* (PO Box 30; ③), *Oyugis Safe Lodge* (PO Box 98; ①) and, on the main road out towards Kisii, *Hotel Ragama* (①) – Oyugis offers little but its pelican-breeding site.

The **pelicanry** (currently free) is reached by leaving the main road (left, southeast) before the Caltex station and continuing (past *Safe Lodge*) up the *murram* in a three-kilometre arc, until you reach two huge fig trees, in a narrow stream-bed 200m from the road on the left. From August to March, you'll see the parent birds wheeling in the air from some distance, and, when you get closer, there's the distinctive smell of pelican guano to guide you. With binoculars you can watch the shaggy **chicks** in their treetop nests ramming their heads down the parents' throats for fish; then, yakking desperately for more, attempting the same manoeuvre on each other. Sadly, the site now risks disappearing under pressure from the rapidly expanding human population around it. Much of the original fencing has been torn down, parts of the reserve have been built on, and elsewhere nesting trees have been felled. Although there are plans to re-protect the area, this will in all probability be too little and far too late.

To Kisii

If you arrive at Oyugis early in the day and are feeling very fit, you can continue on the track past the pelicanry all the way to Kisii, along a route that becomes more and more beautiful as you climb up through dense *shambas* and forests, out onto **Manga ridge** above the town (see p.299). You might be lucky and get a lift some of the way – but don't count on it. If you have your own car, it's a pleasant half-hour drive.

South Nyanza

The territory south of Kisumu is interesting to explore – it's fairly easy to get around, if you're willing to go by *matatu*, and includes a number of small towns, the Lake Victoria islands, a national park and even an archeological site. This section covers the main town of **Homa Bay**, **Ruma National Park**, the newly uncovered site of **Thimlich Ohinga**, the islands of **Rusinga and Mfangano** (perch fishing for the rich; walking and hanging out for the poor), the agreeable little town of **Kendu Bay** and, down near the Tanzanian border, the one-street town of **Migori**.

The **lakeshore** west of Migori is remote and, in parts, beautiful, with **Karungu Bay** a rewarding side trip. In the other direction, **Kihancha**, on the south bank of the Migori River, on another back-country route to Maasai Mara, is reputedly a pretty area.

South Nyanza is largely Luo country, but there are also scattered, rural communities of **Kuria** people down here. The Kuria have an interesting, quasi-matriarchal system found in various parts of Africa, which essentially allows women of means to "marry" younger women in order to have children without the need to live with a man. In practice, it's often a married woman who can't have children who invites a younger woman into her home. The young "bride", in turn, chooses a male partner, often in secret, to father (biologically speaking) her children, who are brought up by the two women without the involvement of the father or the older woman's husband. The older woman is sometimes a widow, sometimes simply a single woman. In any case, she lives like a male elder – attending to light business affairs but essentially waited upon hand and foot from dawn to dusk. It's a system with much to recommend it, especially when it takes care of unmarried mothers (who are barred from marrying men), who come into the family as "wives" – surrogate mothers – and whose children are automatically adopted. Ironically, despite these apparently female-controlled arrangements, it's male children that women-families want – and men who inherit land.

Homa Bay

Travelling down from Kisii, the green, well-watered hills and tightly spaced *shambas* of the Gusii give way to the drier and more open territory of the Luo, where sugar cane, maize and sisal dominate. One of the greatest freshwater lakes in the world lies right in front of you, obscured for most of the day by mist and haze. If you're lucky enough to be travelling after the rains, however, the lake and the colours of the mountains around it are devastatingly beautiful.

The place to head for is the small port town of **HOMA BAY**, the region's main centre and also a good base for visits to Ruma National Park, Rusinga Island and Simbi Lake. At first glance a scruffy and, to some, unremarkable place, it is in fact one of the friendliest and most welcoming towns in Kenya. Whether you're arriving by *matatu* or are driving yourself (in which case picking up hitchers is fun), you can't fail to notice adults as well as kids waving and grinning by the roadsides at the passing *wazungu*.

The town itself admittedly has nothing much of interest, just a few dirty, pot-holed streets and an unusual straw hat-shaped **Catholic cathedral** atop a low hill behind town, with an open-air central altar and great views. It used to have a busy port, which provided the focus for most of the town's activities (fishing, trade and a little tourism), but since June 1997 this, and much of the shoreline around, has been completely hemmed in by over a kilometre of thick, vibrantly green **water hyacinth**. By all accounts the weed infestation happened quite quickly, leading to some boats becoming trapped for several days. Six people actually walked for 4km over the weed to safety, and one woman gave birth to a baby boy – whom she named Victoria Junior – on a trapped boat. Boats to Kisumu and Mbita have been indefinitely suspended (and most of the local boats have been sold), though small convoys of fishing canoes still manage to inch themselves through the weed in the morning into the open lake beyond. The shoreline itself is accessible by turning left just before the defunct pier, where the abandoned *Homa Bay Hotel*'s gardens (the building itself is being eaten by goats) have been turned into a "public nature park", a fun place to meet local people, where colonies of ibis and weaver birds, as well as boys monkeying about, populate the trees. If you're into **traditional Luo music**, Homa Bay is the place to track down tapes of *nyatiti* (lyre), *orutu* (single-stringed bow fiddle) and *onand* (accordion) music, as well as the ubiquitous gospel.

There's a handful of reasonable **accommodation** options, the most modern being the *Hippo Buck Hotel*, 2km out on the Rongo road (PO Box 274; ☎0385/22541 or 22032; B&B ②–③), with clean s/c rooms (no mosquito nets but screened windows), a nice garden and good restaurant (especially fried fish). Look out for live *orutu* and *onand* music here on Friday and Saturday evenings. Opposite the *Hippo Buck* is the much more basic *Hill View Guest Lodge* (PO Box 829; no phone; B&B ②), with small, somewhat dark rooms, all with nets, and shared but clean squat loos (water in buckets). There's a relaxed *nyama choma* bar in the gardens outside. In town itself, the best choice – with excellent views over the lake and Homa Bay – is *Hotel Kavirondo* (PO Box 591; ☎0385/22689; ①), a five-storey building behind the red-and-white metal communications tower next to the signposted *Neem Shade Restaurant*, with breezy s/c rooms with nets (good cold showers, hot water in buckets on request), and doubles with small balconies. There's also a parking compound. *Nyanza Lodge* (①), on the same street as Barclays, has more basic rooms (hold your breath in the shared shower/toilets), reasonable food and safe parking, but the main draw at weekends is its pub, featuring the Victoria Chomeka Original Band.

As to **food**, there are lots of inexpensive *hotelis* almost everywhere. The best is the *Neem Shade Restaurant* in the Salama Building next to *Hotel Kavirondo*: from the pier, head up along the Rongo road, turn left after the market, then take the second right. Also worth trying are: *Snack Hotel* by the Akamba bus office; *Frontline Hotel* across from the *matatu* stage towards the pier, which has huge portions but isn't terribly clean; and *Kasongo Hotel* behind the Migori *matatu* stage, which serves good beans, rice and other staples.

Got Asego

A **hike** up **Got Asego**, the impressive conical hill on the east side of town, is recommended. The hill is the highest of dozens of volcanic plugs (cores of old volcanoes) across the plain; from its table-sized summit, you'll have a 360-degree panorama of lakeshore and surrounding plains. It is remarkable how little of the land is not used – Luo thatched huts are interspersed with tin-roofed homesteads, a patchwork of small plots and agave hedges. Take binoculars and you can see more: clumps of papyrus drifting across the lake beyond the water hyacinth, and traffic along the road where it snakes east to Kendu Bay.

It takes about an hour to reach the top from the centre of town (actual ascent 30–45min), an easy climb but best tackled late in the afternoon (early morning ascents, though cooler, can be treacherous thanks to dew on the rocks). Head up the Rongo road, take the second left after the Total petrol station and turn right up the *murram* road after Homa Bay School. The hill itself is best approached up the northwest ridge, where there's a well-defined footpath. Beware of columns of ants.

Onward from Homa Bay

Matatus leave from the stage near the jetty for Kendu Bay and Kisumu, and from the stage on the main road for Kisii, Migori and Mbita. If you're heading east, the swiftest exit from Homa Bay is probably aboard a Migori *matatu*, which drops you at Rongo on the A1 highway, where you can soon find a Kisii-bound vehicle coming up from the south. Northbound, the road to Kendu Bay looks short on the map, but *matatus* take a good ninety minutes to bump along its rough surface. The road is then paved from Kendu Bay to Kisumu. Plenty of long-distance **buses** start their journeys in Homa Bay, making Nairobi an easy overnight (or daytime) ride. There are two routes: one via Kisii and Kericho, the other via Nakuru, both continuing via Nakuru and Naivasha.

Ruma National Park

Daily 6am–6pm; $15, $5 children/students. Warden: PO Box 420 Homa Bay; ☎0385/22007.

Ruma National Park (previously known as Lambwe Valley Nature Reserve) can be a little tricky to reach – the nearest *matatu* route (Homa Bay to Mbita) skirts the reserve by 11km – but if you're independently mobile and self-sufficient the effort of getting there is usually repaid by animal-watching undisturbed by the presence of other visitors; you're virtually guaranteed the place to yourself.

The Lambwe Valley's 194 square kilometres of tsetse fly-ridden bush is one of the few places in Kenya where you can see **Jackson's hartebeest** and two opposite extremes of antelope: the enormous, horse-like **roan** and the miniature **oribi**. There are about seventy of the beautiful **Rothschild's giraffe** and they're not hard to see above the tall grass. You'll have more difficulty spotting **cheetah** and **leopard**.

Practicalities

To get there, head south out of Homa Bay along the main Rongo–Migori road, and turn off after 3km onto the Mbita road leading southwest; from this (signposted) turning, an eight-kilometre drive along the rough *murram* brings you to a signposted turning to the left, where another *murram* road runs for 11km to the gate and the reserve. If you miss this, the next left turning, 8km further on, will also take you to the gate, though you'll have to ask people directions at the numerous unmarked junctions. You are likely to be greeted by surprised rangers: they get few visitors. There are no facilities of any kind, so although you can camp in the park with your own equipment, you'll need to bring food and water. There are plans to construct a forty-bed **eco-lodge** within the park, which should be ready in theory by the end of 2000: details from the KWS facilities manager (address, p.148).

Work is in progress to make Ruma National Park more accessible to visitors, in order to safeguard its future, but for the present it isn't practical without your own transport. If you're dedicated, your best hope is to talk to the park warden in Homa Bay. You can find him through the manager of the BP petrol station and spare parts store.

Thimlich Ohinga

Thimlich Ohinga is an archeological site of potentially huge significance – "the greatest stone enclosures in East Africa", as the Kisumu Museum bumper stickers declare. The site is the most striking example of an architecture whose remnants are scattered across South Nyanza. Similar to the drystone enclosures of Zimbabwe (of which Great Zimbabwe is the classic example), its main structure consists of a compound about 150m in diameter, inside which are five smaller enclosures – probably used as cattle pens – and at least six house pits, the sites of former dwellings. The walls range in height from 2.5m to 3.5m – higher than those of the seventeenth- and eighteenth-century stone ruins in the Inyanga Highlands in Zimbabwe. Outside the main compound wall on the southeast side, evidence of iron-working has been discovered.

Thimlich Ohinga in Luo means "thick bush with stone enclosures". It's estimated they were built around the fifteenth century by a people whose history has been forgotten. But successive generations of various communities have used stone enclosures and, in some places, modern Luo families have their homesteads inside such walls. It's certainly an unusual and worthwhile site: in up-country Kenya it rates as the equal of Hyrax Hill (see p.245) and is quite absorbing compared to Chetambe's Fort (p.324), but, as usual, if your interest in ruins is limited at best, pass on.

Getting there

You really need your own transport to get to Thimlich. **From Kisii** (105km) or **Homa Bay** (60km), you follow the C20 tarmac Rongo–Homa Bay road as far as Rod Kopany, which is some 15km from Homa Bay and 19km from Rongo. From Rod Kopany the route – unsurfaced – runs southwest, through Mirogi and Ndhiwa to Miranga. Miranga is the limit of what little public transport there is. After Miranga's shops there's a signpost showing the direction of Thimlich Ohinga; look out for following signs which should get you the whole way there.

If you're approaching **from Migori**, take the Isebania/Tanzania road, and after 4km turn off right onto rough *murram*, at the junction for Muhuru Bay, where there is a National Cereals and Produce Board depot. A couple of kilometres from the depot you reach another junction where you take a right and drive straight on through Suna and Macalder, looking out for the Thimlich signposts as you go. The journey is about 55km from the Cereals Board Depot. All these roads necessitate 4WD in wet weather.

Rusinga Island

Far more practical than Ruma National Park or Thimlich Ohinga is a trip to **Rusinga Island**, although the water hyacinth invasion of Homa Bay now means for the time being you can only get here by road. The narrow channel between Mbita and the island was bridged by a **causeway** in 1984, whatever your map may show, so driving around Rusinga is quite feasible, as long as the rains aren't too heavy. The road from Homa Bay has recently been graded, but is still tough on suspensions and can get tricky in the rains. There is a steady stream of converted lorry *matatus* (around Ksh100) from Homa Bay to Mbita throughout the day, but they're always packed, so make sure you get to the stage in plenty of time.

Mbita, straddled on either side of the causeway, is very unprepossessing indeed, but things improve once you get on to the island. The building of the causeway – partly over two dumper trucks which fell into the lake during the operation and couldn't be recovered – has had some unwanted side effects. Vervet monkeys now move onto the island to raid crops, and fish have become scarce on the Kisumu side of Rusinga because the causeway blocks the current, turning the water there into a stagnant pond. A bridge to replace the old chain ferry would have been the best solution to the island's access problem. As it is, the single bit of civil engineering represented by the causeway has ended Rusinga's slight isolation at what many local people feel is an unacceptable cost.

Mbita and around: practicalities

Excepting some *matatus* which run around Rusinga Island, **MBITA** is as far as you can go by public road transport. The last lorry-*matatu* returns to Homa Bay around 3pm. There are, however, some **wooden boats** which connect Mbita daily with various ports on Mfangano Island, Takawiri Island, and Ranalo or Misori on the opposite side of Rusinga Channel, which provides road access northeast via Bondo to Kisumu. Note that these services dry up by mid-afternoon, so if you arrive late, you'll have to stay the night in Mbita (unless you've around Ksh2500 to spare to hire a boat).

Accommodation is limited to three, rather basic, choices, none of which have double rooms. The best of these is *Patroba Ogweno Lodge* (PO Box 315; ☎0385/22184; non-s/c ①, s/c ②), down the alleyway by the *New Foxton* restaurant, whose better rooms are s/c with nets. More characterful, but perhaps not for lone women, is *Viking Lodge* (PO Box 12; ☎0385/22182; ①), on the right side of the *matatu* stage, which has some dingy cells with nets but no s/c, off a lovely bougainvillaea-shaded courtyard which doubles as a bar, with music from 5–10pm. Food here can be ordered in advance. The only other option, and dirt cheap, is the new *Junction Motel*, 1km up the Homa Bay road (no PO Box or phone at present; ①), which is mainly a restaurant (good mutton *nyama choma*) with just two non-s/c rooms: there are plans to expand. Plenty of other cheap *hotelis* provide filling **meals**, but at present you won't find fish on the menu, thanks to a scandal in which local fishermen used toxic chemicals to land their catch – the District Commissioner has banned the sale of cooked fish in all *hotelis* until further notice. Before the ban, the *Calypso Bar* served good tilapia.

If you've an afternoon to while away, there's flourishing birdlife in the vicinity, and doubtless a lot more to be uncovered by adventurous travellers. **Sindo**, 10km south of Mbita, is reckoned a good place to go out in fishing boats, while from the top of **Gemba Hill**, just a few kilometres from the Mbita–Sindo road, there's a superb view across to Homa Bay and down towards Tanzania.

The island

RUSINGA is small and austerely pretty, high crags dominating the desolate, goat-grazed centre, and a single dirt road running around the circumference. Life here is difficult, drought commonplace, and high winds a frequent torment. The occasional heavy rain either washes away the soil or sinks into the porous rock, emerging lower down where it creates swamps. Ecologically, the island is in very dire straits: almost all its trees have been cut down for cooking fuel or to be converted into lucrative charcoal. These conditions make harvests highly unpredictable and most people do some fishing to make ends meet, either selling the catch on to refrigerated lorries or bartering directly for produce with traders from Kisii. And the causeway has forced them to make longer fishing trips. Yet the islanders, in common with their mainland cousins, remain an unfailingly friendly and cheerful bunch, who are more than happy to make contact with wayward *wazungu*.

Aside from its friendliness, the island has two significant claims to fame. It is rich in **fossils**, and was the site of Mary Leakey's discovery of a skull of *Proconsul africanus* (a primitive anthropoid ape), which can be seen in the National Museum. And it was the birthplace of **Tom Mboya** (see Contexts, p.611), civil rights champion, trade unionist and charismatic young Luo politician who was gunned down in Nairobi in 1969, sparking off a crisis that led to over forty deaths in widespread rioting and demonstrations, and was a turning point for the worse in Kenya's independent history.

Tom Mboya's mausoleum lies on family land at **Kasawanga** on the north side of the island, about 7km by the dirt road from Mbita, or roughly 5km directly across the island. You might possibly get a lift from Mbita to Kasawanga (in theory there are five *matatus* a day each way, unless the road gets washed out by heavy rains), but you need to be prepared to walk the whole way there and back if necessary (allow 4hr and take some water). You're likely to find someone to show you the way but Rusinga is so small you're unlikely to get lost. Aim for the crags in the centre (if you're feeling energetic, you could climb the tallest to get a view of the whole island), skirt them to the right and then walk down to rejoin the road on the other side of the Tom Mboya Memorial Health Centre. There's a little *hoteli* here with cold sodas. From here, it's less than 2km to Mboya's mausoleum, the white dome clearly visible just off the road. The mausoleum (open most days to visitors) contains various mementoes and gifts Mboya received during his life. The inscription on the grave reads:

THOMAS JOSEPH MBOYA
August 15th 1930 – July 5th 1969
Go and fight like this man
Who fought for mankind's cause
Who died because he fought
Whose battles are still unwon!

You don't have to know anything about the man to be impressed. In any other surroundings his memorial might seem relatively modest, but on this barren, windswept shore, it stands out like a beacon. Mboya's family live right next door and are happy to see foreign visitors, who rarely come here.

Fifty metres past the Tom Mboya Secondary School, the path to the right takes you through *shambas* of millet and corn to a seasonally grassy lakeside called Hippo Bay. Here you can watch nesting fish eagles as well as, usually, hippos. If you're lucky you may see the pretty and little-known spotted-necked otters that live around Lake Victoria and nowhere else in Kenya.

Also on this side of the island is the amazingly expensive ($350 per person) *Rusinga Island Club* (reservations: PO Box 24513 Nairobi; ☎02/447224, 447228, 447231, fax 447268; closed May and sometimes Christmas; ⑨), the sort of rustic-luxury retreat you would expect, with a high proportion of its clients flying in from a Maasai Mara safari to the nearby airstrip. The main attraction here is sport fishing – Rusinga holds the record for the heaviest Nile perch ever landed – but with water-skiing, windsurfing and guided sightseeing on offer, there's plenty to divert fishing widows and widowers too. It's possible (and a joy) to stay overnight – the club sleeps ten in thatched cottages. Boat excursions (watch the fish eagles for how to catch tilapia in style), activities, meals and drinks are all included in the price.

Mfangano Island

Said to have been inhabited for centuries, enigmatic **Mfangano Island** is out of range of the smallest fishing boats, and entirely without vehicles. The island is populated by a curious mixture of immigrants from all over Kenya, administered by a chief and three sub-chiefs with help from a trio of policemen. Monitor lizards swarm on the sandy shores and **hippos** are much in evidence out in the water.

Larger and more populous than Rusinga, with a similarly rugged landscape but better vegetation cover, Mfangano's greatest economic resource is still the lake itself. Traditional **fishing techniques** are unusual: the islanders fish with floating kerosene lamps hauled shorewards, or towards a boat, to draw in the schools to be netted. Of more immediate interest, however, are the island's **rock paintings**, certainly worth the trip if you're into such things, and a good excuse to get to know the island in any case.

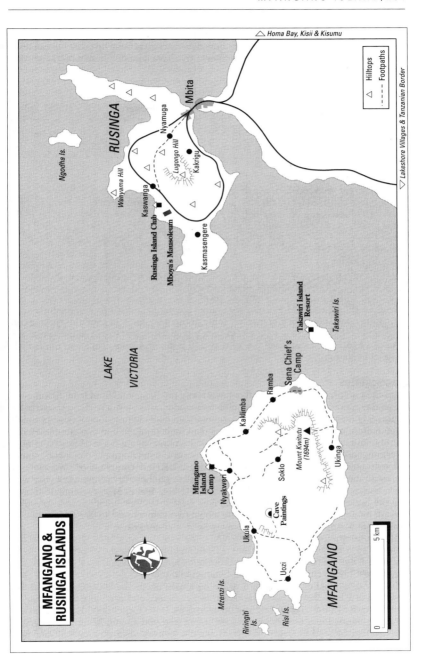

Because there are no vehicles, Mfangano's people rely on a network of temporary **foot-paths** which are constantly changing course. If you arrive at Sena by boat, you can walk all over the island, though it's always easier if you have a guide – Ksh300–500 per day is a fair fee.

The rock paintings

From Ukula (see below), an hour or two's walk into the interior (with a guide) brings you to a high, north-facing bluff on Itone Hill, with startling views out across the island's north coast. Here, in a gently scooped cave, are the **rock paintings**: reddish spirals and whorls, some with rays, up to 50cm across, that could come from any Von Daniken paperback. People will tell you they're very old, but nobody knows who painted them or why, or what they depict. Local people associate the site with supernatural powers and miraculous events, and in some measure fear them, too, which has so far helped prevent the vandalism which has afflicted other rock art sites in Kenya.

The site is still used for traditional rain-making ceremonies, when elders pray to their ancestors to intercede on their behalf. As a result, locals believe that violating traditional practice may lead to something dangerous, so don't be surprised if you find people insisting that you stay put in Ukula for a day or two before setting out: the gods apparently need time to prepare for your arrival. Which explains why, if you go purposefully looking for the paintings, or ask too many questions about them, they'll elude you. But walk as if you didn't care and you'll suddenly come across them. Stories like these suggest the paintings were indeed put on the rock by an earlier and distinctive culture, of which people today have no recollection. If you're really into rock art, the Odengere Hills, also on Mfangano, are unique among Lake Victoria's prehistoric sites in that they have depictions of insects, some of them so fine that even the species can be identified. Experts are at a loss as to their significance. For site-by-site descriptions of Lake Victoria's rock art, see the 1994 (vol.9) issue of *Azania* (copies at the British Institute in Nairobi).

Practicalities

Since the water hyacinth invasion, the diesel **ferry** to Mfangano Island from Kisumu via Homa Bay and Mbita has been indefinitely suspended. Unless you're rich enough to fly in, the only means of access is on the large wooden boats with outboard motors which run a *matatu* service, shuttling local people and their produce between Mbita and the surrounding islands and peninsulas. Most head around Mfangano in an anti-clockwise direction, calling at Sena, Nyakweri and Ukula, others head around clockwise, sometimes dropping in at Takawiri Island and Ukinga. **UKULA** (pronounced "Wakola"), is closest to the rock paintings, and it makes sense to go there first, then work your way back, perhaps over a few days, to Sena. The first boat leaves Mbita around 10–11am, and the last no later than 4pm, which makes day-trips rather pointless unless you've enough money (around Ksh2500) to hire a boat plus skipper for the day. Going back to Mbita from Mfangano, the first boat leaves Sena at around 8am.

It's a ninety-minute crossing to **SENA** – the chief's camp (PO Mfangano Island Chief's Camp, Sena; Radiocall Nairobi ☎3756) and also the capital of Mfangano. Sena has a small *duka*, a post office but no accommodation, as the island's only budget lodging – a rest house run by the chief in Sena – is no more. Unless you're well off (see below), the only option is winging it with the locals: people have camped wild in the past, and at Ukula they've seen the odd traveller before and are more than happy to earn the cost of a B&L for putting you up overnight. Don't forget that Mfangano is desperately poor, without electricity or piped water, and you should bring anything you think you might need. Not surprisingly, Mfangano sees few visitors of any kind and perhaps a handful of travellers each year.

It's another story if you've money to burn: with the success of the exclusive and expensive **Mfangano Island Camp**, a fishing lodge similar to Rusinga's, tourist numbers have increased slightly, but again most of the camp's visitors fly in from the Maasai Mara on a day-trip (fishing and bird-watching in the morning, lunching and lounging in the afternoon) and barely connect with the local people. The camp, a huddle of clay-and-thatch buildings laid out in the shape of a Luo homestead but fitted out in deluxe style, overlooks a private bay and sleeps twelve (reservations through *Governor's Camps*, p.48; FB ⑧, plus around $225pp for the return flight). There's a similar, though less expensive place on **Takawiri Island**, off Mfangano: the *Takawiri Island Resort*, which offers windsurfing, snorkelling and sailing, as well as fishing and bird-watching. Like *Mfangano Island Camp*, it faces west, for unforgettable sunsets. You can get there on a *matatu*-boat from Mbita, or else by light aircraft or on their own cruiser from Kisumu (FB ⑦; reservations through Lake Victoria Game Safaris, PO Box 188 Kisumu; ☎035/45088, fax 44644).

Kendu Bay

KENDU BAY's local fame comes from the curiosity of **Simbi Lake**, about 4km (45 minutes' walk) west of the village: head out of the village on the Homa Bay road and pass the left turn to Oyugis/Kisii. Just over 2km further on, over the river bridge, turn right down the path and walk for another fifteen minutes.

The lake, and the nearby Ondago Swamp, are the recently adopted feeding grounds of a couple of thousand **flamingos**, refugees from Lake Nakuru, where pollution and shrinking food supplies are squeezing the water bird population out. With a steady trickle of naturalists and tourists now coming to Kendu Bay to bird-watch, the villagers are, inevitably, keen for a slice of the action. Among the suggestions that have been made are that the Homa Bay County Council should fence off Simbi Lake, impose admission charges, and make provision for local traders to set up stalls. However, it remains to be seen whether the lake contains enough spirulina algae to support a large flock of flamingos for more than a season or two.

Flamingos or no flamingos, the lake is unquestionably weird: several bright green but changeable acres of opaque water sunk 20–30m below the surrounding land and only a few kilometres from Lake Victoria itself. It has no apparent source and its origins are somewhat mysterious. It looks like a huge meteorite crater with a footpath around the rim.

The **story** goes that an old wandering woman was refused hospitality one rainy night at the village that once occupied the site of the lake. A big beer party was going on and she was ignored. Only one woman would allow her to warm herself and the old woman insisted she and her family leave the village with her. The young woman tried to persuade her husband to come with them, fearing the old lady's revenge for her ill-treatment, but in vain. So the two women left alone. And later that night there was a tremendous cloudburst and the rain came down so hard that the village was swamped to become Simbi Lake. Further variations on the story (there are many) improve on the theme of drunkenness and debauchery to give a Sodom and Gomorrah ring to the tale. Other lakes in Kenya have similar tales of origin.

The little lake's shores are almost devoid of vegetation. Nobody goes out on it in boats and it doesn't look as if they fish there either. It's usually described with the catch-all term "volcanic" and is apparently extraordinarily deep. According to one local belief, visitors should throw money in to avoid bad luck. Whatever the natural explanation, it seems plausible that the area was inhabited when the lake was formed, the disaster accounting for the legends. Similar, though smaller, lakes can be seen east of Kendu Bay along the new road to Kisumu.

If you're heading on to Homa Bay, you might like to see the **Oriang Pottery Centre** in the village of the same name, 2km past the Simbi Lake turning. It's a UNDEP-funded programme, relying on clay from the local river bed.

Practicalities and onward travel

Kendu Bay itself is much smaller than Homa Bay and has a good deal more intrinsic charm. Like Homa Bay, however, it has next to nothing to offer the casual visitor. The ferry dock (a pier partly made of concrete-filled barges) is about a kilometre from the one-street village, currently out of action thanks to the strangling belt of water hyacinth along the shore. One notable building is the gorgeous Masjid Tawakal mosque. You can look around it – though there's not much to see – and climb on the roof.

There are a couple of **B&Ls** in town: *Milimani Bar & Restaurant* (PO Box 77; no phone; ①) has eight very basic non-s/c singles but no showers. Much better is the *Countryside Lodge* (PO Box 184; no phone; B&B ①), with basic non-s/c rooms with nets in peaceful gardens and friendly management; there's no running water, but they have a well, and food can be ordered in advance. The *New Wedero*, a *hoteli* on the Kisumu road near the Oyugis junction, serves unbeatable *mandaazi*.

The *murram* road up to **Oyugis** (on the main A1 highway between Kisii and Kisumu) is generally firm but it sometimes takes a beating in wet weather and becomes, on occasions, impassable. Normally, though, you'll have no difficulty getting a *matatu* up to Oyugis or west to Homa Bay. The obvious alternative escape route is the tarred **lakeshore road** from Kendu Bay to Katito, where it meets the A1 on to Kisumu. This is an excellent, fast highway – another from an Israeli company – which swings beautifully for some 40km, the first 20km close to the lake. There's a wealth of interest in the surrounding Luo countryside, most of it so recently a rural backwater, with scenes of fishing boats and compounds of square, mud-brick-built, thatched houses (a fairly recent change; traditionally they were round). Now that this route has become a lakeside drive, the handful of modern houses – two-storey "villas", complete with tiles and wrought iron – barely look out of place: they suggest a district that people are prepared to invest in.

Migori

MIGORI, down near the Tanzanian border, is basically an ever-expanding roadstead, spread out along 4km of the A1 highway. The main centre of activity seems to be the hospital, where the doctors are adept at treating arrow wounds inflicted during land skirmishes between Gusii, Maasai, Kipsigis and the new Kikuyu settlers. Market days are interesting for the variety of peoples and for traditional activities untainted by tourism. The Maasai people here are far less calculating and aloof than many of those further to the east whose lives have been invaded by cameras and minibuses, but you're likely to be the object of some curiosity. There are two good places to **stay**. Turn left at Shell before the bridge for *Gilly's Hotel* (PO Box 831 Suna-Migori; ☎0387/20523 or 20614, fax 20556; B&B ②). Ignore the bland concrete exterior, as the welcome is warm, and rooms are bright and breezy s/c with nets, the better ones with distant views of the river, and with good breakfasts. *Girango Hotel*, at the south end of town (PO Box 4 Suna-Migori; ☎0387/20608; B&B ②), is marginally cheaper, and has a number of outhouses scattered in pleasant gardens (guarded parking), with a choice of different rooms: cheaper ones are pretty grim, but the better ones are s/c and have nets. Hot water is provided in buckets. There's a popular bar, and a disco weekends too. Worth a mention for **food**, if only for weirdness, is *Njiri Bar & Restaurant*, a bizarre mock-Victorian castellated folly, 2km before Migori.

If you've just arrived **from Tanzania**, there are "direct" (though not non-stop) **buses to Nairobi** leaving at 6am and 7am or in the evening, going via Kisii, Kericho and Nakuru. Lastly, if you're driving, you could consider taking the unsurfaced C13, 4km south of Migori, either east into **Maasai Mara** (p.380), signposted Kehancha, or west to **Mfangano Island** via Ruma National Park (p.290), signposted Muhuru Bay. Note however, that both roads are in a pretty dreadful state, and are especially prone to degradation caused by rains, so should only be attempted in 4WD, and then only in dry weather (the clay gets treacherous when wet).

THE WESTERN HIGHLANDS

The highlands of the west rise all around Lake Victoria in a great bowl. There's superb walking country throughout, in the **Nandi Hills**, for example, or in the little-known **Mau Massif** east of Kericho. But the undoubted highlights are **Saiwa Swamp National Park** and the **Kakamega Forest**, recently accorded national park status of its own. For serious, sensibly equipped hikers, **Mount Elgon** must also be a major temptation, sharing much of Mount Kenya's flora and fauna but none of its popularity. Also wonderful walking country are the high hills of the **Cheranganis**, though, like Elgon, they take some getting to. The highland towns are, on the whole, not arresting. **Kisii** is lively and worth a visit, but **Kericho** ("tea capital of Kenya"), **Eldoret** and **Kitale** are best thought of simply as bases for getting to the real attractions.

Kisii and around

Headquarters of the **Gusii** (or Kisii or Kosova) people, and district town of a region vying with Nyeri in having the fastest-growing population in the country, **KISII** is a suitably fresh, bustling, muddy and rubbish-strewn trading centre in the hills, prosperous and hard-working. For its small size, the town creates terrific noise and energy. It has more lodging houses per head than anywhere else in Kenya (albeit mostly terrible), and enjoys a profusion of excellent fruit and vegetables all year round, especially bananas and sugar cane. Lavishly fertile, the region gets rain all year, in remarkable contrast to the semi-arid lowlands of the lakeshore just a few kilometres away.

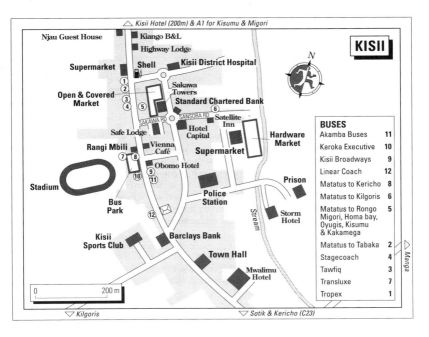

SOME GUSII HISTORY

The Bantu-speaking **Gusii** (after whom the town is named) were only awakened to the brutal realities of British conquest in 1905, when they rebelled – pitching themselves with spears against a machine gun. It was "not so much a battle as a massacre", one of the participants recalled, leaving "several hundred dead and wounded spearsmen heaped up outside the square of bayonets". In 1908, after the District Commissioner was speared in a personal attack, the same thing happened again, only this time the Gusii were trying to escape, not attacking. Crops were burned, whole villages razed to the ground. Churchill telegraphed from the Colonial Office: "Surely it cannot be necessary to go on killing these defenceless people on such an enormous scale."

The Gusii were totally demoralized. In a few brief years, the fabric of their communities had been torn apart, hut taxes imposed, and cattle confiscated to be returned only in exchange for labour. And then came World War I. Kisii was the site of the first Anglo-German engagements in East Africa, and thousands of men were recruited into the hated Carrier Corps by trickery or press gang.

It seems extraordinary that the exceptionally friendly people of Kisii are the grandchildren of the conscripts. The powerful, millennial religious movements which burst among them during the colonial period under the name **Mumboism** may partly account for the very strong ties of community they've maintained against all odds. Prophets and medicine men have always been important here, and even in today's superficially Christianized society, the Gusii have solidly kept their cultural identity. **Witchcraft** and **sorcery** still play important roles in the life of the town and its district. The practice of **trepanning**, for example, which involves tapping a small hole in the skull to relieve headache or mental illness, seems to be as old as the Gusii themselves: it has recently received the ironic laureate of medical journal credibility and the attentions of a German film crew. "Brain operations" are still performed, clandestinely but apparently quite successfully. However, the rising influence of Christianity, as well as occasional abuses of power by witches, has led to spates of **lynchings** of suspected witches and sorcerers (the last in September 1998, when ten people were killed). Residents were reticent to divulge the names of the lynchers to the authorities, which prompted the local police chief to say: "We hope we can get them [the witches] and if possible charge them in court. This way we shall save their lives."

Kisii is also famous for its fine **soapstone**. Surprisingly, there's little of this to be seen in the town itself. The best locality for watching the carvers and making on-the-spot purchases is Tabaka, some way south (see p.298).

Accommodation

You'll find plenty of **places to stay**, although most of them are pretty awful and noisy, especially on Wednesdays and weekends, as many have bars or discos, or else are situated near one (the *Storm* is the exception). For security reasons, women travelling alone are limited to *Kisii Hotel*, *Sakawa Towers* and *Storm Hotel*. You should be prepared for power fluctuations during heavy rain – have some candles handy – and water supplies are uniformly erratic. It's worth staying the night, though, as, once you've settled in, there are several rewarding local **excursions**, and the town itself buzzes day and night with an infectious energy.

Hotel Capital (PO Box 966; ☎0381/20944). Unremarkable and overpriced for what you get, with a noisy bar. Rooms are s/c, but water is not guaranteed. Good views over the busy road. ①.

Highway Lodge (PO Box 910; ☎0381/21213). Utterly squalid, and barely more appetizing than the butchery beside the entrance. It's the cheapest in town, though. ①.

Kiango B&L (PO Box 973; ☎0381/21190). This is a dingy place geared to short-term guests (soap, towel and condom provided), but the balconies compensate, and there's a busy bar-restaurant. Buckets of water are heated for "s/c" rooms on request. ①.

Kisii Hotel, on the road out to Kisumu (PO Box 26; ☎0381/30134 or 20715). First impressions of a certain degree of comfort (certainly compared to the town's other lodgings) vanish like its water supply, which is sporadic, and hot water – if at all – is only available in the mornings. On the plus side, there's an agreeable creaking colonial atmosphere, a half-decent restaurant, and the rooms themselves (some s/c) are large, some with nets and furniture. There's a popular bar (with deafening all-night discos at weekends) and a large, lovely, bird-filled garden. Guarded parking. B&B ②.

Mwalimu Hotel (PO Box 2427; ☎0381/31636). A charmless 1979 block notable mainly for its staggering decrepitude, with most things broken, dirty, damp or caving in. The rooms have views, though, and at least the bar – which keeps you awake at night – plays better music than most. Raucous and very male-oriented discos take over at weekends. B&B ②.

Njau Guest House (PO Box 156; ☎0381/20950). The entrance stinks, but the beds are clean if not much else. Notionally s/c with squat loos, but don't count on the water. ①.

Safe Lodge (PO Box 156; ☎0381/20945). Awful place, woefully misnamed and well past its sell-by. Security is lax, cleanliness leaves much to be desired, and it's above a noisy bar-cum-*nyama choma* joint. Rooms usually rented by the hour. ①.

Sakawa Towers (PO Box 541; ☎0381/21218). Overpriced but a friendly and bright hotel in a block (until recently the tallest building in town) named after a Gusii medicine man and prophet. There are great views of Kisii from the roof. All the rooms are s/c with nets and balconies, but some are cramped and terrifically noisy. Notable also for its one, kinky "suite", which comes complete with a bath (though you'd be unusually lucky to have enough hot water to fill it), two huge animal-skin drums doubling as tables, and a mirror affixed to the headboard of the kingsize bed. Good restaurant and busy first floor bar (with an *askari* at night on the gate leading up to the rooms). B&B ②.

Satellite Inn (PO Box 973; ☎0381/31678). A big, grubby boozer, with large, non-s/c rooms with nets, but otherwise basic. Get one with an external window. There's rooftop *nyama choma*, and a busy first-floor bar which gyrates to *ndombolo* on Friday and Saturday nights. ①.

Storm Hotel (PO Box 973; ☎0381/30649, 30063). Well-run middle-range choice, and the quietest in Kisii (no disco). There's a choice of adequate rooms, all s/c with nets, an outside bar and *nyama choma* joint. B&B ② (suites ③).

Eating

Despite the noxious drain smells, the overflowing **market** is the first base for hungry travellers. The lodgings mostly have dining rooms or restaurants of their own, of which *Sakawa Towers*' is probably the most recommended (Ksh150 for lunch). Despite a dwindling menu, the *Kisii Hotel* is still considered the place where one dines out, especially at lunchtime when it's not raining, when the tables are spread out on the garden lawns. The beer-and-*nyama choma* joint beneath the *Safe Lodge* is Kisii's answer to a Bavarian beer hall, loud and raucous: the meat is usually good. Currently the nicest *hoteli* is the *Obomo Hoteli*, which offers plain food, but good juices and a very pleasant atmosphere (closed Sun). Similarly reliable, for a shot of cholesterol, is *Vienna Café*, opposite *Rangi Mbili*.

Listings

Banks Standard Chartered and Barclays. Don't go near the KCB: they charge outrageous commission.

Earth tremors Kisii lies on a fault line and minor earthquakes are not uncommon – only a slight worry if you're asleep at the top of *Sakawa Towers* hotel at the time.

Football Kisii stadium is the home ground of Shabana FC, now in the First Division.

Garage Rangi Mbili (PO Box 532; ☎0381/20318). A very helpful parts store/workshop if your car is in trouble. Helpful anyway, for that matter – they're eager to meet travellers.

Hospital The main one is Kisii District Hospital (☎0381/20471 or 20473); a private option is the Ram Memorial Hospital.

Kisii Show Held in the first week of July.

Post office Mon–Fri 8am–5pm, Sat 9am–noon. Card- and coinphones outside.

Sports club Swimming pool, tennis, squash, darts, bar, bingo. Saturday discos. A friendly place with temporary membership available.

Onwards from Kisii

Kisii is something of a route focus, with both regional and national bus and *matatu* services passing through. There are plenty of **matatus** leaving throughout the day for Homa Bay, Kericho, Kisumu and Migori, with others to Kakamega, Kilgoris, Oyugis, Rongo and Tabaka. Most leave from the main stage in front of the market: the exceptions are *matatus* for Tabaka, which leave from the Shell station at the north end of town; Kericho, which go from the bus park beside Rangi Mbili; and those for Kilgoris, opposite *Satellite Inn*. There are also useful early morning departures for Narok via the B3, passing the junctions for the C12 and C13 Maasai Mara access roads. **Bus services** are equally numerous: Keroka Exective for Homa Bay–Kisii–Keroka–Nairobi; Kisii Broadways for Isebania, Homa Bay, Kericho, Migori, Naivasha and Nakuru; Linear Coach (☎0381/31322) for Homa Bay–Kisii–Nairobi; Akamba (☎0381/30137) for Nairobi and Homa Bay; Tawfiq (☎0381/31611) on the Homa Bay–Kisii–Nairobi–Mombasa route, as well as Tanzania; Stagecoach (☎0381/31673) for Eldoret, Homa Bay, Kericho, Kisumu, Malaba (on the Ugandan border), Migori, and Mumias; Transluxe for Migori, Sirare, Kisumu, Nairobi and Mombasa; and Tropex (☎0381/30587) for the Migori–Kisii–Kisumu–Eldoret, Sirare–Kisii–Kisumu–Kakamega–Kitale, and Kilgoris–Kisii–Eldoret routes. All Nairobi buses call at Nakuru and Naivasha. The locations of the bus company ticket offices and *matatu* stages are marked on our map.

If you have your own wheels and are headed along the minor but increasingly popular route to **Maasai Mara** via Kilgoris and Lolgorien, note that beyond **Kilgoris**, the road to the Mara is difficult, even with 4WD, and the section down the Oloololo Escarpment can be impossible after rain. Heading for the east end of the reserve, the fastest route is via Sotik and the new road to Bomet and Amala River (see p.386).

Heading south, **Tanzania** is accessible by services to the **border crossing**, variously known as Isebania or Nyabikaye on the Kenyan side, and Serira, Sirare or Siria on the Tanzanian, as well as by daily Tawfiq bus services to Mwanza (on Lake Victoria) and Dar es Salaam (on the coast).

Lastly, if you fancy **cycling**, you can buy an Indian three-speed roadster at the supermarkets in Kisii for under Ksh4000.

Tabaka

TABAKA is one of the most important centres in the world for **soapstone** (steatite) production. Strangely enough, it has never become widely known, and the expected sprouting of signposts and tourist shops is nowhere to be seen. Most of the carvings are bought up by buyers from the curio shops in Nairobi and elsewhere, and on arriving, you might think you've come to the wrong place, it's such a low-key industry.

Getting to Tabaka, it is best to get a **matatu** that goes direct, even if this means waiting around in Kisii. The alternative is hanging around just as long at the halfway point, or a very long walk. If you don't mind the latter, grab any *matatu* heading towards Migori and get out at **Nyachenge**, from where the *murram* road to Tabaka heads off to the southeast (treacherous in wet weather). To get to the soapstone carvers and quarries, continue 5km on the *murram* road, passing the turn for the Tabaka Mission Hospital on your right, then head downhill from the T-junction. The last *matatus* from Tabaka back to Kisii leave at 5pm.

If you're **driving** to Tabaka from Kisii, head out of town to the north and, after 1km, turn left – south – onto the A1 Migori/Isebania road and proceed 17km to a sign indicating (left) the Tabaka Mission Hospital and Kisii Soapstone Carvers Co-operative Society. From here it's a further 5–6km.

The soapstone quarries and carvers

There are two main **quarries** – one on the left, another further down on the right – but there must be vast reserves of stone under the ground all over the district, which provides almost the entire world supply of soapstone. It emerges in a variety of colours and densities: white is easiest to work, shades of orange and pink harder, and rosy-red the hardest and heaviest. A number of families have become full-time carvers, but for most people it's simply a spare-time occupation after agriculture, a way of making a few shillings. You'll even see children walking home from school carving little animals from chips of stone. The professional carvers often specialize: one in inlaid chessboards, another in chess pieces, others in traditional animals (hippos, elephants, lions, fish) and boxes (square, round, duck, tortoise), vases and cups, ashtrays, candlesticks, snake-boxes, napkin rings, egg cups, mugs and more recent designs – human figures, soapstone "Makonde" and various fruit.

There's a number of recommended teams of carvers: ask for anyone from the Mogendi, Abuya or Obonyo families They will usually be happy to show you around, sell you their work, and perhaps give you pieces of stone to try carving yourself: it's great therapy. The stone is dampened to bring up the colour and make it easier to work, then waxed to retain the lustre.

Manga Ridge

This dramatic escarpment **cliff** is two or three hours' walk north of Kisii, wonderful in the early morning – or the late afternoon, as long as you can arrange a ride back again.

Leaving Kisii on the Kericho road, turn left into Manga Road at the bottom of the hill, 500m after Barclays, and follow the road as it sweeps you towards and then alongside the ridge. After about 5km you can cut down one of the tracks across the lush valley to your left and continue straight up the escarpment (several hundred metres high). Beware of snakes lurking among the rocks and grass on the upward scramble. Alternatively, you can continue along the road for a further 5km to come up behind the ridge; from here it's a ten-minute hike up to the edge, where a path follows the cliff for a kilometre or two. Magnificent views out over Kisii and down to Lake Victoria are your reward. It's possible to get *matatus* to Manga from Kisii, but make it clear you want to get off at the ridge.

If you set off early enough, there should be time to walk the whole way around to **Oyugis** (see p.284), through the villages of Manga, Marani and Rioma, a total distance of about 40km. Down at Oyugis you arrive in the town past the pelican breeding site on the right. From Oyugis it's a quick *matatu* hop back to Kisii. A fine walk, this also makes for exuberant **cycling**, through the heart of Gusii-land, as the road loops and swerves in a landscape changing magically with every ridge and valley. Up here you'll find dusty lanes, avenues of cypress trees, grassy verges, old women smoking pipes, and self-contained, reserved, country hamlets, just a few kilometres from the mêlée of Kisii.

Kisii to Kericho

From Kisii to Kericho, the road first snakes up through banana gardens, fields of corn and sugar cane and patches of tea. **Keroka**, the largest town along the way, is an urgent and chaotic community, strung out along the highway. Further along, 43km from Kisii, there's a rarity for the region: an excellent **lodging** in the form of the friendly *Damside Hotel* (PO Box 340 Nyansiongo; ☎0360/32256; ①–②), in a peaceful setting beside a small dammed stream and a pyrethrum field. There's a choice of s/c and non-s/c rooms in *bandas* and cottages, some very basic, dirty and without nets, though the better "Mzungu Cottages", which are individual round *bandas*, are comfortable with clean beds and nets, and you can take meals in the pretty gardens. There are discos most nights.

Seven kilometres from here, just off the road to the south, is **SOTIK**, on a high plateau at the start of the rolling swathe of **tea bushes** that stretches for hundreds of square kilometres up towards the crest of the Mau Escarpment. Sotik is quite a pretty little centre – despite the rutted side streets, you'd almost say well-kept – with its shrubs and borders. The village has a post office, a branch of Barclays (with 24-hour cash machine), petrol, and the usual cluster of shops, bars and eateries. The best of the **lodgings** is the dubiously-named *Hotwax Hotel* (PO Box 126 Sotik; ☎0360/32259; ①–②), a dirty, loud and decrepit three-storey block, whose only attraction is its jumping *ndombolo* sounds disco (Wednesday, Friday and Saturday nights). Otherwise, try the *Al-Karim Hotel* (PO Box 615; ☎0360/32097; ①), on the right past Caltex and the market.

On the approach to Kericho itself, the small *shambas* virtually cease, especially on the eastern side of the road where the land shelves to the Kimugu Valley.

Kericho and the tea country

KERICHO, named after the early English tea planter John Kerich, is Kenya's **tea capital**, a fact that – with much hype from the tourism machine embellished by the presence of the *Tea Hotel* – is not likely to escape you. Its equable climate and famously reliable, year-round afternoon rain showers make it the most important tea-growing area in Africa. While many of the European estates have been divided and reallocated to small farmers since Independence, the area is still dominated by giant tea plantations.

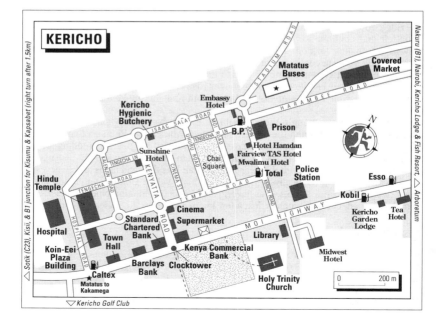

Compact and orderly, Kericho itself seems as neat as the serried rows of bushes that surround it. The central square has shady trees and flowering bushes – a bandstand would make it complete – and even the *matatu* park has lawns around it. It's a gentle, hassle-free place to wander, the people mild-mannered. Clipped, clean and functional, there's little of the shambolic appearance of most up-country towns. And, in many ways, it's an oddity. With so many people earning some sort of salary on the tea plantations or in connection with them, and so few acres under food or market crops, the patterns of small-town life are changed here. Most workers live out on the estates, their families often left behind in the home villages. Kericho is above all an administrative and shopping centre, and a relay point for the needs of the estates: the produce market is small and trading limited. Everything seems to close at 5pm.

In town, there's a substantial Asian population. Many of the streets have a strikingly oriental feel – single-storey *dukas* fronted by colonnaded walkways where the plantation "memsahibs" of forty or fifty years ago presumably did their shopping. This curious, composite picture is completed by the grey stone **Holy Trinity Church**, with its small assembly of deceased planters in a miniature cemetery. Straight out of the English shires and entwined with creepers, it tries so hard to be Norman that it hurts to report it was built only in 1952.

Accommodation

Kericho has a decent number of **places to stay** and you should find something to suit. A couple of the best options are out along the Nairobi road, Moi Highway. You can **camp** at the *Kericho Lodge & Fish Resort* (Ksh150 per person) and at *Kericho Garden Lodge* (Ksh300/tent).

Embassy Hotel, Isaac Salat Rd (PO Box 1505; no phone). Ordinary and basic accommodation, but friendly – marginally the best of the rock-bottom places, but don't eat here. ①.

Fairview TAS Hotel, Moi Rd (PO Box 1260; ☎0361/21507). The entrance, by a busy and characterful *hoteli*-cum-bar, is intimidating, but it should be safe enough (women steer clear though), with basic, none-too-clean rooms (singles only, some s/c) and yukky toilets, but it's quiet at night. ③.

Hotel Hamdan, John Kerich Rd (PO Box 1135; ☎0361/21213). Very basic but cheap. ①.

Kericho Garden Lodge, Moi Highway (PO Box 164; ☎0361/20878). Avoid the grotty singles, but the newer s/c doubles are quite acceptable, clean with hot water, and some look out over the pleasant gardens. Unappetizing food, though, and women may find the atmosphere in the restaurant/bar/TV room off-putting. B&B lower end of ②.

Kericho Lodge & Fish Resort, off Moi Highway (PO Box 25; ☎0361/20035). Take the signposted turning opposite Agip, 700m northeast of the town centre, and follow this track for about 500m. Rather downmarket, alpine chalet in style and atmosphere, and rather dilapidated in appearance, but with a great location above a weir in the Kurungu river good for walks in the lush, tree-filled valley. The rooms themselves are simple but very comfortable, with independent hot water. There's a bar and a pretty awful restaurant. Bed only ③.

Mid West Hotel (PO Box 1175; ☎0361/20611, fax 20615). A large, soulless European-style place and popular conference venue. Nothing special to recommend it, but usually a safe bet if you must have a proper hotel room. There's a new health club with a gym, sauna, steam room (all Ksh150 each), snooker, darts, etc. ③–④.

Mwalimu Hotel, Moi Rd (PO Box 834; ☎0361/21777). Adequate and relatively clean s/c rooms, kept separate from its bar-restaurant. Loos lack seats and toilet paper. Overpriced. B&B ②.

Tea Hotel, Moi Highway (PO Box 75; ☎0361/30004-5, fax 20576; reservations made through *Msafiri*, address p.48). Built, along with the nearby church, in 1952, the *Tea Hotel* formerly belonged to the giant tea corporation Brooke Bond, and it's possible to walk through the gardens to the tea estate beyond and speak with the pickers. It still attracts a few tour groups, though, as well as a steady trickle of travelling businessmen and the occasional dance band using the attached recording studios. The small pool and grassy, well-watered gardens are appealing enough, but the rooms themselves vary greatly: you should aim at getting a bungalow with bath and shower and fireplace. Despite a steady decline in recent years, it can't help being charming and peaceful. Excellent food. Non-resident (dollar) rates are overpriced. B&B ⑤–⑥.

Eating

Kericho has its fair share of cheap and fairly ungastronomic *hotelis*, heavy on the chips and *ugali*: busiest of the *hotelis* is the first-floor *Fairview TAS Hotel*, packed at lunchtimes with workers. The *Sunshine Hotel*, Kenyatta Road, is also popular. If you've a tough stomach, try the ominously named *Kericho Hygienic Butchery* on Isaac Salat Road for its *nyama choma*, behind the dangling carcasses. For altogether classier eating, venture out to the *Tea Hotel*, whose dignified colonial dining room has very reasonable set lunch and dinner menus (Ksh400–500), excellent service and a grand piano which you're free to play. *Kericho Fish Resort* has pretty grim *hoteli* fare, but a great location, whilst the *Mid West* is OK but uninspiring.

Listings

Banks Barclays, Standard Chartered, both with ATMs, plus the KCB are on Moi Highway at the Kisumu end of town.

Car repair Central Garage (☎0361/20061) have a solid reputation.

Library By the *Mid West Hotel*. Not bad at all, though they go for quantity rather than diversity, with about ten copies of each title.

Market Much better at weekends than weekdays, when there's a variety of fruit and vegetables, snacks and spices, at lower-than-expected prices.

Post office Mon–Fri 8am–5pm, Sat 9am–noon.

Swimming pool Clean but chilly, at the *Tea Hotel* (Ksh100).

Taxis A bit of a problem in Kericho: there are very few apart from *matatus*. After dark it's hard to get out much if you don't have your own vehicle or aren't prepared to walk.

Onward travel

Kericho has hassle-free travel options in every direction: **southwest** to Kisii and Migori (near the Tanzanian border), **east** over the Mau Escarpment to Nakuru (route covered in Chapter 3), or **northwest** to Kisumu on Lake Victoria and Kapsabet in the Nandi Hills. *Matatus* for Kakamega leave from the Caltex garage. Heading **south to Maasai Mara** is more problematic, though the first part of the route, from Litein (30km or so from Kericho) to Bomet, follows a fine new road through splendid farming country (see p.386). If you're going **east**, Nairobi and Nakuru buses generally originate in Kisii and pass through Kericho throughout the day (and night): you should have time for a leisurely morning.

Around Kericho

Mostly it's **tea country**. Kenya is the world's third largest producer after India and Sri Lanka, and the biggest exporter to Britain. As you gaze across the dark green hills, you might pause to consider that the land which you now see covered in vast regimented swathes of tea bush, was only a century ago virgin rainforest, only a tiny part of which – Kakamega Forest (p.327) – still survives. The estates were first set up after World War I with tea bushes imported from India and China. Big business as it is – and despite the relative prosperity of Kericho – you can't help feeling that the local population would be better served if this fertile land were given over instead to intensive cultivation of food.

Tea was almost the only sector of the Kenyan economy to benefit from the heavy 1997–98 El Niño rains, which led to a bumper harvest. However, strikes and unrest have afflicted a good part of the industry recently, caused by the usual volatile mixture of high level mismanagement and suspected corruption, and belligerence lower down, specifically by the unregistered Kenya Union of Small-Scale Tea-Owners (KUSSTO). All this risks the possible disintegration of the para-statal Kenya Tea Development Authority, which would only make matters worse.

Unsurprisingly, the estates are not too anxious for visitors (enquire with Brooke Bond Kenya if you like: PO Box 20; ☎0361/20146 or 20149, fax 30506 or 30347), and the *Tea Hotel* no longer provides a guided **tour**. You could also try contacting Kenya Tea Packers (KETEPA) (PO Box 413; ☎0361/20530, fax 20536), but your best bet might be to try to fix something up through chatting to estate workers in town. The factories operate every day except Monday, the day after the pickers' day off.

Tea production is not complicated but it is very labour-intensive. Picking continues throughout the year: you'll see the pickers moving through the bushes in their brilliant yellow-and-green (KETEPA) plastic smocks, nipping off the top two leaves and bud of each bush (nothing more is taken) and tossing them into baskets. Working fast, a picker can collect up to seventy kilos in a day, though half that is a more typical figure; the piece-rate is set at less than three shillings per kilo picked. After withering, mashing, a couple of hours' fermentation and a final drying in hot air, the tea leaves are ready for packing and export. The whole process can take as little as 24 hours.

Kimugu Valley and Chagaik Dam

Down in the **Kimugu Valley**, behind the *Tea Hotel* and *Kericho Lodge & Fish Resort*, you can get some idea of what the land was like before the settlers arrived. The valley is a deep, tangled channel of sprawling trees and undergrowth, with shafts of sunlight picking out clouds of butterflies. The cold brown waters of the Kimugu flow down from Chagaik Dam and allegedly harbour **trout**.

To get to **Chagaik Dam** and the graceful **arboretum** nearby, you'll need a lift in the Nairobi direction, past the KETEPA buildings to the turn marked "Chagaik", about 8km east of town. From there, turn right, then immediately left: it's a five-minute walk to the arboretum – "Founded by Tom Grumbley, Tea Planter 1946–75". Acres of beautiful trees from all over the tropical and subtropical world lead steeply down through well-tended lawns to a lily-covered lake. There are magnificent stands of bamboo on the banks. Entry to this haven of landscaped tranquillity is unrestricted and you can picnic or rest up as long as you like, though there are gardeners around who would probably insist you didn't camp.

Across the lake, thick **jungle** drops to the water's edge. Mysterious splashes and rustles, prolific bird and insect life, and at least one troop of colobus monkeys, are a surprising testament to the tenacity of wildlife in an environment hemmed in on all sides by the alien ranks of the tea bushes.

The Nandi Hills

The journey **from Kericho to Kapsabet** is one of the most varied and spectacular in the west, through country often far wilder than you'd expect: bleak mountainous scrublands and jungle-packed ravines. Midway, you cross the Kano Plains and usually have to change transport at **Chemelil**, a major crossroads on the flat sugar lands. Beyond, the road zigzags into high tea country again, the homeland of the **Nandi**, the fiercest early opponents of the British, and the haunt of a crypto-zoological mystery known as the **Nandi bear** (see box on p.305).

Kapsabet

KAPSABET is the only town of any size before Eldoret but, even here, unless you arrive at the end of the day, there's little point in stopping. There's a branch of Barclays (next to the site earmarked for a new municipal library) and three reasonable **lodgings**. *Kapsabet Hotel* (PO Box 449; ☎0326/2176; ①) is a fairly quiet place but a popular boozer, clean if scruffy and boasting a restaurant that serves mountainous portions of chips. *Keben Hotel* (PO Box 240; ☎0326/2129; ①), above a supermarket, contains three "lodges" on its three floors, *Tanzania, Kenya* and *Uganda*, with rooms named after towns accordingly. Its noisy bar, restaurant, and discos at weekends and holidays make it Kapsabet's main nightspot. The Somali-run *Bogol Inn* (①), on the same side facing the market, serves typically tasty and cheap **food** in its restaurant. Amenities match the very low rates. In the market itself, *Elora Hotel* has fine fried fish. If you're mobile, check out the *Muzungu Hotel* on the Eldoret road, which is a restaurant run by an Italian man and his Kenyan wife – delicious fresh pasta and sauces, and cheap as well.

Eldoret

Although more bustling with trade than Kericho, and somewhat healthier and pleasanter than Nakuru, **ELDORET** has, in all honesty, hardly anything to do or see that couldn't be done or seen in dozens of other highland centres. At first glance, life here seems pleasantly humdrum, at least on the outside: ordinary occupations and careers are actively pursued; the **Uasin Gishu Plateau** all around is reliably fertile cereal, vegetable and stock-raising country; wattle plantations provide the tannin for the town's leather industry; the Raymond textile factory – one of the country's biggest – provides employment, as does a new armaments factory (with a ready market in neighbouring

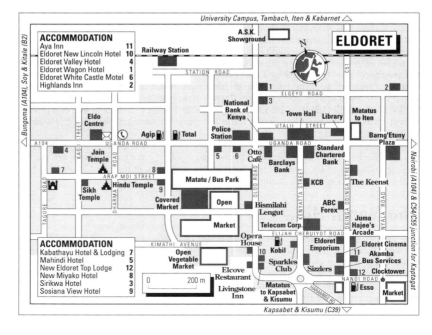

countries); and a centre of higher education, Moi University, has proved a shot in the arm for local schools. The town is also the terminus for the oil pipeline from Mombasa, which Uganda would like to extend to Kampala, and it also has one of the best hospitals in Kenya. Eldoret's prosperity is shown clearly enough by the windows of the Eldoret Jewellers on the main road. In short, this is Kenya's "Middletown"; not very prepossessing perhaps, but with its own momentum for development and, you can be reasonably sure, hardly a tour bus in sight.

The other face of Eldoret is serious **ethnic strife**. In recent years, thousands of refugees from local fighting have flooded the town and its sprawling, poor suburbs. Eldoret – "the town where everyone thinks he is president", according to one disenchanted local – has repeatedly been the focus of conflict between the district's Kalenjin-speakers (who are seen to be – and increasingly are – aligned with Moi and the KANU

THE NANDI AND THE NANDI BEAR

At the end of the nineteenth century, the **Nandi** (one of the Kalenjin-speaking peoples) were probably in the strongest position in their history. Their warriors had drummed up a reputation for such ferocity and daring that much of western Kenya lived in fear of them. Even the Maasai – at a low point in their own fortunes – suffered repeated losses of livestock to Nandi spearsmen, whose prestige accumulated with every herd of cattle driven back to their stockades. The Nandi even crossed the Rift Valley to raid Subukia and the Laikipia Plateau. They were intensely protective of their own territory, relentlessly xenophobic and fearful of any adulteration of their way of life. Foreigners of any kind were welcome only with express permission.

With the killing of a British traveller, Peter West, who tried to cross their country in 1895, the Nandi opened a decade of guerrilla warfare against the British. Above all, they repeatedly frustrated attempts to lay the railway line and keep communications open with Uganda. They dismantled the "iron snake", transformed the copper telegraph wires into jewellery, and took whatever livestock and provisions they could find. Despite increased security, the establishment of forts, and some efforts to reach agreements with Nandi elders, the raiding went on, often costing the lives of African soldiers and policemen under the British. In retaliation, **punitive expeditions** shot more than a thousand Nandi warriors (about one young man in ten), captured tens of thousands of head of livestock, and torched scores of villages. The war was ended by the killing of Koitalel, the *Orkoiyot* or spiritual head of the Nandi who, having agreed to a temporary truce, was then murdered at a meeting with the British. As expected, resistance collapsed (his people had believed Koitalel to be unassailable); the Nandi were hounded into a reserve and their lands opened to settlers.

Traditionally keepers of livestock, the Nandi have turned to agriculture with little enthusiasm and focus instead on their district's milk production: the highest in Kenya. *Shambas*, however, are widespread enough to make your chances of seeing a **Nandi bear** – the source of scores of Yeti-type rumours – remote. Variously said to resemble a bear, a big wild dog or a very large ape, the Nandi bear is believed to have been exterminated in most areas. But in the less accessible regions, on the way up to Kapsabet, many locals believe it still exists: they call it *chemoset*. Exactly what it is is another matter, but it doesn't seem to inspire quite the terror you might expect; the occasional savagely mutilated sheep and cattle reported in the press are probably attributable to leopards. A giant anthropoid ape, perhaps a gorilla, seems the most likely candidate for the *chemoset* and the proximity of the Kakamega Forest may account for the stories. This is a surviving tract of the rain forest that once stretched in a continuous belt across equatorial Africa and is still home to many western and central African species of wildlife (though not, as far as is known, giant apes). The *chemoset* possibly survived up until this century in isolated valleys, even if it is extinct today. Whatever the truth, if you camp out in the Nandi Hills, you won't need reminding to zip your fly sheet.

party) and Kikuyu- and Luo-speaking immigrants (who tend to favour a change of government). None of which is likely to impinge on a casual visit.

Some history

Eldoret was a backwoods post office on Farm 64, later chosen in 1912 as an administrative centre because the farm's soil was poor and the deeds were never taken up by the owner. The name started as Eldare (a river), was then Nandi-ized to Eldaret, and finally misprinted in the *Official Gazette* as Eldoret. Pronunciation is fluid.

Before the town existed, the area was settled by **Afrikaners**; they gave it much of the dour worthiness that seems to have characterized its first half-century and which is perceptible even today, though most of the Boers trekked on after Independence. Modern inhabitants are mainly Kalenjin (Elgeyo and Nandi) but there's also a long-established and respected Asian community (Juma Hajee's supermarket, now a shopping arcade, was the oldest business in the town); in addition there are Somali-speakers, the remnants of a European community, and immigrants from the rest of Kenya.

Eldoret's status as capital of the Kalenjin homelands probably has a great deal to do with its choice as the location for Kenya's newest "international" **airport**, which admittedly only receives occasional French charter flights and four a week from Nairobi. The original projected cost of Eldoret International Airport ran to over $83.3m, but the Kenyan government was forced to scale down the project under tough proposals from the IMF and the World Bank. Sparks flew when Kenya requested a $50m loan for repairs to the Nairobi–Mombasa road (currently in a worse state than ever) – international donors jettisoned the request, arguing that if Kenya could afford a new international airport in an up-country town (not to mention a new presidential jet), it could afford to cover the cost of routine repairs to its principal highway as a matter of priority.

Practicalities

There's no real reason to stay in Eldoret very long, although you might find it a useful stop-over, and it's refreshingly unthreatening and friendly despite its size. The town's affluence is reflected by a wide variety of places to stay, eat and drink – and enough nightlife to see you through an evening or two.

Accommodation

Eldoret has no shortage of **accommodation**. Cheap places tend to be grubby or clearly intended for "short-term guests". You may have to explain to the management the innocent way you intend to spend the night. There are also one or two quaint old haunts from way back. The Reformed Church Centre should agree to you **camping** in the field.

CHEAPER HOTELS AND LODGINGS

Aya Inn, Oginga Odinga St (no phone). A spotless place with a rowdy but good-natured and fun bar attached. Reasonable rates for small s/c rooms with one double bed. ①.

Eldoret Valley Hotel, Uganda Rd (PO Box 734; ☎0321/32314, 33560). For peace and quiet, this is clean and scrupulous, but rather gloomy and somewhat lacking in character. An excellent Somali-style menu compensates. ①.

Kabathayu Hotel & Lodging, Arap Moi St (PO Box 832; ☎0321/22160 or 31073). A simple, clean B&L over a very male-dominated bar: not one for lone women. Good views from the roof terrace and good food to be had nearby – a Somali area. ①.

Mahindi Hotel, Uganda Rd (PO Box 1694; ☎0321/31520). A large, friendly, fairly bright place that allows two to share a single room (ie it's full of prostitutes), so one of the less restful abodes in town. Decent bar. ①.

New Eldoret Top Lodge, corner of Nandi and Oginga Odinga roads (PO Box 703; ☎0321/61564). They will give you a clean room for the whole night, but are not used to doing so. ①.

New Miyako Hotel, Arap Moi St (PO Box 1073; ☎0321/22594). Scruffy and noisy till midnight, but an oft-used stand-by with s/c rooms. Better (but even noisier) rooms have balconies and large windows. ①.

Reformed Church of East Africa Conference and Training Centre, 2km out of town on the Kapsabet road (PO Box 746; ☎0321/32935). Be securely accommodated and cheaply fed, with a minimum of stimulation. ①.

Sosiana View Hotel, Arap Moi St by the transport terminus (PO Box 840; ☎321/33215). A five-storey block with good views but tatty rooms; slightly better ones on second and fifth floors. ①.

MORE EXPENSIVE HOTELS

Eldoret New Lincoln Hotel, Oloo Rd (PO Box 551; ☎0321/22093). With original fixtures and fittings, and a creaking charm that seems to augur imminent collapse, this is Eldoret's most interesting hotel. It's close to Eldoret's transport park and top-volume nightclubs, and it can be noisy if not excessively so. But the New Lincoln is still something of an oasis, with lovebirds chirruping in the courtyard, a pleasant bar and decent food. It's slightly overpriced, and beware of leaving valuables in rooms. ②–③.

Eldoret Wagon Hotel, Elgeyo Rd (PO Box 2408; ☎0321/62270–2, fax 62400). Sunny, and with quiet, comfortable rooms, *nyama choma* bar and safe parking, this gets quite lively at weekends. Much more intimate than the *Sirikwa* opposite. ③.

Eldoret White Castle Motel, Uganda Rd (PO Box 566; ☎0321/33095 or 62773, fax 62209). Although first impressions are very unpromising – a bland modern building on a noisy road – the rooms turn out to be far better than average, and there's a lift after the initial two steps. Overpriced, though. ④.

Highlands Inn, Elgeyo Rd (PO Box 2189; ☎0321/31165). Spacious, presentable and normally quiet, with safe parking, and baths in all rooms but no nets. Outside there's a small kids' playground and an alfresco bar/restaurant serving *nyama choma* and other standards, and another bar and restaurant inside. Very good value. B&B ②.

Sirikwa Hotel, Elgeyo Rd (PO Box 3361; ☎0321/63433, fax 61018; reservations through *Magret International*, Phoenix House, 3rd floor, Kenyatta Ave, PO Box 67440 Nairobi; ☎02/224273, fax 223245). The town's "premier" hotel, this is a monolithic and faintly pompous pile, that would be more at home in Spain than western Kenya, but comfortable if you can ignore the insidious antiseptic smell. Rooms are very good, with real baths, the "superior suites" bizarrely have two bathrooms, and it has a large pool (Ksh75 for day visitors). ⑤–⑦.

Eating and drinking

Eldoret has plenty of good places to grab a bite, with a clutch of established snack places, several places to dine, and one or two evening haunts. For your own supplies, head for the markets west of Oloo Road, or a supermarket: Uchumi at the Eldo Centre, or Eldo Supermarket at Juma Hajee's Arcade.

Baker's Yard, adjacent to Uchumi in the Eldo Centre. Excellent place with biscuits, pies, cakes and pastries as well as bread, and also the place for a quick filter coffee.

Bismilahi Lengut, Oloo Rd. A large, bright eating place near the market.

Elcove, Soko House, Oloo Rd (☎0321/31253) opposite the *New Lincoln*. Run by same people who came up with *The Lantern* in Kitale, and similarly outstanding. The decor is Indian, the menu expansive and imaginative – subtly spiced curries, authentic Chinese, and good shots at Italian – all mostly available. Drinks (including a good house red) are priced to "keep out the riff-raff", according to the owner. Well worth a splurge.

Eldoret Valley Hotel, Uganda Rd. Good Somali food and other fare.

Eldoret Wagon Hotel Elgeyo Rd. Good four-course dinners for Ksh370.

The Keenst, Oginga Odinga St. One of Eldoret's better options, with uniformed waiters and a wide menu. The *nyama choma* is worth a try.

Otto Café, Uganda Rd. Popular *hoteli* with a long and well-priced menu and excellent *mandaazi*. Lives up to its reputation, and the downstairs seating area is one of the few up-country places with real atmosphere.

Sirikwa Hotel (☎0321/31655), Elgeyo Rd. Huge barbecue buffet lunches at weekends for Ksh500 – worth it if you've just spent three days in the Kakamega Forest or up Mount Elgon.

Sizzlers Café, Kenyatta St. A popular American-style joint, offering speedy, high-quality burgers plus ice cream and other desserts.

White Castle Café, Uganda Rd. Traditional Kenyan food such as fried or stewed chicken with chips or *ugali*. Again.

Nightlife

Livingstone Inn (Club Stoney), Oloo Rd, next to the *New Lincoln*. Live visiting band every weekend and midnight shows by dancing troupes.

Sam's Discotheque, Uganda Rd, under the *White Castle Motel*. Middle-of-the-road nightspot with a mixed clientele, always busy. Wednesday is ladies night, Friday soul, Saturday–6am Sunday an all-night jam.

Sparkles Club, Kenyatta St. A far from sparkling, sweaty and run-down disco, but loud and enjoyable, and packed out at weekends.

Opera House (Club Santa Cruz), Oloo Rd. Very firmly established nightspot, with some live acts, and jam sessions Tuesdays until dawn.

Listings

Airport Eldoret International Airport (☎0321/61299 or 63377). There are four Kenya Airways flights a week to Nairobi via Kisumu, on Mon & Wed at 5pm, and Fri & Sun at 6.30pm.

Banks Barclays and Standard Chartered both have ATMs. ABC Forex (banking hours), Zul Arcade, Kenyatta St, has better exchange rates.

Books Oret Bookshop is in the Barng'Etuny Plaza; Eldoret Emporium is on the corner of Elijah Cheruiyot St and Oginga Odinga St; Uchumi supermarket at the Eldo Centre stocks a fair range of paperbacks. The library on Utalii St has a good African history section.

Eldoret show Held in the first week of March.

Hospitals Eldoret Hospital, Makasembo Rd (☎0321/62000–1); Eldoret Municipal Hospital (☎0321/61185); Eldoret District Hospital (☎0321/33472 or 32119).

Pharmacies Asisco Pharmacy, Pandaptai House, Nandi Rd (0321/62496; 7am–midnight); Elgeyo Pharmacy, J. W. Mall, Uganda Rd (☎0321/61974).

Police ☎0321/32222.

Post office Mon–Fri 8am–5pm, Sat 9am–noon. Cardphones outside.

Swimming pool The *Sirikwa Hotel* has a pool (non-residents Ksh75) in its large, dull, grassy gardens. At weekends it's overrun with Kenyans in holiday mood.

Onwards from Eldoret

The main **matatu** enclosure is at the east end of Arap Moi Street, and has services for Kabarnet, Kaptagat and Kakamega, as well as main road services for Kisumu, Kitale and further afield. The Eldoret Express bus stage (for Kitale and Nairobi) is also there. *Matatus* for Iten leave from the stage opposite the library in Oginga Odinga Street, whilst services for Kapsabet and some for Kisumu go from the corner of Oginga Odinga Street and Nandi Road. The Akamba bus office (☎0321/61047) is on Oginga Odinga Street, opposite *Top Lodge*. There are no more passenger trains from Eldoret.

Heading directly towards the **Ugandan border**, there's little to delay your progress to Malaba, two or three hours away, and you no longer need a visa. Bungoma and Webuye, en route, are covered on pp.323 & 324.

Eastbound on the busy A104 road from Eldoret to Nakuru, uphill and then down again, the sombre scenery is pretty with moors and conifers, but the road itself is a fast one.

For **Kakamega Forest** (see p.327) there's a daily noon *matatu* from the main stage (get there early) to Kakamega via the road leading past the *Forest Rest House*; ask for a ticket to Isecheno. Alternatively, you can take any bus or *matatu* going to Kisumu via Kapasabet, and get off at the D267 turning about 20km after Kapasabet (signposted "Kisieni 12km"), from where it's a walk of about three hours to the *Rest House*, or you can catch a bicycle taxi from Shinyalu, 7km up the road.

If you arrived in Eldoret early enough in the day, there are two worthwhile bases outside town to head to for a night or longer.

Kaptagat and the Tambach Escarpment

Naiberi River Campsite, near **Kaptagat** (PO Box 142 Eldoret; ☎Kaptagat 26 or Eldoret ☎0321/31069), is 20km from Eldoret on the well-surfaced C54/C55 road, en route to the Kerio Valley. There's excellent camping by the Naiberi River, a pair of s/c chalets and several *bandas* (②). They also have a restaurant with *hoteli*-style basics at reasonable prices and more expensive Indian specialities. Getting here by public transport is a problem: if you arrive in Eldoret during the week, call the owner on the Eldoret number and transport will be provided. The nearby *Kaptagat Hotel* used to be a good place, too, but it's pretty run-down these days.

If you intend to cross the Rift Valley to Lake Baringo, you'll find a fair number of *matatus* bound for Kabarnet, and a bus which leaves at 10am, using the tarmacked **Tambach Escarpment** route. This is a spectacular journey: from the high pastures and wheat fields of the plateau, the valley suddenly yawns out beneath, some 1500m below. However, the route down to the fluorspar mine at Kimwarer, which passes through Kaptagat and used to be the main way across the valley, no longer sees much traffic. Still worth the effort if you have time, or a solid vehicle of your own, it's an incredible hairpin descent that seems to go on forever. Kerio Valley route details continue on p.264.

Soy

In the other direction (west) out of Eldoret, there's transport towards Kitale by bus, minibus or Peugeot throughout the day, but the **Soy Country Club**, a third of the way there, is nice enough to break your journey for (PO Box 2 Soy; ☎Soy 32037–9; ②). Once a very pukka country retreat, this is a peaceful place to stay, with single-storey wings laid out in classic colonial style, complete with wood-tiled roofs, brick chimneys and a formal garden. It's run-down but the rooms are comfortable enough, and there's a swimming pool (small and rather stagnant; non-residents Ksh40), restaurant and bar. You can camp here cheaply, too. Guests are very rare except at weekends. **SOY** itself is nothing at all – you'll hardly notice it – so if you want to camp at the *Country Club*, bring supplies.

In the Soy area, look out for the famous herd of **Rothschild's giraffe**, now very rare. Most often seen as specks in the distance – barely distinguishable from dead trees – on the dry plain near the junction between the B2 (to Soy) and the A104 (from Eldoret), they occasionally appear near the road. They stand their ground and, for giraffe close-ups, the only place you'll do better is at the Langata Sanctuary near Nairobi, where a number of the Soy animals have been relocated in recent years. Be warned, however, that it's definitely not a good idea to be seen taking photographs near the military barracks to the south of Soy.

Kitale and northward

KITALE is smaller than Eldoret, and not much more exciting, but it has more going for it from a traveller's point of view, primarily because it is the base for visits to **Mount Elgon** and the superb, very underrated, hiking country around Kenya's second giant volcanic cone. It is also an obvious base for the **Cherangani Hills**, and a straightforward departure point for trips to the west side of **Lake Turkana**. There's a **national park** nearby – the little-known but easily accessible **Saiwa Swamp**, where for once the tables are turned on drivers: you can explore on foot only. The town itself boasts a good **regional museum**, one excellent restaurant, and a host of great nightlife possibilities.

The majority of travellers only pass through here on the way to Lake Turkana, which is a shame: unless you're on a tight schedule, the museum, Mount Elgon and Saiwa Swamp, as well Kitale's friendly people (even the streetkids, once you get to know them) add up to a good reason to delay a day or three. The town itself is calm and unprepossessing, with smooth tarmac streets planted with trees, and a lively northern district around and beyond the market, almost a slum in parts, where *wazungu* rarely wander, but where you shouldn't encounter serious problems.

Some history

Originally Quitale, a relay station on the old slave route between Uganda and Bagamoyo in Tanzania, the modern town was founded only in 1920, as the capital of Trans-Nzoia District. When the first settlers arrived (mostly after World War I), this vale of rich grasslands between Mount Elgon and the Cherangani Hills was apparently almost uninhabited. But just a few years earlier it had been a Maasai grazing area, and a group who refer to themselves as "Maasai" still live on the eastern slopes of Elgon. Its present population is a mix of several tribes, including Nandi, Pokot, Marakwet, Sabaot and Sengwer, as well as a few Luhya, Kisii, Kikuyu and Asians. As a result, it has ironically become a focus for these same people fleeing ethnic violence and bloody cattle rustling raids in the surrounding region, especially along the Trans-Nzoia/West Pokot border area, to the northeast of Kitale, and was the venue for **peace talks** held during 1998–99 to try and resolve the problems.

With the arrival of the railway in 1925, the town and the region around it began to flourish, with a fantastic array of fruit, cereals, vegetables and livestock, and all the

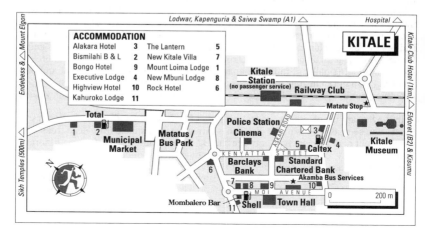

attendant settler paraphernalia of agricultural and flower shows, church fêtes and gymkhanas. This heady era lasted barely forty years, but the region's **agriculture** is still famous: almost anything, including such exotic fruit as apples and pears, can be grown here. The Kitale Show happens each year at the end of October or beginning of November.

Accommodation, eating and drinking

If you're heading north out of town anyway, you may want to stay at **Sirikwa Safaris** (Barnley's House; p.314). If you don't have your own vehicle, allow at least an hour to get there. In Kitale itself there are a number of **cheap lodgings**, down to the usual standard, the most economical up at the grubby north end of town, past the market. The less ornate of the two **Sikh temples** up here also takes travellers; remember to leave a donation. As to **mid-range hotels**, you're spoilt for choice. Note that Kitale suffers from sporadic cuts in its water supply, which affect even the better hotels. If you're **camping**, it's usually OK to use the grounds of the Kitale Museum, but ask the curator first (around Ksh200).

Hotels and lodgings

Alakara Hotel, Kenyatta St (PO Box 1984; ☎0325/20395, fax 30298). A large, clean, bright place with an efficient air, surprisingly good beds, baths in most rooms (cheaper non-s/c rooms available) and 24-hour hot water. The restaurant, too, is good, and the downstairs bar plays "slow dance", supposedly inaudible from the rooms. B&B ②.

Bismilahi B&L, 100m up from the market (PO Box 1191; no phone). Adequate and dirt cheap. ①.

Bongo Hotel, Moi Ave (PO Box 530; ☎0325/20593). Decent, properly furnished s/c rooms, but since the rise of the *Alakara* and *Lantern*, no longer the first choice. Serves up excellent buffet breakfasts. B&B ②.

Executive Lodge, Kenyatta St (PO Box 2275; ☎0325/31698). Secure (no admittance after 11.30pm) but off-puttingly dark, with small and tatty rooms, some s/c. There's a TV room and a reasonable restaurant attached, but at the same price you'd be much better off at the *Alakara* opposite. B&B ②.

Highview Hotel, Moi Ave (PO Box 2925; ☎0325/31570). A friendly highrise, with good, breezy and relatively clean s/c rooms with nets, but sporadic hot water (mornings only), and its four bars can make things noisy at night. B&B ②.

Kahuroko Lodge, Moi Ave, behind the Shell garage (PO Box 2290; ☎0325/31066). Basic lodgings fronted by a bar-restaurant, not for lone women. ①.

Kitale Club, 1km out on the road towards Eldoret (PO Box 30; ☎0325/20030). The site of the old slave quarters (the circle of stones in the car park is said to have surrounded a ring to which they were chained at night), this old colonial club (Ksh200 daily membership) now comes complete with a golf course and pool (Ksh50 extra). It has evidently taken years of trial and error to perfect its unique ambience: for all its pretensions, unless you look and act the part, the atmosphere can be unpleasant, and the service lacking in even the most basic good manners, starting with the hostile receptionist. ④.

The Lantern, Kenyatta St (PO Box 4566; ☎ & fax 30360). Behind its uninviting entrance are the best lodgings in town: calm, clean and welcoming, with parquet floors and proper baths and nets in all rooms. The more expensive "deluxe" doubles are huge and have balconies fronting onto the street. B&B ②–③.

Mount Loima Lodge (PO Box 1517; ☎0325/31929). A little further on from the *Bismilahi* and on the same side, similarly basic and cheap. ①.

New Kitale Villa, Moi Ave (PO Box 4240; ☎0325/31094). Above *Club Villa*, with grotty non-s/c rooms, but it's very friendly and good for a night out – the club plays upbeat sounds day and night. Women on their own might prefer to look elsewhere. ①.

New Mbuni Lodge, Moi Ave (PO Box 951; ☎0325/31022). Cheap and noisy, with a bar and disco upstairs. Non-s/c singles only. ①.

Eating and drinking

The best **food** in Kitale is to be found at *The Lantern* on Kenyatta Avenue, which has a vast, mouth-watering menu, including excellent Chinese and Indian dishes suitable for vegetarians as well as meats and French-style cuisine, red wine and Irish coffees too. Service is professional and unobtrusive, the surroundings pleasant, and the food exquisite, especially if you've been living on a miserable diet of *ugali* and *irio* for a few weeks: recommended for splurge (around Ksh500–600 for a meal excluding drinks). Other dependable options include the *Alakara Hotel*, with a good lunchtime buffet for Ksh350, and the *Kitale Club*, if you can handle the atmosphere and admission fee. *Executive Lodge* is cheaper and has the usual Kenyan fare, chips or *ugali* with everything, and good samosas. The *Bongo Bar and Restaurant*, next door to the hotel, is similar. Cheaper still is *Villa Coffee House (New Kitale Villa)* on Moi Avenue, a clean and bright little place with a good menu. As elsewhere, many restaurants are closed on Sundays.

After dark, there are a number of places providing drink and lively conversation. Currently in with the crowds are the *Bongo*, any one of the *Highview*'s four bars (pool tables in the cellar), and the more sedate *Alakara*, which is an enduring meeting place. All three are generally suitable for women, though you should use your judgement at the *Highview* (some nights are calmer than others). Of the more energetic nightspots (women should go accompanied to these), try *Max* at the *Theatre Club*, opposite the *Kitale Club* (Friday and Saturday nights); the sweaty *Mombalero* opposite the *Bongo*; the *Railway Club*'s old-style dancehall by the station; or the popular *Rock Hotel* disco, at the north end of Kenyatta Street. On Moi Avenue at New Kitale Villa, *Club Villa* is a cheerful and friendly dive with upbeat music and videos day and night, and resident DJs Friday and Saturday nights.

Kitale Museum and the VI Agroforestry Project

Given its location, **Kitale Museum** (daily 8am–6pm; Ksh200) is remarkably successful. Originally the "Stoneham Museum", a collection opened to the public by a Lieutenant Colonel on his Cherangani farm in 1927, it was transferred here in 1972. For the most part, Stoneham's curious collections are just that: collected curiosities in striking contrast to the recent Kenyan additions with more educational motives.

The **ethnographic displays** on Pokot, Elkony (Elgon), Luhya, Maasai, Turkana and Luo are interesting, though perhaps more so if you've seen the stuff in real life and now have a chance to return and see it again. Among the artefacts are Kamba carvings – skin-covered animals and smooth polished abstracts; a Pokot goat bell made from a tortoise shell; Pokot bowls used for collecting blood from cattle; and intricate Turkana belts and beadwork. In the small room to the right of the entrance is a collection of traditional musical instruments (as well as an old piano), which really are becoming museum pieces as younger generations embrace more cosmopolitan musical genres like pop and gospel (though you can buy cassettes of traditional Luhya music in town).

The motley wildlife collection on the walls and downstairs is perhaps best ignored, but the entomology is more interesting – a very fine collection of butterflies and bugs collected in the region in recent years, sadly mostly unlabelled. Incidentally, if you're fed up with the diet of KTN and KBC TV, the museum occasionally screens real celluloid **wildlife documentaries**. They prefer larger groups, though they'd be happy to oblige if you have a special request, are especially keen, or if your visit coincides with one by schoolchildren.

Outside, there are a few display cases containing **snakes**, a **chameleon pit** and the inevitable **tortoise pen**, with its hinged- and leopard-tortoise inmates. Unless it's the mating season, though, it's as boring for you as it must be for them. The recreations of Nandi and Luhya homesteads make an interesting point of comparison with the realities of present-day villages.

Next to the main building, the octagonal **Museum Hall** has some bold murals of Turkana, Maasai, Nandi and Luo domestic life, commissioned by the National Museum and painted by Maggie Kukler. There's occasionally live music or a disco here. The museum also has a craft shop, laboratories and a surprising **nature trail**, which transports you, in a few steps, from suburban Kitale to a chattering, dripping, riverine rain forest with abundant insect and birdlife: look out for Ross's turaco, a large, deep purple species with a square red crest, commoner here than in other forests. If you're lucky, you might also spot colobus and vervet monkeys. The trail follows a stream with a muddy path and rickety footbridges (unsuitable for the infirm), but the forest itself is natural and some of the trees stately. The picnic site, near the end of the trail, is a wonderful place if you can cope with the bugs.

Next door to the museum, the Swedish-backed **VI Agroforestry Project** (PO Box 2006; ☎0325/20139; daily 8am–5pm; free) was set up to educate cultivators in Trans-Nzoia and West Pokot about the basics of tree planting. This accomplished, it has now progressed to concerning itself with the problems of soil erosion and over-grazing, and offers practical advice to farmers on the selection of plant and tree species best adapted to local conditions. There's a small gallery here with well-captioned photographs explaining their work, and, outside, a "demonstration *shamba*" which showcases environmentally sound techniques to increase crop yield.

Onwards from Kitale

As well as the main *matatu* and bus park near the municipal market, there's a smaller gathering opposite Kitale Museum at the road junction heading off to Lodwar, Kapenguria, and Saiwa Swamp. These go to Eldoret, Kimilili, Kiminini, Kakamega and Kisumu. But, if in doubt, go to the main *matatu* stage.

Looking **to the west**: if you're interested in exploring **Mount Elgon** (full details start on p.316), access is a doddle, with three *matatus* daily to the park's Chorlim Gate. If you miss these, the next closest destination is Endebess, reached quickly enough by *matatu* (the route is fast becoming popular as an access route **into Uganda** – get your passport stamped at the District Commissioner's office in Kitale), or you could catch one to Kimilili if you plan to hike outside the confines (and restrictions) of the National Park; you should arrive early in the day if you want to make significant progress up the mountain before dark (Chorlim Gate is a twelve-kilometre walk away). **Southwards**, Kakamega and Kisumu are, with luck, no more than two or three hours away down the A1, a very busy road. As ever, *Akamba* **buses** (☎0325/31732) are the best bet for long hauls back to Nakuru and Nairobi, though with only two buses daily, you may find *Eldoret Express*'s frequent departures more useful: the booking office is a shack in the *matatu*/bus park, and their buses leave from the Total garage 200m along the avenue. It may be worth enquiring at the railway station whether **passenger train services** have resumed along the Kitale–Eldoret–Nairobi line.

Most people setting off from Kitale are **heading north** (route details in Chapter Seven). The road to Lodwar and Kalokol near Lake Turkana is mostly in pretty good condition, although the eighty-kilometre stretch north of Marich Pass has broken up almost completely, making for a very bumpy ride. It's still OK in 2WD so long as you go slowly over the broken sections, and the only cause for concern is flash floods which bar the way for a few hours, occasionally washing away a short stretch. There are several *matatus* a day (no buses) – best caught early, from around 8am – and enough traffic to make hitching a practical option. Remember to take water, and also to stock up provisions, as you'll only find more basic stuff on sale further north (fresh fruit and veg is expensive and of low quality in Lodwar). If you're driving yourself, note that there is nowhere to get fuel between Kapenguria and Lodwar. With a tent, it may be more fun to spend the night before at **Saiwa Swamp National Park** rather than in Kitale itself.

And you could further delay your progress north by stopping over at the Marich Pass Field Studies Centre.

Sirikwa Safaris – Barnley's House

You could also stop off for a day – or quite happily for a week – at the homely **Sirikwa Safaris Guesthouse and Campsite** (PO Box 332 Kitale; c/o Soy Supermarket in Kitale ☎0325/20061), signposted off to the right precisely 23.6km north of Kitale. Situated on a tree-covered hill, there are superb gardens to camp in (Ksh300 per person including firewood, use of a bathroom, *banda* and barbecue facilities), three furnished tents with electricity (③; may be replaced by *bandas* in future) and the Barnley family's fine old house (B&B ④, FB lower end of ⑥), which provides excellent meals, taken with the family, to order. Staff will undertake your washing – most days. Another great draw here are the **guides** (Ksh300/day; Ksh150/day for a porter; Ksh600/day for the ornithologist), for some exceptional bird-watching in the **Cherangani** foothills, and trips further afield to Kongolai escarpment (more bird-watching), Saiwa Swamp and elsewhere. Two- to four-day trips to Marich Pass (p.316) are recommended. The Barnleys themselves are a great source of information on the Cheranganis, invaluable if you fancy spending any time hiking around the area.

Saiwa Swamp National Park

Open daily; $15 adults, $5 children/students, Ksh200 for vehicle; car park; entry on foot. Warden PO Box 753 Chanira ☎Chemeron 22.

Specially created for the protection of the **sitatunga**, a rare and vulnerable semi-aquatic antelope, **Saiwa Swamp National Park** is the country's smallest park. Despite its accessibility – no distance from Barnley's House – it is rarely visited, which is a pity: the requirement that you walk (rather than drive) around the two square kilometres of jungle and swamp, plus the virtual guarantee of seeing the antelope as well as various monkeys and birds, make it an exciting and interesting goal for a day. If you're staying at Barnley's, think about hiring a guide there for the trip – not at all expensive, and really worthwhile.

Game watching

The **sitatunga** (pronounced "statunga") is an unusual antelope with strange splayed and elongated hooves. You probably won't see these because the animal lives most of its life partly submerged in water and weed. It's hard to see quite how the hooves help it "to move freely on the surface of boggy swamps": the theory makes sense, but the design needs more work. Otherwise, the sitatunga is reddish-brown and moth-eaten, with very large, mobile ears and, on the males, horns.

Sitatunga can be found in scattered locations throughout western and central Africa, but only at Saiwa Swamp have they grown really used to humans. They can be watched from the **observation platforms** which have been built in the trees at the side of the swamp – one on the east side, three on the west. The best times are early morning and late afternoon, and the furthest platform is less than a kilometre from the campsite. These lookouts are unmaintained, Tarzan-esque structures enabling you to spy down on the life among the reeds. The park also shelters plenty of **bushbuck**, easily distinguished from the sitatunga by their terrified, crashing escape through the undergrowth as you approach. The sitatunga evidently have steadier nerves, as they pick their way through the morass of water weed regardless of human attention.

A delightful, simple to follow, **early-morning walk** takes you across the rickety duckboards over the swamp and down a jungle path on the eastern shore. Here you're almost bound to see the park's four species of **monkey**: colobus, vervet, blue, and the distinctively white-bearded de Brazza monkey.

Saiwa Swamp is also a great draw for ornithologists, with a number of untypical Kenyan **bird species**, including several turacos (though the great blue is apparently no longer among them), many kingfishers, and the splendid black-and-white casqued hornbill. Most conspicuous of all are the **crowned cranes**, whose lurching flight is almost as risible as their ghastly honking call.

Practicalities

The park – known locally as *Swam'* – lies to the right of the main Kitale–Lodwar road, near the village of **Kipsain** (also known as Kipsoen). *Matatus* and the *Akamba* bus to Kapenguria (7am only) call at the village, which is some 18km from Kitale and off the main road. From here, if you fail to get a lift, it's a poorly signposted five-kilometre walk to the park gates. They have a basic *banda* with firewood (②), and camping is allowed (Ksh200). There are three good sites grouped together, but nothing at all in the way of facilities, apart from a clean, piped water supply at the staff village, plenty of firewood, and a small *duka*, open sporadically. You will need to make a fire, as the swamp mist makes it very chilly up here at night.

Kapenguria, Ortum and the Marich Pass

KAPENGURIA – off the highway north, is surprisingly small given its status as the capital of West Pokot, and notable only for its role of minor notoriety in colonial history (see the background on Kenyatta's trial in Contexts, p.611). If you turn off the main road to visit, you'll find an immaculately tarred main street leading incongruously up through the hovels of "old Kapenguria" to the smarter new town on higher ground, with its hospital, large police station, huge red octagonal Catholic church (stained-glass windows and a spire), and the West Pokot District headquarters.

Also here is the excellent **Kapenguria Museum** (daily 8am–6pm; Ksh200), occupying the prison where Kenyatta and his colleagues were detained during their parody of a trial. Their individually-named cells have been "restored", and contain copies of contemporary press reports, photographs, depositions and the charges laid against each of the men (some almost laughably nebulous). Largely inaccessible during the colonial period, the town was deliberately chosen to hinder the work of the defence lawyers – "a maze of rascalities", one of them called it. All six defendants were found guilty of belonging to Mau Mau and sentenced to seven years in jail with hard labour. Much more visually interesting are the ethnographic displays of Pokot and Cherangani cultures, including well-described photographs of traditional ceremonies (circumcision dances and initiatory groups), musical instruments, and a telling series on the changes wrought by "modern" life. Look out for the chisel for removing teeth, and the small Cherangani horn "for sucking after making incisions on both sides of the head if one has a headache". In the museum grounds are three reconstructed Pokot and Cherangani family compounds, which the museum caretaker will be happy to explain to you. Oddly prescient, given the recent flare-up of ethnic violence and cattle-raiding in West Pokot, is the pastoralist Pokot compound, featuring solid mud roofs which were designed to deflect firebrands flung by raiders.

If you're hungry, the *Talik Hotel* is a worthy target. For **accommodation**, there's a couple of B&Ls down in **Makutano** – the service town for the western Cherangani Hills, at the Kapenguria intersection: the *New Elgonnia Hotel* (PO Box 5; ☎0324/2481; ①), facing Esso, is the more basic, but has some s/c doubles and plays videos in its bar in the afternoons; better is *Elgonnia Springs Hotel*, signposted 300m off the Kitale road 1km south of town (PO Box 132; ☎0324/2284; ①), with small, reasonably clean s/c rooms (long-drop toilets), water most of the time, occasionally hot. You can order food at the bar.

From Makutano/Kapenguria, the road enters the truly spectacular countryside of West Pokot proper, winding up the western ridge of Lenan forest, then plunging steeply to the Marun (or Moruny) river. After some 45km you reach **ORTUM**, beautifully positioned beneath the heights of the Cheranganis, close to the **Marich Pass**, and a good locale to start hiking in the hills. There are at least two cheap **B&Ls** here (*Karumaindo Inn* and *Somtowo Hotel*), and people are pleasantly uninterested in your presence. Of a large number of *hotelis*, the winner is *Rafikis' Hotel*, which serves tasty meals and manages cold sodas despite the absence of electricity. You can do a short **hike to a waterfall**, three hours' walk up from Ortum. Cross the main road beyond the post office, down by the *Karumaindo Inn*, and the first dirt track takes you straight there. Heading into the Kerio Valley (p.264) on the other side of the Cheranganis, *matatus* for Sigor (Thursdays), Lomut (Saturdays) and Chesegon (Wednesdays) coincide with weekly markets, but be aware that these villages were the site of ethnic violence in the run-up to the 1997 general elections, and the road has long had a reputation for armed hold-ups.

An excellent base to make for in this district is the **Marich Pass Field Studies Centre** (PO Box 564 Kapenguria; no phone), beautifully sited on the banks of the Marun River, just north of the small shopping centre of **Marich**, at the junction of the A1 Lodwar and B4 Kerio Valley roads: the centre (signposted) is 1km off the Lodwar road. There's a lovely shaded campsite (Ksh200 per person; one tent available for rent at Ksh100), some very good non-s/c *bandas* with nets (②) and a dorm block (Ksh280 per person). Firewood, stoves and lamps are available for a small fee. The food is basic but impressively plentiful – order well in advance – and drinking water comes pure from the well. Even if you're not staying, it's well worth dropping in for a picnic (daily admission Ksh40), as the centre is surrounded by dense bush, quivering with bird and animal life, and there are guides to help you on excursions around the hills, to Pokot villages and local markets if you have the energy (fixed rates: Ksh240 for 6hr, Ksh360 for 12hr). **Mount Sekerr** (Mtelo) is the peak that looms to the northwest – it's a three-day hike to the top (3354m) and back. Nearer Marich, 3206-metre **Mount Koh** to the southeast is a one-day hike if you've got 4WD to get half way up, two full days otherwise.

Mount Elgon

Straddling the Kenya-Uganda border, the Maasai's **Ol Doinyo Ilgoon** (Breast Mountain) is hidden in clouds most of the time, its precise outline hard to discern. Like Mount Kenya, **Mount Elgon** is an extinct volcano, and around its jagged and much eroded crater rim, the flat-topped peaks crop up like stumpy fingers of an upturned hand. The two mountains are comparable in bulk, but Elgon is lower (below the snowline) and less precipitous – an encouragement, perhaps, if the thought of tackling the "loneliest park in Kenya" was putting you off.

Part of the east side of the mountain is enclosed within the confines of **Mount Elgon National Park**. Outside this zone, however, you're as free to hike and camp as anywhere in Kenya, subject always to the mountain's potentially restricting location on what the authorities have often considered a sensitive border (see box on p.321). **Security problems** in the past mean that to tackle an ascent to the summit, you either need to be convincingly persuasive with the rangers at the gate (not easy), or else have already obtained some sort of official clearance from the KWS headquarters in Nairobi (p.148). Alternatively, hiring the services of an armed ranger at something more than the official Ksh300 per day rate might work, though you'll need to stay on the mountain overnight, which means bringing enough food and shelter for all of you.

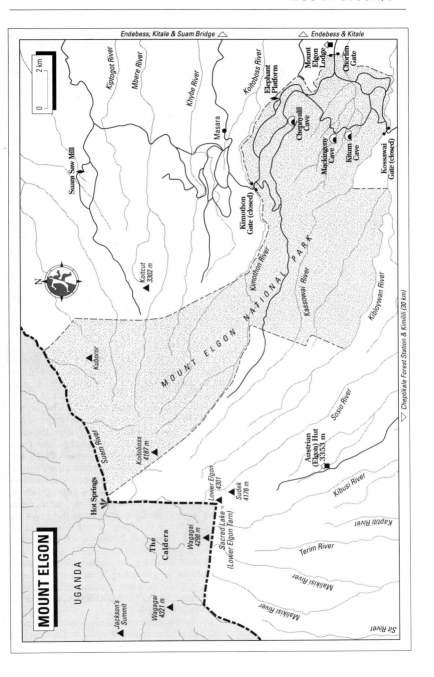

If you do manage to cobble things together, there's invigorating walking country up near the peaks, and the smoothing effects of erosion make hiking relatively easy. The highest peak, **Wagagai** (4321m; there's also another Wagagai nearby, at 4298m), is across the caldera in Uganda, but the most evocatively shaped peaks (Sudek, 4176m; Lower Elgon, 4301m; Koitoboss, 4187m; and Endebess Bluff, 2563m) belong to Kenya. The mountain has good rock-climbing but you must be properly equipped; the best is on the cliffs of Lower Elgon, Sudek and the nearby pinnacles. Again, you'll need clearance from someone in authority. Actually up in the caldera (technically in Uganda), the **warm springs** by the Suam River provide a tempting bath.

Wildlife

Vegetation here is similar to Mount Kenya's, and very impressive, with bamboo and podocarpus forests (the latter more accessible than Mount Kenya's) giving way to open moorland inhabited by the strange statues of giant groundsel and lobelia. **Wildlife** isn't easily seen until you get onto the moors but elephant and buffalo do roam the woods (be extremely wary of both). The best place to see **elephant** used to be the Elephant Platform – herds would congregate here to feed on the acacias – but poaching has made them reclusive. Large numbers of elephant were wiped out by Ugandan poachers in the turbulent 1980s. While the Kenya Wildlife Service is confident that poaching is now under control, and estimates that the elephant population now exceeds 400, it remains to be seen how long they will remain under effective protection. The lions have long gone and, though there are still leopards, you're not likely to see one. The primates are more conspicuous: blue monkeys (found only in western Kenya) and shaggy colobus crash through the forested areas, troops of olive baboons patrol the scrub, and along the Kimothon River there's a scattering of rare de Brazza's monkeys.

The Elkony Caves

Elgon's most captivating attraction is the honeycomb of caves on the lower slopes, inside the national park boundaries. Some of these were long inhabited by one of the loosely related Kalenjin groups, the **Elkony** (whose name, in corrupted form, was given to the mountain), and used both as living quarters and as stock pens at night. There is evidence that the caves may have had a ritual function as well – **Chepnyalil Cave** contains a structure that might have served as an altar or shrine, and its walls are painted with a red-and-white frieze of cattle. The cave is not signposted – from the park gate, head north for 2km to the signposted junction for the Caves (south), Park Gate (east) and Koitoboss Peak (north), and turn right 2.5km towards Endebess Bluff, taking the narrow and overgrown track on the left just before the waterfall. Male circumcision ceremonies among the Luhya people are also linked with the caves (as well as others in the region), where boys spent their month-long initiation period, before returning home as men, covered head-to-toe in the white diatomite powder found nearby (especially visible at Kitum). The Elkony were officially evicted from the caves by the colonial government, who insisted that they live in the open "where they could be counted for tax", but caves with ceilings as high as two-storey buildings were still occupied by extended families within living memory.

Some of the caves are so large and labyrinthine that deep exploration is only possible with navigational aids and breathing apparatus. It is rumoured that there is a route that leads far into the mountain and emerges in Uganda, a secret passage known only to coffee smugglers. The largest and most spectacular cave is **Makingeny**, marked by a cascade falling over the entrance (there's no signpost).

Early explorers believed that some of the caves were man-made, and one report referred to "thousands of chisel and axe marks on the walls". If you actually visit the caves, you'll realise very quickly (from the stench and football-sized droppings, among

---

KITUM CAVE AND THE EBOLA VIRUS

Kitum Cave earned a certain notoriety when it featured as the opening and closing location of *The Hot Zone*, a "true-life thriller" about **Ebola** written in 1994 by an American journalist, Richard Preston. Ebola is a virus so deadly it is scientifically classed as a Level 4 pathogen (HIV is only Level 2). Mercifully, it's rare: the only serious outbreaks in the last twenty years occurred in Zaïre (now Congo) and Sudan in 1976, and then again in April 1995 in Zaïre. In the more recent plague, around 250 people in the Congolese town of Kikwit died after contracting the virus. The manner of death by Ebola is so gruesome that hysterical global media coverage surrounded the outbreak – effectively, the virus liquefies the vital organs of the living victim, and death occurs within days. Scientists have yet to gather any solid data about the origins and means of transmission of the virus, or the identity of its natural host. The link to Kitum Cave is a tenuous, probably meaningless one. Isolated incidences of Ebola infection are reported every few years, and, in two such cases (described in gut-churning detail by Richard Preston in his book), the victims had visited Kitum Cave shortly before they became ill. In an attempt to discover whether the cave harbours the virus in some form, the US Army's Infectious Diseases Unit, in conjunction with the Kenya Medical Research Unit, mounted a research operation in Kitum Cave in 1988. The team made Mount Elgon Lodge their base, donned spaceman-type anti-virus bio-safety suits, and set about making a comprehensive examination of the cave, testing thousands of resident insects, birds, hyraxes, bats, monkeys, baboons, and samples of guano and dung, for Ebola. They found absolutely nothing. Preston's book, going all out for sensationalism, hangs a question mark over the conclusiveness of these findings, but those who know the Elgon area well unanimously write the theory off as irresponsible trouble-stirring.

---

other clues) that generations of elephants were responsible: the well-signposted **Kitum Cave** achieved TV fame as the salt fix of local elephants, which still walk into the caves at night to gouge the salty rock from the walls with their tusks. The elephants, though no longer free to migrate back and forth between Elgon and the Cheranganis as they once did, are still occasional troglodytes. There have been cases of them falling into crevasses or dying under rock falls caused by their over-eager salt-mining.

Planning a trip

In most respects, you should treat a trip up Mount Elgon much as you would one to Mount Kenya (see p.191). However, **altitude** is less of a problem on Elgon and, given several days to climb it, few people will be badly affected by the ascent, except perhaps near the summits. Although access to the National Park is easy, with three *matatus* a day from Kitale, **hiking within the park** is currently restricted to the area immediately west of Chorlim Gate (ie Kitum, Makingeny and Chepnyalil caves, and Endebess Bluff: you're advised to take an armed ranger as a chaperone/guide; Ksh300 per day), and perhaps for this reason it is one of the least-visited national parks in Kenya. It is possible to reach the peak from within the National Park, but for this you need an extremely sturdy, high-slung 4WD, as well as steely nerves, as it's a steep, rocky and extremely muddy ride up to the start of the trail to Koitoboss Peak. Even so, note that the route is often completely impassable (January and February are the best months), and at other times of the year even the area west of Chorlim Gate can be extremely treacherous, with plenty of mud, slippery tyre-ruts and ample opportunities to bog down or even roll your vehicle. Without a car, your only options are seeking special permission (and an armed escort) from the rangers at the gate or, better still, some sort of authorization from KWS headquarters in Nairobi (p.148). Otherwise, the only way up to the summit is via the Kimilili route outside the park, via Cheptikale Forest Station (see p.322).

Timing and guides

Elgon is best from December to March and rather less good in June and July, with the heaviest rains falling during the April to May and August to September periods. This is a lonely mountain, and while there are no specific permanent restrictions on hiking outside the park boundaries (which enclose less than a quarter of the Kenyan slopes), it's probably better not to go up alone. You aren't likely to see anyone else for a day or two, and if something were to happen to you on the heights you can forget about rescue. Men can find **guide-porters** easily enough in villages around the base: just ask around, and expect to pay up to Ksh500 per day. As usual, women travelling alone will be at a disadvantage when it comes to such one-to-one arrangements.

Maps

If you plan more than a look into the park by vehicle, it's useful to have the *Mount Elgon Map & Guide* by Andrew Wielochowski, obtainable in Nairobi or in the UK from Executive Wilderness Programmes, Haulfryn, Cilycwm, Llandovery SA20 0SP (☎01550/721319, fax 720053; £6 including postage within the UK). Survey of Kenya maps are also available, and the 1:125,000 map can be obtained without clearance, though border sensitivity means some other sheets may be restricted at times (see p.149).

Equipment

Take a **compass** and supplies for at least two to three days of self-sufficiency. Suggestions on clothing and equipment can be found in the Mount Kenya section (p.192). A **tent** will enable you to stay up in the peaks area, and a **torch** is essential if you fancy poking about the caves. If you have a vehicle (4WD essential), you can adjust these requirements. The park rangers are often willing to accompany drivers for a fee.

The routes

There are three **routes** up the Kenyan side of Elgon: one directly into the park and two hikes around either side, both passing through fine scenery and neither very severe (the northerly one is currently out of bounds). You should try, if at all possible, to **camp** at one of the sites in the lower half of the park – they're highly recommended as some of the most beautiful in the country – and visit the caves. Of these, *Kapkuro* (or *Kuro*) campsite, the nearest to Chorlim Gate, has a couple of brand new *bandas* available (③), with water and showers.

Mount Elgon Lodge (PO Box 7 Endebess; no phone, but the park gate can take messages on ☎0325/30319; reservations through *Msafiri Inns*, address p.49; B&B ④, FB ⑤), is located 1km outside the park on the track leading to Chorlim Gate (no park fees payable). It has been run at a loss for many years but still manages to stay open, which is good news if you've money for a splash. It's an atmospheric retreat, despite the emptiness: the manorial reception rooms have lovingly polished wood-block floors and quintessentially English garden views, and the bedrooms are comfortable enough (no nets, but the few mosquitoes here aren't malarial). You can choose between one of three original rooms up a creaking flight of stairs ("Cherangani" is the best), or a modern room in the block overlooking the lawns. The water supply is erratic. **Camping** in the grounds is an accepted, and very acceptable, alternative to taking a room (Ksh350 per person, including use of bathroom and showers).

TEMPORARY DIFFICULTIES: SOME NOTES OF CAUTION

Elgon's location occasionally makes it a **sensitive area**. If you plan to go down into the crater and visit the Suam warm springs, remember that they are in Uganda: stories of rebel soldiers have long been rife.

In the 1980s, Elgon was the scene of a number of violent confrontations between elephant poachers and armed park rangers. The last serious outbreak was in 1988 and resulted in several deaths. For some time, Kenyan officials were turning back non-4WD vehicles, even outside the park, and preventing hikers on foot from climbing. You are still required to have 4WD transport if you plan to cover anything more than the area immediately to the west of Chorlim Gate.

The most recent threat to Elgon's status as a hiking attraction is the ethnic strife that has swept the communities of its eastern slopes since the democracy movement gained momentum. The people of Kimilili, Endebess and Kolongolo towns have seen arson, sporadic violence and furious bouts of intimidation directed against non-Kalenjin by gangs of youths of uncertain identity. Currently also causing concern in the same region is a series of bloody cross-border cattle raids, involving heavily armed rustlers. Access up the walking routes may be refused at one point or another, or you may be advised to abandon your attempt. Talk to local people and the park rangers, and take a guide or even an armed ranger.

Direct to the park

Daily fees $15, $5 children/students; $2 to camp. Warden PO Box 753 Kitale; ☎0325/20329.

The only way into the **National Park** is through **Chorlim Gate**, which lies some 12km beyond Endebess. Kimothon and Kossowai gates have been closed and unstaffed for some time – using them risks landing you in a lot of trouble. To reach Chorlim Gate, stock up on petrol at Kitale, and head northwest towards Endebess along the newly resurfaced tarmac road. There's a brown Kenya Wildlife Service signpost marking the left-hand turning to the National Park, 500m after the Kenya Seed Company and ADC compounds. From here a mostly decent *murram* road heads straight to Mount Elgon Lodge and Chorlim Gate (passable with 2WD in dry seasons). If you miss the turning, there's another left turn signposted at Endebess, leading to the same *murram* road (this route is boggier and not for 2WD). *Matatus* run three times a day to the gate from Kitale, and there are frequent services to Endebess, leaving you with a pleasant two-hour walk. Hoping to find a spare seat in a tourist vehicle isn't really an option: with barely a handful of visitors per month you might be in for a long wait.

Once inside the park, the fine (signposted) campsites a few kilometres from the gate are a good target. If you're exceptionally lucky, a night vigil at **Kitum Cave** may be repaid by a visit from the elephants; the bats and the forest are compensation if you're not. You'll need permission from the rangers and a good torch, and be warned that this is a potentially dangerous exercise: plan your escape route well. For **Koitoboss Peak** (4187m), follow the drivable track into the moorlands to the trailhead outside the park (allow 3–4hr to cover the 30km; a ranger should accompany you in your vehicle; 4WD only, and then only safely January–February: ask the rangers whether it's been improved, as there were plans to regrade it). From here it's a three-hour hike to the pass at the southern base of the peak, where there are flat (but cold and windy) places where you can camp. You can then make the one-hour scramble to the top, or take a two- to three-hour diversion to the Suam Springs in the crater.

If you're dreaming about **crossing the mountain into Uganda**, you must inform KWS in Nairobi (p.148) of your plans, who may, or more likely will not, give permission, and help arrange things with the Ugandan parks authorities on the west side of the mountain. At present, you need a pretty good reason for attempting this trek – security concerns on both sides of Mount Elgon are high.

Kimilili and the Western Trail

The **second route** is the most popular with **hikers** (but note caveats: see box on p.321). It begins in **KIMILILI**, a village on the way to Bungoma from Kitale (heading south from Kitale towards Webuye, turn right off the A1 after about 30km; there are frequent *matatus* from Kitale), from where it's a long but invigorating trek up to the moorlands (lifts are scarce). In Kimilili, *Jasho Lodging* (①) is recommended for **rooms**, the *Wanyika Hotel* for **meals**. Kimilili is a lively place on a Thursday, when the **market** attracts rural dwellers from a wide radius. You may be allowed to **pitch a tent** at Kimilili Catholic Secondary School, just outside the town.

The next day, by allowing yourself a good eight to ten hours to cover the 40km, you should be able to reach the Elgon Hut (or Austrian Hut); the hut is disused but it is usually possible to camp near the hut. The first step **up the mountain** is to take a ride by *matatu*, starting as early as possible in the day, from Kimilili to **Kapsakwony**, 7km away (top up with water here if you forgot in Kimilili). At the fork above the village, bear left, then after 2km, turn right at the "Forest Station 25km" signpost. You may get a lift from here, past the Forest Reserve Gate (small fee) to the last village, **Kaberua**, 2.5km further up (see the sign there, "Chepkitale Forest Stn 21km"), but from Kaberua on, you'll almost certainly have to walk. Eight kilometres above Kaberua, the trail gets noticeably worse as it plunges into the cathedral gloom of tsetse-fly-infested bamboo forest. An hour of this and you break into open stands of moss-enveloped giant podocarpus trees ("podos") with spiralling trunks. The trail rolls upwards, you crest a hill, and the entire southern Elgon Ridge system is spread out before you.

The **Chepkitale forest station** has plenty of abandoned buildings for shelter but uncertain water supplies, so it is worth struggling on the last two hours (7km) to the **Elgon Hut**. There's a stream near the hut but little firewood, so remember to collect some on the way. A rough jeep track continues past the hut, but you're unlikely to meet anyone up here.

The **trail** from the hut is well marked with occasional cairns and white blazes: a brisk three to four hours the following morning should see you to **Lower Elgon Tarn**, a good place to camp, from where it's another hour to the top of Lower Elgon itself, the highest peak on the Kenya side. Starting out from the hut, a two-hour hike will bring you up to the ridge that leads up to the peak of Lower Elgon. (Just beyond this, there is a high valley which has the southeast caldera rim, seen from the rear, as its head.)

ELIJA MASINDE'S DINI: THE CULT OF THE ANCESTORS

In the 1940s and 1950s, there was a resurgence of **Bukusu resistance** and nationalism in the *Dini ya Msambwa* (Cult of the Ancestors) movement, spearheaded by the charismatic prophet-rebel, **Elija Masinde**. The heart of the movement was in the Elgon foothills between Kimilili and the Ugandan border. It called for the eviction of all *wazungu* and the transfer of their property to Africans. As the *Dini* spread, there were violent confrontations with colonial forces, and a number of deaths. Masinde was sent into internal exile but, by now a folk hero, his followers kept the sparks of resistance alive throughout the more organized uprising of Mau Mau in the Central Highlands, until Independence was finally obtained. The movement collapsed in the early years of *Uhuru*, when Masinde was allowed home to Kimilili and his continued denouncements of all authority and claims to divine inspiration began to lose their coherence. Until his death in the 1990s, he could still be seen on the streets of Kimilili – a rather terrifying figure shouting at the wind.

There are duiker antelope to be seen bouncing away through the scrub everywhere. Next, you climb a false summit, then dip down, paralleling the series of tabular peaks on your right which form the southern crater lip. From the **tarn**, the trail swerves cruelly up through a gap in the rock wall to put you on the summit of Lower Elgon.

Alternatively, you could make the five-hour trek from the hut to **Koitoboss Peak** and the **Suam warm springs**. To get down to the springs, instead of following the ridge at the two-hour mark, leave the trail and cut across the valley, following the rim to Koitoboss Peak, inside the National Park. Down in the crater, to the left, are the springs. Depending on your supplies and the state of security, you can either turn back to the hut for a second night there or continue around the crater rim to drop down off the mountain on the northeast side, traversing the upper part of the National Park and, ideally, allowing a night camped on the mountain. Note that if you're found in the park, or if you exit through Chorlim Gate, you may have some explaining to do and you'll have to pay park fees at least.

Kimothon route (currently closed)

There's a **third route**, on the north side of the park, which obviates some of the lengthy foot-slogging of the trail from Kimilili, but this has been closed for some years now, and at the last check the park rangers were adamant – with reason – that the route was positively dangerous, in terms of running into armed Ugandan cattle rustlers. If you get caught by rangers on this route, don't expect to be able to talk your way out of trouble: a night or two in detention is more likely, with an outside possibility of deportation. Should the security situation improve, here's the rundown: it starts in Endebess and leads west about 12km up to the village of **Masara** and thence to **Kimothon Forest Station**. It's recommended that you stay the night here and continue the next day on the well-marked trail to Koitoboss and the Elgon hut. Downhill from here, you can follow the Kimilili trail (about 40km, as described above) in reverse. Once you reach Kapsakwony there are *matatus* for the last 7km to Kimilili; it's a ten-hour knee-wobbler of a hike if you want to walk the whole way.

The Uganda road: Webuye, Bungoma and Malaba

This is perhaps the least interesting part of western Kenya to look at: largely monotonous undulating grasslands and sugar fields, dotted here and there with gigantic granite boulders. But it is still the route by which the majority of Africa overland travellers come into the country (when central African security issues permit them to do so), and the most obvious one for those planning to head **out to Uganda**; despite the lack of attractions, it sees a fair number of travellers passing through.

If you're making your way to the south from this district down towards Kakamega and Kisumu, the busy A1 will take you through some fine stands of forest and tropical woodland, heralding the Kakamega Forest zone (see p.327) to the southeast.

Webuye and around

WEBUYE certainly offers very little to attract visitors. It's the site of the giant Panafrican Paper Mills, which dominates the countryside around – with its strong, noxious odour as much as anything else. The explanation for the factory's siting is **Webuye Falls**, gushing through rock clefts behind and above the mills, about 5km from the main road. Formerly known as Broderick Falls, Webuye is a nice spot for a picnic, as long as you have a car for access, but the falls are hardly spectacular. To reach them, turn off the main road at the factory and climb northwards between housing developments and mills, passing a school. From there, the plant (the largest paper factory in Africa), belching smoke across the hot plains, is a powerful statement about change in Kenya.

Webuye has the usual assortment of banks, shops and petrol stations, and if you find yourself in need of a **room**, there are two main options: the *Webuye Motel* on the southeast side of town nearest the factory (PO Box 553; ☎0337/41328; bed only ①–②), has an unexciting selection of rooms, some s/c, some nets, but mostly pretty dingy and musty, all within sniffing distance of the factory and its sirens; and the superior *Park View Hotel*, just up the Kitale road (PO Box 1000; ☎0337/41290; B&B ③), a well-kept and welcoming roadside stop with busy bars and a small pool (Ksh130 for visitors), all rooms s/c with nets, and there's even a sauna (Ksh260 per hour).

Chetambe's Fort

A few kilometres away, on top of the steep scarp that rears up beyond the Kitale road, lies a different kind of monument, the remains of **Chetambe's Fort**. This was the site, in 1895, of a last-ditch stand by the Bukusu group of the Luhya tribe against the motley line-up of a British punitive expedition, which had enrolled Ugandan, Sudanese, Maasai and even other Luhya troops. A predictable – Hotchkiss gun – massacre took place, with negligible losses on the attackers' side. How they managed to storm the scarp in the first place, however, is a mystery: presumably the Bukusu were all inside their walled fort at the top.

With Kenya's historical sites being so few, it's worth the effort to scramble up the steep slope if you're interested. Not surprisingly, perhaps, the "Fort" itself is quite unimpressive: all that remains these days is an overgrown, semicircular ditch, perhaps 100m from end to end. A more convincing reason for going there is to talk to some of the people who live nearby – this is really the only way to weave together the threads of history. You can be shown the site by people who live around it: the compound is just another field now, but one informal guide explained how he used to find bones here when he was young, and women would come here to weep in the evenings. There were even animal sacrifices to the dead warriors. Some "awful machine" had killed them.

If you have your own transport, a roundabout alternative to the slog up the cliffs is to continue following the road which leads past Webuye Falls. The *Nabyole Lodge* up here is quite a good **B&L**, with cold drinks and a restaurant. They'll direct you on to Chetambe's, about 8km further on reasonable *murram*.

Bungoma and into Uganda

The main road to Uganda continues west. The smooth tarmac and dull scenery encourage fast driving, with light vehicles shuddering in the slipstream of thundering lorries. Number-plate spotters will be able to tick off vehicles from all over eastern and central Africa on this one well-pounded stretch.

Sizeable as it is, **BUNGOMA** manages to be unremittingly dull. Unless you're drawn by the siren calls of the *Bungoma Tourist Hotel's* unexpected "sugar-belt style" comforts (PO Box 972; ☎0337/30037 or 20051; ③), there's scarcely any reason to visit the town, as it isn't on the main road. If you do find yourself here, *Grandma's Hotel* (PO Box 225), just 200m south of the A104 Bungoma junction, before you get into the town, is less of a drain on the resources and provides clean, quiet rooms. If you miss this, or find it full, *Hotel Simba B&L* (PO Box 663), has cheap double beds and seems better than the other competition in town. Apart from suggesting that you eat at the *New Yemeni Hotel*, a superior *hoteli*, Bungoma's interest can't be further improved.

Malaba: the Ugandan border

MALABA lies at the end of both the road and the (presently defunct) railway line. While there are usually endless lines of lorries waiting on both sides of the border with **Uganda**, pedestrians have been crossing for some years now without difficulty. Formalities are relatively simple, and British citizens do not currently need a visa, although Americans and some others do.

Arriving in Kenya, note that there are currently no passenger train services: the nearest line is at Kisumu, which has daily services for Nairobi. There's no shortage of unappetizing **B&Ls** along the kilometre of lorry-choked road which is Malaba. While near the border, especially if distracted by the formalities of crossing, don't make the mistake of relaxing your security routines: many people are robbed soon after arriving. There are several bus companies doing the run to Nairobi, of which Akamba (☎0337/20962) have the safest reputation.

Kakamega and Kakamega Forest

KAKAMEGA is the headquarters of the **Luhya**, a loosely defined group of peoples whose only clear common denominator is a **Bantu language**, spoken in more than a score of vernaculars, that distinguishes them from the Luo to the south and the Kalenjin to the east. Numerically, the Luhya (Abaluhya/Luyia) are Kenya's second largest ethnic group, and most are settled farmers.

The town itself was founded as a buying station on the ox trail known as Sclater's Road, which reached here from the coast in 1896. Historically, its only fame came in the 1930s, when gold was discovered nearby and more than a thousand prospectors came to the region. Very few fortunes were made. Today, it's a lively town, but with little to detain casual visitors.

Conversely, the nearby **Kakamega Forest** is one of western Kenya's star attractions; if you have any interest at all in the natural world, it's worth going far out of your way to see. Fortunately, it's fairly easy to get to from Kisumu or, if you've been in the Mount Elgon region, from Webuye along a very scenic stretch of the A1.

Moving on, Akamba buses (☎0331/20743) run daily to Nairobi, via Kapsabet and Nandi Hills at 7.30am, and via Kisumu and Kericho at 7.30pm. There are *matatus* to Kericho, Kisumu, Webuye and sometimes Bungoma.

Kakamega town – practicalities

If you arrive late in the day (or after around 2.30pm in 2WD, when the rain starts to fall), you may want to **stay in town** rather than arrive in the forest after dark. There are several decent lodgings and one or two pleasant places to eat.

Accommodation

Bendera Hotel (PO Box 423; ☎0331/20777). Unexpectedly good B&L – clean and welcoming, with decent-sized s/c rooms. Happily the ear-splitting country and western music from the downstairs bar-restaurant doesn't really filter upstairs. ①.

Franka Hotel (PO Box 621; ☎0331/20086). Plenty of dirty s/c rooms, some with good views, but this place – especially the bar you have to walk through – has the atmosphere of a wide-boys' hangout in the evening and is probably not a good choice for lone women. ①.

Golf Hotel (PO Box 118; ☎0331/30150–3, fax 30155; reservations via *Msafiri Inns*, p.49). A relatively luxurious hotel with its pretensions comically clipped by the vultures hopping over the lawns. All guests become temporary members of the adjacent Sports Club (golf, squash courts) and there's a pool and gift shop. However, non-Kenya resident rates are high. ⑤.

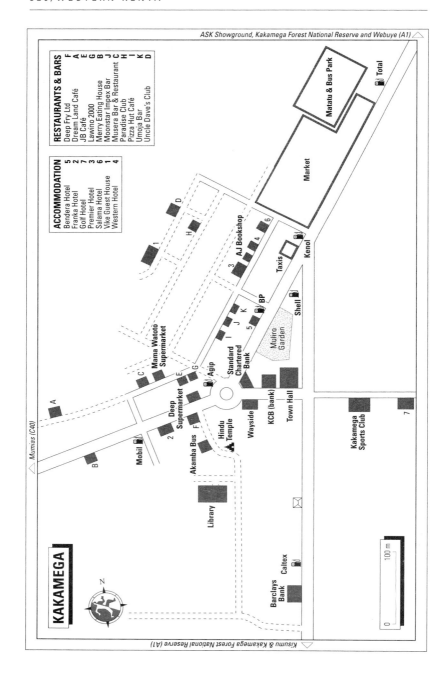

KAKAMEGA

ASK Showground, Kakamega Forest National Reserve and Webuye (A1)

Kisumu & Kakamega Forest National Reserve (A1)

Mumias (C40)

ACCOMMODATION
Bendera Hotel	5
Franka Hotel	2
Golf Hotel	7
Premier Hotel	3
Salama Hotel	6
Vike Guest House	1
Western Hotel	4

RESTAURANTS & BARS
Deep Fry Ltd	F
Dream Land Café	A
JB Café	E
Lawino 2000	G
Merry Eating House	B
Moonstar Impex Bar	J
Musera Bar & Restaurant	C
Paradise Club	I
Pizza Hut Café	H
Umoja Bar	K
Uncle Dave's Club	D

Matatu & Bus Park

Total

Market

AJ Bookshop

Taxis

Kenol

BP

Shell

Muliro Garden

Mama Watoto Supermarket

Standard Chartered Bank

Agip

Deep Supermarket

KCB (bank)

Town Hall

Wayside

Mobil

Akamba Bus

Hindu Temple

Library

Kakamega Sports Club

Caltex

Barclays Bank

N

0   100 m

Premier Hotel, Cannon Awori St (PO Box 1633; no phone as yet). Kakamega's newest option (still being fitted out at the time of writing), with large balconied s/c rooms and a choice of baths or showers. Its bar features Congolese and Luhya *isukuti* music. ③.

Salama Hotel, Cannon Awori St (PO Box 70; ☎0331/20013). Cheap and friendly Somali-run B&L but extremely basic, with tiny slummy rooms off a courtyard at the back of a fly-blown eating place, and worse toilets. On the plus side, you'll experience a side of Kenya – that lived by the vast majority – that's rarely seen by tourists. ①.

Vike Guest House (PO Box 1649; no phone). The best cheapie, with good balconied rooms, all s/c with spotless squat loos and hot water in the morning. It can get loud at night, though, thanks to its ground-floor bar and echoing acoustics. Excellent value. Bed only. ①.

Eating and drinking

In addition to the hotel restaurants, there are some great cheap eats in Kakamega, and plenty of places to drink and listen to music, too. The *Dream Land Café* ("The Pride of the Town") is a generally recommended **eating house**, which offers plentiful, tasty food – great curries – in clean and pleasant surroundings. Recent reports, however, suggest, standards may no longer be quite so high. Also recommended is the *Merry Eating House* where you eat with your fingers (don't be put off by its dingy exterior or tumbledown interior: the fried tilapia is excellent). Other places worth trying include: *Lawino 2000* and the adjacent *JB Café*, both dirt cheap (under Ksh70) and friendly; *Deep Fry Ltd* (no prizes for guessing what it serves); the long list of Kenyan standards at the *Western Hotel*; and *Pizza Hut Café*, a bright little place that only actually has one variety of pizza on the menu, and fairly awful at that, but offers plenty of other choices. For **drinking places** with character, you're spoilt for choice: *Musera Bar and Restaurant* is very mellow; *Moonstar Impex* and *Umoja Bar* are for more hardened boozers; *Bendera Hotel* and the *Wayside* both have good local jukebox sounds. There are two good, and very local, **clubs**, where *wazungu* are a welcome and fascinating rarity: *Uncle Dave's Club* and *Paradise Club*. The *Dream Land Café* has live music Fridays from 6pm.

Listings

Books There's a good bookshop with a few foreign paperbacks on Cannon Awori St. The library is open Mon–Thurs 9am–6pm, Fri 9am–4pm, Sat 9am–1pm; it should have some background on the Kakamega Forest.

Initiation Ceremonies In August every year, Kakamega hosts a mass circumcision and initiation ceremony for boys from all the Luhya speaking communities in the district. It's not certain how much you can get involved, but the party atmosphere should be unmistakeable. Ask locally.

Kakamega Show End of November for three days at the ASK Showground.

Market There's a very lively one next to the bus station. Among the local produce on offer you'll find natural remedies and medicines made from forest plants. Main market days are Wednesday and Saturday.

Supermarkets Mama Watoto near Musera Bar, and Deep Supermarket next to Agip.

Swimming pool A small one at the *Golf Hotel*.

The Kakamega Forest

Kenya Wildlife Service District Warden, PO Box 879 Kakamega; ☎0331/20425 or 30603; free entry.

Some four hundred years ago, the tract of rain forest now called **Kakamega Forest** would have been at the eastern end of a broad expanse of forest stretching west, clear across the continent, virtually unbroken as far as the Atlantic. Three hundred years later, after the advent of the human population explosion and widescale cultivation, the forests everywhere had receded, and had reduced Kakamega to an island of some 2,400 square kilometres, cut off from the rest of the Guineo-Congolan rain forest.

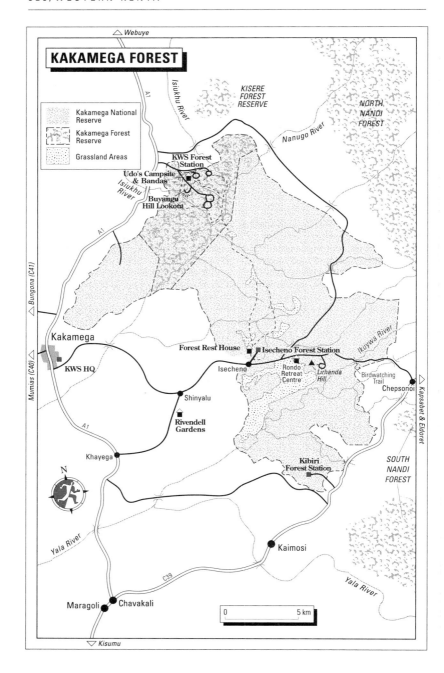

KAKAMEGA FOREST

Today, with an area not surpassing 230 square kilometres, it's a tiny patch of relict equatorial jungle, famous among zoologists and botanists around the world as an example of how an isolated environment can survive cut off from its larger body. The Kakamega Forest is a haven of shadowy gloom for over 300 species of birds, 45 percent of all recorded butterflies in Kenya, seven species of primates and other mammals, as well as snakes, other reptiles and untold varieties of insects. Many of these animals are found nowhere else in East Africa because similar habitats no longer exist. The very real fear among environmentalists now is that even this tiny surviving remnant of rainforest, unique in Kenya, is itself in grave danger of complete elimination.

Although there's talk of building national park style gates "one day", nothing has yet been done: it is indicative of the forest's current plight. Despite a laudable scheme aiming to educate the local population about the forest (see the box below), the lack of any coherent backing or action from the authorities means that the long-term future of the forest isn't looking bright. Pressure from the local people who need grazing for their livestock, land to cultivate, and firewood, amounts to a significant threat. The present area is less than a tenth of what it was at the turn of the century, and its closed canopy cover (which indicates the forest's health and maturity) has dropped from ninety to fifty percent. This has led to the inevitable degradation of the local natural habitat, which in turn has led to some species being threatened, and some – like leopard, which was last seen in 1992 – becoming extinct (the year coincided with an attack by Nandi villagers on the forest cats who, they claimed, had been killing their livestock). Much of the wardens' time is spent patrolling the forest or observing it from lookout points on nearby hilltops, although some newspaper reports in 1998 accused the wardens themselves of adding to the forest's destruction by illegally selling off plots for cultivation. The way things stand, the survival of this unique habitat depends to a considerable degree on the continued support and concern of visitors to the region.

The forest is fragmented, interspersed with open fields of grassland, cultivated stream margins, small settlements and even tea plantations, though the latter have in part been planted by the government in order to both provide a natural protective barrier, as well as to give the locals an alternative source of income to plundering the forest. **Two main areas** can be visited; the first, which has been accessible for many years, is the central **Kakamega Forest Reserve**, lying to the southeast of Kakamega town and somewhat off the beaten track. It is to a part of one of the densest stands in this area that most visitors come, to the **Forest Rest House** in the glade at its edge.

"KEEP OUR FOREST"

Building on groundwork laid by the Kenya Indigenous Forest Conservation Project, the **Kakamega Environmental Education Programme** (KEEP) was set up by the guides at *Forest Rest House* to co-ordinate environmental educational programmes to primary and secondary school children from the local area. This combines lessons with visits to the forest, and it is hoped that by convincing the children of the importance of protecting and preserving the forest, the message will be passed to their parents and other family members. They've started a tree nursery to demonstrate to the children some basic tree-planting techniques, as well giving information on how to recycle waste paper, tins and so on. If enough sponsorship is raised, there are plans to build an office and hall for educational purposes, and to establish a reference library.

They're especially keen to involve environmentalists and other experts in their effort: "to give us ideas, material and mental assistance for our project". If you're interested or can help, contact Wilberforce Okeka, c/o Kakamega Forest Station, PO Box 88 Kakamega, or meet up with him at *Forest Rest House*.

The second section, the recently opened-up **Kakamega Forest National Reserve**, is northeast of the town and very easy to get to.

The central district: Kakamega Forest Reserve

On arriving at *Forest Rest House* (see below for information on getting there), visitors are greeted by an official guide (a member of Kakamega Biodiversity Tour Conservations Operators), whose name should be on the board outside the hut on the path up to the house. You will be given a brief introduction to the region and the conservation work being done by KEEP (see box on p.329; all guides should have a KEEP identity card), which is attempting to educate villagers and schoolchildren on the outskirts of the forest on the importance of preserving it. You may be asked to make a contribution to the effort (Ksh100 minimum), though this is optional – until KWS install their long-talked-about gates, you are not obliged to pay anything for entering or walking in the forest.

It's best to take up the offer of a **guide**, especially if you're a woman on your own (there's one female guide here; otherwise, ask for Wilberforce, Moses or Ben, who are all reliable). Exceptionally for a profession that usually attracts hustlers out for easy money, this lot are professional and knowledgeable (they have to pass an exam before becoming guides). Some are nothing short of encyclopedic and will rattle off the Latin name of any plant or creature you care to enquire about. Their walks are tremendously enjoyable, and they are happy to tailor walks to your particular interests. There is no fixed fee for a guided walk so it's up to you to decide how much to offer: Ksh100 as a minimum per person, and about Ksh200–300 for three hours is about right. Expect a wander along the labyrinthine jungle paths, with birds, monkeys, chameleons and other animals pointed out to you, most of which you would miss on your own. A pair of **binoculars** is more or less indispensable if you're out to watch birds. You'll also find members of the guiding association at Rivendell Gardens and Rondo Retreat Centre.

Among the most common **birds** are the noisy and gregarious black-and-white-casqued hornbill and the very striking, deep violet Ross' turaco. You may also see familiar-looking African grey parrots and, circling above the canopy on the lookout for unwary monkeys, the huge crowned hawk eagle. But Kakamega's avian stars are the **great blue turacos**, glossy, turkey-sized birds looking like dowagers in evening gowns. They're easily located by their raucous calls; a favourite spot at dusk is the grove of very tall trees down by the pumphouse. They arrive each evening to crash and lurch among the branches as they select roosting sites.

The forest draws mammal-watchers as well, particularly for the **monkeys**: troops are often seen at dusk, foraging through the trees directly opposite the *Rest House* verandah. Apart from the ubiquitous colobus, you can see blue monkeys and the much slimmer black-cheeked white-nosed monkey (most easily recognized by its red tail). They're often seen milling around with the hornbills. You may also see pairs of giant forest squirrels capering in the treetops: the deep booming call you sometimes hear in the morning is theirs.

At **night**, armed with a powerful torch, you might catch a glimpse of bushbabies, palm civets, genets or a potto, a slow-moving, lemur-like animal whose name aptly conveys its appearance and demeanour. The forest is also home to several species of fruit bat, of which the hammer-headed fruit bat (*Hypsignathus monstrosus*) is the largest in Africa, with a wingspan of a metre and an enormous head. Other nocturnal Kakamega specialities are the otter shrew, which lives in some of the forest streams, the tree pangolin (a kind of arboreal scaly anteater) and the flying squirrel.

The forest's **reptile life** is legendary, but few people seem to actually see any **snakes** (you're much more likely to come across **chameleons**). Reptiles spend a good deal of time motionless, especially when frightened, and to see any in the dense foliage you have to be well tuned in. Visible or not, however, snakes are abundant and you certainly shouldn't walk in the forest in bare feet or sandals: the gaboon viper, growing to a metre or more in length, and fatter than your arm, is a dangerous denizen of the forest floor. To avoid an encounter, simply walk heavily: they're highly sensitive to vibration and will flee at your seismic approach.

If you have time for more than one daylight walk, you could ask a guide to show you the way to **Lirhanda Hill**, via a trail rich in medicinal plants. You will be shown which leaves, berries and saps the forest dwellers chew, swallow or anoint themselves with to treat various ailments. Lirhanda Hill itself is a lookout point, offering fine views over the whole expanse of forest, with the sombre bulk of Mount Elgon glowering in the distance. Cutting into the hillside near the top is a gold-mining shaft, long disused and now home to a large colony of bats. With a powerful torch and a steely nerve you can grope your way along the tunnel to meet them at close quarters.

GETTING THERE
There are several ways of **getting to** the *Forest Rest House* – beware that maps of Kenya invariably locate the forest incorrectly. If you're **driving**, the easiest road is from **Khayega**, some 10km south of Kakamega on the A1. From here, an earth road leads 7km to Shinyalu. The junction is marked by signposts for the Arap Moi Girls' School and the Office of the President. Keep right at Shinyalu and continue for another 5km, and turn left just after the barrier and a signposted arrow. From here, it's less than a kilometre up the trail to the Rest House. An alternative route from Kakamega turns off to the left at the southern edge of Kakamega town, past the KWS offices, up to Shinyalu, whilst there's a more direct route from Eldoret and Kapsabet starting at Chepsonoi on the C39. Both these routes are in worse condition than the Khayega road. Note that whichever approach you're taking, the surfaces get treacherously slippery in wet weather (especially for low clearance 2WDs): given the relatively metronomic afternoon rains, this limits you to getting there between 10am and 2pm, when the road is at its driest. Even so, 4WD is advisable.

If you're using **public transport**, the best way is to catch the *matatu* that plies once daily in each direction between **Kakamega and Eldoret**, via the village of Shinyalu and the small town of Kapsabet. Either run can leave you right by the *Rest House* trail, marked only by an arrow, but next to a barrier across the main *murram* road – ask to be dropped at **Isecheno**. From here, the *Rest House* is ten minutes' walk away. The *matatu* (called "Musa Maria Mwema") leaves Kakamega around 8am (get there for 7.30am, but check the time the day before, as it used to leave at 7am) from the Kenol petrol station, and passes Isecheno on its way to Eldoret around 8.30–9.15am; the midday run back from Eldoret (from the main *matatu* stage) passes by at about 2.30–3pm.

If you miss "Musa Maria Mwema", there are other routes that involve some footwork. *Matatus* run fairly frequently from Kakamega as far as **SHINYALU** (you can still catch these if you miss "Musa Maria Mwema" in Eldoret by jumping on a *matatu* for Kakamega town), from where it's a lovely two-hour walk to Isecheno, along the road heading left – there's a slim chance of a connecting *matatu* here for Kapsabet, though more likely you'll have to hitch a lift with a passing vehicle, or else hire a *boda boda* bicycle taxi (baggage permitting). Shinyalu itself often has a cattle auction and a major market on Saturdays, when it's worth pausing an hour to soak up the atmosphere of cowboys and corrals in the jungle. It's perfectly possible, of course, to hire a private **taxi** for the trip from Kakamega to the *Rest House* (Ksh600–800), but beware that both taxi drivers and *matatu* touts sometimes overcharge tourists for the run to the forest (especially if it's raining). **From Eldoret**, any bus or *matatu* heading towards Kisumu via Kapsabet, Chavakali and Maragoli will pass the turning for Isecheno at **Chepsonoi**, signposted "Kisieni 12km D267". From the junction it takes about three hours to walk through the gorgeous forest scenery to the *Rest House*.

Moving on, the "Musa Maria Mwema" *matatu* passes the main road barrier between 8.30–9.15am bound for Eldoret, and returns at 2.30–3pm for Kakamega town. Other *matatus* for Kakamega town leave at 7am and 6.45pm. A *matatu* for Khayega leaves the barrier at 2pm. For all these, it's best to double-check times with the guides at the *Rest House*.

ACCOMMODATION

If you're not fussed about luxury, the wooden **Forest Rest House** is a delight. Someone writing in the visitor's book calls it a "budget *Treetops*", a description that scarcely does it justice. Ringed by forest, the *Rest House* has just four first-floor two-bed rooms, with a long verandah facing onto the wall of tropical greenery a few metres away. There are blankets and pillows but no sheets, and you might bring an extra blanket or sleeping bag as it can get decidedly chilly early in the morning. Water supplies are somewhat erratic: when the pump is working, each room has a functioning bathroom and toilet, otherwise you have to fetch water from the pumphouse. There's no electricity and the closest reliable *dukas* are about 3km away on the road to Shinyalu, so it's best to bring your own supplies. For candles and simple staples – bananas, chai, mineral water, biscuits, sodas and occasional beers – there's a small *duka*/canteen on the way to the pumphouse, which is open daily. Here hot meals are cooked to order (given a few hours' notice); the food is generous, reliable and very fresh, and a much better bet than struggling to build your own cooking fire in the campsite or underneath the *Rest House* itself (during the wet season it can rain for days on end).

To be sure of a room – especially at weekends – you can **reserve in advance** (write to: The Forester, PO Box 88 Kakamega, Western Province; rates are very economical, at around Ksh200). Alternatively you can **camp** at the site next to the *Rest House*, or even underneath it (Ksh127 per person), but don't leave tents unattended. In dire straits, other arrangements can be made locally (ask Susie in the canteen about her *bandas*): Kakamega Forest is becoming popular.

There are two alternatives to the *Rest House*. The upmarket option is the **Rondo Retreat Centre**, a fine old 1928 sawmiller's house (location for much of the filming of Harry Hook's *The Kitchen Toto*) about 4km east of the *Rest House* turning (reservations c/o Trinity Fellowship, PO Box 2153 Kakamega; ☎0331/30268, fax 20145; no phone at the centre; ⑦). This is a comfortable base: very fresh and elegant, furnished like an English country house with just enough clutter to make it feel homely, and wonderful bright four-poster bedrooms. Crowned cranes strut about on the cool lawns. The dining room is open to non-residents when the hotel is not fully booked, but the Christian management do not serve alcohol. Arrangements can be made to collect guests from Kakamega town. Much less formal, and a deal cheaper, but a few kilometres out of the forest, is the delightful Swedish-run **Rivendell Gardens**, 1.5km south of Shinyalu off the track to Khayega (reservations essential: PO Box 1136 Kakamega; ☎0331/41316, *gb@net2000ke.com*; B&B ④, FB ⑤). Run by Gunilla Fagerholm and Bertil Lindström, *Rivendell* is a welcoming and relaxed retreat, with an old-looking but actually brand-new wooden ranch house (where you're free to use the living room with the family), a few guest *bandas* (not yet s/c; there will be six eventually) in the gardens, and heaps of things to keep you entertained: games, videos, puppies and rabbits for the children; a trip around the heavens on a telescope; another telescope for bird-watching (at least forty species from the verandah); guides to Kakamega forest; and fascinating trips to nearby villages, including one still engaged in gold mining. Their food is excellent, too, with vegetarians well catered for (try the banana flour burgers), though you need to book a day ahead if you just want to drop in for lunch (Ksh500). There's no electricity in the *bandas*, just hurricane lamps and candles. Wonderfully romantic, even if the occasional "moonshine concerts" on the balcony (Vivaldi, Mozart and Streisand belting from the stereo) are a bit cheesy. Camping is allowed (Ksh200 per tent), and a night in their "African hut" costs Ksh300. They can pick you up from Kakamega.

Kakamega Forest National Reserve

Some 20km north of Kakamega town, there are two turnings off to the right: one is signposted to the Kakamega Forest National Reserve; the other, 50m further on, is signposted "Kenya Wildlife Service Kisere Nature Reserve 6km" and "Kambiri 7km D267". It's the first track you want. The Kakamega Forest National Reserve forest station is 2–3km along the way and you can pick up a guide (belonging to the Kakamega Biodiversity Tour Conservations Operators) to help you orientate yourself if you wish, though they are less knowledgeable than their *Forest Rest House* counterparts and have in the past been prone to scamming (see below). Women on their own might prefer to take a guide from the *Forest Rest House* anyway.

For visitors with their own vehicles, it's easier to get around this part of Kakamega Forest than the central zone. The forest proper is, in fact, a fair walk from the base of the KWS-run *Udo's Bandas and Campsite* (②), named after the ornithologist Udo Savalli. Here there are seven thatched *rondavels* (soon to be upgraded), sleeping five each, and a stream for fresh water, but no food (book through the Kenya Wildlife Service District Warden, PO Box 879 Kakamega; ☎0331/20425 or 30603). As in the central district, all visitors, whether staying or just there for the day, are asked to make a contribution to the forest conservation programme, although this is optional – a recent scam involved charging visitors an "entrance fee" of Ksh100 for every walk they made, guided or not: at present, there is no official fee for entrance to the reserve, so stand firm and demand an official KWS receipt if you think you're being conned.

A number of drivable – and walkable – tracks through the coolness of the forest begin just beyond the forest station. The main trail is well signposted and there are numerous branches and "exit" trails that allow for a relatively quick return when you've had enough of the deep forest. It's not a place you're likely to get lost in, despite its remoteness.

The significant difference between the reserve here and the forest further south is the age of the growth in the reserve: many of the **trees** are colossal (indeed some have plaques inviting you to guess the girth: answers round the back). The climate is generally drier and there's a greater diversity of habitat, including areas of scrub, young forest and ancient forest. It's an impressive area and, as in the southern forest, there's a huge variety of birdlife and many monkeys.

An easy excursion from the forest station is to the **Isiukhu Falls**, a rather feeble waterfall 1.5km away along a rocky path. **Buyangu Hill viewpoint**, a four-kilometre drive or walk from the forest station, is much more worthwhile – a precipice with a spectacular vista east across the forest to the Nandi Escarpment.

The **Kisere Forest Reserve** (as signposted at the turn-off) is a separate area, a small outlying part of the main reserve and home to de Brazza's monkeys among others, with some superb examples of the prized timber tree, the Elgon olive.

Onwards from Kakamega

The obvious routes out of the area lie along the A1 to Kitale or Kisumu. The road **down to Kisumu** is a real roller-coaster, though in relatively good condition (occasional patches of pot-holes), with a final eight-kilometre descent over the picturesque, boulder-strewn Nyando Escarpment, which brings Lake Victoria into view. In clear weather it allows fantastic panoramas across the sugar fields of the Kano plains towards the massif of the Mau and the Kisii hills. Look out for the florid **church** on the left, the headquarters of a local denomination that models itself on the Coptic church, founded in Egypt in the early years of Christianity.

Alternatively, there's a beautiful road **east to Kapsabet** in the Nandi Hills, starting at the bustling rural centre of Maragoli/Chavakali (also spelled Chyvakali and Kyavakali), along the Kisumu road. Note that Maragoli is the "shopping centre" on the A1, while Chavakali, effectively part of the same community, is a kilometre or so off to the east.

Lastly, if you have time and inclination for a diversion far off any beaten track, you could visit the small town of **Mumias**, the sugar belt's biggest processing centre and also one of western Kenya's Muslim strongholds. The road from Kakamega is paved and there's regular transport.

Mumias

MUMIAS was originally *Mumia's*, one of the more important up-country centres, capital of the Luhya-speaking mini-state of **Wanga**, and well established by the middle of the nineteenth century at the head of an important caravan route to the coast. **King Mumia**, who came to power in 1880, was the last King of Wanga. He inherited an army of 10,000 soldiers, half of whom were dispossessed Maasai from the Uasin Gishu Plateau known as the Kwavi. It was this army that was largely responsible for the smashing of Bukusu resistance at Chetambe's Fort fifteen years later (see p.324).

Even at the beginning of Mumia's reign, Europeans were beginning to arrive in the wake of Arab and Swahili slave-traders, who in turn had been settling in since the 1850s with the full accord of the Wanga royal family. The first was Joseph Thomson in 1883, and by 1894 there was a permanent British sub-commissioner or collector of taxes posted here. Mumia had always welcomed strangers, and he allowed the slavers to continue their work on other groups of the Luhya (notably the Bukusu), but he was unprepared for the swift usurpation of his authority by the British, whom he'd assumed were also there to trade. He was appointed "Paramount Chief" of a gradually diminishing state and then, as an old man, was retired without his real knowledge. He died in 1949, aged 100, and with him expired Kenya's first (and only) indigenous, up-country state, almost without notice.

The town's present **mosque** was built in King Mumia's honour and its Koran school is just one of about 25 around the town. Mumias has long been a centre of Islam, famous for its coastal ways, but today women in *buibuis* – the long, black coverall of the coast – are rarely seen. According to the chairman of the Mumias Koran Schools Committee, Islam is losing ground to Catholicism because of sectarian quarrelling between Muslim leaders and because, while mission and government education have an equal standing, the *madrassas* must take second place after school hours. If you're interested, Mumias Mission has published a slim pamphlet outlining their side of the story, and the Catholic church is quite an impressive old building.

The Butere–Kisumu train
Leaving Mumias, a paved road leads directly to Kisumu but, if you have time to spare you might like to hop on the daily **train from Butere**, 12km down the road, instead. This branch line was intended to reach Mumias but never did. The daily train service (no longer steam-hauled since 1988, but nearly as slow and one class only) remains a boon to rural dwellers with more time than money. It leaves Kisumu at 8.45am, arrives in Butere about noon, and returns at 1pm, taking more than three hours to cover barely 60km. A tickets costs Ksh38.

travel details

Kisumu is the west's transport centre. Buses and *matatus* run from there to most major centres in this chapter within half a day. Due to the water hyacinth invasion of parts of Lake Victoria, all scheduled **ferry services** within and from Kenya to Tanzania and Uganda have been suspended indefinitely. There are however a limited number of *matatu*-boat services (no fixed timings, prices or frequencies) from Kisumu to Uganda and Tanzania, and from Mbita to various ports on Mfangano Island. It's a question of enquiring in Kisumu and Mbita.

BUSES

Bungoma to: Nairobi (several daily; 9–10hr); Kisumu (several daily; 2–5hr); Kitale (Mawingo country bus at 5am and 11am; 3hr) via Kimilili.

Eldoret to: Nairobi (hourly; 7–8hr); Kitale (hourly; 2hr).

Kakamega to: Nairobi several runs daily (7–9hr) via Kisumu and Kericho, or via Kapsabet and Nandi Hills.

Kericho to: Nairobi many runs daily; Kisumu several daily (2hr); Kisii several daily (3hr).

Kisumu to: Eldoret several daily runs via Kapsabet (2hr); Kakamega (daily Akamba bus 5.30am; 2hr); Mombasa (2 daily via Nairobi; 14hr); Nairobi (frequent; 5–8hr) via Kericho (2hr) and Nakuru (4–5hr).

Kisii to: Kisumu numerous daily runs (2hr); Mombasa (several daily; 14hr); Migori 2 daily (2pm, 4pm; 2hr) via Homa Bay; Nairobi (6 daily; 7–9hr) via Kericho.

Kitale to: Nairobi several services daily and overnight (8–11hr) via Eldoret and Nakuru; Kapenguria (daily 7am; 1hr).

MATATUS

With nearly half the population of Kenya living in this region, **matatus** are widespread and most minor roads have services. Many also run on bus routes at approximately the same fare, but to even less predictable schedules. As usual, Peugeots move faster than Nissan minibuses, which are faster than vans. Slower vehicles are safer.

Eldoret to: Soy (20min); Kitale (1hr); Malaba (2hr 30min); Nairobi (4–6hr).

Homa Bay to: Rongo (30min); Kendu Bay (1hr 30min); Mbita (2hr).

Kisii to: Homa Bay (1hr); Migori (1hr 30min); Rongo (30min).

Kisumu to: Kakamega (1hr); Kendu Bay (1hr 30min); Kericho (1hr 30min); Kisii (2hr); Kitale (3hr); Nairobi (5–6 hr).

Kitale to: Eldoret (1hr); Kakamega (3hr); Kimilili (45min); Kiminini (20min); Kisumu (3hr); Lodwar (4–5hr).

TRAINS

There are currently no passenger services for Eldoret, Kitale or Malaba. Information through Kenya Railways in Kisumu on ☎035/42211.

Butere to: Kisumu.

Kisumu to: Nairobi (daily 6pm; 12–13hr) via Nakuru (8hr 40min); Butere (daily 8.45am; 3hr 15min).

FLIGHTS

Eldoret to: Nairobi (4 weekly, Kenya Airways via Kisumu; 1hr 45min).

Kisumu to: Nairobi (14 weekly; 1hr).

Connections possible to Mombasa from Nairobi (total flight time 2hr 30min–3hr).

CHAPTER FIVE

THE MOMBASA ROAD AND MAJOR GAME PARKS

T his chapter can't really be said to deal with a region. It covers the well-travelled **route** from **Nairobi to Mombasa** and a number of detours off it, along with six of the country's **major game parks**, most within reasonably easy reach of the capital: Amboseli, Maasai Mara, Meru, Samburu, and Tsavo East and West.

The **Mombasa Highway** is Kenya's most important thoroughfare, yet was in amazingly bad condition even before El Niño threw a tantrum (rehabilitation work is set to continue until 2003), but the scenic interest is marginal for much of the journey and the temptation is to head straight for the coast, stopping only at the **Amboseli** or **Tsavo game parks**. If you have time enough, however, and the inclination to get off the main

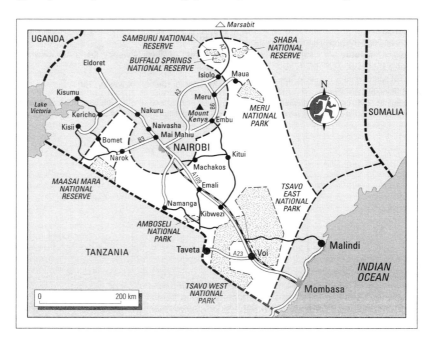

ACCOMMODATION PRICE CODES

Rates for a standard double or twin room. For a full explanation of these rates, see p.47.

① Under Ksh500	(under approx £5/$8)	⑥ Ksh6000–9000	(£60–90/$96–144)*
② Ksh500–1000	(£5–10/$8–16)	⑦ Ksh9000–12,000	(£90–120/$144–192)*
③ Ksh1000–2000	(£10–20/$16–32)	⑧ Ksh12,000–16,000	(£120–£160/$192–256)*
④ Ksh2000–4000	(£20–40/$32–64)	⑨ Over Ksh16,000	(over £160/$256)*
⑤ Ksh4000–6000	(£40–60/$64–96)	* = *usually priced in dollars*	

---

road (a hire car is helpful), there are some rewarding diversions: east into **Akamba country** and the towns of **Machakos** and **Kitui**, or south towards the base of **Kilimanjaro** (the mass of the mountain lies across the border in Tanzania) and the **Taita Hills**. Despite the trail of safari vans towards the parks and coast, these are side roads that are not greatly explored.

The **game parks** in this chapter are, together with the coast, the most visited parts of Kenya – and the archetypal image. This is not to take anything away from their appeal. If you travel around Kenya, it would be absurd not to visit at least one of the parks, for the experience is genuinely fabulous. In the 24,000 square kilometres (10,000 square miles) covered by the six parks, animals, not humans, hold sway. Their seasonal movements, most spectacularly in **Maasai Mara**'s wildebeest migration, are the dominant plots in the drama going on all around. It's not difficult to see the wildlife but it does require patience and an element of luck that makes it exciting – and addictive.

Summaries of the game parks' individual attractions are given in the introduction on p.356. **To visit**, most people will either already be on a safari, or will book one once in Kenya – either from the coast or from Nairobi. The increasingly popular alternative is to **rent a vehicle**, a sensible if quite expensive option if you want to have more than a few days of wildlife viewing, and the freedom of choosing your own route. With a limited budget, a no-frills camping safari is still about the only practical way: there are more details on the ins and outs in Basics, p.64, and plenty of operators listed at the end of the Nairobi and Mombasa sections (pp.134 and 436). It remains possible, though by no means easy, to explore the parks by **hitching around** with whoever you meet and **camping** at designated sites. More specific details are included in the sections on each park.

BETWEEN NAIROBI AND THE COAST

If you take one of the **express buses** for your journey down from Nairobi to Mombasa, you might well end up believing that there's nothing worth stopping for along the way, and, if you take the **train**, you won't see anything anyway as it travels in both directions at night. On the other hand, with a little touch of imagination and, ideally, the luxury of a hired vehicle of some kind for covering the parks, this stretch of the country has a great deal to offer. And any detour into the less well-known parts of **Kamba territory** or down to **Taveta** and the foothills of **Kilimanjaro** should prove a worthwhile antidote to the more purple-rinse excesses of safari-land.

Machakos and Kitui – "Ukambani"

One very good way to start a trip heading towards the coast, if you're in no particular hurry, is to take an excursion right into the heart of **Ukambani**, the land of the Akamba people (adjective and language: Kamba). Buses, *matatus* and Peugeot taxis leave from Nairobi's Country Bus Station (aka "Machakos Airport") for Machakos all the time, although what used to be a journey of a little over thirty minutes is more likely to take ninety minutes, thanks to vastly increased traffic along the two-lane Mombasa road. In addition, there's also at least one company that runs a daily Nairobi–Mombasa service

THE AKAMBA

The largely dry stretch of central Kenya from Nairobi to Tsavo park and north as far as Embu has been the traditional homeland of the Akamba people for at least the last five centuries. They moved here from the regions to the south in a series of vague migrations, in search, according to legend, of the life-saving baobab tree whose fruit staved off the worst famines, and whose trunks held vast quantities of water.

With a diverse economy in better years, including mixed farming and herding as well as hunting and gathering, the Akamba slowly coalesced into a distinct tribe with one Bantu language. As they settled in the hilly parts, the population increased. But drier areas at lower altitudes couldn't sustain the expansion, so **trade** for food with the Kikuyu peoples in the fatter highlands region became a solution to the vagaries of their generally implacable environment.

In return for farm produce, the Akamba **bartered** their own manufactured goods: medicinal charms, extra-strong beer, honey, iron tools, arrowheads and a lethal and much sought-after hunting poison. In the eighteenth and nineteenth centuries, as the Swahili on the coast strengthened their ties inland, **ivory** became the most important commodity in the trade network. With it, the Akamba obtained goods from overseas to exchange for food stocks with the highlands tribes.

Long the **intermediaries** between coast and up-country, acting as guides to Swahili and Arab caravans, leading their own expeditions and settling in small numbers in many parts of what is now Kenya, the Akamba were naturally enlisted by early European arrivals in East Africa. Their broad cultural base and lack of provincialism made them confident travellers and employees, and willing **soldiers and porters**. Even today, the Kenyan army has a disproportionately high Akamba contingent, while many others work as policemen and private *askaris*.

In the early years of **colonialism**, the Akamba were involved in occasional bloody incidents, but these seem to have been more often the result of misunderstandings than anything concerted. The most famous of these blew up after an ignorant official at Machakos cut down a sacred *ithembo* tree to use as a flagpole. On the whole, the Akamba's old trade links helped to ease their relations with the British. Living – and dying – with British soldiers during **World War I** gave them insights into the ways of the Europeans who now ruled them. Together with the Luo and Kikuyu, the Akamba suffered tens of thousands of casualties in white men's wars.

Akamba **resistance to colonialism** was widespread but mostly non-violent. As early as 1911, however, a movement of total European rejection had emerged. Led by a widow named Siotune wa Kathake, it channelled opposition to colonialism into frenetic dancing, during which teenage girls became "possessed" by an anti-European spirit and preached radical messages of non-compliance with the government. Later, in the 1930s, the Ukamba Members Association (one of whose leaders was **Muindi Mbingu**) was formed in order to pre-empt efforts to settle Europeans in Ukambani and reduce Akamba cattle herds by compulsory purchase. Five thousand Akamba marched in peaceful protest to Kariokor market in Nairobi – a show of collective political will that succeeded in getting their cattle returned.

by way of the town. From Machakos, frequent buses and *matatus* continue to Kitui, from where – until a river bridge got washed away by El Niño – you could catch transport to Kibwezi, back on the Mombasa road.

Machakos

The Imperial British East African Company's first up-country post, established in 1889, **MACHAKOS** is ten years older than Nairobi and, in comparison, a striking indication of the capital's rapid growth. "Machakos" is really a corruption of Masaku's, after the headquarters of an Akamba chief of the time. The name is still seen all over town.

Distinctly friendly, and overwhelmingly Kamba, the town has a backdrop of green hills and a tree-shaded, relaxed atmosphere to its old buildings that is quickly endearing, despite the evident poverty in the fringing slums and the rubbish piled up around seemingly every street corner – a sight common to most Kenyan towns. The surrounding Mua Hills have lent their name to a brand of jam from the orchards which thrive on their slopes. The weaving of **sisal baskets** is a more visible industry, though, and a major occupation for many women, either full-time or behind the vegetable stand. Machakos effervesces and it's a great place to stay for a day or two, especially on Monday and Friday, market days, and above all if you are into buying some *vyondo* (baskets). Look for (though you can scarcely miss) the truly splendid and quite venerable **mosque**.

Practicalities

Apart from the many produce markets scattered about town, there are two **supermarkets**: Nafuu and Nova (both open Mon–Sat 8am–8pm & Sun 9am–6pm). The Barclays and Standard Chartered **banks** have ATMs. For **buses and matatus** to Nairobi and Mombasa, head for the main stage in the centre of town. For services to Kitui (with connections there for Embu), the stage is just up on the Embu road, beside the noisy *jua kali* metal workers' area.

The town is rarely visited by tourists, but accommodation and meals are easy. Machakos has the usual range of **eating places**, few of them gastronomically enticing. Three of the best are the *Ivory Restaurant* – chips with everything, but it's all tasty and well served; the enjoyable *Kenny's Boiling Pot*, in the same building as *Masaku Lodge*, with its balcony overlooking the street; and the *T.Tot Hotel*, popular with expats and serving good samosas, *chai* and passion fruit juice. As for **hotels**, the *Masaku Lodge* (PO Box 274; ☎0145/21745; singles only; ①), *T.Ten* (PO Box 841; ☎0145/20157; ①) and *Lalla Salama* by the mosque (PO Box 66; ☎0145/21198; ①) are utterly basic B&Ls, the last with rooms ranging from rank to airy and comfortable (ask to see a selection). There are loads of other budget choices scattered throughout town. The more upmarket options are:

Garden Hotel, ten minutes from the town centre (PO Box 223; ☎0145/20037, fax 21515). Something of an aberration, a totally plush, muzak-piped, "international class" hotel with a health club, sauna, steam bath – and a pool planned for the future. Compared to its Nairobi counterparts, a bargain. Resident Tanzanian band Everest Kings are another bonus (playing Friday and Saturday nights, and Sunday afternoons), almost reason enough in itself to visit Machakos. B&B ④.

Ikuni Hotel (PO Box 1069; ☎0145/21080). A large place with a wide range of rooms, mostly grotty and overpriced singles, but its busy restaurant makes up for it a little. They have discos Wednesday, Friday and Saturday nights, and comedians and traditional dancers Sunday afternoons. Ask for a mosquito net. B&B s/c ③, non s/c ②.

Kafoca Club (Kenya Armed Forces Old Comrades Association; PO Box 595; ☎0145/21933). Despite the uninspiring name, this businessmens' hangout is well run, and fairly wholesome, with a bar and TV-video lounge and a good restaurant which does filling fried platters. S/c rooms way overpriced, non-s/c more reasonable. Safe parking. Bed only, s/c ③, non-s/c ②.

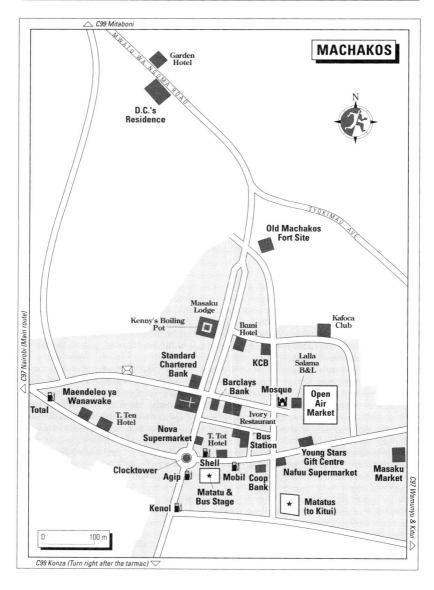

Crafts

For **vyondo**, visit the **market**. The finished articles are much cheaper without the strap (buy lengths of sisal braid and fit your own), and there are reductions if you buy several: the choice of colours is second to none. If you like the genre, it's worth buying sev-

THE MACHAKOS MIRACLE

The whole of Ukambani is prone to **drought** and, according to conventional environmental wisdom, its farms and plots should have blown to dust long ago, especially under ever-increasing population pressure. In the 1930s, when the population was five times less than now, a British Colonial soil inspector condemned the Ukambani hills as "an appalling example" of environmental degradation in which "the inhabitants are rapidly shifting to a state of hopelessness and miserable poverty and their land to a parched desert of rocks, stones and sand."

Sixty years later, it would be unfair to paint the same picture. Instead of relying on cattle herding, as they did in the past, many Akamba have shifted into small-scale agriculture as a means of survival, with surprising results: you even find apples offered for sale by the roadside, an "exotic" fruit otherwise confined to the perennially rain-soaked orchards of Kisii near Lake Victoria. The trick has been the clever use of the little rain which does fall, using small-scale **terracing** and **irrigation techniques** (such as using roads for catchments) learned by Akamba soldiers while serving in India during World War II. So much for the hopelessness of the 1930s; the situation has been turned around so successfully that some have begun calling this "The Machakos Miracle".

eral and posting home a parcel. In connection, the Machakos branch of the women's Maendeleo ya Wanawake organization can be contacted at PO Box 904 (☎0145/21600).

The Young Stars Gift Centre deserves a look, too: they have some splendid wood and goat-skin **drums** – the kind of thing often seen used as tables in hotel lobbies – but volume restrictions may prevent you from sending the large ones home, even if their price (under Ksh1200), and sometimes their timbre, make them irresistible. Less desirable are the East African clothes-moths they frequently harbour – which later hatch in suitably heated living rooms – and the possibility of catching anthrax from them. Be warned that customs officers tend to impound such items on arrival.

On to Kitui

Frequent buses and *matatus* ply this route: the tarmac road passes through some attractive scenery, particularly as you wind down the hill out of Machakos, where high cliffs and chunky, maize-covered hills rise everywhere. **Wamunyu**, en route, was the birthplace of the modern **Kamba carving** industry, evidenced by numerous self-help and co-operative carvers' societies and their shops. Akamba men who served in World War I were introduced to the techniques of wood sculpture by the Makonde ebony carvers on the Tanganyikan coast. Today, the vast majority of carvings in Kenya are produced by Akamba artists, often in workshops far from Ukambani. In Wamunyu, some three thousand people, many of them children, eke out a living with wood carving. The main problem appears to be the middlemen, who take much of the profits: if you're after wood carvings, try to buy them direct from the people who make them. Still, it's a disappointment that the serried ranks of identical antelopes and rhinos don't do justice to the tradition, even if it is a short one. If you want to stay here, there are a number of basic **B&Ls**, the best of which are *Elimu Guest House* (PO Box 171; ☎0141/63291; ①) and *Highway Inn Bar* (①).

Kitui town

KITUI, like Machakos 58km to the west, lies in an impoverished area and, from time to time, is badly hit by drought, with attendant malnutrition and occasional outbreaks of cholera. Despite its proximity to Nairobi, this region at the very edge of the high-

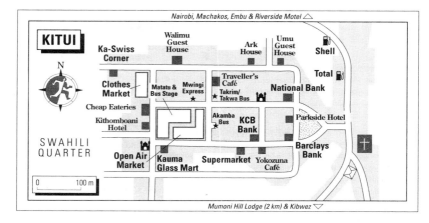

lands is one of Kenya's least developed. The town is small and hasn't any outstanding features of interest, but there's a sizeable Swahili population, descendants of the traders and travellers who crisscrossed Ukambani in the nineteenth century. The town's mango trees were planted then, and the abundance of lodging houses is a reminder of the trading tradition. Kitui was the home village of **Kivoi**, the most celebrated Akamba trader. He commanded a large following which included slaves, and it was he who met the German missionary **Ludwig Krapf** in Mombasa and guided him up to Kitui in 1849, where the European was the first to set eyes on Mount Kenya.

Despite the lack of sights (excepting perhaps Kauma Glass Mart, *the* place for drums and plastic religious icons), the town's atmosphere is the main draw, both a busy market and trading centre with streets lined with arcaded shops, yet also calm, relaxed and unhustly, and an ideal place to get away from more mundane hassles for a few days. The inhabitants are generally very friendly, and making genuine friends here seems easier than elsewhere.

Practicalities

There's nowhere to **stay** in Kitui above the budget category, and nothing much to choose between them, either. Hot water is invariably supplied in buckets. In the town centre, try: *Umau Guest House* (PO Box 202; no phone; ①), which is friendly, with six large s/c rooms with nets and cold showers; the cleaner *Ark House* (PO Box 230; ☎0141/22461; ①), with five s/c rooms around a courtyard; *Kithomboani Hotel* (①), under the same management, with ten cleanish s/c singles only with nets; and *Walimu Guest House* (PO Box 1101; no phone; ①), also s/c, no nets but window screens, with the novelty of breakfast thrown in. The best location is offered by the friendly if none-too-clean *Mumoni Hill Lodge* (PO Box 411; no phone; ①), 2km from the centre down the Kibwezi road just before the end of the tarmac. It's a peaceful retreat with four simple rooms with attached toilets (no showers), a relaxed and somnolent bar, and a lovely setting in large grounds planted with mango trees and plots of maize. They cook food to order, and you can **camp** here, too.

For **food**, you'll find a row of cheap eateries backing on to the Swahili quarter. Other places to try include the bright and clean *Parkside Hotel* on the same side as Barclays bank; *Travellers Café*, which has good snacks and is popular with NGO staff; the popular *Yokozuna Café*; and the *Riverside Motel*, 1500m out of town on the Machakos road in Kalundu Market, serving especially good chicken and fish. The **nightspot** of the moment is the ivy-clad *Ka-Swiss Corner*, with at least three bars (one at least remains open 24hr), music, pool tables and *nyama choma* majoring on chicken. They also have Kitui's most expensive rooms, handy if you plan jiving the night away (PO Box 1070; ☎0141/22485; ②).

Akamba **buses** (☎0141/22052) have daily departures to Nairobi (8.30am) and Mombasa (7pm), both via Machakos. Takrim/Takwa Bus (☎0141/22599) has some cheap fares (Mombasa at 5pm & 6pm; Nairobi twice a day), with connections to Dar es Salaam in Tanzania. Some early morning *matatus* leave for Embu (p.214), but catch them early unless you're happy to spend the day *matatu*-hopping. The road to Embu is only partially tarred to Kangonde (work is in progress to complete this stretch), with fast tarmac and more public transport continuing from Kangonde (on the Thika–Garissa road) via Mwea National Reserve (p.217) to Embu. Scenically dreary in this direction, the road is best travelled coming south towards Kitui, where the town appears as a miraculous oasis of lush greenery after the endless miles of red dust. Heading in the opposite direction, to Kibwezi on the Mombasa road along mostly smooth *murram*, note that the bridge over the Athi River, 120km south of Kitui and 30km short of Kibwezi, was washed away in January 1998 by the El Niño floods, and work has yet to start on its replacement. Previously, it was well served with daily buses and *matatus*, which made the Machakos–Kitui–Kibwezi circuit an attractive proposition.

The Mombasa highway

If you travel down by **bus**, sit on the right of the vehicle for the best of the scenery, from which vantage you may, in exceptionally clear conditions, see **Kilimanjaro** (best in the morning or late afternoon), either on the stretch between the small settlements of Sultan Hamud and Kiboko, or to the south of Tsavo train station. If you **drive** this route yourself, **be careful**. Well before the infamous El Niño rains made their mark, many sections of the road were badly broken up, with the result that some car rental companies now insist you take 4WD. Work has recently started by a Chinese company to resurface the road by around 2003, though it's unlikely the new version will last much longer than its past incarnations. More seriously, the road for the most part is fast and narrow as well as pot-holed, and consequently dangerous: road-users frequently encounter each other with deadly impact. **Driving at night** is ill-advised, as dipped headlights are still something of a novelty, and the highway itself has a reputation for nocturnal hold-ups and car hijacking, though incidents seem to be few and far between. Also be sure to drive with a full fuel tank. **Petrol stations** appear fairly regularly at the settlements between Nairobi and Voi, but supplies thereafter are not guaranteed until Mariakani, 120km further on and just 32km inland from Mombasa. Lastly, note that the current state of the road means you should count on two days to cover Nairobi–Mombasa comfortably, though it is possible in one, exhausting, eight to ten hour drive.

This section does not cover the **Amboseli** or **Tsavo National Parks** – see p.371 and p.360.

Around Emali: Kibiki and Nzaui

Heading southeast from Nairobi, the road runs along the east side of Nairobi National Park, passing at its end the junction for the A104 to Athi River, Namanga, Amboseli and Tanzania, before skirting the Kapiti Plains on your right. Five kilometres after the Athi

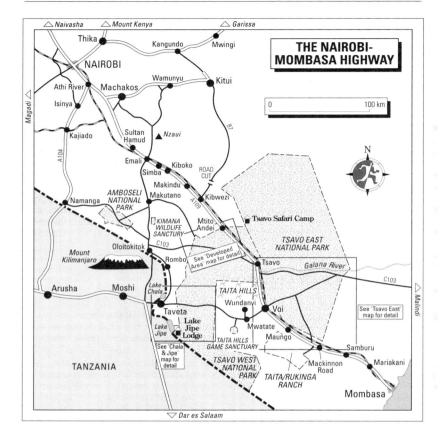

△ Naivasha △ Mount Kenya △ Garissa

THE NAIROBI-MOMBASA HIGHWAY

Thika
NAIROBI
Kangundo
Mwingi
Athi River Machakos Wamunyu Kitui
Isinya
Magadi △
Kajiado
Sultan Hamud ▲ Nzaui
Emali Kiboko ROAD CUT
Simba Makindu
Makutano Kibwezi
Namanga AMBOSELI NATIONAL PARK Mtito Andei ■ Tsavo Safari Camp
KIMANA WILDLIFE SANCTUARY TSAVO EAST NATIONAL PARK
Mount Kilimanjaro Oloitokitok C103
Rombo See 'Developed Area' map for detail
Tsavo Galana River C103
Arusha Moshi Lake Chala TAITA HILLS Wundanyi Voi See 'Tsavo East' map for detail
Taveta Lake Jipe Lake Jipe Lodge Mwatate △ Malindi
See 'Chala & Jipe map for detail' TAITA HILLS GAME SANCTUARY Maungo Samburu
TANZANIA TSAVO WEST NATIONAL PARK TAITA/RUKINGA RANCH Mackinnon Road Mariakani
Mombasa

0 — 100 km

N

△ Dar es Salaam

River junction, there's reasonable **accommodation** at the *Small World Country Club* (PO Box 78 Athi River; ☎0150/22006; ②), a motel-restaurant with basic self-contained *bandas*, secure parking, unexciting snacks (and painfully slow service), and a bar with a disco at weekends. Unfortunately, it pongs rather strongly due to the Kenya Meat Commission's giant butchery in the area.

After here, there's a long drive along smooth tarmac to the truckers' stopover of **Salama**, the first of many one-horse towns on the way to Mombasa, providing lodging, food and beers for truckers and lost-looking Maasai. With a few exceptions (which we've noted), the **B&Ls** in these places (all ①) are very basic, far from clean and, given their clientele, not for lone women. Many double as beer-soaked 24-hour day-and-night clubs, which goes some way in explaining the atrocious driving along the highway. Salama is no exception, as is the next settlement of **Simba**, with its squalid *Simba Lodge*, and **Sultan Hamud** further on, with its marginally more salubrious *Savannah House* (PO Box 100; ☎55 Sultan Hamud). The first centre of any real significance is **EMALI**, 20km further east, which lies on the boundary of Maasai and Akamba territory. There's good accommodation here at the *Kindu Hotel* (PO Box 147 Emali; ☎22 Emali; ①), which also has an unthreatening 24-hour bar and restaurant serving tasty *nyama choma*. Three kilometres beyond Emali, just after the railway flyover, a sharp dog-leg to the right marks the start of the rough mud and *murram* C102, which heads off south to Amboseli's eastern gates. Just beyond here, the small centre of **Kibiki** is the regular Friday venue for a major **cattle market** which attracts hundreds of Maasai herders, as well as Akamba people and Kenya Meat Commission buyers. It's an animated scene and worth a pause if you coincide.

A north turn from Emali leads up into the Machakos Hills with the dramatic **peak of Nzaui**. Enthusiastic reports have been received from hikers who have climbed this steep pinnacle. Without transport, you'll need a *matatu* ride from the Emali crossroads to Matiliku, some 15km from the main road. Nzaui rears up ahead. With luck, you'll find some schoolchildren to guide you up – it's a popular local trip. From the top of the 500-metre precipices on the south face there are sweeping views across the Kamba and Maasai plains to Mount Kilimanjaro. If you have a vehicle, there's also a lazy way up Nzaui from the north, approached from the village of Nziu, further along the same road.

Kiboko and Makindu

There's good **accommodation** at the petrol station oasis of **KIBOKO**, 160km from Nairobi, in the shape of **Hunter's Lodge** (PO Box 77 Makindu; reservations through *Mada Holdings*, Kimathi House, Kimathi Street, PO Box 40683 Nairobi; ☎02/221439, fax 332170; B&B ④). Named after the J.A. Hunter of rhino-potting notoriety (p.369), this promises a lot as a place to stay, with its acacia-backed garden on the banks of the dammed Kiboko (Hippo) River, a tranquil birdlife haven over on the other side. However, the "old rooms" are nothing special for the money, service is sluggish, and the food can be quite ordinary; however, the "new rooms" have verandahs overlooking the small reservoir, which more or less makes up for everything. Ask nicely and they'll probably allow you to camp. It's also a good place to hitch lifts.

Back on the main highway, twenty minutes east of *Hunter's Lodge*, you pass the ostentatious Sikh temple at **MAKINDU**, sometimes strung with what look like Christmas lights, and prettily unmistakable. They give a warm welcome here to travellers who want to stay, on the usual understanding (leave a donation). Of the B&Ls, *Villa Park Lodge* and *Charlie's Inn* are reasonable choices.

Thirteen kilometres further on is the **Makindu Handicrafts Co-operative**, which has blossomed in recent years to provide work for almost fifty active members. Fifteen percent of the takings go to run the place and buy wood; the remainder is divided equally among the carvers. You can watch and photograph members at work, though it has to be said many of their carvings are fairly obnoxious, with "Maasai maidens" and similar panderings more and more prominent. Still, they know their market and the set-up obviously suits the co-op members. There are some nice pieces among the tour-bus fodder, but for a more personal souvenir, the rejects heaped up outside the shop are better value and have more character than the polished creations inside.

The road from here on to Mtito Andei is unusually scenic, with grand, sweeping views south over the Chyulu Hills to the south and glimpses of lava flows and strange rock outcrops just to the north. Large, fantastic **baobabs** dot this stretch of the highway, some, it is said, over a thousand years old. In the past, they were credited with all manner of spiritual powers and associations, and oral history has it that they attracted the Akamba to this area by the sponge-like centres of their trunks, which can hold huge amounts of water and are a vital source of liquid during droughts. As to their strange, ungainly appearance, some legends have it that the baobabs used to be in the habit of walking around the countryside on their roots, until one day God got fed up with their peregrinations and resolved to keep them forever rooted to the soil, by replanting them upside-down. In the low evening sunlight, the baobabs, and the colourfully dressed Akamba women working the tiny plots of maize nestled between them, are one of the highway's most beautiful sights.

Kibwezi: soursops and honey

KIBWEZI is a small Akamba trading centre off the main road at the B7 Kitui junction (this *murram* road is presently cut after 30km at the washed away bridge over the Athi River). The best **accommodation** here is the *MSIP Guest House* (also called the *Danida Guest House*), in a pleasantly shaded, tranquil location: follow the signposts from town for 2km (PO Box 65 Kibwezi; ☎98 Kibwezi; bed only ②). Formerly the headquarters of a Danish irrigation project, it's a friendly stopover, with clean, carpeted s/c rooms with nets, hurricane lamps (electricity only arrived in town in 1998) and cheap food to order. In town, the *New Face Hoteli* offers good food and fantastic murals. Kibwezi also boasts a small **market** where you can often buy spiky green **soursops**, one of those fruits you either love or loathe. Kibwezi is also known for its **honey**, which you'll be offered by countless sellers along the road. When it's good, it's delicious, but try it before buying as some is adulterated with sugar syrup. The art of beekeeping is a Kamba speciality but local custom varies – the honey often has a smokey taste after the bees have been smoked out when the keepers collect it. Bottom price is about Ksh120 for a wine-bottleful. In and around **Kinyambu**, 16km from Kibwezi, you'll see thirty or so grass and brick huts, distinguishable from human dwellings by their lack of windows. Each hut contains up to ten hives, owned and tended by a number of local women's co-operatives, together called "The Kibwezi Honey Project". Along this stretch of the main highway you might also see Maasai cattle herders, here at the northernmost limits of their territory, a strange pastoral contrast with the trucks and buses thundering by.

Mtito Andei to Tsavo

A big sprawl of service stations and snackeries rises out of the dry country at the start of **Tsavo National Park**; it marks **MTITO ANDEI** (which means "Vulture Forest", sometimes softened to "Eagle Forest"). The *Tsavo Inn* (PO Box 20; ☎0147/30342), by the Caltex garage, is a pleasant enough retreat if you don't mind the odd missing bath plug, with a tempting pool (Ksh120 for casual guests), but is overpriced for non-residents: *Rough Guide* readers get resident's rates – just show your copy. **Rooms** in the bungalow rows are large if a little frayed, but have nets and baths (B&B ④ residents, ⑤ non-residents). Don't miss the fascinating 1963 Michelin map in the lobby (there was no tarmac at all to Mombasa in those days). **Camping** should be possible at the gate to Tsavo West National Park (see p.360), 500m away, which is also the best place to try **hitching a lift** around the park. If you want a cheap lodging in town, try the *Okay Safari Lodge* (PO Box 34; ☎0147/30120; ①): clean and basic but loud, and OK for a cold beer or three.

The road between Mtito Andei and Voi is currently being resurfaced, and the diversion is incredibly dusty – roll up your windows. The only place to get anything to **eat** along here is at **Manyani**, 2km past Manyani Gate for Tsavo East National Park. It has a number of very basic *dukas* and *hotelis* serving *githeri* and *ugali* to weary travellers. There's no guarantee of fuel here or at the almost derelict *Maneaters' Motel* (no rooms), by the gulch of the Tsavo River just after Tsavo Gate for Tsavo West National Park (*tsavo* is Kamba for "slaughter"). On the opposite, north, bank, there's the *Riverside* campsite, 500m from the gate – you should be extremely wary of the baboons here as someone who was foolish enough to feed them died after he was savagely mauled. The campsite and motel are in the vicinity of the famous **man-eating lions** that played havoc with the building of the railway in 1898. The two lions seem to have been preternaturally lucky, since they eluded Colonel Patterson's various weapons for nearly a year and ate 28 Indian labourers in that time, as well as the unfortunate Superintendent C. H. Ryall who was dragged off a train carriage by the man-eaters during the hunt. The Field Museum in Chicago has the two stuffed man-eaters on display, and in 1998 organized an absurd research project to some nearby caves, where they had hoped to obtain the remains of Ryall himself: they found nothing. You won't see lions either, but along this section of the road through Tsavo park you may well come across **elephants**. Always a brick-red colour from the soil, they used to be one of the commonest animals on the road, but increased traffic and the gradual erosion of their habitat (by herders, agriculture and the elephants themselves) means you have to be a little lucky to see them.

Voi

The only sizeable town on the road is **VOI**, 5km outside the main gate to Tsavo East National Park, and at the junction for the Taita Hills and Taveta. If you have time to kill, check out the **sisal factory**: you can watch the whole simple process from the crushing of the sisal spikes, through drying and combing, to the final twisting into rope. The town's **market days** are Tuesday and Friday. There are plenty of petrol stations, a branch of Barclays (with ATM), a small supermarket and pharmacy (both in the shopping complex under the *Tsavo Park Hotel*), and plenty of cheap *hotelis*. For **nightlife**, don't miss the cunningly named *Tsavorite Club*, near the market, in a converted sports hall: by day a beer and darts boozer, it livens up at night with discos (Wednesday, Friday & Saturday) and occasional appearances by the incomparable "Cowboy" Ben wa Mumbi's country music, among other delights. There are several excellent **cheap lodgings**.

Ghana Guest House, 500m from the centre on the northside slip road (PO Box 492; ☎0147/30291). A little basic, but friendly and run by women, clean and peaceful (no bar), with some s/c rooms (hot showers), all with nets. ①.

Jumbo Guest House, next to the market square and bus park (PO Box 579; ☎0147/2503). Can be noisy, but cheap enough considering it offers s/c rooms. ②.

Lady Diana Lodge, 2.5km out on the Mtito Andei road (PO Box 368; ☎0147/2534). A red building stuck in the middle of a sisal field, this has cheap, breezy rooms with good views and nets (but only one s/c, with hot water in buckets), food to order (including *nyama choma*), and a disco Friday and Saturday. A taxi out here costs around Ksh150. The *Ikanga Travellers Lodge* on the main road nearby is squalid but plays good reggae in its bar. ①.

Tsavo Park Hotel, right by the bus stop beside the GPO (PO Box 244; ☎0147/30050, fax 30285). New and utterly anomalous, this is a surprisingly plush international standard hotel, with very well appointed and spotless rooms, all with balconies, nets, fans and phones, and satellite TVs planned. There's a gift shop and forex, safe parking, and a (soundproofed) disco underneath. Very swish restaurant (mainly European fare), and cheapish buffet lunches (Ksh450 per person). B&B ④.

Vuria Lodging, 600m from the bus station (PO Box 29; ☎0147/2269). With fans, mosquito nets and real toilets, and a bar downstairs. ①.

The Sagala Hills

An unusual day-trip from Voi – with some lovely walking country largely unvisited by tourists – is the **Sagala hills**, which rise just south of Voi. Five *matatus* run daily from town to **Sagala village**, 20km away: a small rural centre with little more than a store, a small *hoteli* serving nice *chai* and chicken, and a bar opposite the football field. From Sagala, you'll need a local to guide you around – children will be happy to oblige. A 45-minute walk takes you past a small bridge to the even smaller settlement of **Talio**, which has wonderful views of the Taita Hills, Mount Kasigau and the savannah below. There's a small store selling toilet paper, chewing gum and sodas. From here, small paths lead off through the green fields to the base of the hills (1–2hr) where there are other little villages. Apart from some steep rocks which are used by climbers from time to time, and occasional sightings of baboon or mongoose, the main attraction here is the impression of a timeless rural existence yet to be tainted by modernity. Visitors are rare, so please be tactful, especially with a camera, and be generous with your time. In Talio itself, you can either **stay** locally (someone should be happy to earn a few bob by putting you up), or you can pitch a tent somewhere: ask at the school.

Moving on

Leaving Voi, the **train** to Mombasa (1st class Ksh1410, 2nd Ksh1130, 3rd Ksh95) departs at 4.11am; in the other direction, the Nairobi-bound train (1st class Ksh2100, 2nd Ksh1475, 3rd Ksh210) passes through town at 11pm. The branchline train to Taveta (5hr; no 1st class; 2nd Ksh180; 3rd Ksh60) departs Tuesday, Wednesday, Friday and Saturday at 5am, returning at 2.20pm. The station (☎0147/30435) is five minutes' walk south of the market. **Buses** come in all day for both Nairobi and Mombasa, with some (Malindi Bus) continuing on to Malindi. There are at least two daily buses to Taveta, with additional overnight services coinciding with Taveta's market days on Wednesday and Saturday, as well as some *matatus*. Wundanyi in the Taita Hills is served by several *matatus* a day, the last leaving around 5pm. For descriptions of Taveta and the Taita Hills, see pp.349–354.

To the coast

After Voi, the road veers across the relentless **Maungu Plains**, also known as the Taru Desert, a plateau of "wait-a-bit" thorn and occasional baobabs which forms the migratory corridor for wildlife passing from Tsavo East to the foothills of Kilimanjaro. Dull and scenically dreary for much of the year, after heavy rains the plains come alive with colour, and during May and June can be carpeted in white-and-blue convolvulus flowers. Before you get away from the Voi area completely, look out for Kenya's weirdest roadsign, some 14km to the south on the left, erected by the local Round Table association: "The world 24 hours pram pushing record was set here 10th January 1972 – Distance 249.7 miles from start." A kilometre further on, a signposted track on the right takes you to *Ndara Ranch Safari Lodge* (PO Box 3 Voi; ☎0147/30264; B&B ③), a pleasingly decrepit colonial-style place (electricity evenings only, if you're lucky), with seventeen s/c **cottages** with nets, and virtually no guests. Some rooms are tatty, others have huge beds, and there's a swimming pool.

The roadstead of **Maungu** itself, roughly 25km from Voi, has two B&Ls, the better one being the *Susana Lodge* (PO Box 225 Voi; ☎0147/30260; ①), with some very basic s/c rooms, usually with clean beds if not much else, and no electricity or nets. It prides itself, bizarrely, on its hot beers. Ten kilometres down a rough signposted track from Maungu is the ostensibly much posher *Westermann's Safari Camp* (PO Box 88552 Mombasa; ☎011/472155; HB ⑤), which unfortunately is not very appealing, with tiny, dark chalets, no power and little atmosphere. Its guests are almost exclusively German package tourists. Much better is *Galla Camp*: see the box below.

After Maungu, the next place with food (but not much, and no petrol) is **Mackinnon Road**, distinguished by its Sayyid Baghali Shah Pir Padree Mosque, right by the railway track. Past **Samburu** ("butterfly" in Maa; again no fuel supplies) the country is peopled

TAITA AND RUKINGA WILDLIFE CONSERVANCY

Twenty-five kilometres east of Maungu, a right turn opposite Tsavo East's Buchuma Gate (signposted "Taita Ranch HQ") heads off a dusty 16km to **Galla Camp** (PO Box 630 Voi; no phone; reservations through *Savannah Camps & Lodges*, p.50), gorgeously sited on an exposed *kopje* (eroded rock promontory) scampered over by rock hyrax fearful of the eagles circling overhead. The views are spectacular, with a 360° panorama over Taita and Rukinga ranches, the Taita Hills and the distant foothills of Kilimanjaro. Whilst intended primarily for pre-booked visitors on expensive all-inclusive packages (⑨, including game drives), it's also possible simply to drop in unannounced and pay much cheaper rates for self-catering bed space in the permanent tents (⑤). Though rather basic by usual "luxury tented camp" standards, it's comfortable enough, and the views, informal atmosphere, as well as the silence, make for a very relaxing stop-over between Mombasa and Nairobi. If you're not driving, ring Savannah to arrange transport: they can even pick you up from the night train at Voi.

The ranches are part of a privately-run venture which aims to protect wildlife by involving tourists and researchers. The combined area of 680 square kilometres is strategically placed on the migration route of plains game, elephant and lion from the Galana River in Tsavo East to the foothills of Kilimanjaro in Tsavo West. Despite the thickness of the bush, spotting elephants is usually easy (especially from the vantage of the *kopje*), and the nearby water hole – intended primarily for the cattle corral nearby – also attracts baboon, buffalo, gazelle and occasional cheetah and lion. The staff are happy to guide you on walks.

The main purpose of the camp, however, is as a base for visiting the new **Taita Discovery Centre**, 16km west in the neighbouring Rukinga Ranch (access also along 16km of dirt track from Maungu, signposted "Rukinga Ranch") – which is a hands-on educational project with a visitor centre comprising a butterfly farm, live animal house, museum and library, and lab facilities for research students. You can stay there in the bunk-bedded *bandas* (self-catering; ④), or can **camp** in your own tent. There are showers and a bar. Information on the **field courses** (which seem very well thought-out, with plenty of variety) from *Savannah Camps & Lodges*.

mostly by members of the large **Mijikenda** ethnic group, though their distinctive, droopy, thatched cottages are often replaced nowadays by more formal square ones, increasingly also whitewashed and tin-roofed in the coastal manner. The **Duruma** Mijikenda of this district herd cattle, make charcoal and grow a little sisal – there's little else they can do in such a dry region. The small centres of **Maji ya Chumvi** ("salt water"), **Mariakani** ("place of the *mariaka*": the Kamba arrows used in nineteenth-century wars against the Maasai), and Mazeras bring you closer into the coastal domain.

Mazeras is a largely Duruma village and here **the coast** really takes over. The landscape has a quite different cast with its mango trees, lush cultivation of bananas and cassava, and (encouragement for weary travellers) the sublime sight of endless stands of **coconut palms**. For details about Mazeras and the route along the ridge to the north of Mazeras, see p.455. Ahead, the main road plunges with a certain abandon (ie lacking much of its tarmac) down the steep scarp to the Indian Ocean and Mombasa (p.413).

The Taita Hills

A good option, if you have your own car and a spare day or two – or if efforts to hitch into Tsavo proved fruitless – is to head off west from **Voi to Taveta**, a very accessible but largely unvisited region. Apart from being a route into Tanzania, the **Taveta road** has some interesting possibilities to the north and south, while for much of the time the magnificent mass of Kilimanjaro looms on the horizon.

THRUSH UNDER THREAT

Keen ornithologists head for the Taita Hills in search of *Turdus helleri*, the **Taita olive thrush**. This robin-like bird, the size of a European thrush, has a close relative in the ordinary olive thrush of the highlands: olive brown on top, red-breasted and red-billed. The Taita *Turdus* is distinguished by its much darker head and the fact that it appears to live only in the Taita Hills above 1600m – which gives it all of four square kilometres (1000 acres) of potential habitat. As it depends on virgin forest for its survival, the Taita olive thrush is a very rare bird indeed, and may even be extinct. Two or three were seen at Mbololo in 1953, and eight in the Ngangao Forest in 1965; it may also survive on Mount Ngangai. The bird has a bold, liquid warbling song. Good luck with the binoculars.

Wundanyi

To get a glimpse of the less ephemeral **history** of this region, go up into the **Taita Hills**. Several *matatus* pitch through the fertile chasms on a switchback road to the little district capital of **WUNDANYI**. After the sultry, dry plains, you're transported into another world. From the junction at Mwatate, the road twists up 14km into amazingly precipitous and beautiful hills, striped with cliffs, waterfalls and dense cultivation, and highly populated; near the peaks are patches of thick forest. There's notable prosperity up here, and a strong sense of community. Most of the people speak the Taita language, a member of the coastal Bantu family related to Swahili and Mijikenda.

The **Taita people** are welcoming, and Wundanyi is an attractive and enjoyable centre. The conifer trees and a babbling brook running past the football field reinforce the feeling of departure from the thornbush and scrub below. This sense of suspended reality is accentuated by the **cave of skulls** 1.5km outside the town, one of many ancestor shrines in the hills (there's one for each clan). Ask someone to show you the way: it's 500m before the *Mwasungia Scenery Guest House*, hidden in a banana grove just below the road, or ask at the guest house itself. In the niche rest the skulls of 32 Taita ancestors, exhumed from their graves. Traditionally, the shrine was an advice centre where life's perplexities were resolved by consultation with the dead, and was also where sacrifices were made in times of drought to ask the ancestors to intercede for rain: beside the niche is a sacred *mvumo* tree, which always grows near water – a good omen. Christianity has eroded some of the reverence that the Taita once had for these shrines – and traditional dances and rituals have almost completely disappeared – but the niches are left undisturbed nonetheless.

Practicalities

There are three **accommodation** possibilities, the only central one being the basic *Msangachi B&L* (①) near the market. Much better is the charming *Hills View Lodge* (PO Box 1262; ☎0148/2417; ②), 500m before the junction into town, with decent if basic rooms, a nice bar, and a restaurant specializing in fish. The other option, recommended for its helpful owners and lovely location rather than for its facilities, is the cheap, family-run *Mwasungia Scenery Guest House* (PO Box 1026; ☎ c/o Cecilia Mwachala, Wundanyi Prison 0148/2790; ①), 2km from town along a dirt track signposted at the junction at the entrance to town (though you'll have to ask for the building). Rooms are basic, with no electricity or running water, but the welcome is friendly, they can rustle up some food, and this is the best place to settle into if you're interested in finding out more about the Taita: the owner is knowledgeable, and can also take you on walks around the hills to see waterfalls, skull caves (see above), and a cliff-top tree from which villains were once hurled to their fate. There's a choice of good **places to eat**: at the top end of town, near the *matatu* stage, the *New Wundanyi Motel* is recommended for tasty meals and a lively atmosphere – especially emanating from the bar – whilst *Tsavo Hill Café*, overlooking the market, has great service, wicked pizza and good curries. Next to it, the *Dairy Co-op Milk Bar* offers fresh milk, yoghurt, coffee, cakes, "sconze" and *mandaazi*. Downhill, just up from the post office and KCB bank, *Bistro 35 Cafeteria* is bright and cheerful. The big **market days** in Wundanyi are Tuesday and Friday. **Moving on** from Wundanyi, *matatus* to Voi leave in the morning and early afternoon, some continuing on to Mombasa (leave early if headed for Taveta; you'll have to wait at Mwatate).

Taveta and lakes Chala and Jipe

West of the Wundanyi turning at Mwatate, the **road to Taveta** jumps off the tarmac and you follow the railway line through the southern arm of Tsavo West, mostly in a cloud of brilliant red dust. The road was set to be tarmacked a few years back, but the money strangely disappeared – a lamentable state of affairs, especially in contrast to the fast smooth tarmac on the Tanzanian continuation of the road. A number of maps mark a *Murka Lodge* along here, but it has been closed for years and Taveta is the first, and only, place worth stopping at. You're almost certain to see some game on these plains, especially in the rainy season – if you're coming by train, sit on the left for game, or on the right for the looming mass of Kilimanjaro.

Taita Hills Wildlife Sanctuary

The only place attracting much tourist traffic in this district is the 110-square kilometre **Taita Hills Wildlife Sanctuary** (entry $21), which isn't in the Taita Hills at all, but in the hillocky, bosky lowlands 15km beyond Mwatate. It's run by the *Hilton* chain, with two of their lodges and a tented camp acting as bait (all ⑨; reservations: ☎0147/30243 or 30270, fax 30007). The setting of the lodges can't compete with Tsavo or even Amboseli (and they're much more expensive, too), though you can do early-morning **balloon safaris** here (around $400 for 90min). The 24-tent *Safari Hilton Camp* is the least tacky of the three and has a more immediate "bush" feel, with no electricity but a good atmosphere; however children under five aren't welcome here or at *Salt Lick Hilton Safari Lodge*. Most of the visitors here are on fleeting air safaris from coast-hotel holidays. If you're managing without your own transport, there is virtually no chance of getting a lift into the sanctuary itself, though you could walk the half-kilometre from the road to the first hotel, *Taita Hills Hilton Safari Lodge*, just outside the reserve, if you feel like indulging in a *Hilton* meal. Having used the lodge facilities (which include a large pool and water hole game-viewing terraces), you're entitled to free entry to the sanctuary. The lodge itself is a graceless concrete block that could be anywhere.

The sanctuary is well managed and, for most of the year, full of wildlife. Its small size means the rangers always have a good idea of where the animals are hiding out and it's not uncommon to see two dozen species of mammals – among them large numbers of lions, elephants and grazers – in a morning game drive (included in the rates if you're lodging there). During the drier parts of the year, when the animals are not dispersed, *Salt Lick Lodge* on the southern side of the sanctuary provides water hole game-viewing to rival the "tree hotels" of the Central Highlands. But it's for its bizarre **architecture** that *Salt Lick* is most famous: from a distance it looks like a clump of mushrooms sprouting from the swamp. Each of its rooms is a kind of turret on stilts, all of them linked by mock-suspension bridges – there's even a drawbridge at the lobby. This camp ensemble is supposedly in keeping with the area's **World War I** battle history – most of the important Anglo-German engagements in East Africa were fought on these plains.

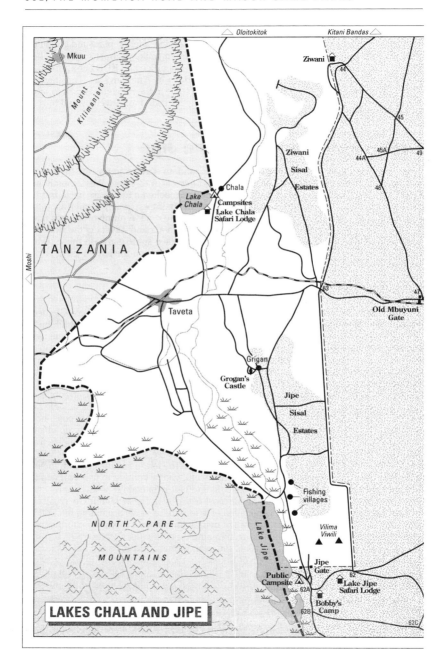

△ Oloitokitok   Kitani Bandas △

Mkuu

Ziwani

44

45

Mount Kilimanjaro

Ziwani

Sisal

Estates

44A   45A

46

49

Chala

Lake Chala

Campsites

Lake Chala Safari Lodge

T A N Z A N I A

△ Moshi

63

47

Old Mbuyuni Gate

Taveta

Grigan

Grogan's Castle

Jipe

Sisal

Estates

Fishing villages

N O R T H   P A R E

Vilima Viwili

M O U N T A I N S

Lake Jipe

Jipe Gate

62

Public Campsite

62A

Lake Jipe Safari Lodge

Bobby's Camp

62B

62C

LAKES CHALA AND JIPE

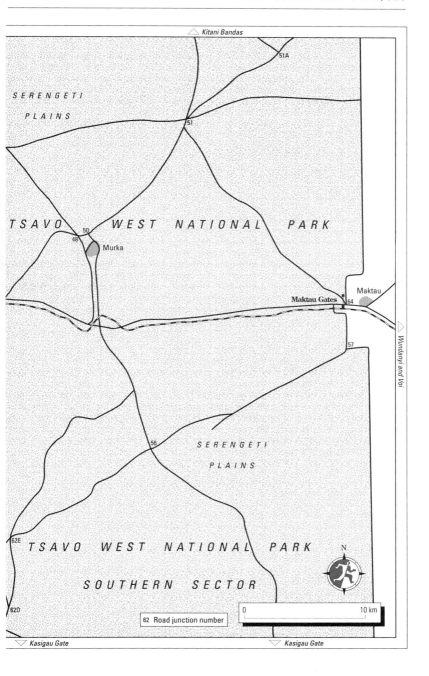

62 Road junction number

Taveta

Somewhat off the beaten track, **TAVETA** is situated on the Tanzania border at the end of the rural corridor running between the northern and southern sections of Tsavo West National Park. Taveta has a mixed population of Taveta, Taita, Maasai, Akamba, Kikuyu and Luo, and even some Makonde (originally from Mozambique, they were brought in in the 1930s to work the sisal estates). Electricity arrived a decade ago, there's a KCB bank (Mon–Fri 8.30am–1pm, Sat 8.30–11am) and a petrol station, and the town is gradually joining metropolitan Kenya. With the recent improvement in East African relations amid talks of resurrecting the East African Union, things look set to change still further. If you're leaving Kenya at Taveta, note that there is a longer walk than you might expect to the Tanzanian side of the frontier – allow at least an hour. For a few moment's reflection, there's a **World War I cemetery** at the entrance to town.

The main **accommodation** options are at the end of the main street, which runs to the right (north) on the other side of the railway level crossing as you enter town. The best option is the nonetheless rather run-down *Chala Hotel* (PO Box 16; ☎0149/2245 or 2212; ③), which has small rooms around an internal courtyard, some with hot water, some with fans, others with nets, but is vastly overpriced for tourists. They serve good, basic food, and have a relaxed TV bar, and the chance to organize local excursions (the *Lake Challa Safari Lodge* is under the same management). In the cheap lodgings bracket (make sure you get a mosquito net), the not-very-salubrious *Livingstone Guest House* is nearby, on the road behind the *Taveta Hotel* (①); cleaner and brighter, 50m further up the road from *Chala Hotel*, is *Kuwoka Lodging House* (PO Box 51; no phone; ①), which features magnificent, gaudy murals in its front restaurant.

The best places to **eat** in town are the *Taveta Hotel*, on the square between the *Chala Hotel* and the bus station, and a couple of restaurants either side of the KCB bank on the street leading to the border post: the *Taveta Border Hotel* (good samosas and chips) and *Golden Fish Hotel*. The local banana stew is also popular, though you might balk at eating eight bananas in one sitting – even if they are smothered with gravy. For something completely different, try the *Taveta Prison Canteen* at the entrance to town, which has sodas and roast meat.

Daily **buses** to Voi, continuing to Mombasa, leave at 8am from outside the Garex office at the main bus and *matatu* stage by the market facing the rail line, with additional 10am services on Wednesdays and Saturdays. The less reliable Tukutendereza Bus (Mombasa daily 8.15am & 10am) leaves from by the level crossing. There are plenty of *matatus*, too. The **train** to Voi departs at 2.20pm on Tuesday, Wednesday, Friday & Saturday (2nd class Ksh180, 3rd Ksh60). There are no train services into Tanzania at present. To explore the **Taveta region** without your own wheels, you'll have to rely on infrequent local *matatus* (better on market days: Wednesday and Saturday in Taveta, Tuesday & Friday at Chumvini) and the occasional private vehicle. Early morning *matatus* continue to Oloitokitok (p.379), near Amboseli National Park, to coincide with its market days on Tuesday and Saturday. If you're driving, note that the **road to Oloitokitok** can be pretty rough going, and is often impassable in the rains.

Lake Chala

Transport isn't such a problem to **Lake Chala**; you could, if necessary, walk most of the twenty-kilometre round trip, and there are **buses** to Chumvini (beyond Chala) on Tuesday, Wednesday, Friday and Saturday. A four-square-kilometre crater lake north of Taveta, Chala has one shore in Kenya and the other in Tanzania. It's right by the road to Amboseli, 8km from the junction outside Taveta and just a ten-minute walk up the slope. Hidden in its crater, it would be easily missed were it not for the signposted turning to **Lake Challa Safari Lodge**, 4km before Chala village (bookings: PO Box 16

Taveta; ☎0149/2245 or 2212; or in Mombasa ☎011/313207, fax 311789; HB ⑤, FB ⑥). Perched on the crater rim, this friendly place sees few visitors, but has some of the most spectacular room views in Kenya – straight over the lake, with Kilimanjaro looming behind.

The lake is a deep and unbelievably transparent blue. It once had a population of harmless dwarf crocodiles (imported from Madagascar by Ewart Grogan; see below), but these have died out and it's inhabited today only by mythical monsters and paddled over by a few fishermen in dugouts (the fishermen live in small caves down by the water's edge, and are happy to chat). You can **camp** for free in a number of places on the rim, with views to die for – the best site is to the right (north) of the lodge, who don't appreciate tents pitched within 200m of their grounds. There are no facilities, but you can eat and drink at the lodge, or use their swimming pool (Ksh200, children Ksh100). If you don't fancy scrambling down the vertiginous crater to the lake, the lodge has installed a flight of steps, access to which costs Ksh50 (children Ksh25). The lake itself is bilharzia-free, which makes for a very pleasant swim. Keep an eye open for the luminous, pink snake that a number of readers have independently reported seeing inside the crater wall, on the path down to the water's edge; watch out, as it may be a red spitting cobra. You may also see green mambas, monitor lizards, large skinks (another lizard), black monkeys and baboons (be wary of the latter, especially when camping).

Lake Jipe

Equally interesting, and totally different, is **Lake Jipe**, 35km south of Taveta. It's fed by Kilimanjaro's snowmelt at its northern end, passing via Lake Chala's underground outlet, as well as by streams flowing to the south from the Pare Mountains, across the border in Tanzania. The Kenyan shore is flat and thickly carpeted in reed beds. Several villages at the northern end make a living from fishing, while Jipe's southeastern shore lies inside Tsavo West National Park.

GROGAN'S CASTLE

Seven kilometres from the Voi–Taveta road, **Grogan's Castle**, a white mansion on an isolated hill rising from the plain along the track to Lake Jipe, deserves a little detour. This extraordinary residence was built in the 1930s by Ewart Grogan, one of the most influential early colonists. His reputation was founded on a walk from the Cape to Cairo which he undertook in 1898, on a notorious public flogging he carried out on three of his servants (nearly killing one of them), and on his wealth: his gilt-edged reputation was such that Grogan was able to dictate terms to the governor before he even arrived in Kenya. At the peak of his prosperity, he owned over 2,500 square kilometres of land.

The "castle" was evidently built as a kind of hacienda for the **sisal estates**. It is totally run-down these days – the only residents of the house are a large colony of bats – but it can be visited if you tip the *askari* (ask for him at the settlement of "Grigan" at the foot of the hill, a one-kilometre walk). It's an enigmatic building, much of it stuck together with aircraft aluminium and tin roofs. There are two enormous circular living rooms with spectacular 360-degree views out towards Kilimanjaro and Lake Jipe. The huge bedrooms have mosquito-screened bed niches, whose steel mesh make them look more like animal cages. On one of the landings an ostentatious cash cupboard is suitably positioned, presumably for the casual display of wealth to passing guests. It will probably end up one day as an expensive lodge, and there are rumours of its having been "grabbed" by the local MP (it seems Grogan left no heirs, at least not in Kenya).

There is no public transport to the lake, indeed very little transport at all. Short of finding a driver in Taveta to take you there, your only option, and by no means an unpleasant one, is to walk. The flat land between the Voi road and the lake is heavily planted under sisal, cotton fields and even coconuts. There are also wide areas of low bush. It is an unusual part of Kenya, rustling with bird and animal life. The Macmillan map, *Tsavo East and West National Parks*, is a useful aid in the area. Driving or walking, head east from Taveta along the Voi road, turning right after 7.5km at the signpost for "Lake Jipe Safari Lodge", 1km beyond the turning for Ziwani Sisal Estate. From here, the track heads straight through the Jipe Sisal Estate to the lakeshore villages, 27km from the junction, passing the unmistakable Grogan's Castle on your right (see box on p.355).

The lakeshore and national park

At **Mukwajoni**, the village 2km before the park gate, you'll find only the most basic provisions (apart from fish), so bring supplies from Taveta. There's nowhere to stay, though someone may be happy to put you up in their hut for a small fee. When exploring the bush around the lakeshore early in the morning, beware of **hippos**: you should keep a sharp eye out, especially between the park gate and the village. A feasible target for a couple of hours' **walk** are the two hills, Vilima Viwili, just outside the park boundary and about 2km east of the track. Once at the lake, the track becomes confused as it heads south towards Tsavo West's **Jipe Gate** (for details of park fees and regulations, see p.360) – keep as close to the lake as you can, as the gate is right on the shore. The rangers here are friendly and have little to do: they also have a **boat** ($5 per person) for a spot of crocodile and hippo-spotting, or for just messing about in. There's a **campsite** just inside the gate ($8 per person), with toilets and showers. Despite the vicious attentions of mosquitos, this is a peaceful and rewarding spot, and a paradise for ornithologists. For something more substantial, the Swiss-run *Bobby's Camp*, 1km from the lake and 500m from the gate, has nine large, simply but comfortably furnished tents under thatched roofs, and meals and drinks available to casual guests (reservations: *Royale Tours & Safaris*, PO Box 99034 Mombasa; ☎011/475255; HB ⑤, FB ⑦ including a game drive). If you're not staying, you might still be able to do a game drive with them around the park to see its unusually angry **elephants** (a probable indication of poaching over the border in Tanzania). *Lake Jipe Safari Lodge*, 5km from the gate on the Maktau track (also inside the park), is a larger and less intimate setup, with rooms in small and not terribly attractive pink *bandas*, but it's currently closed and looking for a buyer.

Leaving the park, you've only really one option, which is a fifty-kilometre drive northeast to the gate at **Maktau**, a small settlement with another gate to Tsavo West's northern sector on the opposite side of the road (you won't need to buy another ticket unless staying another day), a war cemetery, a few *dukas* and nothing else.

THE PARKS

In these animal-rich national parks, the first realization of where you are – among real, uncaptured wildlife – is truly arresting. Which parks to visit can seem at first a pin-in-the-map decision: any of them can provide a store of amazing sight and sound impressions.

Amboseli and **Tsavo** are the two most accessible, with ever-busy game lodges, well-worn trails, large numbers of tourists in the high seasons, and large, if brutally diminished, herds of elephant. Amboseli, with its picture-postcard backdrop of Mount Kilimanjaro and guaranteed **elephants**, is an instant draw, but the flat topography and lack of vegetation cover means you'll be sharing the stunning vistas with dozens of other safari vehicles. Tsavo, in contrast, is huge enough to escape company completely, except at **Mzima Springs**, for which it's worth being part of the crowd if necessary.

Maasai Mara has the most fabled reputation, with horizons of wildlife on every side. Somewhat isolated in the west, it requires a specific, usually there-and-back, visit, but it's well worth the effort (and perhaps the cost), especially during the yearly **wildebeest migration** that takes place sometime between July and November (at its most spectacular in August). The Mara is also *the* place to see **lions** – lots of them. The downside is its popularity: even more than Amboseli, you'll find safari vehicles around almost every corner.

Samburu and **Meru**, on the north side of Mount Kenya, have different varieties of animals, such as northern species or races of giraffe, zebra, antelope and ostrich. Samburu – dry, thorny and split by the Ewaso Nyiro River – is increasingly popular and noted for its **crocodiles** and **leopards**, albeit baited ones. Meru, however, is perhaps the most beautiful Kenyan park – isolated, verdant and surprisingly unvisited.

Practical considerations

Conditions can change rapidly in the parks. The effects of **climate** have led to several temporary closures over recent years and impressions one season may be quite different the next. **Security** is also a consideration, especially in the northern parks and reserves of Meru, Samburu, Shaba and Buffalo Springs, where banditry from the northeast (Chapter Seven) and Somalia occasionally spills over: we've detailed the current situation under each, but you'd be advised to check up on the latest with a reputable travel agent in Mombasa or Nairobi.

It's important, if you want to get as much as possible out of your visit, to have detailed **maps** of the parks. These are often available in the park lodges or on the gates, but not always, and prices are higher than you'll pay in Nairobi. The best map for each park is mentioned in the brief details at the start of each park section, although the Kenya Wildlife Service is currently in the process of putting together its own colour maps and information sheets (available at park gates for $2), which, going by the ones already published (Amboseli, Tsavo, and Nairobi National Park) are as accurate and detailed as you'll need.

The latest **entry fees** for non-residents are also given at the beginning of each park section: the most popular, Amboseli and Maasai Mara, are also the most expensive, followed in price by Tsavo East and West, then Meru, and then the Samburu, Buffalo Springs and Shaba reserves (you have to pay separately for each of these).

For some idea of their current **animal-viewing potential**, the order of enthusiasm in recent travellers' accounts places Samburu and Maasai Mara way out in front, then Amboseli and Tsavo East, followed some way behind by Tsavo West, with Meru last of all. If you're interested in **birds**, you'll find favourable places to watch with your binoculars in all the parks, but it's worth pointing out that Maasai Mara (mostly open plains) is not, on the whole, good for birds, while by contrast Samburu (with its riverine environment) can be exceptionally rewarding.

When to visit

The parks usually get two **rainy seasons** – brief in November or December, more earnest in April and May – but these can vary widely. In Maasai Mara, they can merge together in one season from November to May. Meru also gets heavy rainfall, but it's more scattered. As a general rule, you'll see more animals during the **dry season** when they are concentrated near water and the grasses are low. After the rains break and fill the seasonal watering places, the game tends to disperse deep into the bush. Moreover, if your visit coincides with the rains, you may have to put up with some frustrating game drives, with mud and stranded vehicles. By way of compensation, if your plans include luxury accommodation, you'll save a fortune at lodges and tented camps in the low season (April 1–June 30 and, to a lesser extent, July 1–November 30). Most places reduce their **tariffs** by anything from a third to a half between April and June, with savings particularly spectacular for singles.

Driving

The parks in this chapter are open all year round. If you're **driving** during the rains, remember that none of the park roads are paved and unless you'd be content to keep to the main graded tracks, you will need a 4WD vehicle to venture down the smaller ones: a night spent stuck in the mud in Maasai Mara (a likely enough occurrence if you only have 2WD) isn't recommended, nor is trying to reverse down a boulder-

---

ENVIRONMENTAL CONCERNS

OFF-ROAD DRIVING

Be sensitive to the great damage that can be done to delicate ecosystems by driving off marked roads. Despite the lush, tropical growth after the rains, there's nothing tough about the very seasonal vegetation. Even apparently innocent diversions off the main tracks can scour fragile, root-connected grasslands for years, spreading dust, destroying the integrity of the lowest levels of vegetation, and hindering the life cycles and movements of insects and smaller animals, with consequent disruption to the lives of their predators. Thus a destructive chain reaction is triggered which is difficult to halt. The effects of this are especially visible in Amboseli and Maasai Mara, both of which are now ecologically at risk.

So, use only **signposted roads** and tracks, or ones marked on official maps, though in some areas it can be hard to judge whether you're following an agreed route, or the tracks of others who broke the rule . . . If this means being denied the opportunity to see one of the "Big Five", consider the fact that cheetah, for example, are very sensitive to noise and interference by vehicles, and hunt only by day: when surrounded by minibuses, they may offer great photo-ops (as any brochure shows), but are unable to hunt. Don't be encouraged by those safari minibuses which do go off-road: these are operating illegally and should be reported to the rangers at the gates. If you're with a safari group, agree not to encourage off-track driving for the sake of getting closer to the animals. And don't be afraid to ask the driver to keep to the main route: most are only doing what they perceive their clients want. The scenery and habitats are as important as the animals.

SPEED LIMIT

Stick to the official maximum speed limit posted at the gates, usually 30kph or 50kph. This avoids accidents and prevents too much dust being kicked up.

ANIMAL RIGHTS

Animals have right of way, and are not to be disturbed (even if sitting across the track). This means keeping a minimum distance of 20m, having no more than five vehicles viewing an animal at any one time (wait your turn if there are already five there), no loud noises or flashed headlights, and not following the animals if they start to move away.

DRIVING AT NIGHT

Night driving (usually 7pm–6am) is illegal in all Kenyan parks and reserves without express permission from the warden.

LITTER

Take only photographs and memories, leave nothing behind. Collecting firewood (for camping) is strictly prohibited, as is picking wild flowers.

strewn slope in Tsavo West. In any case, a normal saloon will be shaken to bits on the average park road, and most car-rental companies will insist you have 4WD. If you're driving and can claim residence in Kenya, you can get a special one-year national parks' pass, which allows you multiple entry into all the KWS parks (but not reserves, like Maasai Mara and the Samburu complex). The passengers must also have a pass or pay the usual fees, though there is a couples' pass available. Details are given on p.63 in Basics.

Accommodation in the parks

If you're visiting independently, with or without a vehicle, it may well be worth bringing a **tent** (consider hiring or buying one in Nairobi – see p.146). Without one, Amboseli, Maasai Mara and Samburu are very limiting if you are watching your budget as there is no cheap *banda* accommodation at any of these. In any case, camping out adds to the adventure. If you're visiting the parks on a more comfortable basis and staying in **lodges** or **tented camps**, it would be wise to make **advance reservations** as there's heavy pressure on beds during the peak seasons. Note that if you book via a travel agent, you may be given **discounts** on official "rack rates", sometimes up to ten percent off. Obviously, if you reserve rooms or tents at places in the same hotel group (see p.48), making changes to bookings is easier.

Animal watching

Game viewing soon loses its more self-conscious aspects. Our wildlife colour section will help you identify the larger mammals you're likely to encounter, and the "Wildlife" account on p.630 provides further background reading (see also the "Books" section on p.646). **Rangers** can usually be hired for the day (official KWS rates are Ksh500 per day, or Ksh300 for four hours, though an additional tip is usually expected) and, if you have room, someone with intimate local knowledge and a trained eye is a good companion: knowing some Swahili animal names is a help (see p.633). Most of the lodges and tented camps have their own 4WD vehicles and run regular "game drives". These can be very worthwhile because the drivers usually know the animals and the area. Expect to pay $30–50 per person for scheduled departures and $120–150 for exclusive use of the vehicle for two to three hours.

The usual pattern is two (or sometimes three) game drives a day: at dawn, mid-morning and late afternoon (though if you keep this up for more than a day or two you'll be exhausted). In the middle of the day, the parks are usually left to the animals; you'll be told it's because they are all hiding. A more likely reason is that the midday hours are a lousy time to take pictures. The animals are around, if sleepy, and if you can put up with the heat while most people are safely in the lodges, it can be a tranquil and satisfying time.

To see as much as possible, stop frequently to scan with **binoculars**, watch what the herds of antelope and other grazers are doing (a predator will usually be watched intently by them all), and talk to anyone you meet on your way. The best time of day is sunrise, when nocturnal animals are often still out and about and you might see that weird dictionary leader, the aardvark.

BABOONS: A WARNING

More serious than the occasional robbery in the parks is the continued, unstoppable damage done by those loutish hooligans, **baboons**. A locked vehicle might be safe; an unwatched tent certainly isn't. Insurance companies don't cover such contingencies.

The Tsavo National Parks – East and West

Daily 6am–6.30pm; each park $23 per day/overnight, $8 students/children; private veh cle Ksh200, camping $8 per person. Warden of Tsavo West: PO Box 71 Mtito And (☎0302/22480, 22483 or 22455); warden of Tsavo East: PO Box 14 V (☎0147/30049). No driving after 7pm. Speed limit 30kph Tsavo West, 40kph Tsavo Eas Maps: Macmillan Tsavo East & West National Parks Map at 1cm:4.2km (1988); Surve of Kenya Tsavo West SK78 (1994) and Tsavo East SK82 (1985; out of date for accom modation) at 1cm:2.5km; the KWS colour A3 flyer available at the gate (1998; $2) lack topographical detail, but is bang up-to-date for accommodation and roads.

Biggest by far of Kenyan national parks, and together one of the largest in the worl the combined areas of **Tsavo West** and **Tsavo East** sprawl across 21,000 square kil metres of dry bush country, an area the size of Wales or Massachusetts. **Tsavo East** the larger portion, though all of it north of the Galana River has been closed to the ge eral public for years (poaching there appears to be prevalent). South of the river, th great triangle of flat wilderness with Aruba Dam in the middle has become popula with coastal safari departures, since you can be sure of seeing plenty of animals in very open environment. The traditionally popular part of Tsavo is a mere 1000 squar kilometres, the tall grass-and-woodland **"developed area"** of **Tsavo West**, locate between the Tsavo River and the Mombasa highway. Here, the combination of goo access, excellent facilities and magnificent landscapes attracts tourists in large nun bers, while the well-watered, volcanic soils support wooded grasslands and a gre quantity and diversity of animal life – though it's not always easily observed.

With their numbered junctions and clearly defined *murram* roads and tracks, th Tsavo parks are easy to get around, so long as you have a map. Don't forget the distance involved, however: if you set off somewhere, be sure you have time to get back to bas by nightfall: both parks close their gates at 7pm, and it's illegal to drive around after the

Tsavo West: access and accommodation

If you're looking for a visit outside an organized safari tour and don't have your own ca **Tsavo West** is probably the easiest as well as the cheapest of the big parks to explor From Nairobi or Mombasa, take a bus to **Mtito Andei** (park headquarters and a se vice town for the lodges; see p.346). The gate here is one of the busiest in the countr and your chances of getting a ride are good. *Kilaguni Lodge* should be able to arrang transport if you're coming by public transport, as they have regular evening staff tran ports from the gate. If you get stuck, the rangers are usually helpful and may allow yo to camp just inside, though there's plenty of budget accommodation in Mtito And itself, barely 500m away. The easiest option, of course, is just to **fly in**: contact Eas African Air Charters in Nairobi (p.134), who run flights to the main lodges when ther are enough passengers (around $150 return).

The lack of low-budget **accommodation** – a problem that affects all the main park to some degree – is less of an obstacle in Tsavo West. There are four **campsites** do ted around: one just inside Chyulu Gate, with shower and toilet, and conveniently clos to *Kilaguni Lodge*; another, again with basic shower and toilets, a twenty-minute driv from the Mtito Andei Gate near the park headquarters at Kamboyo Hill; a third ju inside Tsavo Gate; the fourth at Lake Jipe in the far south (p.356). In addition, there ar two recommended and well-equipped self-service **banda camps**, *Kitani* and *Ngulie* which have a number of simple but comfortable chalets, and are miles cheaper – as we as more charming – than the lodges. You have to bring and cook your own food her an attractive proposition if you're sick of *ugali* and chips, or obsequious lodge servic for that matter. Details for both are given below.

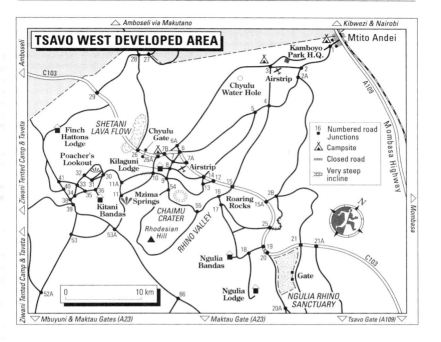

△ *Amboseli via Makutano* △ *Kibwezi & Nairobi*

TSAVO WEST DEVELOPED AREA

Mtito Andei

Kamboyo
Park H.Q.

Airstrip

Chyulu
Water Hole

C103

SHETANI
LAVA FLOW

Finch
Hattons
Lodge

Chyulu
Gate

Poacher's
Lookout

Kilaguni
Lodge

Airstrip

Mzima
Springs

Kitani
Bandas

CHAIMU
CRATER

Rhodesian
Hill

RHINO VALLEY

Roaring
Rocks

Ngulia
Bandas

Gate

Ngulia
Lodge

NGULIA RHINO
SANCTUARY

0   10 km

16	Numbered road Junctions
⚠	Campsite
≈≈	Closed road
⇉	Very steep incline

Ziwani Tented Camp & Taveta
Ziwani Tented Camp & Taveta

Mombasa Highway
△ *Mombasa*
C103

▽ *Mbuyuni & Maktau Gates (A23)* ▽ *Maktau Gate (A23)* ▽ *Tsavo Gate (A109)* ▽

Finch Hattons Tented Lodge, Kampi Ya Simba, 15km northwest of junction 38, 65km from Mtito Andei Gate (PO Box 71 Mtito Andei; ☎0302/22468, fax 22473; reservations PO Box 24423 Nairobi; ☎02/60432–2, fax 604323). Named after the aristocrat who introduced royalty to the bush, *Finch Hattons* must be the suavest and most accomplished of numerous luxury tented camps springing up around Kenya: fine bone china, cut crystal glasses and chandeliers, piped Mozart, impeccable service and food. The camp is sited around the springs and pools of a source of the Loolturesh River, where crocodile and great pink-and-grey hippo splash. The 35 tents are, of course, totally luxurious, with antique commodes, brass lamps and Afghan rugs (rooms 1–7 are best). Not the best place for children as the site and the pools are unfenced, and you may feel rather constricted by the formality of it all. FB ⑨.

Kilaguni Lodge, off junction 8, about 30km from Mtito Andei Gate (PO Box 2 Mtito Andei; ☎02/340000 or 0302/22471, fax 22470; reservations through Express Travel Group, Bruce House, Standard St, PO Box 40433 Nairobi; ☎02/334722–7, fax 334825). The oldest park lodge in Kenya (1962), and still one of the better ones, as much as anything for its prime site by a large (floodlit) water hole and terrific wildlife ambience. There's a busy atmosphere and it's very often full – this is not a quiet place – but it keeps up impeccable service. Good-sized rooms (most facing the wildlife action, with stunning views towards the Chyulu Hills and Kilimanjaro), lush gardens, small pool, petrol. Game drives available (Ksh3500 for a nine-seater Nissan for half a day). Casual visitors welcome (see p.363). Recommended. FB ⑦ low, ⑧ high.

Kitani Bandas (*Kitani Safari Camp* on maps), off junction 36, 12km south of *Kilaguni Lodge*, 8km from Mzima Springs (PO Box 3 Voi; bookings through Let's Go Travel in Nairobi, p.142). In an exposed red-earth site with some shade, the twelve three-bed *bandas* are pleasingly simple and down-to-earth, bliss after the studied excesses of the lodges. Each has a kitchen (with gas cooker), a bathroom (cold water until they finally repair the heater) and mosquito nets. Frequent sightings of buffalo and plains game. Bring all you need, including food and drinks. ④.

Ngulia Safari Lodge, 48km west from Tsavo Gate, off junction 18 (PO Box 42 Mtito Andei; ☎0147/30091, fax 30006; reservations through Kenya Safari Lodges & Hotels, p.49). Somewhat isolated in the more mountainous eastern side of the park close to the rhino sanctuary, this is open-plan and offers tremendous views over the plains far below, but has less immediate wildlife appeal than *Kilaguni*. Still popular and well-maintained despite its age (1969), this is less swish, but friendly and more than adequate. There are two water holes by a terrace, but they rarely attract anything except buffalo who like to sleep there at night during the dry season. Leopards occasionally show up at dusk for a meal of meat tied to a tree by two nervous young men. There's a swimming pool and a pair of high-powered binoculars for scanning the plains. No game drives. Casual visitors welcome (see below). Petrol. FB ⑥ low, ⑦ high.

Ngulia Bandas (*Ngulia Safari Camp* on maps), 18km west of *Ngulia Lodge* between junctions 17 and 18 (bookings through Let's Go Travel in Nairobi, p.142). Like *Kitani*, a delightful place to stay, and popular with Kenyans: you might even strike up a friendship and get a lift around the park for some animal-spotting. Nestled up the heavily vegetated north slopes of Ngulia Hill, this has great views and even its own water hole. The six three-bed *bandas* have bathrooms, showers and kitchens, but no hot water. As with *Kitani*, bring your own food. They have drinking water, but you might feel safer using iodine or chlorine tablets. ④.

Ziwani Tented Camp, on the park's western boundary by junction 44, about 40km south of the "developed area", but most easily reached from the Taveta–Taita Hills road (PO Box 236 Ruiru; ☎0151/21024; reservations through Prestige Hotels, p.49). On a glorious site by a small hippo and crocodile pool, beside a dam in the Sante River, with twenty full-size, permanent tents overlooking the Tsavo River and excellent food. It's quite a distance from the park's main attractions, however, but early-morning guided walks in the bush around the lodge more than compensate. Game drives $21. Less formal and under half the price of its rival, *Finch Hattons*. FB ⑤ low, ⑥ high.

Exploring the "developed area" of Tsavo West

If you are eager to see particular species, Kilaguni's **information centre** (usually open during the high season) should have up-to-date locations of **lion prides** and **cheetahs**, and possibly **leopard sightings**, too. But touring around the rest of Tsavo West is, for the most part, a question of following your inclinations.

The "developed area" is the hilliest sector of any of the parks covered in this chapter, and there's an unending succession of fantastic views across the plains, dotted with volcanic cones and streaked with forest at the water margins. When the animals are abundant – and their numbers fluctuate tremendously, being most visible in the dry seasons – every turn in the track seems to bring you face to face with zebra, giraffe, huge herds of buffalo, casual prides of lions, or methodical, strolling elephants, almost orange from the dust. Among the more unusual animals to look for are the beautiful and shy **lesser kudu** antelope (always, it seems, running away).

In the 1960s, Tsavo had the biggest population of **black rhinos** in Africa – between 6000 and 9000 – and they were a common sight. By 1981, they had been poached to barely 100 individuals (the story is enlarged in the box on p.368). The situation today has improved a little, though most rhinos have been removed to the safety of the **Ngulia Rhino Sanctuary** (4–6pm daily; free, if a ranger accompanies you, he'll expect a tip), where, if you drive around for long enough, you're almost bound to see one (you can always visit the holding pen in the middle of the sanctuary and inspect the latest arrivals).

The trip further on, that takes you around the foot of **Rhodesian Hill**, is recommended too, and **Poacher's Lookout** (also called *Ranger's Lookout*), near *Kitani Bandas*, is a very promising place for a quiet scan with binoculars. There's a thatched shelter here where you can sit in the breeze.

For information on the **southern** part of **Tsavo West**, read the sections on Lakes Chala and Jipe on pp.354–356.

Mzima Springs

The biggest attraction in Tsavo West is **Mzima Springs**, 48km from Mtito Andei and close to both *Kilaguni Lodge* and *Kitani Bandas*. This stream of crystal-clear water was made famous by Alan Root's film *Mzima: Portrait of a Spring*, which followed crocodiles and hippos in their underwater lives. Go very early to avoid the tour-bus atmosphere and you won't be disappointed. The luxuriant growth around the water reverberates noisily with birds and monkeys, and, with luck, some of the night's animal visitors may still be around.

There are **two large pools**, connected by a rush of rapids and shaded by stands of date and raffia palms. The upper (or long) pool is the favoured **hippo** wallow, while the **crocodiles** have retreated to the broader expanse of water lower down. It's worth walking around this lower pool to the right where, if you're stealthy, you have a good chance of seeing them. Just make sure there's not one on the bank behind you. This word of caution applies equally to hippos, but they seem settled in their routine, content to snort and flounder at an irritating point just a little too far from the path for visitors' satisfaction. At the side of the top pool, a circular underwater **viewing chamber** has been built at the end of a short pier. Unless you are exceptionally lucky, all you'll see is a blue swirl of perpetually revolving fish.

Mzima's two **nature trails** (really tree trails) aren't of great interest unless you happen to be a botanist, but it is easy nevertheless to spend a couple of hours in the area. Try to sit for a while completely alone on the bank and you'll begin to piece together the ecological miracle of the place, as the animals and birds forget about your presence. This is where those khaki safari outfits are actually practical.

Mzima Springs has a direct pipeline to Mombasa, completed in 1966, and is the source of most of the city's **drinking water**. Two hundred and fifty million litres of water per day gush out here, filtered to aquarium transparency by the lava of the **Chyulu range** to the north. This dark, largely unexplored, forested ridge creates its own rainfall: the porous rock absorbs the water like a sponge and gravity squeezes it into Mzima.

Plans were mooted in 1952 to build a weir in order to raise the lower pool's level. This would have destroyed the river terrace, however, and by ruining the hippos' "nursery" would probably have caused them to stop breeding. The National Parks trustees stepped in and effectively stalled development, summoning independent engineers to devise a way of taking water from beneath the lava, *above* the spring. There are one or two signs of the pipeline in the area but most are unobtrusive. Mzima has been left whole.

Kilaguni Lodge

While *Kilaguni* is an expensive place to stay, sooner or later you're bound to turn up, and rightly so: a visit (free) is rewarding enough just for the pleasure of sitting on the terrace with a cold beer and watching the enthralling circus going on a few yards away at the **water holes** (neither *Finch Hatton's* nor *Ziwani* encourage day-trippers). Lunches here cost around $18 per person. In the high seasons, casual visitors tend to be herded into a separate "visitors' centre", which has its own bar, restaurant and information desks, but not as much wildlife interest, so try to infiltrate the main reception area anyway, which is open to the panorama of the savannah and Chyulu Hills. Dazzling **birds** hop everywhere, **hyrax** scamper between the tables, and **agama lizards** skim along the walls (the miniature orange and blue dragons are the males in mating drag). In the grass below the terrace lives a colony of **dwarf mongooses**, while pompous **marabou storks** pace slowly up and down awaiting jettisoned bread from the dining room. Out by the water hole, **baboon troops**, **antelope**, **buffalo**, **zebra**, **giraffe** and

elephant provide constant spectacle, with the occasional kill adding tension. At dusk, hundreds of **swallows** swoop back and forth over the human drinkers to their nests in the roof, and, later, **bats** swoop while **genets**, **jackals** and **hyenas** come for the meat scattered under the floodlights: you may get exceptional permission from the warden to drive here at night for this, most likely if you're camping or staying at *Kitani Bandas*.

Ngulia Lodge

The autumn **bird enthusiasts** at *Ngulia Lodge* are far more earnest. The lodge is a stop-over on the annual southern migration of hundreds of thousands of European birds. It seems to be situated on a narrow migration "corridor", but the reasons for its attraction for the birds – apart from its isolated lights – aren't really known. Ornithologists gather in November and early December to band the birds that are trapped in mist nets, and their occasional recapture in places as far afield as Malawi, Iran and Germany slowly helps to build a picture of where the birds are moving to. Perhaps not altogether surprisingly, few are ever caught at *Ngulia* again. Again, admission is free, and you can take lunch or have a dip in the pool (Ksh300).

Lava flows

The **lava** that purifies Mzima's water can be seen in black outcrops all around this part of Tsavo. The **Shetani lava flow** is a spectacular example. Only 200 years old (the Chyulu hills themselves are less than 500 years old), the eruption that spewed it out must have been a cataclysmic event for local people, and it is still the focus of stories about fire and evil spirits (*shetani* means "devil" in Swahili, deriving from the same Arabic linguistic root as "Satan"). Legend has it that many people were buried in the hot lava flow, and their plaintive cries can be heard on certain nights. The local people appease the ghosts by leaving them offerings of food which, of course, are gone by daybreak. There are **caves** here that, despite one or two warnings, are worthy of investigation (you'll need a torch). One of them even has a ladder and a trail of identification plaques by the bones of luckless animal victims who stumbled down.

Chaimu lava flow is fun to walk over, but also dodgy. The lava is brittle, honeycombed and unstable, and very few plants have taken hold yet. It is possible to climb up to the volcano's crater rim, but this can be surprisingly hard work on the scree and shouldn't be attempted in the heat of the day. And beware: when poking around Tsavo's caves and lava zones, you should be alert to the possibility of disturbing large **sleeping animals** as well as **snakes**. Remember, too, that Tsavo's lions have a reputation for ferocity. In the park, you should leave your vehicle at designated nature trails only, or where there's an obvious parking area. And beyond the national park boundaries you should stay on your guard – the animals aren't fenced in.

Tsavo East National Park

Across the highway, the railway, and the apparent natural divide that separates Kenya's northern and southern environments, lies **Tsavo East**. Apart from some tumbled crags and scarps near Voi, this is an uninterrupted plain of flat bush, vast and empty, dotted with the crazed shapes of monstrous baobab trees. It is a forbiddingly enormous reserve and at times over the last couple of decades it has seemed an odd folly, especially since the whole of the sector north of the Galana River – almost two-thirds of the park's area – has been closed to the public due to the long years of war against elephant and rhino poachers (see the box on p.368). Since 1991, however, the situation has changed dramatically: the poaching has been more or less stamped out; the elephants, if not the rhinos, are once again on the increase; and Tsavo East, just a few hours' drive from the charter arrivals hall at Mombasa airport, finds itself very much the centre of tourist attention, especially for budget camping safaris. The **northern sector** is still not routinely open to that kind of tourism, but now by choice rather than necessity: the warden is restricting access to upmarket, low-profile camping and walking parties. Private visits to the northern sector are only possible with express permission from the Rangers' HQ near *Voi Safari Lodge*, and even so you'll probably have to take (and pay for) a ranger for the duration.

Access and getting around
There are presently no scheduled **flights** to the park. Tsavo East has five **gates**, including **Mtito Andei Gate** in the northern sector which only offers access to *Tsavo Safari Camp* (see below). **Buchuma Gate** at the southeastern end is the one most used by safari vans from Mombasa, handy for Aruba Dam but far from the Galana River; remote **Sala Gate** is the one used if you're coming from Malindi; it's 110km due west of Malindi along a seemingly endless dirt road, but there's no public transport further west than Kakoneni, 80km short of the gate, and safari vans are unlikely to offer you a lift without some form of payment. On the western side, **Manyani Gate**, near Mudanda Rock, is little used, but offers a choice of routes into the park. The main gate, and the one you should aim for if hitching, is at **Voi**, about 4km from the town (p.347). The rangers here seem a helpful crowd, with sensible attitudes to lifts and hitching: you can go with them to *Voi Safari Lodge* on their 8pm staff bus. At the gate itself, there's a small educational centre (though the insects in the glass cases look as if they flew in and perished there), and a short **nature trail**, plus a small **staff canteen** with the usual warm beers, sodas, bread and dusty vegetables.

Campsites
There are four public **campsites** in the park, two of them outstanding. The most popular is just 500m inside **Voi Gate**, and plays host to a fair number of organized tours. There are basic toilets, showers and running water, and some unfurnished *bandas* which give additional protection against baboons. You can usually get permission to camp here without a vehicle (it probably depends on how recently a lion was spotted). Apart from its convenience, it provides considerable excitement in the shape of Eleanor, one of Daphne Sheldrick's **elephant orphans**, and her young, male consorts. The elephants, now fending for themselves and completely unafraid of humans, visit the small artificial water hole in front of the cottages every evening. They can, and regularly do, steal food and anything else that appears to be edible. Take care: there's an accident waiting to happen here. There's another site nearby – **Ndolo campsite** – for which you'll need wheels, at the western edge of Kanderi Swamp, off junction 173. The most beautiful campsite, however, is at **Aruba Dam**, about 30km along the north bank of the seasonally meandering Voi River. The dam lake gets visited by thousands of animals; nights can be noisy. Check at the park gates before going, however, as the site may close when the new lodge at Aruba Dam finally opens. The other public campsite is way out on the eastern side of the park, 10km west of junction 176. At Sala Gate, your only option is to camp inside the rangers' compound (for a fee – bargain hard).

Lodges and luxury tented camps
Aruba Lodge, on the north bank of dammed Voi River, off junction 105 (information through Kilimanjaro Safari Club, p.49). Once an obvious focus in Tsavo East, *Aruba Lodge* was derelict throughout the 1990s, but a lease to rebuild and operate it was signed in 1998, which stipulates an opening deadline of the end of 2000. The site is a dream: read the description above.

Crocodile Camp, 9km outside Sala gate (PO Box 81443 Mombasa; ☎0147/30124, fax 30123). One of the few African Safari Club places to admit drop-in visitors, this – like *Tsavo Buffalo Camp* – is right on the river, but larger (fifty beds), and has a more formal, lodge-like feel, with landscaped gardens and imposing public areas. Was good value (④), but the price is set to skyrocket after an upgrade. Lunch Ksh700. No game drives unless pre-booked. FB way overpriced at ⑨.

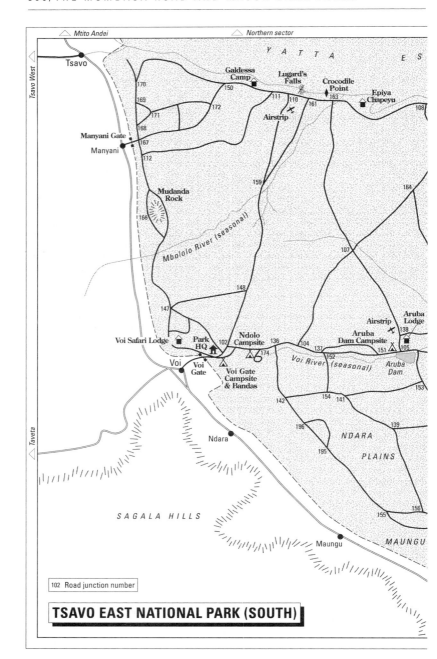

102 Road junction number

TSAVO EAST NATIONAL PARK (SOUTH)

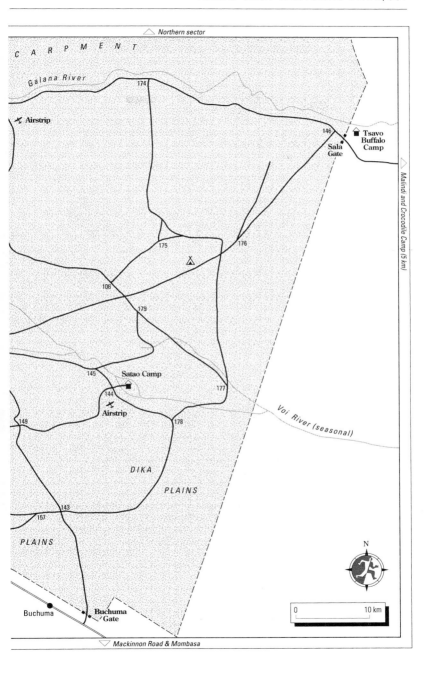

△ Northern sector

C A R P M E N T

Galana River

174

✈ Airstrip

146
Sala
Gate

■ Tsavo
Buffalo
Camp

Malindi and Crocodile Camp (5 km)

175   176

106

179

145   Satao Camp

144

177

✈
Airstrip

149

178

Voi River (seasonal)

D I K A

P L A I N S

143

157

P L A I N S

N

143

0   10 km

Buchuma   ■ Buchuma
             Gate

▽ Mackinnon Road & Mombasa

THE TSAVO POACHING WARS

Saving the elephants . . .

Tsavo East was for a long time the contentious focus for conservation issues. The question of how to manage the elephants – or whether to manage them at all – is still the paramount one, in theory. The policy for years has been to hunt the ivory poachers and allow the elephants to reach a natural balance by starving themselves to a population their habitat could sustain. But the cycles of overpopulation and drought were too long for anyone to know if this was working out or not, and concerns are now being raised about the destruction of Tsavo East's remaining woodland by the pachyderms. Elephants, which are intelligent animals with complex kinship patterns, soon migrate to the increased security of national parks, often assembling in huge herds out of protective instinct.

Such questions have been submerged for many years by the overbearing problem of poaching. In 1972, Tsavo's elephant population was over 17,000. Today it is 8700. The social structure of the herds in many districts has been badly distorted, with many elders wiped out and too many inexperienced younger elephants unable to fend for themselves or to act in a properly mature and sophisticated, elephantine way. Taking account of only natural factors, orphaned infant calves are automatically doomed, while young elephants under ten years have only a fifty–fifty chance of surviving to maturity: over half the present population consists of juveniles under ten years old.

There was a lull in the poaching in the early 1980s, but by the end of the decade any complacency was brutally shattered by an unprecedented slaughter of elephants in their thousands – mostly mature animals with large tusks, but including many with little ivory to offer. The poachers were no longer marginalized Akamba killing an occasional elephant with an old gun or poisoned arrows but a new breed of ivory-hunters, equipped with automatic weapons, going in and wiping out a whole family group in a single attack.

In 1988, it emerged that the Somalian government (as it then was) was mounting a concerted assault on Tsavo's ivory – perhaps in collusion with Kenyan Somalis and park-rangers-turned-poachers – aiming to profit from the tenfold increase in the value of ivory on the world market over the previous three years. Somalia announced it would be exporting 8000 tusks of what it called "confiscated ivory", an incredible figure equivalent to Somalia's own entire elephant herd.

The then Kenya Ministry of Tourism and Wildlife, concerned for the country's tourist image and allegedly covering up for some people on its own payroll, reacted in a curiously defensive way, admitting to poaching tallies far less than the reliable estimates available. President Moi was said to be furious. He personally ordered park rangers to shoot poachers on sight, then beefed up manpower and equipment in the Anti-Poaching Unit and deployed the paramilitary General Service Unit (or GSU, a force more commonly seen on the university campus) into the bush. Ethnic Somalis living near the boundaries of Tsavo East were summarily rounded up and trucked north to Wajir and Mandera, rekindling a bitter resentment which goes back a long way and has nothing to do with poaching.

As the news made the headlines in Kenya, some people started counting the casualties among the defending park staff, a number of whom were also killed. The spectacle unfolding – of a dirty war being fought on the plains amongst mutilated and unmovable elephant corpses, while the tourist minibuses followed each other in search of the perfect picture – was not a glamorous one.

The 1989 international agreement on a five-year ivory trade moratorium (renewed in 1994) had a remarkable effect on the numbers of new elephant corpses being logged in Tsavo. Equally dramatic was the unprecedented aggression with which the Kenyan parks authorities started carrying out their duties under the auspices of the bluntly pragmatic new Director of Wildlife and Conservation Management (which became the Kenya Wildlife Service), Dr Richard Leakey. Leakey obtained huge injections of cash and military equipment for the war: armed men caught in the parks without authority were liable to be shot on sight, which deterred even the most reckless poachers and raised another human rights cloud over the country. Before the 1989 ban, three elephants a day were being killed by poachers; in 1990 fifteen were lost; in 1991 and 1992, almost none. The problem, however, has not disappeared completely – in 1993, 75 were poached, 35 were lost in 1995, 29 the next year, 43 in 1997, and 60 in 1998. Given the parallel rise in the Kenyan elephant population, from 19,000 in 1989 to around 27,000 in 1997, these figures are considered acceptable by KWS. What poaching there is currently seems to centre around the closed northern sector of Tsavo East. Official figures and comment are notable by their absence, fuelling speculation that powerful figures may be involved. More worrying is the pressure from some countries to open up the ivory trade again, which succeeded in 1999 in allowing Zimbabwe, Botswana and Namibia to resume trading in ivory, leading to concerns that this may reopen the floodgates to poachers: despite the increase in their numbers, there is still no guaranteed future for the elephant in Kenya.

...and the rhinos

The black rhinos, of course, are even further down this vicious path to near-annihilation. Their estimated number in Kenya is about 450 (up from 330 in 1989, at the height of the poaching) – that is, somewhere around a quarter of the total population of the species, which remains under a serious and shocking threat of total extinction. More than 95 percent of Kenya's rhino population (most of them in Tsavo) was destroyed in the 1970s. The poaching business suddenly and dramatically escalated when the hunters began buying automatic weapons to slaughter what are essentially quite vulnerable animals.

This escalation wasn't just the result of land pressure and human hardship in the countryside. More significant was a radical expansion of the market for rhino horns – not, as is popularly supposed, in China (where minute quantities of powdered rhino horn are used for tonics and aphrodisiacs – it's hoped that Viagra may stifle this trade), but in Yemen. Oil money made the rhino horn dagger-handle – traditionally the prerogative of the rich – suddenly within reach of thousands of Yemeni men. Many tons of horns were smuggled out of Mombasa in dhows. *Run, Rhino, Run* by Esmond and Chryssee Bradley Martin (see "Books" on p.648) follows this trail in extraordinary and depressing detail.

Yet the savage groundwork was laid long before. After World War II, the Makueni area southeast of Machakos was designated as an Akamba resettlement area. The colonial Kenya Game Department sent in one J.A. Hunter to clear it of unwelcoming rhinos: he lived up to his name, shooting 1088 black rhinos from 50,000 acres. The Akamba didn't take to the scheme and it fizzled out. Today, your chances of seeing black rhinos in the wild in Tsavo are slim. They still hang on in the wilderness sector north of the Galana, where the war between the poachers and the Kenya Wildlife Service has never quite died out.

At the brink of disaster, there are now concentrations of breeding black rhinos in a number of ranches and sanctuaries – notably at Ngulia in Tsavo West, Nakuru, Solio, Lewa Downs, and in Laikipia district to the northwest of Mount Kenya – and saving the rhino has become a national cause.

Epiya Chapeyu, south bank of the Galana River, 5km east of junction 163 (Alphatauri Ltd, PO Box 14653 Nairobi; ☎02/749796 or 750000, fax 750990, *bigi@form-net.com*). Unstuffy Italian-run camp in a lovely location, with apparently frequent visits by a group of immature male elephants, and hippo at night. The twenty tents have bathrooms but no furniture and are closely spaced, the better ones in the front row facing the river. The food is Italian, and they're happy with unannounced guests, even for lunch, so long as they have room. Rates are per person, which makes it good value if you're on your own. Game drives and guided walks in the northern sector possible. Recommended. FB ⑤.

Galdessa Camp, south bank of the Galana River, 4km west of junction 111 (c/o Mellifera Bookings, PO Box 24397 Nairobi; ☎02/574689, fax 564945, *ras@swiftkenya.com*; *www.galdessa.com*). A Swiss-run luxury-tented camp which organizes walking and fishing safaris along the river, plus camel safaris. However, with the surrounding bush vegetation, there's little chance of seeing much wildlife at the camp itself, and the rates are extortionate: $650 for a double. FB ⑨.

Satao Camp (Mukwajuni Camp), east of *Aruba Lodge*, off junction 144 (bookings through Southern Cross Safaris, Ratna Square, Nyali; PO Box 90653 Mombasa; ☎011/471960, fax 471257). A fairly new forty-bed luxury tented lodge, sited on an island in the seasonal Voi River. Well run, with a good atmosphere, and a water hole which attracts elephant, occasional lion and plains game. FB ⑥.

Tsavo Buffalo Camp, 2km outside Sala gate (PO Box 556 Malindi; ☎0147/2549, fax 0123/30715, *coralkey@africaonline.co.ke*). Opened in December 1998, with eight round *bandas* nicely sited on the Galana River, a breezy dining area under a thatch roof, but otherwise not much shade and no game drives. Elephant and hippo are frequently sighted, and it's the cheapest option short of camping. Walk-in lunches Ksh650. Rates are per person (so good value singles). B&B or FB ④.

Tsavo Safari Camp, access through Mtito Andei Gate, then 16km along a dirt track (☎0302/22459–1; reservations through Kilimanjaro Safari Club, p.49; closed mid-April to end June). This tented camp, for pre-booked visitors only, is located on the east bank of the hippo- and croc-filled Athi River, accessed by pulley-powered dinghies. It's a remote and peaceful place, with enthralling birdlife and escorted game-viewing trips. There's a swimming pool, too, and porcupines and hyena come up to the dining area. Accommodation is in 27 "luxury" tents and 9 s/c cottages. FB ⑤ low, ⑦ high.

Voi Safari Lodge, near Voi Gate (Box 565 Voi; ☎0147/30019, fax 30080; reservations through Kenya Safari Lodges & Hotels, p.49). This lodge, a few kilometres away up the hill, is almost as busy as its Tsavo West counterparts, with a magnificent savannah-scape plunging to the horizon and almost guaranteed game viewing from the terrace. The style is agreeable 1970s glam-kitsch: look out for the photo of Miss World 1972. FB ⑤ low, ⑦ high.

Tracking through the park

With minibus safaris increasingly taking in Tsavo East, the emptiness of the park is no longer as overwhelming as it was until recently, but its vast size means you will still have the uninterrupted pleasure of exploring the wilderness, much of the time, completely alone. It's easy to get away off the two or three beaten tracks, and you may find something special – a **serval** perhaps, or a **striped hyena**.

The Voi River's wooded margins often hide a profusion of wildlife: try the **Kanderi Swamp/Ndolo campsite** at junction 173 and the pretty lookout point at junction 174; keep the windows up when driving through the tall grass and undergrowth, not only for security against large animals, but as a defence against the tsetse flies that may mistake your vehicle for a large animal.

Mudanda Rock is particularly recommended at certain times of the year. Like a scaled-down version of Ayers Rock in Australia, it towers above a natural dam which, during the dry season, draws elephants in their hundreds.

As recently as 1990, you were likely to get unforgettable glimpses of the mountainous carcasses of elephants. The elephants of Tsavo, attuned to the potential dangers they face in the bush, have taken to spending much of their time near the lodges and park roads where, shot by cameras, they are relatively safe. Large herds are not uncommon, but, when you see them, you'll notice the scarcity of mature adults.

From Aruba, most people head up towards the **Galana River**, unmistakeable with its fringing cordon of branching doum palms. If you've got permission to visit the northern sector of the park, it's possible to cross the Galana at junction 160 in the dry season, but beware the smoothness of the rock bed, which belies the fact that many unwitting drivers all too easily get stuck in the attempt (note that Suzuki 4WD jeeps are notoriously underpowered, which makes judging your line all the more important). Just to the east of here are the spectacular **Lugard's Falls**, where you can park and clamber around the bizarrely eroded rocks. Even in relatively dry seasons, the force of the falls, which progress from foaming rapids to narrow cascades gounged deep into the bedrock, is quite something. Some safari companies use the falls as a picnic site – apparently with KWS sanction – as evidenced by a litter of plastic wrappers and cigarette butts: please take your rubbish with you.

A kilometre east of the falls, another short diversion takes you to **Crocodile Point**, something of a let-down as the crocs are extraordinarily hard to see until you get up close, which you're no longer allowed to do. Hippos are easier to spot here.

Amboseli National Park

Daily 6am–6.30pm; $27 per day/overnight, $10 students/children; private vehicle Ksh200, no camping. Warden: PO Box 18 Namanga (☎0302/22250–1). No driving after 7pm. Speed limit 40kph. Maps: the most up-to-date is the A3-size KWS Amboseli National Park flyer (1998; $2) available at the gates, which has a useful sketch map of all the tracks, sights and accommodation. More topographical detail is provided on both Macmillan Amboseli National Park Map at 1cm:750m (1988), and Survey of Kenya SK87 at 1cm:500m (1990), but both are dated and many roads have changed.

AMBOSELI is a small and very touristy park. It has suffered badly from off-road driving and its climate makes it a bleak, shimmering plain most of the year. Scenically, however, it is totally redeemed by the stunning spectacle of **Kilimanjaro**, towering over it and (as in those clichéd safari photographs taken with telephoto lenses) appearing almost to fill the sky. Sunrise and sunset are the best times to see the mountain, especially during the rainy season when the air is much clearer, but for the most part it remains tantalizingly shrouded in a thick shawl of cloud. In the right light, the snowy massif, washed coral and orange, is devastatingly beautiful.

On the animal side, Amboseli, like Tsavo, is **elephant** country *par excellence*. You will see large herds, some with big tusks. Predators, apart from hyenas and jackals, are relatively scarce (lions are almost absent, thanks to the revenge wrought by the Maasai upon their expulsion from the park) but good numbers of herbivores are present. In the dry season, most of the animals crowd into the impenetrable marshy areas and patches of acacia woodland where food plants are available. But during and shortly after the rains the picture is different, the animals more dispersed and the landscape greener.

The **erosion** of the grasslands by circling minibuses did much to destroy the park's purpose in the 1980s, turning it into a vehicle-clogged dustbowl that appealed little to animals or tourists. A concerted programme of environmental conservation, road-building and ditch-making was initiated, and this, combined with the toughest approach of any park to off-road driving (including fines and ejections), has improved the situation enormously. In 1992–93, however, heavy rains caused major floods, turning Amboseli into a swamp. The Kenya Wildlife Service responded with a $2 million rehabilitation plan to rebuild park roads and culverts that had been destroyed, but the same thing happened again in 1997–98; these cycles of flood and subsequent drought were amplified by the recurring El Niño effect, and seem to have become nature's way of culling the weakest and least adaptable animals. Unfortunately, this cycle also leaves the park more open to damage by vehicles: even at 10kph, the amount of dust thrown up is astounding.

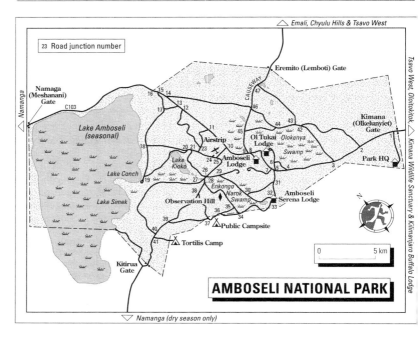

Also troubling the park is relations with the local Maasai, who were evicted from the land they had grazed for centuries when the park was created, in 1973. As a result, some replied by spearing and poisoning animals that strayed outside the park, including rhino and lion, and others became poachers (see "Maasai voices" on p.376). Things have since settled down, and the Maasai are now entitled to a cut of the KWS revenue from tourists. They have also recently started benefiting from a number of upmarket tented camps built on their land outside the park, from which they extract daily entry fees and rent.

The route from Nairobi

The road is tarmac all the way to Namanga on the Tanzanian border, from where it's a very bumpy 76km along rutted *murram* to the park's centre: about four hours' non-stop from Nairobi. Public transport will only take you as far as Namanga (there are a few buses from Nairobi's Country Bus Station), from where you'll have to hitch. As usual, the best chances are with Kenyan weekenders. If you've got the money, it's easier to **fly in**, on the daily 7.30am Airkenya flight from Nairobi's Wilson Airport ($135 return; p.143).

Driving from Nairobi, turn right off the Mombasa highway on to the A104 for Namanga after 23km, just after the dusty Bamburi Cement clinker grinding plant, at the southeastern extremity of Nairobi National Park (p.153). If you're hitching or going by public transport, your first destination is the small town of Athi River, 5km down the Namanga road, reached by bus/*matatu* #110 from Nairobi's KBS bus station. **ATHI RIVER** (also called **Kitengela**) isn't particularly interesting in itself, boasting an export processing zone, cement factory and plenty of dust. There's a colonnaded colonial post office and a Standard Chartered bank, and, if you get stuck here, a few **places to stay**. The *Prince View Motel* (PO Box 97; ☎0150/22321; ②) is the local hot spot and offers good self-contained rooms; couples can share a single, which seems to be the norm around here. Run on similiar ethics is the astonishingly glam-kitsch *Moran Hotel* (PO Box 156; ☎0150/22750; B&B ③), which used to have tacky nightly discos until its owner died, and is now looking rather forlorn and rundown. The overpriced rooms are in tidy little "cottages" out the back, and there's a pool (empty at the last check). There's also a **museum** of sorts, containing a hotchpotch of unlabelled and incredibly dusty artefacts from all over Africa.

Isinya and Kajiado

The road onwards from Athi River through the Kapiti plains is unfortunately pretty dull, broken only by the **Maasai Ostrich Farm** (☎0150/22505–6; Ksh100 including tour), signposted 7km off on the right 15km south of Athi River. Primarily a commercial farm providing meat to local butchers, they also have guided tours of the farm, a swimming pool, limited food and large picnic grounds. There's also the comical attraction of occasional ostrich races; ring ahead for dates.

At **Isinya**, which is now connected with tarmac to the Magadi road (p.182), there's a **Maasai Leatherworking and Handicrafts Centre**. It's touristy, but you can find some unusual work among the beaded key-rings and "marriage necklaces". Check out the handmade shoes and massive, heavy leather bags. If your stomach is strong, you can visit the tannery, and they're happy to see you in the workshops, too. Donations from a church in Folkestone, England, of all places, help Isinya's community.

Further south, in the gentle hills where Maasai country really begins, is the district capital **KAJIADO**, which lies on the Magadi soda railway line. Set among sisal spikes and acacia, it's a friendly market town with a relaxed provincial feel, that provides an ideal stop-over after the hassle of Nairobi. Maasai in all their gear mix with other Kenyans in its busy streets and bars, and the daily **market**, part of which shelters in a modern breeze-block and corrugated iron building near the mosque, is fascinating. The *Kajiado Inn* (①), opposite the train station, has the best **cheap rooms** in town, plus a *nyama choma banda* and a bar-restaurant downstairs. Supposedly more upmarket, but overpriced for its small tatty rooms, is *Embeut Resort* (PO Box 262 Kajiado; ☎0301/21217; B&B ④), 1km back along the Nairobi road, with round s/c *bandas* with nets. There's a *nyama choma* bar, too, which has live music on the last Friday and Saturday of each month (*ndombolo* and other dance). Basic lodgings include *Thayu B&L* (①), at the junction with the Nairobi–Namanga road, which isn't terribly welcoming and tends to be full of drunks, and the weird Maasai *1811–1971 Day and Night Club* (①) which has scrubby rooms but bags of atmosphere. For **cheap eats**, try *Impala Restaurant* opposite the KCB bank, or the bright and breezy *Naitiil Restaurant* (signposted), unfussy but cheap and hygienic. If you're after **nightlife**, there are a number of busy bars and day-and-night clubs: expect inquisitive stares but a friendly if slurred response.

Namanga

The scenic interest picks up after Kajiado, as the road snakes into the hills, giving views of the conical Mount Meru in Tanzania (4565m), and your first glimpses of Kilimanjaro if the sky's clear. **NAMANGA** town sits square on the border, only 130km from Arusha in Tanzania. The petrol station, from where the *murram* road leads off east towards Amboseli, is probably the best place to start if you're trying for a lift into the park.

Namanga River Lodge is the grandest **accommodation** option (PO Box 4 Namanga; ☎67 Namanga; ④): a colonial oddity composed of wooden cabins set amid pretty gardens, it was the halfway house on the old safari trail between Nairobi and Arusha. The

AMBOSELI'S HISTORY

The park has been getting smaller and smaller ever since it was created. It began as part of the Southern Maasai Reserve at the turn of the century. Tourism arrived in the 1940s and Amboseli Reserve was formed as a wildlife sanctuary. Unlike Nairobi and Tsavo national parks, created at the same time and sparsely inhabited, Amboseli's swamps were used by the Maasai to water their herds and they saw no reason not to continue sharing the area with the wildlife and – if necessary – with the tourists. In 1961, the Maasai District Council at Kajiado was given control of the area. But the combined destructive capacities of cattle and tourists began to tell in the 1960s; a rising water table in the following decade brought poisonous alkali to the surface and decimated huge tracts of acacia woodland. Kenyatta declared the 400-square-kilometre zone around the swamps (the present-day Amboseli) a national park, a status that utterly excluded the Maasai and their cattle. Infuriated, they all but exterminated the park's magnificent long-horned black rhinos over the next few years, seizing on Amboseli's tourist emblem with a vengeance (the survivors were moved out by the authorities). They also obliterated a good part of the lion population, which have still not recovered. Not until a piped water supply was set up for the cattle did the Maasai finally give up the portion of land within Amboseli's boundaries. They still, however, periodically pursue lion (which, of course, kill their cattle), although compromise appears to be the order of the day: in the dry seasons, you'll see numerous herds of cattle and their herders encroaching well into the park unhindered, as they always did.

place has a likeable, slightly cranky atmosphere, and has clearly seen better days – the era of baggy trousers and printed frocks seems just around the corner, but it's overpriced for non-Kenyans. Good snacks are served, and you can also happily camp in the garden (Ksh300 per person). Much better value are the s/c rooms (hot water in buckets) at the *Namanga Safari Lodge* next door (PO Box 5 Namanga; ☎29 Namanga; ①), with its pleasantly kitsch garden and bar, reasonable food, and cheaper camping, too (Ksh150 per person). Best of the two basic B&Ls is *Orock County B&L*, at start of track to the River Lodge.

On the main road from Nairobi are several large **tourist emporiums**, including one not far north of Namanga and the other in the town itself, at the big petrol station. Both are packed to overflowing with Maasai bead- and leather-work, as well as Makonde ebony carvings from southern Tanzania and, of course, Kamba animals and Kisii soapstone. They're not especially cheap but, depending on the volume of business, you can strike reasonable bargains and the choice is huge. The glass beads used in the beadwork are not African; they come from the Czech Republic, which exports them to Peru and the Native American reservations as well as East Africa. And don't be misled by the expensive black-and-white marriage necklaces, which are not traditional Maasai ware; nor are the carved animal pendants. As with any art, styles change and innovations are emulated. Among all the trinketry are genuine used articles which tend to attract high prices. For these, you might do better by making offers to people you meet on the road. Bartering clothes or food often works to the benefit of both parties.

Park accommodation

From Namanga, a long, corrugated road – comfortable only at cowboyish high speed, and very slippery when wet – takes you to the park gate. Only one road connects the gate with "Ol Tukai" park centre; a second, which cuts right across Lake Amboseli on many maps, is rarely passable, and even in dry weather risks getting you bogged down in a treacherous version of quicksand: take care. **Arriving**, as most people do, around midday in the dry seasons, Amboseli seems a parched, unattractive place, with

Kilimanjaro disappointingly hazed into oblivion. And heading straight for Ol Tukai, with its lodges, workers, filling station, fences and barriers, doesn't improve first impressions. During the rains, however, it all looks far more impressive, with the lake partially filled, and a number of other seasonal lakes and ponds flanking either side of the road, the occasional home of small flocks of flamingo, pelican, and other migratory species.

Lodges and bandas

If you want to spend the night in Amboseli, you need money: the only budget option is staying at the single **campsite** outside the park, and even then you'll probably need wheels. Otherwise, the closest **rooms** are at the B&L in Kimana (p.379), or the expensive accommodation at *Kilimanjaro Buffalo Lodge* and in the Kimana Community Wildlife Sanctuary (p.379). Wherever you stay, be wary of semi-tame baboons and vervet monkeys, who will grab anything not tied down if it looks tempting, and can give a nasty bite if irritated.

Amboseli Lodge, Ol Tukai area (☎ & fax 0302/22421–2; reservations through Kilimanjaro Safari Club, p.49). After years of mismanagement, the main package destination is finally in good hands. Staff are helpful and friendly, food is good, the cute chalet accommodation is comfortable, but the main draw is the fantastic full-on view of Kilimanjaro from all public areas and some of the rooms. Maasai dancers evenings, and optional cultural talks. Murky green pool, showers and meals (Ksh880 per person) available to casual visitors, as are game drives $35 per person. FB ⑥ low, ⑦ high.

Amboseli Serena Lodge, southern park area (☎0302/22622, fax 22430; reservations through Serena, p.50). Favoured for its location by the Enkongo Narok swamps which attract plenty of wildlife, this is beginning to need a revamp, with slightly tatty rooms and public areas. Thankfully, the pink sugarcube architecture is well hidden behind a jungle of tropical plants and creepers (you can plant trees, if you like, to save future visitors the sight), which encourages a kind of intimate, pseudo-bush feeling accentuated by touches like a stream running through the dining room. You can drop in for lunch (Ksh870), but the pool is for overnight guests only. Game drives $30 per person. Petrol. FB ⑦ low, ⑧ high.

"Drivers' bandas", Ol Tukai area. If you haven't got a vehicle and get dropped off at Ol Tukai, this is the sneaky cheapie, but needs a lot of tact and persuasion before you get admitted, and even then if the management suspect you have money, you'll be obliged to stay in a lodge. Tour drivers pay dirt-cheap B&L-type rates, and once in, you can eat cheaply in the drivers' canteen, and make friends in their bar – a more enlivening experience than the luxury lodges – and you may even be able to arrange a reasonably priced game drive. ①.

Ol Tukai Lodge, Ol Tukai area (☎0302/22623, 22253, fax 22280; reservations through Block Hotels, p.48). The most expensive of Amboseli's three lodges, and deservedly so: built in 1996, with stylish "rustic-safari" architecture, friendly staff (not too formal), and good wooden cottages looking out beyond the fence towards the Amboseli plains (but not Kilimanjaro). Two cottages are designed for the disabled, and there's good access throughout. Nice pool, and educational videos and Maasai dancers most evenings. The headquarters of Cynthia Moss's Amboseli Elephant Research project are nearby. Game drives $35 per person. FB ⑥ low, ⑧ high.

Tortilis Camp, outside the southern park boundary at Kitirua (reservations through Cheli & Peacock Safaris, p.48). This luxury camp has seventeen double "tents" (ie double beds on concrete floors under wicker roofs with en-suite bathroom), with all the amenities you'd expect in a five-star city hotel. Set atop a low hill, it gives stunning views of Kilimanjaro and northern Tanzania as far as Mount Meru. The pool at sunset is quite something, and there's a feeling of intimacy with the wildlife. The camp is managed as a conservation project, which includes paying a proportion of your fee to local Maasai, and the possibility of (unduly expensive) visits to a Maasai *enkang*. Laudable aims, but makes you wonder where the rest of the money ($326 double in high season) is going. Game drives $110 per person/day. FB ⑧ low ⑨ high.

Camping

There are no **campsites** within the park, and only one outside it (Ksh600 per person), accessed from the signposted tracks leading west from *Amboseli Serena Lodge* or south

MAASAI VOICES

The following excerpts are from interviews with Muriankha, at Olgirra Cultural Boma near Tsavo West National Park; Olurei, a Maasai elder from a group ranch near Oloitokitok; Metoe ole Loombaa, a group ranch member near Amboseli National Park; and Ntoros ole Baari, a Maasai elder from the Loita Hills. The interviews, which have been edited but not changed in style or tone from the original translations, were conducted by Ruth McCoy in January 1993. They have subsequently appeared in *No Man's Land* by George Monbiot (see "Books, p.648).

TOURISTS

What is tourism doing to Maasai culture?

Ntoros ole Baari: It is doing a lot of damage; much of Maasai culture is now being tailored to suit the interests of tourists, much of it is fake. Tourists bring a lot of changes to Maasai society, many of which are negative and difficult to cope with. Tourism does provide some financial benefits and cannot be dismissed completely, but we must aim to have culture-friendly tourism.

What do the Maasai feel about being photographed?

Ntoros ole Baari: We don't like it but are forced to accept it as a kind of business. We hate the idea of someone capturing our image for nothing, and sometimes we aren't even prepared for it. People may use our photographs in questionable ways, putting them to uses to which we haven't consented.

WILDLIFE

Would you prefer it if there were no wild animals on your land?

Olurei: Isn't it true that they have their place – the Amboseli National Park? If too many of them come out here and eat our grass, that's bad, but the pastoralists like having some animals around, depending on which ones and the numbers of them. The ones that compete for food with our cattle are the wildebeest and zebra. They bring many other problems, especially when the wildebeest are calving. If their afterbirth enters drinking water or falls on the grass, it can kill cattle through malignant catarrh. Nothing can cure it. It can be devastating. Likewise, when the antelopes give birth, the goats get a sickness of the nose and mouth. This can be very severe as well. And the lions cause us a lot of trouble. From July to September they harass our animals a lot as all the other wildlife has gone into the park.

What do you say to the conservationists who are trying to increase the numbers of wild animals in Maasai-land?

Olurei: It would be really good to have the elephants and rhinos back – there have been very few in recent years. The elephants break down trees, adding to the grass and they dig water holes far from the river where the livestock can water, so they're friends of the herders. And rhinos keep back the thorn bush. But wildebeest and zebra, we don't need any more of them.

The authorities have argued that the Maasai have had to leave Amboseli because they were causing too much damage . . .

Metoe ole Loombaa: No. The Maasai have coexisted with wildlife for a long time and have never caused any damage. We don't eat wildlife, so we never hunt. The manure our cattle were leaving in the park was making the vegetation grow. Now it's completely destroyed and the animals are following us to our ranch to follow our livestock. The park was better off when we were there – you could find rhinos and lions there. But now all the animals have moved out. Poaching was less when we were there.

THE GOVERNMENT AND PARK AUTHORITIES

What problems have the wildlife around Tsavo West National Park caused you?

Muriankha: They've caused a lot of damage. The lions have killed people and are taking livestock. You can see my leg: this was bitten off below the knee by a lion. The weapon we had to protect ourselves was a spear. Now the government doesn't allow us to use it to protect ourselves from wild animals. Sometimes elephants come through here, and although they have not killed anyone, they have done all the damage to our village imaginable. We're helpless; we don't get any assistance. We have to walk a long way to report incidents to the game rangers, and they sometimes come when the animal has already gone.

Has the creation of the Amboseli National Park been a good thing or a bad thing for the Maasai?

Olurei: It's a very bad mistake. The park is where all the animals are in the dry season because of the swamps and the river. But then in the rains, all the animals are out and eat our grass, and only go back into the park in the dry season. The wild animals have a grazing reserve but we don't. I have asked the government to let us in and just recently some conservation people have come and talked to us, but it's the first time they have listened to us. When one of my friends tried to graze in the park, he was grabbed, jailed and fined heavily. They forget the park was made out of our land.

Has the Kenya Wildlife Service done anything in Amboseli to mitigate the effects?

Metoe ole Loombaa: There is no policy of allowing us into the park in times of need. It's all a matter of negotiation, depending on the warden of the day.

Will revenue-sharing and tourist money compensate you?

Metoe ole Loombaa: No, it is not enough compensation as we've lost property and human life. Revenue-sharing can't compare. We're not being helped to earn anything from tourism. KWS isn't assisting us. The problems we are facing cannot be valued against money.

Do you agree with conservationists who say that wildlife and livestock compete in the Mara?

Ntoros ole Baari: The land could easily accommodate both the livestock and wildlife. There are as many wild animals on the Maasai lands as in the reserve. Livestock and wildlife are complementary; wildlife follows the pastoralists' cows wherever they go for their security, as the cows keep the grass down.

What has happened to the Maasai kept out of the Mara?

Ntoros ole Baari: The Maasai are forced to overgraze as so much of their land has been reduced by conservation. By keeping the Maasai out of the reserve, conservationists are in fact contributing to the threat to the environment.

Who in your opinion benefits from the Tsavo West National Park?

Muriankha: It's the government that benefits, as it is a source of permanent income for it during the dry and wet seasons. Those who own the tourist companies and hotels also benefit; the people who live on the land surrounding the park don't benefit and that's what we've been trying to tell the government: we too should benefit from wildlife because we are losing a lot from it, and our livestock is just as crucial to us as wildlife is to the government.

from Observation Hill. It's a fine, wooded site, though no longer overrun with wildlife since it was partially fenced. Apart from warm sodas, a couple of toilets are the only facilities, and even water supplies are unreliable. You're also likely to be hassled by Maasai looking to pose for pictures, offering trinkets or visits to their *enkangs*, or simply demanding cash.

Exploring the park

Small enough to cover easily in two or three game drives in a single day, most of Amboseli is open country with good visibility. Because of this, you escape the nagging feeling you may get in other parks, that you may be in the wrong place and *that's* why you're not seeing any animals – here, you can look everywhere.

A good first stop is **Observation Hill**. Early in the morning, with Kilimanjaro a pervasive sky-filler to the south, the swamps of **Enkongo Narok**, replenished underground from the mountain top, are looped out in a brilliant emerald sash beneath. You can get out and walk around up here, and chat with the heavily armed wardens posted there supposedly to keep a watch on poachers.

There's always a concentration of animals along the swamps and the drivable tracks which closely follow their fringes. The swamps are permanent enough to keep **hippo** here all year and there are hundreds of **elephant** and **buffalo**, plus, predictably, a raucous profusion of **birdlife**. **Lake Kioko**, between Lake Amboseli and Ol Tukai – most easily seen along the track between junctions 21 and 26, is a special oasis, and **Olokenya swamp** with its seasonal lakes north and east of Ol Tukai, is always worth slow exploration, and contained several thousand flamingo at the last visit.

Lions are very rare but **cheetahs** are seen fairly frequently in the woods a little further south and there must be thousands of **giraffe** among the acacias. Look out, too, for the beautifully formed, rapier-horned **fringe-eared oryx** antelope, and **gerenuk** stretching up to forage in the trees.

The open plains are scoured by **zebra** and haphazard, solitary **wildebeest**. The two species are often seen together – a good deal from the zebras' point of view because in a surprise attack the predator usually ends up with the less fleet-footed wildebeest. There are tail-flicking **gazelle** out here, too: the open country provides good protection against lion or cheetah ambushes.

Lastly, if you need a fix of local culture, opinions vary widely about the **Maasai cultural bomas** which are set up just outside the park west of *Amboseli Serena Lodge* (between junctions 33 and 34): after paying a fee (which varies greatly with your perceived ability to pay, from between Ksh300 and $30 per person), you get the right to take as many pictures as you want, and may be treated to a display of traditional dancing, whilst the Maasai get the right to pitch their curios at you with practised persistence. Incidentally, much of the jewellery offered is neither made nor worn by Maasai: only the leather-and-beadwork necklaces and pendants are.

Kimana, Oloitokitok and points onwards

Once in the park, you shouldn't have too much difficulty lining up lifts onwards. If you're **driving**, there are two routes **east out of Amboseli**. One heads through **Eremito Gate** (Iremito, or Lemboti) towards the **Chyulu Hills**, then winds south to Tsavo West along the spine of the lava ridge -- definitely 4WD unless you're feeling reckless. The Chyulus are favourite caving country with long, safe explorations possible. The Cave Exploration Group of East Africa found **Leviathan Cave** here, the longest and deepest lava tube in the world. Before reaching the Chyulus, this route crosses the main C102 *murram* road from Emali (p.344) on the Mombasa highway to Oloitokitok (p.379) at **Makutano**, a tiny featureless Maasai trading centre. There's no problem with the Emali–Oloitokitok road in dry weather, but take care in the wet (4WD only), as it acquires some extremely tricky mud patches, and gets very slippery towards Oloitokitok. There's daily but not terribly frequent **public transport** along this road in both directions.

The second, and more travelled, road (the C103) leaves Amboseli in the southeast through **Kimana Gate** (also called Olkelunyiet), passing the roadstead of **KIMANA** at the junction with the C102 Emali–Oloitokitok road. *Romunja B&L* here has basic rooms (①). As a result of concerns about **security**, you still have to travel in convoy with an official vehicle or armed guard to Tsavo West, although there hasn't been an incident since the early 1990s. The latest schedule is thrice-daily departures in either direction (8.30am, 10.30am & 2.30pm from Ol Tukai and Tsavo's Chyulu Gate; 2–4hr). Otherwise, you can pick up an escort at Ol Tukai, but he'll expect payment. It's possible to circumvent this arrangement if you're headed for Oloitokitok and Taveta, or up the C102 to Emali.

Twelve kilometres out of Amboseli along the C103 is the 200-bed *Kilimanjaro Buffalo Lodge* (☎0302/22263–5; reservations through Kilimanjaro Safari Club, p.49; ⑥ low, ⑦ high). Situated on a substantial Maasai estate, the aim, like *Tortilis Camp*, is for "culture-friendly" tourism: local Maasai are involved in the lodge's management, and provide staff, guides, lectures and dance performances, as well as benefiting directly from receipts. The gardens are landscaped with acacia, pepper and blue gum trees; microlight flights are available over Amboseli from their airstrip, and there's a pool. The highlight is "Hemingway's Viglia" perched high above the property, which offers views over Kilimanjaro, a watering hole and the Chyulu Hills. Accommodation is varied, some with views over Kilimanjaro, others with fireplaces, still others in Maasai-style cottages. It's generally clean but check the bed linen, and the mosquito nets for holes.

Turning left at Kimana, a ten-kilometre drive down the C102 takes you to the sign-posted turning to the **Kimana Community Wildlife Sanctuary** (PO Box 362 Oloitokitok; daily 6.30am–7pm; $10). This is one of a growing number of Maasai group-ranch ventures setting aside land for wildlife conservation and tourism; self-imposed restrictions prohibit any livestock grazing or settlement except in times of severe drought. The 41 square kilometre site was demarcated in 1994 and opened in 1996, helped along by a £10,000 grant from Kuoni Travel, and is advised by the environmental group Friends of Conservation (p.67). The habitat includes plains, acacia woodland, and a wetland area watered by springs whose water holes are frequented by lion, leopard, cheetah and hyena as well as antelope. There are three **campsites** in the sanctuary, the best signposted "Kimana Leopard Camp" from the main road. Two kilometres further up the C102 (1km short of Isinet roadstead), outside the sanctuary but still on ranch land, is the large 112-bed **Kimana Lodge** (☎0302/22258–60; reservations through Kilimanjaro Safari Club, p.49; ⑤ low, ⑦ high; game drives $28 per person), with accommodation in two-room wooden cottages, and the attractions of a hippo pool and a nearby natural spring, which sees the occasional leopard turning up for the meat-bait laid out at night (there are spotlights). The price includes nature walks to the Sinnet Springs.

Oloitokitok and the road to Taveta

Branching off the C103 between the parks at Kimana, you can climb south 15km up the slippery C102 to the Maasai country town of **OLOITOKITOK** right on the border with Tanzania, with Kilimanjaro's jagged satellite peak Mawenzi dead ahead. Oloitokitok (pronounced "Loytoktok") should be nothing to get excited about – just an interesting, bustling little town by the Amboseli–Tsavo circuit. But it is ignored by 99 percent of the tourist minibuses, and it's in a fabulous position, closer to Kilimanjaro than anywhere else in Kenya and high above the plains (altitude 1700m). It is a relaxed and recommended place to settle into if you're interested in finding out more about the Maasai, as this is their easternmost major centre. Oloitokitok is also a border crossing for the Tanzanian town of Moshi a couple of hours away, nestled behind the mountain. And it's close to Kilimanjaro's Kibo Peak, 25km as the crow flies: you can arrange climbing tours up the mountain at *Kibo Slopes Cottages*, and there are enough willing guides and porters in the village, but don't get caught in Kilimanjaro National Park without having paid the fee. The Tanzanians take the offence extremely seriously.

On Tuesdays and Saturdays, when many Maasai are in Oloitokitok centre for the **weekly markets**, there's a fair amount of *matatu* traffic between here and Emali, as well as a service to Taveta (some leave the day before to get to Oloitokitok). At other times, you will have to take potluck with transport – start early. Oloitokitok has a petrol station, a post office and KCB bank (which takes ages to change money), as well as a few **B&Ls** at the top of the hill near the market. Best of these is the Christian-run *Safari's Lodge* (PO Box 291; ☎0302/22088; ①). Otherwise, *Hilltop Lodge* (PO Box 59; ☎0302/22303; ①) and *Mawenzi Safari Inn* (PO Box 365; ☎0302/22306; ①), are both reasonable. *Mwalimu Lodge* in the lower part of town is a serious watering hole. Superior to all is the modern *Kibo Slopes Cottages* (PO Box 218; ☎0302/22091, fax 22427; B&B ④), 1km down a track to the left of the customs post, with good s/c rooms (hot running water morning and evening), some with good views, but overpriced unless you're in a larger group, when the four-bed cottages (④) make sense.

On market days, you can catch a *matatu*-bus to the town of Taveta (p.354), almost 100km away near the southwestern tip of Tsavo West National Park. The route, which skirts the border with Tanzania and the flanks of Kilimanjaro, is far off the beaten track, but scenically rewarding, as well as the shortest and fastest way to get from Amboseli to Voi on the Mombasa road. Even faster, and kinder to your vehicle if you're driving, is the tarmac road on the Tanzanian side, but it's expensive if you haven't got multiple-entry visas for both Tanzania and Kenya. On the Kenyan side, the road is unsurfaced except for the first 9km of soothing tarmac to Illasit (where the tarmac veers off right towards Tanzania: keep going straight), and often becomes impassable in the rains when the fine dust turns to mud. Leaving Oloitokitok, the landscape changes from scrubby cattle pasture to neat – if dusty – plots of sisal and maize plantations, marking the end of Maasai territory. There are only few settlements, acting as market centres for Maasai and Taveta agriculturers, but the next accommodation is 58km away at **Chumvini** (Njukini), where the dogged *Gatanga Guest House* (PO Box 53 Taveta; ☎0149/2639; ①) has some basic non-s/c rooms, a down-at-heel bar with funny murals, a butchery and *nyama choma*. From here, you'll find more frequent transport on to Taveta (daily *matatus*, and buses on Tues, Wed, Fri & Sun). Further on, 10km short of Taveta, is the wonderful aberration of **Lake Chala** – see p.354.

Maasai Mara National Reserve

Daily 6.30am–7pm; $27 per day/overnight, $10 children/students, private vehicle Ksh200, camping Ksh480 per person. Senior warden: PO Box 60 Narok (☎0305/2068 or 2268). No driving after 7pm. Speed limit 40kph. Maps: Survey of Kenya SK86 at 1cm:1km (1987) is preferable to Macmillan's Masai Mara at 1cm:1.25km (1988), but both are out of date and omit newer accommodation; the sketch map you get at the park gate is useless.

For a long list of reasons, **Maasai Mara** is the best animal reserve in Kenya. The panorama sometimes resembles one of those wild animal wall charts, where groups of unlikely looking animal companions are forced into the artist's frame. You can see a dozen different species – or more – at one time: gazelle, zebra, giraffe, buffalo, topi,

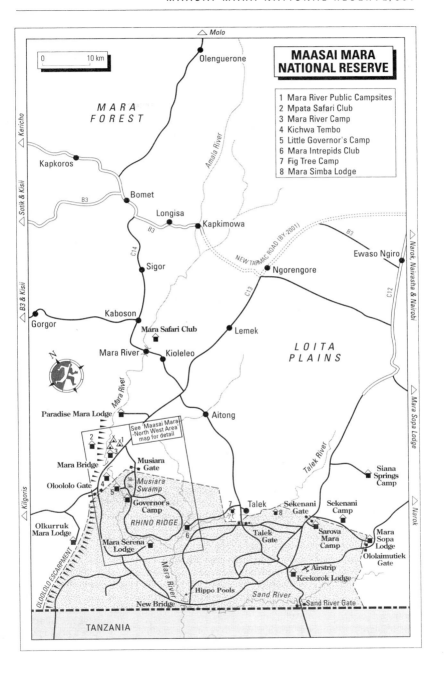

MAASAI MARA
NATIONAL RESERVE

1 Mara River Public Campsites
2 Mpata Safari Club
3 Mara River Camp
4 Kichwa Tembo
5 Little Governor's Camp
6 Mara Intrepids Club
7 Fig Tree Camp
8 Mara Simba Lodge

0   10 km

MARA
FOREST

△ Molo

Olenguerone

△ Kericho

Kapkoros

Bomet

Longisa

Kapkimowa

NEW TARMAC ROAD (BY 2001)

B3

△ Narok, Naivasha & Nairobi

Ewaso Ngiro

Sigor

C14

Ngorengore

C13

Kaboson

Gorgor

Mara Safari Club

Kioleleo

Lemek

LOITA
PLAINS

Mara River

△ B3 & Kisii

△ Sotik & Kisii

Amala River

B3

Mara River

N

Aitong

Paradise Mara Lodge

See 'Maasai Mara
-North West Area'
map for detail

2
1
3

Mara Bridge

Musiara
Gate

Talek River

Siana
Springs
Camp

Ololololo Gate

4
5

Musiara
Swamp

Governor's
Camp

7

Talek

Sekenani
Gate

Sekenani
Camp

△ Kilgoris

RHINO RIDGE

8

Olkurruk
Mara Lodge

Mara Serena
Lodge

6

Talek
Gate

Sarova
Mara
Camp

Mara
Sopa
Lodge

OLOLOLO ESCARPMENT

Mara River

Ololaimutiek
Gate

Airstrip

Keekorok Lodge

△ Narok

Hippo Pools

Sand River

New Bridge

Sand River Gate

△ Mara Sopa Lodge

TANZANIA

kongoni, wildebeest, eland, elephant, hyena, jackal, ostrich, and a pride of lions waiting for a chance.

The reserve is a great wedge of undulating **grassland** nearly 2000m above sea level, watered by one of Kenya's bigger rivers, the Mara. It is in the remote, sparsely inhabited southwest part of the country, snugged up against the border and, indeed, an extension of the even bigger **Serengeti plains** in Tanzania. This is a land of short grasses, where the wind plays with the thick, green mantle after the rains and, nine months later, whips up dust devils from the baked surface.

But Maasai Mara's climate is beneficently predictable, with ample rain, and the new grass supports an annual **wildebeest migration** of up to one and a half million animals from the dry plains of Tanzania. To travel through the reserve in August or September, while the wildebeest are in possession, is a staggering experience, like being caught up in the momentum of a phenomenal historic event. Whether you're watching this or a pride of lions hunting, a herd of elephants grazing in the marsh, or hyenas squabbling with vultures over the carcass of a buffalo, you are conscious all the time of being in a realm apart. There are few places on earth where animals hold such dazzling sway – it's as if you had found yourself in the New York of the natural world.

With its plentiful vegetation and wildlife, and heavy rainfall, the reserve's **ecology** appears at first sight to be relatively resilient to the effect of the huge number of tourists who visit it every year. However, one glance at the clouds of dust rising behind vehicles in the dry season shows up the real fragility of the place. The Mara is the most visited park in Kenya (over 2000 beds in and around the reserve, plus their vehicles), and there are signs that the balance between tourist numbers and wildlife can't be maintained much longer. In parts, erosion gullies started by off-road driving (which turns soil into dust by killing the protective cover of vegetation) has created dust bowls, which themselves begin to spread through the effects of natural wind and water erosion. Similarly, during the rains, many roads become impassable, causing a welter of parallel tracks to appear, many of them knee-deep in mud by the time the rains move on, and which take years to heal.

On entering the reserve, you'll be handed a copy of the relevant **bye-laws** and rules, which should be strictly adhered to, but which sadly in practice rarely are. The Maasai Mara is a beautiful and sensitive environment which can survive only if properly respected, but the first step should really be taken by the reserve authorities in actually bothering to enforce their regulations (at present, a lamentable *laissez faire* prevails).

Getting to the Mara

Part of the reason for the Mara's fantastic spell is its isolation: a trip here is an expedition, and you might as well plan it as such. The vast majority of visitors come on pre-booked safari packages, which invariably work out cheaper than going under your own steam.

If you're organizing it yourself, access is most straightforward, and most expensive (currently $165 return), by the scheduled daily **air services** from Nairobi (see p.143). By all accounts, the twelve-seater flights are thoroughly enjoyable, with plenty of wildlife and the pilot announcing the lodges he would like to land at in his preferred order. Most of the lodges have their own *murram* airstrips, except *Keekorok* and *Mara Intrepids Club* which have tarmac. **Airstrip transfers** to your lodge by jeep costs around $25 per person, with a minimum of four people usually required.

By **road**, however, the rewards are more intimate, including the long **drive** across the Rift Valley from Nairobi, sweeping across dry, stupendous vistas of range lands – the heart of the Maasai country. Cattle are the economic mainstay, but extensive wheat fields are pushing south. While the land often looks empty, if you stop for five minutes, chances are that someone will appear – to request something or to offer a photo pose, or just to pass the time of day.

Whilst the rest of the country's roads took a severe beating in the 1997–98 El Niño rains, the newly resurfaced B3 from Mai Mahiu junction on the old Nairobi-Naivasha road to Narok and Ewaso Ngiro (17km beyond) survived unscathed, with not a pothole in sight. Construction work is currently underway to tarmac the extension of the B3 to Kapkimolwa on the Amala River, which should finally provide year-round 2WD access from Narok to Western Kenya, and make access easier to Maasai Mara's western gates. The C12 which goes from Ewaso Ngiro to the reserve's Sekenani Gate is also being surfaced – at the time of writing, the first 40km were paved, with the remaining 40km being passable by 4WD, and by 2WD in dry weather – allow about two hours to the gate. Note however that the C88 from Naivasha which joins the B3 at Mai Mahiu is in a terrible state: more potholes than tarmac. There's one **accommodation** option at Mai Mahiu, should you get stuck hitching or *matatu*-hopping: *Mount Longonot Transit Hotel*

DRIVING HAZARDS

If you're in a low-clearance, **2WD** car, your only route in and out of the park is via Sekenani Gate, and that only in dry weather. Once in the reserve, only the eastern section (between Sekenani Gate, *Keekorok Lodge*, *Mara Serena Lodge* and *Fig Tree Camp*) is practicable. Don't even dream of trying another route – you're guaranteed to get stuck.

In a **4WD**, your options are wider, but you still have to be an experienced rough-road driver to get much further than usual 2WD territory. Access routes via Talek, Musiara and Oloololo Gates are all possible in dry weather (avoid them in wet), but even then can be exceedingly treacherous, with the main problem being frequent watery **mud pits** across the track. If at all possible, try driving around these, avoiding all areas of mud, whose smooth and apparently firm surface often disguises deep traps from which you can only hope to get towed out. A covering of vegetation usually means a relatively solid surface. If avoiding the pools isn't possible, the most common advice is to aim straight through the centre. There are two ways of tackling them, depending on their appearance. If the pool is large, first kick off your shoes and wade through the entire length of the pool to check its depth and subsurface (better getting muddy than bogged down) – if the water's less than a foot deep, and the subsurface relatively firm (ie your feet only sink in a few inches), you should be able to drive across: engage 4WD, slip into first gear, and drive slowly (but without decelerating) straight through the middle (not at the sides, as you risk getting trapped there in deep mud). Alternatively, if there's a sufficiently hard shoulder on one side, you could try driving across at speed with one wheel on it (beware of toppling over in a Suzuki) – you need good control for this. For smaller pools, gathering up speed on the approach and then barrelling across in second gear usually works, but at the risk of clogging up the carburettor.

On a **swampy black cotton soil** surface, especially during or after rain (which in practice means the land west of *Mara Serena* and *Fig Tree Camp*, and north of *Mara Serena* to Oloololo Gate), you'll need all your wits about you, as even the sturdiest 4WDs have little or no grip on this. The usual way involves a mixture of high-rev driving and luck, which leaves you open to hair-raising spins and sudden, crunching jolts, as well as the possibility of getting bogged down when you lose control. Much better might be to keep in second gear as much as possible, and keep your speed down. Try to keep at least one wheel within a well-defined rut or on more solid ground, as this makes spinning and sideways sliding less likely. Approaching deep mud is really touch and go – drive as fast as you dare (keeping control over the car), never over-steer when skidding (it'll send you into a spin and may get you bogged down), keep the accelerator pressed, and pray.

If you do **get stuck**, stop immediately (spinning the wheels will only get you even more stuck): try reversing once (rev the engine as far as it will go before engaging the gear). If this doesn't work and you don't have sand ladders, you'll just have to wait for another vehicle to pull you out.

(PO Box 9 Mahiu; no phone; B&B ②), 500m down the Narok road, has some unexceptional s/c *bandas*, plus a bar and a bad restaurant.

If you do decide to drive to the Mara, give yourself plenty of time – a good six to seven hours non-stop from Nairobi or Naivasha to the eastern end of the reserve, or all day (9–10hr non-stop) with an early start to the western end. And if you intend to do more than a tank's worth of driving, remember to stock up with cans of **petrol** at the last town you pass through (usually Narok). Although you may be able to buy petrol at one of the lodges (at a price), don't depend on it. Many only keep enough fuel for their own vehicles; others only keep diesel.

Narok

NAROK is the funnel through which almost all road transport enters the Mara. It is the last place to get fuel, a cold drink or almost anything for over 100km before you enter the reserve. First impressions aren't encouraging. *Afrikano*, on the left as you enter from the east, is a tourist trap of the first order, charging exorbitant prices for curios, food and drinks. In the same vein, over the road, a brassy atmosphere pervades the Kobil Service Station and snack bar which, being the first filling station on the way into town, waylays most of the minibuses with its big-game cut-outs, reticulated sunshades and cluster of souvenir shops selling very expensive Maasai paraphernalia (the same stuff is half the price in Nairobi). If you need petrol, the Total station on the far side of town is cheaper and less hassly. When buying petrol, watch the pump counter carefully. If you're **hitching**, the Kobil station is probably the best point to wait and ask. If the direct approach doesn't appeal (there'll be plenty of refusals), try the bridge over the Engare Narok River on the west side of town.

Petrol rip-offs, tourist bazaars and touts aside, Narok is actually quite a lively little place, full of Maasai out shopping or doing business at the market. There's also the small but perfectly formed Narok Maa Cultural Museum (daily 9am–6pm; PO Box 868 Narok; provisional ☎0305/2046; Ksh200), on the right as you come in, which is an excellent introduction to the Maasai (and Samburu) way of life. The walls have a fascinating collection of photographs taken by Maasai women, using disposable cameras given to them for the project, depicting important parts of their daily lives, such as water carrying, milking cattle, and raising children. Considering that it was the first time that any of the women had ever held a camera, the compositions are extraordinarily well-judged. The captions, too, are great: "This photo is showing a bad thing. The women have to carry the heavy water containers all the way. They have to walk for 30km to get water from the wells, because there is no dam in the neighbourhood of their *enkang*" and "This man is milking a cow that has just given birth. Normally I should have done that. It is uncommon for men to milk – they only do it when there are no women around." There are also black-and-white portraits of Maasai taken by Joy Adamson in 1951, as well as helpfully labelled everyday and magical artefacts (look out for the ovine chastity belt, used when there's not much grazing, which puts a solid leather barrier between the ram and his desire). For researchers, there's a storage room containing many more artefacts, though it isn't officially open to the public. There are advanced plans to move the museum to a purpose-built site over on the west side of the river, which may include a campsite and snake park.

PRACTICALITIES

If you're headed for the reserve but arrive in Narok after 4pm, you'll end up having to stay the night here, as you won't have the time to get to get to the reserve by nightfall (gates close at 6.30pm), at least not until the workmen finish tarmacking the road to Sekenani Gate (mid-2000 in theory, in practice unlikely). **Accommodation** is no problem as regards quantity, but quality and cost are anoth-

THE WILDLIFE
OF EAST AND
SOUTHERN AFRICA

A ROUGH GUIDE

T his field guide provides a quick reference to help you identify the larger mammals likely to be encountered in East and Southern Africa. It includes most species that are found throughout these regions, as well as a limited number whose range is more restricted. Straightforward photos show easily identified markings and features. The notes give you clear pointers about the kinds of **habitat** in which you are most likely to see each mammal; its daily rhythm (usually either **nocturnal or diurnal**); the kind of **social groups** it usually forms; and general **tips about sighting** it on safari, its rarity and its relations with humans.

▧ HABITAT ▧ DIURNAL/NOCTURNAL ▧ SOCIAL LIFE ☑ SIGHTING TIPS

Photographs © Bruce Coleman Picture Library. Text © Rough Guides, 1996.

PRIMATES

Baboon *Papio cynocephalus*
◪ open country with trees and cliffs;
adaptable, but always near water
◪ diurnal
◪ troops led by a dominant male
☑ common; several subspecies, including
Yellow and Olive in East Africa and
Chacma in Southern Africa; easily
becomes used to humans, frequently a
nuisance and occasionally dangerous

Eastern Black and White Colobus
Colobus guereza
◪ rainforest and well-watered savannah;
almost entirely arboreal
◪ diurnal
◪ small troops
☑ troops maintain a limited home territory,
so easily located, but can be hard to see at
a great height; not found in Southern
Africa

Patas Monkey *Erythrocebus patas*
◪ savannah and forest margins; tolerates
some aridity; terrestrial except for sleeping
and lookouts
◪ diurnal
◪ small troops
☑ widespread but infrequently seen; can run
at high speed and stand on hind feet
supported by tail; not found in Southern
Africa

Vervet Monkey *Cercopithecus aethiops*
◪ most habitats except rainforest and arid
lands; arboreal and terrestrial
◪ diurnal
◪ troops
☑ widespread and common; occasionally a
nuisance where used to humans

White-throated or Sykes' Monkey/Samango
Cercopithecus mitis/albogularis
- ◩ forests; arboreal and occasionally terrestrial
- ◩ diurnal
- ◩ families or small troops
- ☑ widespread; shyer and less easily habituated to humans than the Vervet

Aardvark *Orycteropus afer*
- ◩ open or wooded termite country; softer soil preferred
- ◩ nocturnal
- ◩ solitary
- ☑ rarely seen animal, the size of a small pig; old burrows are common and often used by warthogs

Spring Hare *Pedetes capensis*
- ◩ savannah; softer soil areas preferred
- ◩ nocturnal
- ◩ burrows, usually with a pair and their young; often linked into a network, almost like a colony
- ☑ fairly widespread rabbit-sized rodent; impressive and unmistakable kangaroo-like leaper

Crested Porcupine
Hystrix africae-australis
- ◩ adaptable to a wide range of habitats
- ◩ nocturnal and sometimes active at dusk
- ◩ family groups
- ☑ large rodent (up to 90cm in length), rarely seen, but common away from croplands, where it's hunted as a pest

PRIMATES – AARDVARK – RODENTS

Bat-eared Fox *Otocyon megalotis*
◫ open country
◫ mainly nocturnal; diurnal activity increases in cooler months
◫ monogamous pairs
☑ distribution coincides with termites, their favoured diet; they spend many hours foraging using sensitive hearing to pinpoint their underground prey

Black-backed Jackal *Canis mesomelas*
◫ broad range from moist mountain regions to desert, but drier areas preferred
◫ normally nocturnal, but diurnal in the safety of game reserves
◫ mostly monogamous pairs; sometimes family groups
☑ common; a bold scavenger, the size of a small dog, that steals even from lions; black saddle distinguishes it from the shyer Side-striped Jackal

Hunting Dog or Wild Dog
Lycaon pictus
◫ open savannah in the vicinity of grazing herds
◫ diurnal
◫ nomadic packs
☑ extremely rare and rarely seen, but widely noted when in the area; the size of a large dog, with distinctively rounded ears

Honey Badger or Ratel
Mellivora capensis
◫ very broad range of habitats
◫ mainly nocturnal
◫ usually solitary, but also found in pairs
☑ widespread, omnivorous, badger-sized animal; nowhere common; extremely aggressive

African Civet *Civettictis civetta*

■ prefers woodland and dense vegetation

■ mainly nocturnal

■ solitary

☑ omnivorous, medium-dog-sized, short-legged prowler; not to be confused with the smaller genet

Common Genet *Genetta genetta*

■ light bush country, even arid areas; partly arboreal

■ nocturnal, but becomes active at dusk

■ solitary

☑ quite common, slender, cat-sized omnivore, often seen at game lodges, where it easily becomes habituated to humans

Banded Mongoose *Mungos mungo*

■ thick bush and dry forest

■ diurnal

■ lives in burrow colonies of up to thirty animals

☑ widespread and quite common, the size of a small cat; often seen in a group, hurriedly foraging through the undergrowth

Spotted Hyena *Crocuta crocuta*

■ tolerates a wide variety of habitat, with the exception of dense forest

■ nocturnal but also active at dusk; also diurnal in many parks

■ highly social, usually living in extended family groups

☑ the size of a large dog with a distinctive loping gait, quite common in parks; carnivorous scavenger and cooperative hunter; dangerous

WEASEL RELATIVES • SPOTTED HYENA

Caracal *Caracal caracal*

open bush and plains; occasionally arboreal

mostly nocturnal

solitary

✔ lynx-like wild cat; rather uncommon and rarely seen

Cheetah *Acionyx jubatus*

savannah, in the vicinity of plains grazers

diurnal

solitary or temporary nuclear family groups

✔ widespread but low population; much slighter build than the leopard, and distinguished from it by a small head, square snout and dark "tear mark" running from eye to jowl

Leopard *Panthera pardus*

highly adaptable; frequently arboreal

nocturnal; also cooler daylight hours

solitary

✔ the size of a very large dog; not uncommon, but shy and infrequently seen; rests in thick undergrowth or up trees; very dangerous

Lion *Panthera leo*

all habitats except desert and thick forest

nocturnal and diurnal

prides of three to forty; more usually six to twelve

✔ commonly seen resting in shade; dangerous

Serval *Felis serval*
- ⊠ reed beds or tall grassland near water
- ⊠ normally nocturnal but more diurnal than most cats
- ⊠ usually solitary
- ☑ some resemblance to, but far smaller than, the cheetah; most likely to be seen on roadsides or water margins at dawn or dusk

Rock Hyrax or Dassie *Procavia capensis*
- ⊠ rocky areas, from mountains to isolated outcrops
- ⊠ diurnal
- ⊠ colonies consisting of a territorial male with as many as thirty related females
- ☑ rabbit-sized; very common; often seen sunning themselves in the early morning on rocks

African Elephant *Loxodonta africana*
- ⊠ wide range of habitats, wherever there are trees and water
- ⊠ nocturnal and diurnal; sleeps as little as four hours a day
- ⊠ almost human in its complexity; cows and offspring in herds headed by a matriarch; bulls solitary or in bachelor herds
- ☑ look out for fresh dung (football-sized) and recently damaged trees; frequently seen at waterholes from late afternoon

CATS – HYRAX – ELEPHANT

Black Rhinoceros *Diceros bicornis*

◪ usually thick bush, altitudes up to 3500m

◪ active day and night, resting between periods of activity

◪ solitary

☑ extremely rare and in critical danger of extinction; largely confined to parks where most individuals are known to rangers; distinctive hooked lip for browsing; small head usually held high; bad eyesight; very dangerous

White Rhinoceros *Ceratotherium simum*

◪ savannah

◪ active day and night, resting between periods of activity

◪ mother/s and calves, or small, same-sex herds of immature animals; old males solitary

☑ rare, restricted to parks; distinctive wide mouth (hence "white" from Afrikaans *wijd*) for grazing; large head usually lowered; docile

Burchell's Zebra *Equus burchelli*

◪ savannah, with or without trees, up to 4500m

◪ active day and night, resting intermittently

◪ harems of several mares and foals led by a dominant stallion are usually grouped together, in herds of up to several thousand

☑ widespread and common inside and outside the parks; regional subspecies include *granti* (Grant's, East Africa) and *chapmani* (Chapman's, Southern Africa, right)

Grevy's Zebra *Equus grevyi*

◪ arid regions

◪ largely diurnal

◪ mares with foals and stallions generally keep to separate troops; stallions sometimes solitary and territorial

☑ easily distinguished from smaller Burchell's Zebra by narrow stripes and very large ears; rare and localized but easily seen; not found in Southern Africa

Warthog *Phacochoerus aethiopicus*
⊠ savannah, up to an altitude of over 2000m
⊠ diurnal
⊠ family groups, usually of a female and her litter
✓ common; boars are distinguishable from sows by their prominent face "warts"

Hippopotamus *Hippopotamus amphibius*
⊠ slow-flowing rivers, dams and lakes
⊠ principally nocturnal, leaving the water to graze
⊠ bulls are solitary, but other animals live in family groups headed by a matriarch
✓ usually seen by day in water, with top of head and ears breaking the surface; frequently aggressive and very dangerous when threatened or when retreat to water is blocked

Giraffe *Giraffa camelopardalis*
⊠ wooded savannah and thorn country
⊠ diurnal
⊠ loose, non-territorial, leaderless herds
✓ common; many subspecies, of which Maasai (*G. c. tippelskirchi*, right), Reticulated (*G. c. reticulata*, bottom l.) and Rothschild's (*G. c. rothschildi*, bottom r.) are East African; markings of Southern African subspecies are intermediate between *tippelskirchi* and *rothschildi*

WARTHOG – HIPPOPOTAMUS – GIRAFFE

African or Cape Buffalo *Syncerus caffer*

⊠ wide range of habitats, always near water, up to altitudes of 4000m

⊠ nocturnal and diurnal, but inactive during the heat of the day

⊠ gregarious, with cows and calves in huge herds; young bulls often form small bachelor herds; old bulls are usually solitary

☑ very common; scent much more acute than other senses; very dangerous, old bulls especially so

Hartebeest *Alcelaphus buselaphus*

⊠ wide range of grassy habitats

⊠ diurnal

⊠ females and calves in small, wandering herds; territorial males solitary

☑ hard to confuse with any other antelope except the topi/tsessebe; many varieties, distinguishable by horn shape, including Coke's, Lichtenstein's, Jackson's (right), and Red or Cape; common, but much displaced by cattle grazing

Blue or White-bearded Wildebeest *Connochaetes taurinus*

⊠ grasslands

⊠ diurnal, occasionally also nocturnal

⊠ intensely gregarious; wide variety of associations within mega-herds which may number over 100,000 animals

☑ unmistakable, nomadic grazer; long tail, mane and beard

Topi or Tsessebe *Damaliscus lunatus*

⊠ grasslands, showing a marked preference for moist savannah, near water

⊠ diurnal

⊠ females and young form herds with an old male

☑ widespread, very fast runners; male often stands sentry on an abandoned termite hill, actually marking the territory against rivals, rather than defending against predators

Gerenuk *Litocranius walleri*

⊠ arid thorn country and semi-desert

⊠ diurnal

⊠ solitary or in small, territorial harems

☑ not uncommon; unmistakable giraffe-like neck; often browses standing upright on hind legs; the female is hornless; not found in Southern Africa

Grant's Gazelle *Gazella granti*

⊠ wide grassy plains with good visibility, sometimes far from water

⊠ diurnal

⊠ small, territorial harems

☑ larger than the similar Thomson's Gazelle, distinguished from it by the white rump patch which extends onto the back; the female has smaller horns than the male; not found in Southern Africa

Springbok *Antidorcas marsupalis*

⊠ arid plains

⊠ seasonally variable, but usually cooler times of day

⊠ highly gregarious, sometimes in thousands; various herding combinations of males, females and young

☑ medium-sized, delicately built gazelle; dark line through eye to mouth and lyre-shaped horns in both sexes; found only in Botswana, Namibia and South Africa

Thomson's Gazelle *Gazella thomsoni*

⊠ flat, short-grass savannah, near water

⊠ diurnal

⊠ gregarious, in a wide variety of social structures, often massing in the hundreds with other grazing species

☑ smaller than the similar Grant's Gazelle, distinguished from it by the black band on flank; the female has tiny horns; not found in Southern Africa

GAZELLES

Impala *Aepyceros melampus*
- ▨ open savannah near light woodland cover
- ◪ diurnal
- ▨ large herds of females overlap with several male territories; males highly territorial during the rut when they separate out breeding harems of up to twenty females
- ☑ common, medium-sized, no close relatives; distinctive high leaps when fleeing; the only antelope with a black tuft above the hooves; males have long, lyre-shaped horns

Red Lechwe *Kobus leche*
- ▨ floodplains and areas close to swampland
- ◪ nocturnal and diurnal
- ▨ herds of up to thirty females move through temporary ram territories; occasionally thousand-strong gatherings
- ☑ semi-aquatic antelope with distinctive angular rump; rams have large forward-pointing horns; not found in East Africa

Common Reedbuck *Redunca arundinum*
- ▨ reedbeds and tall grass near water
- ◪ nocturnal and diurnal
- ▨ monogamous pairs or family groups in territory defended by the male
- ☑ medium-sized antelope, with a plant diet unpalatable to other herbivores; only males have horns

Common or Defassa Waterbuck
Kobus ellipsiprymnus
- ▨ open woodland and savannah, near water
- ◪ nocturnal and diurnal
- ▨ territorial herds of females and young, led by dominant male, or territorial males visited by wandering female herds
- ☑ common, rather tame, large antelope; plant diet unpalatable to other herbivores; shaggy coat; only males have horns

Kirk's Dikdik *Rhincotragus kirki*

▨ scrub and thornbush, often far from water

▨ nocturnal and diurnal, with several sleeping periods

▨ pairs for life, often accompanied by current and previous young

✔ tiny, hare-sized antelope, named after its alarm cry; only males have horns; not found in Southern Africa except Namibia

Common Duiker *Sylvicapra grimmia*

▨ adaptable; prefers scrub and bush

▨ nocturnal and diurnal

▨ most commonly solitary; sometimes in pairs; occasionally monogamous

✔ widespread and common small antelope with a rounded back; seen close to cover; rams have short straight horns

Sitatunga *Tragelaphus spekei*

▨ swamps

▨ nocturnal and sometimes diurnal

▨ territorial and mostly solitary or in pairs

✔ very localized and not likely to be mistaken for anything else; usually seen half submerged; females have no horns

Nyala *Tragelaphus angasi*

▨ dense woodland near water

▨ primarily nocturnal with some diurnal activity

▨ flexible and non-territorial; the basic unit is a female and two offspring

✔ in size midway between the Kudu and Bushbuck, and easily mistaken for the latter; orange legs distinguish it; only males have horns; not found in East Africa

DWARF ANTELOPES - BUSHBUCK ANTELOPES

Bushbuck *Tragelaphus scriptus*

◪ thick bush and woodland close to water

◪ principally nocturnal, but also active during the day when cool

◪ solitary, but casually sociable; sometimes grazes in small groups

☑ medium-sized antelope with white stripes and spots; often seen in thickets, or heard crashing through them; not to be confused with the far larger Nyala; the male has shortish straight horns

Eland *Taurotragus oryx*

◪ highly adaptable; semi-desert to mountains, but prefers scrubby plains

◪ nocturnal and diurnal

◪ non-territorial herds of up to sixty with temporary gatherings of as many as a thousand

☑ common but shy; the largest and most powerful African antelope; both sexes have straight horns with a slight spiral

Greater Kudu *Tragelaphus strepsiceros*

◪ semi-arid, hilly or undulating bush country; tolerant of drought

◪ diurnal when secure; otherwise nocturnal

◪ territorial; males usually solitary; females in small troops with young

☑ impressively big antelope (up to 1.5m at shoulder) with very long, spiral horns in the male; very localized; shy of humans and not often seen

Lesser Kudu *Tragelaphus imberbis*

◪ semi-arid, hilly or undulating bush country; tolerant of drought

◪ diurnal when secure; otherwise nocturnal

◪ territorial; males usually solitary; females in small troops with young

☑ smaller than the Greater Kudu; only the male has horns; extremely shy and usually seen only as it disappears; not found in Southern Africa

Gemsbok *Oryx gazella gazella*

◪ open grasslands; also waterless wastelands; tolerant of prolonged drought

◪ nocturnal and diurnal

◪ highly hierarchical mixed herds of up to fifteen, led by a dominant bull

✔ large antelope with unmistakable horns in both sexes; subspecies *gazella* is one of several similar forms, sometimes considered separate species; not found in East Africa

Fringe-eared Oryx *Oryx gazella callotis*

◪ open grasslands; also waterless wastelands; tolerant of prolonged drought

◪ nocturnal and diurnal

◪ highly hierarchical mixed herds of up to fifteen, led by a dominant bull

✔ the *callotis* subspecies is one of two found in Kenya, the other, found in the northeast, being *Oryx g. beisa* (the Beisa Oryx); not found in Southern Africa

Roan Antelope *Hippotragus equinus*

◪ tall grassland near water

◪ nocturnal and diurnal; peak afternoon feeding

◪ small herds led by a dominant bull; herds of immature males; sometimes pairs in season

✔ large antelope, distinguished from the Sable by lighter, greyish colour, shorter horns (both sexes) and narrow, tufted ears

Sable Antelope *Hippotragus niger*

◪ open woodland with medium to tall grassland near water

◪ nocturnal and diurnal

◪ territorial; bulls divide into sub-territories, through which cows and young roam; herds of immature males; sometimes pairs in season

✔ large antelope; upper body dark brown to black; mask-like markings on the face; both sexes have huge curved horns

ORYXES · ROAN ANTELOPE · SABLE ANTELOPE

Grysbok *Raphicerus melanotis*

🔲 thicket adjacent to open grassland

🔲 nocturnal

🔲 rams territorial; loose pairings

✔ small, rarely seen antelope; two subspecies, Cape (*R. m. melanotis*, South Africa, right) and Sharpe's (*R. m. sharpei*, East Africa); distinguished from more slender Steenbok by light underparts; rams have short horns

Oribi *Ourebia ourebi*

🔲 open grassland

🔲 diurnal

🔲 territorial harems consisting of male and one to four females

✔ localized small antelope, but not hard to see where common; only males have horns; the Oribi is distinguished from the smaller Grysbok and Steenbok by a black tail and dark skin patch below the eye

Steenbok *Raphicerus campestris*

🔲 dry savannah

🔲 nocturnal and diurnal

🔲 solitary or (less often) in pairs

✔ widespread small antelope, particularly in Southern Africa, but shy; only males have horns

Klipspringer *Oreotragus oreotragus*

🔲 rocky country; cliffs and kopjes

🔲 diurnal

🔲 territorial ram with mate or small family group; often restricted to small long-term territories

✔ small antelope; horns normally only on male; extremely agile on rocky terrain; unusually high hooves, giving the impression of walking on tiptoe

er matter. The main *wazungu* den is the shamelessly overpriced *Mpatiany Inn* (PO Box 800; ☎0305/2277, fax 2298; B&B ③), diagonally opposite the market near the mosque, with reasonably modern s/c rooms, hot water in the mornings, and a weirdly funky bar downstairs smooth on soul. Better value, but also overpriced, is the *Transit Hotel* (PO Box 384; ☎0305/2288; ③), opposite the Kobil station, with safe parking but so-so food. A little further up on the same side, also with parking, is the four-storey *Nenkai Plaza Lodging & Restaurant* (no phone; ②), with s/c but rather grubby rooms. Better value is *Kanga Lodge* (no phone; lower end of ②) at the west end of town (turn right at the Agip station and *matatu* stage), with simple but acceptable rooms. Another cheap and basic option is the *Rainbow Café B&L* (PO Box 82; ☎0305/2373; ②), beside the mosque. You can **camp** at the *Members Club* (PO Box 4 Narok; ☎0305/2383; Ksh200), 1km west of the Agip petrol station, which also has a few cheap and basic non-s/c *bandas* in a muddy site (①). Security is uncertain, as there's a rather rough bar here.

For **food and drink**, *Mpatiany* is a safe bet, but otherwise unremarkable. *Mara Bar & Restaurant*, after the post office on the main road, is cheap and has a pleasant first-floor balcony from which to watch the commotion in the street. On the same side, *Hillside Cave Day & Night Club* does good chicken and *kienjeji*, and at night features a bizarre mix of traditionally-garbed Maasai and westernized Kenyans drinking and listening to reggae. A similarly eclectic dive is the *High Life Day & Night Club*, opposite the mosque, which inevitably attracts all the low life. The *Three In One Bar & Restaurant* on the main road features live music at weekends. Barclays Bank (Mon–Fri 9am–3pm, Sat 9–11am) and the **post office** are both on the main road. If you want cheap **beer** in the Mara, stock up now (you'll have to truck back the empties to reclaim the deposit).

Alternative routes to Narok: over the Mau Escarpment

From Lake Naivasha (at the end of the lake road tarmac by Kongoni police station), and **from Nakuru via Njoro**, steep roads twist up over the **Mau Escarpment**. If you're starting out **from further west** you can also get to Narok by the gradually improving Molo–Olenguerone road (see p.253). But this latter route also allows the option of a more direct approach to the west end of the reserve (see overleaf). All these routes are for 4WD only.

The **Mau Range**, not as high but just as massive as the Aberdares, is little known and rarely visited. In the thin, clear air, Maasai and Nandi graze their cattle on luxuriant pastures, and large but steadily shrinking domains of thick, dark forest are still the home to **Okiek hunter-gatherers** (called Dorobo by the Maasai) – though many are mixing the hunt with farming and have moved to the edge of the forest tracts and the margins of Kenya's mainstream economy. It is enrapturing country and highly recommended for **hiking** if you have the time. As a preliminary to Maasai Mara, the Mau is a compelling alternative to the long rolling switchback of the main Mai Mahiu–Narok road. By **matatu**, the Nakuru–Narok route is a little easier than the other two; the village of East Mau, near the peaks, is your first destination.

There's little **accommodation** in the Mau range: **Enangiperi**, for example, roughly the halfway point, has one, very basic "lodging" (more a bed in a barn) and you may find yourself asking, or being invited, to stay with people. This can arouse suspicions in the local authorities, who are very unused to travellers in these parts and are sensitive to the arrival of strangers because of ongoing friction between local people and immigrant farmers and landlords from other parts of Kenya. The region saw some of the bloodiest **ethnic feuding** in the run-up to the 1997 elections, which displaced thousands of families. The scars will take years, if ever, to heal. This shouldn't put you off visiting the region, however – it is wonderful countryside.

Into the reserve from Narok

Once through Narok, you have a choice of routes after 17km. You could branch left for the **C12** road (new tarmac for 30km and then dirt track for 37km: it should all be surfaced within a few years if the authorities are to be believed), which makes its way south towards the Sekenani Gate and the eastern section of the reserve, where *Keekorok Lodge* and the reserve headquarters are the main human focuses. Or turn right, along the **B3** road to **Ngorengore**, for the western end of the reserve, the Mara River, and most of the other lodges and camps. Although the B3 itself (to Amala River) is easily driveable in 2WD in dry weather, this route can be treacherous and uncomfortable during or after rains, and isn't to be contemplated without a 4WD vehicle. In the wet, you're looking at five to six hours' driving and sliding from Narok to the Musiara or Oloololo gates. However, work has already started on tarmacking this road to meet up with the older tarmac at Amala River – check the situation with the *matatu* drivers in Narok. See below for route descriptions from Ngorengore to the reserve.

Into the reserve from the north and west via Bomet and Ngorengore

From Kericho, due north of the reserve, leaving the C23 Kericho–Kisii just before **Sotik**, the route goes via the fast new B3 tarmac highway to Bomet (40km). There's a fair number of *matatus* making this run but nothing much at **BOMET** when you get there. The overblown village consists of just three streets running round the back of the Mobil station, containing a small market, a few meagre *hotelis* and *dukas*, a KCB bank (Mon–Fri 9am–3pm, Sat 9–11am), post office, and three very basic and dirt cheap **lodgings**: *New Paradise Lodge* (①) is over a bar and so is loud; *Kwa-Sisi Lodge* (①) is more secure, and claims to have hot water; *Farmers House* (①), at the end of Bomet on the left just after the Mobil station, is more modern in appearance, but otherwise undistinguished.

Past Bomet, the B3, direction Narok, heads southeast; the tarmac goes just beyond the Amala River (which becomes the Mara River further downstream), although the remaining 57km of dirt track to Ewaso Ngiro, 17km south of Narok, is set to be tarmacked by mid-2000. During the day, most *matatus* only run as far as the Amala River, although there are some early-morning *matatus* from Kisii and one mid-afternoon one from Kericho for Narok. Note that there's no public transport south to the reserve from Ngorengore, and no accommodation at all until the campsites at the reserve gates, so a tent would be handy if you get stuck.

If you're driving, you can follow the unsurfaced B3 past Amala River for about 19km, then turn right at the cluster of *dukas* at **Ngorengore** onto the C13 (4WD only) for Oloololo and Musiara gates at the western side of the reserve. Unless you're an extremely experienced driver, the C13 is for dry weather only, and even then has some very dodgy patches of deep mud along the way (see the box on p.383). Alternatively, you can continue for another 44km from Ngorengore to Ewaso Ngiro and the turning onto the much easier C12 (partly tarmacked, and okay for 2WD in dry weather) for the eastern side via Sekenani Gate. Note however that if it's been raining, even 4WD vehicles find the normally easy B3 hard going, as the wet clay makes escaping from ruts more or less impossible.

It's also possible to head straight for the western side of the Mara from Bomet by turning right off the B3 onto the (unpaved) C14 for Sigor and Kaboson, but this route, though shorter, is very rough, and difficult to navigate (don't even think about it if you haven't got 4WD). You should stop regularly along the way to check with local people that you're on the right track. The first important (and *unmarked*) turning, is about 5km south of Bomet. At Kaboson the C14 continues northwest towards Kilgoris and Kisii; you need to turn off left in order to cross the Mara River and join the C13.

Into the reserve from the west via Kilgoris

From Kisii and South Nyanza, you have two options if you're driving: either going via the new Sotik–Bomet road (see opposite), or alternatively heading south to **Kilgoris** and **Lolgorien** and thence over the extremely rough Oloololo Escarpment to the gate of the same name at the far west of the reserve. Be warned, however, that this route is the worst of the lot, 4WD only, and then only scarcely passable in dry weather.

Into the reserve from Tanzania

On this last route, you're almost certain to be in a private vehicle; there's a twelve-kilometre gap between the Tanzanian formalities and the Kenya Police post at the Sand River Gate, where they'll sign you in and tell you where to go to complete formalities when you reach Nairobi. If you need to change money, there's *Keekorok Lodge*, 10km away, which will do so for you (full details on p.391), but the exchange clerks there have been known to limit this to an unhelpfully small amount like $20, unless you're going to stay at the lodge.

If you're driving out of Kenya to Tanzania in your own vehicle (not a hired car, which is only permitted with certain car rental operators and explicitly stated at the time of booking), you should, if possible, check the formalities in advance at Nyayo House in Nairobi, or at a provincial headquarters like Nakuru or Kisumu. As there are no facilities at Sand River, the police there seem to like photocopies of everything to be left with them, including your log book. As they have no photocopy machine, get these done well in advance.

Camping on a budget

Travellers on a budget aren't well catered for in Maasai Mara. If you can't afford the more expensive lodges and luxury tented camps, there are very few alternatives to do-it-yourself **camping**. Although there are about half a dozen campsites within the reserve itself, access to these is virtually impossible without a guide and your own, very sturdy 4WD transport (they're marked on the *SK86 Survey of Kenya* map). However, the Mara extends far beyond the limits of the reserve, and game is usually in plentiful

---

GROUP RANCH ENTRANCE FEES

Understandably unhappy at having been forced off the reserve lands, a number of Maasai Group Ranches adjacent to the reserve recently decided to create their own **wildlife trusts**, partially supported by KWS and other bodies, primarily to milk their own share of the tourist megabucks which hitherto flowed only into the local Transmara County Council's coffers. On paper, the aims are laudible: to promote the sustainable use of the natural and cultural resources found in the region; to ensure that environmental impacts from tourism are kept at a minimum; and to ensure a more equitable distribution of benefits derived from tourism. In practice, of course, corruption and local power-politics have already come into play, but perhaps it's too early to judge how the schemes are faring.

Although there are no official gates where you can buy the tickets, all of the more upmarket tented camps and lodges situated outside the reserve now insist you buy them, whether you intend to enter the reserve proper or not. In time, it seems likely that even the budget campsites outside the gates will have a person assigned to collect the fees. At least the tickets, which should have a silver hologram set across the central tear, are also valid for the reserve itself, whilst normal reserve tickets bought at the gates are equally valid in the adjacent Group Ranch lands. The Group Ranch tickets cost the same as the reserve tickets: $27 for adults, $10 for students and children.

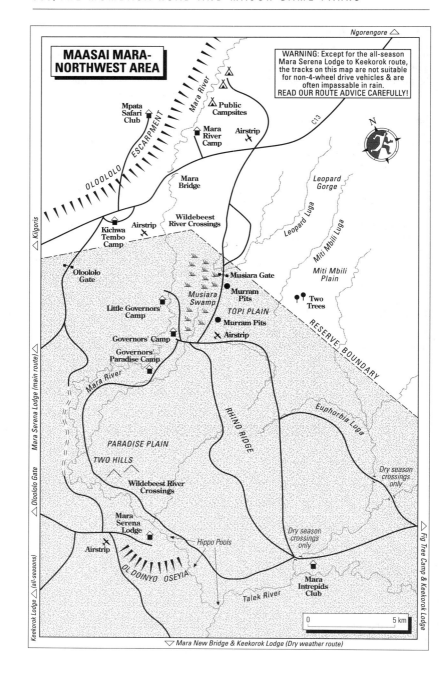

Ngorengore △

MAASAI MARA-
NORTHWEST AREA

WARNING: Except for the all-season
Mara Serena Lodge to Keekorok route,
the tracks on this map are not suitable
for non-4-wheel drive vehicles & are
often impassable in rain.
READ OUR ROUTE ADVICE CAREFULLY!

Mara River

Public
Campsites

Mpata
Safari
Club

C13

Mara
River
Camp

Airstrip

N

OLOOLOLO ESCARPMENT

Mara
Bridge

Leopard
Gorge

Leopard Luga

△ Kilgoris

Wildebeest
River Crossings

Airstrip

Kichwa
Tembo
Camp

Miti Mbili Luga

Oloololo
Gate

Musiara Gate

Miti Mbili
Plain

Murram
Pits

Musiara
Swamp

Little Governors'
Camp

TOPI PLAIN

Two
Trees

Murram Pits

Governors' Camp

Airstrip

Governors'
Paradise Camp

RESERVE BOUNDARY

Mara Serena Lodge (main route) △

Mara River

Euphorbia Luga

PARADISE PLAIN

RHINO RIDGE

TWO HILLS

Dry season
crossings
only

Wildebeest River
Crossings

△ Oloololo Gate

Mara
Serena
Lodge

Dry season
crossings
only

Airstrip

Hippo Pools

△ Fig Tree Camp & Keekorok Lodge

OL DOINYO OSEYIA

Mara
Intrepids
Club

Keekorok Lodge △ (all-seasons)

Talek River

0   5 km

▽ Mara New Bridge & Keekorok Lodge (Dry weather route)

supply north of the boundaries, where most of the campsites are found. But even this is likely to be expensive in future, as the recent introduction of Maasai **Group Ranch entrance fees** (see box) theoretically covers all of the land adjacent to the reserve.

You should remember to be particularly wary of snatch-and-run **baboon raids** at the Mara campsites – baboons are prone to grab anything inviting-looking, whether edible or not, and dash off with it to examine it later. Apparently they have a particular fondness for toothpaste but your camera bag is just as likely a target, if left within reach. You would be asking for trouble if you left your tent unguarded, either from robbery or wreckage by baboons (and probably both). Either pack up each morning or leave someone behind – perhaps a ranger if you can agree about his fee. You should also avoid irritating these loveable simians, as they have been known to attack humans when provoked.

Campsites outside the main gates are found at, clockwise from west to east: Oloololo, Musiara, Talek, Sekenani, Ololaimutiek and Sand River, and generally charge around Ksh200–400 per person per night (exceptions are noted below). Most lack even basic facilities, though drinking water may be available, and you can expect some good-natured pestering by the rangers, who will try to extract money by taking you on game drives in your vehicle – sometimes with success, other times not. With tact, you can sometimes camp in the vicinity of lodges and tented camps located outside the reserve boundaries: a low-key approach (and stressing your self-sufficiency) helps. Be careful, though, as the reserve isn't fenced, and its denizens might get curious (or hungry). The best and some of the rest are as follows.

Musiara Gate has one of the most popular sites. You can camp by a little stream and, while you're safe enough, you're almost guaranteed to hear at close quarters the spine-tingling grunting roars of the Musiara lion prides. The rangers are quite happy to have campers and, if you have your own vehicle, will often be prepared to accompany you after dark for a meal at *Governors' Camp*.

Oloololo Gate's campsite has wonderful views of the escarpment and is also very welcoming. There are three further sites (no facilities) on the east bank of the Mara River, just outside the reserve. These can be booked through the warden in Narok but in practice you can turn up and camp without making prior arrangements. They're hard to locate but better than most of Talek River's, with deep shade from the trees and fewer flies. You're more likely to have to pay Group Ranch fees here, though. There's another recognized site just downstream of *Mara River Camp* on the river bank, reached by turning sharp left before entering the camp. Some lively hippos are found here and the site has the advantage of being close to the road and near the camp. You can also camp at a spectacular vantage point near *Olkurruk Mara Lodge*, high above the reserve an hour's drive from the Oloololo Gate. This is a good site if you're arriving late from the west.

Talek Gate has a large number of campsites along the north bank of the Talek River, east of the gate. Several are the more-or-less permanent territories of camping safari operators – fetch up when a group is in and you may be able to avail yourself of facilities, water and drinks, for a small charge. There have been a few robberies here of late; read the "Security" box on p.390. *Riverside Campsite* is a public site with basic facilities five minutes' walk west of Talek Gate and the bridge, and has a kitchen, showers and latrines. Nearby, the small centre of Talek has a few *dukas* and *hotelis* (*Pilot's Inn* is apparently the best) but no petrol.

Sand River's campsite is perhaps the best, with toilets and fresh water from a stream, and it's nicely located in a spot where animals come to drink at night. The attraction is its isolation: perhaps too isolated, as there have been recent reports of robberies, and the site acquired an unsavoury reputation after the murder here of Julie Ward. The site is within the reserve, so you'll have to pay park fees.

Sekenani Gate has a number of campsites: *Sekenani Gate* campsite itself is pretty basic. Just down the track to the east of the gate, *Olperr Elongo* campsite is much better, as well as cheaper (Ksh250 per person), with toilets, showers and security, tents and equipment for hire, and the option of full-board camping for Ksh1400 per person. It might also have bicycles for hire (for use outside the reserve) at Ksh1000 for a half day. Also here, 2km from the gate, is the fenced-in *Mara Springs Safari Camp* (reservations through *Mountain Rock*, 2nd floor, Jubilee Insurance House, PO Box 40270 Nairobi; ☎ & fax 02/210051, *mtnrock@form-net.com*; $5 per person to camp, $15 per person in

---

SECURITY IN THE MARA

Considering the vast numbers of tourists who pass through Maasai Mara every year, the isolated incidents which are occasionally splashed across the tabloids worldwide – the most notorious being the murder of Julie Ward at Sand River in 1988 – are thankfully just that: isolated and extremely rare. That said, be aware that late 1998 saw a number of robberies from tented camps as well as from basic campsites in and around the Mara, in which one guard was shot dead. Security at all camps has since been stepped up, but, in the unlikely event of finding an intruder in your tent at night, the advice is simply not to resist, or else pretend to be asleep, as one tourist did. You might also consider leaving any unnecessary valuables in a Nairobi hotel safe, and conceal any you might have with you (passport, traveller's cheques etc) in a plastic bag under the tent as you sleep.

---

their tents; *bandas* ④), a little more comfortable, with hot showers, spring water, kitchen and 24-hour security, and the attraction of escorted "ecological and herbal medicine" hikes into the Naunaree hills ($7–15 per person).

Lodges and tented camps

If you're considering treating yourself, either in a safari package or independently, it's worth choosing where you stay carefully, although competition, and demanding clients, keep standards high in every price range. Pressure on the two thousand-odd beds in and around the Mara can be intense, so booking ahead is essential if you want to be sure of your camp or lodge.

With the exception of the very expensive *Mpata Safari Club*, and the cheaper *Paradise Mara Lodge*, the **lodges** and **mid-range tented camps** are all about the same price, and offer pretty much the same level of service. There's nothing intrinsically cheaper about sleeping under canvas: private bathrooms in brick, wood or concrete tent-annexes, hot showers and some remarkably good food in the middle of the wilds naturally hoist prices sky-high. Incidentally, you'll rarely find baths, even in the most expensive places – water is scarce, despite what the state of the roads might tell you, so showers are the order of the day. In the truly astronomic league, there are about half a dozen **luxury tented camps**, which are really little different from their mid-range cousins, with the exception of more pampering service and fewer guests, with game drives included in the price, but even so you'll rarely have the place to yourself despite pretensions of exclusivity. Most of the guests arrive by air, so transfers from the nearest airstrip are also included.

One common **additional cost** is **game drives** in the lodge or camp vehicles, which comes to around $35 per drive (or $70–100 for two or three). The most luxurious of the tented camps have two or three game drives worked into their full-board price. If you fancy **game drives at night** (with spotlights), you'll usually have to stay in one of the places outside the reserve, as driving inside is forbidden between 7pm and 6.30am without special permits. If you're **driving yourself**, it obviously makes most sense to go to a lodge or tented camp with optional game drives. If you have poor luck with animals in your own vehicle, you can always go out on an organized game drive. These are the camps that tend to be favoured by Kenya residents.

Note that **low season rates**, although an attractive fifty–sixty percent off the normal high season rates, usually apply only to the long rains from mid-April to the end of June, when the grass is high and animals difficult to spot. You'll also have problems driving into and around the reserve (courtesy of slippery clay and bogging black cotton soil), which makes getting a flight there and back the only dependable option, especially for places on the western side of the reserve (currently $165 return from Nairobi's Wilson Airport, see p.143).

Lodges: game drives not included

Keekorok Lodge (☎0305/2525–6, fax 2412; reservations through Block, p.48). A large and perennially busy hotel, *Keekorok* is situated in a rather open location, but a good hour closer to Nairobi by road than *Mara Serena*, its main competitor, and handy during the rainy season for access to the plains. The longest-running accommodation in the reserve, it still has high standards, but rooms vary in size and style, and though comfortable, some could do with a refit. There's a pleasant walkway round the back to a bar overlooking a small lake, where there are hippos and monkeys. Balloon flights ($360) lift off daily at 6am, and they can provide game scouts if you have your own vehicle (Ksh500 for two hours). A walk-in African buffet lunch costs $16. ⑤ low, ⑨ high.

Mara Serena Lodge (☎0305/2252, 2059 or 2137; reservations through Serena, p.50). Although the largest hotel in the reserve, this has, perhaps, fewer tour groups and is a touch less streamlined than *Keekorok*. It's located in a quieter area of the reserve and its architecture is more integrated into the surroundings. The design of the lodge is based on a re-creation of two Maasai *enkangs* with smallish but appealing cave-like rooms, up on a ridge with excellent views but little immediate wildlife appeal. Balloons again, and a pool. Reasonable value for money. Incidentally, access to Oloololo Gate is atrocious, whatever your map might say: Sekenani Gate via Keekorok Lodge is the easiest option. ⑤ low, ⑨ high.

Mara Simba Lodge (☎0305/2590 or 2051; reservations PO Box 66601 Nairobi; ☎02/444401–2, fax 444403; or PO Box 84334 Mombasa; ☎011/311093, 316474). Located 5km south of Sekenani Gate, then 7km west, on the east bank of the Talek River. The reserve's newest lodge, and the closest to a coastal resort hotel with its steep *makuti* roofs and wood-framed buildings. The rooms, in six two-storey wood and stone *bandas*, are large, AC, have great showers and views from verandahs over the river. The pool is clean but cool, and there's excellent buffet-style food (vegetarian too). A resident naturalist conducts walking safaris (and night-time game drives) outside the reserve, and there's a floodlight across the river. Downside: they have an overbooking policy, which means that singles may have to share – a bit rich given the price. Petrol. Recommended for the river views. ⑤ low, ⑨ high.

Mara Sopa Lodge (☎0305/2196–7; reservations through Kenya Holidays, PO Box 72630 Nairobi; ☎02/336088 or 336724, fax 223843). By Ololaimutiek Gate on the east side, outside the boundary, with good management. Beautiful, large *banda*-style rooms with huge bathrooms. Pool. Good location for the wildebeest migration. Most guests arrive by air. Currently ⑤ high/low. Was ⑤ low, ⑨ high.

Mpata Safari Club (☎ & fax 0305/2538; reservations through Mpata Investments Inc, 20th Floor, Anniversary Towers, PO Box 58402 Nairobi; ☎02/217017, fax 217016). Up on the northern spur of Oloololo Escarpment overlooking *Mara River Camp*, about 25km from the Mara River Bridge along a pretty dreadful track, and thus most easily accessible by plane. Twenty stone-built *bandas*, including twelve suites, designed by the architects of the *Safari Park Hotel* in Nairobi and totally out of keeping with the area. Each *banda* has, among other comforts, a private verandah and a jacuzzi from which to watch the sunset. The restaurant serves French cuisine and there's a twenty-metre pool. Obvious disadvantages are difficult access, its distance from the reserve proper, and its very high prices. ⑨.

Olkurruk Mara Lodge (☎0305/2493–4 or 2496, fax 2495; reservations through Express Travel Group, Bruce House, Standard St, PO Box 40433 Nairobi; ☎02/334722–7, fax 334825). One of the smallest lodges (small enough to be really friendly), with extraordinary views over the western half of the reserve. Very isolated on Oloololo escarpment and, if you're coming by road, not for the faint-hearted – it's a good hour up from the Mara Bridge and the two western gates, which also means that game trips down to the reserve proper are once-a-day-only or all-day affairs. Thatched, luxury *bandas*, each divided into two twin rooms (rooms no. 1 and no. 4 have the finest outlooks). No pool – as yet. ⑥ low, ⑦ high.

Paradise Mara Lodge (reservations through Safarisun Hotel Management, 7th floor, Hazina Towers, PO Box 41789 Nairobi; ☎02/229262, fax 217154). Opened in 1991, this is upstream on the Mara miles from the reserve, near *Mara Safari Club*. Good game viewing in the vicinity, but the hippos seen from the bar don't quite compensate for few elephants, or predators (cattle are widely grazed here). Rooms are adequate, but small, and there's a pool. The price, though, is almost half that of its competitors. ⑤ low, ⑥ high.

Mid-range tented camps: game drives not included

The following **tented camps** ("mid-range" is purely a relative description: nearly all are luxurious) offer optional game drives and airstrip transfers above their basic, full-board rates. A "package" including three game drives a day adds $60–100 per person per day to the bill. The less accessible western-end places can arrange road transfers from Keekorok Lodge or Sekenani Gates for around $25 per person, usually for four people minimum.

Fig Tree Camp (☎0305/2131 or 2161, fax 2131; reservations through Mada Holdings, 1st Floor, Kimathi House, Kimathi St, PO Box 40683 Nairobi; ☎02/221439 or 218321, fax 332170, *madahold@form-net.com*). Close to Talek Gate and just outside the boundary (but subject to park fees), usually accessible by 2WD in dry seasons. The location is lovely, overlooking an oxbow bend in the Talek River (tents 1–25 occasionally see animals coming to water), and it's unpretentious, which makes a welcome change from the bigger lodges, though the food's nothing special and the showers are weak. There are solid-built rooms as well as comfortable tents (the former in fragrant gardens, the latter overlooking the river), all rather closely spaced, and a small pool and fun treetop bar. Balloon flights ($385), horseback safaris ($30) and game walks ($17) are also available. The friendly, on-site balloon team can always advise on the whereabouts of local wildlife. ⑤ low, ⑦ high.

Kichwa Tembo Camp (☎0305/2465, fax 2501; reservations through Conservation Corporation, p.48). A very highly thought-of Abercrombie & Kent operation and rival to nearby *Governors' Camp* with many loyal repeat guests. Deep in the trees at the foot of the Oloololo Escarpment just outside the reserve, with excellent food and a pleasant pool, and famous for its black-tie dinners. Meryl Streep and Robert Redford stayed here while filming *Out of Africa*. Still, there's something strangely artificial about the place, in sharp contrast to *Siana Springs*, run by the same company. Due to the liveliness of the local fauna, *Kichwa Tembo* (which means "elephant's head") is fenced in. ⑦ low, ⑨ high.

Mara River Camp (☎0305/2186 or 2188; reservations through Savannah Camps and Lodges, p.50). Just outside the reserve 3–4km north of the Mara Bridge on the rough Oloololo Gate–Ngorengore road, on the south bank of the river. With more rustic facilities than most tented camps – plain but wholesome food, water heated over log fires – *Mara River Camp* is rated by enthusiastic naturalists and serious photographers and film-makers (and there's a resident ornithologist who conducts walks). There are sixteen rather closely spaced tents, all with river views: wandering hippos and occasional elephant rule out the possibility of manicured gardens or a pool. Great riverside breakfasts. ⑤ low, ⑨ high.

Sarova Mara Camp (☎0305/2386, 2194, fax 2371; reservations through Sarova, p.50). The most accessible of all the Mara camps and lodges on the main C12 entrance road, just inside the Sekenani Gate. Over seventy well-furnished tents in attractive, jungly gardens, with lily ponds full of fish and families of mongoose populating the shrubberies. Very popular, especially with locals and Indians, as they have a vegetarian menu every day for every meal. There's also a pool. A little too touristy for some, but good value so long as you don't have kids (no reductions). FB ⑤ low, ⑨ high.

Sekenani Camp (☎0305/2454, fax 2458; reservations through Chartered Expeditions Kenya, 3rd Floor, Campus Towers, University Way, PO Box 61542 Nairobi; ☎02/333285, fax 228875). On the reserve boundary 6km southeast of Sekenani Gate (which you have to pass through). Small and select, with fifteen large, very private tents on stilts snuggled up to trees, with baths as well as showers, excellent food and a personal approach. The lack of a pool and reliable electricity dismays some visitors. There's no perimeter fence, so you get escorted to and from the dining area across a rope-and-plank bridge by a spear-wielding Maasai. The camp is run in collaboration with 26 Maasai families, and the policy is to cause as little disruption to wildlife as possible. ⑤ low, ⑨ high.

Siana Springs Camp (☎0305/2553, fax 2429; reservations through Conservation Corporation, p.48). On the site of the former *Cottar's Camp* (an old Kenya residents' favourite), and co-managed with *Kichwa Tembo* – same prices, similar high standards. This complete refit (a lovely pool and sultan-esque tents with every conceivable comfort) is a determined effort to reproduce an old-style mood and manners. The main advantages here – apart from the convenient location, off the main Narok entry road – are the long-established site outside the reserve, shaded by mature trees, with elephant and leopard hides, and a good programme of walking trips in the vicinity, accompanied by a first-rate naturalist. Night game drives by spotlight outside the reserve. Don't forget to zip-up your tent. ⑦ low, ⑨ high.

Luxury tented camps: game drives included

Governors' Camp (☎ & fax 0305/2273; reservations through Governors' Camps, p.49). Located in the woods on a bend in the Mara River on the site of an old hunting camp and close to the fantastic game-viewing of the Musiara marsh (more or less impassable during the rains, as is the track up to

Oloololo Gate), *Governors'* has retained its exclusive "bush" atmosphere despite the large number of tents (38), with no expense spared. Elephants trundle through at night; guards keep watch for more dangerous visitors and escort guests between their tents and the (excellent) restaurant. No pool. Tents 1–3 have no river views, and 25–30 can be noisy. Road access is difficult at the best of times, so guests tend to fly in. Extremely high rates (currently $440 double), and derisory children's reductions. ⑨.

Little Governors' Camp (☎ & fax 0305/2040; same reservations details as main camp). Reached by a two-kilometre drive and then a rope-pulled boat across the Mara, this is the annexe from which the *Governors'* balloons fly. Hidden in the trees by its own water hole, with wonderful bird-watching, it's one of the reserve's smallest and most intimate set-ups, always fully booked in advance of the main camp. It has 27 beds, 3 of them double. No pool, and difficult disabled access (steep steps). There's also an annual encampment called Governors' Paradise Camp – which is set up between *Governors'* and *Little Governors'* in May or June after the long rains. Same rates as *Governors' Camp*. ⑨.

Mara Intrepids Club (☎0305/2168; reservations through Prestige Hotels, p.49). Thirty tents parked on a bluff overlooking the Talek River, just about accessible by road in the rains. Four-poster beds in the "tented suites". Baited leopards come daily, and there's a watchtower and swimming pool. It's also the base for the innovative Night Sight Safaris, an Israeli-run hi-tech outfit which uses ex-army infra-red video cameras and scopes to view game at night ($100 per person, $50 kids, $20 for a video tape of the night's viewing). A stylish way to dispose of your savings. ⑦ low, ⑨ high.

Mara Safari Club (☎0305/2172, fax 2105; reservations through Lonrho, p.48). Very modish tented camp, spaced out in a garden high up on a calm oxbow loop of the Mara River, but over 40km outside the reserve's Oloololo Gate along the terrible Ngorengore road. There are fifty "tents", all the last word in luxury, with four-poster beds, huge marble bathrooms, and verandahs with private views of the river. Hippos wallow and yawn in the chocolatey water below the camp (kept out of the camp by electric fences), while monkeys rampage through the trees on the opposite bank. Facilities include a heated swimming pool – at nearly 2000m not such a bad idea. Balloon flights and visits to Maasai villages are available, but way overpriced (currently $430 in high season) considering the camp's size and location. ⑨.

Around the reserve

Wherever you go there are **animals**. This is the one part of Kenya where the concentrations of game that existed in the nineteenth century can still be seen. The most interesting areas, scenically and zoologically, are **westwards**, signalled by the long ridge of the Oloololo Escarpment. If you only have a day or two, you should spend most of your time here, near the **Mara River**.

It sometimes seems that wherever there are animals there are **people** – in minibuses, in land cruisers, in hired Suzukis, often parked in ravenous, zoom-lensed packs around understandably irritable lions, leopards and cheetahs (the official limit is five vehicles around an animal at any one time, although up to sixteen vehicles (over a hundred people) have been reported around three cheetahs. This popularity is highly seasonal – it can be overbearing around Christmas – but it needn't spoil your visit. If you aren't driving yourself, encourage your tour driver to explore new areas (but not off-road) and perhaps stress you'd rather experience the reserve in its totality than tick off animal species. The reserve is crisscrossed with **tracks** but the level plains tend to encourage off-track driving. So far this hasn't had quite the damaging effect it has in Amboseli – the Mara's ecosystem is less fragile and there's more of it – but there are signs that a balance won't be maintained much longer: look at the stretch along the edge of the forest to the north of *Governors' Camp*, and read the box on "Environmental Concerns" on p.358.

Fast **roads**, with improved, hard-core surfaces and theoretically uncrossable banks and ditches alongside, have been laid in various parts of the reserve, especially the east, and there is now a good all-weather route from Talek Gate to Sekenani Gate, inside the reserve. During the rains, however, and for some weeks after, the western parts of the reserve can be very wet and treacherous. The bolder tracks on our maps

---

VICARIOUS PLEASURES

As usual, if you're not staying in luxury accommodation, a taste of the high life can be had if you drop into a **lodge** for a drink or something to eat (generally expensive: establish the price first). Some of the lodges and camps, *Keekorok* especially, get heavily invaded during the high seasons, and casual visitors have been known to abuse the lodges' hospitality, so these lodges may turn away non-residents. Changing into decent clothes probably won't help – staff know exactly who's who – but discretion and some words of Swahili might. Swimming pools are usually out of bounds. The only shops are lobby gift boutiques. If you're lucky you might find a lodge willing to sell you some fuel, though at high prices. If you don't see pumps or anticipate a refusal, go direct to the oiliest part of the staff compound and ask.

---

should be passable all year round, but the smaller tracks, especially in the northwest, are often waterlogged. Here too, the crossings over the tributaries of the Talek are often impassable: if you're trying to cross the reserve at this time of year, the downstream one, 6km north from the *Mara Intrepids Club*, is the one to aim for, as the camp's Land Rovers may be able to tow you across if the water is high – an experience in a Suzuki that's slightly more exciting than most people want. It's worth noting that the only permanent **east–west route** across the Mara is the long haul via Mara New Bridge on the southern boundary to *Mara Serena*. Heading up from *Mara Serena* to Oloololo Gate, however, the main road skirts the western edge of Olpunyata Swamp, which is completely impassable in wet weather. Similarly dreadful is the shorter but ill-defined jumble of tracks known as the New Mara Serena Road, on the eastern edge of the swamp, for which you'd definitely need a guide in wet weather, and plenty of time in dry.

Visiting Maasai villages

One diversion which you are likely to be offered, especially if you are travelling on an organized safari, is a visit to a **Maasai** *enkang*, usually called, incorrectly, a *manyatta* (see boxes, p.376 and p.396). Forget about the authenticity of tribal life: this is the real world. Many children are sick, many of the young men have fled to the fleshpots, and everyone wants your money. Unprepared and uncomfortable, most visitors find the experience a deeply depressing rip-off –$15–20 each in a group from a lodge or tented camp, or around Ksh400 per person if you arrange it yourself. If you can forget any TV-documentary illusions – and actually sit down and talk to people – the experience can be transformed and full of laughter, as it will be if you have your own children with you (see, for comparison, the accounts of similar meetings with Njemps, Samburu and Elmolo people – p.565 and p.572).

The animals

Big, brunette **lions** are the best-known denizens of the reserve and there are usually several prides living around the **Musiara Swamps**, which are dry much of the year. It is sometimes possible to watch them hunt, as they take very little notice of vehicles. While lions seem to be lounging under every other bush, finding a **cheetah** is much harder (they can often be seen on the *murram* mounds alongside the new Talek–Sekenani road). These are solitary cats – slender, unobtrusive and somewhat shy. When they move, their speed and agility are marvellous. If you are lucky enough to witness a kill (cynicism about such voyeurism is quickly dispelled when you find yourself on the spot), it is likely to take place in a cloud of dust, a kilometre from where the chase began. But cheetahs are vulnerable to too much harassment. Traditionally, they hunt at dawn and dusk (at the same times as tourists are hunting for photographs), but there is evidence that they are turning to a midday hunting pattern when the humans are shaded in the lodges – not a good time of day for the cheetah, which expends terrific energy in each chase and may have to give up if it goes on for more than thirty or forty seconds.

Leopards are rarely seen by visitors, though there are plenty of them. You can give yourself a serious case of risen hair when you come across their footprints down on the sandbanks at the edge of the Mara River outside the reserve boundary. But they are largely nocturnal and prefer to remain well out of sight. You would have to crane your neck at a lot of trees to have much chance of seeing one. Their deep, grating roar at night – a grunt, repeated – is a sound which, once heard, you carry around with you.

If you have a ranger with you, he's certain to know the current news about the **black rhinos** – every calf born is a victory – though finding them is often surprisingly difficult. Check out Rhino Ridge, where a handful of the reserve's surviving *faru* are sometimes obligingly positioned. There are also now a couple of **white rhinos** in the reserve, brought up from South Africa and closely guarded. They seem to be doing well.

Maasai Mara's other heavyweights are about in abundance. The Mara River surges with **hippo**, while big families of **elephant** traipse along the forest margins and spread out into the Musiara marshes when the herbage is thick and juicy. The park is home to an estimated thousand or so elephants, with another five hundred living in the districts beyond its boundaries. **Buffalo** are seen all over and can be menacing when they surround a small Jeep in a thundering herd of several hundred tons. It is the solitary old bulls that you need to watch out for – their reputation (and that of old rhinos) is not exaggerated. Tourists' vehicles get stoved in quite often, so always back off.

Among all these outstanding characters, the herds of humble grazers fade quickly into the background. It's easy to become blasé when one of the much-hyped "big five" (elephant, rhino, buffalo, lion, leopard) isn't eyeballing you at arm's length – but those are the hunter's trophies, not the photographer's. **Warthog** families like rows of dismantled Russian dolls, **zebra** and **gazelle**, odd-looking **hartebeest** and slick, purple-flanked **topi** are all scattered with abandon across the scene. The topi are peculiarly characteristic of Maasai Mara, and there are always one or two in every herd standing sentry on a tussock or an old termite mound. Topi and **giraffe** – whose dream-like, slow-motion canter is one of the reserve's most beautiful and underrated sights – are often good pointers for predators in the vicinity. And the reserve has rare herds of **roan antelope** – swaggering, horse-sized animals with sweeping, curved horns, that you'll see elsewhere only at the Shimba Hills National Park near Mombasa or Ruma National Park near Kisii.

THE WILDEBEEST MIGRATION

It is the annual **wildebeest migration**, however, that plants Maasai Mara in the imagination. With a lemming-like instinct, finally gelled into mass movement, the herds gather in their hundreds of thousands on the withering plains of Serengeti to begin the long, streaming journey northward following the scent of moisture and green grass in the Mara. They arrive in July and August, pouring over the Sand River and into the eastern side of the reserve around *Keekorok*, gradually munching their way westwards in a milling, unsettled mass and turning south again in October. Never the most graceful of animals, wildebeest play up to their appearance with frolicsome, unpredictable behaviour, bucking like wild horses, springing like jack-in-the-boxes, or suddenly sprinting off through the herd for no apparent reason.

The **Mara River** is the biggest obstacle they come up against. Heavy rains falling up on the Mau range where the river rises can produce a sudden brown flood which claims thousands of animals as they try to cross. Like huge sheep (they are, in fact, most closely related to goats), the brainless masses swarm desperately to the banks and plunge

THE MAASAI AND THE MARA

After deep reflection on my people and culture, I have painfully come to accept that the Maasai must change to protect themselves, if not their culture. They must adapt to the realities of the modern world for the sake of their own survival. It is better to meet an enemy out in the open and to be prepared for him than for him to come upon you at home unawares.

Tepilit Ole Saitoti, *Maasai* (Elm Tree Books).

When the first European hunting safaris made the Mara world-famous in the early years of this century, they were ransacking a region recently deserted by the Maasai. Smallpox had ravaged the Maasai communities and rinderpest had torn through their cattle herds. As a consequence, the wild animals had the region virtually to themselves. Traditionally, the Maasai hunted only lion and, in times of famine, eland and buffalo, the "wild cattle". Only the Okiek people (the "Dorobo in Maa", meaning "people without cattle") hunted for a living. The Maasai themselves had always lived in some harmony with the wildlife.

By 1961, after half a century of sport, the white hunters had succeeded in bringing the Mara's lion population down to nine and, to a chorus of alarm, the Maasai Mara Game Reserve was created, to be administered by the Maasai District Council at Narok, exclusively as a game sanctuary – and a tourist attraction. By then, improved medicine and veterinary facilities had eased the old hardships of the traditional Maasai way of life. They were expanding again, and now land was becoming the biggest issue.

Of all Kenya's peoples, the Maasai (also see "Maasai Voices", p376) have received the most attention. Often strikingly tall and slender, dressed in brilliant red cloth, with beads and metal jewellery, and the young men with long, ochred hairstyles, they have a reputation for ferocity, pampered by an arch superiority complex. Traditionally, they lived off milk and blood (extracted, by a close shot with a stumpy arrow, from the jugular veins of their live cattle), and they loved their herds more than anything else, rarely slaughtering a beast. They maintained rotating armies of spartan warriors – the *morani* – who killed lions as a test of manhood. And they opposed all interference and invasion with swift, implacable violence. Their scorn of foreigners was absolute: they called the Europeans, who came swaddled in clothing, *iloridaa enjekat* or "those who confine their farts". They also derided African peoples who cultivated for digging the earth – the Maasai even left their dead unburied – while those who kept cattle were given grudging respect so long as they conceded that all the world's cattle were a gift from God to the Maasai, whose incessant cattle-raiding was thus righteous reclamation of stolen property.

Some of this noble savagery was undoubtedly exaggerated by slave- and ivory-traders, anxious to protect their routes from the Europeans. That said, the Maasai have on the whole been stubbornly conservative, with a disinclination to change their traditional ways which has tended to mark them out as the whipping boys of Kenyan development. At the same time, something close to a cult of the Maasai has been around ever since Thomson walked *Through Maasailand* in 1883. In the early years of the colony, Delamere's obsession with the people and all things Maasai spawned a new term, "Maasai-itis", and with it a motley crop of romantic notions about their ancestors alluding to ancient Romans, Egyptians and even the lost tribes of Israel.

in. Many are fatally injured on rocks and fallen branches; others are skewered by flailing legs and horns. With every surge, more bodies bob to the surface and float downstream. Heaps of bloated carcasses line the banks; injured and dying animals struggle mournfully in the mud, while vultures and marabou storks squat in glazed, post-prandial stupor.

The migration's full, cacophonous impact is awesomely melodramatic – both on the plains where the multitudes graze and cavort, and at the deadly river crossings. This superabundance of meat accounts for the Mara's big lion population. Through it all, the

These days, the tourist industry gives the Maasai a major spot in its repertoire. Maasai dancing is *the* entertainment, while necklaces, gourds, spears, shields, *rungus* (knobkerries), busts (carved by Akamba carvers) and even life-sized wooden *morani* (to be shipped home in a packing case) are the stock-in-trade of the curio and souvenir shops. For the Maasai themselves, the rewards are fairly scant. Cattle are still at the heart of their society; there are dozens of names for different colours and patterns, and each animal among their three million is individually cherished. But they are assailed on all sides: by uplands farmers expanding from the north; by eviction from the tourist/conservation areas within the reserve boundaries to the south; and by a climate of opposition to the old lifestyle from all around. Sporadically urged to grow crops, go to school, build permanent houses, and generally settle down and stop being a nuisance, they face an additional dilemma in squaring these edicts with the fickle demands of the tourist industry for traditional authenticity. Few make much of a living selling souvenirs, but enterprising *morani* can do well by just posing for photos, and even better if they hawk themselves in Nairobi or down on the coast.

Many men persevere with the status of warriorhood, though modern Kenya makes few concessions to it. Arrested for hunting lions, and prevented from building *manyattas* for the *eunoto* transition in which they pass into elderhood, the *morani* have kept most of the superficial marks of the warrior without being able to live the life fully. The ensemble of a cloth tied over one shoulder, together with spear, sword, club and braided hair, is still widely seen, and after circumcision, in their early days as warriors, you can meet young men out in the bush, hunting for birds to add to their elaborate, taxidermic headdresses. But there is considerable local frustration. When the pasture is poor, the *morani* have little compunction about driving their herds into the reserve to compete with the wildlife. All but a few of the Mara's black rhinos have been slaughtered for their horns in the last two decades (though a few more have now been brought in from elsewhere). And there have even been isolated attacks on tourist camps in and around the reserve.

Land is the great issue today. The Maasai have still not fully come to terms with the idea of individual ownership of it, although a promising development for them has been the recent introduction of wildlife reserves run by Maasai Group Ranches (see the box on p.387), which seems at last to be providing a steady source of income from tourism. "Range schemes" – plans for growing wheat or rearing cattle – are also common now, though they are just as likely to benefit newcomers from other parts of Kenya as the local Maasai. The lifestyle is changing: education, MPs and elections, new laws and new projects, jobs and cash, all impinge on the Maasai's lives – with mixed results. The traditional Maasai staple diet of curdled milk and cow's blood is rapidly being replaced by cornmeal *ugali*. Many Maasai have taken work in the lodges and tented camps, while others end up as security guards in Nairobi. For the majority, who continue to live semi-nomadic lives among a welter of constraints, the future would seem to hold little promise. But that stubborn cultural pride – the kind of hauteur that keeps a cattle-owner thoroughly impoverished in cash terms, while he counts his 220 beasts – may yet insulate the Maasai against the social upheavals that seem certain to rock the lives of many Kenyans in the twenty-first century.

spotted hyenas scamper and loiter like psychopathic sheep dogs. Half a million wildebeest **calves** are born in January and February before the migration; two out of three perish without returning to the Serengeti.

Balloon flights

From the ground, the migration of the wildebeest is a compelling phenomenon, bewildering and strangely disturbing, as you witness individual struggles and events – in particular if you have a chance to watch near one of the river crossings. From the air, in a **hot-air balloon**, it resembles an ant's nest. At $360–400 per person for the sixty- to ninety-minute flight plus breakfast with *vin mousseux* (or a Bloody Mary, depending on how you feel) **balloon "safaris"** are the ultimate in bush chic. Just watching the inflation and lift-off at dawn is a spectacular sight, especially at *Little Governors' Camp*, deep in the woods. Balloon trips are run by several of the larger camps and lodges, including *Keekorok, Serena, Siana Springs* and *Fig Tree*. In order to avoid frightening the animals unduly, however, there is now a minimum height below which the balloons are not permitted to fly.

You don't have to be staying at the lodge they fly from: they'll come and pick you up at 5.30am. Operators include:

Adventures Aloft, for flights from *Fig Tree Camp*; reservations through Mada Holdings, 1st floor, Kimathi House, Kimathi St, PO Box 40683 Nairobi (☎02/221439 or 218321, fax 332170, *madahold@form-net.com*). Great staff. Until recently, *Fig Tree* also offered flights in a microlight, whose great advantage over hot-air ballooning was that you were free to take a trip at any time of day – not just at the crack of dawn. Currently suspended, it's worth contacting Mada Holdings in case flights have been resumed.

Balloon Safaris, for flights from *Keekorok Lodge* and *Siana Springs Camp*; reservations through Balloon Safaris Ltd, Wilson Airport, PO Box 43747 Nairobi (☎02/502850–1, fax 501424). From *Keekorok*, the prevailing winds tend to carry the montgolfiers westwards and higher: fine for a grand view, but less satisfactory for animal watching.

Mara Balloon Safaris Ltd, for flights from *Little Governors' Camp*; reservations through Governors' Camps, p.49. The most spectacular take-off site, and the only people to cook your breakfast on the balloon's burners after you land.

Transworld Kenya Ltd, for flights from *Serena Lodge*; reservations through Transworld Kenya Ltd, 5th floor, Corner House, Mama Ngina St/Kimathi St, PO Box 44690 Nairobi (☎02/333129, fax 333488, *transworld@form-net.com*).

The Samburu/Buffalo Springs/Shaba National Reserves

Daily 6.30am–6.30pm; each reserve $15 per day/overnight, $5 students/children; private vehicle Ksh200, camping $8 ($10 in a "special" campsite). District Warden (Samburu): PO Box 53 Maralal (☎0368/2053 or 2412). No driving after 7pm. Speed limit 30kph. Map: Survey of Kenya SK114 Shaba, Samburu and Buffalo Springs at 1cm:500m (1990).

Up in the north of the country, in the hot, arid lowlands beneath Mount Kenya, **Samburu National Reserve** was set up only 25 years ago, a tract of country around the richest stretch of the Ewaso Ngiro (or Uaso Ngiro) River. In this region, the permanent water and the forest shade on the banks draw plentiful wildlife in the dry season and maintain many of the less peripatetic species year-round. While the wildlife spectacle doesn't always match that of the southern parks, the peace and scenic beauty of Samburu is unquestionable and, in the kind of mood swing which only an equatorial region can produce, the contrast with the fertile farming country of the highlands just a few kilometres to the south couldn't be more striking. In the background, the sharp hill of **Koitogor** rises in the middle of Samburu Reserve, making a useful reference point. And on the horizon, 30km to the north, looms the gaunt red block of **Ol Olokwe** mountain. Head up into the scratchy bush in the south of **Buffalo Springs Reserve** and the whole region is spread out before you.

Of the popular game parks, Samburu is usually reckoned the most remote and inaccessible. This has more to do with its location than with present practicalities. On the fringes of what is still called the "NFD" (Northern Frontier District), the combined

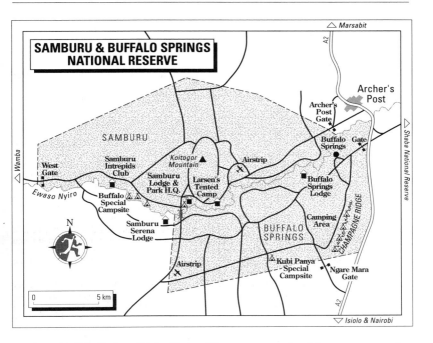

Samburu/Buffalo Springs/Shaba National Reserves were closed for many years after their creation, because of the war against Somali irredentists that flared over northern Kenya in the 1960s and early 1970s. Isolated incidents of banditry have recurred ever since, with major **security concerns** being raised during 1997–98, which saw a number of armed hold-ups of tourist vehicles as well as attacks on locals, some using guns that had apparently been rented out by home guards. Security has since been beefed up within the reserves, but the **road up from Isiolo** is still prone to occasional **banditry** – check the situation with a reputable travel agent in Nairobi, or with the police at the checkpoint just north of Isiolo. Although your chances of running into serious trouble are extremely slim, should you be unlucky enough to get on the wrong end of an AK-47, the usual rule applies: don't resist (though you might consider concealing valuables in the vehicle before leaving Isiolo).

Practicalities

In practical terms, **access** isn't difficult. If you're circling Mount Kenya, Samburu Reserve is close at hand, a couple of hours north of Nanyuki (see p.203). Buses and *matatus* run down onto the hazy plain as far as Isiolo (p.574), as does the tarmac, and, if you don't have wheels, this is normally as far as you can go without hitching, although there are one or two *matatus* which daily venture across the jolting dirt track to Archer's Post. But waiting at the Isiolo police barrier usually gets you a lift into the reserve itself in a few hours. If you're driving independently, Isiolo is a straightforward target. You may be required to wait at the police checkpoint for a convoy to form for the short continuation to the reserve: you won't wait long, as there are plenty of safari vans which cover the stretch every day.

Note that the **daily/overnight fees** chargeable in each reserve apply even if you're only in transit to the other: if you enter, you pay.

Lodges and tented camps

There are five lodges/camps in Samburu/Buffalo, and one in Shaba. They mostly offer very good low-season rates (April to July, except Easter) at fifty–sixty percent of high-season rates for doubles, dropping right down to thirty percent for singles. All prices are for full board.

Buffalo Springs Lodge (PO Box 71 Isiolo; ☎0164/20784; reservations through Motto Tours & Travel, Anniversary Towers, Loita/Monrovia St, PO Box 70739 Nairobi; ☎02/335154 or 334510). On the south side of the river in the more arid Buffalo Springs reserve, this place has fallen on hard times since the collapse of its former parent company in 1998, and when not busy it can feel a rather desolate sort of place. Things aren't helped by its increasingly tatty accommodation: the cottages are OK, but avoid the tents (same price) which are barely adequate. On the plus side, there's good game-viewing across the swamp from the bar (floodlit at night): they bait a crocodile for the cameras, just as other lodges bait leopards. Casual visitors are welcome to use the pool (Ksh200), showers, and bar. Lunch is expensive at $18 per person, but there's Samburu dancing daily at 2.30pm (Ksh200). You can also cash travellers' cheques, at a bad rate. No game drives. ⑤ low, ⑦ high.

Larsens Tented Camp (☎0164/31373–4, fax 31375; reservations through Block, p.48). East of *Samburu Lodge*, this is Samburu's smallest camp, very upmarket and highly recommended if you don't mind the vaguely snooty atmosphere common to all such places, with seventeen en-suite tents facing the river. Game drives are part of the deal, and the food is excellent. No children under seven or children's rates, and no pool (you can use the one at *Samburu Lodge*). ⑦ low, ⑨ high.

Samburu Intrepids Club (reservations through Prestige Hotels, p.49). Upstream of the other lodges and camps on the north bank, an impressive and very luxurious development, and a good deal cheaper than *Larsens*. All 25 tents are on stilts, furnished with unecological mahogany furniture, four-poster beds, fans and electricity. Also offers game drives, camel safaris and bird walks. Good value out of season. ⑤ low, ⑧ high.

Samburu Lodge (☎0164/30762, 30778, fax 30781; reservations through Block, p.48). On the north bank, beautifully located on a heavily wooded broad bend of the river as it passes near the Samburu Reserve headquarters, this is the oldest lodge in the reserves – with rooms of various standards and a pool. Despite a frenetically busy atmosphere around the riverside terraces and crocodile-viewing bars, the glorious setting is hard to fault. Excellent food. Good mechanics and fuel available. ⑥ low, ⑧ high.

Samburu Serena Lodge (☎3900 Radiocall Nairobi; reservations through Serena, p.50). On the south bank, just outside Buffalo Springs Reserve. Well managed, with a good pool and great food, but not one of Serena's best. ⑤ low, ⑦ high.

Sarova Shaba Lodge (☎0164/30638 or 0161/2467; reservations through Sarova, p.50). Downstream on Ewaso Ngiro River in the otherwise empty Shaba Reserve. Immaculate and very attractively landscaped, with a superb swimming pool (Ksh345 for casual visitors) and streams running through public areas (the thick vegetation obscures views of big animals), but the fact that the crystal-clear spring which feeds them was expropriated from the local population (a concrete well was dug for them instead) jars a little. Mosquito-netted rooms with fans, and Samburu ceremonial marriages for those tying the knot around Christmas. Excellent naturalist. Petrol. ⑥ low, ⑦ high.

Campsites

There are four public **campsites** in Buffalo Springs Reserve, not far from the main gate, Ngare Mara, but this Champagne Ridge camping area has a nasty reputation for robberies. If you do stay here, you're strongly advised to take up the offer of night guards which the rangers will probably make – or insist upon. The camps are near the main road and visits by intruders are common. As usual, you also face the hassle of having to pack your tent each day before setting off on the animal trail. If you don't have a vehicle, being dropped off at Champagne Ridge could prove painful if nobody turned up to give you a ride out again. Still, it's a pretty area among the acacias, and it abounds with giraffe and other animals. There's also one "special" campsite in Buffalo Springs – *Kubi Panya*, on the Maji ya Chumvi stream.

Three other sites lie on the north bank of the Ewaso Ngiro river in Samburu, a few kilometres to the west of the bridge and park HQ. Except for the farthest of these – *Buffalo Special* campsite, which has toilets and showers – there are no facilities.

Initially, the best move for the wheel-less is to get to the area of *Samburu Lodge* and **camp** near the park headquarters: not a wonderful site, with no toilets or running water (and the lodge may even make you pay for that commodity), but convenient and legal, if somewhat unhygienic. You can walk to the lodge's riverside bars and restaurant (though if after 6.30pm, get an escort: there are animals everywhere), sometimes flop in the pool (depending on circumstances and numbers: it's occasionally restricted to guests), gloat over the crocodiles in the river below, and peer darkly through binoculars at the regular but brief evening cabaret of leopards retrieving bait from a tree on the far bank. If your finances stretch, you can shell out $30 or so for a two-hour morning or evening game run in one of the lodge's land cruisers, or around $115 for the whole vehicle. Most people camping here without their own vehicles seem to manage to find the occasional ride around the reserve, if only because the opportunities exist to meet travellers with their own transport over a drink.

Note that the **baboons** at the campsite here are beyond being an amusement. Leave your tent and its contents only under guard. The fact that baboons sometimes fall shrill victims to crocs at the water's edge seems less distressing after a day or two spent in the area.

Exploring the reserves

Except during and immediately after the rains, scrubby bush country takes up most of the reserve district, but there are some large acacia thickets, especially in the eastern part of **Buffalo Springs**. Here, the **springs** themselves are a welcome target; these are pools of clear if weedy water, one of which has been sanitized with concrete for the benefit of swimmers and (most of the time) the exclusion of crocodiles. It's always a good idea to check before diving in. *Buffalo Springs Lodge*, a few kilometres away, is low-key and always welcoming for a drink. There's a fine jungly marsh reaching nearly to the terrace, where you'll often see animals.

LEOPARDS AT SAMBURU

Samburu's **leopards** are a regular sight – at least from the terraces at *Samburu* and *Samburu Serena* lodges, both of which have taken to baiting the trees on the opposite banks with haunches of meat. Between drinks and dinner, guests get a floodlit view of the stealthy predator reduced to a giant pussycat. The stampede for cameras doesn't encourage the leopards to stay long, so efforts are made to attach the meat firmly to the tree. It's all pathetically contrived (and you can forget worthwhile pictures or videos at that distance without expensive equipment), but only with luck or dogged persistence will you see a wild leopard other than in such circumstances, and it's hard to blame the hotels for making the most of the local attractions. You should beware, at *Samburu Lodge*, of occasional excursions by the leopards across the river to the human zoo. Several recent sightings on the lodge grounds have been reported early in the evening; hence the signs warning "Do not stray beyond the lit path".

Recent research has shown how little is really known about these cats. For the most part, they live off any small animals that come their way. The popular notion that they consume many baboons is apparently misled: baboon troops will turn on an attacking leopard instantly and, unless surprised, usually manage to fend it off. Less organized monkeys of all kinds, however, are often caught, and in Samburu (for those leopards not on the lodge gravy train), the favourite hunting grounds are the stands of forest and clumps of strange, branching doum palms by the river – these sometimes shake with monkeys. Black-faced vervet and blue monkeys are the commonest inhabitants.

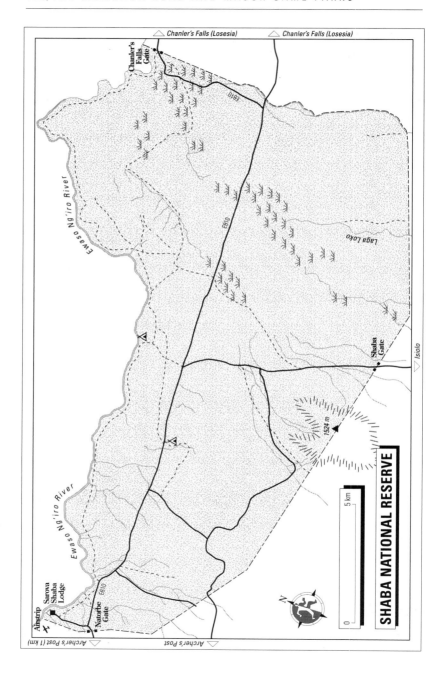

SHABA NATIONAL RESERVE

If Samburu's **wildlife** is occasionally disappointing, it may be fairer to say that the dry country ecosystems are prone to large variations in animal populations as they move in search of water and pasture. Some visitors have tremendous luck and it can provide consistently excellent animal-watching. The best areas, recently, are along the south side of the river in Buffalo Springs Reserve, close to *Samburu Lodge*. Poaching has wiped out the rhino here, but lions are often seen – again, most often in Buffalo Springs.

Meanwhile, the locally burgeoning **elephant herds** have ruined some sections of the riverine forest. The range of rarer, and localized, races and species compensates, though. Common and conspicuous among these are the **reticulated giraffe** with its beautiful jigsaw marking; **Grevy's zebra**, the large, finely striped species that has a bushy mane and outsize ears; the **Somali ostrich**, which has blue rather than pink legs; and the **gerenuk** ("camel head" in Somali), the antelope species that stands on its hind legs to reach the foliage which it feeds upon. Samburu's **birdlife** is diverse and prolific.

Shaba

Across the rutted surface of the Marsabit road lies the **Shaba National Reserve** (more fees to pay), the third of the Samburu district reserves. Unfortunately, if *Sarova*'s grandiose lodge is not within your budget, you'll need a tent to be able to stay the night, as there's no other accommodation. There are theoretically two campsites, though they can be closed if there's been much banditry or cattle raiding; the better one is on the banks of the Ewaso Ngiro, some 9km from Natorbe Gate. Neither have any facilities. Unusually, you are permitted to walk in places (certainly from the airstrip to *Sarova Lodge*): ask the ranger at the gate to point out where. If you've got wheels, you might consider venturing out of the reserve to the east to visit Chanler's Falls, 30km beyond Chanler's Falls Gate on the Ewaso Ngiro river, but double check the security situation first with the rangers – there's no one here except for Samburu herders and, if you're unlucky, heavily-armed raiders.

For **animals**, Shaba is rated the equal of its two neighbours and its **springs** mean that it is better watered. If you can put up with the intense heat, the scenery provides spectacular compensation and the animal-watching is good, with lots of elephants, jackals and a few lions, and plains game including beautifully marked Grevy's zebra and reticulated giraffe, and the gerenuk. The gerenuk rarely if ever drinks, as it manages to extract enough water from morning dew on leaves.

This was also the area where Joy Adamson experimented with the release of hand-reared **leopards**. So, if you're mobile and have a day to spare, Shaba is highly recommended and it's certainly much less visited than Samburu or Buffalo Springs.

Meru National Park

Daily 6am–6.30pm; $20 per day/overnight, $10 students, $5 children; private vehicle Ksh200, camping $8 ($10 in a "special" campsite). Warden: PO Box 11 Maua (☎0164/20613). No driving after 7pm. Speed limit 40kph. Map: Survey of Kenya SK65 at 1cm:1km (1988) has the junctions but campsites and accommodation are out of date. It's not easily available in Kenya (try Prestige Bookshop in Nairobi), so try to order from abroad (see "Maps and advance information" on p.35).

You don't see **Meru National Park** on many safari itineraries. Of the main parks covered in this chapter, it is the least visited – unspoiled and pristine. Abundantly traversed by **streams** flowing into the Tana River on its southern boundary, and luxuriantly rained upon, the rolling **jungle** of tall grass, riverine forest and swamp is lent a hypnotic, other-worldly quality by wonderful stands of prehistoric-looking **doum palms**; and with the high cover they provide, you can never be certain of what's going to be around the next corner.

True, the **animals** aren't always as much in evidence here as they can be in some other Kenyan wildlife parks, but the even more noticeable absence of minibuses and land cruisers more than compensates. After visiting some of the less bushy parks, where the animals can be spotted from miles away, Meru's intimate, unusual landscape is quickly entrancing. Most of the time you really are alone in this surreal wilderness.

Meru is the area where the Adamsons released their most famous lioness **Elsa** back into the wild, and where their later series of experiments with orphaned cheetahs was cut short by the murder of Joy Adamson. Until 1988, you could always guarantee a close encounter with **white rhinos** – close enough to see how they got the name, from the Afrikaans *weit* (meaning wide), a reference to their lugubrious grass-cropping mouths. Unlike black rhinos, they are remarkably good-natured animals. The head keeper of the Meru herd used to encourage visitors to pet them and even sit on them when they were lying down. Morning and evening, the five docile beasts were gently prodded out to graze around the park headquarters and campsites, then brought back at midday to the dust-wallow of their pen to snooze through the heat. The thousands of pounds' worth of horn that they carried on their noses ensured they could never be left unguarded, which required the full-time attention of a team of rangers.

All of this simply wasn't enough to keep them alive. A gang of about thirty **poachers**, armed with automatic rifles, stormed the rhinos' night-time paddock, killing all five, injuring several rangers and escaping with the booty of hacked-off horns.

Be under no illusion: more than a decade later, Meru's location is still potentially dangerous. Lying in the open plains beyond the relative security of the Mount Kenya

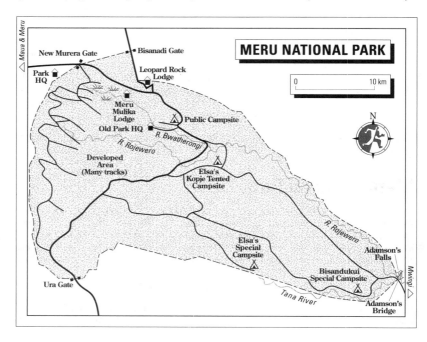

region, it's an easy target – as well as escape route – for the bandits and cattle rustlers who have blighted northeastern Kenya over the past two decades (see Chapter Seven). Things were especially bad in 1988 and 1989, when Somali poachers virtually ruled the park and were mainly responsible for the carnage that tore through other eastern parks and reserves. During their bloody tenure, two French tourists were shot dead when they unwittingly drove into a poachers' hideout. Such was the international outcry that followed their murder, and that of George Adamson in the adjoining Kora National Park a few months later, that the Kenyan government made a huge and successful effort to rout them. Still, although it seems doubtful whether the park will ever see rhinos again, security has been beefed up considerably since the mid-1990s (at a cost of some 12 million shillings), and there have been no incidents involving tourists since then.

Practicalities

If you're **driving**, the last fuel and supplies after Meru (there's no fuel in the park) are in Maua, one hour into the **Nyambeni Hills** on a pretty, paved road, with steep tea terraces and plantations of *miraa*. The park's **New Murera Gate** is about 30km from Maua, down a red *murram* road – the condition of which is sometimes diabolical – with magnificent scenery over your shoulder as you go: the Nyambenis towering above exotic *shambas* of bananas, sugar and corn, and the sky, as often as not, a gaudy cloud-mural of gathering storms. Gradually, as you descend, the scene gives way to the lank grass, termite cathedrals and the scattered trees and streams that characterize the park's savannah. If you fancy an organized tour, both Kimbla Safaris (PO Box 40098 Nairobi; ☎02/891288, fax 891592, *kimbla@form-net.com*) and Africa Expeditions (PO Box 24598 Nairobi; ☎ & fax 02/561054) sometimes include Meru in their overland truck itineraries.

Without your own vehicle, getting to the park isn't easy. From Meru town (p.210), there are frequent buses and *matatus* to Maua, from where other *matatus* run as far as Kiutini – a third of the way between Maua and the park gate. From there, however, you'll have to hitch the remaining 20km, and, even once there, you'll have to rely on the warden taking pity on you and giving you a guided tour, so you might just as well try for a lift with tourists in Maua, or rather about 3km up the hill before it at the junction, but you could stand for literally days without any luck. There a friendly **hotel** at the junction, the *Kiringo Hill Tourist Lodge* (PO Box 300 Maua; ☎0167/21081; B&B ①–②), which has reasonable s/c rooms, better ones in cottages, but little hot water. In **Maua** itself, the best option is the calm *Maua Basin Hotel*, signposted 100m off to the left as you come in (PO Box 452; ☎0167/21519; ②), with a choice of s/c and non-s/c. The *Maua Lodge*, opposite *Kenol* where the *matatus* and buses drop you, is rather more basic (PO Box 343; ☎0167/21117; ①). There's a branch of Barclays, with an ATM being installed, and the *El Niño Memo Pub* is notable for its name, as well as for good, simple food.

At first sight, Maua is an attractively bustling little market town, despite the smouldering piles of rubbish and the glue-sniffing streetkids, unusual in such a remote place. Gorgeously sited at the lower end of a verdant valley planted with maize and *miraa*, sometimes foggy in the morning, it gives way to stunning vistas over the national park and the deserts beyond. Yet there's also a discernable undercurrent of tension in the air, thanks to bitter rivalry between Meru and Somali **miraa traders** which boiled over in January 1999 following the mysterious death in London of the local MP, who also doubled as a *miraa* trader. Locals were quick to blame Somali drug barons for his death, and promptly set about a series of violent protests and revenge attacks, in which several people were killed. The aftermath of this explosion may simmer for years.

Lodges

There are two places currently in operation. The expensive *Elsa's Kopje Tented Camp*, on the former site of Mgwango (or Mughwongo) Camp by junction 19, has recently opened, and promises to be the most exclusive unit in the park, with only 32 beds. The price includes guided walks and day and night game drives (bookings through Cheli & Peacock Safaris, p.48; ⑨). More affordable, though still way out of budget range, is the new thirty-bed *Leopard Rock Lodge* (reservations through Meru Park Adventure Ltd, PO Box 208 Maua; or PO Box 56032 Nairobi; ☎02/246982, fax 212389; ⑥ low, ⑨ high), along the Murera river. There's a swimming pool, and a footpath running along the river (hippo and crocs) and up to the top of Leopard Rock, which used to be visited by lions, not leopards. Activities include game drives, guided bush walks, boat-trips on the Tana River, and visits to Meru farms, *miraa* plantations and a Boran village.

Nearby, 6km from the gate and also in the northern "developed area", will be the new incarnation of *Meru Mulika Lodge* (which may open within this edition's lifetime): its new owners – an American company called Visa Hotels – plan to turn it into a four-star 88-bed lodge – it remains to be seen whether the paradisal charm of the old version will be retained: apart from a pool, it had a wonderful terrace fronting onto the verdant **Mulika Swamp**, where you could watch elephants, oryxes, ostriches and others. There's talk of converting the old park HQ into a lodge, which was news to the rangers at the gate, and tentative plans for an eighty-bed lodge in the adjacent Kora National Park. Up-to-date information on all these developments from Let's Go Travel (p.142), or from the facilities manager at Kenya Wildlife Service (p.148), both in Nairobi.

Bandas and campsites

Thankfully, given the upmarket lurch of the lodges, there is still one remaining *banda* site offering **budget accommodation**, some 18km from the gate near the old park head-quarters at the **public campsite**, on a stretch of open ground running down to a wooded stream. There are toilet and shower blocks, and firewood is plentiful, but bring your own bedding. Otherwise, **camping** is your only option, either here, or at one of eight "special" campsites dotted throughout the park (ask the rangers or the warden which are available, as they tend to open, close and move about fairly regularly), none of which have any facilities except supplies of firewood. There are usually rivers nearby for water.

Exploring the park

Meru's many tracks are mostly sandy and firm; the junctions have useful signposts (useful as long as you have the Survey of Kenya map, and the baboons haven't ripped them off again), and the whole park is uncontaminated by tourism. You're no longer required to take a ranger with you, although it's advisable if you intend exploring south of the "developed area", more to provide radio back-up in case of breakdown than to combat bandits. This is especially important down by the Tana River, where the tracks vary greatly in condition from one season to the next, and some are physically blocked off.

Without going too far, there are still plenty of enticing areas to investigate. The **Rojewero River**, the park's largest stream, is an interesting watercourse: densely overgrown banks flash with birds and monkeys and dark waters ripple with turtles. Large and very visible herds of **elephant**, **buffalo** and **reticulated giraffe** are common, as are, in the more open areas, **gerenuk**, **Grevy's zebra** and **ostrich**. Predators seem scarce, though they may simply be hidden in the long grass – the smaller grazers must have a nerve-wracking time of it here. Large numbers of **leopards** captured in the stock-raising lands of Laikipia (p.558) have been released in the park in recent years, but as usual you have little chance of seeing them.

Onwards to the Tana River

The adjoining **Kora National Park** was the home of George Adamson (of *Born Free* fame), murdered by poachers or cattle-rustlers in August 1989 when he drove through their barricade. The reserve was promptly upgraded to National Park status, but Adamson's grave was subsequently desecrated. Kora, and the three national reserves south and east of Meru – **Bisanadi**, **North Kitui** and **Rahole** – are all in the Land Rover expedition category, a total of 4500 square kilometres of scrub and semi-desert, and the Tana's dense forest where they fringe the river. With the right vehicle and preparations, it would be possible, in theory, to follow the Tana down to Garissa (p.594), by crossing into Kora via the newly constructed Adamson's Falls bridge near Misandukui "special" campsite, then striking out east along the south bank of the Tana. About half way, assuming the track has been repaired (it was washed away years ago), the tiny settlement of **Mbalambala** is a highly rated place for seeing hippo and crocodile.

Regrettably, with the history of bad security in the area, especially around Garissa where attacks and shootings are still common, such a trip would be extremely ill-advised at present and probably impossible: in any case, permission to visit Kora park and the reserves needs first to be obtained from KWS in Nairobi (p.148), and then verified with the warden of Meru National Park (the headquarters are 2km north of New Murera Gate). More likely, and marginally safer, but still subject to obtaining permits, is to head southwest from Adamson's Bridge through North Kitui National Reserve to the village of Mwingi on the Garissa road, along some 150km of badly marked track, which is currently on the brink of famine. A compass, a good map (nigh impossible to find) and a guide who knows the route would all be pretty helpful.

travel details

Road details for the main Nairobi–Mombasa route are given in chapters 1 and 6.

BUSES

Kitui to: Machakos (4 daily; 1hr); Mombasa (daily; 9hr); Nairobi (3 daily; 2hr 30min).

Machakos to: Kitui (4 daily; 1hr); Mombasa (daily; 8hr); Nairobi (frequent; 1hr–1hr 30min); Voi (daily; 5hr).

Maua to: Embu (3 daily; 3hr); Meru (3 daily; 1hr); Nairobi (3 daily; 7hr).

Namanga to: Nairobi (daily; 4hr).

Narok to: Nairobi (2 daily; 4hr).

Taveta to: Mombasa (2 daily; 5hr); Voi (4 daily; 3hr).

Voi to: Malindi (daily; 4hr); Mombasa (frequent; 2hr); Nairobi (frequent; 4–5hr); Taveta (4 daily; 3hr).

MATATUS

Machakos to: Kitui (8 daily; 45min).

Kitui to: Embu (infrequent; 3-4hr); Machakos (8 daily; 45min).

Voi to: Taveta (2–3 daily; 3hr); Wundanyi (4–5 daily; 1hr 30min).

Taveta to: Oloitokitok (market days; 2hr 30min); Voi (2–3 daily; 3hr).

Oloitokitok to: Emali (infrequent; 2–3hr); Taveta (market days; 2hr 30min).

Namanga to: Nairobi (daily; 3hr 30min).

Narok to: Nairobi (daily; 3-4hr).

TRAINS

Taveta to: Voi (2pm Tues, Wed, Fri & Sat; 5hr).

Voi to: Nairobi (11pm daily; 9hr); Mombasa (4.11am daily; 4hr); Taveta (5am Tues, Wed, Fri & Sat; 5hr).

CHAPTER SIX

THE COAST

N early everyone arrives on the coast at **Mombasa**, a much more enjoyable place to spend time than Nairobi. Kenya's second city, it is a tropical centre *par excellence*: steamy, lazy, at times unbelievably dilapidated, but genial. To the north and south there are superb **beaches** and a number of pockets of tourist development – of which the resort strip to the immediate north of the city is the busiest – but the coast is not yet highly developed in the Florida or Spanish *costa* sense. For many visitors (and this is one area where inexpensive package tourism has really taken off) the resort areas represent little more than sun, sea, sand and, even in the AIDS era, sex. You can, of course, have a wonderful time on the beaches doing nothing very much, but there's much more to this part of Kenya than some travel brochures might have you believe – and plenty to do if total lassitude drives you nuts after a few days.

Most obviously, the beaches are the launch pad for one of the most beautiful **coral reefs** in the world, rated in the top three by experienced divers, along with Australia's Barrier Reef and the Red Sea. With breathing apparatus you can do some spectacular dives, including night dives and wreck dives, but with even the most limited equipment – a snorkel and mask (or "goggles"), easily obtained almost anywhere – you can still enter what really is another world, either taking a boat or swimming out to discover sections of reef for yourself. The three most spectacular zones, enclosed in **marine national parks**, are far to the south off Wasini Island, the area between Watamu and Malindi, and in the extreme north, off Kiwaiyu Island.

The string of **islands** that runs up the coast – the main ones being Wasini, Funzi, Chale, Mombasa itself, Lamu, Manda, Pate, Kiwaiyu – are all worth visiting. Apart from their beach and ocean attractions, most of them have some archeological interest, which is also a constant theme on the mainland: the whole coast is littered with the **ruins** of forts, mosques, tombs and even whole towns. Some of these – including **Fort Jesus**, **Lamu** and the ruined town of **Gedi** – are already on the tourist circuit, but there are dozens that have hardly been cleared or investigated and they make for compelling exploration. Fort Jesus Museum in Mombasa has a map of locations.

Nature and wildlife

The hundreds of kilometres of sandy beach that fringe the low-lying coastal strip are backed by dunes and coconut palms, traversed by scores of streams and rivers. Flowing off the plateaus through tumbling jungle, these waterways meander across a

---

ACCOMMODATION PRICE CODES

Rates for a standard double or twin room. For a full explanation of these rates, see p.47.

① Under Ksh500	(under approx £5/$8)	⑥ Ksh6000–9000	(£60–90/$96–144)*
② Ksh500–1000	(£5–10/$8–16)	⑦ Ksh9000–12,000	(£90–120/$144–192)*
③ Ksh1000–2000	(£10–20/$16–32)	⑧ Ksh12,000–16,000	(£120–£160/$192–256)*
④ Ksh2000–4000	(£20–40/$32–64)	⑨ Over Ksh16,000	(over £160/$256)*
⑤ Ksh4000–6000	(£40–60/$64–96)	* = *usually priced in dollars*	

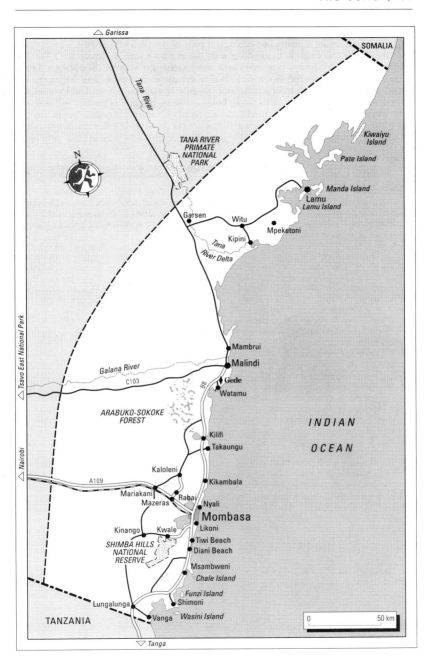

narrow, fertile plain to the sea. In sheltered creeks, forests of **mangrove** trees cover vast areas and create a distinctive ecological zone of tidal mud flats.

Wildlife on the coast is in keeping with the region's lush, intimate feel. The big game of up-country Kenya is more or less absent (though Shimba Hills National Park near Mombasa is an exception), but smaller creatures are abundant. Monkeys are especially common, with troops of baboons regularly seen by the road and vervet and Sykes' monkeys frequently at home in hotel gardens. Birdlife is prolific – if you harbour even a mild interest you should make a point of bringing binoculars. On the reptile front, snakes – brilliant disguise artists – are rarely seen, but lizards skitter everywhere, including upside down on the ceiling at night, and bug-eyed chameleons

---

RESPONSIBLE SNORKELLING, DIVING AND FISHING

Kenya's coral reefs are among the world's most beautiful, and fragile, ecosystems. A reef is a living entity: every branch or cluster of coral consists of thousands if not millions of individual living organisms called polyps, growing ever outwards as the older ones die and become covered in new growth. Coral grows extremely slowly, some species taking over a decade to expand a couple of centimetres.

Solid though it seems, coral is extremely sensitive, and even something as seemingly insignificant as a small change in sea temperature – such as happened in the 1997–98 El Niño event – can have disastrous effects. Even now, many sections of Kenya's reefs have barely begun to recover, and large sections appear grey and dead. Equally disastrous are human pressures, whether through accidental pollution or more deliberate activities. The damage caused by careless trawling and anchoring is obvious. Less obvious are the potentially damaging results of snorkelling and diving.

If you haven't dived for a while, take a refresher course at one of the PADI schools at the beach hotels, and practise your buoyancy control in the safety of a swimming pool. Read the box on "Diving" on p.472.

When mooring a boat, ensure that you use established mooring points to avoid damaging the coral with anchors and chains. If there are no buoys, drop your anchor well away from the reef, and swim in.

Dive and swim carefully, never touching the corals, no matter how solid they appear. Even gentle abrasions can kill some polyps and all coral suffocates if covered with silt or sand thrown up by a careless swipe of fins (flippers) close to the sea floor. For this reason, some companies don't provide fins for snorkellers. If you do wear them, always be aware of where your feet are, and use only your hands to swim when you're close to anything. If you're an inexperienced diver, keep a good distance from the coral to avoid crashing into it.

Don't touch or feed anything. Your actions may cause stress to the animal, and interrupt behaviour. Although several companies encourage it, it's best not to feed fish. In some species, it encourages dependency, can change their behaviour (just like baboons on land, some fish can become aggressive), and it destabilizes the food chain.

Don't collect marine souvenirs. Souvenir collecting of shells, coral and starfish disrupts the ecosystem and is illegal in Kenya, and in most countries, as is all trade in sea-turtle products. Getting caught – whether in Kenya or at your airport of arrival – can land you in serious trouble. Similarly, although they are widely for sale, you shouldn't buy any of these items. With no market, people will stop collecting them. Note that the shellfish will have been killed to provide the shells you're offered.

Big game fishing takes a direct toll on the marine environment by reducing the population of natural predators, kicking off a potentially destructive chain reaction by increasing the populations of their prey, in turn increasing pressure on organisms further down the food chain. Among the game-fishing fraternity, steadily falling catch rates have spurred talk of introducing quotas. It seems likely that regulations will be imposed by law before the boat operators get around to it themselves. If you do go game fishing, you may prefer to tag and release your catch rather than killing and landing it.

waver across the road, sometimes making it to the other side. So do giant millipedes, up to thirty centimetres long, harmless scavengers and known as Mombasa Expresses after the well-known slow train. Insects, including some fierce mosquitoes, are here in full force. But most, including the glorious butterflies of the Jadini and Arabuko-Sokoke forests, are attractive participants in the coast's gaudy show.

Transport to the coast

The **train journey** between Nairobi and Mombasa is, for many people, a highlight of Kenyan travel. While its poor safety record makes it difficult to recommend unreservedly (there have been two serious derailments, with fatalities, in recent years), all the research trips for this book have made frequent use of it. With just one overnight service a day in each direction, at 7pm, the quality of service on board is generally high and, although the carriages need refurbishment, the trip is still a reminder of the era of leisurely rail travel. For full details see p.40. **Buses** from Nairobi to Mombasa go by day as well as night, but most of the road is dull and, at the time of writing (mid-1999) the section from Tsavo to Mombasa is in an appalling state of repair. For coverage of the route, see Chapter Five, p.337.

You can also **fly** to Mombasa, Malindi or Lamu from Nairobi. Flying to Lamu from Nairobi makes sense if you have the cash ($130–187 one way; see "Moving on from Nairobi" on p.138) and not much time, as you avoid retracing your steps between Lamu and Mombasa, but it's not an interesting flight. If you'd like to fly for the fun of it, the Malindi–Lamu hop (see "Travel Details" on p.543) costs $40–65 and gives stunning views over jungle and reef. For details on flying into Mombasa's Moi International Airport, see p.420.

Coast practicalities

There are four main **resort** areas – three to the north and one to the south. The suburban district north of Mombasa, consisting of **Nyali**, **Bamburi**, **Mtwapa** and almost merging into **Kikambala** over on the north side of Mtwapa Creek, is the first, often known as "North Coast"; further north comes **Watamu**, about two hours from Mombasa; and lastly **Malindi**, twenty minutes beyond Watamu. Along the "South Coast", south of Mombasa, **Diani Beach**, forty minutes' drive from the city, is the principal focus, with the lower key **Tiwi Beach** to the north of it. However, most of these places have little that is recognizably Kenyan about them: you're likely to see and meet as many *wazungu* (white people) as Kenyans, and, if you stay at an "all-inclusive" hotel, you won't to see much of "real" Kenya. Apart from the odd small development, however, the rest of the coast is virtually untouched.

The coast is the part of Kenya most affected by the **seasons**. April, May and June are much less busy, and much cheaper, than the rest of the year. While the beaches tend to be damp and the weather muggy and overcast, you can make large savings on

---

TRAVELLING DURING RAMADAN

Islam has been a major influence on the coast, and the annual month of fasting – Ramadan (see p.61 for dates) – is widely observed. Visiting the coast during **Ramadan** might leave a slightly strange impression of a region where everyone is on night shift, but in practical terms it usually makes little difference. If you're travelling on a budget, it can sometimes be difficult to track down a cheap room during the day, if only because everything appears to be closed, but you can usually find a lax restaurant serving food, and you'll do most of your eating after dark in any case. During Id ul Fitr, at the end of Ramadan, and Maulidi al Nebi, the holiday for the prophet's birthday, lodgings often fill up early.

package holidays or, if you're travelling independently, reduce your hotel costs by as much as fifty percent.

As an alternative to hotels, you can stay in **self-catering villas**, **apartments** and **cottages**. There are various options along the beaches north of Mombasa, at Malindi and at Tiwi and Diani beaches, and it's a very sound financial proposition for families or groups. Kenya Villas, Westminster House, Kenyatta Avenue, Nairobi (PO Box 57046; ☎02/338072), act as an agent for many holiday home-owners. Large houses, to sleep eight for example, can be had for under Ksh3000 a night.

One word of warning: tempting as it can be, **sleeping out**, except on the most deserted of beaches, is very unwise. Although the reputation of some areas for daylight theft and more grievous assaults is unfairly exaggerated, to sleep out anywhere near Mombasa or Malindi is asking for trouble – you'll have to find a room or pitch up at one of the handful of recognized campsites.

MOMBASA AND AROUND

Arriving in **Mombasa** by plane or train in the morning, there's ample time, if the heat doesn't fell you, to head straight out to the beaches. But you should consider spending a day or two in Mombasa itself, tuning in to the coast (and to Kenya if you've just jetted in), catching the cadences of "Kiswahili *safi*" (pure Swahili) and looking around Kenya's most historic city. If you have time, there are two worthwhile trips you can make inland to areas that are much less known: **Shimba Hills National Reserve** to the southwest, and, well off the beaten path to the northwest, the **Mijikenda country** between Mazeras and Kaloleni. If you would rather take this latter detour before reaching the

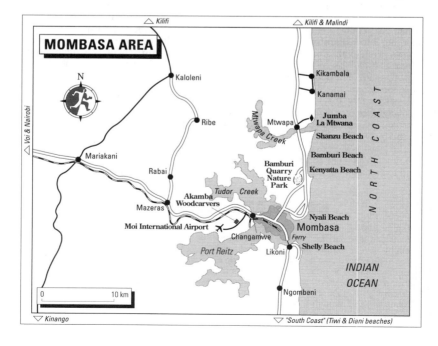

coast proper – and it's a pleasant introduction to the region – buses from Nairobi can drop you at **Mazeras** (see p.349), a simple hitchhike or bus ride away from Mombasa.

Mombasa

Kenya's second city can come as a revelation. There's a depth of history here, and a sense of community which Nairobi lacks. And whereas Nairobi has very clear boundaries between rich and poor districts, things are much more mixed in Mombasa. Sleazy, hot – you're always thirsty – and physically tropical in a way that could hardly be more different from Nairobi, **MOMBASA** is the slightly indolent hub of the coast – a faded, flaking, occasionally charming city that still feels, despite its gentle sprawl, like a small town that was once great.

Mombasa is actually an island, connected to the mainland by two causeways to the west, and by a bridge to the north, but still linked only by ferry to the south. The city is intricate and its streets wriggle deceptively. At its appealing heart is the **Old Town**, a lattice of lanes, mosques and cramped, elderly houses sloping gently down to the once-busy dhow harbour. **Fort Jesus**, an impressive reminder of Mombasa's complicated, bloody past, still overlooks the Old Town from where it once guarded the harbour entrance. It is now a national monument and museum.

Clustered all around you, within easy walking distance, is the whole expanse of downtown, twentieth-century Mombasa, with its wide streets and refreshing lack of high-rise buildings (though their number is steadily growing). While you won't doubt it's a chaotic city – there's only one remaining set of working traffic lights, and every once in a while you'll question how a million people can manage without a predictable water supply or a functioning city council – the atmosphere, even in the commercial centre of one of Africa's busiest ports, is invariably relaxed and congenial. Rush hours, urgency and paranoia seem to be Nairobi's problems (as everyone here will tell you), not Mombasa's. And the gaping, marginal slums that one expects to find outside African cities hardly exist here. True, Likoni and especially Changamwe, on the mainland, are burgeoning suburbs that the municipality has more or less abandoned, but the brutalizing conditions of the Mathare Valley, Kibera and Korogocho shantytowns in Nairobi are absent.

Despite the palms, the sunshine and the happy languor, all is not bliss and perfection: **street crime**, though it hardly approaches Nairobi's level, is a serious problem, and you should be wary of displaying your valuables or accepting invitations to walk down dark alleys. But, as a general rule, Mombasa is a far less neurotic city than Nairobi, and, in stark contrast to the capital, there's nowhere in the centre that could be considered a no-go area. One indication of this is that the city stays awake much later. Climatic considerations may partly explain it, but, at an hour when central Nairobi is empty but for taxis and *askaris*, Mombasans are to be seen strolling in the warm night, old men conversing on the benches in Digo Road, and many shops are still open. The small-town freedoms remain healthy here and it all adds up to a city that is richly satisfying and rewarding to stay in.

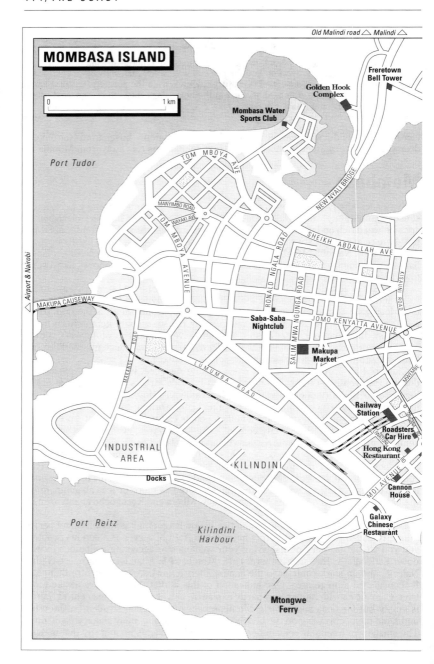

MOMBASA ISLAND

Old Malindi road △ Malindi △

Freetown
Bell Tower

Golden Hook
Complex

Mombasa Water
Sports Club

0   1 km

Port Tudor

TOM MBOYA AVE

MANYIMBO ROAD

TOM MBOYA AVENUE

WAYAKI AVE

NEW NYALI BRIDGE

SHEIKH ABDALLAH AVE

RONALD NGALA ROAD

SALIM MWA NGUNGA ROAD

KISAUNI ROAD

△ Airport & Nairobi

MAKUPA CAUSEWAY

JOMO KENYATTA AVENUE

Saba-Saba
Nightclub

Makupa
Market

MAKINI ROAD

LUMUMBA ROAD

Railway
Station

Roadsters
Car Hire

MWEMBE

Hong Kong
Restaurant

INDUSTRIAL
AREA

KILINDINI

MWEMBE

Cannon
House

MOI AVENUE

Docks

Galaxy
Chinese
Restaurant

Port Reitz

*Kilindini
Harbour*

Mtongwe
Ferry

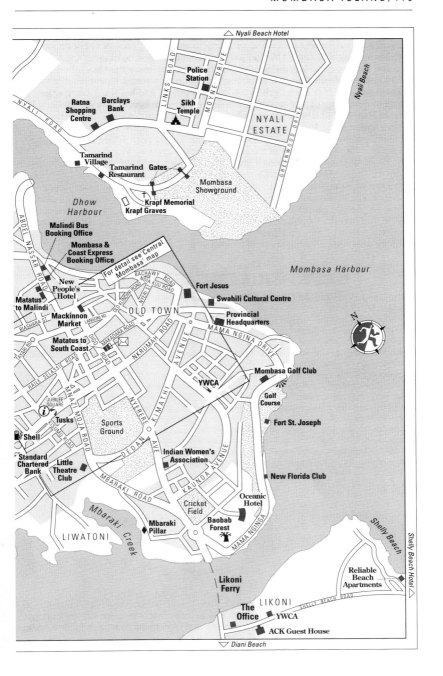

△ Nyali Beach Hotel

Nyali Beach

Police Station

LINKS ROAD

MOYNE DRIVE

GREENWOOD DRIVE

Sikh Temple

NYALI ESTATE

Ratna Shopping Centre

Barclays Bank

NYALI ROAD

Tamarind Village

Tamarind Restaurant

Gates

Mombasa Showground

Dhow Harbour

Krapf Memorial

Krapf Graves

ABDEL NASSER ROAD

Malindi Bus Booking Office

Mombasa & Coast Express Booking Office

For detail see Central Mombasa map

Mombasa Harbour

New People's Hotel

BACHAWY ROAD

NDIA KUU ROAD

NYERERE

Fort Jesus

Matatus to Malindi

OLD TOWN

Swahili Cultural Centre

Mackinnon Market

LANGONI RD.

MAKADARA ROAD

NKRUMAH ROAD

Provincial Headquarters

BIASHARA ROAD

DIGO ROAD

Matatus to South Coast

KIMATHI AVENUE

MAMA NGINA DRIVE

HAILE SELASSIE ROAD

NYERERE AVE

YWCA

Mombasa Golf Club

MANAZI MOJA ROAD

Golf Course

JUBILEE SQUARE

ⓘ

Tusks

Sports Ground

DEDAN

Fort St. Joseph

Shell

Standard Chartered Bank

Little Theatre Club

MBARAKI ROAD

Indian Women's Association

KAUNDA AVENUE

New Florida Club

Cricket Field

Oceanic Hotel

Mbaraki Creek

Mbaraki Pillar

Baobab Forest

MAMA NGINGA

LIWATONI

Shelly Beach

Shelly Beach Hotel

Reliable Beach Apartments

Likoni Ferry

LIKONI

SHELLY BEACH ROAD

The Office

YWCA

ACK Guest House

▽ Diani Beach

Ethnically, Mombasa is perhaps even more diverse than Nairobi. Asian and Arab influence is particularly pervasive, with fifty mosques and dozens of Hindu and Sikh temples lending a strongly Oriental flavour. Still, the largest contingent speaks Swahili as a first language and it is the **Swahili civilization** that, more than any other, accounts for Mombasa's distinctive character. You'll see women wearing head-to-foot *bui-buis* or brilliant *kanga* outfits, men decked out in *kanzu* gowns and hip-slung *kikoi* wraps. The smaller community of settlers and European expatriates figures less prominently here than in Nairobi, but it continues to wield disproportionate economic and social clout.

As a tourist town, Mombasa doesn't go out of its way to please. Indeed, one of its best qualities is its utter lack of pretension. It is principally a port: **Kilindini** harbour takes up most of the western side of the island. Increasingly, too, Mombasa is an industrial city, boasting one of East Africa's major oil refineries (on your right as you arrive by train). In short, Mombasa is not a resort. Visiting sailors are as important to its tourist economy as bona fide tourists, and (a grievous shortcoming) the island has no real beaches. The vast majority of the obvious tourists that you'll see around the place are here only for the purpose of a shopping trip from their north- or south-coast beach hotels. You may not be able to resist the lure of the beaches for too long, but Mombasa deserves a little of your time unless you are in a big hurry; there are few places in the country with such a strong sense of identity.

COASTAL CULTURE: SWAHILI

The coast is where East Africa meets the Classical world. Partly through the intermediary of Islam, with its direct and simple tenets, foreign ideas have shaped the society, language, literature and architecture. More than the pragmatic Portuguese, whose interests seem to have been entirely mercenary, immigrants and traders from Arabia and Asia – once or twice even China – have been a subtle and gradual influence on the coast. They would arrive each year in March or April on the northeast monsoon, the dry *kaskazi* wind, and return in September on the southerly monsoon or *kusi*.

Some, by choice or mishap, would be left behind. Through intermarriage from the earliest times (even before Islam appeared on the scene in the seventh century), a distinct ancient civilization called **Swahili** emerged. Swahili, which is thought to derive from the same Arabic root as *sahel*, meaning edge or coast, is also a language, known to its speakers as **ki-Swahili**. It is one of the more mainstream of the Bantu languages, which are spoken throughout much of Africa south of the equator. Like all old languages used by trading peoples, Swahili contains strong clues about who the people mixed with. Despite popular misconception, Swahili isn't based on Arabic any more than English is derived from Latin, but it is full of words derived from Arabic and peppered with others of Indian, Portuguese and English origin.

The Swahili are not a "tribe" in any definable sense; no less than, say, Americans, they are the result of the mixed heritage reflected in their language. Questions of family background and status in the community have traditionally loomed large: families that trace their roots – not always very plausibly – to foreign shores in the distant past tend to claim superior social status. Nor, predictably, was skin colour ignored. Essentially Muslim, the Swahili interpretation of the religion varies from place to place and according to circumstance: rigidity of form is an alien concept in Swahili culture. Essentially coastal, not all Swahili trade, nor do they all fish – some Swahili groups even avoid eating fish. Coconuts, mixed farming, cattle and goats are all vitally important.

THE TOWNS

Like the language, it was long thought that the towns of the coast began as implants, that is, as Arab, or even Persian, trading forts. It is now known that most were already in existence before any of the great post-Islamic wars and migrations took place in the Middle East. Mombasa, Malindi, Lamu and a host of lesser-known settlements are essentially

Arrival and information

Arriving on the night **train** from Nairobi is the best way: it loops down the steep scarp to the ocean as you wake up to the rustle of starched waiters and the clatter of buckled teapots. When you walk out of the station into the glare of the morning sun, **Haile Selassie Road** is directly ahead, leading in one straight kilometre to the city's main north–south thoroughfare, **Digo Road**. The **Old Town** begins on the far side of Digo Road. To the left of Haile Selassie are markets and bus stations; to the right, a concentration of hotels; then, parallel to it, **Moi Avenue** – the tourist strip. If you pick a taxi out of the swarm awaiting the train's arrival, Ksh100–150 should be the going rate to be taken to any town-centre hotel, no more than a five-minute ride, though you should have no security problems walking.

Arrival by road

Arriving by **bus** or **car** from Nairobi, first impressions can be dismal. You come over the Makupa Causeway with the railway, then diverge from it on the island to head 4km straight down **Jomo Kenyatta Avenue**. Although Mayor Balala had begun to clean things up since taking office (he resigned early in 1999), "shabby" is stil the adjective that comes irresistibly to mind as you bump down this erstwhile showcase avenue: a

---

ancient African towns that have always tolerated and even encouraged peaceful immigration from overseas. The Swahili style has always been to welcome the new and the sophisticated.

With few exceptions, however, any attempt to compromise the independence of these towns was met with violent resistance. The Portuguese were the least successful. When they arrived at the end of the fifteenth century, cultural memories of the Moorish occupation of their own country were still fresh. Accommodation to Islam was not on their agenda and, despite a long acquaintance with the coast, they never established an enduring colonial presence, as they did in Goa on the south Indian coast, further along the same trading route.

THE SLAVE INHERITANCE

Slavery on the coast was originally less a black-and-white moral issue than is commonly assumed. In the past, it was not unusual for people in need to "lend" a member of the family to others in exchange for goods or services. The Mijikenda peoples (see p.456 for more background), for example, maintained close links with the coastal towns, trading their produce, providing armed forces when the towns were under threat, and being supplied in return with overseas trade goods, especially cloth and tools. As traders, the Swahili sometimes accumulated surpluses of grain on the coast at times of severe drought inland. In exchange for food supplies, Mijikenda children would be taken to the towns by their relatives and fostered with Swahili families with whom they had links – to become, in effect, slaves. Later, the children intermarried, or paid off the debt and returned, though a small number were probably sold overseas. But when slavery itself became a major aspect of commerce, and the available foreign goods irresistible (cloth, firearms and liquor from Holland, France, England and America), then any trace of trust in the old arrangement vanished. The weak and defenceless were captured and sold to slavers from the coast (or, in the case of the Akamba who live further inland, beyond the Mijikenda, they sold their own prisoners and insane), often to end up on Dutch or French plantations around the Indian Ocean or in Arabian households. And, with the domination of the Sultan of Oman on the coast in the early nineteenth century, and the large-scale emigration of Arabs to East Africa, slaves from the far interior were increasingly set to work on their truly colonial coastal farms and plantations. When the British formally freed the slaves in 1907, they became part of Swahili society.

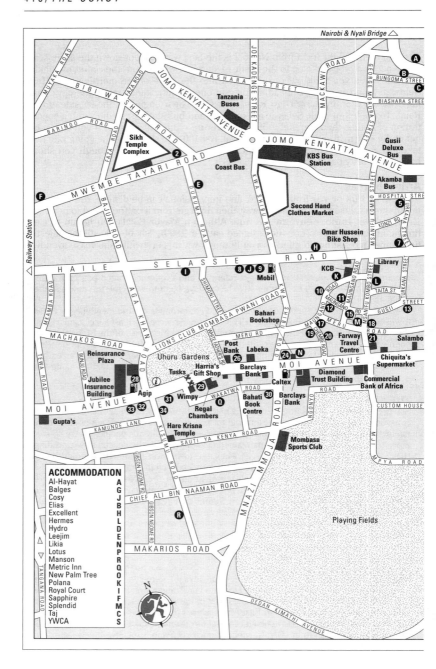

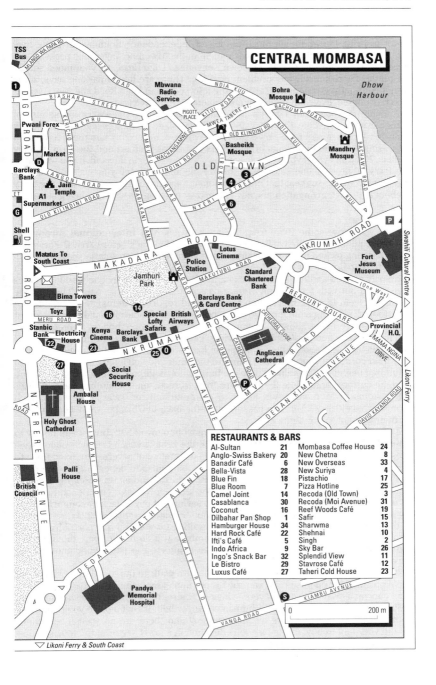

CENTRAL MOMBASA

TSS Bus

Dhow Harbour

Mbwana Radio Service

Bohra Mosque

Pwani Forex

Basheikh Mosque

Mandhry Mosque

Market

OLD TOWN

Barclays Bank

Jain Temple

A1 Supermarket

Shell

Matatus To South Coast

Lotus Cinema

Fort Jesus Museum

Police Station

Jamhuri Park

Standard Chartered Bank

Bima Towers

Swahili Cultural Centre

Barclays Bank & Card Centre

KCB

Toyz

Special Lofty Safaris

British Airways

Stanbic Bank

Electricity House

Kenya Cinema

Barclays Bank

Provincial H.Q.

Camel Joint

Anglican Cathedral

Likoni Ferry

Social Security House

Ambalal House

Holy Ghost Cathedral

Palli House

British Council

Pandya Memorial Hospital

RESTAURANTS & BARS

Al-Sultan	21	Mombasa Coffee House	24
Anglo-Swiss Bakery	20	New Chetna	8
Banadir Café	6	New Overseas	33
Bella-Vista	28	New Suriya	4
Blue Fin	18	Pistachio	17
Blue Room	7	Pizza Hotline	25
Camel Joint	14	Recoda (Old Town)	3
Casablanca	30	Recoda (Moi Avenue)	31
Coconut	16	Reef Woods Café	19
Dilbahar Pan Shop	1	Safir	15
Hamburger House	34	Sharwma	13
Hard Rock Café	22	Shehnai	10
Ifti's Café	5	Singh	2
Indo Africa	9	Sky Bar	26
Ingo's Snack Bar	32	Splendid View	11
Le Bistro	29	Stavrose Café	12
Luxus Café	27	Taheri Cold House	23

0   200 m

▽ Likoni Ferry & South Coast

scene of broken windows, crumbling facades and out-of-date hoardings smothers the street from its inception, via the triumphalist Independence Roundabout to its final disintegration in the diesel-laden environment of the Mwembe Tayari bus parks. If you get out at Mwembe Tayari, walk on down Kenyatta to Digo Road and your mood should lift a little. There's rarely any problem **parking**. There are lots of parking bays, some with meters (charges nominal), around the intersection of Digo Road and Moi Avenue. Don't, of course, leave anything valuable unattended in the car.

Arriving by road from **Dar es Salaam**, you first reach the swarming suburb of Likoni, where you take the ferry to Mombasa island (5min; every 15min [hourly 1am–4am]; passengers free, cars Ksh35). Be **warned**: in recent years there have been increasingly frequent incidents of muggings and sneak-theft around the ferry, usually at dusk. Keep an eye on your vehicle windows while waiting in line and, if you walk onto the ferry while someone else drives the vehicle aboard, leave your valuables inside: there's evidence to suggest that one or two gangs are targeting people just as the ferry is about to depart, giving them the advantage over passengers who risk being stranded.

Arrival by air

By air, you arrive some 10km from the city centre at **Moi International Airport** on the mainland near Port Reitz. Try to change into cool clothes before arrival – essential if you're being picked up from the airport and going straight on safari – as there's really nowhere to do it at the airport. Although the shabby building routinely swarms with the newly arrived and the soon-to-depart, the staff stay admirably cool and formalities are carried out with a minimum of fuss: passport checks take seconds. The luggage carousels seem to work more often than not and reports of items going missing are rare, though pilfering from luggage does occur – take valuables in hand baggage. As at Nairobi, before being allowed on your way, or to meet your holiday representative, you'll usually be gently quizzed about video camcorders, radios, electrical equipment and so on, and also about gifts for people in Kenya. Acknowledge the former and they may be recorded in your passport; admit to the latter and you'll have to pay duty, up to a hundred percent of the value. There are **bank booths** for exchanging money just outside the customs area. Note that if you're flying directly on to Nairobi, you'll be clearing customs in Mombasa. And if you're going straight on safari, you won't touch Mombasa island at all. Vehicles pass through the back of Changamwe, a poor suburb, on their way out to the highway.

There is no airline bus service from the airport into town: KBS **buses** run hourly to Mwembe Tayari, the main bus station. **Taxis**, the best of which are the London-style cabs, have their rates posted and the hassle is generally not severe. The fixed price to the centre of Mombasa is Ksh620, sometimes bargainable, depending on the day's business. Fares are also fixed for the beach resorts, depending on which hotel you're headed for (Diani Beach around Ksh2660; Nyali Beach Ksh900; Tiwi Beach Ksh2100; Shanzu Beach Ksh1500). You'll make a small saving but pay in lack of comfort by taking an unlicensed cab. You can call Airport Taxi Services on ☎011/433211.

You can also arrange to have a rented **car** waiting for you at the airport. Most rental companies that have offices or outlets in Mombasa will do this for you, though you'll usually need to go to their office in town to complete the paperwork and pay the deposit.

If you can handle it, the hour-long four-kilometre **walk** to the road into town (where you'll quickly pick up buses and *matatus*) is not unpleasant; along the road, on the left, is an enormous Kamba woodcarvers' "village", where the art of woodcarving has been reduced to not much more than a human conveyor belt. It isn't a place you're likely to bother visiting unless you are out here anyway and there are no special reductions should you want to buy; it's just a good education in a lowly sector of the tourist industry and, that said, quite entertaining.

AIRPORT DEPARTURES

When you're due to leave, before setting off for **Mombasa airport**, check and double-check the departure time with the airport or the ground agent. Note that if you're coming from a south coast hotel, it can take a surprisingly long time to cross on the Likoni ferry, get through the city and out the other side to the airport. Once at the airport, if you're travelling independently, or suspect you may be in the wrong queue, repeat your destination airport to everyone you deal with. Don't forget you'll have to pay a $20 **departure tax** (cash only, also payable in sterling [£14] or in shillings: currently around Ksh1200). Avoid having any quantity of Kenya shillings left to re-exchange as the rates are poor and the commission swinging, though you are allowed back to the forecourt bank booths from the departure lounge. On a further downbeat note, the duty-free shop has nothing Kenyan that isn't cheaper in town – though it does not accept shillings.

Tourist information

Mombasa's **tourist information** office, operated by the Mombasa and Coast Tourist Association, is on Moi Avenue, near the Tusks (Mon–Fri 8am–noon & 2–4.30pm, Sat 8am–noon; PO Box 99596; ☎011/225428, fax 228208). Although offering little in material terms (apart from brochures and an averagely useful map of Mombasa for Ksh200), the staff are helpful, and can advise you on a range of transport and accommodation matters.

Accommodation

None of the well-known resort hotels is located on Mombasa island, and tour operators almost never offer city hotels, for obvious reasons: there's nothing that could be described as luxury. If real comforts are what you want, the closest option, the *Nyali Beach Hotel*, is a short drive or taxi ride from the centre, on the mainland to the north. This, and subsequent hotels along the North Coast, are covered in the section "North of Mobasa", p.441. At the other end of the scale, the city has a fair scattering of cheap lodgings, but none that really stands out as the obvious focus for budget travellers. There's a YWCA – good for long stays for men as well as women – but no youth hostel and no campsite. Note that **water supplies** in Mombasa are notoriously erratic (you'll see the water carriers with their jingling hand carts all over the city) and many cheap places feature the tell-tale buckets and plastic basins in bathrooms that indicate water often has to be carried up. The tap water – when there is any – is usually safe to drink except in the rainy seasons, when it mixes with sewage and obviously needs boiling and purifying with chlorine tablets or iodine. If in doubt, get bottled water.

Basic lodgings

You might reasonably expect to find a concentration of cheap **lodgings** in the Old Town. Curiously enough, this isn't the case, though most of them cluster in the streets just to the west. All are on the Central Mombasa map on p.418, unless stated.

Al-Hayat Hotel, Digo Rd, above the TSS Bus booking office (PO Box 328; ☎011/229976). A good stand-by, with reasonable rooms, some s/c with fans and balconies, handy for the early-morning bus to Lamu. ①.

Hotel Balges, Digo Rd, across from the junction with Old Kilindini Rd (PO Box 1506; no phone). Dirt cheap, but most rooms are without fans and some lack windows. Not a comfortable place for women alone. ①.

Cosy Guest House, Haile Selassie Rd (PO Box 83011; ☎011/313064). A regular first base for many budget travellers – conveniently close to the railway station – but very basic and with crumbling facilities (no s/c rooms, and the shared bathrooms and toilets are pretty grim). Rooms lack mosquito nets and beds sometimes have only one sheet. ①.

Elias B&L, corner Digo Rd and Bungoma St (PO Box 82577; no phone). Friendly basic lodging with shared showers and toilets. Clean and cheap, and in a good position on the edge of the Old Town. ①.

Excellent Hotel, Haile Selassie Rd (PO Box 90228; ☎011/227683). Big, clean s/c rooms with real baths (but no hot water at the last visit), nets and fans. A reliable first base if you're arriving on the train, but blisteringly noisy on Saturday nights (there's a band on the roof). Slightly overpriced. B&B ③.

Hydro Hotel, corner of Digo and Langoni roads (PO Box 85360; ☎011/223784). Usefully located, friendly old stand-by, but very limited and no longer the place it once was. ②.

Likia Guest House, off Chembe Rd, behind Moi Ave (PO Box 85345; ☎011/223460). Down an unprepossessing back alley, this is a cheap, friendly little place. Fairly hygienic, with clean sheets and fans in most rooms. No mosquito nets though, and the water problems are a pain. ①.

Leejim Hotel, Duruma Rd (PO Box 80094; ☎011/222868). A sizeable place, with reasonable facilities and very friendly, though somewhat lacking in atmosphere. ②.

Metric Inn, Wakatwa Rd, off Moi Ave, on the south side of the Tusks behind *Wimpy* (PO Box 98658; ☎011/222155). B&L with small but acceptable rooms, the more expensive s/c. There's a laid-back bar and restaurant at the front. Bed only ①–②.

New People's Hotel (Mombasa Island map, p.414), Abdul Nassir Rd, right by the main bus and *matatu* offices (PO Box 16639; ☎011/229715). Big, undistinguished and noisy block – the established place to stay if you're taking a bus up to Lamu, Garissa or Malindi in the morning, as they leave from right outside. Past the rough-looking reception, things brighten up upstairs. Singles tend to be dingy and cube-like, but the better s/c doubles facing the street are quite acceptable, despite sagging beds, with real baths (though there's little hot water to fill them). Dirt cheap beds in dorms, too (Ksh130 per person). ①.

Taj Hotel, Digo Rd, entrance on Bungoma St (PO Box 82021; ☎011/313545). A friendly welcome but getting run down, with a very mixed bag of rooms, not all s/c or with nets. The best ones are the doubles on the roof, with a huge shared balcony overlooking the bustling street. ②.

YWCA, corner of Kaunda and Kiambu avenues (PO Box 90214; ☎011/312846). Pleasant ambience with good security, open to men as well as women. Popular with East Africans working or studying in Mombasa, so book ahead (Ksh200 fee). Upstairs rooms are breezier and better, with fans and nets, and sometimes hot water in showers. Cleanish if dilapidated toilets. Funds generated assist local women's projects. For long stays, on HB basis during the week and FB at weekends, they charge under Ksh10,000 per person per month, including laundry. No guests in rooms, no curfew (taxi back from towns costs around Ksh100). Bed only Ksh290 per person. ②.

Mid-range hotels

Head to any of these for basic hotel services, with breakfast included and self-contained rooms, some with air-conditioning. You might care to check your AC unit before choosing the room. Some generate so much water that your windowsill can become a veritable bird bath, attracting all the pigeons in Mombasa. Occasional reports are received of a group of Mombasa hotels in this price range which mistreat their guests and in which theft and prostitution are common and intimidating. The hotels in question are not listed here.

Hotel Hermes, Msanifu Kombo St (PO Box 98419; ☎011/313599). Not a great choice and becoming run-down and boozy (two bars flank the stairwell, open to 11pm). Mostly large rooms, all with fans and AC, though cracks can hinder its effectiveness, and no nets (rooms are sprayed nightly). B&B ③.

New Palm Tree Hotel, Nkrumah Rd (PO Box 90013; ☎011/315272 ext 17). This must have been quite a grand place once upon a time, but it still has bags of charm, despite getting frayed around the edges. Rooms are spacious and clean, all s/c with fans but no nets. There's also a sunny first-floor courtyard with, bizarely enough, sunbeds. Altogether much better than similarly priced competitors. B&B ③.

Hotel Splendid, Msanifu Kombo St (PO Box 90482; ☎011/220967, fax 312769). No longer as splendid as it was: few twin rooms (the best is #42), bathrooms aren't overly clean, and the AC can be noisy. Avoid the small, windowless, interior rooms. On the positive side, there's an elevator, the better rooms have balconies and fans, but nets have to be asked for. Popular for its fourth-floor roof garden bar/restaurant. ③.

Upmarket hotels

Remember that the **resort hotels** are out of town. Compared with Nairobi, the following city hotels tend to be very good value.

Lotus Hotel, corner of Mvita and Cathedral roads (PO Box 90193; ☎011/313207, fax 220673). Overflowing with greenery, with plain but very neat and clean rooms, and located on a quiet corner not far from Fort Jesus, the *Lotus* is the best bet in Mombasa and often full. Every room has AC and a phone. Credit cards accepted. B&B ④.

Manson Hotel, Kisumu Rd (PO Box 83565; ☎011/222356, fax 222420). Newish hotel with large, clean rooms with balconies. TV lounge and bar-restaurant on the ground floor. The welcome isn't warm, but good value overall. ③.

Oceanic Hotel (Mombasa Island map), Mbuyuni Rd, five minutes' walk from the Likoni ferry (PO Box 90371; ☎011/311193, fax 223496). Tired 1960s hulk that has seen better days, and is in need of a good lick of paint, but good value if you're not too fussy, with fine sea views from all rooms, but no beach – catch the ferry for Shelly Beach on the opposite side of the Creek. Murky green pool and scrubby gardens. The adjoining Indian *Swagat* Italian restaurant is quite reasonable, and the *Chandni Nightclub* promises an "Indian musical bonanza". B&B ③, HB ④.

Polana Hotel, Maungano Rd (PO Box 41983; ☎011/222168, fax 314505). 140-room highrise in the centre of the city, offering spacious, clean, comfortable accommodation (AC, phones, satellite TV and baths) – at a price. Great views from the upper floors, and good buffet breakfast (Ksh300 for walk-ins). Casino and room service. B&B ④.

Royal Court Hotel, Haile Selassie Ave (PO Box 41247; ☎011/223379, fax 312398). A six-storey block close to the railway station, with a giant samovar in the stylish reception and faint touches of Swahili decor elsewhere. Elevator access. Twin rooms are a good size and face out over town, but singles are small and lack the views. All have spotless modern tiled bathrooms (with baths and hot water). Good rooftop terrace bar (see "Bars", p.433), which can be loud on Fridays. Good value. B&B ④.

Hotel Sapphire, Mwembe Tayari Rd (PO Box 1254; ☎011/491657, fax 495280). Near the train station, a modern interconnecting five- and ten-storey block. The 110 rooms are all AC, with satellite TV and phones, and the benefit of the only hotel pool in central Mombasa (8am–8pm; day guests pay Ksh200 adults, Ksh150 children). More expensive suites have kitchens. There's also a health club with gym, massage, jacuzzi, steam bath and sauna. Three restaurants (including Chinese and Indian). Annoying piped music throughout. Good value. B&B ④–⑤.

Mombasa's history

Mombasa is one of East Africa's oldest settlements and, so long as you aren't anticipating spectacular historical sites, it's a fascinating place to wander. The island has had a town on it, located somewhere between the present Old Town and Nyali Bridge, for at least 700 years, and there are enough documentary snippets from earlier times to guess that some kind of settlement has existed here for at least 2000 years. Mombasa's own optimistic claim (frequently repeated in the tourist literature) to be 2500 years old comes from Roman and Egyptian adventure stories.

Early tales

Precisely what was going on before the Portuguese arrived is still barely discernible. An armchair traveller, Al-Idrisi, wrote the following in the early twelfth century about a place called *Manfasa* that was in roughly the right location: "This is a small place and a dependency of the Zanj [coastal people]. Its inhabitants work in the iron mines and hunt tigers. They have red-coloured dogs which fight every kind of wild beast and even lions." This sounds most unlikely, but then the history of Mombasa is a series of unlikely episodes. **Ibn Battuta**, the roving fourteenth-century Moroccan, spent a relatively

quiet night here in 1332 and declared the people of the town "devout, chaste and virtu-
ous . . . their mosques . . . strongly constructed of wood . . . the greater part of their diet
. . . bananas and fish". But another Arab writer of a hundred years later found a less
ordered society:

> *Monkeys have become the rulers of Mombasa since about 800 AH [1400 AD]. They even
> come and take the food from the dishes, attack men in their own homes and take away what
> they can find. The master of the house chases the thieving monkey and does not cease cajol-
> ing him until the animal, having eaten the food, gives back the dish or vessel. When the
> monkeys enter a house and find a woman they hold congress with her. The monkeys divide
> into bands each with its own chief and march behind him in an orderly manner. The peo-
> ple have much to put up with.*

Vasco da Gama and other Portuguese visitors

Mombasa had considerably worse depredations to put up with after **Vasco da Gama's**
expedition, full of mercenary zeal, dropped anchor on Easter Saturday 1498. After courtesy gifts had been exchanged, relations suddenly soured and the fleet was prevented
from entering the port. A few days later, richer by only one sheep and "large quantities
of oranges, lemons and sugar cane", da Gama went off to try his primitive diplomacy at
Malindi, and found his first and lasting ally on the coast.

Mombasa was visited again in 1505 by a fourteen-strong fleet. This time, the king of
Mombasa had enlisted 1500 archers from the mainland and stored arsenals of stone
missiles on the rooftops in preparation for the expected **invasion** through the town's
narrow alleys. The attack, pitching firearms against spears, poisoned arrows and
stones, was decisive and brutal. The town was squeezed on all sides and the king's
palace (of which no trace remains) was seized. The king and most of the survivors
slipped out of town into the palm groves which then covered most of Mombasa island,
but 1513 Mombasans had been killed – as against five Portuguese.

The king attempted to save Mombasa by offering to become a vassal of Portugal, but
the request was turned down, the Portuguese unwilling to lose the chance to **loot** the
abandoned town, picking over the bodies in the courtyards and breaking down the
strongroom doors until the ships at anchor were almost overladen. Then, as a parting
shot, they fired the town. The narrow streets and the cattle stalls between the thatched
houses produced a conflagration that must have razed Mombasa to the ground.

In 1528, the Portuguese returned once again to wreck and plunder the new city that
had grown on the ashes of the old. In the 1580s, it happened twice more; on the last
occasion, in 1589, there was a frenzied **massacre** at the hands of the Portuguese and
– coincidentally – a marauding tribe of nomads from the interior called the Zimba
(about whom little is known except their cannibalistic notoriety). The Zimba's unholy
alliance with the Europeans came to a treacherous end at Malindi shortly afterwards,
when the Portuguese, together with the townsfolk and 3000 Segeju archers, wiped
them out.

Remarkably, only two years after this last catastrophe, Mombasa launched a major
land expedition of its own against its old enemy, Malindi. It had finally met a decisive
match. The party was ambushed on the way by Malindi's Segeju allies, who themselves
stormed and took Mombasa, later handing over the town (in which they had little interest) to the Portuguese at Malindi. The Malindi corps transferred to Mombasa, the
Malindi sheikh was grandly installed as sultan of the whole region, and the Portuguese
set to work on **Fort Jesus**, dedicated in 1593.

Fort Jesus

Once completed, the fort became the focus of everything that mattered in Mombasa,
changing hands a total of nine times between the early seventeenth century and 1875.
The first takeover happened in 1631, in a **popular revolt** that resulted in the killing of

every last Portuguese. But the Sultan, lacking support from any of the other towns under Portuguese domination, eventually had to desert the fort and the Portuguese, waiting in Zanzibar, reoccupied it. For the rest of the seventeenth century they continued to hold Mombasa, at first consolidating their control of the Indian Ocean trade.

Meanwhile, however, the **Omani Arabs** were becoming increasingly powerful. And as Dutch, English and French ships started to appear on the horizon, time was clearly running out for the Portuguese trading monopoly. Efforts to bring settlers to their East African possessions failed, and they retreated more and more behind the massive walls of Fort Jesus. Portugal's East African "empire" was under siege, and in 1696–98 Fort Jesus itself was isolated and besieged into submission by the Omanis who, with support from Pate and Lamu, had already taken the rest of the town. After 33 months almost all the defenders – the Portuguese corps and some 1500 Swahili loyalists – had died of starvation or plague.

Under Arab rule

Rapid disenchantment with the new Arab rulers spilled over in 1728 into a mutiny among the fort's African soldiers. The Portuguese were invited back – for a year. Then the fort was again besieged and this time the Portuguese gave up quickly. They were allowed their freedom, and a number were said to have married and stayed in the town. But Portuguese power on the coast was shattered for ever.

The new Omani rulers were the **Mazrui** family. Soon after the return of some kind of normality in Mombasa, they declared themselves independent of Oman, a direct challenge to the **Busaidi** family who had just seized power in the Arabian homeland. Civil war in Oman prevented the Busaidis from doing much about their wayward overseas agents: with the **Nabahani** family in Pate no longer paying much allegiance either, control of what were fast reverting to independent states was increasingly difficult. As usual, though, the lack of unity on the coast prevented any lasting independence.

Intrigue in the Lamu archipelago led to the Battle of Shela (p.517) and Lamu's unwittingly disastrous invitation to the **Sultan of Oman**, Seyyid Said, to occupy its own fort. From here, and by now with British backing, the Busaidis went on to attack Mazrui Mombasa repeatedly in the 1820s.

There was a hiccup in 1824 when a British officer, **Captain Owen**, fired with enthusiasm for defeating the slave trade, extended British protection to Mombasa on his own account, despite official British support for the slave-trading Busaidis. Owen's "Protectorate" was a diplomatic embarrassment and – no surprise – did not last long. The Busaidi government was only installed when the Swahili "twelve tribes" of Mombasa, the traditional inhabitants of the immediate hinterland, fell into a dispute over the Mazrui succession and called in Seyyid Said, the Busaidi leader. In 1840, he moved his capital from Oman to Zanzibar and, with Mombasa firmly garrisoned, most of the coast was soon in his domain.

Surviving members of the Mazrui family went to Takaungu near Malindi and Gazi, south of Mombasa. British influence was sharpened after their guns quelled the mutiny in 1875 of al-Akida, "an ambitious, unbalanced and not over-clever" commandant of the Fort. Once British hegemony was established, they leased the **coastal strip** from the Sultan of Zanzibar and Fort Jesus became Mombasa's prison, which it remained until 1958.

Fort Jesus

Daily 8.30am–6.30pm; Ksh200 adults, Ksh100 children/students; PO Box 82414; ☎011/312839, fax 227297.

Today **Fort Jesus** is a quietly studious museum-monument, surprisingly spacious and tree-shaded inside its giant walls, and retaining most of its original (over the centuries much repaired) character. The curious angular construction was the design of an Italian architect and ensured that assailants trying to scale the walls would always be under crossfire from one of the bastions. It is a classic European fortress of its age.

The best time to visit is probably first thing in the morning; the guidebook on sale is an interesting source of information. Look out especially for the restored **Omani House**, in the far right corner as you enter the fort. Avoiding head contact with the lintel, climb up to the flat roof for a wonderful view over Mombasa. Interesting in their own way, too, are the uncomfortable-looking, wall-mounted **latrines**, which would presumably have been closed in with mats. It is immediately obvious that Fort Jesus was not so much a building as a small, resolutely fortified town in its own right. The ruins of a church, storerooms, and possibly even shops are up at this end and, to judge by some accounts, the main courtyard was at times a warren of simple dwellings. Captain Owen described it in 1824 as being: ". . . a mass of indiscriminate ruins, huts and hovels, many of them built wherever space could be found but generally formed from parts of the ruins, matted over for roofs."

Most of the archeological interest is at the seaward end of the fort, where you'll find the **Hall of the Mazrui** with its beautiful stone benches and eighteenth-century inscription – and a sad quantity of twentieth-century graffiti as well. A nearby room has been dedicated entirely to the display of a huge plaster panel of older **graffiti**, scribbled and etched onto the wall by bored Portuguese sentries. Their subjects are fascinating: ships, figures in armour (including caricatures of the captain of the fort wielding his baton), fish, a chameleon and various motifs. Illiteracy precluded much writing but, oddly enough, there's nothing obscene either (perhaps it has been erased?). The small **café** up here has been serving first-class lime juice for years (or, if you want something to eat, the museum **restaurant**, behind the ticket office, has a lunch dish each day and various snacks).

Fort Jesus Museum

The **museum**, on the eastern side of the fort where the main soldiers' barracks block used to be, is small, but it manages to convey a good idea of the age and breadth of Swahili civilization, and also has a decent display of Mijikenda ethnography (see p.456). Most of the displays are of pottery, indigenous or imported, some from as far afield as China and some of it over a thousand years old. A number of private collections have contributed pieces and there's probably still a wealth of material in private hands. Look out for the big carved door taken from the Mazrui house in Gazi (p.477) and also the extraordinary whale vertebra used as a stool. The museum has a good exhibit on the long-term project to recover as much as possible from the wreck of the *Santo Antonio de Tanna*, which sank in 1697 while trying to break the prolonged siege of the fort. Some 7000 objects have already been brought to the surface, but the bulk of the ship itself remains nine fathoms deep in the harbour.

Around town

From Fort Jesus, the **Old Town** is an easy objective. If you've got the time and the inclination for in-depth exploration, pick up a copy of the guidebook *The Old Town Mombasa*, published by the Friends of Fort Jesus, and available there as well as in some bookshops (see "Listings", p.437). It has a good map, and loads of information on architecture, history and distinguished past residents.

First impressions – of a quarter entirely devoted to gift and **curio shops** – are none too encouraging. But this turns out to be purely the result of Fort Jesus' adjacent car park and tourist appeal, and the shops don't extend far into the Old Town. They are especially ostentatious down at the end of Ndia Kuu Road, where several emporiums are overwhelmingly luxuriant in their displays and multilingual enticements; one or two of them even provide free coffee. Many sell a lot of worthless junk and some deal in shells, including shell lamp stands, ornaments and the like, a trade which operates on the fringes of the law in Kenya. Further west, away from the fort, the stores are smaller, and correspondingly cheaper and less pretentious, with a couple of mouldering genuine antique shops along Kibokini Road. For more about buying crafts, see p.429.

Mosques and other architecture
The Old Town is not in fact that old. Most buildings date from the nineteenth century, and though there may be foundations and even walls that go back many centuries, you'll get a clearer guide to the age of the town from its twenty-odd **mosques**.

The **Mandhry Mosque** on Bachawy Road, founded in 1570, is officially the oldest; rarely open to visitors, it has a striking minaret. The **Basheikh Mosque** on Old Kilindini Road, recently repainted in fresh cream and white, is also acknowledged to be very old – "about 1300", they'll tell you, though this may be exaggerated. Entering the mosques – as long as they aren't locked – is usually all right for men who arrive properly covered and barefoot. Sometimes you may be expected to wash hands and feet as well. Women, however modestly dressed, will as often as not be politely refused.

Much of the other **architecture** in the Old Town is profoundly influenced by the Indian-style Zanzibari tastes of the Busaidi occupiers of the nineteenth century. This is particularly noticeable in the elegant fretwork balconies and shutters still maintained on a few houses, notably on Ndia Kuu. For older relics, you'll have to look further. There are a number of quite ancient tombs along the seafront, especially towards the northern end of the Old Town, some of which have pillars; this is the part of Mombasa considered to be "medieval", or in other words pre-Portuguese.

Returning south along the twisting **seafront road** ("seafront", although the harbour can only be glimpsed), you come to the gigantic mosque of the Bohra Muslims: "Burhani Masjid for Dawoodi Bohra Community", says the sign. In the unassuming setting of the Old Town, it is an imposingly massive edifice.

The dhow harbour
The **dhow harbour** is wildly overrated. There are usually a few boats in port but you can no longer expect to see dozens, let alone hundreds, of dhows, even at the end of the northeast monsoon in April, traditionally the peak time for arrivals. Seasonal variations are less important now that the big *jahazis* have engines. Nor are you likely to have the opportunity to go aboard one of these exotic vessels – a tourist tradition, with coffee and souvenirs, that has died out. Instead, try to imagine how it must once have looked, chat to the many policemen standing around and don't, whatever you do, raise your camera (the harbour is considered a strategically sensitive subject). In fact, you might consider concealing it: muggings and other hassles have become common. Attempting to travel by dhow from Mombasa is, regrettably, an equally discouraging story. Lamu holds more promise (see "Travel Details", p.544).

The Jain temple
Heading up towards Digo Road, you might enjoy stopping by at the **Jain temple**, whose entrance is in Langoni Road (take your shoes off). This sublime creation – intricate icing sugar outside, scrupulously clean and scented within and decorated in dozens of pastel shades – was only built in 1963. Jainism is a Hindu religion closely related to Buddhism and commonest in Gujarat (home of the majority of Kenyan Asians), which prohibits the eating of any kind of animal – in its extreme form, even root vegetables are taboo – and aspires to release adherents from the physical universe and its eternal cycle of death and rebirth. The temple interior is ornamentally and substantially magnificent: the painted figurines of deities in their niches are each provided

with a drain so they can be easily showered down, while around the ceiling, exquisitely stylized pictures portray scenes from a human life, including a familiar snake temptation in a garden.

The Swahili Cultural Centre

The name is promising, but at present the **Swahili Cultural Centre** (free; PO Box 82412; ☎011/227643, fax 227297) offers nothing likely to impress the casual visitor. Located on the quiet east side of Mombasa island, off Mama Ngina Drive next to Mombasa Hospital, the centre is part of a United Nations Development Programme project on the coast, created to alleviate youth unemployment and foster traditional skills. Crafts courses operate in joinery and woodcarving, textile manufacture and embroidery, with associated classes in Swahili design and business management running alongside. It's possible to visit, informally, at any time during the week, though you should go in the morning or late afternoon if you want to find any students there. Let them know in advance if you're coming with a large group. The variety of buildings that make up the centre are set among trees on ancient coral cliffs above Mombasa Harbour, and could become a popular attraction if there was a bit more to do. Meanwhile, embroidery (including some very fine *kofia* skull caps) and a limited selection of carvings are available for sale, at more or less fixed prices.

Walks around Mombasa

For the most part, the rest of Mombasa's pleasures are simple. Strolling, with plenty of cold-drink stops, is a time-honoured Mombasan diversion. You will probably want to see that immortal pair of **elephant tusks** on Moi Avenue. To get to them, you have to run the gauntlet of curio booths that have almost hidden the cool hideaway of Uhuru Gardens on the right, with its Africa-shaped fountain. And when you get there, you may regret your determination to view the tusks close up: they are revealed as grubby aluminium.

More rewarding, if you have the time and inclination for a **long walk**, is the circuit that takes off around the breezy, seaward side of the island down **Mama Ngina Drive**: a fine morning's or evening's walk, when it seems to become the meeting place for half of Mombasa's Indian population. You can get back to town on a *matatu* from the market by Likoni ferry. There are lots of places to sit and watch the waves pounding the coral cliffs through the break in the reef. On the clifftop, protruding from the far side of the golf course (Mombasa Golf Club; ☎011/222620; KGU affiliates Ksh500, others Ksh1000), are the stumpy, insignificant remains of Fort St Joseph, built in 1826 to defend Mazrui Mombasa against the attacks of the Busaidi Omanis. Come down this clifftop promenade at weekends or in the early evening and you'll find plenty of other people doing the same – there are food stalls in several places. At the end of Mama Ngina is an extensive and surprising forest of enormous **baobab trees**, frequently associated with ancient settlements on the coast.

Finally, just to the west of the Likoni ferry roundabout is a huge pillar tomb, the **Mbaraki Pillar**. Supposedly the burial place of a seventeenth-century mainland sheikh, chief of one of the "twelve tribes", its eight-metre height is impressive enough, but it is nevertheless dwarfed by the towers of the nearby molasses refinery.

Beaches and swimming

Mombasa island has no proper beaches of its own. The nearest are **Shelly Beach**, covered in more detail on p.461 (*matatu* or bus from Kenyatta Avenue to the Likoni Ferry, then turn left and walk/hitch 2–3km), and **Nyali Beach**, covered on pp.441–445 (*matatus* from the south end of Abdul Nassir Road, near the junction with Mackawi Road by the mosque, to after Nyali Bridge, then turn right and go 4km). Shelly Beach is relatively uninteresting and narrow, with the reef close to the shore, but fairly peaceful. Nyali is pretty good, crowded at weekends and holidays, and the reef here is much further out. There are several public points of access to Nyali beach, but the easiest is right by the entrance to the *Nyali Beach Hotel*. Most of the time, hotels do not mind if you use their own beaches, bars and restaurants. If it's simply a swim you're after, see "Swimming pools" on p.441.

Shopping

Mombasa is a good city for **shopping**, with a generally wide choice, and fewer hassles as you window-shop than in Nairobi. Once you know where to go for crafts, the business of buying souvenirs improves markedly. For cloth, Mombasa is blessed with Biashara Street.

The main tourist street, as you'll soon discover, is the stretch of Moi Avenue between the Tusks and Digo Road. A number of the retail businesses here are housed in quite old premises, going back to the early years of the twentieth century (look out for Kitui General Stores, which is housed in Old Tusk Lodge, a fine example of an old trading house). However, it's hard to take in the architecture when the pavement is lined with souvenir stalls. Sisal baskets, soapstone, beadwork and fake ebony carvings make up eighty percent of the wares. Those at the Digo Road end of Moi Avenue tend to be the most aggressive at touting their wares, and getting past without stopping is not easy, while, if you do halt, making cool decisions can be fraught. The stalls along Digo Road to the south of the Moi Avenue roundabout are barely any less hassle. The line of stalls on **Chembe Road** seem to be in something of a backwater, and are more fun to deal with.

If you're **buying crafts** in Mombasa, whatever else you do, first go and have a look at Haria's Gift Shop on Moi Avenue, near the Tusks (Mon–Sat 9am–6pm; credit cards accepted). They consistently offer good deals and you may even be able to get things here more cheaply than on the street. Labeka, also on Moi Avenue, is another good store for browsing, with sensible prices and a pleasant, hassle-free environment.

Markets

For a return to earth, visit Mombasa's municipal market, **Mackinnon Market**, which has a splendid abundance of tropical fruit, including such exotics as jackfruit (too big for most people at around 10 kilos) and soursops (a taste you'll either love or hate). Behind the market is a row of stores devoted to spices, coffee and tea – good for bulk turmeric or what-have-you – and several good sweet shops. Apart from the Mackinnon and the big street market off Mwembe Tayari, there's **Makupa market** in the heart of

---

BARGAINING

The usual rules apply when **bargaining** – don't start the ball rolling if you're not in the mood and never offer a price you're not prepared to pay. If you want quite a few items, it's worth browsing for a well-stocked stall and then, as you reach one near-agreement after another with the stallholder, add a new item to your collection. This way you should be able to buy well-finished *vyondo* (sisal baskets) in the range of Ksh200–300, small soapstone items for Ksh50–100, and bracelets and necklaces for a similar price. It's impossible to estimate what you'll pay for carvings as the price depends as much on the workmanship as on the size of the piece. If you expressly *don't* want to purchase ebony (the wood is increasingly rare), you'll run into some amusing conversational one-way streets with stallholders who are a dab hand at "proving" their lumps of dyed acacia wood are ebony.

Majengo, the island's low-income housing district. A colourful, multipurpose market with a busy, rural atmosphere, it's well worth a visit. Go 1500m up Jomo Kenyatta Avenue, then turn left at Salim Mwa Ngunga Road.

Cloth and hardware

Mombasa is also a cheap place to buy the **fabrics** the coast is famous for. Check out the latest *kanga* designs in **Biashara Street**, where they are usually available before anywhere else in Kenya. *Kangas* are distinguished from *kitenges* in that they also carry a printed message, whether "Jambo from Kenya" for the tourists, or more subtle proverbs and sayings in Swahili, still used as a means of communicating messages, either from a husband buying the cloth for his wife or mother-in-law, or by a wife to her husband. Some of the home-produced patterns (usually by "Rivatex") are so good – unusual combinations of brilliant fast colours used to startling effect – they are beginning to make an impact abroad, though prices are usually higher than for imports (Ksh750 for a pair of cotton *kitenge*, for example, as opposed to Ksh400 for an Indian or Indonesian version). Synthetic (nylon) cloth is much cheaper, around Ksh200–300 for *kangas*, Ksh250 for *kikois*, and Ksh450 for Maasai-style checkered wraps. You can also have clothes made to measure (Ksh800 for a dress, for example). It's worth checking prices in several shops before buying, and perhaps going with company so you can bargain for several lots at once: they are always sold in pairs. In the high season, Biashara Street swarms with other tourists looking for "the real Mombasa", so you'll need all your haggling skills; it's actually quite difficult to budge prices more than a token Ksh40–50 for the sake of politeness, as business is just too good.

Beyond Kwavi Road, Biashara Street shifts from textiles to a less gaudy section of **household goods**, such as winnowing trays, coconut graters, palm bags, mats, spoons and furniture. It's more mundane, but just as interesting to browse. For genuine Indian **sarongs**, have a rummage through Old Town.

Eating

The city is full of places to eat, and **street food** is much better – and more available – than in Nairobi. Among the delicacies, try the spicy little kebabs (sometimes chicken, and called "chicken tikka" anyway); young coconuts bursting with juice and lined with soft jelly; and cuplets of *kahawa thungu* (thick bitter coffee, usually flavoured with ginger). Many stalls (mostly open at night) offer what amount to full meals for under Ksh100, including *nyama choma* (roast meat), *muhogo wa nazi*, *samaki wa kupaka*, *chapati*, *marondo*, and pilau. Some also sell cigarettes, sodas, and *miraa*. You'll find them outside *Sky Bar* along Moi Avenue, outside *Casablanca Day & Night Club* nearby on Mnazi Moja Road, at the junction of Nkrumah, Digo and Moi Avenue at *Salambo Disco*, and at Mwembe Tayari bus terminus.

Restaurants

Mombasa is well supplied with good, **cheap restaurants**. Especially if you're newly arrived from up-country, they are one of the city's chief delights, as a discernible cuisine involving coconut, fish, chicken, rice and beans, incorporating spicy Asian flavours, begins to make an impression on your palate. Unfortunately, many Swahili restaurants have closed down, but you'll still find some excellent places stretched out along the north coast, and easily accessible by (24-hour) *matatus* from outside the GPO: the best of these have been listed on p.444 (Nyali) and p.449 (Bamburi to Shanzu).

SWAHILI FOOD

Banadir Café, Kibokoni Rd, Old Town. Basic but satisfying Swahili food – and very cheap.

Recoda, Nyeri St, Old Town. Mombasa's best restaurant for Swahili food and one of its oldest (opened in 1942, partly to record old Mombasa – hence the name and the photos on the walls). Open evenings only, it's a good excuse to throw off any misgivings and plunge into the Old Town after dark. Sitting at pavement tables, choose from a limited but very cheap list of fish, creamed beans, cassava, plantain, *mahamri* and *mushkaki* with salad. If you're not prepared to pick your portion, they'll bring you a never-ending selection though service can sometimes be grumpy and confused. Go early, as by 8pm they're running out of favourites. Ksh150–250 sees most people incapacitated, though you can eat pretty well for half that. Closed Ramadan. There's also a branch at the Moi Ave Tusks, open all day, which leans towards roast meat.

Reef Woods Café, Chembe Rd. Brilliant value and tasty food in this new Swahili place. Ksh50–80.

FAST FOOD, HOTELIS AND UP-COUNTRY COOKING

Bella-Vista, Moi Ave, behind Agip service station by the Tusks (☎011/225848). Established over thirty years, serving up reasonable seafood (and black oysters) and meat grills (*nyama choma*), and some curries. Mains with a drink or two for Ksh250–500. Happy hour 6.30–9pm. Closed Sun.

Blue Fin, Meru Rd. Fish and chips and other dollar-a-meal fry-ups. Open daily.

Blue Room, Haile Selassie Rd. Self-service with lots of spotless aluminium tables, fans and a cool courtyard: very Western, and you pay the price. The pizzas and juices are good, but basics are a little expensive, and service is slow all things considered.

Ifti's Cafe, Hospital St. Self-service cafeteria – a smaller version of the *Blue Room* – with AC, decent if unexciting burgers, chips and sausages (around Ksh120). Daily 9am–10.30pm.

Ingo's Snack Bar, Harbour House, Moi Ave, near the Tusks. Does excellent toasted sandwiches and vegeburgers, and boasts an appetizing salad bar. Prices are similar to the *Blue Room*, but service is better. Open to 11pm.

Lotus Hotel, corner of Mvita and Cathedral roads. Clean and efficient, the food is generally well cooked (though the goat can be a plateful of bones) and the chef is willing to do anything not already on the menu given a day's notice. Try the lightly curried tuna.

Pizza Hotline, Ground Floor, NSSF Building, Nkrumah Rd (☎011/315172). Tasty pizzas and other fast food, with AC.

Sharwma Café, Gusii St (☎011/222742). Roast chicken, pitta bread, sandwiches and curries.

Splendid Hotel, Moi Ave. The rooftop *nyama choma* is fun, and the rooftop itself delightfully airy, but ordering from the general menu can be unpredictable, and is often slow.

INDIAN COOKING

Al-Sultan, Meru Rd. Mughlai cooking, and air-conditioning.

Coconut Restaurant, behind the GPO, across from *Toyz* nightclub. Daily specials of pilau and curries, plus chicken and chips.

Indo Africa, Haile Selassie Ave, next to *Cosy Guest House* (☎011/228524). Much more expensive than the almost adjacent *New Chetna*, and with less choice, but North Indian rather than Gujarati. Decor notable for being absent, though the food is said to be reliably good (and less abdominally-challenging than *New Chetna*'s). Try the prawn or fish masala, or *muttar paneer* (cooked, home-made cheese) for vegetarians. Easily Ksh500 and up. Open daily.

New Chetna, Haile Selassie Ave, next to *Cosy Guest House* (☎011/224477). A long-time favourite for cheap and tasty vegetarian Gujarati dishes at low prices. The eat-all-you-can vegetarian *thali* (Ksh210) is superb. The food can be very hot, so not for the uninitiated. Recommended. Daily 8am–9pm.

Safir, Maungano Rd, behind the *Splendid Hotel*. Indian and Swahili food in a small dining room or at one or two pavement tables. Curries, biriani and pilau for lunch; chicken tikka and tandooris for dinner. Good eating for under Ksh200.

Shehnai Restaurant, Fatemi House, Maungano St (☎011/312492). Mughlai specialities with a good reputation, in a spacious and light interior with somewhat regal furniture. You're spoilt for choice (100 dishes): try *Achar Gosht* (tender mutton cooked in spices and flavoured with pickles), or *Machi Tandoorwalli* – rock cod marinated in spices and grilled in a clay oven. Vegetarian around Ksh450, non-veg Ksh650. Closed Mon.

Singh Restaurant, Mwembe Tayari Rd (☎011/493283). A bit of a walk from the centre of town, but very tasty Punjabi curries when you get there.

Splendid View Restaurant (tucked behind the *Splendid Hotel*, with a view of it). Try the *Faluda* for an extraordinary gastronomic experience.

Stavrose Café, Sheikh Jundani Rd/Maungano Rd (☎011/225216). A small place that's been serving Indian snacks, tikka dishes and kebabs for years. Lunches from around Ksh150–200.

FOREIGN CUISINES

Le Bistro, Moi Ave (daily 9.30am–midnight). Modern and stylish, with very reasonable charcoal-grilled offerings, and economical lunchtime set menus (Ksh200). Around Ksh500.

Galaxy Chinese, Archbishop Makarios Rd, off the far end of Moi Ave (☎011/226132). Good Chinese – they also have branches on Diani Beach and Bamburi Beach.

Hamburger House, Kisumu Rd, just past the Tusks off Moi Ave. Well above average, with an extensive menu.

Hard Rock Café, Nkrumah Rd (Mon–Sat 7.30am–10pm). Always buzzing and not bad at all, despite occasional off days – fancy pizzas, seafood and steaks chosen from hide-behind laminated menus. Around Ksh150–400, with large cocktails (around Ksh200).

Hong Kong, Moi Ave, 350m west of the Tusks, next to "Kenya Toyota" (☎011/226707). Cantonese, with pleasant service and good food: try the chicken cashew, prawn piripiri or sate beef. Around Ksh400. Open daily.

Hunter's Steak Bar, mezzanine floor, Ambalal House (South Tower), Nkrumah Rd (☎011/311156). A very German *kneipe* (pub), with waiters in silly pith helmets and bandoliers, grilled steaks and seafood to the fore. No music, cold AC. Around Ksh1000 a head. Closed 3–6.30pm & Sun.

La Terrazza, at the International Casino, Mbuyuni Rd, Mombasa (☎011/312838). Refined Italian business lunches in mock-rustic surrounds, with views over Kilindini Harbour and the ocean. Seafood specialities, homemade pasta and charcoal-grilled meats, and quick set-lunch menus also. Secure parking, courtesy bus service. Closed Sun lunch.

New Overseas, Moi Ave, 200m west of the Tusks (☎011/230729–30). Excellent-value Cantonese cooking, focusing on seafood, with some more expensive Korean specialities including raw tuna fish *sashimi*. Also notable for its comical robot door-chime, which chants "Welcome" and "Thank you very much" in a Chinese accent. Ksh250–500. Open daily.

New Suriya Restaurant, Nyeri Rd, Old Town. Very similar to the *Recoda* but with Ethiopian food, and pricier.

Tepanyaki, *Golden Hook* complex, over Nyali Bridge on the left (☎011/471217). The only Japanese restaurant on the coast, tepanyaki-style (the stuff is cooked on your table), with *sushi* too. Credit cards accepted. Free transport from North Coast hotels.

SEAFOOD

The two best seafood restaurants are the *Sea Harvest* and *Tamarind*, both on the mainland side of Nyali bridge: see p.444.

Snacks and juice bars

For **snacking**, and the **drinks** you'll probably want to consume ceaselessly, there are corner cafés, hole-in-the-wall juice bars, and confectionery shops all over town.

Anglo-Swiss Bakery, Chembe Rd. The best bakery in Mombasa, and the place to buy something to eat with your coffee at the Mombasa Coffee House.

Camel's Joint, behind the GPO, next to Jamhuri Park. An outdoor place, with ice cream (including "Scud", blended mixed fruit topped with ice cream), juices and snacks.

Luxus Café, Nkrumah Rd, facing Holy Ghost Cathedral. Excellent passion juice and a wonderful shady terrace. Good for simple orders such as sodas, and with a pleasant view of the Holy Ghost Cathedral.

Mombasa Coffee House, Moi Ave. The Kenya Coffee Board's elderly establishment does a good pineapple pie.

Pistachio, Chembe Rd. It's hard to beat this snack bar for the quality of its ice cream and various kinds of coffee, but it isn't cheap. Breakfast is good value however, and they also do lunch dishes. Mon–Sat 7.30am–10pm, Sun noon–10pm.

Taheri Cold House, Nkrumah Rd. Excellent juices and delicious, filling dishes of *chana bateta*. Closed weekends.

Pan shops

Highly characteristic of Mombasa are the Indian **pan shops**, often doubling as tobacconists and corner shops. You have to try *pan* at least once. It's essentially a mildly narcotic dessert, chewed and sucked but not swallowed, consisting of your choice of sweet spices, chopped nuts and vegetable matter, syrup, and white lime, from a display of dishes, all wrapped in a hot-sweet, dark green betel leaf. Pop the triangular parcel in your mouth and munch – it tastes as exotic and unlikely as it sounds – then spit out the pith when you're finished. One of the best *pan* shops is the friendly café-style *Dilbahar* at the corner of Bungoma Street and Digo Road, which also does soft drinks, juices, *lassi*, and sweetly spiced *chai*. It's a lovely calm refuge for a few hours, or a place to read the paper.

Drinking and nightlife

Despite the city's overwhelmingly Muslim population, you won't go thirsty. There are several **nightclubs** too, though you might not guess as much during the day. Always check bills carefully as mistakes are increasingly common.

Bars

Casablanca, Mnazi Moja Rd, just off Moi Ave. This draws a big mixed crowd to a lively terrace, and the prostitutes gather here in force, especially upstairs. They can be a pain – or a laugh – depending on your mood. Cold beers, some (usually good) food, rooms by the hour, or even for the whole night. Food and drinks expensive by local standards.

Excellent Hotel, Haile Selassie Ave. Next door to the hotel, a large and cool old-timers' place. Unlustily, and no prostitutes. There's a live band upstairs on the roof on Saturday nights (free entry).

Hard Rock Café, Nkrumah Ave. This is the island's fanciest bar, selective in its choice of customers because of the relatively high prices, yet still in danger of becoming a pick-up joint.

Le Bistro, Moi Ave. This grillroom is also good for a calm beer (cheaper Tues–Fri 4–8pm), and is generally free of prostitutes. Snooker table. Open daily till midnight.

WALKING IN MOMBASA AT NIGHT

If you don't want to join the throngs in the clubs but don't feel inclined to stay in your room either, **walking after dark** is generally safe in the Old Town and along the main thoroughfares. Around the Old Town, you'll still come across one or two coffee-sellers selling their thick black *kahawa* from traditional high-spouted jugs. Like the men who used to sell glasses of water, their trade has almost died out. At the corner of Langoni and Old Kilindini roads, there's a very good *halwa* shop, normally open late: a hundred grams of fragrantly perfumed almond *halwa* is a fine accompaniment to coffee.

Lotus Hotel, corner of Mvita and Cathedral roads. One of the nicest places in town for a civilized beer, with a comfortable open-air bar as well as an air-conditioned one.

New Palm Tree, Nkrumah Ave. A calm and cool, if somewhat dull, bar, where you can drink at about the lowest prices in the town centre.

Royal Court Hotel, Haile Selassie Ave. Forget the unexceptional ground-floor bar, and head up by lift to the fifth floor, where a flight of steps leads you to a breezy rooftop terrace, great for idle drinks while watching the sunset over town. They usually have a live band here Fridays (currently playing Congolese-style dance hits).

Sky Bar, Moi Ave. Not exactly the place for a quiet drink: there's lots of action, gay as well as straight. You can't avoid company, as the prostitutes are out in force.

Nightclubs and live music

The major tourist hotels are situated outside town and, consequently, so are the flashiest **discos**, though the hotel discos themselves are generally pretty dull: for details of the best of the rest, read the "Nightlife" sections on p.475 (Diani), and p.449 (Bamburi and Shanzu). This, unfortunately, leaves Mombasa itself depleted of high-tech action, and few bands find it worthwhile to play on the island when the resorts pay more. Most of Mombasa's older-style nightclubs at the more disreputable, dock end of Moi Avenue have passed away. The recommendations given below are established and enjoyable. On busy nights (Wed, Fri & Sat), men are charged up to Ksh200 entry, while women are admitted half-price or free.

Mombasa Sports Club, Mnazi Moja Rd. Friday and Saturday are "African nites", with various live bands.

New Florida Nightclub & Casino, Mama Ngina Drive, overlooking the ocean (☎011/313127). Attempts a slick scene, with a choreographed floor show (currently ex-Bolshoi dancers escaping the collapsed rouble) and lots of glitter, but everyone knows what it's really for. While in the essentials it doesn't seem to differ noticeably from its Nairobi namesake – thumping disco, grinding hookers – it does benefit from the terrace by the sea, a pleasant little gaming room (free entry; open from 6pm) and keg beer. It's 2km from the centre, so take a taxi here, or at least back.

New Harbour Hotel, Moi Ave 400m west of the Tusks, at the corner with Liwatoni Rd. One of the few old-time survivors, and the place for visiting Congolese music stars: check the press for details.

Saba-Saba, corner of Jomo Kenyatta Ave and Ronald Ngala Rd (☎011/493877). Often has live music, even in the day, and always provides a sweaty, local atmosphere.

Salambo, Moi Ave (☎011/220180). Open during the day as a dozy bar with very limited snacks, this comes to life at night as the city's only really local disco, with no panderings to tourists or to glitzy style (wonky hallway mirrors excepted). Monday to Saturday there's a mix of *ndombolo*, Congolese

---

BUYING MUSIC CASSETTES

If you harbour even a passing interest in African **music**, Mombasa is as good a place as any to stock up on a few tapes. Prices are low: expect to pay between Ksh150 and Ksh180 for an original cassette, slightly less for dubbed tapes (for imported big names these are invariably low-quality pirates, but the copies of Taarab and traditional music are perfectly legit).

The best place for finding traditional Mijikenda music and Mombasan Taarab, as well as traditional songs from the Wa-Bajuni of Lamu district, is Mbwana Radio Service (☎011/221550), just off Pigott Place in the Old Town. You'll find popular African dance tunes (*soukous*, *ndombolo*) as well as reggae and US soul divas in the street stalls all around town, especially in the streets between Biashara Street and Haile Selassie Road towards Digo Road – just follow your ears. Kikuyu and Kenyan pop, as well as ubiquitous gospel (the cause of the disappearance of traditional music in many parts of the country) is available from the more permanent stuctures: try Zilizopendwa Music Store on George Morura Street.

sounds, funk and reggae, with midnight shows, acrobats, dancing and beauty contests; Sunday features day-long reggae. Open 24 hours.

Toyz, Baluchi St, behind the post office (☎011/313931). Mixed feedback on this, central Mombasa's main club with professional DJs, plastic palm trees and air-conditioning, plus drinks that become more expensive as the night wears on, and a good mix of sounds: you'll hear everything from techno thrash to reggae. Wednesday, Friday and Saturday nights are packed (also many prostitutes), but go on another night and it can be deserted. Live music Sunday afternoons; Sunday evenings are good for dancing without being hassled.

Safari transport and safari operators

Although it doesn't touch Nairobi for variety, you can do most travel-related business in Mombasa, and, with direct charter flights from Europe, Mombasa is increasingly a **safari hub** in its own right, typically for short trips to Tsavo East and Tsavo West aimed at coast-based tourists. For safaris further out, it's easier and cheaper to organize a trip from Nairobi (p.134).

Car rental

Car rental tends to be a little cheaper in Mombasa than in Nairobi if you deal with a local company (Ksh3700–4500 per day for a small saloon rented over a week, including insurance and waivers), but the big multinationals remain expensive (Ksh5000–6000). Read the advice on p.41. You'll find the majority of outlets on Moi Avenue and Nkrumah Road.

Avis, Moi Ave (PO Box 84868; ☎011/223048 or 220465), also at Moi Airport (☎011/433211) and *Serena Beach Hotel* (☎011/485721). Extremely expensive but open to bargaining.

Galu Safaris/Southern Cross Safaris, Ambalal House, Nkrumah Rd (PO Box 99456; ☎011/229520–6, fax 314226). Well priced and has a good reputation.

Glory Car Hire, Trans-Ocean House, Moi Ave (PO Box 85527; ☎011/221159, fax 221196, *glorycarhire@net2000ke.com*). Expensive for a local company, and check the vehicle and small print carefully.

Gupta's, Moi Ave, opposite the Jubilee Insurance Building (PO Box 83451; ☎011/311182, fax 311302). Usually good value, but check the car carefully (as with all companies).

Hertz/UTC, Moi Ave (PO Box 84782; ☎011/316333–4, fax 314549, *utcn@attmail.com*), also at Moi Airport (☎011/433211). Expensive but reliable.

Kuldip's Car Hire, Mji Mpya Rd (PO Box 82662; ☎011/223780, fax 313347). New jeeps, and discounts for cash. Recommended.

Leisure Car Hire, Moi Ave (PO Box 84902; ☎011/313880, fax 228831). Efficient, honest, helpful and sensibly priced. Some Suzuki jeeps.

National Car Rental, Harbour House, Moi Ave (PO Box 86209; ☎011/228318, fax 222139, *natcarma@africaonline.co.ke*). Expensive multinational.

Roadsters Car Hire & Safaris, Tangana Rd (PO Box 90078; ☎011/313483 or 311647, fax 473005). Generally reliable and worth checking out.

Special Lofty Safaris, 1st floor, Hassanali Building, Nkrumah Rd (PO Box 81933; ☎011/220241 or 315789, fax 314397). This safari operator also has some Nissan Sunny's for hire, beating the competition hands-down on price (Ksh2500 per day including 100km).

Unik Car Hire and Safaris, Fatemi Building, Maungano Rd (PO Box 89200; ☎011/226310, fax 311384). Cheap, with some Suzukis jeeps too.

Motorbike rental

If you've got a valid motorcycle driving licence, this is the cheapest option. Scooters for around Ksh1000 per day, Yamaha 600cc for around Ksh2000 per day; prices include 100km.

Fredlink Co. Ltd, High Level Road, 3km from city centre at Shimanzi Industrial Area (PO Box 85976; ☎011/315493).

Pedo Bikes, Kongoni Rd, near Mamba Village roundabout on mainland north of Nyali Bridge (☎011/471193).

Safaris, travel agents and ground handlers

There are a number of safari possibilities from Mombasa apart from an overnight at the Shimba Hills National Park (see p.458). Expect to pay $100 and upwards for a one-day safari (5am pick-up from your hotel) to Tsavo East, including lunch at *Voi Safari Lodge*. Air safaris, even to the Mara, are also quite feasible, though much more expensive (upwards of $400 for two days and one night), although only spending one night you run a higher risk of disappointing game drives. If you're going to Lamu, don't bother with inclusive arrangements: just take a flight there and sort out accommodation when you arrive. Many of the companies listed below also offer half-day **city tours** of Mombasa ($25–35), and day-trips to places like Malindi and Gedi ($100 combined) and Arabuko-Sokoke Forest. Things are much cheaper if you take public transport – full details are given throughout this chapter. The same applies to the much-touted overnight stays in Zanzibar: compare the $500 asking price with the regular $140–168 return airfare (including departure taxes).

Abercrombie & Kent, 3rd floor, Palli House, Nyerere Ave (PO Box 90747; ☎011/316549, fax 314734, *www.abercrombiekent.com*). Impeccable reputation for luxurious tailor-made lodge tours. Expensive. KATO (Kenya Association of Tour Operators).

African Quest Safaris, Palli House, Nyerere Ave (PO Box 40683; ☎011/227052, fax 316501, *aqsltd@africaonline.co.ke*). Large operator doing both camping and lodge safaris, from $100 per day. KATO.

Archer's Tours & Travel (PO Box 84618; ☎011/225362, *archers@africaonline.co.ke*). No frills, rough-and-ready camping safaris. Around $100 per day. KATO.

Big Five, Ambalal House, Mikindani Rd (PO Box 86922; ☎011/311426, fax 311498, *bigfive@form-net.com*). Specializing in expensive lodge air safaris (two nights from $740–770), and lodge safaris by road (two nights at Tsavo and Amboseli $550–590). They're also agents for various dhow trips ($57–100 per person) and day-trips ($25–75 per person), with an overnight at Shimba Hills costing $160 per person. KATO.

Farways Safaricentre, Msanifu Kombo St (PO Box 87815; ☎011/223307, fax 227239). Good value and personal service from a small, long-established company with an excellent network of operator contacts, including car rental, Zanzibar trips, accommodation bookings and safaris.

Hatfield & Holleman, at Sand Island Beach Cottages, Tiwi Beach (PO Box 5516 Diani Beach; ☎ & fax 0127/51233, *hatfield@form-net.com*). Knowledgeable, exclusive and expensive tailor-made safaris, with plenty of ideas to set you dreaming. The general aim is to provide a more complete safari experience than just seeing animals – and includes educational two-way discussions with locals, rangers, and conservationists about local issues, ecosystems, wildlife, and problems faced. It's a new company, but with lots of experience in the field. From $300–500 per person per day.

Pollman's Tours and Safaris, corner of Taveta Rd and Shimanzi Rd (PO Box 84198; ☎011/316732, fax 314502). One of the biggest (you'll see their vehicles everywhere): reliable package tour safaris. Lodge safaris from $200 per day. KATO.

Rhino Safaris, Rhino Building, Nyerere Ave (PO Box 83050; ☎011/311141, fax 315743, *rhinomsa@africaonline. co.ke*). Branch of the respected Nairobi company, but not as immediately impressive. Two nights camping in Tsavo for $270, and a special six-night lodge and luxury tented camp tour in Tsavo and Amboseli for $1055. Half-day Mombasa city tour for $30. KATO.

Somak Holidays, Somak House, Nyerere Ave (PO Box 90738; ☎011/313871, fax 315514, *somak@form-net.com*). Dependable upmarket operation. KATO.

Southern Cross Safaris, Ambalal House, Mikindani Rd (PO Box 99456; ☎011/229520–6, fax 314226, *www.kenya-direct.com/southerncross/*). Branch of the well-respected Nairobi company (p.136), also agents for *Satao Camp* in Tsavo East. Lodge safaris from around $200, and overnights at Shimba ($155–180 depending on the season). KATO.

Special Lofty Safaris, 1st floor, Hassanali Building, Nkrumah Rd (PO Box 81933; ☎011/220241 or 315789, fax 314397). Conscientious operator running its own safaris. They prefer you taking the more expensive but still well-priced "made to order" trips, though they can run camping safaris from about $80 per day. The main draw is their experience and their Land Cruisers (a more personal way of travelling than by Nissan minibus, though they have these too). KATO.

Tour Africa Safaris, ground floor, Social Security House (NSSF), Nkrumah Rd (PO Box 87336; ☎011/316172, fax 316197, *tourafrica@form-net.com*). Well-run and competent travel agency, which also runs its own tailor-made lodge safaris (camping safaris are arranged through other companies). A five-day jaunt in high-class lodges costs $600–800. They also arrange safaris in Tanzania, including the lesser-known national parks, from $90–120 per day camping, or $150–180 in lodges. KATO.

UTC, Moi Ave, PO Box 84782 (☎011/316333-4, fax 314549, *www.unitedtour.com*). This "ground operator" makes the bulk of its business in providing transport and drivers for other companies, but also offers a selection of reasonably priced, tried and tested itineraries. KATO.

Venture Africa, 2nd floor, Canon House II, Bandari Wing, Moi Avenue (PO Box 90217; ☎011/227996–8, fax 228013, *www.venture-africa.com*). Related to the Nairobi outfit, one of the cheapest and appears reliable. KATO.

Moving on from Mombasa

Matatus to most destinations north and west of Mombasa, including Bamburi and Shanzu beaches and Mtwapa Creek, leave from near the GPO on Digo Road. *Matatus* to Malindi congregate at the south end of Abdul Nassir Road, near the junction with Mackawi Road by the mosque. For destinations further afield, its better to catch a bus: details are given overleaf. Information on **sea travel** to Lamu is in "Travel Details" on p.543. The train leaves daily at 7pm (arriving at 8.30am), and costs Ksh3000 in 1st class, Ksh 2100 in 2nd, and Ksh300 in 3rd. Dinner, breakfast and a bed are included in 1st and 2nd class.

Flights
There are no direct scheduled flights from Mombasa to Europe, or elsewhere in Africa excepting Zanzibar and Tanzania: all leave from Nairobi. However, there are a number of direct, non-stop **charter flights**, which you might be able to get a seat on. Airline bookings can either be made direct (see the box on p.439), or through a travel agent: Vogue Tours & Travel, Jubilee Insurance Building, Moi Ave (☎011/221361, fax 316654) are reliable, and can advise on cheap flights back to Europe (currently Gulf Air and Emirates, at under $600 from Mombasa). Don't forget the $20 departure tax on international flights (including Zanzibar) (Ksh100 for flights within Kenya), also payable in sterling (about £12) and shillings (around Ksh1200). Note also that if you're headed for Zanzibar or Tanzania, you'll need to have had a yellow fever jab (and the yellow passport that comes with it). For flight times and prices, see "Travel Details" on p.543.

Listings

American Express c/o Express Travel Group, Nkrumah Rd (PO Box 90631; ☎011/223307, fax 314408).

Banks The best rates are at any of the numerous foreign exchange bureaux springing up around the city, but you need your purchase receipt when changing travellers cheques and few accept VISA cards. Pwani Forex, Digo Rd opposite Mackinnon Market, is efficient (Mon–Sat 8.30am–5pm). Of the banks, the speediest is the Commercial Bank of Africa, Moi Ave (Mon–Fri 8.30am–2.30pm). Otherwise, you'll find branches of Barclays, most with ATM machines for VISA cards, throughout the city (Mon–Fri 9am–3pm, first and fourth Sat of the month 9–11am; Barclays' bureau de change, Moi Ave, Mon–Sat 8.30am–12.30pm & 2–4.30pm). Standard Chartered bank also has ATMs at its Maritime House (Moi Ave) and Treasury Square branches.

MOMBASA BUSES

COAST

Be aware, tourists on coastal bus services, especially Mombasa to Malindi or Nairobi, have been targeted by thieves using drugged food and drink to render their victims unconscious.

Malindi via Kikambala: KBS #11.

Bamburi via Bombolulu: KBS #31.

Kilifi via Kikambala: KBS #39.

Kwale: KBS #34.

Lamu, via Malindi and Kilifi (daily 7–8am; 6–8hr): TSS (cheapest), Faza Express, Tawfiq, Mombasa Liners (who also have a 5.45am departure). For advice about this route, read "Onwards to Lamu" on p.511.

Malindi: Malindi Bus (every 30min; 5am–6.30pm; 90min) and others, from Abdul Nassir Rd.

UP-COUNTRY

Nairobi and the west: competition is fierce over the Mombasa–Nairobi route, with reputations tarnished all round and accidents not uncommon. Note that at the time of writing (mid-1999) the road for much of the way to Nairobi was in a terrible state of repair. Most comfortable and expensive is *The Connection*, which departs daily at 9am, dropping you off at your hotel (Ksh1000; enquiries and reservations through Vogue Tours & Travel, Jubilee Insurance Building, Moi Ave; ☎011/221361, fax 316654). Of the normal buses (Ksh350–400), safest of the lot are Akamba. Mombasa Liners have newish coaches. Most companies run at least one day bus (7–8hr) and one at night (9hr). The night journey can be cold: take warm clothes. Tawfiq's buses go on to Uganda; Akamba connects with its services to western Kenya. Coast Bus can be hair-raising but goes through to Bungoma (5pm; 14hr), Kisumu (6pm; 13hr), Kakamega (6pm; 14hr). Transluxe run direct to Kisii.

Central Kenya: Garissa Express to Maua (5pm; 12hr) and Nyeri (8.30pm; 11hr 30min). Coast Bus and Takrim to Machakos and Kitui (12hr).

Hola and Garissa: From Abdul Nassir Rd: daily at 5.45am on Mombasa Liners and Tawfiq. Garissa Express no longer run to their home town from Mombasa (they go via Nairobi). Mombasa Liners also have a 6.30am bus to Hola.

TANZANIA AND UGANDA

Kampala (Uganda) via Nairobi: Tawfiq (9am).

Dar es Salaam (Tanzania): Various companies from corner Mwembe Tayari Rd/Jomo Kenyatta Ave, and Tawfiq (9am), run several services daily: 14–16hr, via Tanga (7hr).

Bus company booking offices/stages

Akamba Bus, Jomo Kenyatta Ave (☎011/316770).

Coast Bus, Mwembe Tayari Rd (☎011/220158).

Faza Express, Abdul Nassir Rd, next to *New People's Hotel* (☎011/225036).

Garissa Express (Garex), Abdul Nassir Rd (☎011/227201-2).

Goldline, Mwembe Tayari Rd (☎011/220027).

KBS, KBS Bus Station, Jomo Kenyatta Ave (☎011/224851–2).

Malindi Bus, Abdul Nassir Rd (☎011/229662).

Mombasa Liners, Abdul Nassir Rd, next to *New People's Hotel* (☎011/225716).

Takrim, Mwembe Tayari Rd (☎011/495946).

Tawfiq, Abdul Nassir Rd, next to *New People's Hotel* (☎011/433281).

Transluxe, Jomo Kenyatta Ave (no phone).

TSS, Digo Rd, opposite *Elias B&L* (☎011/221839).

Bicycles Mombasa has no bike hire, but buying one is cheap enough: Omar Hussein (Mon–Sat 8.30am–6pm; ☎011/225899) on Haile Selassie Ave near Maungano Rd has a good selection. A three-speed Indian roadster costs Ksh3400, with mountain bikes upwards of Ksh8000.

Bookshops Mombasa has few compared with Nairobi, and most only stock schoolbooks and stationery, so don't rely on finding maps here. Bahati Book Centre, Bahari Bookshop, and Kant Stationers (☎011/225872), all on Moi Ave, are the best.

Cinemas The Kenya, Nkrumah Rd, is the most promising. Otherwise, try the Lotus on Makadara Rd. Both survive on a diet of Indian epics and love stories, with a few American films thrown in. Fort Jesus screens wildlife documentaries (Sunday 7.15pm).

Contraceptives Condoms can be bought in any supermarket or pharmacy. The Family Planning Clinic, which can supply oral contraceptives, is in Mali House, Kenyatta Ave, off Digo Rd (☎011/316937).

Courier services DHL, Ukumbusho House, Treasury Square, Nkrumah Rd (☎011/223933, fax 227837); TNT Express Worldwide, Oriental Building, Nkrumah Rd (☎011/313881); UPS, Ralli House, off Nyerere Ave (☎011/226407, fax 311858).

Dhow cruises Jahazi Marine Ltd (PO Box 89357 Mombasa; ☎011/472213, fax 472414, *jahazi@swiftmombasa.com*) does "cultural trips", sailing around Mombasa in the morning, lunch at their otherwise expensive *Jahazi Restaurant* overlooking Tudor Creek, and afternoons spent at the floating market, visiting a traditional herbalist and dhow builder. They also offer "Mombasa by Night" dhow cruises, including a son-et-lumière performance at Fort Jesus, and a French-style lobster dinner inside served by waiters dressed up as Portuguese, supposedly to remind you of the good old days when the only tourists were heavily armed raiders.

Hospitals Pandya Memorial Hospital, Dedan Kimathi Ave (☎011/314140), is hygienic and efficient, and they also have an ambulance service, as do St John's Ambulance Service (☎011/490625). If

---

AIRLINE COMPANIES

African Express Airways, Ambalal House, Nkrumah Rd (☎011/312820 or 311637, fax 311637). The only jet service to Nairobi, also the cheapest, and may start flights to Zanzibar and Dar es Salaam.

Airkenya, Ambalal House, Nkrumah Rd (PO Box 84700; ☎011/229777, fax 224063; at airport: ☎011/433982, fax 435235).

Coast Air, Moi International Airport (PO Box 84700; ☎011/433320). Charter flights and sightseeing.

Eagle Aviation, mezzanine floor, Ambalal House (North Tower), Nkrumah Rd (PO Box 93926; ☎011/434480–1 or 434504, fax 434249). Some scheduled services, plus package tours to Zanzibar. 10kg baggage allowance.

Kenya Airways, Kenya Airways Terminal, Electricity House, Nkrumah Ave (PO Box 99302; ☎011/221251–9, fax 313815; airport ☎011/433400 or 433541). No flights to Malindi or Lamu (they go direct from Nairobi).

Mombasa Air Safari, Moi International Airport (☎011/433061, fax 434264). Plane charters.

Prestige Air Services, Ambalal House, corner of Nkrumah and Mikindani roads (☎011/221443 or 223073, fax 228157). Charter flights to Lamu (minimum eight passengers; $170 return), more frequent ones to Maasai Mara ($265 return).

The following do not operate flights out of Mombasa but maintain ticketing and reservations offices:

Air Tanzania, 3rd floor, Palli House, Nkrumah Rd (☎011/314752).

British Airways, Trade Bank House, Nkrumah Rd (☎011/312427 or 224206). Can confirm Caledonian Airlines charter flights.

Sabena, Motor Mart Building, Moi Ave (☎011/221995 or 226895).

you're planning to be out in the wilds a lot, Africa Air Rescue (AAR), Harbour House, Moi Ave (☎011/312405) offers short-term membership of its "flying doctors" scheme.

Immigration You can get free visitor's pass extensions at the Provincial Headquarters on Mama Ngina Drive (☎011/311745), but leave enough time, as you always have to wait.

Libraries, Kenya National Library, Msanifu Kombo Rd (Mon–Fri 9.30am–4.30pm); Fort Jesus Museum (archeology; Mon–Fri 8am–12.30pm & 2–4.30pm); British Council, Sheetal Plaza, Mohdar Mohd Habib Rd (Tues–Fri 10am–6pm, Sat 9.30am–1pm; ☎011/223076): has a small air-conditioned library with recent editions of British papers and temporary membership available (Ksh30 per day).

Luggage storage Apart from hotels, the only place to leave bags is the railway station, and their rates seem excessive.

Maps The Survey of Kenya town plan *Mombasa Island and Environs* is useful but it predates the new Nyali Bridge and many street name changes. More up-to-date but not hot on detail is *The Streets of Mombasa Island* map (1998; Ksh200–250). The street-plan book *Mombasa A to Z* (Kenway 1996) is best of all, but out of print: it's worth enquiring in case they do a new edition. If you want to get Survey of Kenya maps of the coast, it's the same story as in Nairobi (see p.149), but autho-rization is unlikely to be given to tourists. The relevant addresses are the Provincial Surveyor's office, 12th Floor, Bima House, Digo Rd (Mon–Fri 9am–12.30pm & 2–4pm), and the DC's office, Room 19, Provincial Headquarters, Mama Ngina Drive, which you must visit if you think it's worth trying to get "the letter of authorization". If you fail, as you probably will, return to Bima House and see if there's anything they can do to help.

Pharmacies The staff at Diamond Arcade Pharmacy, Diamond Arcade, Diamond Trust Building, Moi Ave (Mon–Fri 8am–6pm, Sat 9am–2pm; ☎011/316351), are pleasant and helpful. Yudah Pharmaceuticals, Duruma Rd, are open late (Mon–Fri 9am–10pm, Sat 9am–8pm; ☎011/316028). There's no longer any 24-hour cover in Mombasa: hospital dispensaries can supply necessary drugs and medicaments out of hours.

Post office and telephones (see also "Courier services"). The post office for free poste restante and main services is the General Post Office (GPO) in Digo Rd (Mon–Fri 8am–6pm, Sat 8am–noon). There are cardphones here and a staffed, 24-hour telephone service.

Supermarkets Valu-Plus, Aga Khan Rd and A1 Supermarket, corner of Hospital St and Digo Rd (both Mon–Sat 9am–6pm, Sun 9am–1pm); Chiquitas, Moi Ave (Mon–Sat 8.30am–6.30pm, Sun 9.30am–1pm).

CONSULATES IN MOMBASA

The following diplomatic representatives are mostly honorary appointments; see also the list in the Nairobi chapter (p.150).

Austria, 3rd Floor, Palli House, Nyerere Ave (PO Box 84045; ☎011/313386).

Denmark & Finland, Mr J.H. Nielsen, c/o Comarco, Liwatoni Rd (PO Box 99543; ☎011/316243; residence ☎011/472651).

France, Treasury Square, Nkrumah Rd (PO Box 86103; ☎011/314935).

Germany, 4th floor, Palli House, Nyerere Ave (PO Box 86779; ☎011/314732 or 228781).

Greece, Mr P.Ch. Lagoussis, Dar es Salaam Rd (PO Box 99211; ☎011/224482; residence ☎011/473847).

India, Bank of India Building, Nkrumah Rd (PO Box 90614; ☎011/225286).

Netherlands, Mr L.Van de Lande, Bungalows Rd (PO Box 80301; ☎011/475006, fax 315005; residence ☎011/471250).

Norway, Mrs A. Sondhi, c/o *Reef Hotel*, Nyali (PO Box 82234; ☎011/471771).

Sweden, Mr N.I. Hellman (PO Box 87336; ☎011/316172; residence ☎011/486051).

Switzerland, 8th floor, Ambalal House, Nkrumah Rd (PO Box 85722; ☎011/313403).

Tanzania, 3rd Floor, Palli House, Nyerere Ave (PO Box 1422; ☎011/228596).

USA, Palli House, Nkrumah Rd (☎011/315101).

Theatre The Little Theatre Club (LTC) (PO Box 81143; ☎011/312101) on Mnazi Moja Rd is the occasional venue for the Shangari Players, who put on works by African playwrights. LTC Players occasionally put on African productions, but on the whole they're an outlet for amateur dramatics in the expat/settler community. Seats are about Ksh100 for non-members.

Swimming pools The only one in town is at *Hotel Sapphire* (8am–8pm; Ksh200 adults, Ksh150 children). Further out, you could try the Indian Women's Association, Nyerere Ave, halfway to the Likoni Ferry (during school terms Mon–Fri 5–7.30pm; school holidays Mon–Fri 9am–noon & 2–6.30pm).

Taxis Kenatco, Ambalal House, Nkrumah Rd (☎011/227503) runs reliable 24-hour taxis with fixed prices to the beach hotels. Unlicensed taxis hailed in the street are cheaper if you bargain well.

Tide tables Can be very useful, especially in the Lamu archipelago where ferry departures are dependent upon them; available in bookshops. Daily tables are also published in coastal edition of the *Nation* newspaper, and in *Coastweek*.

Vaccinations The Public Health Department in Msanifu Kombo St gives yellow fever and cholera jabs Wednesday morning and Friday afternoon and typhoid Wednesday afternoon. For women only: yellow fever and cholera Tuesday afternoon, typhoid Monday morning.

Worship The Catholic Holy Ghost Cathdral is on Nyerere Ave. The Anglican Memorial Cathedral is off Nkrumah Rd, down on the right near Fort Jesus.

North of Mombasa

It's easy to get out of Mombasa for the day to explore the nearby **North Coast**. If it's busier, brasher, and generally less pastoral than the **South Coast** (see p.461), there are also more targets for a day-trip up here, with correspondingly less appeal if you simply want to stretch out on the beach. The resorts start just ten minutes' drive from the city centre. Alternatively, if you're on foot, there is ample transport from the Abdul Nassir Road bus and *matatu* area near the *New People's Hotel*. Or simply walk over to the other side of Nyali Bridge and flag down transport. You won't wait long.

Nyali and Nyali Beach

Nyali, the comfortable suburb of Mombasa closest to the town, has a few minor items of interest of its own – apart from three of the North Coast's main hotels. It was the site of **Johan Ludwig Krapf**'s first missionary toehold on the east coast, four years before Livingstone arrived in Africa. Krapf reached Nyali with his wife and baby daughter in May 1844. His wife died of malaria on July 13, their baby the next day. The pathetic graves – still carefully tended by parishioners of St Peter's Church, Nyali – are to be found at the end of the road leading past the *Tamarind Restaurant* (see p.444) and a couple of cement silos. Opposite, on a small knoll, is the stone **Krapf Memorial**.

There's another reminder of the early history of Mombasa in the site of the **Freretown Bell**, at the Nyali Road junction. The bell was erected by the Society of Freed Slaves in the 1880s to warn the people of Freretown (named after Sir Bartle Frere, who founded the freed slave community here) of any impending attack by Arab slavers. The district still has inhabitants who trace the roots of their freed-slave ancestors back to Malawi and Zambia. For years the old bell hung silently under its small stone arch: then, in 1994 it was removed for safekeeping to a nearby Lutheran church, where it is in use, and replaced by a plastic replica – which has now been spirited away.

Behind Nyali Beach and the hotels, you can't miss **Mamba Village** on Links Road (daily 8am–6pm; adults Ksh400, children Ksh250). Nothing to do with poisonous snakes, this is the biggest crocodile (*mamba*) farm in Kenya, with hefty entry fees to the "crocodile trail" and film show. A series of semi-natural pools, created in a disused quarry, houses many thousands of crocodiles at all stages of growth (and a special freaks sideshow of congenitally deformed croc-lets – not a pleasant sight). The overall effect –

MOMBASA: NORTH COAST

Kikambala, △ Kilifi, Watamu & Malindi

MTWAPA

Mtwapa Creek

Prison

Ngomongo Villages

Shanzu Transitional Workshop

Diving Centre

Old Bus Park

School

Shanzu Beach

ACCOMMODATION

Bahari Beach Hotel	22
Baharini Chalets	5
Bamburi Beach Hotel	12
Bamburi Beach Villa	16
Bamburi Chalets	7
Cowrie Shell Beach Apts.	6
Fisherman's Leisure Inn	18
Kenya Beach Hotel	11
Moffat Court Apts.	24
Mombasa Beach Hotel	20
Mombasa Continental Resort	2
Mombasa Safari Inn	1
Mombasa Serena Beach Hotel	3
Neptune Beach Hotel	8
Nyali Beach Holiday Resort	25
Nyali Beach Hotel	27
Nyali Luxury Beach Apts.	26
Ocean View Beach Hotel	15
Petuscha Hotel	4
Plaza Beach Hotel	9
Rami's Beach Cottages	16
Reef Hotel	19
Roy's Pride Rock	21
Severin Sea Lodge	10
Silver Beach Hotel	23
Silver Star Hotel	23
Sonia Apts. Beer Garden	1
Tamarind Village	28
Travellers Beach Hotel	13
Travellers Inn	17
Whitesands Hotel	14

Shops

Diamond Shopping Centre & Shanzu Bazaar

North Quarry Nature Trails

Bamburi Beach

Barclays Bank

Ocean View Shopping Plaza

Bora Bora Disco

Kenyatta Beach

Nguuni Wildlife Sanctuary

Bamburi Cement Factory

RESTAURANTS & BARS

Bamburi Watersports	D
Biene Bar and Restaurant	F
Golden Hook Complex	J
Hong Kong	H
Moorings Restaurant	B
Mtpawa Marine Pub	A
Pirates	E
Prime Time Bar	I
Shanzu Bay Resort	C
Splendid View Café	G
Tamarind Restaurant	K

Bamburi Nature Trail

Planet Centre

0   2 km

Caltex

Bombolulu Cultural Centre

Horse Riding Centre

KISAUNI

Mamba Village Crocodile Farm

KONGOWEA

see 'Mombasa Island' map

Port Tudor

Ratna Shopping Centre

NYALI

Nyali Golf Club

Nyali Beach

MOMBASA ISLAND

Sikh Temple

Police Station

with "croco-burgers" in the snack bar, the 5pm Pavlovian bell-ring feedings, and unlimited saurian souvenirs – is tacky in the extreme, and the crocodile trail sits uneasily with the skin-farming half of the "village", which is not on show. Also part of the saurian empire is the adjacent **Marine Aquarium** (daily 9am–6.30pm; adults Ksh150, children Ksh70), which includes a thirty-minute guided walk around its snake park and gardens, specializing, no great surprise, in the weirdest things they could find, including carnivorous plants and "fishes which blow up for not being eaten" (probably a puffer fish). Also here is the *Mamba International Nightclub* (see p.444). Further down Links Road, the Mamba outfit now also offer **horse-riding** (daily 8–11am & 3–6pm; 1hr beach trips Ksh950; better-value lessons at Ksh2900 for ten 30min stints, or Ksh3900 for ten hour-long rides).

Across the road from *Mamba Village* is **Nyali Golf and Country Club** (PO Box 985678; ☎011/471589), a stuffy sort of place that doesn't go out of its way to welcome non-members. They maintain a dress code for men (shirts with collars, socks) in return for which they offer an ordinary swimming pool, squash, tennis (Ksh1000 for a week's social membership) and, of course, golf (Ksh2000–2200 green fees for non-members or Ksh1000–1100 if playing with a Nyali Club member; caddy Ksh150). A restaurant of the reliable Minar group has opened next door, specializing in Mughlai cuisine (daily; complimentary hotel shuttle service; ☎011/471220). While you're pottering around on Links Road, you might pay a visit to the **Prison Handicraft Showroom**, as unlikely as any a place for handicrafts, but the stuff is usually well-made and cheap. The main public access to the **beach** at Nyali is right by the entrance to *Nyali Beach Hotel*. It gets pretty busy at weekends.

Accommodation

The following **hotel** listings are given from south to north. All the larger hotels can arrange dhow trips, scuba and snorkelling, and trips to Nyali Golf Club, and in the evenings put on cheesy bands and other entertainment. Beaches here are generally narrow, often covered at high tide, and prone to pestering by beach boys. Taxis from Mombasa cost around Ksh600.

Tamarind Village, Cement Silo Rd (PO Box 95805; ☎011/474600–2, fax 474630, *tammsa@africaon-line.co.ke*). Next to the celebrated *Tamarind Restaurant*, this is a luxurious self-service apartment complex with classy touches of Lamu architectural style. Rooms – all en suite with kitchens and AC – overlook Mombasa harbour, and there's a gym, two pools and jacuzzis. No beach. One-bedroom ⑤ low, ⑥ high.

Nyali Beach Hotel (PO Box 90581; ☎011/471551–2, fax 471987, *nyalibh@africaonline.co.ke*; reservations through Block, p.48). Pleasant, bustling and well maintained, this is one of the coast's oldest (1946) and most reputable hotels – establishment in feel but not in any way exclusive. There are two good pools, a jacuzzi and extensive gardens. Good disabled access (lifts and specially designed rooms), daytime kid's club and paddling pool, PADI diving school, and wind surfing and mini-sailing offered for free. Standard rooms are very comfortable, but the only sea views are from the more expensive Palm Wing. Unreasonable phone charges, and overpriced in high season. Discos Wednesday–Saturday. HB ⑥ low, ⑨ high.

Nyali Beach Holiday Resort (PO Box 1874; ☎011/472325, fax 472402). Terracotta-roofed Mediterranean-style development right on the beach, with two pools (one for children; Ksh300/Ksh150 for non-guests). Most of the sixteen rooms face both the pool and the beach, as do the self-catering apartments and "cottages" (four or six people; Ksh5000–8000) equipped with kitchens. All rooms are large, s/c and clean, with AC, nets and TVs. Much better views than Nyali at a fraction of the price. Restaurant and games room, safe parking. Recommended. ③–④ low, ④ high.

Nyali Luxury Beach Apartments, next to Holiday Resorts (PO Box 82843; ☎011/474125, fax 223268). Three four-person self-catering apartments with a pool but no views. Bargaining essential: ⑥ low, ⑦ high.

Moffat Court Apartments, Mt Kenya Rd (PO Box 34126; ☎011/473351 or 472407). Turn right after Mamba Village. A dull modern three-storey block, but cheap, offering sixteen s/c suites and safe parking. Prices bargainable in low season. One bed sleeps two: ③ one-bed, ④ two-bed.

Silver Beach & Silver Star Hotels (☎011/475114, fax 472544; reservations through Prestige Hotels, p.50). Both former African Safari Club establishments, they're now open to all and plans are afoot to merge them (they share the same grounds and facilities). The communal areas are impressive, all meshwork *makuti* ceilings and marble floors, but the feeling of the place is much too formal if you're after a relaxed beach holiday. Unless you've got a long neck, most rooms lack sea views, and the beach, too, is a let-down: small and narrow, bounded by unsightly rubble and concrete defences, and covered at mid- and high-tides. Facilities include two tennis courts, three pools (and paddling pool, but nothing much else for children), sea tricycles, a gym and disco (the *Starion*), and a PADI diving school. The *Silver Star* is probably the only hotel on the coast to offer "aqua jogging", where you're provided with a buoyancy belt and then run on the spot in the pool (Tuesday 5.30pm). *Silver Star* (HB) ④ low, ⑥ high; *Silver Beach* (all-inclusive) ⑤ low, ⑦ high.

Bahari Beach Hotel (PO Box 86693; ☎011/472822, fax 472021, *barahiho@africaonline.co.ke*). Formerly an African Safari Club place (still attracting mainly German clients), built in 1971 and refurbished in December 1997, but lacks the character of more modern places, and can feel a little stuffy. In common with most Nyali hotels, rooms lack sea views (they overlook the manicured gardens instead) and the beach – at the bottom of a small cliff – is just a narrow strip of sand uncovered at low tide. Accommodation is in several two-storey blocks, and rooms are spacious and have balconies. Facilities include a gym, kid's pool and tennis courts. The Ksh1000 day-pass includes lunch, drinks and use of the pool and gym. HB ⑤ low, ⑦ high.

Mombasa Beach Hotel (PO Box 90414; ☎011/471661–5 or 471861, fax 472970; reservations through Kenya Safari Lodges & Hotels, p.48). Despite the clumsy 1970s architecture, there's a good atmosphere here – largely the result of its shady, clifftop location and the fact that it attracts many more African guests than its competitors. Facilities include a safari booking office, tennis courts, and two pools (one huge, the other down at the beach), plus the usual watersports. No disco. Lift access, but no specially designed disabled rooms. HB ⑥ low, ⑥ high.

Roy's Pride Rock (formerly *Kigotho's*), Nyali Rd (PO Box 86178; ☎011/472538 or 472855). Another relatively cheap option set back from the coast (no view), this offers fourteen slightly tatty apartments in separate blocks in the garden, all with fans, equipped with kitchenettes with fridges, and real baths as well as showers. There's also a small pool and a cheap bar-cum-*nyama choma* joint. ③ low, ④ high.

Reef Hotel, Mwamba Drive (PO Box 82234; ☎011/471771, fax 471349, *reefmsa@swiftmombasa.com*). One of Nyali's best, a large and friendly 1972 resort (renovated in 1994), and very much family-oriented, with baby sitters, day-long supervised kid's activities, and a playground and paddling pool to keep them busy. The Garden Wing is a little glum, but there are sea views from the Sea View wing (same price). Superior rooms ($12 per person extra) have minibars and local TV. No disabled facilities, and only some ground floor rooms (no lift). Facilities include a disco, three pools (and pool games), massage, jacuzzi, tennis courts, a PADI diving school and the usual watersports. Courtesy bus to Mombasa. HB ⑤ low, ⑥ high.

Fisherman's Leisure Inn, Mwamba Drive (PO Box 84902; ☎011/474738–9; reservations ☎011/314846, fax 228831). Next to the *Reef Hotel*. Not by the beach, no views and not an obvious choice in its scruffy grounds, this Indian-run place is actually outstanding value, offering a choice of spotless standard rooms (all AC, with nets, TV, phone and minibar) and some huge two-bedroomed apartments, complete with fully equipped kitchenettes and fridges. There's also a pool and jacuzzi, and the *Lobster Pot* restaurant (see below). Recommended. Apartments ⑤ (sleeps four); rooms B&B ④.

Eating and drinking

Anjali's Chinese, Ratna Square Shopping Complex. Fast food and barbecue counter. Not the best, but it's cheap and does the trick. Open Tues–Sat 9am–9pm.

Carnico, at Golden Hook complex, by Nyali Bridge (☎011/471217). The nearest thing to Nairobi's famous *Carnivore* restaurant, serving up vast quantities of the fauna you saw on safari and which you thought was protected, grilled on charcoal. Expensive.

Lobster Pot, Mwamba Drive, at *Fisherman's Leisure Inn*. The Sunday curry lunch buffet here is famous.

Mamba International Nightclub, at Mamba Village (☎011/475180). Huge and popular *makuti*-roofed club, with an expensive sound system and laser light shows (Friday & Saturday midnight & 2am). Wednesdays feature rock, jazz, bhangra or techno, depending on the crowd; Friday plays soul, Congolese sounds and *ndombolo*; Saturdays attract a large Indian and *wazungu* crowd, so techno is the order of the day. On Sunday afternoons (3–10pm) there are family shows, acrobats and jugglers.

Maxim's Bar, at Mombasa Beach Hotel. French-style pretensions, with all the usual overpriced favourites (lobster thermidor and so on); the bouillabaisse Marseillaise (seafood soup) is worth trying.

Roy's Pride Rock. Unfussy *nyama choma* (grilled goat meat) and beer.

Sea Harvest, at the *Golden Hook* complex, by Nyali Bridge (☎011/471217). Classy Lamu-style joint in a prime setting overlooking Tudor Creek, this has the potential to send your finances floating up it (lobster, oysters, calamari . . .), but is highly regarded. Credit cards accepted. Free transport from North Coast hotels.

Tamarind, Cement Silo Rd (☎011/471747 or 474600–2, fax 474630; reservations advisable). From Nyali Bridge, go right at the traffic lights by Freretown Bell Tower, then follow the signs. In a stupendous position, with Mombasa spread out across the creek, the *Tamarind* is one of the best eating houses in Kenya. Go for the seafood platter – excellent value at about Ksh3600 for two; otherwise, the set menu is around Ksh1000 per person. At the jetty below, the same people run the *Nawalilkher* (aka *The Tamarind Dhow*; ☎011/471948, fax 471257), a *jahazi* sailing dhow which has

DHOW TRIPS AND DIVING

For details of **dhow** trip operators, read the box on p.473. Information on **scuba diving** is in the box on p.472.

been converted into Kenya's most expensive dining experience: the two-hour lunch session ($24) sails at 1pm, the four-hour evening bash, including a dance band, departs at 6.30pm ($70; closed Sun). If you've still got cash left over, the *Golden Key Casino* (☎011/471071) on the Tamarind's roof will relieve you of it.

From Nyali Bridge to Kenyatta Beach

Beyond the Freretown Bell and the junction for Nyali – always jostling with people trying to get transport to their shifts at the hotels – the main coast road ploughs through an area of burgeoning suburban growth. Ignored by the resort developers because it's too far from the sea, the primitive living conditions and milling activity here can come as a shock if you're fresh off the plane. Utange Camp (a Somali "intellectuals" refugee camp, full of writers, performers, musicians and their families) is not far away and its inhabitants have imposed an additional burden on the district. This is the Kenya coast that doesn't appear in the brochures. KBS bus #31, and other buses and *matatus* from Mombasa GPO to "Mtwapa" or "Serena" come along this way, as far as Mtwapa town on the other side of Mtwapa Creek. Before you get back to the shore again, there are two very worthwhile objectives to be visited – **Bombolulu** and **Bamburi Quarry Nature Park** – both of them recommended outings whether you're travelling independently or on a package.

Bombolulu

Workshops Mon–Fri 8am–12.45pm & 2–5pm (free); showroom Mon–Sat 8am–6pm (free); Cultural Centre Mon–Sat 8am–5pm (visitors Ksh200, or Ksh540 including transport from your hotel); PO Box 83988 Mombasa (☎011/473571, fax 473570).

Just off the main road 3km north of Nyali Bridge (KBS bus #31 from Abdul Nassir Road in Mombasa, beyond the Malindi buses area), **Bombolulu** (founded 1969) is a crafts training school and manufacturing centre that employs over 260 disabled people, mostly polio victims, in its five handicraft workshops (which you can visit). The **jewellery workshop** is the programme's biggest money-spinner, with hundreds of original designs in metal and local materials (old coins, seeds) now being exported to the USA and Europe – you'll come across them in charity gift catalogues. A more recent development is the opening of a **cultural centre**, incorporating six traditional homesteads from several of Kenya's peoples, around a central restaurant and dance floor, where traditional crafts, cooking and farming are demonstrated while visitors can join in the dances of various tribes (lunchtimes).

Bamburi Quarry Nature Park

Daily 9am–5.30pm; feeding time 4pm; adults Ksh350, children Ksh175.

Five kilometres beyond Bombolulu, the **Bamburi Quarry Nature Park** is the result of an unusual attempt to rehabilitate a giant quarry. The Bamburi Cement Factory (whose giant kilns are visible from miles around) has been scouring the land for limestone here since 1954, at the rate of 35 hectares each year. In 1971, they began a concentrated programme of tree-planting in an effort to rescue the disfigured landscape, to put the small-is-beautiful principle into conservation practice: a modest contribution in a land of vast wildlife parks, but a terrific success. Later, as the project gained momentum, fish-breeding was established, and large numbers of animals and birds introduced, including several **hippos**. There are plenty of **crocodiles** in a setting devoid of Mamba Village's landscaped excesses and quite a comprehensive collection of snakes, including some dangerously unprotected poisonous ones. You'll have the opportunity to get close to a number of other, harmless, creatures, including pelicans, crowned cranes, various antelopes and some splendid giant tortoises.

The walking paths wind through dense groves of casuarina, a tree known for its ability to withstand a harsh environment, across ground which is mostly below sea level, permanently moist with salty water percolating through the coral limestone bedrock. The fish-farming side of the operation experiments with different types of **tilapia**, a freshwater fish highly tolerant of brackish conditions, many tons of which now reach shops and restaurants every year, including the park's own *Whistling Pines Restaurant* (Mon–Wed & Sun 12.30–3pm; Thurs–Sat 12.30–3pm & 7.30–10pm; ☎011/487464 or 485340), which unsurprisingly also dishes up croc meat. KBS **bus** #31 (see "Bombolulu", above) will drop you at Bamburi Nature Trail bus stop, as will *matatus* from the GPO marked "Mtwapa" or "Serena".

On a similar theme, if not as impressive, are the newer **North Quarry Nature Trails** (daily 6am–6pm; Ksh100, children Ksh50), 4km further north (same buses and *matatus*: ask for "Bamburi Beach"), opposite the turning for *Bamburi Beach Hotel*. Intended mainly for joggers and cyclists (there are several looping tracks), there's also a live Butterfly Exhibition Centre (Ksh100 extra). Lastly, if the concept hasn't yet bored you, **Nguuni Wildlife Sanctuary** is the third of Bamburi Cement's sites (pre-booked visits only), good for bird-spotting and for its herds of farmed **eland** and **oryx antelope** (ever wondered where the game meat on your plate came from?). There's also an ostrich farm (ditto).

Kenyatta, Bamburi and Shanzu beaches

These three contiguous stretches of beach are the heart of the "North Coast". If you're out for the day, there should, in most cases, be little difficulty in visiting a hotel and using its beachfront, especially if you buy some drinks or take a meal there. The exceptions are the "all-inclusive" places, which charge steep daily admission (anything up to Ksh3000). The beach itself is entirely public; it's the access to it which has been progressively restricted by the hotel developers. Either way, *Whitesands* and *Mombasa Serena Beach* are perhaps the nicest hotels along this stretch.

One beach that is unquestionably public is **Kenyatta Municipal Beach**, almost the only beach in the country where you'll see droves of ordinary Kenyans by the seaside. There's a great family atmosphere here – and consequently little or no hassle. The beach goes far out at low tide, exposing plenty of coral pools and miles of sand for undisturbed walks. There are sailing boats for hire and trips offered, and at the fringes under the low coconut trees, pedlars sell ice creams and sodas, snacks and drinking coconuts, while others rent out inflated car inner tubes. For many though, the main attraction is *Pirates* (closed Tues; ☎011/486020), a combination of waterslides, restaurant and breezy bar, with a similarly relaxed feel. The slides are a required outing for kids: they're as good as you'll find anywhere, certainly in Africa, consisting of one long, steep and fast one, with a big jump, and one curling and gentle. The slides cost Ksh300 per day for adults, Ksh100 for children. The restaurant (daily except Tues, 10am–midnight) also has two childrens' pools and colourful fountains to splash in, and serves good if not amazingly cheap Mediterranean food. It's also the venue for popular discos (Wednesday, Friday and Saturday), with a mixed crowd and music.

Other attractions

The most unusual of Shanzu's attractions, 1km east of the Mombasa–Malindi road and copiously signosted, are the **Ngomongo Villages** (daily 8.30am–6pm; adults Ksh300, children Ksh150). Like Bamburi Nature Park, this is a reclaimed quarry, but one with a twist: as well as trees, it's been planted with a collection of eleven mock rural homesteads, complete with permanent inhabitants in matching dress, representing the "most colourful tribes of Kenya". Don't expect authenticity, but do expect a fun half-day out in Kenya's only theme park. There are Akamba wood carvers, musicians, herbalists, and the unavoidable crocodile pit, with less common attractions of hands-on activities like archery, Luo-style hook fishing, Turkana-style harpoon fishing, grain pounding, and tree planting. There's also the *Kienyeji Bar & Restaurant*, whose lunchtime African buffet costs Ksh550.

Also worth a visit is the Shanzu Transitional Workshop for Disabled Young Women, 350m east of Ngomongo, run by the Mombasa Girl Guides (Mon–Fri 8am–12.30pm & 2–4.30pm; c/o Mrs D.P. Shah, PO Box 80890 Mombasa; ☎011/223078). Here, fourteen young women between eighteen and twenty years old are currently being trained or employed in practical handicraft skills, turning out a small selection of well-made clothes (great Bermuda shorts), jewellery and leatherwork which is for sale. The idea is to graduate them with enough vocational training to enable them to become self-sufficient in the community. They don't get many visitors, so give them a hand.

Practicalities

The three shopping centres each have adequate, if expensive, supermarkets and pharmacies. The first is a development called The Planet Centre, on the corner of Links Road and the main highway. Ocean View Shopping Plaza, next to the hotel of the same name, has a branch of the efficient Commercial Bank of Africa (Mon–Fri 9.30am–2.30pm). And the shops just north of *Whitesands* include branches of KCB and Barclays **banks** (Mon–Fri 9am–1pm & 3–5pm, Sat 9–11am) and a small **post and telephone office** (Mon–Fri 8am–12.30pm & 2–5pm). You'll find a large cluster of shops at Shanzu, opposite *Mombasa Continental Resort*, with everything including the good Kelele Record Shop which sells African music CDs, and offers email, Internet and telephone services. **Bicycles** can be hired at *Mombasa Safari Inn* at Shanzu, for Ksh100 per hour, Ksh600 for 24hr, or Ksh3500 per week. At Shanzu Bazaar, nearby, there's a clinic (Dr A.S. Buran; ☎011/485238), and an aromatherapy centre (Body-Line Institute; ☎011/486350).

ACCOMMODATION

Between Bamburi Quarry and Mtwapa Creek, more than thirty **beach hotels** throng the six-kilometre shoreline. Most of those that can be booked in the usual way (or in which package tourists may find themselves staying) are marked on our map of the beaches, but seven along Shanzu Beach, run by the Swiss-based African Safari Club company as resorts exclusively for their clients, have been omitted. If you're travelling on a tight budget, you'll find there's nowhere cheap to stay in the vicinity and – unless you're returning to Mombasa – you should forge on to the other side of Mtwapa Creek for some cheap hotels, or continue to the altogether more appealing beach and budget accommodation at Kikambala (see p.452).

The following hotel listings are arranged from south to north.

Travellers Inn (formerly *Piccolo*), Kenyatta Beach (PO Box 87649; ☎011/486113 or 486131, fax 485678). Very small, unpretentious and inexpensive all-inclusive place, with a narrow plot (no gardens to lounge in) and a small pool. The best rooms have bath and balcony and are a good size. Ordinary food and no casual visitors allowed. Current rates are a bargain, but will increase when business picks up. FB (all-inc) ④.

Bamburi Beach Villa, Kenyatta Beach next to *Pirates* (PO Box 82623; ☎011/486161, fax 314553). Mediterranean-style terracotta-roofed self-catering development, with modern two-bedroom "cottages" (sleeping five) with verandahs on the beach, and apartments in three-storey blocks set further back (with views). All have kitchens. There's a pool, and monthly rates are negotiable. Currently no high/low season. Ksh40,000/month; apartments ④ cottages (five people) ⑤.

Rami's Beach Cottages, Kenyatta Beach, next to *Bamburi Beach Villa* (PO Box 90223; ☎011/486575, fax 227221). Older and more characterful than its neighbour: more expensive, slightly run-down and there's no pool. It has three four-bed family cottages. Ksh40,000–50,000 per month; cottages ⑤ low, ⑦ high.

Ocean View Beach Hotel, Bamburi Beach (PO Box 81127; ☎011/485601, fax 314199). An ageing hotel right on the beach, with an informal, if slightly downmarket, atmosphere. Rooms are OK, with AC and nets, but getting tatty. Small but pleasant shaded gardens, and suitable for children (there's a playground, and the pool is equipped with springboard and slide), despite the prostitutes in the bar. There are also some small, long-stay self-catering apartments (Ksh30,000 –35,000/month). HB ④ low, ④ high.

Whitesands Hotel, Bamburi Beach (PO Box 90173; ☎011/485926-9, fax 485652, *whitesands@form-net.com*; reservations through Sarova, p.50). A very impressive, self-confident operation, with not a *makuti* roof in sight. Enormous public areas, with four interconnecting freeform pools (complete with fake beach and island) and busy restaurants. Most of the 340 rooms have sea views of sorts. Slightly more expensive rooms have satellite TV. It has the longest seafront on the Mombasa North Coast, offering jet skiing, scuba diving, windsurfing, pedalos, kayaks, and trips by "banana boat" and catamaran. However, the atmosphere may be too formal for some. HB ⑥–⑦ low, ⑦–⑧ high.

Travellers Beach Hotel, Bamburi Beach (PO Box 87649; ☎011/485121–6, fax 485678, *traveller-shtl@swiftmombasa.com*). Big, fun, package-tour set-up with lots of shops and activities, and a friend-ly atmosphere which compares well to the more formal *Whitesands* glimpsed through the chicken wire fence. You can swim into the lobby then slide out again, but you can't go on the beach at high tide, when it's submerged: four pools make up for that. Facilities include floodlit tennis and AC squash courts, nightclub, children's playground, windsurfing, and a health club with sauna, jacuzzi and steam bath. Dull gardens, and somewhat tenement-like rooms, though spacious and well-appointed with AC and TVs. Good Indian restaurant (*Sher-e-Punjab*, see below). Good value. HB ⑤ low, ⑥ high.

Bamburi Beach Hotel, Bamburi Beach (PO Box 83966; ☎011/485611–8, fax 485900). Unexceptional mid-sized resort hotel with a nice pool, but slow service and dated style (stuffed fish on the walls). On the plus side, all rooms have sea views, and it's a bargain if you're not too fussy. Facilties include PADI diving school, glass-bottomed boats, snorkelling, and squash courts. HB ④ low, ⑤ high.

Kenya Beach Hotel, Bamburi Beach (PO Box 95748; ☎011/485821–2, fax 485574). One of the old generation, circa end-1960s, with the usual *makuti*-roofed reception resembling so many others. It's simpler and smaller than most, but friendly and attracts a mixture of nationalities. Watersports lim-ited to windsurfing, snorkelling and glass-bottomed boats. HB ⑤ low, ⑥ high.

Severin Sea Lodge, Bamburi Beach (PO Box 82169; ☎011/485001, fax 485212, *www.severin-sea-lodge.com*). Large, well-run but expensive resort hotel, with excellent sports and watersports but no beach at high tide. Noted also for its *Imani Dhow* restaurant, which is a converted Zanzibari *jahazi* dhow, rather oddly placed in the gardens when really it should be in the water. "Comfort Class" rooms overpriced in high season. HB ⑤–⑥ low, ⑦–⑧ high.

Plaza Beach Hotel (PO Box 88299; ☎011/485321–4, fax 485325). Rather schizophrenic, combin-ing a spotless white-tiled reception with minimalist decor with tattier areas that need renovation. Rooms are AC. Narrow pool and limited watersports; but well-priced overall. HB ④.

Neptune Beach Hotel, Bamburi Beach (PO Box 83125 Mombasa; ☎011/485701–3, fax 485705, *neptune@africaonline.co.ke*). Slightly downmarket, but refreshingly lacking in pretension, this is a fun package destination with good staff and cheerful atmosphere. Currently a bargain. B&B ④ low, ⑤ high; FB ④ low, ⑤ high.

Bamburi Chalets, next to *Cowrie Shell* (PO Box 84114; ☎011/485706 or 485594). By far the best of the self-catering places, with nine large two-floor cottages (sleeping six people) with fun 1970s styling, plenty of furniture, and well-equipped kitchens, though only three have sea views. Fully ser-viced. Pool, no food. AC, fans, verandahs, and some nets. Rates negotiable (very good value low- and mid-season, overpriced high). ④ low, ⑥ high.

Cowrie Shell Beach Apartments, next to *Baharini Chalets* (PO Box 10003 Bamburi; ☎011/485971, fax 486580). Twelve fully serviced apartments sleeping four, all with kitchens, veran-dahs and views of the sea through the coconut trees, and better equipped than *Baharini*, but about twice as expensive. There's a pool and laundry, but no food (nearest supplies at Shanzu shops), and the beach is partially fenced to discourage beach boys. Discounts for longer stays. Four-person apartment. ④ low, ⑤ high.

Baharini Chalets, Bamburi Beach (PO Box 90371; ☎011/487382 or 486302, fax 223496). The cheapest of three adjacent apartment/chalet complexes tucked in behind a coral rag-rock headland, with a variety of large rooms, all with nets, fans and verandahs. Some have sea views, others have

TURTLES

Several parts of this stretch of beach, notably at *Mombasa Serena* hotel, are popular with **sea turtles** out for a spot of egg-laying. There are educational talks about this endangered species at *Serena* (Monday 7pm), where loud water sports are banned.

cooking facilities. There's also a pool, and a beach restaurant and bar popular with prostitutes. If you're coming by public transport, get off at the *Severin Sea Lodge*. The off-note is the sometimes dodgy clientele. Prices negotiable. ② low, ③ high.

Petuscha Hotel, Shanzu (PO Box 88548; ☎011/485860). Kenyan-German run, with five spotless, modern and comfortable rooms with AC or fans, two with real baths (others with showers), fronting onto a small pool and gardens. Use of homely split-level sitting room with plenty of books. Room only, ③ low, ④ high.

Mombasa Serena Beach Hotel, Shanzu Beach (PO Box 90352; ☎011/220732, fax 485453; reservations through Serena Hotels, p.50). Beautifully put-together in "high-Swahili" style, and very stylishly maintained, this is the most attractive proposition on this stretch of coast, even if the rooms are on the small side. There are loads of activities, most of them free: floodlit tennis and AC squash courts, minigolf, windsurfing, PADI diving school, snorkelling, canoeing, and sailing, and they even take proper care of children. Great food ($18 for a drop-in evening meal). The beach front is popular with beach boys as well as the sea turtles. "Village" HB ⑦ low, ⑧ high; "Garden" HB ⑦ low, ⑧ high.

Mombasa Continental Resort (formerly *Inter-continental*), Shanzu Beach (PO Box 83492; ☎011/486721, fax 485437, *msaconti@africaonline.co.ke*). Not many concessions to (or concerns with) local taste here: bland air-conditioned comfort in robust, international style, based around monolithic accommodation blocks. Happens to be by the sea, but you wouldn't know it. On the bright side, the management are very attentive, and it's one of the few places you can do parascending on the coast (Ksh1500). Other activities include catamarans, windsurfing and diving. HB ⑥.

Sonia Apartments and Beer Garden, Diamond Shopping Centre, Shanzu (PO Box 84963; ☎011/485196, fax ☎313196). Spacious double rooms arrranged around the courtyard restaurant and lively 24-hour bar. All have their own cooking facilities and AC. Fairly basic, but clean enough and friendly. Good value, so long as you don't mind the slightly sleazy atmosphere. ③.

Mombasa Safari Inn, opposite *Mombasa Continental Resort* (PO Box 87458; ☎011/485094). One of the very few cheapies in Shanzu, with modern s/c rooms, and a popular outdoor bar and restaurant (see below). They also rent bicycles. Bed only ②.

EATING, DRINKING AND NIGHTLIFE

Apart from the multifarious attractions of *Pirates* on Kenyatta Beach (see p.446) and the expensive hotel restaurants, there are a good number of other **eating places**, most of which line the unpretty Mombasa–Malindi road. Buses and *matatus* from Mombasa GPO for Mtwapa or "Serena" run past most of the following, both day and night (fares around Ksh20); without haggling, taxis from town cost between Ksh500 (Bombolulu) and Ksh1200 (Shanzu), depending on how far north you're going. The following are listed from south to north.

Prime Time Bar & Restaurant, Bombolulu. A very local dive (bring only money for drinks and the ride back), featuring resident Kamba dance band *Katito*.

Hong Kong, just up from the Planet shopping centre (☎011/4854422 or 486137; daily). Average Cantonese specializing in seafood, in an uninspiring circular dining room. Ksh500–700.

Splendid View Café, 100m up from the *Hong Kong* (☎011/314763 or 487270). This Indian Mughlai is fibbing about the view, unless you count pink chairs and splendidly tacky fantasy paintings on the wall. The food's good though, with unusual daily specials like Baluchistani mutton *sajji* (whole roast leg of lamb), lots of chicken and seafood, and a daily tandoori BBQ. Shaded seating outside, and free transport from North Coast hotels. Under Ksh500 per person. Closed Mon.

Biene Bar and Restaurant (☎011/486439), 100m up from *Splendid View Café* before the entrance to Bamburi Quarry Nature Park. Genuine German cooking (but only Tusker beer), goulash, pork and sausages. Daily specials at Ksh260–310 for a main course. Open 9am–midnight; closed Tues.

Tembo Disco, 100m further on from *Biene* opposite Bamburi Quarry Nature Park (☎011/484074). Garden bar and restaurant open 24hrs, with an underground disco (daily 9pm–6am; women Ksh60, men Ksh120) playing mixed music (some soul, funk and even Motown), with occasional shows and body-building. Taxis wait outside.

Bora Bora Club, at Ocean View Shopping Plaza (nightly from 10pm). Some say it's the best disco on the coast – it's certainly one of the glitziest, with floor shows after midnight and a bevy of prostitutes waiting to way-lay sozzled punters. Busiest Thursday and Saturday.

Jungle Village, Ocean View Shopping Plaza. An upmarket German-run boozer and *nyama choma* joint with a pool. Mon–Fri from 5pm, Sat & Sun from noon.

Bamburi Water Sports, 100m from *Bora Bora* (☎011/485315). On the beach and popular for a Sunday afternoon booze-up), with fresh fish and *nyama choma*, and "African hair stylists" who will plait your hair. The main draw is live weekend music (Friday 5–10pm, Saturday & Sunday 3–9pm) followed by discos. Open daily from 10am; Ksh50.

Rhythms Nightclub, at *Whitesands Hotel*. Cheesy glitzy discos.

Maharajah, next to *Bamburi Beach Hotel*, Bamburi (☎011/485895 or 485977, fax 485861). North Indian Tandoori, with buffet luncheons every Sunday. Free transport from North Coast hotels. Closed Tues.

Sher-e-Punjab, at *Travellers Beach Hotel*. Unusual among hotel restaurants in that this one has acquired quite a reputation for style and quality.

Breakers, at *Bamburi Beach Hotel*, Bamburi. Disco and club, nightly from 11.30am, better than the usual hotel fare, with acrobatic shows.

Beach Corner, at *Baharini Chalets*, Shanzu Beach. The only bar/restaurant on the beach barring those in the big hotels, so very popular, as well as a pick-up joint.

Cha Cha Bar, next to *Petuscha Hotel*, Shanzu. Pleasant and laid-back outdoor bar and restaurant under an octagonal *makuti* roof (around Ksh400 for a meal, Ksh900 for seafood), with less hassly prostitutes than other Shanzu venues. Occasional live music evenings; food daily to 11pm, bar open later.

Mombasa Safari Inn, opposite *Mombasa Continental Resort*. Cheery bar and restaurant (good grills), and relatively cheap, too, with mains under Ksh300, and a full splash for around Ksh400. The bar attracts prostitutes, but the outdoor atmosphere is mellow. Daily 24 hours.

Shanzu Bay Resort, Shanzu Beach (daily 8am–midnight). Sadly underpatronized since the closure of a few nearby hotels, this is a modern *makuti*-thatched bar and restaurant, some way from the beach, serving good African food (no fish though) in a breezy site. Discos (Wednesday, Friday & Saturday nights), and they may reinstate the Sunday afternoon family shows if business picks up.

Mtwapa Marina Pub, Shanzu Beach. Wonderfully sited near the mouth of Mtwapa creek near a huge, grotesquely twisted baobab, this is a lovely place to while away an afternoon, with a bar and meals available, swimming in the creek, and a scuba diving centre. Daily 9am–midnight.

Mtwapa Creek and north

Mtwapa Creek marks the edge of Greater Mombasa, and tropical suburbia – with its scattered villas, supermarkets, clubs and restaurants (and poverty) – is more or less left behind. From here on, the road heads more determinedly, with fewer distractions, up to Kilifi, Watamu and Malindi. Note: if you're **continuing north**, beyond Kikambala, skip to p.482.

Mtwapa

MTWAPA itself is perhaps the most pleasant of the main road settlements, with a more established feel than Bombolulu. There are several fairly rudimentary **hotels**, the best being *Sweet Heart Lodge*, on the right just after the market (☎011/485456; ①). *Glasther Guest House*, 1km north of the bridge, has both s/c and non-s/c rooms (☎011/485853; ①), secure parking and occasional traditional dance performances. But the main reasons to pause in Mtwapa are **boats** and **big fish**: the creek is fast becoming a focus for yachties and game fishermen. Affordable half-day **dhow trips** (no snorkelling, but the

Ksh3450 fee includes a trip up Mtwapa Creek and lunch at their *Aquamarine Restaurant*) are run most days (closed Sun) by Kenya Marineland (PO Box 70; ☎011/485248 or 485866, fax 485075), leaving their jetty at around 9am: turn right at the signboard in Mtwapa 550m north of the bridge, and head along the dirt track for 1.5km, or ring ahead to get picked up from your hotel (free). There's also a 350,000-litre **aquarium** here (Ksh200, including entry to the obligatory reptile and snake park), and a "Maasai Village" for die-hard tourists.

For **food**, the pleasant *makuti*-roofed *Casuarina Nomad*, 300m north of the bridge on the right, has delicious chargrilled meat and seafood. Also good are *Chicken Banda* further up on the left, and *Fayaz* opposite. For upmarket eats, the floating *Moorings Restaurant* is in a fine, breezy location on the north side of the creek, accessible down a track left 300m after the bridge, and has a mainly seafood menu (Tues–Sun 10am–11pm; ☎011/485527; main courses Ksh300–450) and reasonably priced drinks. It's a good place for talk and tales – and to hook up with others, either in person or via the notice board. Similarly stylish, but on dry land, is the excellent *Claudio's Italian Restaurant*, 600m beyond Kenya Marineland, which has wonderful views of the creek as it meets the ocean (daily; ☎011/485368; around Ksh1000). *Aquamarine* at Kenya Marineland itself is overpriced, at nearly Ksh2000 a meal. For **nightlife**, there's a large number of ever-changing disco and live music venues, which rise and fall according to the fashion of the day: just ask around. More dependable are the discos at *Casuarina Nomad* (Tues–Sun 6pm–4am), which usually feature "cocktails" of traditional dancers at weekends, and the more clubbish *Workshop*, overlooking *Moorings Restaurant* on the creekside (Wednesday, Friday and Saturday) that switches on when *Moorings* switches off, around 11pm.

Jumba la Mtwana

A totally different site worth pausing for (and worth a day out of town in its own right) is **Jumba La Mtwana** (daily 8.30am–6.30pm; Ksh200, children Ksh100; ☎011/485543). This national monument, one of three between Mombasa and Malindi, is the ruined centre of a wealthy fourteenth- or fifteenth-century Swahili community. The sign for the 3km access road is 2km north of Mtwapa Creek bridge: if you're travelling by public transport and are dropped off at the junction, you have a good chance of getting a lift.

Jumba la Mtwana means "mansion of the slave", but it has been deserted for some 500 years and probably had a different name in the past. It's a small site in an enchanting setting among baobabs and lawns above the beach. This seems a strange place for

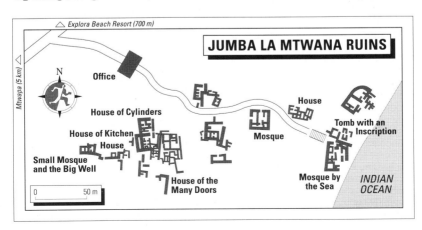

a town, right on an open shore with no harbour, and it's possible the inhabitants were pushed here by raiding parties from inland groups, and relied on Mtwapa Creek as a safe anchorage for the overseas traders who visited yearly. Jumba is fortunate in having good water. But why it was deserted, and by whom, remains a mystery.

Compared with Gedi, further north (see p.490), Jumba's layout is simple. Though it lacks the eerie splendour of that much larger town, it must once have been a sizeable settlement; there were three mosques within the site and a fourth just outside. Most of the population would have lived in mud-and-thatch houses, which have long since disintegrated. In Swahili culture, building in stone (in fact, coral "rag" of different densities) has traditionally been the preserve of certain privileged people, principally the long-settled inhabitants of a town; newcomers would almost always build in less durable materials appropriate to their shorter-term stake in the community. It is believed that building in stone required legal sanction, as it was the material used for mosques.

The best of Jumba's mosques is the **Mosque by the Sea** (a helpful little guidebook which costs Ksh20 is sometimes available at the ticket office – much of this account has been culled from it), which shows evidence of there having been a separate room for women, something which is only nowadays becoming acceptable again in modern mosques. The cistern where worshippers washed is still intact, with coral foot-scrapers set nearby and a jumble of tombs behind the north wall facing Mecca. One of these has a Koranic inscription carved in coral on a panel facing the sea and must have been the grave of an important person:

> *Every soul shall taste death. You will simply be paid your wages in full on the Day of Resurrection. He who is removed from the fire and made to enter heaven, it is he who has won the victory. The earthly life is only delusion.*

The **people of Jumba** seem to have been very religious and hygienic – virtues that are closely associated in Islam. Cisterns and water jars, or at least the remains of them, are found everywhere among the ruined houses, and in most cases there are coral blocks nearby which would have been used to squat on while washing. Latrines are all stone-lined with long-drops. Of course, it is possible that the poorer people of Jumba lived in squalor in their mud huts, yet even the **House of Many Doors**, which seems to have been a fifteenth-century "boarding and lodging", provided guests with private washing and toilet facilities.

Look out for the two **smaller mosques**, each with its well-preserved, carved coral *mihrab* (the arched niche that indicates the direction of Mecca), and for the strange chinks in several walls (in the House of the Cylinders and the Small Mosque), the purpose of which is unknown.

Jumba Beach is a good place to while away an afternoon – in fact late afternoon, when the atmosphere hangs among the ruins like cobwebs, is probably the best time to come. Strange but attractive screw pines grow, aerial-rooted like mangroves, in the sand. You can **camp** or take a **picnic** here, too; there are toilets and showers by the ticket office.

Kikambala

For a day-trip out of Mombasa without your own transport, **KIKAMBALA**, a few kilometres further up the coast, is about as far as you'd want to come (KBS bus #11 Mombasa–Malindi passes the access road junctions regularly). Note that the topography here is very flat: the sea goes out for nearly a kilometre and it's largely impractical for bathing except at high tide, so if you're just coming for the day, consult a tide table before setting off (daily newspapers print this). Much of the coastal strip here is still thickly forested and the beach itself is a glorious white expanse, though it's 2–3km from the highway and there are no *matatus*. The only official **campsite** in the area is at the Kanamai Conference & Holiday Centre, or "Kanamai Youth Hostel". The first low-bud-

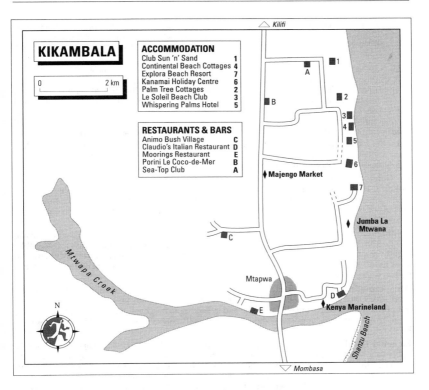

get beach spot north of Mombasa, it makes a good stop-over, and if you plan to stay more than a night you're not utterly marooned: there's usually someone with a vehicle at the site who'll be going to the *dukas* on the main road most mornings and, once or twice a week, if you help with petrol, into Mombasa.

You could also splurge on a day pass at the all-inclusive *Club Sun'n'Sand* (10am–5pm Ksh1400; 5pm–midnight Ksh1800), which is another thirty minutes' walk further north. Unless you happen to be staying at them, the other Kikambala addresses are not worth a special visit.

ACCOMMODATION

The Kikambala **hotels** are virtually the last on the coast north of Mombasa until you reach Kilifi. One downside of being this far out of town, if you haven't got a car, is that taxis into Mombasa cost over Ksh1800 each way. Vehicles normally approach the beach properties from the northern access road (other roads can get tricky in bad weather), 7.4km north of Mtwapa bridge (signposted for "*Sun 'n' Sand*"), and the following places are listed according to their distance from that junction. Coming from the south, it's often quicker to cut in 5.3km north of Mtwapa Bridge, which heads straight to *Kanamai*.

Sea-Top Club & Lodging, 1.7km along northern access road (PO Box 226 Kikambala; ☎0125/32184). Substantial *nyama choma* bar and nightspot with nightly discos featuring Congolese sounds, soul, Caribbean and funk. Decent s/c rooms for weary clients. Fans, but no nets. ①–②.

NK Villa Palm Garden Hotel, 1.8km along northern access road (PO Box 115 Kikambala; ☎0125/32011, fax 32471). Quite an attractive, shady establishment, but plays on its sleazy reputation with low-budget German package tourists. Studio apartments with kitchen and living room. Modest pool. ③.

Club Sun 'n' Sand, 2.1km along northern access road (PO Box 2 Kikambala; ☎0125/32008, fax 32123). One of the oldest hotels on the Kenya coast, originally built in 1932 and recently reopened as an all-inclusive club – it's among the biggest in the country, with nearly 300 bright, functional rooms, furnished with some style. Three large pools, with diving boards, an extended "river" and slides. Lots of activities, including a kids' club. Efficient, pleasant staff make this one of the most popular and regularly recommended club-hotels on the coast. There are several small shops and *dukas* near the gate if the club atmosphere begins to get claustrophobic. ⑤ low, ⑦ high.

Palm Tree Cottages, 2.6km along northern access road (PO Box 82448; ☎0125/26436). Four-bed houses with room for two more in each. Not especially good value and a very uninspiring plot. Four-bed cottages with space for two more beds ④.

Le Soleil Beach Club, 3.2km along northern access road (PO Box 84737 Mombasa; ☎0125/32195–6, fax 32164, *lesoleil@africaonline.co.ke*). More like a tropical office block than a hotel, this is as tacky as it is popular, with a cosmopolitan variety of budget package tourists and tons of activities (and unlimited food and booze) covered in the all-inclusive price. No daily visits. ⑥ low, ⑦ high.

Continental Beach Cottages, 3.6km along northern access road (PO Box 124 Kikambala; ☎0125/32077, fax 32190). Not a great deal of atmosphere, but tranquil enough, with a reasonable, slightly green pool, all set amid lots of tall, established coconut trees. The relatively expensive cottages have TV, AC and nets. Choice of self-catering or eating in the restaurant. Self-catering cottages for two with one double bed. ④.

Whispering Palms Hotel, 3.9km along northern access road (PO Box 5 Kikambala; ☎0125/32004-6, fax 32029, *whispers@africaonline.co.ke*). Peaceful, isolated hideaway for a mix of package tourists from Britain and Europe, but old-fashioned and in need of an overhaul. The grounds are shaded by, at times, quite noisy palm trees. Slightly cheaper than its equivalents closer to Mombasa. B&B ④; FB ⑤.

Kanamai Holiday Centre, 5.3km north of Mtwapa bridge, then 3km along murram (PO Box 46 Kikambala; ☎0125/32101, fax 32048). Big, sprawling but pretty place under the coconuts, run by the National Christian Council of Kenya. The options are beds in dormitories (very basic, B&L level), double-room accommodation (roomy and well furnished, with good fans), or camping pretty much wherever you like (Ksh100 per person). *Kanamai* offers basic meals in the dining room (Ksh80–200) and has a shop with a few provisions, but there's no bar and, for a stay of several days, you should bring supplies. A half-hour stroll north along the sandy lane through the woods brings you to the *Whispering Palms Hotel*, where you can join in all the usual holiday pursuits. ①–②.

Explora Beach Resort, 750m past Jumba ruins (PO Box 43058 Mombasa; ☎011/487430). Totally cut off from the rest of Kikambala by a quarry and a maze of unsignposted tracks, this is what Diani, Tiwi and Nyali might have felt like before the developers moved in: bliss. If you don't mind sacrificing a bit of spit and polish, this is a brilliant place to get away from it all. Cheap and charming, and right on the edge of an exposed cliff overlooking the ocean (steps down to the deserted beach). There are twelve s/c rooms in ramshackle chalets (some with sea views), and food available to order. You can camp here, too (Ksh300 per tent). Rates negotiable. B&B ②.

EATING AND DRINKING

Outside of the hotels, there aren't many **restaurants** and **nightlife** options, though there are a couple of places along the main Mombasa–Malindi road. *Porini Le Coco-de-Mer*, 6.5km north of Mtwapa bridge (daily 10am–11.30pm; ☎0125/32117) is a long-established restaurant set in jungly gardens, and is friendly and laid-back, specializing in Seychelloise cuisine (lots of seafood and chicken, coconut milk and cassava), where a splurge will set you back Ksh600–900. *Animo Bush Village*, 3.3km from Mtwapa bridge and then 1km (signposted) left (PO Box 87118; ☎011/487290) is a former rural nightclub fallen on hard times. It has recently started hosting occasional theatrical productions (in English, Kiswahili and local languages) directed by the veteran coastal thespian Titi Wainaina, but for the most part remains a somnolent bar and *nyama* *choma* joint, with one-off live bands and dancers (Saturday nights and Sunday afternoons). They also provide cleanish s/c rooms with fans (Ksh500).

Inland from Mombasa: Mijikenda country

If you're coming from Nairobi, **MAZERAS** marks the end of the long vistas of scrub; it's perched right on the edge of the steep scarp, amid bananas and coconuts. If you're travelling by road, it isn't a bad idea to break your journey here and savour the new atmosphere; frequent city buses (#35 and #43) run between Mazeras and Mombasa, about thirty minutes away. The *hotelis* serve good, flavourful, coastal *chai* and, for the travel-weary, Mazeras has some delightful **botanical gardens** – bamboo, ponds and green lawns for a snooze in the shade – just a couple of hundred metres back towards Mombasa. Across the road and up the hill a little way is a **mission** and its century-old church, signs of an evangelical presence in the hills behind Mombasa that goes back, remarkably, over 150 years.

For historians of Methodism and the Church Missionary Society or (more likely) connoisseurs of palm wine, the **road to Kaloleni**, 22km north of Mazeras is a required sidetrack; see the map on p.412. It's a beautiful trip in its own right: wonderfully scenic, looping through lush vales with a wide panorama down to the coast on the right and masses of **coconut trees** all around. There are frequent #35 KBS buses from Mombasa to Kaloleni via Rabai, which makes this an easy day-trip away from the coast, especially appealing in the high season if your sense of adventure has become numbed by the influx of tropical paradise-seekers. If a round-trip appeals, arrive in Kaloleni before mid-afternoon and you'll be able to catch a *matatu* further north to Kilifi, and from there back to Mombasa. If you're driving, note that there's no petrol at Mazeras, and only irregular supplies at Kaloleni, so fill up in Mombasa or Mariakani.

Rabai

RABAI, capital of the **Wa-Rabai** Mijikenda and site of the first Christian mission to be established in East Africa, is the first village you come to, 5km from Mazeras. It's also one of only two Mijikenda villages still occupying its original *kaya* (see p.456). A German pastor, the Reverend **Johan Ludwig Krapf**, came here in 1846 after losing his family at Nyali (see p.441), and left his mark on the community when, 41 years later, the imposing **St Paul's church**, now blue and white, was erected. The centre of the village and the church, surrounded by school rooms and sports fields, lie half a kilometre off the main road on the right as you come into Rabai from Mazeras. For the church and museum, fork left after 200m. The first church to have been built (1846–48) now houses the modest **Krapf Memorial Museum** (Mon–Sat 8am–12.30pm & 2–5pm; tip expected; ask for the curator at the last house on your left, which used to be Krapf's house), not the most exciting place in Kenya; it contains a few well-presented photographs but nothing else. The adjacent cottage of Johann Rebmann, Krapf's proselytizing partner, is used as a school room. Between them, the two missionaries managed to explore a great deal of what is now Kenya without the demonstrations of firepower so many of their successors thought necessary. Krapf worked out the grammar of Swahili and produced a translation of the Bible. For all its significance, though, Rabai "centre" has, in all truth, hardly anything to offer, and there's nowhere to stay.

Ribe

RIBE (the Wa-Ribe village) is more substantial than Rabai but harder to get to. Seven kilometres from Rabai, an unmarked track snakes up to the right from a deep valley

THE MIJIKENDA PEOPLES

The principal people of the coastal hinterland region are the **Mijikenda** ("Nine Tribes"), a loose grouping whose Bantu languages are to a large extent mutually intelligible, and closely related to Swahili. They are believed to have arrived in their present homelands in the sixteenth or seventeenth century from a quasi-historical state called Shungwaya, which had undergone a period of intense civil chaos. This centre was probably located somewhere in the Lamu hinterland or in the southwest corner of present-day Somalia. According to oral tradition, the people who left it were the Giriama, the Digo, the Rabai, the Ribe, the Duruma, the Chonyi, the Jibana, the Kauma and the Kambe (not to be confused with the Kamba of the interior).

All these "tribes" now live in the coastal hinterland, with the **Giriama** to the north of Mombasa and **Digo** to the south – the largest and best-known groups. They share a degree of common cultural heritage. Each tribe has a traditional **kaya** central settlement, a fortified village in the forest, usually built on raised ground some kilometres from the coast, but sometimes right by the shore. Some Mijikenda peoples built only one *kaya*; others spawned secondary *kayas* or even whole clusters of *kayas*. The *kayas* still exist, although they are now sacred glades rather than fortified villages, and the dwelling place of ancestral spirits. In theory, they each contain a *fingo* – a charm said to derive from the ancestral home of Shungwaya – but these have nearly all been destroyed or, like the grave posts made from the *brachylinum* tree called *kigango* (*vigango* in the plural) that were also formerly a feature of each *kaya*, stolen for private collections of "primitive art" or loft-converters' ideas of interesting objets d'art.

Today, most *kayas* are run-down, but they are still remembered and visited by one or two elders. While their sacred aspect has ceased to have much relevance for most Mijikenda, their true significance comes out under pressure: when a German hotel developer took a fancy to Chale island (the whole of which is a gazetted *kaya*), he had to "buy" two Digo medicine men to appease the spirits – not best pleased with having their groves smothered in concrete. Nor is their human value the only reason to care about the *kayas*: along with belief in their sacred qualities comes a local conservation tradition. In these forest tracts of between five hectares and three square kilometres nothing has ever been cultivated or disturbed. They represent a biological storehouse of immense diversity, unique along the East African coast. A WWF-backed botanical research programme run by the National Museums of Kenya has been under way for several years to map out the *kaya* ecosystems and to encourage the elders to reassert their authority over

floor: the village is 1.5km along it. Buses stop by the track. If you're driving, continue to a sign (on the right) for a lead mine. There are two bars and *hotelis* and a factory at the junction, which spews its dust over the neighbouring coconut and banana groves. Ribe itself is the second village along the track, about 4km from the main road. It consists of a few small shops and a shady **bar-restaurant** with a courtyard and rooms (①). Another option, just before the turning on the main road (5km north of Rabai), is *Sammy's Rendezvous B&L* (①).

Fifteen minutes' walk away from Ribe, through the *shambas* and dense undergrowth, is a tiny **cemetery**, regularly cleared of weeds and creepers, near the site of Ribe's Methodist mission, itself crumbled to its foundations and now completely overgrown. It isn't hard to find, and it's worth visiting if only to take a look at the pathetic graves of those few missionaries who struggled all the way here before succumbing in what must have been nearly impossible conditions. They were often very young: the Reverend Butterworth, whose carpentry skills ensured him a welcome arrival, died aged 23, just two months after getting there; they used his new tools to make the coffin. It isn't surprising that the cemetery faces out to sea, towards Mombasa, supplies, the mail and new settlers.

each one, something of an urgent matter as many are currently under threat from "land grabbing" developers, usually well-connected and unscrupulous individuals or local politicians. More than twenty *kayas* have so far been gazetted in Kwale district, south of Mombasa, and the process has now started in the Kilifi area. There may be more than fifty altogether, though some could be so small they will disappear under the hoe or the caterpillar tractor before anyone remembers them. It may be possible to visit a *kaya*, but they are by no means tourist attractions: if you're genuinely interested, contact the Coastal Forest Conservation Unit (CFCU) (office is 3km south of Ukunda on the Lungalunga road, signposted to the right; PO Box 86 Ukunda; ☎0127/2518, *cfcu.kwale@swiftmombasa.com*). The possibility that one or two of the old sacred groves might be opened to tourists to generate income still seems some way off. *The Kaya Complex* (Thomas T. Spear, Kenya Literature Bureau, Nairobi 1978) provides interesting reading on the subject.

Like so many other Kenyan peoples, the Mijikenda had age-set systems that helped cut across the divisive groupings of clan and subclan to bind communities together. Much of this tradition has been lost during this century; the installation of a new ruling elders' age-set, for example, required the killing and castration of a stranger.

Economically, the Mijikenda were, and still are, diverse. They were cultivators, herders (especially the Duruma and, at one time, the Giriama), long-distance traders with the interior, makers of palm wine (a Digo speciality now diffused all over Mijikenda-land), hunters and fishermen. They have local market cycles – four-day weeks in the case of the Giriama (days one and two for labour, day three for preparation, and day four, called *chipolata*, for market). They have successfully maintained their cultural identity, warring with the British in 1914 over the imposition of taxes and the demand for porters for World War I, and preserving a vigorous conservative tradition of adherence to their old beliefs in spirits and the power of their ancestors. This is most apparent in the relative ease with which you can pick up cassettes of **traditional music**, especially in Mombasa: wonderful rhythms and some very delicate *chivoti* flute melodies, with only a slight discernable Islamic influence, if at all. If you're really interested and have time to spare, even casual enquiries inland will elicit invitations to weddings or, less likely, funerals, where the old traditions – and music – are still very much centrepieces, despite the Christian veneer. Many Mijikenda, however, have found conversion to Islam a helpful religious switch in their dealings with coastal merchants and businessmen. This conversion seems to be the latest development in the growth of Swahili society.

Kaloleni

The paved road comes to its end at **KALOLENI**. On the way, you pass through dense coconut groves where many of the trees have been initialled to avoid ownership disputes. The tapping of **palm wine** (*tembo*), banned by the government, is still widely practised here, with the **Giriama** section of the Mijikenda leading the field. They call palm wine "the mother of the coconut", since tapping the trees for juice hinders formation of the nuts.

Tapping is done by cutting off the flower stem, binding it tightly and allowing the sap that would have produced new coconuts to collect in a container – usually a baobab pod – tied to the end. Here it ferments rapidly and has to be regularly collected. Variations in the local demand for *tembo*, which is most often drunk at community gatherings like weddings and funerals, and in the coastal market for *copra* (the dried coconut flesh used in soap and oil manufacture), tend to influence the owners of trees in their decision whether to tap or to grow *copra*. You will see trees with the step-notches that enable the tappers to reach the top ending several metres below the crown, indicating that a tree has been left a number of years to develop coconuts.

Palm wine is locally available up and down the coast. In Kaloleni, a beer-bottleful costs just a few shillings. It is best when cold, but rarely is, and you drink it (discreetly) through a reed straw with a coconut-fibre filter.

The only place to **stay** in Kaloleni is the rough-edged *Kaloleni Central Restaurant* (PO Box 34 Kaloleni; no phone; ①) 700m beyond the Kilifi junction at the top end of town opposite the bus terminus: there are four rooms behind its bar/eathouse (*ugali*, fried chicken and goat, chapati and pilau), all very basic, not terribly clean and not s/c, but the sheets are usually fresh (couples sharing have to be a man and a woman, states the manager, concerned about "unholy bonding").

Moving on, there are frequent KBS buses back to Mombasa via Rabai and Mazeras, and less frequent *matatus* up to Kilifi, 40km away (catch these at the bottom of the hill by the Kilifi junction). Lastly, if you've got time and the inclination, it might be worth getting to the Coast Province Herbalists Society, 4.5km along the Kilifi road on the left.

Shimba Hills National Park

Entry $20, students/children $5; warden PO Box 30 Kwale (☎0127/4159 or 4166). Map: Survey of Kenya SK93 at 2.5cm:1km (1980), or Sapra Safari's The Kenya Coast.

Probably Kenya's most underrated wildlife refuge, **Shimba Hills National Park** is less than an hour from Mombasa and, at 500m above sea level, a real refresher after the humidity down below. The hilly park of scattered jungle and grassland is comparatively little visited, which is all to the good: it has a quite wonderful game-viewing lodge and one of the best-situated camping and *banda* sites anywhere.

Kwale and access to the park

The most straightforward option for visiting Shimba is on a **safari from Mombasa** (tickets from most coast hotels and travel agents – about $80–100 for a day-trip, $155–180 for an overnight at *Shimba Lodge*). These prices include park entrance fees but not game drives or nature walks.

If you're **driving**, you'll probably need high clearance 4WD in all but the driest weather and, even so, the southern access road via Kindango Gate is atrocious and often impassable. Note also that Kwale doesn't always have petrol. There are fairly frequent **matatus** and hourly KBS #34 **buses** to **Kwale** from Mombasa's Likoni ferry bus park. The park's **main gate** is some 5km beyond Kwale along an elephant-dunged *murram* road. Here, you can try for **a lift** around the park. Since your best bet is with Mombasans, Sundays and public holidays are the easiest times. The last bus back to Mombasa from Kwale is at 8pm. In case of need, there are two **lodgings** in town. *Garden Guest House* (PO Box 272; ☎0127/4112; B&B ①) is the best, with the advantage of nets.

A third alternative is to enquire about a lift with the **park vehicle**, which usually goes to Kindango Gate on the southeast side of the park to collect gate money on Sunday and Wednesday afternoons. You should be able to get a ride, though people will want *chai*. Ask at the warden's house and offices just outside Kwale.

Moving on from Kwale, a rarely used route away from the coast heads northwest to Mariakani on the Nairobi highway, which is served by a few daily *matatus*. The first and only major town on the way is **Kinango**, where you might have to change vehicle. If you get stuck here, the only **hotel** is the basic *Kinango Silent Rest House* (①). There are *matatus* from here to Mariakani and Likoni.

Shimba Lodge

(PO Box 90581 Mombasa; ☎0127/4077; reservations through Block Hotels, p.48. No children under 7 or children's rates; HB ⑤ low, ⑨ high).

Shimba is a "tree hotel", a kind of coastal *Treetops*, though actually superior in all respects to the original. Check-in is from 3pm, but if you're driving and give advance notice, you can arrive early at the lodge for lunch (Ksh600). It's all intensely atmospheric, as the building, apparently constructed entirely of pitch-dark timber (though it's actually mainly just cladding over the concrete), rises up through the trees and creepers, with aerial plantlife, birds, butterflies and humans all sharing the deep forest glade. The staff are instructed to speak in whispers, and remind guests to do so.

Given the rates, the standard rooms, with shared showers and toilets, might seem a disappointment at first, but when there are bushbabies on the branch outside, the possibility of a leopard, and a sweeping view of the dam and perhaps a fish eagle in the trees opposite, you don't spare too much thought for luxuries. From nearly all the rooms, on three floors, and from several bars and observation platforms, you have views across the small, dammed lake to thick forest. The best feature is the tree-level **walkway**, which runs for 100m or so from one end of the lodge to a platform high above the ground near a small clearing. Hear you can watch elephants, warthogs, forest antelope and monkeys galore – if you're lucky. After dark, spotlights illuminate bushbabies, hundreds of bats and a whirling hailstorm of jungle insects. It's a memorable evening – and the food is good.

The early-evening "sundowner" **nature walk** (4.30pm; Ksh460) is always enjoyable. The next morning there's the option of a proper **game drive** in the park (6am; Ksh730), with the opportunity to see the sable antelope for which Shimba is famous.

Around the park

Predators are rare in Shimba Hills but you may well see **elephant**, especially from the vantage of Elephant Hill or at the nearby Sheldrick Falls, particularly if you go early in the day. There are armed guards at Elephant Hill who will escort you to the falls: it's a very pretty walk but a long pull back up – take water, and swimming gear if you want to swim in the pool. The elephant population in Shimba is estimated at between 500 and 600, up from 300 in 1977: the poaching which decimated Tsavo's herds was thankfully absent here, though this wasn't such good news for the local inhabitants, who increasingly had to put up with their crops and *shambas* being trashed by marauding pachyderms. Just as things were coming to a head (several farmers had been killed trying to defend their livelihoods), a remarkable compromise was reached: the park authorities agreed to electric fence a forty-kilometre stretch of the park's northern boundary adjoining the agricultural lands, and to set up a rapid response unit to deal with rogue elephants, whilst the locals ceded part of their land to form the Mwaluganje Elephant Sanctuary (see p.460): so far, the arrangement seems to be working better than anyone had dared imagine.

Look out also for the park's five **Maasai giraffe**, the product of a tentative experiment. Although Shimba had never had giraffe naturally, a small nucleus was introduced a decade ago after having been rescued from smugglers attempting to take them abroad. Unfortunately, one died in transit, another female died shortly after arrival, and the two males just disappeared, leaving only two females and distraught rangers. Two breeding males were then brought in, one more of the females died, but the other finally gave birth in December 1996, to the delight of everyone. The group now consists of the two males, the female and two young ones. Spurred on by this modest success, **zebra** and **ostrich** have also been introduced. Shimba is best known, however, for its indigenous herds of **sable antelope**, magnificent-looking animals as big as horses, with great, sweeping horns. The park is their only habitat in Kenya. (The similar but even bigger roan antelopes, which were relocated from Western Kenya, died out, it's thought, through lack of necessary minerals.) You are almost certain to see groups of chestnut-coloured sable females but the territorial, jet-black males are more solitary and harder to find. If you have a guide he'll know where to look, but they're most commonly seen in the area overlooking the ocean, between the public campsite and Giriama Point. Another good place to head for is **Makadara picnic site**: there are bats in the toilet and it's supposed to be a good place to see buffalo.

Camping in Shimba Hills

What Shimba Hills may lack in wildlife it more than makes up for with enchanting views in every direction, especially seawards. Haze tends to blot out Mombasa itself but the fringe of Diani Beach is usually visible. The **public campsite** is located at one of the best vantage points in the park, about 3km from the main gate. The four *bandas* here (①) are adequate (though the bedding, lamps, shower and nearby toilet can't be relied on, and the water needs purification), but the setting is sublime: a thickly forested bluff hundreds of metres above the coconut-crowded coastal plain. It is well worth spending the night up here just for the sunrise. If you do, you'll probably have the place to yourself. *Makadara* picnic site is also a good place: its *bandas* are derelict, but you can camp here. *Hunter's Camp* is preferred by locals, but has no facilities whatsoever (book with the rangers); *Pengo Hill* has one basic *banda*, but no bedding or anything else, and **Observation Post** (junction 4A) also has a shelter where you can stay.

Mwaluganje Elephant Sanctuary

To the northwest of Shimba and the area where the "sundowner walks" normally take place, just outside the national park, lies the **Mwaluganje Elephant Sanctuary** ($10). Situated on the slopes of the privately owned Goloni escarpment, it is a remarkable success story of a compromise solution. It was created in 1995 to defuse conflict between the local Duruma farmers and elephants, who had made a habit of trashing their crops and killing farmers attempting to defend their livelihoods. After consultation between the local people, Kenya Wildlife Service, and the Eden Wildlife Trust, 240 square kilometres were set aside for the sanctuary, separated along a third of its boundary from farmland with electric fencing, but left open elsewhere to keep the elephants' migration routes open.

The low-lying areas around the Manolo river are dominated by baobab, while thick *Brachystegia* forest covers the escarpment's flanks, and harbours a surprising wealth of wildlife. You are "guaranteed" to see elephants here and, in time, it is hoped that threatened species can be relocated here from other parts of Kenya. Apart from the prolific birdlife, you might also see zebra, bushbuck, warthog, monkeys and (rarely) leopard.

The gate is 14km beyond Kwale, then 2km along a signposted track to the right (4WD only in the rains). The only **accommodation** in the sanctuary is *Travellers Mwaluganje Elephant Camp* (PO Box 87649 Mombasa; ☎0127/51202–5, fax 51207, *travellershtl@swiftmombasa.com*; ⑥). Most guests come on overnight packages from the coast ($130–140 per person). Set along the shoulder of a low hill facing a well-established elephant trail, there are twenty twin-bedded tents under thatch roofs, each with verandah (watch the elephants walking past), bathrooms and electricity. Escorted game drives are included in the price.

THE SOUTH COAST

A continuous strip of beach runs between Likoni and Msambweni, backed by palms and broken once or twice by small rivers. Along the whole coast south from Mombasa to the Tanzanian border there's just one highly developed resort area, **Diani Beach**. South of Diani, the coast is little known and, in most tour operators' minds at least, nobody stops again until they reach **Shimoni**. This is great news if you have the time to go searching out untrodden beaches by car, bicycle or motorbike (all available to rent), or using the good local public transport.

Most of the people who live along the coastal strip here are **Digo**, and their neat rectangular houses, made of dried mud and coral on a framework of wood, are a distinctive part of the lush roadside scene. Although they belong to the Mijikenda group of peoples, the Digo are unusual in being matrilineal: they traditionally traced descent through the female line, so that a man would, on his death, pass his property on to his sister's sons rather than his own. It is an unusual system with interesting implications for the state of the family and the position of women. However, the joint assault of Islamic and Western values over the last century has shifted the emphasis back towards the male line, and in many ways women in modern Digo society have less freedom and autonomy than they had a hundred years ago.

Likoni and Shelly Beach

Mombasa's Likoni ferry (*matatus* from the post office on Digo Road) makes all the difference: compared with the North Coast, the sense of separation from Mombasa is immediate. More pragmatically, the lack of a bridge has deterred developers and contributed to the South Coast's fairly late arrival in the tour brochures (though Diani is certainly making up for lost time). The ferries (free for foot passengers, Ksh35 for cars) operate around the clock (every 15min, 4am–1am; every hour, 1am–4am; Sat no service 2am–4am). Beware of **pickpockets** here: keep your hands free, don't shake hands, and ensure money belts are secure and can't be cut off from behind.

LIKONI itself is a busy creekside suburb of Mombasa, straggling down the southbound road for a good 3km. A coast road runs off around the headland to the east (see "Mombasa Island" map, p.414), served by infrequent *matatus*, but Shelly Beach – named after its shells – is narrow and has large patches of exposed coral rag rock (bring rubber or plastic soled sandals), and tends to be strewn with seaweed, while the sea here is only feasible for swimming at high tide. Unless you're booked into a hotel already, hop on a bus or *matatu* and make for Tiwi or Diani. Apart from a host of very local (if rough-looking) eateries and good streetfood at Likoni ferry, the only real **restaurant** is the excellent *Island Paradise Bar & Restaurant*, next to *ACK Guest House*, whose tilapia, oddly enough (it's from Lake Victoria, not the Indian Ocean), is very good. For **nightlife**, *Jack City*, to the right as you get off the ferry, is a relaxed reggae club overlooking the creek, used by enough tourists and expats to prevent your presence being too much of a novelty, but not by so many that the locals move elsewhere and the prostitutes move in. *The Office*, another reggae club nearby, is similar.

Accommodation

The following addresses are all Mombasa PO boxes: distances are from the Likoni junction.

ACK Guest House (formerly *CPK Guest House*) (300m; PO Box 96170; ☎011/451619). Even on a low budget, the Anglican Church of Kenya's coastal retreat might seem an odd choice. But it's well

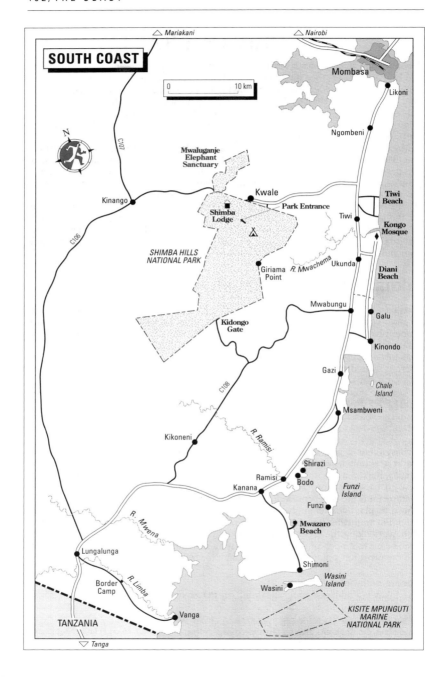

SOUTH COAST

0   10 km

△ Mariakani   △ Nairobi

Mombasa

Likoni

C107

N

Ngombeni

Mwaluganje
Elephant
Sanctuary

Kinango

Kwale

Park Entrance

Tiwi
Beach

Shimba
Lodge

Tiwi

Kongo
Mosque

C106

SHIMBA HILLS
NATIONAL PARK

Giriama
Point

R. Mwachema   Ukunda

Diani
Beach

Mwabungu

Galu

Kidongo
Gate

Kinondo

C108

Gazi

Chale
Island

Msambweni

Kikoneni

R. Ramisi

Shirazi

Ramisi

Bodo

Funzi
Island

Kanana

Funzi

R. Mwena

Mwazaro
Beach

Lungalunga

Shimoni

Border
Camp

R. Limba

Wasini
Island

Wasini

TANZANIA

Vanga

KISITE MPUNGUTI
MARINE
NATIONAL PARK

▽ Tanga

LIKONI AND THE 1997 VIOLENCE

The run-up to the chaotic December 1997 Kenyan general elections was fraught with violence, both in the Rift Valley (which had suffered similarly before the 1992 elections, when some 1000 lives were lost) and – disastrously for Kenya's tourist industry – on the coast. The flashpoint was **Likoni**. For many years the focus for "up-country" immigrants, who had arrived in vast numbers to cash in on the tourist boom, Likoni had also attracted the ire of the government when the – traditionally anti-government voting – immigrants returned an opposition MP to the Likoni seat in 1992.

Over the following years, political and inter-tribal tension between immigrants and the indigenous Digo and Muslim inhabitants worsened, coming to a head in July 1997 when an unauthorized rally calling for constitutional change ended in violence. Shortly afterwards, gangs of thugs armed with guns and machetes started attacking homes, shops and bars. At first, the government blamed a group of "marauding drug addicts and drunks".

Then in August, a raid on Likoni police station by a "mysterious militia" resulted in the deaths of seven policemen and the theft of 44 automatic weapons. In the following hours, seven other people were also found dead. In Likoni, graffiti on the walls of the suddenly almost-deserted town appeared, reading: "Three days to go or you die". Almost one thousand people took refuge in the Catholic Church at Likoni, which itself was attacked two weeks later, two deaths resulting. The subsequent and unusually well-orchestrated violence – including the murder of several members of a band playing at Shelly Beach Hotel – claimed the lives of seventy people, and caused an exodus of immigrants, with around 100,000 people displaced.

Conspiracy theorists were quick to blame KANU ethnic-cleansing and gerrymandering in the run-up to the elections, a claim subsequently given credence first by a police swoop involving the arrests of several high-ranking KANU officials, and then by the findings of the 1998–99 **Akiwumi Clashes Inquiry** which showed that much of the violence had been premeditated by politicians who had paid the thugs, arranged their transport and supplied them with weapons.

run, the better rooms are fine (showers and fans) and good value and, while it's not on the beach, it is handy for Mombasa and south coast transport. There's a good swimming pool (and one for kids), and basic food in the attractive patio dining room overlooking the road, which is a popular meeting place for locals. ②–③.

Childrens' Holiday Resort (3.5km; PO Box 96048; ☎011/451417). An indefinable low-budget bungalow establishment from another age, the *Resort* is a non-profit trust that goes way back, occupying a peaceful, flat sandy site under the coconut palms, right on the beach. Families are preferred but couples and singles aren't excluded. Self-catering only (cooker, fridge and utensils provided), all with electricity, some s/c but most with outside showers and toilets. Nets on request. Bring your own bed linen. Basic but good value: cottages for two-plus. ③.

Reliable Beach Apartments (2.5km; PO Box 82630; ☎011/451595, reservations ☎011/491954). Good-sized apartments on a plot of unsurpassed ugliness, with no facilities apart from a small pool. On a positive note, it's next to the beach. Two-bedroom apartments (up to four people) ④ low, ④ high.

Sea Breeze Beach Cottages (4km; PO Box 90228; ☎011/227683). Not on the beach and overpriced, with somewhat run-down s/c rooms (no nets) and linoleum everywhere. Somnolent bar and murky green pool. The *Children's Holiday Resort* is a far better alternative. ③.

Shelly Beach Club Hotel (2.8km; PO Box 96030; ☎011/451001, fax 451349). An affordable all-inclusive resort (including unlimited booze, until the bar closes at midnight), populated entirely by British package tourists. By no means the most beautiful hotel on the coast and there's refreshingly little pretence to class (starting with the curio stalls outside reception), but it's well run. Rooms are AC; no day visitors. Rates negotiable. ⑥.

YWCA (350m; PO Box 96009; ☎011/451845). Similar to the ACK opposite but not as nice, though it's peaceful, and you don't have to be young, female or even Christian. There are fifty bunks in dorms (ie cheap singles), and one self-catering cottage (three beds). ②–③.

Tiwi Beach

South of Likoni, the first real magnet is **TIWI BEACH**. Popular among budget travellers having a bit of a splash, Tiwi rates as genuine tropical paradise material and attracts lots of Anglo-Kenyan families down from Nairobi. The reef lies just offshore, and there are good snorkelling opportunities at high tide, especially at the northern end. Beach hustlers and all the attendant hassles have mostly yet to arrive, especially in the northern section (fronted by *Sand Island*, *Capricho*, and *Maweni*). With the exception of the large new *Travellers Tiwi Beach Hotel* at its southern end, Tiwi is still cottage territory, with nearly a dozen plots vying with each other for business. The only restaurants as yet are at *Travellers Tiwi Beach Hotel*, *Tiwi Villas* and *Twiga Lodge*, the latter with the best bar. The main drawbacks (some might say its advantages) are the lack of bars, restaurants and nightlife, and its isolation from the rest of the coast. More serious are nagging concerns about security if you're walking anywhere: don't take any valuables.

There are two roads down to the beach from the main South Coast highway. The first, signposted for *Sand Island*, *Capricho* and *Maweni*, is a narrow sandy track some 17km from the Likoni ferry; the second, about 1.5km further south, has a bigger clump of signboards and is much wider, and more reliable for driving in rain. Using either road, you're strongly advised not to walk, certainly if you've all your luggage with you: these access roads through the cashews have seen many *panga*-point robberies. Waiting for a ride won't be a huge problem as there's a fairly frequent taxi service (it should cost Ksh100–300). Or ring ahead and someone should pick you up. Taxis from Mombasa cost about Ksh1600.

In the dry season you can walk to the end of Tiwi Beach and wade across the Mwachema River to Diani Beach and the strange Kongo Mosque, right next to the *Indian Ocean Beach Club*. But check locally that it's safe: there have been one or two incidents of robbery down here, too.

Accommodation

The seasons on Tiwi, as regards prices and availability, are slightly different from other parts of the coast in that they reflect the school holidays of their regular clients. At Christmas, Easter, and in July and August, it's hard to get in anywhere: advance booking is a good idea. The following listings are arranged from north to south. Price codes refer to the cost for two people sharing a one-bedroom cottage, where available; there are always big savings for groups in larger cottages. There's nothing in the real budget range unless you're camping, but the extra expense is well worth it if you choose carefully.

Sand Island Beach Cottages (PO Box 5516 Diani; ☎0127/51233, ☎ & fax 0127/51201, *hatfield@form-net.com*; closed May & June). Long-established and well-maintained, with fully equipped self-catering rustic cottages – all sea-facing – with new kitchen equipment and decent bathrooms. The old Kenya atmosphere is refreshingly informal, with charming family management, and the site is very attractive, with a shifting sand isle exposed with the tides just yards across the water, and safe swimming possible at all times. There's a coral garden nearby, and use of snorkelling equipment is free. The products of a working farm are available, and you can arrange fishing trips with (unpushy) local fishermen on the beach. A nice touch is the possibility of having meals brought to your cottage if you order the day before. Small double to cottages sleeping six. Recommended. ④–⑤.

DHOW TRIPS AND DIVING

For details of **dhow trip operators**, read the box on p.473. Information on scuba diving is in the box on p.472.

Capricho Beach Cottages (PO Box 5177 Diani, ☎0127/51231, fax 51010, *capricho@tiwibeach.com*; office hours 8–11am & 4–5pm; closed May). Where *Sand Island* has the advantage in its beach and ambience, *Capricho* concentrates on flashier amenities – well-designed vault-roofed self-catering cottages with plenty of cool space, and a pool (and no dogs – *Sand Island* love dogs). Bed linen and mosquito nets extra. Marginally more expensive than *Maweni*. Six-person cottage ④; two-person cottage ③.

Maweni Beach Cottages (PO Box 96024 Likoni, ☎0127/51008, fax 51225). A variety of relatively simple self-catering cottages in various positions. Slightly cheaper than either of its northerly neighbours, but more formal and with less charm. The site is conscientiously managed and guarded, and there's a pretty little cove – though *Sand Island*'s and *Capricho*'s beaches are just a short stroll away. Six-person cottage ④; two-person cottage ③.

Tiwi Villas (PO Box 86775 Mombasa; ☎ & fax 0127/51265). A rather schizophrenic place unable to decide whether it's a hotel or cottage complex: the last fridges and cookers were recently removed (an unsubtle way to get you to patronize their restaurant). The seven best cottages have superb sea views, but are cramped, dark and rather basic. There are cheaper rooms at the back of the site. There's no beach, as the site is perched on a coral rock promontory, and the small pool hardly compensates, though you can use the beach next door. Four-person sea-facing cottage ③; double rooms ③.

Coral Cove Cottages (PO Box 96455 Mombasa; ☎0127/51295; ☎ & fax 0127/51062, *www.aussimike.com/coralcove*). From the makers of Nairobi's infamous *Buffalo Bill's*, something rather different: excellent, large, stand-alone cottages with fine new bathrooms and an attractive, palm-shaded beach, all bathed in a laid-back atmosphere provided by low-key but consistently helpful management. Loads of dogs and cats, an aviary and a silly parrot. The beach here is shallow (good for children), and favoured by turtles for laying eggs, so be careful where you step. Free twice weekly transport to Diani for shopping, and fruit, veg and fish vendors call daily. You can rent a cook/housekeeper for Ksh200 per day. The price itself is a bargain: doubles (with barbecue equipment) ②; fully-equipped four-person cottages ③–④.

Twiga Lodge (PO Box 96005 Mombasa; ☎0127/51267). Basic hostel and campsite trading on a reputation established in the

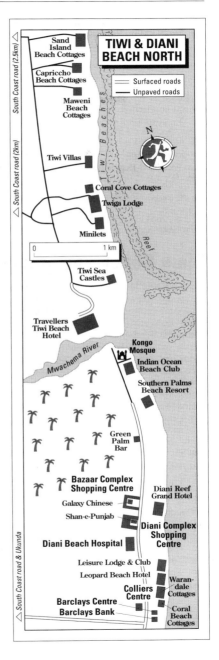

1970s, and still popular with overlanders and budget travellers despite much better competition. The draw of its lively bar aside, it's now just the place you end up if you don't know about the alternatives. For several years it has been beset by security problems, inadequate management and persistently unfriendly staff, and the beach attracts more than its fair share of beach boys. Apart from a variety of dismal cell- or barrack-like rooms (no self-catering facilities, and some lack toilets), you can camp (Ksh150 per person). There's an adequately stocked provisions store and the bar-restaurant does reasonable food. ③.

Minilets. One down from *Twiga Lodge*, but currently closed, which is a real shame: feedback for this was invariably positive, with relaxed and friendly management, helpful staff, and neat chalets prettily scattered down a sloping old coral garden hillside, featuring a swimming pool at the bottom. Worth checking out in case it reopens. ③.

Tiwi Sea Castles (PO Box 96599 Likoni; ☎0127/51229–2, fax 51222). Comfortable rooms, two- and four-bed studios: one of Tiwi's most luxurious developments. B&B ③–④ low, ④–⑤ high.

Travellers Tiwi Beach Hotel, at the south end of Tiwi (PO Box 87649 Mombasa; ☎0127/51202, fax 51207, *travellershtl@swiftmombasa.com*). The beach's only tourist hotel, a large and somewhat impersonal package affair. The main attraction is arguably the longest swimming pool in Kenya, actually a series of pools connected by canals and slides. The public areas are on one side, and rows of three-storey apartment blocks on the other. There's also a nightclub (*Diamonds*, from 9pm nightly), and a good Indian restaurant (*Sher-e-Punjab*; closed Mon lunch). Watersports include waterskiing, windsurfing, snorkelling and scuba diving. Free entry for day visitors. HB ⑤.

Diani Beach and around

DIANI BEACH ought to fulfil most dreams about the archetypal palm-fringed beach: the sand is soft and brilliantly white, the sea is crystal-clear turquoise, the reef is a safe thirty-minute swim or ten-minute boat ride away and, arching overhead, the coconut palms keep up a perpetual slow sway as the breeze rustles through the fronds. Competition for space, however, has begun seriously to mar Diani's paradisal qualities, but the main drawback – common to all of Kenya's major beach resorts – is the droves of hustlers and vendors – the "beach boys" – who had become such a threatening presence a few years back (see box on p.469) that the vast majority of hotel guests virtually never ventured across the boundary from their guarded hotel gardens onto the public sands. Now that "tourist police", as well as the hotels' own security guards (*askaris*) are posted to the area full-time, the beach boys have become more astute and formed themselves into cartels (some worryingly connected to local politicians), and tourists do, once again, dig sandcastles and walk along the strand. Another (minor) drawback is that the beach tends to get covered at high tide, or leaves only a narrow strip of sand. All the beach is open to the public; it's only the access routes that are restricted by some hotels.

If you're coming by public transport **from Mombasa**, first catch a *matatu* from outside the GPO to Likoni ferry (Ksh5), where you have to cross as a foot passenger (free; Ksh35 for private vehicles). Once in Likoni, walk up with the crowd to the well-marked *matatu* stages on the left side, and catch one for "Diani" or "Beach" (Ksh30). Alternatively, get one to Ukunda (Ksh20; see below), and then make a connection down to the beach road – you'll find plenty of transport both day and night. Don't walk, especially if you're burdened with luggage or valuables: the three-kilometre link road has a bad reputation – hard to tell how well-founded – for muggings. Taxis from Mombasa cost around Ksh2100.

Accommodation

Diani now has its own official **tourist information office** (Mon–Fri 8am–1pm & 2–5pm; ☎0127/2227, fax 2156; PO Box 702 Ukunda); the staff are helpful, friendly, and loaded with information. They should have **maps** available, and have compiled lists of most hotels and B&Ls south of Mombasa, complete with prices and contact numbers. They are also the people you should contact if you have serious **complaints** about a hotel or other service. You'll find them at the rear of the building behind the Agip petrol station, 900m south of the junction between Diani Beach Road and the link road from Ukunda.

Running 300m behind the beach, the Diani Beach road feels like Kenya's number-one strip in the high season. Fortunately, thick forest separates the road from the shore, though more of the **Jadini Forest** disappears every year as one new plot after another is cleared, usually not entirely legally. The **tourist hotels** that fill the plots are expensive by Kenyan standards and, if you've been travelling on a budget, the prices will come as a shock. If you're coming from abroad they seem more reasonably priced, and you'll find standards generally high. Most offer low-season reductions, which are generally good value.

The distances in the following listings are from the Ukunda junction on the Diani Beach road, by Barclays Bank.

Camping and budget rooms

Budget accommodation along the beach is sparse and none of the big hotels will entertain campers in their gardens. If you're a family or in a large group, renting a cottage (see below) is invariably better value than taking a room, and gives you the chance to cook up some local food in your own style.

Glory Guest House (500m west of the junction on the way to Ukunda; PO Box 85527; ☎0127/2276). More than adequate unit in this mini-chain of hotels, with a pool. Security appears sound, but caution would nonetheless be advised. B&B ② low, ③ high.

Dan's Camping (1.4km south of the junction, next to *Trade Winds*; PO Box 5019 Diani Beach; ☎ & fax 0127/3405, c/o Janoland Safaris). The former home of Dan Trench who died in 1990, the son of the family which once owned much of the land down here, this was once something of an institution. Unfortunately, despite an attempt to spruce things up a little, it has stubbornly sunk back into its usual state, essentially little more than a basic B&L. The garden is a clutter of luxuriant foliage and fast deteriorating *bandas*, all very basic, not s/c, far from clean and overpriced. Bad security in the past, but no reports of incidents lately. A bicycle fruit-seller arrives every morning from his orchard farm in the bush, and there are fish-sellers on the beach early morning and afternoons: give fish to the manager, who's a dab hand at cooking. Camping Ksh150 per person. ②.

South Fork (1.4km south, then 800m from the road; PO Box 231 Ukunda; ☎0127/3053). Low-budget accommodation and campsite, set back in the bush and fields and a good fifteen-minute walk from the beach at *Trade Winds*. Several large studio rooms (both s/c and non-s/c) and a number of smaller non-s/c rooms, plus a cheap restaurant. Popular disco Saturday nights. Bicycle hire can be arranged, and camping costs Ksh200 per person. Rooms ①, studios ②–③.

Cottages and apartments

As in the Tiwi Beach cottage listings, price codes refer to the cost of the whole cottage if double rooms are not available. As always, the larger cottages offer big savings for groups.

Coral Beach Cottages (300m north; PO Box 168 Ukunda; ☎0127/2413, fax 3138). On a parched, run-down site, this isn't an obvious first choice, especially as only two of its seventeen cottages are up for short-term rent. On the plus side, they face out over the sea, and prices are reasonable. Monthly rates Ksh45,000/60,000. Two/three bedrooms ③–④ low, ④–⑤ high.

Warandale Cottages (600m north; PO Box 11 Ukunda; ☎ & fax 0127/3048 or PO Box 5542 Diani Beach; ☎ & fax 0127/2187). A tangle of different-sized houses and a small pool, all nestled under luxuriant vegetation, this is an exceptionally nice setup – the staff clean and cook for you – and it's good for children. The recent *Fawlty Towers* style bust-up between the owners has led to the farcical sight of two rival booking offices facing each other across the driveway, each handling half the cottages: the Ukunda address handles the good two-bedroom *Mlima* and two other sea-facing cottages; the Diani Beach address has two sea-facing cottages, is considerably cheaper and has monthly rates (Ksh40,000–50,000). Sea-facing, ④–⑤ low, ⑤–⑥ high; non-sea-facing ③–④ low, ④–⑤ high.

Vindigo Cottages (700m south, signposted "Marion Nicholas – Vindigo" opposite Bazaar Centre; PO Box 77 Ukunda; ☎0127/2192). Seven vaguely down-at-heel self-catering cottages in woodland, with a pleasing rustic feel but rather eccentric management. The kitchens are fully equipped and the rooms, though mouldering, are very private, with mosquito-screened windows, fans, electricity, running water in the showers and high-level toilets. Some have lovely views over the beach through the trees. Again, a cook/housekeeper is provided with every cottage, fishermen and fruitsellers call daily and there are three night *askaris*. Pick-ups from Mombasa for a fee. Rates vary according to season, trade, mood and your appearance, and are per cottage. ④.

Wayside Beach Apartments (1.4km south, follow signs to *Trade Winds*; PO Box 83451 Mombasa; ☎0127/3119, fax 487214). Stylish two- to six-bed self-catering apartments in a horseshoe-shaped building around a good pool, set between the main road and *Trade Winds*. Sauna and broken jacuzzi, but it's not located on the beach and is getting tatty. Prices negotiable. Monthly rates Ksh25,000 (one-bed), Ksh45,000 (three-bed). ③ low, ④ high.

Diani Beachalets (6.5km south; PO Box 26 Ukunda; ☎0127/2180). By far the best on Diani, welcoming and homely, run by a charming German woman with a wicked sense of humour and a penchant for cats, as well as visiting duiker antelopes, bushbabies and colobus monkeys. Catering mainly for backpackers, this peaceful refuge is bang on the beach, with a variety of abodes, from simple two-bed *bandas* with fridge, electric light, communal showers and cooking area, to nice, s/c cottages with kitchen, sitting room and verandah. Fresh fish, fruit and veg from pedlars. The beach is pretty well deserted, and the few beach boys there are wary (the Frau calls the tourist police if they get too annoying). Monthly rates Ksh22,500 (two people), Ksh35,000 (four people). Two-bed huts ①; cottages ③–④ low, ④–⑤ high; sea-facing "beachettes" ④ low, Ksh④–⑤ high.

Hotels north of the junction

Generally, the more interesting abodes worthy of major expenditure are to the south of the Ukunda junction – an area which also retains some flicker of pre-hotel times. To the north, the scene is brasher and more despoiled, and there's no forest either. Most hotels provide some sort of nightly entertainment, including uniformly cheesy bands at dinner time.

Leopard Beach Hotel (800m; PO Box 34 Ukunda; ☎0127/3425 or 2111, fax 3424). Mid-range and a touch dated in feel (it was built in the 1970s), but with good facilties. Set in lush gardens with ponds and waterfalls populated by lizards, with friendly staff, a good atmosphere and decent food. Steps down to the beach. Some standard rooms (all AC with minibars) and most cottages have sea views. Facilities include tennis, volleyball, canoeing, windsurfing, snorkelling, glass-bottomed boats and PADI diving school. Good value. ⑤ low, ⑥ high.

Leisure Lodge & Club (1.2km; PO Box 84383 Mombasa; ☎0127/2011–14, fax 2046, *leisure@africaonline.co.ke*). One of the earlier Diani hotels (1971) but recently revamped, and in a striking location on low cliffs hollowed by bat-filled caves. The fine, tree-shaded beach is tucked beneath. There are several pools, an eighteen-hole par 72 golf course opposite the entrance, and a casino in the grounds (which explains the heavier than usual security presence; open daily 9pm–3am). Most standard rooms lack sea views, but have AC, nets and satellite TV; the more expensive "Golf Villas" (⑦) are luxurious, with their own pools, some with sea views. PADI diving school, wind-surfing school, tennis courts. No ocean-swimming at low tide, though the trips to the nearby Kongo River delta are designed to circumvent this. Popular with German and Swiss package tourists. FB from ⑤ low, ⑥ high.

Diani Reef Grand Hotel (1.6km; PO Box 35 Ukunda; ☎0127/2723, fax 2196, *dianireef@formnet.com*). A 1970s construction with over 300 centrally air-conditioned rooms (with minibar, but no fans or nets), this is one of the largest hotels on the coast, with an international accent – fussy public areas, seven restaurants and numerous bars. Uninspiring regular and deluxe rooms in different wings, with not much to distinguish them but the quantity of gold chrome. On a positive note, it's ramped throughout. Facilities include windsurfing, scuba diving school, pedalos and inflatable canoes, the *Regent* casino and *Disco Ngoma* (nightly from 9pm). HB from ⑦ low, ⑧ high.

Southern Palms Beach Resort (2.9km; PO Box 363 Ukunda; ☎0127/3721, fax 3381). Opened in 1992, this is a spacious and well-appointed package hotel with rooms in four-storey blocks with thatched roofs, two fabulous pools (one with jacuzzi and mock desert island, both with water-level bars) that children as well as adults adore, friendly management and staff. PADI diving school, windsurfing, floodlit tennis courts, squash, gym. And for all this, it's a bargain. Recommended. HB ⑤ low, ⑨ high.

BEACH BOYS AND THE TOURIST POLICE

If you're staying in a hotel, spending some peaceful time on the beach can appear virtually impossible. Frustration can set in as the days slip by and you still haven't really been for a swim, or a wander by the shore, because of the hordes of **hustlers** plying their wares, or their camel rides, or their boat trips, or just themselves. Always acknowledge them: ignoring their greetings really is considered very rude. The least painful solution is quickly to strike up a friendship of sorts with one beach boy, to buy at least something, or to go on a boat trip. Once you have a friend, and have done some business, you have some rights, and you'll find you can then stroll on the beach with far fewer hassles from the others. It's not so easy for single women, but the principle for most situations still applies: don't fight it. There is no need, incidentally, to feel physically threatened on the beach. Every hotel has its *askaris* (security guards) posted along the boundary between the plot and the beach, and they usually stay alert to the slightest sign of trouble – which is rare indeed. Apart from the tourist police, there are also KWS rangers patrolling the beaches, though that scheme may be in danger of collapsing through underfunding. One piece of practical advice: if you're bargaining, don't complicate matters by trying to swap clothes for crafts. You'll still be expected to pay some cash, and will end up feeling more ripped off than ever.

Indian Ocean Beach Club (3.6km; PO Box 73 Ukunda; ☎0127/3730, fax 3557; reservations through Block, p.48). Also opened in 1992, this is one of the best hotels on the coast. State-of-the-art rooms, wonderful Lamu-style architecture and attentive management, with most watersports free and swimming possible at all tides in the creek. Fine groves of baobabs in the gardens, and ocean-front rooms don't cost much more. Very grown-up, not ideal for kids, but a great place for a honeymoon. Casual guests welcome (free), but you need permission to use the pool. Stunningly expensive. FB from ⑦ low, ⑨ high.

Hotels south of the junction

Apart from the most popular hotels covered in the following listings, there are several others, and more look set to appear for years to come – to the depreciation, at least in aesthetic terms, of the whole area. Rough tarmac now continues another 4km beyond the end (6.5km south) of the good road, as far as the *Pinewood* on Galu Beach. Distances given are south from the junction.

LTI-Kaskazi Beach Hotel (300m; PO Box 135 Ukunda; ☎0127/3725, fax 2233, *kaskazi@africaonline.co.ke*). Well-run and competitively priced, successfully balancing classy atmosphere with package-tour popularity. Heavy on the Arabic styling, with white-tiled floors, tinkling fountains and soaring *makuti* roofs. One of the few all-inclusive hotels to welcome day visitors (free entry), and consequently has a pleasingly informal feel. Not suitable for the disabled (steps everywhere). There's the sad little ruined seventeenth-century "Diani mosque" in the garden, basically just a old wall. FB all-inc ⑥ low, ⑦ high.

Trade Winds (1.4km). Presently closed due to the collapse of its parent company, this was an unpretentious package hotel – one of the oldest at Diani – right down on the shore, and a favourite haunt of expats. It's likely to reopen during the lifetime of this edition, and should offer competitive rates if nothing spectacular in terms of facilities.

Diani Sea Resort (2km; PO Box 37 Ukunda; ☎0127/3081, fax 3439). Built 1991 and much more cheerful than its neighbouring all-inclusive sister hotel, with consistently good service, nice staff and plenty of things to do. It lacks local style, though: the 170 satellite-TV-equipped rooms are in the same style as *Diani Sea Lodge* and could be anywhere (and most lack views), and the gardens and fountains are formal. Great pool (Ksh300 for casual visitors), gym, tennis and squash courts, crazy golf, windsurfing and PADI diving school. HB ⑦ high.

Diani Sea Lodge (3.5km; PO Box 37 Ukunda; ☎0127/2060, fax 3439). A large, slightly downmarket, Mediterranean-style all-inclusive version of the jointly-owned *Resort*, above. The 125 AC rooms are a let down: despite the good-sized double beds and frame-fitted nets, most are small, in bunga-

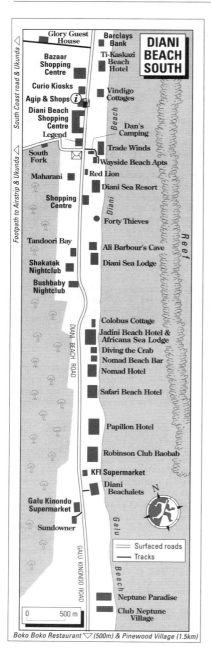

DIANI BEACH SOUTH

Glory Guest House
Barclays Bank
Bazaar Shopping Centre
Ti-Kaskazi Beach Hotel
Curio Kiosks
Agip & Shops ⓘ
Vindigo Cottages
Diani Beach Shopping Centre Legend
Dan's Camping
South Fork
Trade Winds
Maharani
Wayside Beach Apts
Red Lion
Diani Sea Resort
Shopping Centre
Forty Thieves
Tandoori Bay
Ali Barbour's Cave
Shakatak Nightclub
Diani Sea Lodge
Bushbaby Nightclub
Colobus Cottage
Jadini Beach Hotel & Africana Sea Lodge
Diving the Crab
Nomad Beach Bar
Nomad Hotel
Safari Beach Hotel
Papillon Hotel
Robinson Club Baobab
KFI Supermarket
Diani Beachalets
Galu Kinondo Supermarket
Sundowner
Neptune Paradise
Club Neptune Village

South Coast road & Ukunda
Footpath to Airstrip & Ukunda
Diani Beach
Reef
DIANI BEACH ROAD
Galu Beach
GALU KINONDO ROAD

Surfaced roads
Tracks

0   500 m

Boko Boko Restaurant ▽ *(500m) & Pinewood Village (1.5km)*

lows set back in the gardens, and only ten are sea-facing. Pool and childrens' pool, gym, tennis court, crazy golf, windsurfing and PADI diving school. Mainly German clientele. Daily admission Ksh1500. Not the best all-inclusive, but cheap. All-inc ③ low, ⑤ high.

Jadini Beach Hotel (4.2km; PO Box 84616 Mombasa; ☎0127/2622, fax 2269; reservations through Alliance, p.48). Diani's longest established resort hotel (1960s) with high standards and good atmosphere, refurbished in 1991. Busy and cosmopolitan, and good for kids, with its daytime creche and activities. Besides the usual watersports, facilities include a PADI-accredited diving school, three tennis courts, the atmospheric *Jambo Village* restaurant, a petrol station with regular prices, and St Stephen's Chapel for Sunday morning repentance. Most rooms have sea views. Guests can also use the facilities at *Africana Sea Lodge* and *Safari Beach Hotel*. HB ⑤ low, ⑦ high.

Africana Sea Lodge (4.2km; PO Box 84616 Mombasa; ☎0127/2624, fax 2145; reservations through Alliance, p.48). On the same plot as *Jadini*, the *Africana* is sold as a fun hotel for couples, with accommodation in comfortable but unembellished *bandas* (no sea views). It's also the cheapest of the group, and one of the few places which pulls off the balancing act between package tourism and personal service. You can use the facilities at the *Jadini* and *Safari Beach* hotels. HB ⑤ low, ⑦ high.

Nomad Hotel (4.8km; PO Box 1 Ukunda; ☎0127/2155, fax 2391, *nomad@swiftmombasa.com*). Not only the cheapest and least formal of the Diani hotels, with positive and helpful management, but with the best views, too: each of the seventeen twin-bed *bandas* and three cottages (with fans, not AC) has a terrace fronting onto the beach – barely 20m away – the view framed by leaning coconut palms, the odd baobab and the bobbing heads of beach boys. The thatch-and-straw *bandas*, though not luxurious, are cosy, and perched nicely between the palms, some with additional rooms at the back for children, and there are larger and more expensive cottages. There's a good seafood restaurant, too. No pool but a dive school, and forex with good rates. Rates negotiable; recommended. B&B: *bandas* ⑤ low, ⑥ high; cottages ⑥ low, ⑦ high.

Safari Beach Hotel (5.1km; PO Box 90690 Mombasa; ☎0127/2726, fax 2357; reservations through Alliance, p.48). The latest and best of the Alliance hotels, with good sports and watersports facilities (and PADI diving school), excellent food, a disco, and a daily children's programme with full-time staff. The rooms however are unexceptional, set in a confusing complex of identical two-storey *bandas* at the rear of the hotel. HB ⑤ low, ⑦ high.

Papillon Hotel, formerly *Lagoon Reef* (5.5km; PO Box 83058; ☎0127/2627, fax 2216, *onearth@africaonline.co.ke*). Next door and superior to the snooty *Ocean Village Club*, and one of the only few all-inclusives (optional FB) with a really cheerful holiday atmosphere. Staff are helpful and friendly, and there's loads for kids to do, with a playground, children's swimming pool (and a sloping "beach" end on the normal one ideal for toddlers), and a busy daily club organizing painting lessons, beach and forest walks, and pony rides from the hotel's stables. Most rooms have sea views, too. Other activities include scuba diving, catamarans, pedalos and windsurfing, as well as glass-bottomed boats and snorkelling. The gardens have lots of steps. Very good value and free entry to casual visitors. Recommended. FB ⑤, all-inc ⑥.

Robinson Club Baobab (5.9km; PO Box 32 Ukunda; ☎0127/2623, fax 3032, *r.baobab@africaon-line.co.ke*). An elegant and well-kept all-inclusive club (built 1970s), part of the German Robinson chain, located at the end of Diani Beach proper on a coral rock promontory. Unfortunately, only the first row of bungalows have sea views, and casual visitors are kept out by the Ksh4500 daily fee. Nothing much for children, either, and some command of German would be helpful. ⑦ low, ⑨ high.

Neptune Paradise (8.5km, on Galu Beach; PO Box 696 Ukunda; ☎0127/3620, fax 3019, *nep_sc@africaonline.co.ke*). Decent rooms with pink cane furniture in tightly packed regular rows of two-storey *bandas* (no sea views), and an uninteresting long, narrow plot (like the co-owned *Club Neptune Village*) that requires lengthy, shadeless walks. The plot has been extended seawards to the point where there is no beach left at high tide. Scuba diving school, windsurfing, and catamaran trips. Reasonably priced but still overrated. HB ⑤ low, ⑥ high.

Club Neptune Village (8.5km, on Galu Beach; PO Box 517 Ukunda; ☎0127/2728, fax 2354, *nep_sc@africaonline.co.ke*). Jointly owned with *Neptune Paradise*, and no more imaginative. The layout is almost identical, with smaller rooms, the only real difference being that the *Club* is all-inclusive, filled mostly with German clientele. Shares watersports with *Neptune Village*. No casual visitors. ⑥ low, ⑦ high.

Pinewood Village (11km, on Galu Beach; PO Box 190 Ukunda; ☎0127/3128, fax 3131). An extremely stylish condominium on a nearly deserted stretch of beach far to the south of the main Diani strip. Well-thought-out four- or six-bed staffed houses, with direct dial phones, free sporting facilities and laundry, and (unusually) water from their own wells. They aim to avoid nasty hidden extras. Self-cater or use the restaurant. Good value. HB ⑤.

Daytime activities

Enjoying yourself on Diani isn't difficult. You can rent snorkelling gear (about Ksh200) from just about anywhere, and float out across the lagoon to the **reef**. Remember how fiercely the sun is likely to burn and wear a T-shirt unless you're very brown. You need to be a confident swimmer: there are no strong currents nor any real danger, but the reef is 600–1000m away and swimming back on the ebb tide can be tiring. Alternatively, a trip to the reef at low tide on one of the outrigger **canoes** is highly recommended. The crews know all the good (or at least the more reasonable) spots for snorkelling and it shouldn't cost you more than Ksh500–700 for an hour or three. One of the best areas is directly opposite *Robinson Club Baobab*, about 300m out towards the reef, where there is a cluster of coral heads. The sheltered lagoon behind the reef is also ideal for **windsurfing** (Ksh400 per hr).

When you tire of the beach and the sea, or of just lying under the palm trees, you could **rent a bicycle** and go off exploring – from about Ksh600 per day. By *matatu*, Watamu, Malindi or Wasini are easy enough targets for a day out. There's also the eighteen-hole par 72 **golf course** opposite the *Leisure Lodge* (who run it) on the north side of the junction. For details of **dhow trip** operators, see the box below.

Kongo Mosque

For a short excursion with a goal, you could aim for the **Kongo Mosque** at the far north end of the beach, at the mouth of the Mwachema River. It's most easily reached

DIVING ON THE SOUTH COAST

Many South Coast hotels, and a good number along the North Coast, have dive centres, where you can do everything from a basic beginner lesson plus assisted dive ($100) to a full course giving you an internationally recognized (usually PADI) qualification ($350 to "Open Water"; an additional $320 to "Advanced Open Water"). If you already have scuba certification, single dives cost $25–35. You can nearly always take a free dip in the pool wearing diving equipment, to test your affinity: most people find breathing underwater curiously addictive.

Before choosing a centre, take time to compare the equipment of several companies, and ask them about their environmenal policy, safety procedures and general experience. They should at the very least have up-to-date PADI ("Professional Association of Diving Instructors") or BSAC ("British Sub-Aqua Association") accreditation, and ideally be affiliated to Scuba Schools International (SSI). One of the oldest and best established outfits, with an excellent reputation and good equipment, is Diving the Crab, on the beach between Jadini and Nomad hotels on Diani (Blue Wave, PO Box 5011 Diani Beach; ☎0127/3400 or 2369–70, fax 2372), who are also the only company offering state-of-the-art "Nitrox" technology, which mixes nitrogen and oxygen to reduce decompression complications and enable longer dives. If you need more information, contact PADI directly in the United States: 1251 East Dyer Road #100, Santa Ana, CA 92705-5605 (☎+714-540-7234, fax +714-540-2609, www.padi.com).

The Dive Sites of Kenya and Tanzania (see "Contexts" p.648) is highly recommended reading for divers as well as snorkellers. See also the box on "Responsible snorkelling, diving and fishing" on p.410.

through the grounds of the Indian Ocean Beach Club – which gives you the opportunity to visit one of Diani's best-looking hotels. Beyond the boundary fence and inevitable askari, the Kongo Mosque is surrounded by venerable baobabs. Also known as Diani Persian Mosque, the building is enigmatic and disconcerting, with its five heavy wooden doors. There's an electric atmosphere here, the barrel-vaulted mosque brooding like a huge tomb under the trees. It is too complete to be considered a ruin, and has recently been fenced in by local Islamic leaders who have encouraged the community to start using it again, mainly in response to repeated attempts by local politicians to appropriate the mosque and communal land for "development".

Although a sign suggests otherwise, you will, suitably attired and accompanied, be allowed to have a look around. Named after the Kongo Forest, the mosque is thought to be either fourteenth- or fifteenth-century and the one remaining building – maybe the only stone one – of a Wa-shirazi settlement here (see p.479). The river mouth was the first safe anchorage south of Mombasa.

Jadini Forest

For a walk, or a jog (fitness mania overcomes a fair number of visitors), it's more interesting to head south along Diani road. Here there are more hotels, of course, but also, approaching the end of the paving, some wonderful patches of jungly forest comprising the dwindling Jadini Forest. There's the almost obligatory snake park, but if you'd like to search for some animals in the wild rather than support this venture, then any of the tracks leading off to the right will take you straight into magnificent stands of hardwood trees, alive with birds and butterflies, and rocking with vervet and Angolan colobus monkeys. The latter, whose population is estimated at around 1500, have come in for some special attention lately, as concern has mounted over land encroachment and deaths from speeding cars. The resultant campaign, spearheaded by the Wakuluzu Colobus Trust (at Colobus Cottage, 3.7km south; PO Box 5380 Diani Beach; ☎0127/3519, colobus@africaonline.co.ke), has put up warning signs and speedbumps, and – most inventively – the wire, rope

DHOW AND SNORKELLING TRIPS

The following is a list of the main **dhow trip operators**, all of which operate out of the South Coast. Unless stated, all will pick you up from your hotel (South Coast, and North Coast as far as Kikambala), either for free or for a nominal extra charge. For the most part, the dhows are not under sail but are powered by on-board or outboard motors. All can be booked direct, or though your hotel. If you're going to combine a dhow trip with snorkelling, see the box on p.410.

Dolphin Dhow, office at Barclays Centre, Diani Beach (Blue Horizons Adventures, PO Box 85636 Mombasa; ☎ & fax 0127/2094, *www.africaonline.co.ke/dolphin*). Day-long dolphin-spotting trips combined with snorkelling (no flippers provided; bring your own). Early morning pick-ups from North and South Coast hotels. Lunch on board. Dolphin sightings obviously not guaranteed. $90–95.

Funzi Island Club, no walk-in office (PO Box 1108 Ukunda; ☎0127/2044, fax 2346). This expensive hotel also offers dolphin-spotting trips by dhow combined with crocodile spotting on the Ramisi River estuary. No snorkelling. Early morning pick-ups from North and South Coast hotels. $80–90.

Funzi Island Lazy Lagoon, 2.5km down the track from Ramisi through Bodo village (PO Box 90246; ☎011/225546, fax 316458). A variety of personal boat trips, the best-value being the full-day "crocodile canoe" trip up the meandering mangrove estuary of the Ramisi River: meditative, great for bird-spotting, with a seafood BBQ lunch at a beach-side *banda* (Ksh2500 per person). They also have a completely lazy "Bimble in the Bays" trip (Ksh10,000), which features nothing more energetic than lounging about in a boat all day. Price includes transfers from Ukunda market.

Kinazini Funzi Dhow Safaris, Diani Beach Shopping Centre (☎0127/3182 or 3221). Trips with a more cultural bent, with a cruise through Funzi creek and the mangroves, a visit to the ruins on Funzi island, and visits to a local school, a private house and a market place, with lunch on the uninhabited island of Kinazini. Book through *Walter's Inn* in Diani for a 25 percent discount. Ksh4500 per person.

Pilli-Pipa Dhow Safaris, office opposite the *Coral Beach Cottages* turning at Diani Beach (Shimoni Aqua-Ventures, PO Box 5185 Diani Beach; ☎ & fax 0127/2401; office ☎0127/3559 or 0127/52286, *www.pilli-pipa.mf-group.com*). Hugely enjoyable dhow day-trips to Kisiti Marine National Park for outstanding snorkelling (field guides, masks, snorkels and fins provided), with a late lunch of crab claws, fine wine and Swahili food at a private house on Wasini Island. Departures most days at 8.30am from Shimoni jetty (collection can be arranged from both South and North Coast hotels). $95–100.

Shirazi Bay/Club Swahili, office at Barclays Centre, Diani Beach (Exotic Destinations, PO Box 5050 Diani; ☎0127/3502, fax 3389). Day-trips combining an morning mangrove cruise and snorkelling, lunch on Funzi island and a lazy afternoon by the pool, for $99.

SSI East Africa (Blue Wave), (PO Box 5011 Diani Beach; ☎0127/2369–70, fax 2372). Offers mangrove trips (by motorboat; 3-4hr) from *Jadini Beach Hotel* in Diani south to mangrove channels in front of Chale Island, where you might see grey herons, fish eagles, cormorants and kingfishers.

Wasini Island Restaurant & Kisite Dhow Tours, office at *Jadini Beach Hotel*, Diani Beach (PO Box 281 Ukunda; ☎0127/2331 or 3055, fax 3154, *kisite@africaonline.co.ke*). Established over twenty years and environmentally aware, offering day-long dhow and snorkelling trips at Kisite, with a seemingly endless seafood lunch at their restaurant on the north side of Wasini Island upon your hungry return. Costs $60 from Shimoni jetty, or $80–85 including early-morning transport from your hotel. Equipment and field guides are available on board. Scuba diving, if you've already got accreditation, costs an additional $50 for two dives, or $30 per dive for beginners. Dolphin-spotting also possible.

and wood "colobobridges" at known danger spots over the road, which the monkeys quickly learned to use. You can pick up more information at Colobus Cottage, which also has a forest nature trail in its grounds (a guided half-hour walk costs Ksh300). Of the other monkeys, baboons are most common, and are nasty-tempered pests: their nutritious diet of hotel leftovers means they've multiplied greatly, and are not afraid of humans. Keep your distance, as there have been many incidents of unwary tourists getting scratched and bitten. Overly-tame Sykes' monkeys are also becoming a pest.

Snakes you are unlikely to come across. You'll be told the forest is the haunt of leopards, which is extremely unlikely. Come down here at night and you will see eyes in the dark, probably those of bushbabies: it's hard to believe that even leopards would put up with so violent a destruction of their habitat.

Eating, drinking and nightlife

Most of the hotels have snack menus, salad bars and all the rest: if you're on a budget, choose carefully and avoid the dubious temptation of Ksh200 fruit-juice cocktails, and you can still depart satisfied. The following listings, in north-to-south order (distances from the junction), include some of the best, and some of the best-value, places to eat and drink apart from the hotels.

Restaurants

Galaxy, Bazaar Complex Shopping Centre (1.5km north; ☎0127/2529). Classy Chinese restaurant with main dishes from Ksh300. Free pick-up from hotels. Open daily.

Gallo's, Diani Beach Shopping Centre (1km south; ☎0127/3150). Inventive menu with Mexican flavours (main courses around Ksh500) and cheaper options like pizza and pasta. You can ring for take-away orders. They also have a cybercafé and fax services, and a cocktail bar. Free pick-up from hotels. Closed Tues.

Legend (2km south). Monstrous Italian construction, originally intended to be a casino, now operating as a totally over-the-top restaurant and bar with nice espresso – half-acre swimming pool with lifesize elephant models (free use of pool if you buy drinks), boriti poles painted pink and an elderly crooner on white piano accompanied by drum machine.

Maharani (2.5km south; ☎0127/2439). Serving expensive tandoori specialities, this place is palatial in appearance in the evening when lit up. Not the most generous, but exceedingly tasty. Free transport from your hotel. Open daily.

Ali Barbour's Cave (3km south; ☎0127/2033). Bizarrely built inside a deep coral cave: you enter at ground level and descend. Even if you have no intention of disposing of around Ksh3000 for two (with wine) on the lavish French and seafood menu, it's worth dropping in just to have a look. Good food, well presented. Don't wear shorts. Open Mon–Sat from 6pm.

Nomad Restaurant (4.8km south; ☎0127/2155). Attached to the hotel, a quality seafood menu in the "formal" makuti-roofed restaurant by the entrance, with soup served in a large breadroll. More popular is its beach bar (see below).

Boko Boko, 200m past Club Neptune Village (9.3km; ☎0127/2344). Long-established Seychellois restaurant (slightly spicy, Creole cooking) set in a lush garden. Large makuti-cone hall with a few tables. Recommended, and surprisingly reasonable, with main dishes from under Ksh400.

Cheap eating and bars

Green Palm Bar (2.7km north). Opposite the closed Golden Beach Hotel, a popular upmarket place with cocktails under a makuti roof.

Shan-e-Punjab, Diani Complex Shopping Centre (1.4km north; ☎0127/3092). Next to the classier Galaxy, a fairly down-to-earth Indian restaurant and snack bar with an open-air garden, serving African, Punjabi and tourist food. Around Ksh500, with more expensive seafood. It's also something of a local hangout, attracting a fair haul of prostitutes, though not so many as to put off families. Open daily till midnight.

Walter's Inn, Bazaar Shopping Centre (800m south). Big and breezy roadside "pub" – the main local for Diani residents – with keg Tusker and country music under a soaring *makuti* roof. The Austrian manager is helpful for general information, and owns a pig farm and butchery, so the pork and sausages are excellent.

Wiseland (900m south). German-run bar and shaded garden restaurant behind a row of tourist shacks, popular with locals for a quiet drink, snacks and Italian ice cream.

Gallo's, Diani Beach Shopping Centre (1km south). Bar and cybercafé adjacent to the restaurant, popular for coffee and ice cream.

Red Lion Bar & Restaurant (2km south). *Makuti*-meets-Cotswolds, and the closest you'll get on the coast to an English country pub. There's a pleasant beer garden, grill room, and Italian food and ice cream.

Forty Thieves Beach Bar & Restaurant (3km south). This budget beachside hangout is a good place for a daytime drink – a bit of a local watering hole – and perfect in the evening when their beach front is floodlit. Discos on Wednesday, Friday and Saturday (and plenty of barefoot racing around the beach); live band and curry buffet on Sun.

Tandoori Bay, opposite *Diani Sea Lodge* (3.5km south). Down-to-earth Indian place, always popular in the high season.

Nomad Beach Bar (4.8km south). At times wildly popular beach bar down at the water's edge, open 24 hours, with snacks, plenty of booze, a Friday night "locals' night", and famous Sunday lunch curry buffet (Ksh500) – a real family affair, with regular live jazz or a one-man-band.

Sundowner, beside Galu Kinondo supermarket (7km south). A very cheap restaurant and bar, completely unpretentious and not a hustler in sight, with brilliant African food and a laid-back, relaxed atmosphere. The campsite here is closed, but may be worth enquiring about.

Mr T Roof Garden Bar & Restaurant, after Galu Beach (9.2km). A little overpriced for the standard menu of tourist and African food (main dishes Ksh200–300) but it's the breeze and the company that attract the clientele.

Nightlife

To get around Diani Beach at night without your own vehicle, you'll have to rely on getting rides or walking. Hitching up and down the Diani road is generally safe and not too difficult, and, while hotels issue warnings about walking on the beach at night (and there are *askaris* in number to underline them), under a full moon it's a pleasure that's hard to resist. In a group, minus your valuables, and not passing long stretches of bush, you're unlikely to have any problems.

   Giriama dancing is one often touted entertainment – probably not something to go out of your way to find (though the group "Drums of Africa" is exceptionally good), but fun if you happen upon it: a couple of professional troupes work the hotels, performing acrobatically to the accompaniment of superb drumming. You're also likely to happen across **Maasai dancers**, of varying degrees of authenticity; the guttural polyphonic singing is fascinating, though the performances usually end with a "Maasai market" where they flog you overpriced and not necessarily Maasai trinkets. Rarest of all are the **Taarab bands** (see p.668), who sometimes play in hotel dining rooms on special occasions or public holidays. Such entertainment is very seasonal and you won't find much going on when the crowds aren't in occupation. There are several **discos** along the road, each with its own idiosyncrasies. None of them even start to warm up before 11pm. Drinks are priced at hotel rates or a little less, but you'll find they don't sell large beers.

Birimba Casino, Colliers Centre, opposite *Coral Beach Cottages* (300m north). Monte Carlo this ain't, but it has enough one-armed bandits to keep you busy.

Tropicana, behind Agip petrol station (900m south). The oldest disco on Diani, open air, with *makuti* roofs and a basic cement dance floor. Reggae or *soukous* most evenings. Ksh100–150.

South Fork, down the track by the post office (1.4km south). Popular discos Saturday nights.

Shakatak (3.5km south). Wooden dance floor and air-conditioning, but a bit of a dive. Tends to play the heaviest mix on the strip. Ksh100. Closed Mon.

Bushbaby (3.8km south). Open-air club opposite the defunct *Two Fishes Lodge*, which attracts hotel staff as well as intrepid hotel guests in search of local colour. Slightly sleazy, but fun for a bop and they do serve tasty kebabs. Ksh50.

Listings

Finding **food** for self-catering and getting ordinary **business** done in Diani is straight-forward enough, with ambulant fish and fruit sellers on the beach, various stalls along the beach road, and many supermarkets (see below). There's an increasingly heavy scattering of proper shops along the strip, as well as a new **post office**. The main shopping areas on the north side are the Bazaar Complex Shopping Centre (1.6km north of the junction) and Diani Complex Shopping Centre (1.4km). On the south side, the commerce kicks off with the Bazaar Shopping Centre (800m south), with fruit and veg stalls, a curio market and half a dozen safari agents, followed by the Agip petrol station (900m) and Diani Beach Shopping Centre (1km), where vervet monkeys scamper across the designer *makuti*. There are more shops and businesses outside *Diani Sea Resort* and opposite *Diani Sea Lodge*.

Bakery The Austrian *Bungoma Bakery*, behind Agip petrol station, has a good range of fresh European breads.

Banks KCB Bank, Diani Complex (Mon–Fri 9am–3pm, Sat 9am–11am); Barclays (same hours); and the very efficient Commercial Bank of Africa at Diani Beach Shopping Centre (Mon–Fri 8.30am–2pm).

Bicycle and motor bike rental. Unfortunately, the collapse in tourism has also seen off most of bike rental places: try either South Fork (p.468), or arrange an informal deal with the guys at the curio kiosks. Bargain hard (you shouldn't pay more than Ksh600 a day, much less if over a week).

Car rental Glory Car Hire, Diani Beach Shopping Centre (☎0127/3076); Gupta's Car Hire (☎0127/2208; also open Sun 10am–1pm); Leisure Car Hire, by the Agip garage (☎0127/3225); Roadsters Rent-a-Car, outside Diani Sea Resort (☎0127/3267).

Doctors Dr Rekhi, Diani Beach Shopping Centre, recommended (☎0127/3354, emergency ☎0127/2207; Mon–Fri 9.30am–6pm, Sat 9.30am–1pm); Dr Philip Varghese, outside Diani Sea Resort (☎0127/2588 or ☎011/227189; Mon–Fri 9am–12.30pm & 2.30–6pm, Sat 9am–1pm); Dr Lalit D. Kotak, opposite Diani Sea Lodge (Mon–Fri 8.30am–2.30pm, Sat 8.30am–12.30pm).

Hospital Diani Beach Hospital (☎0127/2435-6), next to Diani Complex, is small and modern.

Notice boards Onjiko's Supermarket, behind Agip petrol station, has a reasonable board for buying and selling.

Pharmacy South End Pharmacy, at Diani Beach Shopping Centre.

Post office opposite the junction for *Trade Winds* hotel, 1.4km south of the junction.

Supermarkets Muthaiga Mini Market, Diani Beach Shopping Centre (expensive; Mon–Sat 9am–6.30pm, Sun 10.30am–1pm); Onjiko's, behind Agip (much cheaper but limited range); KFI, just up from *Diani Beachalets* with a good range; and Shan-e-Punjab, Diani Complex (Mon–Sat 9am–7.30pm, Sun 10am–7.30pm), which has the best range of wines and spirits on the South Coast. Galu Kinondo supermarket, at the south end of the beach, is only a basic provision store.

Taxis Most hotels have taxis in their forecourts. There's also a stand at the Agip petrol station.

Telephone, fax and email. There are phones at the post office. More efficient, and sometimes cheaper, with fax and email too, is Diani Telepoint at both the Agip petrol station (fax 0127/3524) and at Colliers Centre beside *Birimbi Casino* (fax 0127/3140), both Mon–Fri 9am–6pm, Sat 9am–3am; phonecalls and faxes to Europe Ksh250 per minute. Phone Home, Bazaar Complex, is competitive; International Call Centre, Bazaar Shopping Centre (daily 8.30am–8pm), charges Ksh290 per min to Europe, Ksh390 per min to the USA; incoming faxes on 0127/3568. *Gallo's* cyber-café, at Diani Beach Shopping Centre, offers fax and email services (*gallos@dianibeach.com*).

Travel agents. There are about half a dozen at Bazaar Shopping, which open and close frequently enough. Don't be taken in by the first one you visit: shop around. At Diani Beach Shopping Centre,

Diani Advice (PO Box 644 Ukunda; ☎ & fax 0127/2548) are independent and good for travel bookings and general travel agent business.

Ukunda

Until a few years ago just a village on the highway, **UKUNDA** is now a scruffily burgeoning town and the main service centre for the resort hotels, with a post office (Mon–Fri 8am–12.30pm & 2–5pm), petrol station, and hundreds of *dukas*. Only marginally touched by tourism, Ukunda has a life of its own, not all of it pleasant: the sprawl is an increasingly deprived area, and along with Likoni (p.463) was a major centre of the ethnic violence that swept the region prior to the 1997 elections, in which some 100,000 "up-country" people were forced to flee. Still, if your holiday isn't otherwise adventurous, it's worth a visit to see something of Kenya a little less unreal than the strip.

If you need accommodation in Ukunda (and if you're on a budget, you could consider staying here and simply catching *matatus* down to the part of the beach you want), there are several cheap **B&Ls**, the best of which is *Corner Guest House* (PO Box 855; no phone; ①), at the junction for the beach road. *Nzeki Guest House* (PO Box 103; no phone; ①) is 500m up the Likoni road, but more quiet is the family-run *Combatto Lodge*, 1.5km along the Likoni road (PO Box 16 Ukunda; ☎0127/2571; ①), with reasonable B&L-standard rooms, awful mattresses, fans and a dozy bar. Located 200m back towards the junction, a more expensive option and the only one with a pool is *Hotel Rock Paradise* (PO Box 81933 Mombasa; ☎0127/2461; all s/c, bed only ②, B&B ③), though at the price you should be able to find a cottage in Diani itself.

For **nightlife**, almost anything here comes as a shock after Diani's more urbane delights: all the bars can seem (and sometimes are) pretty rough places, so go with a Kenyan friend if you can. Currently the best are *Jambo Nightclub*, which has a DJ and a lively crowd; the more mellow *Juhudi Bar*, 600m down the Lungalunga road just before *Total*; and *Casino Bar & Restaurant*, just before that. For long-distance **bus services**, the Arusha Express booking office is 500m down the Lungalunga road opposite *Casino Bar*, with services to Meru and Embu (Chapter Two) and into Tanzania.

Southwards to Shimoni

The Diani Beach road returns to gravel south of the *Pinewood*, although it continues in a drivable condition, through the little village of Kinondo, right down to Chale Point and, 300m offshore, **Chale island**. Chale, until recently an uninhabited beauty spot, has sadly been acquired by a German developer, with the help of two local MPs, despite its being a gazetted Mijikenda *kaya* (see p.456) and not the property of anyone. The resulting, ill-conceived *Chale Paradise Island* (⑧–⑨) has totally disrupted local relations and wiped out acres of natural vegetation. If the ancestors are to be allowed their say, its days are numbered, yet the new owners claim the development has been sensitive, that "only" a third of the island has been built upon and that the other part is a "nature reserve". If you want to see for yourself, you can't avoid bumping into adverts and hoardings for the place all over the South Coast.

Gazi

Down the main coastal highway south of Ukunda, **GAZI** is next, a sleepy little village just off the road. It was once headquarters of the Mazrui leader **Sheikh Mbaruk ("Baruku") bin Rashid**, who acquired a reputation for torturing prisoners after half-suffocating them in the fumes of burning chillies. The story was perhaps intended to discredit him, as he was the principal figure behind the Mazrui Rebellion in 1895, an uprising against British authority that saw Mbaruk flying a German flag at his house and supplying his men with arms donated by the Germans. The British had to send for troops from India; even so, fighting continued for nine months before an Omani puppet regime was re-established and the rebels crushed. Mbaruk died in exile in German Tanganyika.

His mansion is now a primary school, which you can look around out of school hours. More than 150 years old, it was obviously a very grand place – the heavy ceiling timbers show that it once had an upper storey – but it is now sadly neglected. Fort Jesus Museum has plundered its fine front door and unfortunately left an ugly scar. To know where to stop for Gazi, you'll have to ask, as there isn't a sign on the highway. The village itself is on a deep, mangrove-filled bay and has no beach to speak of. "Gazi Beach", about 2km south of the village, is more promising.

Msambweni

Continuing down the road, **MSAMBWENI** is a sizeable village with a famous leprosarium. The road to the beach (there's often a police checkpoint at the junction) goes through the village, following the coast for several kilometres before turning back to the highway. The beach is lovely – low cliffs and less uniformity than Diani – and there are no beach hassles down here, but the tide goes out for miles, with lots of rock pools.

ACCOMMODATION

Several plots at Msambweni have been developed, but in a low-key fashion, with only a few cottages and one or two quasi-exclusive clubs. You really need a car for these, unless you're content to stay in one place the whole time. There are few taxis and the main road is a half-hour walk away.

Club Green Oasis (PO Box 80 Msambweni; ☎0127/52205, fax 52099). The biggest establishment in Msambweni, and a good place to wind down for a couple of days if you can cope with the loud beach discos. Well-looked-after with good food, popular with Germans and Italians. FB from ⑤.

Salima Club (PO Box 9 Msambweni; ☎0127/52032). A hard place to leave (only the prices could possibly shift you). The architect has done some original and beguiling work here on half a dozen staffed, beachfront cottages, with curved passages and atria melding with lush vegetation, all with terraces overlooking the beach. Beautiful pool beneath a baobab. No restaurant. ⑤ low, ⑥ high.

Seascapes Beach Villas (PO Box 77 Msambweni; reservations in Nairobi on ☎02/334280, fax 224952). A newer, more uniform development of six-bed self-service villas, set on the cliffs. ⑤.

Funzi island

If, instead of returning to the main road from Msambweni, you follow the coastline (either on the rough track or the beach), you will eventually reach **Funzi island**, separated from the mainland by a narrow channel that you can walk across at low tide. You can easily camp on the island if equipped for a fair amount of self-sufficiency. Funzi village is at the southern end, about 6km from the mainland, and there are beaches and sections of reef scattered close to the forested shore on both sides of the island. The exclusive *Funzi Island Club* – a tented camp in a grove of mango trees (PO Box 1108 Ukunda; ☎0127/2044, fax 2346; all-inclusive ⑨; closed May & June) – is a place to dream about.

Shirazi (Kifunzi)

The coast highway meanwhile passes through verdant regions of parkland, with borassus, doum and coconut palms (borassus are the ones with a bulge in the trunk) interspersed with swampy dells, before the landscape is firmly established as rolling fields of sugar cane, culminating in **Ramisi**, the coast's main sugar-producing area until the closure of its factory.

On the shore, just before you reach Ramisi, is the tiny and very old settlement of **SHIRAZI**, also known as Kifunzi (which means "little Funzi"). Any of the tracks through the sugar fields on the left of the road will take you to the hamlet – a scattering of houses in the jungle and a small harbour among mangroves. The people of Shirazi call themselves **Wa-shirazi** and are the descendants of a once-important group of the Swahili-speaking people. During the fifteenth and sixteenth centuries, they ruled the coast from Tiwi to Tanga (Tanzania) from their eight settlements on the shore. Around 1620, these towns were captured by the Wa-vumba, another Swahili group. The Wa-shirazi, now scattered in pockets along the coast, speak a distinctive dialect of Swahili. Historians used to think they originally emigrated from Shiraz, in Persia, but it now seems likely that very few of them have Persian ancestry and that the name was adopted for political reasons. Shirazi/Kifunzi, which may be one of the original eight villages, is an important Wa-shirazi centre.

Shirazi, like many villages on the coast, is a backwater in every sense. The people cut a small quantity of *boriti* (mangrove poles) – much less than they used to; they fish and they grow some produce in their garden plots, which are continually being raided by monkeys. But the setting is memorably exotic and worth the three-kilometre walk from the main road. They don't have sodas at Shirazi, but they do have coconuts and tranquillity.

The people who run Funzi Island Fishing Club have a camp on the shore at **Bodo**, just to the southwest of Shirazi. Bodo is a small cargo port, where you can sometimes pick up a ride to Pemba, Tanzania, a seven-hour voyage. See "Travel Details", p.543. This is also from where Kinazini Funzi Dhow Safaris run their **dhow day-trips** (see box on p.473).

There are some unspectacular ruins of walls and a disused well amid tangled foliage just a 100m or so to the south of the village. On the north side is the more interesting hulk of a Friday mosque, its *mihrab* still standing. Elders here describe how earlier inhabitants were routed by the Maasai and fled to the Comoros Islands. They remember when the mosque was still intact, though by the beginning of the twentieth century it had already been abandoned.

Shimoni

There are several buses and *matatus* each day from Mombasa to **SHIMONI**. The turn-off is indicated by a small cluster of tourist signs – you might expect more to be sprouting up all the time, but there has so far been virtually no development down here. A few years back, when Reagan's America enjoyed cosy relations with Kenya, the United States had its eye on getting a naval base on Wasini. This would be a far worse calamity for this remarkable area than the reach of another tentacle of tourism, but thankfully, for the moment, it seems to be on the back burner. For the present, Shimoni and the rocky sliver of Wasini island, just offshore, remain both idyllic and fascinating – a rare combination.

The caves of Shimoni

While you are in Shimoni, you should visit the **caves** after which it was named (*shimo* in Swahili). Shimoni's caves have achieved fame in Kenya, if not much further afield, through singer Roger Whittaker's melodramatic warblings. Whether they were actually used for storing slaves prior to shipment, or whether (as the alternative version has it) they were a secret refuge from Maasai and other raiders, are questions you can ponder as you pick your way around the piles of bat droppings and stinging creepers (beware!) on the floor. Be aware of disturbing the bats: there are not many alternative shelters for them, and if scared away they might never return – so tread lightly, avoid sudden movements, and back off if they start getting unsettled. The path to the caves winds into the jungle from a point directly opposite the jetty. These are coral caves and you descend a ladder through a jagged hole in the ground to reach them. Once down, shafts of sunlight pierce through holes in the forest floor to illuminate the stalactites and dangling lianas quite beautifully. Caving expeditions have found that the cave system extends some 20km underground.

With more time, there are some ruined buildings in Shimoni that might be worth a look (the Imperial British East African Company used to have its headquarters here), including a large two-storey house in the heart of the village near the fish auction house. The auctions themselves are also interesting – there's one every morning – though exciting exhibits like marlin and shark are rarely on the slab.

Accommodation

Although Shimoni is small, the demand for **accommodation** by big-spending game-fishermen has brought two hotels. The Pemba Channel (the Tanzanian island of Pemba lies 50km offshore) is considered one of the world's very best stretches of sea for hunting big fish: it is impressive to think that marlin weighing a quarter of a ton and tiger sharks of close on half a ton race through these waters.

If you're looking for budget accommodation, the only option is the KWS *Camp Eden Bandas*, quite attractive in themselves if you want to experience a real night in the forest. Since Wasini island is an alluring ten-minute boat ride away, there's no other reason to spend the night on the mainland unless you have the transport to get to Mwazaro Beach, down a turning halfway along the rough road between the highway and Shimoni village.

Shimoni Reef Lodge, 500m to the left (east) from village centre (PO Box 82234 Mombasa; Shimoni ☎9, or 011/471771, fax 471349). Part of the *Reef* group of hotels, open all year, and aimed less at sport fishermen than at divers (there's a PADI school here). Excellent accommodation in ten bungalows, rather average food. Sea-water swimming pool. Well priced. HB ④ low, ⑤ high.

Camp Eden Bandas, 500m to the right (west) from the village centre (reservations through KWS, PO Box 55 Ukunda). Wonderful for naturalists, a group of tented *bandas* run by the Kenya Wildlife Service. Has basic facilities (no electricity); bring your own nets. ③.

Pemba Channel Fishing Club, 800m to the right from village centre (PO Box 86952 Mombasa; ☎011/3132749, fax 316875). Essentially for serious anglers, this usually closes for three months at the end of the fishing season in March or April, reopening on August 1. They also welcome non-fishing guests. The diving school is otherwise the main draw, as are its eight-day diving trips aboard the 20-metre *M.Y. Kisiwani* (around $1000). FB ⑦ low/high.

Mwazaro Beach, 7.5km from the main road junction (Shimoni Lobster Company, PO Box 14 Shimoni; no phone). "Where God makes holidays" is how the German owner describes his very low-key development on the east coast of the Shimoni peninsula, exactly halfway between the highway and Shimoni close to the delta of the Ramisi river. Simple *bandas* with good fitted nets, no electricity or private facilities, Zanzibari cooking plus creek and sea trips. Camping Ksh150 per tent plus Ksh100 per person. FB only ④.

Wasini island and offshore

WASINI is easily reached. Between July and April, when *Wasini Island Restaurant* (PO Box 281 Ukunda; ☎0127/2331 or 3055) is open, there's a boat to speed lunchers across the channel for about Ksh200 a load, and this is the going rate for other motorboat operators. Local people use *jahazi*, sailing boat "*matatus*" which – notwithstanding the resentment of the diesel men – you should be able to use, too (Ksh40 each way). This is certainly more fun, but you'll need to haggle determinedly. If you've got a reservation at the restaurant you can often arrange a free transfer in advance.

Only 5km long and 1km across, Wasini has a few hundred inhabitants, and is totally adrift from the mainstream of coastal life, although the recent introduction of telephone wires signals change. There are no cars, nor any need of them: you can walk all the way around the island in a couple of hours on the narrow footpaths through the bush, though few people do. With something of Lamu's cast about it, the island is completely undeveloped, and **Wasini village**, an old Wa-vumba settlement, is built in and around its own ruins. It is a fascinating place to wander and there's even a small pillar tomb which still has its complement of inset Chinese porcelain. The **beach** in front of the village is littered with shells, but don't assume anything: a lot of them have been collected from the reef and dumped here, and people will try to sell them to you, so it wouldn't be wise to treat them as legitimate beachcombings – and, strictly speaking, trade in seashells is illegal in Kenya. Nevertheless, the wealth of interesting items on the shores of Wasini – not just shells but shards of pottery, pieces of glass, scrap metal – add up to a beachcomber's paradise you could explore for hours. Incidentally, locals are getting frustrated by seeing little if any of the tourist bucks rolling into their pockets: if you have a choice, try to buy souvenirs from local hawkers rather than the established gift shops.

Behind the village is a bizarre village green, an area of long-dead **coral gardens** now raised out of the sea but still periodically flooded at spring tides. It is covered in a short swathe of "sea grass" – a tasty vegetable called simply *mboga pwani* (sea vegetable). Walking through the coral grottoes with birds and butterflies in the air leaves a surreal impression of snorkelling on dry land. Exploring the rest of the island is highly recommended: look out for monkeys in the mangroves and parrots in the palms.

Accommodation in Wasini is very limited (more by the island's total reliance on rainwater than by anything else), but there are usually houses for rent for under Ksh200 per day in either the ancient village of Wasini itself or the newer settlement at the other end of the island, **Mkwiro**. There's also a **banda** and **camping site** known as *Mpunguti Lodge* (PO Box 19 Shimoni; no phone; HB ②; FB ③). It's very simple – no electricity, no running water and no nets (but there are very few mosquitoes), though flush toilets and showers have been installed and a second rainwater tank should mean that there is sufficient water for most of the year. The owner has quite an impressive collection of old pottery and ceramics: he's trying to persuade the Fort Jesus people to help him set up a museum. There's magnificent Swahili cooking and you can also **camp** here for Ksh100 per person, but try to bring food (including fruit) and as much drinking water as possible with you, particularly out of season. The owner can also arrange trips to the Marine National Park.

Rather more luxurious, but no less relaxing, is the house used by Pilli-Pipa dhow safaris (p.473) for lunching its day-tripping guests (on succulent crab claws, fried seaweed and other delights). If you contact them in advance, they can pick you up: full-board costs $50 per person (not s/c), and there's the opportunity of snorkelling trips and scuba diving (PO Box 5185 Diani Beach; ☎ & fax 0127/2401, *pilli-pipa@mf-group.com*).

Kisite-Mpunguti Marine National Park

Open daily; $5 (pay rangers who accompany boats or on shore – organized trips include the fee); warden: PO Box 55 Ukunda; Shimoni ☎3.

Wasini has ideal conditions for **snorkelling**, with limpid water all around. Both *Pilli-Pipa* and *Wasini Island Restaurant* (details for both above), a few minutes to the west of the village, run full-day trips in large dhows to the reefs around Kisite island, part of **Kisite-Mpunguti Marine National Park**, which usually has some of the best snorkelling in Kenya. Similar trips, on a more informal, ad hoc basis are run from Mpunguti Lodge, and you can sometimes borrow masks and snorkels from the marine park warden.

The boats normally go out of the Wasini channel to the east, then turn south to pass the islets of **Mpunguti Ya Chini** and **Mpunguti Ya Juu** ("little" and "great") on the port side. Kisite islet, a coral-encircled rock about 100m long, 5km to the southwest, is the routine destination. The best parts of the Kisite anchoring area are towards the outer edge of the main "coral garden". There are fish and sea animals in abundance, including angel fish, moral eel, octopuses, rock cod and some spectacularly large (sixty-centimetre) sea cucumbers. At certain times of the year, however, the water is less clear, and it looks as if repeated anchorings have destroyed much of the coral in at least one small area, where the shallow sea bed is littered with broken ends and grey debris. Ask the crew if you'd like to try to find a better area: **Mako Koke Reef**, the other main part of the park, is about 4km to the west.

Vanga

Kenya's southernmost town, **VANGA** is also the largest of the coastal settlements to have been left alone by the tourist industry. Getting here involves travelling down one of the country's most beautiful, and usually deserted, roads, from the Shimoni junction to Lungalunga, on the Tanzanian border. The seventeen-kilometre *murram* road to Vanga begins, curiously, midway through the Kenyan border post at Lungalunga, where you have to explain your purpose to the officials. There are a couple of lodgings here – *Muthangini Border Lodge* (①) and *Thomas Bar* (①) – but nothing of interest. Turning left, the track skims the Tanzanian border through *shambas* and, as it nears the sea, tunnels through tall forest in deep shade. Vanga itself is in the **mangroves**, approached through the swamp down a causeway which is regularly flooded by spring tides.

Vanga is a largish village with a main street, a number of stores and *hotelis* (the first on the right, the *First and Last*, is the main one), where men come in the evening to chew *miraa* and reflect on the community's isolation. "We have no employment" is a common complaint; the fishing co-operative is the only local provider of a cash income but it isn't always able to buy the entire catch and members are not supposed to sell to anyone else. Many people sell garden produce in Mombasa, which explains the *matatu* departures through the night to ensure early arrival at the markets.

Most people are unlikely to come to Vanga as there isn't anywhere to stay in the town or anything much to do. The big old house on the seafront is a nineteenth-century British customs house, cared for, in theory, by the National Museums of Kenya – in practice falling down. For the less fastidious, dugout canoes can be rented very cheaply for wobbly punting trips through the mangroves. Vanga is a sure antidote to a surfeit of Diani and Malindi: locals are more than willing to accommodate visitors and you may be plied with excellent palm wine.

If you're intent on staying in the area, there is one organized possibility between Lungalunga and Vanga: *Border Camp*, 7km from the Lungalunga customs post (PO Box 167 Lungalunga; no phone). This is a jungle homestead run by a German-Meru couple, with ambitious reforestation and conservation plans (they sell nursery saplings to locals). You can camp here (Ksh200) or sleep in the "treehouse" or in one of the new *banda* rooms (②). The owners are committed to their plans and knowledgeable about the area, which includes nearby lakes and a good variety of flora and fauna, which they are happy to guide you around.

THE NORTH COAST: KILIFI TO MALINDI

From Mtwapa Creek up to **Malindi**, the landscape is a diverse collage, from rolling baobab country and sisal plantations as you near **Kilifi** to groves of cashew trees after it; thick, jungly forest and swamp characterizes Mida Creek, and there's a more compact, populated zone of *shambas* and thicket as you approach Malindi. **Kilifi** and **Takaungu creeks** are stunning – the clash of blue water and green cliffs almost unnatural.

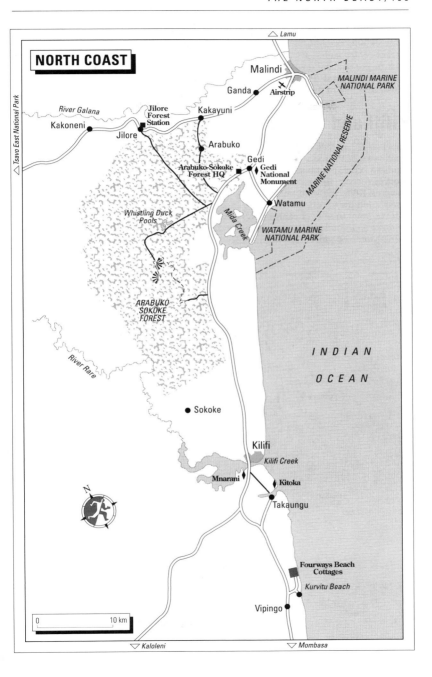

There is wide scope for **beach hunting** along this part of the coast. Malindi and, to some extent, Watamu have been developed, but Kilifi functions largely as a Giriama market-centre and district capital, while Takaungu seems virtually unknown, a throwback to pre-colonial days. There's also superb **snorkelling** at **Watamu** and **Malindi Marine National Parks**. And the ruined town of **Gedi**, deep in the forest near Watamu, is one of the most impressive archeological sites in East Africa.

Kilifi and around

Between Kikambala and Kilifi lies a major **sisal-growing** area, focusing around the small town of **Vipingo** (one or two *dukas* and *hotelis*, but not much else). Across thousands of acres, plumb-straight rows of fleshy-leafed, cactus-like sisal plants stretch in every direction, the surviving **baobab trees** standing out bizarrely (see box below). Towards Kilifi, the road bucks through a hilly area and the baobabs grow more profusely amid the scrub.

If you want **to stay** cheaply on this relatively undeveloped coastline, *Fourways Beach Cottages* is a good target (reservations: 3rd floor, Canon Tower New Wing, PO Box 83365 Mombasa; ☎011/229405, fax 315060; ④). An attractive modern complex of spa-

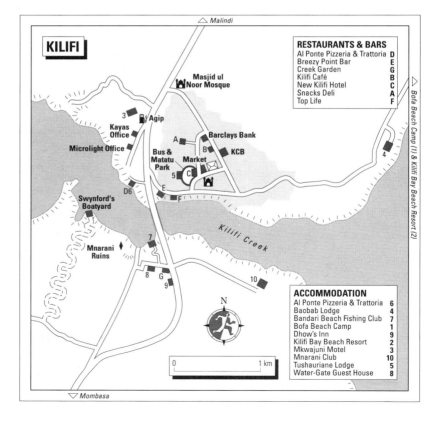

BAOBAB STORIES

The **baobab**'s strange appearance has a number of explanations in mythology. The most common one relates how the first baobab planted by God was an ordinary-looking tree, but it refused to stay in one place and wandered round the countryside. As a punishment, God planted it back again – upside down – and immobilized it. Baobabs may live well over 2000 years, making them among the longest-living organisms. During a severe drought, their large green pods can be cracked open and the nuts made into a kind of flour. The resulting "hungry bread" is part of the common culture of the region.

---

cious self-catering tiled cottages and apartments, most with ocean views, and there's also a restaurant and minimarket (both sometimes closed, so bring your own supplies), and a little pool next to an idyllic stretch of beach. Significantly, the reef is much closer to the shore in this area (Kurvitu Beach) than further south – a plus point for snorkellers. If you're travelling by public transport, ask the bus or *matatu* driver to drop you 1.6km north of Vipingo (18km north of Mtwapa), where you'll see a gravel track off to the right and a small rash of signboards including one for *Fourways* – it's about 3km along. **Be warned** however that this track was the scene of a spate of attacks and robberies on tourists in 1996 – ring beforehand to check the situation.

Takaungu

Ten kilometres before you reach Kilifi, there's a turn-off to the right to **TAKAUNGU**. Although there are two *matatus* most days from Mombasa to Takaungu, the chances of a lift are relatively slim if you get dropped off at the turning. But it is not a long walk (5km) and it gives you time to shed the highway and "the coast" from your mind. Takaungu is enchanting – a quiet, composed village of whitewashed Swahili houses situated on a high bluff above **Takaungu Creek**. There are three mosques and one or two small shops and *hotelis*, but no formal lodgings except for the exceedingly expensive *Takaungu House* (⑨; bookings through Bush Homes of East Africa, p.48); if you want to stay and you speak a little Swahili, people will put you up for a very reasonable price. Food supplies are variable; women will prepare food if you ask, and especially if you supply the ingredients. There's no produce market, but a small fish market by the creek – be there when the catch arrives to get the tasty ones. Takaungu is a place that repays time spent getting to know it: if you just want to kick back and rest up, pass it by and head on to Lamu.

There's a small seaside **beach**, 1km east, through the secondary school. **Takaungu Creek** is startlingly beautiful, the colour of blue Curaçao, and absolutely transparent; the small swimming beach on the stream is covered at high tide, but you can still dive from the rocks. Upstream, the creek disappears between flanks of dense jungle. When you're ready to move on, the tiny, council-operated rowing boat provides a slow and almost free service across the creek to the Kilifi side; from there, it's a five-kilometre (ninety-minute) walk through the sisal fields to Kilifi bridge.

Kilifi and the creek

Kenya's coastline was submerged in the recent geological past, resulting in the creation of the islands and drowned river valleys – the creeks – of today. **KILIFI**, a small but animated place, is on such a creek. When the Portuguese knew it, Kilifi's centre was on the south side of the creek and called **Mnarani**. Together with Kitoka on the north side of Takaungu Creek, and a settlement on the site of the present town of Kilifi, these three constituted the "state" of Kilifi. Mnarani's few **ruins** sit under the trees high above Kilifi Creek, to the west of the old road that led down to the ferry before the bridge was built. Turn left at *Dhows Inn*, then right at the end, where the site is signposted on your left near the old ferry landing – "follow the green posts" (7am–6pm; Ksh200 if there's anyone to collect it). Admittedly, there's not a lot to see apart from a very tall pillar tomb supported by iron props, a couple of mosques and a precipitous well that plummets right down to creek level. The site is archeologically famous mainly for the large number of inscriptions found on its masonry, all in a difficult, and so far untranslated, form of monumental Arabic. Truthfully, however, for the non-buff, Mnarani's most memorable aspect is its superlative position overlooking the creek and, after the visit, cooling down in the creek along with local kids at the jetty.

With the building of the **bridge** in the 1980s, Kilifi's economy was dealt a hard blow. All the creek-side trade made possible by the ferry's endless delays and breakdowns ceased (the ferry itself is now a half-submerged wreck on the Kilifi side), and many bars and *hotelis*, and half the town's lodgings, closed.

Kilifi town

Kilifi is draped along the north side of the creek to the east of the bridge. If you're driving you'll probably pass it by: even most public transport travellers (KBS #39 from Mombasa) only see it from the inside of a bus while more fares are being picked up. But staying the night is not an unpleasant prospect, and while there's not a lot of choice it's certainly a better plan than arriving late in Malindi.

There's little of **sightseeing interest** in Kilifi: its two main **mosques** – one a stumpy shed in the town centre, the other a new and attractively minareted blue, green and white temple, the Masjid ul Noor, at the north junction – more or less sum it up.

If you have time on your hands, you could also enquire about a visit to the **cashew factory** a short distance up the highway (Kenya Cashewnuts Ltd, PO Box 49; ☎0125/22411–4, fax 22040). The nuts are expensive because there are so few of them on the small trees: each one hangs, in an unlikely fashion, from a juicy, pear-shaped, yellow-and-orange fruit – refreshing to suck but inedible. The nut shells are processed to extract an oil used for making preservatives, for waterproofing and even for brake linings.

As for **eating in town**, the **Oloitipitip Market** has a wide range of fruit and vegetables. The *New Kilifi Hotel* (closes 8pm) is a very busy local joint near the bus station, serving good cheap meals and snacks, whilst a good stand-by for snacks and fry-ups is the long established *Kilifi Café*. *Snacks Deli* does fresh juices and tasty bites in fresh, clean surroundings – if it's closed, ask for Eunice. More upmarket, try the superb wood-oven-baked pizzas at *Al Ponte Pizzeria & Trattoria* (see below), in a great creek-side location beside a gigantic gnarled baobab. **Nightlife** is limited to the popular *Bermuda Disco* at *Top Life Garden*, on the north side of the creek by the bridge, the adjacent *Breezy Point* bar, *Dhows Inn* on the south side of the creek (see below), and the adjacent *makuti*-thatched *Creek Garden* bar and restaurant.

There are two **banks** (KCB and Barclays; both Mon–Fri 9am–3pm, Sat 9–11am), and a **post and telephone office** (Mon–Fri 8am–12.30pm & 2–5pm) down near the market. **Moving on**, note that buses to Lamu pass by around 8am (for route details, read the "Onwards to Lamu" section on p.511), and ones to Garissa before 7am. There's lots of transport to Mombasa or Malindi.

ACCOMMODATION

Hotels are thin on the ground, especially if you want to stay in town. For beach accommodation, see the section below.

Al Ponte Pizzeria & Trattoria, barely 1km from the centre (PO Box 1214; no phone). On the north side of the creek by the bridge, this pizzeria has six large s/c rooms with fans and nets and linoleum floors, the better ones with views over the creek. Safe parking. B&B ③.

Bandari Beach Fishing Club, Mnarani, on the south shore of the creek 300m off the road from *Dhows Inn* to the Mnarani ruins (PO Box 508; ☎ & fax 0125/22151). Small, modern German-run guest house that hosts parties of game fishermen; if they have a room, they'll put you up, though it's not exactly stimulating. Difficult parking: get out and ask. HB ③.

Dhows Inn, Mnarani, at the south side of the bridge (PO Box 431; ☎ & fax 0125/22028). Good rooms at this popular upmarket boozer and restaurant with a penchant for country music, especially Kenny Rogers. B&B ②; HB ③.

Mkwajuni Motel, behind the Agip service station off the highway (PO Box 171; ☎0125/22474). More upscale, with good clean rooms with mosquito nets (no fans), a very pleasant open-air bar and restaurant (good coastal food), and the attractive added prospect of manic discos on Wednesdays, Fridays and Saturdays. ①.

Mnarani Club, south side of the creek, entrance near the bridge (PO Box 1008 Kilifi; ☎0125/22747, fax 22200, *www.clubsinternational.com*). An all-inclusive resort, which means no casual visitors, and they don't admit children under sixteen. There's a mixed bag of rooms and few facilities – at the price, you're better off at one of the Kilifi Beach hotels listed below. ⑧.

Tushauriane Lodge, by the bus and *matatu* station (PO Box 259; ☎0125/22486). Ask at the hardware shop on its right side for the owner. The tallest and only option in the town centre, with basic and not terribly clean non-s/c rooms with mosquito nets but no fans – dingy. Unsafe parking. ①.

Water-Gate Guest House, Mnarani, on the road between *Dhows Inn* and Mnarani ruins (no phone). Cheap and cheerful B&L. ①.

Kilifi Creek

Kilifi's seaside-settler/yachtie community tends to hover around the informal bar-restaurant at **Swynford's Boatyard** (☎0125/22479), which is *the* place for making contacts if you have any ideas of Indian Ocean crewing in mind. There's no public transport to this place: if you don't have your own car you'll have to walk, unless you can get a lift. It's a little further up the south side of the creek from the old ferry landing, accessible via a dirt road from the old main road, 1km inland, then right 2km down a steep track to the waterfront. *Swynford's* is a friendly place, with fine views of the creek and the dramatic new bridge. They turn out fresh and simple seafood dishes, including fish and chips and weekend lunch buffets (Ksh400), and there's a notice board for yachties and fishermen to exchange news and trade kit.

Kilifi Beach

The real **beaches** around Kilifi are mostly accessible only through private property, and the best are up on the open coast to the northeast of the town. Along this ten-kilo-

---

THE GIRIAMA AND THE KILIFI KAYAS PROJECT

In recent decades, as the **Giriama** section of the Mijikenda (see p.456) has expanded, Kilifi has become one of their most important towns. Giriama women are quickly noticed by everyone for their unusual **dress**, although it's gradually disappearing. Traditionally a kind of kilt of grass or leaves, it is now made of *kanga* cloth with hips and buttocks accentuated by a bustle of coir fibre stuffed underneath. Older women still occasionally go topless but younger women usually cover up, at least in town. The Mijikenda peoples, and the Giriama especially, are known as great sorcerers and practitioners of witchcraft, and Kilifi is still the frequent scene of accusations that sometimes reach the press. Kilifi is also now the site of an office of the coastal project working to conserve the Mijikenda's sacred groves, or *kayas* (the other office is at Ukunda, see p.477). The main work at present is to identify and gazette the *kayas* of the district, but, in time, it's hoped that tourist visits will be feasible. If you're interested in finding out more about the project, call at the office near the *Mkwajuni Hotel*, or contact them in advance (PO Box 596 Kilifi; ☎0125/22140, *cfcu.kilifi@swiftmombasa.com*).

metre tarred road, however, there are several fairly recent developments. Distances for the following are given from the main Mombasa–Malindi road.

Baobab Lodge (3.2km; PO Box 537; ☎0125/22570, fax 22566; reservations through Mada Holdings, Kimathi House, Kimathi St, PO Box 40683 Nairobi; ☎02/221439, fax 332170, *mada-hold@form-net.com*). Attractively sited amid densely planted gardens and baobabs, in a pleasant position on a bluff above the shore. Tennis courts and a good pool (with lots of shade; Ksh200 for non-residents), but little beach to speak of and no sea-swimming at low tide. The rooms, though, are spacious and well furnished, with AC and fans, but lack sea views. Next door is the *Kilifi Beach Club* for drinks and average food. Closed May and June. B&B ④, FB ⑤.

Kilifi Bay Beach Resort (6.5km; PO Box 537; ☎0125/22264, 22511, fax 22258; reservations as for *Baobab Lodge*). Newly refurbished, and the best of the lot, with a stunning location right on the beach (the best rooms have sumptuous sea views; all have balconies), mature tropical gardens with coconut palms, a freeform pool for when the tide is out, great four-poster beds, spacious *makuti*-roofed communal areas, good service and decent breakfasts. Water sports can be arranged. FB only, ⑤ low, ⑦ high.

Bofa Beach Camp (9.5km – turn right after 8.2km; PO Box 660; ☎0125/22561). Camping and *banda* site at the end of the hard-surfaced beach road, at which you're likely to be the only guests. Having opened, shadeless, in 1992, the site is now beautifully cool and overgrown, and the eight small cottages (s/c, for two or three people) are roomy and clean if already a little run down. The restaurant has drinks and can rustle up food. Gas-cookers available. Given the price and the location, this is highly recommended. Access from Kilifi is the problem – if you're staying over a week, they can pick you up for free (ring ahead); otherwise, take a taxi, hitch part of the way, or walk. Camping Ksh200 per person. B&B ②.

Out of Kilifi: the Arabuko-Sokoke Forest

Forest Visitor Centre near Gedi (8am–4pm; PO Box 1 Gedi; ☎0122/32462; sokoke@ africaonline.co.ke).

Cashew trees line both sides of the road north of Kilifi, but they soon give way to tracts of jungle where monkeys scatter across the road and hornbills plunge into the cover of the trees as you approach. This is the **Arabuko-Sokoke Forest**, the largest patch of indigenous coastal forest left in East Africa. At one time it would have covered most of the coastal hinterland behind the shoreline settlements, part of an ancient forest belt which stretched from Mozambique to Somalia. If you have a car or a few days for some walking, there are some 400 square kilometres to explore, a tiny part of which in the far north (six square kilometres) was declared a national park in 1991.

Much of the forest has been penetrated and cut, as the sawmills you'll come across testify, but several good-sized areas of untouched hardwood forest and stands of rubber trees remain, with efforts to protect them spearheaded by one of Kenya's most energetic and well-organized environmental campaigns, involving the Kenya Wildlife Service, the National Museums of Kenya, and a variety of charities, working together to raise awareness about the forest, and to provide alternative sources of income for the people living around its fringes.

Beside baboons and elephant (usually evidenced by their dung), the forest shelters two rare mammal species: the 35-centimetre-high **Aders' (or Zanzibar) duiker** is a tiny, shy antelope, usually living in pairs, but which you're more likely to see around Gedi, where tourists no longer disturb them as much, and the extraordinary **golden-rumped elephant shrew** (see p.492), which is neither elephant-sized nor a shrew, but does have a comically elephant-like "trunk". It can usually be seen on the walk along the Nature Trail close to the Visitor Centre, or along the sandy tracks further inside the forest, but not for long – it is very speedy. The exceedingly rare **Sokoke bush-tailed mongoose** is unlikely to put in an appearance – there have been no sightings since the mid-1980s. El Niño, which wreaked havoc over most of Kenya in 1997–98, was a boon for Arabuko, seeing an explosion in insect and frog populations, in turn providing a feast for their predators. Unfortunately, the rains also attracted **hippos** from nearby rivers, which caused serious damage (and six deaths) and are presently being tracked by KWS rangers attempting to move them out.

The forest is also home to a glorious variety of butterflies (see Kipepeo Butterfly Farm, p.492) and six globally threatened **bird species**, including the **Sokoke pipit** and the small **Sokoke scops owl**, which is found only in the red-soiled *cynometra* section of the forest, though you'd be lucky to see either through the thick vegetation. The other endangered birds are the Amani sunbird, Clark's weaver, East Coast akalat and spotted ground thrush, all found only here.

Practicalities

Whether driving or walking, head first for the **Forest Visitor Centre**, 1500m south of Gedi and the Watamu junction on the Malindi–Mombasa road, which provides maps and photocopied information sheets at nominal charge, an excellent colour booklet (Ksh350), bird lists and advice for visitors. You might also pick up a copy of the twice-annual *Mbambakofi* news bulletin. Entry to the forest is free, though Kenya Wildlife Service plans to extract fees beginning some time in 2000. The visitor centre is also the place to pick up a **guide** (see below). If you've got a tent, use it: **camping** is permitted, but apart from the main site beside the visitor centre, you must be self-sufficient, and there are restrictions on the lighting of fires.

If you're short of time, there are currently two **driving routes**, both starting at the Mida entrance, 2km south of the visitor centre on the main Mombasa–Malindi road. One goes up to the View Point (see below), the other branches off right to Jilore village on the unsurfaced Malindi–Tsavo East road. If you're going by taxi, haggle well. Before starting, drop in at the Visitor Centre, which has a map of the routes, and can advise you as to whether other roads have reopened (many were rendered impassable by El Niño). The road from the visitor centre itself is extremely difficult.

Much more rewarding – and delightful – is to **walk**; it's best in the morning or late afternoon. Although this isn't the Amazon, a degree of preparation is wise if you plan on venturing far down any of the tracks leading off the main road. Survey of Kenya maps would be useful (the *Kenya Coast* tourist map at the very least), though the visitor centre maps are more than adequate for the main trails. A **compass** is also helpful. Official **ASF guides** are provided at the visitor centre, and cost Ksh300 (per guide, not per person) for a morning or afternoon, Ksh600 for a whole day, and Ksh400 in the evening or at night. All are professional and well-versed in forest ecology. You can also use them for fantastic **night walks** (the chorus of frog calls is awesome), which would otherwise be impossible on your own.

An organized early morning **birdwalk** (Ksh100) leaves the visitor centre on the first Saturday of every month at 6.30am, and there's a **general forest walk** (free) at 8.30am on the last Wednesday. For the masochistic, a cheery group of beer-swilling joggers board vehicles at *Ocean Sports* in Watamu at 5pm most Mondays, Wednesdays and Fridays, for anything between 3km and 10km of self-inflicted suffering, followed by a booze-up back in Watamu.

Going it alone, a numbered **nature trail** takes you from the visitor centre around the first part of the forest, which at the time of writing was spectacularly adorned with the nests of foam-nest tree frogs. You can pick up a guide or explanatory leaflet at the visitor centre. It takes much of a morning, but is an easy walk and excellent introduction to the forest and its (medicinal) uses. Bring water and insect repellant.

OTHER WALKING ROUTES

In the **brachystegia forest** on the way to the View Point, look out for the rare Amani sunbird. From the View Point, which looks east over the forest to Mida Creek and the Indian Ocean, the track continues for another 2km to a second viewing point which looks west onto Cynometra forest and a large exposed escarpment. There are other paths along the western edge of the Whistling Duck Pools (at the junction between the brachystegia and cynomatra forest on the main driving track between the Mida entrance and viewpoints), which are a favourite haunt for white-faced whistling duck, little grebe and open-billed storks, as well as the odd elephant. Little used, but apparently excellent, is the "elephant track" (14km), which passes through both mixed and *brachystegia* forest: it starts at Gedi forest station, heading west for 8km before joining the drivable track to Jilore forest station. A left turn here takes you 5km down to the Mida entrance on the Mombasa–Malindi road.

For details on driving or cycling through the forest from Malindi, see p.509.

Gedi ruins and Kipepeo Butterfly Farm

Ruins open daily 7am–6pm; Ksh200 adults, Ksh100 children; warden: PO Box 5067 Watamu, ☎0122/32065; two paths signposted near Gedi village at the junction of the Malindi and Watamu roads – it's a ten-minute walk.

The Arabuko-Sokoke Forest may partly explain the enigma of **GEDI**. This large, thirteenth- to seventeenth-century Swahili town was apparently unknown to the Portuguese, despite the fact that, for nearly a hundred years, they maintained a strong presence only 15km away in Malindi, at a time when Gedi is judged to have been at the peak of its prosperity. It is not mentioned (at least by the name of Gedi) in any Arabic or Swahili writings either, and, bafflingly, it has to be assumed that, set back from the sea and deep in the forest, it was never noticed.

The **ruins** are confusing, eerie, and, in the late afternoon, hauntingly beautiful. Even if you are resolutely uninterested in seeing any of the other sites on the coast, don't miss this one. Forest has invaded the town over the three centuries since it was deserted, and

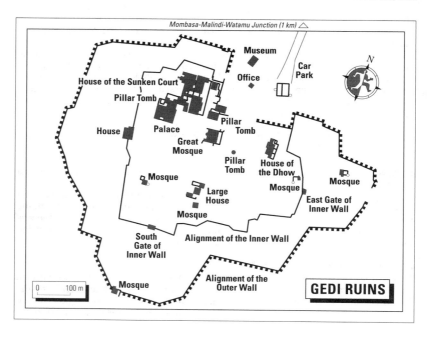

GEDI RUINS

baobabs and magnificent buttress-rooted trees tower over the dimly lit walls and arches. Gedi has a sinister reputation and local people have always been uneasy about it; it has collected an unhealthy share of ghost stories and tales of inexplicable happenings since 1948, when it was opened as a national park and tourists started to visit. Some of this cultural memory may derive from the supposed occupation of the ruins in the eighteenth century by **Oromo**-speaking people (probably ancestors of the Orma, whose present-day territory starts just north of Malindi), a tribe of irrepressible expansionists whose violent and unsettled lifestyle was long a major threat to the coastal communities. This part explains how they got to be known, until recently, as *Galla*, an offensive term which was applied to them by the native Amhara and Mijikenda. The Oromo, it's believed, were the original cause of Gedi's desertion by its inhabitants.

The longer you stay here, the further you seem from an answer to Gedi's anomalies. The display of pottery shards from all over the world in the small **museum** shows that the town must have been actively trading with overseas merchants, yet it is 5km from the sea and 2km from Mida Creek; the coastline has probably moved inland over the centuries, so it might have been further away still. Then, at times of supposed Oromo aggression, sailing into Mida Creek would have been like entering a lobster pot. The reasons for Gedi's location remain thoroughly obscure and its absence from historical records grows more inexplicable the more you think about it.

Gedi tingles spines easily, even today, particularly if you are on your own. James Kirkman, the archeologist who first worked at the site, remembers: "when I first started to work at Gedi I had the feeling that something or somebody was looking out from behind the walls, neither hostile nor friendly but waiting for what he knew was going to happen." Kirkman's booklet, usually available at the entrance gate, has a lot of interesting details as well as a plan of the site, which we've reproduced here. Its directions, however, tend to lead you in circles; it's better just to follow your nose.

The site

The town seems fairly typical of medieval Swahili settlements. It was walled, and originally covered about a quarter of a square kilometre – some 45 acres. The majority of its estimated 2500 citizens, or at least inhabitants, probably lived in mud and thatch huts, long overwhelmed and dissolved by jungle, on the southern, poorer side of town, the side away from Mecca. The palace and the "Stone Town" were in the north. When the site was reoccupied at the end of the sixteenth century, after a hiatus of fifty or so years, a new inner wall was built, enclosing just this prestigious zone.

The **Palace**, with its striking entrance porch, sunken courts and honeycomb of little rooms, is the most impressive single building. The concentration of **houses** to its right is where most of Gedi's interesting finds were made and they are named accordingly: House of the Scissors, House of the Ivory Box, House of the Dhow (with a picture of a dhow on the wall). If you have already been to Lamu, the tight layout of buildings and streets will be familiar, although in Gedi all the houses were single-storey. As usual, sanitary arrangements are much in evidence. Gedi's toilets are all of identical design, and superior to the long-drops you find in Kenya today. While many of the houses have been modified over the centuries, these bathrooms seem original, almost as if the town was purpose-built, like a housing estate. Look out for the **House of the Sunken Court**, one of the most elaborate, with its self-conscious emulation of the palace's courtyards.

Gedi's **Great Mosque**, one of seven on the site, was its Friday mosque, the mosque of the whole town. Compared with other ruined mosques on the coast, this one is very large and had a *minbar*, or pulpit, of three steps in stone, rather than the usual wood construction. Perhaps an inkling of the kind of people who worshipped here – and they were both men and women – and their form of Islam, comes from the carving of a broad-bladed **spearhead** above the arch of the mosque's northeast doorway. Whoever they were, they were clearly not the "colonial Arabs" long believed by European classical scholars to have been the people of Gedi: it's hard to believe that Arabs would have made use of the spear symbol of East African pastoralists.

Nearby is a good example of a **pillar tomb**. These are found all along the coast and are associated with men of importance – chiefs, sheikhs and senior community elders. The fact that this kind of grave is utterly alien to the rest of the Islamic world is further indication that coastal Islam was distinctly African for a long time. Such tombs aren't constructed any more, though there's a nineteenth-century one in Malindi. It looks as if the more recent waves of Arab immigration to the coast have tended to discourage what must have seemed to them an eccentric, even barbaric, style. The **Dated Tomb** next door gives an idea of Gedi's age. Its epitaph reads 802 AH – or AD 1399.

Gedi wildlife

It's easy to spend hours here, and rewarding to walk down some of the well-swept paths through the thick jungle away from the main ruins. In the undergrowth, you catch spooky glimpses of other buildings still unexcavated. And with patience you'll see a **golden-rumped elephant shrew**. The size of a small cat, this bizarre animal resembles a giant mouse with an elongated nose, running on stilts. In one of those mystifyingly evolved animal relationships, it consorts with a small bird, the **red-capped robin chat**, which warns it of danger and picks up insects disturbed by the shrew's snufflings. Your best chance of seeing a shrew is to look for its fluttering companion among the tangle of branches: the shrew will be close by. Gedi also has monkeys, bushbabies, tiny duiker antelope and, according to local belief, a huge, mournful, sheep-like animal that follows you like a shadow down the paths.

Watch out, incidentally, for the *siafu* **ants** that have colonized many of the ruins. They form thick brown columns massing from one hole to another and sometimes gather in enormous clumps. Be careful where you put your feet when stepping over walls. And try not to stand on the walls themselves: they are fragile, and the freedom to walk around Kenya's ruins without restriction isn't likely to continue if they suffer as a result. Incidentally, the **snake farm** near the entrance isn't the best of its kind; just a guide/tout who takes you to a *shamba* (farm) in the forest where a couple of snakes are produced and paraded around the guide's neck.

Kipepeo Project Butterfly Farm

PO Box 58 Gedi, or PO Box 57 Kilifi; ☎ & fax 0122/32380, kipepeo@africaonline.co.ke; daily 8.30am–5pm; Ksh50.

Close by the entrance to Gedi ruins is Kenya's first working butterfly farm, **Kipepeo**. Based on the overseas market for exotic butterflies – for preserved collections and walk-through butterfly "farms" – Kipepeo ("butterfly" in Swahili) supplies local farmers in the Arabuko-Sokoke Forest with newly hatched larvae, which they rear through the caterpillar stages to pupation, selling the pupae back to the project for cash. By linking income generation with the forest, it is hoped to gain the support of the local community for its preservation. The farmers are also responsible for delivering live butterflies for the flight houses. There are three main houses: one with large growing food plants for females to lay eggs, one full of shelves and potted food plants in net cages for hatching larvae, and one for males to flap around while visitors wander among them. The visitor centre provides information on the project and Arabuko-Sokoke Forest in general, and also has local handicrafts on display. Morning is the best time to visit, when the butterflies are most active and you have a chance of seeing them emerging from their pupae.

Watamu

After Gedi, **WATAMU** seems fairly superficial. It consists simply of a small agglomeration of hotels, a strip of beachfront private homes, a compact coconut village of *hotelis* and curio stands, and the **beach**. It tends to cater for package holiday makers staying in the large hotels along it, but there's still plenty for the backpacker – beautiful beaches, a superb marine park and lively young nightlife. Watamu is well-used to tourists: making friends is easy, and you can look around the village without being too badly pestered. The down side of this is the beach boys, who are more in evidence – and more annoying – than those in Malindi, for example.

Although one or two of the hotels are very pleasant, the beach and the coral offshore are really the only justification for visiting Watamu. Fortunately, they are justification enough: this is an exceptional shoreline, with three stunning **bays** – Watamu Bay, the Blue Lagoon and Turtle Bay – separated by raised coral cliffs and dotted with tiny, sculpted coral islets scuttled over by crabs. If you like beach walks, bring a pair of rubber or plastic soled sandals – the coral rock is sharp. Out in the **Watamu Marine National Park**, the submerged crags of living coral gardens are – despite all the visits in glass-bottom boats – as vivid and magically perfect as they must have been for millennia. And despite the high profile of tourism here, there's an easier-going atmosphere than at, say, Diani or Malindi, with fewer security problems than at Malindi and the coastline north and south of Mombasa. Watamu is a good place to go **diving** – or to learn the skill, with at least three diving schools offering one-off dives or approved courses at standard rates (p.498). It's worth knowing, however, that from June to early September **seaweed** is often swept onto the beach and the sea can be murky, while in July it's often too rough to snorkel or dive anyway.

Getting to Watamu is easy: there are reasonably frequent *matatus* from Malindi and the occasional KBS bus ventures here, too. The road from Gedi and the junction runs dead straight for 6km, passes Watamu's **post and telephone office** (Mon–Fri 8am–12.30pm & 2–5pm), then hits the Watamu beach road, which *matatus* scud up and down all the time. Turn left and there's a good **supermarket** and, straight on, a superb little **reptile park**, Bio-Ken, 2km from the junction (daily 9am–noon & 2–5pm; Ksh200). Turn right again for **Watamu village**, *Watamu Beach Hotel*, and a number of smaller hotels.

A right turn at the beach road junction brings you to four main resort hotels – *Blue Bay Village*, *Ocean Sports*, *Hemingways* and *Turtle Bay* – twenty or thirty private homes and, at the end of the narrow bar along which the road runs, the marine park ticket office. And that's Watamu.

Watamu village

Watamu village is a weird mixture of unhurried fishing community and frenzied Germanophile souvenir centre. The traditional rubs elbows with the pseudo-hip; Samburu and Maasai *morani* in full ochred splendour stand around waiting for photographers (and potential female customers); the Jamia Mosque has a notice which reads "All Muslims are Well Come for Prayers. No Trespass. By Management."

The centre of the village is a small **square** at the end of the tarmac road, with a couple of shops and a Barclays bank (Mon–Fri 9am–3pm, bureau de change until 4.30pm). The square's main purpose seems to be to allow the curio-stand owners to size up the latest punters as they arrive (German and Swiss tourists on their way to the *Watamu Beach Hotel* pass this way). But the pressure to buy is relatively subdued and after a couple of visits down here your face, and dress, become known and you can go about

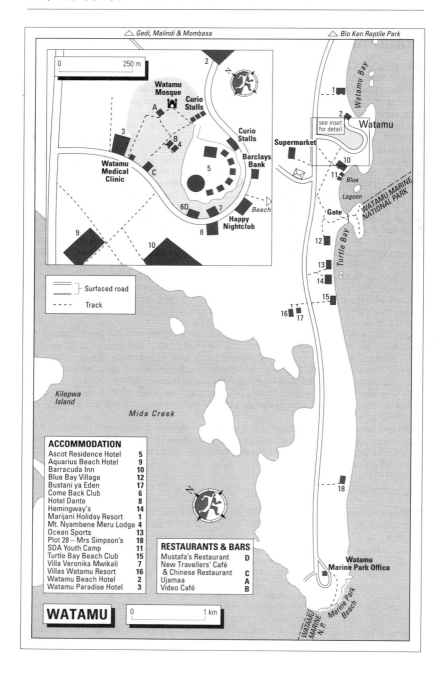

△ Gedi, Malindi & Mombasa   △ Bio Ken Reptile Park

Watamu Bay

Watamu Mosque

Curio Stalls

Curio Stalls

Supermarket

see inset for detail

Watamu

Barclays Bank

Watamu Medical Clinic

Blue Lagoon

WATAMU MARINE NATIONAL PARK

Beach

Gate

Happy Nightclub

Turtle Bay

0   250 m

0   1 km

Surfaced road

---- Track

Kilepwa Island

Mida Creek

ACCOMMODATION

Ascot Residence Hotel	5
Aquarius Beach Hotel	9
Barracuda Inn	10
Blue Bay Village	12
Bustani ya Eden	17
Come Back Club	6
Hotel Dante	8
Hemingway's	14
Marijani Holiday Resort	1
Mt. Nyambene Meru Lodge	4
Ocean Sports	13
Plot 28 – Mrs Simpson's	18
SDA Youth Camp	11
Turtle Bay Beach Club	15
Villa Veronika Mwikali	7
Villas Watamu Resort	16
Watamu Beach Hotel	2
Watamu Paradise Hotel	3

RESTAURANTS & BARS

Mustafa's Restaurant	D
New Travellers' Café & Chinese Restaurant	C
Ujamaa	A
Video Café	B

WATAMU

Watamu Marine Park Office

WATAMU MARINE N.P.   Marine Park Beach

your business with a nod and a smile. Not that there's anything much to be done: apart from a few bars and restaurants, there's little to keep you from the beach.

There are several good **restaurants** on the road into the village. *Watamu Paradise* is good for a splurge and not too expensive, and also has South African wine; *Ascot Hotel* caters mainly to Italians, and has a superb wood-fired pizza oven, and wine at moderate pices; the *Dante* is usually very enjoyable, reasonably priced, and has cheap beer. *New Travellers Cafe & Chinese Restaurant* serves quality Chinese dishes at reasonable prices, and has a sideline in pizzas. *Mustafa's Restaurant* has tasty cheap food (and beer) including traditional favourites like pizza and spaghetti bolognaise. For **bars and nightlife**, try the *Happy Night Club* and the *Come Back Club*, both popular and open till late. More dubious are *Video Café* and *Ujamaa Bar & Restaurant*, essentially pick-up joints posing as a *hoteli* and a pub; the former is very lively, sometimes bordering on rough, shows dodgy kung fu and B-movies and serves lightly spiced Swahili food.

Bicycle rental is offered by a number of outlets, especially in high season when it gets quite competitive (Ksh300–600 per day, depending on season and number of days). Bikes are a great way of getting to know Watamu, with the Gedi ruins and anywhere on the beach road easily reachable in thirty minutes or so.

Should you need any **medical treatment** in Watamu, the Watamu Medical Clinic (Mon–Thurs & Sun 8am–6pm & 8–11pm, Fri 8am–1pm; ☎0122/32241) is on the main road down into the village.

Village accommodation

There's a wide variety of **accommodation** in the few establishments in the village itself – everything from humble and uninviting B&Ls to a pleasant holiday hotel. Bear in mind that some establishments either close or just tick over out of season, remaining open with a skeleton staff. As ever, the tour places are much cheaper if you book them as part of a package. The very central places risk being loud at night thanks to nearby nightclubs.

Ascot Residence Hotel (PO Box 14; ☎0122/32326). Seems to occupy most of the middle of what you feel should be Watamu village. Looks like a very expensive hotel but is very good value, catering mainly for Italians: well-designed rooms with massive beds, fans and patios, and a large dolphin-shaped pool. Good breakfasts. It can become fairly lively in high season, when there's not a lot of privacy. B&B ③.

Come Back Club (☎0122/32408). Typical boozer, with some food and basic accommodation. Fans and nets. B&B ②.

Hotel Dante (PO Box 183; ☎0122/32243). If you're counting the pennies, this might be the one to go for, though it doesn't have the *Veronika*'s shady garden – or breakfasts. Don't let anyone tell you they have a pool: they do, but it's empty. Smallish s/c rooms with fan. ②.

Marijani Holiday Resort (PO Box 282 Watamu; ☎ & fax 0122/32448, *www.muenchen-info.com/kenia/watamu*). A very pleasant surprise: friendly, welcoming, and informal Kenyan-German run place, with superb rooms in two stylish houses. The rooms are very comfortable and exceptionally good value, with huge four-poster beds and spacious nets, fans, and spotless bathrooms (showers). Some have fridges, kitchens or (oddly) sunbeds, and separate kitchens are available. There's also a fully furnished family house (three bedrooms; ④). Safe parking; bicycle rental (Ksh100 per hour); surfboards (Ksh300 per hour). Not on the beach, nonetheless highly recommended. B&B ③.

Mt Nyambene Meru Lodge (no phone). Gloomy rooms are all a single flat rate, averagely clean (though it's hard to tell in the twilight) and dirt cheap. ①.

Sam's Lodge, next to *Video Café* (no phone). Friendly, cheap and unhygienic, but apparently safe, with some two-bed rooms. ①.

Villa Veronika Mwikali (PO Box 57; ☎0122/32083). More or less a B&L, run by an Kikamba-Austrian couple, with fairly ordinary, rather pricey s/c rooms with fans and nets around a courtyard. Little touches, however, like the potted plants and table cloths, and the overall shady, intimate, almost Mediterranean feel of the place help to make it a favourite. ②.

Watamu Paradise Hotel (PO Box 249; ☎0122/32062, fax 32436). Paradise it's not, and a little over-priced, but it's good enough for one night. There are several grades of room: some resemble a B&L, smartened up with whitewash and fancy *kanga* bed covers, with fans and nets; more acceptable are the cottages. The pool doesn't exactly sparkle. The discos are loud and predictably loaded with pros-titutes. ③.

Beach hotels and other accommodation

Several of these establishments focus on watersports, with diving and game fishing on offer. The big fishing competition in the first or second week of March can make accommodation scarce. But in May and June the hotels usually have excellent low-season rates, sometimes available only in packages of seven nights. The following list-ings are arranged from north to south. *Matatus* from Watamu, and some from Malindi, only go as far as *Turtle Bay Beach Club*, though they'll usually drop you further south if you ask.

Watamu Beach Hotel (PO Box 1; ☎0122/32620; African Safari Club). All-inclusive affair whose guests are pre-booked from Germany and Switzerland; day visits are only allowed on payment of Ksh1500 (includes lunch).

Barracuda Inn (PO Box 59; ☎0122/32509, fax 32296). Unusual hotel with impressive *makuti*-vault-ed reception on the shore of the Blue Lagoon, populated mainly by Italians, and well worth consid-ering for an excellent-value getaway break (though note that the second-floor open-air dining ter-race is inaccessible to wheelchairs). The beach outlook is only matched by the *Watamu Beach* and here the scene is more intimate. Ground-floor rooms are more spacious – all have telephones and AC. Nightclub, tennis and pool offered. No credit cards. B&B is half FB rates. FB ⑤ low, ⑦ high.

SDA Youth Camp (PO Box 80; no telephone). Run by the Seventh Day Adventists mainly as a lec-ture place for schoolkids. For those on a really low budget, three simple if very run-down rooms in the main building and a *banda* with a hole in the roof (no nets or fans in any), and a basic but well-equipped kitchen. Dubious water and toilet facilities, but lots of camping space, all set in the dunes under coconuts and casuarinas with a view of the Blue Lagoon you could die for. ①.

Aquarius Beach Hotel (PO Box 96; ☎0122/32069, fax 32512, *aquarius@africaonline.co.ke*; closed off season). Very pleasant if misleadingly named hotel, far from the beach. Rooms have AC plus floor fans. No credit cards. FB ⑤.

Blue Bay Village (PO Box 162; ☎0122/32626, fax 32422, *bluebay@africaonline.co.ke*). Well-estab-lished, again mostly Italian-patronized all-inclusive holiday complex, with beautiful, palmy gardens and a good pool. If you're going to stay, don't compromise – only the deluxe suites (twice the price) are worth the money (standard rooms lack AC). No casual visitors – no great loss. FB standard ⑥, suite ⑧.

Ocean Sports (PO Box 100; ☎0122/32008, fax 32266, *oceansps@africaonline.co.ke*). Slightly macho, impersonal place, whose reputation ("Open Shorts") has sailed before it for years. During holiday times it swarms with young Anglo-Kenyans doing very much their own thing (everything is priced in sterling), but it's right on the beach. Blue marlin trophies gawp from the walls, rooms (fans and AC) are getting run-down, and food is variable: chips with everything. Fine if you like a laddish atmosphere, but not particularly welcoming otherwise. HB ⑥.

Hemingway's (PO Box 267; ☎0122/32624, fax 32256, *hemingways@form-net.com*, reservations through Express Travel Group, PO Box 40433 Nairobi; ☎02/334722–7, fax 334825). Sharing a plot with *Ocean Sports*, the contrast is great. From October to April, landing sharks and marlin is still high on the agenda, but this is a really top-class hotel where the atmosphere tends towards formal and there's nothing much for children. Rooms in the new wing are wonderful, with huge beds, direct-line telephones, fans and AC; all rooms have sea views. Lovely beach with a number of coral outcrops within swimming distance. Food is variable. Snorkelling, dhow cruises, creek fishing and day-trips. HB from ⑦ low, ⑨ high.

Turtle Bay Beach Club (PO Box 457 Malindi; ☎0122/32003, fax 32268, *turtles@africaonline.co.ke*). Expertly run, all-inclusive holiday club, full of happy holidaymakers (mainly British, some German). Lots to do, lots to eat, plenty to drink, and no complaints from anyone it seems, except perhaps Watamu villagers, who don't get much out of it. Cramped gardens. Facilities include PADI diving and windsurfing schools, tennis, minigolf, and a giant chessboard. They also run *Turtle Bay Safari Camp* at Sobo on the Galana River in Tsavo East National Park ($400 per person for a one night/two day safari). You can have a one-day sample of club life for Ksh1500. ⑥ low, ⑦–⑧ high (double over Christmas and New Year).

Bustani ya Eden (PO Box 276; ☎0122/32262). Plain, comfortable chalet-style rooms attached to a locally renowned (not to say notorious) bar-restaurant, with reasonably priced seafood and African dishes. Currently no nightclub licence, but if they get it back, it means the music goes on till late. No beach. B&B ③.

Villas Watamu Resort (PO Box 150; ☎ & fax 0122/32321). Some 400m from the road, a German-run Mediterranean-style self-catering villa development (not a *makuti* roof in sight) with a dramatic line in verandahs and a huge pool, as well as a restaurant. Not overly exciting, and no beach (15min walk), but security is good and the rates, for spacious AC accommodation with TVs and fully equipped kitchens, are very reasonable. Clean and proper. Minimum one week stay. One-bed Ksh7200 per week, Ksh23,400 per month; two-bed Ksh14,400 per week, Ksh37,800 per month.

Plot 28 – Mrs Simpson's (PO Box 33; ☎0122/32023, *jakekh@africaonline.co.ke*). The charming Barbara Simpson has been hosting word-of-mouth guests at her house near the shore for years, helped now by her nephew. She has seven very large rooms for rent (shared bathrooms), some with solar-powered electricity, fans and nets. You're welcome to camp (Ksh200 per person) and, if you're on a budget, you can sleep out on a roof or in the boat shed (Ksh300 per person). Barbara's company and life's worth of African experience are a delight, and her car and small boat are at your disposal – if available. The beach here is deserted, with no beach boys for miles. Exceptional snorkelling trips can be arranged for Ksh500–600 per person (excluding park fee), although you can simply swim out 300m to the nearest reefs, as well as bird-watching trips to Arabuko-Sokoke Forest (Ksh800 per person), the Galana (Sabaki) River and Mida Creek. They can collect you from Malindi. B&B ③, FB ④ per person (including afternoon tea).

Watamu Marine National Park and other excursions

The **Watamu Marine National Park** (daily 6am–6pm; $5, students/children $2; Warden PO Box 335 Watamu; ☎0122/32393) stretches along the coast from the Blue Lagoon to Mida Creek. Its **total exclusion zone** for fishermen has not been greeted with rhapsody all round. On the other hand, tourists come in larger numbers every year and Watamu evidently hasn't gone far wrong in identifying their needs. This is prime **snorkelling** and **diving** territory, highly rated even by professionals, as the reef is in excellent condition and the water usually totally clear. Harmless **whale sharks** visit the area regularly, a highlight for any diver.

If you've never taken a swim before in a shoal of coral fish, the spectacle can be breathtakingly stupendous: every conceivable combination of colour and shape – and a few inconceivable ones – is represented. It seems impossible that fish should take such forms: the ostentatious dazzle of some of them, especially the absurd parrot fish, can be simply hilarious. The most common destination is the "**coral gardens**", a kilometre or two offshore, where the boat drifts, suspended in 5–6m of scintillatingly clear water. Here, over a group of giant coral heads, where fish naturally congregate and where offerings of bread have obviously further encouraged them, you enter the unusual park.

If you can **dive to the sea floor**, you'll get an intense experience of sharing the undersea world with the fish and the coral. Watch out for the small, harmless octopuses that stay motionless until disturbed and then jet themselves across the sea bed – they're brilliant masters of disguise, altering their form, texture and colour to fit their surroundings. Above, the boat's hull creates a deep shadow which, associated with food from the passengers, attracts thousands of fish. As you return to the surface, they move out of the way in mysterious unison, each one avoiding all the others in a kind of natural light show of fantastic beauty. If such adventures aren't your forte, the glass bottoms of the boats provide an alternative view – but it's often a rather obscure and narrow one.

For **visits to the park**, *Ocean Sports* and *Hemingways* both run glass-bottom boat snorkelling trips (around Ksh700, plus $5 park fee). Otherwise, you'll have to haggle with the boatmen along the beach, or outside the park headquarters and ticket office down at the south end of the Watamu road at Temple Point: expect to pay Ksh600–800 per person (including park fees) for a two-hour trip in a glass-bottomed boat combining the coral gardens with a trip along Mida Creek. Masks, snorkels and sometimes fins are provided, but remember to take plenty of sun cream and a T-shirt. Boats wait until everyone has had enough of swimming, so will stay as long as you want to. A four-hour snorkelling trip for two should cost under Ksh2000, including park fees. From the park HQ, a track leads 500m or so to a pretty little beach at Temple Point, with some sun-shades and small boats, by the entrance to Mida Creek. It's all a lot lower-key than Malindi.

Grouper and dolphin spotting – and Sudi Island

At the entrance to Mida Creek is a famous group of caves. Known as the "**Big Three Caves**", these are the meeting place of a school of **giant groupers**, or rock cod, that once numbered only three but are now many more. Up to 2m long and weighing over 300 kilos, these are placid, stationary monsters – thankfully for anyone intrepid enough to dive down 3–4m for a closer look. The site is a good kilometre offshore and there are some moderate currents: boat trips normally only take place at the turn of neap high tides, when visibility, depth and currents give the optimum conditions. You need a permit from the park warden to visit the Big Three Caves: this is usually given freely.

Less predictable sea excursions are also arranged in quest of **dolphins**. These are fairly frequently seen offshore, but it's become accepted practice to pay only a nominal charge for the trip if you're unsuccessful. Check it out before committing yourself. A new excursion, offered by most hotels, is to **Sudi island** in Mida Creek, where a boardwalk takes you right through the mangrove swamps.

Diving and diving schools

From September to April, the **diving** possibilities are extensive at Watamu and you don't need to go far; most of the best dive sites are within thirty minutes of the beach. There are three dive centres, and if you're an experienced diver the best plan is probably to visit all of them and make your own assessment of their competence and suitability. If you're an absolute beginner, go for Aqua Ventures.

The sort of **money** involved, if you're a qualified diver, is something around Ksh7000–8000 for three dives including equipment, much less (around Ksh1500 per dive) with your own equipment. There are reductions if you book a series of dives, and small supplements for night- and wreck-dives. If you haven't dived for a while, you should be asked to do a check-out dive (usually free) or a one-day refresher. Lastly, if you're a beginner, you can do either a one-day, one-dive course (Ksh7000), or opt for the proper PADI course of four dives over five days – leading to certification and your log book – for around $400 inclusive (to "Open Water" level).

Aqua Ventures, Ocean Sports (PO Box 275; ☎0122/32008, fax 32266, *aquav@africaonline.co.ke*). Slightly cheaper than the competitors, and a BSAC school.

Scuba Diving Kenya, next to Blue Bay Village (PO Box 160; ☎0122/32099 or 32423).

Turtle Bay Beach Club (PO Box 457 Malindi; ☎0122/32003, fax 32268).

Malindi and around

When Vasco da Gama's fleet arrived at **MALINDI** in 1498, it met an unexpectedly warm welcome. The king of Malindi had presumably heard of Mombasa's attempts to sabotage the fleet a few days earlier and, no friend of Mombasa himself, he was swift to ally himself with the powerful – and dangerous – Portuguese. Until they finally subdued

Mombasa nearly one hundred years later, Malindi was centre of operations for the Portuguese on the East African coast. Once Fort Jesus was built, Malindi's ruling family was invited to transfer their power base there, which they did, and for many years Malindi was virtually a ghost town as its aristocrats lived it up in Mombasa under Portuguese protection.

Malindi's reputation for hospitality to strangers has stuck, and so has the suggestion of sell-out. As a steadily growing, rock-solid development area for the cultivation of, principally, deutschmarks and lire, the town is slipping towards cultural anonymity: it can't seem to make up its mind whether it wants to be a Mombasa or a Lamu. While retaining a Swahili atmosphere, which Mombasa has partly lost in urban development, it utterly lacks Lamu's self-contained tranquillity. Here is one town in Kenya that would go into precipitate decline were the crutch of tourism removed.

Consequently, whether you enjoy Malindi or not depends, at least in part, on how highly you rate the unsophisticated parts of Kenya, and whether you appreciate a fully fledged resort town for its facilities or loathe it for its tackiness. And of course it depends on when you're here. During the summer holiday season (Malindi's best month, sea- and weather-wise, is August), as well as in December and January, the town can be a bit nightmarish. In a busy high season (and there have been some disappointing ones in recent years) everything African about it seems to recede behind the swarms of window-shopping tourists and Suzuki jeeps. Even so, Malindi at its worst is still relatively placid compared with, say, Spain or the Greek islands, and off-season (reduced here to the long rains only – April to June) can seem positively subdued, as if exhausted. At this time of year, when it is often damp and grey, with piles of seaweed washed ashore, Malindi has the air of a Bournemouth, Bognor or Jersey Shore resort: the faded muddle of an ageing seaside town – garnished with tropical plants. It was opened as a settlers' coastal escape in the 1930s, which in Kenyan terms is a very long time ago, and the last of the sun-wrinkled generation of a bygone era can still be seen walking on Lamu road.

Fortunately, Malindi has some important saving graces. Number one is the **coral reef**. The combined Malindi/Watamu Marine National Parks and Reserve enclose some of the best stretches on the coast. Kisite-Mpunguti, on the south coast, and Kiunga, further north, are reckoned by some connoisseurs to be even better, but the Malindi fish have seen many more strange faces in masks and have become so used to humans that they swarm in front of you like a kaleidoscopic snowstorm. Malindi is a **game-fishing** centre with regular competitions. And it's also a bit of a **surfing** resort, too: good-sized rollers steam into the bay through the long break in the reef during July and August and in early September, whipped up by the southerly monsoon winds which are likely to get you sand-blasted on the beach.

Despite the heavy reliance on tourism, Malindi remains a thriving and ancient town. An interesting old Swahili quarter, one or two "ruins", a busy market, shops, *hotelis* and plenty of lodgings all compensate for the tourist boutiques, beauty salons and real estate agencies. The fact that Malindi has a broad range of places to stay within walking distance of the beach – and a broad range of places to eat and spend money within walking distance of the hotels – gives it a clear advantage over Watamu, Diani or the places north of Mombasa.

Arrival and accommodation

As far as practicalities go, Malindi is uncomplicated. Arriving from the south, the main **bus station** and *matatu* area is about ten minutes' walk south of town along the Mombasa road, from where you can walk, or take a taxi: a cab to the centre shouldn't cost more than Ksh100, or Ksh200–300 to the beach hotels. Coming from Lamu or Garissa, you'll be dropped by the company's booking office in the town centre between the mar-

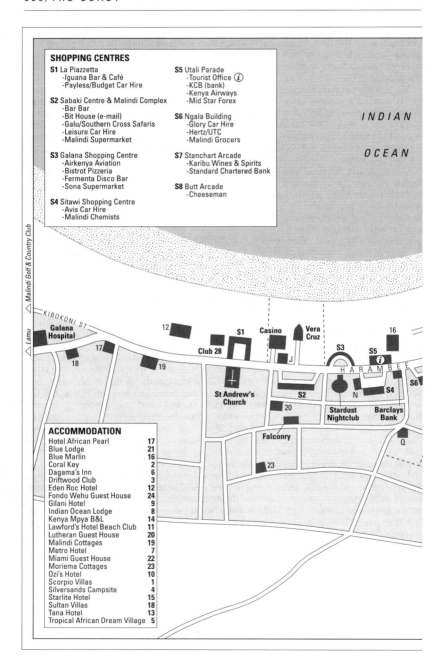

SHOPPING CENTRES

S1 La Piazzetta
  -Iguana Bar & Café
  -Payless/Budget Car Hire

S2 Sabaki Centre & Malindi Complex
  -Bar Bar
  -Bit House (e-mail)
  -Galu/Southern Cross Safaris
  -Leisure Car Hire
  -Malindi Supermarket

S3 Galana Shopping Centre
  -Airkenya Aviation
  -Bistrot Pizzeria
  -Fermenta Disco Bar
  -Sona Supermarket

S4 Sitawi Shopping Centre
  -Avis Car Hire
  -Malindi Chemists

S5 Utali Parade
  -Tourist Office *(i)*
  -KCB (bank)
  -Kenya Airways
  -Mid Star Forex

S6 Ngala Building
  -Glory Car Hire
  -Hertz/UTC
  -Malindi Grocers

S7 Stanchart Arcade
  -Karibu Wines & Spirits
  -Standard Chartered Bank

S8 Butt Arcade
  -Cheeseman

INDIAN

OCEAN

Malindi Golf & Country Club

Lamu

KIBOKONI ST

Galana Hospital

12

S1

Casino

Vera Cruz

16

Club 28

HARAMBEE

S3

S5

(i)

17

18

19

J

St Andrew's Church

S2

N

S4

S6

20

Stardust Nightclub

Barclays Bank

Falconry

Q

23

ACCOMMODATION

Hotel African Pearl	17
Blue Lodge	21
Blue Marlin	16
Coral Key	2
Dagama's Inn	6
Driftwood Club	3
Eden Roc Hotel	12
Fondo Wehu Guest House	24
Gilani Hotel	9
Indian Ocean Lodge	8
Kenya Mpya B&L	14
Lawford's Hotel Beach Club	11
Lutheran Guest House	20
Malindi Cottages	19
Metro Hotel	7
Miami Guest House	22
Moriema Cottages	23
Ozi's Hotel	10
Scorpio Villas	1
Silversands Campsite	4
Starlite Hotel	15
Sultan Villas	18
Tana Hotel	13
Tropical African Dream Village	5

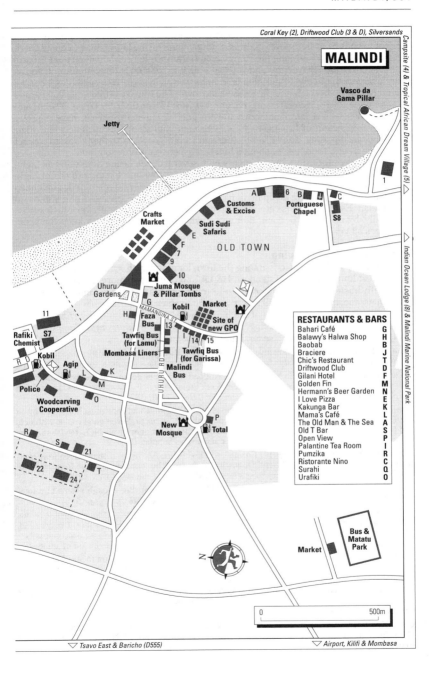

MALINDI

Coral Key (2), Driftwood Club (3 & D), Silversands

Campsite (4) & Tropical African Dream Village (5)

Indian Ocean Lodge (8) & Malindi Marine National Park

Vasco da Gama Pillar

Jetty

Customs & Excise

Portuguese Chapel

Crafts Market

Sudi Sudi Safaris

OLD TOWN

Uhuru Gardens

Juma Mosque & Pillar Tombs

Kobil

Market

Site of new GPO

Faza Bus

Tawfiq Bus (for Lamu)

Mombasa Liners

Tawfiq Bus (for Garissa)

Malindi Bus

Rafiki Chemist

Kobil

Agip

Police

Woodcarving Cooperative

New Mosque

Total

RESTAURANTS & BARS

Bahari Café	G
Balawy's Halwa Shop	H
Baobab	B
Braciere	J
Chic's Restaurant	T
Driftwood Club	D
Gilani Hotel	F
Golden Fin	M
Hermann's Beer Garden	N
I Love Pizza	E
Kakunga Bar	K
Mama's Café	L
The Old Man & The Sea	A
Old T Bar	S
Open View	P
Palantine Tea Room	I
Pumzika	R
Ristorante Nino	C
Surahi	Q
Urafiki	O

Bus & Matatu Park

Market

N

0   500m

Tsavo East & Baricho (D555)

Airport, Kilifi & Mombasa

ket and the messy, noisy high street where the cheapest of the B&Ls are found. The main focus of town is from here up to the misleadingly named Uhuru Gardens (a dusty patch of shade) and then north along the commercial Harambee Road. Malindi **airport** is barely 3km south of the town centre and you can walk into Malindi in forty minutes. If you're lucky, a *matatu* might try its luck, and take you to the main stage; otherwise, taxis charge around Ksh500 to beach hotels, or Ksh300 into town. The **tourist office** is at Utali Parade on Harambee Road (Mon–Fri 8am–4.30pm; PO Box 421; ☎0123/20747, fax 30429), and whilst it doesn't have any hand-outs, they're good for general advice, have a pretty exhaustive collection of brochures to leaf through, and keep lists of hotels and their prices for Malindi, Kilifi, Tana River district and Lamu. They're also the people to contact if you have a serious complaint about a hotel, safari operator or restaurant.

As for **accommodation**, there's plenty of it: several dozen beach hotels and all-inclusive "club resorts", and cottage and villa complexes providing for the crowds of high-season visitors, though over Christmas, room availability may be restricted. The cheap town lodgings, too, tend to fill up in high season, and also during Maulidi and at the end of Ramadan. Establishments catering essentially for tourists generally vary their prices seasonally, by up to fifty percent, though as usual the cheapest places keep the same low prices all year round.

Budget rooms and camping

There are lots of cheap choices among the town lodgings, with some good traveller-oriented guest houses as well as standard **B&Ls**, and one or two more unusual offerings. The youth hostel, still much referred to in travel guides and tourist information, and even on signposts, has been well and truly defunct since the early 1990s. If you want to stay for some time, consider one of the bungalows at the *Lutheran Guest House*. Lastly, beware that solo travellers walking between town and the *Silversands Campsite* have been the victims of muggings several times in recent years.

Blue Lodge, the tall blue building near *Fondu Wehu* (PO Box 209; ☎0123/30246). A standard B&L popular with locals, and perfectly reasonable. Most rooms with fans and nets, some s/c. ①.

Dagama's Inn (PO Box 5073; ☎0123/20196). Not bad if you can get one of the two front rooms with fans (both doubles), but somewhat overpriced, though they also have cheap beds in a dorm (Ksh200 per person), and you can sleep on the roof if they're full. B&B ②.

Fondo Wehu Guest House (PO Box 5805; no phone). Charming and cool guest house run by an English-Giriama family, far from the beach but popular with *wazungu*. Seven good rooms with nets and fans, but not s/c. Healthy breakfasts (and good lunches and dinners available), free laundry, tea and coffee. Bicycle hire planned. Very laid-back and always popular. B&B ②.

Gilani Hotel (formerly Gossip) (PO Box 380; ☎0123/20307). Above the restaurant, entirely overhauled and refreshed, but insufficiently to justify the prices. The four rooms at the front with balconies are the best and only reasons to stay here. Bed only: nets and fans ②, AC ③.

Kenya Mpya B&L, Mama Ngina St (PO Box 209; ☎0123/31658). Big enough rooms in a four-storey block, not all s/c or with fans, with cleanish sheets. Very cheap. ①.

Lutheran Guest House (PO Box 409; ☎0123/21098). Set in a large garden, this has double rooms only (clean and mosquito-netted with fans, some s/c): singles may have to share if they're full. There are also two fully equipped bungalows, each for four people. There's a no-alcohol policy. Rooms B&B ②, bungalows ③, or Ksh4200 per week or Ksh12,000 per month, including utilities.

Metro Hotel (PO Box 352; ☎0123/20902). No fans, no nets – no good reason to stay here unless you're flat broke. Beers are as cheap as they come. A basic sleaze-house and dirt cheap, but not for women. ①.

Miami Guest House (PO Box 998; ☎0123/20329). Spacious and very clean and airy, with a vast *makuti* roof – a posh kind of B&L, with ten s/c and non-s/c rooms, but poor breakfasts. Use of kitchen if required. B&B ②.

Ozi's Hotel (PO Box 60; ☎0123/20218, fax 30421). Very secure and friendly, popular with travellers, but none of the rooms are s/c, which makes it rather overpriced. Next to mosque. Limited free laundry. B&B ②.

Silversands Campsite, 2km from the town centre (PO Box 422; ☎0123/20412). If you're prepared to forego a little comfort in order to camp on the beach then this is the only place (Ksh150 per person). Various *bandas* are also on offer, with great views over the ocean (far surpassing anything offered by the big hotels), but most are ancient, not s/c, and exceedingly grotty. They range from cramped and completely moth-eaten tents with roofs ("green"), to equally dingy huts with mosquito nets ("white"), to more reasonable, small s/c chalets ("*mzuri*"), sometimes discounted for long stays. There's a callbox and a snack and cold drinks store on the site, which is guarded and supervised, though there have nonetheless been reports of thefts from the *bandas* (not helped by sometimes unhelpful management), and the road from town is dangerous after dark. Old-fashioned bikes are available for Ksh200 per day. Many people pay a small fee (Ksh150) to spend the day in the neighbouring *Driftwood Club*. ①–②.

Starlite Hotel, Mama Ngina St, opposite the market (PO Box 194; ☎0123/30424, fax 21225). A good choice if you've just arrived, with helpful staff and large s/c rooms with nets, wonky fans and balconies. Usually clean bar the odd sheet (which they'll replace), hot water 24 hours and a guarded car park. Surprisingly quiet given the central location. B&B ②.

Tana Hotel (PO Box 766; ☎0123/20234, fax 31447). While still quite basic, it's clean and well-kept, with nets as well as fans, though everything is still very stuffy and hot. In addition to ordinary rooms there are three rather dark s/c rooms around a quiet courtyard at the back. Good, busy restaurant with plenty of choice. Bed only: non-s/c ①, s/c ②.

Hotels in the town centre and north

The three main package tour **hotels** (*Blue Marlin*, *Eden Roc* and *Lawford's*) are on the main beach, with newer establishments scattered to the north, and behind the town centre to the west. All have pools, but watersports are very limited (you're usually picked up to be taken to a centre south of the centre): with no reef offshore, there's no snorkelling, and the current makes windsurfing only practicable for the experienced. Distances are from the Uhuru Gardens in the town centre.

Hotel African Pearl (1.7km; PO Box 5835; ☎ & fax 0123/31612). Personable Indian-run hotel, with thirteen s/c rooms in various buildings, three self-catering (with kitchens, but no fridges as yet). The best rooms are characterful and comfortable and have large verandahs. Hot water, nice grounds and a pool, unfortunately sometimes rather murky. Camping possible (no fixed price). Bar and restaurant at the front near the road. Safe parking. Prices negotiable: choose and bargain well and it's good value. B&B ③–④.

Blue Marlin (700m; PO Box 54; ☎0123/20440–1, fax 20459). Much rebuilt, this is where Ernest Hemingway once contemplated game fishing but stayed in the bar instead. It has, appropriately, some Spanish touches, but furnishings and decor are utterly unspecial, and food portions are sometimes snack-sized. Guests – almost entirely package tourists – can use facilities at the jointly owned *Lawford's*. B&B or HB ④.

Eden Roc Hotel (1.5km; PO Box 350; ☎0123/20480, fax 20333). Large old package-tour place, with a calm atmosphere a world away from the clutter of *Blue Marlin* and *Lawford's*, with huge and largely untended gardens stretching several hundred metres down to the dunes and the beach. Friendly if somewhat disorganized management. Very good if you have children – they'll love the grounds (more fun than the manicured and watered lawns more commonly found in such places) – and there's a great playground too (chunky climbing-frames and see-saws), a kid's pool (well away from the boring adult ones), and someone to look after them by day. No watersports on site (you're collected in the morning). Cheaper rooms with fans, and some suites. HB ④–⑤.

Kibokoni Riding Centre (4km; PO Box 857; ☎0123/21273, fax 21030). As you head north out of town along the beach road, the scene becomes one of extreme ostentation. Out of the bush rise vast *makuti* roofs, Malindi's limpet-like status symbols. The last cluster is *Kibokoni*, an ideal retreat for horsey honeymooners, offering excellent rooms with remarkably robust beds constructed from solid tree trunks. ⑤.

Lawford's Hotel Beach Club (300m; PO Box 20; ☎0123/20440–1, fax 20459). Very uninspiring all-inclusive hotel (minimum stay three days), co-owned with the cheaper *Blue Marlin*. If you want to stay in Malindi town centre, however, the location is ideal, and the service is usually good. "Standard" rooms are mediocre: the "superior" ones are much nicer than the superficial surcharge would suggest. Dive centre. All-inclusive ⑤.

Malindi Cottages, Harambee Rd (1.5km; PO Box 992; ☎ & fax 0123/21071). Unexceptional and overpriced rooms in gardens with a green pool, the standard ones (s/c) rather basic but large enough with gale-force fans and clean bathrooms, the self-catering apartments with small verandahs and huge sitting rooms. Rooms ②, two-bedroom cottage ④.

Moriema Cottages (1.5km; PO Box 235; ☎0123/30816). Worth considering if you want to self-cater for a short time – each cottage has gas rings, sink and fridge – but it seems expensive. Cottages come equipped with fans and nets – and furnished with mildewed carpets. B&B ④.

Sultan Villas, Lamu Rd (1.8km; PO Box 704; ☎0123/31668). Seven very comfortable and large apartments in peaceful gardens. Good value. B&B ②.

Hotels south of the town

Suitably protected by reefs, this is where the greatest development has taken place in the last few years, with one **resort hotel** after another reaching almost down to Casuarina Point. Taxis are cheap, and shouldn't cost more than Ksh300 to Casuarina Point, or Ksh200 to the *Driftwood*. Some of the more noteworthy bases follow, listed from north to south (with approximate distances from Uhuru Gardens in the town centre).

Scorpio Villas (1km; PO Box 368; ☎0123/20194, fax 21250, *scorpio@swiftmombasa.com*). An exceptionally well-conceived "village", dense with tropical vegetation. Each villa has a kitchen and dedicated staff and is divided into large rooms, each with its own bathroom and private patio. Eat "at home" or in the restaurant. Great for families and very cosmopolitan. Excellent value (and bargaining is possible). HB ⑤ low, ⑥ high.

Coral Key, just before *Silversands* campsite (2km; PO Box 556; ☎0123/30717, fax 30715, *coralkey@africaonline.co.ke*). Lively and sporty Italian-run resort, with rooms in 38 two-storey brick buildings, some designed for the disabled, but not all AC. Three pools, childrens' pools, and a fine Italian restaurant and pizzeria. Trendy Friday disco, plus gym, watersports, glass-bottomed boat, volleyball, horse-riding, tennis, and a rock climbing wall. They also run *Tsavo Buffalo Camp*, just outside Tsavo East (p.370). HB ④ low, ⑤–⑥ high.

Driftwood Club (2.2km; PO Box 63; ☎0123/20155, fax 30712). Trading on its good food and established reputation among the Anglo-Kenyan community, this is an informal set-up, similar to *Ocean Sports* in Watamu, and excellent value. Prices are non-seasonal, but vary depending on the cooling system, the bathroom arrangements, and which part of the beach the room faces. The two beautiful but expensive four-bed cottages sharing a private pool (⑧) are far from the beach and pretty isolated. Squash court, and diving centre nearby. Cheap day membership (Ksh100) entitles you to use the pool, bar and sunloungers. Half board is good value. B&B ③–④, HB ④–⑤.

Tropical African Dream Village (2.7km; PO Box 939; ☎0123/20711, fax 20788, *tropical@swiftmombasa.com*). The result of a merger of two adjacent hotels, this is a huge all-inclusive *makuti* and tropical garden complex – an Italian-slanted holiday resort with a wide range of watersports available. Loud Euro-rock around one of the two pools penetrates much of the hotel. Rooms in the "Tropical" wing are better but the balconies lack privacy (string tassles separate them). No seasonal rates. All-inclusive (so no day visitors), ⑦.

Indian Ocean Lodge, near Casuarina Point (4km; ☎0123/20394, fax 20394; reservations through Savannah Tours & Lodges, p.50). Set in a small garden on a coral promontory overlooking the bay and a few ancient baobabs, this is a wonderful aberration, definitely a place for a honeymoon, and as expensive as it is exclusive. The lodge consists of just two two-storey Arabic-styled houses, containing five en-suite rooms. Each is huge and extremely luxurious, with magnificent balconies. Service is effortlessly classy, and the common dining room, lounge and terraces are delightfully fitted with antiques. On top of this, the management are refined and friendly. Small pool. Free snorkelling trips, and scuba diving and other excursions can be arranged. No seasonal rates. FB ⑨.

The Town

Other than the beach and the sea, strolling around town is the occupation of most of Malindi's temporary residents, and is not without its idiosyncratic rewards. The old part of Malindi is a half-hour diversion: interesting enough, even though there's nothing specific to see and few of the buildings date from before the second half of the nineteenth century. But the juxtaposition of the earnest and ordinary business of the old town with the near-hysterical *mzungu*-mania only a couple of minutes' walk away on Lamu road produces a bizarre, schizophrenic atmosphere that epitomizes Malindi.

The town has an amazingly salacious reputation which is not entirely home-grown: some European tour operators have in the past been quite inventive in their every-comfort-provided marketing strategies. In the immediate aftermath of the first AIDS-awareness crisis in the late 1980s, there was a massive slump in German tourism to Malindi, but memories are short, it seems: a quick glance at some of the town's bars at night is enough to convince you that the sex safari is back in full swing. Though Germans still come, Italians dominate, and have increased in numbers to the extent that one supermarket even sells Italian canned dog food.

Archeologically, Malindi's offerings are scant. The two **pillar tombs** in front of the Friday mosque on the waterfront are fine upstanding examples of the genre, though the shorter one is only nineteenth-century. This being Malindi, its appearance is usually described as "circumcised". Islamic scholars on the coast tend to dispute the automatic phallic label applied by foreigners.

Malindi's other monuments are Portuguese. **Vasco da Gama Pillar** (1499), down on the point of the same name, makes a good target for a stroll. The **Portuguese Chapel** is a tiny whitewashed cube of a church now covered with *makuti*, whose foundations were laid in the sixteenth century on the site of a Portuguese burial. The most recent Portuguese bequest is the ugly 1959 **Vasco da Gama Monument** on the seaward side of Uhuru Gardens, which contrasts uncomfortably with the "Vasco da Gama = Killer" and "Dagama traitor" graffiti which appeared around town in 1998, on the 500th anniversary of da Gama's arrival in Malindi.

Crafts and shopping

There are two main outdoor areas to head for when you're in the buying mood. Most obvious is the **crafts market** on the seashore below the old town. Naturally, if you stray down here you'll be pounced upon, and leaving without buying anything isn't easy. On the other hand, you can also leave with all sorts of little free gifts if you strike the right bargain. The other area is the **woodcarving co-operative**, in the market in the town centre – a good place for photos. Note there's no bargaining at all in their shop, but you can discuss prices direct with the carvers. There's another similar cooperative near the police station.

Alternatively, for more expensive crafts and the possibility of browsing unhurriedly, try one of the **upmarket shops** along Harambee Road, just to the north of Uhuru Gardens. Prices are naturally very high, but visits are useful for checking comparative values and gauging top prices. At Rasani's Arcade, for example, they have lots of top-quality crafts and objets d'art, including old Lamu silver and jewellery as well as more familiar items available on the street.

Snorkelling and watersports

Not unexpectedly, **snorkelling** ("goggling") and other **watersports** are Malindi's touristic *raison d'être*. Windsurfing, water-skiing, diving and deep-sea game fishing are all cheaper here than at the resorts around Mombasa. Malindi Bay is the main wave-surfing stretch and surfboards are available from all the tourist hotels in town. Unfortunately, all watery activities are marred somewhat by the Galana River's annual outpouring of thousands of tons of prime red topsoil from the up-country plateaus. The cloudy water prevents the growth of coral as far south as Vasco da Gama Point and, ironically, Malindi Bay and the tour-group hotels dotted along it face out across dun-coloured sands to a muddy-brown seascape for much of the year. Murky as it is, this water is not unpleasant to swim in. Note that the shore can get very windy around

September, and in June–July and November the beach becomes covered in seaweed, though many hotels clear their beachfronts daily.

Beach **access** is not a big problem, though the easiest place – and closest to the road – is on the south side of town at Silversands beach. The beach at the town centre and to the north is a good five to ten minutes' walk from the road. There are one or two public access points (see our map) and some hotels are usually willing to allow access for a small fee. *Eden Roc*, for example, charges Ksh100 per day, which allows you use of their pools, plus Ksh100 for a sunbed. The all-inclusive hotels charge much more (*Lawford's* levies Ksh1500), but this does include lunch and free drinks.

Malindi Marine National Park

Daily dawn to dusk; $5 adults, $2 students/children.

Trips out to the **marine park** can be arranged with the boat trip salesmen who make their rounds of *Silversands Campsite* (and elsewhere) most mornings. Alternatively, make your own way down to the **park office** and very pretty beach at Casuarina Point, 5km from town, where you can choose your boat, captain and all. You should find a little room for discussion but won't be able to knock down prices much below the current going rate of Ksh600–700 (excluding park fees) for two hours, especially at peak seasons. Note that your outing may be curtailed if you bargain too ruthlessly. Try to check out the condition of masks and snorkels, and insist on a set for each member of the party. Flippers aren't likely to be up to much (assuming they fit you). The six square kilometres of the **national park** take in the loveliest areas of coral garden, a couple of kilometres offshore, and the trip is worth every shilling you finally agree on. Unless you have a mortal fear of snorkelling or getting wet, don't bother with the **glass-bottomed boats**, which generally have saucepan-sized windows – the **snorkelling** itself, especially if you've never done it before, is sublime, and an experience which will stay with you forever.

With your own or rented gear, of course, you could swim to the reef outside the boundaries of the marine park. All the beachfront hotels from Vasco da Gama Point south as far as *White Elephant Sea Lodge* (3.6km from the town centre) are to the north of the marine park, but the reef is anything from 300–800m offshore.

If you have the qualifications, you can **dive**. The *Driftwood* and *Lawford's* both have dive centres: the one at *Driftwood* is a school. Another school that comes recommended is the well-equipped Diving the Crab, on the beachfront at Tropical African Dream Village (☎0123/20711, fax 20788). Good diving zones to ask about include Shark Point, Tewa, Barracuda Point and Fargialla. Diving isn't generally possible during the rains, as they roughen up the sea beyond the reefs. For general information about diving, see the Watamu account (p.498) and the boxes on p.410 and p.472.

Eating, drinking and nightlife

You're presented with two basic options for **eating** in Malindi. The first is ordinary *hoteli* fare supplemented by a scattering of seriously cheap Indian-style juice and samosa bars in the ramshackle eateries dotted about the market by the Lamu and Garissa bus company offices; the second is a much higher price bracket that includes the big hotels and a small number of more lavish restaurants catering mainly for tourists. If you're buying your own food, you'll find **Malindi Market** is celebrated for fruit and vegetables – second, on the coast, only to Mombasa's.

Basic eateries and bar-restaurants

Bahari Café, town centre near Juma Mosque. Good tasty cheap food in cheerful surroundings, usually with good music too.

Bawaly and Sons Halwa Shop, town centre near Uhuru Gardens. Highly deserving of a mention, a long-established spot to try several varieties of the gooey jelly (of which "Turkish Delight" is a dull relation). Tiny cups of spiced *kahawa* come free.

Golden Fin, back of the town centre. Clean new place with cheap sodas and fried and African food.

Mama's Cafe. Clean, nice decor. Good cheap tasty curries, no beer.

Oasis Gelateria, south side of Malindi, on the beach before *Silversands*. With Italian money flooding into Malindi, a certain scepticism seems in order. But this big new snack bar is simply very good – though more perhaps for the metropolitan touches like cheap soda water on tap, inexpensive homemade bread, delicious omelettes and espresso – than for the forty flavours of ice cream. Sadly, it's part of a huge and hideous time-share complex which has occupied what remained of Silversands public beach. Open daily 9am–11pm.

Open View, by Total roundabout on the outskirts of town. Good local food.

Palantine Tea Room, Mama Ngina St, next to *Kenya Mpya B&L*. Large and busy local eatery; *ugali* or chips with everything. Cheap.

Palm Garden, Harambee Rd. Primarily a bar rendezvous for the sex trade, which also serves inexpensive if very variable curries and seafood. To avoid the prostitutes and rather hustly scene on the front patio, eat in the garden at the back. Always a good place to hit on a Friday, often with live music (about Ksh70 entry), and on Mondays (*Seawaves* band).

Stars and Garters, Harambee Rd, next to Barclays Bank. Brash and busy *makuti*-roofed complex, especially popular for the English football screened on its satellite TVs in the bars. Good range of snacks and fuller meals (mainly Italian), too.

Urafiki Inn. A cheap down-to-earth *hoteli* with the dual bonuses of cold beer and loud but good music.

Upmarket restaurants

Baobab, next to the Portuguese Chapel on the seafront. Expensive seafood (Ksh500–700), curries, Italian and African dishes (Ksh200–300), but well worth patronizing for cheap, cold beer and its sweeping views over the beach and fishing boats. Open daily 8am–11pm.

Bistrot Pizzeria, Galana Shopping Centre, Harambee Rd. Very flashy, with pleasant tables under shade outside.

Braciere, Harambee Rd, near the Casino. Tries to please all with pasta and pizza, curries, and things like lentil and sausage stew for the Germans. Some thatched parasols in courtyard garden. Licensed. From Ksh300.

Driftwood Club, south of Silversands beach (☎0123/20155). Always a good place to eat, but the Ksh500 Sunday curry buffet is worth planning your day around. The salads and chocolate cake are good, too. Much better value than the *Blue Marlin*.

Gilani Hotel, on the seafront. Smart, laid-back and very colourfully decorated eating-house, with a nice terrace on the street. Reasonably priced pasta, curries and seafood.

I Love Pizza, on the seafront (☎0123/20672). Very swish indeed, this is Malindi's classiest restaurant, and the pizzas are really not bad – from around Ksh250. They push their seafood, though, which is also good. Recommended. Open daily 10.30am–3pm & 6.30–10pm.

Ristorante Nino, near the Portuguese Chapel on the seafront (☎0123/31712). Mostly grills, seafood and delicious pizzas cooked in a woodfired oven. Eat in the shaded gardens. From about Ksh300, with a first-rate stuffing costing up to Ksh700 with drinks. Open daily noon–3pm & 7–11pm.

Surahi, at the back of town – see map (☎0123/20911). A fancy Indian restaurant (rated one of Malindi's best) with a limited range of fairly expensive dishes and an uncluttered, cool dining room. Worth a try but not unmissable. Tues–Sun noon–3pm & 7–11pm.

The Old Man & The Sea, on the seafront. High-class, slightly quirky, Italian restaurant. Closed in low season.

Bars and local dives

After dark, especially in high season, Malindi throbs with action. For **live music**, in town try *Mgadini* and *Come Back*, both on the way out of town on the left, before you reach the airport. Out here too, you'll find the *Market Village* club, inside the Malindi Showground, where international African music stars sometimes perform. The entrance price for all these places is nominal – except, of course, when they are hosting someone like Samba Mapangala. Drinks are also cheap and you can usually feast on a half-kilo of *nyama choma*. It's always more fun to go with a Malindi local – though you should have no worries at all about taking a taxi and going on your own.

Bar Bar, Sabaki Centre, Harambee Rd. Yet another pizzeria, with expensive snacks and seating under the designer awning outside. Trendy, and no prostitutes. Live music Wednesday nights.

Chic's Restaurant, at the back of town – see map (☎0123/31430). No food despite the name: popular beer garden, very lively Wednesday, Friday and Saturday nights with local bands (currently *Magazines* on Wednesday, and *Bebabiss* Friday and Saturday) playing from 7pm–midnight.

Hermann's Beer Garden, Harambee Rd, next to *Stars and Garters*. Very German: come for the keg beer and snacks, and to start the evening. Steaks and seafood too. Open daily 8am–1am.

Iguana Bar & Café, La Piazzetta, Harambee Rd. Fashionable place in the pink Italian shopping centre, open 24 hours for drinks (and some dancing at night), snacks and meals. Popular meeting place for locals.

Kakungu Bar, at the back of town – see map. A very local dive with cheap beer, a juke box (almost extinct in Kenya) and a warm welcome.

Old T Bar, next to *Blue Lodge*. Funny name, lively crowd, nicely ramshackle appearance.

Pumzika, near *Fondo Wehu* (open 24 hours). Cheap and friendly local hangout with DJ Wednesday and a band on Saturday.

Urafiki Inn, up the side road opposite *Palm Garden*, past Agip and the police station. Cheerful and unthreatening.

Nightclubs

Hotel discos, a speciality of the south side of Malindi, tend to happen in a different hotel each night through the week, but are rather insipid affairs out of season and the music's rarely anything to rave about. When you're weary of bopping, the *Casino Malindi* has free entry (daily from noon), no dress code and powerful air-conditioning. Play if you want, or just watch the grim-looking Italian bosses tending their novice Giriama croupiers.

Stardust, Harambee Rd (daily 10pm–5am). The biggest and best club, air-conditioned and always busy, but expensive (Ksh400 for *wazungu*, Ksh200 for locals).

Fermenta Disco Bar, Galana Shopping Centre, opposite *Stardust* (from 8pm). Expensive Italian "piano bar" which plays Euro-trash when not inflicting karaoke.

Club 28, Harambee Rd, adjacent to *Eden Roc Hotel*. Originally exclusively for under-28s, this nightclub has its ups and downs, but is a lot smaller than *Stardust*.

Vera Cruz, Harambee Rd (☎0123/31539). Still being built, this promises an "international show" and possibly boogying on the beach. Rooms planned, too.

Moving on from Malindi

The main **bus and matatu park** is a ten-minute walk south of town along the Mombasa road, with frequent services to Gedi, Watamu, Kilifi and Mombasa, and infrequent local *matatus* and buses for points inland. Details of these services are given throughout the text. Bus services to **Lamu** and **northwest to Garissa** start off from Mombasa, and pass by their Malindi booking offices in the centre of town by the market (marked on our map) at around 9am each day. The companies are Faza (☎0123/30224), TSS (no office), Mombasa Liners (no phone) and Tawfiq (☎0123/30850). More details and route information are given on p.543. Garissa (via Garsen and Hola) is served by Tawfiq and Mombasa Liners, which pass through

Malindi around 7.30am (plus an additional 8.30am run to Hola by Mombasa Liners) – for this route, read the route description and **security warning** on p.575 carefully – this is one of the most dangerous roads in Kenya. For both Lamu and Garissa, buy your ticket the day before – otherwise you have an exceedingly uncomfortable standing-up experience to look forward to.

Listings

Airlines Cheapest flights to Lamu are Kenya Airways (Utali Parade, ☎0123/20237 or 20574; airport ☎0123/20192 or 20971), with four weekly flights costing Ksh2500 one-way. They also run (same days) to Nairobi. Much more expensive for Lamu are the daily Airkenya flights (office at Galana Shopping Centre, ☎0123/30808; $65), who also fly to Mombasa (Mon–Sat 4.30pm, Sun 5pm; Ksh1480) and Nairobi (Mon, Wed, Fri & Sun; Ksh5385). You can book flights at their offices, or at any travel agency, though the less reputable of these will charge you more. Prestige Air Services (☎0123/20861) only do charter flights (usually to Lamu, Mombasa and Maasai Mara), but are happy to get you on if there's a seat available (same rates as scheduled flights). Eagle Aviation's flights are now run jointly with Kenya Airways.

Banks Barclays bureau de change (Mon–Fri 9am–4.30pm, Sat 9–11am), KCB and Standard Chartered (both Mon–Fri 9am–3pm, Sat 9–11am). Standard Chartered and Barclays have 24-hour ATMs for visa cards. You should find better rates at Mid Star Forex in Utali Parade. The casino changes money at any time, but at bad rates.

Bicycle rental Available everywhere. *Silversands Campsite* are old hands and their bikes (currently new Indian three-speed clunkers) cost a very reasonable Ksh200 per day or Ksh1200 per week. Other places may have better bikes, but prices are higher.

Car rental Glory Car Hire, Ngala Building, across from the post office (PO Box 994; ☎ & fax 0123/20065), maintains a high profile on the coast and you can leave the vehicle in Nairobi or Mombasa for a supplement. Prices start at Ksh2200 per day plus Ksh14 per kilometre, including insurance: check the vehicle and conditions carefully, though. Also cheap are Galu (see "Travel agents" below) and Leisure Car Hire at Malindi Complex. The multinationals are more expensive: Avis, at Sitawi Shopping Centre (PO Box 197; ☎0123/20513); Payless/Budget, at La Piazzetta centre; and Hertz at UTC (see "Travel Agents" below).

Email services Bit House at Malindi Complex will send emails for Ksh100 plus Ksh50 per attachment.

Horse riding Try the Kibokoni Riding Centre north of town (see p.503). You'll pay around Ksh500 an hour, including a guide, for short bush rides in the vicinity. Beginners can go on a leading rein.

Hospitals There are three in Malindi, but the Galana Hospital on Lamu Rd (at the north end of town on the road to Lamu, just past *Sultan Villas*; ☎0123/2083 or 30575) is the best in an emergency.

Immigration A decrepit-looking office on the waterfront road by the Jumaa Mosque.

Pharmacy Malindi Chemists at Sitawi Shopping Centre; Rafiki Chemist on Harambee Rd, next to Palm Garden.

Post and telephone office The main post office is just off Harambee Rd opposite the police station (Mon–Fri 8am–5pm, Sat 9am–noon), and has a good poste-restante service. The adjacent telephone office is open Mon–Fri 7am–12.30pm & 2–6pm. They sell phone cards for the cardphone, which is cheaper to use than placing a call through the operator. There's also a fax machine.

Supermarkets There are several small places in the shopping arcades up Harambee Road in the town centre, the best – with the widest range – being Sona at Galana Shopping Centre. Try also Malindi Grocers in Ngala Building, and Malindi Supermarket at Malindi Complex. But the cheapest range is at the Jolly Market, 2km south of town at the *Oasis* complex on Silversands beach. Here, you'll find Italian wine from under Ksh200 a bottle, and dairy produce.

Taxis You'll be offered their services everywhere, or you can call one (Baobab Taxis; ☎0123/30499), who promise "negotiable rates".

Travel agents A good scattering along Lamu road and the seafront all offer similar services, including train bookings: try Galu/Southern Cross Safaris, Malindi Complex (☎0123/20493, fax 30032); or UTC/Hertz (☎0123/20069).

Out of Malindi: the Arabuko-Sokoke Forest and Hell's Kitchen

The best way to get around town and its environs is **by bicycle** (several places rent bikes – see "Listings"). If you've been relying on public transport – or organized tour buses – cycling can give you a tremendous lift, enabling you to go virtually anywhere. The flat countryside around Malindi is ideal and Gedi (90min) or Watamu (2hr) are easy objectives, with the guarantee that you'll be blown either there or back by the wind, depending on the time of year.

You might be tempted to head north to what one piece of tourist literature describes as "the Arabian Nights town" of **Mambrui**. True, there's a pretty mosque and the unusual spectacle of cows on the beach, but the very ruinous pillar tomb certainly isn't worth the dust-blown journey and the village itself could hardly be less exciting. The exception might be during the Muslim festival of **Maulidi** (see the box on p.527), when there are street processions and much music. At other times, it's better to head for one of the following.

The northern Arabuko-Sokoke Forest

For immersion in raw nature, drive, or pedal for an hour, along the road out of Malindi towards Tsavo East and, as you near the banks of the Sabaki (or Galana) River, you'll enter the **Arabuko-Sokoke Forest**. To make the most of the day, try setting out early by *matatu*, with your bike on the roof rack. There are several *matatus* daily, and one country bus service, but departure times are unpredictable. Take lots of water. Beware: the sandy tracks on some sections of the routes described below can be very hard going. A car, motorbike or mountain bike is the best solution; an ordinary rented bike may need to be pushed for up to two hours – a punishing slog.

The places to aim for are **Kakayuni** (12km inland from Malindi) and **Jilore** (20km). Kakayuni is the larger of the two and offers a forest road of 10km or so, leading via the small centre of **Arabuko** back to the main Kilifi–Malindi highway. Mostly, however, this path goes through marginal forest lands; continuing to Jilore is more promising. Jilore is a tiny centre, with a scattered collection of huts and one nominal *duka*. The village's position, though, on a ridge overlooking a bend in the Sabaki/Galana River, contrasts impressively with the deep forest into which you now plunge.

The turning for Jilore Forest Station is to the left, just before you reach Jilore village, and the station about 3km down the track. At the first crossroads after the forest station's three huts, turn left: a good trail leads for 16km in a southerly direction to the Kilifi–Malindi highway. If you're doing this trip by car, the track is drivable (though 4WD helps over the deep sand), and it's also clear enough for walkers to follow without getting lost. The track is seldom used by motorists and you're not likely to see other people. Around its halfway mark, the soil changes from red *murram* to a light grey, soft coral sand, signalling the transition back to the coast proper. If you've been pootling along gently on a rented cycle from Malindi, this is pretty well the end of the relaxing bit, where you'll have to start getting off to push. Your eventual emergence onto the main highway, 5–6km south of Gedi, is sudden. Here, you could wait for a short time for a *matatu* straight back to Malindi or, if the day is still young and your energy not completely sapped, turn inland again a couple of kilometres north up the road, where the other track (described above) leads to Arabuko and Kakayuni.

For a short, and much less strenuous, visit to the forest – and more about its natural history – see p.488.

The Marafa Depression: Hell's Kitchen

Northwest of Malindi, the **Marafa Depression** is the remains of a large sandstone ridge, now reduced by wind, rain and floodwater to a series of gorges, where steep gullies and narrow arêtes alternately eat into or jut from the main ridge wall. The colours of the exposed sandstone range from off-white through pale pinks and oranges to deep crimson, all capped by the rich tawny topsoil. It's particularly dramatic at sunset.

"Hell's Kitchen" is the common nickname for this pretty spectacle, though the locals call it *Nyari* – "the place broken by itself" – and tell numerous moralizing **stories** about its dark origins. The village that once stood here was favoured by God with the news of a forthcoming miracle, delivered to the inhabitants by an angel. They were commanded to move on, and all did so, except one old woman who refused to believe such nonsense. The village (and the old lady) disappeared soon after, leaving *Nyari*. Whether that was the miracle is not reported, but it's interesting to note how the story varies according to the teller – in Islamic circles "God talked through an angel", while among traditionalists, "the gods informed a wise woman".

To get there, fork right at the end of Marafa village, and the canyon is about 500m along on the left, invisible until you're right at its edge. At the lip of the gorge the first signs of commercialism – a small car park and a couple of seasonal souvenir stands – don't detract much from the site. It's easy to descend the steep path to the bottom and you can count on spending an hour or two exploring the natural architecture of what looks like an early *Star Trek* set. There's a scattering of *dukas* and *hotelis* among Marafa village's whitewashed, thatched houses, and one basic but very welcoming **hotel**: *Marafa Hell's Kitchen Guest House* (PO Box 6 Madina via Malindi; B&B ②), at the end of the village on the right facing the depression, with clean rooms, beds with mosquito nets, shared toilet and shower, and a pleasant garden. They can also arrange guided walks to Hell's Kitchen, and provide food given some notice.

With a vehicle, you might sensibly combine the Arabuko-Sokoke Forest with a visit to the Marafa Depression by crossing the Galana/Sabaki River – if the bridge across the river at Jilore (marked on some maps) actually existed. In its absence, take the road out of Malindi heading north (which involves a left turn on the other side of the Sabaki bridge) and from there go via **Marikebuni** and **Magarini**. You're looking at a round trip of about 80km, one which – given the vagaries of **public transport** – only drivers can manage in a day. Daily **buses from Malindi** to Marafa leave at 9am, 10am and 11am, returning at 1.30pm, 2.30pm and 4.30pm.

Onwards to Lamu

The **flight to Lamu** (cheapest on Kenya Airways from Malindi; Ksh2500) is an experience not to be missed, and is the usual mode of transport for visitors these days given the dangers of the road. But the **bus journey** is an adventure in its own right and repays you with more than just a cheaper ticket. On a number of occasions throughout the 1990s, it repaid all the occupants of the bus, including its armed escort, with summary eviction from their seats while a gang of bandits (*shifta* is the Kenyan term) made a careful collection of all belongings. On one occasion they stole everyone's clothes, too. More seriously, after a lull of over a year, the bandits struck again in February 1999, randomly spraying one bus with bullets in a failed attempt to get it to stop, injuring two passengers and its armed escort. Security has been stepped up once again, but the banditry has gone on too long for the majority of people, and only the most intrepid or penniless tourists still go by road. Four bus companies presently run the route from Mombasa via Kilifi and Malindi: Faza, TSS, Mombasa Liners and Tawfiq. The price varies according to the perceived state of security along the road: Ksh200–300 from Mombasa when things are considered safe, up to Ksh350–500 when the risk of attack is high. You won't pay much less from Malindi.They're supposed to travel in convoy but, until the last attack, rarely did, so you should find out which are the first buses to leave (currently TSS and Faza), as the bandits tend to target the tail-enders. A seat on the left avoids the sun, but is the side favoured by *shifta*. In any case, buy your tick-

AROUND THE TANA DELTA

If you have your own 4WD vehicle or a little patience, the trip north to Lamu can be stretched over several days, with time to explore the fascinating region around the **Tana Delta**: on the west side, the Pokomo village of **Ngao** and other villages on the river itself; on the east, a dune-shrouded coast and **Kipini**, with the Swahili ruins of **Ungwana, Shaka** and **Mwana** all within 12km. Do however make careful enquiries about any recent bandit attacks in the region before going. If you're genuinely interested, it's suggested you try to see the warden of the museum at Fort Jesus for further information.

As yet almost wholly untouched by tourism, the region to the north of the Tana River Delta – centred around the little fishing village of **Kipini** at the mouth of the Tana and the larger market centre of **Witu**, 21km inland – more than repays the slight hassle of finding a room. Though it's hard to believe, with its lack of electricity, tap water or telephones, **Kipini** was once the headquarters of Tana River District, before it was shifted to Hola at Independence. Nowadays, its erstwhile role is evident only in a mixed population of Orma, Pokomo, Bajuni, Somali and Swahili, who get by on fishing, small-scale farming and some herding. Unfortunately, things look set to change: somebody is selling off communal land to developers, and prime beach front is going cheap. Big time investors are moving in, and have also tried vast agricultural schemes, most failing but displacing many pastoral people in the process. The villagers are currently examining proposals to protect the Tana's ecosystem by putting it under the Ramsar Treaty (which obliges governments and others to protect wetlands of ecological importance), as well as to combat illegal trawlers off the coast, which damage corals, kill turtles and have already caused the disappearance of swordfish. To get a closer look, you can organize local boat rides up the Tana from Kipini – passing crocodiles, and hundreds of birds, such as malachite and pied kingfishers, African fish eagles, and goliath herons. Further upstream is the Ozi Forest.

To get to Kipini, leave the Lamu bus at Witu, where there's a connecting *matatu* to the village. There are no formal **lodgings**, but you should be able to stay with a local family for the price of a B&L; plenty of cheap, wholesome Swahili *hotelis* serve delicious *dalasini* cinnamon tea. Alternatively, you could stay in **Witu** (again, no formal lodgings, though the German NGO, GASP, has an excellent guesthouse which it may let you use), and hire a **bicycle** locally for getting around. From Witu, **buses** for Lamu pass through at around 10am, with Malindi-bound services arriving a little earlier. There are few if any vehicles along the road after 2pm, due to fear of bandits.

You can take a **safari** in the delta with Tana Delta Ltd (PO Box 24988 Nairobi; ☎02/882826, fax 882939; about $200 a day), who also run the expensive *Tana Delta Camp* in the dunes near the ocean (reservations also through Bush Homes of East Africa, p.48; closed April–June, minimum stay 3 nights; ⑨), with six "luxury" double tents and one *banda*. There are boat trips and excellent guided walks available (including mud baths if you're in the mood), as well as canoes and water-skiing, but the price ($530) is very high, especially when you consider you're in one of the poorest regions of Kenya.

et the day before. If you're **driving** your own vehicle, you'll definitely need an armed escort from Minjila junction just south of Garsen to Lamu (the bargainable starting price for two soldiers is Ksh1000), if not from a roadblock north of Malindi at Gongoni. Note that you have to leave your vehicle at Mokowe, in any case, and catch a boat to Lamu.

Installed by a window, you can fully appreciate the flat, gentle, dull landscape, sometimes brown and arid but more usually grey-green and swampy with plenty of large birdlife, which opens out as Malindi's low hills are left behind. At the time of writing, you could still see the floodline left by El Niño up the trunks of the trees after Minjila, in places three to four metres above the soil. Most of the vegetation lower down was killed by the flood (there's now only grass and dead branches), which makes it easier to understand the causes of the famine that swept much of Tana River district in the late 1990s, when an estimated thirty to fifty percent of the region's livestock was lost.

When the scenery palls, the trip is enlivened by the other passengers, by stops at the fly-blown market centres of **Witu** (see below), Mkunumbi and sometimes Mpeketoni for *chai* and a bite to eat, and by occasional flashes of colour: the sky-blue cloaks of **Orma** herders or the red, black and white of shawled **Somali** women. Wonderful **birdlife** and **wild animals** are evident, too: giraffe and antelope, notably waterbuck – even the odd elephant if you look hard enough. And impeccable sources continue to attest to seeing occasional **lions** between Garsen and Mokowe.

The new Chinese-built road is fast tarmac from Malindi to Garsen (p.598). Beyond Minjila – 7km south of Garsen at the junction for the Garissa and Lamu roads (the old road to Lamu from Garsen itself, marked on all maps, was washed away by El Niño) – the tarmac continues for only 20km, before the trundling along the mud-and-*murram* New Garsen Causeway, hurriedly rebuilt in the aftermath of the floods. This is scheduled to be surfaced, too (which would vastly reduce the risk of hold-ups), but the Chinese have pulled out, complaining of the inadequate security provided for them after a spate of *shifta* attacks. If work doesn't resume quickly, the road will inevitably start breaking up, meaning disruptions to bus services as well as increased attacks.

THE LAMU ARCHIPELAGO

A cluster of hot, low-lying desert islands tucked into the coast near the Somalian border, **Lamu** and its neighbours have a special appeal that many find irresistible. While each town or village has its own distinct character, together they epitomize a separate spectrum of Swahili culture. For although the whole coast is – broadly – "Swahili", there's a world of difference between these islands and the coconut beaches of Mombasa and Malindi.

To a great extent the islands are anachronisms. Electricity arrived here only thirty years ago, there are still almost no motor vehicles, and life moves at the pace of a donkey or a dhow. Yet there have been considerable internal changes over the centuries and Lamu itself is now changing faster than ever. Because of its special position in the Islamic world as a much respected Islamic teaching centre, Saudi Arabian direct aid has poured into the island: the hospital, schools and religious centres are all supported by it. At the same time, there have been efforts to open up Lamu beyond its present tourist market, which so far has encompassed only low-budget travellers and short-stay air safaris. Rich foreign sponsors are eagerly sought and several lodging houses have been set up with what is bluntly called "white girl money". Islanders are ambivalent about the future. A string of hotels along the beach, a bridge to the mainland – all seems possible, and all would contribute to the destruction of Lamu's timeless character. Some up-country officials working here might not disapprove: with only two bars, the town is not a popular posting.

But the damage that would be done goes further than spoiling the tranquillity. The Lamu archipelago is one of the most important sources for knowledge about pre-colonial Africa. **Archeological sites** indicate that towns have existed on these islands for at least 1200 years. The dunes behind Lamu beach, for example, are said to conceal the remains of long-deserted settlements. And somewhere close by on the mainland, perhaps just over the border in Somalia, archaeologists expect one day to uncover the ruins of Shungwaya, the town which the nine tribes that comprise the Mijikenda people claim as their ancestral home. The whole region is an academic's delight, a source of endless confusion and controversy, and a place where there is still real continuity between history and modern life.

At least for the present, the islands survive. **Lamu island** itself, most people's single destination, still has plenty to recommend it, despite a serious fire in 1993 and the

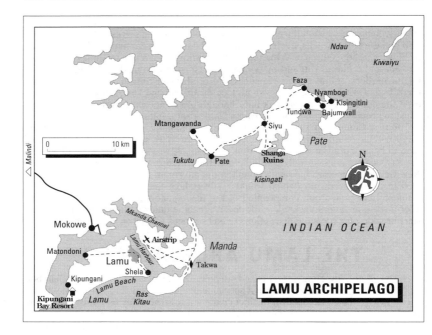

inevitable sprouting of TV satellite dishes. **Manda**, directly opposite, is little visited except for the lifeline it provides with the outside world – the local airstrip; **Pate island** (see p.536), accessible by a scheduled motorboat service, makes a fascinating excursion if you have a week or more in the area. **Kiwaiyu** (see p.542), not quite within the archipelago but exotic and alluring enough to be worth the effort if you have time, is a wisp of a beach island 9km long and less than 1km across, lying to the northeast of the other islands. Those who visit Kiwaiyu normally arrive by private plane, but you can easily reach it by grouping together to charter a dhow in Lamu.

Lamu island

Perhaps best left until the end of your stay in Kenya, **LAMU** may otherwise precipitate a change in your plans as you're gently lulled into a slow rhythm in which days and weeks can pass by unheeded and other objectives can easily be forgotten. For many people, Lamu's deliciously lazy atmosphere is the best worst-kept secret on the coast. Eyes, ears, tongue and nose get a comprehensive work-out here, so that actually *doing* anything is sometimes a problem – like walking through treacle. Hours can be blissfully spent on a roof or a verandah just watching the town go by, its mood swinging effortlessly from one of the day's five prayer calls to the next, from tide to tide, and from dawn to dusk.

If this doesn't hit the right note for you, you may actually rather hate Lamu. Hot, dirty and boring are adjectives that have been applied by perfectly sane, pleasant people, and you can certainly improve your chances of liking the place by not coming here at the tail end of the dry season, when the town's gutters are blocked with dried refuse, the gardens in the houses wilt under the sun and the heat is sapping.

IMPORTANT ADVICE

If you're staying in Lamu a few days only, it's a very good idea to go straight to the appropriate airline office on arrival to **reconfirm** your return seat. There's no guarantee otherwise that your booking will still be there when you come to fly. Buying bus tickets a day in advance is also advisable. Something else to beware of: the **police** in Lamu sometimes organize raids on the guest houses, not just looking for *bangi*, as you might reasonably expect, but to check people's passports. If you're coming to the end of your permitted stay in Kenya, don't outstay it in Lamu: it can prove expensive.

Lamu is something of a **myth** factory. Conventionally labelled "an old Arab trading town", it is actually one of the last viable remnants of the **Swahili civilization** that was the dominant cultural force all along the coast until the arrival of the British. In the late 1960s and early 1970s, Lamu's unique blend of beaches, gentle Islamic ambience, funky old town, and host population well used to strangers, was a recipe which took over where Marrakesh left off. It acquired a reputation as Kenya's Kathmandu: the end of the (African) hippie trail and a stop-over on the way to India. Shaggy foreigners were only allowed to visit on condition they stayed in lodgings and didn't camp on the beach.

Not many people want to camp out these days. The proliferation of good, reasonably priced lodgings in the heart of the town encourages an ethos more interactive than hippie-escapist. Every other traveller you've met along the way seems to end up here, in an ever-recycling community. Happily, travellers and locals cross paths enough to avoid any tedium – though for women travelling without men, this can itself become tedious (see p.529). Having said that, there can hardly be another town in the world as utterly unthreatening as Lamu. Leave your room at midnight for a breath of air and you can stroll past the lantern-lit shopfronts on hushed Harambee Avenue, shopkeepers dozing in front, or tread up the darkest of alleys, where you need fear absolutely nothing. This is an exhilarating experience.

Arrival and orientation

The **bus trip** ends at **Mokowe** on the mainland, where a chugging *mtaboti* (motorboat bus; Ksh30) takes you out around the creek for the thirty-minute ride to the town. They're timed to coincide with the buses, though there are other less frequent services throughout the day. Grab your luggage, ignore the chaotic boat touts pulling you every which way, and jump on the boat which seems fullest – they all go to Lamu. If you **drive** to Lamu yourself, you'll have to leave your vehicle in the car park where it will, by all accounts, be safe: tipping the *askari* beforehand may improve security further. Don't be misled by boys who try to sell you a *mtaboti* charter: just wait for the next public *mtaboti* with everyone else. **Flying** in, planes land on Manda island, across the harbour directly opposite the town; the short boat trip from here (Ksh70, or Ksh100 to Shela) gives a wonderful panorama of Lamu's nineteenth-century waterfront.

Whichever way you arrive, you'll inevitably be met by a **guide**, offering "the best room in Lamu". Much as you might prefer to wander unguided, soaking it all in and tracking down a room yourself, you probably won't escape; unless you've already made a booking, your first hour or so is likely to be full of milling confusion as you're led from one suggested lodging to another through a baffling maze of streets. It's best not to fight this little hustler's ritual: carrying bags gives you away as newly arrived and nobody's going to lead you up an alley and rob you – the town is really too small for that. The guides, who have formed the **Lamu Tour Guides Association**, and who carry small white laminated ID cards, work on commissions from various hotels and guest houses, though some landlords resent the thirty percent commission they have

LAMU IN HISTORY

The undeniably **Arab** flavour of Lamu is not nearly as old as the town itself. It derives from the later nineteenth century when the **Omanis**, and to some extent the **Hadhramis** from what is now Yemen, held political and cultural sway in the town. The first British representatives in Lamu found themselves among pale-skinned slave-owning Arab rulers. The cultural and racial stereotypes that were subsequently propagated have never completely disappeared.

Lamu was established on its present site by the fourteenth century but there have been people living on the island for very much longer than that. The fresh water supplies beneath Shela made the island very attractive to **refugees from the mainland** and people have been escaping here for 2000 years or more – most recently in the 1960s, when Somali secessionists and cattle-raiders caused havoc. It was also one of the earliest places on the coast to attract settlers from the Persian Gulf; there were probably people from Arabia and southwest Asia living and intermarrying here even before the foundation of Islam.

In 1505, Lamu was visited by a heavily armed **Portuguese** man-of-war and the king of the town quickly agreed to pay the first of many cash tributes as protection money. The alternative was the sacking of the town. For the next 180 years Lamu was nominally under Portuguese rule, though the Portuguese favoured Pate as a place to live. In the 1580s, the **Turkish** fleet of Amir Ali Bey temporarily threatened Portuguese dominance, but superior firepower and relentless savagery kept them out and Lamu, with little in the way of an arsenal, had no choice but to bend with the wind – losing a king now and then to the Portuguese executioners – until the Omanis arrived on the scene with fast ships and a serious bid for lasting control.

By the end of the seventeenth century, Lamu's Portuguese predators were vanquished and for nearly a century and a half it had a revitalizing breathing space. This was its **Golden Age**. Lamu became a republic ruled over by the *Yumbe*, a council of elders who deliberated in the palace (now a ruined plot in the centre of town), with only the loosest control imposed by their Omani overlords. This was the period when most of the big houses were built and when Lamu's classic architectural style found its greatest expression. Arts and crafts flourished and business along the waterfront made the town a mag-

to pay on the first night's rent – sometimes for the whole duration of your stay – and refuse to be involved. Others simply tag the commission rather unfairly onto the rate you're paying: to avoid this, make it clear you're only staying for one night, and perhaps move on elsewhere the next morning (when you won't be hassled). If you don't like the guide's choice, ask him to take you to yours: you shouldn't have to pay anything and if you think there's any doubt in his mind, make it clear. Once you've settled on a room – and the landlord has perhaps paid the hustler his tip – you'll be left in peace. It's when he offers to continue to be your guide that you need to decide if you want him around, and discuss openly how much you're prepared to pay for his help if you do. If there are specific things, people or places you want to visit, you should seriously consider it: Ksh200–300 per day would be a very acceptable wage, though if you've a few days, asking other travellers about their recommendations for guides is the best way to avoid disappointment (some of them are far from honest or reliable).

When discovering Lamu for yourself, you shouldn't get lost too easily if you remember that **Harambee Avenue** – the Usita wa Mui or Njia Kuu – runs parallel to and 50m behind the waterfront, and that streets leading into town all climb slightly uphill, but getting lost is rather wonderful anyway. In the listings that follow, the terms Mkomani and Langoni are quite often used. These are the two main parts of Lamu town – Mkomani the northern end and Langoni the southern. If you need a **map** to supplement ours, they sell one at Lamu Museum for Ksh200. Lamu's first **tourist office** net throughout the Indian Ocean. Huge ocean-going dhows rested half the year in the harbour, taking on ivory, rhino horn, mangrove poles and cereals. There was time to compose long poems and argue about language, the Koran and local politics. Lamu became the northern coast's **literary and scholastic focus**, a distinction inherited from Pate. Women achieved a higher status than in the past, though ironically the best known Lamu woman of the time, the poet **Mwana Kupona**, is famous for her "Advice on the Wifely Duty" given to her daughter. The house where she lived for a while is up behind the fort.

For a brief time Lamu's star was in the ascendant in all fields. There was even a famous victory at the **Battle of Shela** in 1812. A combined Pate-Mazrui* force landed at Shela with the simple plan of capturing Lamu – not known for its resolve in battle – and finishing the construction of **the fort** which the Nabahanis from Pate had begun a few years earlier. To everyone's surprise, particularly the Lamu defenders, the tide had gone out and the invaders were massacred as they tried to push their boats off the beach. Appalled at the overkill and expecting a swift response from the Mazruis in Mombasa, Lamu sent to Oman itself for **Busaidi** protection and threw away independence forever. Had the eventual outcome of this panicky request been foreseen, the Lamu *Yumbe* might have reconsidered. Seyyid Said, Sultan of Oman, was more than happy to send a garrison to complete and occupy Lamu's fort – and from this toehold in Africa, he went on to smash the Mazrui traitors in Mombasa, taking the entire coast and moving his own sultanate to Zanzibar.

A stepping stone in the plans of the mighty, Lamu gradually sank into economic collapse towards the end of the nineteenth century as Zanzibar and Mombasa grew in importance. In a sense, it has been stagnating ever since. The building of the Uganda railway from Mombasa, and the banning of slavery, did nothing to improve matters for Lamu in purely economic terms, and it seems that decline has kept up with the shrinking population. However, the new **resettlement programme** on the mainland at Lake Kenyatta (Mpeketoni) is already spinning off new faces to Lamu, and a revived commercialism from up-country has taken root around the market square.

---

* The Mazrui were the Omani family who had set themselves up independently in Mombasa, incurring the wrath of the Busaidi rulers back in Oman.

opened in January 1999 under the DC's office by the waterfront, and consists of desk, chair and (usually absent) man. It remains to be seen what kind of service it will offer.

For details on moving on from Lamu, see p.533.

Accommodation in Lamu town

The better **lodgings** in Lamu town are generally those on the waterfront or those with a height advantage: places on Harambee Avenue tend to be suffocatingly hot. Best known is *Petley's Inn*, but having almost the only bar in town has inflated its reputation. *Petley's* accommodation is not great value and, if you happen to be booked in here on a short package from Nairobi or Mombasa, you should still look for lodging elsewhere, even paying the modest extra from your own pocket. If you want real luxury, *Peponi Hotel*, out on Shela beach, is much more expensive than anything in town and an altogether different prospect. There's also a small number of relatively pricey lodgings and private houses in **Shela** – which has become an alternative, upmarket base to Lamu town, with its own atmosphere. Shela acccommodation is covered on p.530.

In December, January, July and August, and particularly during Maulidi (see the box on p.527), **room availability** can be tight. It's a good idea to book ahead if you can. We've given PO Box and telephone numbers where available; one or two box numbers crop up rather often, indicating common ownership, and several places don't

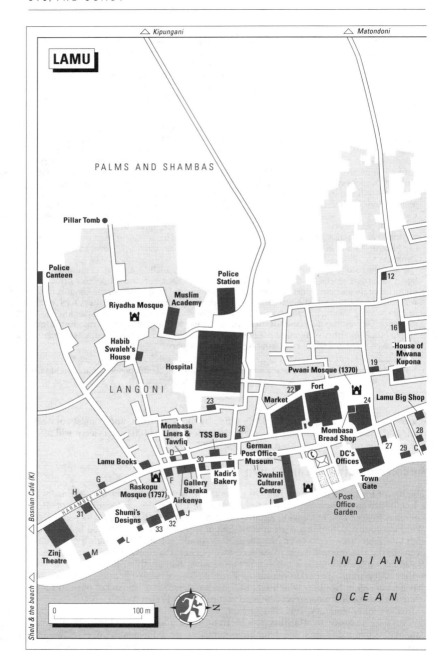

LAMU

△ Kipungani   △ Matondoni

PALMS AND SHAMBAS

Pillar Tomb ●

Police Canteen

Riyadha Mosque

Muslim Academy

Police Station

Habib Swaleh's House

Hospital

LANGONI

Pwani Mosque (1370)

House of Mwana Kupona

12

16

19

Market

Fort

Lamu Big Shop

22

23

24

Mombasa Liners & Tawfiq

TSS Bus

26

28

27   29

Lamu Books

D

30

E

German Post Office Museum

Mombasa Bread Shop

DC's Offices

G

F

Kadir's Bakery

Swahili Cultural Centre

Town Gate

Raskopu Mosque (1797)

Gallery Baraka

Airkenya

Post Office Garden

H

31

Shumi's Designs

J

I

33   32

Zinj Theatre

L

M

INDIAN

OCEAN

△ Bosnian Café (K)

△ Shela & the beach

0   100 m

N

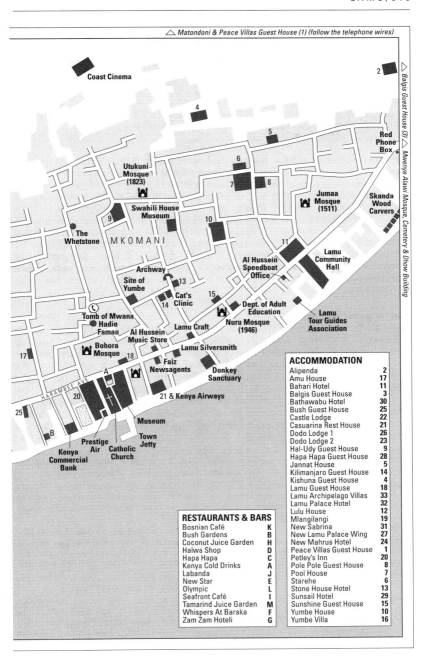

△ Matondoni & Peace Villas Guest House (1) (follow the telephone wires)

Coast Cinema

2

▷ Balgis Guest House (3) ▷ Mwenye Alawi Mosque, Cemetery & Dhow Building

4

5

Red Phone Box

6

Utukuni Mosque (1823)

7   8

Jumaa Mosque (1511)

Skanda Wood Carvers

Swahili House Museum

9   10

The Whetstone   M K O M A N I

11

Lamu Community Hall

Al Hussein Speedboat Office

Archway

Site of Yumbe

13

Cat's Clinic

14

15

Dept. of Adult Education

Lamu Tour Guides Association

Tomb of Mwana Hadie Famau

Al Hussein Music Store

Lamu Craft

Nuru Mosque (1946)

Bohora Mosque

Lamu Silversmith

17

18

Faiz Newsagents

Donkey Sanctuary

HARAMBEE AVE

A

20

21 & Kenya Airways

25

B

Museum

Prestige Air

Town Jetty

Kenya Commercial Bank

Catholic Church

ACCOMMODATION

Alipenda	2
Amu House	17
Bahari Hotel	11
Balgis Guest House	3
Bathawabu Hotel	30
Bush Guest House	25
Castle Lodge	22
Casuarina Rest House	21
Dodo Lodge 1	26
Dodo Lodge 2	23
Hal-Udy Guest House	9
Hapa Hapa Guest House	28
Jannat House	5
Kilimanjaro Guest House	14
Kishuna Guest House	4
Lamu Guest House	18
Lamu Archipelago Villas	33
Lamu Palace Hotel	32
Lulu House	12
Mlangilangi	19
New Sabrina	31
New Lamu Palace Wing	27
New Mahrus Hotel	24
Peace Villas Guest House	1
Petley's Inn	20
Pole Pole Guest House	8
Pool House	7
Starehe	6
Stone House Hotel	13
Sunsail Hotel	29
Sunshine Guest House	15
Yumbe House	10
Yumbe Villa	16

RESTAURANTS & BARS

Bosnian Café	K
Bush Gardens	B
Coconut Juice Garden	H
Halwa Shop	D
Hapa Hapa	C
Kenya Cold Drinks	A
Labanda	J
New Star	E
Olympic	L
Seafront Café	I
Tamarind Juice Garden	M
Whispers At Baraka	F
Zam Zam Hoteli	G

WATER IN LAMU

Before you settle in, try to ascertain the quality of the lodging's **water supply**. You'll soon appreciate the critical problem here: a handful of lodgings seem to have overcome it and advertise 24-hour water as a feature. Lamu is one place where it's quite common to catch hepatitis – an unpleasant and lasting souvenir usually associated with drinking infected water. You should check where the water comes from. If the house or lodging has a long-drop toilet and an open drinking-water cistern in the same bathroom, move on. It only takes one cockroach falling in the water to contaminate it.

---

have phones. Out of season, you may find some places closed. There are no fixed **room prices** in Lamu: it all depends on the season (you can pay up to three times as much in some lodgings in the high-season months as in April or May, the cheapest period), as well as your bargaining skills. In all but a handful of places, the first price you'll be quoted is invariably inflated and needs practised haggling skills to bring down to a reasonable level. And another trend in recent years has been the "gentrification" of a number of erstwhile hippie hangouts – with attendant price increases that outstrip those in the rest of the country. If you like the place, aim to agree a rate for the duration of your stay and pay daily. You may find, at peak times, that some lodge owners insist their prices are fixed – simply a rather unfair bargaining position when rooms are scarce. The price codes given refer to the standard price, without bartering, for a double in high season.

Budget guest houses

These are the lodgings where you really have the opportunity to hone your bargaining skills – there can be huge seasonal variations. How many people you are, how long you intend to stay and when you will actually pay are all useful chips and, unless the town is heaving with travellers, you shouldn't have any problem getting some kind of discount. Everyone who stays in Lamu has their **favourite lodging houses**, determined as much by the owners and staff as by the state of the rooms. The listings given below are fairly comprehensive and include personal favourites and establishments that travellers have regularly recommended. All abbreviations are explained on p.47. Note that "no touts" means you won't be guided here by a hustler – because the establishment in question does not pay commission.

Alipenda, no sign so ask (PO Box 115; ☎ 0121/33395 [c/o their neighbours]; no touts). Some distance from the town centre, but an exceptionally friendly family house, with a good kitchen and three huge guest rooms (all s/c with nets and fans). Room only ① low, ② high.

Balgis Guest House, the tall building next to *Alipenda* (PO Box 210; no phone). No sign except a "Save the Dugong" sticker on the door. Eleven s/c rooms (all with verandahs and ceiling fans) with some Swahili furniture, the best higher up at the front with the benefit of sea breeze. Rooftop restaurant. Has its own well. B&B ③.

Bush Guest House (PO Box 22; no phone). Eight rooms in a tall building accessed from an alley between Harambee Ave and the sea, only two of them s/c, but clean, secure and with nets and fans. Small kitchen and communal lounge overlooking the sea, and a roof where you can sunbathe. Starting price is over the odds, but can be bargained down to ① in low season. B&B ③ low, ③ high.

Castle Lodge (PO Box 10; no phone). Beside the fort, with eight simple rooms, the best two upstairs overlooking the market. Some have fans, all have nets, none are s/c. Cheap. ①.

Casuarina Rest House (PO Box 10; ☎ & fax 0121/33123; no touts). Over the old police station (now Kenya Airways), with a whole variety of rooms from very basic to quite comfortable, in an admirably dreamlike welter of staircases and floors (the best are the two at the front and the two on top). You can sleep on the roof if all the rooms are full. S/c and non-s/c, most with fans. Kitchen available. Excellent waterfront roof terrace. Bargain hard. Room only ② low, ③ high.

Dodo Lodge (PO Box 210; ☎0121/33324). One s/c room only, on the top floor of the owner's house, but very good value with a great view. The other *Dodo* house, nearby, has a number of rooms, is well run and has a good atmosphere. Both ① low, ② high.

Hapa Hapa Guest House (PO Box 213; no phone). Behind the popular eatery of the same name. Two big double rooms at the front and two less appealing singles (not s/c; Ksh300 per person) at the back. Solid walls, but only one room has a fan (and no ceilings) – rooms are open to the *makuti* roof, which keeps a breeze blowing. ②.

Kilimanjaro Guest House, next to the cat clinic (PO Box 17; ☎0121/33179). Darkly atmospheric staircase with heavy stone arches and coral rag walls, in part like a church. The six rooms themselves are unexceptional but perfectly acceptable, all clean and tidy and with nets. The best ones are under the roof, airy and with good views. Use of kitchen, but the "rooftop restaurant" is now just a verandah. Take your key with you to prevent petty pilfering. ②.

Kishuna Guest House, near *Jannat House*. In an inconvenient location, a modern three-storey building with a *makuti*-thatched roof terrace. Reasonable if unexciting. ① low, ② high.

Lamu Guest House (PO Box 240; ☎0121/33338). A well-maintained old house right in the heart of things, owned by the same Indian family for seven generations (175 children saw the world for the first time here, and it's also where Omar Sharif filmed *The Young Indiana Jones*). Not all its twelve rooms are s/c (another five are being converted into an apartment) and have little furniture, but the ceilings are high and there are nets and fans. Inevitably somewhat hot and stuffy given its location, but clean and good value. No kitchen. From ① low, ② high.

Lulu House (PO Box 142; ☎ & fax 0121/33539). A pleasant, if somewhat soulless, purpose-built lodging house, with ten rooms. Breakfast on the roof. S/c and non-s/c. ① low, ② high.

Mlangilangi (PO Box 260; ☎ & fax 0121/33285). A large old Swahili house, nothing fancy and could do with a fair bit of renovation (long promised, but nothing done as yet). There are two doubles (the best on top with views and a balcony), and an entire six-bed apartment for under Ksh2000. The doubles need heavy bargaining. B&B ②–④ low, ③–④ high.

New Sabrina (no phone). Very basic and unappealing B&L with shared bathrooms. Cheap. ①.

Peace Villa Guest House (PO Box 160; ☎0121/33020). A good ten- or fifteen-minute walk from the town centre, out in the sand and palm trees, this is the only place to camp in Lamu town – if you really want to (Ksh100). Most people use the dorms or double rooms (s/c, with fans), but management is slack, and there are reports of swindles regarding dhow trips. ①.

Pole Pole Guest House (PO Box 262; ☎0121/33242 or 32008). Getting a bit run-down, but still pleasant especially if you're used to B&Ls, with a bird's-eye view from the roof – the highest in Lamu. The helpful staff should let you use the kitchen. Nets and fans in most rooms, some not s/c. B&B ② low, ②–③ high.

Sunshine Guest House (PO Box 224; ☎0121/33087). A pleasant, slightly mouldering place with a good terrace and competitive rates. Use of kitchen (with cooker and fridge) is a bonus. Five of the ten rooms are s/c, all have fans and nets over the beds (try and get one without window screens). Bathrooms are a bit grubby, but it remains good value. ① low, ② high.

Talking Trees Village, halfway between Lamu and Shela along the main footpath, 100m from beach beside Lamu Ginners (run by Bush Gardens restaurant (see p.528); talk with them before going). A peaceful and beautiful site (putting aside the barbed-wire fence), but it's nonetheless difficult to see the attraction – a long trudge from either Lamu or Shela. Small *banda* and room in a house, and camping (Ksh200 per person). Food available, and use of kitchen. ①–②.

Lodgings and hotels

Some of these are gems and in most cases worth the extra outlay if you can afford it. Breakfast is usually included.

Amu House (PO Box 230; ☎ & fax 0121/33420). Restored, American-owned stone house with additional rooms on top, built in the same style. Extremely attractive and welcoming. Good value. ③.

Bahari Hotel (PO Box 298; ☎0121/33172, fax 33231). A big lodging on several floors paying token tribute to local styles, with coral rock cladding on the walls. Twenty basic but spacious s/c rooms, with amusing four-poster beds, nets and fans, some with fridges. Always a crowd of travellers. Haggle hard for a good deal. B&B ③ low, ③ high.

Hal-Udy Guest House (PO Box 25; ☎0121/33354). Hidden away at the back of town, a lovely and charming place with a friendly family feel. The six large rooms, accessed up a creaky wooden staircase, all s/c with nets and fans, contain lots of old furniture and four-poster beds. Roof terrace. Use of kitchen. Recommended. B&B ② low, ③ high.

Lamu Archipelago Villas (PO Box 339; ☎0121/33247, fax 33111). Rather unfriendly reception, and the s/c rooms aren't that great. The position, right on the waterfront, is a plus though. Don't take a back room. B&B ③ low, ④ high.

Lamu Palace Hotel (PO Box 421; ☎0121/33272, fax 33104). The biggest thing to hit Lamu's waterfront in years, a three-storey construction incorporating a restaurant terrace and bar. Has 23 s/c rooms, but only four face the sea (no balconies). No nets or fans: all rooms have AC. The seamless tourist-class style appeals to many, but puts off those looking for something more real; look elsewhere and you'll get a better deal for half the price. B&B upper end of ⑤.

New Lamu Palace Wing. Under the same management as *Lamu Palace Hotel*, and seemingly destined for the same prosaic treatment. At present, the eight rooms are a little run-down but pleasingly idiosyncratic, though the potentially great views from the front two rooms are spoilt by mosquito screens. All s/c with fans but no nets, and much cheaper than the hotel. Bed only ③, B&B ④.

New Mahrus Hotel (PO Box 25; ☎ & fax 0121/33001). Rambling old place in a good location, though not on the waterfront, and one of the least Lamu-esque hotels, though it does have its own creaking if run-down charm. Wide variety of rooms and rates. The top floor is "first-class" and nothing special (rooms 1 and 2, overlooking the fort, are the best), the second floor is "second-class" and just ordinary B&L standard, while "third-class" lack s/c. Its rooftop restaurant closed years ago. B&B ①–③.

Petley's Inn (PO Box 4; ☎ & fax 0121/33107). Under the same ownership as *Lamu Palace Hotel*. The eleven rooms have fans and nets (the best two face the sea), but only some are AC, and have been done up in "upmarket-rustic" style – not to everyone's taste. There's a small roof-level swimming pool. The rooftop bar is a lively evening hangout. Overpriced, but they take credit cards. B&B ⑤.

Stone House Hotel (PO Box 193; ☎0121/33544, fax 33149; reservations through Kisiwani Ltd, PO Box 70940 Nairobi; ☎ & fax 02/446384, *kisiwani@swiftkenya.com*). An overly modified eighteenth-century house with orange coral rag-rock stuck on most walls, the rooms furnished in a mixture of Swahili and up-country styles. The thirteen rooms (three not s/c) have phones, but none are as classy as the brochures suggest. Rooftop restaurant. B&B ④.

Sunsail Hotel (PO Box 400; no phone). Brand new conversion in the old stone "Mackenzie" trader's house on the waterfront. Modern intrusion has been kept to a minimum, keeping much of the building's charm. The eighteen rooms have high ceilings and smart tiled bathrooms, but only the two at the front have sea views. Italian food planned. Still not open on last checking, but should be more stylish and better value than either *Lamu Palace* or *Petley's*. B&B ③.

Yumbe House (PO Box 81; ☎ & fax 0121/33101). A lovely conversion, professionally managed, and a positive alternative to *Petley's* if you want some real comfort and style, with guaranteed 24-hour water. Every room has a fridge, but the top room is definitely the best. Singles are good value. *Yumbe Villa* is an annexe a few minutes' walk away. B&B ③ low, ④ high.

House rentals

The following are essentially **private houses**, occupied part of the year by their owners (often *wazungu* Lamu-philes) and for the rest of the year rented out in part or in whole. There's always a kitchen, usually a houseman (though for his services you'll pay an extra negotiated rate), and varying quantities and standards of furnishings. Another possibility is to ask around to find an **empty house** whose caretaker would be willing to let you stay – unofficially – for a reasonable fee. This can work out cheaper than any other arrangement, but bear in mind that the caretaker is sticking his neck out. Finding a private house can seem an impossibility at first, but persist in putting your requirements about and you shouldn't have to wait more than a few days.

Jannat House (PO Box 195; ☎0121/33414). Owned by a Swedish family, so available when they're not there: this is a hugely atmospheric place arranged around a jungly courtyard with much of its original decoration (stuccowork niches and furniture) still intact. All rooms have nets and fans. The better s/c rooms and a nine-bed dorm are upstairs, though the downstairs three- or five-bed suite (not s/c; rooms separated by drapes) is real *Arabian Nights* stuff, and at under Ksh1500, a bargain for families. Nice rooftop verandah with comfy chairs. Recommended. Bed only ②–③.

Pool House (PO Box 48; phone via the museum). An interesting creation and it does have a swimming pool. Less traditional, more an accretion of rooms and architectural ideas. Currently closed for yet more remodelling.

Starehe (PO Box 10; ☎0121/33123). A lovely house, German-owned, with a shady garden. The trouble is finding someone to let you in. ② low, ③ high.

Lamu town

Perhaps surprisingly for so laid-back a corner of Kenya, there's no shortage of things to do in Lamu. The **town** itself is unendingly fascinating to stroll through, with few monuments but hundreds of ancient houses, arresting street scenes and cool corners to sit and rest. And the **museum** outshines all others in Kenya bar the National Museum in Nairobi.

Initially confusing, Lamu is not the random clutter of houses and alleys it appears. Very few towns in sub-Saharan Africa have kept their original **town plan** so intact (Timbuctoo in West Africa is another) and Lamu's history is sufficiently documented, and its architecture well enough preserved, to give you a good idea of how the town developed. The main division is between the **waterfront** buildings and the town behind, separated by **Usita wa Mui**, now Harambee Avenue (actually a narrow alley for the most part). Until around 1830, this was the waterfront, but the pile of accumulated rubbish in the harbour had become large enough by the time the fort was finished to consider reclaiming it; gradually, those who could afford to, built on it. The **fort** lost its pre-eminent position and Lamu, from the sea, took on a different aspect, which included Indian styles such as arches, verandahs and shuttered windows.

Behind the waterfront, the **old town** retained a second division between **Mkomani** district, to the north of the fort, and **Langoni** to the south. These locations are important as they distinguish the town's long-established quarter (Mkomani) from the still-expanding district (Langoni) where, traditionally, newcomers have built their houses of mud and thatch rather than stone or modern materials. This north–south division is found in most Swahili towns and reflects the importance of Mecca, which is due north.

Lamu is divided further into over forty *mitaa* or "**wards**", corresponding to blocks. The names of these suggest a great deal about how the town once looked: they're all listed in *Lamu Town: A Guide* by James Allen (out of print; copies in Lamu Fort Library). *Kinooni* ward ("whetstone corner") boasts to this day a heavy block of stone on the corner for sharpening swords, reputedly imported from Oman. And *Utakuni* ward ("main market") still has a row of shops, even though most of this north side of town is now purely residential.

It is difficult to construct a guided tour of Lamu – serendipity comes to everyone here, and in any event, you're better off exploring in snatches, wandering around whenever you have a spare hour or two – but the following things are worth pursuing whenever you lack the energy for the beach.

Stone architecture

Lamu's **stone houses** are unique, perfect examples of architecture appropriate to its setting. The basic design is an open, topless box enclosing a large courtyard, around which are set inward-facing rooms on two or three floors. These rooms are thus long and narrow, their ceilings supported by close-set timbers or mangrove poles (*boriti*). Most had exquisite carved doors at one time, though in all but a few dozen homes these have been sold off to pay for upkeep. Many also had *zidaka*, plaster-work niches in the walls to give an illusion of extended space, which are now just as rare. Bathroom arrangements are ingenious, with fish kept in the large water storage cisterns to eat the mosquito larvae. On the top floor, a *makuti* roof shades one side. In parts of Lamu these old houses are built so close together you could step across the street from one roof to another.

The private space inside Lamu's houses is inseparable and barely distinguishable from the public space outside: the noises of the town – mosques, donkeys, cats (Lamu is a veritable cat's Calcutta) – percolate into the interiors, encouraged by the constant flow of air created by the narrow coolness of the dark streets and the heat which accumulates on upper surfaces exposed to the sun. To find out more on this, pick up a copy of Usam Ghaidan's book *Lamu: A Study in Conservation* at Lamu Museum giftshop, which has reams of architectural and technical information.

Lamu's museums
All museums daily 7.30am–6pm; Ksh200 adults, Ksh100 children.

In the least spoiled part of Lamu, the regional museum has restored an eighteenth-century house to an approximation of its original appearance – the **House Museum**. Unfortunately, the house is very small and the guided tour included in the entrance fee is extremely brief. Since the house consists only of a small courtyard, two sleeping galleries, two toilets and an upstairs kitchen and roof, this is very poor value. Indeed, there are plenty of private houses, and even a number of guest houses, with superior architectural interest. There's talk of a combined ticket for all Lamu's museums to encourage visits, though that wouldn't make the House Museum any more worthwhile. The old **German Post Office** of the short-lived "Witu-land Protectorate", for long a mouldering wreck, was spruced up with money from the German Embassy and reopened in December 1996 as a museum. Unfortunately, even an ardent philatelist would have difficulty in extracting much interest from its two rooms – just a few old posters, photocopies of German stamps, weighing scales and a sorting rack.

LAMU MUSEUM
The one place you should definitely count on devoting an hour or so to is **Lamu Museum**, built in 1891, which served as the residence of the British colonial governors before Independence. Of Kenya's regional museums, this is the one that best lives up to its name. There's no need to fill spare rooms here with game trophies and trivia; the region's history provides more than enough material.

As you enter, there's a large aerial photo of the town for a fascinating bird's-eye insight. Elsewhere, exhibitions of **Swahili culture** – architecture, boats and boat-building, domestic life and life cycle – are displayed. There are also rooms devoted to the non-Swahili peoples of the mainland: farmers like the **Pokomo**, **Orma** cattle herdsmen and **Boni** hunters. Two magnificent ceremonial **siwa horns**, one in ivory from Pate, the other from Lamu itself in brass, are the prize exhibits – probably the oldest surviving musical instruments in black Africa. The Pate *siwa*, slightly more ancient, dates from between 1690 and 1700. Wooden imitations are on sale all around town.

LAMU FORT ENVIRONMENT MUSEUM
The **fort**, which was begun in 1809 and completed in 1821, seems oddly stranded in its modern-day position, deprived of its role as defender of the waterfront. At least you need no longer worry about accidentally getting it in your camera viewfinder, as was the case until 1984, when it served as a prison. It is now a national monument and is open as a museum. The "temporary exhibition" first installed in 1993, however, is still there, unrefreshed. It's an enthusiastic display of information about the environment and evolution, incorporating local sea life in tanks, but it looks more like an elaborate school project than anything you would expect to find in a public building.

TRADITION AND MORALITY IN LAMU

A number of **old photographs** on display in the museum give the lie to pat pronouncements about "unchanging Lamu". The women's cover-all black **buibui**, for example, turns out to be a fashion innovation introduced comparatively recently from southern Arabia. It wasn't worn in Lamu much before the 1930s when, ironically, a degree of emancipation encouraged women of all classes to adopt the high-status styles of **purdah**. In earlier times, high-born women would appear in public entirely hidden inside a tent-like canopy called a *shiraa*, which had to be supported by slaves; the abolition of slavery at the beginning of this century marked the demise of this odd fashion.

Outsiders have tended to get the wrong end of the stick about Swahili seclusion. While women are undoubtedly heavily restricted in their public lives, in private they have considerable freedom. The notion of **romantic love** runs deep in Swahili culture. Love affairs, divorces and remarriage are the norm, and the *buibui* is perhaps as useful to women in disguising their liaisons as it is to their husbands in preventing them. Which gives a slightly different timbre to the attentions shown by Lamu men to unattached *wazungu* women. Frustration isn't always the reason: money usually is.

All this comes into focus a little when walking the backstreets. You may even bump into some of Lamu's **transvestite** community – cross-dressing men whose community is accepted and long-established and derives from Oman. In fact, the more you explore, the more you realize that the town's conventional image is like the walls of its houses – a severe facade concealing an unrestrained interior.

It's fun to walk round the ramparts of the fort, getting bird's-eye views of the town. Look out for the very interesting set of colour photos of archeological sites in the Lamu archipelago. The town's library is here, too; see "Listings" on p.534.

Mosques

When you start checking out some of Lamu's 23 **mosques**, you'll find that any tone of rigid conformity you might expect is lacking. Most are simple, spacious buildings, as much refuge/men's club as place of prayer. There's no special reason to enter them: their doors are always open and there's little to see. Male visitors, covered up and suitably humble, are normally allowed inside; women are generally excluded. Unfortunately the **Mwenye Alawi Mosque** at the north end of town, once Lamu's only exclusively female mosque, has been taken over by the men, leaving the women to pray at home.

The oldest-known mosque is the **Pwani Mosque**, by the fort, parts of which date back to the fourteenth century. At one time it would have been the place of worship on a Friday for the whole of Mkomani quarter. Lamu's present Friday mosque is the **Jumaa Mosque**, the big one in *Pangahari* ward ("sword-sharpening place").

The star of Lamu's mosques, as well as being one of the youngest, is the sumptuous **Riyadha Mosque** down in Langoni, well to the back of town. It was built at the beginning of the twentieth century and has brought about a radical shift in Lamu's style of Islam, and indeed in the status of Lamu in the Islamic world. It was founded by a descendant of the prophet, or sharif, called **Habib Swaleh**, who came from the Hadramaut (Yemen) to settle in Lamu in the mid-nineteenth century. (His house is close by the mosque, acknowledged with a plaque, but still a more or less empty wattle-and-daub structure, containing a caretaker's bed and a few old papers.) Habib Swaleh and his group introduced a new freedom to the five-times-daily prayers with singing, tambourines and spontaneous readings from the Koran. They attracted a large following, particularly from the slave and ex-slave community, but gradually from all social spheres, even the aristocratic families with long Lamu pedigrees. Some of the other mosques adopted the style but the Riyadha, apart from being Lamu's largest, is still the one most closely associated with this kind of inspirational worship. Non-Muslim men who visit while worship is in session are likely to be invited in and encouraged to sit cross-legged with the rest of the assembly. Any sense of stale ritual is far removed: the atmosphere is light, the music infectious, and more than one *mzungu* has converted to Islam here. The Riyadha is also famous as the spiritual home of Lamu's annual **Maulidi** celebration (see box opposite).

Next to the Riyadha is the big, square **Muslim Academy** – like the Riyadha itself, and so much else in Lamu, heavily under Saudi patronage. Both men and women are allowed to have a look around but there's very little to see. More interesting is the chance to talk to some of the foreign students.

Other sights

After the fort, the only other national monument in Lamu (though you may not believe it when you see it) is the fluted **pillar tomb** behind Riyadha Mosque. This may date from as far back as the fourteenth century, and the occasional visit by a tourist might persuade the families in the neighbourhood that it's worth preserving; it can only be a matter of time before it leans too far and collapses on a passing *mtoto*. In the middle of town by a betel plot is another tomb, that of **Mwana Hadie Famau**, a local woman of the fifteenth or sixteenth century. This has been walled up and lost the porcelain-embedded pillars which would have stood at each corner.

Up along the waterfront you won't miss the **donkey sanctuary**, founded in 1987. Lamu district has over 3000 donkeys and the International Donkey Protection Trust, a Devon-based charity, has put energy and resources into setting up and maintaining this rest home for old and lame beasts that would otherwise perish of exhaustion or end up in a stew. It's not a tourist attraction, but it does rely heavily on donations from visitors and the staff are welcoming (visits daily 9am–12.30pm). If you call in, don't forget to shut the gate behind you. In February 1999, thirty donkeys were "arrested for straying and loitering in the town", and were promptly locked up at the donkey cells.

On a similar theme, but much less agreeable to visit, is the **Lamu Cat Clinic** (Mon–Fri 8am–noon & 2–4pm), on the left up the side street from the donkey sanctuary. The island's cats, which number several tens of thousands, are thought to have originated in Egypt, and were then transported down the coast with early sailors. Some people say that they can talk (possibly if you're on *bhang*), but beware of deliberately insulting them, as many believe that they may be evil *majini* spirits, or else carry the souls of deceased ancestors come to spy on their descendants; the population were understandably suspicious when they found out that the clinic's main aim was to neuter stray cats (akin to castrating your ancestors, in a manner of speaking). However, as the centre's founder relates, one cat's just like another, and he's seen nothing strange, as yet. Unfortunately, the centre itself is in a sorry state: there's cat urine everywhere, the cages are small and their mewing inmates – some have evidently gone mad – are pitiful and underfed: not one for the kids.

Heading north out of town, through *Tundani* ward ("fruit-picking place") and *Weyoni* ward ("donkey racetrack"), you reach the **cemetery**, goal of many religious processions and an interesting short walk. Past suburbs, you come out by the slaughterhouse and rubbish dumps, populated by marabou storks. In the inlet behind them, several large **dhows** and smaller boats are moored. Many are rotting, but one or two are quite new, even unfitted. Tradition notwithstanding, Lamu, rather than Matondoni (see p.531), seems to be the island's main boat-building centre. If you have dreams of owning a dhow (they make great houseboats), a representative price for a forty-foot hull is £4000 ($6500). The price depends entirely on the time the *fundis* take to build it – two years isn't unusual.

MAULIDI IN LAMU

Lamu's annual **Maulidi**, a week-long celebration of Muhammad's birth, sees the entire town involved in processions and dances, and draws in pilgrims from all over East Africa and the Indian Ocean. For faithful participants, the Lamu Maulidi is so laden with *baraka* (blessings) that some say two trips to Lamu are worth one to Mecca in the eyes of God. If you can possibly arrange it, this occasion is the time to be in Lamu, but unless you make bookings, you'll need to arrive at least a week in advance to have any hope of getting a room. Starting dates for the next three years are roughly 27 June 1999, 16 June 2000 and 5 June 2001.

Eating

There are enough **restaurants** and passable *hotelis* in Lamu to enable you to eat out twice a day for a week before going back to your first port of call. And nowhere else in Kenya is there such a concentration of eating places with an overwhelmingly budget-traveller clientele. Unfortunately, the rock-bottom prices of only a few years ago are rising fast and some places are already expensive by Kenyan standards. It's still possible to eat fully for as little as Ksh50 for the basics, but you can easily pay twenty times as much in some of the waterfront eating houses. Again, prices really rocket in the peak seasons.

A fine balance has been achieved between what is demanded and what can be supplied: yoghurt, fruit salad, pancakes, muesli, milkshakes and puréed fruit juices have become Lamu specialities. Superb lobster and crab dishes, oysters, swordfish and delicious shark are also on many menus – it's a nice change to find a fishing town where you can actually eat seafood relatively cheaply. A number of ordinary **hotelis** serving the up-country staples – beans, curries, pilau, steak, chicken, chips, eggs, even *ugali* and *karanga* – crowd along Harambee Avenue, particularly down in Langoni. Meat is notoriously stringy: several of the tourist-oriented places receive regular supplies from Malindi by plane.

If you spend any time in Lamu, you'll probably run into someone offering you a "genuine" Swahili **dinner at home**: at its best, this is a great way of seeing how the majority of Lamu's inhabitants live, and the food can be delicious. On the other hand, it can also feel a little contrived, and the price demanded at the end (which, like everything in Lamu, depends mainly on your perceived ability to pay) might not necessarily be any cheaper than having eaten in a decent restaurant.

If you enjoy doing your own **cooking** (several lodgings have kitchens you can use) a whole new world starts to open up. Try, for example, cooking fish in coconut: any restaurant will show you how to grate out the flesh and strain off the cream from the coconut to use it as a basis for sauces, using a conical coconut basket. Tamarind is another good complement to fish. The rebuilt **produce market** in front of the fort – run for the most part by up-country women – has everything you'll need, with separate sections for meat, fish, and fruit and veg; for fresh fish or shellfish, get there very early. By 9am all the interesting ones have been sold. Check out also the "**crab and loster market**", little more than a pair of weighing scales over a ditch in an alley, south along the shore just in from the last building ("Hodi Hodi"). Lamu has wonderful **fruit** and is famous for its enormous, aromatic **mangoes**, but you should also try the unusually sweet and juicy **grapefruit**. While you're here, you might also find one of Lamu's traditional exports: **betel** is the green vine you see trailing out of all the empty plots in town. The sweet-hot tasting leaves are wrapped around other ingredients, including white lime and betel nut, which stains the teeth red, to make *pan*. Rather sweeter, the *halwa* shop is on Harambee Avenue in Langoni, and there's a good bakery facing the

---

DRINKING AND SMOKING

In the old days, when *Petley's* restricted its roof to guests, and casual drinkers in the downstairs bar were sneered at, they often used to "run out" of **beer**; people would buy it direct from the Kenya Breweries depot, or go to the police canteen. Nowadays, although you can always get a drink (bottles of rot-gut Safari "whisky", totally colourless, as well as expensive bottles of wine, appear out of nowhere if you spread the word), only *Petley's* (5pm–midnight daily) or the *Lamu Palace* (all day) have alcohol licences. At other places, you can sometimes order "ice-cold tea".

More common is **bhang** (marijuana), but be aware that *bhang* is illegal in Kenya, and if caught in possession, you risk up to eight years in jail (recently reduced from fifteen) and not a lot of sympathy from your embassy. There have been reports of beach boys working in tandem with the police.

---

right side of the fort. Lamu Big Shop grocers on Harambee Avenue just north of the fort has slightly odd opening hours (8.45am–12.45pm, 5–7.45pm & 8.45–11pm).

Lastly, try the tiny mutton kebabs (wrapped in a chapati) and cakes which are sold along Harambee Avenue at night, around the corner from the *Casuarina*: They cost next to nothing and are usually delicious.

Hotelis and cheap eating

Bathawabu Hotel, Harambee Ave, Langoni. Dead cheap, busy local *hoteli*.

Bosnian Café, Harambee Ave, Langoni. Cheap hole-in-the-wall *hoteli* for snacks and the cheapest juices in town.

Halwa shop, Harambee Ave, Langoni. Lamu's main outlet for the sticky confection, just Ksh120 per kilo; nameless and unidentified except for its blue door (there's a wooden plaque for Al-Hussein boat charters next to it), but once you've been you'll never forget the hot kitchen and the huge copper vat.

New Star, Harambee Ave, Langoni. Unchanged for two decades, in a large and tatty *makuti*-roofed shelter. One of the few restaurants catering even-handedly to travellers and locals, and one of the cheapest in town. Especially good for breakfast before an early-morning walk to the beach. Daily 5.30am–10.30pm.

Seafront Café, next to the Swahili Cultural Centre (open to midnight). A very cheap little *hoteli* and travellers' restaurant with good and bad days, offering coconut fish or beans, rice, pilau and *karanga*. Fill up for Ksh100.

Zam Zam Hoteli, Harambee Ave, Langoni. Cheap *hoteli* with rarely a *mzungu* to be seen.

Cafés and tourist restaurants

Bush Gardens, on the waterfront, competing for the same business as *Hapa Hapa* but more upmarket. A seafood and kebab place with a popular following and a charming proprietor, though food quality varies from very average to first-rate. Not as costly as you might expect. Worth patronizing for the garlic bread alone. Daily 7am–10pm.

Coconut Juice Garden, Harambee Ave. Best juices and shakes on Lamu; you can order any combination you want – orgasmic coconut and banana, wonderful passionfruit and pawpaw, and a pint of avocado with extra ice cream is lunch in itself. They also do solid food.

Hapa Hapa, on the waterfront. Popular and friendly, very central rendezvous – the food is generally good, occasionally excellent, and there are its famous pint jugs of freshly pressed juices and milkshakes (Ksh50). More down-to-earth than *Bush Gardens*, and a good place to while away the hours at any time of day.

Kenya Cold Drinks, Harambee Ave, town centre. Standard, unexciting meals and snacks (little seafood), and no marked prices so ask before you eat.

Labanda, at the southern end of the waterfront. Usually busy with a breezy first-floor terrace, but quite basic and very unpredictable: sometimes inspired (try the "Monster Crab" with rice for Ksh300), other times pretty dreadful for both food and service. Open daily till 10pm.

Lamu Palace Restaurant, at the southern end of the waterfront. This impressive restaurant (or rather the *makuti*-roofed part at the back) used to be the *Equator*, the town's fanciest establishment. It's still quite reliable and often does realistically priced all-you-can eat seafood buffets as well as the more expensive crab and lobster staples. However, it can feel rather uncomfortable spending all this money just yards away from the impoverished waterfront.

Olympic, at the southern end of the waterfront. Popular for juices and snacks.

Petley's Inn. The rooftop bar and restaurant does genuinely good food at prices that are not grossly inflated, but it's loud: if only they wouldn't play the same few tapes night after night.

Stone House Rooftop Restaurant. Upmarket eats, sometimes very good, but the "rooftop" doesn't have much of a view and it lacks the atmosphere of the waterfront places.

Tamarind Juice Garden, waterfront, Langoni. Good juices and shakes, a little pricier than most.

Whispers at Baraka, Harambee Ave, Langoni (☎0121/33355). Pretentious it may be (it comes with a *parfumerie*, "Baraka Gallery" gift shop and invitation-only "artistes' colony"), but it's not easy to resist real espresso and wonderful cakes and pastries, unless you're really counting the pennies. Expensive. Daily 9am–9pm, closed 2–4pm low season; closed May–June.

Around the island: beaches and beyond

The one place everyone goes on Lamu is, of course, the **beach**, which more than repays the slight effort of getting there. The walk is enlivened by the village of Shela, at the start of the beach 3km south of Lamu town, one of three villages on the island. Don't take any valuables if you walk here – there have been muggings in the past. Alternatively, you can go to the beach the easy way, by dhow ferry (Ksh100 from the airport; Ksh50 from Lamu; fares increase after 6pm; Ksh200 minimum for a motorboat). Fewer people see the **interior** of Lamu island itself, which is a pity, as it's a pretty, if rather inhospitable, reminder of how remarkable it is that a town exists here at all. Much of it is patched into *shambas* with the herds of cattle, coconut palms, mango and citrus trees that still provide the bulk of Lamu's wealth. The two villages you might head for are Matondoni and Kipungani.

   Dhow trips with a beach barbecue are the stock-in-trade of the waterfront hustlers, and as such hard to avoid even if you wanted to; always fun, they also give you the chance to see the ruins of Takwa on Manda island (see p.535).

Shela Beach

A usually deserted twelve-kilometre sickle of white sand, splashed by bath-warm sea and backed by empty **sand dunes**, Lamu's **beach** is the real thing; you half expect Robinson Crusoe to come striding out of the heat haze. Unprotected by a reef, the sea here has some motion to it for once: it is one of the few places on the coast where, at certain times of the year, you can body-surf (August is probably best). Beyond *Peponi Hotel*, it's also a beach where formerly, on your private square kilometre, you could sometimes dispense with a swimming costume. Not any more. There were two rapes a few years ago, muggings are no longer unheard of, and there is now a two-man Kenya Navy security post in the dunes. Women may also find that wanderers along the beach can be a nuisance. Stay in shouting distance of other sunbathers and preferably go to the beach in company.

   Beware of the **sun**, a more likely assailant. There's absolutely no cover and you'll find that the cooling breeze is too strong for erecting a sunshade. You'll need to take a drink or a bag of grapefruit and some skin protection. Coconut oil, sold in town, is used by some to avoid drying out, but you need a deep tan to begin with, otherwise it fries your skin. Ordinary sunscreen cream is available in town. Lastly, and perhaps obviously, bear in mind that if you walk for miles along the beach in the early morning, you'll have to do it back again in the heat of the day.

   Getting to the beach, you can either walk the pleasant shoreline from Lamu's harbour down to Shela village (40min at low tide; 60min at high tide, when you take the track that veers inland after the last of the dhows) and then head as far down the sands as you like, or you can take a motorboat or dhow to *Peponi* (Ksh50). The third option you might be tempted to try – striking out across the *shambas* behind town and heading direct for the middle of the beach, is actually a time-consuming and exhausting short cut that involves wading through deep sand. If you walk along the shore, on arrival at Shela you can collapse into the *Bahari Restaurant* for a drink or a bite to eat, or head straight for the cold beers at *Peponi*.

Shela

SHELA, once a thriving settlement, is now in limbo, midway between rural decline and upmarket tourist boom. Its people, who trace their ancestry back to Manda island and speak a dialect of Swahili quite distinct from Lamu town's, are gradually leaving the village, many of them going to Malindi; a number of fine old houses have been bought by foreigners and converted into ravishing holiday homes, decked in bougainvillea and empty most of the year (some can be rented; see below). While it's an utterly hedonistic place to lounge away a few days, you won't have the thrill of staying among the mosques and street life of Lamu town itself.

Shela's only sight is the strange, much-photographed **Friday mosque**, built in 1829, which stands out for its rocket-shaped minaret, unusual in East Africa. If you're suitably dressed and bare-footed, ask politely to go up to the top.

The gaggle of beach boys playing football at low tide, or loafing around the hotel terrace sizing up the latest speedboat tourist arrivals from Manda airstrip, are part of the limited **gay scene**. The atmosphere of an embryonic Key West is beginning to pervade Lamu, and *Peponi* ("Heaven"), its only international-class hotel, is the natural venue.

ACCOMMODATION

If you seriously want to spend all your time on the beach, **staying** in Shela seems the obvious solution, and there are several quite stylish possibilities, although, unlike Lamu town, there's nowhere in the really cheap price categories. Equally restrictive, there are virtually no **restaurants** aside from those in the hotels, though there are one or two samosa vendors on the beach and the odd seasonal beach café. Of these, *Treasure Dune Café* is good: clean, cheap and fun, serving up tamarind juice, fruit salads and chapati.

HOTELS

Bahari Guest House, 100m north of *Peponi* (PO Box 59; ☎0121/33091). You pay for the location here, which, above the sea-lapped restaurant of the same name, is immaculate. The five rooms (three s/c), are simple but nicely done and just about give good value in low season. High season rates however are overpriced, so bargain hard. Kitchen. B&B ③ low, ⑤ high.

Island Hotel (PO Box 179 Lamu; ☎0121/33290, fax 33568; reservations through Kisiwani Ltd, PO Box 70940 Nairobi; ☎ & fax 02/446384, *kisiwani@swiftkenya.com*; closed May to mid-June). Fifteen spacious, attractively furnished rooms, and a restful atmosphere. Rustic luxury just about sums it up, and the penthouse is especially appealing – almost open-air, like sleeping on the roof but in privacy and comfort. Fans in all rooms and nets on frames. Good, reasonably priced rooftop restaurant – the *Barracuda* – candelit at night, with mild but tasty Swahili curries, grilled fish, and vegetarian dishes, plus juices and snacks all day, but no alcohol licence. Non-seasonal rates. B&B or HB ⑤, including boat transfer from airport.

Kijani House (PO Box 266; ☎0121/33235, fax 33237; closed May and June). Pretty and comfortable French-owned hotel, well-run but not as luxurious as you might imagine from their brochure – and their high prices. The superior rooms are excellent (1, 3, 4 and 5 are best), but the standard ones are overpriced. Small pool. Non-seasonal rates. B&B ⑥, FB ⑦–⑧.

Peponi Hotel (PO Box 24; ☎0121/33154, fax 33029, *peponi@africaonline.co.ke*; closed May and June). Shela's main beachfront focus, where everyone stops in for a cold drink (or a good single malt). It is fabulously situated, features windsurfing and a PADI diving school, and offers superb food and service. The best rooms have the high numbers, from 21 upwards, but the standard rooms (in the four undistinguished block-like structures across from the main building), are just that – if you can afford to stay, then pay the extra for rooms in the main house. Non-seasonal rates. B&B ⑦–⑧, FB ⑧–⑨.

Shela Pwani Guest House (PO Box 59; ☎0121/33540). Stylish, roomy house, co-owned with the *Bahari*, overlooking *Peponi*. The five rooms here (all s/c) offer various options, but all, by Shela standards, are a good deal, with their old furniture, antique stuccowork and soft light. The top rooms are brilliant. B&B ③ low, ④ high.

Shela Rest House (c/o *Casuarina Guest House* in Lamu). Up past *Island Hotel*, turn first right and then left (it's easier with someone to show the way). Eight rooms, only two s/c, all very different, including a funny one on a converted balcony with only curtains for privacy (and security). Even without haggling, these are the cheapest rooms in Shela. ③.

Shela White House, at the top of the alley leading past *Shela Pwani* (PO Box 305; ☎0121/33091, fax 33542). Five s/c rooms in a stand-alone three-storey house, of which two are sea-facing, and three are s/c. They can cook food to order, or you can use the kitchen. Roof terrace. B&B ③ low, ④ high.

HOUSE RENTAL

If you're looking to **rent a house**, there are a dozen or more private houses available from time to time, most of which will cost you a fortune unless you're in a big group and can share the cost. Ask for *Jasmin House* (good for kids as it has a large garden), *White Rock*, or *Nyumba ya Giovanna* (Giovanna's House, opposite *Shela Rest House*). The following are mostly renovated townhouses:

Beach House (reservations PO Box 39486 Nairobi; ☎02/442171, fax 445010; UK bookings through Scott Dunn World ☎0181/672 1234, fax 767 2026, *shela@africaonline.co.ke*). Right on the seafront, this purpose-built villa is the last major building before the beach proper. Sleeps ten and features an "infinity pool", a team of staff, and wonderful sea views. Just the one drawback: $7000 per week.

Bustani Square (Going Places, PO Box 14776 Nairobi; ☎02/442312–3, fax 446402, *going-places@swiftkenya.com*). At the north end of the village about 100m from the sea, in its own gardens. Sleeps four, terrace with views, services of a cook and houseman included. $1200 per week.

Kisimani House (reservations in Nairobi on ☎02/882409). Ostensibly the oldest house in Lamu, sleeps eight and has house staff. From $1400 per week.

Palm House (reservations PO Box 39486 Nairobi; ☎02/442171, fax 445010, *shela@africaonline.co.ke*). Set well back from the sea behind the mosque; sleeps ten and has house staff. The elegant modern interior owes little to Swahili style. From $2800 per week.

Shela House (reservations PO Box 39486 Nairobi; ☎02/442171, fax 445010, *shela@africaonline.co.ke*). Adjacent to *Palm House*, and pretty similar in having been so thoroughly renovated that it's lost much of its original charm. Sleeps ten, house staff. From $4200 per week.

Matondoni and Kipungani

MATONDONI is the most talked-about destination on Lamu apart from Shela and the beach. It's a fine walk if you start early, with a hot return made more bearable by the prospect of a cold drink at the end – the soft sand track isn't fun in blazing sunshine. A sane, enjoyable alternative is to go by **donkey**: fix up a beast through your guest house reception, or you can take one of the sand dhows on its trip from Lamu jetty to Matondoni, get some lunch and walk back along the line of the telephone wires. In truth, Matondoni itself is not wildly exciting and its fame as the district's principal dhow-building centre seems misplaced.

If you really want to look **around the whole island**, proceed from Matondoni to **KIPUNGANI**, one hour's walk from the end of the beach (4hr from Shela village). This is the halfway mark on the round-the-island walk; the whole trip takes eight or nine hours at least. It is useful to know the state of the tides for the stretch from Matondoni to Kipungani, as you can take a direct route through the mangroves at low tide (but don't get caught out!). Kipungani has an upmarket **hotel**, 1.5km before the

---

SWAHILI PROVERBS AND SAYINGS

The Swahili are renowned for the imagery, rhythm and complexity of their **proverbs**. *Kangas* always have some kind of adage printed on one side and these are often traditional Swahili saws. The first of these few – an admonishment to be patient – is the one you will most often hear.

Haraka, haraka: haina baraka – Haste, haste: there's no blessing in it.

Nyumba njema si mlango – A good house isn't (judged by) its door [ie, don't judge by appearances].

Mahaba ni haba, akili ni mali – Love counts for little, intelligence is wealth.

Faida yako ni hasara yangu – Your gain is my loss.

Haba na haba kujaza kibaba – Little by little fills the jug.

Kuku anakula sawa na mdomo wake – A chicken eats according to her beak [interpretations invited].

Mungu alitolandika, haliwezi kufutika – What God has written cannot be erased.

Heri shuka isiyo kitushi, kama shali njema ya mauwa – Better an honest loincloth than a fancy cloak (of shame).

Mke ni nguo, mgomba kupalilia – A wife means clothes (like) a banana plant means weeding.

---

village, in the shape of *Kipungani Bay Resort* (Lamu office under *Casuarina Guest House*: ☎ & fax 0121/33432; reservations through *Prestige Hotels*, p.49; closed after Easter to early July), a delightful "desert island" complex of fourteen simple mat-and-*makuti* thatch *bandas* up on the beach, with bar and restaurant decorated with driftwood and the products of beachcombings. It's expensive (FB ⑨), but with justification; the food is superb and the welcome, service, and sense of blissful isolation are everything you could ask for. The views over the sands and channel are exceptional, and there's a pool, too, though children risk getting thoroughly bored. Excursions, windsurfing and snorkelling trips are all on offer. You can get there direct from Lamu town by speedboat (30min). Check first with the office in Lamu if you want to go for lunch (Ksh1000).

Dhow trips

Where the hotel hustlers left off after you settled in, the dhow-ride men take up the challenge. You'll be persistently hassled until you agree to go on a trip and then, as if the word's gone out, you'll be left alone. The truth is that your face quickly becomes familiar to anyone whose livelihood depends upon *wazungu*.

In fact the **dhow trips** are usually a lot of fun and, all things considered, very good value. The simplicity of Swahili sailing is delightful, using a single lateen sail that can be set in virtually any position and never seems to obstruct the view. Sloping past the **mangroves**, with their primeval-looking tangle of roots now at eye level, hearing any number of squeaks and splashes from the small animals and birds that live among them, is quite a serene pleasure.

Basically, the **price** you pay will depend on where you want to go, for how long, and how much hard work it's going to be for the crew. Agree on the price beforehand (a full day with lunch for less than Ksh300 is unlikely, but out of season, you might get a couple of hours for Ksh100), then gather as large a group as is practicable and pay up afterwards. Try also to agree on who's supplying food and drink apart from any fish you might catch (funny, but the guests rarely catch fish; it's the crew who keep hauling them up). Whatever you pay, chances are it'll be much cheaper than any equivalent trip taken in Malindi or Watamu.

A couple of pertinent **practical points**: cameras of the more expensive kind are easily damaged on dhow trips; wrap them up well in a plastic bag. And take the clothes and drinks you'd need for a 24-hour spell in the Sahara – you'll burn up and dry out otherwise. Dhow crews think it's all very amusing.

DHOW DESTINATIONS
There are limitless possibilities for dhow trips, though only a short "menu" is usually offered. One variation which is not especially recommended is a dhow trip to Matondoni: these tend to end up being over-organized when you get there. The cheapest trip is a slow sail across Lamu harbour and up Takwa "river", fishing as you go, followed by a barbecue on the beach at **Manda island**, then back to town. This might commence with some squelching around in the mud under the mangroves, digging for huge bait-worms. If the trip is timed properly against the tides, you can include a visit to **Takwa ruins**, or, for rather more money, you can stay the night on the beach behind the ruins and come back the next day. This is usually done around full moon. Few sailors are prepared to venture out into the ocean, so Takwa has to be approached from the landward side up the creek, and this can only be done at high tide – and if misjudged can mean a long wait at Takwa before you can set off again.

A further variation has you sailing south down Lamu harbour, past the headland at Shela and out towards the ocean for some **snorkelling** over the reefs on the southwest corner of Manda around **Kinyika rock**. Snorkel and mask are normally provided, but bringing your own is obviously much better; note that the snorkelling here, though excellent, is difficult for beginners, as there are strong currents at all but neap tides, and the sudden swells can make keeping your position virtually impossible.

Moving on from Lamu

Most visitors come and leave by plane, not so much for convenience as for safety: the road down to Malindi, especially the first section to Minjila near Garsen, has always been prone to bandit attack, which resumed on buses in February 1999 after a year's lull.

Nonetheless, four **bus companies** currently run daily to Mombasa via Malindi and Kilifi: Faza Express, Mombasa Liners, Tawfiq and TSS. All leave between 7.30am and 8am: the ferries to Mokowe are timed to connect. They're supposed to travel in convoy but rarely do unless there's been a recent attack, so you run a marginally lesser risk of being shot by taking the first bus to leave (currently TSS or Faza). Buy tickets the day before or earlier to be sure of a seat: the booking offices are all at the south end of Harambee Avenue near *New Star Restaurant* (daily 8.30am–12.30pm, 2.30–4.30pm & 7–8.30pm). Prices vary according to competition and the state of security: in early 1999, TSS were cheapest (Ksh200 to Mombasa), while the more comfortable Mombasa Liners charged Ksh300. Prices can almost double when bandits are deemed a serious risk. Lastly, if you're headed for Garissa, you may have time to get off at Minjila and catch the Mombasa Liners bus to Hola (you'll probably miss the convoy to Garissa), but it would be easier spending a night in Malindi and changing there.

Playing it safe, Kenya Airways, under *Casuarina Guest House* (Mon–Fri 8am–12.15pm & 2–5pm, Sat morning only; ☎0121/32040) has four weekly **flights** to Nairobi (2hr 10min; Ksh5500) via Malindi (Mon, Thur & Sat 12.40pm, Wed 1.40pm; 25min; Ksh2500). Airkenya, on Harambee Avenue between Gallery Baraka and *Whispers* (daily 8am–12.30pm & 1.30–6pm; ☎0121/33445) has daily flights to Mombasa at 3.45pm (1hr 10min; $85) via Malindi ($65). They also fly daily to Kiwaiyu (2.50pm; $110 return). Prestige Air, under the casuarinas next to the church (☎0121/33055), may have spare seats on a charter (you won't pay more than Airkenya). Eagle Aviation flights are now operated by Kenya Airways. **Tickets** should be booked or reconfirmed as early as possible. Cancelling tickets you've already got from Mombasa, Malindi or Nairobi is a big pain, as refunds are usually only available from the issuing agent. The connecting boats to the airport on Manda cost Ksh70 from Lamu, Ksh100 from Shela.

Listings

Bank KCB is the only bank in Lamu (Mon–Fri 9am–3pm, Sat 9–11am), is reasonably efficient, and charges Ksh20 commission per travellers cheque, and one percent on cash (check your receipt before signing). You can also get cash advances on VISA cards, but the commission (five percent) is swingeing, and we've received reports of them charging up to fifteen percent.

Books (see also "Library") Try the museum for a small selection of new and souvenir books, and the stand next to *Hapa Hapa* for the best secondhand choice. There's a book exchange at the *Peponi Hotel* in Shela.

Cinemas The Zinj Theatre on Harambee Ave in Langoni screens American or Indian films (9pm nightly, plus women-only showings on Wed & Sun at 2.30pm; Ksh20). Coast Cinema shows videos.

Clothes and tailors A number of shops along Harambee Ave will run up clothes very cheaply in a day or so. The easiest way to end up with something that fits is to provide a model garment. Shumi's Design, on the waterfront in Langoni, is recommended. Langoni is the place to hunt out *kangas* and *kikois*.

Crafts and souvenirs Woodcarving shops are mostly found along Harambee Ave in Mkomani. Model dhows, chests, furniture and *siwa* horns are all attractive but bulky. Beautifully hand-carved safari chairs are also a hassle to carry but worth the effort for the prices. Some of the shops selling jewellery and trinkets have some genuinely old and interesting pieces. Look out for tiny lime caskets in silver, earlobe plugs in buffalo horn or silver, and old coins. A recommended silversmith is Lamu (Slim) Silversmith on Harambee Ave just up from the donkey sanctuary. They'll make jewellery for you; bargain hard. There are also expensive but unusual jewellery pieces at Gallery Baraka at the southern end of Harambee Ave (Mon–Sat 9am–1pm & 3.30–7.30pm). The Swahili Cultural Centre (closed Sat; 8am–1pm & 3–6pm) has a small selection of not terribly inspiring dresses and bags made by trainee girls working above the German Post Office, and a few other curios.

Dhows to Mombasa See "Travel Details" on p.544.

Discos There's usually a disco every Friday at the *Civil Servants' Club*, about 1km south of the GPO, entrance on the waterfront, and every Saturday at the *Police Canteen* (ask at the police station). The *Full Moon Party* (where you go to Manda Island for a beach barbecue) is "fun but used by dhow boat captains as an excuse to smoke pot and seduce white girls", says one visitor.

Email Lamu Internet Spider, at *New Mahrus Hotel*, is the only provider, and it shows: a stinging Ksh200 to send an email, an astronomical Ksh70 per minute (Ksh50 after 6pm) to surf the Net.

Fax Several guest houses now have fax machines. The going rate for a page to Europe or America is about Ksh500.

Film From Faiz newsagents on Harambee Ave.

Health Be more than ordinarily careful about the water you drink. Malaria can also be a problem: if you get a fever go straight to the hospital. For your teeth, you can buy toothbrush sticks (*msuake*) from the market.

Henna painting A number of women around town offer this attractive dye-painting for hands and feet. The best have portfolios of designs to choose from. Expect to pay around Ksh200 for both hands or both feet. If done properly, your hands or feet will be bound in cloth for twelve hours and the design should stay for up to six months. Try "Hodi Hodi" at the south end of the port by the lobster and crab market.

Hospital The new hospital (☎0121/33012) is one of the best in Kenya attracting patients from a huge part of northeastern Kenya, but treatment is often woefully inadequate. There are several private clinics – ask around.

Immigration In the District Commissioner's (DC's) offices on the waterfront. Go there before your pass expires – it shouldn't cost anything.

Library The town library is on the top floor of the fort (Mon–Fri 8.30am–12.30pm & 2–5.30pm, Sat 10–12pm; ☎0121/33201; five-day pass Ksh100). It's a surprisingly good collection, with lots on Lamu, as well as a sixteenth-century Koranic manuscript.

Music cassettes Al-Hussein Hand Craft, on Harambee Ave, has tapes of Taarab, traditional Wa-Bajuni and Mijikenda music.

Newspapers and magazines Tide tables, film and film processing too (Ksh600 to develop and print 36 exposures), all from Faiz, at the northern end of Harambee Ave. Newspapers get snapped up quickly in Lamu: try New Cold Drinks before 10am.

Photocopying Faiz newsagents on Harambee Ave, and the shop opposite, both have machines (Ksh5 for A4).

Police The days of hassle are long gone. Don't fail to stand still, however, if you're on the waterfront whenever the national flag is lowered, or you'll find yourself "in discussion" with them. Lamu is also a favourite place to trap *wazungu* who have failed to extend their visitor's permit (see "Immigration").

Post and telephone office Open Mon–Fri 8am–5pm, Sat 8–11.30am. Poste restante available. The international cardphone is handy – when they have phone cards for sale.

Safe deposit At the bank.

Speedboat charter Not exactly in keeping with the spirit of Lamu's lifestyle, it certainly gets you from A to B effectively, but drinks diesel fuel at an unbelievable rate, which makes it expensive. *Al Hussein*, which comfortably seats four, plus captain and "small captain", can be chartered at their office on Harambee Ave in Mkomani (PO Box 156; ☎0121/33509). Rates are currently around Ksh5000 for Pate, Ksh12,000 to Kiwaiyu, and Ksh8000 to Faza. In Shela, *Peponi Hotel* offers a similar service, at similar prices.

Spices and herbs There's a good little shop opposite Raskopu mosque in Langoni.

Swahili lessons Being suffused in Swahili culture, Lamu is a good place to learn but as yet nothing is organized. Get in touch with the Department of Adult Education on Harambee Ave, and see if they can help, or ask at Lamu Museum.

Travel agents Lamu Archipelago Tours at the hotel of the same name (PO Box 12; ☎0121/33368, fax 33500); Tawasal Tours (PO Box 248; ☎ & fax 0121/33533, *www.tawasal.com*), at *Milimani Guest House*, a ten-minute walk inland from the fort (ask), specializes in ecological and educational trips for college groups. As ever, prices depend on how much they think they can squeeze out of you.

Windsurfing At Peponi in Shela. About Ksh500 per hour, Ksh1500 for a half-day.

Manda island

Practically within shouting distance of Lamu town, **Manda** – with almost no fresh water – is almost uninhabited and, apart from being the site of the main airstrip on the islands, and the location of the old ruined town of **Takwa** (favourite destination of the dhow trip operators) is not much visited either. Significant archeologically for the ruins of Takwa and Manda, the north side of the island is also the location of the very exclusive *Blue Safari Club*, a more or less private establishment catering for heads of state and similar clients (it charges $1000 in high season). Altogether different is the *Manda Beach Club*, run by the same people as Chale Island (p.477), which has already managed to offend Shela's inhabitants with its loud disco music, floodlights at night, and by the purchase of a plot of land at Shela for the sole purpose of piping water over to Manda. The former hotel at Ras Kitau, facing Lamu island, is abandoned.

The island is crisscrossed with paths through the jungle, should you be taken by the urge to spend a day there. But go soon. Rumours have been flying around the archipelago that either an American naval facility, or a new seaport for northeast Kenya, or a gas terminal for the finds around Garissa, is going to be built on Manda. The hoteliers and farmers were given notice to leave a few years back and the dredgers started clearing the channels. For the moment it's all quietened down again, although the US dredger crews have returned and are hunkered down in Lamu. **Motorboats** frequently make the crossing from Lamu town to the Manda **airstrip jetty** – where they sell "duty-free mangoes" in the "departure lounge" – and there's nothing to stop you using them if you want to visit the island.

ELEPHANTS AHOY!

One of the strangest wildlife spectacles in Kenya – which you're most unlikely to see unless you organize an expedition especially and have plenty of time to wait – is the sight of **elephants swimming** between the mainland and Manda Island, with only their trunks and flapping ears above the water. Some forty to fifty members of the much larger mainland Dodora herd have a traditional migratory route which takes them just before the onset of the long rains (usually one day in March) across the narrow Mkanda channel to Manda island. The mangrove leaves amply supplies their food and salt requirements, but there's no water. Amazingly, the elephants have somehow learned that by rolling in the ground, they make troughs which then catch the rain. Despite the herd's proximity to Somalia and that country's rampant elephant poaching, their unusual migration perhaps explains how they continue to survive – even from the air, the elephants are almost impossible to see, thanks to the luxuriant cover of the mangroves – and on the ground, you could be within yards of one without seeing it, its presence signalled only by steaming dung.

Takwa ruins

Whether you make a flying visit to **Takwa** (daily 8am–6pm; Ksh200), a thirty-minute boat ride from Lamu, or sleep out on the beach behind it (there are some shelters), the site is well worth seeing. A flourishing town in the sixteenth and seventeenth centuries, it was deserted, as usual, for no one knows what reason, and is in many respects reminiscent of Gedi. As at other sites, toilets and bathrooms figure prominently in the architecture. In Islam, cleanliness is so close to godliness as to almost signify it – the Takwans must have been a devout community. The doors of all the houses face north towards Mecca, as does the main street with the **mosque** at the end of it. The mosque is interesting for the pillar at one end which suggests it was built on a tomb site (that of a founder of the town perhaps?), and for the simple lines of its *mihrab*, so different from the ornate curlicues of later designs. Another impressive **pillar tomb** stands alone, just outside the town walls, its date translating to about 1683. It has a very ancient significance and still occasionally attracts pilgrims from Shela (some of whom claim descent from Takwa), who come to pray for rain.

Takwa has been thoroughly cleared but, in order to preserve it for the future, hardly excavated at all. What has been found, however, suggests an industrious, healthy, well-balanced community. They lived in an easily defensible position with a wall all around the town, the ocean on one side behind the dunes and mangroves on the other. Despite this, they appear to have left in a panic and, as usual, there's ample room for conjecture about why. In this sense, most of Kenya's ruined towns are very different from those of the classical world, although influenced by them. Part of their great appeal lies in the open debate that still continues about who, precisely, their builders and citizens were, and why they so often left in such evident haste. And there's always the fascinating possibility that old Swahili manuscripts will turn up to explain it all.

Pate island

Only two hours by ferryboat from Lamu, totally unaffected by tourism and rarely visited, **Pate island** has some of the most impressive ruins anywhere on the coast and a clutch of old Swahili settlements which, at different times, have been as important as Lamu or more so. There are few places on the coast as memorable.

Pate is mostly low-lying and almost surrounded by mangrove swamps; no two maps of it ever agree (ours on p.514 shows only the permanent dry land, not the ever-changing mangrove forests that surround it in the shallow sea), so getting on and off the island requires deft awareness of the tides. This apparent remoteness coupled with a lack of information deters travellers but, in truth, Pate is not a difficult destination, and, in purely physical terms, it's an easier island to walk around than Lamu, with none of the exhausting soft sand.

A *matatu* **motorboat** (one of three plying the route) leaves daily except Friday, about one hour before high tide (which can be very early in the morning), from the municipal jetty at Lamu. On reaching the **Mkanda Channel**, you pass the ferry making the return trip; the Mkanda is navigable only at high tide, and even then it can be a close call when the boat is overloaded, as it usually is. The boat, sometimes accompanied by dolphins, then calls at a deserted spot called **Mtangawanda** (the dock for Pate town, which takes 2–3hr from Lamu), followed by **Faza** at the northern end of the island, which is up to four hours away from Lamu, finally docking at Kijinitini (Kisingitini), thirty minutes further on.

The obvious plan, having walked to Pate town from Mtangawanda dock (1hr, though you'll need directions after 45min for the minor side track; it gets slippery in the rains, so watch out), is to walk through **Siyu** to Faza, returning to Lamu by ferry from there. You could also do this in reverse, of course, but there is a major drawback in that the boat might not pick you up at Mtangawanda on its return if, as often happens, it's full. The walk itself can be done in a day if the tides force an early start, but you may well find yourself wanting to stay longer and breaking for at least a night in Siyu.

Two other possibilities include catching a dhow from Mtangawanda to Pate town instead of walking, though arriving at low tide means you'll have to wade through shal-

---

HISTORY OF PATE

According to its own **history**, the *Pate Chronicle*, the town was founded in the early years of Islam with the arrival of Arabian immigrants. This statelet is supposed to have lasted until the thirteenth century, when another group of dispossessed Arab rulers – the **Nabahani** – arrived to inject new blood into Pate. The story may have been embellished by time but archeological evidence does support the existence of a flourishing port on the present site of Pate as early as the ninth century; probably by the fifteenth century the town exerted a considerable influence on most of the quasi-autonomous settlements along the coast, including Lamu. As usual, the claims of the royal line to be of overseas extraction were by now more political than biological in nature.

The first **Portuguese** visitors were friendly, trading with the Pateans for the multi-coloured silk cloth for which the town had become famous, and they also introduced gunpowder, which enabled wells to be easily excavated, a fact which must have played a part in Pate's rising fortunes. During the sixteenth century, a number of Portuguese merchants settled and married in the town. But as Portugal tightened its grip and imposed taxes relations quickly deteriorated. There were repeated uprisings and reprisals until, by the mid-seventeenth century, the Portuguese had withdrawn to the security of Fort Jesus in Mombasa. Even today, though, several families in Pate are said to be *Wa-reno* (from the Portuguese *reino*: kingdom), meaning of Portuguese or part-Portuguese descent.

During the late seventeenth and eighteenth centuries, having thrown out the old rulers and avoided domination by new invaders like the Omani Arabs, Pate underwent a **cultural rebirth** and experienced a flood of creative activity similar to Lamu's. The two towns had a lively relationship, and were frequently in a state of war. At some time during the Portuguese period, Pate's harbour had started to silt up and the town began to use Lamu's, which must have caused great difficulties. In addition, Pate was ruled by a Nabahani king who considered Lamu part of his realm. The disastrous Battle of Shela of 1812 (see p.517) marked the end of Lamu's political allegiance to Pate and the end of Pate as a city-state.

low waters which are favoured by stingrays – or you can catch a connecting *mtaboti* ferry at Mtangawanda for Siyu (1hr).

Practicalities

The daily motorboat (except Fridays) leaves Lamu in time to catch a high tide in the Mkanda Channel about an hour later. The fare to Mtangawanda is around Ksh50. **Tide tables** could be useful here, and don't be dissuaded by hustlers who insist the service doesn't operate and offer their dhow instead. Keep asking – it sometimes seems there's a conspiracy of silence on this one. You can, of course, choose to take a dhow to Pate, and even up to Kiwaiyu. If you have the time, and some companions, it's a fine trip, for which you should allow a good four to five days in all. Alternatively, if you have less time but can afford to spend a lot more, you might look into taking a speedboat (see "Listings", p.535) which would enable you to reach Pate town direct, from the south, at high tide, in less than half an hour. But you'd have to wait until the next high tide to get out of Pate creek, unless the speedboat went round to Mtangawanda or Siyu, leaving you to walk. There are many possible permutations.

Accommodation on Pate island is rarely a problem but, with no proper lodgings, a **tent** is a useful back-up. Normally, you'll be invited to stay by someone almost as soon as you arrive in a village. It is wise to take **water** with you (five litres if possible) as Pate's supplies are unpredictable and it's often very briny. As for **food**, most islanders live on home-produced food and staples brought from Lamu and, although there are a few small shops on the island, it's a good idea to have some emergency provisions. These make useful gifts as well. **Mosquitoes** and flies (especially in May and June) are a serious menace on Pate. The shops sell mosquito coils but, during the day, you may be glad to have some repellent.

If you plan on spending several days on Pate, and you're interested in the archeology of the region, you should ask for **advice** and **contact names** from Lamu Museum and Lamu Fort, and don't forget to have a good look at the photo display at the latter.

Pate town

From the dock at Mtangawanda (which has the only **beach** in the vicinity – watch out for sharks), a narrow **footpath** leads to Pate through thick bush; ask for the *ndia ya Pate*, the "path to Pate". Once on the trail it's easy to follow. You cross a broad, tidal "desert", pockmarked with fiddler crab holes, then climb a slight rise to drop through thicker bush, and arrive after an hour on the edge of town.

Despite its small size, you would hardly describe **PATE** as a village. Yet, reduced to the status of sub-location, its only link with government an assistant chief, its sole provision a primary school, the town is today a mere shadow of its former self. But at least its inhabitants are said to remain the richest on the island, thanks to their cash crop, **tobacco**, possibly introduced by the Portuguese and certainly grown here longer than anywhere else on the coast.

There's no electricity, no alcohol and obviously no cars. After Lamu it comes as a series of surprises. The town plan is pretty much the same – a maze of narrow streets and high-walled houses – but here the streets are made of earth, and the houses are built of coral and dried mud, unplastered and somehow forbidding. The overall layout is confusing, with little slope, as in Lamu, to help direction. Pateans do, in fact, refer to the "upper" and "lower" parts of town – Kitokwe and Mitaaguu respectively. The lower part is down near the town dock, which is only briefly underwater at high tide. This part of town is said to be richer and more welcoming. There's a house which sometimes lets out rooms in this quarter: ask for the *nyumba ya Abala Hassan* or *nyumba ya Abdullah* (Abala Hassan's house, or Abdullah's house). There are no fixed prices (but it shouldn't be much over ①, including food), and Abdullah himself is very friendly and welcoming. The house is clean, has great views from the top rooms, and the food is filling. He can also arrange a guide for looking round the island.

If you arrive from Mtangawanda in the "upper" part of town – reputedly poorer and less friendly – you're likely to be struck immediately by the *Wa-pate* – the **people**, and notably the women. Brilliant, determined ladies, with short, bushy hair and rows of gold earrings, stare out directly, unhidden by *buibuis*. Some wear nineteenth-century American gold dollars or half-dollars, though these reminders of the great Yankee trading expeditions have become so valuable that many have been sold. Big **earlobe plugs** made of silver, gold or buffalo horn can also be seen, as well as nose-rings. If you speak any Swahili, you're likely to find the dialect here unrecognizable. *Wazungu* are rare, and, after Lamu's studied repose, Pate is arrestingly upfront in its dealings with foreigners.

Unless you can stay at one of the houses mentioned above, you may find yourself in the sticky position of bargaining with a family for **bed and board**, a predicament with not much room for manoeuvre. It's not unusual to be somewhat peremptorily offered a room, brought a dish of food and left to your own devices. At night, the town resounds with the chimes of dozens of big old **wall clocks**, further reminders of American trade here in the nineteenth century, which, juxtaposed with the muezzins' calls to prayer, sound thoroughly bizarre.

The Nabahani ruins

More layers are peeled off Pate's enigmatic exterior when you start to explore the ruins of the **Nabahani** town just outside the modern one. The acres of walls, roofless buildings, tombs, mosques and unidentifiable structures are fascinating, the more so perhaps because this isn't an "archeological site" in the commonly expected mould. Tobacco farmers work in the stony fields between the walls.

Boys will guide you around the ruins for a small payment, but don't expect anyone to take you at night: although it's very beautiful in a full moon, you'll have to go alone because the locals are afraid of the *djinn* and ghosts living there. Most impressive are the **Mosque with Two Mihrabs** (one for men and one for women?), a nearby house that still has a facing of beautiful *zidaka* (niches) on one wall, and the remains of a sizeable mansion. This last building, you'll be told, is a **Portuguese house**. Certainly, the worn-down stumps of bottle glass projecting from the top of one of its walls do lend it a curiously European flavour, and in the plaster on another wall are scratched two very obvious galleons. Its ceiling slots are square for timbers rather than round for *boriti*, as elsewhere in the ruins.

Shards of pottery and household objects lie in the rubble everywhere but many of the interiors of the buildings are so clogged with tangled roots and vegetation that getting in is almost impossible. It is worth persevering, however: the sense of personal discovery is exciting and immensely satisfying if you can ignore the mosquitoes that silently home in on bare skin when you walk through the weeds.

Many of the walls and buildings have already been demolished to obtain lime for tobacco cultivation. Without weighty financial backing, it's hard to see how the National Museums of Kenya (NMK) could ever preserve the remains of old Pate as well as compensate the farmers. Gradually, tragically, it is all returning to the soil. In the meantime, see it – and photograph it – while you still can.

Siyu

The **path from Pate to Siyu** is a slightly tricky eight kilometres. Having set off in the right direction, the first half-hour is fairly straightforward; if in doubt, bear right. You come to a crossroads (easily missed unless you look backwards) and turn right. This narrow red dirt path soon broadens into a track known as the *barabara ya gari* (the "motor highway" – there was once a car); it takes you to a normally dry tidal inlet where you veer left a little before continuing straight on through thick bush for another hour to reach Siyu.

Wherever the bush on either side is high enough you may come across gigantic **spider's webs** strung across the path. The matching spiders are brightly coloured, non-hairy, and merely waiting for insects, but they are nevertheless intimidating. Fortunately they have the sense to build their webs well out of the way.

Siyu town

SIYU is even less well-documented than Pate. Still less accessible by sea, the town was a flourishing and unsuspected centre of Islamic scholarship from the seventeenth to the nineteenth century and apparently something of a **sanctuary** for Muslim intellectuals and craftsmen. While Lamu, Pate and other trading towns were engaged in political rivalry and physical skirmishing, Siyu never had its heart in commerce or maritime activities, and never attracted much Portuguese attention. Instead, there was enormous devotion to **Koran-copying, book-making, text illumination**, and cottage industries like the **woodcarving** and **leatherwork** for which it's still famous locally. Siyu **sandals** are said to be absolutely the best, though plastic flip-flops have forced almost all the makers out of business. Siyu **carved doors** are among the most beautiful of all Swahili doors, with distinctive guilloche patterns and inlays of ground shell.

The sources of wealth and stability for Siyu's florescence are a little mysterious, but the town's agricultural base obviously supported it well and it was probably the largest settlement on the island in the early nineteenth century, with up to 30,000 inhabitants. In 1873, the British vice consul in Zanzibar could still describe it as "the pulse of the whole district".

These days you wouldn't know it. Less than 4000 people live here, and signs of the old brilliance are hard to find. Siyu lost its independence and presumably much of its artistic flair when the sultan of Zanzibar's Omani troops first occupied the fort in 1847 – though it was twenty years before the Omanis were able to hold it for more than a brief spell. Built in the early nineteenth century (no one knows for sure by whom), **Siyu Fort** is the town's most striking building and indeed, in purely monumental terms, the most imposing building on the whole island. Substantially renovated, it is one of the few surviving traces of the glory days. It's freely accessible, though watch out for dangers like the well and the unstable walls. Around the outskirts of Siyu on the south side are a number of quite impressive **tombs**. The big domed tomb with porcelain niches dates from 1853.

Most of Siyu's houses today conform to the "open-box" plan typical of the Kenyan coast: yellowish mud with a ridged *makuti* roof, open at each end. These houses stand, each on its own, with no real streets to connect them, so, although it's larger than Pate, Siyu feels far more like a village. The cultural isolation of these communities from each other, a separateness which continues to this day, is easily appreciated after arriving in Siyu from Pate. There are still few *buibuis* here but there's much less jewellery in evidence and the atmosphere is altogether less severe.

For **accommodation**, it helps if you've had a word with the museum people in Lamu.

Shanga ruins

You'll need the help of a qualified guide if you hope to visit the ruins of **SHANGA**, a large Swahili town at least 1000 years old, which would be almost impossible to find unaided. Expect to pay around a couple of hundred shillings for a guide. Shanga is on the south coast of the island, about an hour's walk from Siyu. You have to fight your way, literally, through the undergrowth when you arrive at the site. The most impressive sight is the white pillar tomb, eminently phallic, which you come to first. The very large Friday mosque nearby and a second mosque nearer the sea are only the most obvious of innumerable other remains in every direction.

In 1980, Shanga was largely cleared, and partly excavated, by a team from the NMK, with Cambridge University archeologists and Operation Drake participating. More recently, London University excavated the site. What they found is a walled site of thirteen acres, with five access gates and a cemetery outside the walls containing 340 stone tombs. There was even a sea wall. Inside the town, 130 houses were surveyed, together with what looks to have been a palace similar in some respects to the one at Gedi. Shanga is believed to have been occupied from the ninth to the fourteenth century and, like Gedi, no very convincing reasons have been found for why it should have been abandoned, nor why it was never mentioned by travellers and traders of the time.

Limited work has been done here to restore some of the plaster in a set of wall niches and on the fluted pillar tomb, but on the whole the clearing and excavating only seems to have encouraged the jungle. Getting from one ruin to the next isn't easy. Dangerously camouflaged **wells** and **snakes**, both common, add further to the Shanga experience. If you walk on down to the sea – and assuming you have a certain capacity for hardship in paradise – there's said to be a beautiful **beach** and some ideal camping spots.

Faza

Siyu to **FAZA** is a shorter walk than from Pate to Siyu and more interesting, through waist-high grass, fertile *shambas* and sections of bush. It takes about two hours, but you'll need guidance, at least as far as the airstrip inherited from a 1980s oil-prospecting venture. From there it's straightforward. An hour or so out of Siyu, you reach the first *shambas*. There are usually people on the path; if you catch up with someone from behind, announce your presence before trying to pass. Strangers are rare and you could give someone – especially an old person – quite a fright.

On a coast of islands, it's not surprising that Faza itself is almost an island, surrounded by tidal flats and mangroves. A secondary school, health centre, police station (with nothing to do) and even a post office and telephone exchange have made Faza the most important settlement on Pate island. There's even a Land Rover ambulance donated by Saudi Arabia, the only vehicle on the island. Every few years a lodging house opens, but the lack of visitors forces them to close sooner or later. There's a very unprepossessing council guest house which is available in theory. **Private accommodation**, though, is easy to find. Fishing is the commonest occupation, with much of the catch going to a cold room at Kisingitini, from where it's shipped to Mombasa. Faza suffered a serious fire in 1990, which razed many houses to the ground and caused devastation. Today, you would hardly know.

As a contemporary Kenyan rural centre, Faza makes an interesting place to walk around and you're almost certain to have plenty of time to fill before the boat leaves. One part of the village is devoted exclusively to cattle stalls, but goats run everywhere, ruining the efforts of the primary school headmaster to prevent soil erosion on the badly rutted and sloping football field. A fine evening stroll takes you across the mud on a new concrete causeway to the thickets on the "mainland", where the island's expanding secondary school is located. From Faza you could, if you wanted, walk on to the **other villages** on the island, all fairly modern and bunched together within forty minutes of Faza: Kisingitini, Bajumwali, Tundwa (Chundwa), and the closest, Nyambogi.

Faza's history and archeology

Archeologically Faza has less to offer than its neighbours. It was one of the most defiant Swahili towns over any attempts to usurp its independence; it was razed by the Pate army after a dispute over water rights in the fifteenth century, and again by the Portuguese in 1586 after collaborating with the Turkish fleet of Amir Ali Bey. On this occasion the entire population was massacred and the head of Faza's king was taken to Goa in a barrel of salt to be paraded triumphantly in the streets. Faza's unfortunate history may partly account for its relative lack of ruins, but one success is commemorated in the **tomb** of Seyyid Hamed bin Ahmed al-Busaidy (also known as Amir Hamad), commander-in-chief of the sultan of Zanzibar's forces, who met his death in 1844 under a hail of arrows. He was on an expedition against Siyu and Pate, and retreating to the relative safety of Faza when he was ambushed by a party of Siyu bowmen. His grave (*kaburi*), with a long epitaph, lies just outside Faza.

There are several ruined mosques around Faza, including the very crumbled Kunjanja Mosque. The ruins of the eighteenth-century **Mbwarashally Mosque** (also known as the Shala Fatani Mosque) merit a visit, however. Now theoretically protected by the National Museums of Kenya, the mosque – barring its *mihrab* – is just a pile of rubble; the *mihrab*, however, turns out to incorporate exquisite and unusual heart motifs, including the *shahada* (the Islamic creed) inscribed within an inverted heart shape.

Kiwaiyu

From Faza you're within striking distance of the desert island retreat of **Kiwaiyu**, about an hour by *mtaboti*, if you can find one. It is likely, however, that a group dhow charter in Lamu would be a cheaper way to visit Kiwaiyu. For Ksh2000–3000 a day, you can charter a small dhow for four or five days, including breakfast and dinner, snorkelling and fishing gear, and plenty of fresh water. Split this price among five or six people and it becomes very cheap. The best advice is to form an enthusiastic group around the lodgings in Lamu, then start direct negotiations, as soon as possible, with whoever is going to be running the show. Too often, arrangements are made with dhow hustlers that owners and crew can't or won't honour.

You can expect to spend 24 to 36 hours on the journey in each direction, depending on wind, tides and the skill of the crew – though with the wind behind you it's possible to get up to Kiwaiyu in under eight hours. The snorkelling around the **Kiunga Marine National Reserve** is nice enough, though not as consistently good as Malindi/Watamu, but the experience of sailing, the nights under the stars, and the acquaintance of the Swahili crew are altogether highly recommended.

On Kiwaiyu, **budget travellers** stay at the reasonable *Kasim's* camping and *banda* site, near the beach on the inshore coast of the island just a few hundred metres north of **Kiwaiyu village**. *Kasim's* consists of several palm-mat *bandas*, plus a couple of unusual tree houses (②; camping Ksh150). Most people just drag one of the cane beds down onto the beach and sleep under the stars. The village has limited provisions in a couple of shops, but most people eat what is prepared each day and served in the little "dining room".

Five minutes south of *Kasim's* is the village, a quiet, rural place but friendly enough. A further ten minutes south, you come to the "Italian cold store" – a stalled shellfish export project with attached accommodation, which looks like a long-term investment that's being ignored. Ten minutes' walk further still, you reach a house on the high southern tip of the island. This is a fishing camp (the plane you may have seen parked near the village belongs to the owner) but it's strictly private and does not provide accommodation to walk-in visitors. From here, the superb, ocean-facing beach, with the reef close offshore, is just a scramble down the sandy hillside. There are one or two first-class **snorkelling** spots off this southern tip of the island, with huge coral heads and a multitude of fish. Ask for precise directions as it's possible to spend hours looking and still miss them. You'll need good footwear to survive the dead coral reef.

Luxury lodges

There are two **luxury lodges** at Kiwaiyu. The one on the island itself is *Munira Island Camp*, about 2km north of Kiwaiyu village, a group of *bandas* planted on the crest of the island to catch the breeze (bookings through *Peponi Hotel* in Shela, or PO Box 40088 Nairobi; ☎02/512543, fax 512213, *bigblue@africaonline.co.ke*; FB ⑨). "Mike's Bandas", as the establishment is also known, is very laid-back and civilized, and there's plentiful birdlife in the vicinity. It's a favourite with Anglo-Kenyans and those who find even *Peponi* too busy. Return transfers are Ksh12,000 by speedboat from *Peponi*, $80 by dhow, or free from *Kiwaiyu Safari Village*, the other lodge, on the mainland a little further north.

Kiwaiyu Safari Village (bookings in Nairobi on ☎02/503030, fax 503149; all-inclusive ⑨) is nestled on a prisitne, palm-shaded beach across the channel from the northern end of Kiwaiyu, within the gazetted Kiunga National Marine Reserve. The pristine combination of exclusive, palm- and grass-thatch cottages (all S/C) and excellent food and watersports makes for a romantic getaway at a very high price (from around $600/day for two).

Kenya's northeastern corner

There is nothing to keep you from visiting the **far northeastern coastal region** by land if you're determined – nothing, that is, apart from roaming Somali guerillas and other desperados, armed to the teeth. Make careful enquiries before you set off: at the time of writing (mid-1999), firm advice to the contrary was being proffered by both locals, and by bandits in the form of a spate of attacks on local villages.

If things have quietened down, you could *matatu*-hop from the jetty at Mokowe to **Hindi** (the road there has been partially fenced-in against bandits, without much success), then leave the Malindi to Mombasa route and head for the Somalian border at **Dar es Salaam/Shakani**. On the way, you pass the sweetly named **Mundane Hills**, but back on the coast things should improve. There are plenty of Swahili ruins, including the **walled city of Ishakani**, partly cleared by the National Museums of Kenya, and a reportedly pretty coastal road leading back south to the headland opposite Kiwaiyu. In the dry season it's certainly worth slogging up here with a Suzuki. If you go, let us know.

travel details

More detailed information on various transport companies, prices and schedules are included in the "Moving on" sections throughout this chapter.

BUSES

Buses operate in both directions with the same frequency.

Mombasa to: Dar es Salaam (14–16hr), via Tanga (7hr); Garissa via Kilifi, Malindi, Garsen and Hola (2–3 daily; 8–10hr); Lamu via Kilifi and Malindi (5 daily; 7–8hr); Kampala (daily via Nairobi; 24hr); Malindi via Kilifi (hourly; 90min); Nairobi and the west (frequent; 7–9hr).

MATATUS

Frequent services between various points on the **main coast road** (Malindi–Vanga). Less frequent services from Mombasa to Kwale. Limited services north of Malindi.

TRAINS

For booking details, see "Moving on from Mombasa" (p.437)

Mombasa to: Nairobi (daily at 7pm; 13hr 30min).

HITCHING

Mombasa to: Lamu (difficult and not worthwhile); Malindi and Likoni to Diani Beach (straightforward enough); Nairobi (take a bus to Mazeras and hitch from there).

FLIGHTS

As well as the scheduled **flights** listed below, you can get spare seats on chartered aircraft operated by Eagle Aviation and Prestige Air Services. Fares quoted (1999) are one-way, with returns usually costing double or fractionally less.

Malindi to: Lamu (Airkenya daily; 35min; $65/Eagle Aviation charters $65); Kiwaiyu (Airkenya daily; 6hr 10min including stop-over in Lamu; $120); Maasai Mara (Eagle Aviation charters; 2–3hr; $145); Mombasa (Airkenya daily; 25min; Ksh1480); Nairobi (Kenya Airways 4 weekly; 1hr 15min; Ksh5385).

Mombasa to: Kilimanjaro (Eagle Aviation 3 weekly; 1hr 10min; $110); Kiwaiyu (Airkenya daily; 6hr 45min including stop-over in Lamu; $140); Lamu (Airkenya daily; 1hr 10min; $85); Maasai Mara (Eagle Aviation daily 8.30am; 2–3hr; $145); Malindi Airkenya (daily; 25min; Ksh1480); Nairobi (Jomo Kenyatta) (African Express Airways 2 daily; Ksh4200); Nairobi (Wilson Airport) (Airkenya 1–3 daily; 1hr 15min; Ksh5375/Kenya Airways 8 daily; Ksh5755); Zanzibar (Eagle Aviation 2 weekly; 40–60min; $50/Kenya Airways 5 weekly; $64).

Lamu to: Kiwaiyu (Airkenya daily; 10min; $55); Malindi (Airkenya daily; 35min; $65/Kenya Airways 4 weekly; Ksh2500); Mombasa (Airkenya daily; 1hr 10min; $85); Nairobi (Airkenya daily; 1hr 30min; $187/Kenya Airways 4 weekly; 2hr 10min; $130).

SEA TRAVEL

For **Indian Ocean voyages**, check the Mombasa Yacht Club or, more likely, Moorings at Mtwapa Creek or Swynford's Boatyard in Kilifi for crewing possibilities. There are no passenger services to Asia.

Dhows from Mombasa to Lamu or beyond are difficult if not impossible to find, though your best change is May–September when the gentle southeasterly Kuzi wind replaces the northeasterly Kas Kazi. Passengers are sometimes taken but there are no hard and fast rules for getting pas-

sage. The stumbling block – at least the first one – is that dhows have no passenger insurance, so any passage is effectively illegal and a proportion of the fee you negotiate will be needed for official "*chai*". **Dhows from Lamu to Mombasa** are relatively straightforward, once you've found an agreeable captain and assuming it's the right time of year (roughly once a week from December–March). There's a protocol: first you should go to the District Commissioner's secretary's office (first floor on the right, opposite the town jetty) for a form absolving the captain and the government of all responsibility in the case of mishap. Then take one copy to him, which he'll present to customs, on the first floor across the courtyard, when he files his crew and passenger manifest. They'll tell you it's a 36-hour trip to Mombasa but count on some doldrums and allow up to three or even four days. Bring fruit and anything else you anticipate needing to break the monotony of unvarying fish and ugali meals. You should get a passage for less than Ksh1000.

Bodo (small village near Shirazi) to: Pemba (Tanzania); frequent cargo dhow; 7hr; Ksh800; exit stamp needs to be arranged at Mombasa or Lungalunga before embarkation.

Mombasa to: Europe (difficult: ask around the ships' captains at Kilindini; Mediterranean Shipping Company's monthly service through the Suez canal to Livorno and the UK is available if you have the money; see p.437); Lamu (Catamaran ferry service *MV Sepideh* operated by Zanzibar Sea Ferries; many agents on the Kenya coast; around $100); Tanzania (Pemba, Zanzibar, Dar es Salaam; catamaran ferry service *MV Sepideh*; $50–60; also cargo vessels *MV Maendeleo* and *MV Mapinduzi*, which you can trace by asking at the port).

CHAPTER SEVEN

THE NORTH

There is one half of Kenya about which the other half knows nothing and seems to care even less.

Negley Farson, *Last Chance in Africa*

K enya is rarely thought of in terms of desert, but **the North** – over half the country in area – is exclusively arid land, burned out for more than ten months of the year. The old Northern Frontier District (still called NFD by many) remains one of the most exciting and adventurous parts of Africa for independent travel: a vast tract of territory, crisscrossed by ancient migration routes, and still tramped by the nomadic Samburu, Boran, Rendille, Gabbra, Turkana, and Somali herders.

The target for most travellers is the wonderful jade splash of **Lake Turkana**, very remote in feel and highly unpredictable in nature (when British sailors first ventured out on it, they reckoned it could turn "rougher than the North Sea"). To get there, you have the option of organized camping safaris, as well as *matatus* and lorries up from the hub of highlands Kenya. Elsewhere in the north, travelling can be harder going, usu-

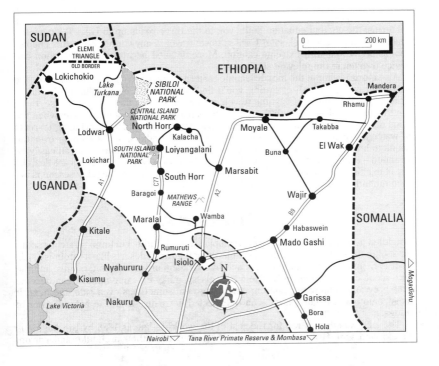

ally by gut-shaking lorries, with heat and dust constant, the water often briny and useless for washing. But the **desert towns** have their own rewards, not least in the bewilderment of arriving and finding places so little known yet so important to an enormous compass of countryside and population.

Because of the layout of the **roads** and **tracks** that radiate north from the central highlands, you'll need to make a decision about which "spokes" to cover: there are few east–west routes. Don't be over-ambitious. Bus and *matatu* services are patchy at best, whilst lorries and hitching can work out, but are exhausting. If you're driving, water, enough fuel and mechanical know-how should be your priorities since you'll need to be almost self-sufficient. Note however that **cattle-rustling**, **tribal feuding**, **armed banditry**, and **shootings** have become commonplace in many parts of the region, especially east of the Isiolo–Marsabit–Moyale road and north of Garsen, which has, effectively, been a no-go zone for tourists since the late 1980s: read the warning on p.575. Most people on business, and relief workers, now fly there and back, and cannot conceive why a tourist would even want to go there, let alone by land transport. In practical terms, the current situation limits you to the three roads up to Lake Turkana, the Mathews Range, and (less safe) Garissa town: travel to anywhere else in this chapter should be treated with extreme caution. More detailed background information and advice is given in the relevant sections.

A **seasonal** factor in the mostly Islamic eastern parts of the region is **Ramadan** (see p.61): during the month of fasting you'll find many *hotelis* closed during the day – which, with the efforts of daytime travel, can be hard to handle. And, of course, there are the annual **rains**. Though the landscape is parched for most of the year, when the rains do come (usually around May) they can have dramatic effect, bringing torrents of water along the ravines, tearing away fords and bridges, and sweeping over the plains to leave an ooze of mud and new shoots. In these conditions, you can easily be stranded – even along the paved road up to Lodwar. However, if your plans are flexible, it's an exciting time to explore. Driving your own vehicle during the rainy season is not recommended unless you've got 4WD and experience.

TURKANA

Straddled at its northern end by the Ethiopian border, **Lake Turkana** stretches south for 250km through Kenya's arid lands, bisecting the rocky deserts like a turquoise sickle. It is hemmed in by sandy wastes and by black-and-brown volcanic ranges, and the lake scene changes constantly. The water, glassy, milky blue one minute, can become slate-grey and choppy or a glaring emerald green, sometimes even jade, the next. It feels remote and hallucinatory – an unexpected departure from the natural order of things.

The lake was discovered for the rest of the world as late as 1888 by the Austrians **Teleki** and **von Hohnel**, who named it "Rudolf" after their archduke and patron.

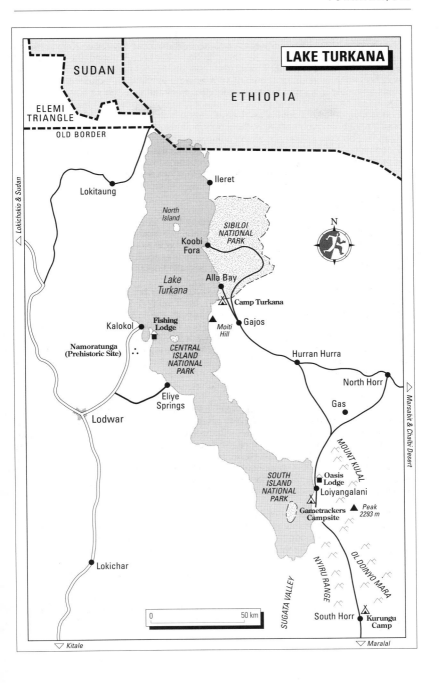

LAKE TURKANA

Later, it became eulogized as the "Jade Sea" in John Hillaby's book about his camel trek. The name "Turkana" only came into being during the wholesale Kenyanization of place names in the 1970s. By then, it had also been dubbed the "Cradle of Mankind", the site of revelatory fossil discoveries in the field of human evolution. And it was becoming something of a spiritual mecca for atavists, an excuse for a week of riotous assembly in a safari lorry or a dignified weekend in a Cessna and a lakeshore lodge.

But to depict Lake Turkana as "Kenya's latest touristic discovery" as one or two glossies would have you believe is, thankfully, a monstrous piece of hype: there are two lodges, one on each shore (the western one is currently closed), catering for perhaps a dozen people between them at any one time. Otherwise there are a handful of B&Ls, one or two windy campsites and that's it. As yet, the only **asphalt** – that certain sign of imminent change – is the crooked finger that reaches north from **Kitale** to **Lodwar** and on to **Kalokol** on the western shore.

Ecology and climate

Lake Turkana is the biggest permanent desert lake in the world, with a shoreline longer than the whole of Kenya's sea coast. Yet today it has been reduced to a mere sliver of its former expanse. Like some gigantic sump, with rivers flowing in but no outlet available, a staggering three metres of water depth **evaporates** from its surface each year (nearly a centimetre a day). As a result, it is alkaline, though not inimical to some aquatic life.

In common with other lakes with no outflow, the **water level** is subject to sometimes wild fluctuations: from the mid-1980s to 1997, the level receded steadily, leaving parts of the 1980s shoreline over 8km from the lake. But the 1997–98 El Niño rains, combined with completion of both the Turkwel Dam hydroelectric scheme in Kenya and River Omo irrigation projects in Ethiopia, have led to a six-metre rise in the lake level in the space of less than a year, and at the time of writing (mid-1997) it was still rising. The effect of this has been relief all round, as fish stocks have recovered from years of drought and former fishing villages rediscover their vocation. Yet less than 10,000 years ago the lake surface was 150m higher, and spread south as far as the now desolate Suguta Valley.

This mammoth inland sea fed the headwaters of the Nile, which accounts for the presence of enormous **Nile perch** (sometimes weighing over 100kg) and Africa's biggest population of **Nile crocodiles** – between 10,000 and 22,000 of them. Turkana is one of the few places where you can still see great stacks of them basking on sand banks. There is a profusion of **birdlife**, too, including European migrants seen most spectacularly on their way home between March and May. And **hippos**, widely hunted and starved from many of their former lakeshore haunts through lack of grazing, still manage to hang on in fairly large numbers, though you won't see many unless you go out of your way.

Climatically, Turkana is devastatingly hot and dry for ten months of the year, and unpleasantly muggy during the rains. It is notorious for its strong easterly **winds** which, while not incessant, puff and gust energetically most of the time and occasionally become demonic. The winds, more than hippos or crocodiles, are the cause of most accidental deaths of local people on the lake.

The **people** you are most likely to meet are **Turkana** (p.551) on the western and southern shores of the lake round to Loiyangalani, **Samburu** (p.565) south of Loiyangalani, **Elmolo** (p.572) to the north of Loiyangalani, and **Gabbra** (p.580) to the east. The Turkana and Samburu are pastoral people with great reverence for their cattle, the Gabbra herd camels, while the Elmolo are traditionally property-less hunters and fishers.

Getting there

There are **three road routes** to Turkana: one to the western shore from Kitale and two to the east shore from Maralal and Marsabit (the latter very remote). There is no route connecting the east and west shores: the volcanic **Suguta Valley** forms a blazing hot barrier.

The **western approach** from **Kitale to Lodwar** is the one used by most independent travellers without their own vehicles. There is no bus, but there are a number of crammed **matatus** to Lodwar every morning, and some in the afternoon.

On the east, the **Maralal–Loiyangalani route** is the one used by nearly all of the Turkana **camping safari** lorries (the main operators are Gametrackers and Safari Camp Services, see p.135). If you can afford $400–500 or so for a week-long trip, it has definite advantages: magnificent scenery and that sense of adventure that comes only from travel into a desert.

The third route, from **Isiolo to Loiyangalani** via **Marsabit** and **North Horr**, is feasible if you are prepared to wait around for days for lifts, first from Isiolo to Marsabit, and then on to North Horr. But it's not much used and you should be prepared to give up the idea after a day or two if nothing is going your way. The safari firm Gametrackers uses this route for their longer Turkana Bus trips via the Chalbi Desert, and may give you a lift (route details are given on p.585).

A last option is **flying**. As there are no scheduled flights, the price is variable but always expensive, costing around $1000 for hiring a plane, so obviously it works out much cheaper in a group. Ask around at Nairobi's Wilson airport, or try one of the companies listed on p.134. Although flying here destroys much of the sense of the lake's isolation, and it doesn't give enough time to explore, the flight itself – low down between the Aberdares and Mount Kenya – is sublime.

North to Lodwar and the western lakeshore

From Kitale, a number of **matatus** leave for Lodwar in the early morning (the first at around 6am), with the last stragglers leaving just after midday, taking about seven hours. Check the going rate with other passengers, as *wazungu* are frequently ripped off on this route. Alternatively you might try **hitching** – there are plenty of trucks and jeeps bound for the aid centre at Lokichokio, northwest of Lodwar near the Sudanese border, and stopping a vehicle is not too difficult, though you'll have to bargain hard for the price. It's worth taking some water for this trip: everyone who does it has a different story to tell of punctures, breakdowns and inexplicable delays.

The best part of the journey is the beginning – covered in Chapter Four – as you pass **Saiwa Swamp National Park** (p.314) then go through the green valleys of **Trans-Nzoia** and **West Pokot** towards **Kapenguria** (p.315), site of the trial of Kenyatta and five colleagues in 1953. Kapenguria, or rather the turn-off for it at Makutano, is reputedly a good place for lining up lifts, with a relief supply lorry passing through daily at around 3pm. The ride costs around Ksh300 for a place in the back, not the fastest way, but with great views. Beyond Makutano, the road scales a neck of the Cherangani Hills (p.267), then plunges headily along their northern slopes, following a tributary of the Turkwel River before slipping through the defiles of the **Marich Pass** (p.316) with its excellent *banda* and camp site, and down onto the scorching south Turkana plains.

The last **petrol station** and bank before Lodwar are at Makutano. From the thorny wilderness of the **Turkana plains** beyond, it's hard to extract much of scenic interest unless you're a desert aficionado, though the regular stops to pick up increasingly wild-looking passengers maintain gently heightening expectations about the far north you're heading into.

Once down on the plains, the tarmac begins to break up, but not so badly as to necessitate 4WD: just drive slowly to avoid destroying anything. There is a possible detour to the **Nasalot National Reserve** ($15 adults, $5 children/students; access by car only – Ksh200 extra – unless you arrange a walking escort with the rangers at the gate), which bounds the northern slopes of the mountains and the southern fringes of the thorny wilderness of the south Turkana plains. From the gate, 6km off the Lodwar road (signposted on the left), the winding paved route drops several hundred metres into the heat, with plunging precipices and spectacular views all round, to the **Turkwel Gorge** and **hydroelectric dam**.

As the reserve is mostly covered with thick bush, **spotting animals** isn't all that easy: the elephants here, though larger than their southern cousins, hide themselves pretty well, and your best chance of seeing them is on the paved road at dawn or dusk. You'd be unusually fortunate to see any of the reserve's lion and leopard. Otherwise, the diminutive dikdik antelopes are plentiful, if shy – you'll see them bounding into the bushes ahead of you, and there are also buffalo and warthogs. Camping is not allowed, but there are some extremely good value **bandas** by the dam (Ksh300 per three bedroom), where you can also go swimming.

Beyond Nasalot back on the main A1 Lodwar road, another detour to the right takes you to the **South Turkana National Reserve** (free entry, though there are plans to extract charges as for Nasalot), which lacks Nasalot's scenic grandeur, but is where the elephant migrate to between March and July.

Lodwar

For most Kenyans, mention of **LODWAR** conjures up remote and outlandish images of the badlands, an aberrant place where anything could befall you. And the Turkana District capital is, to put it mildly, a wild town: unformed, loud, and somehow incongruous in this searing wilderness. During the 1980s it became Kenya's desert boom town, the lake's fishing, the possibility of oil discoveries and the new road from Kitale all encouraging inward migration. This expansion has now all but fizzled out and the harsher realities of economics – too many people, too little money – have asserted themselves: children plead for "shillingi" wherever you go, and the wannabe "guides" and hustlers are more persistent than elsewhere.

While **Turkana people** predominate, **Luo** and **Luhya** have also arrived in search of opportunities. As the exhaustion of farming country in the south drives people further and further afield in the quest for land and work, Lodwar and the area around it is becoming increasingly attractive to pioneers and cowboys of all sorts. The distinct and lasting impression is of a town with a high population of men. Newspapers arrive with the first *matatu* each afternoon, eight hours after the rest of the country have received theirs. All around the shady trees in the centre of town, men sit reading them, discussing the daily stories, trying to reduce the **isolation** felt here. When news of the August 1982 "coup" came through, the police in Lodwar immediately freed all the prisoners and relaxed with beer for the rest of the day. It's that sort of town.

The Turkana have been able to go south more easily with the tarmac road, though elders who don't speak English or Swahili tend to get pushed around and taken advantage of. Coming north, there's a lot of overpriced fruit and vegetables from Kitale (shrivelled apples and oranges in the grocery stores) and all the little signs of affluence – radios, bicycles, stereos, factory furniture – that still draw in the people from the boondocks. And then there's the tourists. Hand-me-down trinkets are suddenly worth a day's wages – or a week's, with the right customer – and wrist knives are worth making again, even if they'll probably never be used in earnest (AK-47s are rather more effective). To be frank, Lodwar has become rather sad. Whispers about **oil** in the north have long since ceased; most of the NGOs pulled out as the famine receded in the late

THE TURKANA

Until very recently, **the Turkana**, the main people of the western shore of the lake, had very little contact with the outside world, or even with the Republic of Kenya. You'll still see older people in more remote parts wearing very few clothes or, in some cases, animal skins; and some of the head-loads carried by Turkana women seem little short of miraculous. Linguistically, the Turkana are related to the Maa-speaking Samburu and Maasai. Indeed, along the northwest shore of the lake, the people are probably an old mixture of Turkana and Samburu, although, like the Luo (also distantly related by language), the Turkana did not traditionally practise circumcision. They moved east from their old homeland around the present-day borders of Sudan and Uganda in the seventeenth century. The desolate region between the lake and the Ugandan border which they now occupy is barely habitable land, and their daily struggle for existence has profoundly influenced the shape of their society and, inevitably, helped create the funnel into modern Kenya which Lodwar, with its road, has become.

The Turkana are more individualistic than most Kenyan peoples and they show a disregard for the ties of clan and family that must have emerged through repeated famines and wars: some anthropologists have begun to suggest that loyalty to particular **cattle brands** is a more important indicator of identity than blood or lineage. Although essentially **pastoralists**, always on the move to the next spot of grazing, they do grow crops when they can get seed and when the rains are sufficient. Often the rains fail, notably during the prolonged drought of the early 1980s, which took a terrible toll of children. The situation has eased since then, but life is still very much a matter of day-to-day survival, aided here and there by hand-outs from the UN and other agencies. With characteristic pragmatism, the Turkana have scorned the taboo against fish so prevalent among herders, and **fishing** is a viable option that is increasingly popular.

Turkana **bellicosity** is infamous in Kenya (Turkana migrants to the towns of the south are frequently employed as *askaris*). Relations with their neighbours – especially the Merille to the north of the lake, the Samburu to the south, and the Pokot to the southwest – have often been openly aggressive. British forces were engaged in the gradual conquest of the Turkana – the usual killings, livestock raids and property destruction – and they succeeded, at some cost, in eventually disarming them of their guns in the 1920s. But the Merille, meanwhile, were obtaining arms from Abyssinia's imperial government, and they took savage advantage of the Turkana's defenceless position. When war was declared by Italian-held Abyssinia in 1940, the British rearmed the Turkana, who swiftly exacted their revenge on the Merille. They were later disarmed again. Now, it is the Turkana who are the victims once again: in the far north, heavily armed Toposa raiders from Sudan are thought to have killed almost ten thousand Turkana in recent years.

Violence is no longer in the air down at **Ferguson's Gulf** – though you might see older Turkana men with scars on their arms and chests to indicate who they've killed: females on the left upper arm and chest, males on the right. Turkana directness is unmistakable in all their dealings with *wazungu*. They are, for example, resolute and stubborn bargainers (even if you're not interested in buying), while offers of relatively large sums for photos often leave them stone cold – not necessarily from any mystical fear of the camera, but because of a shrewd estimation of what the market will stand, and hence, presumably, of their own reputation. Unlike the Maa-speaking warriors, the Turkana rarely pose for photos for a living, although the exceptions are increasing in number.

1980s (though the war in Sudan seems to be gradually drawing them in again), and the only dream left lies in tourists' pockets.

Practicalities

Lodwar is an incredibly hot, dusty town most of the year, but for a day or two you may find the rough, frontier atmosphere exhilarating, especially after the faintly parochial air of the highlands. There's a KCB **bank** (which changes travellers cheques, though you might have to wait for hours), a **post office** (Mon–Fri 8am–1pm & 3–5pm, Sat 9am–noon; international calls are theoretically possible) and a number of places to stay.

Most presentable of the town centre **lodgings** is the *Turkwel Lodge* (PO Box 14; ☎0393/20166 or Lodwar 900; bed only ①, B&B in cottages ②), a fairly clean place with the very definite luxury of fans in each room, nets in most, a good restaurant and a bar popular with expats, with a disco Fridays and Saturdays (free before 9pm). This is where officials and aid workers stay. A sign in the rooms says: "We hope your stay with us will be quite nice": it's certainly quite noisy, with Congolese tunes thumping out until the early hours. The *Nature Hotel* opposite (PO Box 123; ☎0393/21040 or 21252) should be a worthy competitor when it finally finishes its s/c *bandas*; it currently has a half-decent restaurant and a bar. Considerably cheaper and less salubrious are: *Africana Lodge* (PO Box 99; ☎0393/21254; ①), with some s/c rooms; *Air Fan Lodge* (PO Box 433; no phone; ①), non-s/c rooms only but all have fans (dependent on the dodgy electricity) and some nets in a basic, secure compound; *New Lodwar Tourist Hotel* (PO Box 266; ☎0393/21027; ①), which has some s/c rooms and the virtue of lacking a bar, so is quiet at night; and the *Salama* (①), which has working fans in all rooms, ice-cold sodas and beer, and fresh *miraa* at Ksh120 a kilo – the downside is its dirty, almost squalid, rooms. At rock-bottom prices are the *Beer Garden* (PO Box 19; ☎0393/21218; ①), a relaxed sort of place to collapse into after a heavy session, and the rooms behind the *New Chamunga B&L*'s lurid bar (perhaps the cheapest singles in the country at Ksh80).

There are two **lodgings outside town**: the best, far outshining any of the other offerings, is *Nawoitorong Guest House* (PO Box 192; ☎0393/21208, fax 21572, *edfrhp@imul.com*; rooms B&B ①; cottages B&B ③; camping Ksh100 per person), signposted 1km south over the Turkwel bridge, then 1.5km east. This is part of the Turkana Women's Conference Centre, a co-operative which rehabilitates and cares for widows, single mothers and drought victims; male tourists can stay as well as women. Starting with four women in 1984 who began baking bread, it has progressed in leaps and bounds, currently employing over 35 women in its guesthouse, bakery, and in firing bricks. It uses the proceeds to educate Turkana women about basic issues such as health and hygiene, unwanted pregnancies, HIV and leadership skills, and it also provides shelter for needy women and their children. Perched on a slight hill, and shaded by acacias, *Nawoitorong* has a lot to recommend it, especially if you're staying more than one night. Solar-powered lighting is supplemented by kerosene lamps, there are good showers, they still bake their own bread, and serve occasionally excellent food. The non-s/c rooms in the main compound are spotless and have great mosquito nets, but lack privacy and can be noisy; better but more expensive are the three stand-alone s/c cottages.

On the left along the track to *Nawoitorong* is the *Lodwar Club* (PO Box 123; ☎0393/21252; ③), with five s/c rooms with some nets and ceiling fans, in a modern but already mouldering block, and optional use of kitchen facilities. In the dusty garden, a crocodile snaps behind a worryingly flimsy fence. There's also an underused *nyama choma* bar. The **swimming pool** at the "Project" next door can be used by anyone for a Ksh80 fee.

There are a few reasonable *hotelis* in town for **food**. *Hotel Salama* is good all round; the *Africana* has good chapatis (and many tourists); *Mombasa Hotel* has hot, spicy food as well as omelettes and pasta (open 24hr); *New Safari Hotel* serves pilau, fried meat and *mboga*; the Somali-run *Rafiki Hotel* also has pilau and some pasta (open 24hr); *New Lodwar Tourist Hotel* has chicken and *kienyeji*; the *Beer Garden* has *nyama choma*; and *Delicious Café* is the only place to eat *irio*. All are fast and cheap. More upmarket are the *Nature Hotel* and *Turkwel Lodge*, which both do pepper steaks, various kinds of grilled meat and the usual rubbery chicken. **Drinking** can be done virtually anywhere, and the range of bottled beers available, often cold, beats that of most highlands towns: *Nature Hotel* and *Turkwel Lodge* are the most refined. For more characterful drinking try: the *Beer Garden* and *DM's Corner Bar* (both relaxed and mellow); the *New Chamunga B&L* (lurid seats and clientele); *Lodwar Rest House Bar* (*ndombolo* music till late); *Bahati Bar* (drink till you drop); and the *Salama*, where you can also chew *miraa* (the effect combined with beer is something like a tequila OD without the spins – allegedly).

Apart from just hanging around and taking in the scene, there's not a lot to do in Lodwar. If you have the time and some spare energy, you can **hike** up one of the hills behind the town (the guides from *Nawoitorong Guest House* are best). Lodwar's canopy of acacias makes it surprisingly invisible below, but the view stretches for miles. For **handicrafts**, you'll find good woven baskets on sale at *Nawoitorong*, as well as in the town's streets, where boys will also offer you Turkana trinkets. If you plan any walking, pick up a pair of invaluable **5000-mile shoes** (flip-flops made from old truck tyres), which are comfortable and virtually unbreakable – they're made by the old men outside *DM's Corner Bar*.

Note, when heading **back to Kitale** by *matatu*, you will have to book your seat – and almost certainly pay for it – the evening before. Most leave at midnight, connecting nicely with buses returning to Nairobi, though you may be lucky and find some during the day.

Kalokol

Ferguson's Gulf is the only easily accessible place to head for on the lakeshore, though accommodation is a problem if you don't have a tent as the expensive lodge here is more often closed than open. The village you want initially is called **KALOKOL** (formerly known as Lokwar Kangole). There are several *matatus* making the trip from Lodwar; if you're hitching, try the Kobil station or wait further up along the road.

There is little point in visiting Kalokol for its own sake. It has a surprising amount of hassle for such a small place (600 or so permanent inhabitants), and only one basic **lodging**: *Kalokol Tours Lodge & Hotel* (PO Box 3; ☎18 Kalokol; ①), which is overrun by

---

THE DANCING STONES OF NAMORATUNGA

During the one- to two-hour journey to Kalokol, look out for the **standing stones of Namoratunga**, 15km before Kalokol on the right, some fifty metres off the road. They're easy to miss, being only a small cluster of metre-high cylindrical stones similar to the sacks of foraging sold by the Turkana, with the curious oddity that the Turkana have the habit of balancing small rocks on top of the large stones. Like a miniature Stonehenge, the pillars are a spiritual focus and, usually in December, they're the scene of a major gathering of Turkana clans. The stones pre-date the arrival of the Turkana, but little is known about them, even by the Turkana (the name "namoratunga" is used by them to describe any standing stone site). One theory, that the stones were aligned with the positions of important stars in Eastern Cushitic astronomy and were therefore used to determine the dates of ritual ceremonies, appears to have been discounted. Some people call them "dancing stones", following a legend which had a small tribe of people dancing on the site. When strangers arrived (possibly the Turkana), the dancers pleaded with the visitors not to laugh at them, a plea which they ignored, with the result that the dancers were turned to stone. More plausible reasons for their existence might be the concentration of haematite and copper ore around the site, the smelting of which (for making weapons) may have acquired ritual significance in the past. Uphill from the stones you'll find several raised rock cairns covering ancient graves, some perfectly delineated with larger regular stones. It's fascinating, and all rather mysterious.

> ### A FISHY STORY
>
> In the late 1970s, **Kalokol** acquired a big Norwegian-aided fish-filleting and freezing plant and many Turkana came to the co-operative there looking for a livelihood. Altogether, as many as 20,000 homed in on the lake's fishing opportunities in the early 1980s. Many were persuaded to give up their herds, but thousands of animals were driven down to the lakeshore while their owners looked for work, bringing ecological disaster to the area around Kalokol and Lodwar. Firewood gathering and over-grazing were the main causes, coupled with the prolonged drought that afflicted much of sub-Saharan Africa at that time. The project was a failure almost from the beginning. The plant's electricity requirements could not possibly be met with the local supply; it ran the cold rooms for just two days. Then the trawler sank. And as these major setbacks were being contemplated, the diversion of water for irrigation of water from the Omo River in Ethiopia, and the construction of the Turkwel Dam in south Turkana, began to decrease the lake's supply, leaving the Norwegian jetty high and dry several kilometres from the shore. Compounded by plummeting fish stocks, the project was finally abandoned amidst bitter recriminations and accusations of corruption and mismanagement. The joke, if there is one – and a lesson to all NGOs – is that the Norwegians had only considered *freezing* the fish: as soon as the project was jettisoned, the locals moved in, broke the factory's windows, and embarked on the glaringly obvious solution that had eluded the Europeans – inside the shaded, breezy hulk of the factory, they simply laid out their fish to dry.

irritating wannabe guides. It does however have space to pitch a tent (Ksh50) and also offers **camel safaris** (the catch being that you have to buy the camel, only to resell it later at half the price). Unless you're a seasoned bargainer, you can forget their offers of boat trips, as the prices are ridiculously high – far better to enquire with the fishermen on the lakeshore proper, 4km to the east. As to **guides**, you will certainly be offered their services in Kalokol, if not already in Lodwar, but beware, they can be expensive, and stories circulate regarding theft.

While **food** supplies have improved a little with the opening of a few *dukas*, Kalokol doesn't have a lot in this line and it's not a bad idea to bring at least some fruit with you from Kitale or Lodwar. Water supplies, too, are erratic, and iodine or purifying tablets are essential (there was an outbreak of cholera in October 1998 which killed seventeen people). *Skyways Hotel* serves good meals and has the edge over *Kalokol Tours Lodge & Hotel*, whose menu ("big fish, medium fish, small fish, smaller fish. . . ") is mostly wishful thinking.

The village is especially good for buying **Turkana crafts** and souvenirs: wonderful (and far too big) baskets, sharp wrist knives and finger knives, rich-smelling, oiled head stools, ostrich shell necklaces, and a whole array of snuff and tobacco horns made of cowhorn (traditionally) or pieces of plastic piping. When you've had enough, transport of one sort or another usually leaves at midnight for Kitale, and a number of *matatus* leave throughout the day for Lodwar.

Ferguson's Gulf

To visit the lake, you might want to pay something to one of the children in the village as a guide, though it's easy to find your own way there (just follow the road east for 4km). Having been dry for much of a decade, the El Niño rains of 1997–98 once again filled **Ferguson's Gulf**: before the rains, the nearest lakeshore had been a wild 9km walk from Kalokol.

Simply being by the lake fills the time here, with the constantly mutating background of the western shore across the bay, as well as the closer prospect of Turkana fishermen, hundreds of species of birds, and the occasional glimpse of crocodile or hippo on the water surface. From a distance, the activity at the water's edge seems silent since the wind whips the sound away westwards, lending the whole scene a bizarre, dreamlike quality. Down on the shore you can talk with the children who follow you everywhere, and who often speak good English. If you make friends, you can be taken looking for snakes (be careful), to see *changaa* brewing (always by women) or, if you're lucky, to a dance. Ordinary teenagers' and children's dances happen several times a week, but are best when there's a full moon: the boys tie cans of stones to their ankles and pretend to ignore the girls' flirting.

Swimming is generally fine and pleasantly warm and while the crocodiles are often big, they seldom attack (there are few, in any case, near Ferguson's Gulf). They are not rated as man-eaters, since they haven't been widely hunted. This is apparently because their skins aren't up to standard due to the alkaline water. Hippos are certainly much more to be feared, as are the lake's peculiarities of climate. The tales surrounding the two human skulls that lay (and may still lie) in the sand below the lodge are varied, but they are probably the result of drowning accidents on the remote eastern coastline. One of them was certainly far from ancient. They're a very effective reminder of the precariousness of life here.

The lodge and Longech

It's about 6km through scrub and palm groves from Kalokol to the *Lake Turkana Fishing Lodge* (currently closed): after 4km, turn left at the (defunct) Italian fishing project sign and continue for another 2km. From the jetty at the end, you have to get a boat to the lodge. If, as seems likely, the lake waters begin once again to recede, the crossing should become fordable by foot (ignore the children screaming "Crocodile! Crocodile!" and trying to get you in their boats – unless you want a short boat trip and a new friend).

The lodge has been opening and closing sporadically for many years now, and has had several different owners: you're advised to check out the situation at the Kobil station in Lodwar, the owner of which is currently the lodge's proprietor. The lodge itself is perched at the end of a sandy spit, offering shade, shelter from the fan-heater wind and a beautiful view across the lake. It caters mostly to weekend visitors who arrive by air, and midweek it's invariably empty. Its **campsite** has moved down to the mainland by the defunct Italian fishing project (a rotten Ksh500 per person), though with the amount of hassle you can expect from local kids this isn't likely to appeal for very long in any case. Alternatively, people may give you bed space in **LONGECH**, the village that stretches a couple of kilometres down the former shoreline, for a small fee or for a trade of some of your belongings. Fresh or dried fish is usually available but the only other food is the lodge's expensive set menu.

When you're tired of wandering around Longech, being mobbed by toddlers, watching the fishermen paddling out on their waterlogged rafts, and the pied kingfishers hovering and plunging over the shallows, there are a few active things to do. If you're feeling rich and macho, you can rent **fishing** rods and the lodge's boat and, with luck, land several hundred pounds of Nile perch: by all accounts, though, the perch don't play properly and almost line up to be landed. Fishermen rate the tiger fish as more of a fighter. The lodge will cook your catch for you (or some of it) and you can add your mark to the fishermen's tales on the walls of the bar.

Central Island National Park

A trip to **Central Island National Park** is highly recommended. This is one of two island national parks in the lake (the other is the less accessible South Island). Central Island is a unique triple volcano poking gauntly out of the water; the island covers just five square kilometres, most of which is taken up by two crater lakes (a third has dried up) hidden behind its rocky shores. One of the lakes is the only known habitat of an ancient species of tilapia, a reminder of the time when Lake Turkana was connected to the Nile. The island is the nesting ground for big colonies of water birds but, like some African Galapagos, it really belongs to the reptiles. Crocodiles breed here in the largest concentration in Africa, and at the right time of year (usually April–May) you can witness the newly hatched croc-lets breaking out of the nests and sprinting with loud squeaks down to the crater lake where they'll pass their first season. The vegetation is scant, but some of the sheltered lees are overgrown with thick grass and bushes for a short period each year, and the nests are dug beneath this foliage.

Boat trips are expensive. When it was last open, boats from the lodge (90min–2hr each way) cost the better part of $120 for a nine-passenger vessel and $55 for a boat that took up to four only. Alternatively, *Kalokol Tours Lodge & Hotel* can arrange a trip, but expect to pay extra for "guiding fees" and transport from and back to Kalokol. Forget their astronomical starting price (Ksh10,000): you should aim to bargain down to around Ksh3000. The only other option is to walk south, down the lakeshore in front of Longech, and try to hire a fishing boat for the trip. It's worth knowing that the park game warden, who accompanies the lodge's boat trips, will normally want to intervene at this point and generally makes it impossible for you to make the trip privately – in fact the most recent reports suggest the villagers aren't interested. A national parks' entry fee of $15 each ($5 students/children) will also be demanded which, in view of the activities of some of the national parks staff in the area (croc hunting), leaves a bitter taste. If you find a boat, the best plan is to go immediately rather than make arrangements in advance. Do be sure, however, that it is thoroughly lake-worthy and that the crew know what they are doing: vicious squalls can blow up fast and it's at least 10km to the island. Taking your own compass might be a good idea.

Boats across the lake

Also worth enquiring about, both in Lodwar and Kalokol, is whether the Fisheries Commission boat to **Loiyangalani** on the eastern side of the lake has been reinstated. This used to leave at the end of each month to collect taxes and fees, taking upwards of eight hours and charging a small fortune for a lift. You may also be able to **rent a boat** with a helmsman at Ferguson's Gulf or Eliye Springs (see below) for the same trip, but unless you offer a more than substantial sum (something over Ksh10,000) the fishermen may not consider the risk as being worthwhile. Also just about accessible from here are the remote archaeological sites of **Koobi Fora** and **Sibiloi National Park** (see p.571), 48km due east across the lake, though be warned that unless you can be sure of the boatman waiting for you for the return leg, you will need to be entirely self-sufficient for several days, perhaps even for weeks, as there is only extremely infrequent private transport from there to Loiyangalani. Enquire at *Kalokol Tours Lodge & Hotel* for the boats (starting price Ksh15,000, which should be bargained hard), and check the state of the boat before you go. Alternatively, enquire about the National Museums' boat, which supposedly leaves once a month.

Eliye Springs

Eliye Springs, 66km south of Lodwar, used to be *the* place for travellers on the lakeshore and still attracts the occasional overland truck and self-sufficient 4WD weekenders. **Getting there** and back is the main problem. Failing a lift in Lodwar (where you might wait for days), you might **rent a vehicle** (4WD advisable) with driver at around Ksh1500 for the round trip. However, if you'll be staying overnight or longer at Eliye Springs, don't count on the vehicle coming back to pick you up. It's a long walk back.

Alternatively, you could **walk** from Ferguson's Gulf or Kalokol: just follow the coast for 55 or so sweltering kilometres, and take plenty of drinking water. There may be a

Dutch-run **campsite** about halfway, apparently with working fans in its *bandas*. There are crocodiles along the shore for much of the way, which makes a night walk ill-advised. Another possible route from Kalokol is a little shorter (45–50km); it cuts across the desert inland and this *is* really only feasible overnight, preferably by moonlight. A guide will cost around Ksh1200, and it's quite an adventure – bring plenty of water. The only other possibility is to **rent a boat** to or from Ferguson's Gulf for up to Ksh500 per hour; the boat seats four, and the trip takes four to six hours. If you're only going one-way, you may still have to pay for the return leg regardless.

Eliye Springs itself readily compensates for the hassles of the journey – a paradisal place with rustling doum palms watered by hot springs, with gorgeous views, and nothing to do except lounge about and swat flies. The *bandas* (③; camping Ksh200), although run-down, are adequate and have comfortable beds. There is also a pool fed by the springs (though swimming in the lake here is quite safe) and a bar; meals can be prepared if ordered in advance.

Onwards from Lodwar: Lokichokio

It's possible, but by no means easy, to explore the region of Turkana **north of Ferguson's Gulf** and **Lodwar**. A paved road (in bad condition) turns left across the river outside town and goes up to **Lokitaung**, branching left after about 60km for **Lokichokio** (Lokichoggio, often called just **Loki**) and the Sudanese border. Travel here is strictly in convoy but even this does not guarantee safety: 1996 saw an upsurge in shootings and armed banditry on this road, with several fatalities, one just 7km from Lodwar. The current wisdom is that you should get to where you're going before 3pm, as bandit attacks after then are more likely. If you do get held up, give them what they want. Clearly, travel here is not advisable. If you want go anyway, *matatus* leave Lodwar early in the morning and foreign relief vehicles may also consider giving you a lift. Alternatively, you might try approaching Trackmark Aviation at Wilson Airport in Nairobi (p.143), who operate daily NGO flights to Lokichokio.

Loki itself, an unremittingly dry and rocky place with steel freight containers lining the road, is even more of a cowboy town than Lodwar, with an eclectic mix of rough international types, businessmen, tribal Turkana, haggard relief workers, doctors, pilots, nurses, missionaries and shady arms-dealers. And beer. Loki is the major UN aid centre for southern Sudanese fleeing the civil war in Sudan (there's a big refugee hospital), and the main supply centre for NGOs within Sudan, with hundreds of personnel, Kenya's busiest airfield, and numerous bars for tired and frustrated relief workers. Ironically enough, Loki is also the centre for arms-running into Sudan: poke around some of the *dukas*, and you'll find AK-47s, ammunition and even bombs openly for sale. There's no accommodation for travellers, so you have to arrange matters with the aid workers (which can be expensive). The refugee centre itself is at **Kakuma**, 108km south of Loki on the Lodwar road.

Maralal, the Mathews and East Turkana

This is the exciting route to Lake Turkana. Anyone who has been up to **Loiyangalani** will talk your ear off telling you about the adventures they had on the way. It is one of the most exhilarating and remote journeys you can make.

From Nairobi, the distance is a good deal shorter than to the west coast, but even full tilt on the rough roads it's a full two-day **drive**. Saloon cars can make it as often as not, though vicious bedrock greets many a sump, and the car-rental companies aren't enthusiastic, but to be sure of arriving you'll need 4WD (a long-wheel-base Suzuki jeep is ideal) and spare petrol. Even then, if you go during the rainy season, you could be held up for 24 hours or more at several points.

The obvious solution is a **camping safari**, though, as with any group travel, this has its limitations. Still, a week isn't long enough for irritations to detract from the experience and most people thoroughly enjoy these trips, coming back loaded with amazing souvenirs and photographs, and stories of weird and wonderful encounters. A major drawback is the brevity of organized trips and the fact that they therefore run to a rough timetable. The oldest, and many think the best, outfit is Safari Camp Services' **Turkana Bus**, which runs every other Saturday throughout the year. They have loads of experience – and with the ancient Bedford lorries they use, they need it. Gametrackers also use Bedfords (or Land Cruisers if the group size is small); their fortnightly round trips (departing Fridays) via the Chalbi Desert are unique and highly recommended, and their lakeside campsite, 7km south of Loiyangalani, is pretty close to paradise (Safari Camp Services use a site at Loiyangalani itself, away from the lake).

If your budget is tight but you have time and a flexible attitude, and don't want a spoon-fed adventure, the maximum exposure to Turkana and the north comes from travelling completely independently. This may require some patience, especially at **Baragoi**, the terminus for **public transport**, where you'll have to line up a lift.

The routes to Maralal

Three roads lead to **Maralal**, the Samburu district town at the end of the first stage of the trip north.

Nyahururu to Maralal: C77

The easiest route, the **C77**, rolls up from Nyahururu via Rumuruti: tarmac to Rumuriti, decent *murram* but dull scenically to Maralal. Each morning at least one **bus** and sometimes a *matatu* or three leave Nyahururu. The C77 bounds over the ranching and cereal country of **Laikipia**, settled after World War I by British soldiers, but once a Maasai stronghold. Most of the settlers have left, and it's a bleak, somewhat forlorn region, racked by inter-tribal violence since the 1991 change-over to multiparty democracy. Cattle rustling is also prevalent, which only complicates matters. All this is extremely unlikely to affect tourists, as most of the incidents have taken place in remote villages.

Rumuruti (onomatopoeic Maa for "mosquito") is hardly noticeable any more; it merely marks the end of the paved road. The road to Rumuruti was built in the early 1980s for a minister who lives there and needed to be able to get to and from Nairobi without using a tractor. Maralal was connected with electricity at the same time, because, say the cynics, it would have been too obvious if the lines had only gone to his house. There's some very good game country in the vicinity, and for **night stops** in Rumuruti you might check out the *Tumaini Country Restaurant* which has rooms and claims: "We are famous for making people happy", or try *Mama Kanyi Guest House* with cheap s/c rooms (both ②). Equally inviting is the dilapidated *Laikipia Club* with its improbable efforts to preserve the old values. The best place, however, is the cheap self-service cottage accommodation at *Kifuko Bandas* (c/o Cape Chestnut Ltd, fax 0176/32208; ②–③), 10km southeast of Rumuriti along a rough dirt track; check first in Rumuruti, or at Let's Go Travel in Nairobi (p.142), whether they're still open.

The road follows the **Ewaso Narok River** (see the "Laikipia" map on p.206) for some way beyond Rumuruti into Samburu-land proper, where the two other routes described below join it. Passing *Bobong Campsite* on a bluff to the left, then the turn-off (after 27km) for the luxurious but extraordinarily expensive *Colcheccio Lodge* – it costs $560–610 for a double – sited on its bank (reservations through Tandala Ltd, PO Box

24397 Nairobi; ☎02/568804, fax 564945, *royal.africasaf@commsol.sprint.com*; or through Let's Go Travel in Nairobi, p.142; ⑨), the road climbs, broad and stony, towards Maralal's plateau. At **Suguta Marmar**, 20km south of Maralal, there's little more than a livestock auction yard, a police checkpoint, a few cheap *hotelis* and the basic *Checkpoint B&L* (①).

Lake Baringo to Maralal: D370

The second route is the lonely but well-constructed *murram* road from the **Rift Valley**, which in its earlier stages has breathtaking views back over Lake Baringo and some fascinating Pokot villages on the way. It's only a D road, but don't be discouraged for that reason from driving it (there have been occasional hold-ups at gunpoint along the way). There are no buses, and you'd be lucky to find a *matatu*. For the best chances of **hitching** success, ask at Lake Baringo Club or wait at the Kampi ya Samaki junction (see p.263).

Isiolo to Maralal: A2 and C79/C78

The maddeningly corrugated **A2** comes up from **Isiolo** past Archer's Post (p.580), then heads off left as the **C79** past the turn for Wamba, where it becomes the **C78**. Despite a continuation of the A2's washboard surface, the C79/78 has everything to recommend it scenically, including some magnificent desert buttes and sweeping views over the valley of the Ewaso Ngiro River, which flows on through Samburu. From 1992 until 1994 there were a few isolated incidents of **banditry**, but these appear to have ceased. The garishly decorated "Babie Coach" runs this route (Isiolo–Maralal), leaving one or the other town every other day, usually packed full of Samburu warriors. *Matatus* run daily in both directions. Your best chances of **hitching** a ride are at the Samburu lodges inside the national reserve (see p.400), or at the Isiolo police barrier.

Maralal

Some of the Laikipia settlers would have dearly liked to set themselves up around the cool, conifer-draped highlands of **MARALAL**. But even before British administrators made this the district capital, Maralal had been a spiritual focus for the **Samburu people** and, despite some dithering, the colonial administrators didn't accede to the settlers' demands.

Maralal is a peculiar town, spread with exaggerated spaciousness around a depression in the hills. Samburu people crowd its dusty streets, with a brilliant collage of skins, blankets, beads, brass, and iron, and a special smell, too – of sour milk, fat, and cattle. The main hotel is called *Buffalo Hotel*. The place sets itself up for Wild West comparisons and the climate is appropriate – unbelievably dusty, almost always windy, and, at 2220m, sharp enough at night for log fires and braziers. All it needs is wolves – and even there hyenas fill the role.

Of course, the regular arrival of safari lorries means that Maralal has plenty of persistent souvenir salesmen. Yet despite this (or perhaps because of it – very few *wazungu* stay more than a few hours), it's a good place to get to know the Samburu and especially worthwhile on Christian holidays. Many Samburu around the town have become Catholics and the colourful procession on Palm Sunday – mostly thousands of women, waving branches and leaves – is riveting.

A notable resident of Maralal until recently was the travel writer and Arabist **Wilfred Thesiger**, who had made the town his home and had adopted a number of orphaned boys. Thesiger made his name with his accounts of the Shiite Arabs of the southern Iraqi marshes and the Bedu of the Arabian peninsula, and followed up these achievements with several books on Kenya, notably *My Kenya Days*. Among the Samburu he

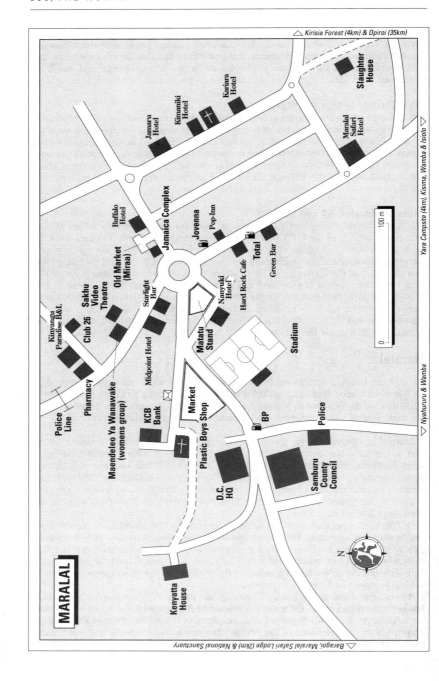

MARALAL

Kirisia Forest (4km) & Opiroi (35km)

Slaughter House

Kariara Hotel

Maralal Safari Hotel

Jamaru Hotel

Kimaniki Hotel

Buffalo Hotel

Jamaica Complex

Jovenna

Pop-Inn

Total

Green Bar

Yare Campsite (4km), Kisima, Wamba & Isiolo

Old Market (Miraa)

Sakhu Video Theatre

Starlight Bar

Nanyuki Hotel

Hard Rock Cafe

Club 26

Kinyangu Paradise B&L

Pharmacy

Midpoint Hotel

Matatu Stand

Stadium

Police Line

Maendeleo Ya Wanawake (womens group)

KCB Bank

Market

Plastic Boys Shop

BP

Police

Nyahururu & Wamba

D.C. HQ

Samburu County Council

Kenyatta House

N

Baragoi, Maralal Safari Lodge (2km) & National Sanctuary

100 m

found equally congenial companions for his old age, and was well respected throughout the district.

If you forget to visit the liberally signposted **Kenyatta House**, don't fret. The fact that Kenyatta was detained here in 1961 before his final release doesn't really improve the interest of this unexceptional and empty bungalow. It seems a pity it's a national monument and not some family's home.

Guides and crafts

On arriving in Maralal, you'll invariably attract a flock of persistent and annoying "guides" offering evening excursions to see **traditional dancing** in nearby *manyattas*, or else visits to local **Samburu witch doctors** and **blacksmiths** and a nearby **Turkana village**. Bear in mind that many wily con artists are at work in town, so use your judgement before accepting, making it absolutely clear how much you are prepared to pay, and bringing plenty of chewing tobacco and *miraa* for the old men. The reason behind this unwelcome attention is the town's high unemployment, caused by a massive influx of previously nomadic herders following the drought of 1982–85 and the subsequent explosion in cattle rustling, which led many Turkana and Samburu to lose their livestock.

An attempt to tame the guides by organizing them into disciplined groups is the **Plastic Boys' Co-operative Self Help Group**, so named after the street children who used to make dolls and trinkets using plastic bags and cartons. They have now progressed, under the guidance of the Kenya Wildlife Service and various NGOs, to carving and selling woodcrafts, spears and other touristy items. Their shop is in the market, and they should be able to sort you out with some of the more reliable guides, should you need one. For more "authentic" souvenirs, the women's group Maendeleo Ya Wanawake has a shop selling distinctly used calabashes, headrests and dolls. They can also point you in the right direction should you want Samburu beadwork.

Maralal National Sanctuary and Safari Lodge

Maralal Safari Lodge (PO Box 70; ☎0368/2060; bookings: 2nd floor, Windsor House, Muindi Mbingu St, PO Box 15020 Nairobi; ☎02/211124, fax 211125), signposted 2–3km out of town on the Lake Turkana road, is comfortable and under-subscribed – and very attractive with its huge wooden chalet-style rooms (B&B ⑦). Your patronage is welcome in the bar and restaurant, and you can sit on the terrace to watch the animals from the surrounding **Maralal National Sanctuary** and Yamo Forest (zebra, baboon, impala, eland, warthog, buffalo and hyena) filing up the hill to the concrete water hole a few metres away.

Accommodation

Setting aside the excellent lodge, Maralal has a large number of **cheap lodgings**, the more acceptable of which are listed here; the mid-range Yare Safari Club also has **camping** facilities.

Buffalo Hotel (PO Box 28; ☎0368/2028). The main travellers' haunt, decent, but more expensive than usual and not for light sleepers – its infamous back bar closes when the last punter hits the floor. No s/c. ①.

Green Bar (PO Box 7). Friendly with a decent restaurant. Singles only. ①.

Jamaru Hotel (PO Box 245; ☎0368/2215). Maralal's largest, rather spartan but with a good, busy restaurant, and some s/c rooms too. ①–②.

Kariara Hotel (PO Box 68). The cheapest and best in town, this is also Maralal's only two-storey hotel. It has basic but clean rooms, festooned with bougainvillea, all with mosquito nets; bring your own padlock. Get a room on top – on a good morning you can see Mount Kenya. ①.

Kimaniki Hotel (PO Box 117; ☎0368/2444). Rooms behind a noisy bar-disco to suit night owls. ①.

Kinyangu Paradise B&L (PO Box 193; ☎0368/2297). Another local joint, its bar is open till midnight and frequented by Samburu and Turkana tribesmen. Cheap and reasonable. ①.

Midpoint Hotel (PO Box 93; ☎0368/2221). Acceptable if not overly clean, with hot water (not s/c) and food available. Singles only. ①.

Yare Safari Club and Campsite (PO Box 281 Maralal; ☎0368/2295; in Nairobi ☎ & fax 02/214099, *www.iconnect.co.ke/~travelkenya*). Just over 4km down the Isiolo road, beyond Wilfred Thesiger's old home, *Yare* is Maralal's main tourist centre, with some beautiful thatched *bandas*, a good restaurant and well-stocked bar, and pleasant campsite next to a camel pen (Ksh200 per person; under Ksh100 for tent hire). There's a resident Samburu blacksmith who plays superb Samburu guitar, camels available for hire ($3 per hour including handler), and walks can be arranged ($20 per day). Longer camel safaris can also be organized, as can mountain biking treks. B&B ③.

Eating, drinking and entertainment

Maralal boasts a surprising number of good **restaurants** as well as the usual run of cheap and filling eating houses. The popular Somali-run *Pop-Inn Hotel* is easily the best, with a great atmosphere, breakfasts, pilau and *dengo* (a delicately spiced stew of root vegetables and small beans). Also recommended is the anomalous *Hard Rock Café* which specializes in beefburgers, chips, espresso coffee and brains (oh yes). *Maralal Safari Hotel* serves *githeri* to Samburu warriors with lolloping reggae in the background. *Jamaica Complex Hotel* is big on *nyama choma*, whilst the *Nanyuki Hotel*, by the *matatu* stand, has huge portions of Swahili food (*mchele* stew a speciality) at criminally low prices. The *Midpoint Hotel* and *Kinyangu Paradise B&L* are also recommended.

A night spent in Maralal's numerous **bars** can be exhilarating, infuriating, dangerous or just plain daft. *Buffalo Hotel* is the best of the lot: a heady place with skulking ex-pats, wheedling con merchants and a host of bizarre local nutcases. Round the back is its late-night video bar with enough footage of reggae and soukous bands to drown in – unless they're showing *Delta Force* or *King Solomon's Mines* yet again. There's a real **cinema** opposite the *Starlight Bar* which usually gets in some genuine celluloid on Saturdays. The bar itself is a straightforward drinking den full of broken stools and fallen pride. Predictably enough, *Jamaica Complex* resounds to baseline slow jam and rootsy reggae, while *Kimaniki* hosts the dancey *Club 24* from Friday to Sunday. The similar *Club 26* is almost opposite *Kinyangu Paradise B&L*.

Other practicalities – and moving on

If you're **continuing north**, note that Maralal is the last place where you can rely on supplies of **petrol**, and **change money** – at the smart KCB bank (Mon–Fri 8.30–2.30am, Sat 8.30–10.30am), at *Yare Safari Club*, or at the *Maralal Safari Lodge* (where they don't have much cash). If **beer** is important to you (and it can assume great importance up in the desert), then stock up on that before following the route described next.

MARALAL INTERNATIONAL CAMEL DERBY

The Maralal International **Camel Derby** provides for a strange weekend at the end of July. Anyone may enter, or just spectate, as dozens of competitors from East Africa, Europe, China, Australia and South Africa battle it out over 11km amateur and 42km professional stages. Entry fees are very reasonable: amateur class, including camel and handler, is Ksh1900; professional Ksh2500. There's also a locally-run funfair, marathon, and javelin and *rungu* (club) throwing contests, as well as a possible tie-in with a Kenya Mountain Bike series race. The event is based at the *Yare* site. For more details, contact Yare Safari Club or the Organizing Committee, Maralal Festival and Camel Derby, PO Box 281 Maralal; ☎02/214099, fax 32709; *travelkenya@iconnect.co.ke*.

If you don't have your own vehicle, you may find a source of **rides onward** at *Yare* or the lodge, but you're more likely to catch vehicles by staying in town and spreading the word at the petrol stations. Let it be known you are willing to travel in the back of a lorry – many people will assume you're not. Supply lorries do go up to Loiyangalani and your chances of scoring a lift – eventually, even if it takes you a week – are good. Two Land Rover *matatus* leave for Baragoi around noon (the northernmost limit of public transport), and for Nyahururu and Isiolo at 10am or 11am. Nakuru is served daily by Nyayo Bus. There are early morning *matatus* for Nairobi, otherwise catch one to Rumuruti or Nyahururu, and change there. Goldline Bus for Nairobi leaves nightly at 2am.

Wamba and the Mathews Range (Lenkiyio Hills)

In terms of the vastness of the north, the **Mathews Range** is virtually on Maralal's doorstep. The range, most of which is a forest reserve, is impressively wild hill country, with Mathew Peak (Ol Doinyo Lenkiyio) rising to 2375m. Lower down, the mountains are heavily cloaked in forest and thick bush; unusual vegetation includes "living fossil" cycad plants, giant cedars and podocarpus. Among the animal life, you can look out for (but shouldn't expect to meet) small numbers of black rhinos – every one of them known and tracked, for its own safety, by forest guards and their Samburu staff – and really outstanding butterflies. This is first-rate walking and exploring country for hardy travellers, but you need to be fully self-sufficient, which includes having all your food requirements.

First target is **WAMBA**, a one-street town 5km off the C78/79 highway, roughly midway between Maralal and Isiolo. You can get the odd *matatu* here from Maralal, or use the Babie Coach which passes by the Wamba turning just after midday (heading out from Maralal one day, coming back from Isiolo the next). Wamba's main focus is its large, modern Catholic hospital outside town. *Saudia Lodge* (①), in town, is pretty well the only **B&L**, with clean, pleasant and very cheap rooms. There are a few *dukas*, though they have no fuel and little in the way of fresh food, only basic fruit or veg. You might try *Imani Bar & Restaurant* which serves the usual limited range of stews and a reasonable *githeri*.

The big mountain you can see outside town (9km to the peak as the crow flies) is **Warges**. Guides from Wamba will take you up there, though they'll stress how full of wild animals it is and how much their lives (not yours of course) are at risk. If you have a serious interest in witchcraft, one of Kenya's most respected **witch doctors** lives in the shadow of the mountain. Forget the town guides – he is resolutely *not* a tourist attraction; instead, make discreet enquiries with the Kenya Wildlife Service rangers who regularly pass through Wamba, or else, if your Maa is good enough, with one of the young Samburu *morani*, but make sure you are accompanied by someone who really knows the place.

Kitich Camp and campsite

The main route from Wamba, however, is towards the expensive bush-luxury *Kitich Camp* and the nearby KWS station campsite. If you're four-wheel-driving, you basically set off towards Barsaloi (Parsaloi) along a rough road that commences just half a kilometre along the Wamba access road. From here you drive 15km, then turn right and do a further 17km to **Ngilai** (follow the yellow stones). Some 6km further, you fork left to ford the **Ngeng River**. With the mountains looming all around, this is the way into the heart of the Mathews: the campsite is a couple of kilometres up the track on the other side, and *Kitich Camp* some 4km further north. Note that there's no fuel along the way and normally none for sale at Kitich.

If you're on foot, find a guide in Wamba and set off cross-country, direct to Ngilai, crossing several *luggas*, and seeing almost nobody on the way. The distance is about

30km and an exhausting day's walk; double-check in Wamba whether the site is still open. Ngilai has a Lutheran mission (2km out of the centre to the north) and a single shop, which may put you up for the night if you can't make the final 8km to the campsite before nightfall.

The **campsite** is pleasant and shady, with showers and toilet, and water available from the nearby pools. Note that there is no food available at the campsite and, while you can go angling in the river, there's a limit to how much catfish a person can stand. Unfortunately, **Kitich Camp**, nestled unobtrusively on the river bank beneath towering giant figs, doesn't go out of its way to welcome travellers, and a night here – at $650 – is exceptionally expensive.

If you want to walk any distance, you're strongly advised to take a guide, either from the camp or from the campsite (where they'll seek you out if you're camping). There are some fine **excursions**, including short walks up the valley to wonderful, deep, rock pools where you can swim. The area around the Ngeng Valley is thick with wildlife. There are elephants everywhere, buffaloes, hyenas, leopards and plenty of more innocuous game. You really have to watch yourself, especially if you go down near the river. It's a lot of fun, but take care.

North from Maralal: into Samburu-land

The first stretch of the road **north from Maralal** climbs higher into the **podocarpus forests** of the national sanctuary, before dropping down into the scorching Suguta Valley. The northern boundary of the sanctuary has been scarred by the wholesale burning of much of its valley sides, presumably to make way for cattle pasture. Other theories posit the local administration police ("Home Guard"), or Kenya Police Reserves (heavily armed Samburu herders) as responsible, suggesting that they remove the natural cover which facilitates the **cattle rustling** raids that have become endemic in the 1990s between the Samburu and their northern Turkana neighbours. The raids come to a head at the end of the year and during the dry months of January and February, as Samburu herders take their livestock up north towards Baragoi on the Samburu-Turkana border. Once in the Suguta valley, stolen cattle are difficult to retrieve due to the valley's exceptionally high temperatures (up to 60°C), lack of water and the rough terrain.

Twenty kilometres from Maralal, a detour to the left takes you through the village of **Poror**, past a large wheat-farming project, and, after 6km, to the dramatic scimitar edge of the **Losiolo Escarpment**. The Rift Valley is, by its nature, bordered from end to end by vertiginous escarpments and each one seems more impressive than the last. But Losiolo is not just an escarpment, it's a colossal amphitheatre dropping down to Suguta Valley, 2000m below. Try to get here very early in the morning – it is awesome. From Poror, the road north is increasingly rough and hot as it drops down through the Samburu Hills on to the Lopet Plateau. Settlements from hereon are few but evenly scattered: the first is **Morijo**, which has a few basic *chai* kiosks, one or two Somali-run *dukas*, a mission and a police station. **Marti**, 20km further north, is much the same.

Baragoi

Sitting 37km north of Marti is **BARAGOI**, in the heart of the barren Elbarta plains, watered only occasionally by run-off from the Samburu Hills and Ndoto Mountains. The river which skirts the town is dry for much of the year, and in times of drought the pits which are dug into it by women fetching water can reach depths of over 6m. It's a blistering, dusty and unforgiving land, dotted here and there with sun-bleached bones and populated only by red-robed semi-nomadic herders armed with spears or bows and

THE SAMBURU

The **Samburu** are historically close to the Maasai. Their languages are nearly the same (both Maa) and culturally they are virtually indistinguishable to an outsider. Both came from the region around present-day northwest Turkana in the seventeenth century: the Samburu turned east, establishing themselves in the mountain pastures and spreading across to the plains; the Maasai continued south.

Improvements in health and in veterinary care over the last century have swelled the Samburu population and the size of their herds. Many in the driest areas of their range in the northeast have turned to camel herding as a better insurance against drought than cattle. Since livestock is the basis of relations between in-laws (through the giving of "bridewealth" from the husband to his wife's family), having camel herds has disrupted patterns of marriage and initiation into new generations because camel herds increase more slowly than cattle herds. And the reality on the ground is all about twice as confusing as it sounds on paper. Memories, recording every transaction over successive generations, are phenomenal (the Samburu have only just begun to acquire writing).

The Samburu age-set system, like many others in Africa, is a complicated arrangement to which a number of anthropologists have devoted lifetimes of investigation. Essentially it's a gerontocracy (rule by old men) and the elders are assured, by the system they manipulate, of having the first choice of young women to marry. The promiscuous and jingoistic – but, by Samburu reckoning, still juvenile – warriors are forced to wait, usually until their thirties, before initiation into elderhood, marriage and children brings them a measure of real respect. In turn, they perpetuate the system on their own sons, who have everything to gain by falling in line and much to lose if they withdraw their stake in the tradition, perhaps by going to Nairobi or the coast to look for work.

For women the situation is very different. They are married at fifteen or sixteen, immediately after their clitoridectomy and before they have much chance to rebel. But they may continue affairs with their *morani* boyfriends, the unmarried juniors of their new, much older husbands. This polygamy in itself seems to be an important motivating force for the whole generation system. For the warriors and their girlfriends, there's a special young people's language – a vocabulary of conspiratorial songs and idioms – which has to be modified with the initiation of every age-set, so that it's kept secret from the elders.

This highly intricate system is now beginning to collapse in many areas, with a widespread disruption of pre-colonial ways; even the circumcision initiation of boys to warriorhood is less of a mass ceremony. While herds are still the principal criterion of wealth, people in some areas are turning to agriculture: after the rains you can see planting holes at the roadside in certain places, with corn the main crop. There are enormous problems for such initiatives, especially when there's no aid or government support, but they do show that the standard stereotypes don't always fit. As for the *morani* warriors, opportunities for cattle-raiding and lion-killing have diminished with more efficient policing of their territories, although there are still annual clashes with the Turkana in the north of Samburu-land. For some, tourist hunting has taken over. You can even see *morani* in full rig striding past the hotels on the Indian Ocean beaches.

arrows to protect their cattle, goats and camels against the endemic rustlers (*ngorokos*). "Stealing cattle is very important to us. It is a way of life" admits the Baragoi Ward Councillor.

First settled in the 1930s, Baragoi retains its original function as the region's major livestock market, attracting both Samburu and Turkana for whom the town also marks the invisible boundary between their respective grazing lands. Yet things have changed a lot over the last few years. A construction boom has spawned dozens of one-storey cinder-block buildings in which half a dozen new hotels, numerous bars and restaurants have taken root. A clue to this sudden expansion lies in the name of a bar at the north end of the village: *Bosnia Wines & Spirits*. Shortly after the UN resolved to send peace-keepers to former Yugoslavia, a 900-strong Kenyan battalion was despatched to help patrol a ceasefire line around the self-proclaimed (now defunct) Serbian Republic of Krajina. News of the detachment spread quickly, particularly of the astronomical sums to be made serving in UNPROFOR (soldiers were paid up to $1200 a month, compared with the average Kenyan monthly wage of perhaps $70). Samburu warriors from around Baragoi and Lesriken, 25km east, were quick to enlist for the second and third missions to Bosnia, the last of which returned in 1994.

The rewards were indeed beyond belief for the veterans, and for men who in the past had been expected to kill a lion in order to prove their manhood, the ferocity of the fighting left them unfazed. What did shock them, however, were the atrocities they witnessed, committed against ordinary civilians and now the subject of war crimes tribunals.

The Bosnian experience has not been without its problems. For some, sudden wealth has led to alcoholism as hard spirits have become affordable, and even cocaine abuse, and on arriving in Baragoi you'll be assailed by the usual band of desperate types, madmen and "guides" who missed out on their brothers' good fortunes. Unpleasant though the reception is, weather the storm (the locals will help you out of any serious trouble) and you'll find that Baragoi is a fascinating place, well worth a day or two of anyone's time.

The livestock market

Despite the UN money, life for the majority remains a hard and restless search for water and pasturage, often violently conflicting with other herders grazing the same territory. Down off Bosnia Street to the northwest of town is the **livestock market**. It's a gentle, unhurried affair where old men with gnarled hands and ostrich plumes in their hair play *ngiles* (*mbau*) with stones and seeds on "boards" carved out of the bone-dry earth as they wait for business to arrive. Here, Samburu deal with Rendille and Turkana, some of whom may have spent up to seven days walking their livestock south from the lake. In turn the Samburu, and sometimes Turkana, trek eastward for five or six days to reach Isiolo where, with luck, they resell their animals at a profit.

If the herder is of **courting** age (Samburu *moran*; Turkana *lmoli*), Isiolo is also where he buys the beads, necklaces and bangles with which to woo his bride. Once back home, he will not only present her with these gifts but mime and sing the attributes of the animals which will provide him and his family with their means of survival. For these semi-nomads, animals are the source of all wealth, and the young herder must represent them favourably to attract the attention and confidence of a bride. To this end, he selects a single castrated bull, camel or goat which he then mimics, indicating with his hands and gestures its size, colour, the shape of its horns, even its temperament. There's a comical side to all this, too, for even the poorest herder, whose beast may only be a goat with lopsided horns, must dance to attract a spouse and does this by raising a few smiles with a self-deprecating parody of his goat. Dances are held almost nightly in the *manyattas* on the outskirts of town, wild and hugely enjoyable events at which you are bound to be made welcome. Cameras, of course, are generally not acceptable. Ask around at the market or else try one of the *manyattas* behind the primary school.

Practicalities

The best **accommodation** in town is the basic but clean *Morning Star Guest House* (PO Box 37; singles only, ①) with a decent restaurant and bar. *Bosnia Wines & Spirits* (①), also singles only, is spartan but clean and cheap; the beds are narrow but have the benefit of nets. *Mount Ngiro B&L* (②) distinguishes itself in having the only doubles in Baragoi; it's full-board only and comparatively expensive, though bargaining is possible.

The *Morning Star* has a pleasant courtyard and good, scalding *chai*, but by far the best **bar and restaurant** is *Zaire Hotel* on Nachola Road, a colourful and cheerful place, open till 11pm, with Baragoi's only really cold drinks, Congolese music and the weird sight of Samburu and Turkana herders in full rig supping tea and nibbling scones. It may have rooms to let in future. For simple and filling staples like *githeri*, *Flora Hotel*, *Al-Mukaram* and *Wid-Wid Hotel* are all cheap.

There are no official **money-changing** facilities, but there is a **post office** (Mon–Fri 8am–5pm), an **Oxfam** office and a decent **car mechanic** (Dalfer Welders, opposite the post office). Emergency **petrol supplies** can be had, at a price, from Mount Ngiro Supplies. There's been talk for years of a new Bosnia-financed petrol station at the head of Bosnia Street, but nothing substantial as yet.

Moving on from Baragoi

Baragoi marks the end of **northbound** public transport, which means you have to line up a lift with supply lorries, mission jeeps and the like. The police station on the north side of town is helpful, but be prepared to wait for several days. You might also find a Turkana Bus safari lorry to take you to Loiyangalani: a generous tip for the driver and cook(s) is in order. Going **south to Maralal** is easy if uncomfortable: two Land Rover *matatus* leave daily from outside the post office (7am & 9am).

South Horr and Kurungu Camp

Baragoi marks the end of the forbidding Elbarta plains, as the road now climbs into ravine and mountain country, fantastically green if there's been rain. Some 30km from Baragoi, a track to the left towards Nyiru, signed by a red gas cylinder, leads to Desert Rose Camel Safaris (p.137), who organize luxury camel treks of six days or more in the surrounding *luggas* and hills and up to Lake Turkana, with vehicle back-up and two nights at their *Desert Rose Lodge* (FB ⑨).

There's a positive jungle all year round at the oasis village of **SOUTH HORR** (*horr* means "flowing water"), wedged tightly between the Nyiru and Ol Doinyo Mara mountains. With its pleasantly somnolent atmosphere, ample shade and relaxed herders lounging under the trees, it's a great place to bunk down for a night or three, and making friends is easy despite the language barrier. There are a few cheap *hotelis* and cold drinks at *Nhiro Serima Bar*, but only rarely beer. If you stay the night, you've a choice of half a dozen basic **B&Ls** (all ①). There is good, dirt-cheap **camping** at the *Forest Department Campsite*, located up a rough trail to the left of the road a kilometre before South Horr. Facilities consist of long-drops, an *askari*, and a river for drinking water, bathing and washing the dust out of your clothes. This site, a short walk from South Horr village where most vehicles stop, is a good base for meeting up with supply or mission vehicles in hopes of a lift north.

Well worth a visit in the village itself is SALTLICK (Semi-Arid Lands Training and Livestock Improvement Centres Kenya), which concerns itself with supporting the local pastoralist Samburu communities via honey-production projects and cash-crop experiments involving the Senegalese acacia gum tree; it's a mine of information on Samburu culture. For a more intimate experience, you might try asking about the **camel market** which is held on occasions a few kilometres south of the village at a roadside well.

Kurungu Camp

For a place to bump into motorized tourists, the delightful **Kurungu Camp**, 6km past the village along the sandy, vegetation-festooned track, is preferable to Loiyangalani. This is a well-kept **campsite** operated by Safari Camp Services (p.135), surrounded by flowering bushes and shaded by distinguished old trees. The *bandas* are derelict and supplies of cold drinks can't be relied on, but there are bucket showers. Camping out here (about Ksh100 per person) is fabulous.

It's worth spending a couple of nights at Kurungu and exploring the **mountain forest** around you – it hides lots of wildlife, including elephants and buffaloes, and bursts with birds and butterflies. You can be guided by Samburu *morani* up the lower slopes or, more ambitiously, on the stiff hike up to **Nyiru peak**, which has stunning views over Lake Turkana. If you entertain thoughts of any more daring expeditions in the region, **camel hire** should cost in the region of Ksh600–1000 per beast per day. Be careful if you're embarking on anything way off the beaten track. Many men who will sell themselves as **guides** have led surprisingly sheltered lives; they don't know the desert like the backs of their hands any more than you do. Real knowledge and experience are sought after and more expensive.

At Kurungu, you are also likely to have the (mixed) pleasure of **Samburu dancing**, especially if on an organized safari. For about Ksh200–300, you are allowed into the arena to take as many pictures of the dancers as you want, although they do not mask their displeasure. Scepticism is briefly swamped by the hour-long jamboree that follows. A troupe of *morani* go through an informal dance programme, flirtatiously threatening the audience with whoops and pounces. Young women and girls join in – sometimes with the evident disapproval of older Samburu onlookers – to be propositioned with whisks of the men's ochred hair-dos. Meanwhile, there's the constant offering of necklaces, trinkets, spears, pouches and more photo poses, to be negotiated individually with those who are too old or too young to dance.

The *morani* dance and dance and no one feels the money was badly spent. But is it authentic? Does it mean anything? What do *they* think? It's extremely difficult to disentangle motives from relations, and better to forget about the fleeting illusion of "authenticity" on these occasions, accepting the dances for what they are: vivid, funny, dynamic entertainment.

Down to the lake

After South Horr, the track winds down between the Nyiru Range to your left and the Ol Doinyo Mara mountains to the right, before opening onto featureless plains of black lava with the massif of Kulal dominating the northern horizon. The lava is hard and jagged – a vicious test for tyres – and the track itself, pummelled to a fine dust, can become a quagmire after a rainstorm. This is Turkana territory. The numerous **stone circles** and **cairns** around here are the remains of settlements and burial sites, which, with a keen eye, you'll learn to recognize all over the region. Most distinctive are the low semicircular constructions, which you'll see in use as you approach the lake: these serve as shelters against the viciously hot wind that blows almost incessantly off the flanks of Kulal. The burial cairns are by no means as ancient as they appear, as traditionally neither the Turkana nor Samburu (who migrated from this area a few hundred years ago) buried their dead, but instead simply left the bodies out in the open for wild animals to eat. The more important members of the community, such as blacksmiths and respected elders, were sometimes buried under cairns, or were left in a hut whose door would be walled up. The site would be abandoned and thereafter never again be used for human habitation. Since Independence and the rise in the power of Christian missions, however, both Turkana and Saburu are now obliged to bury their dead.

Just when you were beginning to wonder, **Lake Turkana** appears as the road drops away in front: a stunning vista of shot blues and greens, with the black, castellate silhouette of South Island hanging as if suspended between lake and sky. Descending a little further along a viciously rocky stretch of road known to drivers as The Staircase, you pass several safe bays for swimming, a few tiny temporary fishing settlements and, an hour or so later, Loiyangalani.

Loiyangalani and around

LOIYANGALANI – "the place of the trees" – is a vague agglomeration of grass huts, mud huts, tin shacks, a police station, a school, a pair of campsites, "the mission" and "the lodge". It's a small community far from metropolitan Kenya, without newspapers and often without beer (a real measure of its isolation). The land around is mostly barren and stony, scattered with the carcasses of livestock, with palm trees and acacias clustered around the settlement's life source, a **hot spring** of fresh water. This empties into two pools near the police station, one for men, the other for women.

The village came into being in the early 1960s with the *Oasis Lodge* and its airstrip, and the Italian mission to the **Elmolo** people, a small group who live by hunting and fishing on the southeastern lakeshore. Somali raiders ransacked both establishments in 1965, but since then the two institutions have been left alone. The mission is now starting to thrive and its net of influence has reached most of Loiyangalani's more permanent inhabitants, especially the children who come to the school.

For all its apparent drabness, the village isn't dull. When you've had enough of haggling for artefacts and fantastic quartz, onyx, amethyst, and other semi-precious stones collected from Kulal – as well as the odd fossil – you can wander over to the springs and the school. You'll inevitably pick up a cluster of teenagers – Turkana, Elmolo, Samburu, Rendille – eager to practise their English. Swahili has never made much impact up here and English is the usual teaching medium. Education is perhaps the most positive of the major influences – including state interference, Christianity and tourist money – bringing pressure to bear on local customs and traditions.

The **mission**, while changing the structure of traditional society (through conversions to Catholicism, which have been particularly effective among the Elmolo), is at the same time helping to make local people sufficiently independent to resist unwanted change and to make choices about their future, by helping to set up income-generating schemes such as the shops, some of the boats and a new service station. Some of the Italian missionaries are extremely open and informative and, although you can't be assured they'll have any time to meet you, the chance to talk to them about Loiyangalani may well arise if you're around for a few days. For non-Christians, however, the whole concept of missionaries and their work can be difficult to swallow: for all their schools and clinics, it's difficult to escape the feeling that these people – for so long "untouched" by the outside world – managed very well with their original beliefs and traditions, which formed the basis of their society, cosmology and human relations. With Christianity now ascendant, the old structures are breaking down fast and some risk being lost completely (the Elmolo lost their language in March 1998 following the death of its last speaker, for example). By preferring to convert children, rather than their more obstinate parents, the deeper morality of the well-meaning missionaries is questionable at best. More positively, there's a small library at the mission, which you're free to use.

Loiyangalani's **"beach"** is a grubby strip a couple of kilometres down the road. People do swim, but the dingy water is hardly enticing. Many of the loose stones on the shore also shelter scorpions (not serious) and carpet vipers (very serious).

In the evenings, **dances** often take place around Loiyangalani: informal, energetic, pogo-ing performances for fun, always worth checking out. Track them down by the booming sound of collective larynxes. It's the girls who ask the boys to dance, and you're welcome to join in (no cameras or torches unless permission is expressly given and paid for: usually Ksh300 per person).

Practicalities

The German-run *Oasis Lodge* (PO Box 14829 Nairobi; ☎2 Loiyangalani; reservations through Bunson Travel, address p.48; FB ⑦; closed mid-May to mid-July) tries to be exclusive, and certainly charges as though it was. There's a Ksh300 daily entrance fee to casual visitors to discourage them from drinking the entire stock of beer; the fee at least entitles you to swim in its two, jealously guarded pools. The **accommodation**, however, in windblown and rather basic "chalets", is certainly not worth the expense. More useful is the lodge's **car-rental service**, ideal for visiting Sibiloi National Park (see below), but the prices are very high (upwards of $200 per day including driver). Similarly expensive are its hiking trips up Kulal and around (around $100 per person per day). Fishing boats can be rented for Ksh2500 per hour, with fishing licences an additional Ksh500. You're advised to bargain hard for all the lodge's services, and to double-check on any price before taking anything on.

Much more down to earth is the **B&L** run by "Mama Changa" (the charming "Mrs Bead", who doesn't speak English), who, apart from supplying much of the Turkana's beadwork necklaces and bracelets, has eighteen cleanish but perfectly adequate rooms round the back of the misnamed *Cold Drink Hotel* (its fridge broke down in 1984), each with a kerosene lamp and free drinking water (①). This is the place to meet up with other travellers and drivers, should there be any. Totally different in style but equally pleasant and recommended is *Mosaretu Camp*, adjacent to *Oasis Lodge*, which is run by the local branch of the women's Maendeleo Ya Wanawake movement. Apart from camping (Ksh150–200 per tent; watch out for snakes and scorpions), they have five traditional thatched *bandas* (①) under the palm trees, with mosquito nets, mattresses and food-aid sacks used for roofing ("USA CORN: Not to be Sold"). There are toilets and showers, and a kitchen is being built. Other **camping** possibilities include the near-derelict *El Molo Lodge* at the head of the airstrip, which recently disposed of the remaining beds and mattresses in its concrete *bandas* (there are plans to redo them, but don't hold your breath). You can camp anywhere in the lush gardens (Ksh200 per person), and there's a bonus of a pool (also Ksh200 per person), a charcoal fridge for coolish sodas, and clear drinking water (iodine or chlorine tablets nonetheless advisable). The nearby *Sunset Strip* is used by *Safari Camp Services*' "Turkana Bus", but has less shade than *El Molo*. The palm trees here are mainly useful for giving shelter from the wind lashing down from the fortress bulk of Kulal, but the site is marred by the high wire perimeter fence – built to allow you to leave your gear with some confidence. There are toilets and showers. Last but not least, 7km to the south of Loiyangalani on the lakeshore (a long hot walk) is probably Lake Turkana's most perfect campsite, operated by Gametrackers for their Turkana safaris, with thatched *bandas* facing out over the lake. There's no shade, but the *bandas* are a delight, the lake swimming is wonderful and the views unparalleled. They use it for only two or three days a week, so you may be able to do a deal with the caretaker.

Food is more difficult. The *Cold Drink Hotel* is nothing special, and has a propensity to charge "*wazungu*" rates" (ie multiply by three). Food is cheaper and drinks colder from the modestly-named *Hilton Hotel* opposite and *South Island Hotel* a little further down. If there are beers in town, you'll find them either at *El Molo Hotel* (warm) or *Cold Drinks Shop* (who do have a fridge) at the south end of the village.

South Island National Park

If you want to visit **South Island National Park** ($15, $5 students/children), you should ask about a trip at the lodge first, but spread the word and you may find a much cheaper means of getting there. It's a thirty-kilometre round trip, so the weather needs to be fair. By all accounts it's one of the weirdest places to stay a night, in the unlikely event of the warden allowing you to do so; its volcanic vents, rising some 300m above sea level, give out a ghostly luminous glow that has long put off local fishermen from venturing there.

Mount Kulal

On dry land, you could make a stab at climbing **Mount Kulal**, if you have the energy. There are two summits, joined by a narrow and dicey ridge. The climb itself, once you're on the right track, is straightforward enough, but talk to some gem-hunters who may guide you up. And note that, although Kulal seems to tower over Loiyangalani, two days is barely enough to walk to the base and back: you really will need transport unless you're very determined and suitably equipped. The views from the top are fabulous, with the lake on one side and the searing Chalbi Desert on the other, and bird-watchers have the added incentive of a rare species of **white-eye** peculiar to the mountain. Bring all the **water** you will need, as there are no supplies on the mountain.

Elmolo Bay

At **Elmolo Bay**, 8km north of Loiyangalani, lives the last viable community of **Elmolo people**. To visit them, you pay a fixed fee per person, depending on the size of your party (around Ksh300–400), to the headman, to be given the freedom of the village, including the right to take photos and a trip to the island opposite the bay to look for crocodiles. During the week, the children are nearly all at school in Loiyangalani; they come home at the weekend, which is the best time to visit. Impromptu dances start, little hands are slipped engagingly into yours for a walk around the low, grass huts. Older people stare rather blankly from the entrances. The ground is a litter of fishbones, string, shreds of cloth. Someone sets up a stall of beadwork and gourds – apparently identical to what you could find up and down the Rift Valley. It's a novel, disturbing experience which contrives to be stage-managed and voyeuristic at the same time. Because of their friendliness, their small number and the increased interest shown in them, the Elmolo risk being taken advantage of by tourists. However, the usual rules apply: ask before you take pictures and be generous with your time and your wallet.

Over on the island – which, because of Lake Turkana's lowering, you can now reach by a causeway – you should see **crocodiles** if you walk softly and approach the far shore cautiously. On the island's stern, rocky beaches, the remains of Elmolo fish picnics and old camps can be found everywhere; one find was a nearly fossilized hippo tusk from some long-ago feast. Today, a hippo hunt has to be organized discreetly (strictly speaking, hunting hippos is illegal) and usually takes place further north on the marshier shores below Moiti Hill. Hippos have gone from Loiyangalani.

Sibiloi National Park

Sibiloi National Park (daily fee $15, $5 students/children) provides a powerful temptation to go further north – even for jumping ship if you came up to Turkana by safari tour. **Access** is the main problem, as vehicles heading there from Loiyangalani are extremely rare (a two-week wait might be considered lucky). If you have enough money (upwards of $200per day), the easiest way is to hire one of *Oasis Lodge*'s battered Land Rovers (with driver). With your own vehicle (high clearance 4WD essential for the first section along the northern flanks of Mount Kulal), a full day's drive might get you there, but be sure to get precise directions from as many people as you can beforehand in Loiyangalani, as most maps are useless. From the Loiyangalani–North Horr road, turn left after some 45km, after the road begins to drop down from Mount Kulal's rocky shoulder. From here, a completely desolate track heads due north for 40km to the settlement of Hurran Hurra, where a left should get you to the camel watering-point and settlement of Gajos, another 40km northwest. Another left here (heading west, then northwest) begins to drop down towards the lake and the national park itself. **Camp Turkana**, near the shore just south of Alia Bay, marks the park's south-

THE ELMOLO

The people of Loiyangalani with the best claim to be the original inhabitants are the **Elmolo**. In Kenya, they're famous for being famous. Dubbed "the smallest tribe in the world" (in number, not size), they are the only hunter-gatherer community in the country who can be visited quite easily (for a price) and who don't resent the intrusion. The Elmolo call themselves *el-Des*, but their usual name comes from the Samburu *loo molo onsikirri*, "the people who eat fish". They once inhabited South Island, but now occupy a couple of islands in Elmolo Bay, and a few gatherings of grass huts on the torrid shores 8km north of Loiyangalani. Most of the 600-strong community live here, partly by **fishing** and the occasional heroic crocodile or hippo hunt (officially banned), partly by **cash receipts** from tourist visitors.

The Elmolo are enigmatic. At the time of Teleki's discovery of the lake, they spoke a **Cushitic** language, the family of languages to which Somali and Rendille belong. Recent linguistic research on historical migrations points to their having arrived on the shores of Lake Turkana at a very early time – perhaps over 2000 years ago. They seem to have no tradition of livestock-herding, which might have been kept up if they had turned, like the Turkana, to fishing as a supplement. Today they speak **Samburu** (the last Elmolo-speaker died in March 1998) and have started to intermarry with them. This, as well as the mission's influence, has been quite significant in raising their numbers (from less than 200 twenty years ago) and also in diluting their cultural identity. Once strictly monogamous, polygamy isn't uncommon now and they also send some children to the school in Loiyangalani as weekly boarders. On the slope, right behind the village, a new Catholic church looms.

All this signals the final curtain for a culture and history that has been largely ignored or denied. The conventional wisdom about hunter-gatherers in Kenya is that they are often the descendants of pastoralists who lost their herds. But if the Elmolo are, as some say, pastoral Rendille who took to fishing in order to survive, then it's strange that they have never tried to replace their herds. For without herds, they could never hope to pay bridewealth for wives from their non-fishing neighbours in the traditional way. A better explanation, and one favoured by the Elmolo themselves, is that their people have always been fishermen and hunters, and, until very recently, pressures from other tribes, particularly the Turkana, had pushed them almost to the point of annihilation.

By the the end of the twentieth century, the Elmolo fishing culture was beginning to rub off on other ethnic groups and now the Samburu have started to eat fish. As long as thirty years ago, Peter Matthiessen wrote in *The Tree Where Man was Born*:

> *The Samburu and Turkana may linger for weeks at a time as guests of the Llo-molo, who have plenty of fish and cannot bear to eat with all these strangers hanging around looking so hungry. Other tribes, the Llo-molo say, know how to eat fish better than they know how to catch them . . . "We have to feed them," one Llo-molo says, "so that they will feel strong enough to go away."*

The Elmolo are a charming and hospitable people, and how they survive in their chosen environment is almost beyond belief. Outwardly similar in dress and appearance to the other people of the area, they are slightly smaller, but the bowed legs which are supposed to be the characteristic result of their diet seem to be confined to the older people – you might have thought all that fish would give them strong bones.

Incidentally, if you think you're being offered **children for sale**, which two concerned readers have written to Rough Guides about, here's the explanation: when a mother hands you her child, then asks for money (anything up to Ksh5000), she's not selling her offspring, but simply wants you to sponsor the child's education with a large wad of cash.

ern boundary, with the National Museums' base of Koobi Fora another 10km further up. Getting back down without your own transport is a matter of waiting for any southbound transport: the museums people are obviously the best bet for this.

Apart from **flying in** (around $1000 return from Nairobi's Wilson Airport: you have to negotiate with the pilots), an alternative way of getting there is by boat from

Ferguson's Gulf on the lake's western shore, near Kalokol (p.554): prices vary according to your bargaining skills and perceived ability to pay, though around $200–300 for a return crossing is probably normal (you may have to pay more, however, to convince your boatman to wait longer than one night for the return leg if you're into an extended stay, and he'll expect you to arrange all his food and accommodation requirements, too). There's also an infrequent National Museums supply boat from here.

Discoveries in human prehistory

Sibiloi was created to protect the sites of numerous remarkable **hominid fossil** finds that have been made since 1968 by Richard Leakey's, and latterly Kamoya Kimeu's, team from the University of Nairobi. The park, more than 1600 square kilometres of rock desert and arid bush, is an exceptional source because many of the fossils are found on the surface, blown clean by the never-ending wind. The finds set back the dates of intelligent, co-operative, tool-making behaviour among hominids further and further all the time, but most of the species concerned are assumed to have died out. The crucial discoveries that will link humankind to our prehuman ancestors have yet to be made. One striking find made at Sibiloi in 1972 was "1470", the skull of a *Homo habilis* over two million years old, believed to be a direct ancestor of modern *Homo sapiens*. Sibiloi was declared a national park a year later. As more and more discoveries are made here (currently nearing 200), on the other side of the lake (where excavations have yielded the earliest australopithecine known, *Australopithecus anamensis*, dated between 4.2 and 3.9 million years), in southern Ethiopia and at Olduvai in northern Tanzania, evolutionary theories are beginning to flesh out.

The so-called **museum** at the "expedition" headquarters in Alia Bay, where some of the fossils (including part of a one-and-a-half-million-year-old elephant) are supposedly displayed *in situ*, isn't easily traced: all that was found recently were empty ranger buildings and unhelpful staff. There are no real facilities for visitors and, apart from water supplies, you need to be self-sufficient. In Nairobi, you might try contacting Safari Camp Services (see p.135) who organize occasional specialist tours to Sibiloi for visiting US paleontologists, archeologists and anthropologists, guided by experts in the field.

Animal life

At times, Sibiloi has a surprising wealth of **wildlife**. Indeed, until the 1930s, there were large numbers of elephant living here. Rainless years, ivory hunters, and especially the increase in the herds of livestock, contributed to their demise. But lion, cheetah, hyena, both kinds of zebra (the ordinary Grant's and the finer-striped, taller Grevy's), giraffe, ostrich, Grant's gazelle, topi, kudu and gerenuk all occur here, though there's no guarantee you'll see much. Because of the protection from hunters, hippos and crocodiles are numerous. The tree cover is minimal. The closest you're likely to come to finding

THE KOOBI FORA FIELD SCHOOLS

Possibly the best way of visiting the archeological sites is by coinciding your trip with one of two six-week **field schools** organized by the National Museums of Kenya in tandem with Rutdgers University in the USA. Approximate dates are from June to mid-August, and from mid-August to September. The first two weeks involve "ecological tours" around Nairobi and other national parks, followed by four weeks of rooting around at Koobi Fora with the experts where you're taught excavation methods and fossil analysis. Some places are awarded as bursaries, but unless you're an especially deserving case, the fees are upward of $1000: enquiries to Mr Karega Munene, Director of Koobi Fora Field School, PO Box 40658 Nairobi (☎02/742131, fax 741424).

trees is the petrified forest of stone trunks, reminders of the lush vegetation of the lakeshore in prehistoric times.

THE NORTHEAST

Northeastern Kenya has a single and limited travel circuit: up through **Isiolo** to **Marsabit Mountain and National Park**. It's well worth doing, especially as it's the only route in the northeast currently considered relatively safe.

Beyond, or east of Marsabit, the few towns – Moyale, Mandera, Wajir and Garissa – are remote administrative outposts, ostensibly controlling land essentially peripheral to the onward thrust of development and change, but in reality rarely exerting any real influence for more than a few dozen kilometres around. Few travellers ever make it up here (we'd be interested to hear from those who have) and the rewards if you venture out into these districts are hard to pin down. Savagely hot, rebarbative wastelands unfold for hours on end as you truck your way along interminable dirt roads to towns that can at first seem devastatingly anticlimactic. But there is, as ever, fascination in the regional population: the Somalis, Rendille and Boran, who live by herding their camels and cattle, moving from well to well, crisscrossing the deserts on old migration routes. Being among them is a reward in itself. They tend to be stern and indifferent until you break the ice, and then the kindness and hospitality they show are astonishing. The dusty, fly-blown towns, too, take on distinctive characters as you get to know them; their atmosphere little resembles that of down-country Kenya.

Travel throughout the northeast has a special quality. The normal stimuli of passing scenery, animals, people and events fleetingly witnessed is replaced with a massive open sky, shimmering greenish-brown earth, and just occasionally a speck of movement – some camels, a pair of ostriches, a family moving on with their donkeys. It is a sparse, absorbingly simple landscape. And not the least of its attractions is the restful absence of hassle and shove, and a solitude hardly found anywhere else.

But, except for the Marsabit run, this is travel almost entirely for its own sake. If you decide to go all the way to **Moyale** or **Mandera** (the two towns at the end of the route "spokes"; read the warning opposite and on p.589), the greatest reward is in getting there. Retracing the journey in the opposite direction is a more dubious pleasure, but one you will have to do from Mandera (Somalia still being embroiled in its bloody civil war). A visit to Moyale has more purpose, as it offers the possibility of a brief visit to **Ethiopia**, and is the only recognized crossing into that country and beyond (the route up into famine- and war-ravaged Sudan from the western side of Lake Turkana is obviously ill-advised). Incidentally, the road up from Moyale to Addis Ababa is entirely surfaced. There are generally no special conditions attached to crossing for a few hours to wander around. Crossing the border at Mandera into Somalia is, for the foreseeable future, a dangerous and pointless exercise, as the town on the other side has ceased to exist and Somalia is lawless and without a government.

Isiolo

ISIOLO is the hub for travel to Marsabit, Moyale, Wajir and Mandera, and is the northeast's most important town; there's no problem getting here from the Mount Kenya region and it's perfectly safe to do so (though for travel beyond Isiolo, read the warning opposite, and the advice in the relevant route details).

Southernmost of the "Northern Frontier" towns, Isiolo is on the border between two different worlds – the fertile highlands and the desert. A measure of the untamed badlands beyond is given by the three military training schools based here: Infantry,

---

INSECURITY IN THE NORTHEAST - A WARNING

The **northeast** of Kenya has long been known for lawlessness, but what was sometimes dismissed as only the exaggerated fear and ignorance of "down-country" Kenyans, acquired a starker and more brutal reality in the 1990s.

Since the flight of Somali dictator Siad Barre in 1991, and that country's anarchic disintegration into warring fiefdoms, northeastern Kenya has borne the full brunt of Somalia's desperate refugee crisis. Because the border is largely an uncontrolled one, the war itself occasionally spills over too. The situation has recently been further complicated by Somali clans such as the Degodia acquiring automatic weapons and then using the confusion to settle old scores with neighbouring clans, recently escalating to fully-fledged massacres of whole villages. There's also the largely unknown quantity of the "Oromo Liberation Front", which claims parts of Kenya and Ethiopia as the Oromospeaking peoples' homeland, and which has been blamed for a number of civilian massacres. There are also the ever-present and increasingly cold-blooded bandits who attack vehicles, even when travelling under armed escort.

All this has recently been made more volatile by the prolonged drought which has affected most of the region since 1996 (El Niño's floods notwithstanding), claiming thirty to fifty percent of the region's livestock and its first human lives in 1999.

Whatever the complicated situation on the ground, you can be sure of one thing: there are more people than before with guns, ammunition and little else. Armed attacks on remote villages and even on armed convoys have become commonplace, averaging – through the end of 1998 and the first half of 1999 – one major attack a week. Of these, two-thirds involved fatalities. Presumably, many other non-fatal incidents were simply never reported. Given the low volume of traffic in the region, any form of land travel therefore poses a serious risk.

The military presence in the northeast is pervasive: roadblocks, vehicle searches and armed escorts are part of everyday life and you should be sure your passport is in order for the duration of your trip. For all this, however, the military presence is also almost entirely ineffective. Of all the incidents reported during the period of our research, not one resulted in an arrest, nor was a single head of cattle ever returned to its owner. Indeed, some accuse the police of being complicit in the crimes.

We've endeavoured to note the current security situation for all parts of this chapter, but you're strongly advised to seek advice on the ground before travelling anywhere covered in the following pages. Be aware that the situation can change very quickly and unpredictably: for example, the area between Isiolo and Archer's Post, including Samburu and Buffalo Springs National Reserves, was considered safe for several years before 1997, after which it suffered repeated attacks on villages and tourists. Though the situation in the parks there is now calmly controlled by the KWS, things could easily change again.

In summary, the main likely no-go area for the foreseeable future (certainly within this edition's lifetime) is the entire region north and east of Garissa up to the Ethiopian and Somali borders, in practical terms meaning everything east of the Isiolo–Marsabit–Moyale road, including Wajir, Habeswein, El Wak, and Mandera. Areas where extreme caution are advised are the roads from Mwingi to Garissa, Garsen to Garissa, and the last 30km before entering Moyale. Areas currently regarded as relatively safe, but which have been unsafe in the past, include the Isiolo–Marsabit–Moyale road itself, Archer's Post to Maralal, the road from Malindi to Garsen and Lamu, and the road from Kangonde to Mwingi. The only definitely safe road in this section is from Mount Kenya to Isiolo. Use your judgement, and ask advice everywhere you go, but bear in mind that the region has never been declared a safe zone by the government, even since before Independence. Independent driving at night, incidentally, is not only the height of folly, but also illegal.

Combat Engineering and Artillery, as well as a tank regiment. Isiolo is a frontier in every respect. The terrific **Somali influence** here is something you'll notice everywhere you travel in the northeast. Isiolo is one of their most important towns in Kenya

△ *Samburu, Marsabit & Wajir*

ISIOLO

Livestock Market

N

Talent Lodge

★ **Akamba Bus** **Mashallah Hotel**

BP

Jamhuri Lodging

Barclays Bank

Matatus (for east)

Total

Jeddah Hotel

Savannah Inn

KANSAN ROAD

Nanyuki Guest House

Frontier Green Café

Salama Restaurant

Bomen Hotel

Al-Hilal Café

Silver Bells Hotel

Mocharo Lodge

Jamia Mosque

District Commissioner (D.C.)

Pasoda Lodge

Coffee Tree Hotel

Covered Market

Matatu Stand

SHANTY TOWN

Produce Market

Caltex

Utamaduni

Playing Field

Matatu Stand (for south)

0   200 m

Hotel Classica

✚ **Catholic Church**

▽ *Meru & Nanyuki*

because it was here that many veteran Somali soldiers from World War I were settled. Recruited in Aden and Kismayu, they gave up their nomadic lifestyle to become livestock and retail traders.

But **the town** is really a cultural kaleidoscope, with Boran, Meru, Samburu and some Turkana inhabitants as well as the Somalis. To someone newly arrived from Nanyuki or Meru, the upland towns seem ordinary in comparison. Women from the irrigated *shambas* around Isiolo sell cabbages, tomatoes and carrots in the busy market. Cattle owners, nomadic camel traders and merchants exchange greetings and the latest news from Nairobi and Moyale. In the livestock market, goats scamper through the alleys. Hawkers stroll along the road raising their Somali swords and strings of bangles to the minibuses heading up to Samburu National Reserve (see p.398). And, in the shade, energetic *miraa*-chewing and hanging around are the major occupations. *Miraa* has a long history in Somali culture, and the Nyambeni Hills, where most of the Kenyan crop is grown, are just 30km away (p.405).

Practicalities

Arriving here is particularly exotic at night. The 8.30pm bus from Nairobi doesn't get in till about 2am, and the town can be seen glittering out on the plain far below for an hour or more beforehand. During Ramadan, lanterns glow along the pavements for the *miraa* sellers and most of the shops are still open. You can find a B&L or sleep on the bus until dawn. For **changing money**, Barclays' extravagant Foreign Legion fortress is still the only bank in town (Mon–Fri 8.30am–1pm, Sat 8.30am–11am), and there's a **post office** (Mon–Fri 8am–1pm & 2–5pm).

Accommodation

Isiolo boasts one reasonable, mid-range **hotel**. Of the more humble **lodgings**, all are cheap, and several surprisingly good value. If for some reason Isiolo doesn't appeal, there's a good place 10km south of town in the form of the shaded *Rangeland Hotel* (☎0165/2340; ②), which also has a small playground for children.

Bomen Hotel (PO Box 67 Isiolo; ☎0165/2389, fax 2225). The best and most expensive in town: clean, polite and serving good breakfasts. Rooms lack fans, but are s/c and have nets, and hot water mornings and evenings. ③.

Hotel Classica (PO box 334; ☎0165/2098), on the south side of town, opposite the gargantuan Catholic church. A newish place with comfortable beds in s/c rooms (hot water), but already showing signs of old age. Safe parking. ①.

Jamhuri Lodging (PO Box 88; ☎0165/2065). Newly renovated, clean, courteous and mellow – currently the most popular cheap place. Laundry facilities. Not s/c. ①.

Jeddah Hotel (PO Box 335; ☎0165/2264). The newest in town, on the same street and similar to the *Jamhuri*, also clean and secure. ①.

Mashallah Hotel (PO Box 378; ☎0165/2142). Clean, functional, Somali-run apartment block with both s/c and cheaper non-s/c. Not terribly welcoming. Doubles and singles. ①.

Mocharo Lodge (PO Box 106; ☎0165/2385). Good value, safe parking. Recommended. ①.

Nanyuki Guest House (PO Box 451; ☎0165/2168). Reasonable and dirt cheap, with spartan rooms, nets, fresh cold milk, dry-cleaning facilities and safe parking. ①.

Pasoda Lodge (PO Box 62; ☎0165/2162). Quiet and clean, with inexpensive meals. All rooms s/c with nets. Safe parking. ②.

Silver Bells Hotel, between the *Bomen* and *Pasoda* (PO Box 247; ☎0165/2251). Clean, quiet and mid-priced, with a grubby cocktail bar which sells only beer and soda. ①.

Talent Lodge (PO Box 174; ☎0165/2262). Basically a boozer with cheap rooms, pleasant but sometimes dirty. ①.

Eating and drinking

Somali *hotelis* provide excellent **food**, day and night. Now that you're in the northeast, you'll see pasta (usually spaghetti) appearing quite prominently on menus – one of the better Italian bequests to the Somalis.

Al-Hilal Café. Pretty good – especially noted for its samosas – and it has some ultra-cheap accommodation.

Bomen Hotel. The *nyama choma* at the patio bar is worthwhile for meat-eaters.

Coffee Tree Hotel. Down-to-earth eats.

Frontier Green Café. A brilliant, tree-filled garden-restaurant with disco (Wednesday, Friday and Saturday), fluorescent spider's webs and UV tubes – in outlandish contrast with the rest of the town. Long popular for its good spiced *chai* for next to nothing a glass. The bar is open 24hr.

Interfast Food Takeaway. Under *Mashallah Hotel*, unexciting but adequate.

Salama Restaurant. The best in town – especially for an early breakfast or their very good spaghetti.

Talent Lodge. A worthwhile move on a hot afternoon for a cold beer on their rooftop terrace, though the broken bottles and legless chairs somewhat mar the atmosphere.

Crafts, salesmen and other distractions

Isiolo is one of the best places to buy **bracelets** of copper, brass and aluminium. Prices are generally around Ksh50 for the simple ones, up to Ksh100 for the heavier, more complicated designs, if you can bargain effectively (starting prices are much higher). In the tourist low season, you may present the day's only opportunity for a sale, so prices can drop even further. Short "Somali swords" in red leather scabbards are also much in evidence. The "sharp boys" who mob you near the markets will invariably offer to guide you to one of the few blacksmiths in town to watch the fascinating process of twisting the wires for the bangles. Profits come from buying rough bangles, then polishing and selling them. If you go, you're generally expected to make a purchase and tip a few shillings to the boys. While the bangle and knife salesmen throng as soon as you sit down for a *chai*, their approach is rarely aggressive (though see the note about tyre-spiking below). Women offer small wooden dolls with woven hair, which in the past were given to young girls as both toys and fertility charms. Some of the former "sharp boys" have recently teamed up to start the **Utamaduni Self-Help Group** (PO Box 16; office in the market opens Mon–Fri 3–5.30pm), which aims to organize and rehabilitate homeless and orphaned youth in community-based projects (for example by building small bridges over sewage ditches). Though some of their members are still a little rough around the edges, it's a laudable venture, and the best place to get a **guide** for visiting local *manyattas* (they must have an ID card; you should pay between Ksh500–800 for a full day). For trips further afield, test the guide first on a one-day trip in the environs of Isiolo before trusting him on a longer journey.

If you're at a loose end in the evening, the Comix Cinema, up near the Pasoda, and the one next to the *Savannah Inn*, has a **video screen** with an endless mix of movies you'd forgotten about, plus more up-to-date war, ninja and kung-fu fare. Finally, you can ask at the *Bomen Hotel* for the man who runs one-hour camel rides: tourists pay up to Ksh600, others Ksh200–300.

Moving on from Isiolo

Isiolo is a great town for passing the time. Memorable conversations are one of its strong points, although the street boys are a hassle and being reeled into slurred soliloquies with men drunk on *changaa* or stoned on *miraa* can get tiresome. However, when heading north or east, waiting in Isiolo is a predictable part of the trip.

The only public transport onwards from Isiolo is to Wamba and Maralal via Archer's Post, details for which are given below. Otherwise, there are no buses and only limited *matatu* services north or east from Isiolo, so your only options for travel to Marsabit, Moyale, Wajir and Mandera are either **self-drive**, which is ill-advised for all but the most experienced, well-equipped and mechanically-skilled driver (and you have to travel in convoy, except to Maralal, Archer's Post and Samburu and Shaba national reserves), or **hitching a ride** with a truck, also in convoy. If you're lucky, you might get a lift with one of the mission or aid vehicles, but even these rarely venture further than Kalacha or Wajir and are, in any case, often too wary to give lifts to strangers. Note if you're driving that Isiolo is the last **fuel** stop until Maralal, Marsabit or Wajir, and beware also that tyre spikers were until recently at work at Isiolo police barrier: while you stamp about, change your wheel and arrange for your puncture to be repaired, an army of souvenir peddlers pitch their gear at you.

Back to Nairobi via the Central Highlands

If you're travelling by **bus**, Akamba has two daily services via Nanyuki, Kiganjo, Nyeri and Karatina, departing at 7.30am and 8pm, arriving in Nairobi at 1pm and 2am respectively. Their office is in the *Maendeleo Hotel* building. The cheaper Eastern Express, opposite Barclays Bank, has one daily departure at 7.30am, which doesn't stop in Nyeri, and has a reputation for insane drivers. For *matatus* you have to be at the market stage before sunrise – last departures at 6am are not unheard of.

North to Marsabit and Moyale

For many years this route was considered highly dangerous due to traditional **bandit-ry**, but things appear to have calmed down a little over the last three years, with only occasional incidents now being reported, mainly on lone vehicles travelling (illegally) out of convoy. The main trouble spots at the time of writing were the first 40-odd kilo-metres to Archer's Post (sporadic highway-style hold-ups of tourist vehicles bound for the Samburu national reserves, so don't dawdle), and the approach to Moyale, which is subject to more frequent raids from neighbouring Ethiopia. **Matatus** go as far as Archer's Post, which is only helpful if you're visiting Samburu or Shaba national reserves (see p.398). Otherwise, try for trucks at the **police roadblock** 3km north of Isiolo at the **end of the tarmac**, by the junction for Wajir, where drivers sign their vehi-cles out of town. There are usually a few heading up to Moyale daily, and most take pas-sengers (for a fee): you'll have to stand on top of the load along with the other, usually male, passengers, although given the state of the roads, this is actually more comfort-able than sitting down. Alternatively, Gametrackers' Turkana Bus passes through Archer's Post early in the morning every other Sunday, which – if the driver's amenable – can take you as far as Marsabit, probably for a fee. If you do get a lift, the 262km to Marsabit takes seven to ten hours, with the next leg to Moyale (245km) anything from ten hours to two days, depending on the state of the road and the frequency of hold-ups, natural or otherwise. Trucks charge upwards of Ksh800.

Northeast to Wajir and Mandera

This road has been extremely dangerous since 1995, and should not be attempted for any reason. Transport is strictly in **convoy**, escorted by heavily-armed soldiers and police. Even so, **attacks** on armed convoys have been increasing in intensity, and fatalities are common enough: the bandits here have ditched the usual formalities, preferring to shoot up the vehicles first, and then take what they want. If you're not dissuaded, Land Rover *matatus*, departing from under the tree beside *Maendeleo Hotel*, only ply as far as Mado Gashi, 160km short of Wajir along the increasingly terrible B9 (due for "rehabilitation", apparently), though they occasionally venture further when security seems better. You may find a further connection here, or you may not. Departure times are sporadic and often they do not depart at all. Otherwise, **hitching** a lift with an armed convoy is the only option. Early morning is the time for this, again, at the **police checkpoint**, although *miraa* sales can add hours to journey times. You'd be wise to secure the lift, and the price, the night before. The 352km to Wajir should take around nine hours unless the convoy leaves late, in which case a night in Mado Gashi, where the armed guard is changed, is likely. Wajir to Mandera should, again, take nine hours, again assuming minimal hold-ups. Be warned, again, that this is the most dangerous leg of the trip – in fact one of the most perilous roads in Kenya – and incidents are common, averaging one a week in 1999. If you're still determined, it's a wild and often extremely uncomfortable journey but worth it for the subsequent feeling of elation at having survived.

West to Maralal

Still considered by some to be a trifle dangerous (there were a few isolated incidents of banditry in the early 1990s, and the stretch to Archer's Post has experienced armed hold-ups lately), the **Isiolo–Archer's Post–Maralal** run is served by the wacky Babie Coach, a converted Bedford lorry which operates a daily run between Isiolo and Maralal (or vice versa), leaving one town at around 9am to reach the other five to six hours later – though you could stop off in Wamba (p.563) to explore the grandly mys-terious Mathews Range. On the days that Babie Coach is on its homebound run to Isiolo, you may find the odd *matatu* going to Maralal. If you're **driving** the route your-self, bring enough fuel for the whole journey – there are no supplies at Wamba.

To Marsabit – and North Horr

No matter the speed, this is a fantastically uncomfortable trip, with rocks, ruts and corrugations that shake smaller vehicles to breaking point. Somewhat unbelievably, the road is said to have been surfaced at least three times in the past, all the way to Moyale – not a trace of which remains.

Passing over the usually dry Ewaso Nyiro River and a police barrier, you hit the agglomeration of shiny-roofed shacks and rows of *dukas* which is **ARCHER'S POST**. This is as far north as you'll get by *matatu*, although lifts into Samburu and Shaba national reserves may be forthcoming from Kenya Wildlife Service personnel, who frequent a number of particularly good bars. There are some **rooms** here, too, should you fail: try *Accacia Shade Inns*, which also has a **campsite** (with no guarantee of security). There's no **petrol** available; the nearest is an expensive trip to either *Samburu Lodge* or *Sarova Shaba Lodge* in the reserves. Finally, advertising "hard and pertinent facts about the Samburu people", **Samburu Cultural Centre** (daily 10am–4pm; PO Box 548 Isiolo), half a kilometre from Archer's Post market along the Samburu National Reserve road, has a small **ethnographic museum** and *manyatta*, complete with ironmongery, woodwork and beadwork for sale, displays of dancing, and more.

PEOPLES OF THE NORTHEAST

Identities in the northeast can be confusing. The largest group are the **Boran**, part of the **Oromo peoples** (formerly called Galla, an Amhara term of abuse), whose homeland was near the Bale Mountains in Ethiopia, from where they suddenly exploded out, in all directions, in the sixteenth century. The pastoral Boran developed and flourished in what is now southern Ethiopia, but Menelik's conquest of the area and the oppressive Amhara regime caused some of them to move down to the lowlands (much less suitable for their cattle) of northern Kenya; the first Boran arrived in Marsabit only in 1921. Similarly recent Ethiopian immigrants to the region between Marsabit and Moyale are the **Burji**, an agricultural people who were called down by colonial administrators in the 1930s who wanted crops grown to feed themselves. The Burji took quickly to Western education and trade, and as a result dominated Marsabit politically in the first decade after Independence. As is common throughout out the world in relations between pastoralists and agriculturalists, there is little love lost between the nomadic Boran and the settled Burji.

At around the time of the Oromo expansion, another group of people - the forefathers of the Gabbra - arrived in northern Kenya, causing havoc in the region, only to be themselves pressured by the ensuing expansion of **Muslim Somalis** from the east. The ancestors of the **Gabbra** became "Boranized" to the extent that they changed their language and adopted Boran customs. Although most Boran and Gabbra, especially those who adopted a more sedentary life, have adopted Somali styles in dress and culture, they eschew Islam, in preference for their own religions. The **Rendille**, to the northwest of Marsabit, look and act like Samburu, with whom they are frequently allied; they speak a language close to Somali but have non-Muslim religious beliefs. They normally herd camels rather than cattle and, to a great extent, continue to roam the deserts, facing the prospect of settling down without any enthusiasm at all and visiting Marsabit only for vital needs or a brief holiday.

In Marsabit itself, distinctions other than superficial ones are increasingly hard to apply as people intermarry, more children are sent to school, and down-country ideas – and Christian missionaries – percolate up the road. Still, language and religious beliefs remain significant in deciding who does what and with whom, and outside the town, individual tribal identities are as strong – and potentially bloody – as they have ever been.

North of Archer's Post, the road veers northwest and for thirty minutes the great mesa – over 2000m – of **Ol Olokwe Mountain** (or Ol Doinyo Sabache) spreads massively across the horizon in front of you. If you're travelling independently with a vehicle, it can be climbed. If you fancy something more organized and worthy, **Namunyak Wildlife Conservation Trust** (PO Box 88 Wamba; information and bookings from Let's Go Travel in Nairobi, p.142) is a community-wildlife venture set-up in 1995 to preserve some 300 square kilometres of land around the mountain for the benefit of local Samburu. They offer walking safaris up the mountain led by Samburu *morani*, rich ground for bird-spotters with frequent sightings of Gambaga flycatcher, shining sunbird, the tiny cisticola, stone partridge, and Kenya's largest nesting colony of Ruppell's vultures. You might also see dikdik, klipspringer, Chandler's mountain reedbuck, rock hyrax, vervet monkey, olive baboon, and (very rarely) leopard and elephant.

For several hours beyond Ol Olokwe you roar across the flat **Kaisut Desert**. **Laisamis** isn't much of a break – a low windblown cluster of tin-roofed huts and Samburu, offering sodas and toothbrush sticks to passers-by – and the Losai National Reserve – which you have just crossed – isn't any different from the rest of the scenery. The **approach to Marsabit**, though, is unmistakable. The road begins to climb and suddenly you're on a hilly island in the desert, a region of volcanic craters, lush meadows and forest. The branches of the trees on the steep slopes are disguised by swathes of Spanish moss, looking at first glance like algae-covered rocks in shades of grey and green.

Marsabit town

MARSABIT is a surprise: it's hard to prepare yourself, after the flat dustlands, for this fascinating hill oasis, in the desert but not of it. Rising a thousand metres above the surrounding plains, *Saku*, as the mountain is known by locals, is permanently green, well watered by the clouds which form and disperse over it in a daily cycle. The high forest is usually mist-covered until late morning, the trees a characteristic tangle of foliage and lianas.

The town is capital of the largest administrative district in the country, as well as a major meat- and livestock-trading centre. It is small and intimate in feel; walking around, you're always bumping into familiar faces. The lively cultural mix in the main market area is the biggest buzz: transient **Gabbra** herdsmen and **Boran** with their prized short-horn cattle, women in the printed shawls and chiffon wraps of **Somali** costume rubbing elbows with ochred **Rendille** wearing skins, high stacks of beads and wire, and fantastic braided hairstyles. There are government workers here, too, from other parts of Kenya, and a scattering of **Ethiopian immigrants** (mainly Burji) and refugees. For some Marsabit background, try Mude Dae Mude's novel *The Hills are Falling* (Transafrica, Nairobi 1979), now out of print but you might still find a copy in Nairobi. If you're interested in **traditional music**, ask for George's Music Store in Marsabit: George is happy to answer queries, and has a great selection of cassettes.

Accommodation

Kenya Lodge & Hotel (PO Box 176; ☎0183/2221; ①) used to be an outstanding **place to stay**, but has been getting decidedly rundown since its Ethiopian owners left: no longer clean, but still relatively modern and cosy, and cheap. Other places include the large but rather miserable *Marsabit Highway Hotel* (PO Box 110; ☎0183/2236; ①), with a bakery below (fresh bread every afternoon), and some self-contained rooms with double beds; the *Badassa Hotel*, an unexceptional B&L with a decent *hoteli* (①); the *Al-Jazeera*, which offers extremely cheap and peaceful accommodation and very safe parking (①); and the clean, Muslim-run *Al-Bandir Hotel* (①). A little further out, by the market, are two more cheap B&Ls, *Greenshade Hotel* and *Marsabit Hotel*. Whichever you choose, ask about **hot water** before moving in: night temperatures can drop very low (by some accounts, *Marsabit* means "place of cold") and lukewarm showers are no fun. New boreholes mean that the town is currently well supplied with water, and electricity is generally reliable (unless the diesel-powered generator breaks down). If you want **to camp**, head for the National Park's main gate (see below).

Other practicalities

For **changing money**, the KCB is open Monday to Friday 9am–1pm and Saturday morning 9–11am. There's also a **post office** (Mon–Fri 8am–1pm & 2–5pm), and several reasonable places to **eat and drink**. For Ethiopian food and a varied menu of Kenyan food, visit the *Al-Bandir Restaurant*; the *Al-Jazeera* serves decent meals, too. Or simply head for the market. There is very cheap food in a lively atmosphere at any time of day from the *hotelis*: hefty pancakes, *githeri*, *Mandaazi* and *nyama choma*. The *hotelis* double as butchers so you can select your own slab for roasting from the carcasses hanging up. There's a well-stocked grocery next

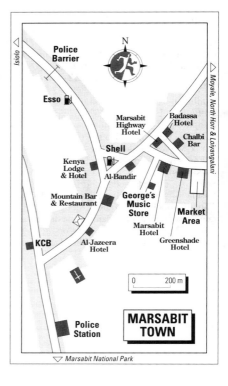

to the *Kenya Lodging*. If you're thirsty, the *Mountain Bar & Restaurant* (PO Box 20; ☎0183/1342) is the die-hards' drinking den, with a melange of characters and the occasional dispute over prostitutes – or try the *Chalbi Bar B&L*, opposite the *Marsabit Highway Hotel*.

Walks out of town

There are a number of trips you can make on foot from Marsabit in a few hours or less – particularly good restoratives if you haven't got your own vehicle and failed to get into the National Park (see below). The easiest, with rewarding views, is the short walk up to the big wind-powered **generator** on a hill just west of the town. Turn left just before the police barrier and simply follow the path.

A longer excursion takes you up to the **VOK transmitter** behind the town, an excellent morning or afternoon hike through lush forest with magnificent panoramas of the whole district from the top. There are wells up here, too (see below). During the rainy season, everything is tremendously green and you walk over flowering meadows through clouds of butterflies.

From there, you should be able to see the closest sizeable crater, **Gof Redo**, about 5km north of the town in the fork of the roads to Moyale and North Horr. Follow either road from where they fork for about 3km, then turn left or right accordingly for a one-kilometre cross-country walk. The crater is quite a favoured hideout for greater kudu, and there's a population of cheetah around here too, not infrequently seen from a vehicle (but likely to flee if you're on foot). You can scramble down the crater wall. Gof Redo can't really be missed, but a friend from town would be reassuring.

Even easier is a walk to the **"singing wells"** at Ulanula (called Hulahula by some). These are less exotic than they sound, but they're still a good excuse to explore. Ulanula is a conical peak to the right of the Isiolo road, about 6km from town. Leaving Marsabit, you cross two bridges, then turn left and climb 200–300m up a narrow, tangled ravine. A concrete holding-tank, visible from the road, gives the place away. Behind it are two natural wells, the first with a wooden trough in front, the second longer and apparently deeper, containing a fluctuating depth of brown, frog-filled water. A silent pumphouse stands by.

The **singing** is done not by the wells but by the Boran herders who use them. When the water is low, human chains are formed to get it out with luxuriantly leaking leather buckets: singing helps the work. At the driest times of the year you may be lucky and witness this, but try to get here early. Animals are usually driven to the wells after dawn, and it's a brisk 75-minute walk from town. Go out there in the late afternoon, though, and you should get a lift back with one of the day's vehicles up from Isiolo.

Onward from Marsabit

One or two trucks do occasionally spend the night in Marsabit, to or from Moyale or Isiolo. Otherwise, the convoy to Moyale usually passes in the afternoon, and that towards Isiolo anytime between 5pm and 11pm. The best place to wait is at the **police checkpoint**, 300m from the Esso garage on the Isiolo road. Ask around the petrol stations if you are trying to hitch a lift to Loiyangalani; with your own tent, your first target is Kalacha, otherwise aim for North Horr. If you are **driving**, supplies of petrol are usually available.

Marsabit National Park

Daily fees: $15, students/children $5; map – Survey of Kenya Marsabit National Reserve SK 84 at 1cm:1km.

Having made the long journey to Marsabit, you'll certainly want to get into the **park**. The forest is wild and dense, its two crater lakes idyllically beautiful. Except during the long rains (March–June), there's a good chance you'll see some of the long-tusked Marsabit **elephants**, relatives of the famous Ahmed – a big tusker to whom Kenyatta gave "presidential protection", with elephant guards tracking him day and night (now replicated in fibreglass in the National Museum in Nairobi). Marsabit's new king is Mohammed, his tusks estimated at a cool 45kg each side. The park is also renowned for its **greater kudu** antelope and there's a very wide range of other wildlife. Between the nearly impenetrable forests of the peaks and the stony scrub desert at the base of the mountain, however, you'll need a little luck for sightings. This is a rewarding park but one where you have to look hard.

Practicalities

The park's **main gate** is at the edge of town, past the bank and the District Commissioner's office. It is not often visited and you may be in for a long wait if you want a lift around its forest tracks. On the other hand, the inverse law of hitching will probably come into play when a vehicle does arrive. In addition, government officers and soldiers garrisoned in town drive up to the **lodge** (see below) fairly frequently; this short trip, with the view over the first lake – Gof Sokorte Dika – and its forested rim, is a lot better than nothing. You might also be able to convince an armed ranger to escort you to the first lake (say Ksh500) – it's a wonderful walk through the forest, with clouds of butterflies and the occasional mouth-drying encounter with buffalo or elephant.

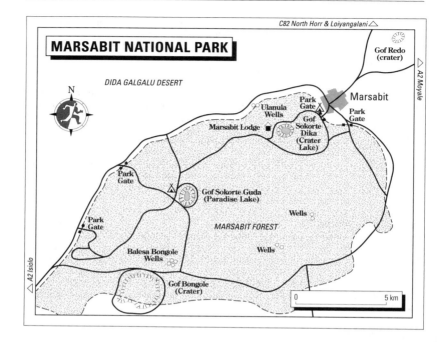

If you venture to **drive in the park** without 4WD, make sure you can get back out. Some of the tracks in the forest are steep and tend to be muddy.

There's a **campsite** near the main gate (100m down the hairpin to the left of the ranger's house) which is free in theory, although the rangers may request a small fee, especially if you wish to use the new toilet and shower block. It's a wonderfully shaded place overrun with baboons swinging on the lianas.

There are several other places to camp in the park. Gof Sokorte Guda (Lake Paradise), a stunning, dark pool a kilometre across for much of the year, has wonderful sites on its crater rim, where a night would be chilly and thrillingly spent – lion, leopard and the rare and shaggy striped hyena are all seen and heard from time to time. This *Lake Paradise Special Campsite* costs $10 per person (plus park entry fee), but does not include the Ksh500 or so "guiding fee" for the obligatory accompanying ranger.

Marsabit Lodge is sadly now closed and falling rapidly into dereliction, though it may be sold to a private developer (information from Kenya Tourist Development Corporation, 11th floor, Utalii House, PO Box 42013 Nairobi; ☎02/229751–4, fax 227815). This is a pity because of the exquisite beauty of its location on the shore of Gof Sokorte Dika and the outstanding views from all its rooms. Elephants are no longer common visitors since the salt that lured them is no longer laid out.

Marsabit's fauna

Your animal count in the park will very much depend on the season of your visit. Good rains can encourage the grazers off the mountain and out into the temporarily lush desert, and the predators (always far fewer) will follow. **Elephants** especially are tremendous wanderers, sometimes strolling into town, causing pandemonium. More problematically, the people of Marsabit have been encouraged to cultivate around the base of the mountain, at the same time creating a barrier to the elephants' free movement and unintentionally providing them with free lunches.

The **birdlife** in the park is amazing: almost 400 species have been recorded, including 52 different birds of prey. Very rare **lammergeiers** (bearded vultures) are thought to nest on the sheer cliffs of Gof Bongole, the largest crater, which has a drivable track around its ten-kilometre rim. Marsabit is also something of a **snake** sanctuary, with some very large cobras – this isn't a place to go barefoot or in sandals.

To Kalacha and North Horr

Reaching North Horr from Marsabit is getting easier, though continuing the logical next step down to Lake Turkana and Loiyangalani is still somewhat difficult. There is a more or less regular passenger lorry which leaves Marsabit "often", as well as mission, Education Department, commercial and aid vehicles.

En route, **MAIKONA** is a friendly Gabbra settlement on the fringes of the **Chalbi Desert**, with a thriving daily market for goats and cattle (the camels which become ubiquitous from here on tend to be traded at Isiolo). As with all the villages up here, keep your camera out of sight, and ask permission if you want to take **photographs**: belief in the camera's evil eye is prevalent. *Kamkunji Hotel* may have one or two rooms. Some 5km north is a small, seemingly miraculous oasis pond of blue water with a sweet green grass fringe. It's the last fresh water until **KALACHA**, a regular night stop for some of the longer Turkana expeditions (Gametrackers stay here). It's the neatest village in all Africa, with its "streets" defined by rows of carefully placed stones, and litter, if there were any, is quickly blown away by the furnace wind. There's a church designed by a German architect, two very basic *dukas*, a bar that sells very hot beer, and the humble but friendly *Bismillahi Hotel* which has rooms. But the real treat is the remarkably good mission-run **campsite** – dusty and barren yet with decent showers and even a rather inventive swimming pool/water tank, that subsequently feeds an irrigation system. The water, pumped up by a windmill, is sporadically chlorinated. Local Gabbra cluster to sell their wares and to pick up what useful items they can.

From Kalacha to North Horr, the track streaks out over blinding white salt pans and shifting quicksands, ducks behind straggly oasis clusters of half-dead palm trees, and finally loses itself in a vast orange expanse rimmed only by the floating hulks of very distant mountains. The exact path of the road varies annually, and in April is often impassable when the rains bring with them a circus of flamingos. **NORTH HORR**, when you finally reach it, is a welcome haven, with a handful of *dukas*, the Somali *Al-Rachid Hotel*, opposite the mosque, for traditional fare, rooms at the *Mandera Central Hotel*, and even a red phone box that works. From here on down to Loiyangalani, the terrain becomes even tougher as the road painfully climbs the volcanic foothills of Mount Kulal, but the view from the top, looking down over the lake far away, can be spellbinding.

To Moyale and beyond

From Marsabit, the **journey to Moyale** takes between five and nine hours depending on the vehicle. For the first three of these you descend from the mountain's greenery past spectacular craters – Gof Choba is the whopper on the left – to the forbidding black moonscape of the **Dida Galgalu Desert**. Dida Galgalu means "plains of darkness", according to one Boran story. Another account derives it from Galgalu, a woman buried here after she died of thirst trying to cross it. The road arrows north for endless miles, then cuts east across watercourses and through bushier country beneath high crags on the Ethiopian frontier. En route, you pass a new refugee centre at Lugga Walde (or Walda), 80km before Moyale (a UN and American IRC charity camp), and the turning to the small village of **Sololo** on the Ethiopian border, arrestingly sited between soaring peaks, which can be climbed for stunning views over the northern plains and Ethiopian highlands. Sololo has a mission, which may let you camp in their grounds, and a single lodging/brothel (the *Treetop*). Note that the road to Sololo, and the last stretch into Moyale, sees occasional **armed hold-ups**, though nothing as vicious as those around Garissa and Wajir: again, the usual rule applies – travel in convoy, and don't resist.

There are some magnificent, towering **termite mounds** along the northern part of the route, a sight that is quintessentially African, yet one which can be quickly taken for granted, like leafless trees in a northern winter. And, as the distances roll away, the 250km from Marsabit to Moyale is resolved as just a few bends, a couple of scenery changes. Over spaces that would take days to cover on foot you can see where you have been and where you are going – the pastoralists' conservatism hallowed by the landscape.

The road bends north again and winds up through the settlements of Burji farmers – an agricultural people who emigrated from Ethiopia earlier in the twentieth century – past their beautifully sculpted houses and sparse fields, to Moyale.

Moyale

Straddling the Ethiopian border, **MOYALE** makes Marsabit look like a metropolis. Though the town is growing rapidly, and was recently supplied with electricity, the centre is small enough to walk around in fifteen minutes. You'll find several sandy streets, a pretty mosque, a few *dukas*, a bar, a camel-tethering ground, two petrol stations (one of which occasionally belies its defunct appearance), a big police station, a fairly large market area, a new KCB bank and an incredibly slow post office – five weeks to Europe. Moyale is not much to write home about in fact, and there's not a lot to do except wander around, perhaps try some camel milk (very rich and creamy) and pass the time of day with everyone else, with or without the aid of *miraa*. Note that there have been a number of shootings in town recently involving "Ethiopian bandits", with the local population as victims. It's a regular enough occurrence, it seems, judging by the practised haste of the shopkeepers in sealing up their businesses on hearing even distant gunfire.

The most interesting aspect of Moyale is its **architecture** – at least, the good number of traditionally built houses which are still standing (the rest were bombed and shelled during World War II, after which the good citizens of Moyale clubbed together for "less fortunate people", contributing £80 to the colony's "Food for Britain Fund"). The Boran build in several styles, including circular mud-and-thatch huts, but in town the houses are rectangular, of mud and dung on a wood frame, with a flat or slightly tilted roof projecting 1–2m to form a porch, supported by sturdy posts and tree trunks. The roof is up to 50cm thick, a fantastic accretion of dried mud, sticks, scrap, and vegetation. Chickens and goats get up there, improving the roof's fertility, and every time it rains another layer of insulating herbage springs up. As a result, the houses are cool while the outside temperature hovers above 30°C for most of the year (July and August are cooler).

Practicalities

Accommodation is very limited and all firmly in the budget category. The most established B&L is *Barissah Hotel* (①), which shares frontage with the bar. The *Barissah* has a dozen dark cubes around an earth compound, and, while it's hardly clean, it is friendly enough. The **restaurant** has *karanga* and *chapatis* every evening, 24-hour *malayas*, and a permanent supply of warm tea. You need to bring a padlock, and "showers" (a basin of water) have to be ordered.

A second lodging, where family and guests share the same roof, is *Bismillahi B&L* (①), across the way from the *Barissah* behind the Esso pumps. It's slightly more expensive, and facilities here don't match the *Barissah*'s, but the food is good. *Silent Lodge* (①), just outside town near the police barrier, has clean, three-bedded rooms and is perhaps the most promising place. There are other B&Ls on the main street, past the mosque.

The water in Moyale can be briny at times and it's worth bringing a few litres of drinking water up from Marsabit. You can obtain **clean water** in Moyale from the Ministry of Water.

Into Ethiopia

The most interesting prospect in Moyale is to cross the valley into **Ethiopia** (see box on p.588) and spend a few hours, or even a night, there. For Kenyans and Ethiopians, the border is an open one. For foreigners there are just a few formalities on the Kenyan side, none on the Ethiopian side, and crossing is easy. Doubtless the situation depends much on the latest directives from Nairobi and Addis, and on relations between the two governments, which have generally been good, although local tensions are currently high between competing clans in the district, exacerbated by Ethiopian pastoralists who have encroached on the Kenyan side.

You can increase your chances by ensuring your Kenyan visa (if you have one) is a multiple-entry type, thus allowing you back in again. Naturally, an Ethiopian visa wouldn't hinder your progress either, though the embassy in Nairobi is not likely to concede that entry through Moyale would be permitted (by the rule book, tourists go into Ethiopia only by air through Addis Ababa). As temptation, however, the Ethiopians have trumped the Kenyans and have built a smooth tarmac road from the border all the way to Addis.

Onward travel from Moyale – the theory

The following routes are ill-advised at present: read the box on p.575.

Unless you were lucky enough to have a visa and be given clearance to travel overland to Addis Ababa, you'll probably be thinking about **returning to Marsabit and Isiolo** on the next truck or, if your thirst for adventure is still not quenched, getting to **Wajir** and **Mandera**. You can also find occasional food-aid transport trucks heading straight down to **Mombasa via Garissa**.

In Moyale, the police are very helpful and will let you know if any GKs (government vehicles) are going your way. Only GK vehicles can travel when they like; others have to go in escorted convoy. One possibility is hitching a ride to Buna (about halfway to Wajir), where there is a mission, and then finding another vehicle to Wajir.

The track from Moyale to Wajir is infrequently used, often impossible after rain, and passes through some of the most dangerous country in Kenya, scene of the infamous Bagalla Massacre (p.590). The track along the Ethiopian border to Mandera has been virtually abandoned.

Moyale to Wajir

Until 1994, this route was covered by the now-defunct Mandera Express. The eight- to twelve-hour journey is made very rarely these days, usually by convoy. Should you manage a lift, the route passes through the pretty, northern borderlands (much woodland, lots of wildlife) towards Takabba, cutting back south before it reaches that village and passing through **Buna**; from there, Wajir is monotonously and uneventfully reached in a few hours. There are police checks at every little settlement along the way.

A FEW HOURS IN SOUTHERN ETHIOPIA

First you visit the Kenyan police sentry box down the hill, where you may be told that, strictly speaking, your intentions are unlawful and if their senior officer got to hear of it ... The usual arrangement applies, so have some small notes with you. From here the road up the hill to **Ethiopia** is wide and invitingly tarred, though used almost exclusively by pedestrians and livestock. At the Ethiopian post they will ask you if you have an entry visa and, if you have, your passage should be straightforward. Otherwise, explain you're just visiting briefly and go to see the customs and immigration officials at the office on the right as you go up the hill. After they've made one of two phone calls you should be allowed in. On no account go on up the hill if you haven't seen the immigration officer. You may well be given permission to stay the night, but note that customs searches are thorough. Probably the best plan is to take a room in Kenya and leave your gear there.

Ethiopian Moyale is larger than its Kenyan counterpart and noticeably more prosperous – a result, it seems, of the paved road to Addis, some piped water, and a long-established electricity supply. There are several bars, a hotel that wouldn't look out of place in a small town in Greece, lots of simple stores, and plenty of eating places. The market buzzes colourfully with camels and goats, piles of spices, flour and vegetables. Otherwise life here seems much the same as over the border, but easier. As a back-door view of Ethiopia, however, it may be no more representative than the other side of town is of Kenya.

But never mind that; there are some new tastes to try. A good place to **eat** *njera* and *wat*, the Ethiopian equivalent of *karanga na chapati*, is the *Negussie Hotel* (up the hill, take the first left past the wooden slogan "bridge", then the first right). *Njera* is soft, unleavened millet bread, with an uncanny resemblance to a dish cloth, sometimes delicious, other times not. *Wat* is a spicy stew that can be made of any kind of meat or vegetables. The *Negussie* also has a bar serving Ethiopian beer or white wine from Awash Wineries, not for sensitive palates but cheap enough. You can pay for everything in Kenya shillings; the Ethiopian currency is the *birr*.

If you are **staying the night**, head for the state-chain *Bekele Molla Hotel*, about 2km from the border. The bar here appears to be the focus of night-time action for hundreds of kilometres and the rooms are clean and nominally self-contained. *Zibib*, on sale in the bar, is Ethiopian *ouzo* and easily drunk. If your bill seems to bear the wrong date, that's because the Amharic calendar is eight years behind the Gregorian one.

English will serve you much better than Swahili, which is spoken by very few people. The people in this part of Ethiopia are mainly **Boran** and **Konso**, not Amhara, but an Amharic word worth remembering is thank you – *amaser-genalehu*.

Moyale to Mandera

This route tells the same story, with the once six-times-monthly bus suspended indefinitely. This is a region well beyond the reach of the Kenyan Armed Forces and travel here is ill-advised (for want of any concrete information rather than specific reports of attacks). Should you somehow find a vehicle, it takes two days to cover the severe track, with a night stop in the small centre of **Takabba**. Vehicles that use the track along the border, rather than via Takabba (mostly lorries), are driving illegally, and your comfort tends to be ignored: it gets cold in the back at night and there are no food supplies of any kind between Moyale and **Rhamu**. Your personal security is in the lap of the gods.

From Isiolo to Wajir

The following route is ill-advised at present: read the box opposite.

Undoubtedly the hottest, wildest, most remote route in the country, Kenya seems all but left behind when you set off from Isiolo for **Wajir** and **Mandera**. The journey unfolds predictably enough, with the truck running full tilt for hours on end in a cloud of dust across a sizzling pancake of sand, gravel and meagre scrub. The road stretches, empty in both directions, to indiscernible melting points on the horizon.

Mado Gashi and Habaswein

Land Rover *matatus* are currently most unlikely to venture farther than **MADO GASHI**, and even this may be one step too far – most end up 80km short at **Garba Tula**, leaving you to hitch a lift with the convoys from Isiolo. By truck, a late departure usually means a night stop at Mado Gashi, a witheringly unappealing Somali and "Somali-ized" Boran village which is a crossroads for coast, northeast, and Central Highlands traffic. The Boran, like the Samburu more recently, for long bore the brunt of Somali atrocities, but they got wise in the early 1990s, acquired automatic weapons, and now everyone's shooting everyone. The people here aren't exactly unfriendly but the long stares, more than at most places, can be a little intimidating.

While there are numerous **lodgings**, the village has no electricity or running water, so they're spartan and generally dirty; marginally preferable is *Mount Kenya Lodge* at the Isiolo end of town. If you're exceptionally lucky, Mado Gashi's "**cinema**" will be showing something: one of the *chai* shops has a generator and a projector, and a small killing is made whenever the owner gets some reels. The impact of such entertainment on a community like this has to be seen to be believed.

The only settlement of any size between here and Wajir is **HABASWEIN**. This is located right on the edge of the Lorian "swamp", the seasonal flood plain where the Ewaso Nyiro River sheds the rain that falls on the north and east sides of Mount Kenya.

Wajir

First impressions of **WAJIR** are of its size, a fair amount of construction going on, whitewashed, blue, and yellow buildings, and a feeling of Araby in the air which genuinely reflects the town's considerable Arab population. The place has a real gravity of its own, electricity (albeit rationed) and running water, and the "legionary" castellated fortress for which it's famous.

Some background

Like most major settlements in the northeast, Wajir's significance comes largely from its **wells**. More than a hundred of them are scattered across seventy square kilometres of desert, providing the basis of a livelihood for the **Somali** people of the region through their milk camels. At the last count, the region supported some 2.3 million camels as well as 2.8 million cattle, although the recent **drought** may have considerably

---

EAST FROM ISIOLO – A WARNING

The Isiolo–Wajir–Mandera route has been closed at times recently and is heavily patrolled and garrisoned by the army (see also the box on p.575), but with seemingly little effect. Along with the roads north and east from Garissa, this road – especially around Wajir – has seen some of the bloodiest attacks and massacres in recent years, and is to be avoided completely. Isiolo is the furthest extent of "normal" traffic and, by the time you get there, you're likely to know whether you're allowed to proceed at all. At the latest reckoning (1999), the entire section from Mado Gashi to Mandera was reckoned highly unsafe. Keep your ear to the ground and ask everyone you meet about the latest news. If you're serious about visiting this region, you might consider taking a *miraa* plane from Nairobi Wilson airport – there are several daily departures to Wajir, Mandera and back again.

reduced their number; unsurprisingly, the wells have always been bitterly fought over and jealously protected. Conflict between Somali clans and clan sections over water rights is probably as old as the clans themselves. Feuds are never forgotten: vengeance and blood money are traditional elements in the struggle for survival in this inimical environment.

In 1984, tensions were running higher than usual and parliamentary balance had gone awry with some sections feeling unrepresented by the town's two Somali MPs. Amid accusations of atrocities between rival clans, the regional administration announced an amnesty for those Somalis who surrendered their guns. Wajir's notoriety stems from this point, when thousands of men and boys of the Degodia clan were rounded up and interned by the authorities in a fenced military airstrip at Wagala, west of the town, for refusing to comply. Hundreds subsequently died of exposure or dehydration or were killed trying to escape. A local tragedy of catastrophic proportions, the **massacre** left many families without their menfolk.

The provincial officials held to blame for the massacre were transferred and there were some attempts to bring improvements to the town's services, but the bitterness remained, especially in the vast and uncontrolled hinterland. Throughout the 1990s, things became steadily worse, with a string of attacks, bloody cattle-rustling raids, reprisals, armed hold-ups and shootings along the region's few roads filling the newsprint back in Nairobi. Things came to a head in the summer of 1998, when the Degodia were ordered by the authorities to leave the district. They refused. At 6am on October 24, 1998, several hundred raiders armed with machine guns, machetes, hand-grenades – and even phosphorous bombs, according to subsequent medical reports – unleashed a 48-hour orgy of killing on a number of isolated Degodia settlements and water-points some 200km west of Wajir, murdering around 300 villagers in what became known as the **Bagalla Massacre**. News of the atrocity reached Wajir four days later, by which time the 17,500 stolen cattle, and 74 abducted teenage girls, were presumed to have crossed the border into Ethiopia. First reports blamed the Ethiopian Oromo Liberation Front (OLF) guerrillas, but others pinned the blame on the Oromo-speaking Borana – long-time rivals of the Degodia – who were said to have hired the mercenaries to avenge the deaths of nine Borana herders earlier that month. There were also reports that the militia-men had camps within Kenya at Ambalo, Uraan, Kiniisa and Makutano in Moyale district. The Kenyan police and army seem extremely reluctant, or unable, either to prevent the attacks or to pursue the raiders, effectively leaving the vast tract of territory between Marsabit, Moyale, Mandera and Wajir to the mercy of whoever wields the gun.

The Town

The **market area** on the west side of town is fascinating and well worth wandering around. Quite different from any market you'll have seen before in Kenya, it's a maze of Somali *herio* (grass and stick huts) and wooden shelters. There's a wide assortment of locally made domestic odds and ends including beautiful and simple pottery incense burners for scenting clothing. Fruit and vegetables are in short supply and fairly uninteresting: you'll usually find oranges and sometimes slashes of brilliant red watermelon, though often on the main street between the *Nairobi* and the *Kulan* hotels rather than in the market itself. On the next street up you'll see **tailors** sitting under the trees at their treadle machines in a scene duplicated in thousands of towns across Africa. There's also a **craftsmen's quarter** of metal workers and other artisans around the big new mosque on the way out to Isiolo.

If you'd like to visit some **wells**, the closest are just a little north of town past a flurry of street activity, the administrative departments and the post office. Obviously the activity around the wells depends on the condition of the pasture in the region, and for much of the year the big herds of camels are out in the desert on clan grazing grounds. But when they are here at the wells the scene is memorable. While out wandering, you may also come across some newcomers to the town, a herd of **reticulated giraffes**. These, pestered out of their browsing grounds in the bush by the disruption to the region brought about by the Somali civil war, have taken to the streets of Wajir for security. They are completely tolerated.

Lastly, and equally bizarrely, there's a **squash club** in town, now called the Gamia (Camel) Club, though originally christened the Royal Wajir Yacht Club. It was named thus to bring a bit of a smile to the faces of the British officials posted here in the 1940s and 1950s. Wajir, otherwise, isn't exactly a bundle of laughs.

Practicalities

Finding **somewhere to stay** in the town is no problem. You'll probably end up in the *Nairobi Hotel* (①–②), desperate for shade, a cold drink or ten, food, a shower and sleep: it has it all. The *Malab Hotel* (Box 323; ☎0136/21211; ①–②), right by the bus stop, is reportedly excellent, with fans as well as mosquito nets. There are a number of other lodgings: the *Kulan* is good value with decent, rather basic food; and the *Pastoralist Guest House* (①–②) has been recommended, with a pleasant courtyard, half-asleep service, and New Blue Omo washing powder instead of soap: the normal stuff is useless in the town's hard water.

Because of Wajir's very high **water table** (only 10m below the surface), mosquitoes are a terrible menace here, and you should come adequately prepared with your favourite repellent. For the same geological reason, long-drop toilets are not in use, but there's not much you can do to prepare yourself for the horror of the *kimbo* tins. Avoid drinking the water if you can.

The **food** is generally pretty good in Wajir, with many places offering pasta, pilau rice (*mchele*) and the distinctive, delicious, spiced black tea of the northeast called *strungi*. The main pastime in Wajir seems to be chewing *miraa*, but you'll probably soon get tired of that (or at least your jaws will). Although **alcohol** is officially banned in town, it is available if you ask the right people discreetly: there used to be one or two **bars** with cheap AFCO (armed forces) beer on the eastern, administrative, side of town: try the *Soweto* for mixed Somali/administration company.

There's a KCB **bank** (Mon–Fri 8.30am–1pm & Sat 9–11am), a **post office** (Mon–Fri 8am–1pm & 2–5pm, Sat 8am–1pm) and part-time **petrol station**.

The best place to wait for **trucks** to Mandera is outside the police station. **Flights** from Wajir airfield (used to transport relief supplies to Somalia) to Nairobi are operated by Blue Bird Aviation, with 5.30pm flights on Wednesday and Saturday (Ksh10,000 one-way); they also run to Mandera (same days, around 2pm; Ksh10,400 one-way).

Onwards to Mandera

The following route is ill-advised at present: read the box on p.589.

While it's not a journey for sybarites or weak bladders (vehicles roll non-stop for hours), the final desperate kick from Wajir up to Mandera takes you as far from Nairobi as you can get, which for many people is not an altogether unattractive proposition.

El Wak and Rhamu

About halfway from Wajir to Mandera is **EL WAK** (The Wells of God) and a scramble of people eager to buy whatever *miraa* the bus travellers have for sale. There used to be a camel corps here, but the police today seem to have abandoned the dromedary as a way of getting around. Should you end up spending the night here – and it is amazing how many unscheduled night stops you'll make in the northeast – the bed and board on offer at the only **lodging** is pretty insalubrious.

Another possible overnighter is **RHAMU** (confusingly, often pronounced "Lamu"). Renowned for its mosquitoes, it's right on the Ethiopian border by the seasonal Daua River. There's a National Christian Council of Kenya centre here where you can.

From Rhamu, the **paved road**, which has been an on-and-off affair since El Wak, is continuous to Mandera but in a very sorry state indeed. The road is straight and largely empty, with the barren fastnesses of Ethiopia rising up remotely on the left, but it's one of the most dangerous in Kenya as it crosses, unperplexed, a series of steep north–south ridges with a broadside lack of regard for gradient. Shattered hulks of vehicles litter the slopes, having stalled and rolled backwards. If you are in the back of a heavily laden lorry, it is worth at least finding a suitable position for leaping off. Some of the slopes have been circumvented by zigzags and the worst of them are being levelled. There's ample compensation for an unpredictable journey in the startling quantities of wildlife that's often to be seen along this way, including ostriches, warthogs, giraffes and gazelles.

If your vehicle makes the Wajir–Mandera connection by way of the Somalian border route, you veer to the right after El Wak and make straight for Mandera via the village of **Arabia**: an insane route to take without the protection of heavy armour.

Mandera

More than 1000km from Nairobi and only half that to Mogadishu (capital of Somalia), **MANDERA** nestles at the tip of a much disputed salient of Kenyan territory, wedged uncomfortably between Ethiopia and Somalia. The town, more even than Wajir, has only the most tenuous lifeline to Nairobi – and this thanks mainly to one or two daredevil light aircraft operators who fly in daily shipments of *miraa*. The same planes collect and deliver mail, messages (Mandera has telephones but only just) and government workers. You can drive up, of course, if you're prepared to run the gauntlet of armed hold-ups along the way (a very high risk). Note also that parts of the road up from Wajir were washed away by El Niño flash floods and have yet to be repaired; and there's no petrol at all along the 418km from Wajir (none at El Wak).

Because of the difficulties of land communication with Nairobi, the town formerly relied heavily and uneasily on food supplies from Somalia. As at Moyale, the **border** here was always virtually an open one for local people. Since the destruction of Bula Hawa – the town on the Somali side of the border – and the arrival of tens of thousands of refugees, supplies are less easy to come by and the trade in Kenyan *miraa* for food (rice, sugar, pasta, milk powder and flour), supplied as foreign aid to Somalia and sold into Kenya, has vastly declined, while the needs of Mandera's swollen population have dramatically increased.

The town itself lacks the established atmosphere of Wajir and makes its southerly neighbour look positively urbane. The Girls' Secondary School, for example, is the only one in the entire district (25,000 square kilometres) and it has just a few dozen students.

The heart of Mandera consists of a cluster of Somali *bula* (hamlets) interspersed with administrative buildings. At the time of writing, however, Mandera is effectively a giant **refugee camp**, overrun by victims of the war in Somalia. Tens of thousands of people (more than Mandera's own population) cram into a huge area of *herio* huts and shelters spread across the wasteland between the airstrip and the centre of the town. Their presence makes Mandera tense and the army is much in evidence.

Practicalities

Mandera has critical **water problems** outside of the rainiest months of the year, December and April and, in recent years, drought has once or twice forced many residents and herders to flee into Ethiopia in search of water and pasture, leaving the Somali refugees behind them. All the town's water is supplied by the Daua River. If you can choose a time to visit the town, however, come in August for the annual Agricultural Society of Kenya (ASK) show, when Mandera gets a rare chance to blow its own trumpet.

A Mandera branch of the **KCB** bank has opened (Mon–Fri 8.30am–1pm, Sat 8.30–11am), but so far it doesn't seem to have set off the sweeping changes in the region you might expect. (Whether changing money or not, though, the air-conditioning makes it a fine place to hang out.) They're as helpful as possible, but they have to radio Nairobi for the day's rates and the transaction can take hours (which can be spent watching the *miraa* barons come and go with their colossal wads).

There are few lodgings, their continued existence permanently threatened by the instability of the town. The only decent ones are the *Jabane* (④), which is close to the middle of things, offers fans, showers and towels, and does the best food, and the *Mombasa Inn* (④), next door, which is a little more basic and not as comfortable. The *Mandera County Council Resthouse* (④) is a third option, a surprise with its neat, self-contained rooms, fans and clean water. It's hard to resist after the journey, though you'll score better on conversation and local immersion down at the cheaper places: the *Resthouse* is just a bit far from the town centre. The *New Iftin* (④) and the *Mombasa Inn* (④) both have restaurants – scruffy, rapid-turnover joints swirling with old chits and face-stuffing patrons.

Mandera's **market** is the town's focus and, like Wajir's, a bustling maze of huts and shelters – liveliest around 9 or 10am after the *miraa* arrives – with small stores and *hotelis* all around. You'll also find **arms dealers** here, doing a roaring trade. For a **beer** (Kenyan Tusker or an Ethiopian St. George), try either *The Parliament* or the *Members' Club*, the only licence holders in town, who share a building and compete on the strength of the tapes they play. Both are open after about 4pm. To post letters from this far corner of Kenya, you can use the **post office** (Mon–Fri 7.30am–12.30pm & 2.30–4.30pm, Sat 7.30am–12.30pm), but post takes at least four days just to reach Nairobi, and at bad times it might sit there for weeks. To send something faster, go down to the airstrip in the morning and hand it to the pilot when the plane comes in.

Moving on from Mandera

Getting on the **plane** to return to Nairobi is quite an entertainment: amid the confusion of activity centring on the pilot and the *miraa* big shots, the potential passengers vie for seats – or rather places, since some of the seats have been removed. The big bales of *miraa* are off-loaded, sped into town in a Land Rover and exchanged for huge volumes of banknotes, which are then brought back to the pilot for the purchase of the next consignment. The scene is fraught with confusion but if there's a seat you'll be offered it by the Somali charterer, not the pilot. There are usually two or three flights a day, but during public holidays and Ramadan – when lots of *miraa* is chewed – there's a whole flock. The price falls between $70 and $120 for the two- to three-hour flight, which usually stops at Wajir before clipping past the peaks of Mount Kenya to Nairobi's Wilson Airport. More reliable, if expensive, is the twice-weekly flight run by Blue Bird Aviation, which leaves for Nairobi via Wajir on Wednesday and Saturday at 4.30pm (Ksh13,650 one-way).

Apart from the plane, there used to be two **bus** services back to the hub of Kenyan life. These, however, have been discontinued due to bandit raids; if the situation improves, the buses should return. As it is, if you want to travel anywhere from Mandera without flying, **trucks** (invariably in convoy) are your only option. Try around the big tree by the police station. Again, read the warning on p.589.

Garissa

GARISSA, North Eastern Province's capital, is the least interesting of the desert towns, relatively close to Nairobi and Mombasa, and visibly influenced by both. Still, it comes across as a friendly, unhustly place and it has its ethnic interest: a large Somali contingent who live more or less harmoniously with their non-Somali neighbours, many of whom are coastal Muslims. Garissa was, until recently, the lowest bridging point across the **Tana River**. While the Tana is not mighty, the view of the loop of brownish-red water where it flows under the new bridge just outside town is quite impressive, especially after rain: a sullen reminder of Kenya's water and erosion problems, when you suddenly realize this is the biggest river you've seen in the country. However, severe drought in the area (1995, and from 1997 to date) has severely hit livestock (the government estimates that thirty to fifty percent of the region's cattle had been lost by mid-1998); wily local businessmen have cashed in by selling grass cut from the river banks to the desperate herders.

The easiest – and safest – way to Garissa is by bus from Nairobi (details on p.140), though there are occasionally long delays as police search for *miraa* and bribes. The rangelands flanking the highway are prime cattle-rustling territory, however, but hold-ups – which used to be common – appear to have been deterred by the armed escorts which travel with the convoys up from Mwingi, 200km to the west.

Garissa hovers uncertainly between coast, up-country and desert. Before the current security problems beset it, it was sometimes in the news for various serpentine encounters – a large python was found in the District Commissioner's office and a cobra in a school toilet. They were probably fleeing the heat: this is Kenya's hottest town and often unflaggingly humid as well. During the day the thermometer rarely leaves the 32–37°C zone.

GARISSA - A WARNING

Do not attempt to travel east of Garissa by road. Fatal incidents, some as close as 5km from town, are frequent (once a week on average, sometimes three). The bandits here have dispensed with the usual "Your money or your life" formalities, and simply spray the vehicle and its passengers with bullets to bring it to a halt, whether it's a relief truck or a heavily guarded bus. The armed escorts appear to have little deterrent effect (seventeen police and security officers were killed in one week in September 1998, which led to protesters rioting in Garissa). These incidents, at first greeted with outraged headlines in the Kenyan press, now merit little more than a short paragraph on an inside page.

Travel can be reckoned to be anything from slightly risky to highly dangerous on: the **A3 road** via Dadaab and its refugee camps to Liboi near the Somali border; **the C81** north to Mado Gashi and on to Wajir; and on the **track due north of Garissa** to Sankuru (where some maps mark the defunct *Sankuru Safari Lodge*).

Other roads out of Garissa – the A3 west to Mwingi, and the B8 south to Garsen via Bura and Hola – both require armed escorts, or you should travel in convoy (leaving early in the morning). Check the situation for these roads wherever you can: mostly safe, they do see the occasional attack, no less bloody than those north and east of Garissa.

If you're driving, the usual rule is to get wherever you're going by 3pm – attacks thereafter seem more likely, and if your car breaks down after then, you've little chance of a lift.

You'll probably want to take the first transport out of Garissa, but if you have some time to kill, stroll down to the **Tana bridge** in the late afternoon and watch Kenya's precious topsoil flowing to the ocean. You can sometimes see hippos from here and even crocodiles (Garissa District has a high incidence of death by *mamba*), and there are signs warning you about the banks where they lurk. It's likely you'll meet some friendly Somali youngsters to take you around.

Practicalities

The best **lodging** is the *Nairobi Guest House*, Miraa Road, next to the Tana River Express booking office, with good cheap rooms, but not s/c (①). *New Safari Hotel* (PO Box 56), a clean B&L with running water, mosquito nets (bring your own door padlock), has a good restaurant doing *mkate mayai* each evening. The *Green Garissa Hotel* is very basic, without running water, while the cut-price beer and gloomy, self-contained rooms at the *Garissa Guest House* (PO Box 55; ☎0131/2019) aren't worth the longish walk. *Kenya Hotel and Lodging* has a busy restaurant but its rooms are unappetizing. *New Silver Cafe* in the main street near the mosque has very good meals, and you can sit outside on the verandah and watch the street life. Just over the Tana bridge on the right is a row of *hotelis* and **bars** that come alive in the evenings. (Be careful about taking photographs by the bridge: the local police don't approve.)

The town has a **bank** (Mon–Fri 8.30am–noon, Sat 8.30–11am), a pretty good **market** and **petrol stations**.

Moving on from Garissa

See the boxes on p.575 and p.589 about transport difficulties and security in the region. As ever, the situation is fluid and you are advised to thoroughly check out your plans before travelling further. At the time of writing, **Gantaal Bus Service** was running a thrice-weekly service to Wajir, escorted Beirut-style with "technicals" (a high-powered machine gun mounted on a Land Rover) and over a dozen heavily armed policemen in jungle fatigues and carrying hand grenades. Despite all this, an attack in February 1999 left twelve passengers dead, and the service seems likely to be suspended. There may be a service to **Liboi** via Dadaab, but it's pointless going there (the Somali border is closed) and the risk of banditry is high (the aid lorries bound for the refugee camps between the two towns are a tempting and frequent target). **Nairobi** has four weekly connections with Garissa (out on Mon, Wed, Fri & Sat; back from Garissa on Tues, Thurs, Sat & Mon). Buses arrive at and depart from a spot opposite the KBS terminus in Eastleigh. All the Nairobi-bound buses (6–7hr) from Garissa depart at 6.30am in an armed convoy.

To **Mombasa** and **Malindi**, Mombasa Lines and Tawfiq share the route, with 6.30am departures from the Kobil station, or from outside the *New Safari Hotel*. If you're heading for Lamu, get off at **Minjila** junction, 7km south of **Garsen** (not in Garsen itself – the Lamu-bound road from here was washed away by El Niño), where you'll have to wait for a lift (you'll have missed the daily buses from Malindi, which pass by before midday; there's a good YWCA nearby if you get stuck). Alternatively, just continue to Malindi, and catch the Lamu bus the next day.

Down the Tana to Garsen

The route down to the coast from Garissa runs through Orma and Pokomo country – low-lying, flat, and densely bush-covered. The Orma **cattle herders** of this region are invariably swathed in distinctive, brilliant, deep-blue cloth, a much-favoured colour which was being imported along the coast over a thousand years ago. Don't expect much of the Tana's remaining pockets of **riverine forest** to grace the scene, however, much less the river itself, as for most of the way the gravelled road isn't close. The bus calls at **BURA**, a desolate resettlement area, whose **irrigation scheme** attracted tens of thousands of former herders as farmers in the early 1990s, but was completely destroyed by flooding late in 1997 – the rains were twenty times heavier than usual – with disastrous consequences. The floods themselves caused an outbreak of a new strain of **Rift Valley fever (RVF)**, a rapidly fatal haemorrhaging disease normally restricted to cattle but which jumped the species barrier to humans, decimating herds and killing hundreds of people. Subsequently, the 1998 rains failed, and at the time of writing (mid-1999) **drought** and **famine** was affecting the whole of Bura district and much of northeastern Kenya besides. Of the seven dammed water sources in the area, six are now dry, and the one remaining is so rank as to be unusable.

Next comes **HOLA**, site of an infamous massacre during the dying days of the colonial period. Not far from the river and consisting more or less entirely of grass huts, with an animated main street, it's a nice place to spend a day or two. **Arawale National Reserve** lies on the opposite bank of the river, and was set up as a refuge for the seriously threatened **hirola antelope** (or Hunter's hartebeest). Its total African population has dwindled from 14,000 in 1976 to about 350 today, most living in the Garissa and Tana River districts. The population in neighbouring Somalia is believed to have been wiped out by persistent drought and war. In response, in 1996 the World Wildlife Fund together with KWS revived a translocation programme which had begun in 1963 when 30 animals were moved to Tsavo East National Park. Since 1996, another 35 animals have joined them and their descendants, bringing the Tsavo population to around a hundred.

You can get a free ride across the Tana in a Pokomo dugout. There are no roads within the reserve, which presupposes 4WD and a tent, but at present a visit would be illadvised – the road skirting its eastern side (from Bura to Ijara trading centre) sees occasional shootings on vehicles by bandits. For **accommodation**, all four options are along the street where the buses drop you, none rising above very basic B&L standard (all ①), and few, if any, have double rooms. The best of these is the *New Safari Inn* (PO Box 22), for a clean, quiet, friendly stay and good cakes. And there's evening entertainment, too: the Riverway Cinema shows American and Indian films on a tiny screen under the stars.

Tana River Primate National Park

No charges at present.

On the map, getting to the **Tana River Primate National Park** – main refuge of two of Kenya's rarest and most beautiful monkeys – doesn't look easy without your own vehicle. In fact, with only a small degree of perseverance, you can find your way to the river and the research headquarters (make prior enquiries with the Kenya Wildlife Service in Nairobi if possible). **Mnazini** is the easiest place to head for if you're without wheels: the 6.30am bus from Garissa makes the side trip down to the village itself, 6km from the main road (so long as the area isn't flooded). If the district is flooded, you'll almost certainly find yourself being carried by poled canoe from just down the Mnazini track all the way to the village itself: it takes about an hour. Regarding **security**, the reserve itself appears relatively secure, and is guarded by a special team of armed KWS rangers. However, the village of **Wenje**, just to the north, has acquired local notoriety as the base for a gang of bandits who operate in the area: take local advice if you're driving.

Mnazini is a fine, coastal-style village beneath mango trees. There are no lodgings but *hotelis* will take you in for the night once you've cleared it with the sub-chief and the headman. One of the **village shops** also has most of what you're likely to need for a few days' stay in the reserve. Beyond Mnazini, there's nothing in the way of food but occasional fruit and garden vegetables.

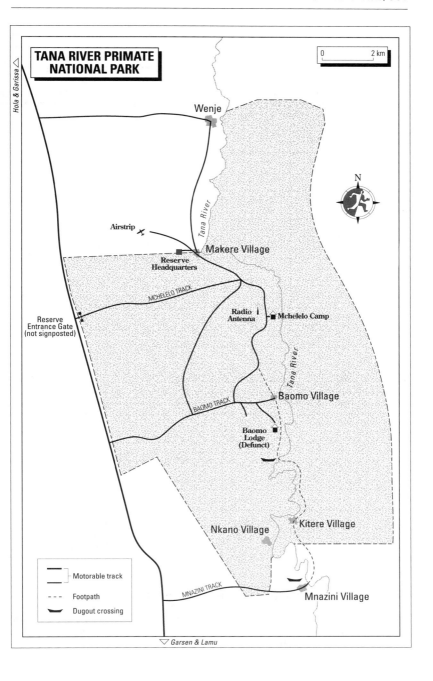

Nobody in the area knows Tana River Primate National Park by that name. Locals all refer to **Mchelelo**, the site of the primate research headquarters. The twelve-kilometre walk to get there involves two river crossings over the Tana's meanders, and there's no way you'd find the route through the **bush** and **gallery forest** unguided. Pokomo **guides** are happy to help and not hustling.

Depending on water levels, you may find you can wade across. If you need a boat, it shouldn't normally cost anything. You enter the forest at Kitere and walking thereafter becomes much more pleasant in the cool shade.

Reserve practicalities

Mchelelo campsite is small, secluded, and ravishingly pretty, with a shower and long drop. It's the site of a National Museums of Kenya research camp and the primatologists here are not used to visitors. If you don't have a letter from the NMK (and preferably an introduction and advance warning sent ahead; address on p.107) you may not be able to stay here. In that case they are likely to direct you on to the park headquarters at **Makere**.

If you're **driving**, the Baomo or Mchelelo tracks to the river are the ones to use, though the latter doesn't seem to be signposted from the road. It's also possible to approach the reserve from **Wenje** village, to the north. The track to Baomo is indicated on the road, but *Baomo Lodge* itself, while it still appears on some maps, is abandoned.

If you're lucky, you'll be made reasonably welcome at Makere, or at least allowed to camp. It has to be reiterated, however, that they don't have organized facilities for visitors – and you may even be given a section of fully armed rangers on the anti-poaching force to accompany you, in military fashion, as you walk the paths looking for monkeys and watching the area's superb birdlife. One or two young guides from Makere village will also help to locate the primates, as will the KWS rangers.

Wildlife

The reserve's protected inhabitants include **Tana River red colobus** and **Tana River crested mangabey** monkeys, both extremely rare and vulnerable. These species occur more commonly in the rain forests of western Uganda and Congo, and are indicative of the time, centuries ago, when these great forests covered the whole of Africa – west to east. In the meantime, continued encroachment on the forest threatens both species of monkey; the colobus very rarely leaves the trees.

Your chances of seeing groups of both monkeys are good. The forest areas are fairly restricted, even within the reserve, and it's not difficult to find them in a day or two. Other wildlife in the area includes blue monkeys, baboons, Grevy's and Burchell's zebra, oryz, lesser kudu, various squirrels and even lions, giraffe and buffalo; on the east side of the park you can see elephants, and there's also a small seasonal population of the endangered Hunter's hartebeest, or hirola, here (see above). At one time it was possible to make raft and boat trips on the sluggish river, dodging large numbers of hippos and crocodiles, but such adventures haven't operated as commercial safaris for years (see the Tana Delta box, p.512, for some details about something like this further downstream). You're likely to find local people willing to take you.

Garsen and connections to Lamu and Malindi

If you're coming from the north and are heading for Lamu, note that the road east from Garsen no longer exists, since it was washed away by El Niño. Instead, ignore your map and leave the bus at the **Minjila** junction, 7km south of Garsen, from where a new tarmac road heads off across the Tana delta. As you'll arrive too late to catch the daily Faza Express bus from Malindi (which passes the junction before midday without going to Garsen), your only hope is hitching. If you have no luck, don't worry: 1km north of the junction, back towards Garsen, the *YWCA* (PO Box 32 Garsen; no phone; ①) is a good place to stay, with ten five-bed dorms, and food available if you order in advance. The centre is mainly used as a base for the Tana River Women's Development Programme, which trains and educates local women in crafts and basic skills to raise their standard of living.

GARSEN itself isn't anyone's favourite place, and something of a dead-end now that the Lamu road by-passes it. There's no electricity or bank, but there is petrol, a post office and police station (pick up an armed escort here if you're heading north in your own vehicle – around Ksh1000 for two guards). There are two lodgings and no short-age of *hotelis*. The *3-in-1 Lodging and Restaurant* (PO Box 16; ①) lacks some basic amenities but is reasonably clean, with a passable restaurant. If the restaurant has gone further downhill, check out the *Happy Family Restaurant & Hotel* (①), right by where the buses stop, which has some grubby rooms and happily subverts its name with bright murals of gun-toting bandits on its walls. For telephones, more reliable and quicker than the post office is the service run by Garsen Agrochemist, 20m along from the *Happy Family*. In season, incidentally, Garsen's mangoes are reckoned to be some of the best and cheapest in Kenya.

Moving on to Malindi, Mombasa Liners and Tawfiq buses pass by daily at around 3pm. Garissa-bound, catch them between 9am and 10am.

travel details

Because of their importance, particulars about **road transport** are given throughout the chapter. On the main axes – Kitale–Lodwar, Nyahururu–Baragoi, Isiolo–Moyale and Nairobi–Garissa – you will rarely be stuck for a ride too long. Least frequented is the route up to Loiyangalani and this, together with Isiolo–Moyale and Isiolo–Wajir–Mandera, has no bus service. For the northeast, see the box on p.594.

BUSES

This indicates the minimum service you can expect in the north. The reverse service applies on each route with the same frequency. Arrival times are not guaranteed. Because of the security position, the routes from Moyale to Mandera and Wajir, and from Wajir to Mandera have been discontinued.

Garissa to: Malindi (in convoy; 2 daily; 11hr); Mombasa (in convoy to Malindi; 2 daily; 14hr); Nairobi: (in convoy from Mwingi; 8 weekly; 10hr); Wajir (currently suspended).

Isiolo to: Maralal (every 2 days).

Nyahururu to: Maralal (daily; 90min).

FLIGHTS

Flights to Wajir and Mandera Hitching a lift on the daily charter from Nairobi's Wilson Airport to Mandera is harder than getting a lift back again because *miraa* is a more profitable cargo than passengers. There are regular scheduled flights run by Blue Bird Aviation (p.143) connecting Nairobi with Wajir and Mandera on Wed and Sat (Ksh14,625 return to Wajir, Ksh20,800 return to Mandera).

Flights to Lake Turkana are usually part of all-inclusive weekend packages at around $500–700 per person at either Ferguson's Gulf (*Fishing Lodge*) or Loiyangalani (*Oasis Lodge*). Otherwise, contact one of the plane charter companies listed on p.134.

PART THREE

THE
CONTEXTS

THE HISTORICAL FRAMEWORK

The picture of Kenya's past that the first Europeans formed – a multitude of primitive peoples with no appreciable history – has been brushed aside in this century. Techniques have been found for tracing past events and migrations by combining oral traditions and comparing languages. Nevertheless, Kenya's precolonial past is still the subject of endless conjecture and, up-country, it's difficult for the traveller to keep much sense of it – especially since the physical record in ancient architecture is virtually nonexistent. On the coast, settlement ruins, old documents and the Islamic tradition help considerably to retain the feeling of a long past. What follows, up to the colonial period, is a much condensed overview, intended to pull together the historical accounts of individual peoples that are given throughout the guide. More emphasis here is given to the firmer history of the last hundred years or so.

THE CRADLE OF MANKIND

Kenya could be the place where human beings first evolved. The oldest remains belonging indisputably to **ancestral hominids** have been found on the shores of Lake Turkana. But it's hard to say whether this is conclusive proof: older finds made elsewhere could suddenly turn the theory upside down.

The east African **Rift Valley**, however, is ideal territory for the search for human origins: volcanic eruptions have repeatedly showered thick layers of ash and cinders over fossil beds, building up strata that can be reliably used to compare ages. The **Leakey** family have been instrumental in much of the work that has been done. Olduvai Gorge in Tanzania, was the first major site to disclose evidence of human prehistory, and Louis Leakey and his wife, Mary, worked there from the 1930s. Their son, Richard, went on to explore the Turkana region and found even older fossils, putting Kenya in the spotlight of scientific attention. A suggestion in support of the "cradle of mankind" idea

is that the Rift Valley's very formation – a major event on the earth's crust, which began some twenty million years ago – may have been the environmental spark that was the catalyst for human evolution.

At any rate, while current research pushes the dates back further and further, it hasn't answered the biggest question: if this is the cradle, who were the parents? The search for an **evolutionary line** linking humans directly with more primitive primates is still the number-one priority. Theories change so fast that books published in the 1960s and early 1970s contain ideas that today have been completely overturned. The "**ape-men**" australopithecines are no longer regarded as ancestors of *Homo sapiens* and it is now known that our own ancestors shared evolutionary time with them in east Africa. The fossil skull 1470 (its catalogue number), discovered by **Bernard Ngeneo** in 1972 and now in the National Museum in Nairobi, is evidence of this. Between two and three million years old, it's an example of *Homo habilis*, "handy man", a direct human ancestor.

Until Ngeneo's discovery, it was thought that while the massive, plant-munching *Australopithecus boisei* did eventually die out, its slighter, higher-brow neighbour *A. africanus* survived, adapting and evolving into the *Homo* line. Now it's believed all three species lived on the savannah and forest margins at the same time. A recent flood of discoveries of *Homo* fossils shows that the evolutionary line that eventually led to human beings was already established as long as five million years ago. Most spectacular in recent years has been the discovery of the nearly complete 1.5-million-year-old skeleton of a twelve-year-old boy of the species *Homo erectus*, our immediate ancestor. It was *erectus* ("upright" man – though in fact the australopithecines probably spent most of their time upright, too) who developed **speech**, discovered how to make **fire** and improved enormously on the **tool-making** efforts of *Homo habilis*. **Olorgasailie** and **Kariandusi** are two "hand axe" sites, probably belonging to *Homo erectus*, which have been used within the last five hundred thousand years. And it was *erectus* who, if the "cradle" theory is right, spread the humanoid gene pool to Asia, Europe and the rest of Africa, where, over the next few hundred thousand years, *Homo sapiens* emerged on the scene.

EARLY INHABITANTS

Real history begins with the **hunter-gatherers**. Numbering probably fewer than a hundred thousand, living in small units of several families, and either staying in one place for generations or moving through the country according to the dictates of the seasons, these earliest human inhabitants may have been related to the ancestors of present-day Pygmy and Bushman peoples, and probably spoke "click" languages similar to those spoken by the Bushmen today (Khoi and San). Remnant hunter-gatherer groups still live in remote parts of Kenya – the **Boni** on the mainland north of Lamu, the **Sanye** along the Tana River and the **Okiek** and **Dorobo** in parts of the highlands – but their languages have mostly been adopted from neighbouring peoples. The hunting and gathering way of life is one that has persisted in the cultural memories of most Kenyan peoples, and some of the groups who still practise it may have veered away from farming or herding societies in times of hardship.

The earliest distinct migration to Kenya was of **Cushitic**-speaking people from the Ethiopian Highlands. Occasional hunters and gatherers themselves, they were also livestock herders and farmers; over the centuries, they filled the areas that were too dry for a purely subsistence way of life. They also absorbed many of the previous inhabitants through intermarriage. Having herds and cultivating land brought up questions of ownership, inheritance and water rights, and an elaboration of social institutions and customs to deal with them. The Cushites left evidence of their settlements in burial cairns and living sites at places like **Hyrax Hill**, near Nakuru. Stone cairns and hollow depressions in the ground are found all over the Kenya Highlands and in the Rift Valley, especially out in the dry areas towards Lake Turkana. The same people may have built the **irrigation works** still used today along the Elgeyo Escarpment, west of Lake Baringo. They had a strong material culture, using stone, particularly obsidian, to produce beautiful arrowheads, knives and axes, and they made a whole range of pottery utensils.

The **Somali** and **Rendille** of the northeast are the main groups still speaking Cushitic languages, though their arrival in Kenya was more recent. Today, only the Boni still speak a language related to the Southern Cushitic of the first farmers and herders, although the Boni themselves are hunter-gatherers. For the most part, the earliest Cushites were absorbed by peoples who came later and they adopted new languages and customs. The changes were not all one-sided, however: **circumcision** and **clitoridectomy**, practised by the early Cushites, became important cultural rituals for many of the peoples who succeeded and absorbed them.

For present-day Kenya, the most important arrivals began to reach the country in the first few centuries AD. From the northwest and the headwaters of the Nile came the **Nilotic**-speaking ancestors of the **Kalenjin**; from the west and the south came speakers of **Bantu** languages, forebears of today's **Kikuyu**, **Gusii**, **Akamba** and **Mijikenda**, among others. (Bantu, a word coined by twentieth-century linguists, derives from the common stem for "person" – *ntu* – and the plural prefix *ba*. The word is not found in any of the six hundred contemporary Bantu languages, spread across the continent, but it may have been the one used for "people" in the original proto-language before it diversified.)

The new arrivals brought not just themselves and their languages, but also new technologies, including iron-working. **Iron** had enabled the Bantu to spread from the Nigeria/Cameroon area across central Africa, clearing the virgin forests and hoeing the ground for their crops. Eastwards, they encountered new Asian food crops – bananas, yams and rice – which had arrived in east Africa by way of the Indonesian colonization of Madagascar. This new diversity of foods helped people to settle permanently in chosen regions. The Kalenjin consolidated in the Western Highlands. The Bantu were particularly successful and, as their broad economic base took hold across the southern half of Kenya, their languages quickly spread. Herding, hunting, fishing and gathering were important supplements to the agricultural mainstay, while trade conducted with their exclusively pastoral or hunter-gatherer neighbours, especially in iron tools, carried their influence further.

By about 1000 AD, Kenya's Stone Age technology had been largely replaced by an Iron Age one, and, as human domination of the country increased, the beginnings of real specialization in agriculture and herding set in among the peoples.

Down on **the coast**, Bantu immigrants mixed, over several hundred years, with the longer-established Cushitic-speaking inhabitants and with a continuous trickle of settlers from Arabia and the Persian Gulf. With the advent of Islam, this melange gradually gave rise to a distinct culture and civilization – **Swahili** – speaking a Bantu language laced with foreign vocabulary. The Swahili were Kenya's link with the rest of the world, trading animal skins, ivory, agricultural produce and slaves for cloth, metals, ceramics, grain, ghee and sugar, with ships from the Middle East, India and even China. The Swahili were the first Kenyans to acquire firearms. They were also the first to write their language (in the Arabic script) and the first to develop complex, stratified communities based on town and countryside. Swahili history is covered in more depth in Chapter Six.

LATER ARRIVALS

New **American crops** – corn, cassava and tobacco – spread through Kenya after the Portuguese arrived at the beginning of the sixteenth century. They undoubtedly increased the country's population capacity, while enabling a greater degree of permanent settlement and providing new trade goods.

At about this time, a pastoral **Nilotic**-speaking people, distantly related to the earlier Kalenjin arrivals, began a migration from the northwest. These were the first **Luo**-speakers who, some generations earlier, had left their homeland (around Wau in southern Sudan) for reasons that were probably largely economic. In the alternately flooded and parched flatlands around the Nile, unusual conditions could be catastrophic. The Luo ancestors were always on the move, herding, planting, hunting or fishing. Politically, they had a fairly complex organization, as, for months on end, while the Nile flooded, communities would be stranded in concentration along the low ridges. Several good years might be followed by drought, and population pressure then forced less dominant groups to go off in search of water and pasture. The overall trend was southwards. Groups of migrants picked up other, non-Luo-speakers on the way, gradually assimilating them through intermarriage and language change, always drawing attention with the impressive regalia and social standing of their *ruoth* – the Luo kings.

On the shores of Lake Victoria, where they finally settled, sleeping sickness is thought to have wiped out many of the Luo herds. But they were pragmatic, resourceful people, whose background of mixed farming and herding during the era of migration supported them. They turned to agriculture and, increasingly, to fishing.

Towards the end of the seventeenth century, another Nilotic, pastoral people, the **Turkana**, appeared in Kenya. Linguistically closer to the Maasai Nilotes, they seem to have shared the Luo resilience to economic hardship and they, too, have (recently) turned to fishing. Also like the Luo, and almost unique among Kenyan peoples, they have never practised circumcision.

The Maa-speakers – **Maasai** and **Samburu** – were the last group to arrive in Kenya, and their rise and fall had far-reaching effects on neighbouring peoples. Moving southwards from the beginning of the seventeenth century, their nomadic pastoral lifestyle enabled them to expand swiftly and, in a few generations, they were transformed from an obscure group into a dominant force in the region. Culturally, they borrowed extensively from their neighbours, especially the **Kalenjin**. Kalenjin words and cultural values were adopted, including circumcision, the age-set system and some ancient (originally probably Cushitic) taboos against eating fish and certain wild animals. It is likely that much of the "traditional" Maasai appearance also owes something to these contacts. The Maasai migration was no slow spread. Their cattle were periodically herded south and other peoples were raided en route to enlarge the herds; by 1800, they were widely established in the Rift Valley and on the plains, everywhere between Lake Turkana and Kilimanjaro. In response to Maasai dominance, many of the Bantu peoples adopted their styles and customs. Initiation by genital mutilation, probably already practised by most Bantu-speakers, was imbued with a new significance – especially for the Kikuyu – by intermarriage and close, if not always peaceable, relations with the Maasai.

Severe **droughts** in the nineteenth century pushed the Maasai further and further afield in search of new pastures, bringing them into conflict, and trade, with other peoples. Drought, disease and rinderpest epidemics (which killed off their cattle) were also responsible for a series of civil wars between different Maasai sections in the second half of the nineteenth century.

These **Maasai civil wars** disrupted the **trading networks** which had been set up between the coast and the interior, mainly by Swahili, Mijikenda, Akamba and Kikuyu. Dutch, English and French goods were finding their way up-country, and American interests were already being served nearly two centuries ago, as white calico cloth (still called *amerikani* today) became a major item of profit. From western Kenya and Uganda, **slaves** were being exported in exchange for foreign commerce in the last throes of the slave trade's existence. Largely in response to slavery and widespread fighting, the first **missionaries** installed themselves up-country (the earliest went inland from Mombasa in 1846). Throughout this period, the Maasai disrupted movements through their territories and attacked Swahili slavers, Bantu traders and explorer-missionaries alike. The Maasai *morani* were specifically trained for raiding – a kind of guerrilla warfare – but, while their reputation lived on, they were bitterly divided among themselves and not organized on anything like a tribal scale.

By the time Europe had partitioned the map of Africa, the Maasai, who could have been the imperialists' most intractable enemies, were unable to retaliate effectively. The Kalenjin-speaking **Nandi** of the Western Highlands, who had begun to take the Maasai's place as Kenya's most feared adversaries, put up the stiffest resistance. They were organized to the extent of having a single spiritual leader, the *orkoiyot*, who ruled what was in effect a theocracy. Their war of attrition against the British delayed advances for a number of years. But the Nandi did not have the territorial advantage that would have helped the Maasai, and the murder of their *orkoiyot*, **Koitalel**, by the British, destroyed their military organization.

THE INVASION: 1885–1902

All Kenya's peoples resisted colonial domination to some degree. In the first twenty years of British attempts to rule, tens of thousands were killed in ugly massacres and manhunts, and many more were made homeless. Administrators – whose memoirs (see "Books", p.648) are the most revealing background for that period – all differed in their ideas of the ultimate purpose of their work and the best means of imposing British authority.

British interests in east Africa at the close of the last century had sprung from the European power struggle and the "scramble for Africa". The 1885 Berlin Conference chopped the continent into arbitrary spheres of influence. Germany was awarded what was to become Tanganyika; Britain got Kenya and Uganda. In 1886, formal agreements were drawn up and Kilimanjaro was ceded to Victoria's grandson, the Kaiser, giving each monarch a snowcapped equatorial mountain.

But rivalry wasn't far beneath the red tape and Germany clearly had Uganda earmarked. Sir William Mackinnon, who for a decade had been pressing for a licence to start trading, was now given permission to start commercial operations with his Imperial British East Africa Company (IBEAC) in 1888. The company officers – mostly young and totally inexperienced English clerks – established a series of trading forts at fifty-mile intervals in a line connected by a rough ox-track leading from Mombasa into Uganda. Machakos, Murang'a and Mumias all began as IBEAC stations. **Uganda** was the focus of interest, since Kenya – decimated by drought, locusts, rinderpest and civil war – seemed largely a deserted wasteland. And Uganda was strategically important for **control of the Nile** – which had long been a British preoccupation. Conspiring foreign powers were mentioned darkly in the House of Lords. Britain's claim was in danger of lapsing if Uganda could not be properly garrisoned and supplied. It was also a centre for the **slave trade** that Britain, in need not of slaves but of new markets, was committed to wiping out. And in the back of many minds was the kind of sentiment expressed by the London *Times* in 1873:

> There seems no reason not to believe that one of the finest parts of the world's surface is going to waste under the shroud of malaria which surrounds it, and under the barbarous anarchy with which it is cursed. The idea dawns upon some of us that some better destiny is yet in store for a region so blessed by nature, and the development of Africa is a step yet to come in the development of the world.

In the end, the practicability of developing "some better destiny" for Uganda proved out of reach.

With the bankruptcy of the IBEAC and its failure to establish any kind of administration, the

British government formally stepped into the breach in 1885 and declared a **protectorate** over Uganda and Kenya. Having acquired the region in a haphazard lottery, the government was now forced to do something with it. A useful gesture was required: Her Majesty's government decided to build a **railway**. This classic, valedictory piece of Victorian engineering took six years to complete and cost the lives of hundreds of Indian labourers. Financially, it was a commitment which grew out of all proportion to the likely returns and continued to grow long after the last rail was laid. But its completion transformed the future of east Africa. From now on, the supply lines were secure and the interior only a month's journey from Europe by ship and rail. Suddenly, the prospects for developing the cool, fertile Kenya highlands looked much more attractive than the distant unknowns of Uganda and its powerful kingdoms.

More immediately, the railway physically divided the **Maasai** at a time when they were already disunified and moving into alliances with the British. Their grazing lands, together with the regions of the **Kalenjin** and **Kikuyu** on the lower slopes of the highlands, were to become the heartland of white settlerdom.

THE KENYA COLONY

While the government, typically, dragged its feet, the story circulated that Kenya might be a land of opportunity: a new New Zealand, or even a Jewish homeland. A party of Zionists was in fact escorted around Kenya but declined the offer. It was Sir Charles Eliot, the Protectorate's second governor, who was the main mover behind the **settlement scheme**. While there was an undercurrent of consideration for "the rights of natives" which shouldn't be forgotten, the growing clamour of voices claiming the support of British taxpayers – who had met the bill for the railway – outweighed any altruism. Eliot's extravagant reports on the potential of BEA (British East Africa) were published and, willy-nilly, government policy was directed towards getting the settlers in and making the railway pay. Landless aristocrats, middle-class adventurers, big-game hunters, ex-servicemen and Afrikaners (the farming land was also advertised in South Africa) began to trickle up the line. Using ox-wagons to get to the tracts of bush they had leased, they started their farms from scratch. Lord Delamere, gover-

nor himself for a time, was their biggest champion. In the years leading up to World War I, the trickle of settlers became a flood and by 1916 the area "alienated" to **Europeans** had risen to 15,000 square kilometres of the best land. Imported livestock was hybridized with hardy, local breeds; coffee, tea, sisal and pineapples were introduced and thrived; European crops flourished in super-abundance and cereals soon covered vast areas.

Nearly half the land worth farming was now in the hands of **settlers**, but it had rapidly become clear that it was far from empty of local inhabitants. Colonial invasion had occurred at a low point in the fortunes of Kenya's peoples and, unprepared for the scale of the incursion, they were swiftly pushed aside into "native reserves" or became "squatters" without rights. As populations recovered, serious land shortages set in. The British appointment of "chiefs" – whose main task was to collect a tax on every hut – had the effect of diverting grievances against colonial policy onto these early collaborators and laying the foundations of a class structure in Kenyan society. Without a money economy, employment was the only means available to pay taxes and, effectively, a system of forced labour had been created. The whole apparatus quickly became entrenched in a series of **land and labour laws**. A poll tax was added to the hut tax; all African men were compelled to register to facilitate labour recruitment; squatters on alienated land were required to pay rent, through labour; and cash cropping on African plots was discouraged or banned (coffee licences, for example, were restricted to white farmers). The highlands were strictly reserved for white settlement, while land not owned by Europeans became Crown Land, its African occupants "tenants at will" of the Crown and liable to summary eviction.

Asians, too, were excluded from the highlands. While the leader of Kenya's Indians, **A.M. Jeevanjee**, had called for the transformation of Kenya into the "America of the Hindu", the proposal never came near consideration by the British. Barred from farming on any scale – except in the far west, where they developed sugar cane as an important crop – Indians concentrated on the middle ground, setting up general stores (*dukas*) across the country, investing in small industries and handling services.

WORLD WAR I

World War I had a number of profound effects, although there were comparatively few battles in Kenya itself. Some 200,000 African porters and soldiers were conscripted and sent to Tanganyika (German East Africa), where one in four of them died. Those who returned were deeply influenced by the experience. They had seen European tribes at war with each other, they had experienced European fallibility, and witnessed the kind of organization used to overcome it.

General von Lettow Vorbeck, the German commander, waged a dogged campaign against British forces despite the fact that his own were vastly outnumbered, with the aim of engaging as much manpower as possible and taking the heat off German forces in Europe. He earned a respectable place in the history books as a result. Nevertheless, the Germans lost the war – and Tanganyika – to the British, and the Crown's commitments in east Africa were suddenly multiplied.

Sir Edward Northey, governor of Kenya at the time of armistice, pushed his **Soldier Settlement Scheme** through without difficulty. Its aim, to double the settler population in Kenya to nine thousand and increase revenue, seemed promising enough to a government sapped by war. But the Soldier Settlement Scheme was bitterly resented by Africans, particularly those who had fought beside the soldiers and were now excluded from their gains.

EARLY NATIONALISM AND REACTION

Political associations sprang up among those with a mission education and ex-servicemen: the Kikuyu Association, the Young Kikuyu Association and the Young Kavirondo Association. **Harry Thuku,** secretary of the Young Kikuyu Association, realized its potential and re-formed it as the East Africa Association in order to recruit on a nationwide basis. The hated registration law by which every African was obliged to carry a pass – the *kipande* – was a prime grievance, but tax reduction, introduction of land title deeds and wage increases were demanded as well. Alliances were built up with embittered Indian associations and 1921 saw a year of **protests** and rallies. These culminated in Thuku's detention, **violent suppression** and the shooting by police of 25 demonstrators at a mass rally calling for Thuku's release. He remained in detention for eleven years.

The Indian constituency eventually secured two nominated seats (not elected) on the Legislative Council. Africans, meanwhile, remained voiceless, landless, disenfranchised and segregated by the colour bar.

As the settlers became established, they began to contribute appreciably to the income of **the colony** (which Kenya had officially become in 1920). Most of them seem to have believed that they were in at the beginning of a long and glorious pageant of white dominion. Indeed, settler self-government, along Canadian or South African lines, was a declared aim. African demands were hardly heeded by the authorities, but the Colonial Office was in a difficult position over the **Indians**, who were already British subjects and whose demands for equal rights they had trouble in refuting. Tentative proposals to give them voting rights, allow unrestricted immigration from India and abolish segregation caused alarm and indignation among the settlers. Their **Convention of Associations**, already arguing the case for white home rule, formed a "Vigilance Committee", which worked out detailed military plans for rebellion, including the kidnapping of the governor and the deportation of the Indians. Sensing a crisis, the Colonial Office drew up a white paper and a grudging settlement was reached that allowed five Indians and one Arab to be elected to the Legislative Council (the colony's local government), as opposed to eleven Europeans.

The primacy of African "interests", admirably reiterated yet again in the Devonshire Declaration, was still denied any real expression, least of all by Africans themselves. A system of de facto **apartheid** was being practised. It was in this climate in the 1920s and 1930s that, floating above their economic troubles, the settlers had their heyday – the **Happy Valley life** so appallingly and fascinatingly depicted in *White Mischief* and other books.

EDUCATION, KENYATTA AND THE KIKUYU

The opportunities available to Africans came almost entirely through **mission schools** at first. Again, there was conflict between government and settlers on the question of **educa-**

tion. The Colonial Office was committed, on paper at least, to the general development of the country for all its inhabitants, while the white farmers were on the whole adamant that raising educational standards could only lead to trouble. A crude form of Swahili had become the language of communication between Africans and Europeans. But the teaching of English was a controversial issue that hard-liners foresaw eventually rebounding on government and settlers alike. In frustration, self-help **Kikuyu independent schools** were set up in the 1930s, primarily in order to teach their own children English.

Whether barring access to English education would ultimately have made any difference is debatable, but by the late 1930s there were already enough educated Africans to pose the beginnings of a serious challenge to white supremacy. One of these was **Jomo Kenyatta**.*

After Thuku's imprisonment and the subsequent bloodshed at Nairobi in 1921, the East African Association was dissolved. It was succeeded by the **Kikuyu Central Association** (**KCA**), which Kenyatta joined in 1928. The KCA was the spearhead of **nationalism** and lobbied hard for a return of alienated land, the lowering of taxes and for elected African representatives on the Legislative Council. It also protested against missionary efforts to outlaw "**female circumcision**", on the grounds that the church was attempting to undermine Kikuyu culture. This last conflict led to a leadership crisis in the KCA and for a number of years threatened to swamp other issues. But Kenyatta spent most of the period between 1931 and 1946 in Britain, campaigning for the KCA, studying anthropology under Malinowski at the London School of Economics and writing his homage to the Kikuyu people, *Facing Mount Kenya*.

Kenya survived the 1929 stock market crash and the resulting world **trade slump** as the colonial government became increasingly committed to the struggling settlers it was now bailing out. Exports fell catastrophically; coffeeplanting by non-whites was still prohibited and

*Kenyatta, born in the late 1890s, went to a mission school and was baptized a Christian. He was also circumcised, and initiated into Kikuyu adulthood. His name was adopted from the shop he ran in Nairobi, Kenyatta Stores, which in turn was named after the traditional beaded belt (kenyatta) he always wore.

the tax burden continued to be placed squarely on Africans. Faced with this crisis, even some of the settlers began to accept that large-scale changes were in order. Just as awareness was growing that the economy could not survive indefinitely unless Africans were given more of a chance to participate in it, Kenya was thrown into World War II.

WORLD WAR II – AND MAU MAU

Perhaps not surprisingly, soldiers were easily recruited into the **King's African Rifles** when Italian-held Ethiopia (then Abyssinia) declared war on Kenya. Volunteers wanted money, education and a chance to see the world; conscripts, filling the quotas assigned to their chiefs, faced a life at home or on the reserve that was no better. Propaganda immediately succeeded in casting Hitler's image as the embodiment of all racist evil. Some Africans thought the war, once won, would improve their position in Kenya. They were partly right. Military campaigns in Ethiopia and Burma owed much of their success to African troops and during the war their efforts were glowingly praised by Allied commanders.

On the soldiers' return, a new awareness, more profound than that felt by the returning porters and *askaris* of World War I, came upon them. The white tribes of Europe had fought the war on the issue of self-determination; the message wasn't lost on Africans. Yet still, in almost every other sphere of life, they were demeaned and humiliated. The KCA had been banned at the outbreak of war, allegedly for supporting the Italian fascists, and African political life was subdued. Real change, for 99 percent of the population, was still a dream.

Kenya's food-exporting economy had done well out of the war and it was clear the colony could make a major contribution to Britain's recovery. The post-war Labour government encouraged economic expansion without going far to include Africans among the beneficiaries of the investment. Industrialization gathered momentum and there was a rapid growth of towns. There was also further promotion of **white immigration** – a new influx of European settlers arrived soon after the war – and greater power was given to the settlers on the Legislative and Executive Councils. Population growth and intense **pressure on land** in the rural areas were leading to severe disruptions of traditional community life as people were shunted into the reserves or else left their villages to search for work in the towns. On the political front, militant **trade unionism**, dominated by ex-servicemen, gradually usurped the positions of those African leaders who had been prepared to work with the government.

POSTWAR AFRICAN POLITICS

A single African member, Eliud Mathu, was appointed to the Legislative Council in 1944. More significant, however, was the formation of the **Kenya African Union (KAU)**, a consultative group of leaders and spokesmen set up with the governor's approval to liaise with Mathu. The KAU's first president was Harry Thuku, but it was **Kenyatta's return** from England in 1946, to an unexpectedly tumultuous hero's welcome, that signalled a real departure for African political rights and the birth of a new current of nationalism. KAU was transformed into an active political party – and ran straight into conflict with itself. The **radicals** within the party wanted sweeping changes in land ownership, equal voting rights and abolition of the pass law. The **moderates** were for negotiation, educational improvement, multiracial progress and a gradual shift of power. Nor were the moderates convinced that their own best interests lay in confronting the British head on: they had all achieved considerable ambitions in the settler economy. Kenyatta was ambitious himself, but the Europeans mistrusted his intentions and rumour-mongered about his communist connections, his visit to Russia during his time abroad and his personal life.

Despite Kenyatta's efforts to steer a middle course, KAU became increasingly radical and Kikuyu-dominated. While he angled to give the party a multi-tribal profile to appease the settlers, he also managed to sacrifice some moderates in the leadership for the sake of party unity. But there were defections as well. Several radicals, including **Dedan Kimathi**, joined an underground movement and took **oaths** of allegiance against the British. Betrayal of the movement was punished by execution and collaborators with the government faced the same threat. Oathing groups emerged secretly all around the Central Highlands and, by 1952, a central committee was organized to co-ordinate activities.

THE MAU MAU REBELLION

The question of how much the KAU leadership was involved in what came to be known as **Mau Mau** (from *muma*, a traditional Kikuyu oath) is one that reappeared time after time in the years leading to and after Independence. Certainly Mau Mau attracted large numbers of young men from the rural periphery of towns like Nyeri, Fort Hall and Nairobi, and they used Kenyatta's name in their propaganda. Many members had taken part in strikes in the late 1940s: they were mobilized into violent action by the shortage of land on the reserves and the contrast with the new-found success of the settlers. There was a burning desire to oust the Europeans from the "White Highlands". The Mau Mau oath-takers called themselves the **Land and Freedom Army. Ex-soldiers** who had fought for the British, many of whom had learned guerrilla warfare in Burma, were crucial to their military effort.

Kenyatta played a delicate political game, condemning strikes and even oath-taking but ready to seize on any chance to exploit the situation. In 1952, incensed by simmering African nationalism and random outbursts of violence on white farms, the settlers pressured the government into declaring a **state of emergency**. Mau Mau was banned and all African nationalist organizations were proscribed. Kenyatta and other KAU leaders were arrested, convicted of founding and managing Mau Mau – on the flimsiest evidence – and sent into internal exile. For the next four years, while "**The Emergency**" blazed and African political life was brought, once again, to a virtual standstill, the full weight of British military muscle was brought to bear against the revolt, barely forty years since the era of "punitive expeditions".

Thousands of **British troops** were sent to Kenya. To them, every African was a potential terrorist, every homestead a Mau Mau hide-out. As the troops moved in, the hard-core guerrillas fled into the forest and lived off the jungle for months on end, launching surprise attacks at night. They relied on considerable support from the Kikuyu homesteads for supplies, intelligence reports and stolen weapons. Under emergency powers, a policy of "villagization" was enforced and tens of thousands of Kikuyu were relocated to "secure villages" or detained in barbed-wire concentration camps. At one point, one-third of the entire male Kikuyu population was being held in detention. It was during this period that the cluster of closely related small tribes known today as the Kalenjin, acquired their name, which means "I tell you" in their common language, Nandi. Forging together the Nandi, Pokot, Elgeyo, Marakwet, Tugen and others under a single umbrella, it was largely the creation of the colonial authorities, seeking to recruit and reinforce support against the Kikuyu-dominated Mau Mau.

The **end of the revolt** came with the British capture and execution of Dedan Kimathi, the Land and Freedom Army's commander-in-chief. Helicopters and defoliant were brought in to flush out the last pockets of resistance, but in any case morale was low. The Western press made much of Mau Mau atrocities, though a total of just 32 European civilians and about 50 troops were killed in the struggle. For Africans, the figure was around 13,000 men, women and children, mainly Kikuyu. Many of these, uncommitted to Mau Mau, yet living in key locations as far as the British were concerned, were caught, sometimes literally, in the crossfire.

The authorities described Mau Mau as a tribal uprising, a meaningless explosion of tension. Paranoid settlers perceived an external communist threat in the revolt. Some observers went so far as to call it a Kikuyu civil war between those established on the reserves and others – the guerrillas – newly displaced from European farms. And while Akamba, Maasai, Luo, Meru and Embu did join the Land and Freedom Army, its membership was overwhelmingly Kikuyu-speaking. As a focus for nationalism, the revolt served as a political barometer: the tension between the loyalists and the rebels and their sympathizers was the fulcrum on which Kenyan politics was to swing in the years leading up to and after Independence. Jomo Kenyatta was in many ways lucky to have been forced to sit out the period in detention.

INDEPENDENCE – *UHURU*

With the emergency over, the KAU leaders still at liberty set about exploiting the European fear of a repeat episode. Anything that now delayed the fulfilment of African nationalist aspirations could be seen as fuel for another revolt. There was no longer any question of a Rhodesia-style, white-dominated Independence. Settlers, mindful of the **preparations for independence** taking place in other African countries, began

rallying to the cry of multi-racialism in a vain attempt to secure what looked like a very shaky future.

At the 1960 Lancaster House Conference in London, African representatives won a convincing victory by pushing through measures to give them majorities in the Legislative Council and the Council of Ministers. Members, all nominated by the colonial authorities, included **Tom Mboya**, the prominent and charismatic Luo trade unionist, and the radical politician **Oginga Odinga** (another Luo), as well as **Daniel Arap Moi** and the Mijikenda leader **Ronald Ngala**. A new constitution was drawn up and eventual access to the White Highlands was accepted. The declaration promised that "Kenya was to be an African country": the path to Independence was guaranteed. **Macmillan** was saying as much in his "Wind of Change" speech given to the South African parliament at the time the Lancaster House Conference was meeting.

The settlers perceived a "calamitous betrayal", with universal franchise and African-dominated independence expected within ten years. (In fact, it happened earlier than anticipated.) Minority tribal associations, meanwhile, foresaw troubles ahead if the **Kikuyu-Luo elite** achieved independence for Kenya at the cost of the smaller constituencies. In 1960, the Kenya African National Union (**KANU**) was formed. Soon after, a second, more moderate party, the Kenya African Democratic Union (**KADU**), was created, with Britain's help, to federate the minority, largely rural-based, political associations in a broad defensive alliance against Kikuyu-Luo domination. One of KADU's leading members was Daniel Arap Moi.

Elections were held in 1961 and KANU emerged with nineteen seats against KADU's eleven. But KANU refused to form a government until Kenyatta was released. Settlers began to leave the country, selling their farms and evacuating before the predicted collapse of European privilege – or even holocaust – that some feared if the "leader unto darkness and death" were set free.

A temporary coalition government was formed, composed of KADU, European and Asian members. Kenyatta was duly released and, six months later, a member resigned his seat, making room for him on the Legislative Council. In 1962, Kenyatta became Minister for

Constitutional Affairs and Economic Planning – a wide portfolio – in a new coalition government formed out of the KADU alliance and KANU. Despite a second London conference to try to reach an agreement about the federal constitution demanded by KADU, the question was left in the air. Independence elections the following year (though the Somalis of the northeast, who had no wish to be in Kenya, boycotted them) seemed to answer the constitutional question. KANU emerged with an even greater lead and a mandate for a non-federal structure. On June 1 – **Madaraka Day** – Kenyatta became Kenya's first prime minister. And on December 12, 1963, control of foreign affairs was handed over and Kenya became formally **independent**.

THE KENYATTA YEARS – *HARAMBEE*

It was barely sixty years since the pioneer settlers had arrived. Many of them – those who hadn't panicked and sold out – were now determined to stay and risk the future under an **African government**. Despite his unjust seven years in detention, Kenyatta turned out to have more consideration for their interests than could have been foreseen. He held successful meetings with settlers in his home village; his bearded, genial image and conciliatory speeches assuring them of their rights and security quickly earned him the respected title *Mzee* (Elder) and wide international support. Many Europeans retained important positions in administration and the judiciary.

Milton Obote and Julius Nyerere, leaders of newly independent Uganda and Tanzania, held talks with Kenyatta on setting up an **East African Community** to share railways, aviation, postal services and telecommunications, and customs and excise. This was formally inaugurated in 1967. There was a mood of optimism: it looked very much as if Kenya had succeeded against all the odds.

But there were urgent issues to contend with. **Land reform** and the rehabilitation of freedom fighters and detainees were the most pressing. Large tracts of European land were bought up and a programme to provide small plots to landless peasants was rapidly instigated. Political questions loomed large as well. On December 12, 1964, Kenya became a republic, its head of state no longer the Queen, but rather President Kenyatta. KADU was dissolved "in the interests of national unity", its leaders absorbed into the ruling KANU party. There was, it seemed, no longer any need for an opposition: everyone was on the same side and Kenya was henceforth a de facto one-party state. For the sake of "national security", British troops were kept on, initially to quell a revolt of ethnic Somalis in the northeast and an army mutiny in Nairobi. A defence treaty has kept a British force at Nanyuki ever since.

There was heavy emphasis on co-operation and unity. The spirit of *harambee* (pulling together) was endorsed by Kenyatta at all his public appearances. *Harambee* meetings became a unique national institution, fund-raising events at which – in a not untraditional way – donations were made by local notables and politicians towards self-help health-care and educational programmes. During the 1960s and 1970s, hundreds of *harambee* schools were built and equipped in this way. But the ostentatious gifts, and particularly the guaranteed press coverage the next day with donors listed in order of value, sometimes reduced the *harambee* vision of community development to an exercise in patronage and competitive status-seeking.

On the **economic front**, the first decade of Independence saw remarkable changes and rapid growth. Although only a quarter of the country gets enough rainfall to make it agriculturally reliable, the settlers' fairly broad-based crop-exporting economy was a powerful springboard for development; one, moreover, that wasn't difficult to transfer to predominantly African control. While many large landholdings were sold *en bloc* to African investors, smaller farmers did begin to contribute significantly to export earnings through coffee, tea, pyrethrum and fruit.

Industrialization proceeded at a slower pace. Kenya's mineral resources are very limited and the country relies heavily on oil imports. **Foreign investment** wasn't especially beneficial, as investors were given wide freedoms to import equipment and technical skills and to re-export much of the profit.

Growth, rather than a radical redistribution of wealth, was the government's main concern. Although by 1970 more than two-thirds of the European mixed farming lands were occupied by some 50,000 Africans, and the overall standard of living had improved considerably, income disparities were greater than ever. And 16,000 square kilometres of ranch lands and plantations remained largely in foreign hands.

From the outset, it was clear that the fruits of Independence were not going to be shared fairly. Kikuyu-Luo domination – but particularly Kikuyu – was irksome and strongly resented by other groups. It was perhaps inevitable that the people who had lost most and suffered most under British rule should expect to receive the most benefits from Independence. However, many Kikuyu had also been able to take advantage, as far as it was possible, of the settler economy by earning wages, setting up businesses and sending their children to school.

The resettlement programme was abandoned in 1966, its objectives "largely attained". But many peasants, having been squatters on European farms, were now "illegal squatters" on private African land. Thousands migrated to the towns where unemployment was already a serious problem. Kenya was becoming a class-divided society.

POLITICAL OPPOSITION . . . AND REACTION

It was in this climate that KANU's leadership split. **Oginga Odinga**, the party vice-president, resigned in 1966 to form the socialist **Kenya People's Union (KPU)** and 29 MPs joined him. The ex-guerrilla Bildad Kaggia became deputy head of the KPU and a vocal agitator for poorer Kikuyu. Kenyatta and Mboya closed ranks in KANU and prepared for political conflict. KPU was anti-capitalist and claimed to speak on behalf of the masses, who it maintained had been betrayed by *Uhuru*. On foreign affairs it was firmly non-aligned. Denouncing the opposition, KANU – led in this respect by Tom Mboya – stressed the need for close ties with the West, for commercial enterprise and foreign investment, and for economic conditions that would attract foreign aid. Ideologically, KANU talked of "African socialism". KPU's stand was claimed to be divisive: the country should be pulling together to fight the triple evils of poverty, ignorance and disease. KPU was barely tolerated for three years, its members harassed and detained by the security forces, its activities obstructed by new legislation and constitutional amendments.

In KANU, Odinga was succeeded (briefly) in the post of vice-president by Joseph Murumbi

and then, with behind-the-scenes encouragement from the British government's Foreign and Commonwealth Office in London (which wanted to avoid a radical in the job), by Daniel Arap Moi.

Odinga had strong, grassroots support in the Luo and Gusii districts of western Kenya. But **Tom Mboya**'s supporters came from an even broader base, including many poor Kikuyu. By the end of the 1960s, speculation was mounting about whether he would be able to take over the presidency on Kenyatta's death. As the *Mzee's* right-hand man he was widely tipped to succeed – a possibility that alarmed Kenyatta's Kikuyu supporters. The republic's second political **assassination*** decided the matter: Mboya was gunned down by a Kikuyu assassin in central Nairobi on July 5, 1969. No high-level complicity in the murder was ever brought to light, but Mboya's death was a devastating blow to Kenya's fragile stability, setting off shock waves along both class and tribal divisions. There was widespread fighting and rioting between Kikuyu and Luo, fuelled by years of rivalry and growing feelings of Luo exclusion from government. During a visit by Kenyatta to Kisumu – where he attended a public meeting at which Odinga and his supporters were present – hostility against his entourage was so great that police opened fire, killing at least ten demonstrators.

The KPU was immediately banned and Odinga detained without trial. Although the constitution continued to guarantee the right to form opposition parties, non-KANU nominations to parliament were, in practice, forbidden. There was a resurgence of oath-taking among Kikuyu, Meru and Embu, pledging to maintain the Kikuyu hold on power. The Kikuyu contingent in the army was strengthened and a new force of shock troops, the General Service Unit (GSU), was recruited under Kikuyu officers; independent of police and army, it was to act as an internal security force. In the early 1970s, Kikuyu control – of the government, the administration, business interests and land – gripped tighter and tighter.

Internationally, however, Kenya was seen as one of the safest African investments – a model of stability and democracy only too happy to allow the multinational corporations access

---

*The first was that of Pia Gama Pinto, an outspoken Goan communist politician who was killed in 1965.

to its resources and markets. The development of the tourist industry helped give the country a bright and positive profile. And, in comparison with most other African countries, some still fighting for independence and others beset by civil war or paralysed by drought, Kenya's future looked healthy enough.

But in achieving record economic growth, foreign interests often seemed to crush indigenous ones. An elite of rich profiteers – nicknamed the **Wabenzi** after the Mercedes Benz they favoured – extracted enormous private gains out of transactions with foreign companies. Nepotism was blatant and Kenyatta himself was rumoured to be one of the richest men in the world. For the mass of Kenyan people, life was hardly any better than before Independence. Graduates poured out of the secondary schools with few prospects of using their qualifications; population increase was (and remains) the highest in the world; and, most damaging of all, land distribution was still grossly unfair in a society where land was the basic means of making a living for nearly all.

In 1975, in the first ever explicit public attack on the Kikuyu monopoly of power, the radical populist MP **J.M. Kariuki** warned that Kenya could become a country of "ten millionaires and ten million beggars". He was arrested for his pains, then, some weeks later, was found murdered in the Ngong Hills. Reaction was stunned and a massive turnout at his funeral was followed by angry **student demonstrations**. Kariuki's appeal had derived from unimpeachable honesty and forthrightness and a stubborn perseverance in addressing the issues of economic and social justice. He riled his opponents by his sincerity and his refusal to espouse any easily shot-down ideology. Although a Kikuyu himself, from a non-ruling northern clan, a former Mau Mau detainee and at one time a close associate of Kenyatta, he was unquestionably a threat to the Kikuyu power base. A parliamentary report on his death had two prominent names deleted at Kenyatta's demand. "Kariuki's death", wrote the then outspoken *Weekly Review*, "instils in the minds of the public the fear of dissidence, the fear to criticize, the fear to stand out and take an unconventional public stance." Kenyatta and the Kikuyu clique meant business. In the following years, a number of other MPs were detained. The burning issue of

landlessness was no longer one many people were prepared to shout about.

As criticism at home was suffocated, foreign criticism of the direction Kenya was taking began to grow. Early in 1975, a series of bomb explosions in Nairobi – attributed to a "poor people's" liberation group – drew attention to the country: the foreign press carried reports of entrenched **corruption** from the president and his family down. Kariuki's murder and, later, a parliamentary row over ivory smuggling in which Kenyatta was heavily implicated, refocused attention on Kenya. But the government was far from inviting serious condemnation from the West. Kenya was seen, despite its formal non-alignment, as a staunchly anti-communist ally of Britain and America, and a recipient of massive grants and loans (for which, in return, foreign investors were allowed to reap handsome profits). And, as was rightly pointed out, there was no clear successor to the president nor any effective opposition worth cultivating.

Kenyatta had retreated into dictatorial seclusion, propped up by close Kikuyu cronies, among them Chief Koinange and Charles Njonjo, who ten years later was to cause a political storm. As parliament, and even the cabinet, took an increasingly passive role in decision-making, the pronouncements from the *Mzee*'s "court" began to be accompanied by vague suggestions of threats to his government from unspecified foreign powers. By 1977, the **East African Community** had ceased to function. Its structure had always favoured Kenya as the strongest member, and it was wracked by mistrust between Kenya and Tanzania, then further torn by Idi Amin's 1971 coup in Uganda. Kenya finally seized the lion's share of community assets, mostly ships and rolling stock in the territory at the time. Hostility towards socialist policies in Tanzania, delayed elections, further detentions and growing allegations of corruption formed the sullen backdrop to **Kenyatta's death**, in bed, on August 28, 1978.

KENYA IN THE 1980S – *NYAYO*

The passing of the *Mzee* took Kenya by surprise. There was a nationwide outpouring of grief and shock. Mourners filed past the coffin for days. For many, however, there was also a profound sense of relief and anticipation. An era was over and the future might better reflect the ideals of twenty years earlier.

Fears about the succession proved unfounded as vice-president **Daniel Arap Moi** smoothly assumed power with the help of Mwai Kibaki and Charles Njonjo. He quickly gathered popular support with moves against corruption in the civil service (where the mass of Kenyans felt it most), his stand against tribal nepotism (he himself comes from a minority group, the Kalenjin), and the release of all Kenyatta's political prisoners. The press, too, traditionally circumspect and conservative, relaxed a little. Moi assured Kenya and the world that, while he would not be making radical departures from Kenyatta's policies, the more blatant iniquities of the old guard's paternalistic system would be ironed out.

But the honeymoon was short. Odinga and other ex-KPU MPs were prevented from standing in the general elections of 1979. **Student protests**, focusing on the anniversary of Kariuki's murder, began again; the closing of the university became an annual event. On the international scene, the whole Indian Ocean region became strategically important with the fall of the Shah of Iran and the Soviet invasion of Afghanistan. Kenya developed significantly closer ties with the **United States**, extending military facilities to American vessels in exchange for gifts of grain after a failure of the harvest in 1983. Ironically, the country's own surplus had been exported the previous year.

In the first year or two of his presidency, Moi's **Nyayo** (footsteps) philosophy of "peace, love and unity" in the wake of Kenyatta found wide appeal, and his apparent honesty and outspoken attacks against tribalism impressed many, making him friends abroad. But the failure to make any adjustments in economic policy in favour of the rural and urban poor soon resulted in strong, if muted, criticism at home.

THE COUP ATTEMPT

Two major events rocked the government in the 1980s. On Sunday August 1, 1982 – three months after constitutional amendments were pushed through by Njonjo to make Kenya officially a one-party state (to prevent Oginga Odinga registering a new political party, the Kenya Socialist Alliance) – sections of the Kenya Air Force attempted a **military coup**. Kenyans woke to the sound of continuous Bob Marley on the radio, a repeated coup broadcast and, in Nairobi at least, sporadic gunfire. There

was widespread confusion for several hours. The People's Redemption Council, who had taken the radio station, were unknown: there had been no lead-up. Most of the army was on military exercise in the north, and at first the Air Force rebels were in control. During the course of the day, hundreds of shops, especially in Nairobi, were looted, mostly by civilians. Asians, particularly, suffered huge losses: Asian women were raped and many Asian homes ransacked.

By the end of the day, the "coup" had disintegrated into a free-for-all. But as it became clear that there was no prearranged support among other armed forces, the army and the GSU consolidated against the KAF, shooting hundreds of men, raping and killing women and patrolling the streets on the lookout for rebels. Dozens of students were killed. The government announced 159 deaths, but witnesses claim to have seen more bodies on a single street.

In the immediate aftermath of the coup attempt, thousands of airmen were arrested and the service itself was disbanded. The university, believed to be a "breeding ground for subversion", was dissolved. Fourteen airmen were sentenced to death though only two, who had fled to asylum in Tanzania, were eventually executed when handed back to Kenya. There had been considerable Luo involvement in the attempt to seize power and Oginga Odinga was once again placed under house arrest.

THE NJONJO AFFAIR AND AFTER

Foreign investors held their breath and tourist bookings slumped, but postmortems of the uprising faded as the country was distracted by a new political drama – the **"Njonjo affair"**. In May 1983, Moi announced to parliament that he had evidence that a foreign power was grooming a senior colleague to take over as president. The charges were unspecific but the Attorney General **Charles Njonjo**'s name was mentioned and he rapidly fell from grace. A member of the Kikuyu elite who had shored up Kenyatta, Njonjo was a skilled politician with a wide circle of influence outside Kenya. His name was often linked with apartheid South Africa and Israel and, during the judicial inquiry into his activities, it was alleged that he had embezzled KANU money, and that he was privy to the coup attempt and also to another in the Seychelles. More crucially, there was intense rivalry between Njonjo and **Mwai Kibaki**, the sober and respected vice-president, over the question of succession.

The case, which filled the papers for over a year, was brought to a close with the purge from KANU of Njonjo's associates. He himself was ordered to pay back misappropriated funds, but was eventually granted a pardon by the president on Independence Day 1984, with the understanding that his political life was terminated.

Whatever lay behind it – most likely Njonjo's designs on the presidency – the Njonjo affair succeeded in distracting the public and easing away the volatility engendered by the coup attempt. Oginga Odinga and a number of other political detainees were released. More broadly, provincial administration was increasingly "de-tribalized", with officials working away from their home areas. And, on another front, a complete restructuring of the educational curriculum put new emphasis on technical and vocational studies.

For university candidates, a new quasi-military **National Youth Service** programme was launched, with students engaged in public works across the country. Student unrest continued, however. Twelve students were killed in February 1985 when the GSU broke up a meeting on the campus, ostensibly about canteen food, but considered subversive by the authorities. And on the other side of the political fence, KANU "youth wingers" began taking the law into their own hands, forming vigilante groups to attack criminal suspects and those suspected of "causing disunity".

KENYA TODAY

Economically, Kenya has come a long way since Independence. But, with the population today standing at nearly four times what it was forty years ago (8 million then; around 30 million today), the rate of increase in the standard of living is levelling off, and by some indexes has actually declined in the last two decades. Politically, any improvement in Kenya's position is more open to question. While the last ten years has seen a dramatic shift from the formal one-party state to a multi-party system, this has not been accompanied by great improvements in government accountability or rule of law. On the contrary, the international reputation the country enjoyed in the 1960s and 1970s has been steadily eroded by countless examples of human rights abuses during the two decades-plus of Daniel Arap Moi's presidency, and appears to have bottomed out with the second multi-party elections of 1997.

Some of Kenya's outstanding shortcomings include: a **corrupt judicial system**, as reported by the organization African Rights; some of the worst prisons in the world, (more than 800 prisoners died in detention in 1995 according to the Kenya Human Rights Commission); systematic **torture** of criminals and political prisoners (Amnesty International); massive **corruption** throughout the economy, from the small bribes needed to obtain routine forms to backhanders and fraud on a gigantic scale (several ongoing financial investigations); criminal **underinvestment** in infrastructure, including Kenya Railways, which resulted in a major, fatal train derailment in March 1999; and **anti-intellectualism** in the KANU government that seriously jeopardizes the viability of all higher education – colleges and universities frequently close for long periods as a result of student unrest.

DEVELOPMENT AND TOURISM

Kenya is largely agricultural, and heavily reliant on the fortunes of **coffee** and **tea** on the world markets: it is the world's biggest tea exporter after Sri Lanka, and together the crops account for just over half the country's export earnings. **Horticulture** – especially cut flowers, soft fruit and vegetables air-freighted to European supermarkets – accounts for around twenty percent of hard currency earnings.

Kenya has no oil reserves and, despite the building of alternative **energy** providers like the Turkwel Dam scheme and the geo-thermal power station at Lake Naivasha, still has to import three-quarters of its energy requirements.

While the country's imports continue to outstrip its exports, servicing the national debt – around $7billion – costs Kenya a far smaller proportion of export earnings than many poor countries have to surrender. **Development** is, however, deeply dependent on foreign aid grants and loans. When they are not under suspension for non-compliance with IMF and World Bank conditions, few African countries receive as much. In society, there are persistent spectres: a fresh half-million **school leavers** each year competing for only 70,000 new jobs in the swelling towns; an unwieldy, obstructive **bureaucracy**; minimum wage rises that trail behind inflation; parastatal organizations that are notoriously corrupt and resistant to change; and repeated chronic failures of the government to respond positively to instances of ethnic strife and crime that hinder foreign investment and disrupt tourism. The average yearly income of around £180 ($300) is currently dropping at a rate of around seven percent each year, and it's officially acknowledged that nearly half of all Kenyans are underfed.

Natural factors, too, have been important in trimming economic growth. The savage **drought** of 1984, poor rains in 1992, and El Niño **flooding** in 1997 and 1998 have repeatedly resulted in near-famine conditions in many parts of the north and east. In January 1999, the government started buying emergency food stocks from maize farmers in the Rift Valley, which was the only region to have done well out of the El Niño weather. While the bad years tend to be balanced by bumper harvests in the good years, there's a continuing chronic shortage of storage facilities to help smooth the troughs, and therefore little confidence that similar disasters won't recur.

In the **tourist industry** – now the biggest earner of foreign exchange – the first sign of serious disquiet among foreign tour operators was the attention given to Kenya's **AIDS** problem in the late 1980s. Highlighted by the British

RICHARD LEAKEY AND THE KENYA WILDLIFE SERVICE

Although now internationally renowned as a wildlife conservationist, **Richard Leakey** rose to prominence as a **paleontogist** from the shadows of his eminent parents Mary and Louis Leakey. They had made the first really significant finds in the history of early human evolution, at Olduvai Gorge in Tanzania, but Richard went on to make even more remarkable discoveries at Koobi Fora near Lake Turkana. He published several books and eventually became head of the National Museums of Kenya in Nairobi.

In 1989, facing an international outcry over the poaching of elephants and the serious impact that was already having on the tourist industry, President Moi hired Leakey to take charge of the **Kenya Wildlife Service**. Leakey's first move was a characteristically bold one: he invited the world's press to watch Moi ignite Kenya's US$3 million stockpile of confiscated ivory – producing the most memorable photo opportunity of the Moi presidency. With Moi's solid support, Leakey created anti-poaching units, briefed to shoot to kill any poachers apprehended in the parks, and transformed the KWS from a demoralized sector of the civil service into what one senior member of staff called "the most radical institution in Africa". The World Bank and other donors were so impressed they gave over US$140 million in grants. The

poaching stopped, the elephants and rhinos were saved from the brink of extinction, and Kenya's international image was partially restored.

But Leakey's success went too far for some local politicians, particularly in Maasai-land. His confrontational approach to the balance of human and animal needs in the parks – all humans out – infuriated many. And he was incorruptible: the KWS had dried up completely as a source of patronage.

In June 1993, on a routine flight at the controls of his Cessna plane, Leakey crashed, losing both legs in the accident. Foul play was suspected, but not proven. (At the time, he'd been bitterly opposed to the grabbing of a 200-square-kilometre chunk of the Tana River Delta initially earmarked for the world's largest wetlands reserve, the Tana River Delta Wetlands Reserve.) Within months he was walking on artificial limbs, anxious to get back to work. But there had been a mood change in his employers. The Minister of Tourism, Noah Katana Ngala, announced that a secret probe had found evidence of corruption and serious mismanagement at the KWS. No more bitter irony could be imagined. In January 1994, Leakey called a press conference and publicly announced his **resignation**.

Leakey's departure wasn't just the result of refusing to countenance graft. The KWS had become a ruthless organization to work for, in

Army's ban on some coastal resorts for soldiers on leave, and the rumour that the virus could be spread by mosquitoes, the scare caused bookings, particularly from Germany, to crash.

Further adverse publicity damaged the industry in Britain as the case of **Julie Ward**, whose murder in the Maasai Mara was at first clumsily covered up, unfolded for month after month. At the time of writing (mid-1999) the case was being heard in London. In isolated but widely reported incidents, several other tourists were murdered in the 1990s.

In the run-up to the 1992 election, **political violence** and ethnic cleansing caused a slump in tourism. Worse was to come in 1997, with massive disruption to the coastal economy, first by pre-election violence and the forced expulsion of tens of thousands of up-country workers from south of Mombasa, and then by the actual closure of many hotels as tourists stayed away.

Two serious **train crashes** on the chronically underfunded Nairobi–Mombasa line (one

attributed to flood damage, the other, in March 1999, to poor maintenance) resulted in dozens of casualties, including a number of tourists). Added to this catalogue of calamity, the imposition of expensive **visas** for British travellers damaged Kenya's standing still further.

Elephant poaching, too, has seriously damaged Kenya's tourist industry. While the ivory scandals which smeared Kenyatta's family have not been repeated under Moi's presidency, the scale of the slaughter from the mid-1980s on far exceeded anything during Kenyatta's rule. In 1989, Kenya announced a major offensive on **ivory smuggling** and succeeded in persuading most importing countries, including the USA, Britain, Hong Kong and Japan, to place a blanket ban on any further consignments. The Wildlife Service, under the new directorship of **Richard Leakey**, took brutal control of the situation, hunting down poachers and protecting the herds, thus salvaging at least a fragment of which failure to come up to Leakey's standards could mean lack of prospects and poor financial rewards. However, it was the intense campaign of vilification by certain Maasai politicians that was the crucial factor in engineering his downfall.

Leakey's replacement was **David Western**, a milder, less charismatic figure who was able to find a modus operandi that seemed to be producing results acceptable both to local people and to conservationists. His park fee reforms were widely praised.

Leakey, meanwhile, entered politics. In May 1995 he joined a group of opposition intellectuals and applied to register a new party, **Safina**, announcing that Kenya needed a solution to its manifold failures. "If KANU and Mr Moi will do something about the deterioration of public life, corruption and mismanagement, I'd be happy to fight alongside them. If they won't, I want somebody else to do it." The party's application was turned down and it was only registered days before the 1997 elections, too late to put forward a presidential candidate. Leakey was denounced by Moi, accused of being a racist colonial, bent on destabilizing Kenya with foreign backers. There is no doubt that Leakey commands support and respect overseas, earned by his thick-skinned energy rather than diplomatic skills. But, unfortunately for Moi, Leakey is a Kenyan, born and bred, and only the most shameless hypocrisy is likely to remove this thorn from KANU's side. Remarkably, after Leakey's political ambitions were curtailed by Moi, he accepted the KWS role for a second time, after David Western was sacked in 1998.

Western has always disagreed with Leakey's view that parks were self-contained ecosystems, which would eventually need fencing. He talked instead of a "strategy of decentralization, addressing problems of human–wildlife conflict" He received widespread support and the reasons for his dismissal are not crystal clear, though it's widely presumed that he fell out with the KANU hierarchy by failing to draw the international limelight that comes so easily to Leakey. KWS's finances went from surplus to debt within Western's first year, growing steadily worse each year. Poaching, too, began to reappear, and the Samburu game parks became a haven for bandits. KWS suffered a partial pull-out of international donor support, and Leakey's reappointment is quite possibly the only solution. Another controversial figure, the Kikuyu business tycoon **Charles Njonjo**, was made KWS chairman.

Leakey's challenges now involve rejuvenating KWS from its current dire state, eradicating the re-emerging poaching and rehabilitating the crumbling infrastructure. The crux, though, is how to fit humans, especially the Maasai, into the equation: overcoming his misanthropic reputation may be Leakey's biggest challenge.

Kenya's reputation in conservation and tourism circles.

THE POLITICAL CLIMATE

Back in 1987, an **Amnesty International** report roundly condemned Kenya's human rights record; an American congressional delegation was "stunned" by the mistreatment of political detainees and the fears expressed by Kenyans – as well as by its own abrupt treatment at the hands of the Kenyan Special Branch. The USA's strategic geopolitical relationship with Kenya is no longer so special, nor so strategic, as to prevent it from openly criticizing the country, and there has been a dramatic chill in relations between Washington and Nairobi since the end of the 1980s, largely as a result of the outspokenness on human rights of the former American ambassador **Smith Hempstone**.

During the **one-party era**, however, Moi always appeared firmly in control and it was never clear why opposition of any kind was dealt with so harshly. Despite efforts to throttle all dissent, the groundswell of resentment continued to grow. An opposition group, **Mwakenya** (a Swahili acronym for Union of Nationalists to Liberate Kenya), one of several murky organizations mounting anti-government campaigns, attracted attention through its pamphlets, calling for the replacement of the Moi government, new democratic freedoms and an end to corruption and Western influence. While Mwakenya barely identified itself and didn't appear to pose any serious threat to the government, hundreds of people were arrested in the late 1980s. Their defence lawyers tended, in turn, to get arrested themselves. As reported by Amnesty, a number of detainees died in custody and prisoners were routinely tortured and kept in waterlogged cells beneath Nyayo House in Nairobi.

The development of an **underground opposition** in Kenya wasn't surprising. For years public meetings of more than five people were only permitted with police approval (rarely granted). Dissent, even within the sole party, KANU, was crushed, and further illiberal measures were adopted by the government, including the change from secret balloting at elections to a public be-seen-and-counted **queue-voting** system, in which voters lined up behind the candidate of their choice. The government also passed a law empowering it to dismiss judges.

As power became increasingly concentrated in fewer and fewer hands – and whose hands became a topic for rumour – only the **church** and a few powerfully connected politicians dared to question the government. President Moi, a regular churchgoer, has always sought to avoid confrontations with senior clergy – though the suspicious death of one clergyman in a head-on collision on the A104 (see below) was partly instrumental in pushing the government into conceding to the demands for a multi-party system.

THE PATH TO MULTI-PARTY DEMOCRACY

It was the grisly murder in February 1990 of **Robert Ouko**, the Luo foreign minister, at his farm near Kisumu, that sparked off the first explosion of **civil unrest** in a rolling crisis that has beset the government ever since. Ouko, a stout Moi supporter who enjoyed excellent personal relations with governments in both Britain and the USA, was widely viewed as a potential successor to the presidency, and was backed by Britain for the vice-presidency in 1988.

When Ouko's death was reported, a week of **rioting** shook the country, although it was most violent in Kisumu, Ouko's home town. It is widely believed that his murder was the work of government bullies exceeding their briefs to threaten him (a parallel has been drawn with the murder of J.M. Kariuki in 1975). Ouko's popularity with the foreign press and the suave and articulate contrast he made with the president – combined with his threat to expose corruption – were the likely motivating factors.

Although the riots of February 1990 dismayed the government, July of that year saw Central Highlands towns in **violent tumult** as public opposition to the government mounted in the wake of demands for a multi-party system by three heavyweight public figures. The former

cabinet minister **Kenneth Matiba**, together with the then radical **Raila Odinga** (son of the much-respected veteran of the political scene, Luo leader Oginga Odinga) and the ex-mayor of Nairobi, **Charles Rubia**, declared themselves for a multi-party system and denounced the violent mass evictions that had recently taken place in the Nairobi slum of Muoroto: the three were subsequently detained without charge for over a year. Several human rights and pro-democracy lawyers were also arrested, while one who escaped arrest, **Gibson Kamau Kuria**, was given refuge in the US embassy. A Nairobi **pro-democracy rally** on July 7 (banned by the government) degenerated into attacks on buildings and security forces. There were dozens of deaths in street battles with armed police. President Moi blamed "hooligans and drug addicts" for the explosion.

Ouko's murder and the July 7 Saba Saba (Swahili for the seventh day of the seventh month) riots were followed by the gravely embarrassing death in a road accident of the outspoken **Bishop Alexander Muge** on his return from a visit to western Kenya. Muge's car collided head-on with a lorry which veered onto the wrong side of the road. The Archbishop, who had spoken out forcefully against the Muoroto evictions, had been warned against his visit to Luo-land in the most menacing terms by the Minister for Labour, who subsequently resigned from the cabinet.

In this hostile, nervous climate, the government came down hard on **journalists**, virtually stifling local newspapers and accusing the foreign press, and particularly the **BBC** in Nairobi, of mischief-making. The corporation was just the latest in a notorious line-up of divergent – and diversionary – "enemies" of Kenya, including the Ku Klux Klan and Colonel Gaddafi.

Relations with the international community plummeted. Against all the prevailing trends in Africa, Moi's stubborn resistance to adopting a multi-party system riled his overseas backers. He seemed barely aware of the end of the Cold War and the hard reassessment of aid distribution taking place among the rich countries.

In 1991, the steady build-up of an opposition lobby became so powerful it could not be dismantled and jailed, member by member. For the first time ever, the threat to the government looked substantial and set to endure. The Luo leader **Oginga Odinga** – effectively Kenya's elder statesman – set up the **Forum for the Restoration of Democracy (FORD)** in association with his son Raila Odinga and a committed group of lawyers, chief among whom was the influential chairman of the Law Society, **Paul Muite**. FORD quickly attracted government opponents from all quarters and was soon established as a mass movement for change, far removed from the shadowy, ideology-laden opposition movements of the previous decade, such as Mwakenya. Kenneth Matiba and Charles Rubia, recently released from detention, both joined FORD, and the long-time government critic **Martin Shikuku**, dissatisfied with KANU and sensing a sea-change in Kenyan politics, also joined, having defected from the ruling party.

The response to FORD, at home and overseas, was mixed. President Moi, in typically charming, uncompromising mood, referred to the movement as "rats" that would be "crushed", and blamed the energetic Nairobi diplomatic corps – and in particular the American ambassador of the time – for supporting anti-government forces. But this foreign support was not unanimous: the British High Commission kept their heads down and, in London, the Foreign Office quietly – but unconstructively – opined that multi-party democracy might bring about tribal clashes.

ETHNIC VIOLENCE

At least 3000 people have been killed in violence between different **language groups** in the Rift Valley, western Kenya and on the coast since the early 1990s. And at least 300,000 people have been displaced, nearly all of them non-Kalenjin, in ethnic cleansing.

For years, any reference to multi-party politics by KANU leaders was accompanied by dire warnings of the bloody consequences for tribal harmony of such a system. Once the government was forced into a corner on the issue by foreign aid donors, the prophecy was quickly realized. Ethnic allegiance swamped the new political order before it had even consolidated, so that the opposition parties were unable to formulate policies and election strategies that were free of ethnic considerations. Every move involved calculations of ethnic voting. FORD-Kenya tried the hardest to be ethnic-free, but KANU still seemed to be pulling the strings.

The **Kikuyu**, **Luo** and **Luhya** have been emigrating from their densely populated parts of Kenya for decades, buying marginal farmlands in the **Rift Valley** and other normally unproductive areas, trying to apply their farming techniques among the local Kalenjin and Maa-speakers and benefiting from local aid and subsistence initiatives. In most towns, at least until recently, it has been Kikuyu traders who ran many of the shops and small businesses.

The victims of the early attacks in various parts of Rift Valley Province described organized gangs of youths terrorizing non-Kalenjin homesteads and villages while local police arrived too late to do anything or just stood by. As KANU politicians warned that the Kalenjin should watch their backs for attacks by "outsiders", so their predictions were soon coming true. The KANU "policy", if

such it was, began to work, as Kikuyu vigilante groups began to retaliate and, in turn, provided spurious justification for Kalenjin fears. In electioneering terms, however, it proved totally counterproductive, as the government lost more votes from disgust with their inaction than it gained from forcing opposition voters out of marginal KANU constituencies. Probably the aim was simply to demonstrate to the world at large, through the media, that multi-partyism in Africa leads to tribal violence. In this – to the Moi government's lasting shame, and despite all the evidence of its fabrication – it succeeded.

In 1992, although the opposition had feared that an early election date would defeat it in its disorganized infancy, as the delays on setting the date continued against the background of ethnic violence (while Moi declared he was waiting for everything to be "all right in the country"), it began to look like the government agenda was to *allow* tribal divides to set in firmly in advance of the election. Accusations of **majimboism** – the creation of ethnic blocks – began to fly.

The violence in 1992 and 1997/8 was not so much the "clashes" or "fighting" (certainly not "tribal war") of newspaper headlines, as unprovoked attacks, muggings and vandalism. The perpetrators, who carried spears, *pangas*, bows and arrows and clubs – but rarely guns – looted property, stole livestock, burned houses, and beat up or killed anyone who got in their way. Their message was, "Get off our land", and thousands of victims moved to refugee camps outside Eldoret and other big towns. Now the people of the affected communities, while often cynical about government pronouncements, have been drawn willy-nilly into conflict with each other.

By the end of 1991, however, Kenya's immediate future was increasingly out of Moi's control. John Troon, the ex-Scotland Yard man hired by Moi to investigate Ouko's murder, revealed that the greatest suspicion fell on the president's closest advisor **Nicholas Biwott**, and his internal security chief, **Hezekiah Oyugi**. Biwott and Oyugi were both sacked and then arrested (they were later released "for lack of evidence", but not reinstated).

In the wake of this damaging news, the **Paris group** of donor nations suspended balance-of-payment support to Kenya for six months, pending economic and political reforms. Moi got the message. Within days he announced there would be multi-party elections for the next parliament and a free vote for the presidency, though he made it clear that multi-partyism had been foisted upon him and he saw no good could come of it. The constitutional amendment that had legalized the one-party state in 1982 was repealed and the stage was set for the registration of opposition parties and the first, legal, mass rallies.

THE 1992 ELECTIONS

There were convulsions in KANU. Many, if not all, ministers faced losing their seats in a free election. Among those who quickly resigned was former vice-president **Mwai Kibaki**, who formed the **Democratic Party** (DP) which soon found support among the Kikuyu and in parts of the east and northeast.

The government, however, had dealt itself a good hand before the elections were announced. Kenya's first-past-the-post electoral system and KANU's popularity in underpopulated districts (leading to huge overrepresentation for the areas of KANU support) were both very helpful. As, too, was the overwhelming (if more or less obligatory) support for KANU from the media, particularly the radio. But the party in power had some aces up its sleeve that were only revealed weeks before polling day.

To begin with there was the **voter registration scandal**. Since the previous election, in 1988, between three and four million young people had turned 18. Few of them had received national identity cards, a prerequisite of voter registration, and there were unexplained delays in issuing the cards in time for the elections, at least in many non-KANU-voting areas. Then, parliament quietly passed a law that almost

guaranteed Moi's continued presidency whatever the outcome of the general elections. To win the presidency, the candidate had to have at least 25 percent of the vote in five out of the eight provinces. Barring unexpected, huge reversals, only one man would achieve that.

Another new law came into force shortly before the election specifying the president had to form a government entirely from his own party (an anti-coalition law). Having split the opposition, this was nice timing.

FORD was finding the transformation from opposition lobby group to **political party** very hard to manage. As a party it was promiscuous in the welcome it extended to every ex-KANU minister who made the leap. Within weeks, the contest for the leadership of FORD and the nomination for a presidential candidate was in full swing.

Less than six months old, the FORD party began to disintegrate. There had always been a division between the established opposition, fronted by Oginga Odinga and led by Paul Muite and his lawyers' circle, and the newer opposition of displaced KANU people and establishment and business figures out of favour with the ruling party. Three months before the election, FORD split into FORD-Kenya (FORD-K; presidential candidate Odinga) and FORD-Asili (FORD-A; candidate Kenneth Matiba).

In parts of Kikuyu-land, **FORD-K** earned the nickname FORD-Kihii (*kihii* means an uncircumcized boy), an ethnic jibe against FORD-Kenya's Luo supporters. With the split, the ethnic divisions of multi-party politics were revealed. It became impossible to enter the political arena without constant reference to the language groups of the politicians and their supporters. Of all the parties, FORD-K were the most ardent in their rejection of tribally based politics. With Odinga, a Luo, as presidential candidate and Muite, a Kikuyu, as his running mate, the country's two largest ethnic groups were well represented. FORD-K was intellectually the strongest party, too, with a radical programme, but pragmatic economic policies, drawn up by an impressive group of economists, including expat businesspeople.

FORD-A was the big, centrist, Kikuyu party, with major support from business, its leader Matiba a serious threat to KANU. During Matiba's year of incarceration he had suffered two strokes and been refused permission to

CORRUPTION AND THE IMF

Corruption in Kenya is so widespread – infecting every strand of society – that it is accepted by the majority of people as the way things are, rather than as an aberration. That, however, is not the view of Kenya's bankers, led by the IMF.

The release in 1996 of some US$730 million-worth of aid to Kenya, followed the actions of the sober and apparently committed Minister of Finance, **Musalia Mudavadi**. Mudavadi's willingness to toe the IMF line had not been warmly approved of by Moi, but it had given Kenya's parlous finances some much needed breathing space. Mudavadi ultimately fell out with the IMF and lost his job after the 1997 election: his replacement, **Simeon Nyachae**, was more hawkish and less appeasing. Nyachae, however, also lost his job, in 1999, ostensibly because he refused to stand up against the IMF, but allegedly because he was getting too close on the heels of people near the top who owed billions of shillings to the banks.

The collapse of the IMF talks with Mudavadi, during the run-up to the elections in 1997 (with the fund demanding action on rampant **corruption**, and the government offering to do very little) led to the suspension of a $220m tranche of aid. Moi had balked at the austerity measures demanded, but finally implemented them: they included cutting funds for education and health care, laying off public employees and removing food subsidies.

In October 1997, a presidential advisor, **Joshua Kulei** was accused by *Finance* magazine of having amassed a fortune of £100 million. Allegations in the follow-up issue, which included details about Moi's son Gideon, didn't make the newsstands. The Kulei allegations had first appeared in the *Rift Valley Times*, whose publisher and writer were promptly locked up.

But the most sensational scandal of recent years has been **Goldenberg**. Between November 1990 and December 1992, Goldenberg International, with a monopoly on exports of gold and diamonds from Kenya, was granted a 35 percent export bonus by the government. The company claimed to have exported over £49 million worth of gold and diamonds, thus claiming £17m from the treasury in export bonuses. Kenya, of course, has no gold or diamonds. The fraud undermined the value of the Kenya shilling and those allegedly involved, including Asian businessman Kamlesh Pattni, have still not been brought to book. An early political casualty of the affair was George Saitoti – he must have given his approval – who lost his job as finance minister. Saitoti held the vice-presidency for a couple of years until 1997. The Goldenberg trial finally got underway in March 1998.

travel abroad for treatment. There was thus a well-founded fear in KANU about his personal animosity towards key figures in the ruling party.

The **Democratic Party**, despite support from a range of backgrounds, never looked, in the 1992 elections, like a serious contender to win the presidency or a majority in parliament, as its opposition credentials were suspect, leader Mwai Kibaki having only recently resigned from KANU. This was to change dramatically in the following five years.

There were opposition efforts until the last minute to forge tactical alliances in order to oust Moi and KANU. But, in the climate of mutual suspicion and risk-assessment, none materialized. KANU, meanwhile, having started 1992 in disarray, was looking stronger again by the end of the year. By **printing billions of shillings**, the government was able to buy support for KANU on a massive scale. Encouraged by the largesse, there were a number of significant returns to the KANU fold as the divisions among the opposition became clearer and a

KANU victory less unthinkable. Many had no deep-seated opposition to KANU, just a deep-rooted fear of being on the losing side.

On the coast, the banned fundamentalist **Islamic Party of Kenya** was something of a wild card. Khalid Salim Ahmed **Balala**, the IPK leader, spent much of the run-up to, and aftermath of, the election in detention, held on the trumped-up charge of "imagining" the death of President Moi.

At the last minute, the election date was switched from December 7 to **December 29**, the worst possible date for a good voter turnout. It was sure to favour the rural rather than the urban, the unemployed rather than those in work (who had registered to vote at their places of work rather than in their home villages, where many would be over Christmas), and, on balance, KANU over the opposition.

And so it turned out. Voting was low and, when the boxes were finally counted after several days, KANU had 100 seats out of the total of 188. Seventeen of these were returned "unopposed" as the opposition candidates had been physically prevented from presenting their nomination papers. There was, undoubtedly, widespread ballot-stuffing and fraud, but, with only 200 local and foreign election monitors to check 7000 ballot boxes, little to prevent it. In the presidential race, Moi received 1.9 million votes to the opposition candidates' combined 3.2 million.

The first session of Kenya's new multi-party parliament was suspended for two months, a slap in the face for opposition MPs whose disgust with the outcome of the election had at first led to a call to boycott their seats. The two months gave KANU a chance to buy back a number of MPs into the party (as a result there were a number of by-elections in western Kenya, usually accompanied by violence) and to try to come up with some sort of strategy for dealing with the superior intellectual and rhetorical strengths of the opposition.

KANU had lost all but one of its cabinet ministers to opposition candidates and, with a total lack of people of ministerial calibre on the government back benches, Moi was put in the extraordinary position of having to offer defeated cabinet ministers their posts back as nominated MPs (the Kenyan parliament at the time had 200 seats – 188 of which were elected seats and 12 of which were nominated, the latter in the president's gift). KANU has almost no MPs from the Kikuyu or Luo communities.

THE AFTERMATH OF THE ELECTIONS

Despite the bad taste left by the elections, the international community was little better impressed with the divided opposition parties, who, acting together, could easily have defeated KANU. The **IMF** and **World Bank** decided that there had, in the end, been much support for the incumbents and, after a false start – with a row in which Moi called their economic demands "suicidal and dictatorial" – agreement was reached with foreign donors to pick up the aid programme, two years after it had ceased.

In November 1993 donor nations finally agreed around US$500 million in new aid, although this did little to refill the badly depleted coffers pilfered since the end of the 1980s. The aid was contingent on stringent conditions, foremost among them a dramatic raft of privatizations of nationalized industries, including post

and telecommunications, the railways and the national produce and cereals board. Privatization was demanded partly out of obedience to economic theory, partly in an effort to reduce the cash available for siphoning off for political patronage.

In the **FORD-K party**, the activities of its elderly leader alarmed some of the membership. Oginga Odinga's agreement with Moi in 1993 to seek a partnership with the government to improve the economy and infrastructure in western Kenya, rather than going all-out to topple KANU, was judged a sell-out, and when it was further revealed that the old man had received at least Ksh2 million from the director of the scandal-ridden financial institution **Goldenberg International** (see box on p.623), the FORD-K party was torn apart. As a result, the hard-line younger FORD-K activists, including Oginga's son Raila Odinga, quit the party. Oginga Odinga died in January 1994, his departure hailed by KANU as a sad day for Kenya. State TV and President Moi paid him moving tributes and KANU offered to help meet funeral and other expenses.

FORD-A, meanwhile, steadily declined in confidence and credibility while its own ageing leader, Kenneth Matiba (today its sole MP) made increasingly wild accusations and pronouncements, including a bluntly racist attack on Kenyan Asians whom he accused of plundering the country.

Early in 1995, the ex-Kenya Wildlife Service chief, **Richard Leakey**, (recently sacked from his conservation post by Moi) joined lawyer Paul Muite to form a new political party, **Safina** ("The Ark"), with the intention of binding together the fragmented opposition. Moi's reaction was unsubtle: "What do I say to Leakey? I say no, no and no to any white man who wants to lead Kenya". Safina's application to register as a legal party was turned down and, at a meeting in Nakuru, Leakey and party leaders were beaten up.

There now followed two years of economic slowdown; strikes by teachers and nurses; mass demonstrations for constitutional reform; breakdown of relations with the IMF (which led to a run on the Kenya shilling); IMF and World Bank insistence on reforms and good governance; KANU in-fighting for succession, with Moi manoeuvring for control; and the many-headed opposition repeatedly splitting and reforming in a variety of brief experimental alliances. Senior figures in the three main parties (Martin Shikuku, now the leader of FORD-A; DP leader Mwai Kibaki; and Michael Wamalwa of FORD-K) finally agreed to work together as an **alliance**, which would put forward a single presidential candidate. Richard Leakey co-ordinated the alliance and raised funds. But Kenneth Matiba's ambitions for the presidency, not to mention those of Martin Shikuku, should the alliance not work out, were clear signals that the opposition would be in no better a state of united readiness than in 1992. When Moi finally unbanned Safina it was too late for the party to organize a presidential candidate.

But at the same time as the opposition was left awry, the run-up to the 1997 elections saw internal divisions in Moi's KANU beginning to show. A rift began to appear between the vehemently anti-Kikuyu **KANU A** – dominated by Maasai strong-man William Ntimama and Simeon Nyachae, a politician from the Kisii region widely seen in his camp as a possible successor to Moi – and the more wily **KANU B**, led by George Saitoti and Nicholas Biwott, who foresaw little future for the party, post-Moi (1997–2002 is his last term in office), without the involvement of the Kikuyu. Moi leans towards KANU B and appears to place great trust in Biwott, his former personal assistant from the Keiyo Kalenjin sub-group, who styles himself "Total Man".

For most of 1997, Kenyan politics polarized between KANU hardliners and the National Convention Executive Committee (NCEC) – a coalition of religious leaders, unionists and student activists – and the country was kept guessing as Moi swung between conciliation and hardline, man-the-barricades rhetoric.

By June 1997, the opposition, and particularly students, were howling for reforms in advance of the elections. Rallies were called for July 7, a date commemorating the 1990 Saba Saba pro-democracy rally. The police response, included the **storming of the University**, left more than a dozen dead after protests around the country, and included the beating up of elderly churchmen and the savage cudgelling of women with babies, witnessed by millions of TV viewers.

There were protests from all Kenya's big aid donors and outraged depositions from Nairobi's diplomatic community. Moi reacted in panic.

Although he refused to talk to the NCEC, he agreed to meet with the parliamentary opposition in a grouping that came to be known as the **Inter-Party Parliamentary Group**. Reforms to the law and the unbanning of most opposition parties were suddenly on the agenda, and Moi regained the initiative.

Repression alternated with promises of reform through the rest of year, accompanied by a series of national strikes, until, in November 1997, the Constitutional (Amendment) Bill passed its final reading in parliament. The **reforms** saw the long overdue removal of the archaic sedition laws – the Chief's Act and the Public Order Act, two pieces of legislation that were designed to restrict basic freedoms of movement and speech. In the context of the Moi government, these laws, along with the Societies Act, were effectively exploited to emasculate and cower the opposition, restricting its operations, especially in areas considered to be KANU zones. Reforms, forced upon Moi, like multi-partyism five years earlier, had been brought about by mass action, the falling out with the IMF, increasing international isolation, and the fear in Moi's camp that the youth in particular would take Mobutu's downfall in Zaire as encouragement to pull down their own president (the two dictators have often been compared). The new laws also provide for equal access to state media by the opposition – in theory. But people can still only associate with institutions that are registered: the Societies Act bans true freedom of association.

Despite the impending reforms, Mombasa erupted in violence in August 1997, when two police stations were attacked, six policemen killed, weapons stolen and dozens of up-country people later killed and thousands more expelled by armed gangs who terrorized the district of **Likoni**. Notices circulated "reclaiming" the coast for its indigenous inhabitants, and demanding the largely Kikuyu newcomers – who tend to support the opposition – return to their home districts. For once, the police acted on the side of the victims of what was widely presumed to be a resumption of government-inspired ethnic cleansing, and arrested two local KANU party chiefs.

THE 1997 ELECTIONS

The elections were held, once again, on December 29, though this time they were beset

WANGARI MAATHAI AND THE GREEN BELT MOVEMENT

One of the government's most outspoken and consistently credible critics is the former chairwoman of the National Council of Women of Kenya, Professor **Wangari Maathai**. A founding member of FORD, she was also the instigator, in 1977, of the **Green Belt Movement**, Kenya's remarkable grassroots environmental lobby. The Green Belt Movement has planted more than 12 million tree saplings around the country and is responsible for a transformation in environmental awareness, especially among the rural poor, and particularly among women, who have done most of the planting. Unlike Maendeleo Ya Wanawake, which, over the years, has come to be seen as essentially a tool of KANU, the Green Belt movement is not aligned with any political party.

In March 1992, Maathai, on hunger strike in Uhuru Park with the wives and mothers of political prisoners, demanding their release, was clubbed unconscious by police, and she later became involved in the commission of inquiry over ethnic violence in the Rift Valley.

Articulate and trenchant, Maathai has clashed directly with President Moi over his plans for a high-rise development in Uhuru Park, and most recently has spearheaded the demonstrations against the destruction of Nairobi's Karura Forest. She has often accused the government of corruption and the misappropriation of aid funds. After her colleague John Makanga was violently arrested in 1993, and she received death threats, Maathai went into hiding. She came out to receive the 1993 Edinburgh Medal, awarded for an outstanding contribution to humanity through science.

Wangari Maathai claims to have no political ambitions, but her charisma, her fame and her impeccably nationalist and internationalist views must make her a leading candidate for Kenya's — and Africa's — first woman president or prime minister.

from start to finish by **organizational chaos** and **severe weather**: two returning officers, and their ballot boxes, were swept away in a flooded river. Many polling stations opened late, or not at all; ballot papers were delivered to the wrong constituency, or were insufficient for the number of queuing voters; electoral commission staff walked out of polling stations in protests over pay; and boxes remained uncollected.

The **vote**, predictably, split along ethnic lines, with the Kalenjin constituencies of the Rift Valley, along with the Maasai and Samburu, the Somali, Turkana, coastal and many Luhya and Kisii constituencies, largely voting for Moi and KANU. Mwai Kibaki's Democratic Party performed extremely well in the Kikuyu areas, even better than expected given it was five years since he had left KANU. In the Kikuyu heartland, not even Jomo Kenyatta's son, Uhuru Kenyatta, (a Moi family business associate), could win a seat for KANU in his Gatundu South constituency. In the presidential race, Moi polled 2.4 million votes against Kibaki's 1.9 million.

Charity Ngilu, the daughter of a minister in the Ebenezer Gospel Church, who had been expected to do well with her Social Democratic Party, put over a feisty, honest and hard-working image: "Ngilu beats up official" headlined one newspaper, about a hapless official she suspected of tampering with voter forms. But her support was largely limited to her Kamba ethnic base. **Raila Odinga**, too, with his National Development Party, was well supported, but only locally, in Luo-land.

Mwai Kibaki and Raila Odinga both called for a rerun of the presidential election, and Kibaki challenged the election results through the courts. Paul Muite and Richard Leakey's Safina party accepted the results, however, and Leakey quit politics soon afterwards (see box on p.618).

An unfolding postscript to the elections has been the **succession question**, and the wooing by KANU of Michael Wamalwa's FORD-K and Raila Odinga's NDP, both with their grassroots support in the west. This **Luo-Luhya alliance with KANU,** with the patronage flowing from Nairobi, appears to be another twist in Moi's continued determination to control the country, even after his departure. Whether the alliance can last is another matter.

Like his father in the earlier part of the decade, the stance of the once radical Raila Odinga on anti-corruption and non-tribalism has been considerably eroded; he rarely speaks out against graft or land theft and has made public statements about the danger of a Kikuyu threat. He has even publicly compared himself to Mandela, casting Moi as Kenya's De Klerk. On this startling analysis, how KANU plans to draw in the **Kikuyu**, as the strong men of KANU-B would prefer – rather than take them on, at the next elections in 2002 – is hard to conceive.

THE TURN OF THE MILLENNIUM

Kenya today is, in many respects, a harsh and bitter country below the surface. Very little makes sense, socially and politically, beyond calculations of **personal interest** for those powerful figures whose voices are heard. The reality of civic life in Kenya is one of interminably drawn-out court cases, pointless public enquiries, corruption on a scarcely believable scale and flagrant police brutality every day, in every town. Kenyans, rich and poor, have been badly let down.

The horrific August 1998 **bombing** of the American Embassy, by presumed Islamic fundamentalists, in which more than 250 people were killed and 5000 injured, led to a suspension of ordinary faction fighting and a genuine mood of public reconciliation. Charles Njonjo, a figure in the political wasteland for fifteen years, took up the chair of the disaster fund. There was even a noticeable upswing in Kenya's fortunes in the international tourist market as the world sympathized with a poor country struggling blamelessly with a familiar pattern of events.

But the lull was short-lived. As the dust settled, business as usual was quickly resumed. The judicial inquiry into ethnic clashes has resumed its grindingly slow process. There were more than 100 further killings, mostly of Kikuyu, in Laikipia and Nakuru districts, in January 1999. The police made no arrests. There is ceaseless pressure on the elderly Daniel Moi to appoint a vice-president. Moi is doing his fifth and final term of office, heightening pressure for nomination of his successor.

Ethnicity is dangerously to the fore. Questions of prior **rights over land** are being brought up across the country, in every sphere of life, even when there is little history of dispute, in order to raise the political temperature and increase KANU's leverage. **Majimboism** (see box) is widely debated. Ethnic violence continues sporadically in the Rift Valley and the government seems powerless or unwilling to stop it.

MAJIMBOISM

The infamous **majimboism** (federalism) debate that is related to the constitutional reform exercise has become vigorous in recent years. Coastal legislators, who have long pioneered the crusade, now claim to have released a blueprint for a federal government system. In July 1998, a number of MPs from Central Province – Kenya's most prosperous region – uncharacteristically plunged into the fray with a call for their own *jimbo* (federal state) called Kirinyaga. The MPs not only advocated the creation of a region that would bring the economically powerful "Gema" (Kikuyu, Embu and Meru) communities together, but also suggested Nairobi as their *jimbo*'s headquarters.

The possibility of the country's capital city becoming the headquarters of Kenya's most developed *jimbo* shook majimboists into a serious rethink. Three Coast MPs – Mathias Keah (KANU), Emmanuel Karisa Maitha (DP) and Suleiman Shakombo (Shirikisho Party) – advocated a system that would address "all socio-economic and political issues". "What we want is *jimbo* for political, economic and social development which will ensure that all the people residing in the region benefit from the resources and improve their standards of living."

The **Shirikisho Party**, founded on the eve of the 1997 elections, is an exclusively coastal outfit whose main agenda is to fight for *majimbo* (plural) and the rights of the coastal peoples. The party was at one time threatened with deregistration for allegedly promoting violence, and has occasionally found itself in bad light, especially in relation to the August 1997 Likoni killings that culminated in the death of over 100 people, and the displacement of tens of thousands of others. Up-country people – mainly Kikuyu, Luo, Luhya and Kamba – bore the brunt of the attacks. The violence, officially attributed to the locals' grievances over the up-country peoples' alleged monopoly of land ownership, jobs and business, seriously afflicted the tourist industry which is the region's sole economic mainstay. Consequently, many hotels and tourist resorts in the region closed down, rendering thousands of workers jobless. A religious link to the *majimbo* quest in both the Coast and North-Eastern provinces is already being floated by opponents of the system. Church leaders in particular are wary of the crusade, pointing out that a large majority of the legislators calling for majimboism in the two regions are Muslims.

In the worst-affected communities, it has occasionally led to a resurgence of Kikuyu **oathing** (see p.610), a particularly powerful form of secret social sanction, binding the oathers together and almost guaranteeing revenge attacks on members of opposing ethnic groups.

The current ethnic rifts are mirrored by long-existing **economic disparities** that need to be addressed. The supporters of KANU (mostly Kalenjin, Maasai, Samburu, people of the northeast, and some small coastal ethnic groups) include most of Kenya's most marginalized communities, who have benefited most from the KANU government's limited hand-outs and subsistence support. Because of their poor, often pastoral, economies, they tend to lag behind in educational opportunities. In contrast, the opposition – ethnically dominated heavily by the Kikuyu and Luo – is based in the most economically developed regions and communities, where ambitions constantly outstrip the limited rewards that Kenya can offer to educated and business-minded people.

Perhaps Kenya will hold together if the country can remain a political patchwork – with the KANU-supporting marginal districts separated from each other by fertile opposition regions of high population density. But the drawing-in by KANU of Raila Odinga's largely Luo supporters and Michael Wamalwa's FORD-K, with its Luhya support base – both from the west of Kenya, and bordering Moi's Rift Valley heartland – may

THE CHALLENGE OF PRESS FREEDOM

In March 1999, the veteran KANU politician and Minister of Home Affairs, **Shariff Nassir**, twice publicly threatened the press with "problems" if they persisted in "printing lies" and "criticizing the government". The press duly responded by reporting his threats verbatim, together with essays pointing out that Kenya had progressed, however shakily, from dictatorship to an era of democracy, and that the threats were those of a man clearly out of step with the times. The infamous **sedition laws** which had previously gagged the media were repealed in 1997, and Nassir's threats were shrugged off. This would have been unthinkable in the bad old days, when the editors would have been imprisoned and copies of the offending papers impounded.

However, after so many decades of dictatorship and press control, Kenya's new-found freedoms are far from guaranteed. Although established high circulation dailies like the **Nation** and **Standard** seem able to criticize with relative impunity, the government is still a dab hand at more sinister forms of censorship. In March 1998, the newly-appointed Information and Broadcasting Minister Joseph Nyagah accused an unnamed section of the press of "taking advantage" of the lax laws to conduct a "vicious campaign" to undermine presidential authority and national stability. At the end of the month, Moi himself ordered the closure of the *Star* newspaper, for having reported on the armed forces. At the same time, the *Nation* group's radio and TV licence was cancelled, allegedly due to a dispute with a local businessman, but the *Nation* claimed the decision demonstrated "a deep-seated fear of truth in public life and the values of free expres-

sion". The *Nation* was sanctioned early in 1999, for publishing a leaked document from the Akiwumi tribal clashes inquiry, for which it was banned from reporting for a month. Other papers are treated less kindly: the editors and owners of the magazines **Finance** and **Law Monthly**, both of which favour scandalous headlines accusing one politician or another of corruption, repeatedly face arrest and the impounding of their presses or files, as does the long-suffering editor of **Kenya Confidential**, who seems to spend more time in jail than out, the last time for an article headlined "Kenya Police: a Monstrous Disaster".

Despite this far from perfect environment, the advances in press freedom over the last few years are remarkable, and have played an instrumental part in pushing Kenya from dictatorship towards democracy. With donor pressure still very much on Kenya to comply with their conditions of more openness and democracy, these press freedoms seem likely to continue – at least as long as the donors keep up the pressure. However, the government's control over the executive and judiciary remains tight and Nassir's threats, at present taken lightly by the press, may still be realized.

Whatever the climate for local journalists, there is no doubt that Kenya is one of the best places in Africa in which to work as a **foreign correspondent**. Based mostly at Chester House in Nairobi, (and largely unimpeded if not greatly encouraged), foreign reporters put Kenya, more than most other African countries, under intense international scrutiny. Responding to their reports in a robust, credible fashion, however, has never been the government's strong point.

shift Kenya's political centre of gravity away from Nairobi altogether. And the possibility that an east African regional power base is being constructed in **Eldoret** is the disturbing conclusion that may have to be drawn from the opening of its redundant international airport and bullet factory. (There's an interesting chink of light in the Kalenjin armour with which Moi is shielding himself in the town: the Nandi. Many Nandi don't accept the Kalenjin label foisted on them – they are the largest "Kalenjin" group, all of whom speak the same language, Nandi. Increasing numbers of Nandi in Eldoret, their main home, are refusing to have any truck with KANU.)

Kenya finds itself in a disastrous predicament, and any sense of stability is illusory. More than ever before, resolving the linked problems of landlessness, unemployment and poverty – the root causes of Kenya's internal conflicts – must remain the priority. It would be refreshing if the KANU government were to initiate pragmatic reforms to its practices, by actively prosecuting the embezzlers of Kenya's precious public funds, and by putting humanity plainly at the top of its agenda, signalling a genuine concern for the country's people. The brute realities of the international economic order make these tasks difficult for the best-intentioned governments. But, after nearly four decades in power, it is clear that the KANU government is incapable of addressing these issues independently. Perhaps the best that can realistically be hoped for is that it avoids completely alienating the opposition parties and the international community. Without their involvement, Kenya's future, on current form, is not bright.

WILDLIFE

Despite the tremendous losses of the twentieth century, Kenya teems with wildlife. In one place or another, not just inside the protective boundaries of the forty-odd parks and reserves, it is possible to see almost all of the country's big animals. Even outside the parks, if you travel fairly widely, you're almost certain to note various gazelles and antelopes, zebra and giraffe – even hippo, buffalo, crocodile and elephant. Monkeys and baboons can be seen almost anywhere and are a regular menace.

If this impression of abundant wild animals slightly alarms you, rest assured that, outside the park boundaries, any danger is minimal. The big cats are hardly ever seen, and man-eating lions and enraged elephants are no more a realistic

cause for concern than the few remaining rhinos, which live entirely within the parks; buffalos, though plentiful, are only really dangerous when solitary. For lonely hikes – on Mount Kenya, Mount Elgon and the Aberdares, for example – hiring a guide is sometimes a good idea. Statistically, however, your chances of being attacked by a wild animal in Kenya are very small.

The country's **birdlife** is even more noticeable than its mammals, and astonishingly diverse, attracting ornithologists from all over the world and converting many others as well. Superb starlings, iridescent relatives of our own subtler species, are everywhere, but there are over a thousand species in all, ranging from the thumb-sized red-cheeked cordon bleu to the ostrich.

This introduction to Kenya's habitats, mammals, birds, reptiles and amphibians supplements our full-colour guide to "The Wildlife of East and Southern Africa" in the centre of this book, which will prove useful in identifying the main species of mammals likely to be seen on safari. For more detailed coverage, a good full-length field guide is very valuable – some recommended **books** are listed on p.647.

FOREST AND WOODLAND HABITATS

Several forest types are present in Kenya, including montane, coastal and lowland dry forests.

HIGHLAND FORESTS

The highlands support rich montane forests, which give way to agricultural lands as you approach Nairobi. The characteristic landscape

GETTING INVOLVED

CERT, the Campaign for Environmentally Responsible Tourism, PO Box 4246, London SE21 7ZE. Lobbies to educate tour operators and tourists in a sensitive approach to travel.

East African Wildlife Society, 2nd Floor, Museum Hill Centre, Museum Hill Rd, Nairobi (☎02/748170, fax 02/746868). They publish an excellent bi-monthly magazine, *Swara*, and your subscription funds worthwhile conservation work.

Friends of Conservation, PO Box 74901 Nairobi (☎02/339537 or 02/243976); Sloane Square House, Holbein Place, London SW1W 8NS,

(☎0171/730 7904); 1520 Kensington Rd, Oakbrook, Illinois, IL 60521 (☎708 954 3388).

Save the Rhino, 105 Park St, London W1Y 3FB.

Tourism Concern, Stapleton House, 277–281 Holloway Rd, London N7.Campaigns for the rights of local people to be consulted in tourist developments affecting their lives. They produce a quarterly magazine of news and articles.

Tusk Trust, 19 Amner Rd, London SW11 6AA.

Worldwide Fund for Nature (WWF), Panda House, Weyside Park, Godalming, Surrey GU7 1XR, UK.

in the highlands is patches of evergreen forest separated by vast meadows of grasses – often wire grass and Kikuyu grass.

The highland forest is quite limited in extent in Kenya; it is typically found above 1500m, and also on isolated massifs. It bears some resemblance to lowland forest, but contains different tree species and does not normally grow as tall and dense. Typical trees of this forest include **camphor**, **Juniperus procera** (the "cedar" tree of east Africa) and **podocarpus**. The better-developed forests are found on the wetter, western slopes of the massifs. Above the forest line, stands of giant bamboo are found at altitudes of over 2500m. Along the lower, drier edge of the highlands, trees grow less high and are dotted in fields of tall grass; various species of olive tree are commonly found here.

The **main highland forest areas** are to be found on Mount Kenya, Mount Elgon, the Mau escarpment, the Aberdares and Mount Marsabit. **Mount Kenya** displays a mountain summit plant community (known as **Afro-Alpine**), which bears a strong similarity to that found on other high east African mountains (there's more on Mount Kenya's high-altitude flora on p.196). The highest part of the montane forest belt, at altitudes over 2900m, is characterized by a giant form of St John's wort. Above this, giant heather and *Proteus* trees form a heather belt, whilst at even higher altitudes, open marshy moorland is found, dominated by tussock grasses, giant groundsel and giant lobelia. Higher still, the tree groundsel comes into its own (this has an upper limit of 4460m).

Several species of **near-endemic birds** are associated with the highland forest habitat. These are Jackson's francolin (a game bird of high-altitude forest undergrowth), the dazzling golden-winged sunbird (golden-yellow wings and long, yellow tail streamers) and Hartlaub's turaco. Other typical birds of these forests and streams include African black duck, mountain buzzard, bar-tailed trogon, white-starred robin, mountain warbler and mountain wagtail.

THE KAKAMEGA FOREST

West of the Rift Valley, the 240 square kilometres of Kakamega forest, and a few adjacent outliers, are examples of the Guineo-Congolian **equatorial forest**, which is more typically a feature of central and west Africa and is now very restricted within Kenya. For this reason,

many bird and plant species not encountered elsewhere in Kenya are found here – it's a memorable experience to be in the forest at first light when the shafts of morning sun spear their way through the tallest boughs of the semi-evergreen trees.

LOWLAND AND COASTAL FOREST AND WOODLANDS

Very few areas of **lowland rain forest** are left in Kenya, mainly restricted to the coastal strip, and the banks of the lower Athi and Tana rivers. The soils of these forests quickly lose their fertility when cleared for agriculture, and many of the areas that remain are degraded.

Lowland woodland areas are found inland of the coastal forest strip and away from the rivers. Woodlands are defined as more open forest areas with the ground flora dominated by grasses and the forest canopy covering as little as twenty percent of the area. Trees in such woodlands may average only 4–5m high.

The rain forests, all threatened by human incursions, include **Witu forest** near Lamu, the **Mida-Gedi forest**, the **Sabaki river forest** near Malindi, forest fragments in the **Shimba Hills** and the **Ramisi river forest** on the southern coast.

The most important area of natural forest is the **Arabuko-Sokoke forest**, which lies slightly inland along the western side of the main coast road, south of Malindi and north of Kilifi. Arabuko-Sokoke is unique in that it comprises a largely unbroken block of 420 square kilometres of coastal forest, consisting of *Brachystegia* woodland (containing a huge variety of birdlife), dense *Cynometra* forest, and zones of mixed lowland rain forest that are very rich in plants, mammals and insects.

Large areas of the coastal plain are covered in moist, tree-scattered grasslands. On the beach itself, tall **coconut palms** and the rather weedy-looking **casuarina** (known as whistling pine) dominate the high-tide line.

GRASSLAND

Grassland with scattered trees (wooded savannah) covers vast areas in Kenya, both in the **Lake Victoria basin** (which includes the Mara), and **south and east of Mount Kenya** at elevations of 1000–1800m. This type of ecosystem prevails because of regular fires.

Many of the trees that persist are broad-leaved and deciduous, protected from fire damage by their corky bark. In areas with a similar altitude, but with more erratic rainfall, a thin scattering of tall, flat-topped acacia trees, along with shorter acacias, occurs amongst the grassland, producing the archetypal imagery of the east African landscape.

DESERT AND SEMI-DESERT

Typical desert and semi-desert flora comprises **thornbush and thicket**. Thirty kilometres inland from the Indian Ocean, beyond the fringes of the Arabuko-Sokoke forest and others, is the eastern edge of the **Nyika wilderness**, which stretches west to the edge of the highlands. Nyika is characterized by an often impenetrably thick growth of stunted, thorny trees, which are grey for most of the year, but become green during the rainy season. Scaly-barked species such as acacia and euphorbia species occur in this plant community.

Desert grass-bush and the drier **desert scrub** communities cover nearly seventy percent of the land area of Kenya, mainly in the east, north and northeast. These areas are at low altitude (below 600m) and have unreliable rainfall, suffering long droughts, a lack of regular flowing water and strong wind exposure. Vegetation is sparse and scrubby, with bushes and occasional, widely scattered tall trees, mainly baobab, *mwangi* and *mgunga* (acacia) trees. Much of the ground free of bushes is covered by dispersed bunches of grass and other low shrubs. However, much of the soil surface here is bare.

The true desert habitat is drier still and plant life is very limited in some areas. Many of the trees and bushes (if present at all) are dwarf. Large areas are bare, stony desert with a thin and patchy growth of desert grasses and perhaps a few bushes along dry river margins or dry water courses.

WET HABITATS

The Kenyan coast is dominated by two major habitat types, sandy beach and mangrove forest. There are also some offshore rocky islands and coral reefs along the coast, which provide refuge for birds, but there are no breeding sites of pelagic seabirds (birds of the open ocean) in the country. Many species of shore birds

(waders) are found in tidal creeks and estuaries, for example at Mida Creek, on the Sabaki estuary, and also on the Lamu archipelago. One unique wader species, the **crab plover** – a pied wader which runs to catch crabs for food – over-winters at Mida Creek.

LAKES

The savannah of the **Great Rift Valley** is dotted with bird-rich lakes, ranging from the two fresh-water lakes – Naivasha and Baringo – to intensely saline ones like Magadi and Bogoria. The Rift Valley acts as a magnet to passage and wintering birds.

The vast expanse of **Lake Victoria** is an example of an oligotrophic lake – fed mainly by rainwater falling on to the lake's surface, rather than being fed by rivers and streams. As a result, it has a relatively low nutrient concentration. A feature of the lake is its papyrus beds and marshlands which harbour birds not found elsewhere in Kenya.

RIVERS

There are very few permanent riverine habitats in Kenya, because the country is so dry, but those river systems which exist are extremely attractive to birds and mammals. The best examples of such rivers are the **Tana** and **Athi-Galana-Sabaki** systems.

MANGROVE FOREST

Marine mangrove swamps are found in many parts of the coast. The largest tracts, and the areas from which most mangrove poles (*boriti*) are cut for the building trade, are in the Lamu archipelago, but all the coastal creeks are more or less bordered by mangroves (*mkoko* in Swahili). There are also areas of saline grassland on the landward side of some of the mangrove thickets. Although fun to travel through by boat, mangrove forests are not noted for their faunal diversity. One unusual animal you're bound to see is the **mudskipper**, a fish on the evolutionary road to becoming an amphibian.

MAMMALS

Kenya has more than a hundred species of large native mammals. The majority of species are vegetarian grazers, browsers and foragers at the lower end of the food chain – animals such as monkeys, rodents and antelopes. The big preda-

SWAHILI ANIMAL NAMES

Bweha	Jackal	*Nigri*	Warthog
Bweha masigio	Bat-eared fox	*Nsya*	Duiker
Choroa	Oryx	*Nungu*	Porcupine
Chui	Leopard	*Nyamera*	Topi
Dondoo	Steinbok, grysbok	*Nyani*	Baboon
Duma	Cheetah	*Nyati*	Buffalo
Faru	Rhinoceros	*Nyegere*	Ratel
Fisi	Hyena	*Nyoka*	Snake
Fisi maji	Otter	*Nyumbu*	Wildebeest
Fungo	Civet	*Paa*	Suni antelope
Kalasinga	De Brazza's monkey	*Paka*	Cat
Kamandegere	Springhare	*Pala hala*	Sable antelope
Kanu	Genet	*Pimbi*	Rock hyrax
Kiboko	Hippopotamus	*Pofu*	Eland
Kima	Monkey	*Punda*	Horse, ass
Komba	Bushbaby	*Punda milia*	Zebra
Kongoni	Hartebeest	*Sange*	Elephant shrew
Korongo	Roan antelope	*Sibamangu*	Caracal
Kuru	Waterbuck	*Simba*	Lion
Mamba	Crocodile	*Sunguru*	Hare, rabbit
Mbega	Colobus monkey	*Swala granti*	Grant's gazelle
Mbwa mwitu	Hunting dog	*Swala pala*	Impala
Mdudu	Insect, bug	*Swala tomi*	Thomson's gazelle
Mondo	Serval	*Swala twiga*	Gerenuk
Muhanga	Aardvark	*Tandala*	Kudu
Ndege	Bird (also means plane)	*Taya*	Oribi
Ndovu	Elephant	*Tohe*	Reedbuck
Nguchiro	Mongoose	*Tumbili*	Vervet monkey
Nguruwe	Pig, hog	*Twiga*	Giraffe

tors are fewer in species and tend to be the dominant topic of conversation at game lodges. Everyone remembers seeing lions for the first time or cheetahs. To see a leopard is often a personal goal, and a highlight. Once you get the bug, you'll be looking out for a lone striped hyena, rather than the common and gregarious spotted version, or for a serval cat rather than a cheetah. But don't ignore the less glamorous animals. There can be just as much satisfaction in spotting a shy, uncommon antelope, or in noting rarely observed behaviour, as in ticking off one of the more obvious predatory status symbols.

PRIMATES

There are twelve species of primates in Kenya, excluding *Homo sapiens*. They range from the pint-sized, slow-motion, lemur-like potto, found in Kakamega forest, to the baboon. Kenya no longer has any great apes (the family to which the gorilla and the chimpanzee belong), although they probably only became extinct in the western forests, of which Kakamega is a relic, in the last five hundred years, during which time the region was widely settled by humans. The legend of the Nandi Bear (see p.305) is probably connected with those passed-down memories. A new **chimpanzee sanctu-**

The **cross-references** given below lead to pages in our colour guide to "The Wildlife of East and Southern Africa" in the centre of this book.

Black-and-white colobus

ary has recently been established at Sweetwaters in Laikipia, "stocked" with chimps from Jane Goodall's famous Gombe Stream reserve in Tanzania.   Today, the primate you are certain to see almost anywhere in Kenya, given a few trees, is the **vervet** (p.2), a small, lightweight monkey that has no difficulty adjusting to the presence of humans and, if possible, their food. The vervet is one of the guenons – typical African monkeys, with distinctive facial markings and hairstyles, all wonderfully adapted to a life on the prowl for fruits, leaves, insects and just about anything else small and tasty. Almost as common in certain areas, notably on the coast, is **Sykes' monkey** (p.3). At Diani Beach, a number of Sykes' troops have become notoriously accustomed to stealing food from hotel dining tables, and large males will even raid bedrooms. Up-country populations of Sykes' (or blue) monkey appear to be more timid.

It is up-country where you are most likely to see the beautiful, leaf-eating **black and white colobus monkeys** (p.2) – although they can also be spotted in the Diani forest. They are usually found high in the tree canopy; look out for the pure white young. The related Tana River red colobus is only found in the remote Tana River Park, which also shelters the dwindling population of Tana River crested mangabeys, a partly ground-dwelling monkey with a characteristic Mohican-style crest of hair. Other rare or more localized monkeys include: the red-tailed guenon of the far west; the stocky but distinguished looking De Brazza's monkey, with its white goatee, found almost exclusively in Saiwa Swamp National Park; and the **Patas monkey** (p.2), a moustachioed plains runner of the dry northwest and Laikipia.

If you stay in a game lodge, you are quite likely to see **bushbabies** at night, as they frequently visit dining rooms and verandahs. There's a large, cat-sized species (the greater galago) and a small bushbaby not much bigger than a kitten (the lesser galago). Both are engaging animals, with sensitive, inquisitive fingers and large eyes and ears to aid them in their hunt for insects and other small animals.

On safari you'll have plenty of opportunities to watch **baboon troops** (p.2) up close. Large males can be somewhat intimidating in size and manner, disconcertingly so towards women. Troops average forty to fifty individuals, who spend their lives, like all monkeys, in clear, but mutable social relationships. Rank and precedence, physical strength and kin ties all determine an individual's position in this mini-society led by a dominant male. The days are dominated by the need to forage and hunt for food (baboons will consume almost anything, from a fig tree's entire crop to a baby antelope found in the grass). Grooming is a fundamental part of the social glue during times of relaxation. When baboons and other monkeys perform this massage-like activity on each other, the specks which they pop into their mouths are sometimes parasites – notably ticks – and sometimes flakes of skin.

RODENTS – AND HYRAXES

Rodents aren't likely to make a strong impression on safari, unless you're lucky enough to do some night game drives – or preferably walks. In that case you may see the bristling back end of a **crested porcupine** (p.3) or the frenzied leaps of a **spring hare** (p.3), dazzled by headlights or a torch. In rural areas off the beaten track you may occasionally see hunters taking home **giant rats** or **cane rats** – shy, vegetarian animals, which make good eating. Kenya has several species of **squirrel**, the most spectacular of which are the giant forest squirrel, with its splendid bush of a tail, and the nocturnal flying squirrel – which actually glides, rather than flies, from tree to tree, on membranes between its outstretched limbs. Both these squirrels are most likely to be seen in Kakamega forest. Very widespread, however, are the two species of **ground squirrel** – striped and unstriped – which are often seen, dashing along the track in front of the vehicle, in Tsavo National Park and the Samburu reserves.

Rock hyraxes (p.7), which you are certain to see at Hell's Gate National Park and on Mount Kenya, look like they should be rodents. In fact the rock hyrax and closely related tree hyrax are technically ungulates (hoofed mammals) and form a classificatory level entirely their own. Their closest living relatives are elephants, with which they share distant common ancestry. Present-day hyraxes are pygmies compared with some of their prehistoric ancestors, which were as big as a bear in some cases. Rock hyraxes live in busy, vocal colonies of twenty or thirty females and young, plus a male. In a few places they are extremely tame and wait to be fed by passing hikers. Usually, however, they are timid in the extreme – not surprising in view of the wide range of predators that will take them.

CARNIVORES

Kenya's carnivores are some of the most exciting and easily recognizable animals you'll see. Although often portrayed as fearsome hunters, pulling down plains game after a chase, many species do a fair bit of scavenging and all are content to eat smaller fry when conditions dictate or the opportunity arises.

Of the large cats, **lions** (p.6) are the easiest species to find. Lazy, gregarious and physically large – up to 1.8m in length, not counting the tail, and up to a metre high at the shoulder – they rarely make much effort to hide or to move away, except on occasions when a large number of tourist vehicles intrude. They can be seen in nearly all the parks and reserves, and their presence is generally the main consideration in determining whether you're allowed out of your vehicle or not. Popular parks where lions are normally absent are Hell's Gate and Lake Bogoria (you can hike in both); parks which are inhabited by lions, but in which you can generally hike, include the Aberdares and Mount Kenya. "Man-eating" lions appear from time to time but seem to be one-off feline misfits. Normally, lions hunt co-operatively, preferring to kill very young, old or sick animals, and making a kill roughly once in every two attacks. When they don't kill their own prey, they will steal the kills of cheetahs or hyenas.

Leopards (p.6) may be the most feared animals in Kenya. Intensely secretive, alert and wary, they live all across the country except in the most treeless zones. Their unmistakable call, likened to a big saw being pulled back and forth, is unforgettable. Although often diurnal in the parks, they are strictly nocturnal wherever human pressures impinge, and sometimes survive on the outskirts of towns and villages, carefully preying on different domestic animals to avoid a routine. They tolerate nearby human habitation and rarely kill people unprovoked. Accidents do occur, however, and disturbed individuals occasionally take to human-hunting – or are forced to become "man-eaters" through infirmity. For the most part, leopards live off any small animals that come their way, pouncing from an ambush and dragging the prey up into a tree where it may be consumed over several days. Monkeys, especially the relatively less organized species such as colobus and vervet, are frequent prey. Baboons, unless very unlucky, are usually able to mob a leopard to defend the troop. The spots on a leopard vary from individual to individual, but they always appear in the form of rosettes. Melanistic (black) leopards are known as panthers or black panthers, and seem to be more common in some areas (Mount Kenya and the Aberdares, for example) than others.

In the flesh, the **cheetah** (p.6) is so different from the leopard, it's hard to see how there could ever be any confusion. Cheetahs are lightly built, finely spotted, with small heads and very long legs. Unlike leopards, which are highly arboreal, cheetahs never climb trees. Cheetahs live alone, or sometimes briefly form a pair during mating. Hunting is normally a solitary activity, down to eyesight and an incredible burst of speed that can take the animal up to 100kph (70mph) for a few seconds. Cheetahs can be seen in any of the large, up-country parks, though Nairobi National Park is as easy a place to find them as any.

Other large, Kenyan cats include the beautiful part-spotted, part-striped **serval** (p.7), found in most of the parks, though somewhat uncommon; and the aggressive, tuft-eared **caracal** (p.6), a kind of lynx, which is seen even less often than the serval, favouring drier zones like Tsavo East and the Samburu complex.

The biggest carnivore after the lion is the **spotted hyena** (p.5); it is also, apart from the lion, the meat-eater you will most often see. Although considered a scavenger *par excellence*, the spotted hyena is a formidable hunter, most often found where antelopes and zebras are present. Exceptionally efficient consumers, with immensely strong teeth and jaws, spotted hyenas eat virtually every part of their prey, including bones and hide and, where habituated to humans, often steal shoes, unwashed pans and refuse from tents and villages. Although they can be seen by day, they are most often active at night – when they issue their unnerving, whooping cries. Clans of twenty or so animals are dominated by females, which are larger than the males and compete which each other for rank. Curiously, female hyenas' genitalia are hard to distinguish from males', leading to a popular misconception that they are hermaphroditic. Not surprisingly, in view of all their attributes, the hyena is a key figure in local mythology and folkore.

In comparison with the spotted hyena, you are not very likely to see a **striped hyena**. A usually solitary animal, it's slighter and much rarer than its spotted relative, though occasionally glimpsed very early in the morning.

The commonest members of the dog family in Kenya are the **jackals**. The black-backed or silver-backed jackal (p.4) and the similar side-striped jackal, can be seen just about anywhere, both species usually in pairs. The golden jackal is most likely to be seen in the Mara. **Bat-eared foxes** (p.4) are also not uncommon, and

unmistakable in appearance. However, the unusual and rather magnificent **hunting dog** (p.4) is now more or less extinct in Kenya, having been present in reasonable numbers thirty years ago. Canine distemper has played a big role in their decline, as have human predation and habitat disruption.

Among smaller predators, the unusual **honey badger** or **ratel** (p.4) is related to the European badger and has a reputation for defending itself extremely fiercely. Primarily an omnivorous forager, it will tear open bees' nests (to which it is led by a small bird, the honey guide), its thick, loose hide rendering it impervious to their stings. **Genets** (p.5) are reminiscent of slender, elongated cats (they were once domesticated around the Mediterranean, but cats proved better mouse-hunters). In fact they are viverrids, related to mongooses. and are frequently seen after dark around national park lodges, where they live a semi-domesticated existence.

Most species of **mongoose** (p.5) are also tolerant of humans and, even when disturbed out in the bush, can usually be observed for some time before disappearing. Their snake-fighting reputation is greatly overplayed: in practice they are mostly social foragers, fanning out through the bush like beaters on a shoot, rooting for anything edible – mostly invertebrates, eggs, lizards and frogs.

The **civet** (p.5) is a stocky animal, resembling a large, terrestrial genet. It was formerly kept in captivity for its musk (once a part of the raw material for perfume), which is secreted from glands near the tail. Civets aren't often seen, but they are predictable creatures that can be seen wending their way along the same paths at the same time night after night.

ELEPHANTS

Elephants (p.7) are found throughout Kenya. Almost all the big plains and mountain parks have their populations. These are the most engaging of animals to watch, perhaps because their interactions, behaviour patterns and personality have so many human parallels. Like people, they lead complex, interdependent social lives, growing from helpless infancy, through self-conscious adolescence, to adulthood. Babies are born with other cows in close attendance, after a 22-month gestation. The calves suckle for two to three years, from the mother's two breasts between her front legs.

Lioness

Elephants' basic family units are composed of a group of related females, tightly protecting their babies and young and led by a venerable matriarch. It's the matriarch that's most likely to bluff a charge – though occasionally she may get carried away and tusk a vehicle or person. Bush mythology has it that elephants become embarrassed and ashamed after killing a human, covering the body with sticks and grass. They certainly pay much attention to the disposal of their own dead relatives, often dispersing the bones and spending time near the remains. Old animals die in their seventies or eighties, when their last set of teeth wears out and they can no longer feed.

Seen in the flesh, elephants seem even bigger than you would imagine – you'll need little persuasion from those flapping, warning ears to back off if you're too close – but they are at the same time surprisingly graceful, silent animals on their padded, carefully placed feet. In a matter of moments, a large herd can merge into the trees and disappear, their presence betrayed only by the noisy cracking of branches as they strip trees and uproot saplings.

Managing the elephant population (see the "Poaching Wars" box on p.368) leads to arcane ecological puzzles in which new factors keep emerging; current wisdom suggests that elephants are in a way "architects" of their environment. Overpopulation is usually the result of old migration routes being cut off, forcing the animals into unnatural reserves – like the Mara – where their massive appetites can appear to be destructive. Adults may consume up to 170kg of plant material daily – that works out at well over a hundred tons of foliage through the Mara's collective elephant gut every day. However, this foliage destruction by crowded herds also puts new life into the soil. Acacia seeds sprout much better after being eaten and dunged by elephants than if they simply fall to the ground. Dung beetles gratefully tackle the football-sized elephant droppings, break them into pellets and pull them into their burrows where the seeds germinate. Elephants also dig up dried-out water holes with their tusks (they're either right- or left-tusked, in the same way as humans favour one hand or the other), providing moisture for other animals.

RHINOS

There are two species of **rhinoceros** (p.8) found in Africa – the hook-lipped or black rhino,

and the much heavier wide-lipped or white rhino. Both are on the brink of extinction in the wild. The shape of their lips is far more significant than any alleged colour difference, as it indicates their respective diets (browsing for the black rhino, grazing for the white) and favoured habitats (thick bush and open grassland respectively).

Rhinos give birth to a single calf, after a gestation period of fifteen to eighteen months, and then the baby is not weaned until it is at least a year, sometimes two years, old. Their population growth rate is slow compared with most animals – another factor contributing to their predicament.

White rhinos have been extinct for several hundred years in Kenya, but reintroduced animals (principally from South Africa) have always done well – when allowed the chance to do so out of the telescopic sights of poachers.

The smaller black rhinos were, until the mid-1970s, a fairly common sight in most of the parks. In the 1960s, Amboseli, for example, had hundreds of magnificent black rhinos, some with graceful, long upper horns over a metre in length. The facts behind their rapid and depressing decimation are given in some detail on p.369.

Today, there are fewer than 500 black rhinos in Kenya, and just a few dozen white rhinos. You can see black rhinos in Maasai Mara, Lake Nakuru, Nairobi, Aberdares and Mount Kenya national parks and Ngulia Rhino Sanctuary in Tsavo West. White rhinos can be seen in Maasai Mara and Lake Nakuru. Small numbers of both species can also be encountered at private ranches in northern Kenya, especially in Laikipia, north of Mount Kenya. Such is the threat to their survival, the exact location of rhino groups is not always made widely known.

HIPPOS

Hippopotami (p.9) are highly adaptable, and found throughout Kenya wherever rivers or freshwater lakes are deep enough for them to submerge in and have a surrounding of suitable grazing grass. By day they need to spend most of their time in water to protect their thin, hairless skin from dehydration.

Hippos can be found everywhere from the humid estuary of the Tana River to the chilly mountain district of Nyahururu, including the briny Lake Nakuru in the central Rift Valley and Lake Turkana in the semi-desert of the northwest. After dark, hippos leave the water to spend the whole night grazing, often walking up to 10km in one session. In the Maasai Mara, they wander across the savannah; at Lake Naivasha they plod through farms and gardens; and everywhere they are rightly feared.

Hippos are reckoned to be responsible for more human deaths in Africa than any other animal. These occur mostly on the water, when boats accidentally steer into hippo pods, but they can be aggressive on dry land, too, charging and slashing with their fearsomely long incisors. They can run at 30kph if necessary and have a small turning circle. Although uncertain on land (hence their aggression when cornered), they are supremely adapted to long periods in water. Their nostrils, eyes and ears are in exactly the right places and their clumsy feet become supple paddles – as can be seen from the underwater observatory at Mzima Springs in Tsavo West National Park, for example.

ZEBRAS

Zebras (p.8) are closely related to horses and, together with wild asses, form the equid family. Of the three species of zebra, two live in Kenya. Burchell's has thick stripes and small ears and is found in suitable habitats in most parts of the country, while Grevy's is a large animal with very fine stripes and big, saucer-like ears, restricted to Tsavo East and the northern parks and reserves.

Burchell's zebras found in Kenya are mostly the *granti* subspecies and often called Grant's

Burchell's zebra

zebras. In the far north, they have a tendency to have a very short mane, or even to lack a mane. In Tsavo West and other parts of southern Kenya, they tend to exhibit the "shadow striping" typical of the species in southern Africa (fawn stripes between the black ones). In Amboseli and the Mara, Burchell's zebras gather in migrating herds up to several thousand strong, along with wildebeest and other grazers. In contrast, Grevy's zebras live in small territorial herds.

PIGS

The commonest wild pig in Kenya is the **warthog** (p.9), regularly sighted throughout Kenya up to altitudes of over 2000m. Quick of movement and nervous, warthogs are notoriously hard to photograph as they're generally on the run through the bush, often with the young in single file, tails erect. They shelter in holes in the ground, usually old aardvark burrows. They live in family groups, usually of a mother and her litter of two to four piglets, or occasionally two or three females and their young. Boars join the group only to mate. Boars are distinguishable from sows by their prominent face warts, which are thought to be defensive pads protecting their heads during often violent fights. Although a favourite prey animal of large cats – and humans – the warthog's survival doesn't appear to be threatened, although its rooting and wallowing behaviour brings it into conflict with farmers.

Two other much rarer pigs, both nocturnal, live in Kenya: the huge, dark-coloured **giant forest hog**, a bristly, big-tusked pig which lives in the highlands and is most likely to be seen from a tree hotel on Mount Kenya or in the Aberdares; and the **red river hog** or **bush pig** which is very rarely seen, though not uncommon in dense forest, close to agriculture and river margins.

GIRAFFES

The tallest mammals on earth, **giraffes** (p.9) are common and unmistakable. Their daylight hours are spent browsing on the leaves of trees too high for other species; acacias and combretums are favourites. At night they lie down and ruminate. Non-territorial, they gather in loose leaderless herds. Bulls test their strength while in bachelor herds. When a female comes into oestrus, which can happen at any time of year,

Maasai giraffe

the dominant male mates with her. She will give birth after a gestation of approximately fourteen months. Over half of all young, however, fall prey to lions or hyenas in their early years.

Kenya has three types of giraffe, differentiated from each other by their pattern and the configuration of their short horns. Most often seen is the **Maasai giraffe**, with two horns and a very broken pattern of dark blotches on a buff or fawn background. This is the giraffe you'll see in Maasai Mara, Amboseli and Tsavo West. Roughly north of the Nairobi–Mombasa road (a natural dividing line) lives the dramatically patterned **reticulated giraffe**, which normally has three or five horns and boldly defined chestnut patches on a very pale background. The more solidly built **Rothschild's giraffe**, which has a pattern more like crazy paving (also with well-defined blotches) and usually two horns, is found only in parts of western Kenya (and over the border in Uganda). There's disagreement among zoologists over whether any of the giraffe's subspecies should be accorded the status of separate species – particularly concerning the reticulated giraffe – but they all interbreed.

HOLLOW-HORNED RUMINANTS

This category of mammals includes buffalo and all the antelopes – exemplified by the 28 two-toed cud-chewers illustrated on pp.10–16 of our colour wildlife guide. The **buffalo** itself (p.10) is a very common and much-photographed safari animal, closely related to the domestic milk- and meat-producing cow. Buffalos live in herds of 100 to 300 and rarely make much effort to move when vehicles approach. Indeed, they

aren't troubled by close contact with humans, and you don't have to read the papers in Kenya long before finding an example of buffalos trampling crops or goring a farmer.

The rather ungainly **hartebeest** family (p.10) includes one of the rarest antelopes in Kenya, Hunter's hartebeest of the lower Tana river. The Coke's hartebeest or kongoni, however, is found widely in southern Kenya, and **topi** (p.10) are practically emblematic of the Maasai Mara, their main habitat. The white-bearded **wildebeest** (p.10) is also particularly associated with the Mara. Their spectacular annual migration through the reserve is described on p.395.

Of the **gazelles**, the most obvious are **Thomson's** and **Grant's** (both p.11), easily seen at the roadside in many parts of southern Kenya. The range of Grant's gazelle extends further north to encompass the northern parks (Samburu, Meru) where "Thommies" are absent. The **gerenuk** (p.11) is an unusual browsing gazelle able to nibble from bushes standing on its hind legs (its name is Somali for "giraffe-necked"). Although considered an arid land specialist, its range encompasses most of Kenya east of the Rift Valley. The **impala** (p.12), although not a gazelle, is closely related and very common throughout much of Kenya.

The **reedbuck** and **waterbuck** (p.12) are related to each other, both spending much time in or near water. The common or Bohor reedbuck has a patchy distribution in southern Kenya, whereas the waterbuck is common in many central and southern areas.

Some of the smallest antelopes in the world are quite easily seen in Kenya. **Kirk's dikdik** (p.13) is a common miniature antelope found all over the country, measuring no more than 40cm in height, which usually pairs for life. The **suni**, which is uncommon, but can be encountered almost anywhere in forest cover, is even smaller (32cm). Other small Kenyan antelopes – all fairly widespread but nowhere common – include the surprisingly aggressive **steenbok** (p.16) which, despite a height of only 50cm, defends itself furiously against attackers; the **oribi** (p.16), with its rather charming foreplay (when the female is in oestrus, the male pushes his head under her hindquarters and pushes her along on her forelegs like a wheelbarrow race); and the **klipspringer** (p.16), which has hooves wonderfully adapted for scaling near-vertical cliffs.

The duikers (from the Dutch for "diver", referring to their plunging into the bush) are larger – the **common duiker** (p.13) is around 60cm high – though they appear smaller because of their hunched posture. The common duiker is found throughout the country in many habitats, but most duikers are more choosy and prefer plenty of dense cover and thicket. These include the tiny Zanzibar duiker, whose range in Kenya is restricted to the Arabuko-Sokoke forest, the widespread red duiker and blue duiker, and the more localized black-fronted duiker (Mount Kenya and Mount Elgon) and yellow-backed duiker (Mau forest).

Kenya's big antelopes are the *Tragelaphinae* – twisted-horn bushbuck types – and the *Hippotraginae* – horse-like antelopes. The **bushbuck** itself (p.14) is notoriously shy – a loud crashing through the undergrowth and a flash of a chestnut rump are all most people witness. The **bongo** is a particularly impressive member of this group, now confined to the highlands of Mount Kenya, the Aberdares (where it's sometimes seen at tree hotels), and possibly the Cheranganis and Mau escarpment. The **sitatunga** (p.13) is a smaller relative, semi-aquatic by nature, found in Kenya only in remote corners of the Lake Victoria shoreline and at the very accessible Saiwa Swamp National Park, where they are easy to see. Also easily seen, almost anywhere in the country, is the huge, cow-like **eland** (p.14), with its distinctive

dewlap. The two species of kudu are not uncommon where they exist at all, but they are very localized. Both are browsers. You're most likely to see **greater kudu** (p.14) at Lake Bogoria or Marsabit and **lesser kudu** (p.14) in Tsavo West or East, but neither species in the Mara.

The horse-like antelopes include the very fine **fringe-eared oryx** (p.15), which is found almost everywhere except the Mara; the massive **roan antelope** (p.15), restricted to the Mara and the Lambwe valley in western Kenya (after an abortive relocation attempt to Shimba Hills, southwest of Mombasa); and the handsome **sable antelope** (p.15) which lives, and thrives, only in the Shimba Hills.

OTHER MAMMALS

Of Kenya's other mammals, you're not likely to see more than a glimpse. Rarest of all is the **dugong**, the marine mermaid-prototype, of which there are believed to be seven or eight individuals remaining, drifting in the shallows around the Lamu archipelago.

The insectivorous **elephant shrews** are worth looking out for, simply because they are so weird. Your best chance of a sighting is of the golden-rumped elephant shrew, at Gedi on the coast (see p.492).

The **aardvark** (p.3) is one of Africa's – indeed the world's – strangest mammals, a solitary termite-eater weighing up to 70kg. Its name, Afrikaans for "earth pig", is an apt description, as it holes up during the day in large burrows – excavated with remarkable speed and energy – and emerges at night to visit termite mounds within a radius of up to 5km, to dig for its main diet. It is most likely to be common in bush country well scattered with tall termite spires.

Pangolins are equally unusual – nocturnal, scale-covered mammals, resembling armadillos and feeding on ants and termites. Under attack, they roll themselves into a ball. The ground pangolin, the only species found in Kenya (most pangolins are arboreal), lives mainly in savannah districts.

Kenya's many **bats** will usually be a mere flicker over a water hole at twilight, or sometimes a flash across the headlights at night. The only bats you can normally observe in any meaningful way are fruit bats hanging from

Greater kudu

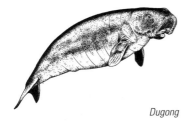

Dugong

their roosting sites by day. The hammer-headed fruit bat, sometimes seen in Kakamega forest, has a huge head and a wing span of over a metre.

BIRDS

Kenya boasts the second-highest country bird list – after the Congo – in Africa, at over 1070 species (this compares with no more than 300 for Britain and around 600 for North America). Nearly eighty percent of Kenya's birds are thought to breed in the country, with the remainder breeding during the northern summer in the Palaearctic region (Europe, north Africa and Asia north of the Himalayas) but wintering in tropical Africa. Many of these are familiar British summer visitors, such as swallows, nightingales and whitethroats, which have to negotiate or skirt the inhospitable Sahara on their migration. In winter, the migrant terns and waders can seem to dominate Kenya's shore-lines, and the Palaearctic swallows and warblers may comprise a large proportion of the birds in bushland habitats.

If you're a novice **bird-watcher**, Kenya is an excellent place to start. No amount of wildlife documentaries can do justice to the thrill of glimpsing your first colourful bee-eaters overhead (twelve species have been recorded in Kenya, three or four of which you might expect to encounter), watching rollers and shrikes swoop from perches to hunt insects, or seeing groups of vultures wheeling and dipping in the skies overhead as they prepare to arrive at a kill. The wide variety and accessibility of habitats makes bird-watching in Kenya highly rewarding. The keenest independent bird-watchers might expect to encounter over 600 species in a four-week period, whereas some of the organized bird-watching tour groups, living and breathing

birds for a three-week period, might record over 700 species in that time; one tour group holds the African record of 797 species in 25 days. However, even for those just dipping into the hobby or with limited time and choice of itineraries, Kenya offers some wonderful surprises.

Interesting bird records from the country can be submitted to the **Bird Committee** at Nature Kenya (formerly the East Africa Natural History Society), PO Box 44486, Nairobi (☎02/749957 or 741049). Another useful contact is the **African Bird Club** (c/o BirdLife International, Wellbrook Court, Girton Rd, Cambridge CB3 0NA, UK), who do an excellent regular bulletin and occasional well-produced monographs and itineraries. See also "Bird-watching in Nairobi" on p.149.

DISTRIBUTION

Only a few species of birds are found throughout Kenya. Three which will become familiar to sharp-eyed visitors are the **laughing dove**, the **African drongo** (an all-black crow-like bird with a forked tail) and the **grey-headed sparrow**. Most other species have well-defined distributions dependent on habitat type, itself a reflection of altitude and rainfall patterns.

Part of Kenya's bird diversity can be explained by the large numbers of species reaching the edge of their known ranges inside its borders. These include birds originating in the Horn of Africa but having their western or southwestern limits in Kenya (for example, the Somali bee-eater), species widespread in southern Africa which reach their northern limits here (such as the rufous-bellied heron), coastal species which are confined to the east (for example, the mangrove kingfisher), species from west African equatorial forests whose ranges just overlap the forest patches in west Kenya (for example, the grey parrot), and species occurring along the southern edge of the Sahel which reach the extreme southeast of their range in Kenya (for example, the Abyssinian roller).

Many Kenyan birds display two more or less separate populations, one on the coast, the other in the highlands. This is determined by habitat: the coastal areas tend to have much less rain than the highlands, and are much hotter with a more severe dry season. In some species, such as the widespread speckled mousebird, two distinct races are evolving.

ENDEMIC AND NEAR-ENDEMIC SPECIES

Of over a thousand species of bird found in Kenya, there are only six **endemic species** (that is, species found only in Kenya). Although these species are unlikely to be encountered by the novice and can be difficult to identify, their existence serves to emphasize Kenya's remarkable birdlife. They comprise two species of cisticola (small, skulking species, found in dense vegetation), a species of lark found only in the Marsabit and Isiolo areas, Sharpe's pipit (found in high grasslands in western and central Kenya), Clarke's weaver (found only in and around the Arabuko-Sokoke forest), and Hinde's pied babbler (found in the vicinity of Kianyaga near Embu).

Many birdwatchers are attracted to Kenya by the large number of **near-endemic species**, confined to northeast Africa, for which Kenya offers a reasonably accessible chance of a sighting. These include Heuglin's bustard, the Somali bee-eater (a very pale, open-country bee-eater found in the north and often noted at Samburu), Hartlaub's turaco (a green species of turaco, only found in highland forests in east Africa), and the small Sokoke Scops owl found most easily around the Arabuko-Sokoke forest.

LARGE WALKING BIRDS

Several species of large, terrestrial (or partly terrestrial) birds are regularly seen on safari. Their size and common form of locomotion (though the secretary bird and marabou stork can both fly perfectly well, and the ground hornbill is not flightless) makes them the birds most frequently spotted by non-ornithologists.

The locally common, distinctive **ostrich** is found in dry, open plains and semi-desert. The world's biggest bird, at up to 2.5m high, it is virtually absent from the coastal strip, but can readily be seen in Nairobi National Park and most others.

The **secretary bird** is a large, long-tailed, long-legged bird, grey-white in colour with a scraggy crest (the quills of which gave it its name), black on the wings and black "stockings". A bird of dry, open bush and wooded country, often seen in pairs, it is most commonly noticed stalking prey items which it has disturbed from grassland. Prey includes beetles, grasshoppers, reptiles and rodents, sometimes up to the size of a hare. Secretary birds are

Secretary bird

scarce in west Kenya and at the coast, but can be seen easily in Nairobi National Park.

The **marabou** is a large, ugly stork, up to 1.2m in height, with a bald head and a dangling, pink throat pouch. Most specimens look as if they're in an advanced state of decomposition. The marabou flies with its head and neck retracted (unlike other storks) and is often seen in dry areas, including towns, where it feeds on small animals, carrion and refuse.

Another reasonably common walking bird is the **ground hornbill**. This impressive creature lives in open country and is the largest hornbill by far, black with red face and wattles, bearing a distinct resemblance to a turkey. It's not uncommon to come across pairs, or sometimes groups, of ground hornbills, especially in the Mara, trailing through the scrub on the lookout for small animals. They nest among rocks or in tree stumps. (The other hornbills are covered below.)

FLAMINGOS AND IBISES

Many visitors to Kenya are astounded by their first sight of **flamingos** – a sea of pink on a soda-encrusted lake, which, together with the salt-rich smell of the lake and the stench of the birds' guano, powerfully evokes east Africa. Two species are found in Kenya, the greater flamingo and the lesser flamingo. Both are birds of the Rift Valley lakes and adjacent areas, and both are colonial nesters.

Much the commoner of the two is the **lesser flamingo**, smaller, pinker and with a darker bill than its greater relative. The Rift Valley population of lesser flamingos, with over a million birds gathering at one time at Lakes Bogoria and Nakuru, is one of only three populations in Africa. This species is nomadic, moving in relation to fluctuating food supplies, water levels and alkalinity. Flocks can leave or arrive at an area in a very short period of time – an estimated 400,000 birds have been recorded leaving Lake Bogoria over a seven-day period. Lesser flamingos feed by filtering suspended aquatic food, mainly blue-green algae that occurs in huge concentrations on the shallow, soda lakes of the Rift.

Greater flamingos may occur in their thousands but are considerably fewer in number than the lessers. They are bottom feeders, filtering small invertebrates as well as algae. Although greaters tend to be less frequently nomadic than their relatives, they are more likely to move away from the Rift Valley lakes to smaller water bodies and even the coast.

The most widely distributed **ibis** species (stork-like birds with downcurved bills) is the **sacred ibis**, which occurs near water and human settlements. It has a white body with black head and neck, and black tips to the wings. Also frequently encountered is the **Hadada ibis**, a bird of wooded streams, cultivated areas and parks in southern Kenya. It is brown with a green-bronze sheen to the wings, and calls noisily in flight.

WATER BIRDS

Most large water bodies, apart from the extremely saline lakes, support several species of **ducks and geese**, many of which breed in Europe, but overwinter in Africa.

Several species of **herons, storks and egrets** occur in areas with water, or can be observed overflying on migration. The commonest large heron is the black-headed heron, which can sometimes be found far from water. Mainly grey with a black head and legs, the black heron can be seen "umbrella-fishing" along coastal creeks and marsh shores: it cloaks its head with its wings whilst fishing, which is thought to cut down surface reflection from the water, allowing the bird to see its prey more easily.

The **hamerkop** is a brown, heron-like bird with a sturdy bill and mane of brown feathers, which gives it a top-heavy, slightly prehistoric appearance in flight, like a miniature pterodactyl. Hamerkops are widespread near water and build large, conspicuous nests that are often taken over by other animals, including owls, geese, ducks, monitor lizards or snakes.

GUINEAFOWL

Four species of these large, grey game birds are found in Kenya. The **vulturine guineafowl** is a bird of very arid areas, recognized by the long tapered feathers hanging from the base of the neck over a royal blue chest. The well-known **helmeted guineafowl**, a bird of moister areas, has a bony yellow skull protrusion (hence its name). The crested and the Kenya crested guineafowl are both birds of thickets.

BIRDS OF PREY

Kenya abounds with birds of prey – kites, vultures, eagles, harriers, hawks and falcons. Altogether, over 75 species have been recorded in the country, several of which are difficult to miss.

Six species of **vulture** range over the plains and bushlands of Kenya and are often seen soaring in search of a carcass. All the species can occur together, and birds may travel vast distances to feed. The main differences are in feeding behaviour: the lappet-faced vulture, for example, pulls open carcasses; the African white-backed feeds mainly on internal organs; the hooded vulture mainly picks from bones.

Two other birds of prey that are firmly associated with east Africa are the **bateleur**, an eagle that is readily identified by its silver wings, black body, chestnut red tail, stumpy

African vulture

body shape and wedge-shaped tail; and the **fish eagle**, whose haunting calls render a sense of emptiness and space to many a wildlife television documentary. Fish eagles are generally found in pairs near water, often along lake shores.

CRANES AND BUSTARDS

Kenya's national bird, the **crowned crane**, is found in the south and west of the country. It is a distinctive, elegant bird, the head crowned with an array of yellow plumes. Crowned cranes are often seen feeding on cultivated fields or in marshy areas.

Some nine species of **bustard** occur in the plains and grasslands of Kenya. These large, open-country species are long-legged and long-necked and are very well camouflaged among the browns and yellows of their African back-drop. The heaviest flying bird in the world, the Kori bustard, is commonest in the Rift Valley highlands. Bustards are affected by intensive, small-scale agricultural and human presence, and several species have undergone a decline in Kenya.

Crowned crane

PARROTS AND LOVEBIRDS

Eight species of *Psittacidae* have been recorded in Kenya, three of which are introduced. The parrot species that you're most likely to see is the **brown parrot**, which occurs in wooded areas in the west of the country. Lovebirds are small, green, hole-nesting birds (like small par-rots) and are readily seen in the acacias around Lake Naivasha, where a feral breeding popula-tion of **yellow-collared lovebirds** has

become established. This species has been introduced to Kenya from Tanzania, and hybridizes with the introduced and very similar **Fischer's lovebird**.

GO-AWAY BIRDS AND TURACOS

These distinctive, related families are found only in Africa. Medium-sized and with long tails, most **go-away birds** and **turacos** have short rounded wings. They are not excellent fliers, but are very agile in their movements along branches and through vegetation. Many species are colourful and display a crest. The largest, the magnificent **great blue turaco** (blue above, and green and brown below) is found only in the western forests in Kenya – notably at Kakamega, where it is one of the largest species in the forest. Other turacos are generally green or violet in colour, and all are confined to thickly wooded and forest areas. Open-country species, such as the widely dis-tributed and common **white-bellied go-away bird** (go-aways are named after their call), are white or grey in colour.

MOUSEBIRDS

Three species of mousebird are found in Kenya. Their name derives from their rapid scampering through thick tangles of branches using unusu-ally adapted claws. They can be identified by their slight crests and their long, tapering tails. Generally grey or brown in colour, they're noisy and feed actively in quite open vegetation. The **speckled mousebird** is a very common species throughout southern Kenya, often found in small groups at forest margins and in subur-ban gardens.

ROLLERS, SHRIKES AND KINGFISHERS

A family of very colourful and noticeable birds of the African bush, **rollers** perch on exposed bushes and telegraph wires and hawk flying insects. They take their name from their impres-sive courtship flights – a fast dive with a rolling and rocking motion, accompanied by raucous calls. Many have a sky-blue underbody and sandy-coloured back; long tail streamers are a distinctive feature of several Kenyan species. The **lilac-breasted roller** is a common and conspicuous species.

Shrikes are found throughout Kenya. Fierce hunters with sharply hooked bills, they habitually sit on prominent perches, and take insects, reptiles and small birds.

Kingfishers are some of Kenya's most colourful and noticeable birds, with eleven species found here. They range in size from the tiny **pygmy kingfisher**, which feeds on insects and is generally found near water, to the **giant kingfisher**, a shy fish-eating species of wooded streams in the west of the country. Several kingfishers eat insects rather than fish and they can often be seen perched high in trees or on open posts in the bush where they wait to pounce on passing prey. A common and widespread insectivorous species is the **chestnut-bellied kingfisher**.

HORNBILLS

Named for their long, heavy bills, surmounted by a casque or bony helmet, hornbills generally have black and white plumage. Their flight consists of a series of alternate flaps and glides. When in flight, hornbills may be heard before they are seen, the beaten wings making a "whooshing" noise as air rushes through the flight feathers. Many species have bare areas of skin on the face and throat and around the eyes, with the bill and the casque often brightly coloured, their colours changing with the age of the bird. Thirteen species have been recorded in Kenya, most of them omnivorous, but tending largely to eat fruit. Several species are common open-country birds; **silvery-cheeked hornbills** are sometimes seen in Nairobi. Hornbills have interesting breeding habits: the male generally incarcerates the female in a hollow tree, leaving a hole through which he feeds her while she incubates the eggs and rears the young. (The unusual ground hornbill is covered under "Large walking birds", above.)

WOODPECKERS

The abundance of trees within such a variety of habitats in Kenya means that many species of woodpecker (up to fourteen) are present. One species you're almost certain to encounter is the sparrow-sized **cardinal woodpecker**.

SUNBIRDS

Sunbirds are bright, buzzy, active birds, feeding on nectar from flowering plants, and distributed throughout Kenya, wherever there are flowers, flowering trees and bushes. Over 35 species have been recorded in the country, with many confined to discrete types of habitat. Common species in the Nairobi area are **variable** and **scarlet-chested sunbirds**. Males are brightly coloured and usually identifiable, but many of the drabber females require very careful observation to identify them.

STARLINGS

The glorious orange and blue starlings which are a common feature of bushland habitats – usually seen feeding on the ground – belong to one of three species. The **superb starling** is the most widespread of these, found everywhere from remote national parks to gardens in Nairobi. It can be identified by the white band above its orange breast. Similar starlings are the larger **golden-breasted**, often seen in Tsavo National Park, and **Hildebrand's** (also orange-breasted), which is commonest around Machakos but can be encountered all over southern Kenya.

WEAVERS AND WHYDAHS

These small birds are some of the commonest and most widespread of all Kenyan birds. Most male **weavers** have some yellow in the plumage, whereas the females are rather dull and sparrow-like. In fact, many species appear superficially very similar; distinctions are based on their range and preferred type of habitat. Weavers nest in colonies and weave their nests into elongated shapes, which can be used to help in the identification of the species. Many nests are situated close to water or human habitation and sometimes hang suspended. The **golden palm weaver** is the species you'll commonly see on the coast, often in hotel gardens.

Whydahs are also known as widow birds. The **paradise whydah** has extremely ornate tail feathers, with the central pair of tail feathers flattened and twisted into the vertical. Male paradise whydahs are mainly black in colour, and perform a strange bouncing display flight to attract females.

REPTILES AND AMPHIBIANS

There is only one species of crocodile in Kenya – the big **Nile crocodile** which, left to grow, can reach 6m or more in length and is considered a cunning and dangerous animal. You'll see them in the Mara river, in the Tana, at

Mzima Springs in Tsavo West, in great numbers in Lake Turkana and, if you take the trouble to look, in many other rivers and large bodies of water.

Kenya has many species of **snakes**, some of them quite common, but your chances of seeing a wild specimen here are more remote than in Australia or the USA, or even certain parts of Europe. In Kenya, as all over Africa, snakes are both revered and reviled and, while they frequently have symbolic significance for local people, that is quite often forgotten in the rush to hack them to bits with a *panga* upon their discovery. All in all, snakes have a very hard time surviving in Kenya: their turnover is high and their speed of exit from the scene when humans show up is remarkable. If they fascinate you, wear boots and go softly. If you hate them, be sure to tread firmly and they will flee on detecting your bad vibrations.

Common **non-poisonous species** of snakes include the rock python (a constrictor, growing up to 5m or more in length), the egg-eating snake and the sand boa. Common **poisonous species** include the green and black mambas (fast, agile, arboreal snakes), the boomslang, the spitting cobra and the dangerous puff adder, which is probably responsible for more bites than any other, on account of its sluggish disposition.

Tortoises are quite frequently encountered on park roads in the morning or late afternoon. Some, like the leopard tortoise, can be quite large, up to 50cm in length, while the hinged tortoise (which not only retreats inside its shell but shuts the door, too) is much smaller – up to 30cm. In rocky areas, look out for the unusual pancake tortoise, a flexible-shelled species that can put on quite a turn of speed but, when cornered in its fissure in the rocks, will inflate to wedge itself inextricably, to avoid capture. Terrapins or turtles of several species are common in ponds and slow-flowing streams. On the coast, sea turtles breed and it's not unusual to see them from boats during snorkelling trips.

Lizards are common everywhere, harmless and often colourful. The commonest are **rock agamas**, the males often seen in courting "plumage", with brilliant orange heads and blue bodies, ducking and bobbing at each other. They live in loose colonies often near human habitation; one hotel may have hundreds, its neighbours none. The biggest lizards, **Nile monitors**,

Jackson's chameleon

grow to nearly 2m in length and are often seen near water. From a distance, as they race off, they look like speeding baby crocodiles. The other common monitor, the smaller savannah monitor, is less handsomely marked.

A large, docile lizard you may come across is the **plated lizard**. This intelligent, mild-mannered reptile is often found around coastal hotels, looking for scraps from the kitchen or pool terrace. At night on the coast, the translucent little aliens on the ceiling are **geckoes**, catching moths and other insects, and worth encouraging. By day, their minuscule relatives, the day geckoes (velvet grey and yellow), patrol coastal walls. In the highlands you may come across prehistoric-looking three-horned **Jackson's chameleons** creeping through the foliage – and there are several other species, living in most parts of the country, which you are most likely to see squashed flat on the road.

In the **amphibian** world, night-time is usually the right time. Unless you make an effort to track down the perpetrators of the frog chorus down by the lodge water pump, you will probably only come across the odd toad, sitting under a footpath light, waiting for insects to drop on to the ground. There are, however, dozens of species of frogs and tree frogs, ranging from the common squeaker to the red and black rubber frog.

BOOKS

Having a **field guide**, especially to the hundreds of species of birds that will pass your way, makes a huge difference to travelling on safari. The Collins field guides are sometimes out of print (o/p) and not published in the US, but American readers can safely assume they'll be available in Kenya.

COLLINS FIELD GUIDES

Michael Blundell, *Wild Flowers of East Africa* (Harper Collins, o/p). Botanical companion in the series.

Jean Dorst and Pierre Dandelot, *Larger Mammals of Africa* (HarperCollins). Readable and accessible with lively illustrations, though it tends to favour classifying many races as separate species.

T. Haltenorth and H. Diller, *Mammals of Africa* (HarperCollins). A rival for Dorst and Dandelot, which tends to find fewer species in the variety of mammals out there. With its superabundance of detail, this might look like first choice, but the somewhat stylized paintings are less meaningful than Dorst and Dandelot's when you're thumping through the bush, and much of the text is superfluous for all but the professional zoologist.

Ber van Perlo, *Birds of Eastern Africa* (HarperCollins). An essential pocket guide, providing clear colour illustrations and distribution maps for every species known to occur in east Africa, though little by way of descriptive text. Overall, an improvement on Williams's now outdated and less user-friendly bird guide (see below).

Chris Stuart and Tilde Stuart, *Field Guide to the Larger Mammals of Africa* (New Holland/Ralph Curtis). Good field guide published in the late 1990s.

John Williams, *Birds of East Africa* (HarperCollins). The standard spotter's tome.

John Williams, *Field Guide to the Butterflies of Africa* (HarperCollins). Exotic and useful – if you can get hold of a copy.

John Williams, *National Parks of East Africa* (HarperCollins). Covers parks, reserves, mammals and birds, but there's too much space devoted to long lists of fauna, and the practical details for the parks are too dated to be of any use.

OTHER FIELD GUIDES

Ray Moore, *Where to Watch Birds in Kenya* (Transafrica Press, available in Kenya and sometimes in the UK). Invaluable tips and background for the devoted bird-watcher.

Dave Richards, *Photographic Guide to the Birds of East Africa* (New Holland). Over three hundred colour photos.

Nigel Wheatley, *Where to Watch Birds in Africa* (Christopher Helm/Princeton Univeristy Press). Tight structure and plenty of useful detail make this a must-have for serious bird-watchers in Africa; 25 pages on Kenya.

Zimmerman, Turner and Pearson, *A Field Guide to the Birds of Kenya and Northern Tanzania* (UK only, Adlard Coles Nautical, 1999). Comprehensive coverage in a brand new paperback edition.

Richard Trillo and Tony Stones.
With thanks to Tony Pinchuck for extra mammal input.

BOOKS

There is a substantial volume of reading matter on Kenya, though much of the European output has been fairly lightweight and the more scholarly works tend to be indigestible. You might want to subscribe to *The Journal of African Travel Writing*, a twice-yearly, 100-page publication ($10 yearly, PO Box 346 Chapel Hill, NC 27514, USA, *www.unc.edu/ottotwo/*) which always contains a catholic selection, from poetry and anecdotes to lit crit.

For pre-departure reading, the growing body of **Kenyan literature** provides a good foretaste. Some of the following titles may be most easily available in Kenya (for imports in the UK, try the Africa Book Centre, 38 King St, London WC2E 8JT; ☎0171 240 6649, fax 497 0309; *africabooks@dial.pipex.com*). British and American publishers are given in the order UK/US. Note that UP means University Press. It's worth visiting libraries and secondhand bookshops to find those titles which are out of print (o/p) – or were at the time of writing, mid-1999. Most useful of all, of course, are the **Internet bookstores**, such as *amazon.com*, *amazon.co.uk* and *BOL.com*, which will *try* to get just about anything, and are cheap and convenient if you know exactly what you want.

TRAVEL AND GENERAL ACCOUNTS

Bartle Bull, *Safari: A Chronicle of Adventure* (UK & US Penguin, 1992). A great, macho slab of a book, jammed with photos. It's grotesque but utterly compelling – even if the cruelty and foolish waste of the hunting era, so recently past, is emotionally wearing.

Negley Farson, *Behind God's Back* (o/p). An American journalist's account of his long overland journey across Africa on the eve of World War II. A lively book if you can stomach the alarming shifts between criticism of the colonial world and participation in its worst prejudices.

Dick Hedges, *Tilda's Angel* (UK only, Book Guild, 1994). If you want to know all about the man behind Safari Camp Services and the Turkana Bus, this is for you. Good on what makes Anglo-Kenyans tick.

John Hillaby, *Journey to the Jade Sea* (UK only, Constable, 1993, o/p). An obvious one to read before a trip to Lake Turkana. Hillaby's account of his walk in the early 1960s is dated and not always informative – an adventure, as he writes, "for the hell of it", with sprinklings of tall stories and descriptions of loony incompetence.

David Lamb, *The Africans* (US only, Vintage, 1987). There's really no contest between Lamb, a *Los Angeles Times* hack, and Marnham (see below) for a contemporary view of the continent. *The Africans* has been something of a best seller, but Lamb's fly-in, fly-out technique is a muddled, statistical rant, couched in Cold War rhetoric; even when ostensibly uncovering a pearl of wisdom, he can be unpleasantly offensive.

Patrick Marnham, *Fantastic Invasion: Dispatches from Africa* (o/p). Although written in the 1970s, nothing since has matched this withering and devastatingly sharp collection, which includes several essays on Kenya. An excellent book, which tunnels beneath the mountain of dross written about Africa.

Peter Matthiessen, *The Tree Where Man Was Born* (Harvill, 1998/Petersmith, 1997). Wanderings and musings of the Zen-thinking polymath in Kenya and northern Tanzania, first published in 1972. Enthralling for its detail on nature, society, culture and prehistory, and beautifully written, this is a gentle, appetizing introduction to the land and its people.

George Monbiot, *No Man's Land* (UK only, Macmillan, 1994, o/p). A journey through Kenya and Tanzania, providing a shocking exposé of Maasai dispossession and a major criticism of the wildlife conservation movement. Some of the interviews on p.396 were used in the book.

Dervla Murphy, *The Ukimwi Road* (Flamingo, 1994/Overlook, 1995). Murphy's bike ride from Kenya to Zimbabwe becomes – for her – a trip through lands lost to AIDS and neo-colonialism.

Shiva Naipaul, *North of South* (Penguin Twentieth Century Classics, 1996/Penguin 1997). A fine but caustic account of the late Naipaul's life and travels in Kenya, Tanganyika and Zambia in the 1970s. Always readable and sometimes hilarious, the insights make up for the occasionally angst-ridden social commentary and some passages that widely miss the mark.

Craig Packer, *Into Africa* (UK & US, Chicago UP, 1994). A professor of ecology, evolution and behaviour, Packer puts it all to good use in day-by-day reflections during an eight-week field trip.

Joyce Poole, *Coming of Age with Elephants* (Hodder & Stoughton, 1996/Hyperion, 1997). Deeply sympathetic account of studying the social and sexual behaviour of elephants in Amboseli.

Keith B. Richburg, *Out of America; a Black Man Confronts Africa* (Basic Books, 1997/Harcourt Brace, 1998). Nairobi bureau chief for the *Washington Times* from 1991–94 (Somalia, Rwanda, Kenya's elections...), Richburg discovered that he was American, not African, and preferred it that way. A rather depressing read – and partial by the nature of its author: journalists need stories, and that usually means bad news – and unfortunately likely to stoke the flames of moral relativism.

Rick Ridgeway, *The Shadow of Kilimanjaro* (Bloomsbury 1999/Henry Holt & Co, 1998). The American adventurer and filmmaker took a walk in 1997 through the bush from Kilimanjaro to Mombasa – mostly through Tsavo West and East, along the Tsavo-Galana River. Robust, readable and full of passionate enthusiasm for the wild country and the wildlife.

Wilfred Thesiger, *My Kenya Days* (Flamingo, 1995/Moorehouse, 1994, o/p). The account of thirty-odd years in northern Kenya by a very strange man indeed – an old Etonian noble savage with no interest in modern Africa, wedded to his own ego and a reactionary, glamour-laden view of his tribal companions.

Daisy Waugh, *A Small Town in Africa* (UK only, Mandarin, 1995). A year in the life of Isiolo.

Evelyn Waugh, *A Tourist in Africa* (US only, Greenwood Press, 1977, o/p). First published in 1960, Waugh's diary of a short trip to Kenya, Tanganyika and Rhodesia is determinedly arrogant and uninformed, but funny, too – and brief enough to consume at a single sitting.

TRAVEL BIBLIOGRAPHIES

Oona Strathern, ed, *Traveller's Literary Companion: Africa* (In Print Publishing, 1994/Passport Books, 1995, o/p). Brief selections of literature from or about virtually every African country, including a good raft of Kenyan pieces.

Louis Taussig, *Resource Guide to Travel in Sub-Saharan Africa: Vol 1 East and West Africa* (Hans Zell, 1994/KG-Saur, 1994). The definitive guide to the guides and much more. Extraordinarily detailed country-by-country coverage of every published source of interest to travellers or expatriates, as well as bookstores, libraries, mapping institutes, children's resources and conservation societies, to list just a few.

EXPLORERS' ACCOUNTS

The following explorers' books deal largely with Kenya and make for interesting pre-departure reading.

J. Ludwig Krapf, *Travel and Missionary Labors in Africa* (first published 1860, Frank Cass, o/p/ International Specialized Book Services, 1968). The account of the first missionary at Mombasa, and the first European to set eyes on Mount Kenya.

C.H. Stigand, *The Land of Zinj* (first published 1912, US only, Bibilo Distribution Centre o/p).

Joseph Thomson, *Through Maasailand: To the Central African Lakes and Back* (first published 1885, 2 vols, Frank Cass, 1968/ International Specialized Book Services. 1968).

COLONIAL WRITERS

Not surprisingly perhaps, settler society produced few notable authors. Karen Blixen was the literary prima donna.

KAREN BLIXEN

Isak Dinesen (Karen Blixen), *Out of Africa* (Penguin, 1999/Vintage, 1989). This has become something of a cult book, particularly in the wake of the movie. First published in 1937, it describes Blixen's life (Dinesen was a nom de plume) on her Ngong Hills coffee farm between the wars. Read today, it seems to hover uncertainly between contemporary literature and historical document. It's an intense read – lyrical, introspective, sometimes obnoxiously and intricately racist, but worth pursuing and never superficial, unlike the film. Karen Blixen's own *Letters from Africa 1914–1931* (trans. Anne Born, US only, Chicago UP, 1984) gives posthumous insights.

Peter Beard, *Kamante's Tales from Out of Africa* (UK & US, Chronicle Books, 1998, o/p). Fascinating photos of Blixen and friends, as well as an unnecessarily condescending handwritten text by the grandsons of Kamante (her houseboy in Kenya), transcribing the memories of one of the principal characters in *Out of Africa*.

Linda Donelson *Out Of Isak Dinesen In Africa: The Untold Story* (UK & US, Coulsong List, 1998). Diligently researched and thoughtfully written account of Karen Blixen's years in Kenya that brings a complex personality to life.

Judith Thurman, *Isak Dinesen: The Life of a Story Teller* (Penguin, 1984/Picador 1995). A biography that sets the record straighter and was the source of much of the material for the *Out of Africa* film.

OTHER WORKS OF THE COLONIAL ERA

Harry Hook, *The Kitchen Toto* (Faber, 1987, o/p). By way of an antidote to a surfeit of settlers' yarns, this screenplay tells the story of Mwangi, a Kikuyu houseboy caught up in the early stages of the Mau Mau rebellion. Writerdirector Hook's movie is as keen as a country *panga* and draws masterful performances from a largely unknown cast.

Elspeth Huxley, *The Flame Trees of Thika* (Pimlico, 1998/Viking 1981, o/p); *The Mottled Lizard* (Pimlico, 1999/Penguin o/p). Based on her own childhood, from a prolific author (d.1997) who also wrote numerous works on colonial history and society, including *White Man's Country* (o/p), a biography of the settlers' doyen, Lord Delamere, and *Out in the Midday Sun: My Kenya* (o/p), both as readable, if also predictable, as any. *Nine Faces of Kenya* (UK only, Harvill, 1991), is a somewhat dewy-eyed anthology of colonial east African ephemera. More interesting is the collection of her mother's letters, *Nellie's Story* (o/p), which includes some compelling coverage of the Mau Mau years from the pen of a likably eccentric settler.

Beryl Markham, *West with the Night* (Penguin, 1988/Northpoint, 1985). Markham made the first east–west solo flight across the

Atlantic. This is her first and last book about her life in the interwar Kenya colony, drawing together adventures, landscapes and contemporary figures. Not great literature, but highly evocative.

Richard Meinertzhagen, *Kenya Diary 1902–1906* (UK only, Eland, 1983, o/p). The haunting day-to-day narrative of a young British officer in the protectorate. Meinertzhagen's brutal descriptions of "punitive expeditions" are chillingly matter-of-fact and make the endless tally of his wildlife slaughter pale inoffensively in comparison. As a reminder of the savagery that accompanied the British intrusion, and a stark insight into the complex mind of one of its perpetrators, this is disturbing, highly recommended reading. Good photos, too.

Errol Trzebinski, *The Lives of Beryl Markham* (Mandarin, 1994/Norton, 1995). In which, among much else, it is suggested that Markham did not, and could not, have written *West with the Night*.

KENYAN FICTION IN ENGLISH

Although a number of authors have written in the older languages of Kenya, English still predominates as the medium for artistic expression, a situation which creates dilemmas for writers struggling both to reach a readership at home and to find viable channels for publication.

Ngugi wa Thiong'o, *Decolonising the Mind: The Politics of Language in African Literature* (UK & US, Heinemann, 1986). Ngugi has long been closely associated with attempts to move Kenyan literature and African literature in general towards expression in the readers' mother tongues (see box opposite).

J. Roger Kurtz, *Urban Obsessions, Urban Fears: the Postcolonial Kenyan Novel* (James Currey, 1999/Africa World Press, 1999). Explores the relationship between Kenyan fiction in English and the city of Nairobi. Includes a comprehensive bibliography of all the Kenyan novels in English since Ngugi's *Weep Not, Child* was first published in 1964.

PROSE COLLECTIONS

African Short Stories, edited by Chinua Achebe and C.L. Innes (UK & US, Heinemann, 1985). A collection which treats its material geographically, including Kenyan stories from

Jomo Kenyatta, Grace Ogot, Ngugi and a spooky offering (*The Spider's Web*) from Leonard Kibera, brother of Sam Kahiga (a short story by whom appears on p.662).

Two Centuries of African English, edited by Lalage Bown (UK & US, Heinemann, o/p). Includes non-fiction extracts from the work of J. M. Kariuki (*Mau Mau Detainee* – see p.654), Ali Mazrui on intellectuals and revolution, Githende Mockerie and R. Mugo Gatheru recounting their childhoods, and Tom Mboya on Julius Nyerere, first president of Tanzania.

Unwinding Threads: Writing by Women in Africa, edited by Charlotte H. Bruner (UK & US, Heinemann, 1983). Also geographical, with succinct introductions to each region. East Africa features Kenyan writers Charity Waciuma and the excellent Grace Ogot, whose *The Rain Came* is a bewitching mystery myth, combining traditional Luo tales with her own fiction in a perplexingly "Western" form. There's a new Heinemann collection edited by Bruner, entitled *African Women's Writing*.

NOVELS AND SHORT STORIES

Thomas Akare, *The Slums* (UK & US, Heinemann, 1981, o/p). A bleaker read than Mwangi, but also more humane. Without quotation marks, the dialogue melds seamlessly into the narrative; no doubts about the authentic rhythms of Kenyan English here. But much is assumed to be understood and there's much that won't be, unless you're sitting under a 25-watt light bulb in a River Road Boarding & Lodging.

Sam Kahiga, *Flight to Juba* – Short Stories (Longman, Kenya); *The Girl from Abroad* (UK & US, Heinemann, o/p). Vital, exasperating, obnoxious and plain crazy – a writer to love to hate (see excerpted story, p.662).

Bramwell Lusweti, *The Way to the Town Hall* (Macmillan, Kenya). Enjoyable satire aimed at small-town politicians and businessmen. A Swahili dictionary (to translate the characters' names!) is a help.

Marjorie Oludhe Macgoye, *Victoria* and *Murder in Majengo* (UK only, Macmillan, 1993).

NGUGI WA THIONG'O

Ngugi wa Thiong'o, the dominant figure of modern Kenyan literature, currently lives in the USA: although his books in English are not banned in Kenya, his political sympathies are not welcome.

Ngugi's work is art serving the revolution – didactic, brusque, graphic and unsentimental. His novels, especially the later ones, are unforgiving: the touch of humour that would leaven the polemic rarely comes to the rescue. Powerful themes – exploitation, betrayal, cultural oppression, the imposition of Christianity, loss of and search for identity – drive the stories along urgently. Characters deal with real events and the changes of their time, struggling to come to terms with the influences at work on their lives.

Ngugi's style is heady, idealistic and undaunted, never teasing or capricious. Disillusioned with English ("Whom do I write for?"), his first work in Kikuyu, in collaboration with Ngugi wa Mirii, was the play *Ngahiika Ndeenda* (*I will Marry When I Want*, Heinemann, 1982), and its public performance by illiterate peasants at the Kamiriithu Cultural Centre in Limuru got him detained for a year. He'd found his mark. Ngugi's work in the Kikuyu language is now banned, or rarely available, in Kenya.

Most of Ngugi's writings in English are published in the paperback Heinemann African Writers series. Try *Secret Lives* (Heinemann, 1975) for short stories, *Weep Not, Child* (Heinemann, 1964) for a brief but glowing early novel, or, for the mature Ngugi, *Petals of Blood* (Heinemann 1977/EP Dutton, 1991) – a richly satisfying detective story that is at the same time a saga of wretchedness and struggle (see p.659 for an excerpt). Others include *The River Between* (Heinemann, 1965), on the old Kikuyu society and the coming of the Europeans; *A Grain of Wheat* (Heinemann, 1965), about the eve of Independence; *Devil on the Cross* (Heinemann, 1982, written in detention on scraps of toilet paper); and *Matigari* (The Patriots). *Matigari*, first published in Kikuyu by Heinemann in 1986 (published in the US by Africa World Press, 1998), had a remarkable effect in the Central Highlands. Rumours circulated that a man, Matigari, was spreading militant propaganda against the government. The police even tried to track him down, before realizing their mistake and confiscating all copies of the book.

Apart from *I will Marry When I Want*, Ngugi has written two other plays, *The Black Hermit* and *The Trial of Dedan Kimathi* (with Micere Mugo). Academic works include *Moving the Centre* (James Currey, o/p/Heinemann Inc, o/p), a collection of essays. Ngugi's contribution to Kenyan literature – and liberation literature – is enormous, and delving in is rewarding, if not always easy.

Two novels – available in one volume – putting a Luo woman's view on life in Kenya from one of the country's few published women writers.

Ali Mazrui, *The Trial of Christopher Okigbo* (UK & US, Heinemann, o/p). A clever "novel of ideas" from the US-based political scientist, who always succeeds in infuriating both critics of Kenya and its supporters. His book, *Cultural Forces in World Politics* (James Currey, 1990/Heinemann, 1991) is a survey of cultural and political ideas which also addresses the issues surrounding Salman Rushdie's *Satanic Verses*.

David Mulwa, *Master and Servant* (UK only, Longman, 1987 o/p). Growing up in colonial Kenya: a funny and affecting string of episodes.

Mude Dae Mude, *The Hills are Falling* (Kenya Literature Bureau, Nairobi). Life from Marsabit to Nairobi.

Meja Mwangi, *Going Down River Road; Carcase for Hounds; Kill Me Quick* (all in Heinemann's African Writers series, UK & US, the latter two titles now o/p). Mwangi is lighter and more accessible than Ngugi, his fiction infused with the absurdities of urban (Nairobi) slum life. *Going Down River Road* (1976) is the best known: convincing scenes, chaotic action and sharp dialogue (though it's never clear whether the English/American street cool is meant to be real, or an effort to render the Swahili-Kikuyu "Sheng" slang of the slums). Great *in situ* reading. Mwangi was shortlisted for the Commonwealth Writers' Prize, with *Striving for the Wind* (1992), set in a rural rather than urban location.

Kenneth Watene, *Sunset on the Manyatta* (East African Publishing House, Nairobi, 1974). A Maasai man in Germany.

KENYAN POETRY

The oldest form of written poetry in Kenya is from the coast. Inland, poetry in the sense of written verse is a recent form. But oral folk literature was often relayed in the context of music, rhythm and dance.

SWAHILI POETRY

Swahili poetry reads beautifully even if you don't understand the words. Written for at least 300 years, and sung for a good deal longer, it's one of Kenya's most enduring art forms. An *Anthology of Swahili Poetry* has been compiled

and rather woodenly translated by **Ali A Jahadmy** (Heinemann o/p). Some of Swahili's best-known classical compositions from the Lamu archipelago are included, with pertinent background.

There's a more enjoyable anthology of romantic and erotic verse, *A Choice of Flowers*, with **Jan Knappert**'s idiosyncratic translations and interpretations (UK & US: Heinemann o/p), and the same linguist's *Four Centuries of Swahili Verse* (UK & US, Darf, 1988), which expounds and creatively interprets at much greater length. A translation of an exquisite poem from the latter is included on p.666.

KENYAN POETRY IN ENGLISH

Poems of Black Africa, edited by Wole Soyinka (UK only, Heinemann, 1975). A hefty and catholic selection. Its Kenyan component includes the work of Abangira, Jared Angira, Jonathan Kariara and Amin Kassam.

Heinemann Book of African Poetry (UK & US, Heinemann, 1990). Includes the work of Kenyan poet Marjorie Oludhe Macgoye.

KENYA IN MODERN WESTERN FICTION

Kenya has been the setting for the work of a number of recent writers.

Justin Cartwright, *Masai Dreaming* (Picador, 1994/Random House, 1995). A compelling novel juxtaposing a film-maker's vision of Maasai-land with the barbarities of the Holocaust, linked by the tapes of a Jewish anthropologist.

Jeremy Gavron, *Moon* (UK only, Penguin, 1997). Vivid short novel about a white boy growing up on a farm during the Emergency.

Martha Gellhorn, *The Weather in Africa* (Eland, 1984/Hippocrene, o/p). Three absorbing novellas, each dealing with aspects of the Europe–Africa relationship, set on the slopes of Kilimanjaro, in the "White Highlands" of Kenya and on the tourist coast north of Mombasa. Highly recommended.

David Lambkin, *The Hanging Tree* (Penguin, 1997/Counterpoint, 1998). A human-nature-through-the-ages saga which makes a good yarn – in fact, several yarns.

Paul Meyer, *Herdsboy* (US only, Northwest Publishing, 1993). American tourist "finds herself captive of a native tribe". A pacey first novel, set in Samburu-land, that overcomes that jacket description.

Maria Thomas, *Come to Africa and Save Your Marriage* (Serpent's Tail, 1989/Soho Press, 1995). Most of these tales are set in Kenya or Tanzania. Thomas's characters are solid, but the stories leave a wearying aftertaste as if there were nothing positive to be had from the expatriate experience. Her first novel, *Antonia Saw the Oryx First* (same publishers, 1988/1993), is painfully detailed – a good antidote to *Out of Africa*.

HISTORY AND PEOPLES

There's a good range of background reading on Kenyan history and a large number of anthropological works on different peoples. Few of the latter are mentioned here. In the UK, the best source for specialist ethnographic titles is probably the School of Oriental and African Studies Library in London (see p.35).

KENYA IN AFRICAN HISTORY

Basil Davidson, *Let Freedom Come: Africa in Modern History* (Penguin o/p/Little, Brown o/p). Lucidly argued and very readable summary of nineteenth- and twentieth-century events.

Christopher Hibbert, *Africa Explored: Europeans in the Dark Continent 1769–1889* (o/p). Entertaining read, devoted in large part to the "discovery" of east and central Africa.

Alan Moorehead, *The White Nile* (Penguin, 1973/Adventure Library, 1995). A riveting account of the search for the source and European rivalries for control in the region.

Roland Oliver and J. D. Fage, *A Short History of Africa* (Penguin, 1990/Penguin US, 1988). Dated, but still the standard paperback introduction.

KENYA IN GENERAL

Jeffrey A. Fadiman, *When We Began There Were Witchmen* (US only, California UP, 1994). Recounts the story of the Meru people from their mythical origins in Shungwaya in northeastern Kenya to the decimation of Meru culture by a tiny handful of missionaries and colonial administrators.

Fedders and Salvadori, *People and Cultures of Kenya* (UK only, Transafrica and Rex Collings o/p). A useful tribe-by-tribe introduction.

Cynthia Salvadori's *Through Open Doors: A View of Asian Cultures in Kenya* (Kenway Publications o/p) combines a stack of lively and readable erudition with fascinating marginal notes and sketches – superlative.

Terry Hirst, *The Struggle for Nairobi* (Mazingira Institute, Kenya). Sort of large-format "Nairobi for Beginners" that manages to make town planning (or the lack of it) fascinating, bringing together a mass of otherwise hard-to-get information about the city's growth.

Kenya's People (series of ten pamphlets, Evans, Kenya). Simple and reliable background on ten of Kenya's peoples. Aimed at Kenyan secondary schools, they're pitched just right for culturally uninitiated visitors.

Jomo Kenyatta, *Facing Mount Kenya* (first published 1962, US only, Vintage). A traditional, functionalist, anthropological monograph, but written by a member of the society in question – in this case, the Kikuyu – under the supervision of Bronislaw Malinowski at the London School of Economics, shortly before World War II. One of the few scholarly works ever written on traditional Kikuyu culture, this is as interesting for the insights it offers on its author as for its quite readable content. Good Kikuyu glossary.

Maxon and Ofcansky, *Historical Dictionary of Kenya* (US only, Scarecrow Press, 1999). From a reliable series that covers nearly every African country, this is an A to Z of Kenya's history. Includes an extensive bibliography.

William R. Ochieng, *A History of Kenya* (Macmillan, Kenya, o/p). Somewhat pedestrian but the best general overview from prehistory to 1980, with useful maps and photos to show the way. *A Modern History of Kenya 1895–1980* (Evans, o/p) covers the twentieth century in eight chapters – solid enough up to the middle of Kenyatta's reign.

William R. Ochieng, ed, *Themes in Kenyan History* (James Currey, 1991/Ohio UP o/p). A new collection of writings by historians and other academics, all teaching in Kenyan universities.

Thomas Spear and Richard Waller, eds, *Being Maasai* (James Currey, 1993/Ohio UP, 1993). Articles about Maasai identity – a subtle and interesting field, and vital reading for anyone concerned with the ethnic politics of modern Kenya.

COASTAL HISTORY

G. S. P. Freeman-Grenville, *The East African Coast* (Oxford UP, o/p). If you're heading for the coast, this is fascinating – a series of accounts from the first century to the nineteenth – vivid and often extraordinary.

Sarah Mirza and Margaret Strobel, *Three Swahili Women* (US only, Indiana UP, 1989). Three histories of ritual, three women's lives. Born between 1890 and 1920 into different social backgrounds, these biographies document enormous changes from the most important of neglected viewpoints.

James de Vere Allen, *Swahili Origins: Swahili Culture and the Shungwaya Phenomenon* (James Currey, 1993/Ohio UP, 1993). The life work of a challenging and readable scholar, bound to raise a fascinating field of study to new prominence.

PROTECTORATE AND COLONIAL KENYA

James Fox, *White Mischief* (UK only, Vintage, 1998). Investigative romp through the events surrounding the notorious unsolved murder of Lord Errol, one of Kenya's most aristocratic settlers, at Karen in 1941. Well told and highly revealing of British Kenyan society of the time. Michael Radford's 1987 film version is equally enjoyable, and a good deal more stimulating than the *Out of Africa* movie.

Charles Miller, *The Lunatic Express* (Westlands Sundries, Kenya, o/p). The story of that railway. Miller narrates the drama of one of the great feats of Victorian engineering – as bizarre and as madly magnificent as any Wild West epic – adding weight with a broad historical background of east Africa from the year dot. The same author's *The Battle for the Bundu* (UK only: Macmillan o/p) follows a little-known corner of World War I, as fought out on the plains of Tsavo between British Kenya and German Tanganyika – immensely readable.

Errol Trzebinski, *The Kenya Pioneers* (Heinemann, 1985 o/p/Norton o/p). Despite academic pretensions, this is something of a paean to the early settlers.

THE MAU MAU REBELLION

Bruce Berman, *Control and Crisis in Modern Kenya* (James Currey, 1990/Ohio UP, 1991). A study of the growth of state control, from the 1890s through to interwar crisis and postwar disintegration.

Donald L. Barnett and Karari Njama, *Mau Mau from Within: Autobiography and Analysis of Kenya's Peasant Revolt* (Monthly Review Press o/p). An account based on personal recollections.

Robert B. Edgerton, *Mau Mau: An African Crucible* (I B Tauris, o/p). An account of the revolt based on guerrillas' testimonies. Includes explorations of the role of women and class formation in modern Kenya.

Frank Furedi, *The Mau Mau War in Perspective* (James Currey, 1989/Ohio UP, 1989). Furedi analyses, using new archival sources, the continued struggle for land redistribution once the struggle for Independence had been won.

Tabitha Kanogo, *Squatters and the Roots of Mau Mau 1905–63* (James Currey, 1987/Ohio UP, 1987). Delves into the early years of the "White Highlands" to show how resistance, and the conditions for revolt, were built into the relations between the settler land-grabbers and the peasant farmers and herders ("squatters") they usurped. Strong on the role of women in the Mau Mau movement.

J. M. Kariuki, *Mau Mau Detainee: The Account by a Kenya African of His Experience in Detention Camps* (Oxford UP o/p/Books on Demand, Michigan UP o/p). A remarkably forbearing account of life and death in the detention camps. Kariuki's vision for the future of Kenya and his loyalty to Kenyatta have a special irony after his assassination in 1975. Recommended.

David Throup, *Economic and Social Origins of Mau Mau* (James Currey, 1987/Ohio UP, 1988). An examination of the story from the end of World War II, covering the colonial mentality and differences in efficiency between peasant cash-cropping and more wasteful plantation agriculture.

AFTER INDEPENDENCE

Jean Davison, *Voices from Mutira: Change in the Lives of Rural Gikuyu Women 1910–1995* (US only, Lynne Rienner, 1996). Rich, unselfconsciously moving and particularly interesting for the attitudes it documents on brideprice and genital mutilation.

Anthony Howarth, *Kenyatta: A Photographic Biography* (East African Publishing House,

Nairobi, o/p). A roughly hewn biography composed of an amalgam of black-and-white photographs, news clippings and quotations. It doesn't pretend to be exhaustive, but manages to capture the spirit of the leader and the struggle for Independence.

Kenneth King, *Jua Kali Kenya* (James Currey, 1996/Ohio UP, 1996). First serious study of Kenya's important informal sector – the self-employed fixers and manufacturers who work under the "hot sun" (the *jua kali*). Great photos.

Tom Mboya, *The Challenge of Nationhood* (UK & US, Heinemann, 1970). The vision of Kenya's best-loved statesman – and a Luo – assassinated in 1969 for looking like a clear successor to Kenyatta.

Andrew Morton *Moi: the Making of an African Statesman* (UK & US, Michael O'Mara, 1998). Strange subject for the author of *Diana: Her True Story* and a strangely compelling book is the result. While it would be impossible to deny this is a sycophantic biography – Morton's reported conversations with Moi usually dry up just as the reader formulates the critical question – simply getting access to the notoriously defensive president was remarkable in itself. The research is here; there are insights, but also too many factual inaccuracies (including the notion that "the Kalenjin are a homogenous tribe": a political hot potato Morton swallows whole) not to cast a shadow of doubt over the whole account.

Jeremy-Murray Brown, *Kenyatta* (US only, E.P. Dutton o/p), and **David Goldsworthy** *Tom Mboya: The Man Who Kenya Wanted to Forget* (US only, Africana, 1982), are the two big biographies: both weighty and deeply researched.

Ngugi wa Thiong'o, *Detained – A Writer's Prison Diary* (UK only, Heinemann, 1981). A retrospective of Kenya's history up to 1978, woven into the daily routine of political detention during Kenyatta's last year. Ngugi discourses widely and, while his reflections are occasionally pedantic or obscure and sometimes written with almost religious fervour, he hits home often. His *Barrel of a Pen: Resistance to Repression in Neo-Colonial Kenya* (US only, Africa World Press, 1983) hones some of his points sharply (see also the box on p.651).

Oginga Odinga, *Not Yet Uhuru* (UK only: Heinemann o/p). The classic critique of Kenya's direction at the time it was written.

Bethuel Ogot and William Ochieng, eds, *Decolonization and Independence in Africa 1940–93* (James Currey, 1995/Ohio UP, 1995). The standard work on these years, asking how much Kenya's – and other countries' – difficulties are linked to the colonial past and the process of growing away from it.

Geoff Sayer, *Kenya: Promised Land?* (Oxfam GB, 1998/Humanities Press International, 1998). Concise, readable essays – newspaper-article length with good photography, properly captioned – that get right to the point about the issues that make Kenya the fascinatingly problematic place it is.

WorldFocus Kenya (Heinemann). Children's introduction to the country – one of a series for the seven-plus age group – written with style and intelligence, and incorporating good photos and case studies of real people.

ARTS

Most works dealing with the arts cover the whole continent.

Jane Barbour and Simiyu Wandibba, *Kenyan Pots and Potters* (Oxford UP, o/p). This comprehensive description of pot-making communities includes techniques, training, marketing and sociological perspectives.

Roy Braverman, *Islam and Tribal Art* (Cambridge UP, o/p). A useful paperback text for the dedicated.

Susan Denyer, *African Traditional Architecture* (UK only, Holmes & Meier, 1983). Useful and interesting, with hundreds of photos (most of them old) and detailed line drawings.

Frank Willett, *African Art* (Thames & Hudson 1994/Thames & Hudson 1993). An accessible volume; good value, with a generous illustrations–text ratio.

Geoffrey Williams, *African Designs from Traditional Sources* (UK & US, Dover, 1971). A designer's and enthusiast's sourcebook, from the copyright-free publishers.

MOUNTAIN, HIKING AND DIVING GUIDES

The following should prove detailed enough for most purposes. See also the Mount Kenya "Guidebooks and Maps" section on p.195.

Paul Clarke, *Mountains of Kenya* (Mountain Club of Kenya,1993: African Books Collective/

Alpenbooks). A detailed and practical guide, comprehensively updated since its earlier incarnation and well worth buying if you plan to do any Kenyan hiking.

David Else, *Trekking in East Africa* (UK & US, Lonely Planet, 1998). Well-produced guide to hiking in the region, with good coverage of Mount Kenya and less extensive coverage of other areas.

Guide Book to Mount Kenya and Kilimanjaro (Mountain Club of Kenya,1991: African Books Collective/Alpenbooks). For fully equipped alpinism, this is indispensable.

Anton Koornhof, *The Dive Sites of East Africa* (New Holland). Highly recommended if you're at all taken by snorkelling or diving, with detailed text on each and every major site in Kenya, Tanzania and Zanzibar, beautifully illustrated and with thoughtful sections on environmental matters. One to make you dream.

COFFEE-TABLE BOOKS

Mohamed Amin, *Cradle of Mankind* (Camerapix, 1989). Stunning photographs of the Lake Turkana region, by the award-winning maverick photo-journalist Amin, killed in the Comoros plane hijack in 1997.

Mohamed Amin, *Portrait of Kenya* (Camerapix, 1991). Splendid coffee-table glamour.

Anne Arthus-Bertrand and Anne Spoerry, photos by Yann Arthus-Bertrand, *Kenya from the Air* (Thames and Hudson, 1994/Vendome, 1994). Superb images of the country from the eagle's viewpoint.

Mitsuaki Iwago, *Serengeti* (US only, Chronicle, 1987). Stunning scenes and portraits from Serengeti (the Tanzanian continuation of the Maasai Mara) from a master photographer. Simply the best volume of wildlife photography ever assembled, this makes most glossies look feeble. If you're trying to persuade someone to visit east Africa – or if any aesthetic argument were needed to preserve the parks and animals – this is the book to use.

David Keith Jones, *Shepherds of the Desert* (UK only, Hamish Hamilton 1984). Brilliant photos (many in black and white), with a text more lucid and less superficial than most glossies; this book concerns itself only with northern Kenya.

Brian Jackman and Jonathan Scott, *The Marsh Lions* (Elm Tree o/p/Godine o/p). Beautifully produced and painstakingly researched study of the lions and other animals around the Musiara Marsh in Maasai Mara.

Tepilit Ole Saitoti and Carol Beckwith, *Maasai* (Harvill, 1991/Abradale Press, 1990). *The* Maasai coffee-table book; some photos are too much to take at reading distance. Exquisite but largely staged portraits of Maasai culture (and even Beckwith's camera can't disguise the tourist souvenirs in the background). Variably interesting, chauvinistic text, which plays the cult value of the Maasai for all it's worth.

WRITING FROM KENYA

Very little Kenyan literature appeared in print before World War II. But while east Africa has tended to lag behind the rest of the continent in modern forms – the novel, short stories, drama and modern poetry – there's a rich tradition of oral literature and a specifically coastal Swahili verse culture that put African stories into writing as long as three hundred years ago.

THE ORAL TRADITION IN PRINT

*With the exception of the coast, precolonial Kenyan literature was entirely oral, and stories were passed – and modified – from generation to generation. These **folk tales**, commonly told by the leaders of the community to the children, were very often "trickster" tales about animals. While they frequently contained a moral, their main purpose was to entertain.*

THE HARE'S PRACTICAL JOKE

A long, long time ago, there were two people who were very good friends. One was Mr. Hare and the other Mr. Hyena. They used to visit each other and on each of these visits, the Hare used to carry in his bag some honey and sweetened meat. He used to put his little finger in the bag and give his friend to lick. Said the Hare: "Brother, I have something very, very sweet in my bag here. Take it and see for yourself." The Hyena liked it very much.

"Hi, Hi, Brother Hare, give me some more, more I say. It is very, very . . ."

"No, no, this is a sweetness that you must have a little at a time."

And the same thing happened day after day for many days. One day, the Hare came on as usual and said:

"Brother Hyena, may I give you something very, very sweet, sweeter than sweetness itself?"

"Yes, my good friend, I'd love some very, very much." And the Hare gave his sweetened finger to the Hyena to lick.

"Oh, Hare, my very good friend do give me more."

"No, no, old man, you cannot eat much of this sweetness. It is a sweetness that must be eaten sparingly."

"But brother, where do you get much much sweetness?"

"I get it from those mountains you see above our heads," pointing at the white clouds. "Once you eat this sweetness you should never pass piss or shit because then the sweetness gets lost."

"Then what do people do so that they do not pass out piss or shit after they have eaten this sweetness?"

"Ah, Mr. Hyena, that is very simple, they have their bottoms sewn up and if you want, I can do the sewing up for you."

"Yes, yes, do sew it up for me." And the Hare sewed the Hyena's bottom.

They took three bags each and the Hare led the way to the sweetness that never passes. Now the Hyena ate the honey, the honeycombs and the dead bees. Then the Hare said: "Now that we have filled our stomachs and our bags let us go home." Now when they were on the way, the Hyena went down to the stream to drink some water. And when he drank he just dropped down like a stump of a tree. He stayed and stayed and stayed there; his eyes popping out like sweet potatoes. He stayed there for so many days, until he thought he was going to die.

One day he saw the Eagle coming down to drink some water – said he:

"Good Brother Eagle, help me."

"Hi, brother, how shall I help you?"

"Come round behind me at my bottom end. You will see a string going right through it, prick it and pull carefully because I feel pain. I was sewn up by the Hare and he did a very bad thing."

Now as soon as the Eagle touched this string a flood of piss and shit rushed out and covered the Eagle and the piss was like a mountain with the Eagle as the core.

One day there was a heavy rain which washed away the piss and shit, slowly by slowly until the Eagle emerged with a scratch on the neck. He flew away swearing revenge on the Hyena. For many days he and the Hyena played hide and seek until one day the Hyena, being the foolish person, forgot that he was the sworn enemy of the Eagle. The Eagle being clever did not want a physical contact with the Hyena. He knew very well that the Hyena was stronger than him. Now he started to show the Hyena the choice pieces of meat that he carried in his bag and every day he gave a little to the Hyena saying: "Brother, I carry this kind of meat, have a bite" and the Hyena said: "Brother Eagle, these delicacies, this choice meat you give me, where does it come from?"

"Now, Brother Hyena, these delicacies, the choice meats are very, very many. If you like, I can take you where they come from. But," continued the Eagle, "it is impossible to get that meat alone. You must come too. Now go and collect all your people. Let them bring bags, tins and drums. Then we shall bring as much meat as will last for three years."

The Hyena was very happy and he ran to collect all his people. Panting: "Do you see all that meat above? My friend brings it to me every day. Now this friend has told me to collect all my people so that we can go and fetch this meat. Let each one of you bring tins, bags or drums and I, with your permission, will ask the Eagle to mention the day on which we can go."

Said all Hyenas: "Hi, we also would like to eat the white choice meat."

All the Hyenas of that country had gathered together and when they saw the Eagle coming towards them they said: "Now, Brother Eagle, let us go to get this meat. Tell us when we can go".

The Eagle said, "We shall go on the third day from today. Be ready."

On that day the Hyena gathered and the Eagle arranged them in a line according to age, the smallest one being put at the back. The Eagle was right in front. He said to the Hyena behind him: "Now, Brother, hold tight to the feathers of my tail," and the Hyena held tight. "Everybody hold each other's tail," he shouted and then he flew up, up, up, and heading to the choice meats in the sky. Now when they had gone very high, the Eagle asked:

"Are you all clear off the ground?"

"No, no, some are still touching the ground." He flew, flew and flew.

"Can you see the earth?"

"Yes, yes, we can see it." The Eagle was waiting to hear that all the Hyenas could no longer see the earth.

"Can you see the earth?"

"We see it dimly now." The Eagle flew and flew.

"Do you still see the earth?"

"We see only black, black darkness, we cannot tell where the earth is."

The Eagle knew then that the distance from the earth was very, very great. Then he said to the Hyena behind him:

"Hi, hi, my friend, a scratch, a scratch on my back wing," and the Hyena behind let go the tail feathers of the Eagle. Suddenly the whole line of Hyenas went tumbling down. Kuru Kuru Kuru like the sound of thunder. Some Hyenas crushed their limbs, their bones and died instantly. Some died before they reached the earth. Only the last Hyena was left, but she acquired a limp in the leg which she carries to this day.

Reprinted from Kikuyu Folktales, *edited and translated by Rose Gecau. By permission of Kenya Literature Bureau.*

HARE AND HORNBILL

Hare and Hornbill were great friends. One day Hare said: "My friend, we have looked for girls all over this land, and there are none that are good enough for you and me. Let us go up to Skyland, perhaps we will find some suitable ones."

Hornbill replied: "I know it is getting a bit late for us to get married, but you know my problem, you know I have this terrible thing!"

"You mean your chronic diarrhoea? But that is nothing to worry about." Hare produced a cork of the right size and blocked up Hornbill's anus.

The two friends made preparations for the journey, and after saying good-bye to their families, Hare got on Hornbill's back and they flew up through the clouds into Skyland. There was a big marriage dance. Hare and Hornbill put on their dancing costumes and went straight into the arena. Hornbill danced gracefully, touching the ground lightly and moving his wings up and down to the rhythm of the drums. His neck swayed this way and that way, and his eyes sparkled with love. Hare danced as best he could, but he could not follow the rhythm of the dance, and sang out of tune; moreover, his big ears looked funny. Beautiful girls fought to dance before Hornbill, but none came anywhere near Hare; and when he approached the girls they ran away from him. That night Hornbill slept with a very pretty girl. Hare slept cold.

The next day Hornbill won two girls; Hare again slept cold. The next night when Hornbill was asleep, resting beside his fourth lover, Hare tip-toed into the house and unhooked the cork. Three days' accumulation of diarrhoea spewed out and flooded the entire house. The stench rose like smoke and the dancers fled from the arena, and Hornbill woke up, and in great shame flew down through the clouds, leaving Hare behind.

There was much commotion as the Skylanders tried to find out what had happened. Hare denied all knowledge of the cause of the trouble.

"But where is your handsome friend?" they asked.

"I am also looking for him," said Hare, adding, "I must find him otherwise it will be a bit difficult to return to earth."

When they failed to find Hornbill the Skylanders decided to get rid of Hare by lowering him down to earth on a rope of plaited grass. The girls cut many heaps of grass. They made the rope and tied one end around Hare's waist and continued to plait the other end as Hare was lowered downwards. The Skylanders gave Hare a drum and told him, "As soon as you reach the earth beat this drum very hard so that the girls may stop plaiting the rope." Hare thanked the Skylanders, said good-bye and began his homeward journey.

Hare descended slowly through the clouds, but on seeing the faint tips of the highest mountain he hit the drum very hard. The skylanders stopped plaiting and dropped the rope. Hare came hurtling down like a falling stone. But just before hitting the ground he cried to the smallest black ants, "Collect me! Collect me! Collect . . ."

Hare hit the ground and broke up into many many very small pieces. The smallest black ants collected the pieces and put them together again, and Hare became alive. But today when Hare is running you hear his chest making crackling sounds, because the bones of his chest were not put together properly.

Reprinted from Hare and Hornbill, *a collection of folk tales edited and translated by Okot p'Bitek. By permission of Heinemann Educational Books.*

PETALS OF BLOOD

Ngugi wa Thiong'o *is Kenya's best-known writer and one of the country's most consistent-*ly outspoken critics. The following extract from the satirical *Petals of Blood has been taken from the middle of the book. The people of Ilmorog, a village in the Rift Valley, are beginning to appreciate the power and influence of the New Kenya.*

CHANGES COME TO ILMOROG

Munira folded the newspaper and went to Wanja's place to break the news. He felt for her and Nyakinyua. He did not expect favours. He just wanted to take her the news. And to find out more about it. She was not at her Theng'eta premises. Abdulla told him that she had gone to Nyakinyua's hut. Munira walked there and found other people. News of the threatened sale must have reached them too. They had come to commiserate with her and others similarly affected, to weep with one another. They looked baffled: how could a bank sell their land? A bank was not a government: from whence then, its powers? Or maybe it was the government, an invisible government, some others suggested. They turned to Munira. But he could not answer their question. He only talked about a piece of paper, they had surrendered to the bank. But he could not answer, put to sleep, the bitter scepticism in their voices and looks. What kind of monster was this bank that was a power unto itself, that could uproot lives of a thousand years?

He went back and tried to drink Theng'eta, but it did not have the taste. He remembered that recently he had seen Wambui carting stones to earn bread for the day and he wondered what would happen to the old woman. She was too old to sell her labour and sweat in a market.

"The old woman? Nyakinyua?" Munira echoed Karega's question, slowly. "She died! She is dead!" he added quickly, almost aggressively, waking up from his memories.

Karega's face seemed to move.

Nyakinyua, the old woman, tried to fight back. She tramped from hut to hut calling upon the peasants of Ilmorog to get together and fight it out. They looked at her and they shook their heads: whom would they fight now? The Government? The Banks? KCO? The Party Nderi? Yes who would they really fight? But she tried to convince them that all these were one and that she would fight them. Her land would never be settled by strangers. There was something grand, and defiant, in the woman's action

– she with her failing health and flesh trying to organise the dispossessed of Ilmorog into a protest. But there was pathos in the exercise. Those whose land had not yet been taken looked nervously aloof and distant. One or two even made disparaging remarks about an old woman not quite right in the head. Others genuinely not seeing the point of a march to Ruwaini or to the big City restrained her. She could not walk all the way, they told her. But she said: "I'll go alone . . . my man fought the white man. He paid for it with his blood . . . I'll struggle against these black oppressors . . . alone . . . alone . . ."

What would happen to her, Munira wondered.

He need not have worried about her. Nyakinyua died peacefully in her sleep a few days after the news of the bank threat. Rumour went that she had told Wanja about the impending journey: she had said that she could not even think of being buried in somebody else's land: for what would her man say to her when she met him on the other side? People waited for the bank to come and sell her land. But on the day of the sale Wanja redeemed the land and became the heroine of the new and the old Ilmorog.

Later Munira was to know.

But at that time only Abdulla really knew the cost: Wanja had offered to sell him her rights to their jointly owned New Building. He did not have the money and it was he who suggested that they sell the whole building to a third person and divide the income between them.

So Wanja was back to her beginnings.

And Mzigo was the new proud owner of the business premises in Ilmorog.

Wanja was not quite the same after her recent loss. For a time, she continued the proud proprietor of the old Theng'eta place. Her place still remained the meat-roasting centre. Dance steps in the hall could still raise dust to the roof, especially when people were moving to their favourite tunes:

How beautiful you are, my love!
How soft your round eyes are, my honey!
What a pleasant thing you are,
Lying here
Shaded by this cedar bush!
But oh, darling,
What poison you carry between your legs!

But Wanja's heart was not in it. She started building a huge wooden bungalow at the lower end of her shamba, some distance from the shanty town that was growing up around Abdulla's shop, the lodgings and the meat-roasting centre, almost as a natural growth complement to the more elegant new Ilmorog. People said that she was wise to invest in a building the money remaining after redeeming her grandmother's shamba: but what was it for? She already had a hut further up the shamba, hidden from the noise and inquisitive eyes of the New Ilmorog by a thick natural hedge. She went about her work without taking anybody into her confidence. But it was obvious that it was built in the style of a living house with several spacious rooms. Later she moved in: she planted flower gardens all around and had electric lights fixed there. It was beautiful: it was a brave effort so soon after her double loss, people said.

One night the band struck up a song they had composed on their first arrival. As they played, the tune and the words seemed to grow fresher and fresher and the audience clapped and whistled and shouted encouragement. The band added innovations and their voices seemed possessed of a wicked carefree devil.

This shamba girl
Was my darling
Told me she loved my sight.
I broke bank vaults for her,
I went to jail for her,
But when I came back
I found her a lady,
Kept by a wealthy roundbelly daddy,
And she told me,
This shamba-lady girl told me,
No, Gosh!
Sikujui
Serikali imebadilishwa
Coup d'état!

They stopped to thunderous handclaps and feet pounding on the floor. Wanja suddenly stood up and asked them to play it again. She started dancing to it, alone, in the arena. People were surprised. They watched the gyrations of her body, speaking pleasure and pain, memories and hopes, loss and gain, unfulfilled longing and desire. The band, responding to the many beating hearts, played with sad maddening intensity as if it were reaching out to her loneliness and solitary struggle. She danced slowly and deliberately toward Munira and he was remembering that time he had seen her dancing to a juke-box at Safari Bar in Kamiritho. As suddenly as she had started, she stopped. She walked to the stage at the bandstand. The "house" was hushed. The customers knew that something big was in the air.

"I am sorry, dear customers, to have to announce the end of the old Ilmorog Bar and meat-roasting centres, and the end of Ilmorog Bar's own Sunshine Band. Chiri County Council says we have to close."

She would not say more. And now they watched her as she walked across the dusty floor toward where Munira was sitting. She stopped, whirled back, and screamed at the band. "Play! Play! Play on. Everybody dance — Daaance!" And she sat down beside Munira.

"Munira, wouldn't you like to come and see my new place tomorrow night?"

Munira could hardly contain himself. So at long last. So the years of waiting were over. It was just like the old days before Karega and the roads and the changes had come to disturb the steamy peaceful rhythm in Ilmorog, when he was the teacher.

The next day he could not teach. He could not talk. He could hardly sit or stand still in one place. And when the time came, he walked to her place with tremulous hands and beating heart. He had not been inside the new house and he felt it an honour that she had chosen him out of all those faces.

He knocked at the door. She was in. She stood in the middle of the room lit by a blue light. For a second he thought himself in the wrong place with the wrong person.

She had on a miniskirt which revealed just about everything, and he felt his manhood rise of itself. On her lips was smudgy red lipstick: her eyebrows were pencilled and painted a luminous blue. What was the game, he wondered? He thought of one of the many advertisements he had earlier collected: Be a platinum blonde: be a whole new you in 100% imported hand-made human hair. Wanja was a really new her.

"You look surprised, Mwalimu. I thought you always wanted me," she said, with a false seductive blur in her voice. Then in a slightly changed voice, more natural, which he could

recognise, she added: "That's why you had him dismissed, not so? Look now. They have even taken away my right, well, our right to brew. The County Council says our licence was sold away with the New Building. They also say our present premises are in any case unhygienic! There's going to be a tourist centre and such places might drive visitors away. Do you know the new owner of our Theng'eta breweries? Do you know the owner of the New Ilmorog Utamaduni Centre? Never mind!" She had, once again, changed her voice: "But come: what are you waiting for?" She walked backwards: he followed her and they went into another room — with a double bed and a reddish light. He was hypnotized. He was angry with himself for being tongue-tied and yet he was propelled toward her by the engine-power of his risen body and the drums in the heart. Yet below it all, deep inside, he felt a sensation of shame and disgust at his helplessness.

She removed everything, systematically, piece by piece, and then jumped into bed.

"Come, come, my darling!" she cooed from inside the sheets.

He was about to jump into bed beside her and clasp her to himself, when she suddenly turned cold and chilly, and her voice was menacing.

"No, Mwalimu. No free things in Kenya. A hundred shillings on the table if you want high-class treatment."

He thought she was joking, but as he was about to touch her she added more coldly:

"This is New Kenya. You want it, you pay for it, for the bed and the light and my time and the drink that I shall later give you and the breakfast tomorrow. And all for a hundred shillings. For you. Because of old times. For others it will be more expensive."

He was taken aback, felt the wound of this unexpected humiliation. But now he could not retreat. Her thighs called out to him.

He took out a hundred shillings and handed it to her. He watched her count it and put the money under the mattress. Now panic seized him. His thing had shrivelled. He stood there and tried to fix his mind on the old Wanja, on the one who had danced pain and ecstasy, on the one who had once cried under watchful moonbeams stealing into a hut. She watched him, coldly, with menace, and then suddenly she broke out in her put-on, blurred, seductive voice.

"Come, darling. I'll keep you warm. You are tonight a guest at *Sunshine Lodge*."

There was something pathetic, sad, painful in the tone. But Munira's thing obeyed her voice. Slowly he removed his clothes and joined her in bed. Even as the fire and thirst and hunger in his body were being quenched, the pathetic strain in her voice lingered in the air, in him, in the room everywhere.

It was New Kenya. It was New Ilmorog. Nothing was free. But for a long time, for years to come, he was not to forget the shock and the humiliation of the hour. It was almost like that first time, long ago, when he was only a boy.

Indeed, changes did come to Ilmorog, changes that drove the old one away and ushered a new era in our lives. And nobody could tell, really tell, how it had happened, except that it had happened. With a year or so of the new Ilmorog shopping centre being completed, wheatfields and ranches had sprung up all around the plains: the herdsmen had died or had been driven further afield into the drier parts, but a few had become workers on the wheatfields and ranches on the earth upon which they once roamed freely. The new owners, masterservants of bank power, money and cunning came over at weekends and drove in Landrovers or Range Rovers, depending on the current car fashion, around the farms whose running they had otherwise entrusted to paid managers. The peasants of Ilmorog had also changed. Some had somehow survived the onslaught. They could employ one or two hands on their small farms. Most of the others had joined the army of workers who had added to the growing population of the New Ilmorog. But which New Ilmorog?

There were several Ilmorogs. One was the residential area of the farm managers, County Council officials, public service officers, the managers of Barclays, Standard and African Economic Banks, and other servants of state and money power. This was called Cape Town. The other – called New Jerusalem – was a shanty town of migrant and floating workers, the unemployed, the prostitutes and small traders in tin and scrap metal. Between the New Jerusalem and Cape Town, not far from where Mwathi had once lived guarding the secrets of iron works and native medicine, was All Saints church, now led by Rev. Jerrod Brown. Also somewhere between the two areas

was Wanja's *Sunshine Lodge*, almost as famous as the church.

The shopping and business centre was dominated by two features. Just outside it was a tourist cultural (Utamaduni) village owned by Nderi wa Riera and a West German concern, appropriately called Ilmorog African Diamond Cultural and Educational Tours. Many tourists came for a cultural fiesta. A few hippies also came to look for the Theng'eta Breweries which, starting on the premises owned by Mzingo, had now grown into a huge factory employing six hundred workers with a number of research scientists and chemical engineers. The factory also owned an estate in the plains where they experimented with different types of Theng'eta plants and wheat. They brewed a variety of Theng'eta drinks: from the pure gin for export to cheap but potent drinks for workers and the unemployed. They put some in small plastic bags in different measures of one, two and five shillings' worth so that these bagfuls of poison could easily be carried in people's pockets. Most of the containers, whether plastic or glass bottles, carried the famous ad, now popularized in most parts of the country through their sales vans, newspapers and handbills: POTENCY – Theng'a Theng'a with Theng'eta. P=3T.

The breweries were owned by an Anglo-American international combine but of course with African directors and even shareholders. Three of the four leading local personalities were Mzigo, Chui and Kimeria.

Long live New Ilmorog! Long live Partnership in Trade and Progress!

Reprinted from Petals of Blood. *By permission of Heinemann Educational Books.*

SHORT STORY – SAM KAHIGA

Short stories are immensely popular in Kenya and you'll find stacks of well-thumbed, short romantic novels at any second-hand bookstall. **Sam Kahiga**'s *energetic, exasperatingly racy style, sprinkled with a combination of British and American idioms, is strange at first, but his stories are revealing about the values of modern, urban Kenya.*

A HIGH VOLTAGE AFFAIR

At school I was afflicted by that chronic laziness that is often the lot of young students who think they are especially clever and can pass any exam through sheer genius. After getting my "O" levels with nine points and no sweat at all, I went to Strathmore College for "A" levels. I remember my goal then – to be a nuclear physicist. And if that was too advanced for the Third World then I'd compromise gracefully, step down, and just be a bloody good research scientist. The Third World could do with some of those.

Well my "A" levels were a disaster. What could I blame it on? Girls, booze or drugs? I blame it on the lot – plus the sort of risky confidence that comes after you've been top of the class too many times. Of my days in Strathmore I remember the movies and the parties rather than what happened in the labs. Except for jokingly trying to invent a drug that could give one a trip I hardly applied myself. And when the final results came out I realized that I was on a bad trip that just wouldn't end up in the university. It was bad, shocking, in fact.

Guys whose IQs were nowhere near as high as mine got called up to the university. As for me I was bad news in academic circles. Trying to save face I applied feverishly to foreign universities. My daddy could afford to send me to one. But no foreign university seemed interested. I kept trying until my daddy casually let me know that if I was intending to go abroad I would have to get the dough myself. That's what is known as fatherly affection.

Let me explain his attitude, for I understood it perfectly. My daddy (his friends and enemies call him GM) was no kid-spoiler. Although he could afford to send me round the world seven times he wasn't going to help because I had proved I was a failure. If I had failed at home I would not succeed abroad. I realized from his acid comments that he knew about the kind of life I had led at Strathmore – girls, booze, drugs. Could he then seriously think of sending me to America, that modern Babylon and hippy headquarters.

"Go on your own," said GM. He had turned a blind eye to my mischief until I let him down and failed to make it to the university. And GM is not the kind of man you let down and get away with it. He himself had never failed. Where he couldn't work his way out smoothly he bulldozed. If the front door was closed he tried the back door. That was the way he made his millions in the construction business.

Sons of poor men were going to university, so why not GM's first-born? He felt betrayed. What

was it that he had not done for me? My pocket money had been two hundred and fifty bob a month. And he had told me to buy any book that I wanted. So why had I not gone to university?

GM had never even been to high school because he had been born too many years before the fruit of independence ripened. When independence came he was just a mason grade three. We lived at Shauri Moyo. GM grabbed his share of the fruit and we moved off to Lavington where I had my own motor-cycle and a couple of rooms to myself which were a mess of wires, novels and beat music that made my mother ill. The smell of my strange "cigarettes" made her ill too, but mothers are like that. You have to be patient with them.

I agree that GM spoilt me. But all the money and stuff he showered on me was on the understanding, which I did until this hazy "A" levels. In fact I did more. For instance at seventeen I was the maintenance man around the place, the little genie who knew what was wrong with the TV, the fridge or even his car. GM couldn't even change his own spark plugs. He trusted me to tune and service his car and considered me the last word in wiring. Now you can begin to understand about the two hundred and fifty bob pocket money. I spent most of it on cocaine.

After I had failed GM didn't want to see me around. He is a very unforgiving man. He had dug up my Strathmore background and it had shocked him so much that he didn't want me to even touch his car.

What finally broke up our relationship was when the disciplinarian daddy in him came to the surface and he thought he could teach me a physical lesson just because my room smelt of something strange. He sniffed and realized that it was grass.

The rest is embarrassing. Let's just say that there was yet another side of me that he hadn't known. I had a panther's reflexes that had come from picking up all that one needs to know about judo and karate. I didn't hurt him at all but he stared at me from the floor with great surprise. Through his gaping mouth I saw a little film of blood on his small white teeth – nothing serious.

After that there was nothing else to do except pack. The mansion at Lavington was a bit too small for both of us.

Somehow I feel that this background is important before I tell the story that follows.

When I went to the Power Institute to train as a technician for the Power Company I went on my own ticket. The exams accompanying the interview were tough and gruelling to most of the boys but I sailed through, although I was half-starving. They accepted me at the Power Institute on my own merit, not a millionaire's influential word. It is important that this is understood.

Every young boy carries in his heart the soft-focus image of a woman he could love, serve and die for. I'm still not sure whether she eventually turns up, this ever youthful, totally compliant dream girl whom you want to set on a pedestal and worship. She is mutable, changing with your fancy and experience, but something remains constant about her, whether you are twelve or forty.

This constancy I guess is the subservience to your ego. She will love you no matter what happens, no matter who else is there. She loves you when you are vomiting into the toilet bowl and sticks by your side as you piss into a dark alley. She will be petite and cuddlesome when you are in a gentle mood and you want her to be like that. She will have an Afro hairdo if that's what you want. She's a virgin, nobody ever touched her before. Sometimes her breasts are small, sometimes her breasts are large. Sometimes she's innocent, sometimes she's master of the Kama Sutra, a deep well of erotic knowledge.

The first time she came to me in the flesh (or was it her more mundane twin sister?) was at the Power Institute at the beginning of the second year. My thoughts were hardly on love but on electro-magnetic forces, watts, ohms and coulombs. Instead of breasts I was thinking of turbines and transformers and the only kick I ever got during those sober, sombre months was the flow of electrons through me whenever I was fool enough to step on a live wire. In short, I was immersed in electricity, my biggest love since childhood. I hadn't seen anybody for a year – nobody mattered. For companions I had watts, coils and ohm's law. If I needed a drink, coke was enough, thanks. The hostel supplied the grub. There wasn't much else I felt I needed.

Then during Easter we had a dance at the hostel and this chick came along with one of the boys. I remember I was pretty lonesome hanging around the stuffy room with my coke and yet expecting nothing from all the bull-shit. To make things worse it was raining badly outside and I couldn't walk back to the hostel even if I had wanted to.

What is dancing? I asked myself. Some hang-over from some primitive era. Some sort of savage convolution totally outside the realm of scientific discipline. I wanted to go home but the damn rain was falling. When I looked out of the window the world was suddenly lit up by the taut gnarled roots of a devilish lightning flash. "Jupiter's thunder-bolt." "God's footstep." To scientists: atmospheric electric phenomena. I wanted to go to bed.

She was very pretty but couldn't have been with a worse man. Mbote was rude, coarse and argumentative. He was a slum child and he was proud of the fact. No efforts at all to be a gentleman. The girl he was with was a lady from the toe up to the rich mass of black hair. And if I wasn't wrong she was trying to catch my eye.

I put my ginger ale on the ledge of a window (tired of cokes by now). I singled her out from the rest of the clumsy humanity, forgave her for imperfections and danced with her to a slow number.

"What's your label?" I asked.

"I beg your pardon?"

"The name. What's your name?"

"Esther."

"Esther what?"

"Mbacia."

Esther Mbacia. I was a bit annoyed with her for looking like my dream girl while going around with a guy like Mbote. My dream girls are supposed to be my own. They shouldn't be wandering around among crude wolves. They might get eaten. I wouldn't have been surprised if she ended up in Mbote's cubicle.

"You didn't tell me your name, but I know you," she said. "You are GM's son, aren't you?"

"So?" I asked coldly.

"I used to see you when you were in Strathmore. I was then in Kenya High. You know, when you had that motor-cycle." I couldn't help grinning.

"Your girl-friend was my classmate, Edith." Edith, a grass addict.

"Mbacia," I said. "Is your father the Mbacia? Mbacia Enterprises?"

"Happens to be," she said.

"Oh."

"Oh, what?"

"Nothing."

We laughed together. And then I saw the livid angry eyes of Mbote staring at me over the rim of his glass of alcoholic poison. He was mixing everything, the only way he could get drunk cheaply. He had drunk changaa ever since he was a small boy in Majengo slums, so beer to him was mere water.

"Your boyfriend looks angry and dangerous," I said.

"He's not my boyfriend," said Mbacia's daughter.

There might have been a fight that night had I been just any other boy. But my reputation was good. They knew my reflexes. Mbote was a dreaded street fighter who bullied almost everybody else but he knew I could paralyse him by just touching a nerve. Neatly, with no glasses being broken. He didn't want that. I didn't want to be unfair so I gave her a date and went to bed.

So that's how the tragic triangle started. Poor slum boy grabs a rich girl, wants to make her happy in his own rude way. Rich boy comes along with polished karate and his father's millions behind him and poor boy has no chance. The fact that I was broke most of the time didn't worry her one bit. In fact it seemed to add to my attraction. GM's son, but always broke. How funny!

I liked serious movies but also liked seeing Chinese movies to improve on my karate. She liked ice-cream, chewing gum and I'm not quite sure what else. I liked her. A girl doesn't have to have a line of interest to be liked. I still don't know her line of interest. She doesn't share my passion for turbines and transformers but so what? So nothing. She was high voltage. There were electrostatic forces in her breasts. When she smiled at me the electrons flowed. She was my cathode and I was her anode.

She was Mbote's heartbreak. Poor slum boy, son of a Majengo prostitute, he had never had any love in his life. He thought he had found it in Esther. Esther thought she had found it in me. The eternal triangle.

He came to me one night when I was reading and knocked on the door of my cubicle. He was totally drunk. I threw him out. I threw him out because he called me a hybrid.

"Just because you are a hybrid and she's a hybrid you feel you must cross-breed. To keep the millions in one family."

"Get the hell out," I said. But I had to remove him physically.

What I think shattered him was my bringing Esther to the end of term dance. At first he was vulgar and insulting, though not talking to us directly. I heard the words "hybrid" and "cross-breeding" and tried to take no notice. Then I saw that he was staring at us silently, no longer speaking. The jilted lover: why not just find a girl? Why let this thing play on his complexes? I wished I could give him the girl but I was already in love with her. Or maybe there was this vacuum in my soul that she very conveniently filled. Sometimes it's difficult to distinguish love from the flight from loneliness.

The following morning was Sunday and that was when the nightmare began. Most of the boys had already gone home and the hostel was almost deserted.

With a towel around my loins I went into the shower room. Mbote who was waiting for that move came and locked the door with a key. Standing outside the door he told me a lot of things. How he had loved and how I had ruined his chances.

"What's the point of locking the door?"

"I want to kill you."

The shower was running, the warm water caressing my skin. He was going to kill me. He must be joking. And yet I knew how reckless he was, the kind of strange practical jokes he used to play on people. Better watch out.

"Look Mbote, Esther is mine," I said, wearily.

"You snatched her. You rich people think you can snatch everything. You think you are smart. You'll pay for it."

"How?"

"I want to make you dance. You like dancing I'll make you dance."

"Look, open the door and stop being stupid. What are you up to?"

"When you come out of there you won't be alive."

"Why?"

"The shower room is wired. I'm just about to give you a thousand volts." I got the idea. I broke into a sweat. I stared at the wet floor of my death cell. The water would conduct the electricity from wherever the terminals were.

"Open the door and don't be stupid," I cried and that was the last thing I said before the current shot up through my bare feet and shot me up to the ceiling. I screamed, then hit the floor unconscious.

SWAHILI POETRY

Swahili poetry is Kenya's oldest written literature, recorded in Arabic script since the seventeenth century and in the Roman alphabet since the turn of this century. The oldest poems are praise and wedding songs from the oral tradition and narrative epics relating the early years of Islam. There's a wide variety of forms, but the rhythms and rhymes are not too unfamiliar to Western ears. Swahili, with its infinite capacity for allusion and imagery, has produced some beautiful verse. **Shaaban Robert**, who died in 1962, is probably the greatest twentieth-century Swahili poet. This lament for his wife was written in the *shairi* metre of sixteen syllables to the line.

AMINA

Amina unmejitenga, kufa umetangulia,	Amina, you have withdrawn yourself, you led the way in dying,
Kama ua umefunga, baada ya kuchanua,	Like a flower you have closed, after having opened first,
Nukuombea mwanga, peponi kukubaliwa.	I pray for you, my light, that you may be welcomed in paradise.
Mapenzi tuliyofunga, hapana wa kufungua.	The love we made between us, no one ever will undo it.
Nilitaka unyanyuke, kwa kukuombea dua,	I had hoped that you would rise again, and I prayed for you,
Sikupenda ushindike, maradhi kukuchukua,	I did not want you to be defeated, and be carried away by the disease,
Ila kwa rehema yake, Mungu amekuchagua.	But by His mercy, God has chosen you.
Mapenzi tuliyofunga, hapana wa kufungua.	The love we made between us, no one ever will undo it.
Majonzi hayaneneki, kila nikikumbukia,	My grief is indescribable, every moment I remember,
Nawaza kile na hiki, naona kama ruia,	I keep thinking this and yonder I see things as if I were dreaming,
Mauti siyasadiki kuwa, mwisho wa dunia.	I did not believe in death first, that it was the end of the world, this life.
Mapenzi tuliyofunga, hapana wa kufungua.	The love we made between us, no one ever will undo it.
Nasadiki haziozi, roho hazitapotea,	I believe that souls don't perish, they cannot be lost forever,
Twafuata wokozi, kwa mauti kutujia,	We pursue salvation's pathway, when death's angel comes to meet us,
Nawe wangu mpenzi, Peponi utaingia.	And you, my beloved partner, you will enter heaven's gateway.
Mapenzi tuliyofunga, hapana wa kufungua.	The love we made between us, no one ever will undo it.
Jambo moja nakumbuka, sahihi ninalijua,	Just one thing I do remember, one I know for sure and truly,
Kuwa sasa umefika, ta'bu isikosumbua,	That you have now reached the place where no suffering can plague you,
Kwayo nimefurahika, nyuma nilikobakia.	Therefore do I still feel gladdened, here where I am left behind.
Mapenzi tuliyofunga, hapana wa kufungua.	The love we made between us, no one ever will undo it.
Ninamaliza kutunga, kwa kukuombea dua,	I have finished my composing, while for you I pray,
Vumbi tena likiunga, roho likirudishiwa,	When dust is rejoined together, when the soul returns into it,
Mauti yakijitenga, mapenzi yatarejea.	While the power of death retires, then our love will be returning.
Mapenzi tuliyofunga, hapana wa kufungua.	The love we made between us, no one ever will undo it.

Translated by Jan Knappert, 1979. Reprinted from *Four Centuries of Swahili Verse*, by permission of the translator.

Hospital. The first week was a blank. The next one I began to recognise people – chaps from the Power Institute, GM, Esther.

The third week I was fine and that was when they told me that Mbote had electrocuted himself when I was in a coma. The cops had come for him and rather than face the law he had taped electric wires to his head. He had turned on the switch, died instantly and made headlines for the first and last time.

I try to look on it all to see why and how it happened but I'm still not strong enough to sort out little psychological details. Or perhaps my mind just refuses to work. I saw a picture of Mbote's mother in the papers and she was wailing, saying he was a good boy. I take my own refuge behind public opinion for that's all I can

do. Public opinion has it that Mbote was crazy to try and electrocute GM's son. He was quite right to electrocute himself, though. But he shouldn't go round trying to electrocute heirs to millions. (GM wants to know if I need bodyguards.)

It all depresses me. When my heart is really low I call up Esther on the phone.

"Doctor says I need lots of therapy, girl, and only you can give it to me. So come over quick."

She always does. I told you she's high voltage – if you see what I mean. Maybe she really *is* hybrid.

Reprinted from the collection Flight to Juba *by permission of Longman Kenya.*

MUSIC

Although its music is less well known abroad than that of a number of other African countries, Kenya's home-grown musical vitality is there if you listen. And Nairobi's audiences and recording facilities have long been a draw for musicians from all over east and central Africa, bringing to the city a pan-African musical flavour.

TRADITIONAL MUSIC

All the people of Kenya have **traditional musical cultures**; some have survived more intact than others into the twenty-first century. If you are prepared to persevere a little, you can usually buy cassettes locally, though the quality is often dire.

Music in Kenya has always been used to accompany **rites of passage**, from celebrations at a baby's birth to songs of adolescence and warriorhood. There were songs for all ceremonies and events – marriage, harvests, solar and lunar cycles, festivities, religious rites – and there were songs for death, too.

Nowadays, the majority of Kenyans are Christian, notably in the centre and west of the country, though missionary activity continues in the far north and west, bordering Uganda, Sudan and Ethiopia. Gospel now reigns supreme; sadly not the uplifting version of the southern United States, but a tinny, synthesized and homogenous form which in many areas has all but obliterated traditional music.

Among the Kikuyu (Kenya's largest tribe) and the Kalenjin (who comprise much of the government), traditional music is almost extinct. And elsewhere, to hear anything at all you need a lot of time and patience, and effectively would need to live with a people for several weeks to gain their trust and respect before being allowed to witness what can still be very sacred events. With perseverance, too, it is possible to find tapes of traditional music.

The following is a very brief tribe-by-tribe run-down of more easily encountered traditional music and instruments. Obviously, there's much more available if you know where to search and what to ask for: essential **reading** for this is George Senoga-Zake's *Folk Music of Kenya* (Uzima Press, Nairobi 1986). Other works on music are thin on the ground, though most bookshops stock a reasonable selection of school textbooks, some of which provide a handy introduction to the subject.

AKAMBA

Best known for their skill at drumming, the **Akamba** tradition is sadly now all but extinct. To record anything, you'll have to go well off the beaten track in Ukambani, as there's next to nothing either in Machakos or Kitui. There's only one commercial cassette available (*Akamba Drums*, Tamasha), which covers many styles and has some interesting sleeve notes, which you can order from the Zanzibar Curio Shop in Nairobi.

BAJUNI

The **Bajuni** are a small ethnic group living in the Lamu archipelago and on the nearby mainland, and are known musically for an epic women's work song called *Mashindano Ni Matezo*. One of only very few easily-available recordings of women singing in Kenya, this is gradually hypnotic counterpoint singing, punctuated by metallic rattles and supported by subdued drumming. You can find it in Lamu, Kilifi or Mombasa.

BORANA

The **Borana**, who live between Marsabit and the Ethiopian border, have a rich musical tradition. Cassettes are difficult to obtain; either spread the word in Isiolo, or in Marsabit. The Arab influence is readily discernible, as are more typically Saharan rhythms. Most distinctive is their use of the *chamonge* guitar, nowadays a large cooking pot loosely strung with metal wires. On first hearing it, you'd be forgiven for thinking that it is funky electric guitar, or some old earthy precursor to the blues.

CHUKA

Sadly practically extinct, **Chuka** music from the east side of Mount Kenya – like that of the Akamba – is drumming genius. Your only hope is to catch the one remaining band (who currently play at the Mount Kenya Safari Club near Nanyuki), or pale imitations in coastal holiday resorts.

GUSII

Gusii music is certainly Kenya's oddest. The favoured instrument is the *obokano*, an enormous version of the Luo *nyatiti* lyre which is pitched at least an octave below the human voice, and which at times can sound like roaring thunder. They also use the ground bow, essentially a large hole dug in the ground over which an animal skin is tightly pegged. The skin has a small hole cut in the centre, into which a single-stringed bow is placed and plucked: the sound defies description. Spread the word and you should be able to pick up recordings in Kisii easily enough.

LUHYA

Luhya music has a clear Bantu flavour, easily discernible in the pre-eminence of drums. Of these, the *sukuti* is best-known, sometimes played in ensembles, and still used in rites of passage such as circumcision. Tapes are easily available in Kakamega and Kitale, and in some River Road shops in Nairobi.

LUO

The **Luo** are best-known as the originators of *benga* (see p.672). Their most distinctive musical instrument is the *nyatiti*, a double-necked eight-string lyre with a skin resonator which is also struck on one neck with a metal ring tied to the toe. It produces a tight, resonant sound, and is used to generate sometimes long and remarkably complex hypnotic rhythms. Originally used in the fields to relieve workers' tiredness, a typical piece begins at a moderate pace, and quickens progressively, the musician singing over the sound. The lyrics cover all manner of subjects, from politics and change since the *wazungu* arrived, to moral fables and age-old legends. Look out also for recordings of *onand* (accordion) and *orutu* (a single-stringed fiddle).

MAASAI

The nomadic lifestyle of the **Maasai** tends to preclude the carrying of any large instruments, and as a result their music is one of the most distinctive in Kenya, characterized by a total lack of instruments, and some astonishing polyphonous multi-part singing – both call-and-response, sometimes with women included in the chorus, but most famously in the songs of the *morani* warriors, where each man sings part of a rhythm, more often than not from his throat (rather like a grunt), which together with the calls of his companions create a pattern of rhythms. The songs are usually competitive (expressed through the singers alternately leaping as high as they can) or bragging – about how the singer killed a lion, or rustled cattle from a neighbouring community. The Maasai have retained much of their traditional culture, so singing is still very much used in traditional ceremonies, most spectacularly in the *eunoto* circumcision ceremony in which boys are initiated into manhood to begin their ten- to fifteen-year stint as *morani*.

Even in Narok and Kajiado, the main Maasai urban centres in Kenya, most tourists staying in big coastal hotels or in game park lodges in Amboseli and Maasai Mara will have a chance to sample Maasai music in the form of groups of *morani* playing at the behest of hotel management. Cassettes are difficult to find: there's a Maasai variant of gospel music (from Arusha in Tanzania) available in Narok, and an excellent little music store in Oloitokitok, but otherwise your only hope is to record the music yourself.

MIJIKENDA

The **Mijikenda** of the coast have a prolific musical tradition which has survived Christian conversion and is readily available on tape throughout the coastal region. Performances can occasionally be seen in the larger hotels. Most of the music available is from the Giriama section of the Mijikenda, who live inland of Malindi. Like the Akamba, the Mijikenda are superb drummers and athletic dancers. The music is generally light and overlaid with complex rhythms, impossible not to dance to. Look out also for the *kiringongo* music of the Chonyi people, which features the xylophone (an instrument otherwise unknown in Kenya).

TAPE COMPILATIONS OF TRADITIONAL MUSIC AVAILABLE IN KENYA

Bomas of Kenya: Songs of our African Heritage (ZAIT 511). Includes pieces from the Kikuyu, Mijikenda (Digo and Giriama), Embu, Akamba, Samburu, Borana, Luo and Luhya tribes.

Folk Music of East Africa (Philips CPKLP 102). Accompanies the book (out of print) *Musical Instruments of East Africa* by Graham Hyslop. Includes music from the Luhya, Kuria, Mijikenda (Digo) and Swahili peoples.

Gonda Traditional Entertainment "Second Step" (Tamasha CPOLP 327). Music from the Mijikenda and Taita people.

Muziki Wa Kiasili (Folk Music of Kenya) (ZAIT 503). Contains Luo, Gusii, Luhya, Kuria and Mijikenda music.

Traditional Music of East Africa Vol.I (C/Trad Vol 1). Includes Kikuyu dances, *nyatiti* (Luo), *litungu* (Luhya), Akamba singing and drums, Giriama and Digo dances.

Traditional Music of East Africa Vol.II (C/Trad Vol 2). Includes Akamba, Luo, Kikuyu and Luhya music.

Traditional Musical Instruments of Kenya, Vol 1 (Tamasha CPOLP 321). Melodic and percussive instruments including: *nyatiti* (Luo lyre), *chivoti* and *nzumari* (Mijikenda flutes), *marimba* (Mijikenda xylophone), *orutu* (single-string Luo fiddle), *sukuti* (Luhya drums), *sengenya* and *chakacha* (Mijikenda drums) and *mbeni* (Akamba drums).

SAMBURU

Despite its having been discovered by tourists and authors of glossy coffee-table books, there are no commercial recordings of **Samburu** music except on the occasional compilation. Like their Maasai cousins, whose singing it closely resembles, Samburu musicians make a point of not playing instruments, though if you delve a little deeper (like asking the blacksmith at Yare Safari Camp in Maralal, for example), you'll find that they're being conservative with the truth. They do play small pipes, and also a kind of guitar with a box resonator and loose metal strings – which seems to be related to the *chamonge* of the Borana further north. But these are played purely for pleasure, or to soothe a crying baby, and are thus not deemed "music" by Samburu. Listen out also for the sinuously erotic rain songs sung by women in times of drought. For cassettes, ask around at the lodges and campsites in Samburu/Buffalo Springs National Reserves, or – better still – in Maralal.

TURKANA

Until the 1970s, the **Turkana** were one of Kenya's remotest tribes, and in large part are still untouched by Christian missionaries. Their traditional music is based loosely on a call-and-response pattern. The main instrument is a kudu antelope horn with or without finger holes, but most of their music is entirely vocal. A rarity to look out for are the women's rain songs, sung to the god Akuj during times of drought. As traditional music is still played on ceremonial occasions (and being nomadic, the Turkana have no electricity or tape recorders), finding cassettes is extremely difficult; it's a question of asking around in Loiyangalani. You're usually welcome to join performances in Loiyangalani for a small fee – just ask.

Jens Finke

NGOMA, AND THE ARRIVAL OF THE GUITAR

Kenya's oldest musical tradition is **ngoma**, still the central term used to describe all the facets of a musical performance, including the accompanying dances. *Ngoma* in most Bantu languages of Kenya refers to a specific kind of **drum** and a related dance, but more broadly the term refers to drums in general and a genre of music using drums as its main instruments.

Although an inter-ethnic *ngoma* called *beni* (band) emerged on the coast around the turn of the century and spread inland (you can still witness this anachronistic, marching-band form on special occasions in Lamu), *ngoma* music today is essentially ethnic, related to a specific language group and using the respective vernacular and local dance rhythms. *Ngoma* also provides most of the music used during the lifecycle festivities (birth, initiation and circumcision, marriage and death), whether in the town or the country. You can buy *ngoma* music on singles. Look out for recordings by Luhya **sukuti** groups: the *sukuti* is the central drum of these ensembles.

From the early 1950s on, with society rapidly changing, the coming of recording and broadcasting, and the introduction of new instruments – especially the **guitar** – an acoustic guitar-based music developed as accompaniment to songs sung in **Swahili**. Perhaps the most important artist of this "first generation" of guitarists was **Fundi Konde**. A basis for Swahili-language popular music had already been laid by the *beni* groups flourishing in east African towns during the first half of the century. *Beni* songs, as well as the new guitar songs, featured the strong and critical social commentary so beloved of Kenyans. The songs are usually in the form of a short story and may comment on an actual political or social topic, or perhaps recount a personal experience of the musician. Romantic lyrics are almost non-existent, even in songs dealing with men and women.

The guitar styles themselves developed out of different instrumental techniques and musical perceptions, but they were influenced by the records available at the time, mainly from other parts of Africa. Kenyan musicians of the period cite the finger-picking style of **Jean Bosco Mwenda** and **Losta Abelo**, both from Katanga (today, Shaba Province in the Congo), and **George Sibanda**, from Bulawayo in Zimbabwe, as important inspirations. From this period, the notables of Kenya's acoustic guitar styles are **John Mwale**, **George Mukabi** (directly out of the Luhya *sukuti* tradition) and **Isaya Mwinamo**.

The 1960s saw the introduction of **electric guitars** as well as larger groups (of three to four guitars). **Kwela** and **twist** were the rage, coming from, or via, southern Africa. These were the days of the **Equator Sound Band** (Equator being the main record label), featuring the songs of **Daudi Kabaka**, **Fadhili William**, **Nashil Pichen** and **Peter Tsotsi**.

MODERN KENYAN STYLES

It isn't very meaningful to speak of Kenyan pop as a genre. There are really a number of styles that borrow freely and influence each other in a cross-fertilization that gives the music its unifying Kenyan flavour. What is fundamental, though, is the prominent role of guitars and guitar solos. The Earthworks' compilations *Guitar Paradise of East Africa* and *Kenya Dance Mania*, along with Rounder Records' *The Nairobi Beat*, provide ample evidence, with an excellent cross-section of Kenyan pop spanning the last thirty years. Another ingredient in the Kenyan mix is the **cavacha** rhythm popularized in the mid-1970s by Congolese groups such as Zaiko Langa Langa and Orchestra Shama Shama. A sense of this rhythm is conveyed by Bo Diddley's distinctive beat, the "shave-and-a-haircut, six-bits" rhythm which closely approximates *cavacha*. This rapid-fire percussion, usually on the snare or high hat, quickly took hold in Kenya and continues to underlie a great sweep of Kenyan music from the Kalambya Sisters to Les Wanyika and Orchestra Virunga. Many Kenyan musicians direct their efforts towards their own linguistic groups and perform most of their songs in one of Kenya's indigenous languages. Alongside this regional/ethnic orientation – often simply referred to as "tribal" in Kenya itself – are two other local pop music varieties: one consisting of songs with lyrics in Swahili, or the Congolese language Lingala,

TARABU MUSIC

Tarabu, the main popular music of the coastal **Swahili** people, deserves special mention. It has a long tradition in the festive life of the Swahili and is also the general music of entertainment of the coastal communities. But the music has strong Arabic-Islamic overtones in instrumentation, especially in the haunting vocals. Earlier *tarabu* (*taarab*, *tarab*) groups used the full Arabic orchestra, including the lute-like *oud* and violins. Today the main instruments are mandolin or guitar and either an Indian harmonium or a small electronic organ/piano, plus a variety of local, Arabic or Indian drums. Indian movies, with their strong musical component, are very popular among the coastal people and under their influence many features of Indian music have entered *tarabu*. From as early as the 1940s *tarabu* has been sung not only in Swahili but also in Urdu/Hindi. Many of the lead singers and bandleaders of *tarabu* groups are women, almost unique in Kenyan traditional music. The focus of *tarabu* is intricately rhythmic poetry and, in this, **Juma Balo** is one of its masters. Leading female voices are **Malika** and **Zuhura**, while mixed-sex vocals are the feature of the **Black Star** and **Lucky Star Musical Clubs**, originally from Tanzania.

aimed at a national and largely urban audience, and the other propelled by foreign tourism and Kenyans with a taste for international pop.

BENGA BANDS

The end of the 1960s and early 1970s was a time of transition in Kenyan music. While the African Eagles and others continued to play their brands of Swahili music, many top Kenyan groups, such as the Ashantis, Air Fiesta and the Hodi Boys, were playing Congolese covers and international pop, especially soul music, in the Nairobi clubs. But it was also at this time that a number of musicians were beginning to define the direction of the emerging **benga** style, which, perhaps more than anything else, became Kenya's most characteristic pop music.

Although the word and what it represents originated with the Luo people of western Kenya, *benga*'s transition to a popular style has been so pervasive that practically all the local bands, Luo or otherwise, play variants of it, and today most of the regional or ethnic pop groups refer generally to their music as *benga*. As a pop style, *benga* dates back to the 1950s when musicians began adapting traditional dance rhythms and the string sounds of the *nyatiti* and *orutu* to the acoustic guitar and later to electric instruments. During its heyday much of the early *benga* was exported to west and southern Africa where it was very popular.

Throughout the 1970s and into the 80s, *benga* music dominated Kenya's recording industry and, although the whole industry is in serious decline, it remains an important force.

Luo

By any measure, the most famous **Luo** *benga* group is **Shirati Jazz** led by **D.O. (Daniel Owino) Misiani**. Born in Shirati, Tanzania, just south of the Kenyan border, he has been playing *benga* since the mid-1960s. His style is characterized by soft, flowing and melodic two-part vocal harmonies, a very active, pulsating bass line that derives at least in part from traditional *nyatiti* and drum rhythms, and stacks of invigorating guitar work, the lead alternating with the vocal.

Misiani may be a "*benga* wizard", but *benga* is not his exclusive property and, contrary to the impression you might receive in London or New York record shops, there are many other important *benga* artists. Pioneering Luo names include Colella Mazee and Ochieng Nelly – either together or separately in various incarnations of **Victoria Jazz** and the **Victoria Kings** – as well as George Ramogi and his Continental Luo Sweet Band. All are still active in Kenya except for Ramogi who died in 1997. Two other Luo groups that have been quite popular in recent years also lost their leaders in 1997. Okatch Biggy (Elly Otieno Okatch) of Heka Heka and Prince Jully (Julius Okumu) of the Jolly Boy's Band both died. Of all these *benga* groups, Misiani's Shirati is one of the few that can find sufficient work to make it a full-time profession. For most, music is a part-time job in addition to the homestead farm, wage employment, or a small business.

One Luo name which didn't fit neatly into any of these stylistic categories is **Ochieng Kabaselleh** and his **Luna Kidi Band**. His songs were mostly in Luo, but sometimes with a liberal seasoning of Swahili and English. Likewise, the melodies and harmonies are from the Luo *benga* realm but the rhythm, guitar work, and horns suggest influences from the Congolese/Swahili-dominated sound. Kabaselleh, who languished in prison for several years (for "subversion"), returned to the music world with a flood of new releases in the 1990s. In 1997, Kabaselleh and group toured the USA and recorded his first international CD release, *From Nairobi with Love*. In 1998, he suddenly died, a victim of complications related to diabetes. Some of his most interesting music of the 1980s is available in a collection called *Sanduku ya Mapendo* (A Loadful of Love) from Equator Heritage Sounds.

Luhya

The **Luhya** highlands to the north of Luo-land are home to many of Kenya's most famous guitarists and vocalists. Daudi Kabaka, despite his renowned early career, struggles today with only the occasional hotel gig and few recording opportunities. The humorous social commentary of **Sukuma bin Ongaro** has made him a giant of the current scene, although mainly among his fellow Luhya-speakers. **Shem Tube**, however, is an artist who straddles both past and present in his music, though it's his musical past which has given him a popular following in the UK and Europe.

In 1989, GlobeStyle Records released *Abana ba Nasery* (The Nursery Boys), a compilation of songs by Tube and his group in the *omutibo* style. With two acoustic guitars (playing high and low), and rhythm played on a Fanta bottle, the *Abana ba Nasery* collection offers a glimpse of a musical era of the 1960s and early 1970s which has largely vanished. Coming together as a trio in the early 1960s, Abana ba Nasery were innovators, blazing a path for Kenyan pop to follow. While using traditional Luhya rhythms and melody lines, their two-guitar line-up and three-part vocal harmonies (and the Fanta bottle) were a hint of things to come. Abana's style from the 1960s contains the major elements of today's contemporary pop sound in Kenya: the central position of the solo guitar in Kenya's electric groups is anticipated in Shem Tube's solos of twenty-five years ago. Justo Osala's guitar parts in the lower ranges are like the rhythm and bass parts in today's electric bands. Even Enos Okola's Fanta rhythms are a precursor of the modern drum kit.

While Abana's first CD release created tremendous interest – a rootsy but very accessible African sound – the compatibility of their music with strands of European folk tradition is clear in their second CD release, recorded by GlobeStyle in London: *Nursery Boys Go Ahead!* Guest artists included members of the Oyster Band and Mustaphas as well as Ron Kavana and Tomás Lynch. Although it's an all-acoustic recording, several songs on this collaborative effort are true rockers – which is not out of character with the group on their home turf. Although they've never earned enough money to buy their own electric guitars and amps, Abana ba Nasery have had a string of local hits as an electric band under the stage names Mwilonje Jazz and Super Bunyore Band (listen, for example, to Super Bunyore's "Bibi Joys" on the *Nairobi Beat* compilation).

Kikuyu

As Kenya's largest ethnic group, the **Kikuyu**-speaking people of Central Province and Nairobi are a major market force in Kenya's music industry. Perhaps because of this large "built-in" audience, few Kikuyu musicians have tried to cross over into the national Swahili or English-language markets. On the international scene, Kikuyu-language music is conspicuously absent, but for the few songs that have made it onto some of the compilation CDs. Kikuyu melodies are quite distinct from those of the Luo and

Luhya of western Kenya, and their pop manifestations also differ significantly in harmonies and rhythm guitar parts. In contrast to Luo and Luhya pop, women vocalists play major roles as lead and backing singers for Kikuyu groups. Many of the top groups have women's auxiliaries – duos and trios invariably called the something-or-other sisters. While Kikuyu pop music has a traditional melodic structure, there is a good deal of stylistic variety and innovation. Most often, Kikuyu pop takes the form of the *benga/cavacha* style, but popular alternatives are also based on country and western, reggae and Congolese soukous.

The king of Kikuyu pop is **Joseph Kamaru**, who has been making hit records since the release of *Celina* in 1967, performed, on one guitar and maracas, with his sister Catherine Muthoni. Since then he has carved a small empire – which includes his **Njung'wa Stars** band and the Kamarulets dancers, two music shops and a recording studio. He sees himself as a teacher, expressing the traditional values of his culture, as well as contemporary social commentary, in song. In the early 1990s his recording, *Mahoya ma Bururi* (Prayers for the Country), gently criticized the Kenya government but resulted in his shop being raided and the banning of the song from the airwaves. Kamaru takes pride in his lyrics for going beyond trivial matters. "My songs are not like other peoples' 'I love you, I love you,' they keep on singing – No, no, no! My songs are not that way. I can compose a love song but very deep, a grown-up loving."

In the period following *Mahoya ma Bururi*, Kamaru's popularity was steadily on the rise: his band was fully booked, playing his regular and "X-rated, Adults Only" shows to packed nightclub crowds. Thus his announcement in 1993 that he had been "born again" came as a bombshell for his fans. Much to their disappointment, Kamaru abandoned the pop music scene to devote his efforts to evangelistic activities and gospel music promotion.

Kamaru may not write songs for teenage lovers but someone who does, and who became famous in the process, is hit-maker **Daniel "DK" (Councillor) Kamau**. Kamau released his first three records in 1967 while still at school, and continued with a highly successful career through the 1970s. He is regarded as having brought Kikuyu music into the *benga* mainstream, but it wasn't until 1990 that he returned to the stage with a new **Lulus Band**. In Kenya's rapidly changing political climate, the councillor struck a responsive chord with his fans and the population at large with his Top Ten hit, FORD Fever (about the newly formed opposition party). DK has continued to address political and human rights issues: in partnership with singer-composer Albert Gacheru, his 1993 cassette, *Clashes – Mbara ya Molo na Narok*, denounces the ethnic violence in the highlands of western Kenya. Both DK and Gacheru are still active in Kenya's music scene (Gacheru is the Chairman of the Music Composers Association) but the piercing political commentary of the early 1990s was largely missing from the general elections of 1997 (where the return of the ruling party seemed a foregone conclusion).

With Kamaru's departure from the pop market, at least a part of the void has been filled by one of the rare female headliners in Kikuyu pop, **Jane Nyambura**. Known these days simply as Queen Jane, she's a staunch advocate for the inclusion of traditional folk forms and local languages within contemporary pop. The "language problem", the use of tribal languages in her music, has severely limited her radio exposure – and that of all musicians singing in local languages. (Such music is deemed "tribal" in official circles and usually heard only on the few local language stations.) In an interview for the *Sunday Nation*, she was adamant: "It is nonsense to argue that music in local dialects promotes tribalism, for music knows no language. I fail to understand how a government can allow the promotion of imported music as happens here while muffling works by its own sons and daughters."

Kamba

East and southeast of Nairobi is a vast, semi-arid plateau, the home of the **Kamba** people, linguistically close relations of the Kikuyu. Kamba pop music is firmly entrenched in the *benga/cavacha* camp. Although distinctive melodies distinguish Kamba pop from other styles of *benga*, there are other special Kamba features. One is the delicate, flowing, merry-go-round-like rhythm guitar that underlies many Kamba arrangements. While the primary guitar plays chords in the lower range, the second guitar plays a fast pattern of notes that mesh with the rest of the instrumentation to fill in the

holes. This gentle presence is discernible in many of the recordings of the three most famous Kamba groups: the **Kalambya Boys & Kalambya Sisters**, **Peter Mwambi and his Kyanganga Boys** and **Les Kilimambogo Brothers Band**, formerly led by Kakai Kilonzo.

These groups dominated Kamba music from the mid-1970s. Mwambi, although he can get into some great guitar solos, has a following that comes largely from within the Kamba community: his musically simple, pulsing-bass drum style may not have enough musical variation to keep non-Kamba speakers interested.

The Kalambya Sisters are a different story. Backed by Onesmus Musyoki's Kalambya Boys Band, the Sisters (now disbanded) were famous, even notorious, throughout Kenya and they even had a minor hit in Europe with *Katelina*. This relates the comic plight of a young woman, Katelina, who likes to drink the home-brew *uki*, but gets pregnant with annual regularity in the process. The soft, high-pitched, feline voices of the Sisters whine engagingly in unison over the delightfully sweet guitar work of Musyoki and the Boys (check out their style in *Kopulo Onesi* on *The Nairobi Beat* CD). After a ten-year absence from the studio, Musyoki returned to record *Sweet Sofia* in 1993, while founding sister, Mary Nduku, now leads the **Mitaboni Sisters**.

To reach a larger audience, a number of local-language artists have turned to Swahili, which is widely spoken throughout east and central Africa. Kakai Kilonzo and Les Kilimambogo Brothers band were always identified as a "Kamba" band, but once Kakai started recording in Swahili, the group enjoyed widespread popularity in Kenya. With socially relevant lyrics, a good dose of "merry-go-round" guitar and a solid dance-beat backing, Les Kilimambogo were national favourites until Kakai's death in 1987.

These days, a new generation of musicians, relative newcomers to the Kamba hall of fame, is drawing most of the limelight away from the old guard. The **Katitu Boys Band** have come to dominate the Kamba cassette market. Leader David Kasyoki, a former guitarist with Mwambi's Kyanganga Boys, won the 1992 Singer of the Year award for *Cheza na Katitu* (Dance with Katitu). Other groups of the new Kamba generation include Kimangu Boys Band, Kiteta Boys, and Mutituni Boys Band.

BIG-NAME BANDS

The **big-name bands** in Kenya can usually muster sufficiently large audiences for shows in sprawling, ethnically diverse towns like Nairobi, Nakuru or Mombasa. Unlike the groups with a particular ethnic leaning, the national performers can appeal to a broad cross-section of the population with music which tends to be either a local variant of the **Congolese** sound or **Swahili music**, a Kenyan-Tanzanian hybrid sound unique to Kenya.

In both Congolese and Swahili popular music, rumba has always been a major ingredient. Songs typically open with a slow-to-medium rumba that ambles through the verses, backed by a light percussion of gentle congas, snare and high hat. Then, three or four minutes into the song, there's a transition – or more often a hiatus. It's goodbye to verses and rolling rumba as the song shifts into high gear. A much faster rhythm, highlighting the instrumental parts, especially solo guitar and brass, takes over with a vengeance.

There are some significant points of divergence in the Swahili and Congolese styles. The tempo of Swahili music is generally slower, even in the fast section. Swahili music over the last twenty-five years has been particularly faithful to this two-part structure although, today, both Swahili and Congolese musicians often dispense with the slow rumba portion altogether. While the Congolese musicians are famous for their vocals and their intricate harmonies, Swahili groups are renowned for their demon guitarists and crisp, clear guitar interplay.

While "Swahili pop" is usually associated with Swahili lyrics, it isn't distinguished by the language. In fact one of the greatest Swahili hits of all time, *Charonyi Ni Wasi*, is not in Swahili but in the closely related Taita language. Similarly, Nairobi's Congolese scene has become less Lingala as it has moved from the near-exclusive use of that Congolese language twenty-five years ago to a preponderance of Swahili lyrics today. Nearly all the songs on the recent *Feet on Fire* CD from the immensely popular Orchestra Virunga are in Swahili, helping to guarantee popularity with a mass audience. As for Lingala songs, while few Kenyans understand the lyrics, their mysterious incomprehensibility and a veneer of Gallic sophistication gives them a certain sex appeal.

Most of the Swahili and Congolese music produced in Kenya originated with the multinational giants like Polygram and CBS/Sony or was put out by independent labels run by British or Asian Kenyans. When European and American interest in African music began to emerge in the early 1980s, it was these companies with their international connections that put out the first, tantalizing sounds from Nairobi. Although they were also involved in the vernacular language scene, the early Kenyan recordings released in London were drawn from the big names and featured artists such as Super Mazembe, Orchestra Makassy, Orchestra Virunga, Lessa Lassan, Issa Juma and Lovy Longomba. Of these, all but the Tanzanian-born Issa Juma came from Congo (then Zaire) – there wasn't a Kenyan among them – and it wasn't until several years later, after Shirati Jazz had made their first British tour, that Kenya achieved an international reputation for its indigenous *benga* dance music.

THE CONGOLESE CONNECTION

Congolese musicians have been making musical waves in Kenya since the late 1950s. It was the Congolese OS Africa Band that opened Nairobi's famous *Starlight Club* on Nairobi Hill (now defunct) back in 1964. But it wasn't until the mid-1970s, after the passing of the American soul craze, that music from Congo began to dominate the city nightclubs. One of the first musicians to settle in Kenya during this period was **Baba Gaston**. The rotund Gaston had already been in the business for twenty years when he arrived in Nairobi with his group Baba National in 1975. A prolific musician and father (he had twelve children), he stole the scene until his retirement as a performer and recording artist in 1989. Gaston died in Moshi of cardiac arrest in 1997.

In the mid-1970s, at about the same time Baba Gaston was just getting settled in Nairobi, the Congolese group Boma Liwanza was already on the scene at the *Starlight Club* and the popular Bana Ngenge were about to leave Nairobi for a year in Tanzania. Super Mazembe had just completed their migration from (then) Zaire to Kenya by way of Zambia and Tanzania. And soon to follow were Samba Mapangala and Les Kinois, though they stopped along the way in Uganda for a couple of years – and had a near-fatal encounter with the army – before moving to Nairobi in 1977. With the break-up of Les Kinois in 1980, some members moved to Mazembe, while Samba began putting together his first version of **Orchestra Virunga**. The famous "Malako" recordings included several members of Bana Ngenge, including vocalist Fataki Lokassa and the late Lawi Somana, who went on to lead Tabu Ley's Afrisa.

Meanwhile, despite their rising popularity in 1982–83, Super Mazembe began to fragment. The group's versatile lead singers Lovy Longomba and Kasongo wa Kanema (of "Kasongo" and "Shauri Yako" fame) quit the band – Kasongo to team up with Virunga and Lovy to front his own group, Super Lovy, and later Bana Likasi.

By 1984, Samba Mapangala's line-up had experienced a number of changes in personnel but was still going strong. It wasn't long, however, before Virunga also ran into the Kenya Immigration Department. With extensions to their work permits refused, Virunga were soon out of money and falling apart.

Out of Virunga's misfortune came **Ibeba System**. It was led by ex-Virunga guitarist Sammy Mansita and other Virunga/Kinois alumni including Siama Matuzungidi on guitar, Johnny-Ko Walengo on bass, and vocalists Kasongo wa Kanema and Coco Zigo Mike. Lovy Longomba also did a spell with Ibeba System before setting off to Dar es Salaam to join Afriso Ngoma. When Ibeba first took over from Virunga at the *Starlight*, the group was a virtual clone of the Virunga sound. Over several years performing at the *JKA Resort Club* they became one of Nairobi's most accomplished club acts with a good mix of their own soukous and covers of African pop.

The ultimate Congolese crossover band in Nairobi, and darlings of Kenya's young elite, were **Vundumuna**. The group formed in 1984 with guitarist **Tabu Frantal** of Boma Liwanza and Shika Shika, Ugandan vocalist Sammy Kasule, and bassist Nsilu wa Bansilu of Bana Ngenge and Virunga. Vundumuna quickly gained institutional status at the *Carnivore*, packing in the crowds with their Wednesday and Saturday night performances. With the best equipment in the city, they presented a clean, hi-tech sound fusing Congolese soukous, *benga* rhythms, and elements of Western jazz. Their flawless horn arrangements blended beautifully with leader **Botango Bedjil**'s (B.B. Mo-Franck)

keyboards and Frantal's guitar. After three LPs and riding a crest of popularity, the future was looking bright until, once again, the Immigration Department struck. The group played its farewell concert at the *Carnivore* in late 1986 and, since then, they have worked abroad in places as far afield as Japan and Oman. In between jobs, they returned to Kenya – several band members have Kenyan wives and children – and they have been allowed to play short stints as guest performers.

The vacuum created by the loss of Vundumuna set the stage for the return of Orchestra Virunga to Nairobi in 1988. Kenyans were hungry for top flight Congolese music. With work permits suddenly no longer a problem, Virunga made a triumphant entry into *Garden Square Nightclub*. They had no trouble immediately recapturing the abundant enthusiasm they left behind after their untimely departure from the music scene three years prior. With a captivating stage show, they played dazzling renditions of all their familiar hits. New compositions like *Safari* and *Vunja Mifupa* joined the list of favourites. Sadly, in 1993, Samba gave up on the local nightclub scene and disbanded the group. He still performs for special events in Kenya, tours abroad and makes records. Although the musicians continue to change, nothing has altered Samba Mapangala's formula for brilliant music – a catchy, not over-complex melody, faultless vocal harmonies, innovative, interlocking guitar lines and superbly crafted horns floating over light, high-tensile percussion.

Samba Mapangala was not the only one disillusioned by the business of music in Nairobi. By the early 1990s, Nairobi's status as an island of opportunity for Congolese musicians had fallen flat. With harder economic times, a declining record industry, fewer live music venues and restrictive work rules for foreign musicians, Nairobi had become a departure point for greener pastures. Some musicians headed for neighbouring countries but others followed Vundumuna's lead and signed up to play abroad.

Since the mid-1990s however, the Congolese music scene has once again been on the upswing with a host of new names and new places to work. Some Congolese names on the current scene are **Senza Musica**, **Choc la Musica**, **Station Japan**, **Tshiakatumaba International** and **Bilenge Musica**. The latter have a CD release called *Rumba Is Rumba* (Kelele Records) that, in terms of quality, places them among the top soukous bands anywhere. The name of vocalist Coco Zigo Mike was originally included in this list as leader of Losako la Musica. Sadly, he died in 1998 at the age of 39. "Prince Cocozigo", as he was known, sang in the late-70s band Viva Makale, and later in Orchestra Virunga, Ibeba System, and Moreno Batamba's Orchestra Moja One.

SWAHILI BANDS: THE TANZANIAN INFLUENCE

Songs with **Swahili lyrics** are part of the common currency of east African musical culture. Kenya's own brand of Swahili pop music has its origin in the Tanzanian pop styles of the 1970s but, since that time, the Kenyan variety has followed a separate evolutionary path from the Tanzanian mainstream.

In addition to the stylistic features it shares with the Congolese sound (light, high-hat-and-conga percussion and a delicate two/three-guitar interweave), the Kenyan Swahili sound is instrumentally sparse, allowing the bass to fill in gaps, often in syncopated rhythms. Trumpets and saxes are common in recorded arrangements but usually omitted in club performances because of the extra expense.

One of the first groups to migrate to Kenya was Arusha Jazz, the predecessor of what is now the legendary **Simba Wanyika Original** ("Simba Wanyika" means "Lion of the Savanna"). Founded by Wilson Peter Kinyonga and his brothers George and William, the group began performing in Mombasa in 1971. The following year, they began recording for Phonogram (Polygram), making a name for themselves with single releases such as *Eliza Wangu* (My Eliza), *Jose Twende Zaire* (Jose Let's Go to Zaire) and *Mama Suzie*. In 1975, the three brothers, along with Tanzanian recruit Omar Shabani on rhythm and Kenyan Tom Malanga on bass, shifted their base to Nairobi and released their first album, *Jiburudisheni na Simba Wanyika* (Chill Out with Simba Wanyika). Over their twenty-year history in Nairobi (to 1995), the group were favourites of the city's club scene and made scores of recordings.

Despite George Kinyonga's death in 1992, the band continued to perform, but following the death of Wilson Kinyonga in 1995, Simba Wanyika rapidly collapsed.

The Kinyonga brothers had been its essential ingredient, maintaining a consistent, instantly recognizable style over this period despite several major changes in personnel. Interestingly, their most widely circulated recordings outside Kenya present a rather different sound from their typical recordings for Polygram in Nairobi. In both their international releases, *Simba Wanyika Original: Kenya Vol I* and *Pepea*, the group has taken a page from the *benga* handbook and quickened the pace considerably — though the vocal and instrumental parts are indeed "original" Simba Wanyika of great guitars, creamy sax (on "Vol I") and pleasing, listener-friendly vocal lines. For purists interested in Simba Wanyika's Polygram sound, the albums *Haleluya* and *Mapenzi Ni Damu*, recorded before and after *Kenya Vol I*, are more representative of their local, live sound. George Peter's *Pole* cassette, released under the name of his own band Orchestra Jobiso, features alternative versions of several of their most famous songs, with the rougher Nairobi versions sounding quite different from the more polished, Dutch-produced *Pepea*. There's a striking contrast in the vocals, for example, placed distinctly out front on *Pepea* but further back and with a ton of echo in the *Pole* mix. The Kenyan version also has stronger congas and high hat and the luxury of a pair of saxophones. But like the differences between various Mazembe and Makassy productions of a decade before, it's hard to say that either the Kenyan or European version is superior.

The Wanyika name is famous in East Africa not only for Simba Wanyika, but for several other related bands that emerged from the Wanyika line. The first big split occurred in 1978 when the core of supporting musicians around the Kinyonga brothers left Simba Wanyika to form **Les Wanyika**. Among those who made the move were rhythm guitarist "Professor" Omari Shabani, bass player Tom Malanga, drummer Rashid Juma and vocalist Issa Juma, who had only joined Simba Wanyika a month before. The group added another crucial member in Tanzanian lead guitar player John Ngereza, who had been playing in Kenya with the Congolese group Bwambe Bwambe. After six months' practice, Les Wanyika began performing at *Garden Square* and soon found fame across Kenya with their massive hit *Sina Makosa* (It's Not My Fault) which was quickly followed by singles such as *Paulina*, *Pamela*, and *Kajituliza Kasuku*.

Under Ngereza's leadership, Les Wanyika have remained one of Nairobi's top bands. While cut from the same mould as the Simbas, Les Wanyika have distinguished themselves with imaginative compositions and arrangements, a typically lean, clean sound and the delicious blend of Professor Omari's rhythm-guitar mastery with Tom Malanga's bass. The sparse percussion majors on the high hat and a muted, pulsing kick drum. This lean instrumentation provides the backing for vocalist and lead guitar player Ngereza, who alternates between the two roles. During vocal choruses, there's solid vocal backing in multi-part harmonies from Mohamed Tika and other Swahili session vocalists. Some of the finest examples of their work are found on the *Dunia Kigeu-geu* compilation, released in Kenya in 1985.

John Ngereza knows the Kenyan music market and is not afraid to adapt to changing times. In the early 1990s, as Kenyan tastes embraced disco music, Les Wanyika were there with a remake of their greatest hits into two disco medleys. *Les Les Non-Stop '90* was locally quite successful and carried over into their next album, *Kabibi* – an unfortunate departure into the dismal realm of international disco crossover. Mercifully, Ngereza abandoned this course on his following cassette releases and, in returning to classic Les Wanyika form, has consistently been in Kenya's Top Ten charts with each new release. His inclusion as a guest artist on Orchestra Virunga's 1997 US tour has finally brought him some international exposure outside Africa as well as his first international CD in 1998 entitled *Amigo*. A sad note to the Les Wanyika story, however, is the death in 1998 of Professor Omari, whose brilliant rhythm guitar was a mainstay of the Les Wanyika sound and who composed many of the group's early hits.

An important figure in the Wanyika story is Tanzania-born **Issa Juma**, who quickly established a name for himself in Kenya as a premier vocalist in the early days of Les Wanyika. Mention his name today and many Kenyans will immediately think of "Sigalame", a character from his 1983 single of the same name and now a part of Kenyan vocabulary. *Sigalame* is Issa Juma's most famous song, not because of the music, which is generic *cavacha*, but because of its entertaining lyrics. Sigalame is a mysterious character who has disappeared from family and friends but is rumoured to be living in Bungoma doing "business". What kind of business? ("Biashara gani?") With so many illegal activities to choose from, it was up to the listener to answer.

As one of the most productive recording artists of the 1980s, Issa Juma released many numbers in the style of Swahili-*benga* fusion heard in *Sigalame*. Yet, he has been perhaps the most versatile and creative of the Swahili artists in his willingness to take his music in different directions.

Although the Wanyika bands have been dominant in Swahili music, it is not their exclusive domain. Foremost among other Tanzanians and Kenyans performing in the Swahili style are the **Maroon Commandos**. Still members of the Kenya Army, the Commandos are one of the oldest performing groups in the country. They first came together in 1970, although they had a serious setback with deaths of several band members in a road accident in 1972. In the mid-1970s, the group was mainly a "covers band" playing the current hits of Zaire (now Congo). But by 1977 they had come out as a strong force in the Swahili style with the huge Taita-language hit *Charonyi Ni Wasi*, recently released again in Kenya. Within their genre, the Commandos do not limit themselves to any sort of rigid formula. Like many of the Swahili groups, they use trumpets and sax liberally but they're also quite experimental and have at various times added a keyboard and innovative guitar effects and, at their most creative, mingle Swahili and *benga* styles.

TOURIST AND INTERNATIONAL POP

International influences have always been a part of Kenyan music, but where Kenyan pop meets the tourist industry, such as on the Kenyan coast, another distinct brand of music can be heard in all the hotels. Down on the coast, north and south of earthy Mombasa, are the tourist resorts, where a successful band can make a living just playing hotel gigs. **Tourist pop bands** typically have highly competent musicians, relatively good equipment and, overall, a fairly polished sound. In live performances, they play a schizophrenic mixture of old Congolese rumba tunes as warmups, popular international covers, a few Congolese favourites of the day, greatest hits from Kenya's past, and then some original material that leans heavily towards the American/Euro-pop sound but with lyrics relating to local topics.

The most successful Kenyan group in this realm has been a perennial favourite, the excruciatingly named **Them Mushrooms**. Strictly speaking, the Mushrooms graduated from the coastal hotel circuit when they moved to Nairobi in 1987. Their music, however, lives on at the coast, highlighted by their crowning achievement, the tourist anthem *Jambo Bwana* with its refrain, *Hakuna Matata* – no problems. TM have several different versions of the song, and while they are proud to take credit for this insidiously infectious bit of fluff, they have much more serious intentions in the world of music.

At their inception, in 1972, the Mushrooms were a reggae band without an audience. However, as they gravitated toward the hotel circuit for work, they changed their style to a more "commercial" sound encompassing international covers, African pop standards, a little soca and reggae, and some Kenyan variants of *benga* and the coastal *chakacha* rhythm. As they moved to Nairobi and the famous *Carnivore* restaurant in 1987, their polished sound established them as a favourite among the wel-to-do nightclub set.

The Mushrooms are without doubt Kenya's most active band today, with at least fifteen albums to their credit. They now own and operate one of the better studios in Kenya. Over their twenty-five (plus) years, they have produced a series of highly successful collaborations, highlighting quite diverse artists, including pioneering musician Fundi Konde, *taarab* star Malika and the Kikuyu singer Jane Nyambura. Their recent work has taken them back to their first love, reggae, with the CD *Kazi Ni Kazi* (Work Is Work), released internationally on the Kelele label.

The Mushrooms' long-time counterparts in the hotel circuit, **Safari Sound**, have also joined the reggae club with another Kelele release called *Mambo Jambo*. This group already has the distinction of having Kenya's best-selling album ever in *The Best of African Songs*, a veritable greatest hits of hotel classics that includes *Malaika* – a beautiful composition about ill-starred love, first sung by Fadhili William, and rarely given the soulful treatment it deserves (see box on p.682).

THE EVOLVING MUSIC SCENE

Although Kenya has a rich musical tradition, it has always been a struggle on the part of musicians to gain recognition and respect. Kenyans seem to be of two minds on this: on one side, they speak fondly of the great names in Kenyan pop and their songs, and they relish all the local music around them on the streets – in restaurants, buses and bars. On the other hand, they often speak disparagingly about Kenyan music in comparison with music from neighbouring Tanzania, Congo, Europe or America. Institutionally, little has been done to help Kenyan musicians. Cassette piracy and the lack of local sources for affordable instruments and supplies are two of the major **problems** facing musicians. Kenyan radio does not give them much support either, especially if their songs are recorded in a local language.

These days, musicians playing *benga*, Swahili pop, or Congolese music face stiff competition on the airwaves and in the music shops. Many of Kenya's younger generation of musicians take their inspiration from rap, R&B, house, reggae and dancehall genres, not simply copying international styles but blending elements of Euro-American pop with local Kenyan melodies, lyrics and rhythms.

For the first time in several years, there seems to be some genuine enthusiasm for local music in this niche. There is also a sense of anticipation of much greater things to come. The 1998 CD, *Kenyan: The First Chapter*, seems to be an expression of such optimism. The disc is a showcase for several of the pioneers in this new music. Hardstone, Hart and Shadz O'Blak are represented, but so are another half-dozen newcomers, most receiving their first exposure on CD and radio. It's hard to predict who will be most successful, but for the moment this is one of the bright spots in the local scene.

DISCOGRAPHY

o = CD

COMPILATIONS

o **Before Benga Vol. 1: Kenya Dry** (Original Music, US). o **Before Benga Vol. 2: The Nairobi Sound** (Original Music, US). Both the acoustic collection on *Kenya Dry* and the electric *Nairobi Sound* provide an excellent cross-section of guitar music from the 1950s to the 70s. These are styles that have largely disappeared in Kenya.

o **Guitar Paradise of East Africa** o **Kenya Dance Mania** (Earthworks/Stern's, UK). These two CDs provide an excellent introduction to Kenya's various styles, although not always the best or most representative material from the artists. Highlights on *Guitar Paradise* include the classic hit *Shauri Yako* by Super Mazembe as well as Kabaselleh Ochieng's *Achi Maria*. On *Kenya Dance Mania* are some Kenyan classics of the 1970s and 80s including Les Wanyika's *Sina Makosa* and Maroon Commandos' *Charonyi Ni Wasi* (recently revived in Kenya).

o **Kapere Jazz Band & Others** *Luo Roots: Musical Currents from Western Kenya* (GlobeStyle, UK). Today's versions of the traditional music of the Luo people, suggesting the foundations of the *benga* style.

o **The Most Beautiful Songs of Africa** (ARC Music, UK). At first glance, the title and "touristy" photographs on the cover would be enough to turn away any serious collector of east African music. In fact, it's quite a good collection of (largely) 1970s Kenyan and Tanzanian music. The mix is totally eclectic with the Congolese dance sounds of Super Mazembe (with *Kasongo* and *Shauri Yako*) and Bopol Mansiamina, *taarab* music of the coast, Tanzanian dance music from Afro 70 and Western jazz, not to mention one of Miriam Makeba's best versions of the Swahili song, *Malaika* (the version that served as the model for Angelique Kidjo's rendition).

o **The Music of Kenya and Tanzania** [The Rough Guide] (World Music Network, UK). A superb collection of Kenyan and Tanzanian music, it samples traditional and popular styles, including *taarab* from the coastal region. Kenyan artists include Simba Wanyika (of Tanzanian origin), Victoria Kings, D.O. Misiani and Shirati Jazz, Abana ba Nasery, Henry Makobi, Ogwang Lelo Okoth with Paddy J. Onono and Zein Musical Party.

o **The Nairobi Beat: Kenyan Pop Music Today** (Rounder, US). This is a collection of mid-Eighties music put together by the author of this article for Rounder Records. A fine cross-section of pop music

varieties, it showcases some of the best examples of regional *benga* styles: Luo, Kikuyu, Kamba and Luhya, plus a couple of Swahili and Congolese dance tunes for good measure.

o **The Secret Museum of Mankind, Music of East Africa, Ethnic Music Classics: 1925–48** (Yazoo, US). This compilation, with selections from throughout East Africa, provides a fascinating window onto traditional and popular sounds reflecting local styles (mainly of the 1930s and 40s).

o **Top Hits from Kenya** (Gefraco, France). Unfortunately, what the title doesn't say is that these hits represent a very narrow segment of the Kenyan market: tourist music. The artists are unnamed but most of them are or were active on the Kenya coast. For the most part, this has an international pop sound quite different from what most Kenyan bands are playing. If you've experienced the beach hotels and their music, you may find this CD taking you right back to the beach (or the *Carnivore Restaurant* in Nairobi).

ARTISTS
ABANA BA NASERY

From western Kenya, this trio keeps alive a style of music they pioneered in the 1960s and early 70s.

o *Abana Ba Nasery: Classic Acoustic Recordings from Western Kenya* (GlobeStyle, UK). These are the original recordings made back in the late Sixties and early Seventies. A charming collection of finger-picking acoustic guitar music from Bunyore, Kenya.

o *!Nursery Boys Go Ahead! The Guitar and Bottle Kings of Kenya* (GlobeStyle, UK/Xenophile, US). This CD captures the crisp ABN sound in new recordings made on their 1991 tour to the UK. It also places the trio in some interesting collaborations with European artists, some of which really get rockin'.

BILENGE MUSICA

This group of eight Congolese musicians came together in Nairobi in early 1996 under the leadership of Didie Double-weight. Individually, they've played with some of Congo's most famous musicians and groups including Sam Mangwana, Koffi Olomide, Viva la Musica and Tanzanian-based Maquis Original and Carnival Band.

o *Rumba is Rumba* (Kelele, Germany). But for Swahili language lyrics in several of the songs, this is mainstream Congolese soukous all the way – and that's not bad. The sound is reminiscent of Wenge Musica and the production at Sync Sound Studios in Nairobi is first-rate, as usual.

OGUTA BOBO

Not much is known about the late Oguta Bobo Otange, but that he's a compelling accordion player from among the Luo of western Kenya and his music covered the gamut of topics from serious social commentary to the lighter side of love.

o *Rujina Kalando* (Equator Heritage Sounds, US). Squeeze-box fanatics: here's your chance to get some rare recordings of African accordion with Oguta Bobo singing and playing. The songs are traditional in melody and rhythm but contemporary in lyrics of the time (the 1960s). And, for those who understand Luo, the songs are filled with humour.

SAM CHEGE'S ULTRA-BENGA
A University of Nairobi graduate in 1990 and with postgraduate studies in the US, Sam Chege is not the typical Kenyan musician. Raised by his grandmother in rural central Kenya, Chege received a solid grounding in Kikuyu music and the oral tradition.

o **Kickin' Kikuyu-Style** (Original Music, US). *Kickin* is a great example of Kikuyu *benga* music, with its solid pulsing kick drum, interlocking guitars (with seriously delayed reverb), providing an interesting contrast to the Luo *benga* of D.O. Misiani, George Ramogi, or Victoria Kings. Lively, fun music with excellent sound quality.

HARDSTONE
At heart, Hardstone is a rapper in Kikuyu and Jamaican English. He's one of the new breed of young Kenyan artists (he was born in 1977) pursuing musical interests in international pop.

o *Nuting but de Stone* (Kelele Records, Germany). This CD joins Caribbean ragga, American urban sounds, and African lyrics and rhythms in a superbly produced package that ranges from ragga to R&B with many stopping points along the way.

H.N. OCHIENG' KABASELLEH & THE LUNNA KIDI BAND
From the area around Lake Victoria, Kabaselleh (died 1998) was one Kenyan bandleader whose music is always a little bit different – an interesting mix of Luo *benga*, Swahili rumba and Congolese influences.

o *Sanduku ya Mapendo* (Equator Heritage Sounds, US). A collection of five of Kabaselleh's double-sided singles from the 1980s – a fine example of his fusion of *benga*, rumba and soukous.

FUNDI KONDE
One of Kenya's most renowned early guitarists and the creator of many of what Kenyans consider "the classics". His heyday was the 1950s, but he was rediscovered by Kenyans in the 1990s through his collaboration with Them Mushrooms in new releases of his music.

o *Fundi Konde Retrospective Vol. 1 (1947–56)* (RetroAfric, UK). Many of the tunes are rumbas, though a couple sound as though they are precursors to reggae.

LES WANYIKA
Les Wanyika are the last of the great Swahili rumba bands in the "Wanyika" lineage dating back to the early 1970s.

o *Amigo* (Clifford Lugard Productions, US). After years of hit recordings on cassette and LP, John Ngereza's band finally broke through with a CD release of Swahili rumba with the great guitar interweave and some very cool horn/sax combinations.

SAMBA MAPANGALA & ORCHESTRA VIRUNGA
Orchestra Virunga have long been one of Kenya's most exciting groups and Samba one of Kenya's most gifted talents.

o *Virunga Volcano* (Earthworks/Stern's, UK). This disc isn't representative of Kenyan music. The first CD from Samba Mapangala and Orchestra Virunga. In a class all of its own, this is the perfect album, with each song like a story that develops over a ten-minute period, exploring different combinations of rhythm, melody and harmony right through to the finish. As fresh and enticing today as it was when created back in the early 1980s.

o *Feet On Fire* (Stern's Africa, UK). First-rate Samba Mapangala in the east African groove, recorded on the 1991 UK tour.

o *Vunja Mifupa* (Lusam, US). Samba's latest CD is also one of his best. Tracks to watch out for are "Confusion" and "Wabingwa", with its evolution of guitar riffs.

D.O. MISIANI & SHIRATI BAND
One of the founding fathers of *benga* music, Daniel Owino Misiani is still playing after more than thirty years.

o *Benga Blast!* (Earthworks/Stern's, UK) o *Piny Ose Mer/The World Upside Down* (GlobeStyle, UK). Fine collections from the definitive name in Luo *benga*, the first (being the rough, unpolished sound of the old Pioneer House studios) in mono.

AYUB OGADA
Ayub Ogada has been exploring and bridging cultural boundaries over the last two decades.

o *En Mana Kuoyo* (Real World, UK). This begins with Luo tradition: the *nyatiti* harp, praise songs and indigenous rhythms. Then he infuses his own creative genius for a quiet, largely acoustic CD with beautiful melodies and captivating rhythms.

GEORGE RAMOGI AND C.K. DUMBE DUMBE JAZZ BAND
Since the early 1960s, George Ramogi helped fashion the sound of Luo pop music with his *benga* and rumba styles.

SWAHILI POP LYRICS

Jambo Bwana
by Teddy Kalanda Harrison

Jambo, jambo Bwana	Greetings, greetings Bwana
Habarai gani?	How are you doing?
Nzuri sana	Very well
Wageni mwakaribishwa	Visitors, you are all welcomed
Kenya yetu	In our Kenya
Hakuna matata	There are no problems
Kenya ni nchi nzuri	Kenya's a beautiful country
Hakuna matata	There are no problems
Nchi ya kupendeza	A pleasing country
Hakuna matata	There are no problems
Nchi ya maajabu	A country of wonders
Hakuna matata	There are no problems
Nchi yenye amani	A country of peace
Hakuna matata	There are no problems

Malaika
Authorship disputed, first popularized by Fadhili William

Malaika, nakupenda malaika	Angel, I love you angel
Malaika, nakupenda malaika	Angel, I love you angel
Nami nifanyeje, kijana mwenzio	And me? What shall I, your boyfriend, do?
Nashindwa na mali sina wee	If I weren't struggling for money
Ningekuoa malaika	I would marry you angel
Nashindwa na mali sina wee	If I weren't struggling for money
Ningekuoa malaika	I would marry you angel
Pesa zasumbuwa roho yangu	Money is the source of my heartache
Pesa zasumbuwa roho yangu	Money is the source of my heartache
Nami nifanyeje, kijana mwenzio	And me? What shall I, your boyfriend, do?
Nashindwa na mali sina wee	If I weren't struggling for money
Ningekuoa malaika	I would marry you angel
Nashindwa na mali sina wee	If I weren't struggling for money
Ningekuoa malaika	I would marry you angel
Kidege, hukuwaza kidege	Little bird, I'm always dreaming of you, little bird
Kidege, hukuwaza kidege	Little bird, I'm always dreaming of you, little bird
Nami nifanyeje, kijana mwenzio	And me? What shall I, your boyfriend, do?
Nashindwa na mali sina wee	If I weren't struggling for money
Ningekuoa malaika	I would marry you angel
Nashindwa na mali sina wee	If I weren't struggling for money
Ningekuoa malaika	I would marry you angel

o *1994 USA Tour-Safari ya Ligingo* (Dumbe Dumbe Records, US). In 1994, a small group of Kenyans in the United States pooled their resources to bring Ramogi and band to the US to perform. Authentic *benga* with moments of greatness.

SIMBA WANYIKA ORIGINAL
One of Kenya's favourite Swahili rumba bands since the early 1970s, the deaths of both of the founding brothers, George and Wilson Peter Kinyonga recently wound up the band.

o *Pepea* (Kameleon Records/Stern's, Netherlands/ UK). Their only solo CD, this is superbly produced, allowing the band to shine on some of their biggest hits of the previous twenty years. Highly recommended.

THEM MUSHROOMS

Them Mushrooms have sprouted in several forms over their 25-years-plus history. Since 1993, they've returned to their reggae origins.

o *Them Mushrooms* (Rags Music, UK). After the first two songs, *Jambo Bwana* and *Mushroom Soup*, the remainder of the CD is the Mushrooms' remakes of classic Kenyan tunes from the 1950s and 60s.

o *Kazi Ni Kazi* (Kelele Records, Germany). The Mushrooms have fully entered the reggae camp in this CD and they certainly sound at home.

VICTORIA KINGS

One of the great *benga* groups from Luo country, western Kenya, they started in the early 1970s with Ochieng Nelly as bandleader, soon joined by long-time musical partner Collela Mazee. One of the top-selling recording groups of the golden age of *benga* in the late 1970s and early 80s.

o *The Mighty Kings of Benga* (GlobeStyle, UK). A different perspective on *benga* (ie not Shirati Jazz) and a very good compilation.

Adapted from contributions by Doug Paterson and Werner Graebner to the Rough Guide to World Music: Africa (1999).

A BEGINNER'S GUIDE TO SWAHILI

Surprisingly, perhaps, Swahili is one of the easiest languages to learn. It's pronounced exactly as it's written, with the stress nearly always on the penultimate syllable. And it's satisfyingly regular, so even with limited knowledge you can make yourself understood and construct simple sentences.

In Kenya, you'd rarely be stuck without Swahili, but it makes a huge difference to your perceptions if you try to speak it. People are delighted if you make the effort (though they'll also tend to assume you understand more than you do). Don't forget that for many Kenyans Swahili is another foreign language they get by in, like English. For travels further afield in east Africa, and especially in Tanzania, some knowledge of Swahili is a very useful backup.

The language has spread widely from its coastal origins to become the lingua franca of east Africa and it has tended to lose its richness and complexity as a result. Up-country, it is often spoken as a second language with a minimum of grammar. On the coast, you'll hear it spoken with tremendous panache: oratorical skills and punning (to which it lends itself with great facility) are much appreciated. Swahili is a Bantu language (in fact one of the more mainstream of the family), but it has incorporated thousands of foreign words, the majority of them Arabic. Far more of this Arabic inheritance and borrowing is preserved on the coast. The "standard" dialect is derived from Zanzibar Swahili, which the early missionaries learned and first transcribed into the Roman alphabet. **Written Swahili** is still not uniform and you'll come across slight variations in spelling, particularly on menus.

PRONUNCIATION

Once you get the hang of voicing every syllable, **pronunciation** is easy. Each vowel is syllabic. Odd-looking combinations of consonants are often pronounced as one syllable, too. *Mzee*, for example, is pronounced "mz-ay-ay" (rhyming with "hey!") and *shauri* (troubles, problem) is pronounced "sha-oor-i". Nothing is silent.

You'll often come across an "**m**" where it looks out of place: this letter can precede any other. It's almost always pronounced as one syllable with the letter(s) that follow it: eg *mnyama* – animal; *mbwa* – dog; *mboga* – vegetables. Just add a bit of an "m" sound at the beginning; "mmmb-oga". Don't say "erm-bwa" or "mer-boga"– you'll be misunderstood. The letter "n" can precede a number of others and gives a nasal quality.

For memorizing, it often helps to ignore the first letter or syllable. Thousands of nouns, for example, start with "ki" (singular) and "vy" (plural), and they're all in the same noun class.

A as in **A**rthur
B as in **b**ed
C doesn't exist on its own
CH as in **ch**urch, but often sounds like a "t", a "dj", or a "ky"
D as in **d**onkey
DJ as in py**j**amas
DH like a cross between **dh**ow and **th**ou
E between the "e" in **E**dward and "ai" in **ai**ling
F as in **f**an
G as in **g**ood
GH at the back of the throat, like a growl; nearly an "r"
H as in **h**armless, sometimes contracted from KH as in lo**ch**
I like the "e" in **e**vil
J as in **j**ug
K as in **k**iosk, sometimes like soft "t" or "ch"
KH a "k" but breathier
L as in **l**ullaby, but often pronounced "r"
M as in **M**artian
MN one syllable, eg *mnazi* (coconut), "mna-zi"
N as in **n**onsense
NG as in wro**ng**, but sometimes pronounced with no "g" sound at all
O as in **o**range, never as in "open" or "do"
P as in **p**enguin
Q doesn't exist (except in early Romanized texts; now "k")
R as in **r**apid, or rolled as in the French *rapide*
S as in **S**amson
T as in **t**iny
TH as in **th**anks, never like the "th" in them
U as in l**u**te
V as in **v**ictory
W as in **w**obble
X doesn't exist
Y as in **y**ou
Z as in **z**ero

ELEMENTARY GRAMMAR

Noun classes put people off Swahili. They are something like the genders in French or Latin in that you alter each adjective according to the class of noun. In Swahili you add a prefix to the word. Each class covers certain areas of meaning and usually has a prefix letter associated with most of its nouns. For example, words beginning "ki" or "ch" (singular), and "vi" or "vy" (plural) are in the general class of "things", notably smallish things (eg *kitoto* – small child, infant). Words beginning "m" in the singular and "wa" in the plural are people (eg *mtu/watu* – person/people; *mtalii/watalii* – tourist/s). Words beginning "m" (singular) and "mi" (plural) are often trees and plants (eg *mti*, *miti* – tree/s), or have connections with life.

Most abstract nouns begin with "u" (eg *uhuru* – freedom, *utoto* – childhood). There are seven or eight classes (and plurals for each), but this gives you some idea.

Prefixes get added to adjectives, so you get *kiti kizuri* – a good chair; *mtu mzuri* – a good person; *miti mizuri* – lovely trees. Really correct Swahili, with everything agreeing, isn't much spoken except on the coast, and you can get away with murder. But once you've grasped the essential building blocks – the root meanings and the prefixes, suffixes and infixes of one or two letters which turn them into words – it becomes a very creative language to learn.

VERBS

There are a few exceptions and irregularities, but the **verb system** is basically straightforward and makes conversational Swahili a realistic goal even for convinced non-linguists.

to want	*ku-taka*	to see, to meet	*ku-ona, ku-onana*
to come	*kuja*, irregular; the infinitive "ku" part stays with the root	to look	*ku-tazama*
		to hear	*ku-sikia*
		to buy	*ku-nunua*
to go	*kwenda*, ie ku-enda but, again, *usually* keeps the "ku" part	to know	*ku-jua*
		to think	*ku-fikiri*
		to like/love	*ku-penda*
to eat	*ku-la*	to be able (can)	*ku-weza*
to drink	*ku-nywa*	to give	*ku-pa*
to sleep	*ku-lala*	to bring	*ku-leta*
to be tired	*ku-choka*	to be/become	*ku-wa*
to stay	*ku-kaa*	to come from	*ku-toka*
to say, speak	*ku-sema*	to have	*ku-wa na* (lit. "to be with")

PRONOUNS

me, I	*mimi, ni*	us, we	*sisi, tu*
you	*wewe, u*	you (pl.)	*ninyi, m*
him/her	*yeye*	them, they	*wao, wa*
she/he	*a*		

TENSES

present tense	*-na-*	future tense	*-ta-*
past tense	*-li-*	just past, or still going on	*-me-*

EXAMPLES OF PRONOUNS, VERBS AND TENSES

she wanted	*a-li-taka*	have they gone?	*wa-me-kwenda?*
I'm tired	*ni-me-choka*	she said...	*a-li-sema...*
we will sleep	*tu-ta-lala*	can I...?	*ni-na-weza...?*
did you hear?	*u-li-sikia?*	I will bring	*ni-ta-leta*
they like...	*wa-na-penda...*	we are staying (at/in)...	*tu-na-kaa...*
are you (pl.) going?	*m-na-enda?*	I know	*ni-na-jua*
has he come?	*a-me-kuja?*		

For the present tense of "to have", you can say *mimi nina gari* (I am with a car/I have a car) or just *nina gari, una gari, ana gari*, etc.

WORDS AND PHRASES

The words and phrases listed here are all in common usage but Swahili (like English) is far from being a homogeneous language, so don't be surprised if you sometimes get some funny looks. And, for lack of space for explanation, there are a number of apparent inconsistencies; just ignore them unless you intend to learn the language seriously. These phrases should make you understood at least.

USEFUL GREETINGS

Jambo or *Hujambo*	Hello, good day, how are you? (multi-purpose greeting, means "Problems?")	*Kwaheri/ni* *Asante/ni* *sana* *Bwana*	Goodbye to one/many Thank you to one/many very (a common emphasis) Mister, the equivalent of *Monsieur* in French
Jambo or *Sijambo* *Habari?*	(the response) No problems How are things? (literally "News?")	*Mama*	like the French *Madame* or *Mademoiselle*, for adult women
Nzuri *Hodi!*	Fine, good, terrible Hello? Anyone in? (said on knocking or entering)	*kjana* *mtoto* *Jina lako nani?*	youth, teenager (pl. *vijana*) child, kid (pl. *watoto*) What's your name?/What
Karibu	Come in, enter, welcome (also said on offering something)	*Unaitwaje?*	are you called?

BASICS

My name is/I am called...	*Jina langu/Nina itwa...*	now	*sasa*
Where are you from?	*Unatoka wapi?*	soon	*sasa hivi*
Where are you staying?	*Unakaa wapi?*	why?	*kwa nini?*
I am from...	*Ninatoka...*	because. . .	*kwa sababu. . .*
I am staying (at/in)...	*Ninakaa...*	who?	*nani?*
See you!	*Tutaonana!* (lit. "We shall meet")	what? which?	*nini?* *gani?*
yes	*ndiyo* (lit. "it is so")	true	*kweli*
no	*hapana* (a general negative); *la* (Arabic – heard mostly on the coast)	and/with or (it) is/(they) are	*na* *au* *ni* (a useful little con nector when you
I don't understand	*Sifahamu/Sielewi*		can't think of an
I don't speak Swahili, but...	*Sisemi kiswahili, lakini...*		alternative, eg *njia ni nzuri* – the road
How do you say... Swahili?	*Unasemaje kwa* in *kiswahili...?*	isn't it?	is good) *siyo?* (equivalent of
Could you repeat that?	*Sema tena* (lit. "speak again")		French *n'est-ce pas?*)
Speak slowly	*Sema pole pole*	I'm British/American/	*Mimi Mwingereza/*
I don't know	*Sijui*	German/ French/Italian	*Mwamerika/*
where (is)?	*wapi?*		*Mdachi/*
here	*hapa*		*Mfaransa/Mwitalia.*
when?	*lini?*		

DAILY NEEDS

Where can I stay?	*Naweza kukaa wapi?*	toilet, bathroom	*choo, bafu*
Can I stay here?	*Naweza kukaa hapa?*	washing water	*maji ya kuosha*
room/s	*chumba/vyumba*	hot/cold water	*maji moto/baridi*
bed/s	*kitanda/vitanda*	I'm hungry	*Nina njaa*
chair/s	*kiti/viti*	I'm thirsty	*Nina kiu*
table/s	*meza*	Is there any...?	*Iko...?* or *Kuna...?*

DAILY NEEDS

Yes there is...	Iko..., or Kuna...	fifty cents	sumni
No there isn't any	Haiko..., or Hakuna...	Reduce the price,	
How much?	Ngapi?	come down a little!	Punguza kidogo!
money	pesa	shop	duka
What price...?	Bei gani...?	bank	benki
How much is...?	Pesa ngapi...?	post office	posta
I want...	Nataka...	café, restaurant	hoteli
I don't want...	Sitaki...	telephone	simu
Give me/Bring me		cigarettes	sigara
(can I have?)	Nipe/Niletee	I'm ill	Mimi mgonjwa
again/more	tena	doctor	daktari
enough	tosha/basi	hospital	hospitali
expensive	ghali sana	police	polisi
cheap (also "easy")	rahisi	tip, bribe	"chai"

TRAVEL AND DIRECTIONS

bus/es	bas, basi/mabasi	Stop!	Simama!
car/s, vehicle/s	gari/magari	Where are you going?	Unaenda wapi?
taxi	teksi	To where?	Mpaka wapi?
bicycle	baiskeli	From where?	Kutoka wapi?
train	treni	How many kilometres?	Kilometa ngapi?
plane	ndege	I'm going to...	Nenda...
boat/ship	chombo/meli	Move along,	Songa!/Songa kido
petrol	petroli	squeeze up a little	go!
road, path	njia/ndia	Let's go, carry on	Twende, endelea
highway	barabara	straight ahead	moja kwa moja
on foot/walking	kwa miguu	right	kulia
When does it leave?	Inaondoka lini?	left	kushoto
When will we arrive?	Tutafika lini?	up	juu
slowly	pole pole	down	chini
fast, quickly	haraka	I want to get off here	Nataka kushuka hapa
Wait!/		The car has broken down	Gari imevunjika
Hang on a moment!	Ngoja!/Ngoja kidogo!		

TIME, CALENDAR AND NUMBERS

What time is it?	Saa ngapi?	Monday	jumatatu	20	ishirini
four o'clock	saa nne	Tuesday	jumanne	21	ishirini na moja
quarter past	na robo	Wednesday	jumatano	30	thelathini
half past	na nusu	Thursday	alhamisi	40	arobaini
quarter to	kasa robo	Friday	ijumaa	50	hamsini
minutes	dakika	Saturday	jumamosi	60	sitini
early	mapema	Sunday	jumapili	70	sabini
yesterday	jana	1	moja	80	themanini
today	leo	2	mbili	90	tisini
tomorrow	kesho	3	tatu	100	mia moja
daytime	mchana	4	nne	121	mia moja na ishirini
night time	usiku	5	tano		na moja
dawn	alfajiri	6	sita	1000	elfu
morning	asubuhi	7	saba		
last/this/next	wiki iliopi	8	nane		
week	ta/hii/ijayo	9	tisa		
this year	mwaka huu	10	kumi		
this month		11	kumi na moja		
(lit. "moon")	mwezi huu	12	kumi na mbili		

SIGNS

Danger	*Hatari!*	Fierce dog!	*Mbwa mkali!*
Warning	*Angalia!/Onyo!*	No entry!	*Hakuna njia!*

WORDS WORTH KNOWING

good	*-zuri* (with a prefix at the front)	problems, hassles	*wasiwasi, matata*
bad	*-baya* (ditto)	No problem	*Hakuna wasiwasi/Hakuna matata*
big	*-kubwa*		
small	*-dogo*	friend	*rafiki*
a lot of	*-ingi*	sorry, pardon	*samahani*
other/another	*-ingine*	It's nothing	*Si kitu*
not bad	*si mbaya*	Excuse me	
OK, right, fine	*sawa*	(let me through)	*Hebu*
fine, cool	*safi*	What's up?	*Namna gani?*
completely	*kabisa*	If God wills it	*Inshallah* (heard often on the coast)
just, only	*tu (kitanda kimoja tu* – just one bed)	please	*Tafadhali* (rare up-country and not heard much on
thing/s	*kitu/vitu*		the coast either)

And two phrases you're more likely to hear than to ever say:

Take a picture of me!	*Piga picha mimi!*	Help the poor!	*Saidia maskini!*

BOOKS AND COURSES

There are several of published teach-yourself **courses** around. *Teach Yourself Swahili* by Joan Russel (Teach Yourself Books, 1995) is solid. For the analytical approach, the best book is probably *Simplified Swahili* by Peter M Wilson (Longman, 1985). *Kiswahili kwa Kitendo* ("Swahili by Action", US only, Africa World Press, 1988) is the best bet if you find ordinary grammars indigestible. The course by Joan Maw, *Swahili for Starters* (Oxford University Press, 1999), is good. As for phrasebooks, the *Rough Guide Swahili phrasebook dictionary* (1998) is one of the best.

OTHER LANGUAGES

The following brief lists are intended only for introductions and as a springboard for communication. If you'll be spending time in a particular linguistic region, you may be surprised at how difficult it is to track down usable primers and phrasebooks for these languages. Very little material exists for non-native speakers of African languages, though you can make some progress if you're prepared to struggle (with a dictionary) with short novels or the Bible and the like. Try the sources on p.35 for further ideas. However, even the library of the School of African and Oriental Studies is rather bereft of user-friendly material.

LUO (LAKE VICTORIA)

How do you do?	*Iriyo nade?*	5	*Abich*
Response:	*Ariyo maber!*	6	*Auchiely*
Thank you	*Erokamano*	7	*Abiriyo*
1	*Achiel*	8	*Aboro*
2	*Ariyo*	9	*Ochiko*
3	*Adek*	10	*Apar*
4	*Angwen*		

MAA (MAASAI)

Greetings to a man:	*Lo murrani! Supa!*	3	*Okuni*
Response:	*Ipa!*	4	*Oonguan*
Greetings to a woman:	*Na kitok! Takuenya!*	5	*Imiet*
Response:	*Iko!*	6	*Ile*
Thank you (very much!)	*Ashe (naleng!)*	7	*Oopishana*
Goodbye!	*Sere!*	8	*Isiet*
1	*Obo*	9	*Ooudo*
2	*Aare*	10	*Tomon*

KIKUYU (CENTRAL HIGHLANDS)

How are things?	*Kweruo atia?*	1	*Imwe*
Fine!	*Ni kwega!*	2	*Igiri*
How are you?	*Waigua atia?*	3	*Ithatu*
Are you well? (pl.)	*Wi mwega/Muri ega?*	4	*Inya*
Response:		5	*Ithano*
("Nothing wrong")	*Asha, ndi mwega*	6	*Ithathatu*
Goodbye		7	*Mugwanja*
(when you're leaving)	*Tigwo na wega*	8	*Inyanya*
Goodbye		9	*Kenda*
(when you're staying)	*Thii na wega*	10	*Ikumi*

GLOSSARY

These words are all in common usage. Remember, however, that plural forms often have different beginnings.

AFCO Armed Forces Catering Ordnance

ASK Agricultural Society of Kenya

ASKARI policeman, security guard

BANDA any kind of hut, usually round and thatched

BARABARA main road

BOMA a fort or defensive stockade, often used to mean a small village or cluster of huts

BORITI mangrove poles, used on the coast for building and exported to the Gulf states for the same purpose

BUIBUI the black cover-all cloak and scarf of Swahili women

BWANA Mister, a common term of address

CHAI not just tea, but also the common term for a tip, or more often a small bribe or persuasion

CHOO toilet (pronounced *cho*)

DUKA shop, store

DUKA LA DAWA chemist

ENGKANG Maasai village (see "Manyatta")

FORD Forum for the Restoration of Democracy

FUNDI mechanic, craftsman, expert

GARI car

GEMA the ethnic grouping of Gikuyu (Kikuyu), Embu and Meru

GK Government of Kenya

HARAMBEE "pull together" – the ideology of peaceable community development espoused by Kenyatta. *Harambee* meetings are local fund-raising gatherings – for schools, clinics, etc – but they've come in for some criticism in recent years as politicians vie to contribute the most money.

HOTELI small restaurant, *chai* shop, café

JUA KALI "hot sun" – open-air car repairer's yard or small workshop

KANGA printed cotton sheet used as a wrap, often incorporating a motto

KANISA church

KANU Kenya African National Union, Kenya's ruling political party

KBC Kenya Broadcasting Corporation

KIKOI brightly coloured woven cloth

LAIBON Maasai spiritual leader, with the status of regional headman

LUGGA dry river valley (usually in the north)

MAENDELEO progress, development

MAGENDO corruption, bribery, abuse of power

MAJIMBOISM the creation of federal blocks in formerly heterogeneous regions – these days associated with ethnic cleansing

MAKONDE beautifully worked Tanzanian wood carving, typically in ebony and representing entwined spirit families – much copied in the tourist markets

MAKUTI palm-leaf roof common on the coast

MALAIKA angel

MALAYA prostitute

MAMA common term of address for married women

MANAMBA *matatu* tout, "turnboy"

MANYATTA temporary cattle camp, often loosely used for a village (Maasai)

MASKINI the poor, beggars (*Saidia maskini!* – "Help the poor!")

MATATU pick-up taxi, usually full to overflowing

MIRAA mildly narcotic herb grown in Nyambeni Hills, chewed to assuage hunger and stay awake – much used by bus, *matatu* and long-distance lorry drivers, and during Ramadan.

MKENYA Kenyan citizen (pl. *wakenya*)

MORAN man in the warrior age group of Maasai or Samburu (pl. *morani*)

MSIKITI mosque

MTALI tourist (pl. *watali*)

MUNGU God

MURRAM red or black clay soil, usually referring to a road

MWANANCHI person, peasant, worker (pl. *wananchi*, the people)

MZEE old man: "*the* Mzee" is Kenyatta

MZUNGU white person (pl. *wazungu*)

NCCK National Christian Council of Kenya

NGO non-governmental organization

NGOMA dancing, drumming, party, celebration

NJIA road, path

NYAYO "footsteps" – the follow-in-his-footsteps philosophy of post-Kenyatta Kenya propounded by President Moi

PANGA multi-purpose short machete carried everywhere in the countryside

PESA lit. "silver", money, "cash"

SAFARI journey of any kind

SHAMBA small farm, plot

UHURU freedom, independence

UKIMWI AIDS

ULAYA Europe

WATU literally "people", but often used slightly disparagingly by expats and Anglo-Kenyans, especially when referring to their staff

INDEX

Stay in touch with us!

ROUGH*NEWS* is Rough Guides' free newsletter. In four issues a year we give you news, travel issues, music reviews, readers' letters and the latest dispatches from authors on the road.

I would like to receive ROUGH*NEWS*: please put me on your free mailing list.

NAME ....

ADDRESS ....

Please clip or photocopy and send to: Rough Guides, 62–70 Shorts Gardens, London WC2H 9AB, England or Rough Guides, 375 Hudson Street, New York, NY 10014, USA.

ROUGH GUIDES: Travel

Amsterdam
Andalucia
Australia

Austria
Bali & Lombok
Barcelona
Belgium &
  Luxembourg
Belize
Berlin
Brazil
Britain
Brittany &
  Normandy
Bulgaria
California
Canada
Central America
Chile
China
Corfu & the
  Ionian Islands
Corsica
Costa Rica
Crete
Cuba
Cyprus
Czech & Slovak
  Republics

Dodecanese
Dominican
  Republic
Egypt
England
Europe
Florida
France
French Hotels &
  Restaurants 1999
Germany
Goa
Greece
Greek Islands
Guatemala
Hawaii
Holland
Hong Kong
  & Macau
Hungary
India
Indonesia
Ireland
Israel & the
  Palestinian
  Territories
Italy
Jamaica
Japan
Jordan

Kenya
Laos
London
London
  Restaurants
Los Angeles
Malaysia,
  Singapore &
  Brunei
Mallorca &
  Menorca
Maya World
Mexico
Morocco
Moscow
Nepal
New England
New York
New Zealand
Norway
Pacific Northwest
Paris
Peru
Poland
Portugal
Prague
Provence & the
  Côte d'Azur
The Pyrenees
Romania

St Petersburg
San Francisco
Sardinia
Scandinavia
Scotland
Scottish Highlands
  & Islands
Sicily
Singapore

South Africa
Southern India
Southwest USA
Spain
Sweden
Syria
Thailand
Trinidad & Tobago
Tunisia
Turkey
Tuscany & Umbria
USA
Venice
Vienna
Vietnam
Wales
Washington DC
West Africa
Zimbabwe &
  Botswana

AVAILABLE AT ALL GOOD BOOKSHOPS

ROUGH GUIDES: Mini Guides, Travel Specials and Phrasebooks

MINI GUIDES

Antigua
Bangkok
Barbados
Big Island of
  Hawaii
Boston
Brussels
Budapest

Seattle
Sydney
Tokyo
Toronto

TRAVEL SPECIALS

First-Time Asia
First-Time Europe
More Women Travel

Dublin
Edinburgh
Florence
Honolulu
Jerusalem
Lisbon
London
  Restaurants
Madrid
Maui
Melbourne
New Orleans
St Lucia

PHRASEBOOKS

Czech
Dutch

Egyptian Arabic
European
French
German
Greek
Hindi & Urdu
Hungarian
Indonesian
Italian
Japanese

Mandarin
  Chinese
Mexican Spanish
Polish
Portuguese
Russian
Spanish
Swahili
Thai
Turkish
Vietnamese

AVAILABLE AT ALL GOOD BOOKSHOPS

ROUGH GUIDES:
Reference and Music CDs

REFERENCE
Classical Music
Classical:
100 Essential CDs
Drum'n'bass
House Music
Jazz
Music USA

Opera
Opera:
100 Essential CDs
Reggae
Reggae:
100 Essential CDs
Rock
Rock:
100 Essential CDs
Techno
World Music
World Music:
100 Essential CDs
English Football
European Football

Internet
Millennium

ROUGH GUIDE MUSIC CDs
Music of the
Andes
Australian
Aboriginal
Brazilian Music
Cajun & Zydeco

Classic Jazz
Music of Colombia
Cuban Music
Eastern Europe

Music of Egypt
English Roots
Music
Flamenco
India & Pakistan
Irish Music
Music of Japan
Kenya & Tanzania
Native American
North African
Music of Portugal

Reggae
Salsa
Scottish Music
South African
Music
Music of Spain
Tango
Tex-Mex
West African Music
World Music
World Music Vol 2
Music of
Zimbabwe

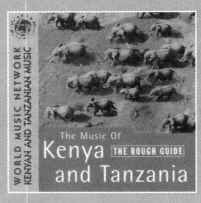

FIG TREE CAMP
MASAI MARA

Fig Tree is one of the traditional camps of the Masai Mara. Beautifully located on the banks of Talek River, Fig Tree offers a choice of both Tents and Cabins. Game Walks, Horse Safaris and Night Game Drives are part of the many activities available.

ADVENTURES ALOFT
MASAI MARA, KENYA

Adventures Aloft Balloon Safaris fly daily from Fig Tree Camp and from Siana Springs in the Masai Mara. Flights over the Masai Mara are celebrated with a champagne breakfast on the Mara plains. Free transfers from surrounding lodges and camp sites can be arranged.

KILIFI BAY BEACH RESORT
KILIFI

Kilifi Bay Beach Resort lies 55 km north of Mombasa, and is home to one of the finest beaches on the Kenya coastline. The Resort has fifty rooms, two swimming pools, three bars and two restaurants. The Kilifi Bay is perfect for those looking for privacy and personalised service.

Oakwood Hotel

OAKWOOD HOTEL
NAIROBI - KIMATHI STREET

A lovely little hotel in the heart of the city. The hotel is tastefully furnished with an old world charm. All rooms are en suite with T.V. and in house movies.

MADA HOTELS CENTRAL RESERVATIONS:
1ST FLOOR KIMATHI HOUSE, KIMATHI STREET
P. O. BOX 40683, NAIROBI KENYA
TEL:(254-2) 221439/218321   FAX:(254-2) 332170
E- mail: madahold@form-net.com

If you need a
more personalised
and individual service
for Safaris to Kenya, we
believe we can give you
the very best.

From the heights of snowcapped Mount Kenya on the equator down
through the highlands, rain forest and plains to the beautiful Indian Ocean,
Let's Go Travel are the knowledgeable experts who will tailor
Kenyan Safaris exactly to your requirements.
Please phone us on Nairobi 340331 or fax Nairobi 336890 and you
will receive our most prompt attention.
With Branch offices in Arusha - Tanzania & Kampala - Uganda.

Let's Go Travel Caxton House, Standard St. (Next to main G.P.O.,
Opposite Bruce House.) P.O.Box 60342, Nairobi, Kenya
Tel: 340331/213033 **Fax:** (254-2) 336890/214713
E-mail: info@letsgosafari.com **Internet:** www.letsgosafari.com

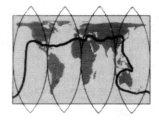

SAVANNAH CAMPS & LODGES

P.O. BOX 48019 NAIROBI, KENYA FEDHA TOWERS, STANDARD STREET
TEL # 331191/229009 FAX # 254-2-330698

MARA RIVER CAMP
DELAMERE CAMP
LERAI TENTED CAMP

GALLA CAMP
SANGARE TENTED CAMP
INDIAN OCEAN LODGE

A SELECTION OF SMALL TENTED CAMPS & LODGES ON PRIVATE LAND IN SOME OF KENYA'S MOST SCENIC WILDLIFE AREAS.

LOOKING FOR A SAFARI FROM MOMBASA ?

........then let the experience and expertise of **GAMEWATCH** help you make your choice.

T wo or three day Tsavo tours, by jeep or mini-bus, are our speciality. Other itineraries available.

S ome packages require you to vacate your beach hotel accommodation whilst away on safari. We do <u>not</u>.

A sk about our "private" safaris for families and friends. You'll be pleasantly surprised by our..........

V alue-for-money prices (children from just £79).

O rganise your safari in the U.K....pre-booking makes sense.

For further details, and our colour brochure, contact Phil or Anita Pope at
GAMEWATCH SAFARIS on 01761-437654

**HOSTELLING
INTERNATIONAL**

The last word in accommodation

Safe reliable accommodation
from $8 a night at over 4500 centres
in 60 countries worldwide

http://www.iyhf.org

the perfect getaway vehicle

low-price holiday car rental.

rent a car from holiday autos and you'll give yourself real freedom to explore your holiday destination. with great-value, fully-inclusive rates in over 4,000 locations worldwide, wherever you're escaping to, we're there to make sure you get excellent prices and superb service.

what's more, you can book now with complete confidence. our £5 undercut* ensures that you are guaranteed the best value for money in holiday destinations right around the globe.

drive away with a great deal, call holiday autos now on **0990 300 400** and quote ref RG.

holiday autos miles ahead